Visit the Student Site for

Understanding World Societies

bedfordstmartins.com/mckayworldunderstanding

FREE Online Study Guide

Get instant feedback on your progress with

- Chapter self-tests
- Key terms review
- Map quizzes
- Timeline activities
- Note-taking outlines
- Chapter study guide steps

FREE History Research and Writing Help

Refine your research skills and find plenty of good sources with

- A database of useful images, maps, documents, and more at *Make History*
- A guide to online sources for history
- Help with writing history papers
- A tool for building a bibliography
- Tips on avoiding plagiarism

THE CONTEMPORARY WORLD

ARCTIC OCEAN

NORWAY
SWEDEN
FINLAND
ESTONIA
LATVIA
LITHUANIA
DEN.
NETH.
GERMANY POLAND
BEL.
LUX. CZ.
SLK.
AUS. HUNG.
SWITZ. ITALY
SLN.
CR.
B.H.
MO. KO.
ALB.
MAC.
GREECE

RUSSIAN FEDERATION

BELARUS
UKRAINE
MOLDOVA
ROMANIA
SE.
BULGARIA
GEORGIA
TURKEY
ARMENIA
AZERBAIJAN

KAZAKHSTAN
UZBEKISTAN
KYRGYZSTAN
TURKMENISTAN
TAJIKISTAN
AFGHANISTAN

MONGOLIA

CHINA

N. KOREA
S. KOREA

JAPAN

PACIFIC OCEAN

TUNISIA
MALTA
CYPRUS
SYRIA
LEBANON
ISRAEL
West Bank
IRAQ
Gaza Strip
JORDAN
IRAN
PAKISTAN

BHUTAN
NEPAL

Taiwan

ALGERIA
LIBYA
EGYPT

KUWAIT
BAHRAIN
SAUDI ARABIA
QATAR
UNITED ARAB
EMIRATES
OMAN

BANGLADESH
INDIA
MYANMAR
(BURMA)
LAOS
VIETNAM
THAILAND
CAMBODIA

Mariana Is.
(U.S.)

Guam
(U.S.)

MARSHALL
IS.

NIGER
CHAD
SUDAN
ERITREA
YEMEN
DJIBOUTI

PHILIPPINES

NIGERIA
BENIN
TOGO
CENTRAL
AFRICAN REP.
SOUTH
SUDAN
ETHIOPIA
SOMALIA

MALDIVES
SRI
LANKA

BRUNEI

PALAU

FEDERATED STATES
OF MICRONESIA

CAMEROON
EQ.
GUINEA
GABON
CONGO
UGANDA
RWANDA
KENYA
DEM. REP. OF
THE CONGO

MALAYSIA

SINGAPORE

NAURU
KIRIBATI

TUVALU

SÃO
TOMÉ
& PRÍNCIPE
BURUNDI
TANZANIA
COMOROS
SEYCHELLES

INDONESIA

PAPUA
NEW
GUINEA

SOLOMON
IS.

ANGOLA
ZAMBIA
MALAWI

INDIAN OCEAN

TIMOR
LESTE

VANUATU
FIJI

NAMIBIA
BOTSWANA
ZIMBABWE
MADAGASCAR
MAURITIUS

New Caledonia
(Fr.)

AUSTRALIA

MOZAMBIQUE
SWAZILAND
SOUTH
AFRICA
LESOTHO

NEW
ZEALAND

Tasmania
(Aust.)

ANTARCTICA

20°E   40°E   60°E   80°E   100°E   120°E   140°E   160°E

ABBREVIATIONS

ALB.	ALBANIA
AUS.	AUSTRIA
BEL.	BELGIUM
B.H.	BOSNIA AND HERZEGOVINA
CR.	CROATIA
CZ.	CZECH REPUBLIC
DEN.	DENMARK
HUNG.	HUNGARY
KO.	KOSOVO
LUX.	LUXEMBOURG
MAC.	MACEDONIA
MO.	MONTENEGRO
NETH.	NETHERLANDS
SE.	SERBIA
SLK.	SLOVAKIA
SLN.	SLOVENIA
SWITZ.	SWITZERLAND

Understanding World Societies

A BRIEF HISTORY

Understanding World Societies

A BRIEF HISTORY

VOLUME 2 **Since 1450**

John P. McKay
University of Illinois at Urbana-Champaign

Bennett D. Hill
Late of Georgetown University

John Buckler
Late of University of Illinois at Urbana-Champaign

Patricia Buckley Ebrey
University of Washington

Roger B. Beck
Eastern Illinois University

Clare Haru Crowston
University of Illinois at Urbana-Champaign

Merry E. Wiesner-Hanks
University of Wisconsin–Milwaukee

BEDFORD/ST. MARTIN'S
Boston • New York

FOR BEDFORD/ST. MARTIN'S

Publisher for History: Mary Dougherty
Executive Editor for History: Traci M. Crowell
Director of Development for History: Jane Knetzger
Senior Developmental Editor: Laura Arcari
Production Editor: Katherine Caruana
Senior Production Supervisor: Dennis J. Conroy
Executive Marketing Manager: Jenna Bookin Barry
Editorial Assistant: Victoria Royal
Production Assistant: Elise Keller
Copyeditor: Susan Moore
Indexer: Leoni Z. McVey
Cartography: Mapping Specialists, Ltd.
Photo Researchers: Carole Frohlich and Elisa Gallagher, The Visual Connection Image Research, Inc.
Permissions Manager: Kalina K. Ingham
Senior Art Director: Anna Palchik
Text Designer: Boynton Hue Studio
Cover Designer: Donna Lee Dennison
Cover Art: Head of a Jamaican Girl by Augustus Edwin John. © The Gallery Collection/Corbis.
Composition: Jouve
Printing and Binding: RR Donnelley and Sons

President, Bedford/St. Martin's: Denise B. Wydra
Presidents, Macmillan Higher Education: Joan E. Feinberg and Tom Scotty
Director of Marketing: Karen R. Soeltz
Production Director: Susan W. Brown
Associate Production Director: Elise S. Kaiser
Managing Editor: Elizabeth M. Schaaf

Library of Congress Control Number: 2012932453

Copyright © 2013 by Bedford/St. Martin's

Manufactured in the United States of America.

7   6   5   4   3   2
f   e   d   c   b   a

For information, write: Bedford/St. Martin's, 75 Arlington Street, Boston, MA 02116   (617-399-4000)

ISBN 978-1-4576-1867-3 (Combined edition)
ISBN 978-1-4576-1873-4 (Volume 1)
ISBN 978-1-4576-1874-1 (Volume 2)

Understanding World Societies grew out of many conversations about the teaching, study, and learning of history in the last decade. This book sets out to solve a number of problems that students and instructors face. First, we knew that many instructors wanted a world history text that introduced students to overarching trends and developments but that also re-created the lives of ordinary men and women in appealing human terms. We also recognized that instructors wanted a text that presented cutting-edge scholarship while simultaneously showing that history is a discipline based on interpretation and debate. At the same time, we understood that despite the fact that many students dutifully read their survey texts, they came away overwhelmed and confused about what was most important. We knew too that convenience was important to students, and that having digital choices and cost-saving format options was valuable to today's students. We also came to realize that a growing number of instructors thought that their students needed a brief text, either because instructors were assigning more supplemental reading or because they thought their students would be better able to grasp key concepts given less detail. Finally, many instructors wanted a text that would help students focus as they read, that would keep their interest in the material, and that would encourage students to learn historical thinking skills.

With these issues in mind, we took a hard look at the course from a number of different directions. We reflected on the changes in our own classrooms, reviewed state-of-the-art scholarship on effective teaching, consulted learning experts and instructional designers, and talked to students and instructors about their needs. We looked at how many people are teaching online, and listened to instructors' wish lists for time-saving support materials. The product of these efforts is a textbook designed to address all of these concerns: *Understanding World Societies: A Brief History*. With this book, we offer something new—an abridged world history that focuses on important developments, combined with an innovative design and pedagogy orchestrated to work together to foster students' comprehension and historical thinking. This brief narrative with distinctive pedagogy will help your students grasp important developments and begin to think like historians.

Narrative

We believe the study of world history in a broad and comparative context is an exciting, important, and highly practical pursuit. It is our conviction, based on considerable experience in introducing large numbers of students to world history, that a book reflecting current trends in scholarship can fascinate readers and inspire an enduring interest in the long human experience. Our approach has been twofold.

First, we have made social and cultural history the core elements of our narrative. We seek to re-create the lives of ordinary people in appealing human terms, and also highlight the interplay between men's and women's lived experiences and the ways that men and women reflect on these to create meaning. Second, we have made every effort to strike an effective global and regional balance. Thus we have adopted a comprehensive regional organization with a global perspective that is clear and manageable for students. So for example, students are introduced in depth to East Asia in Chapter 7, while at the same time the chapter highlights the cultural connections that occurred via the Silk Road and the spread of Buddhism. We study all geographical areas while stressing the links among cultures, political units, and economic systems, for it is these connections that have made the world what it is today. We make comparisons and connections across time as well as space, for understanding the unfolding of the human story in time is the central task of history.

In response to the calls for a briefer, less detailed text, in developing *Understanding World Societies*, we shortened the narrative of the parent text, *A History of World Societies*, by 25 percent. We condensed and combined thematically related sections and aimed throughout the text to tighten our exposition while working hard to retain topical balance, up-to-date scholarship, and lively, accessible writing. The result is a brief edition that preserves the narrative flow, balance, and power of the full-length work, and that allows students to better discern overarching trends and connect these with the individuals who animate the past. And in response to the changing needs of instructors and students, we offer a variety of e-book options—including some that make it easy for instructors to customize the book for their unique classroom needs.

Pedagogy and Features

In trying to create a text that would help students grasp key concepts, maintain their interest in reading, and help them develop historical-thinking skills, we then joined this brief narrative with an innovative design and unique pedagogy. *Understanding World Societies'* chapter architecture supports students' reading, helps them to identify key themes and ideas, and shows them how to think like historians. All chapters open with a succinct statement about the main themes and events of the chapter, designed to establish clear learning outcomes. Chapters are organized into three to six main sections, with **section headings crafted as questions** to facilitate active reading and to emphasize that history is an inquiry-based discipline. **Quick review questions** at the end of each major section prompt students to check their comprehension and reflect on what they've read. **Chapter-opening chronologies** underscore the sequence of events, and definitions in the margins highlight **key terms**, providing on-the-page reinforcement and a handy tool for review. **Chapter locators** across the bottom of each two-page spread keep students focused on where they are in the chapter and helps them see how the material they are reading connects to what they have already reviewed and to what is coming next.

We also reconsidered the traditional review that comes at the end of the chapter. Each chapter includes a **"Connections"** conclusion that provides an insightful synthesis of the chapter's main developments and draws connections and comparisons between countries and regions that explain how events relate to larger global processes such as the influence of the Silk Road, the effects of the transatlantic slave trade, and the ramifications of colonialism. Each chapter ends with a three-step **Chapter Study Guide** that encourages students to move beyond a basic knowledge of what happened and moves them toward a deeper synthesis of how events relate to each other. In essence, the chapter-review sections provide the tools to help students develop the skills of historical analysis and interpretation while also helping them to read and think critically. Students can also test their mastery of the reading using the Online Study Guide and via Learning Curve, a game-like interface that helps students test their historical knowledge at their own pace.

We hope that this combination of design and pedagogy will help students to grasp meaning as they read and also model how historians think, how they pose questions, and how they answer those questions with evidence and interpretation.

Other features of the book further reinforce historical thinking, expand upon the narrative, and offer opportunities for classroom discussion and assignments. In our years of teaching world history, we have often noted that students really come alive when they encounter stories about real people in the past. Thus, each chapter includes an **"Individuals in Society"** biographical essay that offers a brief study of an individual or group, informing students about the societies in which they lived. The spotlighting of individuals, both famous and obscure, underscores the book's attention to cultural and intellectual developments and highlights human agency. Biographical essays in *Understanding World Societies* include features on Lord Mengchang, who in the third century B.C.E. rose to rule the Chinese state of Qi; Hürrem of the Ottoman State, a slave concubine and imperial wife who lived in the sixteenth century; and Henry Meiggs, a nineteenth-century speculator who built and lost fortunes in South America.

Each chapter also includes a primary source feature, **"Listening to the Past,"** chosen to extend and illuminate a major historical issue considered in each chapter through the presentation of a single original source or several voices on the subject. Each opens with an introduction and closes with "Questions for Analysis" that invite students to evaluate the evidence as historians would. Selected for their interest and importance, and carefully fitted into their historical context, these sources allow students to observe how history has been shaped by individuals. Documents include sixth-century biographies of Buddhist nuns; Katib Chelebi on the spread and practice of smoking tobacco in the Ottoman Empire; and the Burmese opposition politician Aung San Suu Kyi's 1991 "Freedom from Fear" speech.

Rounding out the book's feature program is the **"Global Trade"** feature, essays that focus on a particular commodity, exploring the world trade, social and economic impact, and cultural influence of that commodity. Each essay is accompanied by a detailed map showing the trade routes of the commodity. Topics range from pottery to slaves, and from oil to arms.

We are particularly proud of the illustrative component of our work—the art and map program. Although this is a brief book, over 300 illustrations, all contemporaneous with the subject matter, reveal to today's visually attuned students how the past speaks in pictures as well as in words. Recognizing students' difficulties with geography, we also offer 100 full-size, full-color maps and 79 spot maps. Each chapter includes a **"Mapping the Past"** activity that helps improve students' geographical literacy and a **"Picturing the Past"** visual activity that gives students valuable skills in reading and interpreting images.

The new directions in format and pedagogy that are the hallmark of *Understanding World Societies* have not changed the central mission of the book since it first appeared in its original format, which is to introduce students to the broad sweep of world history in a fresh yet balanced manner. As we have made changes, large and small, we have always sought to give students and teachers an integrated perspective so that they could pursue—on their own or in the classroom—those historical questions that they find particularly exciting and significant. We hope students would then take the habits of thinking developed in the history classroom with them, for understanding the changes of the past might help them to handle the ever-faster pace of change in today's world.

Acknowledgments

It is a pleasure to thank the many editors who have assisted us over the years, first at Houghton-Mifflin and now at Bedford/St. Martin's. At Bedford/St. Martin's, these include: development editor Laura Arcari; associate editor Robin Soule; editorial assistant Victoria Royal; executive editor Traci Crowell; director of development Jane Knetzger; publisher for history Mary Dougherty; photo researcher Carole Frohlich; text permissions editor Heather Salus; Katherine Caruana, production editor, with the assistance of Elise Keller and the guidance of managing editor Elizabeth Schaaf and assistant managing editor John Amburg. Other key contributors were designer Cia Boynton, copyeditor Susan Moore, proofreaders Anne True and Angela Morrison, indexer Leoni McVey, and cover designer Donna Dennison. We would also like to thank president Denise Wydra and co-president of Macmillan Higher Education Joan E. Feinberg.

Many of our colleagues at the University of Illinois, the University of Washington, the University of Wisconsin-Milwaukee, and Eastern Illinois University continue to provide information and stimulation, often without even knowing it. We thank them for it. The authors also thank the many students they have taught over the years. Their reactions and opinions helped shape this book. Merry Wiesner-Hanks would, as always, also like to thank her husband Neil, without whom work on this project would not be possible. Clare Haru Crowston thanks her husband Ali, and her children Lili, Reza, and Kian, who are a joyous reminder of the vitality of life that we try to showcase in this book. Roger Beck is thankful to Ann for keeping the home fires burning while he was busy writing and to the World History Association for all past, present, and future contributions to his understanding of world history.

Each of us has benefited from the criticism of his or her co-authors, although each of us assumes responsibility for what he or she has written. We'd like to especially thank the founding authors, John P. McKay, Bennett D. Hill, and John Buckler, for their enduring contributions and for their faith in each of us to carry on their legacy.

Brief Contents

16 The Acceleration of Global Contact 1450–1600   406

17 European Power and Expansion 1500–1750   434

18 New Worldviews and Ways of Life 1540–1790   464

19 Africa and the World 1400–1800   492

20 The Islamic World Powers 1300–1800   518

21 Continuity and Change in East Asia 1400–1800   546

22 Revolutions in the Atlantic World 1775–1815   576

23 The Revolution in Energy and Industry 1760–1850   606

24 Ideologies of Change in Europe 1815–1914   632

25 Africa, Southwest Asia, and the New Imperialism 1800–1914   666

26 Asia in the Era of Imperialism 1800–1914   694

27 Nation Building in the Americas and Australia 1770–1914   720

28 World War and Revolution 1914–1929   750

29 Nationalism in Asia 1914–1939   780

30 The Great Depression and World War II 1929–1945   806

31 Global Recovery and Division Between Superpowers 1945 to the Present   838

32 Independence, Progress, and Conflict in Asia and the Middle East
1945 to the Present   868

33 The Global South: Latin America and Africa 1945 to the Present   896

34 A New Era in World History   924

Index   I-1

Contents

Preface   ix

Maps, Figures, and Tables   xxv

Special Features   xxvii

Versions and Supplements   xxix

How to Use This Book   xxxii

Introduction: The Origins of Modern World Societies   xxxix

16 The Acceleration of Global Contact

1450–1600   406

How did trade link the peoples of Africa, Asia, and Europe prior to 1492?   408
   The Trade World of the Indian Ocean   408
   Peoples and Cultures of the Indian Ocean   409
   Trade with Africa and the Middle East   409
   Genoese and Venetian Middlemen   412

How and why did Europeans undertake voyages of expansion?   412
   Causes of European Expansion   413
   Technology and the Rise of Exploration   414
   The Expanding Portuguese Empire   414
   Christopher Columbus's Voyages to the Americas   416
   Later Explorers   417
   Spanish Conquest in the New World   420

What was the impact of conquest?   422
   Colonial Administration   422
   The Impact of European Settlement on the Lives of Indigenous Peoples   423
   The Columbian Exchange   424
   Sugar and Early Transatlantic Slavery   425
   The Birth of the Global Economy   425

How did expansion shape values and beliefs in Europe and the Americas?   427
   New Ideas About Race   427
   Michel de Montaigne and Cultural Curiosity   428
   William Shakespeare and His Influence   430
   Religious Conversion in the New World   430

Connections   431

Chapter Study Guide   432

Individuals in Society *Zheng He*   410

Listening to the Past *Columbus Describes His First Voyage*   418

Global Trade *Silver*   428

17 European Power and Expansion
1500–1750   434

How did European states respond to the crises of the seventeenth century?   436
    Crises Among Peasants and the Urban Poor   436
    The Return of Serfdom in Eastern Europe   436
    The Thirty Years' War   437
    Achievements in State Building   439

How did the absolutist monarchies of France and Spain fare in this era?   439
    The Foundations of Absolutism   439
    Louis XIV and Absolutism   440
    Life at Versailles   441
    French Finances   442
    Louis XIV's Wars   442
    The Decline of Absolutist Spain   442

How did absolutism develop in Austria, Prussia, and Russia?   444
    The Austrian Habsburgs   445
    Prussia in the Seventeenth Century   445
    The Consolidation of Prussian Absolutism   446
    Mongol Rule in Russia and the Rise of Moscow   447
    The Tsar and His People   448
    The Reforms of Peter the Great   449

Where and why did constitutionalism triumph?   452
    Absolutist Claims in England   452
    Religious Divides and Civil War   452
    The Puritan Protectorate   454
    Restoration of the English Monarchy   454
    Constitutional Monarchy   455
    The Dutch Republic in the Seventeenth Century   455

How did European nations compete to build new colonies in the Americas?   458
    Colonial Expansion of Northern European Powers   458
    Mercantilism and Colonial Wars   459
    Life in the Colonies   459

Connections   461

Chapter Study Guide   462

Listening to the Past   *A German Account of Russian Life*   450

Individuals in Society   *Glückel of Hameln*   456

18 New Worldviews and Ways of Life
1540–1790   464

What was revolutionary about the scientific revolution?   466
    Scientific Thought Through the Early 1500s   466
    Origins of the Scientific Revolution   467
    Copernican Hypothesis   468
    Proving Copernicus Right   468
    Newton's Synthesis   469
    Bacon, Descartes, and the Scientific Method   470
    Medicine, the Body, and Chemistry   471
    Science and Society   471

What were the core principles of the Enlightenment?   472
    The Emergence of the Enlightenment   472
    The Influence of the Philosophes   473
    Enlightenment Across Europe   475
    Urban Culture and Life in the Public Sphere   476
    Late Enlightenment   477

What did enlightened absolutism mean?   478
    Reforms in Prussia, Russia, and Austria   478
    Jewish Life and the Limits of Enlightened Absolutism   479

How did consumerism and the Atlantic economy influence Enlightenment ideas?   482
    A Revolution in Consumption and Daily Life   482
    The Atlantic Economy   483
    Identities and Communities of the Atlantic World   484
    Race and the Enlightenment   488

Connections   489

Chapter Study Guide   490

Individuals in Society   *Moses Mendelssohn and the Jewish Enlightenment*   481

Listening to the Past   *Denis Diderot's "Supplement to Bougainville's Voyage"*   486

19 Africa and the World
1400–1800   492

What kinds of states and societies coexisted in early modern West Africa?   494

    The West Coast: Senegambia and Benin   494

    The Sudan: Songhai, Kanem-Bornu, and Hausaland   496

    The Lives of the People of West Africa   497

    Trade and Industry   499

How did the arrival of outsiders impact East Africa?   500

    Muslim and European Incursions in Ethiopia, ca. 1500–1630   500

    The Swahili City-States and the Arrival of the Portuguese, ca. 1500–1600   501

What were the causes and consequences of the transatlantic slave trade?   503

    The Institution of Slavery in Africa   503

    The Transatlantic Slave Trade   506

    Impact on African Societies   512

Connections   515

Chapter Study Guide   516

Listening to the Past   *Duarte Barbosa on the Swahili City-States*   504

Global Trade   *Slaves*   508

Individuals in Society   *Olaudah Equiano*   510

20 The Islamic World Powers
1300–1800   518

How were the three Islamic empires established?   520

    The Ottoman Turkish Empire's Expansion   520

    The Ottoman Empire's Use of Slaves   523

    The Safavid Empire in Persia   525

    The Mughal Empire in India   526

What characterized the cultural flowering of the Islamic empires?   528

    The Arts   528

    City and Palace Building   529

    Gardens   530

    Intellectual Advances and Religious Trends   532

    Coffeehouses and Their Social Impact   533

How were non-Muslims treated in the Islamic empires?   534

How did shifts in global trading patterns affect the Islamic empires?   536

    European Rivalry for Trade in the Indian Ocean   537

    Merchant Networks in the Islamic Empires   538

    From the British East India Company to the British Empire in India   539

What factors led to the decline of central power in the Islamic empires?   540

Connections   543

Chapter Study Guide   544

Individuals in Society   *Hürrem*   524

Listening to the Past   *Katib Chelebi on Tobacco*   530

21 Continuity and Change in East Asia

1400–1800   546

What sort of state and society developed in China under the Ming?   548
The Rise of Zhu Yuanzhang and the Founding of the Ming Dynasty   548
Problems with the Imperial Institution   549
The Mongols and the Great Wall   550
The Examination Life   551
Everyday Life in Ming China   553
Ming Decline   554

How did the Manchus build on Ming accomplishments?   555
The Rise of the Manchus   555
Competent and Long-Lived Emperors   556
Imperial Expansion   557

How did war and political instability shape Japan in the Middle Ages?   558
Muromachi Culture   558
Civil War   558
The Victors: Nobunaga and Hideyoshi   559

What was life like in Japan during the Tokugawa peace?   559
Tokugawa Government   560
Commercialization and the Growth of Towns   561
The Life of the People in the Edo Period   562

How did the arrival of Europeans change the Asian maritime sphere?   565
Zheng He's Voyages   565
Piracy and Japan's Overseas Adventures   566
Europeans Enter the Scene   567
Christian Missionaries   570
Learning from the West   571
The Shifting International Environment in the Eighteenth Century   572

Connections   573

Chapter Study Guide   574

Individuals in Society *Tan Yunxian, Woman Doctor*   552

Listening to the Past *Keinen's Poetic Diary of the Korea Campaign*   568

22 Revolutions in the Atlantic World

1775–1815   576

What factors combined to spark revolutions in the Atlantic world?   578
Social Change   578
Growing Demands for Liberty and Equality   579
The Seven Years' War   580

How did American colonists forge a new, independent nation?   581
The Origins of the Revolution   582
Independence from Britain   583
Framing the Constitution   583

What were the causes and consequences of the French Revolution?   584
Breakdown of the Old Order   584
The Formation of the National Assembly   585
Popular Uprising and the Rights of Man   586
A Constitutional Monarchy and Its Challenges   589

How and why did the French Revolution take a radical turn?   590
The International Response   590
The Second Revolution and the New Republic   591
Total War and the Terror   592
The Thermidorian Reaction and the Directory   594

How did Napoleon assume control of France and much of Europe?   595
Napoleon's Rule of France   595
Napoleon's Expansion in Europe   596
The Grand Empire and Its End   597

What led to the creation of the independent state of Haiti in 1804?   599
Revolutionary Aspirations in Saint-Domingue   599
The Outbreak of Revolt   600
The War of Haitian Independence   601

Connections   603

Chapter Study Guide   604

Listening to the Past *Abbé de Sieyès, "What Is the Third Estate?"*   588

Individuals in Society *Toussaint L'Ouverture*   602

23 The Revolution in Energy and Industry

1760–1850   606

How and why did Britain industrialize between 1780 and 1850?   608
   Origins of the British Industrial Revolution   608
   The First Factories   609
   The Steam Engine Breakthrough   611
   The Coming of the Railroads   613
   Industry and Population   613

When and how did industrialization spread beyond Britain?   615
   National and International Variations   615
   The Challenge of Industrialization in Continental Europe   616
   Agents of Industrialization   618
   Government Support and Corporate Banking   618
   The Situation Outside of Europe   619

What were the social consequences of industrialization?   620
   The New Class of Factory Owners   620
   The New Factory Workers   621
   Work in Early Factories   622
   Working Families and Children   623
   The Sexual Division of Labor   624
   The Early Labor Movement in Britain   626
   The Impact of Slavery   628

Connections   629

Chapter Study Guide   630

Individuals in Society **Josiah Wedgwood**   612

Listening to the Past **The Testimony of Young Mine Workers**   626

24 Ideologies of Change in Europe

1815–1914   632

How was European conservatism challenged between 1815 and 1848?   634
   The European Balance of Power   634
   Coerced Conservatism After 1815   635
   Liberalism and the Middle Class   635
   The Growing Appeal of Nationalism   637
   The Birth of Socialism   638

What led to the revolutions of 1848 and why did they fail?   639
   Liberal Reform in Great Britain   639
   Revolutions in France   640
   The Revolutions of 1848 in Central Europe   641

How did nation building transform Italy, Germany, and Russia?   643
   Cavour, Garibaldi, and the Unification of Italy   644
   Bismarck and German Unification   645
   The Modernization of Russia   648

How did urbanization impact cities, society, and ideas?   649
   Taming the City   649
   New Social Hierarchies and the Middle Classes   651
   The People and Occupations of the Working Classes   651
   The Changing Family   652
   Science for the Masses   653
   Cultural Shifts   657

How did nationalism and socialism shape politics before 1914?   658
   Trends in Suffrage   659
   The German Empire   659
   Republican France   659
   Great Britain and the Austro-Hungarian Empire   660
   Jewish Emancipation and Modern Anti-Semitism   661
   The Socialist Movement   662

Connections   663

Chapter Study Guide   664

Individuals in Society **Giuseppe Garibaldi**   646

Listening to the Past **Mrs. Beeton's Guide for Running a Victorian Household**   654

25 Africa, Southwest Asia, and the New Imperialism

1800–1914   666

How did slavery, Islam, and imperialism shape Africa's development?   668
  Trade and Social Change   668
  Islamic Revival and Expansion in Africa   669
  The Scramble for Africa, 1880–1914   672
  Southern Africa in the Nineteenth Century   674
  Colonialism's Impact After 1900   675

What were the causes and consequences of European empire building?   677
  Causes of the New Imperialism   677
  A "Civilizing Mission"   680
  Critics of Imperialism   680
  African and Asian Resistance   681

How and why did Ottoman and Egyptian leaders reform their states?   682
  Decline and Reform in the Ottoman Empire   682
  Egypt: From Reform to British Occupation   684

How did Western industrialization change the world economy?   686
  The Rise of Global Inequality   687
  The World Market   687

What explains global migration patterns in this period?   689

Connections   691

Chapter Study Guide   692

Listening to the Past *A French Leader Defends Imperialism*   678

Individuals in Society *Muhammad Ali*   685

Global Trade *Indigo*   688

26 Asia in the Era of Imperialism

1800–1914   694

What were the consequences of British rule for India?   696
  The Evolution of British Rule   696
  The Socioeconomic Effects of British Rule   696
  The British and the Indian Educated Elite   697

Why were most but not all Southeast Asian societies colonized?   699
  The Dutch East Indies   700
  Mainland Southeast Asia   700
  The Philippines   702

What factors contributed to China's decline in the nineteenth century?   702
  The Opium War   702
  Internal Problems   704
  The Self-Strengthening Movement   704
  Republican Revolution   705

How did Japan respond to the challenges posed by the West?   706
  The "Opening" of Japan   707
  The Meiji Restoration   707
  Industrialization   709
  Japan as an Imperial Power   710

Why did people move into and out of Asia in the nineteenth century?   712
  Westerners to Asia   712
  Asian Emigration   713

What common experiences did Asian societies share in this era?   716

Connections   717

Chapter Study Guide   718

Individuals in Society *José Rizal*   701

Listening to the Past *Fukuzawa Yukichi, Escape from Asia*   710

27 Nation Building in the Americas and Australia

1770–1914   720

How did Latin American nations fare after independence?   722
   The Origins of the Revolutions Against Colonial Powers   722
   Resistance, Rebellion, and Independence   725
   The Aftermath of Independence   726
   Neocolonialism and Its Socioeconomic Effects   727
   The Impact of Immigrants from Europe, Asia, and the Middle East   731

How did the United States become a world power?   732
   Manifest Destiny and Its Consequences for Native Americans   733
   Women's Roles in White Settlements   735
   Black Slavery in the South   735
   The Civil War and Its Impact   735
   Industrialization and the Formation of Large Corporations   738
   Immigrants and Their Reception   739

What factors shaped the development of Canada?   740

How did Australia evolve from penal colony to nation?   742
   A Distant Land Turned Penal Colony   742
   An Economy Built on Wool, Gold, and Immigrant Labor   744
   The Shaping of a Government and a National Identity   745

What common forces shaped the Americas and Australia?   745

Connections   747

Chapter Study Guide   748

Listening to the Past *Mary Seacole on Her Early Life*   728

Individuals in Society *Henry Meiggs, Promoter and Speculator*   730

28 World War and Revolution

1914–1929   750

How did European conflicts lead to global war?   752
   The Bismarckian System of Alliances   752
   The Outbreak of War   754
   Stalemate and Slaughter   755
   The War Becomes Global   757

What made World War I a "total war"?   759
   Mobilizing for Total War   759
   The Social Impact   759
   Growing Political Tensions   763

How did war lead to revolution in Russia?   764
   The Fall of Imperial Russia   764
   The Provisional Government   764
   Lenin and the Bolshevik Revolution   765
   Dictatorship and Civil War   766

What were the global consequences of the war?   767
   The End of the War   768
   The Treaty of Versailles   768
   American Rejection of the Versailles Treaty   770

How did leaders seek to re-establish peace and stability?   770
   Germany and the Western Powers   771
   Hope in Foreign Affairs   772
   Hope in Democratic Government   772

How were postwar anxieties reflected in art and science?   773
   Uncertainty in Philosophy and Religion   773
   The New Physics   774
   Freudian Psychology   774
   Twentieth-Century Literature   774
   Modern Architecture, Art, and Music   775
   Movies and Radio   776

Connections   777

Chapter Study Guide   778

Listening to the Past *The Experience of War*   760

Individuals in Society *Vera Brittain*   762

29 Nationalism in Asia
1914–1939   780

How did World War I stimulate nationalism in Asia?   782
　Asian Reaction to the War in Europe   782
　The Mandates System   783
　Nationalism's Appeal   784

What forces shaped nationalism in the Middle East?   784
　The Arab Revolt   786
　The Turkish Revolution   787
　Modernization Efforts in Persia and Afghanistan   790
　Gradual Independence in the Arab States   791
　Arab-Jewish Tensions in Palestine   791

What characterized the Indian independence movement?   792
　British Promises and Repression   792
　The Roots of Militant Nonviolence   793
　Gandhi's Resistance Campaign in India   794

What nationalist struggles emerged in East and Southeast Asia?   795
　The Rise of Nationalist China   795
　China's Intellectual Revolution   797
　From Liberalism to Ultranationalism in Japan   798
　Japan Against China   800
　Striving for Independence in Southeast Asia   802

Connections   803

Chapter Study Guide   804

Listening to the Past *Resolution of the General Syrian Congress at Damascus* 788

Individuals in Society *Ning Lao, a Chinese Working Woman* 799

30 The Great Depression and World War II
1929–1945   806

Why did the Great Depression spread around the world?   808
　The Economic Crisis   808
　Mass Unemployment   809
　The New Deal in the United States   810
　The European Response to the Depression   810
　Worldwide Effects   811

How did totalitarianism differ from conservative authoritarianism?   812
　Conservative Authoritarianism   813
　Radical Totalitarian Dictatorships   813

What characterized Stalin's rule in the Soviet Union?   814
　From Lenin to Stalin   814
　The Five-Year Plans   815
　Life and Culture in Soviet Society   816
　Stalinist Terror and the Great Purges   817

How did Italian fascism develop?   817
　The Seizure of Power   817
　The Regime in Action   818

What were the goals of Hitler and his Nazi regime?   819
　The Roots of Nazism   819
　Hitler's Road to Power   820
　The Nazi State and Society   820
　Hitler's Popularity   821
　Aggression and Appeasement, 1933–1939   822

What led to World War II and how did the Allies prevail?   824
　Hitler's Empire in Europe, 1939–1942   824
　The Holocaust   826
　Japan's Asian Empire   826
　The Grand Alliance   832
　The War in Europe, 1942–1945   832
　The War in the Pacific, 1942–1945   833

Connections   835

Chapter Study Guide   836

Individuals in Society *Primo Levi* 827

Listening to the Past *Ultranationalist Pamphlet for Japanese Students* 828

31 Global Recovery and Division Between Superpowers

1945 to the Present   838

What were the causes of the Cold War? 840
  The Origins of the Cold War 840
  West Versus East 841

How did western Europe recover after World War II, and why did progress stall? 843
  The Postwar Challenge 843
  Building Europe and Decolonization 844
  The Changing Class Structure and Social Reform 845
  Economic and Social Dislocation, 1970–1990 847

How did the Soviet Union dominate eastern Europe in the postwar era? 848
  Stalin's Last Years 848
  Limited De-Stalinization and Stagnation 849
  The Impact of Reform on Everyday Life 849
  The Gorbachev Era 850
  The Revolutions of 1989 851
  The End of the Cold War and Soviet Disintegration 855

What factors shaped social and political developments in postwar America? 856
  America's Economic Boom and Civil Rights Revolution 856
  Youth and the Counterculture 857
  The Vietnam War 858
  Détente and a Return to Cold War Tensions 859

How did Japan become a global power after its defeat in World War II? 859
  Japan's American Revolution 859
  "Japan, Inc." 860
  Japan in the Post–Cold War World 860

What opportunities and challenges did Europe face after the Cold War? 861
  Common Patterns and Problems 861
  Recasting Russia Without Communism 861
  Postcommunist Reconstruction in Eastern Europe 863
  Unity and Identity in Western Europe 863

Connections 865

Chapter Study Guide 866

Global Trade *Oil* 846

Listening to the Past *A Solidarity Leader Speaks from Prison* 852

Individuals in Society *Václav Havel* 854

32 Independence, Progress, and Conflict in Asia and the Middle East

1945 to the Present   868

What explains East Asia's economic success after World War II? 870
  The Communist Victory in China 870
  Mao's China 871
  The Limits of Reform 872
  The Asian "Economic Tigers" 875
  Political and Economic Progress in Southeast Asia 876
  The Reunification of Vietnam 877

How have India, Pakistan, and Bangladesh fared since independence? 877
  The End of British India 878
  Pakistan and the Creation of Bangladesh 880
  India Since Independence 882

How has religion shaped Middle Eastern politics since 1945? 883
  The Arab-Israeli Conflict 884
  The Palestinian Quest for Independence 885
  Egypt: Arab World Leader 887
  A Fractured Lebanon 888
  Challenges to Turkey's Secularism 890
  Revolution and War in Iran and Iraq 890

Connections 893

Chapter Study Guide 894

Individuals in Society *Liu Xiaobo* 874

Listening to the Past *Aung San Suu Kyi, "Freedom from Fear"* 878

Contents   **xxiii**

33 The Global South: Latin America and Africa

1945 to the Present   896

How did Latin American states develop after World War II?   898
    Economic Nationalism in Mexico and Brazil   899
    Communist Revolution in Cuba   900
    From Authoritarianism to Democracy in Latin America   902
    Pan–Latin American Unity   906

What factors influenced decolonization in sub-Saharan Africa?   906
    The Growth of African Nationalism   907
    Achieving Independence with New Leaders   908
    Ghana Shows the Way   908
    French-Speaking Regions   909

What common features characterize independent African states since 1960?   910
    Striving for National Unity   910
    Nigeria, Africa's Giant   912
    The Struggle in Southern Africa   913
    Political Reform in Africa Since 1990   915

How have writers depicted the experience of the emerging world?   920

Connections   921

Chapter Study Guide   922

Individuals in Society *Eva Perón*   904

Listening to the Past *Nelson Mandela, The Struggle for Freedom in South Africa*   916

34 A New Era in World History   924

How has global politics changed since 1989?   926
    The United Nations   926
    Preemptive War in Iraq   927
    Complexity and Violence in a Multipolar World   929
    The Terrorist Threat   930
    Weapons of Mass Destruction   933

What are the consequences of increasing global interdependence?   936
    Multinational Corporations   936
    Industrialization and Modernization   937
    Agriculture and the Green Revolution   938
    The Economics and Politics of Globalization   940

What are the causes and consequences of worldwide urbanization?   942
    Rapid Urbanization   942
    Overcrowding and Shantytowns   942
    Rich and Poor   943
    Urban Migration and the Family   944
    Urbanization and Agriculture   944

How have developments in science and technology changed the world?   945
    The Medical Revolution   945
    Population Change: Balancing the Numbers   945
    Global Epidemics   946
    Environmentalism   947
    Mass Communication   948

What social problems do women and children face?   949
    Women: The Right to Equality   949
    Children: The Right to Childhood   950

Connections   951

Chapter Study Guide   952

Individuals in Society *The Dalai Lama*   928

Listening to the Past *The United Nations Millennium Project Report*   930

Global Trade *Arms*   934

Chapter Endnotes   EN-1

Index   I-1

Maps

Chapter 16

Map 16.1 The Fifteenth-Century Afroeurasian Trading World 411

Map 16.2 Overseas Exploration and Conquest in the Fifteenth and Sixteenth Centuries 415

Map 16.3 Seaborne Trading Empires in the Sixteenth and Seventeenth Centuries 426

Map 16.4 The Global Silver Trade 429

Spot Map Portuguese Expansion into Africa 414

Spot Map Columbus's First Voyage to the New World, 1492–1493 416

Spot Map Invasion of Tenochtitlán, 1519–1521 420

Spot Map The Transatlantic Slave Trade 425

Chapter 17

Map 17.1 Europe After the Thirty Years' War 438

Map 17.2 Europe After the Peace of Utrecht, 1715 444

Map 17.3 The Growth of Austria and Brandenburg-Prussia to 1748 446

Map 17.4 Seventeenth-Century Dutch Commerce 457

Spot Map The Expansion of Russia, to 1725 447

Spot Map The English Civil War, 1642–1649 454

Chapter 18

Map 18.1 The Partition of Poland, 1772–1795 480

Map 18.2 The Atlantic Economy in 1701 485

Spot Map The Pale of Settlement, 1791 479

Chapter 19

Map 19.1 West African Societies, ca. 1500–1800 494

Map 19.2 East Africa in the Sixteenth Century 501

Map 19.3 The International Slave Trade 509

Spot Map West African Trade Routes 499

Spot Map Cape Colony, ca. 1750 506

Spot Map The Slave Coast of West Africa 507

Chapter 20

Map 20.1 The Ottoman Empire at Its Height, 1566 522

Map 20.2 The Safavid Empire, 1587–1629 526

Map 20.3 India, 1707–1805 536

Map 20.4 The Muslim World, ca. 1700 541

Spot Map Empire of Timur, ca. 1405 520

Spot Map The Mughal Empire, 1526–1857 527

Chapter 21

Map 21.1 The Qing Empire, ca. 1800 556

Map 21.2 Tokugawa Japan, 1603–1867 560

Map 21.3 East Asia, ca. 1600 567

Spot Map Ming China, ca. 1600 548

Spot Map Hideyoshi's Campaigns in Japan and Korea, 1537–1598 559

Chapter 22

Map 22.1 European Claims in North America and India Before and After the Seven Years' War, 1755–1763 581

Map 22.2 Napoleonic Europe in 1812 598

Map 22.3 The War of Haitian Independence, 1791–1804 601

Spot Map Loyalist Strength in the Colonies, ca. 1774–1776 583

Spot Map Areas of French Insurrection, 1793 592

Spot Map German Confederation of the Rhine, 1806 596

Chapter 23

Map 23.1 The Industrial Revolution in England, ca. 1850 613

Map 23.2 Continental Industrialization, ca. 1850 617

Spot Map Cottage Industry and Transportation in Eighteenth-Century England 608

Chapter 24

Map 24.1 Europe in 1815 636

Map 24.2 The Unification of Italy, 1859–1870 644

Map 24.3 The Unification of Germany, 1866–1871 647

Spot Map The Crimean War, 1853–1856 648

Spot Map The Russian Revolution of 1905 649

Chapter 25

Map 25.1 The Partition of Africa 671

Map 25.2 The Indigo Trade 689

Spot Map The Struggle for South Africa, 1878 675

Spot Map Ottoman Decline in the Balkans, 1818–1830 682

Spot Map The Suez Canal, 1869 686

Chapter 26

Map 26.1 Asia in 1914 698

Map 26.2 Emigration Out of Asia, 1820–1914 714

Spot Map The Great Mutiny/Great Revolt, 1857 696

Spot Map Chinese Rebellions, 1851–1900 704

Spot Map Japanese Expansion, 1875–1914 712

Chapter 27

Map 27.1 Latin America in ca. 1780 and 1830   724

Map 27.2 Indian Cession of Lands to the United States, 1784–1890   734

Map 27.3 Slavery in the United States, 1861   737

Map 27.4 The Dominion of Canada, 1871   741

Map 27.5 Australia   743

Chapter 28

Map 28.1 European Alliances at the Outbreak of World War I, 1914   752

Map 28.2 The Balkans, 1878–1914   754

Map 28.3 The First World War in Europe   756

Map 28.4 Territorial Changes in Europe After World War I   769

Spot Map The Schlieffen Plan   755

Spot Map The Russian Civil War, 1917–1922   767

Spot Map French Occupation of the Ruhr, 1923–1925   771

Chapter 29

Map 29.1 The Partition of the Ottoman Empire, 1914–1923   785

Map 29.2 The Chinese Communist Movement and the War with Japan, 1927–1938   796

Spot Map Afghanistan Under Amanullah Khan   790

Spot Map India, ca. 1930   794

Spot Map The Spanish-American War in the Philippines, 1898   802

Chapter 30

Map 30.1 The Growth of Nazi Germany, 1933–1939   823

Map 30.2 World War II in Europe and Africa, 1939–1945   825

Map 30.3 World War II in the Pacific   831

Spot Map Italy's Ethiopian Campaign, 1935–1936   822

Spot Map Vichy France, 1940   824

Spot Map The Holocaust, 1941–1945   826

Chapter 31

Map 31.1 Cold War Europe in the 1950s   842

Map 31.2 The Oil Trade, ca. 1900–1975   847

Map 31.3 Russia and the Successor States   855

Map 31.4 The European Union, 2011   864

Spot Map Postwar Territorial Changes in Eastern Europe   841

Spot Map The Korean War, 1950–1953   843

Spot Map The Vietnam War, 1964–1975   858

Chapter 32

Map 32.1 The New States in Asia   870

Map 32.2 The Partition of British India, 1947   880

Map 32.3 Palestine, Israel, and the Middle East   885

Map 32.4 Abrahamic Religions in the Middle East and Surrounding Regions   891

Spot Map Asian "Economic Tigers"   875

Spot Map The 2006 Israel-Lebanon War   889

Chapter 33

Map 33.1 Authoritarian Governments in Latin America   903

Map 33.2 Decolonization in Africa, 1947 to the Present   911

Spot Map Cuba   900

Spot Map South African Native Land Act of 1913   913

Spot Map Second Congo War, 1998 to the Present   919

Chapter 34

Map 34.1 The Arms Trade   935

Map 34.2 The Global Distribution of Wealth, ca. 2010   941

Map 34.3 People Living with HIV/AIDS Worldwide, ca. 2010   947

Spot Map Iraq, ca. 2010   929

Figures and Tables

Figure 19.1 Estimated Slave Imports by Destination, 1501–1866   507

Figure 19.2 The Transatlantic Slave Trade, 1501–1866   514

Thematic Chronology Key Events of the French Revolution   585

Figure 23.1 Railroad Track Mileage, 1890   614

Table 23.1 Per Capita Levels of Industrialization, 1750–1913   616

Thematic Chronology Latin America, ca. 1760–1900   726

Thematic Chronology Key Events of the Russian Revolution   765

Thematic Chronology Events Leading to World War II   830

Thematic Chronology Nationalism in Black Africa   907

Special Features

Listening to the Past

Columbus Describes His First Voyage   418

A German Account of Russian Life   450

Denis Diderot's "Supplement to Bougainville's Voyage"   486

Duarte Barbosa on the Swahili City-States   504

Katib Chelebi on Tobacco   530

Keinen's Poetic Diary of the Korea Campaign   568

Abbé de Sieyès, "What Is the Third Estate?"   588

The Testimony of Young Mine Workers   626

Mrs. Beeton's Guide for Running a Victorian Household   654

A French Leader Defends Imperialism   678

Fukuzawa Yukichi, Escape from Asia   710

Mary Seacole on Her Early Life   728

The Experience of War   760

Resolution of the General Syrian Congress at Damascus   788

Ultranationalist Pamphlet for Japanese Students   828

A Solidarity Leader Speaks from Prison   852

Aung San Suu Kyi, "Freedom from Fear"   878

Nelson Mandela, The Struggle for Freedom in South Africa   916

The United Nations Millennium Project Report   930

Václav Havel   854

Liu Xiaobo   874

Eva Perón   904

The Dalai Llama   928

Global Trade

Silver   428

Slaves   508

Indigo   688

Oil   846

Arms   934

Individuals in Society

Zheng He   410

Glückel of Hameln   456

Moses Mendelssohn and the Jewish Enlightenment   481

Olaudah Equiano   510

Hürrem   524

Tan Yunxian, Woman Doctor   552

Toussaint L'Ouverture   602

Josiah Wedgwood   612

Giuseppe Garibaldi   646

Muhammad Ali   685

José Rizal   701

Henry Meiggs, Promoter and Speculator   730

Vera Brittain   762

Ning Lao, a Chinese Working Woman   799

Primo Levi   827

Adopters of *Understanding World Societies: A Brief History* and their students have access to abundant extra resources, including documents, presentation and testing materials, the acclaimed Bedford Series in History and Culture volumes, and much much more. See below for more information, visit the book's catalog site at bedfordstmartins.com/mckayworldunderstanding/catalog, or contact your local Bedford/St. Martin's sales representative.

Get the Right Version for Your Class

To accommodate different course lengths and course budgets, *Understanding World Societies: A Brief History* is available in several different versions and e-book formats, which are available at a substantial discount.

- Combined edition (Chapters 1–34) — available in paperback and e-book formats
- Volume 1: To 1600 (Chapters 1–16) — available in paperback and e-book formats
- Volume 2: Since 1450 (Chapters 16–34) — available in paperback and e-book formats

The online, interactive **Bedford e-Book** can be examined or purchased at a discount at bedfordstmartins.com/ebooks. Your students can also purchase *Understanding World Societies* in other popular e-book formats for computers, tablets, and e-readers.

Online Extras for Students

The book's companion site at bedfordstmartins.com/mckayworldunderstanding gives students a way to read, write, and study by providing plentiful quizzes and activities, study aids, and history research and writing help.

FREE *Online Study Guide*. Available at the companion site, this popular resource provides students with quizzes and activities for each chapter, including multiple-choice self-tests that focus on important concepts; flashcards that test students' knowledge of key terms; timeline activities that emphasize causal relationships; and map quizzes intended to strengthen students' geography skills. Instructors can monitor students' progress through an online Quiz Gradebook or receive e-mail updates.

FREE *Research, Writing, and Anti-plagiarism Advice*. Available at the companion site, Bedford's **History Research and Writing Help** includes the textbook authors' **Suggested Reading** organized by chapter; **History Research and Reference Sources**, with links to history-related databases, indexes, and journals; **More Sources and How to Format a History Paper**, with clear advice on how to integrate primary and secondary sources into research papers and how to cite and format sources correctly; **Build a Bibliography**, a Web-based tool known as The Bedford Bibliographer that generates bibliographies in four commonly used documentation styles; and **Tips on Avoiding Plagiarism**, an online tutorial that reviews the consequences of plagiarism and features exercises to help students practice integrating sources and recognize acceptable summaries.

Resources for Instructors

Bedford/St. Martin's has developed a rich array of teaching resources for this book and for this course. They range from lecture and presentation materials and assessment tools to

course management options. Most can be downloaded or ordered at bedfordstmartins
.com/mckayworldunderstanding/catalog.

HistoryClass for Understanding World Societies, now with LearningCurve. HistoryClass, a Bedford/St. Martin's Online Course Space, puts the online resources available with this textbook in one convenient and completely customizable course space. There you and your students can access an interactive e-book and primary source reader; maps, images, documents, and links; chapter review quizzes, including **LearningCurve**, a game-like adaptive quizzing system that provides students with immediate feedback; interactive multimedia exercises; and research and writing help. In HistoryClass you can get all of our premium content and tools and assign, rearrange, and mix them with your own resources. For more information, visit yourhistoryclass.com.

Bedford Coursepack for Blackboard, WebCT, Desire2Learn, Angel, Sakai, or Moodle. We have free content to help you integrate our rich materials into your course management system. Registered instructors can download coursepacks easily and with no strings attached. The coursepack for *Understanding World Societies: A Brief History* includes book-specific content as well as our most popular free resources. Visit bedfordstmartins.com/coursepacks to see a demo, find your version, or download your coursepack.

Instructor's Resource Manual. The instructor's manual offers both experienced and first-time instructors tools for preparing lectures and running discussions. It includes chapter review material, teaching strategies, and a guide to chapter-specific supplements available for the text.

Computerized Test Bank. The test bank includes a mix of fresh, carefully crafted multiple-choice, matching, short-answer, and essay questions for each chapter. It also contains the Review, Visual Activity, Map Activity, Individuals in Society, and Listening to the Past questions from the textbook and model answers for each. The questions appear in Microsoft Word format and in easy-to-use test bank software that allows instructors to easily add, edit, re-sequence, and print questions and answers. Instructors can also export questions into a variety of formats, including WebCT and Blackboard.

The Bedford Lecture Kit: **PowerPoint Maps, Images, Lecture Outlines, and i>clicker Content**. Look good and save time with *The Bedford Lecture Kit*. These presentation materials are downloadable individually from the Instructor Resources tab at bedfordstmartins.com/mckayworldunderstanding/catalog and are available on ***The Bedford Lecture Kit*** **Instructor's Resource CD-ROM**. They provide ready-made and fully customizable PowerPoint multimedia presentations that include lecture outlines with embedded maps, figures, and selected images from the textbook and extra background for instructors. Also available are maps and selected images in JPEG and PowerPoint formats; content for i>clicker, a classroom response system, in Microsoft Word and PowerPoint formats; the Instructor's Resource Manual in Microsoft Word format; and outline maps in PDF format for quizzing or handing out. All files are suitable for copying onto transparency acetates.

Make History — **Free Documents, Maps, Images, and Web Sites**. *Make History* combines the best Web resources with hundreds of maps and images, to make it simple to find the source material you need. Browse the collection of thousands of resources by course or by topic, date, and type. Each item has been carefully chosen and helpfully annotated to make it easy to find exactly what you need. Available at bedfordstmartins .com/makehistory.

Videos and Multimedia. A wide assortment of videos and multimedia CD-ROMs on various topics in world history is available to qualified adopters through your Bedford/St. Martin's sales representative.

Package and Save Your Students Money

For information on free packages and discounts up to 50%, visit bedfordstmartins.com /mckayworldunderstanding/catalog, or contact your local Bedford/St. Martin's sales representative.

Bedford e-Book. The e-book for this title can be packaged with the print text at a discount.

Sources of World Societies, **Second Edition**. This two-volume primary source collection provides a rich selection of sources to accompany *Understanding World Societies: A Brief History*. Each chapter features five to six written and visual sources that present history from well-known figures and ordinary individuals alike. A Viewpoints feature highlights two or three sources that address the same topic from different perspectives. Document headnotes and reading and discussion questions promote student understanding. Available free when packaged with the print text.

Sources of World Societies e-Book. The reader is also available as an e-book. When packaged with the print or electronic version of the textbook, it is available for free.

The Bedford Series in History and Culture. More than one hundred titles in this highly praised series combine first-rate scholarship, historical narrative, and important primary documents for undergraduate courses. Each book is brief, inexpensive, and focused on a specific topic or period. For a complete list of titles, visit bedfordstmartins .com/history/series. Package discounts are available.

Rand McNally Historical Atlas of the World. This collection of over seventy full-color maps illustrates the eras and civilizations of world history from the emergence of human societies to the present. Available for $3.00 when packaged with the print text.

The Bedford Glossary for World History. This handy supplement for the survey course gives students historically contextualized definitions for hundreds of terms — from *abolitionism* to *Zoroastrianism* — that they will encounter in lectures, reading, and exams. Available free when packaged with the print text.

World History Matters: A Student Guide to World History Online. Based on the popular "World History Matters" Web site produced by the Center for History and New Media, this unique resource, edited by Kristin Lehner (The Johns Hopkins University), Kelly Schrum (George Mason University), and T. Mills Kelly (George Mason University), combines reviews of 150 of the most useful and reliable world history Web sites with an introduction that guides students in locating, evaluating, and correctly citing online sources. Available free when packaged with the print text.

Trade Books. Titles published by sister companies Hill and Wang; Farrar, Straus and Giroux; Henry Holt and Company; St. Martin's Press; Picador; and Palgrave Macmillan are available at a 50% discount when packaged with Bedford/St. Martin's textbooks. For more information, visit bedfordstmartins.com/tradeup.

A Pocket Guide to Writing in History. This portable and affordable reference tool by Mary Lynn Rampolla, now also available as a searchable e-book, provides reading, writing, and research advice useful to students in all history courses. Concise yet comprehensive advice on approaching typical history assignments, developing critical reading skills, writing effective history papers, conducting research, using and documenting sources, and avoiding plagiarism — enhanced with practical tips and examples throughout — have made this slim reference a bestseller. Package discounts are available.

A Student's Guide to History. This complete guide to success in any history course provides the practical help students need to be effective. Author Jules Benjamin introduces students to the nature of the discipline, teaches a wide range of skills from preparing for exams to approaching common writing assignments, and explains the research and documentation process with plentiful examples. Package discounts are available.

How to use this book to figure out what's really important.

16

The Acceleration of Global Contact

1450–1600

The **chapter title** tells you the subject of the chapter and identifies the time span that will be covered.

The **chapter introduction** identifies the most important themes, events, and people that will be explored in the chapter.

Before 1500 Europeans were relatively marginal players in a centuries-old trading system that linked Africa, Asia, and Europe. Elite classes everywhere prized Chinese porcelains and silks, while wealthy Chinese wanted ivory and black slaves from East Africa and exotic goods and peacocks from India. African people wanted textiles from India and cowrie shells from the Maldives. Europeans craved spices and silks, but they had few desirable goods to offer their trading partners.

The Indian Ocean was the locus of these desires and commercial exchanges, which sparked competition among Arab, Persian, Turkish, Indian, African, Chinese, and European merchants and adventurers. They fought each other for the trade that brought great wealth. They also jostled with Muslim scholars, Buddhist teachers, and Christian missionaries, who competed for the religious adherence of the peoples of Sumatra, Java, Borneo, and the Philippine Islands.

The European search for better access to Asian trade goods led to a new overseas empire in the Indian Ocean and the accidental discovery of the Western Hemisphere. With this discovery South and North America soon joined an international network of trade centers and political empires, which Europeans came to dominate. The era of globalization had begun, creating new forms of cultural exchange, assimilation, conversion, and resistance. Europeans sought to impose their cultural values on the peoples they encountered while struggling to comprehend them and their societies. The Age of Discovery from 1450 to 1650, as the time of these encounters is known, laid the foundations for the modern world as we know it today.

Mexica Noble This image from the early-seventeenth-century indigenous *Codex Ixtlilxochitl* shows a Mexica noble holding flowers and a tube of tobacco in his right hand. His jewelry and decorated cape emphasize his wealth and social standing. (Codex Ixtlilxochitl, Facsimile edition by ADEVA, Graz, Austria)

Memorizing facts and dates for a history class won't get you very far. That's because history isn't just about "facts." It's also about understanding cause and effect and the significance of people, places, and events from the past that still have relevance to your world today. This textbook is designed to help you focus on what's truly significant in the history of world societies and to give you practice in thinking like a historian.

Chapter Preview

▶ How did trade link the peoples of Africa, Asia, and Europe prior to 1492?

▶ How and why did Europeans undertake voyages of expansion?

▶ What was the impact of conquest?

▶ How did expansion shape values and beliefs in Europe and the Americas?

The **Chapter Preview** lists the questions that open each new section of the chapter and will be addressed in turn on the following pages. You should think about answers to these as you read.

Each section has tools that help you focus on what's important.

How did trade link the peoples of Africa, Asia, and Europe prior to 1492?

Historians now recognize that a type of world economy, known as the Afroeurasian trade world, linked the products and people of Europe, Asia, and Africa in the fifteenth century. Prior to 1492, the West was not the dominant player in world trade. Nevertheless, wealthy Europeans were eager consumers of luxury goods from the East, which they received through Venetian and Genoese middlemen.

The Trade World of the Indian Ocean

The Indian Ocean was the center of the Afroeurasian trade world, serving as a crossroads for commercial and cultural exchanges between China, India, the Middle East, Africa, and Europe (Map 16.1). From the seventh through the fourteenth centuries, the volume of this trade steadily increased, declining only during the years of the Black Death.

Merchants congregated in a series of multicultural, cosmopolitan port cities strung around the Indian Ocean. Most of these cities had some form of autonomous self-government, and mutual self-interest had largely limited violence and attempts to monopolize trade. The most developed area of this commercial web was made up of the ports surrounding the South China Sea. In the fifteenth century the port of Malacca became a great commercial entrepôt (AHN-truh-poh), a trading post to which goods were shipped for storage while awaiting redistribution to other places.

The Mongol emperors opened the doors of China to the West, encouraging Europeans to do business there. After the Mongols fell to the Ming Dynasty in 1368, China entered a period of agricultural and commercial expansion, population growth, and urbanization. Historians agree that China had the most advanced economy in the world until at least the start of the eighteenth century.

China also took the lead in exploration, sending Admiral Zheng He's fleet as far west as Egypt. (See "Individuals in Society: Zheng He," page 410.) From 1405 to 1433, each of his seven expeditions involved hundreds of ships and tens of thousands of men. The purpose of the voyages was primarily diplomatic, to enhance China's prestige and seek tribute-paying alliances. The voyages came to a sudden halt after the deaths of Zheng and the emperor who initiated his voyages, probably due to court opposition to their high cost and contact with foreign peoples.

By ending large-scale exploration on China's part, this decision marked a turning point in history. Nonetheless, Zheng He's voyages left a legacy of increased Chinese trading in the South China Sea and Indian Ocean. Following Zheng He's voyages, tens of thousands of Chinese emigrated to the Philippines, where they acquired commercial dominance of the island of Luzon by 1600.

Another center of Indian Ocean trade was India, the crucial link between the Persian Gulf and the Southeast Asian and East Asian trade networks. Trade among ports bordering the Indian Ocean was revived in the Middle Ages by Arab merchants who circumnavigated India on their way to trade in the South China Sea. The need for stopovers led to the establishment of trading posts at Gujarat and on the Malabar coast, where the cities of Calicut and Quilon became thriving commercial centers.

The inhabitants of India's Coromandel coast traditionally looked to Southeast Asia, where they had ancient trading and cultural ties. Hinduism and Buddhism arrived in Southeast Asia from India during the Middle Ages, and a brisk trade between Southeast Asian and Coromandel port cities persisted from that time until the arrival of the Portuguese in the sixteenth century. India it system. Most of the world's pepper was grown in India, and Indian cotton and silk textiles were also highly prized.

Peoples and Cultures of the Indian Ocean

Indian Ocean trade connected peoples from the Malay Peninsula (the southern extremity of the Asian continent), India, China, and East Africa, among whom there was an enormous variety of languages, cultures, and religions. In spite of this diversity, certain sociocultural similarities linked these peoples, especially in Southeast Asia.

For example, by the fifteenth century, inhabitants of what we call Indonesia, Malaysia, the Philippines, and the many islands in between all spoke languages of the Austronesian family, reflecting continuing interactions among them. A common environment led to a diet based on rice, fish, palms, and palm wine. In comparison to India, China, or even Europe after the Black Death, Southeast Asia was sparsely populated. People were concentrated in port cities and in areas of intense rice cultivation.

Another difference between Southeast Asia and India, China, and Europe was the higher status of women in the region. Women took the primary role in planting and harvesting rice, giving them authority and economic power. At marriage, which typically occurred around age twenty, the groom paid the bride (or sometimes her family) a sum of money called bride wealth, which remained under her control. This practice was in sharp contrast to the Chinese, Indian, and European dowry, which came under the husband's control. Property was administered jointly, in contrast to the Chinese principle and Indian practice that wives had no say in the disposal of family property. All children, regardless of gender, inherited equally.

Respect for women carried over to the commercial sphere. Women participated in business as partners and independent entrepreneurs, even undertaking long commercial sea voyages. When Portuguese and Dutch men settled in the region and married local women, their wives continued to play important roles in trade and commerce.

In contrast to most parts of the world other than Africa, Southeast Asian peoples had an accepting attitude toward premarital sexual activity, and no premium was placed on virginity at marriage. Divorce carried no social stigma, and it was easy if a pair proved incompatible. Either the woman or the man could initiate a divorce, and common property and children were divided.

Trade with Africa and the Middle East

On the east coast of Africa, Swahili-speaking city-states engaged in the Indian Ocean trade, exchanging ivory, rhinoceros horn, tortoise shells, copra (dried coconut), and slaves for textiles, spices, cowrie shells, porcelain, and other goods. Peopled by confident and urbane merchants, East African cities were known for their prosperity and culture.

Mansa Musa This detail from the Catalan Atlas of 1375 depicts a king of Mali, Mansa Musa, who was legendary for his wealth in gold. European desires for direct access to the trade in sub-Saharan gold helped inspire Portuguese exploration of the west coast of Africa in the fifteenth century. (Bridgeman-Giraudon/Art Resource, NY)

Chapter Chronology

1450–1650	Age of Discovery
1492	Columbus lands on San Salvador
1494	Treaty of Tordesillas ratified
1518	Atlantic slave trade begins
1519–1521	Spanish conquest of Aztec capital of Tenochtitlán
1533	Pizarro conquers Inca Empire
1571	Spanish found port of Manila in the Philippines
1580	Michel de Montaigne's *Essays* published
1602	Dutch East India Company established

The **Chapter Chronology** shows the sequence of events and underlying developments in the chapter.

bride wealth In early modern Southeast Asia, a sum of money the groom paid the bride or her family at the time of marriage, in contrast to the husband's control of dowry in China, India, and Europe.

Key terms in the margins give you background on important people, ideas, and events. Use these for reference while you read, but also think about which are emphasized and why they matter.

The Chapter Study Guide provides a process that will build your understanding and your historical skills.

Visit the FREE Online Study Guide to do these steps online and to check how much you've learned.

Chapter 16 Study Guide

To do these exercises online, go to bedfordstmartins.com/mckayworldunderstanding.

STEP 1
Identify the key terms and explain their significance.

Step 1

GETTING STARTED

Below are basic terms about this period in global history. Can you identify each term below and explain why it matters?

TERMS	WHO (OR WHAT) AND WHEN	WHY IT MATTERS
bride wealth, p. 409		
caravel, p. 414		
Ptolemy's *Geography*, p. 414		
Treaty of Tordesillas, p. 418		
conquistador, p. 420		
Mexica Empire, p. 420		
Inca Empire, p. 422		
viceroyalties, p. 423		
encomienda system, p. 423		
Columbian exchange, p. 424		

STEP 2
Analyze differences and similarities among ideas, events, people, or societies discussed in the chapter.

Step 2

MOVING BEYOND THE BASICS

The exercise below requires a more advanced understanding of the chapter material. Examine the nature and impact of Spanish exploration and conquest in the Americas by filling in the chart below with descriptions of the motives behind Spanish expansion across the Atlantic. Next, identify key Spanish conquests and discoveries and the institutions of Spanish rule in the Americas. Finally, describe the impact of Spanish conquest in the New World and Europe. When you are finished, consider the following questions: How do the motives you listed help explain the course of Spanish expansion in the New World? Were the ambitions of the men who carried out Spain's conquests always consistent with those of the crown? What intended and unintended consequences resulted from Spanish expansion?

MOTIVES	CONQUESTS AND DISCOVERIES	INSTITUTIONS OF SPANISH RULE	IMPACT IN THE NEW WORLD AND EUROPE

Step 3

PUTTING IT ALL TOGETHER

Now that you've reviewed key elements of the chapter, take a step back and try to see the big picture. Remember to use specific examples from the chapter in your answers.

STEP 3
Answer the big-picture questions using specific examples or evidence from the chapter.

THE AFROEURASIAN TRADE WORLD BEFORE COLUMBUS

- Which states were at the center of global trade prior to 1492? Why?
- Why were Europeans at a trading disadvantage prior to 1492? How did geography limit European participation in world trade? What role did Europe's economy and material culture play in this context?

DISCOVERY AND CONQUEST

- In your opinion, what was the most important motive behind European expansion? What evidence can you provide to support your position?
- What was the Columbian exchange? How did it transform both Europe and the Americas?

CHANGING VALUES AND BELIEFS

- How did European expansion give rise to new ideas about race?
- How did expansion complicate Europeans' understanding of themselves and their place in the world?

LOOKING BACK, LOOKING AHEAD

- If Europe was at the periphery of the global trading system prior to 1492, where was it situated by the middle of the sixteenth century? What had changed? What had not?
- What connections can you make between our own experience of globalization in the twenty-first century and the experience of globalization in the sixteenth century? In what ways are the experiences similar? In what ways do they differ?

In Your Own Words Imagine that you must explain Chapter 16 to someone who hasn't read it. What would be the most important points to include and why?

ACTIVE RECITATION
Explain the important points in your own words to make sure you have a firm grasp of the chapter material.

433

The Origins of Modern World Societies

World historians increasingly begin their exploration of the human past millions of years ago, when in eastern Africa humans evolved from a primate ancestor. Humans migrated out of Africa in several waves, walking along coasts and over land, eventually spreading across much of the earth. Their tools were initially multipurpose sharpened stones and sticks, but gradually they invented more specialized tools that enabled them to obtain food more easily, make clothing, build shelters, and decorate their surroundings. Environmental changes, such as the advance and retreat of the glaciers, shaped life dramatically.

The Earliest Human Societies, to 2500 B.C.E.

Studying the physical remains of the past, scholars constructed a model of time and gave labels to eras according to the primary materials out of which tools that survived were made. (Constructing models of time is called "periodization.") Thus the earliest human era became the Stone Age, the next era the Bronze Age, and the next the Iron Age. They further divided the Stone Age into the Old Stone Age, or Paleolithic, during which people used stone, bone, and other natural products to make tools, and they gained food largely by foraging, that is, by gathering plant products, trapping or catching small animals and birds, and hunting larger prey. This was followed by the New Stone Age, or Neolithic, which saw the beginning of agricultural and animal domestication. People around the world adopted agriculture at various times, though some never did, but the transition between the Paleolithic and the Neolithic is usually set at about 9000 B.C.E., the point at which agriculture was first developed.

In the Paleolithic period, people lived in small groups of related individuals, moving through the landscape in the search for food. Most had few material possessions, and social and gender hierarchies were probably much less pronounced than they would become later. Beginning around 50,000 B.C.E. people in many parts of the world began to decorate their surroundings and the objects they made, often with vivid representations of animals and people, and sometimes with symbols. These, and careful burials of the dead, suggest that people had developed ideas about supernatural or spiritual forces beyond the visible material world.

Beginning about 9000 B.C.E. people living in the Near East, and then elsewhere, began to plant seeds and raise certain animals, selectively breeding both plants and animals to make them more useful to humans. This domestication of plants and animals, called the Agricultural Revolution, was the most important change in human history. Crop-raising began as horticulture, in which people—often women—used hand tools to plant and harvest. Animal domestication began with sheep and goats, which were often herded from place to place so that they could eat the available vegetation, an economic system called pastoralism. The domestication of large animals such as cattle and water buffalo led to plow agriculture, through which humans could raise much more food. Agriculture required more labor than did foraging, but it allowed the human population to grow far more quickly.

The division of labor that plow agriculture required led to growing social hierarchies between those who could afford the new tools and products and those who could not. Plow agriculture also strengthened differentiation based on gender. Men became more associated with the world beyond the household and women with the domestic realm. Neolithic agricultural communities developed technologies to meet their needs, including pottery, cloth-weaving, and wheeled vehicles, and they often traded with one another for products that they could not obtain locally. In some parts of the world, production and trade included copper and bronze, although most tools continued to be made of stone, bone, and wood.

Although today's complex world seems very different from that of the earliest human societies, some aspects of life in the Neolithic, or even the Paleolithic, were very slow to change. Foraging, horticulture, pastoralism, and agriculture have been the primary economic activities of most people throughout the entire history of the world. Though today there are only a few foraging groups in very isolated areas, there are significant numbers of horticulturalists and pastoralists, and just a century ago the vast majority of the world's people still made their living directly through agriculture. The social patterns set in early agricultural societies—with most of the population farming the land, and a small number of elite who lived off their labor—lasted for millennia.

The Ancient World, 3500 B.C.E.–500 C.E.

Ten thousand years ago, humans were living in most parts of the planet. They had designed technologies to meet the challenges presented by deep forests and jungles, steep mountains, and blistering deserts. As the climate changed, they adapted, building boats to cross channels created by melting glaciers, and finding new sources of food when old sources were no longer plentiful. In some places the new sources included domesticated plants and animals, which allowed people to live in much closer proximity to one another than they had as foragers.

That close proximity created opportunities, as larger groups of people pooled their knowledge to deal with life's challenges, but it also created problems. Human history from that point on can be seen as a response to these opportunities, challenges, and conflicts. As small villages grew into cities, people continued to develop technologies and systems to handle new issues. They created structures of governance based on something beyond the kin group to control their more complex societies, along with military forces and taxation systems to support the structures of governance. In some places they invented writing to record taxes, inventories, and payments, and they later put writing to other uses, including the preservation of stories, traditions, and history.

Writing, first developed around 3000 B.C.E., was perhaps the most important of these new technologies. Written sources provide a wider range of information about past societies than is available from physical evidence alone, which means that we know much more about the societies that left written records than about those that did not. Writing was developed to meet the needs of the more complex urban societies that are often referred to as civilizations, and particularly to meet the needs of the state, a new structure of governance distinct from tribes and kinship groups. In states, a small share of the population is able to coerce resources out of everyone else, and leaders gain and maintain power through organized violence, bureaucracies, systems of taxation, and written laws. These laws generally created more elaborate social and gender hierarchies.

Mesopotamia and Egypt

States first developed in Mesopotamia, the land between the Euphrates and Tigris Rivers. Starting in the southern part of Mesopotamia known as Sumer, sustained agriculture reliant on irrigation resulted in larger populations, a division of labor, and the growth of cities. Priests and rulers invented ways to control and organize these complex societies, including armies, taxation systems, and cuneiform writing. Conquerors from the north unified Mesopotamian city-states into larger empires and spread Mesopotamian culture over a large area. The most significant of these was the Babylonian empire, which under King Hammurabi in 1790 B.C.E. developed a written code of law and expanded trade connections.

During the third millennium B.C.E., a period known as the Old Kingdom, Egypt grew into a cohesive state under a single ruler in the valley of the Nile, which provided rich farmland and an avenue of communication. The Egyptians developed powerful be-

The Golden Calf According to the Bible, Moses descended from Mount Sinai, where he had received the Ten Commandments, to find the Hebrews worshipping a golden calf, which was against Yahweh's laws. In July 1990 an American archaeological team found this model of a gilded calf inside a pot. The figurine, which dates to about 1550 B.C.E., is strong evidence for the existence of the cult represented by the calf in Palestine. (Harvard Semitic Museum, Ashkelon Excavations)

liefs in life after death, and the focal point of religious and political life was the pharaoh, a god-king who commanded the wealth, resources, and people of Egypt. For long stretches of history Egypt was prosperous and secure in the fertile Nile Valley, although at times various groups migrated in seeking better lives or invaded and conquered. Very often these newcomers adopted aspects of Egyptian religion, art, and politics, and the Egyptians adopted aspects of the newcomers' cultures, such as the techniques for making and casting bronze of the Hyksos. During the period known as the New Kingdom (ca. 1550–1070 B.C.E.), warrior-pharaohs expanded their power beyond the Nile Valley and created the first Egyptian empire, during which they first fought and then allied with the iron-using Hittites. After the collapse of the New Kingdom, the Nubian rulers of Kush conquered Egypt, and another group, the Phoenicians, came to dominate trade in the Mediterranean, spreading a letter alphabet.

For several centuries after the collapse of New Kingdom Egypt, a Semitic people known as the Hebrews or the Israelites controlled a small state on the western end of the Fertile Crescent. Their most important legacy was not political, but rather a new form of religious belief, Judaism, based on the worship of a single all-powerful god, Yahweh. The Hebrews wrote down their religious ideas, traditions, laws, advice literature, prayers, hymns, history, and prophecies in a series of books, which came to define the Hebrews as a people. This group of books, the Hebrew Bible, describes the Covenant between Yahweh and the Hebrew people. It sets out laws and traditions that structured Hebrew society and family life. Reverence for these written texts was passed from Judaism to the other Western monotheistic religions that grew from it, Christianity and Islam.

In the ninth century B.C.E. the Assyrians began a rise to power from northern Mesopotamia, creating an empire by means of often brutal military conquest. Assyria's success was also due to sophisticated, farsighted, and effective military tactics, technical skills, and organization. From a base in what is now southern Iran, the Persians established an even larger empire, developing effective institutions of government and building roads. Though conquerors, the Persians, unlike the Assyrians, usually respected their subjects and allowed them to practice their native customs, traditions, and religions. Around 600 B.C.E. a new religion based on the teachings of the prophet Zoroaster grew in Persia. This religion emphasized the individual's responsibility to choose between good and evil.

The Greeks

The people of ancient Greece developed a culture that fundamentally shaped the civilization of the western part of Eurasia. The Greeks were the first in the Mediterranean and neighboring areas to explore most of the philosophical questions that still concern thinkers today. Going beyond mythmaking, the Greeks strove to understand the world in logical, rational terms. The result was the birth of philosophy and science, subjects as important to many Greeks as religion. Drawing on their day-by-day experiences, the Greeks also developed the concept of politics, and their contributions to literature still fertilize intellectual life today.

The history of the Greeks is divided into two broad periods: the Hellenic, roughly the time between the founding of the first complex societies in the area that is now the Greek islands and mainland, about 3500 B.C.E., and the rise of the kingdom of Macedonia in the north of Greece in 338 B.C.E.; and the Hellenistic, the years from the reign of Alexander the Great (336–323 B.C.E.) through the spread of Greek culture from Spain to India (ca. 100 B.C.E.). During the Hellenic period Greeks developed a distinctive form of city-state known as the polis and made lasting cultural and intellectual achievements. During the Hellenistic period Macedonian and Greek armies defeated the Persian Empire and built new cities and kingdoms. During their conquests they blended their ideas and traditions with those of the societies they encountered, creating a vibrant culture.

In its earliest history, Greece's mountainous terrain and lack of navigable rivers led to political fragmentation. The Greeks developed the independent city-state, known as the polis, in which individuals governed themselves without elaborate political machinery. The two most important polises were Sparta and Athens, which formed new social and political structures. Sparta created a military state in which men remained in the army most of their lives, and women concentrated on raising healthy soldiers. After much social conflict, Athens created a democracy in which male citizens both voted for their leaders and had a direct voice in an assembly. As was the case in all democracies in ancient Greece, women, slaves, and outsiders could not be citizens.

In the classical period, between 500 and 336 B.C.E., Greek civilization reached its highest peak in politics, thought, and art, even as it engaged in violent conflicts. The Greeks successfully defended themselves from Persian invasions but nearly destroyed themselves in the Peloponnesian War, which pitted Sparta and its allies against Athens and its allies. In the last half of the fifth century B.C.E. the brilliant Athenian leader Pericles turned Athens into the showplace of Greece by sponsoring the building of temples and other buildings. In other artistic developments, wealthy Athenians paid for theater performances in which dramatists used their art in attempts to portray, understand, and resolve life's basic conflicts. This period also saw the rise of philosophy; and Socrates, Plato, and Aristotle began a broad examination of the universe and the place of humans in it.

In the middle of the fourth century B.C.E. the Greek city-states were conquered by King Philip II and his son Alexander, rulers of Macedonia to the north of Greece. A brilliant military leader, Alexander conquered the entire Persian Empire, along with many territories to the east of Persia. He also founded new cities in which Greek and local populations mixed. His successors continued to build cities and colonies, which became powerful instruments in the spread of Greek culture and in the blending of Greek traditions and ideas with those of other peoples. The mixing of peoples in the Hellenistic era influenced religion, philosophy, and science. In the scholarly realm, advances were made in mathematics, astronomy, and mechanical design.

The Greek world was largely conquered by the Romans, and the various Hellenistic monarchies became part of the Roman Empire. In cultural terms the lines of conquest were reversed: the Romans derived their alphabet from the Greek alphabet, though they changed the letters somewhat. Roman statuary was modeled on Greek, and it was often, in fact, made by Greek sculptors, who found ready customers among wealthy Romans. Furthermore, the major Roman gods and goddesses were largely the same as Greek ones, though they had different names. The influence of the ancient Greeks was not limited to the Romans. Art and thought in northern India was shaped by the blending of Greek and Buddhist traditions. Later during the Renaissance, European thinkers and writers made conscious attempts to return to classical ideals in art, literature, and philosophy. These influences continued in America when political leaders from the Revolutionary era on decided that important government buildings should be modeled on the Parthenon or other temples, complete with marble statuary of their own heroes.

The Romans

Like the Persians under Cyrus and the Macedonians under Alexander, the Romans conquered vast territories. Their singular achievement lay in their ability to incorporate conquered peoples into the Roman system. Roman history is usually divided into two periods. The first is the republic (509–27 B.C.E.), the age in which Rome grew from a small group of cities in the middle of the Italian peninsula to a state that ruled much of the

Mediterranean. The second period is the empire (27 B.C.E.–476 C.E.), when the republican constitution gave way to rule by a single individual.

In its earliest development, Roman culture was influenced by the Etruscans, people who established permanent settlements in northern and central Italy. The Etruscans introduced Romans to urbanism, industry, trade, and the alphabet. In 509 B.C.E. the Romans won independence from Etruscan rule and continued to expand their territories. They also established a republic, which functioned through a shared government of the people directed by the senate, summarized by the expression SPQR — *senatus populusque Romanus*, meaning "the Roman senate and people." In the resolution to a social conflict known as the Struggle of the Orders, nobles and ordinary people created a state administered by magistrates elected from the entire population and established a uniform law code.

In a series of wars the Romans conquered the Mediterranean, creating an overseas empire that brought them unheard of power and wealth. Yet social unrest came in the wake of the war, opening unprecedented opportunities for ambitious generals who wanted to rule Rome like an empire. Civil war ensued, and it appeared as if the great politician and general Julius Caesar would emerge victorious, but he was assassinated by a group of senators. After his assassination and another period of civil war, his grand-nephew Augustus finally restored peace and order to Rome, and then he assumed control as a single individual.

Augustus's success in creating solid political institutions was tested by the ineptness of some leaders who followed him, but later in the first century C.E. Rome entered a period of political stability, prosperity, and relative peace that lasted until the end of the second century C.E. During this period, later dubbed the *pax Romana*, the city of Rome became the magnificent capital of the empire. The Roman provinces and frontiers also saw extensive prosperity in the second century through the growth of agriculture, trade, and industry,

Ara Pacis In the middle years of Augustus's reign, the Roman senate ordered a huge altar, the Ara Pacis, built to honor him and the peace he had brought to the empire. This was decorated with life-size reliefs of Augustus and members of his family, prominent Romans, and other people and deities. One side shows a goddess figure, most likely the goddess Peace herself, with twin babies on her lap, surrounded by symbols of fertility and dominance, thus linking the imperial family with continued prosperity. (Scala/Art Resource, NY)

among other factors. As the Roman Empire expanded eastward from Europe, it met opposition, yet even during the fighting, commerce among the Romans and peoples who lived in central and southern Asia thrived along a series of trade routes.

One of the most significant developments during the time of Augustus was the beginning of Christianity. Christianity was a religion created by the followers of Jesus of Nazareth (ca. 3 B.C.E.–29 C.E.), a Jewish man who taught that belief in his divinity led to eternal life. His followers spread their belief across the Roman Empire, transforming Christianity from a Jewish sect into a new religion. Christian groups were informal at first, but by the second century they began to develop hierarchical institutions modeled on those of Rome. At first many pagans in the Roman Empire misunderstood Christian practices and rites, and as a result, Christians suffered sporadic persecution under certain Roman emperors. Gradually, however, tensions between pagans and Christians lessened, particularly as Christianity modified its teachings to make them more acceptable to wealthy and educated Romans.

In terms of politics and economics, the prosperity of the Roman Empire in the second century C.E. gave way in the third century to a period of civil war, barbarian invasions, and conflict with foreign armies. These disrupted agriculture, trade, and production, and they damaged the flow of taxes and troops. At the close of the third century the emperor Diocletian ended the period of chaos, in part because he recognized that the empire had become too great for one man to handle. He therefore divided it into a western and an eastern half. Diocletian and his successor, Constantine, also took rigid control of the struggling economy, but their efforts were not successful. Free tenant farmers lost control of their lands, exchanging them for security that landlords offered against barbarians and other threats. Meanwhile, tolerance of Christianity grew, and Constantine legalized the practice of this religion throughout the empire. The symbol of all the changes in the empire became the establishment of its new capital, Constantinople, the New Rome.

From the third century onward the Western Roman Empire slowly disintegrated. The last Roman emperor in the West, Romulus Augustus, was deposed by the Ostrogothic chieftain Odoacer (OH-duh-way-suhr) in 476, but much of the empire had already come under the rule of various barbarian tribes well before this. Thus despite the efforts of emperors and other leaders, by the fifth century the Western Roman Empire no longer existed, a development that scholars who focus on Europe have long seen as one of the great turning points in history.

India

The vast subcontinent of India, protected from outsiders by the towering Himalayan Mountains to the north and by oceans on its other borders, witnessed the development of several early civilizations, primarily in the richly cultivated valley of the Indus River, which flows about 1,980 miles before reaching the ocean. Only in the northwest—the area between modern Afghanistan and Pakistan—was India accessible to invasion. The northwest was also the area of the earliest civilization in India, the Harappan, which built large cities mostly of brick. After the decline of this civilization, the Aryans, a nomadic Indo-European people, entered India by way of the Khyber Pass around 1500 B.C.E. They were able to establish dominance over large regions, including the eastern regions of the Ganges River. By 500 B.C.E. the Aryans ruled a number of large kingdoms in which cities were the centers of culture. The period of Aryan rule saw the evolution of a caste system designed to denote birth or descent and to distinguish Aryan from non-Aryan and rulers from the ruled. The four groups, or castes, that emerged—the *Brahman* (priests), the *Kshatriya* (warriors), the *Vaishya* (peasants), and the *Shudra* (serfs)—became the dominant features of Indian society. Persons without a place in this hierarchical strata or who lost their caste status because of some violation of ritual were *outcastes*.

Through the Khyber Pass in 513 B.C.E. the Persian King Darius I entered India and conquered the Indus Valley. The Persians introduced techniques for political administration and for coin minting, and they brought India into commercial and cultural contact with the sophisticated ancient Middle East. From the Persians the Indians adopted the Aramaic language and script, and they adapted that script to their needs and languages. In 326 B.C.E. the Macedonian king Alexander the Great invaded the Indus Valley, but his conquests had no lasting effect. Under Ashoka (r. 269–232 B.C.E.), ancient India's greatest ruler, India enjoyed a high degree of peace and stability, but from 180 B.C.E. to 200 C.E. the region suffered repeated foreign invasions. There was no dominant unifying state and regional cultures flourished. In the northwest rulers such as the Shakas and Kushans came from outside India.

Ancient India's most enduring legacies are the three great religions that flowered in the sixth and fifth centuries B.C.E.: Hinduism, Jainism, and Buddhism. One of the modern world's largest religions, Hinduism holds that the Vedas—hymns in praise of the Aryan gods—are sacred revelations and that these revelations prescribe the caste system. Religiously and philosophically diverse, Hinduism assures believers that there are many legitimate ways to worship Brahma, the supreme principle of life. India's best-loved hymn, the *Bhagavad Gita*, guides Hindus in a pattern of life in the world and of release from it.

Jainism derives from the teachings of the great thinker Vardhamana Mahavira (ca. 540–468 B.C.E.), who held that only an ascetic life leads to bliss and that all living things are too sacred to be destroyed. Nonviolence is a cardinal principle of Jainism. Thus a Jain who wishes to do the least violence to life turns to vegetarianism.

Mahavira's contemporary, Siddhartha Gautama (ca. 563–483 B.C.E.), better known as the Buddha, was so deeply distressed by human suffering that he abandoned his Hindu beliefs in a search for ultimate enlightenment. Meditation alone, he maintained, brought that total enlightenment in which everything is understood. Buddha developed the "Eightfold Path," a series of steps of meditation that could lead to *nirvana*, a state of happiness attained by the extinction of self and human desires. Buddha opposed all religious dogmatism and insisted that anyone, regardless of sex or class, could achieve enlightenment.

Gandharan Frieze Depicting the Buddha This carved stone from ca. 200 C.E. is one in a series portraying scenes from the life of the Buddha. From the Gandharan kingdom (located in what is now modern Pakistan), this frieze depicts the Buddha seated below the bo tree, where he was first enlightened. (Freer Gallery of Art, Smithsonian Institution, Washington, D.C., Purchase, F1949.9b)

He attracted many followers, and although Buddhism split into several branches after his death, Buddhist teachings spread throughout India to China, Japan, Korea, and Vietnam. Buddhism remains one of the great Asian religions and in recent times has attracted adherents in the West.

China

Chinese civilization, which developed initially along the Huang He (Yellow) River, was quite a bit farther away from the ancient Middle East than India, and it had much less in the way of contact with other early civilizations. Still, the Shang dynasty, ca. 1200 B.C.E., shared features of other early civilizations, such as bronze technology, cities, and writing. The writing system China developed, with separate symbols for each word, had no connection to the writing systems of other parts of Eurasia and became a key feature of Chinese culture.

The Chinese always looked back on the Zhou period (ca. 1000–256 B.C.E.) as their classical age, when social and political ideas were perfected. After a few centuries, however, political unity was lost and China consisted of many states, large and small, that made alliances with each other but who also frequently fought each other. Political disorder seems to have stimulated philosophy, and this became the period when "one hundred schools of thought contended." Compared to Indian religious speculation, Chinese thinkers were more secular than religious in outlook. Interested primarily in social and economic problems, they sought universal rules of human conduct, from the level of the family up to that of the state. Ancient China witnessed the development of Confucianism, Daoism, and Legalism—philosophies that profoundly influenced subsequent Chinese society and culture.

Confucius (551–479 B.C.E.) was interested in orderly and stable human relationships, and his thought focused on the proper duties and behavior of the individual in society. Confucius considered the family the basic unit within society. Within the family, male was superior to female, age to youth. If order is to exist in society, he taught, order must start at the level of the family. Those who help the king govern should be gentlemen, by which he meant men who exhibited the virtues of loyalty, sincerity, deference, generosity, and commitment. Only gentlemanly conduct, which involved a virtuous and ethical life, would lead to well-run government and peaceful conditions in society at large. Self-discipline, courtesy to others, punctiliousness in service to the state, justice to the people—these are the obligations and behavior expected of the Confucian gentlemen. Confucius minimized the importance of class distinctions and taught that even men of humble birth, through education and self-discipline, could achieve a high level of conduct and become gentlemen. The fundamental ingredient in the evolution of the Chinese civil service, Confucianism continued to shape Chinese government up to the twentieth century.

Daoism treated the problems of government very differently. In the two books, *Laozi* and *Zhuangzi*, each named after a Daoist master, earnest efforts to perfect society were ridiculed. Daoism maintained that people would be happier only if they abandoned the world and reverted to simpler ways. Daoists insisted that the best government was the least active government. Public works and government services require higher taxes, which lead to unhappiness and popular resistance. According to the Daoists, the people should be kept materially satisfied and uneducated. A philosophy of consolation, Daoism was especially popular among those who were frustrated by the political system.

Legalism is the name given to a number of related political theories originating in the third century B.C.E. The founders of Legalism proposed pragmatic solutions to the problems of government, exalted the power of the state, and favored an authoritarian ruler who would root out dissent. They argued that laws should be made known, the penalties for infractions should be clear and harsh, and that they should apply to everyone in society, even the close relatives of the ruler. Though Legalism seemed too harsh to many, it did contribute to the Chinese system of centralized bureaucratic rule.

In the third century B.C.E. the state of Qin adopted Legalism and then set out to defeat all of the other states, thus unifying China. The Qin government made efforts to achieve uniformity at many levels—standardizing weights and measures, writing systems, and laws. It even tried to do away with ideas it disapproved by collecting and burning books. The new dynasty was called *Qin* (chin), from which the Western term "China" derives. Under the Qin Dynasty and its successor, the Han, China achieved a high degree of political and social stability and economic prosperity. On its northern border, however, the Qin and the Han faced tough military opponents in the Xiongnu (SHUNG-noo), pastoralists who excelled at horsemanship.

The period of the Han Dynasty (206 B.C.E.–220 C.E.) witnessed notable intellectual achievements. First, many of the books that had been burned by the Qin were reconstructed from memory or hidden copies. These texts came to be known as the *Confucian Classics*. Scholars piously studied these books and worked to make them widely accessible as standards of moral behavior. Second, historical writing developed. The historian Sima Qian (145–ca. 85 B.C.E.) produced the *Records of the Grand Historian*, a massive and comprehensive survey of earlier Chinese civilization. These two sets of writings left a permanent impact on Chinese thought and peoples.

The Islamic World, 600–1400

One of the most important developments in world history—one whose consequences obviously redound to our own day—was the rise and remarkable expansion of Islam in the early Middle Ages. Muhammad (ca. 570–632), a devout merchant of Mecca in present-day Saudi Arabia, called on his followers to return to god. Even before Muhammad's death his teachings spread through Arabia, uniting the tribes there. Within two centuries his followers controlled Syria, Palestine, Egypt, Iraq, Iran, northern India, Spain, and southern France, and his beliefs were carried eastward across Central Asia to the borders of China. In the ninth, tenth, and eleventh centuries the Muslims created a brilliant civilization centered at Baghdad in Iraq and Córdoba in Spain.

Muhammad believed that God sent him messages or revelations. These were later collected and published as the Qur'an, from an Arabic word meaning "reading" or "recitation." On the basis of God's revelations to him, Muhammad preached a strictly monotheistic faith based on the principle of the absolute unity and omnipotence of God. Since God is all-powerful, believers must submit to him. *Islam* means "submission to God," and the community of Muslims consists of those who have submitted to God by accepting the final revelation of his message as set forth by Muhammad. (Earlier revelations of God, held by Muslims to be the same God worshipped by Jews and Christians, had come from the prophets Abraham, Moses, and Jesus, whose work Muslims believe Muhammad completed.)

The Arabs carried their religion to the east and west by military conquest. Their own economic needs, the political weaknesses of their enemies, a strong military organization, and the practice of

Separating Men and Women in a Mosque In this mid-sixteenth-century illustration of the interior of a mosque, a screen separates the women, who are wearing veils and tending children, from the men. The women can hear what is being said, but the men cannot see them. (Bodleian Library, University of Oxford, Ms. Ouseley Add 24, fol. 55v)

establishing army camps in newly conquered territories made possible their rapid expansion. In time, many of those in the conquered lands converted to Islam.

The assassination of one of the caliphs, or successors of Muhammad, led to a division within the Islamic community. When the caliph Ali (r. 656–661) was murdered, his followers claimed that because he was related by blood to Muhammad, and because Muhammad had designated him leader of the community prayer, he had been Muhammad's prescribed successor. These supporters of Ali were called *Shi'ites*, or *Shi'a*, partisans of Ali; they claimed to possess special divine knowledge that Muhammad had given his heirs. Other Muslims adhered to traditional beliefs and practices of the community based on precedents set by Muhammad. They were called *Sunnis*, a term derived from the Arabic *Sunna*, a collection of Muhammad's sayings and conduct in particular situations. This schism within Islam continues today. Sufism, an ascetic movement within Islam that sought a direct and mystical union with God, drew many followers from all classes.

Long-distance trade and commerce, which permitted further expansion of the Muslim faith, played a prominent role in the Islamic world, in contrast to the limited position it held in the heavily agricultural medieval West. The Black and Caspian Seas, the Volga River giving access deep into Russia, the Arabian Sea and the Indian Ocean, and to a lesser extent the Mediterranean Sea — these were the great commercial waterways of the Islamic world. Goods circulated freely over them. Muslim commercial tools such as the bill of exchange, the check, and the joint stock company were borrowed by Westerners. Many economic practices basic to capitalism were used by Muslim merchants and businessmen long before they became common in the West.

Long-distance trade brought the wealth that supported a gracious and sophisticated culture in the cities of the Muslim world. Baghdad in Iraq and Córdoba in Spain, whose streets were thronged with a kaleidoscope of races, creeds, customs, and cultures and whose many shops offered goods from all over the world, stand out as superb examples of cosmopolitan Muslim civilization. Baghdad and Córdoba were also great intellectual centers where Muslim scholars made advances in mathematics, medicine, and philosophy. The Arabs translated many ancient Greek texts by writers such as Plato and Aristotle. When, beginning in the ninth century, those texts were translated from Arabic into Latin, they came to play an important part in the formation of medieval European scientific, medical, and philosophical thought. Modern scholars consider Muslim civilization in the period from about 900 to 1200 among the most brilliant in the world's history.

Asia, 300–1400

Between about 300 and 1400 the various societies of Asia continued to evolve their own distinct social, political, and religious institutions. But also in these years momentous changes swept across Asia. Buddhism spread from India to Central Asia, China, Korea, Japan, Southeast Asia, and Tibet. Arab conquerors and their Muslim faith reached the Indian subcontinent. The Turks, moving westward from the Chinese border, converted to Islam. China, under the Tang and Song Dynasties, experienced a golden age. Japan emerged into the light of written history. The Mongols formed a confederation of the tribes of the steppes of Inner Asia that had extraordinary success in conquering cities from Korea and China to Persia, Baghdad, and Russia. These centuries witnessed cultural developments that have molded and influenced later Asian societies.

India

Under the Gupta kings, who ruled from around 320 to 500, India enjoyed a great cultural flowering. Interest in Sanskrit literature — the literature of the Aryans — led to the preservation of much Sanskrit poetry. A distinctly Indian drama appeared, and India's greatest poet, Kalidasa (ca. 380–450), like Shakespeare, blended poetry and drama. Mathematicians arrived at the concept of zero, essential for higher mathematics, and scientific thinkers wrestled with the concept of gravitation.

The Gupta kings succeeded in uniting much of the subcontinent. They also succeeded in repulsing an invasion by the Huns, but the effort exhausted the dynasty. After 600 India reverted to the pattern of strong local kingdoms in frequent conflict. Then, between 600 and 1400, India suffered repeated invasion as waves of Arabs, Turks, and Mongols swept down through the northwest corridor. The most successful of these were Turks from the area of modern Afghanistan, who held power in Delhi for three centuries and managed to turn back the Mongols. By around 1400 India was as politically splintered as it had been before Gupta rule. Under their rule Islam became dominant in the Indus Valley (modern Pakistan). Elsewhere Hinduism resisted Islam.

One other development had a lasting effect on Indian society: the proliferation and hardening of the caste system. Early Indian society had been divided into four major groups. After the fall of the Guptas, further subdivisions arose, reflecting differences of profession, trade, tribal or racial affiliation, religious belief, even place of residence. By 800 India had more than three thousand castes, each with its own rules and governing body. As India was politically divided, so castes served to fragment it socially.

China

Scholars consider the period between 580 and 1200, which saw the rule of Tang and Song Dynasties, as China's golden age. In religion, political administration, agricultural productivity, and art, Chinese society attained a remarkable level of achievement. This era was followed by the rise of the Mongols, which in time engulfed China.

Merchants and travelers from India introduced Buddhism to China from the first century C.E. on. Scholars, rulers, the middle classes, and the poor all found appealing concepts in Buddhist teachings, and the new faith won many adherents. China distilled Buddhism to meet its own needs, and Buddhism gained a place next to Confucianism and Daoism in Chinese life.

The Tang Dynasty, which some historians consider the greatest in Chinese history, built a state bureaucracy unequaled until recent times for its political sophistication. Tang emperors subdivided the imperial administration into departments of military organization, maintenance and supply of the army, foreign affairs, justice, education, finance, building, and transportation. To staff this vast administration, an imperial civil service developed in which education, talent, and merit could lead to high office, wealth, and prestige. So effective was the Tang civil service and so deeply rooted did it become in Chinese society that it lasted until the twentieth century.

Under the Song Dynasty (960–1279), greatly expanded agricultural productivity, combined with advances in the technology of coal and iron and efficient water transport, supported a population of 100 million. (By contrast, Europe did not reach this figure before the late eighteenth century.) Greater urbanization followed in China. Political stability and economic growth fostered technological innovation, the greatest being the invention of printing. Tang craftsmen invented the art of carving words and pictures into wooden blocks, inking the

Woman Attendant The Song emperors were patrons of a still-extant temple in northern China that enshrined a statue of the "holy mother," the mother of the founder of the ancient Zhou Dynasty. The forty-two maids who attend her, one of whom is shown here, seem to have been modeled on the palace ladies who attended Song emperors. (© Cultural Relics Press) blocks, and then pressing them onto paper. The invention of movable type followed in the eleventh century. As would happen in Europe in the fifteenth century, the invention of printing lowered the price and increased the availability of books and contributed to the spread of literacy. Printing led to the use of paper money, replacing the bulky copper coinage, and to developments in banking. The highly creative Tang and Song periods also witnessed the invention of gunpowder, originally used for fireworks, and the abacus, which permitted the quick computation of complicated sums. In the creation of a large collection of fine poetry and prose, and in the manufacture of porcelain of superb quality and delicate balance, the Tang and Song periods revealed an extraordinary literary and artistic flowering.

Shipbuilding advanced, and large ships were used both for war and for trade. Trade expanded as Japan and Korea eagerly imported Chinese silks and porcelains. The Muslims shipped Chinese goods across the Indian Ocean to East African and Middle Eastern markets. Southern China participated in a commercial network that stretched from Japan to the Mediterranean.

The thirteenth century witnessed the violent and amazingly fast creation of the Mongol Empire, the largest continuous land empire in world history. The Mongols were a steppe nomadic people in north-central Asia who had fought largely among themselves until about 1200. A shortage of pasture land for their sheep, goats, and cattle, and the rise of a great warrior-leader, Chinggis Khan (1162–1227), who united the steppe peoples and led them to conquer and absorb one neighbor after another, led to their extraordinary expansion. Building a vast army of loyal followers to whom he displayed great generosity, and using a policy of terror as a weapon of war, Chinggis swept across Central Asia into northern China. In 1215, he burned Beijing, and many Chinese governors quickly submitted. Chinggis then turned westward, and destroyed the Persian Empire, massacring hundreds of thousands of people. Under Chinggis's sons, the Mongols won control of Kievan Russia and Moscow, looted cities in Poland and Hungary, and established the Khanate of the Golden Horde. Chinggis's grandson Khubilai (r. 1260–1294) completed the conquest of China and overran Korea. The Mongols viewed China as their most important conquest; Mongol rule extended over most of East Asia, which they called the Great Khanate. They even invaded, but did not conquer, Japan. The Chinese called the period of Mongol rule the Yuan Dynasty. In 1368 Hungwu, the first emperor of the Ming Dynasty, restored Chinese rule.

Japan

The chain of islands that constitutes Japan entered the light of written history only in sporadic references in Chinese writings, the most reliable set down in 297 c.e. Because the land of Japan is rugged, lacking navigable waterways, and because only perhaps 20 percent of it is arable, political unification by land proved difficult until modern times. The Inland Sea served both as the readiest means of communication and as a rich source of food; the Japanese have traditionally been fishermen and mariners.

Early Japan was divided into numerous political units, each under the control of a particular *clan*, a large group of families claiming descent from a common ancestor and worshipping a common deity. In the third century c.e. the Yamato clan gained control of the fertile area south of modern Kyoto near Osaka Bay and subordinated many other clans to it. The Yamato chieftain proclaimed himself emperor and assigned specific duties and functions to subordinate chieftains. The Yamato established their chief shrine in the eastern part (where the sun-goddess could catch the first rays of the rising sun) of Honshu, the largest of Japan's four main islands. Around this shrine local clan cults sprang up, giving rise to a native religion that the Japanese called *Shinto*, the "Way of the Gods." Shinto became a unifying force and protector of the nation.

Through Korea two significant Chinese influences entered Japan and profoundly influenced Japanese culture: the Chinese system of writing and record keeping, and Buddhism. Under Prince Shotoku (574–622), talented young Japanese were sent to Tang

China to learn Chinese methods of administration and Chinese Buddhism. They returned to Japan to share and enforce what they had learned. The Nara era of Japanese history (710–794), so called from Japan's first capital city north of modern Osaka, was characterized by the steady importation of Chinese ideas and methods. Buddhist monasteries became both religious and political centers, supporting Yamato rule.

Perhaps because Buddhist temples had too much power in Nara, in 794 the imperial family removed the capital to Heian (modern Kyoto), where it remained until 1867. A strong reaction against Buddhism and Chinese influences followed, symbolized by the severance of relations with China in 838. The eclipse of Chinese influences liberated Japanese artistic and cultural forces. A new Japanese style of art and architecture appeared. In writing, Japanese scholars produced two *syllabaries*, sets of phonetic signs that stand for syllables instead of whole words or letters. Unshackled from Chinese forms, Japanese writers created their own literary styles and modes of expression. The writing of history and poetry flowered, and the Japanese produced their first novel, *The Tale of Genji*, a classic of court life by the court lady Lady Murasaki written over several years (ca. 1000–1010).

The later Heian period witnessed the breakdown of central authority as aristocrats struggled to free themselves from imperial control. In 1156 civil war among the leaders of the great clans erupted. By 1192 the Minamato clan had defeated all opposition. Its leader Yoritomo (1147–1199) became *shogun*, or general-in-chief. Thus began the Kamakura Shogunate, which lasted from 1185 until 1333.

In addition to the powerful shogun, a dominant figure in the new society was the *samurai*, the warrior who by the twelfth century exercised civil, judicial, and military power over the peasants who worked the land. The samurai held his land in exchange for his promise to fight for a stronger lord. In a violent society strikingly similar to that of western Europe in the early Middle Ages, the Japanese samurai, like the French knight, constituted the ruling class at the local level. Civil war among the emperor, the leading families, and the samurai erupted again in 1331. In 1338 one of the most important military leaders, Ashikaga Takauji, defeated the emperor and established the Ashikaga Shogunate, which lasted until 1573. Meanwhile, the samurai remained the significant social figure.

By 1400, the continents of Africa, Asia, and Europe experienced considerable cultural contact with one another. Chinese silks passed across the Great Silk Road to southwestern Asia and Europe. The religious ideals of Buddhism spread from India to China and Korea. The expansion of Islam—across northern Africa and into the Iberian Peninsula, down the east coast of Africa, across Central Asia and into northern India, and through the Malay Archipelago—led to rich commercial contacts. Religious and philosophical ideas, artistic and architectural models, and scientific and medical learning flowed across these international trade routes. The centuries (ca. 1100–1300) that witnessed the European religious-military-imperialistic expeditions to the Middle East known as the Crusades led to the slow filtering of Muslim (and ancient Greek) medical and architectural knowledge to Europe. By way of Islam, features of Chinese technology (such as paper manufacture) and nautical information (such as the compass and the astrolabe) reached Europe.

African Societies And Kingdoms, 1000 B.C.E.–1500 C.E.

Africa is a huge continent with many different climatic zones and diverse geography. The peoples of Africa are as diverse as the topography. Groups relying on herd animals developed in the drier, disease-free steppe regions well-suited to domesticated animals, while agricultural settlements developed in the wetter savanna regions. In the tropical forests of central Africa and arid zones of southern Africa, hunter-gatherers dominated. Along the coasts and by lakes and rivers, maritime communities grew whose inhabitants relied on fishing and trade for their livelihood.

Because the peoples south of the Sahara are generally described as "black" Africans, the inappropriate concept of race has engendered fierce debate over just who is African. For example, since the days of ancient Greece, historians have debated whether Egypt, because of its proximity to the Mediterranean, should be identified as part of Africa or part of the Mediterranean world. Race as a concept for determining one's "Africanness" has today generally been discredited as extremist.

Agriculture began very early in Africa. Knowledge of plant cultivation arrived in the Nile Delta in Egypt about the fifth millennium B.C.E. Settled agriculture then traveled down the Nile Valley and moved west across the Sahel to the central and western Sudan. Early societies across the western Sudan were profoundly affected as they switched from hunting and gathering in small bands to form settled farming communities. Populations increased significantly in this rich savanna zone that was ideally suited for grain production. Blood kinship brought together families in communities governed by chiefs or local councils. Animistic religions that recognized ancestral and nature spirits developed. The nature spirits were thought to dwell in nearby streams, forests, mountains, or caves.

Settled agriculture developed independently in West Africa. From there it spread to the equatorial forests. The spread of agriculture was related to the expansion of Bantu-speaking peoples, who originated in the Benue region, the borderlands of modern Cameroon and Nigeria. In the second millennium B.C.E. they began to spread south and east into the forest zone of equatorial Africa, eventually spreading across all of central and southern Africa. Possessing iron tools and weapons, domesticated livestock, and a knowledge of settled agriculture, these Bantu-speakers assimilated, killed, or drove away all the previous inhabitants of these regions.

Lines of trade and communication linked many parts of Africa with each other and with other parts of the world. The peoples of North Africa were closely connected with the Middle Eastern and European civilizations of the Mediterranean basin. Similarly, the peoples of the Swahili coast of east Africa participated in trade with Arabia, the Persian Gulf, India, China, and the Malay Archipelago.

Between 700 and 900, a network of caravan routes running south from the Mediterranean coast across the Sahara to the Sudan developed. Arab-Berber merchants exchanged manufactured goods for African gold, ivory, gum, and slaves from the West African savanna. The most essential component in the trans-Saharan trade was the camel. The camel made it possible for great loads to be hauled across vast stretches of hot, dry desert. The Berbers of North Africa endured these long treks south and then north again across the Sahara. To control this trade they fashioned camel saddles. This gave them great political and military advantage. The primary items of trade were salt from the north and gold from the south, although textiles, fruit, ivory, kola nuts, gum, beads, and other goods were also prized by one side or the other. Enslaved West Africans, males and females, were also traded north to slave markets in Morocco, Algiers, Tripoli, and Cairo.

The trans-Saharan trade had three important effects on West African society. First, it stimulated gold mining. Second, it increased the demand for West Africa's second most important commodity, slaves. Third, the trans-Saharan trade stimulated the development of large urban centers in West Africa, such as Gao, Timbuktu, Koumbi Saleh, Sijilmasa, and Jenne. In the period after 700 it had a fourth major effect, introducing Islam to West African society. Conversion led to the involvement of Muslims in African governments, bringing efficient techniques of statecraft as well as advanced scientific knowledge and engineering skills. Between the ninth and fifteenth centuries, Islam greatly accelerated the development of the African kingdoms. Through the trans-Saharan trade, Africans living in the Sahel zone of West Africa became part of the larger world of Islam.

The period from 800 to 1450 witnessed the flowering of several powerful African states. In the western Sudan, the large empires of Ghana (ca. 900–1100) and Mali (ca. 1200–1450) arose. Each had an elaborate royal court, a massive state bureaucracy, a sizable army, a sophisticated judicial system, and a strong gold industry. Indeed, the fame of Ghana rested on gold, and when the fabulously rich King Mansa Musa of Mali (r. ca. 1312–1337), a devout Muslim, made a pilgrimage to Mecca, his entourage included one hundred elephants, each carrying one hundred pounds of gold.

Mali's strength rested on two fundamental assets. First, its strong agricultural and commercial base provided for a large population and for enormous wealth. Second, Mali had two rulers, Sundiata and Mansa Musa, who combined military success with exceptionally creative personalities. The city of Timbuktu developed into a great center for scholarship and learning. Architects, astronomers, poets, lawyers, mathematicians, and theologians flocked there. Intermarriage between Arab and North African Muslim intellectuals and traders and local women brought into being a group of racially mixed people. The necessity of living together harmoniously, the traditional awareness of diverse cultures, and the cosmopolitan atmosphere of Timbuktu all contributed to a rare degree of racial toleration and understanding.

Meanwhile, the East African coast gave rise to powerful city-states such as Kilwa, Mombasa, and Mogadishu, which maintained a rich maritime trade with India, China, and the Muslim cities of the Middle East; like the western Sudan, the East African cities were much affected by Muslim influences. Like East Africa, South Africa was made up of city-states, chief among them Great Zimbabwe, which flourished between the eleventh and fifteenth centuries. Located at the southernmost reach of the Indian Ocean trade network, these city-states exchanged their gold for the riches of Arabia and Asia. Somewhat more isolated, the kingdom of Aksum in Ethiopia utilized its access to the Red Sea to trade north to the Mediterranean and south to the Indian Ocean.

The East African city-states and the kingdoms of the western Sudan were both part of the world of Islam. Arabian merchants brought Islam with them as they settled along the East African coast, and Berber traders brought Islam to West Africa. Differing from its neighbors, Ethiopia formed a unique enclave of Christianity in the midst of Islamic societies. The Bantu-speaking peoples of Great Zimbabwe were neither Islamic nor Christian, and they practiced indigenous forms of worship such as animism.

The Americas, 2500 B.C.E.–1500 C.E.

The first humans settled in the Americas between 40,000 and 15,000 B.C.E., after emigrating from Asia. The melting of glaciers 13,000 to 11,000 years ago separated the Americas and Afroeurasia, and the Eastern and Western Hemispheres developed in isolation from one another. There were many parallels, however: in both hemispheres people initially gathered and hunted their food, and then some groups began to plant crops, adapting plants that were native to the areas they settled. Techniques of plant domestication spread, allowing for population growth. In certain parts of both hemispheres, efficient production and transportation of food supplies led to the growth of cities, and to larger political entities such as states and empires.

In the Americas, all the highly varied environments, from polar tundra to tropical rain forests, came to support human settlement. About 8000 B.C.E., people in some parts of the Americas began raising crops as well as gathering wild produce. Maize became the most important crop, with knowledge about its cultivation spreading out from Mesoamerica — consisting of present-day Mexico and Central America — into North and South America.

Agricultural advancement led to an increase in population, which allowed for greater concentrations of people and the creation of the first urban societies. In certain parts of North and South America, towns dependent on agriculture flourished. Some groups in North America began to build large earthwork mounds, while others in Mesoamerica and South America practiced irrigation. The Olmecs created the first society with cities in Mesoamerica, with large ceremonial buildings, an elaborate calendar, and a symbolic writing system.

The urban culture of the Olmecs and other Mesoamerican peoples influenced subsequent societies. Especially in what became known as the classical era (300–900 C.E.), various groups developed large states centered on cities, with high levels of technological and intellectual achievement. Of these, the Maya were the longest-lasting, creating a complex written language, multiple-crop milpas or fields and raised beds for agriculture,

Aztec Adolescents This scene of adults supervising the tasks that young people at each age (indicated by dots) were expected to learn appeared in a painted book made by Mexica artists in the middle of the sixteenth century. It includes Nahuatl and Spanish words, including "dos [two] tortillas," the basic amount of food the artists thought was appropriate for these adolescents. (The Bodleian Library, University of Oxford, MS Arch. Selden. A.1, fol. 60r)

roads connecting population centers, trading practices that built unity among Maya communities as well as wealth. They also made striking works of art. Peoples living in North America built communities that were smaller than those in Mesoamerica but many also used irrigation techniques to enhance agricultural production and built earth-work mounds for religious purposes.

In Mesoamerica, the Aztecs, also known as the Mexica, built a unified culture based heavily on the heritage of earlier societies and distinguished by achievements in engineering, sculpture, and architecture, including the streets, canals, public squares, and aqueduct of Tenochtitlán (tay-oh-tee-way-KAHN), the most spectacular and one of the largest cities in the world in 1500. In Mexica society, religion was the dynamic factor that transformed other aspects of the culture: economic security, social mobility, education, and especially war. War was an article of religious faith, providing riches and land, sacrificial victims for ceremonies honoring the Aztec gods, warriors for imperial expansion, and laborers. Aztec society was hierarchical, with nobles and priests having special privileges.

In the Andes, Inca achievements built on those of cultures that preceded theirs, including the Moche and Chavin civilizations. Moche, Chavin, and Inca cultures made their home in the valleys along the Peruvian coast and in the Andean highlands, cultivating food crops and cotton. The Incas, who began as a small militaristic group, eventually created the largest empire in South America in the fifteenth century, and they conquered surrounding groups. The Incas' far-flung empire stretched along the Andes, kept together through a system of roads, along which moved armies and administrators. The Incas achieved imperial unification by imposing their gods on conquered peoples, forcing local chieftains to participate in the central bureaucracy, and pursuing a policy of colonization. The imperial expansion that increased the Incas' strength also caused stress. Andean society was dominated by clan groups, and Inca measures to disrupt these groups and move people great distances created resentment.

Europe, 500 to 1500

In the fifteenth century, scholars in Europe began the practice of dividing European history into different periods. They called the time of Greece and Rome the ancient or classical era, and the thousand-year period between the fall of the Western Roman Empire and their own day (what they considered the modern period) the Middle Ages. This three-part division—ancient, medieval, and modern—has been very influential, even in areas beyond Europe.

The Middle Ages

The transition from ancient to medieval was a slow process, not a single event. The primary agents in this process of change were the barbarian tribes whose migrations broke the Roman Empire apart. The barbarians brought different social, political, and economic structures with them. Although Greco-Roman art and architecture still adorned the land and people continued to travel on Roman roads, the roads were rarely maintained, and travel itself was much less secure than during the empire. Merchants no longer traded over long distances, so people's access to goods produced outside their local area plummeted. There was intermarriage and cultural assimilation among Romans and barbarians, but there was also violence and great physical destruction.

The Eastern Roman Empire, called the Byzantine Empire, did not fall to barbarian invasions, however. During the sixth and seventh centuries the Byzantine Empire survived waves of attacks, owing to effective military leadership and to fortifications around Constantinople. From this strong position Byzantine emperors organized and preserved Roman institutions, and the Byzantine Empire lasted until 1453, nearly a millennium longer than the Roman Empire in the West. In particular, the emperor Justinian oversaw creation of the *Code*, which distilled the legal genius of the Romans into a coherent whole, eliminated outmoded laws and contradictions, and clarified the law itself. Just as they valued the law, the Byzantines prized education, and because of them many masterpieces of ancient Greek literature survived to influence the intellectual life of the modern world. In mathematics and science, the Byzantines passed Greco-Roman learning on to the Arabs.

Along with Byzantium, the Christian Church was an important agent of continuity in the transition from ancient to medieval in Europe. Christianity gained the support of the fourth-century emperors and gradually adopted the Roman system of hierarchical organization. The church possessed able administrators and leaders whose skills were tested in the chaotic environment of the end of the Roman Empire in the West. Bishops expanded their activities, and in the fifth century the bishops of Rome, taking the title "pope," began to stress their supremacy over other Christian communities. Monasteries offered opportunities for individuals to develop deeper spiritual devotion and also provided a model of Christian living, methods that advanced agricultural development, and places for education and learning. Missionaries and church officials spread Christianity within and far beyond the borders of what had been the Roman Empire, transforming a small sect into the most important and wealthiest institution in Europe, North Africa, and the eastern Mediterranean.

Christian thinkers reinterpreted the classics in a Christian sense, incorporating elements of Greek and Roman philosophy and of various pagan religious groups into Christian teachings. Missionaries and priests got pagan and illiterate peoples to understand and become more accepting of Christianity by preaching the basic teachings of the religion, stressing similarities between pagan customs and beliefs with those of Christianity, and introducing the ritual of penance and the veneration of saints.

Classical and Christian traditions modified those of barbarian society, although barbarian political systems were very different from those of Rome. Barbarians generally had no notion of the state as we use the term today; they thought in social, not political, terms. The basic social unit was the tribe, made up of kin groups formed by families.

Family groups lived in small agriculture-based villages, where there were great differences in wealth and status. Most barbarian kingdoms were weak and short-lived, though the kingdom of the Franks was relatively more unified and powerful. Rulers first in the Merovingian Dynasty of the fifth century, and then in the Carolingian of the eighth century, used military victories, strategic marriage alliances, and the help of the church to enhance their authority.

The Frankish kingdom broke down in the late ninth century, and continental Europe was fractured politically. No European political power was strong enough to put up effective resistance to external attack, which came from many directions. Vikings from Scandinavia carried out raids for plunder along the coasts and rivers of Europe. They traveled as far as Iceland, Greenland, North America, and Russia. In many places they set up permanent states, as did the Magyars, who came into central Europe from the east. From the south came Muslims, who conquered Sicily and drove northward into Italy. All these invasions as well as civil wars weakened the power of kings, and local nobles became the strongest powers against external threats. They established a new form of decentralized government, later known as feudalism, and similar to that of Japan in the era of the samurai. Common people turned to nobles for protection, paying with their land, labor, and freedom.

Beginning in the last half of the tenth century, the invasions that had contributed to European fragmentation gradually ended, and domestic disorder slowly subsided. Feudal rulers began to develop new institutions of law and government that enabled them to assert their power over lesser lords and the general population. Centralized states slowly crystallized, first in western Europe in the eleventh century, and then in eastern and northern Europe as well. An era of relative stability and prosperity followed, generally known as the "High Middle Ages," which lasted until climate change and disease brought calamity in the fourteenth century.

At the same time that rulers expanded their authority, energetic popes built their power within the Western Christian church. They asserted their superiority over kings and emperors, though these moves were sometimes challenged by those secular rulers. Monasteries continued to be important places for learning and devotion, and new religious orders were founded. Meanwhile, Christianity expanded into Europe's northern and eastern regions, and Christian rulers expanded their holdings in Muslim Spain. On a more personal scale, religion structured people's daily lives and the yearly calendar.

A papal call to retake the holy city of Jerusalem from the Muslims led to nearly two centuries of warfare between Christians and Muslims. Christian warriors, clergy, and settlers moved out in all directions from western and central Europe, so that through conquest and colonization border regions were gradually incorporated into a more uniform European culture. The enormous popular response to the pope's call reveals the influence of the papacy and a new sense that war against the church's enemies was a duty of nobles. The Crusades were initially successful, and small Christian states were established in the Middle East. They did not last very long, however, and other effects of the Crusades were disastrous: Jewish communities in Europe were regularly attacked; relations between the Western and Eastern Christian Churches were poisoned by the Crusaders' attack on Constantinople; and Christian-Muslim relations became more uniformly hostile than they had been earlier.

For most people, the High Middle Ages did not bring dramatic change. The vast majority of medieval Europeans were rural peasants who lived in small villages and worked their own and their lords' land. Peasants led hard lives, and most were bound to the land, although there were some opportunities for social mobility. Nobles were a tiny fraction of the total population, but they exerted great power over all aspects of life. Aristocratic values and attitudes, often called chivalry, shaded all aspects of medieval culture. Medieval towns and cities grew initially as trading centers and recruited people from the countryside with the promise of greater freedom and new possibilities. They also became centers of production, and merchants and artisans formed guilds to protect their livelihoods. Not everyone in medieval towns and cities shared in the prosperity, however; many residents lived hand to mouth on low wages.

The towns that became centers of trade and production in the High Middle Ages also developed into cultural and intellectual centers. Trade brought in new ideas as well as merchandise, and in many cities a new type of educational institution — the university — emerged from cathedral and municipal schools. Universities developed theological, legal, and medical courses of study based on classical models and provided trained officials for the new government and church bureaucracies. People also wanted permanent visible representations of their piety, and church and city leaders supported the building of churches and cathedrals as symbols of their Christian faith and their civic pride. Cathedrals grew larger and more sumptuous, with high towers, soaring arches, and exquisite stained-glass windows in a style known as Gothic. New types of vernacular literature arose in which poems, songs, and stories were written down in local dialects.

In the fourteenth century the prosperity of the High Middle Ages ended. Bad weather brought poor harvests, which contributed to an international economic depression and fostered disease. The Black Death caused enormous population losses and had social, psychological, and economic consequences. Additional difficulties included the Hundred Years' War between England and France, which devastated much of the French countryside and bankrupted England; a schism among rival popes that weakened the Western Christian Church; and peasant and worker frustrations that exploded in uprisings. These revolts were usually crushed, though noble landlords were not always successful in reasserting their rights to labor services instead of cash rents.

The Renaissance and the Reformation

While Europe suffered greatly in the fourteenth century, a new culture was beginning to emerge in southern Europe. First in Italy and then elsewhere, scholars, writers, and artists thought that they were living in a new golden age, later termed the Renaissance, French for *rebirth*. The word *renaissance* was used initially to describe art that seemed to recapture, or perhaps even surpass, the glories of the classical past, and then came to be used for many aspects of life of the period. The new attitude diffused slowly out of Italy, with the result that the Renaissance "happened" at different times in different parts of Europe.

The Renaissance was characterized by self-conscious awareness among fourteenth- and fifteenth-century Italians, particularly scholars and writers known as humanists, that they were living in a new era. Key to this attitude was a serious interest in the Latin classics, a belief in individual potential, and a more secular attitude toward life. Humanists opened schools for boys and young men to train them for active lives of public service, but they had doubts about whether humanist education was appropriate for women. As humanism spread to northern Europe, religious concerns became more pronounced, and Christian humanists set out plans for the reform of church and society. Their ideas were spread to a much wider audience than those of early humanists as a result of the development of the printing press with movable metal type, which revolutionized communication. Interest in the classical past and in the individual shaped Renaissance art in terms of style and subject matter. Also important to Renaissance art were the wealthy patrons who helped fund it.

Social hierarchies in the Renaissance developed new features that contributed to the modern social hierarchies of race, class, and gender. The distinction between free people and slaves was one such hierarchy. Although in the Renaissance slavery in Europe was not limited to Africans, increasing numbers of black Africans entered Europe as slaves to supplement the labor force, and black skin color was increasingly viewed as a mark of inferiority. In terms of class, the medieval hierarchy of orders based on function in society intermingled with a new hierarchy that created a new social elite whose status was based on wealth. In regard to gender, the Renaissance debate about women led many to discuss women's nature and proper role in society, a discussion sharpened by the presence of a number of ruling queens in this era. Nevertheless, women continued to lag behind men in social status and earnings.

During the Renaissance, the feudal monarchies of medieval Europe gradually evolved into nation-states. Beginning in the fifteenth century rulers in western Europe used aggressive methods to build up their governments, reducing violence, curbing unruly nobles, and establishing domestic order. They emphasized royal majesty and royal sovereignty and insisted on the respect and loyalty of all subjects. War and diplomacy were important ways that states increased their power, but so was marriage. Because almost all of Europe was ruled by hereditary dynasties, claiming and holding resources involved shrewd marital alliances.

Religious reformers carried out even more dramatic changes than did humanists, artists, or rulers. Calls for reform of the Christian Church began very early in its history and continued throughout the Middle Ages, but in the sixteenth century these calls gained wide acceptance. The Western Christian Church, generally known as the Roman Catholic Church, had serious problems that stretched from local parishes and monasteries to the pope in Rome. Many individuals and groups were discontented with the power and wealth of the church, and even with some basic church teachings. This discontent helps explain why the ideas of one reformer, Martin Luther, found such a ready audience. Luther and other Protestants developed a new understanding of Christian doctrine that emphasized faith, the power of God's grace, and the centrality of the Bible. Protestant ideas were attractive to the literate middle classes, and they spread rapidly through preaching, hymns, and the printing press. The progress of the Reformation was shaped by the political situation in the Holy Roman Empire, the decentralization of which allowed the Reformation to spread. In England the king's need for a church-approved divorce triggered the break with Rome, and a Protestant church was established. Protestant ideas also spread into France and eastern Europe. In all these areas, a second generation of reformers, most prominently John Calvin, developed their own theology and plans for institutional change.

The Roman Catholic Church responded slowly to the Protestant challenge, but by the middle of the sixteenth century the papacy was leading a movement for reform within the church that became known as the Catholic Reformation. Popes supported improvements in education for clergy, banned the selling of church offices, established a special court to deal with suspected heretics, and required bishops to live in their territories rather than in palaces in Rome. Every diocese, the territory governed by a bishop, was supposed to establish a seminary for training clergy. In terms of doctrine, popes and the general council of the church that met at Trent (1545–1563) reaffirmed existing Catholic teachings on the importance of tradition as well as Scripture and the importance of good works as well as faith. New religious orders such as the Jesuits and the Ursulines spread Catholic ideas through teaching, and in the case of the Jesuits through missionary work.

Religious differences led to riots, civil wars, and international conflicts in the later sixteenth century. In France and the Netherlands Calvinist Protestants and Catholics attacked each other, and religious differences mixed with political and economic grievances. Long civil wars resulted, with the civil war in the Netherlands becoming an international conflict. War ended in France with the Edict of Nantes, in which Protestants were given some civil rights, and in the Netherlands with the division of the country into a Protestant north and a Catholic south. The era of religious wars was also marked by the most extensive witch persecutions in European history, as both Protestants and Catholics tried to rid their cities and states of people they regarded as linked to the Devil.

The Renaissance and the Reformation are often seen as key to the creation of the modern world. The radical changes of these times contained many elements of continuity, however. Artists, humanists, and religious reformers looked back to the classical era and early Christianity for inspiration, viewing those times as better and purer than their own. Political leaders played important roles in cultural and religious developments, just as they had for centuries in Europe and other parts of the world.

The events of the Renaissance and Reformation thus were linked with earlier developments, and they were also closely connected with another important element in the modern world: European exploration and colonization, which you will study in depth in Chapter One of this book. Renaissance monarchs paid for expeditions' ships, crews, and supplies, expecting a large share of any profits gained and increasingly viewing overseas territory as essential to a strong state. Only a week after Martin Luther stood in front of Emperor Charles V at a meeting of German rulers in the city of Worms declaring his independence in matters of religion, Ferdinand Magellan, a Portuguese sea captain using Spanish ships, was killed by indigenous people in a group of islands off the coast of Southeast Asia. Charles V had provided the backing for Magellan's voyage, the first to circumnavigate the globe. Magellan viewed one of the purposes of his trip as the spread of Christianity, and later in the sixteenth century institutions created as part of the Catholic Reformation, including the Jesuit order, would operate in European colonies overseas as well as in Europe itself. The islands where Magellan was killed were later named the Philippines, in honor of Charles's son Philip. The desire for fame, wealth, and power that was central to the Renaissance, and the religious zeal central to the Reformation, were thus key to the European voyages and to colonial ventures as well.

Understanding World Societies

A BRIEF HISTORY

16

The Acceleration of Global Contact

1450–1600

Before 1500 Europeans were relatively marginal players in a centuries-old trading system that linked Africa, Asia, and Europe. Elite classes everywhere prized Chinese porcelains and silks, while wealthy Chinese wanted ivory and black slaves from East Africa and exotic goods and peacocks from India. African people wanted textiles from India and cowrie shells from the Maldives. Europeans craved spices and silks, but they had few desirable goods to offer their trading partners.

The Indian Ocean was the locus of these desires and commercial exchanges, which sparked competition among Arab, Persian, Turkish, Indian, African, Chinese, and European merchants and adventurers. They fought each other for the trade that brought great wealth. They also jostled with Muslim scholars, Buddhist teachers, and Christian missionaries, who competed for the religious adherence of the peoples of Sumatra, Java, Borneo, and the Philippine Islands.

The European search for better access to Asian trade goods led to a new overseas empire in the Indian Ocean and the accidental discovery of the Western Hemisphere. With this discovery South and North America soon joined an international network of trade centers and political empires, which Europeans came to dominate. The era of globalization had begun, creating new forms of cultural exchange, assimilation, conversion, and resistance. Europeans sought to impose their cultural values on the peoples they encountered while struggling to comprehend them and their societies. The Age of Discovery from 1450 to 1650, as the time of these encounters is known, laid the foundations for the modern world as we know it today.

Mexica Noble This image from the early-seventeenth-century indigenous *Codex Ixtlilxochitl* shows a Mexica noble holding flowers and a tube of tobacco in his right hand. His jewelry and decorated cape emphasize his wealth and social standing. (Codex Ixtlilxochitl, Facsimile edition by ADEVA, Graz, Austria)

Chapter Preview

▸ How did trade link the peoples of Africa, Asia, and Europe prior to 1492?

▸ How and why did Europeans undertake voyages of expansion?

▸ What was the impact of conquest?

▸ How did expansion shape values and beliefs in Europe and the Americas?

How did trade link the peoples of Africa, Asia, and Europe prior to 1492?

Historians now recognize that a type of world economy, known as the Afroeurasian trade world, linked the products and people of Europe, Asia, and Africa in the fifteenth century. Prior to 1492, the West was not the dominant player in world trade. Nevertheless, wealthy Europeans were eager consumers of luxury goods from the East, which they received through Venetian and Genoese middlemen.

The Trade World of the Indian Ocean

The Indian Ocean was the center of the Afroeurasian trade world, serving as a crossroads for commercial and cultural exchanges between China, India, the Middle East, Africa, and Europe (Map 16.1). From the seventh through the fourteenth centuries, the volume of this trade steadily increased, declining only during the years of the Black Death.

Merchants congregated in a series of multicultural, cosmopolitan port cities strung around the Indian Ocean. Most of these cities had some form of autonomous self-government, and mutual self-interest had largely limited violence and attempts to monopolize trade. The most developed area of this commercial web was made up of the ports surrounding the South China Sea. In the fifteenth century the port of Malacca became a great commercial entrepôt (AHN-truh-poh), a trading post to which goods were shipped for storage while awaiting redistribution to other places.

The Mongol emperors opened the doors of China to the West, encouraging Europeans to do business there. After the Mongols fell to the Ming Dynasty in 1368, China entered a period of agricultural and commercial expansion, population growth, and urbanization. Historians agree that China had the most advanced economy in the world until at least the start of the eighteenth century.

China also took the lead in exploration, sending Admiral Zheng He's fleet as far west as Egypt. (See "Individuals in Society: Zheng He," page 410.) From 1405 to 1433, each of his seven expeditions involved hundreds of ships and tens of thousands of men. The purpose of the voyages was primarily diplomatic, to enhance China's prestige and seek tribute-paying alliances. The voyages came to a sudden halt after the deaths of Zheng and the emperor who initiated his voyages, probably due to court opposition to their high cost and contact with foreign peoples.

By ending large-scale exploration on China's part, this decision marked a turning point in history. Nonetheless, Zheng He's voyages left a legacy of increased Chinese trading in the South China Sea and Indian Ocean. Following Zheng He's voyages, tens of thousands of Chinese emigrated to the Philippines, where they acquired commercial dominance of the island of Luzon by 1600.

Another center of Indian Ocean trade was India, the crucial link between the Persian Gulf and the Southeast Asian and East Asian trade networks. Trade among ports bordering the Indian Ocean was revived in the Middle Ages by Arab merchants who circumnavigated India on their way to trade in the South China Sea. The need for stopovers led to the establishment of trading posts at Gujarat and on the Malabar coast, where the cities of Calicut and Quilon became thriving commercial centers.

The inhabitants of India's Coromandel coast traditionally looked to Southeast Asia, where they had ancient trading and cultural ties. Hinduism and Buddhism arrived in Southeast Asia from India during the Middle Ages, and a brisk trade between Southeast Asian and Coromandel port cities persisted from that time until the arrival of the Portuguese in the sixteenth century. India itself was an important contributor of goods to the world trading system. Most of the world's pepper was grown in India, and Indian cotton and silk textiles were also highly prized.

Peoples and Cultures of the Indian Ocean

Indian Ocean trade connected peoples from the Malay Peninsula (the southern extremity of the Asian continent), India, China, and East Africa, among whom there was an enormous variety of languages, cultures, and religions. In spite of this diversity, certain sociocultural similarities linked these peoples, especially in Southeast Asia.

For example, by the fifteenth century, inhabitants of what we call Indonesia, Malaysia, the Philippines, and the many islands in between all spoke languages of the Austronesian family, reflecting continuing interactions among them. A common environment led to a diet based on rice, fish, palms, and palm wine. In comparison to India, China, or even Europe after the Black Death, Southeast Asia was sparsely populated. People were concentrated in port cities and in areas of intense rice cultivation.

Another difference between Southeast Asia and India, China, and Europe was the higher status of women in the region. Women took the primary role in planting and harvesting rice, giving them authority and economic power. At marriage, which typically occurred around age twenty, the groom paid the bride (or sometimes her family) a sum of money called **bride wealth**, which remained under her control. This practice was in sharp contrast to the Chinese, Indian, and European dowry, which came under the husband's control. Property was administered jointly, in contrast to the Chinese principle and Indian practice that wives had no say in the disposal of family property. All children, regardless of gender, inherited equally.

Respect for women carried over to the commercial sphere. Women participated in business as partners and independent entrepreneurs, even undertaking long commercial sea voyages. When Portuguese and Dutch men settled in the region and married local women, their wives continued to play important roles in trade and commerce.

In contrast to most parts of the world other than Africa, Southeast Asian peoples had an accepting attitude toward premarital sexual activity, and no premium was placed on virginity at marriage. Divorce carried no social stigma, and it was easy if a pair proved incompatible. Either the woman or the man could initiate a divorce, and common property and children were divided.

Trade with Africa and the Middle East

On the east coast of Africa, Swahili-speaking city-states engaged in the Indian Ocean trade, exchanging ivory, rhinoceros horn, tortoise shells, copra (dried coconut), and slaves for textiles, spices, cowrie shells, porcelain, and other goods. Peopled by confident and urbane merchants, East African cities were known for their prosperity and culture.

bride wealth In early modern Southeast Asia, a sum of money the groom paid the bride or her family at the time of marriage, in contrast to the husband's control of dowry in China, India, and Europe.

Mansa Musa This detail from the Catalan Atlas of 1375 depicts a king of Mali, Mansa Musa, who was legendary for his wealth in gold. European desires for direct access to the trade in sub-Saharan gold helped inspire Portuguese exploration of the west coast of Africa in the fifteenth century. (Bridgeman-Giraudon/Art Resource, NY)

Chapter Chronology

1450–1650	Age of Discovery
1492	Columbus lands on San Salvador
1494	Treaty of Tordesillas ratified
1518	Atlantic slave trade begins
1519–1521	Spanish conquest of Aztec capital of Tenochtitlán
1533	Pizarro conquers Inca Empire
1571	Spanish found port of Manila in the Philippines
1580	Michel de Montaigne's *Essays* published
1602	Dutch East India Company established

INDIVIDUALS IN SOCIETY

Zheng He

IN 1403 THE CHINESE EMPEROR YONGLE ordered his coastal provinces to build a vast fleet of ships, with construction centered at Longjiang near Nanjing. The inland provinces were to provide wood for the ships and float it down the Yangzi River. Thirty thousand shipwrights, carpenters, sailmakers, ropers, and caulkers worked in a frenzy. As work progressed, Yongle selected a commander for the fleet. The emperor chose Zheng He (1371–1433), despite fearing that the thirty-five-year-old was too old for so politically important an expedition. The decision rested on Zheng's unquestioned loyalty, strength of character, energy, ability, and eloquence. These qualities apparently were expected to compensate for Zheng's lack of seamanship.

The southwestern province of Yunnan, where Zheng was born, had a large Muslim population, and he was raised in that faith. When the then prince Zhi Di defeated the Mongols in Yunnan, Zheng's father was killed in the related disorder. The young boy was taken prisoner and, as was the custom, castrated. Raised in Zhi Di's household, he learned to read and write, studied Confucian writings, and accompanied the prince on all military expeditions. By age twenty Zheng was not the soft, effeminate stereotype of the eunuch; rather he was "seven feet tall and had a waist five feet in circumference. His cheeks and forehead were high . . . [and] he had glaring eyes . . . [and] a voice loud as a bell. . . . He was accustomed to battle." Zheng must have looked imposing. A devout Muslim, he persuaded the emperor to place mosques under imperial protection after a period of persecution. On his travels, he prayed at mosques at Malacca and Hormuz. Unable to sire sons, he adopted a nephew. When Zheng became a naval commander under Yongle, he was the first eunuch in Chinese history to hold such an important position.

The fleet for Zheng's first expedition was composed of 317 ships, including junks, supply ships, water tankers, warships, transports for horses, and patrol boats, and carried twenty-eight thousand sailors and soldiers; it was the largest naval force in world history before World War I. Because it bore tons of beautiful porcelains, elegant silks, lacquer ware, and exquisite artifacts to be exchanged for goods abroad, it was called the "treasure fleet."

Between 1405 and 1433, Zheng led seven voyages, which combined the emperor's diplomatic, political, geographical, and commercial goals (see Map 16.1). During the voyages he worked toward Yongle's goal of securing China's hegemony over tributary states and collecting pledges of loyalty from them. Zheng also sought information on winds, tides, distant lands, and rare plants and animals, and he sailed as far west as Egypt to gather it. Because smallpox epidemics had recently hit China, another purpose of his voyages was to gather pharmacological products. An Arab text on drugs and therapies was secured and translated into Chinese. He also brought back a giraffe and mahogany, a wood ideal for ships' rudders because of its hardness.

Just before his death, Zheng recorded his accomplishments on stone tablets. The expeditions had unified "seas and continents . . . the countries beyond the horizon from the ends of the earth have all become subjects . . . and the distances and routes between distant lands may be calculated," implying that China had accumulated considerable geographical information. From around the Indian Ocean, official tribute flowed to the Ming court as a result of Zheng's efforts. A vast immigration of Chinese people into Southeast Asia, sometimes called the Chinese diaspora, came into being after the expeditions. Immigrants carried with them Chinese culture, including social customs, diet, and practical objects of Chinese technology — calendars, books, scales for weights and measures, and musical instruments. With legends collected about him and monuments erected to him, Zheng became a great cult hero.

Source: Louise Levathes, *When China Ruled the Seas: The Treasure Fleet of the Dragon Throne, 1405–1433* (New York: Oxford University Press, 1996).

QUESTIONS FOR ANALYSIS

1. What do the voyages of the treasure fleet tell us about China in the fifteenth century?
2. What was Zheng He's legacy?

Zheng He (right), voyager to India, Persia, Arabia, and Africa. (From Lo Monteng, *The Western Sea Cruises of Eunuch San Pao*, 1597)

Map 16.1 The Fifteenth-Century Afroeurasian Trading World After a period of decline following the Black Death and the Mongol invasions, trade revived in the fifteenth century. Muslim merchants dominated trade, linking ports in East Africa and the Red Sea with those in India and the Malay Archipelago. The Chinese admiral Zheng He's voyages (1405–1433) followed the most important Indian Ocean trade routes, hoping to impose Ming dominance of trade and tribute.

West Africa also played an important role in world trade. In the fifteenth century most of the gold that reached Europe came from Sudan in West Africa and, in particular, from the kingdom of Mali near present-day Ghana. Transported across the Sahara by Arab and African traders, the gold was sold in the ports of North Africa. Other trading routes led to the Egyptian cities of Alexandria and Cairo, where the Venetians held commercial privileges.

Inland nations that sat astride the north-south caravan routes grew wealthy from this trade. In the mid-thirteenth century the kingdom of Mali emerged as an important player on the overland trade route. In later centuries, however, the diversion of gold away from the trans-Sahara routes would weaken the inland states of Africa politically and economically.

Gold was one important object of trade; slaves were another. Arabic and African merchants took West African slaves to the Mediterranean to be sold in European, Egyptian, and Middle Eastern markets and also brought eastern Europeans to West Africa as slaves. In addition, Indian and Arabic merchants traded slaves in the coastal regions of East Africa.

The Middle East served as an intermediary for trade between Europe, Africa, and Asia and was also an important supplier of goods for foreign exchange, especially silk and cotton.

Two great rival empires, the Persian Safavids and the Turkish Ottomans, dominated the region, competing for control over western trade routes to the East. By the mid-sixteenth century the Ottomans had established control over eastern Mediterranean sea routes to trading centers in Syria, Palestine, Egypt, and the rest of North Africa. Their power also extended into Europe as far west as Vienna.

Genoese and Venetian Middlemen

Compared to the East, Europe constituted a minor outpost in the world trading system, for European craftsmen produced few products to rival those of Asia. However, Europeans desired luxury goods from the East, and in the late Middle Ages such trade was controlled by the Italian city-states of Venice and Genoa. In exchange for European products like Spanish and English wool, German metal goods, Flemish textiles, and silk cloth made with imported raw materials, the Venetians obtained luxury items like spices, silks, and carpets. They accessed these from middlemen in the eastern Mediterranean and Asia Minor. Because Eastern demand for these European goods was low, Venetians made up the difference by earning currency in the shipping industry and through trade in firearms and slaves.

Venice's ancient trading rival was Genoa. By the time the Crusades ended around 1270, Genoa dominated the northern route to Asia through the Black Sea. From then until the fourteenth century, the Genoese expanded their trade routes as far as Persia and the Far East.

In the fifteenth century, with Venice claiming victory in the spice trade, the Genoese shifted focus from trade to finance and from the Black Sea to the western Mediterranean. Located on the northwestern coast of Italy, Genoa had always been active in the western Mediterranean, and when Spanish and Portuguese voyages began to explore the western Atlantic (see page 414), Genoese merchants, navigators, and financiers provided their skills to the Iberian monarchs.

A major element of both Venetian and Genoese trade was slavery. Merchants purchased slaves, many of whom were fellow Christians, in the Balkans of southeastern Europe. After the loss of the Black Sea trade routes—and thus the source of slaves—to the Ottomans, the Genoese sought new supplies of slaves in the West, eventually seizing or buying and selling the Guanches (indigenous peoples from the Canary Islands), Muslim prisoners and Jewish refugees from Spain, and by the early 1500s both black and Berber Africans. With the growth of Spanish colonies in the New World, Genoese and Venetian merchants became important players in the Atlantic slave trade.

Italian experience in colonial administration, the slave trade, and international trade and finance served as a model for the Iberian states as they pushed European expansion to new heights. Mariners, merchants, and financiers from Venice and Genoa—most notably Christopher Columbus—played crucial roles in bringing the fruits of this experience to the Iberian Peninsula and to the New World.

Quick Review
What goods did each of the major participants in the Afroeurasian trade system supply?

How and why did Europeans undertake voyages of expansion?

In the fifteenth and early sixteenth centuries, Europeans launched new voyages of exploration, commerce, and conquest out of a desire to spread Christianity, to undo Italian and Ottoman domination of trade with the East, and to tap entirely new sources of wealth. Ultimately, their efforts landed them in the New World.

Causes of European Expansion

Europeans sought to expand their international reach for many reasons. By the middle of the fifteenth century, Europe was experiencing a revival of population and economic activity after the lows of the Black Death. This revival created demands for luxury goods, especially spices, from the East. However, the conquest of Constantinople by the Ottomans gave the Muslim empire control of trade routes to the east and blocked the fulfillment of European demands. Europeans thus needed to find new sources of precious metal to trade with the Ottomans or to find trade routes that bypassed the Ottomans.

Religious fervor was another important catalyst for expansion. The passion and energy ignited by the Christian reconquista of the Iberian Peninsula encouraged the Portuguese and Spanish to continue the Christian crusade. In 1492 Spain conquered Granada, the last remaining Muslim state on the Iberian Peninsula. Just seven months later, Columbus departed across the Atlantic.

Combined with eagerness to gain wealth and to spread Christianity were the desire for glory and the urge to chart new waters. Scholars have frequently described the European discoveries as a manifestation of Renaissance curiosity about the physical universe. The journals kept by European voyagers attest to their motives and fascination with the new peoples and places they visited. When the Portuguese explorer Vasco da Gama reached the port of Calicut, India, in 1498 and a native asked what he wanted, he replied, "Christians and spices."[1]

Eagerness for exploration was heightened by a lack of opportunity at home. After the reconquista, young men of the Spanish upper classes found their economic and political opportunities greatly limited. The ambitious turned to the sea to seek their fortunes.

Whatever the reasons, the voyages were made possible by the growth of government power. The Spanish monarchy was stronger than before and in a position to support foreign ventures. In Portugal explorers also looked to the monarchy, to Prince Henry the Navigator in particular (page 414), for financial support and encouragement. Monarchs shared many of the motivations of explorers. In addition, competition among European monarchs was an important factor in encouraging the steady stream of expeditions that began in the late fifteenth century.

Ordinary men chose to join these voyages to escape poverty at home, to continue a family trade, or to find better lives as illegal immigrants in the colonies. However, common sailors were ill-paid, and life at sea meant danger, hunger, and overcrowding. For months at a time, 100 to 120 people lived and worked in a space of 1,600 to 2,000 square feet.

The people who stayed at home had a powerful impact on the process and a strong interest in it. Royal ministers and factions at court influenced monarchs to provide or deny support for exploration. The small number of people who could read served as an audience for tales of fantastic places and unknown peoples. One of the most popular books of the time was the fourteenth-century text *The Travels of Sir John Mandeville*, which purported to be a firsthand account of the author's travels

The Travels of Sir John Mandeville The author of this tale claimed to be an English knight who traveled extensively in the Middle East and Asia from the 1320s to the 1350s. Although historians now consider the work a skillful fiction, it had a great influence on how Europeans understood the world at the time. This illustration, from an edition published around 1410, depicts Mandeville approaching a walled city on the first stage of his voyage to Constantinople. (© British Library Board, Add 24289, f14v)

in the Middle East, India, and China. These fantastic tales of cannibals, one-eyed giants, men with the heads of dogs, and other marvels were believed for centuries. Columbus took a copy of Mandeville and the equally popular and more reliable *The Travels of Marco Polo* on his voyage in 1492.

Technology and the Rise of Exploration

Technological developments in shipbuilding, navigation, and weaponry provided another impetus for European expansion. In the course of the fifteenth century, the Portuguese developed the caravel, a small, light, three-mast sailing ship. The caravel was maneuverable, sturdy, and could be sailed with a small crew. When fitted with cannon, it could dominate larger vessels.

Great strides in cartography and navigational aids were also made during this period. Around 1410 Arab scholars reintroduced Europeans to Ptolemy's *Geography*. Written in the second century, the work synthesized the geographical knowledge of the classical world. It represented a major improvement over medieval cartography, showing the world as round and introducing the idea of latitude and longitude to plot position accurately. It also contained significant errors. Unaware of the Americas, Ptolemy showed the world as much smaller than it is, so that Asia appeared not very distant from Europe.

The magnetic compass enabled sailors to determine their direction and position at sea. The astrolabe, an instrument invented by the ancient Greeks and perfected by Muslim navigators, was used to determine the altitude of the sun and other celestial bodies. It permitted mariners to plot their latitude, that is, their precise position north or south of the equator.

Like the astrolabe, Europeans borrowed much of the technology for their voyages from the East. Gunpowder, the compass, and the sternpost rudder were Chinese inventions. The lateen sail, which allowed European ships to tack against the wind, was a product of the Indian Ocean trade world. Advances in cartography also drew on the rich tradition of Judeo-Arabic mathematical and astronomical learning in Iberia. In exploring new territories, European sailors thus called on techniques and knowledge developed over centuries in China, the Muslim world, and trading centers along the Indian Ocean.

The Expanding Portuguese Empire

Portugal was a small and poor nation on the margins of European life. Yet Portugal had a long history of seafaring and navigation. Blocked from access to western Europe by Spain, the Portuguese turned to the Atlantic, whose waters they knew better than did other Europeans.

In the early phases of Portuguese exploration, Prince Henry (1394–1460), a younger son of the king, played a leading role. A nineteenth-century scholar dubbed Henry "the Navigator" because of his support for the study of geography and navigation and for the annual expeditions he sponsored down the western coast of Africa.

Portugal's conquest of Ceuta, an Arab city in northern Morocco, in 1415 marked the beginning of European overseas expansion. In the 1420s, under Henry's direction, the Portuguese began to settle the Atlantic islands of Madeira (ca. 1420) and the Azores (1427). In 1443 they founded their first African commercial settlement at

Portuguese Expansion into Africa

caravel A small, maneuverable, three-mast sailing ship developed by the Portuguese in the fifteenth century that gave the Portuguese a distinct advantage in exploration and trade.

Ptolemy's *Geography* Second century C.E. work that synthesized the classical knowledge of geography and introduced the concepts of longitude and latitude. Reintroduced to Europeans in 1410 by Arab scholars, its ideas allowed cartographers to create more accurate maps.

Map 16.2 Overseas Exploration and Conquest in the Fifteenth and Sixteenth Centuries

The voyages of discovery marked a dramatic new phase in the centuries-old migrations of European peoples. This map depicts the voyages of the most significant European explorers of the period.

ANALYZING THE MAP Consider the routes and dates of the voyages shown. How might the successes of the earlier voyages have contributed to the later expeditions? Which voyage had the most impact, and why?

CONNECTIONS Do you think the importance of these voyages was primarily economic, political, or cultural? Why?

Arguin in North Africa. By the time of Henry's death in 1460, his support for exploration was vindicated by thriving sugar plantations on the Atlantic islands, the first arrival of enslaved Africans in Portugal (see page 425), and new access to African gold.

The Portuguese next established trading posts and forts on the gold-rich Guinea coast and penetrated into the African continent all the way to Timbuktu (Map 16.2). By 1500 Portugal controlled the flow of African gold to Europe.

The Portuguese then pushed farther south down the west coast of Africa. In 1487 Bartholomew Diaz (ca. 1451–1500) rounded the Cape of Good Hope at the southern tip, but was forced to turn back. A decade later Vasco da Gama (ca. 1469–1524) succeeded in rounding the Cape while commanding a fleet in search of a sea route to India. With the help of an Indian guide, da Gama reached the port of Calicut in India. He returned to Lisbon with spices and samples of Indian cloth. Thereafter, a Portuguese convoy set out for passage around the Cape every March.

Lisbon became the entrance port for Asian goods into Europe, but this was not accomplished without a fight. Muslim-controlled port city-states had long dominated the rich spice trade of the Indian Ocean, and they did not surrender it willingly. Portuguese conquest of a number of these cities laid the foundation for Portuguese imperialism in the sixteenth and seventeenth centuries. The acquisition of port cities and their trade routes brought riches to Portugal but had limited impact on the lives of Asian peoples beyond Portuguese coastal holdings. In the meantime, Spain also had begun the quest for an empire.

Christopher Columbus's Voyages to the Americas

The westward voyages of Christopher Columbus (1451–1506), a native of Genoa, embodied a long-standing Genoese ambition to circumvent Venetian, and then Portuguese, domination of eastward trade. Columbus was knowledgeable about the sea. He had worked as a mapmaker, and he was familiar with the most advanced navigational innovations of his day. The success of his first voyage to the Americas, which took him across the Atlantic to the Caribbean in thirty-three days, owed a great deal to his seamanship.

Columbus was also a deeply religious man. He had witnessed the Spanish conquest of Granada and shared fully in the religious and nationalistic fervor surrounding that event. Like the Spanish rulers and most Europeans of his age, he understood Christianity as a missionary religion that should be carried to places where it did not exist.

Although the spread of Christianity was an important goal, Columbus's primary objective was to find a direct ocean trading route to Asia. Inspired by the stories of Mandeville and Marco Polo, Columbus also dreamed of reaching the court of the Mongol emperor, the Great Khan (not realizing that the Ming Dynasty had overthrown the Mongols in 1368). Based on Ptolemy's *Geography* and other texts, he expected to pass the islands of Japan and then land on the east coast of China.

Columbus's First Voyage to the New World, 1492–1493

Before Columbus could begin his voyage he needed financing. Rejected for funding by the Portuguese in 1483 and by Ferdinand and Isabella in 1486, he finally won the support of the Spanish monarchy in 1492. The Spanish crown agreed to make him viceroy over any territory he might discover and to give him one-tenth of the material rewards of the journey. With this backing, Columbus and his small fleet left Spain on August 3, 1492. He landed in the Bahamas, which he christened San Salvador, on October 12, 1492.

On his arrival in the Bahamas Columbus believed he had found some small islands off the east coast of Japan. In a letter he wrote to Ferdinand and Isabella on his return to Spain, Columbus described the natives as handsome, peaceful, and primitive. Believing he was in the Indies, he called them "Indians," a name that was later applied to all inhabitants of the Americas. Columbus concluded that they would make good slaves and could quickly be converted to Christianity. (See "Listening to the Past: Columbus Describes His First Voyage," page 418.)

Scholars have identified the inhabitants of the islands as the Taino (TIGH-noh) people, speakers of the Arawak language, who inhabited Hispaniola (modern-day Haiti and the Dominican Republic) and other islands in the Caribbean. Columbus received reassuring reports from Taino villagers of the presence of gold and of a great king in the vicinity.

From San Salvador, Columbus sailed southwest, believing that this course would take him to Japan or the coast of China. He landed instead on Cuba on October 28. Deciding that he must be on the mainland of China near the coastal city of Quinsay (now Hangzhou), he sent a small embassy inland with letters from Ferdinand and Isabella and instructions to locate the grand city.

The landing party found only small villages. Confronted with this disappointment, Columbus focused on trying to find gold or other valuables among the peoples he had discovered. The sight of Taino people wearing gold ornaments on Hispaniola seemed to prove that gold was available in the region. In January, confident that its source would soon be found, he headed back to Spain to report on his discovery.

Over the next decades, the Spanish would follow a policy of conquest and colonization in the New World (see pages 420–422). On his second voyage, Columbus forcibly subjugated the island of Hispaniola and enslaved its indigenous peoples. On this and subsequent voyages, he brought with him settlers for the new Spanish territories. Columbus himself, however, had little interest in or capacity for governing. Arriving in Hispaniola on this third voyage, he found revolt had broken out against his brother. A royal expedition sent to investigate returned the brothers to Spain in chains. Although Columbus was quickly cleared of wrongdoing, he did not recover his authority over the territories.

To the end of his life in 1506, Columbus believed that he had found small islands off the coast of Asia. He never realized that he had found a vast continent unknown to Europeans, except for a fleeting Viking presence centuries earlier. He could not know that the lands he discovered would become a crucial new arena for international trade and colonization, with grave consequences for native peoples.

Later Explorers

The Florentine navigator Amerigo Vespucci (veh-SPOO-chee; 1454–1512) realized what Columbus had not. Writing about his discoveries on the coast of modern-day Venezuela, Vespucci was the first to describe America as a continent separate from Asia. In recognition of Amerigo's bold claim, the continent was named for him.

World Map of Diogo Ribeiro, 1529 This map integrates the wealth of new information provided by European explorers in the decades after Columbus's 1492 voyage. Working on commission for the Spanish king Charles V, mapmaker Diogo Ribeiro incorporated new details on Africa, South America, India, the Malay Archipelago, and China. Note the inaccuracy in his placement of the Moluccas, or Spice Islands, which are much too far east. This "mistake" was intended to serve Spain's interests in trade negotiations with the Portuguese. (Biblioteca Apostolica Vaticana, BORG.III)

Columbus Describes His First Voyage

On his return voyage to Spain in February 1493, Christopher Columbus composed a letter intended for wide circulation and had copies of it sent ahead to Isabella, Ferdinand, and others when the ship docked at Lisbon. Because the letter sums up Columbus's understanding of his achievements, it is considered the most important document of his first voyage.

❝ Since I know that you will be pleased at the great success with which the Lord has crowned my voyage, I write to inform you how in thirty-three days I crossed from the Canary Islands to the Indies, with the fleet which our most illustrious sovereigns gave me. I found very many islands with large populations and took possession of them all for their Highnesses; this I did by proclamation and unfurled the royal standard. No opposition was offered.

I named the first island that I found "San Salvador," in honour of our Lord and Saviour who has granted me this miracle. . . . When I reached Cuba, I followed its north coast westwards, and found it so extensive that I thought this must be the mainland, the province of Cathay.* . . . From there I saw another island eighteen leagues east-wards which I then named "Hispaniola."† . . .

Hispaniola is a wonder. The mountains and hills, the plains and meadow lands are both fertile and beautiful. They are most suitable for planting crops and for raising cattle of all kinds, and there are good sites for building towns and villages. The harbours are incredibly fine and there are many great rivers with broad channels and the majority contain gold.‡ The trees, fruits and plants are very different from those of Cuba. In Hispaniola there are many spices and large mines of gold and other metals.§ . . .

The inhabitants of this island, and all the rest that I discovered or heard of, go naked, as their mothers bore them, men and women alike. A few of the women, however, cover a single place with a leaf of a plant or piece of cotton which they weave for the purpose. They have no iron or steel or arms and are not capable of using them, not because they are not strong and well built but because they are amazingly timid. All the weapons they have are canes cut at seeding time, at the end of which they fix a sharpened stick, but they have

not the courage to make use of these, for very often when I have sent two or three men to a village to have conversation with them a great number of them have come out. But as soon as they saw my men all fled immediately, a father not even waiting for his son. And this is not because we have harmed any of them; on the contrary, wherever I have gone and been able to have conversation with them, I have given them some of the various things I had, a cloth and other articles, and received nothing in exchange. But they have still remained incurably timid. True, when they have been reassured and lost their fear, they are so ingenuous and so liberal with all their possessions that no one who has not seen them would believe it. If one asks for anything they have they never say no. On the contrary, they offer a share to anyone with demonstrations of heartfelt affection, and they are immediately content with any small thing, valuable or valueless, that is given them. I forbade the men to give them bits of broken crockery, fragments of glass or tags of laces, though if they could get them they fancied them the finest jewels in the world.

I hoped to win them to the love and service of their Highnesses and of the whole Spanish nation and to persuade them to collect and give us of the things which they possessed in abundance and which we needed. They have no religion and are not idolaters; but all believe that power and goodness dwell in the sky and they are firmly convinced that I have come from the sky with these ships and people. In this belief they gave me a good reception everywhere, once they had overcome their fear; and this is not because they are stupid — far from it, they are men of great intelli-gence, for they navigate all those seas, and give a marvellously good account of everything — but be-cause they have never before seen men clothed or ships like these. . . .

In all these islands the men are seemingly content with one woman, but their chief or king is allowed more than twenty. The women appear to work more than the men and I have not been able to find out if they have private property. As far as I could see what-ever a man had was shared among all the rest and

---

Treaty of Tordesillas The 1494 agreement giving Spain everything west of an imaginary line drawn down the Atlantic and giving Portugal everything to the east.

To settle competing claims to the Atlantic discoveries, Spain and Portugal turned to Pope Alexander VI. The resulting Treaty of Tordesillas (tor-duh-SEE-yuhs) in 1494 gave Spain everything to the west of an imaginary line drawn down the Atlantic and Portugal everything to the east. This arbitrary division worked in Portugal's favor when in 1500 an expedition led by Pedro Alvares Cabral, en route to India, landed on the coast of Brazil, which Cabral claimed as Portuguese territory.

Spain had not given up the search for a western passage to Asia. In 1519 Charles V of Spain commissioned Ferdinand Magellan (1480–1521) to find a direct sea route to the spices of the Moluccas, islands off the southeast coast of Asia. Magellan sailed southwest across this particularly applies to food. . . . In another island, which I am told is larger than Hispaniola, the people have no hair. Here there is a vast quantity of gold, and from here and the other islands I bring Indians as evidence.

In conclusion, to speak only of the results of this very hasty voyage, their Highnesses can see that I will give them as much gold as they require, if they will render me some very slight assistance; also I will give them all the spices and cotton they want. . . . I will also bring them as much aloes as they ask and as many slaves, who will be taken from the idolaters. I believe also that I have found rhubarb and cinnamon and there will be count- less other things in addition. . . .

So all Christendom will be delighted that our Redeemer has given victory to our most illustrious King and Queen and their renowned kingdoms, in this great matter. They should hold great celebra- tions and render solemn thanks to the Holy Trinity with many solemn prayers, for the great triumph which they will have, by the conversion of so many peoples to our holy faith and for the temporal benefits which will follow, for not only Spain, but all Christendom will receive encouragement and profit.

This is a brief account of the facts.

Written in the caravel off the Canary Islands.**

15 February 1493

At your orders

THE ADMIRAL »

Source: J. M. Cohen, ed. and trans., *The Four Voyages of Christopher Columbus* (Penguin Classics, 1958), pp. 115–123. Copyright © J. M. Cohen, 1969, London. Reproduced by permission of Penguin Books Ltd.

*Cathay is the old name for China. In the logbook and later in this letter Columbus accepts the native story that Cuba is an island that they can circumnavigate in something more than twenty-one days, yet he insists here and during the second voyage that it is in fact part of the Asiatic mainland.

†Hispaniola is the second largest island of the West Indies; Haiti occupies the western third of the island, the Dominican Republic the rest.

Christopher Columbus, by Ridolfo Ghirlandaio. Friend of Raphael and teacher of Michelangelo, Ghirlandaio (1483–1561) enjoyed distinction as a portrait painter, and so we can assume that this is a good likeness of the older Columbus. (Scala/Art Resource, NY)

‡This did not prove to be true.

§These statements are also inaccurate.

**Actually, Columbus was off Santa Maria in the Azores.

QUESTIONS FOR ANALYSIS

1. How did Columbus explain the success of his voyage?
2. What was Columbus's view of the Native Americans he met?
3. Evaluate his statements that the Caribbean islands possessed gold, cotton, and spices.
4. Why did Columbus cling to the idea that he had reached Asia?

the Atlantic to Brazil, and after a long search along the coast he located the treacherous strait off the southern tip of South America that now bears his name (see Map 16.2). After passing through the strait, his fleet sailed up the west coast of South America and then headed west into the Pacific toward the Malay Archipelago. Some of these islands were conquered in the 1560s and named the Philippines for Philip II of Spain.

Terrible storms, disease, starvation, and violence haunted the expedition, and only one of Magellan's five ships returned to Spain. Magellan himself was killed in a skirmish in the Philippines. In 1522 the sole remaining ship, with only eighteen men aboard, returned to Spain, having traveled from the east by way of the Indian Ocean, the Cape of Good

Hope, and the Atlantic. The voyage—the first to circumnavigate the globe—had taken close to three years.

Despite the losses, this voyage revolutionized Europeans' understanding of the world by demonstrating the vastness of the Pacific. Magellan's expedition also made Spain rethink its plans for overseas commerce and territorial expansion. Clearly, the westward passage to the Indies was too long and dangerous for commercial purposes. Thus Spain soon abandoned the attempt to oust Portugal from the Eastern spice trade and concentrated on exploiting its New World territories.

The English and French also set sail across the Atlantic during the early days of exploration, in their case to search for a northwest passage to the Indies. In 1497 John Cabot (ca. 1450–1499), a Genoese merchant living in London, discovered Newfoundland. The next year he returned and explored the New England coast. These forays proved futile, and at that time the English established no permanent colonies in the territories they explored. Early French exploration of the Atlantic was equally frustrating. Between 1534 and 1541 Frenchman Jacques Cartier (1491–1557) made several voyages and explored the St. Lawrence region of Canada, searching for a passage to the wealth of Asia. When this hope proved vain, the French turned to a new source of profit within Canada itself: trade in beavers and other furs. French fisherman also competed with the Spanish and English for the teeming schools of cod they found in the Atlantic waters around Newfoundland.

Spanish Conquest in the New World

After Columbus's voyages Spanish explorers penetrated farther into the New World. This territorial expansion began in 1519, when the Spanish governor in Cuba sent an expedition, under the command of the **conquistador** (kahn-KEES-tuh-dor) Hernando Cortés (1485–1547), to what is now Mexico. Accompanied by six hundred men, sixteen horses, and ten cannon, Cortés was to launch the conquest of the **Mexica Empire**. Its people were later called the Aztecs, but now most scholars prefer to use the term *Mexica* to refer to them and their empire.

The Mexica Empire was ruled by Montezuma II (r. 1502–1520) from his capital at Tenochtitlán (tay-nawch-teet-LAHN), now Mexico City. Larger than any European city of the time, it was the heart of a sophisticated, advanced civilization.

Soon after Cortés landed on the Mexican coast on April 21, 1519, his camp was visited by delegations of Mexica leaders bearing gifts and news of their great emperor. Impressed by the wealth of the local people, Cortés decided to defy his orders from the governor in Cuba, which restricted him to trading and exploration, and set up a settlement, Veracruz, under his own authority. He then burned his ships to prevent any disloyal or frightened followers from returning to Cuba.

The Mexica state religion necessitated constant warfare against neighboring peoples to secure captives for religious sacrifices and laborers for agricultural and building projects. Conquered peoples were required to pay tribute to the Mexica state through their local chiefs. Realizing that he could exploit dissension over this practice to his own advantage, Cortés forged an alliance with the Tlaxcala (tlah-SKAH-lah) and other subject kingdoms. In October a combined Spanish-Tlaxcalan force occupied the city of Cholula and massacred many thousand inhabitants. Strengthened by this display of power, Cortés made alliances with other native kingdoms. In November 1519, with a few hundred Spanish men and some six thousand indigenous warriors, he marched on Tenochtitlán.

conquistador Spanish for "conqueror"; Spanish soldier-explorer, such as Hernando Cortés and Francisco Pizarro, who sought to conquer the New World for the Spanish crown.

Mexica Empire Also known as the Aztec Empire, a large and complex Native American civilization in modern Mexico and Central America that possessed advanced mathematical, astronomical, and engineering technology.

Invasion of Tenochtitlán, 1519–1521

Gulf of Mexico

Texcoco • Otumba • • Zautla • Jalapa
• • • • Tlaxcala • Veracruz
Tenochtitlán • Cholula

→ Cortés's original route, 1519
→ Cortés's retreat, 1520
→ Cortés's return route, 1520–1521

Picturing the Past

Doña Marina Translating for Hernando Cortés During His Meeting with Montezuma

In April 1519 Doña Marina (or La Malinche as she is known in Mexico) was among twenty women given to the Spanish as slaves. Fluent in Nahuatl (NAH-wha-tuhl) and Yucatec Mayan (spoken by a Spanish priest accompanying Cortés), she acted as an interpreter and diplomatic guide for the Spanish. She had a close relationship with Cortés and bore his son, Don Martín Cortés, in 1522. This image was created by Tlaxcalan artists shortly after the conquest of Mexico and represents one indigenous perspective on the events. (The Granger Collection, New York)

ANALYZING THE IMAGE What role does Doña Marina (far right) appear to be playing in this image? Does she appear to be subservient or equal to Cortés (right, seated)? How did the painter indicate her identity as non-Spanish?

CONNECTIONS How do you think the native rulers negotiating with Cortés might have viewed Doña Marina? What about a Spanish viewer of this image? What does the absence of other women suggest about the role of women in these societies?

Montezuma refrained from attacking the Spaniards as they advanced toward his capital and welcomed Cortés and his men into Tenochtitlán. Other native leaders attacked the Spanish, but Montezuma relied on the advice of his state council, itself divided, and on the dubious loyalty of tribute-paying communities subjugated by the Mexica. Montezuma's long hesitation proved disastrous. When Cortés took Montezuma hostage, the emperor's influence over his people crumbled.

During the ensuing attacks and counterattacks, Montezuma was killed. The Spaniards and their allies escaped from the city and began gathering forces and making new alliances against the Mexica. In May 1510 Cortés led a second, much larger assault on Tenochtitlán. The Spanish victory in late summer 1521 was hard-won and greatly aided by the effects of smallpox, which had weakened and reduced the Mexica population. After the defeat of Tenochtitlán, Cortés and other conquistadors began the systematic conquest of Mexico. Over time a series of indigenous kingdoms fell under Spanish domination, although not without decades of resistance.

Inca Empire The vast and sophisticated Peruvian empire centered at the capital city of Cuzco that was at its peak from 1438 until 1532.

More surprising than the defeat of the Mexicas was the fall of the remote Inca Empire in Peru. Like the Mexicas, they had created a vast empire that rivaled that of the Europeans in population and complexity. However, by the time of the Spanish invasion the Inca Empire had been weakened by a civil war over succession and an epidemic of disease, possibly smallpox.

The Spanish conquistador Francisco Pizarro (ca. 1475–1541) landed on the northern coast of Peru on May 13, 1532, the very day Atahualpa (ah-tuh-WAHL-puh) won control of the empire after five years of fighting his brother for the throne. As Pizarro advanced across the Andes toward Cuzco, the capital of the Inca Empire, Atahualpa was also heading there for his coronation.

Atahualpa sent envoys to greet the Spanish and invite them to meet him in the provincial town of Cajamarca. His plan was to lure the Spaniards into a trap, seize their horses and ablest men for his army, and execute the rest. Instead, the Spaniards ambushed and captured him, collected an enormous ransom in gold, and then executed him in 1533.

Quick Review
How did previous knowledge of and experience with the Afroeurasian trade system shape European expansion in the fifteenth and early sixteenth centuries?

The Spanish then marched on to Cuzco, profiting once again from internal conflicts to form alliances with local peoples. When Cuzco fell in 1533, the Spanish plundered immense riches in gold and silver.

As with the Mexica, decades of violence and resistance followed the defeat of the Incan capital. Nevertheless, the Spanish conquest opened a new chapter in European relations with the New World. It was not long before rival European nations attempted to forge their own overseas empires.

What was the impact of conquest?

The growing European presence in the New World transformed its land and its peoples forever. Violence and disease wrought devastating losses, while surviving peoples encountered new political, social, and economic organizations imposed by Europeans. Although the exchange of goods and people between Europe and the New World brought diseases to the Americas, it also gave both the New and Old Worlds new crops that eventually altered consumption patterns across the globe.

As important, for the first time, a truly global economy emerged in the sixteenth and seventeenth centuries, and it forged new links among far-flung peoples, cultures, and societies. The ancient civilizations of Europe, Africa, the Americas, and Asia confronted each other in new and rapidly evolving ways. Those confrontations often led to conquest, forced migration, and brutal exploitation, but they also contributed to cultural exchange and renewal.

Colonial Administration

Columbus, Cortés, and Pizarro had claimed the lands they had discovered for the Spanish crown. How were these lands governed? Already in 1503, the Spanish had granted the port of Seville a monopoly over all traffic to the New World and established the House of Trade to oversee economic matters. In 1524 Spain added to this body the Royal and Supreme

Council of the Indies, with authority over all colonial affairs subject to approval by the king. Spanish territories themselves were divided into **viceroyalties** or administrative divisions (see Map 16.2).

Within each territory, the viceroy, or imperial governor, exercised broad military and civil authority as the direct representative of Spain. The viceroy presided over the *audiencia* (ow-dee-EHN-see-ah), a board of judges that served as his advisory council and the highest judicial body. Later, King Charles III (r. 1759–1788) introduced the system of intendants to Spain's New World territories. These royal officials possessed broad military, administrative, and financial authority within their intendancies, smaller divisions within each viceroyalty, and were responsible not to the viceroy but to the monarchy in Madrid.

The Portuguese governed their colony of Brazil in a similar manner. After the union of the crowns of Portugal and Spain in 1580, Spanish administrative forms were introduced. Local officials called *corregidores* (kuh-REH-gih-dawr-eez) held judicial and military powers. Royal policies placed severe restrictions on Brazilian industries that might compete with those of Portugal and Spain.

Spanish Viceroyalties in the New World
New Spain: Created in 1525 with Mexico City as its capital
Peru: Created in 1542 with Lima as its capital
New Granada: Created in 1717 with Bogotá as its capital
La Plata: Created in 1776 with Buenos Aires as its capital

viceroyalties The name for the four administrative units of Spanish possessions in the Americas: New Spain, Peru, New Granada, and La Plata.

The Impact of European Settlement on the Lives of Indigenous Peoples

Before Columbus's arrival, the Americas were inhabited by thousands of groups of indigenous peoples with different languages and cultures. These groups ranged from hunter-gatherer tribes organized into tribal confederations to large-scale agriculture-based empires connecting bustling cities and towns.

The lives of these indigenous peoples were radically transformed by the arrival of Europeans. In the sixteenth century perhaps two hundred thousand Spaniards immigrated to the New World. To work the cattle ranches, sugar plantations, and silver mines these settlers established, the conquistadors first turned to the indigenous peoples.

The Spanish quickly established the **encomienda system**, in which the Crown granted the conquerors the right to employ groups of Native Americans as laborers or to demand tribute from them in exchange for providing food and shelter. In practice, the encomiendas (ehn-koh-mee-EHN-duhz) were a legalized form of slavery.

encomienda system A system whereby the Spanish crown granted the conquerors the right to forcibly employ groups of Indians; it was a disguised form of slavery.

The new conditions and hardships imposed by conquest and colonization resulted in enormous native population losses. The major cause of death was disease. Having little or no resistance to diseases brought from the Old World, the inhabitants of the New World fell victim to smallpox, typhus, influenza, and other illnesses. Another factor behind the decline in population was overwork. Unaccustomed to forced labor, native workers died in staggering numbers. Moreover, forced labor diverted local people from tending to their own crops, leading to malnutrition, reduced fertility rates, and starvation. Malnutrition

Silver Mine at Potosí The incredibly rich silver mines at Potosí (in modern-day Bolivia) contributed to the intensification of the African slave trade. In New Spain millions of indigenous laborers suffered brutal conditions and death in the silver mines. (Courtesy of The Hispanic Society of America)

Español con India,
Mestizo.

Mestizo con Española,
Castizo.

5

6

Mulato con Española,
Morisco.

Morisco con Española,
Chino.

Mixed Races The unprecedented mixing of peoples in the Spanish New World colonies inspired great fascination. An elaborate terminology emerged to describe the many possible combinations of indigenous, African, and European blood, which were known collectively as *castas*. This painting belongs to a popular genre of the eighteenth century depicting couples composed of individuals of different ethnic origin and the children produced of their unions. (Schalkwijk/Art Resource, NY)

and hunger in turn lowered resistance to disease. Finally, many indigenous peoples also died through outright violence in warfare.[2]

The Franciscan Bartolomé de Las Casas (1474–1566) documented the brutal treatment of indigenous peoples at the hands of the Spanish, claiming that "of three millions of people which Hispaniola itself did contain, there are left remaining alive scarce three hundred persons."[3] Las Casas and other missionaries asserted that the Indians had human rights, and through their persistent pressure the Spanish emperor Charles V abolished the worst abuses of the encomienda system in 1531.

The pattern of devastating disease and population loss established in the Spanish colonies was repeated everywhere Europeans settled. The best estimate is that the native population declined from roughly 50 million in 1492 to around 9 million by 1700. It is important to note, however, that native populations and cultures did survive the conquest period, sometimes by blending with European incomers and sometimes by maintaining cultural autonomy.

For colonial administrators the main problem posed by the astronomically high death rate was the loss of a subjugated labor force to work the mines and sugar plantations. The search for fresh sources of labor gave birth to the new tragedy of the Atlantic slave trade (see page 425).

The Columbian Exchange

Columbian exchange The exchange of animals, plants, and diseases between the Old and the New Worlds.

The travel of people and goods between the Old and New Worlds led to an exchange of animals, plants, and diseases, a complex process known as the Columbian exchange. As we have seen, the introduction of new diseases to the Americas had devastating consequences. But other results of the exchange brought benefits not only to the Europeans but also to native peoples.

Everywhere they settled, the Spanish and Portuguese brought and raised wheat with labor provided by the encomienda system. Grapes and olives brought over from Spain did well in parts of Peru and Chile. Perhaps the most significant introduction to the diet of Native Americans came via the meat and milk of the livestock that the early conquistadors brought with them, including cattle, sheep, and goats. The horse enabled both the Spanish conquerors and native populations to travel faster and farther as well as to transport heavy loads.

In turn, Europeans returned home with many food crops that became central elements of their diet. Crops originating in the Americas included tomatoes as well as many varieties of beans, squash, pumpkins, and peppers. One of the most important of such crops was maize (corn). By the late seventeenth century maize had become a staple in Spain, Portugal, southern France, and Italy, and in the eighteenth century it became one of the chief foods of southeastern Europe. Even more valuable was the nutritious white potato, which slowly spread from west to east—to Ireland, England, and France in the seventeenth century, and to Germany, Poland, Hungary, and Russia in the eighteenth, contributing everywhere to a rise in population.

While the exchange of foods was a great benefit to both cultures, the introduction of European pathogens to the New World had a disastrous impact on the native population. The wave of catastrophic epidemic disease that swept the Western Hemisphere after 1492 can be seen as an extension of the swath of devastation wreaked by the Black Death in the 1300s, first on Asia and then on Europe. The world after Columbus was thus unified by disease as well as by trade and colonization.

Sugar and Early Transatlantic Slavery

As Portuguese explorers began their voyages along the western coast of Africa, one of the first commodities they sought was slaves. In 1444 the first ship returned to Lisbon with a cargo of enslaved Africans. While the first slaves were simply seized by small raiding parties, Portuguese merchants soon found that it was easier to trade with African leaders, who were accustomed to dealing in slaves captured through warfare with neighboring powers. From 1490 to 1530 Portuguese traders brought between three hundred and two thousand black slaves to Lisbon each year.

In this stage of European expansion, the history of slavery became intertwined with the history of sugar. Originally sugar was an expensive luxury that only the very affluent could afford, but population increases and greater prosperity in the fifteenth century led to increasing demand. The establishment of sugar plantations on the Canary and Madeira Islands in the fifteenth century testifies to this demand.

Sugar was a particularly difficult crop to produce for profit. Sugar cultivation was extremely labor intensive and, because sugarcane has a virtually constant growing season, there was no fallow period when workers could recuperate. The demands of sugar production were increased with the invention of roller mills to crush the cane more efficiently. Yields could be augmented, but only if a sufficient labor force was found to supply the mills. Europeans solved the labor problem by forcing first native islanders and then enslaved Africans to perform the backbreaking work.

The transatlantic slave trade began in 1518 when Spanish king Charles I authorized traders to bring African slaves to New World colonies. The Portuguese brought the first slaves to Brazil around 1550; by 1600 four thousand were being imported annually. After its founding in 1621, the Dutch West India Company transported thousands of Africans to Brazil and the Caribbean, mostly to work on sugar plantations. In the late seventeenth century, with the chartering of the Royal African Company, the English got involved in bringing slaves to Barbados and other English colonies in the Caribbean and mainland North America.

Before 1700, when slavers decided it was better business to improve conditions, some 20 percent of slaves died on the voyage from Africa to the Americas.[4] The most common cause of death was dysentery induced by poor-quality food and water, lack of sanitation, and intense crowding. On sugar plantations, death rates among slaves from illness and exhaustion were extremely high, leading to a constant stream of new shipments of slaves from Africa. Driven by rising demands for sugar, cotton, tobacco, and other plantation crops, the tragic transatlantic slave trade reached its height in the eighteenth century.

The Transatlantic Slave Trade

■ Main sources of slaves
■ Main destinations of slaves
← Slave trade route

The Birth of the Global Economy

With Europeans' discovery of the Americas and their exploration of the Pacific, the entire world was linked for the first time in history by seaborne trade. The opening of that trade brought into being three successive commercial empires: the Portuguese, the Spanish, and the Dutch.

Map 16.3 Seaborne Trading Empires in the Sixteenth and Seventeenth Centuries By the mid-seventeenth century trade linked all parts of the world except for Australia. Notice that trade in slaves was not confined to the Atlantic but involved almost all parts of the world.

The Portuguese were the first worldwide traders. In the sixteenth century they controlled the sea route to India (Map 16.3). From their fortified bases at Goa on the Arabian Sea and at Malacca on the Malay Peninsula, ships carried goods to the Portuguese settlement at Macao in the South China Sea. From Macao Portuguese ships loaded with Chinese silks and porcelains sailed to the Japanese port of Nagasaki and to the Philippine port of Manila, where Chinese goods were exchanged for Spanish silver from New Spain. Throughout Asia the Portuguese traded in slaves. Back to Portugal they brought Asian spices that had been purchased with textiles produced in India and with gold and ivory from East Africa. They also shipped back sugar from their colony in Brazil, produced by African slaves whom they had transported across the Atlantic.

Becoming an imperial power a few decades later than the Portuguese, the Spanish were determined to claim their place in world trade. This was greatly facilitated by the discovery of silver, first at Potosí in modern-day Bolivia and later in Mexico. Silver poured into Europe through the Spanish port of Seville, contributing to steep inflation across Europe. Demand for silver also created a need for slaves to work in the mines. (See "Global Trade: Silver," page 428.)

The Spanish Empire in the New World was basically land-based, but across the Pacific the Spaniards built a seaborne empire centered at Manila in the Philippines. The city of Manila served as the transpacific bridge between Spanish America and China. In Manila, Spanish traders used silver from American mines to purchase Chinese silk for European markets.

In the seventeenth century the Dutch challenged the Spanish and Portuguese Empires, emerging by the end of the century as the most powerful worldwide seaborne trading power. The Dutch Empire was built on spices, and the Dutch East India Company was founded in 1602 with the stated intention of capturing the spice trade from the Portuguese.

The Dutch set their sights on gaining direct access to and control of the Indonesian sources of spices. In return for assisting Indonesian princes in local squabbles and disputes with the Portuguese, the Dutch won broad commercial concessions. Through agreements, seizures, and outright war, they gained control of the western access to the Indonesian archipelago in the first half of the seventeenth century. Gradually they achieved political domination over the archipelago itself. By the 1660s the Dutch had managed to expel the Portuguese from Ceylon and other East Indian islands, thereby establishing control of the lucrative spice trade.

> **Quick Review**
> What factors contributed to the precipitous drop in American indigenous populations following European conquest?

How did expansion shape values and beliefs in Europe and the Americas?

The age of overseas expansion heightened Europeans' contacts with the rest of the world. These contacts gave birth to new ideas about the inherent superiority or inferiority of different races, in part to justify European participation in the slave trade. Two great writers of the period both captured and challenged these views. The essays of Michel de Montaigne epitomized a new spirit of skepticism and cultural relativism, while the plays of William Shakespeare reflected his efforts to come to terms with the cultural complexities of his day. Religion became another means of cultural contact, as European missionaries aimed to spread Christianity in both the New World and East Asia, with mixed results.

New Ideas About Race

At the beginning of the transatlantic slave trade, most Europeans would have thought of Africans, if they thought of them at all, as savages and barbarians. They grouped Africans into the despised categories of pagan heathens or Muslim infidels. As Europeans turned to Africa for new sources of slaves, they drew on beliefs about Africans' primitiveness and barbarity to defend slavery and even argue that enslavement benefited Africans by bringing the light of Christianity to heathen peoples.

Over time the institution of slavery fostered a new level of racial inequality. Africans gradually became seen as utterly distinct from and wholly inferior to Europeans. In a transition from rather vague assumptions about African's non-Christian religious beliefs and general lack of civilization, Europeans developed increasingly rigid ideas of racial superiority and inferiority to safeguard the growing profits gained from plantation slavery. Black skin became equated with slavery itself as Europeans at home and in the colonies convinced themselves that blacks were destined by God to serve them as slaves in perpetuity.

After 1700 the emergence of new methods of observing and describing nature led to the use of science to define race. From referring to a nation or an ethnic group, henceforth "race" would be used to describe supposedly biologically distinct groups of people whose physical differences produced differences in culture, character, and intelligence, differences that justified the enslavement of "inferior" races.

GLOBAL TRADE

Silver

Silver in vast quantities was discovered in 1545 by the Spanish, at an altitude of fifteen thousand feet, at Potosí in unsettled territory conquered from the Inca Empire. A half-century later, 160,000 people lived in Potosí, making it about the size of the city of London. In the second half of the sixteenth century the mine (in present-day Bolivia) yielded perhaps 60 percent of all the silver mined in the world. From Potosí and the mines at Zacatecas and Guanajuato in Mexico, huge quantities of precious metals poured forth.

Mining became the most important industry in the colonies. The Spanish crown claimed the quinto, one-fifth of all precious metals mined in South America, and gold and silver yielded the Spanish monarchy 25 percent of its total income. Seville was the official port of entry for all Spanish silver, although a lively smuggling trade existed.

The real mover of world trade was not Europe, however, but China, which in this period had a population approaching 100 million. By 1450 the collapse of its paper currency led the Ming government to shift to a silver-based currency. Instead of rice, the traditional form of payment, all Chinese now had to pay their taxes in silver. The result was an insatiable demand for the world's production of silver.

Japan was China's original source, and the Japanese continued to ship large quantities of silver ore until the depletion of its mines near the end of the seventeenth century. The discovery of silver in the New World provided a vast and welcome new supply for the Chinese market. In 1571 the Spanish founded a port city at Manila in the Philippines to serve as a

bridge point for bringing silver to Asia. Throughout the seventeenth century Spanish galleons annually carried 2 million pesos (or more than fifty tons) of silver from Acapulco to Manila, where Chinese merchants carried it on to China. Even more silver reached China through exchange with European merchants who purchased Chinese goods using silver shipped across the Atlantic.

In exchange for silver, the Chinese traded high-quality finished goods much desired by elites across the world, including fine silks, porcelain, and spices. To ensure continued demand for their products, enterprising Chinese merchants adapted them to Western tastes.

Silver had a mixed impact on the regions involved. Spain's immense profits from silver paid for the tremendous expansion of its empire and for the large armies that defended it. However, the easy flow of money also dampened economic innovation. It exacerbated the rising inflation Spain was already experiencing in the mid-sixteenth century. When the profitability of the silver mines diminished in the 1640s, Spain's power was fundamentally undercut.

China experienced similarly mixed effects. On the one hand, the need for finished goods to trade for silver led to the rise of a merchant class and a new specialization of regional production. On the other hand, the inflation resulting from the influx of silver weakened the finances of the Ming Dynasty. As the purchasing power of silver declined in China, so did the value of silver taxes. The ensuing fiscal crisis helped bring down the Ming and led to the rise of the Qing in 1644. Ironically, the two states that benefited the most from silver also experienced political decline as a direct result of their reliance on it.

Silver ore mined at Potosí thus built the first global trade system in history. Previously, a long-standing Afroeurasian trading world had involved merchants and consumers from the three Old World continents. Once Spain opened a trade route across the Pacific through Manila, all continents except Australia and Antarctica were enduringly linked.

Michel de Montaigne and Cultural Curiosity

Racism was not the only possible reaction to the new worlds emerging in the sixteenth century. Decades of religious fanaticism, bringing civil anarchy and war, led both Catholics and Protestants to doubt that any one faith contained absolute truth. Added to these doubts was the discovery of peoples in the New World who had radically different ways of life. These shocks helped produce ideas of skepticism and cultural relativism in the sixteenth and seventeenth centuries. Skepticism is a school of thought founded on doubt that total certainty or definitive knowledge is ever attainable. Cultural relativism suggests that one culture is not necessarily superior to another, just different. Both notions found expression in the work of Frenchman Michel de Montaigne (MEE-shel duh mahn-TAYN; 1533–1592).

Montaigne developed a new literary genre, the essay—from the French essayer, meaning "to test or try"—to express his thoughts and ideas. Published in 1580, Montaigne's Essays consisted of short personal reflections. Intending to be accessible to ordinary people, Montaigne wrote in French rather than in Latin and used an engaging conversational style.

Map 16.4 The Global Silver Trade

Silver remained a crucial element in world trade through the nineteenth century. When Mexico won independence from Spain in 1821, it began to mint its own silver dollar, which became the most prized coin in trade in East Asia. By the beginning of the twentieth century, when the rest of the world had adopted gold as the standard of currency, only China and Mexico remained on the silver standard, testimony to the central role this metal had played in their histories.

Montaigne's essay "On Cannibals" reveals the impact of overseas discoveries on his consciousness. In contrast to the prevailing views of the time, he rejected the notion that one culture is superior to another. Speaking of native Brazilians, he wrote:

> *I find that there is nothing barbarous and savage in this nation [Brazil], . . . except, that everyone gives the title of barbarism to everything that is not according to his usage; as, indeed, we have no other criterion of truth and reason, than the example and pattern of the opinions and customs of the place wherein we live.*[5]

In his own time and throughout the seventeenth century, few would have agreed with Montaigne's challenging of European superiority. The publication of his ideas, however, contributed to a basic shift in attitudes. Montaigne inaugurated an era of doubt. "Wonder," he said, "is the foundation of all philosophy, research is the means of all learning, and ignorance is the end."[6]

William Shakespeare and His Influence

In addition to marking the introduction of the essay as a literary genre, the period fostered remarkable creativity in other branches of literature. England—especially in the late sixteenth and early seventeenth centuries—witnessed remarkable literary expression.

The undisputed master of the period was the dramatist William Shakespeare, whose genius lay in the originality of his characterizations, the diversity of his plots, his understanding of human psychology, and his unsurpassed gift for language. Born in 1564, Shakespeare was a Renaissance man with a deep appreciation of classical culture, individualism, and humanism.

Like Montaigne's, Shakespeare's work reveals the impact of new connections between Europeans and peoples of other cultures. The title character of *Othello* is described as a "Moor of Venice." In Shakespeare's day, the word *moor* referred to Muslims of Moroccan or North African origin, including those who had migrated to the Iberian Peninsula. It could also be applied, though, to natives of the Iberian Peninsula who converted to Islam or to non-Muslim Berbers in North Africa. To complicate things even more, references in the play to Othello as "black" in skin color have led many to believe that Shakespeare intended him to be a sub-Saharan African. This confusion in the play reflects the uncertainty in Shakespeare's own day about racial and religious classifications.

The character of Othello is both vilified in racist terms by his enemies and depicted as a brave warrior, a key member of the city's military leadership, and a man capable of winning the heart of an aristocratic white woman. Shakespeare's play thus demonstrates both the intolerance of contemporary society and the possibility for some individuals to look beyond racial stereotypes.

Shakespeare's last play, *The Tempest*, displays a similar interest in race and race relations. The plot involves the stranding on an island of sorcerer Prospero and his daughter, Miranda. There Prospero finds and raises Caliban, a native of the island, whom he instructs in his own language and religion. After Caliban's attempted rape of Miranda, Prospero enslaves him, earning the rage and resentment of his erstwhile pupil. Modern scholars often note the echoes between this play and the realities of imperial conquest and settlement in Shakespeare's day. It is no accident, they argue, that the playwright portrayed Caliban as a monstrous dark-skinned island native who was best-suited for slavery. However, Shakespeare himself borrows words from Montaigne's essay "On Cannibals," suggesting that he may have intended to criticize, rather than endorse, racial intolerance.

Religious Conversion in the New World

Converting indigenous people to Christianity was a key ambition for all European powers in the New World. Galvanized by the desire to spread their religion and prevent any gains by Protestants, Catholic powers actively sponsored missionary efforts. Franciscans, Dominicans, Jesuits, and members of other religious orders who accompanied the conquistadors and subsequent settlers established Catholic missions throughout Spanish and Portuguese colonies. Later French explorers were also accompanied by missionaries who preached to the Native American tribes with whom they traded.

Rather than a straightforward imposition of Christianity, conversion entailed a complex process of cultural exchange. Catholic friars were among the first Europeans to seek understanding of native cultures and languages as part of their effort to render Christianity comprehensible to indigenous people. In addition to spreading Christianity, missionaries taught indigenous peoples European methods of agriculture and instilled loyalty to colonial masters. In turn, Christian ideas and practices in the New World took on a distinctive character. For example, a sixteenth-century apparition of the Virgin Mary in Mexico City, known as the Virgin of Guadalupe, became a central icon of Spanish-American Catholicism.

Missionaries' success in the New World varied over time and space. In Central and South America large-scale conversion forged enduring Catholic cultures in Portuguese and Spanish colonies. Conversion efforts in seventeenth-century North America were less effective due to the scattered nature of settlement and the lesser integration of native people into the colonial community. On the whole, Protestants were less active than Catholics as missionaries, although some dissenters like Quakers and Methodists did seek converts among native people. Efforts to Christianize indigenous peoples in the New World were paralleled by missionary work by the Jesuits and other orders in the Far East.

Quick Review
How did the discovery and colonization of the New World change Europeans' sense of themselves and their place in the world?

Connections

JUST THREE YEARS separated Martin Luther's attack on the Catholic Church in 1517 and Ferdinand Magellan's discovery of the Pacific Ocean in 1520. Within a few short years western Europeans' religious unity and notions of terrestrial geography were shattered. Old medieval certainties about Heaven and earth collapsed. In the ensuing decades Europeans struggled to come to terms with religious differences among Protestants and Catholics at home and with the multitudes of new peoples and places they encountered abroad. While some Europeans were fascinated and inspired by this new diversity, too often the result was violence. Europeans endured decades of religious civil war, and indigenous peoples overseas suffered massive population losses as a result of European warfare, disease, and exploitation. Tragically, both Catholic and Protestant religious leaders condoned the trade in slaves that was to bring suffering and death to millions of Africans.

Even as the voyages of discovery contributed to the fragmentation of European culture, they also factored into state centralization and consolidation in the longer term. Henceforth, competition to gain overseas colonies became an integral part of European politics. Spain's investment in conquest proved spectacularly profitable, and yet, the ultimate result was a weakening of its power. Over time the Netherlands, England, and France also reaped tremendous profits from colonial trade, which helped them build modernized, centralized states.

The most important consequence of the European voyages of discovery was the creation of enduring contacts among five of the seven continents of the globe—Europe, Asia, Africa, North America, and South America. From the sixteenth century onward, the peoples of the world were increasingly entwined in divergent forms of economic, social, and cultural exchange. Our modern era of globalization had begun.

- **For a list of suggested readings for this chapter, visit** *bedfordstmartins.com/mckayworldunderstanding*.

- **For primary sources from this period, see** *Sources of World Societies*, Second Edition.

- **For Web sites, images, and documents related to topics in this chapter, see Make History at** *bedfordstmartins.com/mckayworldunderstanding*.

Chapter 16 Study Guide

To do these exercises online, go to bedfordstmartins.com/mckayworldundersanding.

 Step 1

GETTING STARTED
Below are basic terms about this period in global history. Can you identify each term below and explain why it matters?

TERMS	WHO (OR WHAT) AND WHEN	WHY IT MATTERS
bride wealth, p. 409		
caravel, p. 414		
Ptolemy's *Geography*, p. 414		
Treaty of Tordesillas, p. 418		
conquistador, p. 420		
Mexica Empire, p. 420		
Inca Empire, p. 422		
viceroyalties, p. 423		
encomienda system, p. 423		
Columbian exchange, p. 424		

 Step 2

MOVING BEYOND THE BASICS
The exercise below requires a more advanced understanding of the chapter material. Examine the nature and impact of Spanish exploration and conquest in the Americas by filling in the chart below with descriptions of the motives behind Spanish expansion across the Atlantic. Next, identify key Spanish conquests and discoveries and the institutions of Spanish rule in the Americas. Finally, describe the impact of Spanish conquest in the New World and Europe. When you are finished, consider the following questions: How do the motives you listed help explain the course of Spanish expansion in the New World? Were the ambitions of the men who carried out Spain's conquests always consistent with those of the crown? What intended and unintended consequences resulted from Spanish expansion?

MOTIVES	CONQUESTS AND DISCOVERIES	INSTITUTIONS OF SPANISH RULE	IMPACT IN THE NEW WORLD AND EUROPE

PUTTING IT ALL TOGETHER

Now that you've reviewed key elements of the chapter, take a step back and try to see the big picture. Remember to use specific examples from the chapter in your answers.

THE AFROEURASIAN TRADE WORLD BEFORE COLUMBUS

- Which states were at the center of global trade prior to 1492? Why?

- Why were Europeans at a trading disadvantage prior to 1492? How did geography limit European participation in world trade? What role did Europe's economy and material culture play in this context?

DISCOVERY AND CONQUEST

- In your opinion, what was the most important motive behind European expansion? What evidence can you provide to support your position?

- What was the Columbian exchange? How did it transform both Europe and the Americas?

CHANGING VALUES AND BELIEFS

- How did European expansion give rise to new ideas about race?

- How did expansion complicate Europeans' understanding of themselves and their place in the world?

LOOKING BACK, LOOKING AHEAD

- If Europe was at the periphery of the global trading system prior to 1492, where was it situated by the middle of the sixteenth century? What had changed? What had not?

- What connections can you make between our own experience of globalization in the twenty-first century and the experience of globalization in the sixteenth century? In what ways are the experiences similar? In what ways do they differ?

In Your Own Words Imagine that you must explain Chapter 16 to someone who hasn't read it. What would be the most important points to include and why?

17

European Power and Expansion

1500–1750

The seventeenth century was a period of crisis and transformation in Europe. What one historian described as the long European "struggle for stability" that originated with conflicts sparked by the Reformation in the early sixteenth century and continued with economic and social breakdown was largely resolved by 1680.[1] To meet the demands of war, armies grew larger, taxes increased, and new bureaucracies came into being. Thus at the same time that powerful governments were emerging and evolving in Asia—such as the Qing Dynasty in China, the Tokugawa Shogunate in Japan (see Chapter 21), and the Mughal Empire in India (see Chapter 20)—European rulers also increased the power of the central state.

Important differences existed, however, in terms of which authority within the state possessed sovereignty—the Crown or privileged groups. Between roughly 1589 and 1715 two basic patterns of government emerged in Europe: absolute monarchy and the constitutional state. Almost all subsequent European governments have been modeled on one of these patterns, which have also influenced greatly the rest of the world in the past three centuries.

Constitutional or absolutist, European states sought to further increase their power through colonial expansion. Jealous of the silver that had flowed into Spain from the New World, England, France, and the Netherlands vied for new acquisitions on the mainland and in the Caribbean.

Louis XIV Representations of royal power emphasized the aristocratic bearing, elegance, and innate authority of absolutist kings. This was one of Louis XIV's favorite portraits of himself. He liked it so much that he had many copies. (Louvre/Giraudon/The Bridgeman Art Library)

Chapter Preview

▶ How did European states respond to the crises of the seventeenth century?

▶ How did the absolutist monarchies of France and Spain fare in this era?

▶ How did absolutism develop in Austria, Prussia, and Russia?

▶ Where and why did constitutionalism triumph?

▶ How did European nations compete to build new colonies in the Americas?

How did European states respond to the crises of the seventeenth century?

Historians often refer to the seventeenth century as an "age of crisis." After the economic and demographic growth of the sixteenth century, Europe was challenged by population losses, economic decline, as well as social and political unrest. These difficulties were partially due to climate changes that reduced agricultural productivity. But they also resulted from religious divides, increased taxation, and war. Peasants and the urban poor were hit especially hard and often took direct action in an attempt to relieve their own suffering. In the long run, however, governments proved increasingly able to impose their will on the populace, growing in size and power over the course of the century.

Crises Among Peasants and the Urban Poor

In the seventeenth century a period of colder and wetter climate throughout Europe, dubbed the "little ice age" by historians, meant a shorter growing season with lower yields. Scarce food led to famine and the diseases caused by malnutrition, resulting in a drop in Europe's population.

When food prices were high, industry also suffered because consumers had little money to purchase goods. In turn, low wages and widespread unemployment further exacerbated economic problems. The urban poor and peasants were the hardest hit by the economic crisis. When the price of bread rose beyond their capacity to pay, they frequently expressed their anger by rioting. In towns they invaded bakers' shops to seize bread and resell it at a "just price." In rural areas they attacked convoys taking grain to the cities.

The Return of Serfdom in Eastern Europe

While economic and social hardship was common across Europe, important differences existed between east and west. In the west the demographic losses of the Black Death allowed peasants to escape serfdom as they acquired enough land to feed themselves and the livestock and ploughs necessary to work their land. In eastern Europe, however, the Black Death had the opposite effect. Before the arrival of the plague, starting in about 1050, rulers and nobles in sparsely populated eastern Europe had attracted new settlers by offering them land on excellent terms and granting them much personal freedom. But in the fourteenth century eastern lords addressed labor shortages caused by the Black Death by restricting the right of their

Estonian Serfs in the 1660s The Estonians were conquered by German military nobility in the Middle Ages and reduced to serfdom. The German-speaking nobles ruled the Estonian peasants with an iron hand, and Peter the Great reaffirmed their domination when Russia annexed Estonia. (Mansell Collection/Time Life Pictures/Getty Images)

Chapter 17 European Power and Expansion • 1500–1750

436

CHAPTER LOCATOR

How did European states respond to the crises of the seventeenth century?

peasants to move to take advantage of better opportunities elsewhere. Moreover, lords steadily took more and more of their peasants' land and arbitrarily imposed heavier and heavier labor obligations.

Between 1500 and 1650 the consolidation of serfdom in eastern Europe was accompanied by the growth of commercial agriculture, particularly in Poland and eastern Germany. As economic expansion and population growth resumed after 1500, eastern lords increased the production of their estates by squeezing surpluses out of the impoverished peasants. They then sold these surpluses to foreign merchants, who exported them to western Europe.

The worsened conditions for serfs in eastern Europe reflected the fact that eastern lords enjoyed much greater political power than their western counterparts. In the late Middle Ages, the noble landlord class had greatly increased its political power at the expense of the ruling monarchs. Moreover, the western concept of a king as one who protects the interests of all his people was not well developed in eastern Europe before 1650.

With the approval of weak kings, landlords in eastern Europe systematically undermined the medieval privileges of the towns and the power of the urban classes. The populations of the towns and the urban middle classes declined greatly. This development both reflected and promoted the supremacy of noble landlords in most of eastern Europe in the sixteenth century. Although noble landlords held onto their powers in the seventeenth century, kings increased their authority during this period (see pages 444–452).

The Thirty Years' War

In the first half of the seventeenth century, the fragile balance of life was violently upturned by the ravages of the Thirty Years' War (1618–1648). Leading up to the war were conflicts between Catholics and Protestants in the Holy Roman Empire. Although the emperor was Catholic, Protestantism had started to take hold in parts of the empire, including Germany, and clashes resulted. In 1555 the two religious groups came to an uneasy truce under the Peace of Augsburg, which officially recognized Lutheranism and allowed political authorities in each German territory to decide whether the territory would be Catholic or Lutheran. But the truce deteriorated as the faiths of various areas shifted. Lutheran princes felt compelled to form the Protestant Union (1608), and Catholics retaliated with the Catholic League (1609). Dynastic interests were also involved; the Spanish Habsburgs strongly supported the goals of their Austrian relatives: the unity of the empire and the preservation of Catholicism within it.

The war is traditionally divided into four phases: the Bohemian phase (1618–1625), the Danish phase (1625–1629), the Swedish phase (1630–1635), and the French phase (1635–1648). The division of the war into phases reflects the shifting alliances between central European territories and a variety of outside powers that characterized the conflict. In each phase, a different set of religious and political issues predominated.

The 1648 **Peace of Westphalia** that ended the Thirty Years' War marked a turning point in European history. The treaties that established the peace not only ended conflicts fought

Chapter Chronology

ca. 1500–1650	Consolidation of serfdom in eastern Europe
1533–1584	Reign of Ivan the Terrible in Russia
1589–1610	Reign of Henry IV in France
1598–1613	Time of Troubles in Russia
1612–1697	Caribbean islands colonized by France, England, and the Netherlands
1620–1740	Growth of absolutism in Austria and Prussia
1642–1649	English civil war, ending with the execution of Charles I
1643–1715	Reign of Louis XIV in France
1651	First of the Navigation Acts
1653–1658	Oliver Cromwell's military rule in England (the Protectorate)
1660	Restoration of English monarchy under Charles II
1665–1683	Jean-Baptiste Colbert applies mercantilism to France
1670	Charles II agrees to re-Catholicize England in secret agreement with Louis XIV
1670–1671	Cossack revolt led by Stenka Razin
1682	Louis XIV moves court to Versailles
1682–1725	Reign of Peter the Great in Russia
1683–1718	Habsburgs push the Ottoman Turks from Hungary
1685	Edict of Nantes revoked
1688–1689	Glorious Revolution in England
1701–1713	War of the Spanish Succession

Peace of Westphalia The name of a series of treaties that concluded the Thirty Years' War in 1648 and marked the end of large-scale religious violence in Europe.

Map 17.1 **Europe After the Thirty Years' War** Which country emerged from the Thirty Years' War as the strongest European power? What dynastic house was that country's major rival in the early modern period?

over religious faith but also recognized the independent authority of more than three hundred German princes (Map 17.1), reconfirming the emperor's severely limited authority. The Augsburg agreement of 1555 became permanent, adding Calvinism to Catholicism and Lutheranism as legally permissible creeds.

The Thirty Years' War was probably the most destructive event for the central European economy and society prior to the world wars of the twentieth century. Perhaps one-third of urban residents and two-fifths of the rural population died, leaving entire areas depopulated. Trade in southern German cities was virtually destroyed. Agricultural areas also suffered catastrophically. Many small farmers lost their land, allowing nobles to enlarge their estates and consolidate their control.[2]

438

Chapter 17   European Power and Expansion • 1500–1750

CHAPTER LOCATOR

How did European states respond to the crises of the seventeenth century?

Achievements in State Building

In this context of economic and demographic depression, monarchs began to make new demands on their people. Traditionally, historians have distinguished between the absolutist governments of France, Spain, eastern and central Europe, and Russia and the constitutionalist governments of England and the Dutch Republic. More recently, historians have emphasized commonalities among these powers. Despite their political differences, all these states sought to protect and expand their frontiers, raise new taxes, consolidate central control, and compete for the colonies opening up in the New and Old Worlds.

Rulers who wished to increase their authority encountered formidable obstacles. Travel by horse on unpaved roads was slow; it took weeks to convey orders from the central government to the provinces. Rulers also suffered from lack of information about their realms, making it impossible to police and tax the population effectively. Local power structures presented another obstacle. Nobles, the church, town councils, guilds, and other bodies held legal privileges that could not easily be rescinded. In some kingdoms many people spoke a language different from the Crown's, further augmenting their sense of autonomy.

Nonetheless, over the course of the seventeenth century both absolutist and constitutional governments achieved new levels of central control. This increased authority focused on four areas in particular: greater taxation, growth in armed forces, larger and more efficient bureaucracies, and the increased ability to compel obedience from subjects.

> **Quick Review**
> How did European states take advantage of seventeenth-century economic and political conditions to consolidate their authority?

How did the absolutist monarchies of France and Spain fare in this era?

Kings in absolutist states claimed exclusive power to make and enforce laws, denying any other institution or group the authority to check their power. Louis XIV of France is often seen as the epitome of an absolute monarch. In truth, his success relied on collaboration with nobles, and thus his example illustrates both the achievements and the compromises of absolutist rule.

As French power rose in the seventeenth century, Spain faded. Once the fabulous revenue from American silver declined, Spain's economic stagnation could no longer be disguised, and the country faltered under weak leadership.

The Foundations of Absolutism

Louis XIV's absolutism had long roots. In 1589 his grandfather Henry IV (r. 1589–1610), the founder of the Bourbon dynasty, acquired a devastated country. Civil wars between Protestants and Catholics had wracked France since 1561. Poor harvests had reduced peasants to starvation, and commercial activity had declined drastically.

Henry IV inaugurated a remarkable recovery by keeping France at peace during most of his reign. Although he had converted to Catholicism, he issued the Edict of Nantes, allowing Huguenots (French Protestants) the right to worship in 150 traditionally Protestant towns. He sharply lowered taxes and improved the country's infrastructure, building new roads and canals as well as repairing the ravages of years of civil war. Despite his efforts at peace, Henry was murdered in 1610 by a Catholic zealot.

How did the absolutist monarchies of France and Spain fare in this era?

How did absolutism develop in Austria, Prussia, and Russia?

Where and why did constitutionalism triumph?

How did European nations compete to build new colonies in the Americas?

439

After the death of Henry IV his wife, the queen-regent Marie de' Medici, headed the government for their eldest son, nine-year-old Louis XIII (r. 1610–1643). In 1628 Armand Jean du Plessis—Cardinal Richelieu (1585–1642)—became first minister of the French crown. Richelieu's maneuvers allowed the monarchy to maintain power within Europe and within its own borders despite the turmoil of the Thirty Years' War.

Cardinal Richelieu's domestic policies were designed to strengthen royal control. He extended the use of intendants, commissioners for each of France's thirty-two districts who were appointed directly by the monarch, to whom they were solely responsible. They recruited men for the army, supervised the collection of taxes, presided over the administration of local law, checked up on the local nobility, and regulated economic activities in their districts. As the intendants' power increased under Richelieu, so did the power of the centralized French state.

Under Richelieu, the French monarchy also acted to repress Protestantism within its borders, seeing it as a threat to royal authority. Richelieu did not aim to wipe out Protestantism in the rest of Europe, however. His main foreign policy goal was to destroy the Catholic Habsburgs' grip on territories that surrounded France. Consequently, Richelieu supported Habsburg enemies, including Protestants (see page 437). For the French cardinal, interests of state outweighed religious considerations.

In 1642 Cardinal Jules Mazarin (1602–1661) succeeded Richelieu as chief minister for the next child-king, the four-year-old Louis XIV. Along with the regent, Queen Mother Anne of Austria, Mazarin continued Richelieu's centralizing policies. His struggle to increase royal revenues to meet the costs of the Thirty Years' War led to the uprisings of 1648–1653 known as the Fronde. In Paris, magistrates of the Parlement of Paris, the nation's most important law court, were outraged by the Crown's autocratic measures. These so-called robe nobles (named for the robes they wore in court) encouraged violent protest by the common people. As rebellion spread outside Paris and to the sword nobles (the traditional warrior nobility), civil order broke down completely, and young Louis XIV had to flee Paris. In 1651 Anne's regency ended with the declaration of Louis as king in his own right. Much of the rebellion died away, and its leaders came to terms with the government. Humiliated by his flight from Paris during the Fronde, Louis was determined to avoid any recurrence of rebellion when he assumed personal rule at Mazarin's death in 1661.

Fronde A series of violent uprisings early in the reign of Louis XIV triggered by growing royal control and oppressive taxation.

Louis XIV and Absolutism

In the long reign of Louis XIV (r. 1643–1715) the French monarchy reached the peak of absolutist development. Louis believed in the doctrine of the divine right of kings: God had established kings as his rulers on earth, and they were answerable ultimately to him alone. However, kings could not simply do as they pleased. They had to obey God's laws and rule for the good of the people. To symbolize his central role in the divine order, when he was fifteen years old Louis danced at a court ballet dressed as the sun, thereby acquiring the title "Sun King."

Louis worked very hard at the business of governing. He ruled his realm through several councils of state and insisted on taking a personal role in many of the councils' decisions. He refused to have a prime minister and he selected councilors from the recently ennobled or the upper middle class, stating that "the public should know, from the rank of those whom I chose to serve me, that I had no intention of sharing power with them."[3] Despite increasing financial problems, Louis never called a meeting of the Estates General, the traditional French representative assembly composed of the three estates of clergy, nobility, and commoners. His subjects had no means to form united views or exert joint pressure on the monarch.

Although personally tolerant, Louis hated division within the realm and insisted that religious unity was essential to the security of the state. He thus pursued the policy of

Chapter 17   European Power and Expansion • 1500–1750

440

CHAPTER LOCATOR

How did European states respond to the crises of the seventeenth century?

Protestant repression launched by Richelieu and, in 1685, revoked the Edict of Nantes.

Despite his claims to absolute authority, there were multiple constraints on Louis's power. As a representative of divine power, he was obliged to rule in a way that seemed consistent with virtue and benevolent authority. He had to uphold the laws issued by his royal predecessors. Moreover, he also relied on the informal collaboration of nobles. Without their cooperation, it would have been impossible for Louis to extend his power throughout France or wage his many foreign wars (see page 442). His need to elicit noble cooperation led him to revolutionize court life at his palace at Versailles.

Life at Versailles

Through most of the seventeenth century, the French court had no fixed home, following the monarch to his numerous palaces and country residences. In 1682 Louis moved his court and government to the palace at Versailles, in the countryside southwest of Paris. The palace quickly became the center of political, social, and cultural life. The king required all great nobles to spend at least part of the year in attendance on him there. Since he controlled the distribution of state power and wealth, nobles had no choice but to obey and compete with each other for his favor at Versailles.

Louis XIV Receiving Ambassadors from Siam The kings of France and Siam (today's Thailand) sent ambassadors to each other's courts in the 1680s. This engraving commemorates Louis XIV's reception of the second Siamese diplomatic mission at Versailles, a visit that aroused great excitement and enthusiasm throughout western Europe. (Private Collection/Photo © Luca Tettoni/The Bridgeman Art Library)

Louis further revolutionized court life by establishing an elaborate set of etiquette rituals to mark every moment of his day, from waking up and dressing in the morning to removing his clothing and retiring at night. He required nobles to serve him in these rituals, and they vied for the honor of doing so. These rituals may seem absurd, but they were far from meaningless or trivial. The king controlled immense resources and privileges; access to him meant access to power and wealth. Courtiers sought these rewards for themselves and their family members and followers. A system of patronage—in which a higher-ranked individual protected a lower-ranked one in return for loyalty and services—flowed from the court to the provinces. Through this mechanism Louis gained cooperation from powerful nobles.

Although they were denied public offices and posts, women played a central role in the patronage system. At court the king's wife, mistresses, and other female relatives recommended individuals for honors, advocated policy decisions, and brokered alliances between noble factions. Noblewomen played a similar role among courtiers, bringing their family connections into their marriages to form powerful social networks.

Louis XIV was also an enthusiastic patron of the arts. He commissioned many sculptures and paintings for Versailles as well as performances of dance and music. Louis loved the stage, and in the plays of Molière and Racine his court witnessed the finest achievements in the history of the French theater.

French Finances

Louis's controller general, Jean-Baptiste Colbert (1619–1683), understood that France's ability to build armies and fight wars depended on a strong economy. Colbert's central principle was that the wealth and the economy of France should serve the state. To this end, from 1665 to his death in 1683, Colbert rigorously applied mercantilist policies to France.

Mercantilism is a collection of governmental policies for the regulation of economic activities by and for the state. It derives from the idea that a nation's international power is based on its wealth, specifically its supply of gold and silver. To accumulate wealth, a country always had to sell more goods abroad than it bought. Thus, to reduce imports Colbert insisted that French industry should produce everything needed by the French people.

To increase exports, Colbert supported old industries and subsidized new ones. To encourage the purchase of French goods, he abolished many domestic tariffs and raised tariffs on foreign products. In 1664 Colbert founded the Company of the East Indies with hopes of competing with the Dutch for Asian trade. Colbert also sought to increase France's control over and presence in New France (Canada) (see page 458).

During Colbert's tenure as controller general, Louis was able to pursue his goals without massive tax increases and without creating a stream of new offices. The constant pressure of warfare after Colbert's death, however, undid many of his economic achievements.

Louis XIV's Wars

Louis XIV kept France at war for thirty-three of the fifty-four years of his personal rule. François le Tellier, Marquis de Louvois, Louis's secretary of state for war, created a professional army in the employ of the French state, and over the course of the seventeenth century, the French army nearly tripled in size. As in so many other matters, Louis's model was followed across Europe.

During this long period of warfare Louis's goal was to expand France to what he considered its natural borders. His armies managed to make considerable progress toward this goal, but by the beginning of the 1680s Louis had reached the limit of his expansion. The wars of the 1680s and 1690s brought no additional territories but placed unbearable strains on French resources. Colbert's successors resorted to desperate measures to finance these wars, including devaluation of the currency and new taxes.

Louis's last war resulted from a dispute over the rightful successor to the Spanish throne. In 1700 the childless Spanish king Charles II (r. 1665–1700) died. His will bequeathed the Spanish crown and its empire to Philip of Anjou, Louis XIV's grandson. The will violated a prior treaty by which the European powers had agreed to divide the Spanish possessions between the king of France and the Holy Roman emperor. Claiming that he was following both Spanish and French interests, Louis broke with the treaty and accepted the will, thereby triggering the War of the Spanish Succession (1701–1713).

In 1701 the English, Dutch, Austrians, and Prussians formed the Grand Alliance against Louis XIV. War dragged on until 1713, when it was ended by the Peace of Utrecht. This series of treaties allowed Louis's grandson Philip to remain king of Spain on the understanding that the French and Spanish crowns would never be united. France surrendered large territories overseas to England (Map 17.2; see also page 459). In 1714 an exhausted France hovered on the brink of bankruptcy. It is no wonder that when Louis XIV died on September 1, 1715, many subjects felt as much relief as they did sorrow.

The Decline of Absolutist Spain

By the early seventeenth century signs of Spanish decline were becoming evident. Between 1610 and 1650 Spanish trade with the colonies in the New World fell 60 percent due to

mercantilism A system of economic regulations aimed at increasing the power of the state based on the belief that a nation's international power was based on its wealth, specifically its supply of gold and silver.

Peace of Utrecht A series of treaties, from 1713 to 1715, that ended the War of the Spanish Succession, ended French expansion in Europe, and marked the rise of the British Empire.

CHAPTER LOCATOR

Spanish Troops The long wars that Spain fought over Dutch independence, in support of Habsburg interests in Germany, and against France left the country militarily exhausted and financially drained by the mid-1600s. In this detail from a painting by Peeter Snayers, Spanish troops—thin, emaciated, and probably unpaid—straggle away from battle. (Prado, Madrid/Index/The Bridgeman Art Library)

competition from colonial industries and from Dutch and English traders. At the same time, the silver mines that filled the Spanish Empire's treasury started to run dry, and the quantity of metal produced steadily declined after 1620.

In Madrid, royal expenditures constantly exceeded income. To meet state debt, the Spanish crown repeatedly devalued the coinage and declared bankruptcy, which resulted in the collapse of national credit and the contraction of commerce and manufacturing. To make matters worse, the Crown expelled some three hundred thousand Moriscos, or former Muslims, in 1609, significantly reducing the pool of skilled craftsmen.

Spanish aristocrats, attempting to maintain an extravagant lifestyle they could no longer afford, increased the rents on their estates. High rents and heavy taxes drove the peasants from the land, leading to a decline in agricultural productivity. In cities wages and production stagnated.

The Spanish crown had no solutions to these dire problems, and Spain's situation worsened with internal conflicts and military defeats over the course of the seventeenth century. In 1640 Spain faced serious revolts in Catalonia and Portugal. A long and costly war with France over Mantua (1628–1658) ended with the Treaty of the Pyrenees of 1659, under the terms of which Spain was compelled to surrender extensive territories to France. And in 1688 the Spanish crown reluctantly recognized the independence of Portugal. With these losses the era of Spanish dominance in Europe ended.

Quick Review
What role did economic factors play in the rise of France and the fall of Spain?

Map 17.2 Europe After the Peace of Utrecht, 1715

The series of treaties commonly called the Peace of Utrecht ended the War of the Spanish Succession and redrew the map of Europe. A French Bourbon king succeeded to the Spanish throne. France surrendered the Spanish Netherlands (later Belgium), then in French hands, to Austria and recognized the Hohenzollern rulers of Prussia. Spain ceded Gibraltar to Great Britain, for which it has been a strategic naval station ever since. Spain also granted Britain the *asiento*, the contract for supplying African slaves to America.

ANALYZING THE MAP Identify the areas on the map that changed hands as a result of the Peace of Utrecht. How did these changes affect the balance of power in Europe?

CONNECTIONS How and why did so many European countries possess scattered or discontiguous territories? What does this suggest about European politics in this period? Does this map suggest potential for future conflict?

How did absolutism develop in Austria, Prussia, and Russia?

Rulers in eastern and central Europe and in Russia also labored to build strong absolutist states in the seventeenth century. But they built on social and economic foundations far different from those in western Europe, namely serfdom and the strong nobility who

444 Chapter 17 European Power and Expansion • 1500–1750

CHAPTER LOCATOR How did European states respond to the crises of the seventeenth century?

benefited from it. The endless wars of the seventeenth century allowed monarchs to increase their power by building large armies, increasing taxation, and suppressing representative institutions. In exchange for their growing power, monarchs allowed nobles to remain unchallenged masters of their peasants.

The Austrian Habsburgs

In 1521 Habsburg emperor Charles V ceded his Austrian territories to his brother Ferdinand I, thus permanently separating the dynasty into Austrian and Spanish branches. Like all of central Europe, the Austrian Habsburgs emerged from the Thirty Years' War impoverished and exhausted. Their efforts to turn the weak Holy Roman Empire into a real state had failed. Defeat in central Europe encouraged the Austrian Habsburgs to focus inward and eastward in an attempt to unify their diverse holdings.

Habsburg victory over Bohemia during the Thirty Years' War was an important step in this direction. Ferdinand II (r. 1619–1637) drastically reduced the power of the Bohemian Estates, the largely Protestant representative assembly. He also confiscated the landholdings of Protestant nobles and gave them to his supporters. After 1650 a large portion of the Bohemian nobility was of recent origin and owed its success to the Habsburgs.

With the support of this new nobility, the Habsburgs established direct rule over Bohemia. Under their rule the condition of the enserfed peasantry worsened substantially, and Protestantism was stamped out. These changes were important steps in creating absolutist rule in Bohemia.

Ferdinand III (r. 1637–1657) continued to build state power. He centralized the government in the empire's German-speaking provinces, which formed the core Habsburg holdings. For the first time, a permanent standing army was ready to put down any internal opposition.

The Habsburg monarchy then turned east toward Hungary, which had been divided between the Ottomans and the Habsburgs in the early sixteenth century. Between 1683 and 1699 the Habsburgs pushed the Ottomans from most of Hungary and Transylvania. The recovery of all the former kingdom of Hungary was completed in 1718 (Map 17.3).

The Hungarian nobility, despite its reduced strength, effectively thwarted the full development of Habsburg absolutism. Throughout the seventeenth century Hungarian nobles repeatedly rose in revolt against the Habsburgs. In 1703, with the Habsburgs bogged down in the War of the Spanish Succession, the Hungarians rose in one last patriotic rebellion under Prince Francis Rákóczy (RAH-coht-see).

Rákóczy and his forces were eventually defeated, but the Habsburgs agreed to restore many of the traditional privileges of the Hungarian aristocracy in return for the country's acceptance of hereditary Habsburg rule. Thus Hungary was never fully integrated into a centralized Habsburg state. Despite checks on their ambitions in Hungary, the Habsburgs made significant achievements in state building elsewhere by forging consensus with the church and the nobility.

Prussia in the Seventeenth Century

In the fifteenth and sixteenth centuries the Hohenzollern family ruled parts of eastern Germany as the imperial electors of Brandenburg and the dukes of Prussia, but they had little real power.

When he came to power, twenty-year-old Frederick William (r. 1640–1688), later known as the Great Elector, was determined to unify his three provinces and enlarge them by diplomacy and war. These provinces were Brandenburg; Prussia, inherited in 1618; and scattered holdings along the Rhine inherited in 1614 (see Map 17.3). Each had

How did the absolutist monarchies of France and Spain fare in this era?

How did absolutism develop in Austria, Prussia, and Russia?

Where and why did constitutionalism triumph?

How did European nations compete to build new colonies in the Americas?

445

Map 17.3 The Growth of Austria and Brandenburg-Prussia to 1748 Austria expanded to the southwest into Hungary and Transylvania at the expense of the Ottoman Empire. It was unable to hold the rich German province of Silesia, however, which was conquered by Brandenburg-Prussia.

Junkers The nobility of Brandenburg and Prussia; they were reluctant allies of Frederick William in his consolidation of the Prussian state.

its own representative assembly, or estates, and taxes could not be levied without their consent. The estates of Brandenburg and Prussia were dominated by the nobility and the landowning classes, known as the Junkers.

In 1660 Frederick William persuaded Junkers in the estates to accept taxation without consent in order to fund a permanent army. They agreed to do so in exchange for reconfirmation of their own privileges, including authority over the serfs. Opposition from the towns was crushed ruthlessly.

Thereafter, the estates' power declined rapidly, for the Great Elector had both financial independence and superior force. State revenue tripled during his reign, and the army expanded dramatically. In 1701 the elector's son, Frederick I, received the title of king of Prussia (instead of elector) as a reward for aiding the Holy Roman emperor in the War of the Spanish Succession.

The Consolidation of Prussian Absolutism

The son of the first king of Prussia, Frederick William I (r. 1713–1740) completed his grandfather's work, eliminating the last traces of parliamentary estates and local self-government. Frederick William firmly established Prussian absolutism and transformed Prussia into a

CHAPTER LOCATOR

How did European states respond to the crises of the seventeenth century?

military state. Twelfth in Europe in population, Prussia had the fourth largest army by 1740. The Prussian army was the best-trained in Europe, astonishing foreign observers with its precision, skill, and discipline.

Despite his restrictive rule, Frederick William and his ministers built an exceptionally honest and conscientious bureaucracy to administer the country and foster economic development. Nevertheless, Prussians paid a heavy and lasting price for bureaucratic and military achievements. Civil society became rigid and highly disciplined. As a Prussian minister later summed up, "To keep quiet is the first civic duty."[4] Thus the policies of Frederick William I, combined with peasant bondage and Junker tyranny, laid the foundations for a highly militaristic country.

Frederick II (r. 1740–1786), commonly known as Frederick the Great, built masterfully on the work of his father. When the young Maria Theresa of Austria inherited the Habsburg crown, Frederick invaded Austria's rich, mainly German province of Silesia, defying solemn Prussian promises to respect the Pragmatic Sanction, a diplomatic agreement that had guaranteed Maria Theresa's succession. In 1742, as other powers vied for her lands in the European War of the Austrian Succession (1740–1748), Maria Theresa was forced to cede almost all of Silesia to Prussia. In one stroke Prussia had doubled its population. Now Prussia unquestionably towered above all the other German states and stood as a European Great Power.

Mongol Rule in Russia and the Rise of Moscow

Absolutism in Russia had its roots in two hundred years of rule under the Mongols. In the thirteenth century the Mongols conquered Kievan Rus, the medieval Slavic state centered first at Novgorod and then at Kiev, a city on the Dnieper River, which included most of present-day Ukraine, Belarus, and part of northwest Russia. The princes of the Grand Duchy of Moscow, a principality within Kievan Rus, became particularly adept at serving the Mongols. They loyally put down uprisings and collected the khan's taxes. Eventually the Muscovite princes were able to destroy the other princes who were their rivals for power. Ivan III (r. 1462–1505), known as Ivan the Great, successfully expanded the principality of Moscow eastward toward the Baltic Sea and westward to the Ural Mountains and the Siberian frontier.

By 1480 Ivan III felt strong enough to stop acknowledging the Mongol khan as his supreme ruler. To legitimize their new autonomy, he and his successors declared themselves to be autocrats, meaning that they were the sole source of power. The Muscovite state also borrowed Mongol institutions such as the tax system, postal routes, and the census. Loyalty from the highest-ranking nobles, or **boyars**, helped the Muscovite princes consolidate their power.

Another source of legitimacy lay in Moscow's claim to the political and religious inheritance of the Byzantine Empire. After the empire's capital, Constantinople, fell to the Turks in 1453, the princes of Moscow saw themselves as the heirs of both the caesars (or emperors) and of Orthodox Christianity. The title *tsar*, first taken by Ivan IV in 1547, is a contraction of *caesar*.

Moscow, ca. 1300
Gains by 1505
Gains by 1584
Gains by 1725
Major battle

SWEDEN
FINLAND
URAL MTS.
St. Petersburg
Novgorod
POLAND-LITHUANIA
Moscow
Cossacks
Kiev
Poltava 1709
Cossacks
CAUCASUS MTS.

The Expansion of Russia, to 1725

boyars The highest-ranking members of the Russian nobility.

Russian Peasant An eighteenth-century French artist visiting Russia recorded his impressions of the daily life of the Russian people in this etching of a fish merchant pulling his wares through a snowy village on a sleigh. Two caviar vendors behind him make a sale to a young mother standing at her doorstep with her baby in her arms. (From Jean-Baptiste Le Prince's second set of Russian etchings, 1765. Private Collection/www.amis-paris-petersbourg.org)

The Tsar and His People

Developments in Russia took a chaotic turn with the reign of Ivan IV (r. 1533–1584), the famous Ivan the Terrible. Ivan's reign was successful in defeating the remnants of Mongol power, adding vast new territories to the realm, and laying the foundations for the huge multiethnic Russian empire. After the sudden death of his beloved first wife, Anastasia Romanov, however, Ivan began a campaign of persecution against those he suspected of opposing him. Many were intimates of the court from leading boyar families, whom he killed along with their families, friends, servants, and peasants. To further crush the power of the boyars, Ivan created a new service nobility, who received noble titles and estates in return for serving in the tsar's army.

Ivan also moved toward making all commoners servants of the tsar. During Ivan's reign, growing numbers of peasants fled toward wild, recently conquered territories to the east and south. There they joined free groups and warrior bands known as Cossacks. In the 1580s Ivan's government began to forbid peasants to leave their masters, a first step toward the imposition of serfdom on all peasants.

Simultaneously, Ivan bound urban traders and artisans to their towns and jobs so that he could tax them more heavily. These restrictions checked the growth of the Russian middle classes. From nobles down to merchants and peasants, all the Russian people were thus brought into the tsar's service. Ivan even made use of Cossack armies in forays to the southeast, forging a new alliance between Moscow and the Cossacks.

Following Ivan's death, Russia entered a chaotic period known as the Time of Troubles (1598–1613). While Ivan's relatives struggled for power, the Cossacks and peasants rebelled against nobles and officials. This social explosion from below brought the nobles together. They crushed the Cossack rebellion and elected Ivan's grandnephew, Michael Romanov,

Cossacks Free groups and outlaw armies originally comprising runaway peasants living on the borders of Russian territory from the fourteenth century onward. By the end of the sixteenth century they had formed an alliance with the Russian state.

the new hereditary tsar (r. 1613–1645). (See "Listening to the Past: A German Account of Russian Life," page 450.)

Although the new tsar successfully reconsolidated central authority, uprisings continued. One of the largest rebellions was led by the Cossack Stenka Razin, who in 1670 attracted a great army of urban poor and peasants, killing landlords and government officials and proclaiming freedom from oppression. In 1671 this rebellion was defeated.

Despite the turbulence of the period, the Romanov tsars, like their Western counterparts, made several important achievements during the second half of the seventeenth century. After a long war, Russia gained land in Ukraine from Poland in 1667 and completed the conquest of Siberia by the end of the century. Territorial expansion was accompanied by growth of the bureaucracy and the army. Exploitation of Siberia's natural resources funded the Romanovs' bid for Russia's status as a Great Power. Thus, Russian imperialist expansion to the east paralleled the Western powers' exploration and conquest of the Atlantic world in the same period.

The Reforms of Peter the Great

Peter the Great (r. 1682–1725) embarked on a tremendous campaign to accelerate and complete the process of state building. In 1697 the tsar, who was fascinated by foreign technology, led a group of Russian elites on an eighteen-month tour of western European capitals. Traveling unofficially to avoid lengthy diplomatic ceremonies, Peter met with foreign kings and experts. He was particularly impressed with the growing power of the Dutch and the English, and he considered how Russia could profit from their example. He soon had reason to apply what he had learned.

Suffering initial defeat in war with Sweden in 1701, Peter responded with measures designed to increase state power and strengthen his armies. He required all nobles to serve in the army or in the civil administration—for life. Peter also created schools and universities to produce skilled technicians and experts. Furthermore, he established a military-civilian bureaucracy with fourteen ranks, and he decreed that all had to start at the bottom and work toward the top. Drawing on his experience abroad, Peter sought talented foreigners and placed them in his service. These measures gradually combined to make the army and government more powerful and efficient.

Peter also greatly increased the service requirements of commoners. He established a regular standing army of peasant-soldiers commanded by officers from the nobility. Taxes on peasants to fund the military and other government spending increased threefold during Peter's reign. Serfs were arbitrarily assigned to work in the growing number of factories and mines that supplied the military.

In 1709 Peter's new war machine was able to crush the army of Sweden in Ukraine at Poltava in one of the most significant battles

Peter the Great This compelling portrait by Grigory Musikiysky captures the strength and determination of the warrior-tsar in 1723, after more than three decades of personal rule. In his hand Peter holds the scepter, symbol of royal sovereignty, and across his breastplate is draped an ermine fur, a mark of honor. In the background are the battleships of Russia's new Baltic fleet and the famous St. Peter and St. Paul Fortress that Peter built in St. Petersburg. (Bildarchiv Preussischer Kulturbesitz/The Bridgeman Art Library)

How did the absolutist monarchies of France and Spain fare in this era?

How did absolutism develop in Austria, Prussia, and Russia?

Where and why did constitutionalism triumph?

How did European nations compete to build new colonies in the Americas?

449

LISTENING TO THE PAST

A German Account of Russian Life

Seventeenth-century Russia remained a remote and mysterious land for western and even central Europeans, who had few direct contacts with the tsar's dominion. Westerners portrayed eastern Europe as more "barbaric" and less "civilized" than their homelands. Thus they expanded eastern Europe's undeniably harsher social and economic conditions to encompass a very debatable cultural and moral inferiority.

Knowledge of Russia came mainly from occasional travelers who had visited Muscovy and sometimes wrote accounts of what they saw. The most famous of these accounts was by the German Adam Olearius (ca. 1599–1671), who was sent to Moscow on three diplomatic missions in the 1630s. These missions ultimately proved unsuccessful, but they provided Olearius with a rich store of information for his Travels in Muscovy, *from which the following excerpts are taken. Published in German in 1647 and soon translated into several languages (but not Russian), Olearius's unflattering but well-informed study played a major role in shaping European ideas about Russia.*

▌▌ The government of the Russians is what political theorists call a "dominating and despotic monarchy," where the sovereign, that is, the tsar or the grand prince who has obtained the crown by right of succession, rules the entire land alone, and all the people are his subjects, and where the nobles and princes no less than the common folk—townspeople and peasants—are his serfs and slaves, whom he rules and treats as a master treats his servants. . . .

If the Russians be considered in respect to their character, customs, and way of life, they are justly to be counted among the barbarians. . . . The vice of drunkenness is so common in this nation, among people of every station, clergy and laity, high and low, men and women, old and young, that when they are seen now and then lying about in the streets, wallowing in the mud, no attention is paid to it, as something habitual. If a cart driver comes upon such a drunken pig whom he happens to know, he shoves him onto his cart and drives him home, where he is paid his fare. No one ever refuses an opportunity to drink and to get drunk, at any time and in any place, and usually it is done with vodka. . . .

The Russians being naturally tough and born, as it were, for slavery, they must be kept under a harsh and strict yoke and must be driven to do their work with clubs and whips, which they suffer without impatience, because such is their station, and they are accustomed to it. Young and half-grown fellows sometimes come together on certain days and train themselves in fisticuffs, to accustom themselves to receiving blows, and, since habit is second nature, this makes blows given as punishment easier to bear. Each and all, they are slaves and serfs. . . .

Because of slavery and their rough and hard life, the Russians accept war readily and are well suited to it. On certain occasions, if need be, they reveal themselves as courageous and daring soldiers. . . .

Although the Russians, especially the common populace, living as slaves under a harsh yoke, can bear and endure a great deal out of love for their masters, yet if the pressure is beyond measure, then it can be said of them: "Patience, often wounded, finally turned into fury." A dangerous indignation results, turned not so much against their sovereign as against the lower authorities, especially if the people have been much oppressed by them and by their supporters and have not been protected by the higher authorities. And once they are aroused and enraged, it is not easy to appease them. Then, disregarding all dangers that may ensue, they resort to every kind of violence and behave like madmen. . . . They own little; most of them have no feather beds; they lie on cushions, straw, mats, or their clothes; they sleep on benches and, in winter, like the non-Germans [natives] in Livonia, upon the oven, which serves them for cooking and is flat on the top; here husband, wife, children, servants, and maids huddle together. In some houses in the countryside we saw chickens and pigs under the benches and the ovens. . . . Russians are not used to delicate food and dainties; their daily food consists of porridge, turnips, cabbage, and cucumbers, fresh and pickled, and in Moscow mostly of big salt fish which stink badly, because of the thrifty use of salt, yet are eaten with relish. . . .

The Russians can endure extreme heat. In the bathhouse they stretch out on benches and let themselves be beaten and rubbed with bunches of birch twigs and wisps of bast (which I could not stand); and when they are hot and red all over and so exhausted that they can bear it no longer in the bathhouse, men and women rush outdoors naked and pour cold water over their bodies; in winter they even wallow in the

in Russian history. Russia's victory against Sweden was conclusive in 1721, and Estonia and present-day Latvia came under Russian rule for the first time. The cost was high: warfare consumed 80 to 85 percent of all revenues. But Russia became the dominant power in the Baltic and a great European power.

After his victory at Poltava, Peter channeled enormous resources into building a new Western-style capital on the Baltic to rival the great cities of Europe. Originally a Swedish

450

Chapter 17   European Power and Expansion • 1500–1750

CHAPTER LOCATOR

How did European states respond to the crises of the seventeenth century?

The brutality of serfdom is shown in this illustration from Olearius's *Travels in Muscovy*. (University of Illinois Library, Champaign)

snow and rub their skin with it as if it were soap; then they go back into the hot bathhouse. And since bathhouses are usually near rivers and brooks, they can throw themselves straight from the hot into the cold bath. . . .

Generally noble families, even the small nobility, rear their daughters in secluded chambers, keeping them hidden from outsiders; and a bridegroom is not allowed to have a look at his bride until he receives her in the bridal chamber. Therefore some happen to be deceived, being given a misshapen and sickly one instead of a fair one, and sometimes a kinswoman or even a maidservant instead of a daughter; of which there have been examples even among the highborn. No wonder therefore that often they live together like cats and dogs and that wife-beating is so common among Russians. . . .

In the Kremlin and in the city there are a great many churches, chapels, and monasteries, both within and without the city walls, over two thousand in all. This is so because every nobleman who has some fortune has a chapel built for himself, and most of them are of stone. The stone churches are round and

vaulted inside. . . . They allow neither organs nor any other musical instruments in their churches, saying: Instruments that have neither souls nor life cannot praise God. . . .

In their churches there hang many bells, sometimes five or six, the largest not over two hundredweights. They ring these bells to summon people to church, and also when the priest during mass raises the chalice. In Moscow, because of the multitude of churches and chapels, there are several thousand bells, which during the divine service create such a clang and din that one unaccustomed to it listens in amazement. 🙶

Source: G. Vernadsky and R. T. Fisher, Jr., eds., *A Source Book for Russian History from Early Times to 1917*, vol. 1 (New Haven: Yale University Press, 1972), pp. 249–251. Reprinted by permission of Yale University Press.

QUESTIONS FOR ANALYSIS

1. How did Olearius characterize the Russians in general? What evidence did he offer for his judgment?
2. How might Olearius's account help explain Stenka Razin's rebellion (page 449)?
3. On the basis of these passages, why do you think Olearius's book was so popular and influential in central and western Europe?

outpost, St. Petersburg was designed to reflect modern urban planning with wide, straight avenues, buildings set in a uniform line, and large parks. Each summer, twenty-five to forty thousand peasants were sent to provide construction labor in St. Petersburg without pay.

There were other important consequences of Peter's reign. For Peter, modernization meant westernization, and both Westerners and Western ideas flowed into Russia for the first time. He required nobles to shave their heavy beards and wear Western clothing. He

How did the absolutist monarchies of France and Spain fare in this era?

How did absolutism develop in Austria, Prussia, and Russia?

Where and why did constitutionalism triumph?

How did European nations compete to build new colonies in the Americas?

451

also required them to attend parties where young men and women would mix together and freely choose their own spouses, in defiance of tradition. From these efforts a new elite class of Western-oriented Russians began to emerge.

Peter's reforms were unpopular with many Russians. For nobles, one of Peter's most detested reforms was the imposition of unigeniture—inheritance of land by one son alone—cutting off daughters and other sons from family property. For peasants, the reign of the tsar saw a significant increase in the bonds of serfdom, and the gulf between the enserfed peasantry and the educated nobility increased.

Quick Review
Why did accomplishments in state building in eastern Europe so often come at the expense of towns, merchants, and the peasantry?

Where and why did constitutionalism triumph?

constitutionalism A form of government in which power is limited by law and balanced between the authority and power of the government, on the one hand, and the rights and liberties of the subject or citizen, on the other; it includes constitutional monarchies and republics.

republicanism A form of government in which there is no monarch and power rests in the hands of the people as exercised through elected representatives.

While France, Prussia, Russia, and Austria developed absolutist states, England and the Netherlands evolved toward **constitutionalism**, which is the limitation of government by law. Constitutionalism also implies a balance between the authority and power of the government, on the one hand, and the rights and liberties of the subjects, on the other.

Despite their common commitment to constitutional government, England and the Dutch Republic represented significantly different alternatives to absolute rule. After decades of civil war and an experiment with **republicanism**, the English opted for a constitutional monarchy in 1688. For their part, the Dutch rejected monarchical rule in 1648, when their independence from Spain was formally recognized. Instead, they adopted a republican form of government in which elected estates (assemblies) held supreme power.

Absolutist Claims in England

In 1603 the immensely popular Queen Elizabeth (r. 1558–1603) died without leaving a direct heir. As had been agreed before her death, her Scottish cousin James Stuart succeeded her as James I (r. 1603–1625). King James was well educated and had thirty-five years' experience as king of Scotland. But he was not as interested in displaying the majesty of monarchy as Elizabeth had been. Urged to wave at the crowds who waited to greet their new ruler, James complained that he was tired and threatened to drop his breeches "so they can cheer at my arse."[5]

James's greatest problem stemmed from his absolutist belief that a monarch has a divine right to his authority and is responsible only to God, arguing that "There are no privileges and immunities which can stand against a divinely appointed King." Such a view ran counter to the long-standing English idea that a person's property could not be taken away without due process of law. James I and his son Charles I (r. 1625–1649) considered such constraints a threat to their divine-right prerogative. Consequently, at every meeting of Parliament between 1603 and 1640, bitter squabbles erupted between the Crown and the House of Commons. Charles I's attempt to govern without Parliament (1629–1640) and to finance his government by emergency taxes brought the country to a crisis.

Religious Divides and Civil War

Puritans Members of a sixteenth- and seventeenth-century reform movement within the Church of England that advocated purifying it of Roman Catholic elements.

Religious issues also embittered relations between the king and the House of Commons. In the early seventeenth century increasing numbers of English people felt dissatisfied with the Church of England. Many **Puritans** believed that the Reformation had not gone far

452   Chapter 17 European Power and Expansion • 1500–1750

CHAPTER LOCATOR

How did European states respond to the crises of the seventeenth century?

Puritan Occupations These eight engravings depict typical Puritan occupations and show that the Puritans came primarily from the artisan and lower middle classes. The governing classes and peasants made up a much smaller percentage of Puritans, and most generally adhered to the traditions of the Church of England. (Visual Connection Archive)

enough. They wanted to "purify" the Anglican Church of Roman Catholic elements, including crown-approved bishops.

James I responded to such ideas by declaring, "No bishop, no king." For James, bishops were among the chief supporters of the throne. His son and successor, Charles I, further antagonized subjects with opposing religious views. Not only did Charles marry a Catholic princess, but he also supported the policies of Archbishop of Canterbury William Laud (1573–1645). In 1637 Laud attempted to impose elements of Anglican church organization in Scotland. The Presbyterian Scots rejected these efforts and revolted. To finance an army to put down the Scots, King Charles was compelled to summon Parliament in November 1640.

Charles had ruled from 1629 to 1640 without Parliament, financing his government through stopgap levies considered illegal by most English people. Most members of Parliament believed that such taxation without consent amounted to despotism. Consequently, they were not willing to trust the king with an army. Moreover, many supported the Scots' resistance to Charles's religious innovations. Accordingly, this Parliament, called the Long Parliament because it sat from 1640 to 1660, enacted legislation that limited the power of the monarch and made government without Parliament impossible.

In 1641 the House of Commons passed the Triennial Act, which compelled the king to summon Parliament every three years. The Commons also impeached Archbishop Laud and then threatened to abolish bishops. King Charles, fearful of a Scottish invasion, reluctantly accepted these measures. The next act in the conflict was precipitated by the outbreak of rebellion in Ireland. In 1641 the Catholic gentry of Ireland led an uprising in response to a feared invasion by anti-Catholic forces of the British Long Parliament.

Without an army, Charles I could neither come to terms with the Scots nor respond to the Irish rebellion. After a failed attempt to arrest parliamentary leaders, Charles left London for the north of England, where he recruited an army. In response, Parliament formed its own army, the New Model Army. During the spring of 1642 both sides prepared for war.

How did the absolutist monarchies of France and Spain fare in this era? | How did absolutism develop in Austria, Prussia, and Russia? | **Where and why did constitutionalism triumph?** | How did European nations compete to build new colonies in the Americas?

453

The English civil war (1642–1649) pitted the power of the king against that of the Parliament. After three years of fighting, Parliament's New Model Army defeated the king's armies at the battles of Naseby and Langport. Charles refused to concede defeat. Both sides jockeyed for position, waiting for a decisive event. This arrived in the form of the army under the leadership of Oliver Cromwell, a member of the House of Commons and a devout Puritan. In 1647 Cromwell's forces captured the king and dismissed members of the Parliament who opposed Cromwell's actions. In 1649 the remaining representatives, known as the Rump Parliament, put Charles on trial for high treason. Charles was found guilty and beheaded on January 30, 1649.

The English Civil War, 1642–1649

The Puritan Protectorate

With the execution of Charles, kingship was abolished. The question then became how the country would be governed. One answer was provided by philosopher Thomas Hobbes (1588–1679). Hobbes held a pessimistic view of human nature and believed that, left to themselves, humans would compete violently for power and wealth. The only solution, as he outlined in his 1651 treatise *Leviathan*, was a social contract in which all members of society placed themselves under the absolute rule of a monarch who would maintain peace and order.

Hobbes's longing for a benevolent absolute monarch was not widely shared in England. Instead, a commonwealth, or republican government, was proclaimed. Theoretically, legislative power rested in the surviving members of Parliament, and executive power was lodged in a council of state. In fact, the army that had defeated the king controlled the government, and Oliver Cromwell controlled the army. Though called the **Protectorate**, the rule of Cromwell (1653–1658) was a form of military dictatorship.

Protectorate The English military dictatorship established by Oliver Cromwell following the execution of Charles I (1653–1658).

The army prepared a constitution, the Instrument of Government (1653), that invested executive power in a lord protector (Cromwell) and a council of state. It provided for triennial parliaments and gave Parliament the sole power to raise taxes. But after repeated disputes, Cromwell dismissed Parliament in 1655. Cromwell divided England into twelve military districts, each governed by a major general. Reflecting Puritan ideas of morality, Cromwell's state forbade sports, kept the theaters closed, and censored the press.

On the issue of religion, Cromwell favored some degree of toleration, and all Christians except Roman Catholics had the right to practice their faith. Cromwell had long associated Catholicism in Ireland with sedition and heresy, and he led an army there to reconquer the country in August 1649. Following Cromwell's reconquest, the English banned Catholicism in Ireland, executed priests, and confiscated land from Catholics for English and Scottish settlers. These brutal acts left a legacy of Irish hatred for England and had little success in discouraging Catholicism.

The Protectorate collapsed when Cromwell died in 1658 and his ineffectual son succeeded him. Fed up with military rule, by 1660 the English were ready to restore the monarchy.

Restoration of the English Monarchy

The Restoration of 1660 brought to the throne Charles II (r. 1660–1685), eldest son of Charles I, formerly exiled in the Netherlands. Both houses of Parliament were also restored, together with the established Anglican Church. The Restoration failed to resolve two seri-

CHAPTER LOCATOR

How did European states respond to the crises of the seventeenth century?

ous problems, however. What was to be the attitude of the state toward Puritans, Catholics, and dissenters from the established church? And what was to be the relationship between the king and Parliament?

To answer the first question, Parliament enacted the **Test Act** of 1673 against those outside the Church of England, denying them the right to vote, hold public office, preach, teach at or attend the universities, or even assemble for meetings. In politics Charles II set out to work with Parliament, but this resolve did not last. Finding that Parliament did not grant him an adequate income, in 1670 Charles entered into a secret agreement with his cousin Louis XIV. The French king promised to subsidize Charles's income, and in return Charles would relax the laws against Catholics, gradually re-Catholicize England, and convert to Catholicism himself. When the details of this treaty leaked out, a great wave of anti-Catholic sentiment swept England.

When James II (r. 1685–1688) succeeded his brother, the worst fears of English anti-Catholics were realized. In violation of the Test Act, James appointed Roman Catholics to positions of authority. And he went further; attempting to broaden his base of support with Protestant dissenters and nonconformists, James granted religious freedom to all.

Seeking to prevent the return of Catholic absolutism, a group of eminent persons in Parliament and the Church of England offered the English throne to James's Protestant daughter Mary and her Dutch husband, Prince William of Orange. In December 1688 James II fled to France. Early in 1689 William and Mary were crowned king and queen of England.

Test Act Legislation passed by the English parliament in 1673 to secure the position of the Anglican Church by stripping Puritans, Catholics, and other dissenters of the right to vote, preach, assemble, hold public office, and attend or teach at the universities.

Constitutional Monarchy

The English call the events of 1688 and 1689 the Glorious Revolution because it replaced one king with another with a minimum of bloodshed. The revolution also established the principle that sovereignty, the ultimate power in the state, was divided between king and Parliament and that the king ruled with the consent of the governed. This principle was enshrined in a Bill of Rights, which was formulated in direct response to the attempts by the Stuart kings to impose absolute rule on England.

The Glorious Revolution and the concept of representative government found its best defense in political philosopher John Locke's *Second Treatise of Civil Government* (1690). Locke (1632–1704) maintained that a government that oversteps its proper function — protecting the natural rights of life, liberty, and property — becomes a tyranny. By "natural rights" Locke meant rights basic to all men because all have the ability to reason. Under a tyrannical government, he argued, the people have the natural right to rebellion.

Although the events of 1688 and 1689 brought England closer to Locke's ideal, they did not constitute a democratic revolution. The Glorious Revolution placed sovereignty in Parliament, and Parliament represented the upper classes.

The English Bill of Rights
Laws to be made by Parliament
No suspension of laws by the Crown
Parliament to be called every three years
No taxes without the approval of Parliament
Independence of the judiciary established
No standing army in peacetime
Limitations placed on the rights of Catholics

The Dutch Republic in the Seventeenth Century

In the late sixteenth century the seven northern provinces of the Netherlands fought for and won their independence from Spain. The independence of the Republic of the United Provinces of the Netherlands was recognized in 1648 in the treaty that ended the Thirty Years' War. In this period, often called the "golden age of the Netherlands," Dutch ideas and attitudes played a profound role in shaping a new and modern worldview. At the same time, the United Provinces developed its own distinctive model of a constitutional state.

Rejecting the rule of a monarch, the Dutch established a republic, a state in which power rests in the hands of the people and is exercised through elected representatives. An oligarchy

How did the absolutist monarchies of France and Spain fare in this era?

How did absolutism develop in Austria, Prussia, and Russia?

Where and why did constitutionalism triumph?

How did European nations compete to build new colonies in the Americas?

455

INDIVIDUALS IN SOCIETY

Glückel of Hameln

IN 1690 A JEWISH WIDOW IN THE SMALL GERMAN town of Hameln in Lower Saxony sat down to write her autobiography. She wanted to distract her mind from the terrible grief she felt over the death of her husband and to provide her twelve children with a record "so you will know from what sort of people you have sprung, lest today or tomorrow your beloved children or grandchildren came and know naught of their family." Out of her pain and heightened consciousness, Glückel (1646–1724) produced an invaluable source for scholars.

She was born in Hamburg two years before the end of the Thirty Years' War. In 1649 the merchants of Hamburg expelled the Jews, who moved to nearby Altona, then under Danish rule. When the Swedes overran Altona in 1657–1658, the Jews returned to Hamburg "purely at the mercy of the Town Council." Glückel's narrative unfolds against a background of the constant harassment to which Jews were subjected — special papers, permits, bribes — and in Hameln she wrote, "And so it has been to this day and, I fear, will continue in like fashion."

When Glückel was "barely twelve," her father betrothed her to Chayim Hameln, and they married when she was fourteen. She describes him as "the perfect pattern of the pious Jew," a man who stopped his work every day for study and prayer, fasted, and was scrupulously honest in his business dealings. Only a few years older than Glückel, Chayim earned his living dealing in precious metals and in making small loans on pledges (pawned goods). This work required constant travel to larger cities, markets, and fairs, often in bad weather, always over dangerous roads. Chayim consulted his wife about all his business dealings. As he lay dying, a friend asked if he had any last wishes. "None," he replied. "My wife knows everything. She shall do as she has always done." For thirty years Glückel had been his friend, full business partner, and wife. They had thirteen children, twelve of whom survived their father, eight then unmarried. As Chayim had foretold, Glückel succeeded in launching the boys in careers and in providing dowries for the girls.

Glückel's world was her family, the Jewish community of Hameln, and the Jewish communities into which her children married. Her social and business activities took her across Europe, from Amsterdam to Berlin, from Danzig to Vienna; thus her world was far from narrow or provincial. She took great pride that Prince Frederick of Cleves, later king of Prussia, danced at the wedding of her eldest daughter. The rising prosperity of Chayim's businesses allowed the couple to maintain up to six servants.

Glückel was deeply religious, and her culture was steeped in Jewish literature, legends, and mystical and secular works. Above all, she relied on the Bible. Her language, heavily sprinkled with scriptural references, testifies to a rare familiarity with the Scriptures.

Students who wish to learn about seventeenth-century business practices, the importance of the dowry in marriage, childbirth, Jewish life, birthrates, family celebrations, and even the meaning of life can gain a good deal from the memoirs of this extraordinary woman who was, in the words of one of her descendants, the poet Heinrich Heine, "the gift of a world to me."

Source: *The Memoirs of Glückel of Hameln* (New York: Schocken Books, 1977).

QUESTIONS FOR ANALYSIS

1. Consider the ways in which Glückel of Hameln was both an ordinary and an extraordinary woman of her times. Would you call her a marginal or a central person in her society? Why?
2. How might Glückel's successes be attributed to the stabilizing force of absolutism in the seventeenth century?

Although no images of Glückel exist, Rembrandt's *The Jewish Bride* suggests the mutual devotion of Glückel and her husband for one another. (Rijksmuseum-Stichting Amsterdam)

456 Chapter 17 European Power and Expansion • 1500–1750

CHAPTER LOCATOR   How did European states respond to the crises of the seventeenth century?

of wealthy businessmen called regents handled domestic affairs in each province's estates, or assemblies. The provincial estates held virtually all the power. A federal assembly, or States General, handled foreign affairs and war, but all issues had to be referred back to the local estates for approval, and each of the seven provinces could veto any proposed legislation.

In each province, the estates appointed an executive officer, known as the stadholder, who carried out ceremonial functions and was responsible for military defense. Although in theory freely chosen by the estates, in practice the reigning prince of Orange usually held the office of stadholder in several of the seven provinces of the republic.

The political success of the Dutch rested on their commercial prosperity. The moral and ethical bases of that commercial wealth were thrift, frugality, and religious toleration. Jews enjoyed a level of acceptance and assimilation in Dutch business and general culture unique in early modern Europe. (See "Individuals in Society: Glückel of Hameln," page 456.) In the Dutch Republic, toleration paid: it attracted a great deal of foreign capital and investment.

The Dutch came to dominate the shipping business by putting profits from their original industry—herring fishing—into shipbuilding. They boasted the lowest shipping rates and largest merchant marine in Europe (Map 17.4). Trade and commerce brought the Dutch the highest standard of living in Europe, perhaps in the world.

stadholder The executive officer in each of the United Provinces of the Netherlands, a position often held by the princes of Orange.

Quick Review
How did constitutionalism in England and the Netherlands differ? How would you explain the differences you note?

Map 17.4 **Seventeenth-Century Dutch Commerce** Dutch wealth rested on commerce, and commerce depended on the huge Dutch merchant marine, manned by perhaps forty-eight thousand sailors. The fleet carried goods from all parts of the globe to the port of Amsterdam.

How did the absolutist monarchies of France and Spain fare in this era?

How did absolutism develop in Austria, Prussia, and Russia?

Where and why did constitutionalism triumph?

How did European nations compete to build new colonies in the Americas?

457

How did European nations compete to build new colonies in the Americas?

As Spain's power began to weaken in the early seventeenth century, the Dutch, English, and French seized their opportunity, ruthlessly vying to claim their own territories in the New World. Conflicts over access to trade with the Americas mounted in the seventeenth century, but by the early eighteenth century England had won a series of concessions that enabled it to dominate trade across the Atlantic.

Life in the colonies was shaped by many factors, including the absence or presence of European women. Complex ethnic and cultural identities emerged due to the mixing of European, indigenous, and African peoples.

Colonial Expansion of Northern European Powers

In the sixteenth century the Spanish and Portuguese dominated colonization of the Americas (see Chapter 16). In the early seventeenth century, however, England, France, and the Netherlands profited from Spain's weakness to challenge its dominion. Unlike Spain, where the royal government financed exploration and directly ruled the colonies, England, France, and the Netherlands left colonization largely to chartered companies endowed with monopolies over settlement and trade in a given area.

Founded at Jamestown in 1607, Virginia, the first successful English colony, produced tobacco for a growing European market. Indentured servants obtained free passage to the colony in exchange for several years of work and the promise of greater opportunity than in England. In the 1670s Carolina was settled by English colonists from the Caribbean island of Barbados, who found conditions suitable for large rice plantations. During the late seventeenth century enslaved Africans replaced indentured servants as laborers on tobacco and rice plantations, and a harsh racial divide was imposed.

For the first settlers on the coast of New England, the reasons for seeking a new life in the colonies were more religious than economic. Many of these colonists were radical Protestants escaping Anglican repression. The small and struggling outpost of Plymouth Colony (1620) was followed by Massachusetts Bay Colony (1630), which grew into a prosperous settlement. Religious disputes in Massachusetts led to the dispersion of settlers into the new communities of Providence, Connecticut, Rhode Island, and New Haven. Because New England lacked the conditions for plantation agriculture, slavery was always a minor element of life there.

Whereas the Spanish established wholesale dominance over Mexico and Peru, English settlements hugged the Atlantic coastline. This did not prevent conflict with the indigenous inhabitants over land and resources. The haphazard nature of English colonization also led to conflicts of authority within the colonies. As the English crown grew more interested in colonial expansion, efforts were made to acquire the territory between New England in the north and Virginia in the south. The goal was to unify English holdings and minimize French and Dutch competition on the Atlantic seaboard. The results of these efforts were the mid-Atlantic colonies: the Catholic settlement of Maryland (1632); New York, captured from the Dutch in 1664; and the Quaker colony of Pennsylvania (1681).

The French established colonies in present-day Canada and then moved farther south. In 1608 Samuel de Champlain founded the first permanent French settlement at Quebec as a post for trading beaver pelts with Native American peoples. Louis XIV's economic minister, Jean-Baptiste Colbert, established direct royal control over New France (Canada) and sent colonists to enlarge its population. Although the population of the French settlements was always minuscule compared with that of British North America, the French were energetic

458 Chapter 17 European Power and Expansion • 1500–1750

CHAPTER LOCATOR

How did European states respond to the crises of the seventeenth century?

and industrious traders and explorers. In 1673 the Jesuit Jacques Marquette and the merchant Louis Joliet sailed down the Mississippi and claimed possession of the land on both sides of the river as far south as present-day Arkansas. In 1682 Robert de La Salle traveled the Mississippi to the Gulf of Mexico, opening the way for French occupation of Louisiana.

In the first decades of the seventeenth century, English and French captains also defied Spain's hold over the Caribbean Sea (see Map 18.2 on page 485), with both England and France seizing control of a number of important islands. These islands acquired new importance after 1640, when the Portuguese brought sugar plantations to Brazil. Sugar and slaves quickly followed in the West Indies (see page 425), making the Caribbean plantations the most lucrative of all colonial possessions.

Not content with challenging the Portuguese in the Indian Ocean, the Dutch also aspired to a role in the Americas. Founded in 1621 in a period of war with Spain, the Dutch West India Company aggressively sought to open trade with North and South America and succeeded in taking possession of portions of Brazil and the Caribbean. The Dutch also successfully interceded in the transatlantic slave trade, bringing much of the west coast of Africa under their control.

Dutch efforts to colonize North America were less successful. The colony of New Netherland, governed from New Amsterdam (modern-day New York City), was hampered by lack of settlement and weak governance, and it was easily captured by the English.

Mercantilism and Colonial Wars

European powers in the seventeenth century shared a mercantilist view of economics (see page 442). In England the desire to increase both military power and private wealth resulted in the mercantile system of the Navigation Acts. Oliver Cromwell established the first of these laws in 1651, and the restored monarchy of Charles II extended them in 1660 and 1663. The acts required most goods imported into England and Scotland (Great Britain after 1707) to be carried on British-owned ships with British crews or on ships of the country producing the article. Moreover, these laws gave British merchants and shipowners a virtual monopoly on trade with British colonies.

Navigation Acts Mid-seventeenth-century English mercantilist laws that greatly restricted other countries' rights to trade with England and its colonies.

The Navigation Acts were a form of economic warfare. Their initial target was the Dutch, who were far ahead of the English in shipping and foreign trade in the mid-seventeenth century. In conjunction with three Anglo-Dutch wars between 1652 and 1674, the Navigation Acts seriously damaged Dutch shipping and commerce. By the late seventeenth century the Netherlands was falling behind England in shipping, trade, and settlement.

Thereafter France was England's most serious rival in the competition for overseas empire. Rich in natural resources, allied with Spain, and home to a population three or four times that of England, France was continental Europe's leading military power. But the War of the Spanish Succession, the last of Louis XIV's many wars (see page 442), tilted the balance in favor of England. The 1713 Peace of Utrecht forced France to cede its North American holdings in Newfoundland, Nova Scotia, and the Hudson Bay territory to Britain. Spain was compelled to give Britain control of its West African slave trade and to let Britain send one ship of merchandise into the Spanish colonies annually. These acquisitions primed Britain to take a leading role in the growing Atlantic trade of the eighteenth century, including the transatlantic slave trade (discussed in Chapter 19).

Life in the Colonies

Many factors helped shape life in European colonies, including locations of settlements, indigenous cultures and practices, as well as the cultural attitudes and official policies of the European colonizers. Women played a crucial role in the creation of new identities

6. De Español y Negra Mulato.

Mulatto Painting

The caption in the upper left corner of this mid-eighteenth-century painting identifies the family as being composed of a Spanish father and a black mother, and their child is described as "mulatto." The painting was number six in a series of sixteen images by the painter Jose de Alcibar, each showing a different racial and ethnic combination. The series belonged to a popular genre in the Spanish Americas known as *castas* paintings, which commonly depicted sixteen different forms of racial mixing. (Attrib. Jose de Alcibar, 6, De *Espano y Negra, Mulato*, ca. 1760–1770. Denver Art Museum: Collection of Frederick and Jan Mayer. Photo © James O. Milmoe)

ANALYZING THE IMAGE How would you characterize the relations among mother, father, and child as shown in this painting? Does the painter suggest power relations within the family? What attitude does the painter seem to have toward the family?

CONNECTIONS Why do you think such paintings were so popular? Who do you think the audience might have been, and why would viewers be fascinated by such images?

and the continuation of old ones. The first explorers formed unions with native women, through coercion or consent, and relied on them as translators, guides, and intermediaries in the formation of alliances with indigenous powers. As settlement developed, the character of each colony was influenced by the presence or absence of European women. Where women and children accompanied male colonists, as in the British colonies and the Spanish mainland colonies, new settlements took on European languages, religion, and ways of life. Where European women did not accompany male settlers, as on the west coast of Africa and most European outposts in Asia, local populations largely retained their own cultures, to which male Europeans acclimatized themselves.

Most women who crossed the Atlantic were Africans, who constituted four-fifths of the female newcomers before 1800.[6] Wherever slavery existed, masters profited from their power to engage in sexual relations with enslaved women. The mixing of indigenous people with Europeans and Africans created whole new populations, ethnicities, and complex

460 Chapter 17 **European Power and Expansion • 1500–1750**

CHAPTER LOCATOR

How did European states respond to the crises of the seventeenth century?

self-identities. In Spanish America the word *mestizo*—*métis* in French—described people of mixed Native American and European descent. The blanket terms *mulatto* and *people of color* were used for those of mixed African and European origins. With its immense slave-based plantation system, large indigenous population, and relatively low Portuguese immigration, Brazil developed a particularly complex racial and ethnic mosaic.

Quick Review
How did northern European colonial efforts in the Americas differ from earlier Spanish and Portuguese efforts?

Connections

THE SEVENTEENTH CENTURY represented a difficult passage between two centuries of dynamism and growth in Europe. On one side lay the sixteenth century's religious enthusiasm and strife, overseas discoveries, rising populations, and vigorous commerce. On the other side stretched the eighteenth century's renewed population growth, economic development, and cultural flourishing. The first half of the seventeenth century was marked by the spread of religious and dynastic warfare across Europe, resulting in death and widespread suffering. Recurring crop failure, famine, and epidemic disease contributed to a stagnant economy and population loss. In the middle decades of the seventeenth century, the very survival of the European monarchies established in the Renaissance appeared in doubt.

With the re-establishment of order in the second half of the century, maintaining stability was of paramount importance to European rulers. While a few nations placed their trust in constitutionally limited governments, many more were ruled by monarchs proclaiming their absolute and God-given authority. The ability to actually assume such power depended on cooperation from local elites. In this way, both absolutism and constitutionalism relied on political compromises forged from decades of strife.

As Spain's power weakened, other European nations bordering the Atlantic Ocean sought their own profits and glory from overseas empires. Henceforth, war among European powers would include high-stakes conflicts over territories and trade in the colonies. European rulers' increased control over their own subjects thus went hand in glove with the expansion of European power in the world.

The eighteenth century was to see these power politics thrown into question by new Enlightenment aspirations for human society, which themselves derived from the inquisitive and self-confident spirit of the scientific revolution. These movements—both of which would have long-lasting influence worldwide—are explored in the next chapter. By the end of the eighteenth century, demands for real popular sovereignty, colonial self-rule, and slave emancipation challenged the very bases of order so painfully achieved in the seventeenth century. Chapter 22 recounts the revolutionary movements that swept the late-eighteenth-century Atlantic world, while Chapters 25, 26, and 27 follow the story of European imperialism and the resistance of colonized peoples into the nineteenth century.

- **For a list of suggested readings for this chapter, visit** *bedfordstmartins.com/mckayworldunderstanding*.

- **For primary sources from this period, see** *Sources of World Societies*, Second Edition.

- **For Web sites, images, and documents related to topics in this chapter, see Make History at** *bedfordstmartins.com/ mckayworldunderstanding*.

Chapter 17 Study Guide

To do these exercises online, go to bedfordstmartins.com/mckayworldunderstanding.

 Step 1

GETTING STARTED

Below are basic terms about this period in global history. Can you identify each term below and explain why it matters?

TERMS	WHO (OR WHAT) AND WHEN	WHY IT MATTERS
Peace of Westphalia, p. 437		
Fronde, p. 440		
mercantilism, p. 442		
Peace of Utrecht, p. 442		
Junkers, p. 446		
boyars, p. 447		
Cossacks, p. 448		
constitutionalism, p. 452		
republicanism, p. 452		
Puritans, p. 452		
Protectorate, p. 454		
Test Act, p. 455		
stadholder, p. 457		
Navigation Acts, p. 459		

Step 2

MOVING BEYOND THE BASICS

The exercise below requires a more advanced understanding of the chapter material. Examine the growth of state power in France, Prussia, Austria, Russia, and England by filling in the chart below by describing developments in each state in four areas where seventeenth-century governments achieved new levels of control: taxation, the armed forces, bureaucracies, and the ability to compel obedience from subjects. When you are finished, consider the following questions: Why did seventeenth-century governments place so much emphasis on increasing their military power? How did the growth of the state in England differ from the growth of the state in absolutist France, Prussia, Russia, and Austria?

	TAXATION	ARMED FORCES	BUREAUCRACIES	CONTROL OVER SUBJECTS
France				
Prussia				
Austria				
Russia				
England				

PUTTING IT ALL TOGETHER

Now that you've reviewed key elements of the chapter, take a step back and try to see the big picture. Remember to use specific examples from the chapter in your answers.

ABSOLUTIST MONARCHIES AND THE SEVENTEENTH-CENTURY CRISIS

- How did life for Europe's peasants change during the seventeenth century? Why was peasant life harder in eastern Europe than in western Europe?

- How and why did Louis XIV try to co-opt and control the French aristocracy? In practice, how "absolute" was his rule?

- Compare and contrast absolutism in Austria, Prussia, and Russia. What common problems and challenges did would-be absolutist rulers face in each of these three states?

CONSTITUTIONAL STATES AND THE SEVENTEENTH-CENTURY CRISIS

- Why did the efforts of English monarchs to build an absolutist state fail? What groups and institutions in English society were most responsible for the triumph of constitutionalism?

- Compare and contrast the constitutional governments of England and the Netherlands. What role did merchant elites and commercial interests play in each state?

COMPETITION FOR EMPIRE

- Why did northern European powers enter the competition for New World land and resources in the seventeenth century?

- How did England come to dominate the Atlantic economy over the course of the seventeenth century?

LOOKING BACK, LOOKING AHEAD

- How did the strong, centralized states of the second half of the seventeenth century differ from their fifteenth- and sixteenth-century counterparts? What new powers and responsibilities did seventeenth-century states take on?

- How might the state-building efforts of European powers in the seventeenth century have contributed to the acceleration of globalization that characterized the eighteenth and nineteenth centuries?

In Your Own Words Imagine that you must explain Chapter 17 to someone who hasn't read it. What would be the most important points to include and why?

Step 3

18

New Worldviews and Ways of Life

1540–1790

Intellectual developments of the sixteenth through eighteenth centuries created the modern worldview that the West continues to hold — and debate — to this day. In the sixteenth century, European scholars began to develop new ways of understanding the natural world, later characterized as a "scientific revolution." Whereas medieval scholars looked to classical works and the Bible, seventeenth-century natural philosophers, as they called themselves, performed experiments and relied on mathematical calculations.

Eighteenth-century philosophers extended the use of reason from nature to human society. Self-proclaimed members of an "Enlightenment" movement, they wished to bring the same progress to human affairs that their predecessors brought to the understanding of the natural world. While the scientific revolution ushered in modern science, the Enlightenment created concepts of human rights, equality, progress, and tolerance that still guide Western societies. At the same time, some Europeans used their new understanding of reason to explain their own superiority, thus rationalizing attitudes now regarded as racist and sexist.

The expression of new ideas was encouraged by changes in the material world. With the growth of population, the revitalization of industry and growing world trade, Europeans began to consume at a higher level. Feeding the growth of consumerism was the expansion of transatlantic trade and lower prices for colonial goods, often produced by slaves. During the eighteenth century, ships crisscrossing the Atlantic circulated commodities, ideas, and people to all four continents bordering the ocean. As trade became more integrated and communication intensified, an Atlantic world of mixed identities and shared debates emerged.

> **Free People of Color**
> A sizable mixed-race population emerged in many European colonies in the Americas, often descendants of unions between masters and enslaved African women. The wealthiest of the free people of color, as they were called, were plantation owners with slaves of their own. (Unknown artist, *Portrait of a Young Woman*, late 18th Century, pastel, 16 x 12 inches, Saint Louis Art Museum, Museum Purchase 186:1951)

Chapter Preview

▶ What was revolutionary about the scientific revolution?

▶ What were the core principles of the Enlightenment?

▶ What did enlightened absolutism mean?

▶ How did consumerism and the Atlantic economy influence Enlightenment ideas?

What was revolutionary about the scientific revolution?

A noted historian has said that the scientific revolution, which lasted roughly from 1540 to 1690, was "the real origin both of the modern world and the modern mentality."[1] Through new methods of investigating the physical world, Western society began to come to a new understanding of astronomy, physics, and medicine based on both experimentation and reasoning.

Scientific Thought Through the Early 1500s

The term *science* as we use it today came into use only in the nineteenth century. Prior to the scientific revolution, many different scholars and practitioners were involved in aspects of what came together to form science. One of the most important disciplines was natural philosophy, which focused on fundamental questions about the nature of the universe, its purpose, and how it functioned. In the early 1500s natural philosophy was still based primarily on the ideas of Aristotle. Medieval theologians such as Thomas Aquinas brought Aristotelian philosophy into harmony with Christian doctrines. According to the revised Aristotelian view, a motionless earth was fixed at the center of the universe and was encompassed by ten separate concentric crystal spheres in which were embedded the moon, sun, planets, and stars. Beyond the spheres was Heaven. Angels kept the spheres moving in perfect circles.

Aristotle's cosmology made intellectual sense, but it could not account for the observed motions of the stars and planets and, in particular, provided no explanation for the apparent backward motion of the planets. The great second-century Greek scholar Ptolemy offered a theory for this phenomenon. According to Ptolemy, the planets moved in small circles, called epicycles, each of which moved in turn along a larger circle. Ptolemaic astronomy was less elegant than Aristotle's and required complex calculations, but it provided a surprisingly accurate model for predicting planetary motion.

Aristotle's views, revised by medieval philosophers, also dominated thinking about physics and motion on earth.

natural philosophy An early modern term for the study of the nature of the universe, its purpose, and how it functioned; it encompassed what we call "science" today.

The Aristotelian Universe as Imagined in the Sixteenth Century A round earth is at the center, surrounded by spheres of water, air, and fire. Beyond this small nucleus, the moon, the sun, and the five planets were embedded in their own rotating crystal spheres, with the stars sharing the surface of one enormous sphere. Beyond, the heavens were composed of unchanging ether. (Image Select/Art Resource, NY)

Aristotle had distinguished sharply between the world of the celestial spheres and that of the earth—the sublunar world. The sublunar realm was made up of four imperfect, changeable elements: air, fire, water, and earth. The spheres, however, consisted of a perfect, incorruptible "quintessence," or fifth essence. Aristotle and his followers also believed that a uniform force moved an object at a constant speed and that the object would stop as soon as that force was removed. Both of these views would be challenged based on new observations and analysis of the physical world.

Origins of the Scientific Revolution

Why did Aristotelian teachings give way to new views about the universe? The first important driver of the scientific revolution was the medieval university. In the fourteenth and fifteenth centuries leading universities established new professorships of mathematics, astronomy, and physics (natural philosophy) within their faculties of philosophy. Although the prestige of the new fields was low, a permanent community of scholars was now focused on investigating scientific problems.

Medieval scholarship in the universities was based on the study of ancient texts. Contact with Muslims in Spain and Sicily brought awareness of many ancient texts that survived only in Arabic versions, and these were translated into Latin in the twelfth century. In some instances, such as mathematics and astronomy, the translations were accompanied by learned commentaries that went beyond ancient learning. Arabic and Persian mathematicians, for example, invented algebra, the concept of the algorithm, and decimal point notation, while Arabic astronomers improved on measurements recorded in ancient works.

Second, the Renaissance also stimulated scientific progress. Renaissance patrons played a role in funding scientific investigations, as they did art and literature. The goal of exploration in late fifteenth and sixteenth centuries was not only to find wealth and Christian converts but also to increase Europeans' knowledge about the wider world. In addition, Renaissance artists' turn toward realism and their use of geometry to convey three-dimensional perspective encouraged scholars to practice close observation and to use mathematics to describe the natural world. Furthermore, the Renaissance rise of printing provided a faster and less expensive way to circulate knowledge across Europe.

The navigational problems of long sea voyages in the age of overseas expansion were a third factor in the scientific revolution. To help solve these problems, inventors developed many new scientific instruments, such as the telescope, barometer, thermometer, pendulum clock, microscope, and air pump. Better instruments, which permitted more accurate observations, often led to important new knowledge.

Finally, recent historical research has focused on the contribution of practices now regarded as far beyond the realm of science. For most of human history, interest in astronomy was inspired by the belief that the changing relationships between planets and stars influenced events on earth. Many of the most celebrated astronomers were also astrologers. Centuries-old practices of magic and alchemy also remained important traditions for participants in the scientific revolution. The idea that objects possessed hidden or "occult" qualities that allowed them to affect other objects was a particularly important legacy of the magical tradition. Such hidden qualities helped inspire an important new law of physics (see pages 469–470).

Chapter Chronology

ca. 1540–1690	Scientific revolution
ca. 1690–1789	Enlightenment
ca. 1700–1789	Growth of book publishing
1720–1780	Rococo style in art and decoration
1740–1748	War of Austrian Succession
1740–1780	Reign of the empress Maria Theresa
1740–1786	Reign of Frederick the Great of Prussia
ca. 1740–1789	French salons led by elite women
1762–1796	Reign of Catherine the Great of Russia
1765	Philosophes publish *Encyclopedia: The Rational Dictionary of the Sciences, the Arts, and the Crafts*
1780–1790	Reign of Joseph II of Austria
1791	Establishment of the Pale of Settlement

Copernican Hypothesis

The first great departure from the medieval understanding of the physical world system was the work of the Polish cleric and astronomer Nicolaus Copernicus (1473–1543). In the course of his study of astronomy, Copernicus came to believe that Ptolemy's cumbersome system detracted from the majesty of a perfect creator. He preferred an ancient Greek idea: that the sun, rather than the earth, was at the center of the universe.

Without questioning the Aristotelian belief in crystal spheres or the idea that circular motion was divine, Copernicus theorized that the stars and planets, including the earth, revolved around a fixed sun. Fearing the ridicule of other astronomers, Copernicus did not publish his *On the Revolutions of the Heavenly Spheres* until 1543, the year of his death.

The Copernican hypothesis presented a revolutionary view of the universe and brought sharp attacks from religious leaders, especially Protestants, who objected to the Copernican hypothesis on the grounds that it contradicted scripture. Catholic reaction was milder at first. The Catholic Church had never held to literal interpretations of the Bible, and not until 1616 did it officially declare the Copernican hypothesis false.

Copernican hypothesis The idea that the sun, not the earth, was the center of the universe.

Proving Copernicus Right

One astronomer who agreed with Copernicus was the Danish astronomer Tycho Brahe (TEE-koh BRAH-hee; 1546–1601). Aided by grants from the king of Denmark, Brahe built the most sophisticated observatory of his day.

Upon the king's death, Brahe acquired a new patron in the Holy Roman emperor Rudolph II and built a new observatory in Prague. In return for the emperor's support, he pledged to create new and improved tables of planetary motions. For twenty years Brahe observed the heavens, compiling much more complete and accurate data than ever before. His limited understanding of mathematics and his sudden death in 1601, however, prevented him from making much sense out of his data.

It was left to Brahe's young assistant, Johannes Kepler (1571–1630), to rework Brahe's mountain of observations. A brilliant mathematician, Kepler was inspired by his belief that the universe was built on mystical mathematical relationships and a musical harmony of the heavenly bodies.

Kepler was convinced that Brahe's data could not be explained by Ptolemy's astronomy. Abandoning the Ptolemaic system, Kepler developed three revolutionary laws of planetary motion. First, he demonstrated that the orbits of the planets around the sun are elliptical rather than circular. Second, he demonstrated that the planets do not move at a uniform speed in their orbits. When a planet is close to the sun it moves more rapidly, and it slows as it moves farther away from the sun. Finally, Kepler's third law stated that the time a planet takes to make its complete orbit is precisely related to its distance from the sun.

Kepler's work demolished the old system of Aristotle and Ptolemy, and in his third law he came close to formulating the idea of universal gravitation (see page 470). Kepler was not, however, the consummate modern scientist that his achievements suggest. His duties as court mathe-

Galileo's Telescope Among the many mechanical devices Galileo invented was a telescope that could magnify objects twenty times (other contemporary telescopes could magnify objects only three times). Using this telescope, he obtained the empirical evidence that proved the Copernican system. (Scala/Art Resource, NY)

TVBVM OPTICVM VIDES GALILAEII INVENTVM,ET OPVS,QVO SOLIS MACVLAS,
ET EXTIMOS LVNAE MONTES, ET IOVIS SATELLITES,ET NOVAM QVASI
RERVM VNIVERSITATE PRIMVS DISPEXIT A.MDCIX.

matician included casting horoscopes, and his own diary was based on astrological principles. He also wrote at length on cosmic harmonies and explained, for example, elliptical motion through ideas about the music created by planetary motion. His career exemplifies the complex interweaving of rigorous empirical observations and mystical beliefs in the emerging science of his day.

While Kepler was unraveling the mysteries of planetary motion, a young Florentine named Galileo Galilei (1564–1642) was challenging old ideas about motion on earth. Galileo's great achievement was the elaboration and consolidation of the experimental method. Rather than speculate about what might or should happen, Galileo conducted controlled experiments to find out what actually did happen.

In his famous acceleration experiment, he showed that a uniform force—in this case, gravity—produced a uniform acceleration. Through another experiment, he formulated the **law of inertia**. According to this law, rest is not the natural state of objects. Rather, an object continues in motion forever unless stopped by some external force, such as friction. His discoveries thus proved Aristotelian physics wrong.

Galileo also applied the experimental method to astronomy. On hearing details about the invention of the telescope in Holland, Galileo made one for himself. He quickly discovered the first four moons of Jupiter, which clearly suggested that Jupiter could not possibly be embedded in an impenetrable crystal sphere as Aristotle and Ptolemy maintained. This discovery provided new evidence for the Copernican theory, in which Galileo already believed. Galileo then pointed his telescope at the moon. He wrote in 1610 in *Siderus Nuncius*:

> By the aid of a telescope anyone may behold [the Milky Way] in a manner which so distinctly appeals to the senses that all the disputes which have tormented philosophers through so many ages are exploded by the irrefutable evidence of our eyes, and we are freed from wordy disputes upon the subject.[2]

A new method of learning and investigating was being developed, in which scholars relied more on observable evidence and critical thinking than on established authority. This method proved useful in any field of inquiry. A historian investigating documents of the past, for example, is not so different from a Galileo studying stars and rolling balls.

Within the Catholic world, expressing public support for Copernicus was increasingly dangerous. In 1616 the Holy Office placed the works of Copernicus and his supporters on a list of books Catholics were forbidden to read. Thus, out of caution, Galileo kept quiet about his beliefs, until in 1623 he saw new hope with the ascension of Pope Urban VIII, a man sympathetic to developments in the new science. However, Galileo's 1632 *Dialogue on the Two Chief Systems of the World* went too far. Published in Italian and widely read, this work openly lampooned the traditional views of Aristotle and Ptolemy, and it also defended those of Copernicus. In 1633 Galileo was tried for heresy by the papal Inquisition. Imprisoned and threatened with torture, the aging Galileo recanted.

law of inertia A law formulated by Galileo that states that motion, not rest, is the natural state of an object, and that an object continues in motion forever unless stopped by some external force.

Newton's Synthesis

Despite the efforts of the church, by about 1640 the work of Brahe, Kepler, and Galileo had been largely accepted by the scientific community. But the new findings failed to explain what forces controlled the movement of the planets and objects on earth. That challenge was taken up by English scientist Isaac Newton (1642–1727).

Newton's towering accomplishment was a single explanatory system that integrated the astronomy of Copernicus, as corrected by Kepler's laws, with the physics of Galileo and his predecessors. Newton did this through a set of mathematical laws that explain motion and mechanics. These laws were published in 1687 in Newton's *Mathematical Principles of Natural Philosophy* (also known as the *Principia*).

The key feature of the Newtonian synthesis was the law of universal gravitation. According to this law, each body in the universe attracts every other body in a precise mathematical relationship, whereby the force of attraction is proportional to the quantity of matter of the objects and inversely proportional to the square of the distance between them. The whole universe was unified in one majestic system. Newton's synthesis prevailed until the twentieth century.

Bacon, Descartes, and the Scientific Method

One of the keys to achieving a better understanding of the world was the development of better ways of obtaining knowledge. Two important thinkers, Francis Bacon (1561–1626) and René Descartes (day-KAHRT; 1596–1650), were influential in describing and advocating for improved scientific methods based, respectively, on experimentation and mathematical reasoning.

The English politician and writer Francis Bacon was the greatest early propagandist for the new experimental method. Rejecting the Aristotelian and medieval method of using speculative reasoning to build general theories, Bacon argued that new knowledge had to be pursued through empirical research. The researcher who wants to learn more about leaves or rocks, for example, should not speculate about the subject but should rather collect a multitude of specimens and then compare and analyze them to derive general principles. Bacon's contribution was to formalize the empirical method, which had already been used by Brahe and Galileo, into the general theory of inductive reasoning known as empiricism.

empiricism A theory of inductive reasoning that calls for acquiring evidence through observation and experimentation rather than reason and speculation.

On the continent, more speculative methods retained support. In 1619, the French philosopher René Descartes discovered that there was a perfect correspondence between geometry and algebra. He also figured out that geometrical spatial figures could be expressed as algebraic equations and vice versa. A major step forward in the history of mathematics, Descartes's discovery of analytic geometry provided scientists with an important new tool.

Descartes used mathematics to elaborate a highly influential vision of the workings of the cosmos. Drawing on ancient Greek atomist philosophies, Descartes developed the idea that matter was made up of identical "corpuscles" (tiny particles) that collided together in an endless series of motions. All occurrences in nature could be analyzed as matter in motion. Descartes's mechanistic view of the universe depended on the idea that a vacuum was impossible, so that every action had an equal reaction, continuing in an eternal chain reaction. Although Descartes's hypothesis about the vacuum was proved wrong, his notion of a mechanistic universe intelligible through the physics of motion proved highly influential.

Descartes's greatest achievement was to develop his initial vision into a whole philosophy of knowledge and science. Descartes began by pointing out that impressions of the world gained through the senses can sometimes be proved wrong. Thus, they can be doubted. Only things about which there can be no doubt should be accepted as truths, Descartes argued, and from these truths, or general principles, people can arrive at additional truths. This process of moving from general principles to specific truths is known as deductive reasoning. Descartes's reasoning ultimately reduced all substances to "matter" and "mind" — that is, to the physical and the spiritual. His view of the world as consisting of two fundamental entities is known as Cartesian dualism.

Cartesian dualism Descartes's view that all of reality could ultimately be reduced to mind and matter.

Both Bacon's inductive experimentalism and Descartes's deductive mathematical reasoning had faults. Bacon's inability to appreciate the importance of mathematics and his obsession with practical results clearly showed the limitations of antitheoretical empiricism. Likewise, some of Descartes's positions—he believed, for example, that it was possible to deduce the whole science of medicine from a set of foundational first principles—demonstrated the inadequacy of rigid, dogmatic rationalism. Although insufficient on their own, Bacon's and Descartes's extreme approaches are combined in the modern scientific method, which began to crystallize in the late seventeenth century.

Frontispiece to *De Humani Corporis Fabrica* (*On the Structure of the Human Body*) The frontispiece to Vesalius's pioneering work, published in 1643, shows him dissecting a corpse before a crowd of students. This was a revolutionary new hands-on approach for physicians, who usually worked from a theoretical, rather than a practical, understanding of the body. Based on direct observation, Vesalius replaced ancient ideas drawn from Greek philosophy with a much more accurate account of the structure and function of the body. (© SSPL/Science Museum/The Image Works)

Medicine, the Body, and Chemistry

The scientific revolution, which began with the study of the cosmos, soon inspired renewed study of the microcosm of the human body. For many centuries the ancient Greek physician Galen's explanation of the body carried the same authority as Aristotle's account of the universe. According to Galen, the body contained four humors. Illness was believed to result from an imbalance of these humors.

Swiss physician and alchemist Paracelsus (1493–1541) was an early proponent of the experimental method in medicine and pioneered the use of chemicals and drugs to address what he saw as chemical, rather than humoral, imbalances. Another experimentalist, Flemish physician Andreas Vesalius (1514–1564), studied anatomy by dissecting human bodies. In 1543, Vesalius issued *On the Structure of the Human Body*, revolutionizing the understanding of human anatomy. The experimental approach also led English royal physician William Harvey (1578–1657) to discover the circulation of blood in 1628.

Irishman Robert Boyle (1627–1691) founded the modern science of chemistry. Following Paracelsus's lead, he undertook experiments to discover the basic elements of nature, which he believed was composed of infinitely small atoms. Boyle was the first to create a vacuum, and he discovered Boyle's law (1662), which states that the pressure of a gas varies inversely with volume.

Science and Society

The rise of modern science had many consequences. First, it led to the rise of a new and expanding social group—the international scientific community. Members of this community were linked together by common interests and shared values as well as by journals and learned scientific societies. Second, as governments intervened to support and sometimes direct research, the new scientific community became closely tied to the state and its agendas. National academies of science were created under state sponsorship in London in 1662, Paris in 1666, Berlin in 1700, and later across Europe.

Some things did not change in the scientific revolution. For example, new "rational" methods for approaching nature did not question traditional inequalities between the sexes—and may have worsened them in some ways. When Renaissance courts served as centers of learning, talented noblewomen could find niches in study and research. But the rise of a professional scientific community raised barriers for women because the new academies that furnished professional credentials did not accept female members.

There were, however, a number of noteworthy exceptions. In Italy, universities and academies did offer posts to women. Moreover, women across Europe were allowed to work as makers of wax anatomical models and as botanical and zoological illustrators. They were also very much involved in informal scientific communities, attending salons (see page 477), participating in scientific experiments, and writing learned treatises.

The scientific revolution had few consequences for economic life and the living standards of the masses until the late eighteenth century, when its insights helped create new manufacturing technologies. Instead, it was first and foremost an intellectual revolution. For more than a hundred years its greatest impact was on how people thought and believed.

Finally, there is the question of the role of religion in the development of science. All Western religious authorities opposed the Copernican system to a greater or lesser extent until about 1630, by which time the scientific revolution was definitely in progress. The Catholic Church was initially less hostile than Protestant and Jewish religious leaders, and Italian scientists played a crucial role in scientific progress right up to the trial of Galileo in 1633. Thereafter, the Counter-Reformation church became more hostile to science, a change that helped account for the decline of science in Italy after 1640. At the same time, Protestant countries—especially those lacking a strong religious authority capable of imposing religious orthodoxy on scientific questions—became quite "pro-science." Such countries included the Netherlands, Denmark, and England.

Quick Review
Why did the thinkers of the scientific revolution think that the study of nature was important? What was the impact of their discoveries?

What were the core principles of the Enlightenment?

The scientific revolution was the single most important factor in the creation of the new worldview of the eighteenth-century Enlightenment. This worldview grew out of a rich mix of diverse and often conflicting ideas. Despite the diversity, three concepts stand at the core of Enlightenment thinking: the crucial importance of the use of reason, the scientific method, and a belief in both the possibility and desirability of human progress.

Enlightenment The influential intellectual and cultural movement of the late seventeenth and eighteenth centuries that introduced new ways of thinking based on the use of reason, the scientific method, and progress.

The Emergence of the Enlightenment

The European Enlightenment (ca. 1690–1789) gained strength gradually and did not reach maturity until about 1750. Yet it was the generation that came of age between the publication of Newton's *Principia* in 1687 and the death of French king Louis XIV in 1715 that tied the crucial knot between the scientific revolution and a new outlook on life. Talented writers of that generation popularized hard-to-understand scientific achievements for the educated elite.

This new generation came to believe that the human mind itself is capable of making great progress. Medieval and Reformation thinkers had been concerned primarily with sin and salvation. The humanists of the Renaissance had emphasized worldly matters (especially art and literature), but their inspiration came from the classical past. By contrast, Enlightenment thinkers came to believe that their era had gone far beyond antiquity and that fresh intellectual progress was possible.

The excitement of the scientific revolution also generated doubt and uncertainty, as Europeans of the late seventeenth century began to question long-standing religious assumptions and practices. In the wake of the devastation wrought by the Catholic-Protestant struggle of the Thirty Years' War, some people asked whether ideological conformity in religious matters was really necessary. Others skeptically asked if religious truth could ever be known with absolute certainty and concluded that it could not.

The most famous of these skeptics was the French Huguenot Pierre Bayle (1647–1706). Bayle critically examined the religious beliefs and persecutions of the past in his *Historical and Critical Dictionary* (1697). Demonstrating that human beliefs had been extremely varied and often mistaken, he concluded that nothing can ever be known beyond all doubt, a view known as skepticism.

Some Jewish scholars participated in the early Enlightenment movement. The philosopher Baruch Spinoza (1632–1677) believed that mind and body are united in one substance and that God and nature were two names for the same thing. He envisioned a deterministic universe in which good and evil were merely relative values. Few of Spinoza's radical writings were published during his lifetime, but he is now recognized as among the most original thinkers of the early Enlightenment.

Out of this period of intellectual turmoil came John Locke's *Essay Concerning Human Understanding* (1690), often viewed as the first major text of the Enlightenment. In this work Locke (1632–1704) insisted that all ideas are derived from experience. According to Locke, the human mind at birth is like a blank tablet, or tabula rasa, on which the environment writes the individual's understanding and beliefs. Human development is therefore determined by education and social institutions, for good or for evil. The *Essay Concerning Human Understanding* passed through many editions and translations and, along with Newton's *Principia*, was one of the dominant intellectual inspirations of the Enlightenment.

The rapidly growing literature about non-European lands and cultures was another cause of questioning among thinkers. In the wake of the great discoveries, Europeans were learning that the peoples of the world had their own very different beliefs and customs. The countless examples of cultural differences discussed in travel accounts helped change the perspective of educated Europeans. They began to look at truth and morality in relative, rather than absolute, terms. If anything was possible, who could say what was right or wrong?

The Influence of the Philosophes

By the time Louis XIV died in 1715, many of the ideas that would soon coalesce into the new worldview had been assembled. Yet Christian Europe was still strongly attached to its established political and social structures and its traditional spiritual beliefs. By 1775, however, a large portion of western Europe's educated elite had embraced many of the new ideas. This acceptance was largely the work of a group of French intellectuals known as the philosophes.

To appeal to the public and get around the censors, the philosophes produced works filled with satire and double meanings to spread their message. One of the greatest philosophes, the baron de Montesquieu (mahn-tuhs-KYOO; 1689–1755), pioneered this approach in *The Persian Letters* (1721). This satirical work consisted of letters supposedly written by two Persian travelers, Usbek and Rica, who as outsiders see European customs in unique ways and thereby allow Montesquieu a vantage point for criticizing existing practices and beliefs.

After writing *The Persian Letters*, Montesquieu settled down on his family estate to study history and politics. Disturbed by royal absolutism under Louis XIV and inspired by the example of the physical sciences, Montesquieu set out to apply the critical method to the problem of government in *The Spirit of the Laws* (1748).

In *The Spirit of the Laws*, Montesquieu argued for a separation of powers, with political power divided among a variety of classes and legal estates holding unequal rights and privileges. Montesquieu was no democrat; he was apprehensive about the uneducated poor, and he did not question the overarching sovereignty of the French monarch. But he was

philosophes A group of French intellectuals who proclaimed that they were bringing the light of knowledge to their fellow creatures in the Age of Enlightenment.

Picturing the Past

Enlightenment Culture

An actor performs the first reading of a new play by Voltaire at the salon of Madame Geoffrin in this painting from 1755. Voltaire, then in exile, is represented by a bust statue.
(Réunion des Musées Nationaux/Art Resource, NY)

ANALYZING THE IMAGE Which of these people do you think is the hostess, Madame Geoffrin, and why? Using details from the painting to support your answer, how would you describe the status of the people shown?

CONNECTIONS What does this image suggest about the reach of Enlightenment ideas to common people? To women? Does the painting of the bookstore on page 476 suggest a broader reach? Why?

concerned that royal rule in France was drifting into tyranny and believed that strengthening the influence of intermediary powers was the best way to prevent it.

The most famous philosophe was François-Marie Arouet, who was known by the pen name Voltaire (1694–1778). Voltaire's early career was turbulent, and he was arrested on two occasions for insulting noblemen. To avoid a prison term in France, Voltaire moved to England for three years, and there he came to admire English liberties and institutions.

Returning to France, Voltaire met Gabrielle-Emilie Le Tonnelier de Breteuil, marquise du Châtelet (1706–1749), a gifted woman from the high aristocracy. Madame du Châtelet invited Voltaire to live with her at Cirey in Lorraine and became his long-time companion (under the eyes of her tolerant husband). Passionate about science, she studied physics and mathematics. She published scientific articles and translations, including the first French translation of Newton's *Principia*.

While living at Cirey, Voltaire wrote works praising England and popularizing English scientific progress. Yet, like almost all of the philosophes, Voltaire was a reformer, not a revolutionary, in social and political matters. He pessimistically concluded that the best form of government was a good monarch, since human beings "are very rarely worthy to govern themselves." Nor did Voltaire believe in social and economic equality. The only realizable equality, Voltaire thought, was that "by which the citizen only depends on the laws which protect the freedom of the feeble against the ambitions of the strong."[3]

Voltaire's philosophical and religious positions were much more radical than his social and political beliefs. Voltaire believed in a deistic God. Drawing on Newton, Voltaire envisioned a mechanistic universe in which God acted like a great clockmaker who built an orderly system and then stepped aside and let it run. Above all, Voltaire and most of the philosophes hated all forms of religious intolerance, which they believed often led to fanaticism and savage, inhuman action.

The ultimate strength of the philosophes lay in their number, dedication, and organization. Their greatest and most representative intellectual achievement was a group effort—the seventeen-volume *Encyclopedia: The Rational Dictionary of the Sciences, the Arts, and the Crafts*, edited by Denis Diderot (1713–1784) and Jean le Rond d'Alembert (1717–1783).

Completed in 1765, the *Encyclopedia* contained hundreds of thousands of articles by leading scientists, writers, skilled workers, and progressive priests, and it treated every aspect of life and knowledge. Science and the industrial arts were exalted, religion and immortality questioned. Intolerance, legal injustice, and out-of-date social institutions were openly criticized. The *Encyclopedia* also included thousands of articles describing non-European cultures and societies. Summing up the new worldview of the Enlightenment, the *Encyclopedia* was widely read, especially in less-expensive reprint editions, and it was extremely influential.

Enlightenment Across Europe

Enlightenment thought took on distinctive forms in different European countries. Even within each nation, reform-minded philosophers and writers formed their own societies and cliques with contrasting interests and points of view.

The Scottish Enlightenment, centered in Edinburgh, was marked by an emphasis on pragmatic and scientific reasoning. A key figure was David Hume (1711–1776), whose carefully argued religious skepticism had a powerful impact at home and abroad. Building on Locke's teachings on learning, Hume argued that the human mind is really nothing but a bundle of impressions. Since our ideas ultimately reflect only our sense experiences, our reason cannot tell us anything about questions that cannot be verified by sense experience, such as questions about the origin of the universe or the existence of God. Paradoxically, Hume's rationalistic inquiry ended up undermining the Enlightenment's faith in the power of reason.

Another Scottish philosopher, Adam Smith (1723–1790), was a pioneer of the new field of political economy. Inspired by the possibilities of growing world trade, Smith developed the general idea of freedom of enterprise and established the basis for modern economics in his groundbreaking work, *Inquiry into the Nature and Causes of the Wealth of Nations* (1776). In it, he argued that government intervention in the economy was unnecessary and undesirable, and that the pursuit of self-interest in a competitive market would be sufficient to improve the living conditions of citizens, a view that quickly emerged as the classic argument for **economic liberalism**.

In most of central and eastern Europe, reform-minded thinkers rejected the deism of Voltaire and the skepticism of Hume. Instead, they tried to integrate the findings of the scientific revolution with the teachings of established churches. In Germany, Gottfried Leibniz (GAHT-freed LIGHB-nuhtz; 1646–1716) tried to reconcile philosophy with faith by arguing that God allowed evil to exist as a means of allowing imperfect humans to exercise free will. He further argued that, despite the existence of pain and suffering, our world must be the best of all possible worlds since it was created by an omnipotent and benevolent God.

economic liberalism The theory that the pursuit of self-interest in a competitive market suffices to improve living conditions, rendering government intervention unnecessary and undesirable, associated with Adam Smith.

Immanuel Kant (1724–1804), a professor in East Prussia and the greatest German philosopher of his day, took up the question of the age when he published a pamphlet in 1784 titled *What Is Enlightenment?* Kant answered, "*Sapere Aude* (dare to know)! 'Have the courage to use your own understanding' is therefore the motto of enlightenment." He argued that if serious thinkers were granted the freedom to exercise their reason publicly in print, enlightenment would almost surely follow. Kant nonetheless epitomized the cautious eastern European attitude toward state authority. He insisted that in their private lives, individuals must obey all laws, no matter how unreasonable, and should be punished for "impertinent" criticism.

Urban Culture and Life in the Public Sphere

A major stimulant to Enlightenment thought was urbanization. More and more people migrated to the city, especially after 1750, and urban life gave rise to new institutions and practices that encouraged the spread of Enlightenment ideas. From about 1700 to 1789, the production and consumption of books grew significantly, and the types of books people read changed dramatically. The proportion of religious and devotional books published in Paris declined after 1750; history and law held constant; the arts and sciences surged.

Reading more books on many more subjects, the educated public increasingly approached reading in a new way. The result was what some scholars have called a reading revolution. The old style of reading was centered on a core of sacred texts. Reading was

The French Book Trade Book consumption surged in the eighteenth century and along with it, new bookstores. This appealing bookshop in France with its intriguing ads for the latest works offers to put customers "Under the Protection of Minerva," the Roman goddess of wisdom. Large packets of books sit ready for shipment to foreign countries. (Musée des Beaux-Arts, Dijon/Art Resource, NY)

patriarchal and communal, with the father of the family slowly reading texts aloud. Now reading involved a broader field of books that constantly changed. Reading became individual and silent, and texts could be questioned. Subtle but profound, the reading revolution ushered in new ways of relating to the written word.

The conversation, discussion, and debate encouraged by an urban milieu played a critical role in the Enlightenment. Paris set the example that other French and European cities followed. In Paris from about 1740 to 1789, a number of talented, wealthy women presided over regular social gatherings named after their elegant private drawing rooms, or **salons**. There they encouraged the exchange of ideas between great aristocrats, wealthy middle-class financiers, high-ranking officials, and noteworthy foreigners.

Elite women also exercised great influence on artistic taste. Soft pastels, ornate interiors, sentimental portraits, and starry-eyed lovers protected by hovering cupids were all hallmarks of the style they favored. This style, known as rococo, was popular throughout Europe from 1720 to 1780. During this period, women were also closely associated with the rise of the novel as a literary genre, both as authors and readers. The novel helped popularize a new cult of sensibility, which celebrated strong emotions and intimate family love. Some philosophes championed greater rights and expanded education for women, claiming that the position and treatment of women were the best indicators of a society's level of civilization and decency.[4]

While salon membership and artistic pursuits were largely restricted to the well-born and the exceptionally talented, a number of institutions emerged for the rest of society. Lending libraries served an important function for people who could not afford their own books. The coffeehouses that first appeared in the late seventeenth century became meccas of philosophical discussion. In addition, book clubs, Masonic lodges (groups of Freemasons, a secret egalitarian society that existed across Europe), and journals all played a part in creating a new **public sphere** that celebrated open debate informed by critical reason. The public sphere was an idealized space where members of society came together to discuss the social, economic, and political issues of the day.

Enlightenment philosophes did not direct their message to peasants or urban laborers. Most believed that educating the masses was an impractical and potentially dangerous process. There is some evidence, however, that ordinary people were not immune to the words of the philosophes. At a time of rising literacy, book prices were dropping in cities and towns, and many philosophical ideas were popularized in cheap pamphlets. Moreover, even illiterate people had access to written material through the practice of public reading. Although they were barred from salons and academies, ordinary people were nonetheless exposed to the new ideas in circulation.

Late Enlightenment

After about 1770 a number of thinkers and writers began to attack the Enlightenment's faith in reason and progress. The most famous of these was the Swiss intellectual Jean-Jacques Rousseau (1712–1778). Like other Enlightenment thinkers, Rousseau was passionately committed to individual freedom. Unlike them, however, he attacked rationalism and civilization as destroying, rather than liberating, the individual. Warm, spontaneous feeling, Rousseau believed, had to complement and correct cold intellect. Moreover, he asserted, the basic goodness of the individual and the unspoiled child had to be protected from the cruel refinements of civilization. Rousseau's ideals greatly influenced the early romantic movement, which rebelled against the culture of the Enlightenment in the late eighteenth century.

Rousseau's major contribution to political theory, *The Social Contract* (1762), was based on two fundamental concepts: the general will and popular sovereignty. According to Rousseau, the **general will** is sacred and absolute, reflecting the common interests of all

salons Regular social gatherings held by talented and rich Parisian women in their homes, where philosophes and their followers met to discuss literature, science, and philosophy.

public sphere An idealized intellectual space that emerged in Europe during the Enlightenment. Here, the public came together to discuss important social, economic, and political issues.

general will A concept associated with Rousseau, referring to the common interests of all the people, who have replaced the power of the monarch.

people, who have displaced the monarch as the holder of sovereign power. The general will is not necessarily the will of the majority, however. At times the general will may be the authentic, long-term needs of the people as correctly interpreted by a far-seeing minority. Little noticed before the French Revolution, Rousseau's concept of the general will appealed greatly to democrats and nationalists after 1789.

What did enlightened absolutism mean?

enlightened absolutism
Term coined by historians to describe the rule of eighteenth-century monarchs who, without renouncing their own absolute authority, adopted Enlightenment ideals of rationalism, progress, and tolerance.

Although Enlightenment thinkers were often critical of untrammeled despotism and eager for reform, their impact on politics was mixed. Outside of England and the Netherlands, especially in central and eastern Europe, most believed that political change could best come from above—from the ruler—rather than from below. Encouraged and instructed by proponents of the Enlightenment, some absolutist rulers tried to reform their governments in accordance with Enlightenment ideals. The result was what historians have called the enlightened absolutism of the later eighteenth century.

Reforms in Prussia, Russia, and Austria

In 1740 Frederick II (r. 1740–1786) of Prussia, known as Frederick the Great, initiated the War of the Austrian Succession (1740–1748) to contest the right of a woman, Maria Theresa, to inherit the Habsburg throne. After a bold military victory, Frederick the Great acquired almost all of the province of Silesia from Austria, albeit without unseating Maria Theresa from her throne. Influenced by the philosophes, Frederick tolerantly allowed his subjects to believe as they wished in religious and philosophical matters. He promoted the advancement of knowledge, improving his country's schools and permitting scholars to publish their findings. He also sought to improve life for ordinary people with innovations in agriculture and industry.

Frederick's most fundamental reforms were to the legal system. Under his reign, Prussia's laws were simplified, torture of prisoners was abolished, and judges decided cases quickly and impartially. Prussian officials became famous for their hard work and honesty. However, Frederick did not free the serfs of Prussia; instead, he extended the privileges of the nobility over them.

Frederick's reputation as an enlightened prince was rivaled by that of Catherine the Great of Russia (r. 1762–1796), one of the most remarkable rulers of her time. When she was fifteen years old Catherine's family ties to the Romanov dynasty made her a suitable bride for the heir to the Russian throne. Catherine profited from her husband's unpopularity, having him murdered so that she could be declared empress of Russia.

Never questioning that absolute monarchy was the best form of government, Catherine set out to rule in an enlightened manner. She had three main goals. First, she worked hard to continue Peter the Great's efforts to bring the culture of western Europe to Russia (see pages 449–452). To do so, she patronized Western architects, sculptors, musicians, and philosophes and encouraged Russian nobles to follow her example. Catherine's second goal was domestic reform. She restricted the practice of torture and allowed limited religious toleration. She also tried to improve education and strengthen local government. The philosophes applauded these measures and hoped more would follow.

These hopes were dashed by a massive uprising of serfs in 1733 under the leadership of a common Cossack soldier named Emelian Pugachev. Although Pugachev was ultimately captured and executed, his rebellion shocked Russian rulers and put an end to any inten-

Maria Theresa The empress and her husband pose with eleven of their sixteen children at Schönbrunn palace in this family portrait by court painter Martin Meytens (1695–1770). Joseph, the heir to the throne, stands at the center of the star on the floor. Wealthy women often had very large families, in part because they, unlike poor women, seldom nursed their babies. (Réunion des Musées Nationaux/Art Resource, NY)

tions Catherine might have had about reforming the system. After 1775 Catherine gave the nobles absolute control of their serfs and extended serfdom into new areas. In 1785 she formally freed nobles from taxes and state service. Therefore, under Catherine the Russian nobility attained its most exalted position, and serfdom entered its most oppressive phase.

Catherine's third goal was territorial expansion, and in this respect she was extremely successful. Her armies subjugated the last descendants of the Mongols and the Crimean Tatars, and began the conquest of the Caucasus, on the border between Europe and Asia. Her greatest coup was the partition of Poland, which took place in stages from 1772 to 1795 (Map 18.1).

Maria Theresa (r. 1740–1780) of Austria also established reforms in her nation, although traditional power politics was a more important motivation for her than were Enlightenment teachings. Her more radical son, Joseph II (r. 1780–1790), drew on Enlightenment ideals, earning the title of "revolutionary emperor." Most notably, Joseph abolished serfdom in 1781. When Joseph died at forty-nine, the Habsburg empire was in turmoil. His brother Leopold II (r. 1790–1792) canceled Joseph's radical edicts in order to re-establish order.

Jewish Life and the Limits of Enlightened Absolutism

Perhaps the best example of the limitations of enlightened absolutism are the debates surrounding the possible emancipation of the Jews. Europe's small Jewish populations lived under highly discriminatory laws. For the most part, Jews were confined to tiny, overcrowded ghettos, excluded by law from most business and professional activities, and they could be ordered out of a kingdom at a moment's notice.

In the eighteenth century, an Enlightenment movement known as the **Haskalah** emerged from within the European Jewish community. This movement was led by the Prussian philosopher Moses Mendelssohn (1729–1786). (See "Individuals in Society: Moses Mendelssohn and the Jewish Enlightenment," page 481.) Christian and Jewish Enlightenment philosophers, including Mendelssohn, began to advocate for freedom and civil

The Pale of Settlement, 1791

Haskalah A Jewish Enlightenment movement led by Prussian philosopher Moses Mendelssohn.

Mapping the Past

Map 18.1 The Partition of Poland, 1772–1795

In 1772 the threat of war between Russia and Austria arose over Russian gains from the Ottoman Empire. To satisfy desires for expansion without fighting, Prussia's Frederick the Great proposed dividing parts of Poland among Austria, Prussia, and Russia. In 1793 and 1795 the three powers partitioned the remainder, and Poland ceased to exist as an independent nation.

ANALYZING THE MAP Of the three powers that divided the kingdom of Poland, which benefited the most? How did the partition affect the geographical boundaries of each state, and what was the significance? What border with the former Poland remained unchanged? Why do you think this was the case?

CONNECTIONS Why was Poland vulnerable to partition in the later half of the eighteenth century? What does it say about European politics at the time that a country could simply cease to exist on the map? Could that happen today?

rights for European Jews. In an era of growing reason and tolerance, they argued, restrictions on religious grounds could not stand.

Arguments for tolerance won some ground, especially under Joseph II of Austria. Most monarchs, however, refused to entertain the idea of emancipation. In 1791 Catherine the Great established the Pale of Settlement, a territory including modern-day Belarus, Lithuania, Latvia, Moldava, Ukraine, and parts of Poland, in which most Jews were required to live until the Russian Revolution of 1917.

Quick Review
What aspects of their states and societies did enlightened absolutists attempt to reform, and which did they tend to leave alone? Why?

IN 1743 A SMALL, HUMPBACKED JEWISH BOY WITH a stammer left his poor parents in Dessau in central Germany and walked eighty miles to Berlin, the capital of Frederick the Great's Prussia. According to one story, when the boy reached the Rosenthaler Gate, the only one through which Jews could pass, he told the inquiring watchman that his name was Moses and that he had come to Berlin "to learn." The watchman laughed and waved him through. "Go Moses, the sea has opened before you."*

In Berlin the young Mendelssohn studied Jewish law and eked out a living copying Hebrew manuscripts in a beautiful hand. But he was soon fascinated by an intellectual world that had been closed to him in the Dessau ghetto. There, like most Jews throughout central Europe, he had spoken Yiddish—a mixture of German, Polish, and Hebrew. Now, working mainly on his own, he mastered German; learned Latin, Greek, French, and English; and studied mathematics and Enlightenment philosophy. Word of his exceptional abilities spread in Berlin's Jewish community (the dwelling of 1,500 of the city's 100,000 inhabitants). He began tutoring the children of a wealthy Jewish silk merchant, and he soon became the merchant's clerk and later his partner. But his great passion remained the life of the mind and the spirit, which he avidly pursued in his off-hours.

Gentle and unassuming in his personal life, Mendelssohn was a bold thinker. Reading eagerly in works of Western philosophy dating back to antiquity, he was, as a pious Jew, soon convinced that Enlightenment teachings need not be opposed to Jewish thought and religion. He concluded that reason could complement and strengthen religion, although each would retain its integrity as a separate sphere.† Developing this idea in his first great work, "On the Immortality of the Soul" (1767), Mendelssohn used the neutral setting of a philosophical dialogue between Socrates and his followers in ancient Greece to argue that the human soul lived forever. In refusing to bring religion and critical thinking into conflict, he was strongly influenced by contemporary German philosophers who argued similarly on behalf of Christianity. He reflected the way the German Enlightenment generally supported established religion, in contrast to the French Enlightenment, which attacked it.

Mendelssohn's treatise on the human soul captivated the educated German public, which marveled that a Jew could have written a philosophical masterpiece. In the excitement, a Christian zealot named Lavater challenged Mendelssohn in a pamphlet to accept Christianity or to demonstrate how the Christian faith was not "reasonable." Replying politely but passionately, the Jewish philosopher affirmed that his studies had only strengthened him in his faith, although he did not seek to convert anyone not born into Judaism.

Rather, he urged toleration in religious matters and spoke up courageously against Jewish oppression.

Orthodox Jew and German philosophe, Moses Mendelssohn serenely combined two very different worlds. He built a bridge from the ghetto to the dominant culture over which many Jews would pass, including his novelist daughter Dorothea and his famous grandson, the composer Felix Mendelssohn.

*H. Kupferberg, *The Mendelssohns: Three Generations of Genius* (New York: Charles Scribner's Sons, 1972), p. 3.

†D. Sorkin, *Moses Mendelssohn and the Religious Enlightenment* (Berkeley: University of California Press, 1996), pp. 8 ff.

QUESTIONS FOR ANALYSIS

1. How did Mendelssohn seek to influence Jewish religious thought in his time?
2. How do Mendelssohn's ideas compare with those of the French Enlightenment?

Lavater (right) attempts to convert Mendelssohn, in a painting of an imaginary encounter by Moritz Oppenheim. (akg-images)

How did consumerism and the Atlantic economy influence Enlightenment ideas?

The new practices of debate and sociability brought by the Enlightenment took place within a rapidly evolving material world. A rising European population in the eighteenth century furnished more skilled hands to produce finished goods as well as more consumers to purchase these products. Consumerism was fed by an increasingly integrated Atlantic economy that circulated finished European products, raw materials from the colonies, and enslaved peoples from Africa. Over time, distinctive Atlantic communities and identities were constituted by the peoples, goods, and ideas that crisscrossed the ocean.

In turn, the contents of Enlightenment thought were shaped by the material world in which they emerged. Enlightenment thinkers drew inspiration from accounts of New World encounters as well as from the economic possibilities of colonial trade. As Adam Smith himself declared, "The discovery of America and that of a passage to the East Indies by the Cape of Good Hope, are the two greatest and most important events recorded in the history of mankind."[5] Enlightenment thinkers also used science and reason to establish a racial hierarchy that placed whites at the top, helping to justify slavery.

A Revolution in Consumption and Daily Life

One of the most important developments of eighteenth-century Europe was the emergence of a fledgling consumer culture. Many purchasers of consumer goods were from the upper and upper-middle classes, but a boom in cheap reproductions of luxury items provided affordable goods for city dwellers of modest means. This "consumer revolution," as it has been called, created new expectations for comfort and self-expression, dramatically changing European daily life in the eighteenth century.

Food was one of the chief areas of advance. Using Enlightenment techniques of observation and experimentation, a group of scientists, government officials, and

The Consumer Revolution From the mid-eighteenth century on, the cities of western Europe witnessed a new proliferation of consumer goods. Items once limited to the wealthy few—such as fans, watches, snuffboxes, umbrellas, teapots, and ornamental containers (right)—were now reproduced in cheaper versions for middling and ordinary people. The fashion for wide hoopskirts was so popular that the armrests of the chairs of the day, known as Louis XV chairs (left), were specially designed to accommodate them. (jar: Victoria & Albert Museum, London/The Bridgeman Art Library; chair: Louvre/Réunion des Musées Nationaux/Art Resource, NY)

a few big landowners devised new agricultural practices and tools that raised crop yields dramatically, especially in England and the Netherlands. These included new forms of crop rotation, better equipment, and selective breeding of livestock. The controversial process of enclosure, fencing off common land to create privately owned fields that increased agricultural production, allowed a break with traditional methods, but at the cost of reducing poor farmers' access to land.

Colonial plants also provided new sources of calories and nutrition. Introduced into Europe from the Americas—along with corn, squash, tomatoes, and many other useful plants—the humble potato provided an excellent new food source. Together, these improvements in agriculture led to a rapid growth of population, especially after 1750.

One of the most remarkable dietary changes in the eighteenth century was the greater consumption of sugar, tea, coffee, tobacco, and chocolate. Previously expensive and rare luxury items, they became dietary staples for people of all social classes, especially in Britain. This was possible because new surpluses in production provided by slave labor in the New World lowered the price of many of these items.

Greater demand for manufactured clothing was another major factor behind the growth of consumption. Shrewd entrepreneurs made fashionable clothing seem more desirable, while legions of women entering the textile and needle trades made it ever cheaper. As a result, eighteenth-century western Europe witnessed a dramatic rise in the consumption of clothing, particularly in large cities. Colonial economies again played an important role in lowering the cost of materials, such as cotton and vegetable dyes, largely due to the unpaid toil of enslaved Africans. Cheaper copies of elite styles made it possible for working people to aspire to follow fashion for the first time.

Changes in outward appearances were reflected in inner spaces as new attitudes about privacy and individuality also emerged. In 1700 the cramped home of a modest family consisted of a few rooms, each of which had multiple functions. For example, the same room might be used for sleeping, receiving friends, and working. In the eighteenth century rents rose sharply, making it impossible to gain more space, but families began attributing specific functions to specific rooms and putting barriers up to divide rooms into separate spaces.

New levels of comfort and convenience accompanied this trend toward more individualized ways of life. Books and prints, now available at lower prices, decorated shelves and walls. Improvements in glassmaking provided more transparent glass, which allowed daylight to penetrate into gloomy rooms. Cold and smoky hearths were replaced by more efficient and cleaner coal stoves. All these changes made rooms warmer, better lit, more comfortable, and more personalized.

The scope of the new consumer economy should not be exaggerated. These developments were concentrated in large cities in northwestern Europe and in the colonial cities of North America. Even in these centers elites benefited the most from the new modes of life. The eighteenth century did, however, lay the foundations for one of the most distinctive features of modern Western life: societies based on the consumption of goods and services obtained through global markets in which many individuals' identities and self-worth are shaped through the goods they consume.

The Atlantic Economy

The consumer revolution fed on the dynamic growth of trade across the Atlantic Ocean. Commercial exchange in the Atlantic is often referred to as the triangle trade, designating a three-way transport of goods: European commodities, like guns and textiles, to Africa; enslaved Africans to the colonies; and colonial goods, such as cotton, tobacco, and sugar, back to Europe. This model highlights some of the most important flows of trade but significantly oversimplifies the picture. For example, a brisk intercolonial trade also existed,

enclosure The controversial process of fencing off common land to create privately owned fields that increased agricultural production at the cost of reducing poor farmers' access to land.

with the Caribbean slave colonies importing food in the form of fish, flour, and livestock from the northern colonies and rice from the south, in exchange for sugar and slaves (Map 18.2). Moreover, the Atlantic economy was inextricably linked to the older trade systems centered on the Indian and Pacific Oceans.

Across the eighteenth century the economies of European nations bordering the Atlantic Ocean relied more and more on colonial exports. In England, sales to the mainland colonies of North America and the West Indian sugar islands—with an important assist from West Africa and Latin America—soared from £500,000 to £4 million. Exports to England's colonies in Ireland and India also rose substantially from 1700 to 1800.

At the core of this Atlantic world was the misery and profit of the Atlantic slave trade (see pages 506–512). The brutal practice intensified dramatically after 1700 and especially after 1750 with the growth of trade and demand for slave-produced goods. English dominance of the slave trade provided another source of large profits to the home country.

The French also profited enormously from colonial trade in the eighteenth century, even after losing their vast North American territories to England in 1763. The French Caribbean colonies provided immense fortunes in plantation agriculture and slave trading. By 1789 the population of Saint-Domingue (sehn daw-MEHNG) included five hundred thousand slaves, whose labor had allowed the colony to become the world's leading producer of coffee and sugar and the most profitable plantation colony in the New World.[6] The wealth generated from colonial trade fostered the confidence of the French merchant classes, and merchants soon joined other elite groups clamoring for more political power.

The third major player in the Atlantic economy, Spain, also saw its colonial fortunes improve during the eighteenth century. Its mercantilist goals were boosted by a recovery in silver production, which had dropped significantly in the seventeenth century. Spanish territory in North America expanded significantly in the second half of the eighteenth century. At the close of the Seven Years' War (1756–1763), Spain gained Louisiana from the French, and its influence extended westward all the way to northern California through the efforts of Spanish missionaries and ranchers.

Identities and Communities of the Atlantic World

As contacts among the Atlantic coasts of the Americas, Africa, and Europe became more frequent, and as European settlements grew into well-established colonies, new identities and communities emerged. The term *Creole* referred to people of Spanish ancestry born in the Americas. Wealthy Creoles and their counterparts throughout the Atlantic colonies prided themselves on following European ways of life.

Over time, however, the colonial elite came to feel that their circumstances gave them different interests and characteristics from those of their home population. Also, they began to turn against restrictions from their home countries: Creole traders and planters increasingly resented the regulations and taxes imposed by colonial bureaucrats, and such resentment would eventually lead to revolutions against colonial powers (discussed in Chapter 27).

Enlightenment ideas thrived in the colonies. The colonies of British North America were deeply influenced by the Scottish Enlightenment, with its emphasis on pragmatic approaches to the problems of life. Following the Scottish model, leaders in the colonies adopted a moderate, "common-sense" version of the Enlightenment that emphasized self-improvement and ethical conduct.

Northern Enlightenment thinkers often depicted the Spanish American colonies as the epitome of the superstition and barbarity they contested. The Catholic Church strictly controlled the publication of books there, just as it did on the Iberian Peninsula.

Map 18.2 The Atlantic Economy in 1701 The growth of trade encouraged both economic development and military conflict in the Atlantic basin. Four continents were linked together by the exchange of goods and slaves.

CHAPTER LOCATOR

What was revolutionary about the scientific revolution?

What were the core principles of the Enlightenment?

What did enlightened absolutism mean?

How did consumerism and the Atlantic economy influence Enlightenment ideas?

485

LISTENING TO THE PAST

Denis Diderot's "Supplement to Bougainville's Voyage"

Denis Diderot (1713–1784) was born in a provincial town in eastern France and educated in Paris. Rejecting careers in the church and the law, he devoted himself to literature and philosophy. In 1749, sixty years before Charles Darwin's birth, Diderot was jailed by Parisian authorities for publishing an essay questioning God's role in the creation and suggesting the autonomous evolution of species. Following these difficult beginnings, Diderot's editorial work and writing on the Encyclopedia *were the crowning intellectual achievements of his life and, according to some, of the Enlightenment itself.*

Like other philosophes, Diderot disseminated Enlightenment ideas through various types of writing, ranging from scholarly articles in the Encyclopedia *to philosophical treatises, novels, plays, book reviews, and erotic stories. His "Supplement to Bougainville's Voyage" (1772) was a fictional account of a European voyage to Tahiti inspired by the writings of traveler Louis-Antoine de Bougainville. In this passage, Diderot expresses his own loathing of colonial conquest and exploitation through the voice of an elderly Tahitian man. The character's praise for his own culture allows Diderot to express his Enlightenment idealization of natural man, free from the vices of civilized societies.*

❝ He was the father of a large family. When the Europeans arrived he looked upon them with scorn, showing neither astonishment, nor fear, nor curiosity. On their approach he turned his back and retired into his hut. Yet his silence and anxiety revealed his thoughts only too well; he was inwardly lamenting the eclipse of his countrymen's happiness. When Bougainville was leaving the island, as the natives swarmed on the shore, clutching his clothes, clasping his companions in their arms and weeping, the old man made his way forward and proclaimed solemnly, "Weep, wretched natives of Tahiti, weep. But let it be for the coming and not the leaving of these ambitious, wicked men. One day you will know them better. One day they will come back, bearing in one hand the piece of wood you see in that man's belt, and, in the other, the sword hanging by the side of that one, to enslave you, slaughter you, or make you captive to their follies and vices. One day you will be subject to them, as corrupt, vile and miserable as they are. . . ."

Then turning to Bougainville, he continued, "And you, leader of the ruffians who obey you, pull your ship away swiftly from these shores. We are innocent, we are content, and you can only spoil that happiness. We follow the pure instincts of nature, and you have tried to erase its impression from our hearts. Here, everything belongs to everyone, and you have preached I can't tell what distinction between 'yours' and 'mine'. . . . If a Tahitian should one day land on your shores and engrave on one of your stones or on the bark of one of your trees, *This land belongs to the people of Tahiti*, what would you think then? You are stronger than we are, and what does that mean? When one of the miserable trinkets with which your ship is filled was taken away, what an uproar you made, what revenge you exacted! At that moment, in the depths of your heart, you were plotting the theft of an entire country! You are not a slave, you would rather die than be one, and yet you wish to make slaves of us. Do you suppose, then, that a Tahitian cannot defend his own liberty and die for it as well? This inhabitant of Tahiti, whom you wish to ensare like an animal, is your brother. You are both children of Nature. What right do you have over him that he does not have over you? You came; did we attack you? Have we plundered your ship? Did we seize you and expose you to the arrows of our enemies? Did we harness you to work with our animals in the fields? We respected our own image in you.

"Leave us our ways; they are wiser and more decent than yours. We have no wish to exchange

---

Nonetheless, educated elites were well aware of the new currents of thought, and the universities, newspapers, and salons of Spanish America produced their own reform ideas. In all European colonies, one effect of Enlightenment thought was to encourage colonists to criticize the policies of the mother country and aspire toward greater autonomy.

Not all Europeans in the colonies were wealthy or well-educated. Numerous poor and lower-middle-class whites worked as clerks, shopkeepers, craftsmen, and plantation managers. Whether rich or poor, however, white Europeans usually made up a small proportion of the population. Since most European migrants were men, much of the colonial population of the Atlantic world descended from unions—forced or through consent—of European men and indigenous or African women. Colonial attempts to establish and systematize racial categories greatly influenced developing Enlightenment thought on racial differences (see page 488).

In the Spanish and French Caribbean, as in Brazil, many masters acknowledged and freed their mixed-race children, leading to sizable populations of free people of color.

This image depicts the meeting of French explorer Louis-Antoine de Bougainville with Tahitians in April 1768. Of his stay on the island, Bougainville wrote: "I felt as though I had been transported to the Garden of Eden. . . . Everywhere reigned hospitality, peace, joy, and every appearance of happiness." Diderot's philosophical tract was a fictional sequel to Bougainville's account. (Unknown artist, *Tahitians presenting fruit to Bougainville attended by his officers.* PIC T2996 NK5066 LOC7321, National Library of Australia)

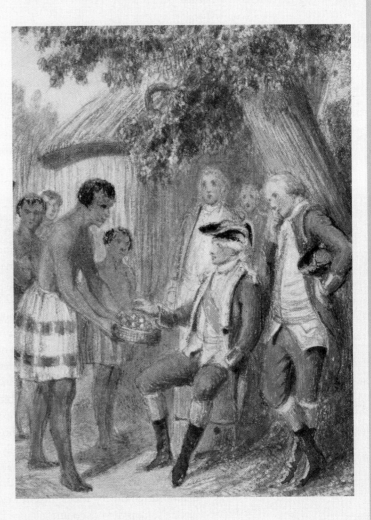

what you call our ignorance for your useless knowledge. Everything that we need and is good for us we already possess. Do we merit contempt because we have not learnt how to acquire superfluous needs? When we are hungry, we have enough to eat. When we are cold, we have enough to wear. You have entered our huts; what do you suppose we lack? Pursue as far as you wish what you call the comforts of life, but let sensible beings stop when they have no more to gain from their labours than imaginary benefits. If you persuade us to go beyond the strict bounds of necessity, when will we finish our work? When will we enjoy ourselves? We have kept our annual and daily labours within the smallest possible limits, because in our eyes nothing is better than rest. Go back to your own country to agitate and torment yourselves as much as you like. But leave us in peace. Do not fill our heads with your factitious needs and illusory virtues. . . ." 🙺

Source: Edited excerpts from pp. 41–43 in Denis Diderot, *Political Writings*, translated and edited by John Hope Mason and Robert Wokler. © 1992 by Cambridge University Press.

QUESTIONS FOR ANALYSIS

1. On what grounds does the speaker argue for the Tahitians' basic equality with the Europeans?
2. What is the good life, according to the speaker, and how does it contrast with the European way of life? Which do you think is the better path, and why?
3. In what ways could Diderot's thoughts here be seen as representative of Enlightenment ideas? Are there ways in which they are not?
4. How realistic do you think this account is? Does it matter? How might defenders of colonial expansion respond to Diderot's criticism?

Advantaged by their fathers, some became wealthy landowners and slaveholders in their own right. Their prosperity provoked a backlash from the white population in French colonies, with new race laws prohibiting nonwhites from marrying whites and forcing them to adopt distinctive attire. In the British colonies of the Caribbean and the southern mainland, masters tended to leave their mixed-race progeny in slavery, maintaining a stark discrepancy between free whites and enslaved people of color.[7] British colonial law forbade marriage of Englishmen and women to Africans or Native Americans.

Restricted from owning land and holding many occupations in Europe, Jews were eager participants in the new Atlantic economy and established a network of mercantile communities along its trade routes. Jews were considered to be white Europeans and thus ineligible to be slaves, but they did not enjoy equal status with Christians. For example, restrictions existed on the number of slaves they could own in Barbados in the early eighteenth century.[8] The status of Jews adds one more element to the complexity of Atlantic identities.

Race and the Enlightenment

Encounters in the Atlantic world—either personal or experienced through memoirs, travel literature, and other sources—had a strong impact on Enlightenment philosophers' views on race. Although most Europeans had little direct contact with Africans, educated writers were well aware of the growth of the slave trade and may have encountered individuals of African descent living in European cities.

Alongside intensified interaction with non-European peoples, another primary catalyst for new ideas about race was the urge to classify nature unleashed by the scientific revolution and its insistence on empirical observation. As scientists developed more elaborate taxonomies of plant and animal species, they also began to classify humans into hierarchically ordered "races" and to investigate the origins of race. The French naturalist Georges-Louis Leclerc, Comte de Buffon (1707–1788), argued that humans originated with one species that then developed into distinct races due largely to climatic conditions. Enlightenment thinkers such as David Hume and Immanuel Kant (see pages 475–476) helped popularize these ideas.

In *On the Different Races of Man* (1775), Kant claimed that there were four human races, each of which had derived from a supposedly original race of "white brunette" people. According to Kant, the closest descendants of the original race were the white inhabitants of northern Germany. As they acquired new physical characteristics from their local climate and geography, the other races had degenerated both physically and culturally from this origin.

Using the word *race* to designate biologically distinct groups of humans was new. Previously, Europeans grouped other peoples into "nations" based on their historical, political, and cultural affiliations, rather than on supposedly innate physical differences. Europeans had long believed they were culturally superior. The new idea that racial difference was physical and innate rather than cultural taught them they were biologically superior as well. In turn, scientific racism helped legitimate and justify the tremendous growth of slavery that occurred during the eighteenth century.

Racist ideas did not go unchallenged. *Encyclopedia* editor Denis Diderot penned a scathing critique of European arrogance and exploitation in the voice of Tahitian villagers. (See "Listening to the Past: Denis Diderot's 'Supplement to Bougainville's Voyage,'" page 486.) Scottish philosopher James Beattie (1735–1803) responded directly to claims of white superiority by pointing out that Europeans had started out as savage as nonwhites and that many non-European peoples in the Americas, Asia, and Africa had achieved high levels of civilization. German thinker Johann Gottfried von Herder (1744–1803) criticized Kant, arguing that humans could not be classified into races based on skin color and that each culture was as intrinsically worthy as any other.

One popular idea, among Rousseau and others, was that indigenous peoples of the Americas represented prime examples of "natural man," the being who embodied the essential goodness of humanity uncorrupted by decadent society. Other popular candidates for utopian natural man were the Pacific Island societies explored by Captain James Cook and others from the 1770s on (see pages 742–743).

There are clear parallels between the use of science to propagate racial hierarchies and to defend social inequalities between men and women. French philosopher Jean-Jacques Rousseau used women's "natural" passivity to argue for their passive role in society, just as other thinkers used non-Europeans' "natural" inferiority to defend slavery and colonial domination. The new powers of science and reason were thus marshaled to imbue traditional stereotypes with the force of natural law.

Quick Review
What changes in daily life, trade, and colonial interaction accompanied and shaped the new worldview of the Enlightenment?

Connections

HAILED AS THE ORIGIN of modern thought, the scientific revolution must also be seen as a product of its past. Borrowing in part from Arabic translators and commentators, medieval universities gave rise to important new scholarship. In turn, the ambition and wealth of Renaissance patrons nurtured intellectual curiosity and encouraged scholarly research and foreign exploration. Religious faith also influenced the scientific revolution, inspiring some thinkers to understand the glory of God's creation, while bringing censure and personal tragedy to others. Natural philosophers following Copernicus pioneered new methods of observing and explaining nature while drawing on centuries-old traditions of mysticism, astrology, alchemy, and magic.

Enlightenment ideas of the eighteenth century were a similar blend of past and present, progressive and traditional, homegrown and influenced by other cultures. Enlightenment thinkers advocated universal rights and liberties but also preached the biological inferiority of non-Europeans. Their principles served as much to bolster authoritarian regimes as to inspire revolutionaries to fight for human rights. Although the Enlightenment fostered critical thinking about everything from science to religion, most Europeans, including many prominent thinkers, remained devout Christians.

The achievements of the scientific revolution and the Enlightenment are undeniable. Key Western values of rationalism, human rights, and open-mindedness were born from these movements. With their new notions of progress and social improvement, Europeans would embark on important revolutions in politics and industry (discussed in Chapters 22 and 23). Nonetheless, some critics have seen a darker side. For them, the mastery over nature permitted by the scientific revolution now threatens to overwhelm the earth's fragile equilibrium, and the Enlightenment belief in the universal application of reason can lead to arrogance and intolerance, particularly intolerance of other people's spiritual, cultural, and political values. Such vivid debate about the legacy of these intellectual and scientific developments testifies to their continuing importance in today's world.

As the era of European exploration and conquest gave way to colonial empire building, the eighteenth century witnessed increased consolidation of global markets and bitter competition among Europeans for the spoils of empire. The eighteenth-century Atlantic world thus tied the shores of Europe, the Americas, and Africa in a web of commercial and human exchange, including the tragedy of slavery, discussed in Chapter 19. The Atlantic world maintained strong ties with trade in the Pacific and the Indian Oceans.

- **For a list of suggested readings for this chapter, visit** *bedfordstmartins.com/mckayworldunderstanding*.

- **For primary sources from this period, see** *Sources of World Societies*, Second Edition.

- **For Web sites, images, and documents related to topics in this chapter, see Make History at** *bedfordstmartins.com/ mckayworldunderstanding*.

Chapter 18 Study Guide

To do these exercises online, go to bedfordstmartins.com/mckayworldunderstanding.

Step 1

GETTING STARTED

Below are basic terms about this period in global history. Can you identify each term below and explain why it matters?

TERMS	WHO (OR WHAT) AND WHEN	WHY IT MATTERS
natural philosophy, p. 466		
Copernican hypothesis, p. 468		
law of inertia, p. 469		
law of universal gravitation, p. 470		
empiricism, p. 470		
Cartesian dualism, p. 470		
Enlightenment, p. 472		
philosophes, p. 473		
economic liberalism, p. 475		
salons, p. 477		
public sphere, p. 477		
general will, p. 477		
enlightened absolutism, p. 478		
Haskalah, p. 479		
enclosure, p. 483		

Step 2

MOVING BEYOND THE BASICS

The exercise below requires a more advanced understanding of the chapter material. Examine the contributions of key figures of the scientific revolution by filling in the chart below with descriptions of the scientific discoveries of the figures listed. Be sure to include both concrete discoveries and contributions to the development of the scientific method. When you are finished, consider the following questions: How did these thinkers build off of each other's discoveries and insights? What common goals did they share?

	DISCOVERIES AND CONTRIBUTIONS
Nicolaus Copernicus	
Tycho Brahe	
Johannes Kepler	
Francis Bacon	
René Descartes	
Galileo Galilei	
Isaac Newton	

PUTTING IT ALL TOGETHER

Now that you've reviewed key elements of the chapter, take a step back and try to see the big picture. Remember to use specific examples from the chapter in your answers.

THE SCIENTIFIC REVOLUTION

- What was revolutionary about the scientific revolution? How did the study of nature in the sixteenth century differ from the study of nature in the Middle Ages?

  - What role did religion play in the scientific revolution? How did religious belief both stimulate and hinder scientific inquiry?

THE ENLIGHTENMENT AND ENLIGHTENED ABSOLUTISM

- How did the scientific revolution contribute to the emergence of the Enlightenment? What new ideas about the power and potential of human reason were central to both developments?

- What connections can you make between the state-building ambitions of central and eastern European absolute monarchs and their embrace of Enlightenment reforms?

CONSUMERISM AND THE ATLANTIC WORLD

- How did the growth and consolidation of the Atlantic economy shape the everyday lives of eighteenth-century Europeans?

- How did Enlightenment thinkers deal with issues of gender and race? How did New World encounters shape their thinking?

LOOKING BACK, LOOKING AHEAD

- How did medieval and Renaissance developments contribute to the scientific revolution? Should the scientific revolution be seen as a sharp break with the past, or the culmination of long-term, gradual change?

- At the beginning of the chapter, a noted historian was quoted as saying that the scientific revolution was "the real origin both of the modern world and the modern mentality." Do you agree or disagree with this characterization? Why?

In Your Own Words Imagine that you must explain Chapter 18 to someone who hasn't read it. What would be the most important points to include and why?

19

Africa and the World

1400–1800

African states and societies of the early modern period — from the fifteenth through the eighteenth centuries — comprised a wide variety of languages, cultures, and kinds of economic and political development. Kingdoms and stateless societies coexisted throughout Africa, from the small villages of the Senegambia to the kingdom of Songhai and its renowned city of Timbuktu in West Africa, and from the Christian state of Ethiopia to the independent city-states of the Swahili coast in East Africa. So too by the fifteenth century had Africans developed a steady rhythm of contact and exchange. Across the great Sahara, trade goods and knowledge passed back and forth from West Africa to North Africa and beyond to Europe and the Middle East. The same was true in East Africa, where Indian Ocean traders touched up and down the African coast to deliver goods from Arabia, India, and Asia and to pick up the ivory, gold, spices, and other products representing Africa's rich natural wealth. In the interior as well, extensive trading networks linked African societies across the vast continent.

Waist Pendant of Benin Worn by Royalty European intrusion in Africa deeply affected the diverse societies of Africa. The facial features, the beard, and the ruffled collar on this Edo peoples' artifact dating from the sixteenth to the nineteenth centuries are clearly Portuguese, but the braided hair is distinctly African. (Image copyright © The Metropolitan Museum of Art/Art Resource, NY)

Modern European intrusion into Africa beginning in the fifteenth century profoundly affected these diverse societies and ancient trading networks. The intrusion led to the transatlantic slave trade, one of the greatest forced migrations in world history, through which Africa made a substantial, though involuntary, contribution to the building of the West's industrial civilization. In the seventeenth century an increasing desire for sugar in Europe resulted in an increasing demand for slave labor in South America and the West Indies. In the eighteenth century Western technological changes created a demand for cotton and other crops that required extensive human labor, thus intensifying the West's "need" for African slaves.

Chapter Preview

▶ **What kinds of states and societies coexisted in early modern West Africa?**

▶ **How did the arrival of outsiders impact East Africa?**

▶ **What were the causes and consequences of the transatlantic slave trade?**

What kinds of states and societies coexisted in early modern West Africa?

In mid-fifteenth-century Africa, Benin and a number of other kingdoms flourished along the two-thousand-mile west coast between Senegambia and the northeastern shore of the Gulf of Guinea (Map 19.1). Further inland, in the region of the Sudan, the kingdoms of Songhai, Kanem-Bornu, and Hausaland benefited from the trans-Saharan caravan trade, which along with goods brought Islamic culture to the region. These West African kingdoms maintained their separate existences for centuries. Stateless societies existed alongside these more centralized states. Despite their political differences and whether they were agricultural, pastoral, or a mixture of both, the cultures of West Africa equally faced the challenges presented by famine, disease, and the slave trade.

The West Coast: Senegambia and Benin

The Senegambian states possessed a homogeneous culture and a common history. For centuries Senegambia served as an important entrepôt for desert caravan contact with North African and Middle Eastern Islamic civilizations. Through the transatlantic slave trade, Senegambia came into contact with Europe and the Americas. Thus Senegambia felt the impact of Islamic culture to the north and of European influences from the maritime West.

Mapping the Past

Map 19.1 West African Societies, ca. 1500–1800

The coastal region of West Africa witnessed the rise of a number of kingdoms in the sixteenth century.

ANALYZING THE MAP What geographical features defined each of the kingdoms shown here? Consider rivers, lakes, oceans, deserts, and forests. How might these have impacted the size and shape of these kingdoms?

CONNECTIONS Compare this map to the spot map of the slave coast of West Africa on page 507. Consider the role that rivers and other geographical factors played in the development of the West African slave trade. Why were Luanda and Benguela the logical Portuguese sources for slaves?

The Senegambian peoples spoke Wolof, Serer, and Pulaar, which all belong to the West African language group. Both the Wolof-speakers and the Serer-speakers had clearly defined social classes: royalty, nobility, warriors, peasants, low-caste artisans such as blacksmiths and leatherworkers, and enslaved persons. This enslaved class consisted of individuals who were pawned for debt, house servants who could not be sold, and people who were acquired through war or purchase. Senegambian slavery varied from society to society but generally was not a benign institution. In some places, slaves were considered chattel property and were treated as harshly as they would be later in the Western Hemisphere.

The word chattel originally comes from a Latin word meaning head, as in "so many head of cattle." It reflects the notion that enslaved people are not human, but subhuman, like beasts of burden, like animals. Thus, they can be treated like animals. But in Senegambia and other parts of Africa, many enslaved people were not considered chattel property. That is, unlike livestock or other common property, they could not be bought and sold. What is more, unlike in the Americas, where slave status passed forever from one generation to the next, in Africa the enslaved person's descendants were sometimes considered free, although the stigma of slavery could attach to the family.

Senegambia was composed of stateless societies, culturally homogeneous ethnic societies where kinship and lineage groups tended to fragment communities. These societies comprised small groups of villages without a central capital. Among these stateless societies age-grade systems evolved. Age-grades were groups of teenage males and females whom the society initiated into adulthood at the same time. Age-grades cut across family ties, created community-wide loyalties, and provided a means of local law enforcement, because each age-grade was responsible for the behavior of all its members.

The typical Senegambian community was a small, self-supporting agricultural village of closely related families. Fields were cut from the surrounding forest, and the average six- to eight-acre farm supported a moderate-size family. Village markets for produce exchange offered opportunities for receiving outside news and for social diversion. Social life was centered around the family, and government played a limited role, interceding mostly to resolve family disputes and conflicts between families.

Alongside West African stateless societies were kingdoms and states ruled by kings who governed defined areas through bureaucratic hierarchies. The kingdom of Benin emerged in the fifteenth and sixteenth centuries in what is now southern Nigeria (see Map 19.1). Over time the position of its oba, or king, was exalted, bringing stability to the state. In the later fifteenth century the oba Ewuare strengthened his army and pushed Benin's borders as far as the Niger River in the east, westward into Yoruba country, and south to the Gulf of Guinea. During the late sixteenth and seventeenth centuries the office of the oba evolved from a warrior-kingship to a position of spiritual leadership.

At its height in the late sixteenth century, Benin controlled a vast territory, and European visitors described a sophisticated society. A Dutch visitor in the early 1600s, possibly Dierick Ruiters, described the capital, Benin City, as possessing a great, wide, and straight

Chapter Chronology

1400–1600s	Salt trade dominates West African economy
ca. 1464–1591	Songhai kingdom dominates the western Sudan
1485	Portuguese and other Europeans first appear in Benin
1493-1528	Muhammad Toure governs and expands kingdom of Songhai
1498	Portuguese explorer Vasco da Gama sails around Africa
ca. 1500–1900	Era of transatlantic slave trade
1502–1507	Portuguese erect forts at Kilwa, Zanzibar, and Sofala on Swahili coast
1529	Adal defeats Ethiopian emperor and begins systematic devastation of Ethiopia
1543	Portuguese defeat Muslims in Ethiopia
1571–1603	Idris Alooma governs kingdom of Kanem-Bornu
1591	Moroccan army defeats Songhai
1658	Dutch allow importation of slaves into Cape Colony
1680s	Famine from Senegambian coast to Upper Nile
1789	Olaudah Equiano publishes autobiography

chattel An item of personal property; a term used in reference to enslaved people that conveys the idea that they are subhuman, like animals, and therefore may be treated like animals.

age-grade systems Among the societies of Senegambia, groups of men and women whom the society initiated into adulthood at the same time.

oba The title of the king of Benin.

The Oba of Benin The oba's palace walls were decorated with bronze plaques that date from about the sixteenth to the eighteenth centuries. This plaque vividly conveys the oba's power, majesty, and authority. The necklace (or choker) is his symbol of royalty. His warrior attendants surround and protect him and carry his royal regalia. (Museum für Völkerkunde/Kunsthistorisches Museum, Vienna)

main avenue down the middle, with many side streets crisscrossing it. The visitor entered the city through a high, well-guarded gate framed on each side by a very tall earthen bulwark, or wall, with an accompanying moat. There was also an impressive royal palace. Visitors also noted that Benin City was kept scrupulously clean, and it had no beggars and that public security was so effective that theft was unknown. The period also witnessed remarkable artistic creativity in ironwork, carved ivory, and especially bronze portrait busts. In 1485 Portuguese and other Europeans began to appear in Benin in pursuit of trade, and over the next couple of centuries Benin grew rich from the profits made through the slave trade and the export of tropical products. Its main European trading partners were the Dutch and Portuguese. In the early eighteenth century tributary states and stronger neighbors nibbled at Benin's frontiers, challenging its power.

The Sudan: Songhai, Kanem-Bornu, and Hausaland

The Songhai kingdom, a successor state of the kingdoms of Ghana (ca. 900–1000) and Mali (ca. 1200–1450), dominated the whole Niger region of the western and central Sudan (see Map 19.1). The imperial expansion of Songhai (song-GUY) began during the reign of the Songhai king Sonni Ali (r. ca. 1464–1492) and continued under his successor, Muhammad Toure (r. 1493–1528). From his capital at Gao, Toure extended his rule as far north as the salt-mining center at Taghaza in the western Sahara and as far east as Agades and Kano. A convert to Islam, Toure returned from a pilgrimage to Mecca impressed by what he had seen there. He tried to bring about greater centralization in his own territories by building a strong army, improving taxation procedures, and replacing local Songhai officials with more efficient Arabs in an effort to substitute royal institutions for ancient kinship ties.

Taghaza A settlement in the western Sahara, the site of the main salt-mining center.

We know little about daily life in Songhai society because of the paucity of written records and surviving artifacts. Some information is provided by Leo Africanus (ca. 1465–1550), a Moroccan captured by pirates and given as a slave to Pope Leo X. Leo Africanus became a Christian, taught Arabic in Rome, and in 1526 published an account of his many travels, including a stay in the Songhai kingdom.

As a scholar, Africanus was naturally impressed by Timbuktu, the second city of the empire, which he visited in 1513. "Here [is] a great store of doctors, judges, priests, and other learned men, that are bountifully maintained at the King's court," he reported.[1] Many of these Islamic scholars had studied in Cairo and other centers of Muslim learning.

Songhai under Muhammad Toure seems to have enjoyed economic prosperity. The elite had large amounts of money to spend, and expensive North African and European luxuries were much in demand. The existence of many shops and markets implies the development of an urban culture. At Timbuktu, merchants, scholars, judges, and artisans constituted a distinctive bourgeoisie. The presence of many foreign merchants, including Jews and Italians, gave the city a cosmopolitan atmosphere.

Slavery played an important role in Songhai's economy. On the royal farms scattered throughout the kingdom, enslaved people produced rice—the staple crop—for the royal granaries. Slaves could possess their own slaves, land, and cattle, but they could not bequeath any of this property; the king inherited all of it. Muhammad Toure greatly increased the number of royal slaves. He gave slaves to favorite Muslim scholars, who thus gained a steady source of income. Slaves were also sold at the large market at Gao, where traders from North Africa bought them in order to resell them in Cairo, Constantinople, Lisbon, Naples, Genoa, and Venice.

Despite its considerable economic and cultural strengths, Songhai had serious internal problems. Islam never took root in the countryside, and Muslim officials alienated the king from his people. Muhammad Toure's reforms were a failure. He governed diverse peoples who were often hostile to one another, and no cohesive element united them. Finally, the Songhai never developed an effective method of transferring power. Revolts, conspiracies, and palace intrigues followed the death of every king. Muhammad Toure himself was murdered by one of his sons. His death began a period of political instability that led to the kingdom's slow disintegration.

In 1582 the Moroccan sultanate began to press southward in search of a greater share of the trans-Saharan trade. In 1591 a Moroccan army of three thousand soldiers—many of whom were slaves of European origin equipped with European muskets—crossed the Sahara and inflicted a crushing defeat on the Songhai at Tondibi, spelling the end of the Songhai Empire.

East of Songhai lay the kingdoms of Kanem-Bornu and Hausaland (see Map 19.1). Under Idris Alooma (r. 1571–1603), Kanem-Bornu subdued weaker peoples and gained jurisdiction over an extensive area. Well-drilled and equipped with firearms, camel-mounted cavalry and a standing army decimated warriors fighting with spears and arrows. Idris Alooma perpetuated a form of feudalism by granting land to able fighters in return for loyalty and the promise of future military assistance. Meanwhile, agriculture occupied most people. Kanem-Bornu shared in the trans-Saharan trade, shipping eunuchs and young girls to North Africa in return for horses and firearms.

A devout Muslim, Idris Alooma built mosques at his capital city of N'gazargamu and substituted Muslim courts and Islamic law for African tribunals and ancient customary law. His eighteenth-century successors lacked his vitality and military skills, however, and the empire declined.

Between Songhai and Kanem-Bornu were the lands of the Hausa, an agricultural people who lived in small villages. Hausa merchants traded slaves and kola nuts with North African communities across the Sahara, and obscure trading posts evolved into important Hausa city-states like Kano and Katsina, through which Islamic influences entered the region. Kano and Katsina became Muslim intellectual centers and in the fifteenth century attracted scholars from Timbuktu. As in Songhai and Kanem-Bornu, however, Islam made no strong imprint on the Hausa masses until the nineteenth century.

The Lives of the People of West Africa

The negative effects of the transatlantic slave trade (see page 506) on West Africa's population profoundly affected marriage patterns and family structure. Wives and children were highly desired because they could clear and cultivate the land. They also brought prestige, social support, and security in old age. The result was intense competition for women, inequality of access to them, an emphasis on male virility and female fertility, and serious tension between male generations. Polygyny was almost universal.

Queen Mother and Attendants As in Ottoman, Chinese, and European societies, the mothers of African rulers sometimes exercised considerable political power because of their influence on their sons. African kings granted the title Queen Mother as a badge of honor. In this figure, the long beaded cap, called "chicken's beak," symbolizes the mother's rank, as do her elaborate neck jewelry and attendants. (Image copyright © The Metropolitan Museum of Art/Art Resource, NY)

Men acquired wives in two ways. First, some couples simply eloped and began their union. More commonly, a man's family gave bride wealth to the bride's family as compensation for losing her productive and reproductive abilities. She was expected to produce children, to produce food through her labor, and to pass on the culture in the raising of her children. Because it took time for a young man to acquire the bride wealth, all but the richest men delayed marriage until about age thirty. Women married at about the onset of puberty.

The easy availability of land in Africa reduced the kinds of generational conflict that occurred in western Europe, where land was scarce. Competition for wives between male generations, however, was fierce. On the one hand, tradition stressed respect for the elderly. On the other hand, West African societies were not based on rule by elders as we think of them today, as few people lived much beyond forty. Young men possessed the powerful asset of their labor, which could easily be turned into independence where so much land was available.

"Without children you are naked" goes a Yoruba proverb, and children were the primary goal of marriage. Just as a man's virility determined his honor, so barrenness damaged a woman's status. A woman might have six widely spaced pregnancies in her fertile years; the universal practice of breast-feeding infants for two, three, or even four years may have inhibited conception. Long intervals between births due to food shortages also may have limited pregnancies and checked population growth. The harsh climate, poor nutrition, and infectious diseases also contributed to a high infant mortality rate.

Both nuclear and extended families were common in West Africa. Nuclear families averaged only five or six members, but the household of a Big Man (a local man of power) included his wives, married and unmarried sons, unmarried daughters, poor relations, dependents, and scores of children. Extended families were common among the Hausa and Malinke peoples. Where one family cultivated extensive land, a large household of young adults, children, and slaves probably proved most efficient.

In agriculture men did the heavy work of felling trees and clearing the land; women then planted, weeded, and harvested. Between 1000 and 1400, cassava (manioc), bananas, and plantains came to West Africa from Asia. Cassava required little effort to grow and became a staple food, but it had little nutritional value. In the sixteenth century the Portuguese introduced maize (corn), sweet potatoes, and new varieties of yams from the Americas. Fish supplemented the diets of people living near bodies of water.

Disease posed perhaps the biggest obstacle to population growth. Malaria, spread by mosquitoes and rampant in West Africa, was the greatest killer, especially of infants. West Africans developed a relatively high degree of immunity to malaria and other parasitic diseases. Acute strains of smallpox introduced by Europeans certainly did not help population growth, nor did venereal syphilis, which possibly originated in Latin America. As in Chinese and European communities in the early modern period, the sick depended on folk medicine. African medical specialists, such as midwives, bonesetters, exorcists using religious methods, and herbalists, administered a variety of treatments. Still, disease was common where the diet was poor and lacked adequate vitamins.

The devastating effects of famine, often mentioned in West African oral traditions, represented another major check on population growth. Drought, excessive rain, swarms of locusts, and rural wars that prevented the cultivation of land all meant later food shortages. In the 1680s famine extended from the Senegambian coast to the Upper Nile, and many people sold themselves into slavery for food. In the eighteenth century "slave exports" reached their peak in times of famine, and ships could fill their cargo holds simply by offering food.

Trade and Industry

As in all premodern societies, West African economies rested on agriculture. There was some trade and industry, but population shortages encouraged local self-sufficiency, slowed transportation, and hindered exchange. There were very few large markets, and their relative isolation from the outside world and failure to attract large numbers of foreign merchants limited technological innovation.

For centuries, black Africans had exchanged goods with North African merchants in centers such as Gao and Timbuktu. That long-distance trans-Saharan trade was conducted and controlled by Muslim-Berber merchants using camels. The two primary goods exchanged were salt, which came from salt mines in North Africa, and gold, which came mainly from gold mines in modern-day Mali.

West African Trade Routes

SAHARA

Taghaza

Timbuktu   Gao

Niger R.

Benin City

NIGER DELTA

→ Trade route

As elsewhere around the world, water was the cheapest method of transportation, and many small dugout canoes and larger trading canoes plied the Niger and its delta region (see Map 19.1). On land West African peoples used pack animals (camels or donkeys) rather than wheeled vehicles; south of the Sahara, only a narrow belt of land was suitable for animal-drawn carts. Such difficulties in transport severely restricted long-distance trade, so most people relied on the regional exchange of local specialties.

West African communities had a well-organized market system. At informal markets on riverbanks, fishermen bartered fish for local specialties. More formal markets existed within towns and villages or on neutral ground between them. Markets also rotated among neighboring villages on certain days. Local sellers were usually women; traders from afar were men.

Salt had long been one of Africa's most critical trade items, and the salt trade dominated the West African economies in the fifteenth, sixteenth, and seventeenth centuries. The main salt-mining center was at Taghaza in the western Sahara. In the most wretched conditions, slaves dug the salt from desiccated lakes and loaded heavy blocks onto camels' backs. **Tuareg** warriors and later Moors (peoples of Berber and Arab descent) traded their salt south for gold, grain, slaves, and kola nuts. **Cowrie shells**, imported from the Maldives in the Indian Ocean by way of Gujarat and North Africa, served as the medium of exchange. Gold continued to be mined and shipped from Mali until South American bullion flooded Europe in the sixteenth century (see page 425). Thereafter, its production in Africa steadily declined.

West African peoples engaged in many crafts, such as basket weaving and pottery making. Ironworking became hereditary in individual families; such expertise was regarded as family property. The textile industry had the greatest level of specialization. The earliest

Tuareg Along with the Moors, warriors who controlled the north-south trans-Saharan trade in salt.

cowrie shells Imported from the Maldives, they served as the medium of exchange in West Africa.

fabric in West Africa was made of vegetable fiber. Muslim traders introduced cotton and its weaving in the ninth century. By the fifteenth century the Wolof and Malinke regions had professional weavers producing beautiful cloth, but this cloth was too expensive to compete in the Atlantic and Indian Ocean markets after 1500.

How did the arrival of outsiders impact East Africa?

East Africa in the early modern period faced repeated incursions from foreign powers. At the beginning of the sixteenth century Ethiopia faced challenges from the Muslim state of Adal, and then from Europeans. The wealthy Swahili city-states along the southeastern coast of Africa were also confronted with European intrusions in the sixteenth century. For such cities, the arrival of the Portuguese in 1498 proved catastrophic, and the Swahili coast suffered economic decline as a result.

Muslim and European Incursions in Ethiopia, ca. 1500–1630

Coptic Christianity Orthodox form of Christianity from Egypt practiced in Ethiopia.

At the beginning of the sixteenth century the powerful East African kingdom of Ethiopia extended from Massawa in the north to several tributary states in the south (Map 19.2), but the ruling Solomonic dynasty faced serious external threats. Alone among the states in northeast and eastern Africa, Ethiopia was a Christian kingdom that practiced Coptic Christianity, an orthodox form of the Christian faith that originated in Egypt in 451. By the early 1500s Ethiopia was an island of Christianity surrounded by a sea of Muslim states.

Adal, a Muslim state along the southern base of the Red Sea, began incursions into Ethiopia, and in 1529 the Adal general Ahmad ibn-Ghazi inflicted a disastrous defeat on the Ethiopian emperor Lebna Dengel (r. 1508–1540). Ahmad followed up his victory with systematic devastation of the land; destruction of many Ethiopian artistic and literary works, churches, and monasteries; and the forced conversion of thousands to Islam. Lebna Dengel fled to the mountains and appealed to Portugal for assistance. A Portuguese force of four hundred men under Christovao da Gama came to his aid, but Dengel was killed in battle before the Portuguese arrived. The Muslim occupation of Christian Ethiopia, which began around 1531, ended in 1543, after a joint Ethiopian and Portuguese force defeated a larger Muslim army at the battle of Wayna Daga.

No sooner had the Muslim threat ended than Ethiopia encountered three more dangers. The Galla, Cushitic-speaking peoples, moved northward in great numbers, occupying portions of Harar, Shoa, and Amhara. The Ethiopians could not defeat them militarily, and the Galla were not interested in assimilation. For the next two centuries the two peoples lived together in an uneasy truce. Simultaneously, the Ottoman Turks seized Massawa and other coastal cities. Then the Jesuits arrived and attempted to force Roman Catholicism on a proud people whose Coptic form of Christianity long antedated the European version. The overzealous Jesuit missionary Alphonse Mendez tried to revamp the Ethiopian liturgy, rebaptize the people, and replace ancient Ethiopian customs and practices with Roman ones. Since Ethiopian national sentiment was closely tied to Coptic Christianity, violent rebellion and anarchy ensued.

In 1633 the Jesuit missionaries were expelled. For the next two centuries, hostility to foreigners, weak political leadership, and regionalism characterized Ethiopia. Civil conflicts between Galla and Ethiopia erupted continually. The Coptic Church, though lacking strong authority, survived as the cornerstone of Ethiopian national identity.

The Swahili City-States and the Arrival of the Portuguese, ca. 1500–1600

The word Swahili means "People of the Coast" and refers to the people living along the East African coast and on the nearby islands. Although predominantly a Bantu-speaking people, the Swahili have incorporated significant aspects of Arabic culture. Roughly 35 percent of Swahili words come from Arabic. By the eleventh century the Swahili had accepted Islam, which provided a common identity and unifying factor for all the peoples along coastal East Africa. Living on the Indian Ocean coast, the Swahili also felt the influences of Indians, Indonesians, and Persians.

Swahili civilization was overwhelmingly maritime. A fertile, well-watered, and intensely cultivated stretch of land extending down the coast yielded rice, grains, citrus fruit, and cloves. The region's considerable prosperity, however, rested on trade and commerce. The Swahili acted as middlemen in an Indian Ocean–East African economy that might be described as early capitalism. They exchanged ivory, rhinoceros horn, tortoise shell, inlaid ebony chairs, and inland slaves for Arabian and Persian perfumes, toilet articles, ink, and paper, and for Indian textiles, beads, and iron tools. In the fifteenth century the cosmopolitan city-states of Mogadishu, Pate, Lamu, Mombasa, and especially Kilwa enjoyed a worldwide reputation for commercial prosperity and high living standards.[2]

The arrival of the Portuguese explorer Vasco da Gama (see Map 16.2 on page 415) in 1498 spelled the end of the Swahili cities' independence. Lured by the spice trade, da Gama wanted to build a Portuguese maritime empire in the Indian Ocean. Swahili rulers responded in different ways to Portuguese intrusion. Some, such as the sultan of Malindi, quickly agreed to a trading alliance with the Portuguese. Others, such as the sultan of Mombasa, were tricked into commercial agreements. Still other Swahili rulers totally rejected Portuguese overtures, and their cities were subjected to bombardment. To secure alliances made between 1502 and 1507 the Portuguese erected forts at the southern port cities of Kilwa, Zanzibar, and Sofala. These fortified markets and trading posts served as the foundation of Portuguese commercial power on the Swahili coast. (See "Listening to the Past: Duarte Barbosa on the Swahili City-States," page 504.)

The Portuguese presence in the south did not yield the expected commercial fortunes. Rather than accept Portuguese commercial restrictions, the residents deserted the towns, and the town economies crumbled. Large numbers of Kilwa's people, for example, immigrated to northern cities. The gold flow from inland mines to Sofala slowed to a trickle. Swahili noncooperation successfully prevented the Portuguese from gaining control of the local coastal trade.

Map 19.2 East Africa in the Sixteenth Century In early modern times, the Christian kingdom of Ethiopia, first isolated and then subjected to Muslim and European pressures, played an insignificant role in world affairs. But the East African city-states, which stretched from Sofala in the south to Mogadishu in the north, had powerfully important commercial relations with Mughal India, China, the Ottoman world, and southern Europe.

Swahili Meaning "People of the Coast," the term used for the people living along the East African coast and on nearby islands.

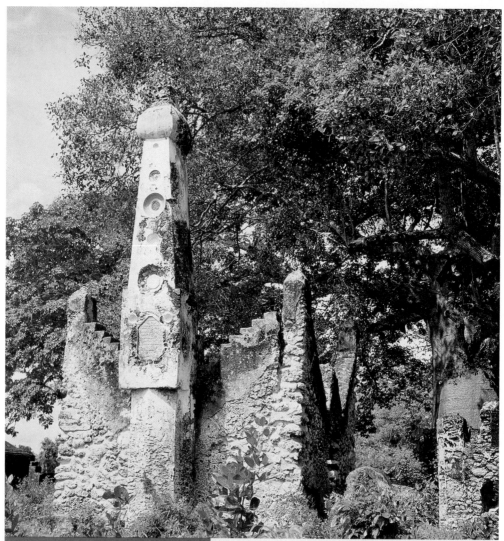

Chinese Porcelain Plates

Embedded in an eighteenth-century Kunduchi pillar tomb, these Chinese plates testify to the enormous Asian-African trade that flourished in the fourteenth to sixteenth centuries. Kunduchi, whose ruins lie north of Dar es Salaam in present-day Tanzania, was one of the Swahili city-states. (Werner Forman/Art Resource, NY)

ANALYZING THE IMAGE How many Chinese plates can you identify? What features identify this as a tomb?

CONNECTIONS Why would a Muslim African want a Chinese plate embedded in his tomb? What does this suggest about his status, occupation, and wealth?

In 1589 Portugal finally won an administrative stronghold near Mombasa. In the late seventeenth century pressures from the northern European maritime powers—the Dutch, French, and English, aided greatly by Omani Arabs—combined with local African rebellions to bring about the collapse of Portuguese influence in Africa. A Portuguese presence remained only at Mozambique in the far south and Angola on the west coast.

Quick Review
How did Muslim and Portuguese incursions destabilize East African societies and states?

What were the causes and consequences of the transatlantic slave trade?

The exchange of peoples captured in local and ethnic wars within sub-Saharan Africa, the trans-Saharan slave trade with the Mediterranean Islamic world beginning in the seventh century, and the slave traffic across the Indian Ocean all testify to the long tradition and continental dimensions of the African slave trade before European intrusion. As a consequence of European intrusion, however, the trans-Saharan slave trade became less important than the transatlantic trade, which witnessed an explosive growth during the seventeenth and eighteenth centuries. The millions of enslaved Africans forcibly exported to the Americas would have a lasting impact on African society, and it would lead ultimately to a wider use of slaves within Africa itself.

The Institution of Slavery in Africa

Islamic practices strongly influenced African slavery. African rulers justified enslavement with the Muslim argument that prisoners of war could be sold and that captured people were considered chattel, or personal possessions, to be used any way the owner saw fit. Between 650 and 1600, black as well as white Muslims transported perhaps as many as 4.82 million black slaves across the trans-Saharan trade route.[3] In the fourteenth and fifteenth centuries the rulers and elites of Mali and Benin imported thousands of white Slavic slave women, symbols of wealth and status, who had been seized in slave raids from the Balkans and Caucasus regions of the eastern Mediterranean by Turks, Mongols, and others.[4]

Meanwhile, the flow of black people to Europe, begun during the Renaissance, continued. In the seventeenth and eighteenth centuries as many as two hundred thousand Africans entered European societies. Some arrived as slaves, others as servants; the legal distinction was not always clear. Eighteenth-century London, for example, had more than ten thousand blacks, most of whom arrived as sailors on Atlantic crossings or as personal servants brought from the West Indies. In England most were free, not slaves. London's black population constituted a well-organized, self-conscious subculture, with black pubs, black churches, and black social groups assisting the black poor and unemployed. Some black people attained wealth and position, the most famous being Francis Barber, manservant of the sixteenth-century British literary giant Samuel Johnson and heir to Johnson's papers and to most of his sizable fortune.

In 1658 the Dutch East India Company (see page 426) began to allow the importation of slaves into the Cape Colony, which the company had founded on the southern tip of Africa in 1652. Over the next century and a half about 75 percent of the slaves

Below Stairs The prints and cartoons of Thomas Rowlandson (1756–1827) testify to the sizable numbers of blacks in eighteenth-century London, where they worked in naval and military as well as domestic service. Here the household cook, maid, and footman relax before the kitchen fire. Interracial marriages were not uncommon. (Courtesy of the Trustees of the British Museum)

LISTENING TO THE PAST

Duarte Barbosa on the Swahili City-States

The Portuguese writer, government agent, and traveler Duarte Barbosa made two voyages to India. Arriving first in 1500, he acted for five years as interpreter and translator in Cochin and Cananor in Kerala (in southwestern India on the Malabar Coast), returning to Lisbon in 1506. On his second trip to India in 1511, he served the Portuguese government as chief scribe in the factory of Cananor (a factory was a warehouse for the storage of goods, not a manufacturing center) and as the liaison with the local Indian rajah (prince). Barbosa returned to Portugal around 1516. In September 1519 he began his greatest adventure, setting off with Ferdinand Magellan to circumnavigate the globe. Magellan was killed in a battle with native forces in the Philippines. Barbosa then took joint command of the expedition, but was himself killed in the Philippines less than a week after Magellan, on May 1, 1521.

On the basis of his trips around the Indian Ocean in 1518, Barbosa completed his Libro de Duarte Barbosa (The Book of Duarte Barbosa), *a geographical and ethnographic survey of peoples, lands, and commerce from the Cape of Good Hope to China. It was based largely on his personal observations. First published in Italian, the book won wide acclaim in Europe, and modern scholars consider its geographical information very accurate. The excerpts below describe some of the city-states along the East African coast of Swahili.*

Sofala

❝ And the manner of their traffic was this: they came in small vessels named *zambucos* from the kingdoms of Kilwa, Mombasa, and Malindi, bringing many cotton cloths, some spotted and others white and blue, also some of silk, and many small beads, grey, red, and yellow, which things come to the said kingdoms from the great kingdom of Cambaya [in northwest India] in other greater ships. And these wares the said Moors who came from Malindi and Mombasa paid for in gold at such a price that those merchants departed well pleased; which gold they gave by weight.

The Moors of Sofala kept these wares and sold them afterwards to the Heathen of the Kingdom of Benametapa, who came thither laden with gold which they gave in exchange for the said cloths without weighing it. These Moors collect also great store of ivory which they find

hard by Sofala, and this also they sell in the Kingdom of Cambaya at five or six cruzados the quintal. They also sell some ambergris, which is brought to them from the Hucicas, and is exceeding good. These Moors are black, and some of them tawny; some of them speak Arabic, but the more part use the language of the country. They clothe themselves from the waist down with cotton and silk cloths, and other cloths they wear over their shoulders like capes, and turbans on their heads. Some of them wear small caps dyed in grain in chequers and other woollen clothes in many tints, also camlets and other silks.

Their food is millet, rice, flesh and fish. In this river as far as the sea are many sea horses, which come out on the land to graze, which horses always move in the sea like fishes; they have tusks like those of small elephants in size, and the ivory is better than that of elephants, being whiter and harder, and it never loses colour. In the country near Sofala are many wild elephants, exceeding great (which the country-folk know not how to tame) ounces, lions, deer and many other wild beasts. It is a land of plains and hills with many streams of sweet water. . . . ❞

Kilwa

❝ Going along the coast from this town of Mozambique, there is an island hard by the mainland which is called Kilwa, in which is a Moorish town with many fair houses of stone and mortar, with many windows after our fashion, very well arranged in streets, with many flat roofs. The doors are of wood, well carved, with excellent joinery. Around it are streams and orchards and fruit-gardens with many channels of sweet water. It has a Moorish king over it. From this place they trade with Sofala, whence they bring back gold, and from here they spread all over . . . the seacoast [which] is well-peopled with villages and abodes of Moors.

Before the King our Lord sent out his expedition to discover India the Moors of Sofala, Cuama, Angoya and Mozambique were all subject to the King of Kilwa, who was the most mighty king among them. And in this town was great plenty of gold, as no ships passed towards Sofala without first coming to this island. . . .

brought into the colony came from Dutch East India Company colonies in India and Southeast Asia or from Madagascar; the remaining 25 percent came from Africa. Some of those enslaved at the Cape served as domestic servants or as semiskilled artisans, but most worked as field hands and at any other menial or manual forms of labor needed by their European masters.

The slave population at the Cape was never large, although from the early 1700s to the 1820s it outnumbered the European free burgher population. When the British ended slav-

This town was taken by force from its king by the Portuguese, as, moved by arrogance, he refused to obey the King our Lord. There they took many prisoners and the king fled from the island, and His Highness ordered that a fort should be built there, and kept it under his rule and governance. Afterwards he ordered that it should be pulled down, as its maintenance was of no value nor profit to him, and it was destroyed by Antonio de Saldanha. . . . 》

Malindi

《 . . . Journeying along the coast towards India, there is a fair town on the mainland lying along a strand, which is named Malindi. It pertains to the Moors and has a Moorish king over it; the which place has many fair stone and mortar houses of many storeys, with great plenty of windows and flat roofs, after our fashion. The place is well laid out in streets. The folk are both black and white; they go naked, covering only their private parts with cotton and silk cloths. Others of them wear cloths folded like cloaks and waist-bands, and turbans of many rich stuffs on their heads.

They are great barterers, and deal in cloth, gold, ivory, and divers other wares with the Moors and Heathen of the great kingdom of Cambaya; and to their haven come every year many ships with cargoes of merchandize, from which they get great store of gold, ivory and wax. In this traffic the Cambay merchants make great profits, and thus, on one side and the other, they earn much money. There is great plenty of food in this city (rice, millet, and some wheat which they bring from Cambaya), and divers sorts of fruit, inasmuch as there is here abundance of fruit-gardens and orchards. Here too are plenty of round-tailed sheep, cows and other cattle and great store of oranges, also of hens.

The walls of the sultan's palace sit silently amidst the ruins at Gedi, a historic Swahili site a few miles south of Malindi on the Kenyan coast. Founded in the late thirteenth or early fourteenth century, it survived as a thriving trading community until the early seventeenth century. Although it was not a major Swahili town, excavations have uncovered iron lamps from India, scissors from Spain, a Chinese Ming vase, Persian stoneware, and Venetian beads. Some homes had bathrooms with running water and flush toilets, and the streets had drainage gutters. The dated tomb in the cemetery has 1399 incised in its plaster wall. (Ariadne Van Zandbergen/Lonely Planet Images)

The king and people of this place ever were and are friends of the King of Portugal, and the Portuguese always find in them great comfort and friendship and perfect peace, "and there the ships, when they chance to pass that way, obtain supplies in plenty." 》

Source: Dames, Mansel Longworth, trans., *The Book of Duarte Barbosa, Volume 1* (London: Bedford Press, 1918).

QUESTIONS FOR ANALYSIS

1. What seems to have impressed Barbosa? What was his attitude toward the various peoples he saw? What Portuguese or Western prejudices do you discern?
2. What was the Portuguese relationship to the Swahili city-states at the time Barbosa saw them?
3. What was the source of Sofala's gold? Of Sofala's and Malindi's ivory? What did the Indian kingdom of Cambaya use ivory for?

ery in the British Empire in 1834, there were around thirty-six thousand slaves in the Cape Colony. In comparison, over three hundred thousand enslaved Africans labored on the Caribbean island of Jamaica, also a British slaveholding colony at the time.

Although in the seventeenth and eighteenth centuries Holland enjoyed a Europe-wide reputation for religious toleration and intellectual freedom (see page 455), in the Cape Colony the Dutch used a strict racial hierarchy and heavy-handed paternalism to maintain control over enslaved native and foreign-born peoples. The offspring of a freeman and an enslaved woman remained enslaved. Because enslaved males greatly outnumbered enslaved females in the Cape Colony, marriage and family life were almost nonexistent. And, because there were few occupations requiring special skills, those enslaved in the colony lacked opportunities to earn manumission.

The savanna and Horn regions of East Africa experienced a great expansion of the slave trade in the late eighteenth century and the first half of the nineteenth century. Exports of slaves from these areas and from the eastern coast of Africa amounted to perhaps thirty thousand a year. Why this demand? Merchants and planters wanted slaves to work the sugar plantations on the Mascarene

Cape Colony, ca. 1750

Islands, located east of Madagascar, the clove plantations on Zanzibar and Pemba, and the food plantations along the Kenyan coast. The eastern coast also exported enslaved people to the Americas, particularly to Brazil. In the late eighteenth and early nineteenth centuries, precisely when the slave trade to North America and the Caribbean declined, the Arabian and Asian markets expanded. Only with colonial conquest of Africa by Great Britain, Germany, and Italy after 1870 did suppression of the trade begin. Enslavement, of course, persists even today. (See "Global Trade: Slaves," page 508.)

The Transatlantic Slave Trade

Although the trade in African people was a worldwide phenomenon, the transatlantic slave trade involved the largest number of enslaved Africans. This forced migration of millions of human beings, extending from the early sixteenth to the late nineteenth centuries, represents one of the most inhumane, unjust, and shameful tragedies in human history. It also immediately provokes a troubling question: Why Africa? Why, in the seventeenth and eighteenth centuries, did enslavement in the Americas become exclusively African?

European settlers first enslaved indigenous peoples, the Amerindians, to mine the silver and gold discovered in the New World (see page 426). When they proved ill suited to the harsh rigors of mining, the Spaniards brought in Africans. Although the Dutch had transported Indonesian peoples to work as slaves in the Cape Colony in South Africa, the cost of transporting Chinese or Pacific island peoples to the Americas was far too great.

One scholar has argued that a pan-European insider-outsider ideology prevailed across Europe. This cultural attitude permitted the enslavement of outsiders but made the enslavement of white Europeans taboo. According to this theory, a similar pan-African ideology did not exist, as Africans had no problem with selling Africans to Europeans.[5] Several facts argue against the validity of this theory. English landlords exploited their Irish peasants with merciless severity; French aristocrats often looked on their peasantry with cold contempt; and Russian boyars treated their serfs with casual indifference and harsh brutality. These and other possible examples contradict the existence of a pan-European ideology or culture that opposed the enslavement of white Europeans. Moreover, the flow of white enslaved Slavic peoples from the Balkans into the eastern Mediterranean continued unabated during the same period.

Another theory holds that in the Muslim and Arab worlds by the tenth century, an association had developed between blackness and menial slavery. The Arab word *abd*, or "black," had become synonymous with *slave*. Although the great majority of enslaved persons in the Islamic world were white, a racial element existed in Muslim perceptions: not all slaves were black, but blacks were identified with slavery. In Europe, after the arrival of tens of thousands of sub-Saharan Africans in the Iberian Peninsula during the fifteenth century, Christian Europeans also began to make a strong association between slavery and black

Africans. Therefore, Africans seemed the "logical" solution to the labor shortage in the Americas.[6]

Another important question relating to the African slave trade is this: Why were African peoples enslaved in a period when serfdom was declining in western Europe, and when land was so widely available and much of the African continent had a labor shortage? The answer seems to lie in a technical problem related to African agriculture. Partly because of the tsetse fly, which causes sleeping sickness and other diseases, and partly because of easily leached lateritic soils (containing high concentrations of oxides), farmers had great difficulty using draft animals. Tropical soils responded poorly to plowing, and most work had to be done with the hoe. Productivity, therefore, was low. In precolonial Africa, the individual's agricultural productivity was low, so his or her economic value to society was less than the economic value of a European peasant in Europe. Enslaved persons in the Americas were more productive than free producers in Africa. And European slave dealers were very willing to pay a price higher than the value of an African's productivity in Africa.

The incidence of disease in the Americas also helps explain African enslavement. Smallpox took a terrible toll on Native Americans, and between 30 and 50 percent of Europeans exposed to malaria succumbed to that sickness. Africans had developed some immunity to both diseases, and in the Americas they experienced the lowest mortality rate of any people, making them, ironically, the most suitable workers for the environment.

In 1500 a Portuguese fleet en route to India around Africa sailed too far west into the Atlantic and made landfall on the coast of modern Brazil. Its commander, Pedro Cabral, immediately claimed the land for King Manuel I, the Portuguese monarch. Colonization began in the early 1530s, and in 1551 the Portuguese founded a sugar colony at Bahia. Between 1551 and 1575, before the North American slave traffic began, the Portuguese delivered more African slaves to Brazil than would ever reach British North America (see Figure 19.1). Portugal essentially monopolized the slave trade until 1600 and continued to play a large role in the seventeenth century, though the trade was increasingly taken over by the Dutch, French, and English. From 1690 until the British House of Commons abolished the slave trade in 1807, England was the leading carrier of African slaves

Population density and supply conditions along the West African coast and the sailing time to New World markets determined the sources of slaves. As the demand for slaves rose, slavers moved down the West African coast from Senegambia to the more densely populated hinterlands of the Bight of Benin and the Bight of Biafra. The abundant supply of Africans to enslave in Angola, the region south of the Congo River, and the quick passage from Angola to Brazil and the Caribbean established that region as the major coast for Portuguese slavers.

The great majority of enslaved Africans were intended for the sugar and coffee plantations extending from the Caribbean islands to Brazil. Angola produced 26 percent of all African slaves and 70 percent of all

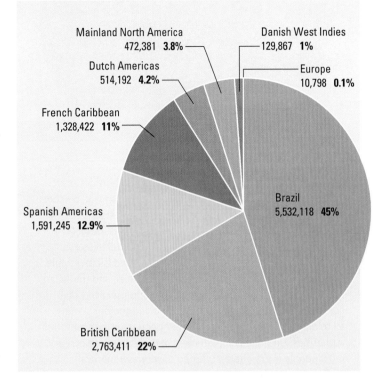

Figure 19.1 **Estimated Slave Imports by Destination, 1501–1866**
Brazil was the single largest importer of African slaves from 1501 to 1866. But when taken cumulatively, the British, French, Dutch, and Danish colonies of the Caribbean rivaled the much larger colony of Brazil for numbers of slaves imported from Africa. **Source:** Data from Emory University. "Assessing the Slave Trade: Estimates," in *Voyages: The Trans-Atlantic Slave Trade Database*. 2009. http://www.slavevoyages.org.

The Slave Coast of West Africa

GLOBAL TRADE
Slaves

Slaves are people who are bound to servitude and often traded as property or as a commodity. Most societies, with the remarkable exception of the Aborigines in Australia, have treated people as goods and have engaged in the slave trade. Those who have been enslaved include captives in war, persons convicted of crimes, persons sold for debt, and persons bought and sold for sex. The ancient Greek philosophers, notably Aristotle, justified slavery as "natural." The Middle Eastern monotheistic faiths — Judaism, Christianity, and Islam — while professing the sacred dignity of each individual, and the Asian religious and sociopolitical ideologies of Buddhism and Confucianism, while stressing an ordered and harmonious society, all tolerated slavery and urged slaves' obedience to established authorities. Until the Enlightenment of the eighteenth century, most people everywhere accepted slavery as a "natural phenomenon."

Between 1500 and 1900 the transatlantic African slave trade accounted for the largest number of people bought and sold. As such, and because of ample documentation, it has tended to identify the institution of slavery with African blacks. From a global perspective, however, the trade was far broader.

Slaves came from all over the world and included people of all races. The steady flow of white women and children from the Crimea, the Caucasus, and the Balkans in the fourteenth to eighteenth centuries for domestic, military, or sexual services in Ottoman lands, Italy, and sub-Saharan Africa; the use of convicts as galley slaves in the Venetian, French, Spanish, and Turkish navies; the enslavement of peoples defeated in war by Aztec, Inca, Sioux, Navajo, and other indigenous peoples of the Americas; the various forms of debt slavery in China and in Russia (where the legal distinction between serf and slave before 1861 was very hazy); the traffic of Indonesian and Pacific island peoples for slave labor in Dutch South Africa; and the trans-Saharan stream of Africans to Mediterranean ports that continued at medieval rates into the late nineteenth century — all were different forms of a worldwide practice. Although these forms sometimes had little in common with one another, they all involved the buying and selling of human beings who could not move about freely or enjoy the fruits of their labor.

The price of slaves varied widely over time and from market to market, according to age, sex, physical appearance, buyers' perceptions of the social characteristics of each slave's ethnic background, and changes in supply and demand. The Mediterranean and Indian Ocean markets preferred women for domestic service; the Atlantic markets wanted strong young men for mine and plantation work, for example. We have little solid information on prices for slaves in the Balkans, Caucasus, or Indian Ocean region. Even in the Atlantic trade, it is difficult to determine, over several centuries, the value of currencies, the cost and insurance on transported slaves, and the cost of goods exchanged for slaves. Yet the gold-encrusted cathedrals of Spain and the elegant plantation houses of the southern United States stand as testimony to the vast fortunes made in the slave trade.

How is the human toll of slavery measured? Transformations within societies occurred not only because of local developments but also because of interactions among regions. For example, the virulent racism that in so many ways defines the American experience resulted partly from medieval European habits of dehumanizing the enemy (English versus Irish, German versus Slav, Christian versus Jew and Muslim) and partly from the movement of peoples and ideas all over the globe. American gold prospectors in the 1850s carried the bigotry they had heaped on blacks in the Americas to Australia, where it conditioned attitudes toward Asians and other peoples of color. Racism, like the slave trade, is a global phenomenon.

Middle Passage African slaves' voyage across the Atlantic to the Americas, a long and treacherous journey during which slaves endured appalling and often deadly conditions.

Portuguese slaves. Trading networks extending deep into the interior culminated at two major ports on the Angolan coast, Luanda and Benguela. The Portuguese acquired a few slaves through warfare but secured the vast majority through trade with African dealers. Whites did not participate in the inland markets, which were run solely by Africans.

Almost all Portuguese shipments went to satisfy the virtually insatiable Brazilian demand for slaves. The so-called Middle Passage was the horrific journey experienced by Africans from freedom to enslavement in the Americas. Here is an excerpt from a Portuguese doctor's 1793 report on conditions in Luanda before the voyage across the Atlantic had begun. Be sure to note in this and subsequent quotations how the enslaved peoples are clearly considered, and treated, as chattel:

> The dwelling place of the slave is simply the dirt floor of the compound, and he remains there exposed to harsh conditions and bad weather, and at night there are only a lean-to and some sheds . . . which they are herded into like cattle. . . .

Map 19.3 The International Slave Trade

For all the cries for human rights today, the slave trade continues. The ancient Indian Ocean traffic in Indian girls and boys for "service" in the Persian Gulf oil kingdoms persists, as does the sale of African children for work in Asia. In 2011 an estimated 12 to 27 million people globally are held in one form of slavery or another. The U.S. State Department estimates that 15,000 to 18,000 enslaved foreign nationals are brought to the United States each year and, conservatively, perhaps as many as 50,000 people, mostly women and children, are in slavery in America at any given time. They have been bought, sold, tricked, and held in captivity, and their labor, often as sex slaves, has been exploited for the financial benefit of masters in a global enterprise.

> And when they reach a port . . . , they are branded on the right breast. . . . This mark is made with a hot silver instrument in the act of paying the king's duties, and this brand mark is called a carimbo. . . .
> In this miserable and deprived condition the terrified slaves remain for weeks and months, and the great number of them who die is unspeakable.[7]

Conditions during the Middle Passage were even worse. Olaudah Equiano (see "Individuals in Society: Olaudah Equiano," page 510) describes the experience of his voyage as a captured slave from Benin to Barbados in the Caribbean:

> At last, when the ship we were in had got in all her cargo [of slaves], they made ready with many fearful noises, and we were all put under deck. . . . The stench of the hold while we were on the coast was so intolerably loathsome that it was dangerous to remain there for any time, and some of us had been permitted to stay on the deck for the fresh air; but now that

INDIVIDUALS IN SOCIETY

Olaudah Equiano

THE TRANSATLANTIC SLAVE TRADE WAS A MASS movement involving millions of human beings. It was also the sum of individual lives spent partly or entirely in slavery. Most of those lives remain hidden to us. Olaudah Equiano (1745–1797) represents a rare ray of light into the slaves' obscurity.

In his autobiography, *The Interesting Narrative of the Life of Olaudah Equiano* (1789), Equiano says that he was born in Benin (modern Nigeria) of Ibo ethnicity.* His father, one of the village elders (or chieftains), presided over a large household that included "many slaves," prisoners captured in local wars. One day, when all the adults were in the fields, two strange men and a woman broke into the family compound, kidnapped the eleven-year-old Olaudah and his sister, tied them up, and dragged them into the woods. Brother and sister were separated, and Olaudah was sold several times to various dealers before reaching the coast. As it took six months to walk there, his home must have been far inland. The sea, the slave ship, and the strange appearance of the white crew terrified the boy (see page 509). Equiano's master took him to Jamaica, to Virginia, and then to England, where he placed him in the custody of a kind family. They gave him the rudiments of an education, and he was baptized a Christian.

Equiano soon went to sea as a captain's boy (servant), serving in the Royal Navy during the Seven Years' War. On shore at Portsmouth, England, after one battle, Equiano was urged by his master to read, study, and learn basic mathematics. This education served him well, for after a voyage to the West Indies, his master sold him to a Philadelphia Quaker, Robert King, who was a rum and sugar merchant. Equiano worked as a clerk in King's warehouse, as a longshoreman loading and unloading cargo ships, and at sea where he developed good navigational skills; King paid him for his work. Equiano became an entrepreneur himself, buying and selling small goods in the islands and mainland ports. Determined to buy his freedom, Equiano had amassed enough money by 1766, and King signed the deed of manumission. Equiano was twenty-one years old; he had been a slave for ten years.

Equiano returned to London and used his remaining money to hire tutors to teach him hairdressing, mathematics, and how to play the French horn. When money was scarce, he found work as a merchant seaman, traveling to Portugal, Nice, Genoa, Naples, and Turkey. He even participated in an Arctic expedition.

Equiano's *Narrative* reveals a complex and sophisticated man. He had a strong constitution and an equally strong char-

acter. His Christian faith undoubtedly sustained him. The very first thought that came to his mind the day he was freed was a passage from Psalm 126: "I glorified God in my heart, in whom I trusted."

Equiano loathed the brutal slavery he saw in the West Indies and the vicious racism he experienced in the North American colonies. He respected the fairness of Robert King, admired British navigational and industrial technologies, and had many close white friends. He once described himself as "almost an Englishman." He was also involved in the black communities in the West Indies and in London. Equiano's *Narrative* is a well-documented argument for the abolition of slavery and a literary classic that went through nine editions before his death.

Olaudah Equiano's *Narrative*, with its horrific descriptions of slavery, proved influential, and after its publication Equiano became active in the abolition movement. He spoke to large crowds in the industrial cities of Manchester and Birmingham in England, arguing that it was in the business interests of manufacturers to support abolition, as Africa was a huge, virtually untapped market for English cloth. Though he died in 1797, ten years before its passage, Equiano significantly advanced the abolitionist cause that led to the Slave Trade Act of 1807.

Source: *Equiano's Travels: The Interesting Narrative of the Life of Olaudah Equiano*, ed. Paul Edwards (Portsmouth, N.H.: Heinemann, 1996).

*Recent scholarship has re-examined Equiano's life and raised some questions about his African origins and his experience of the Middle Passage. To explore the debate over Equiano's authorship of the African and Middle Passage portions of his autobiography, see Vincent Carretta, *Equiano, the African: Biography of a Self-Made Man* (New York: Penguin, 2007).

QUESTIONS FOR ANALYSIS

1. How typical was Olaudah Equiano's life as a slave? How atypical?
2. Describe Equiano's culture and his sense of himself.

Olaudah Equiano, 1789, dressed as an elegant Englishman, his Bible open to the book of Acts. (National Portrait Gallery, Smithsonian Institution/Art Resource, NY)

Peddlers in Rio de Janeiro A British army officer sketched this early-nineteenth-century scene of everyday life in Rio de Janeiro, Brazil. The ability to balance large burdens on the head meant that the person's hands were free for other use. Note the player (on the left) of a musical instrument originating in the Congo. On the right a woman gives alms to the man with the holy image in return for being allowed to kiss the image as an act of devotion. We do not know whether the peddlers were free and self-employed or were selling for their owners. (From "Views and Costumes of the City and Neighborhood of Rio de Janeiro, Brazil," in *Drawings Taken by Lieutenant Henry Chamberlain, During the Years 1819 and 1820* [London: Columbian Press, 1822])

the whole ship's cargo were confined together it became absolutely pestilential. The closeness of the place and the heat of the climate, added to the number in the ship, which was so crowded that each had scarcely room to turn himself, almost suffocated us. This produced copious perspirations, so that the air soon became unfit for respiration from a variety of loathsome smells, and brought on a sickness among the slaves, of which many died, thus falling victims to the improvident avarice, as I may call it, of their purchasers. This wretched situation was again aggravated by the galling of the chains, now become insupportable, and the filth of the necessary tubs [of human waste], into which the children often fell and were almost suffocated. The shrieks of the women and the groans of the dying rendered the whole a scene of horror almost inconceivable.[8]

Although the demand was great, Portuguese merchants in Angola and Brazil sought to maintain only a steady trickle of slaves from the African interior to Luanda and across the ocean to Bahia and Rio de Janeiro: a flood of slaves would have depressed the American market. Rio, the port capital through which most enslaved Africans passed, commanded the Brazilian trade. Between 1795 and 1808, approximately 10,000 Angolans per year stood in the Rio slave market. In 1810 the figure rose to 18,000; in 1828 it reached 32,000.[9]

The English ports of London, Bristol, and particularly Liverpool dominated the British slave trade. In the eighteenth century Liverpool was the world's greatest slave-trading port. In all three cities, small and cohesive merchant classes exercised great public influence. The cities also had huge stores of industrial products for export, growing shipping industries, and large amounts of ready cash for investment abroad.

Slaving ships from Bristol plied back and forth along the Gold Coast, the Bight of Benin, Bonny, and Calabar looking for African traders who were willing to supply them with slaves. Liverpool's ships drew enslaved people from Gambia, the Windward Coast, and the Gold Coast. British ships carried textiles, gunpowder and flint, beer and spirits, British and Irish linens, and woolen cloth to Africa. A collection of goods was grouped together into what was called the **sorting**. An English sorting might include bolts of cloth, firearms, alcohol, tobacco, and hardware; this batch of goods would be traded for an enslaved individual or a quantity of gold, ivory, or dyewood.[10]

European traders had two systems for exchange. First, especially on the Gold Coast, they established factory-forts (for more on factory-forts, see page 537). These fortified trading posts were expensive to maintain but proved useful for fending off European rivals. Second, they used **shore trading**, in which European ships sent boats ashore or invited African dealers to bring traders and enslaved Africans out to the ships.

The shore method of buying slaves allowed the ship to move easily from market to market. The final prices of those enslaved depended on their ethnic origin, their availability when the shipper arrived, and their physical health when offered for sale in the West Indies or the North or South American colonies.

Supplying slaves for the foreign market was controlled by a small, wealthy African merchant class, or it was a state monopoly. By contemporary standards, slave raiding was a costly operation: gathering a band of raiders and the capital for equipment, guides, tolls, and supplies involved considerable expense. Only black African entrepreneurs with sizable capital and labor could afford to finance and direct raiding drives. They exported enslaved men and women because the profits on exports were greater than the profits to be made from using labor in the domestic economy.

The transatlantic slave trade that the British, as well as the Dutch, Portuguese, French, Americans, and others, participated in was part of a much larger trading network that is known in history as the "triangle trade." European merchants sailed to Africa on the first leg of the voyage to trade European manufactured goods for enslaved Africans. When they had filled their ships' holds with enslaved peoples, they headed across the Atlantic on the second leg of the voyage, the Middle Passage. When they reached the Americas, the merchants unloaded and sold their human cargoes and used the profits to purchase raw materials — cotton, sugar, indigo — that they then transported back to Europe, completing the third leg of the commercial triangle.

Enslaved African people had an enormous impact on the economics of the Portuguese and Spanish colonies of South America and in the Dutch, French, and British colonies of the Caribbean and North America. But the importance of the slave trade extended beyond the Atlantic world. The expansion of capitalism, as well as the industrialization of Western societies, Egypt, and the nations of West, Central, and South Africa — all related in one way or another to the traffic in African people.

Impact on African Societies

What economic impact did European trade have on African societies? Africans possessed technology well suited to their environment. Over the centuries, they had cultivated a wide variety of plant foods; developed plant and animal husbandry techniques; and mined, smelted, and otherwise worked a great variety of metals. Apart from firearms, American tobacco and rum, and the cheap brandy brought by the Portuguese, European goods presented no novelty to Africans. They found foreign products desirable because of their low prices. Traders of handwoven Indian cotton textiles, Venetian imitations of African beads, and iron bars from European smelters could undersell African manufacturers. Africans exchanged slaves, ivory, gold, pepper, and animal skins for those goods.

sorting A collection or batch of British goods that would be traded for a slave or for a quantity of gold, ivory, or dyewood.

shore trading A process for trading goods in which European ships sent boats ashore or invited African dealers to bring traders and slaves out to the ships.

The African merchants who controlled the production of exports gained the most from foreign trade. Dahomey's king, for example, had a gross income in 1750 of £250,000 (almost U.S. $33 million today) from the overseas export of his fellow Africans. A portion of his profit was spent on goods that improved his people's living standard. Slave-trading entrepôts, which provided opportunities for traders and for farmers who supplied foodstuffs to towns, caravans, and slave ships, prospered. But such economic returns did not spread very far.[11] International trade did not lead to Africa's economic development. Africa experienced neither technological growth nor the gradual spread of economic benefits in early modern times.

As in the Islamic world, women in sub-Saharan Africa also engaged in the slave trade. In Guinea these women slave merchants and traders were known as *nhara*, a corruption of the Portuguese term *senhora*, a title used for a married woman. They acquired considerable riches, often by marrying the Portuguese merchants and serving as go-betweens for these outsiders who were not familiar with the customs and languages of the African coast.

The intermarriage of French traders and Wolof women in Senegambia created a métis, or mulatto, class. In the emerging urban centers at Saint-Louis, members of this small class adopted the French language, the Roman Catholic faith, and a French manner of life, and they exercised considerable political and economic power. However, European cultural influences did not penetrate West African society beyond the seacoast.

The political consequences of the slave trade varied from place to place. The trade enhanced the power and wealth of some kings and warlords in the short run but promoted conditions of instability and collapse over the long run. In the Kongo kingdom, which was located in parts of modern Angola, the Republic of the Congo, and the Democratic Republic of the Congo, the perpetual Portuguese search for Africans to enslave undermined the monarchy, destroyed political unity, and led to constant disorder and warfare; power passed to the village chiefs. Likewise in Angola, which became a Portuguese proprietary colony (a territory granted to one or more individuals by the Crown for them to govern at their will), the slave trade decimated and scattered the population and destroyed the local economy. By contrast, the military kingdom of Dahomey, which entered into the slave trade in the eighteenth century and made it a royal monopoly, prospered enormously. Dahomey's economic strength rested on the slave trade. The royal army raided deep into the interior, and in the late eighteenth century Dahomey became one of the major West African sources of slaves. When slaving expeditions failed to yield sizable catches and when European demand declined, the resulting depression in the Dahomean economy caused serious political unrest. Iboland, inland from the Niger Delta, from whose great port cities of Bonny and Brass the British drained tens of thousands of enslaved Africans, experienced minimal political effects. A high birthrate kept pace with the incursions of the slave trade, and Ibo societies remained demographically and economically strong.

What demographic impact did the slave trade have on Africa? Between approximately 1501 and 1866, more than 12 million Africans were forcibly exported to the Americas, 6 million were traded to Asia, and 8 million were retained as slaves within Africa. Figure 19.2 shows the estimated number of slaves shipped to the Americas in the transatlantic slave trade. Export figures do not include the approximately 10 to 15 percent who died during procurement or in transit.

The early modern slave trade involved a worldwide web of relationships among markets in the Middle East, Africa, Asia, Europe, and the Americas. But Africa was the crucible of the trade. There is no small irony in the fact that Africa, which of all the continents was most desperately in need of population because of its near total dependence on labor-intensive agriculture and pastoralism, lost so many millions to the trade. Although the British Parliament abolished the slave trade in 1807 and traffic in Africans to Brazil and Cuba gradually declined, within Africa the trade continued at the levels of the peak years of the transatlantic trade, 1780–1820. In the later nineteenth century, developing

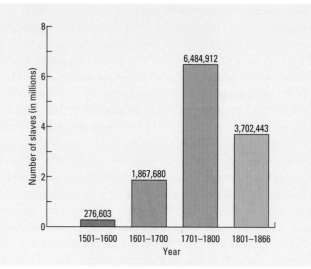

Figure 19.2 **The Transatlantic Slave Trade, 1501–1866**
The volume of slaves involved in the transatlantic slave trade peaked during the eighteenth century. These numbers show the slaves who embarked from Africa, and do not reflect the 10 to 15 percent of enslaved Africans who died in transit. **Source:** Data from Emory University. "Assessing the Slave Trade: Estimates," in *Voyages: The Trans-Atlantic Slave Trade Database.* 2009. http://www.slavevoyages.org.

African industries, using slave labor, produced a variety of products for domestic consumption and export. Again, there is irony in the fact that in the eighteenth century European demand for slaves expanded the trade (and wars) within Africa, yet in the nineteenth century European imperialists defended territorial aggrandizement by arguing that they were "civilizing" Africans by abolishing slavery. But after 1880 European businessmen (and African governments) did not push abolition; they wanted cheap labor.

Markets in the Americas generally wanted young male slaves. Asian and African markets preferred young females. Women were sought for their reproductive value, as sex objects, and because their economic productivity was not threatened by the possibility of physical rebellion, as might be the case with young men. Consequently, two-thirds of those exported to the Americas were male, one-third female. As a result, the population on the western coast of Africa became predominantly female; the population in the East African savanna and Horn regions was predominantly male. The slave trade therefore had significant consequences for the institutions of marriage, the local trade in enslaved people (as these local populations became skewed with too many males or too many females), and the sexual division of labor. Although Africa's overall population may have shown modest growth from roughly 1650 to 1900, that growth was offset by declines in the Horn and on the eastern and western coasts. While Europe and Asia experienced considerable demographic and economic expansion in the eighteenth century, Africa suffered a decline.[12]

Quick Review
Why did the transatlantic slave trade intensify in the early modern period and what were the consequences for Africa?

Connections

DURING THE PERIOD from 1400 to 1800 many parts of Africa experienced a profound transition with the arrival of Europeans all along Africa's coasts. Ancient trade routes, such as those across the Sahara Desert or up and down the East African coast, were disrupted. In West Africa trade routes that had been purely internal now connected with global trade networks at European coastal trading posts. Along Africa's east coast, the Portuguese attacked Swahili city-states in their effort to take control of the Indian Ocean trade nexus.

The most momentous consequence of the European presence along Africa's coast, however, was the introduction of the transatlantic slave trade. For more than three centuries Europeans, with the aid of African slave traders, enslaved millions of Africa's healthiest and strongest men and women. Although many parts of Africa were untouched by the transatlantic slave trade, at least directly, areas where Africans were enslaved experienced serious declines in agricultural production, little progress in technological development, and significant increases in violence.

As we will see in Chapters 20 and 21, early European commercial contacts with the empires of the Middle East and of South and East Asia were similar in many ways to those with Africa. Initially, the Portuguese, and then the English, Dutch, and French, did little more than establish trading posts at port cities and had to depend on the local people to bring them trade goods from the interior. Tropical diseases, particularly in India and in Southeast Asia, took heavy death tolls on the Europeans as they did in tropical Africa. What is more, while it was possible for the Portuguese to attack and conquer the individual Swahili city-states, Middle Eastern and Asian empires — such as the Ottomans in Turkey, the Safavids in Persia, the Mughals in India, and the Ming and Qing Dynasties in China — were, like the West African kingdoms, economically and militarily powerful enough to dictate terms of trade with the Europeans.

Resistance to enslavement took many forms on both sides of the Atlantic. In Haiti, as discussed in Chapter 22, resistance led to revolution and independence, marking the first successful uprising of non-Europeans against a colonial power. At the end of the nineteenth century, as described in Chapter 25, Europeans used the ongoing Arab-Swahili slave raids from Africa's eastern coast far into the interior as an excuse to invade and eventually colonize much of central and eastern Africa. The racial discrimination that accompanied colonial rule in Africa would set the stage for a struggle for equality that would lead to eventual independence after World War II.

- **For a list of suggested readings for this chapter, visit** *bedfordstmartins.com/mckayworldunderstanding*.

- **For primary sources from this period, see** *Sources of World Societies*, Second Edition.

- **For Web sites, images, and documents related to topics in this chapter, see Make History at** *bedfordstmartins.com/ mckayworldunderstanding*.

Chapter 19 Study Guide

To do these exercises online, go to bedfordstmartins.com/mckayworldundunderstanding.

 Step **1**

GETTING STARTED
Below are basic terms about this period in global history. Can you identify each term below and explain why it matters?

TERMS	WHO (OR WHAT) AND WHEN	WHY IT MATTERS
chattel, p. 495		
age-grade systems, p. 495		
oba, p. 495		
Taghaza, p. 496		
Tuareg, p. 499		
cowrie shells, p. 499		
Coptic Christianity, p. 500		
Swahili, p. 501		
Middle Passage, p. 508		
sorting, p. 512		
shore trading, p. 512		

Step **2**

MOVING BEYOND THE BASICS
The exercise below requires a more advanced understanding of the chapter material. Compare and contrast early modern West and East Africa by filling in the chart below with descriptions of key aspects of each region. When you are finished, consider the following questions: What were the most important differences between West African and East African states? What role did governments in each region play in regulating commerce? What role did slavery and the slave trade play in each region? How did outsiders shape the development of each region?

	POLITICAL ORGANIZATION	ECONOMY AND COMMERCE	RELATIONSHIP TO EUROPE AND THE MUSLIM WORLD	SLAVERY AND THE SLAVE TRADE
West Africa				
East Africa				

PUTTING IT ALL TOGETHER

Now that you've reviewed key elements of the chapter, take a step back and try to see the big picture. Remember to use specific examples from the chapter in your answers.

WEST AFRICA

- What was the relationship between stateless societies and the dominant states of West Africa?

- How did the slave trade shape marriage patterns and family structure in West Africa?

EAST AFRICA

- What was the legacy for Ethiopia of early modern conflicts between Muslims, Coptic Christians, and Roman Catholics?

- Why was the arrival of the Portuguese an economic disaster for East Africa?

THE AFRICAN SLAVE TRADE

- What economic forces, both inside Africa and in the larger Atlantic world, contributed to the growth of the transatlantic slave trade?

- How and why did enslavement in the Americas become exclusively African?

LOOKING BACK, LOOKING AHEAD

- How did the transatlantic slave trade build on earlier African labor practices and commercial connections? How were older patterns of trade and exchange disrupted by the demand for African slaves in the Americas?

- What connections can you make between the colonization and exploitation of Africa by industrialized nations in the nineteenth and twentieth centuries and the transatlantic slave trade?

In Your Own Words Imagine that you must explain Chapter 19 to someone who hasn't read it. What would be the most important points to include and why?

20

The Islamic World Powers

1300–1800

After the decline of the Mongol Empire in the mid-fourteenth century, powerful new Islamic states emerged in south and west Eurasia. By the sixteenth century the Ottoman Empire, centered in Anatolia; the Safavid (sah-FAH-weed) Empire in Persia; and the Mughal (MOO-guhl) Empire in India controlled vast territories from West Africa to Central Asia, from the Balkans to the Bay of Bengal.

Lasting more than six centuries (1299–1922), the Ottoman Empire was one of the largest, best-organized, and most enduring political entities in world history. In Persia (now Iran) the Safavid Dynasty created a Shi'a state and presided over a brilliant culture. In India the Mughal leader Babur and his successors gained control of much of the Indian subcontinent. Mughal rule inaugurated a period of radical administrative reorganization in India and the flowering of intellectual and architectural creativity. Although these three states were often at war with each other, they shared important characteristics and challenges. For instance, their ruling houses all emerged from Turkish tribal organizations, and they all had to adapt their armies to the introduction of firearms. Over time, they became strongly linked culturally, as merchants, poets, philosophers, artists, and military advisers moved relatively easily across their political boundaries. Before the end of this period, Europeans were also active in trade in these empires, especially in India.

Persian Princess
The ruling houses of the Islamic empires were great patrons of art and architecture. This depiction of a princess in a garden is from an early-seventeenth-century palace built by Shah Abbas of the Safavid Dynasty in Persia.
(Giraudon/The Bridgeman Art Library)

Chapter Preview

▶ How were the three Islamic empires established?

▶ What characterized the cultural flowering of the Islamic empires?

▶ How were non-Muslims treated in the Islamic empires?

▶ How did shifts in global trading patterns affect the Islamic empires?

▶ What factors led to the decline of central power in the Islamic empires?

How were the three Islamic empires established?

Before the Mongols arrived in Central Asia and Persia, another nomadic people from the region of modern Mongolia, the Turks, had moved west, gained control over key territories from Anatolia to Delhi in north India, and contributed to the decline of the Abbasid caliphate in the thirteenth century. The Turks had been quick to join the Mongols and were important participants in the armies and administrations of the Mongol states in Persia and Central Asia. In these regions, Turks far outnumbered ethnic Mongols.

As Mongol strength in Persia and Central Asia deteriorated in the late thirteenth to midfourteenth centuries, the Turks resumed their expansion. In the late fourteenth century the Turkish leader Timur (1336–1405), also called Tamerlane, built a Central Asian empire from his base in Samarkand that reached into India and through Persia to the Black Sea. After his death his sons and grandson fought each other for succession. By 1450 his empire was in rapid decline, and power devolved to the local level. Meanwhile, Sufi orders (groups of Islamic mystics) thrived, and Islam became the most important force integrating the region. It was from the many small Turkish chiefs that the founders of the three main empires emerged.

The Ottoman Turkish Empire's Expansion

Ottomans Ruling house of the Turkish empire that lasted from 1299 to 1922.

Anatolia The region of modern Turkey.

The Ottomans took their name from Osman (r. 1299–1326), the chief of a band of seminomadic Turks that had migrated into western Anatolia while the Mongols still held Persia. The Ottomans gradually expanded at the expense of other small Turkish states and the Byzantine Empire (Map 20.1). Although temporarily slowed by defeat at the hands of Timur in 1402, the Ottomans quickly reasserted themselves after Timur's death in 1405.

Osman's campaigns were intended to subdue, not to destroy. The Ottomans built their empire by absorbing the Muslims of Anatolia and by becoming the protector of the Orthodox Church and of the millions of Greek Christians in Anatolia and the Balkans. In 1326 they took Bursa in western Anatolia, and in 1352 they gained a foothold in Europe by seizing Gallipoli. In 1389 at Kosovo in the Balkans, the Ottomans defeated a combined force of Serbs and Bosnians. And in 1396 on the Danube River in modern Bulgaria, they crushed King Sigismund of Hungary. After the victories in the Balkans, the Ottomans added to their military strength by obtaining slave troops. These troops were outfitted with guns and artillery, and they were trained to use them effectively.

sultan An Arabic word originally used by the Seljuk Turks to mean authority or dominion; it was used by the Ottomans to connote political and military supremacy.

In 1453, during the reign of Sultan Mehmet II (r. 1451–1481), the Ottomans conquered Constantinople, capital of the Byzantine Empire. The Byzantine emperor, Constantine IX Palaeologus (r. 1449–1453), with only about ten thousand men, relied on Constantinople's circular walls and stone fortifications for defense. Although Mehmet II had more than a hundred thousand men and a large fleet, iron chains spanning the city's harbor kept him out. Nevertheless, Turkish ingenuity and up-to-date technology eventually decided the battle. Mehmet's army carried boats over steep hills to come in behind the chains blocking the harbor and then bombarded the city with cannon from the rear.

Once Constantinople was theirs, the Ottoman sultans considered themselves successors of both the Byzantine and Seljuk Turk emperors, and they

Empire of Timur, ca. 1405

quickly absorbed the rest of the Byzantine Empire. In the sixteenth century they continued to expand through the Middle East and into North Africa.

To begin the transformation of Constantinople (renamed Istanbul) into an imperial Ottoman capital, Mehmet appointed officials to adapt the city administration to Ottoman ways and ordered wealthy residents to participate in building mosques, markets, fountains, baths, and other public facilities. The city's population had declined in the decades before the conquest, and the conquest itself had decreased it further. Therefore, Mehmet transplanted inhabitants of other territories to the city, granting them tax remissions and possession of empty houses. He wanted them to start businesses, make Istanbul prosperous, and transform it into a microcosm of the empire.

Gunpowder, which was invented by the Chinese and adapted to artillery use by the Europeans, played an influential role in the expansion of the Ottoman state. In the first half of the sixteenth century, thanks to the use of this technology, the Ottomans gained control of shipping in the eastern Mediterranean, eliminated the Portuguese from the Red Sea and the Persian Gulf, and supported Andalusian and North African Muslims in their fight against the Christian reconquest of Muslim Spain. In 1514, under the leadership of Selim (r. 1512–1520), the Ottomans turned the Safavids back from Anatolia. The Ottomans also added Syria and Palestine (1516) as well as Egypt (1517) to their empire, giving them control of the holy cities of Islam. Next they extended their rule across North Africa to Tunisia and Algeria. Selim's rule marks the beginning of four centuries when most Arabs were under Ottoman rule.

Suleiman (r. 1520–1566) extended Ottoman dominion to its widest geographical extent (see Map 20.1). Suleiman's army crushed the Hungarians at Mohács in 1526. Three years later the Turks besieged the Habsburg capital of Vienna. This target proved impossible to attain, however, perhaps because the Ottomans had reached the logistical limit of their expansion, as some scholars argue.

From the late fourteenth to the early seventeenth centuries, the Ottoman Empire was a key player in European politics. In 1525 Francis I of France and Suleiman struck an alliance; both believed that only their collaboration could prevent Habsburg domination of Europe. The Habsburg emperor Charles V retaliated by seeking an alliance with Safavid Persia. Suleiman renewed the French agreement with Francis's son, Henry II (r. 1547–1559), and this accord became the cornerstone of Ottoman policy in western Europe. Suleiman also allied with the German Protestant princes, forcing the Catholic Habsburgs to grant concessions to the Protestants. Ottoman pressure thus contributed to the official recognition of Lutheran Protestants at the Peace of Augsburg in 1555 and the consolidation of the national monarchy in France.

In eastern Europe to the north of Ottoman lands stood the Grand Duchy of Moscow. In the fifteenth century Ottoman rulers did not regard it as a threat. But in 1547 Ivan IV (the Terrible) brought the entire Volga region under Russian control (see Map 20.1). In 1557 Ivan's ally, the Cossack chieftain Dimitrash, tried to take Azov, the northernmost Ottoman

Chapter Chronology

1299–1326	Reign of Osman, founder of the Ottoman Dynasty
1299–1922	Ottoman Empire
1336–1405	Life of Timur
ca. mid-1400s	Coffeehouses become center of Islamic male social life
1453	Ottoman conquest of Constantinople
1501–1524	Reign of Safavid Shah Isma'il
1501–1722	Safavid Empire
1520–1558	Hürrem wields influence in the Ottoman Empire as Suleiman's concubine and then wife
1520–1566	Reign of Ottoman sultan Suleiman I; period of artistic flowering in Ottoman Empire
1521	Piri Reis produces *Book of the Sea*, a navigational map book
1526–1857	Mughal Empire
1556–1605	Reign of Akbar in Mughal Empire
1570	Ottomans take control of Cyprus
1571	First major Ottoman defeat by Christians, at Lepanto
1587–1629	Reign of Shah Abbas; height of Safavid power; carpet weaving becomes major Persian industry
1631–1648	Construction of Taj Mahal under Shah Jahan in India
1658–1707	Reign of Aurangzeb; Mughal power begins to decline
1763	Treaty of Paris recognizes British control over much of India

What characterized the cultural flowering of the Islamic empires?

How were non-Muslims treated in the Islamic empires?

How did shifts in global trading patterns affect the Islamic empires?

What factors led to the decline of central power in the Islamic empires?

521

Mapping the Past

Map 20.1 The Ottoman Empire at Its Height, 1566

The Ottomans, like their great rivals the Habsburgs, rose to rule a vast dynastic empire encompassing many different peoples and ethnic groups. The army and the bureaucracy served to unite the disparate territories into a single state.

ANALYZING THE MAP Trace the coastlines of the Ottoman Empire. What were the major port cities of the empire? Which regions were encompassed within the empire at its height?

CONNECTIONS If the Ottoman Empire is compared to Europe of the same period (see Map 17.1 on page 438), which had more of its territory near the sea? How did proximity to the Mediterranean shape the politics of Ottoman-European relations in this period?

fortress. Ottoman plans to recapture the area succeeded in uniting Russia, Persia, and the pope against the Turks.

Competition with the Habsburgs and pirates for control of the Mediterranean led the Ottomans to conquer Cyprus in 1570 and settle thousands of Turks from Anatolia there. In response, Pope Pius V organized a Holy League against the Turks, which had a victory in 1571 at Lepanto off the west coast of Greece with a squadron of more than two hundred Spanish, Venetian, and papal galleys. Still, the Turks remained supreme on land and quickly rebuilt their entire fleet.

To the east, war with Safavid Persia occupied the sultans' attention throughout the sixteenth century. Several issues lay at the root of the long and exhausting conflict: religious antagonism between the Sunni Ottomans and the Shi'a Persians, competition to expand at each other's expense in Mesopotamia, desire to control trade routes, and European alliances. (For more on the Shi'a faith, see page 525.) Finally, in 1638 the Ottomans captured Baghdad, and the treaty of Kasr-I-Shirim established a permanent border between the two powers.

The Ottoman political system reached its classic form under Suleiman I. All authority flowed from the sultan to his public servants: provincial governors, police officers, military generals, heads of treasuries, and **viziers**. Suleiman ordered Lütfi Paşa (d. 1562), a poet and juridical scholar of slave origin, to draw up a new general code of laws that prescribed penalties for routine criminal acts such as robbery, adultery, and murder. It also sought to reform bureaucratic and financial corruption, such as foreign merchants' payment of bribes to avoid customs duties, imprisonment without trial, and promotion in the provincial administration because of favoritism rather than ability. The legal code also introduced the idea of balanced government budgets. The head of the religious establishment was given the task of reconciling sultanic law with Islamic law. Suleiman's legal acts influenced many legal codes, including that of the United States. Today, Suleiman's image appears in the chamber of the U.S. House of Representatives, along with the images of the Athenian lawmaker Solon, Moses, and Thomas Jefferson.

viziers Chief assistants to caliphs.

The Ottoman Empire's Use of Slaves

The power of the Ottoman central government was sustained through the training of slaves. Slaves were purchased from Spain, North Africa, and Venice; captured in battle; or drafted through the system known as **devshirme**, by which Christian families in the Balkans were compelled to sell their boys. As the Ottoman frontier advanced in the fifteenth and sixteenth centuries, Albanian, Bosnian, Wallachian, and Hungarian slave boys filled Ottoman imperial needs. The slave boys were converted to Islam and trained for the imperial civil service and the standing army. The brightest 10 percent entered the palace school, where they were prepared for administrative jobs. Other boys were trained for military service. Known as **janissaries** (Turkish for "recruits"), they formed the elite army corps. The devshirme system enabled the Ottomans to apply merit-based recruitment to military and administrative offices at little cost and provided a means of assimilating Christians living in Ottoman lands.

devshirme A process whereby the sultan's agents swept the provinces for Christian youths to become slaves.

janissaries Turkish for "recruits"; they formed the elite army corps.

The Ottoman ruling class consisted partly of descendants of Turkish families who had formerly ruled parts of Anatolia and partly of people of varied ethnic origins who rose through the bureaucratic and military ranks, many beginning as the sultan's slaves. In return for their services to the sultan, they held landed estates for the duration of their lives. The ruling class had the legal right to use and enjoy the profits, but not the ownership, of the land. Because all property belonged to the sultan and reverted to him on the holder's death, Turkish nobles, unlike their European counterparts, did not have a local base independent of the ruler. The absence of a hereditary nobility and private ownership of agricultural land differentiates the Ottoman system from European feudalism (discussed in Chapter 14).

Another distinctive characteristic of the Ottomans was the sultan's failure to marry. From about 1500 on, the sultans did not contract legal marriages but perpetuated the ruling house through concubinage. A slave **concubine** could not expect to exert power the way a local or foreign noblewoman could (with a notable exception; see "Individuals in Society: Hürrem," page 524). When one of the sultan's concubines became pregnant, her status and her salary increased. Because succession to the throne was open to all the sultan's sons, fratricide often resulted upon his death, and the losers were blinded or executed.

concubine A woman who is a recognized spouse but of lower status than a wife.

Slave concubinage paralleled the Ottoman development of slave soldiers and slave viziers. All held positions entirely at the sultan's pleasure, owed loyalty solely to him, and

What characterized the cultural flowering of the Islamic empires?

How were non-Muslims treated in the Islamic empires?

How did shifts in global trading patterns affect the Islamic empires?

What factors led to the decline of central power in the Islamic empires?

523

INDIVIDUALS IN SOCIETY

Hürrem

HÜRREM (1505?–1558) WAS BORN IN THE WESTERN Ukraine (then part of Poland), the daughter of a Ruthenian priest, and was given the Polish name Aleksandra Lisowska. When Tartars raided, they captured and enslaved her. In 1520 she was given as a gift to Suleiman on the occasion of his accession to the throne. The Venetian ambassador (probably relying on secondhand or thirdhand information) described her as "young, graceful, petite, but not beautiful." She was given the Turkish name Hürrem, meaning "joyful."

Hürrem apparently brought joy to Suleiman. Their first child was born in 1521. By 1525 they had four sons and a daughter; sources note that by that year Suleiman visited no other woman. But he waited eight or nine years before breaking Ottoman dynastic tradition by making Hürrem his legal wife, the first slave concubine so honored. For the rest of her life, Hürrem played a highly influential role in the political, diplomatic, and philanthropic life of the Ottoman state. First, great power flowed from her position as mother of the prince, the future sultan Selim II (r. 1566–1574). Then, as the intimate and most trusted adviser of the sultan, she was Suleiman's closest confidante. During his frequent trips to the far-flung corners of his multiethnic empire, Hürrem wrote him long letters filled with her love and longing for him and her prayers for his safety in battle. She also shared political information about affairs in Istanbul, the activities of the grand vizier, and the attitudes of the janissaries. At a time when some people believed that the sultan's absence from the capital endangered his hold on the throne, Hürrem acted as his eyes and ears for potential threats.

Hürrem was the sultan's contact with her native Poland, which sent more embassies to Istanbul than any other power. Through her correspondence with King Sigismund I, peace between Poland and the Ottomans was maintained. When Sigismund II succeeded his father in 1548, Hürrem sent congratulations on his accession, along with two pairs of pajamas (originally a Hindu garment but commonly worn in southwestern Asia) and six handkerchiefs. Also, she sent the shah of Persia gold-embroidered sheets and shirts that she had sewn herself, seeking to display the wealth of the sultanate and to keep peace between the Ottomans and the Safavids.

The enormous stipend that Suleiman gave Hürrem permitted her to participate in his vast building program. In Jerusalem (in the Ottoman province of Palestine), she founded a hospice for fifty-five pilgrims that included a soup kitchen that fed four hundred pilgrims a day. In Istanbul Suleiman built and Hürrem endowed the Haseki (meaning "royal favorite concubine") mosque complex and a public bath for women near the Women's Market.

Perhaps Hürrem tried to fulfill two functions hitherto distinct in Ottoman political theory: those of the sultan's favorite and of mother of the prince. She also performed the conflicting roles of slave concubine and imperial wife. Many Turks resented Hürrem's interference at court. They believed she was behind the execution of Suleiman's popular son Mustafa on a charge of treason to make way for her own son to succeed as sultan.

Source: Leslie P. Pierce, *The Imperial Harem: Women and Sovereignty in the Ottoman Empire* (New York: Oxford University Press, 1993).

QUESTIONS FOR ANALYSIS

1. How does Hürrem compare to powerful women in other places, such as Empress Wu in China, Isabella of Castile, Catherine de' Medici of France, Elizabeth I of England, Mary Queen of Scots, or any other you know about?
2. What was Hürrem's "nationality"? What role did it play in her life?

Hürrem and her ladies in the harem. (Bibliothèque nationale de France)

Music in a Garden This illustration of a courtly romance depicts several women in a garden, intently listening to a musician, with cups of a beverage in their hands.
(Biblioteca Vaticana Apostolica, VAT.AR.388)

thus were more reliable than a hereditary nobility, as existed in Europe. Great social prestige, as well as the opportunity to acquire power and wealth, was attached to being a slave of the imperial household. Suleiman even made it a practice to marry his daughters to top-ranking slave-officials.

The Safavid Empire in Persia

With the decline of Timur's empire after 1450, Persia was controlled by Turkish lords, with no single one dominant until 1501, when fourteen-year-old Isma'il (1487–1524) led a Turkish army to capture Tabriz and declared himself **shah** (king).

The strength of the early **Safavid** state rested on three crucial features. First, it had the loyalty and military support of Turkish Sufis known as **Qizilbash** (KIH-zil-bahsh). The shah secured the loyalty of the Qizilbash by granting them vast grazing lands, especially on the troublesome Ottoman frontier. In return, the Qizilbash supplied him with troops. Second, the Safavid state utilized the skills of urban bureaucrats and made them an essential part of the civil machinery of government.

The third source of Safavid strength was the Shi'a faith, which became the compulsory religion of the empire. The Shi'a believed that leadership among Muslims rightfully belonged to the Prophet Muhammad's descendants. Because Isma'il claimed descent from a line of twelve infallible imams (leaders) beginning with Ali (Muhammad's cousin and son-in-law), he was officially regarded as their representative on earth. Isma'il recruited Shi'a scholars outstanding in learning and piety from other lands to instruct and guide

shah Persian word for "king."

Safavid The dynasty that encompassed all of Persia and other regions; its state religion was Shi'ism.

Qizilbash Nomadic Sufi tribesmen who were loyal to and supportive of the early Safavid state.

What characterized the cultural flowering of the Islamic empires?

How were non-Muslims treated in the Islamic empires?

How did shifts in global trading patterns affect the Islamic empires?

What factors led to the decline of central power in the Islamic empires?

525

Map 20.2 The Safavid Empire, 1587–1629 In the late sixteenth century the power of the Safavid kingdom of Persia rested on its strong military force, its Shi'a Muslim faith, and its extraordinarily rich trade in rugs and pottery. Many of the cities on the map, such as Tabriz, Qum, and Shiraz, were great rug-weaving centers.

ulama Religious scholars whom Sunnis trust to interpret the Qur'an and the Sunna, the deeds and sayings of Muhammad.

his people, and he persecuted and exiled Sunni **ulama**. To this day, Iran remains the only Muslim state in which Shi'ism is the official religion.

Safavid power reached its height under Shah Abbas (r. 1587–1629), who moved the capital from Qazvin to Isfahan. His military achievements, support for trade and commerce, and endowment of the arts earned him the epithet "the Great." In the military realm, he adopted the Ottoman practice of building an army of slaves, who could serve as a counterweight to the Qizilbash, who had come to be considered a threat. He also increased the use of gunpowder weapons and made alliances with European powers against the Ottomans and Portuguese. In his campaigns against the Ottomans, Shah Abbas captured Baghdad, Mosul, and Diarbakr in Mesopotamia (Map 20.2). After Shah Abbas, however, Safavid power was sapped by civil war between tribal factions vying for control of the court.

The Mughal Empire in India

Mughal A term meaning "Mongol," used to refer to the Muslim empire of India, although its founders were primarily Turks, Afghans, and Persians.

Of the three great Islamic empires of the early modern world, the **Mughal** Empire of India was the largest, wealthiest, and most populous. Extending over 1.2 million square miles at the end of the seventeenth century, with a population between 100 and 150 million,

Mughal territory
- In 1525
- Added, by 1539
- Added, by 1605
- Added, by 1707
- Lost, by 1707

The Mughal Empire, 1526–1857

and with fabulous wealth and resources, the Mughal Empire surpassed the other two by a wide margin. In the sixteenth century, only the Ming Dynasty in China could compare.

In 1504 a Turkish ruler named Babur (r. 1483–1530) captured Kabul and established a kingdom in Afghanistan. An adventurer who claimed descent from Chinggis Khan and Timur, Babur moved southward in search of resources to restore his fortunes. In 1526, with a force that was small but was equipped with firearms, Babur defeated the sultan of Delhi at Panipat. Babur's capture of the cities of Agra and Delhi, key fortresses of the north, paved the way for further conquests in northern India. Although many of his soldiers wished to return north with their spoils, Babur decided to stay in India.

During the reign of Babur's son Humayun (r. 1530–1540 and 1555–1556), the Mughals lost most of their territories in Afghanistan. Humayun went into temporary exile in Persia, where he developed a deep appreciation for Persian art and literature. The reign of Humayun's son Akbar (r. 1556–1605) may well have been the greatest in the history of India. A boy of thirteen when he succeeded to the throne, Akbar pursued expansionist policies. Under his leadership, the Mughal state took definitive form and encompassed most of the subcontinent north of the Godavari River. The once independent states of northern India were forced into a centralized political system under the sole authority of the Mughal emperor.

Akbar replaced Turkish with Persian as the official language of the Mughal Empire. To govern this vast region, Akbar developed an administrative bureaucracy centered on four co-equal ministers: for finance and revenue; the army and intelligence; the judiciary and religious patronage; and the imperial household, whose jurisdiction included roads, bridges, and infrastructure throughout the empire. In the provinces, imperial governors, appointed by and responsible solely to the emperor, presided over administrative branches modeled on those of the central government. The government, however, rarely interfered in the life of village communities. Whereas the Ottoman sultans and Safavid shahs made extensive use of slaves acquired from non-Muslim lands for military and administrative positions, Akbar used the services of royal princes, nobles, and warrior-aristocrats. Initially these men were Muslims from Central Asia, but to reduce their influence, Akbar vigorously recruited Persians and Hindus.

Akbar's descendants extended the Mughal Empire farther. His son Jahangir (r. 1605–1628) consolidated Mughal rule in Bengal. Jahangir's son Shah Jahan (r. 1628–1658) launched fresh territorial expansion. Faced with revolts by the Muslims in Ahmadnagar and the resistance of the newly arrived Portuguese in Bengal, Shah Jahan not only crushed this opposition but also strengthened his northwestern frontier. Shah Jahan's son Aurangzeb (r. 1658–1707), unwilling to wait for his father to die, deposed him and confined him for years in a small cell. A puritanically devout and strictly orthodox Muslim, as well as a skillful general and a clever diplomat, Aurangzeb ruled more of India than did any previous Mughal emperor, having extended the realm deeper into south India. His reign, however, also marked the beginning of the empire's decline. His non-Muslim subjects were not pleased with his religious zealotry, and his military campaigns were costly. In the south resistance to Mughal rule led to major uprisings. (For more on Aurangzeb's rule, see page 535.)

Quick Review

What common characteristics linked the Islamic empires of the early modern period?

What characterized the cultural flowering of the Islamic empires?

How were non-Muslims treated in the Islamic empires?

How did shifts in global trading patterns affect the Islamic empires?

What factors led to the decline of central power in the Islamic empires?

What characterized the cultural flowering of the Islamic empires?

All three Islamic empires presided over an extraordinary artistic and intellectual flowering. Artistic and intellectual advances spread from culture to culture, probably because of the common Persian influence on the Turks since the tenth century. This exchange was also aided by common languages. Persian was used as the administrative language by the Mughals in India, and Arabic was a lingua franca of the entire region because of its centrality in Islam. In Ottoman lands both Persian and Arabic were literary languages, but Turkish slowly became the lingua franca of the realm.

The Arts

One of the arts all three empires shared was carpet making. Carpet designs and weaving techniques demonstrate both cultural integration and local distinctiveness. Turkic migrants carried their weaving traditions with them as they moved but also readily adopted new motifs, especially from Persia. In the Safavid capital of Isfahan alone, factories employed more than twenty-five thousand weavers. Women and children often were employed as weavers, especially of the most expensive rugs, because their smaller hands could tie tinier knots.

Another art that spread from Persia to both Ottoman and Mughal lands was miniature painting, especially for book illustration. This tradition had been enriched by the many Chinese artists brought to Persia during the Mongol period. There was also an interplay

Persian "Ardabil" Carpet, ca. 1540 The Persians were among the first carpet weavers of ancient times and perfected the art over thousands of years. This wool carpet, reputably from the Safavid shrine at Ardabil, is one of only three signed and dated carpets from the Safavid period, when Persian carpet making was at its zenith. Hand-knotted and hand-dyed, it was royally commissioned with a traditional medallion design, consisting of a central sunburst medallion surrounded by radiating pendants. Mosque lamps project from the top and bottom of the medallion. Inscribed on the carpet is an ode by the fourteenth-century poet Hafiz: "I have no refuge in this world other than thy threshold / My head has no resting place other than this doorway." (Victoria & Albert Museum, London/The Art Archive at Art Resource, NY)

between carpets and miniature painting. Naturalistic depictions of flowers, birds, and even dragons appear in both book illustrations and carpets.

Akbar enthusiastically supported artists who produced magnificent paintings and books in the Indo-Persian style. In Mughal India, as throughout the Muslim world, books were regarded as precious objects. Time, talent, and expensive materials went into their production, and they were highly coveted because they reflected wealth, learning, and power. Akbar reportedly possessed twenty-four thousand books when he died.

City and Palace Building

In all three empires strong rulers built capital cities and imperial palaces as visible expressions of dynastic majesty. With annual state revenues of about $80 million (at a time when Elizabeth I of England could expect $150,000 and Francis I of France perhaps $1 million) and thousands of servants, Suleiman had a lifestyle no European monarch could begin to rival. He used his fabulous wealth to adorn Istanbul with palaces, mosques, schools, and libraries, and the city reached about a million in population. The building of hospitals, roads, and bridges and the reconstruction of the water systems of the great pilgrimage sites at Mecca and Jerusalem benefited his subjects. Safavid Persia and Mughal India produced rulers with similar ambitions.

Shah Abbas made his capital, Isfahan, the jewel of the Safavid Empire. He had his architects place a polo ground in the center and surrounded it with palaces, mosques, and bazaars. A seventeenth-century English visitor described one of Isfahan's bazaars as "the surprisingest piece of Greatness in Honour of commerce the world can boast of." Besides splendid rugs, stalls displayed pottery and fine china, metalwork of exceptionally high quality, and silks and velvets of stunning weave and design. A city of perhaps 750,000 people, Isfahan also contained 162 mosques, 48 schools, 273 public baths, and the vast imperial palace. Private houses had their own garden courts, and public gardens, pools, and parks adorned the wide streets.

Akbar in India was also a great builder. The birth of a long-awaited son, Jahangir, inspired Akbar to build a new city, Fatehpur-Sikri, to symbolize the regime's Islamic foundations. The city combined the Muslim tradition of domes, arches, and spacious courts with the Hindu tradition of flat stone beams, ornate decoration, and solidity. Completed in 1578, the city included an imperial palace, a mosque, lavish gardens, and a hall of worship, as well as thousands of houses for ordinary people. Unfortunately because of its bad water supply, the city was soon abandoned.

Of Akbar's successors, Shah Jahan had the most sophisticated interest in architecture. Because his capital at Agra was cramped, in 1639 he decided to found a new capital city at Delhi. In the design and layout of the buildings, Persian ideas predominated, an indication of the number of Persian architects and engineers who had flocked to the subcontinent. The walled palace-fortress alone extended over 125 acres. In 1650, with living quarters for guards, military officials, merchants, dancing girls, scholars, and hordes of cooks and servants, the palace-fortress housed 57,000 people. It also boasted a covered public bazaar (comparable to a modern mall). It was probably the first roofed shopping center in India, although such centers were common in western Asia. Beyond the walls, princes and aristocrats built mansions and mosques on a smaller scale. With its fine architecture and its population of between 375,000 and 400,000, Delhi gained the reputation of being one of the great cities of the Muslim world.

Shah Jahan's most enduring monument is the Taj Mahal. Between 1631 and 1648 twenty thousand workers toiled over the construction of this memorial in Agra to Shah Jahan's favorite wife, who died giving birth to their fifteenth child. One of the most beautiful structures in the world, the Taj Mahal is both an expression of love and a superb architectural blending of Islamic and Indian culture.

What characterized the cultural flowering of the Islamic empires? | How were non-Muslims treated in the Islamic empires? | How did shifts in global trading patterns affect the Islamic empires? | What factors led to the decline of central power in the Islamic empires?

529

Katib Chelebi (1609–1657) was an Ottoman civil servant who spent much of his time as an accountant for the Turkish army, accompanying it on several important campaigns. Over time he became passionate about learning and pursued not only Islamic law but also ancient Greek philosophy, geography, and modern European sciences. He wrote several important books, including a bibliographical encyclopedia. The book of essays from which the following extract comes also discusses such contemporary issues as coffee, singing, opium, shaking hands, bowing, and bribery.

❝ Sometime in the latter half of the ninth century of the Hijra, after some Spanish ships had discovered the New World, the Portuguese and English were exploring its shores to find a passage from the Eastern to the Western Ocean. They came to an island close to the mainland, called in the Atlas "Gineya." A ship's doctor, who had been smitten with a lymphatic disorder, due to the influence of the sea air on his natural temperament, decided to try and cure it with hot and dry things, in accordance with the laws of treatment by opposites. When his ship reached that island, he noticed a kind of leaf was burning. He smelled it, and as it was hot of scent he began to inhale it, using an instrument resembling a pipe. It did him good, so he took a large quantity of the leaf and used it throughout their stay. The ship's company saw this and, regarding it as a beneficial medicine, followed the doctor's example and loaded themselves up with the leaf. One saw another and they all began to smoke. When the ship arrived in England, the habit spread, through France to the other lands. People tried it, not knowing its origin, and not considering that it was smoked for a serious purpose. Many became addicts, putting it in the category of stimulating drugs. It has become a thing common to East and West, and no one has succeeded in suppressing it.

From its first appearance in Turkey, which was about the year 1010/1601, to the present day, various preachers have spoken against it individually, and many of the Ulema [ulama] have written tracts concerning it, some claiming that it is a thing forbidden, some that it is disapproved. Its addicts have replied to the effect that it is permissible. After some time had elapsed, the eminent surgeon Ibrāhīm Efendi devoted much care and attention to the matter, conducting great debates in the Abode of the Sultanate, that is, in the city of Istanbul, giving warning talks at a special public meeting in the mosque of Sultan Mehmed, and sticking copies of fetwas [fatwas] onto walls. He troubled himself to no purpose. The more he spoke, the more people persisted in smoking. Seeing that it was fruitless, he abandoned his efforts. After that, the late Sultan Murad IV, towards the end of his reign, closed down the coffeehouses in order to shut the gate of iniquity, and also banned smoking, in consequence of certain outbreaks of fire. People being undeterred, the imperial anger necessitated the chastisement of those who, by smoking, committed the sin of disobedience to the imperial command. Gradually His Majesty's severity in suppression increased, and so did people's desire to smoke, in accordance with the saying, "Men desire what is forbidden," and many thousands of men were sent to the abode of nothingness.

When the Sultan was going on the expedition against Baghdad, at one halting-place fifteen or twenty leading men of the Army were arrested on a charge of smoking, and were put to death with the severest torture in the imperial presence. Some of the soldiers carried short pipes in their sleeves, some in their pockets, and they found an opportunity to smoke even during the executions. At Istanbul, no end of soldiers used to go into the barracks and smoke in the privies. Even during this rigorous prohibition, the number of smokers exceeded that of the non-smokers.

After that Sultan's death, the practice was sometimes forbidden and sometimes allowed, until the Sheykh al-Islam, the late Baha'i Efendi, gave a fetwa ruling that it was permissible, and the practice won renewed popularity among the people of the world. Occasional reprimands from the Throne to smokers have generally been disregarded, and smoking is at present practiced all over the habitable globe. Such are the vicissitudes undergone by tobacco.

Now there are a number of possible ways of considering the subject, which we shall briefly set forth.

(1) The first possibility is that the people may be effectively prevented from smoking and may give it

Gardens

Many of the architectural masterpieces of this age had splendid gardens attached to them as well. Gardens represent a distinctive and highly developed feature of Persian culture. They commonly were walled, with a pool in the center and geometrically laid-out flowering plants. Identified with paradise in Arabic tradition, gardens served not only as centers of prayer and meditation but also as places of leisure and revelry. Although first limited to the ruler's court, gardening soon spread among the wealthy citizens.

A man is smoking a long pipe in one of the stalls in a bazaar depicted in this seventeenth-century Turkish painting. (The Granger Collection, New York)

up. This possibility must be set aside, for custom is second nature. Addicts are not made to give up in this way. . . .

(2) Is this tobacco found to be good or bad by the intelligence? If we set aside the fact that addicts think it good, common sense judges it to be bad. . . .

(3) Its good and harmful effects. As to its harmful effects there is no doubt. It ends by becoming a basic need of the addict, who does not consider its evil consequences. Its harmful physical effect too is established, for tobacco is medically noxious in that it makes turbid the aerial essence. . . .

(4) Is it innovation? It may be conceded that it is innovation in the eyes of the sacred law, for it appeared in recent times, nor is it possible to class it as "good innovation." That it is innovation in the light of intelligence is sure, for it is not a thing that has been seen or heard of by the intelligent ever since the time of Adam. . . .

(5) Is it abominable? There is no word of justification for this, in reason or in law. . . . It is perhaps not irrelevant to point out that the scent of burning tobacco has curative uses as an inhalant. But an evil odor arises in the mouth of the heavy smoker. . . .

(6) Is it canonically forbidden? It is written in the manuals of jurisprudence that in any particular matter where there is no decisive ruling in the law, the jurisconsult may exercise his own discretion. He may, according to one point of view, bring together all relevant circumstances, consider them, and make his own deductions. Yet the following course is preferable: not to declare things forbidden, but always to have recourse to any legal principle that justifies declaring them permitted, thus preserving the people from being laden with sins and persisting in what has been prohibited.

(7) Is it canonically indifferent? As the rise of smoking is of recent occurrence, there is no explicit treatment or mention of it in the legal manuals. This being so, some say that in accordance with the principle that permissibility is the norm — i.e., that in the absence of a clear prohibition things are permitted — smoking is permitted and lawful.

Source: Katib Chelebi, *The Balance of Truth*, trans. G. L. Lewis (London: George Allen and Unwin, 1957), pp. 50–58.

QUESTIONS FOR ANALYSIS

1. What do you learn about social life in the Ottoman Empire from this essay?
2. What can you infer about the sorts of arguments that were made by Islamic jurists in Katib Chelebi's day?
3. How open-minded was Katib Chelebi? What evidence from the text led you to your conclusion?

After the incorporation of Persia into the caliphate in the seventh century, formal gardening spread west and east through the Islamic world, as illustrated by the magnificent gardens of Muslim Spain, southern Italy, and later southeastern Europe. The Mongol followers of Timur took landscape architects from Persia back to Samarkand and adapted their designs to nomad encampments. When Timur's descendant Babur established the Mughal Dynasty in India, he adapted the Persian garden to the warmer southern climate.

Because it evoked paradise, the garden played a large role in Muslim literature. Some scholars hold that to understand Arabic poetry, one must study Arabic gardening. The

What characterized the cultural flowering of the Islamic empires?

How were non-Muslims treated in the Islamic empires?

How did shifts in global trading patterns affect the Islamic empires?

What factors led to the decline of central power in the Islamic empires?

531

Isfahan Tiles The embellishment of Isfahan under Shah Abbas I created an unprecedented need for tiles, as had the rebuilding of imperial Istanbul after 1453, the vast building program of Suleiman the Magnificent, and a huge European demand. Persian potters learned their skills from the Chinese. By the late sixteenth century Italian and Austrian potters had imitated the Persian and Ottoman tile makers. (© Victoria & Albert Museum, London/V&A Images)

literary subjects of flowers and gardens provided basic themes for Hispano-Arab poets. The secular literature of Muslim Spain, rife with references such as "a garland of verses," influenced the lyric poetry of southern France, the troubadours, and the courtly love tradition.

Intellectual Advances and Religious Trends

Between 1400 and 1800, the culture of the Islamic empires underwent many changes. Particularly notable were new movements within Islam as well as advances in mathematics, geography, astronomy, and medicine. Building on the knowledge of earlier Islamic writers and stimulated by Ottoman naval power, the geographer and cartographer Piri Reis produced a map incorporating Islamic and Western knowledge that showed all the known world (1513). His *Book of the Sea* (1521) contained 129 chapters, each with a map incorporating all Islamic (and Western) knowledge of the seas and navigation as well as describing harbors, tides, dangerous rocks and shores, and storm areas. In the field of astronomy, Takiyuddin Mehmet (1521–1585), who served as the sultan's chief astronomer, built an observatory at Istanbul. He also produced *Instruments of the Observatory*, which catalogued astronomical instruments and described an astronomical clock that fixed the location of heavenly bodies with greater precision than ever before.

There were also advances in medicine. Under Suleiman the imperial palace itself became a center of medical science, and the large number of hospitals established in Istanbul and throughout the empire testifies to his support for medical research and his concern for the sick. Abi Ahmet Celebi (1436–1523), the chief physician of the empire, founded the first Ottoman medical school, which served as a training institution for physicians of the empire.

In the realm of religion, the rulers of all three empires drew legitimacy from their support for Islam, at least among their Muslim subjects. The Sunni-Shi'a split between the Ottomans and Safavids led to efforts to define and enforce religious orthodoxy on both sides. For the Safavids this entailed suppressing Sufi movements and Sunnis, even marginalizing—sometimes massacring—the original Qizilbash warriors, who had come to be seen as politically disruptive. Sectarian conflicts within Islam were not as pronounced in Mughal lands, perhaps because even though the Mughals ruled over both Sunni and Shi'a subjects, these subjects were greatly outnumbered by non-Muslims, mostly Hindus.

Sufi fraternities thrived throughout the Muslim world in this era, even when the states tried to limit them. In India, Sufi orders also influenced non-Muslims. The mystical Bhakti movement among Hindus involved dances, poems, and songs reminiscent of Sufi practice. The development of the new religion of the Sikhs (seeks) also was influenced by Sufis. The Sikhs traced themselves back to a teacher in the sixteenth century who argued that God did not distinguish between Muslims and Hindus but saw everyone as his children. Sikhs rejected the caste system (division of society into hereditary groups) and forbade alcohol and tobacco, and men did not cut their hair (covering it instead with a turban). The Sikh movement was most successful in northwest India, where Sikh men armed themselves to defend their communities.

Despite all the signs of cultural vitality in the three Islamic empires, none of them adopted the printing press or went through the sorts of cultural expansion associated with it in China and Europe. Until 1729 the Ottoman authorities prohibited printing books in Turkish or Arabic. Printing was not banned in Mughal India, but neither did the technology spread, even after Jesuit missionaries printed Bibles in Indian languages beginning in the 1550s. The Islamic authorities in each of these empires did not want to see writings circulate that might unsettle society and religious teachings.

Coffeehouses and Their Social Impact

In the mid-fifteenth century a new social convention spread throughout the Islamic world—drinking coffee. Arab writers trace the origins of coffee drinking to Yemen Sufis, who sought a trancelike concentration on God to the exclusion of everything else and found that coffee helped them stay awake. Most Sufis were not professional holy men but were employed as tradesmen and merchants. Therefore, the use of coffee for pious purposes led to its use as a business lubricant—an extension of hospitality to a potential buyer in a shop. Merchants carried the Yemenite practice to Mecca in about 1490. From Mecca, where pilgrims were introduced to it, coffee drinking spread to Egypt and Syria. In 1555 two Syrians opened a coffeehouse in Istanbul.

Objections to Coffeehouses
Coffee is intoxicating, making it analogous to wine, prohibited to Muslims
Coffee drinking was an innovation and therefore a violation of Islamic law
Coffeehouses encouraged political discussions, facilitating sedition
Coffeehouses attracted unemployed soldiers, riffraff, and other low types, encouraging immoral behavior, such as gambling, using drugs, and soliciting prostitutes
The musical entertainment that coffeehouses provided encouraged debauchery

Coffeehouses provided a place for conversation and male sociability; there a man could entertain his friends cheaply and more informally than at home. But coffeehouses encountered religious and governmental opposition, with some officials contending that coffeehouses were a threat to public health, order, and morality. On the other hand, the coffee trade was a major source of profit that local notables sought to control.

Although debate over the morality of coffeehouses continued through the sixteenth century, their eventual acceptance represented a revolution in Islamic life: socializing was no longer confined to the home. Ultimately, because the medical profession remained divided on coffee's harmful effects and because religious authorities could not prove that coffeehouses violated religious law, coffee drinking could not be forbidden. In the seventeenth century coffee and coffeehouses spread to Europe. (For reaction to another new product that spread quickly despite opposition, see "Listening to the Past: Katib Chelebi on Tobacco," page 530.)

Quick Review

What role did the rulers of the Islamic empires play in the cultural flowering of their societies?

How were non-Muslims treated in the Islamic empires?

Drawing on Qur'anic teachings, Muslims had long practiced a religious toleration unknown in Christian Europe. Muslim rulers for the most part guaranteed the lives and property of Christians and Jews on their promise of obedience and the payment of a poll tax.

In the case of the Ottomans, this tolerance was extended not only to the Christians and Jews who had been living under Muslim rule for centuries but also to the Serbs, Bosnians, Croats, and other Orthodox Christians in the newly conquered Balkans. The Ottoman conqueror of Constantinople, Mehmet, nominated the Greek patriarch as official representative of the Greek population. This and other such appointments recognized non-Muslims as functioning parts of the Ottoman society and economy. In 1454 Rabbi Isaac Sarfati sent a letter to the Jews in the Rhineland, Swabia, Moravia, and Hungary, urging them to move to Turkey because of the good conditions for Jews there. A massive migration to Ottoman lands followed. When Ferdinand and Isabella of Spain expelled the Jews in 1492 and later, many immigrated to the Ottoman Empire.

The Safavid authorities made efforts to convert Armenian Christians in the Caucuses, and many seem to have embraced Islam, some more voluntarily than others. Nevertheless, the Armenian Christian Church retained its vitality, and under the Safavids Armenian Christians were prominent merchants in long-distance trade (see page 539).

Babur and his successors acquired even more non-Muslim subjects with their conquests in India. Over time, the number of Indians who converted to Islam increased, but the Mughal rulers did not force conversion. Akbar went the furthest in promoting Muslim-Hindu accommodation. He celebrated important Hindu festivals and he wore his uncut hair in a turban as a concession to Indian practice. Also, Akbar twice married Hindu princesses, one of whom became the mother of his heir, Jahangir. Eventually, Hindus totaled 30 percent of the imperial bureaucracy. In 1579 Akbar abolished the **jizya**, the poll tax on non-Muslims that guaranteed their protection. These actions, especially the abolition of the jizya, infuriated the ulama, and serious conflict erupted between them and the emperor. Ultimately, Akbar issued an imperial decree declaring that the Mughal emperor had supreme authority, even above the ulama, in all religious matters. This statement, resting on a policy of benign toleration, represented a severe defeat for the Muslim religious establishment.

Some of Akbar's successors, above all Aurangzeb, sided more with the ulama. Aurangzeb appointed censors of public morals in important cities to enforce Islamic laws against gambling, prostitution, drinking, and the use of narcotics. He forbade sati—the self-immolation of widows on their husbands' funeral pyres—and the castration of boys to be sold as eunuchs. He also abolished all taxes not authorized by Islamic law. To replace the lost revenue, in 1679 Aurangzeb reimposed the tax on non-Muslims. Aurangzeb's reversal of Akbar's

Emperor Akbar in the City of Fatehpur-Sikri In 1569 Akbar founded the city of Fatehpur-Sikri (the City of Victory) to honor the Muslim holy man Shaykh Salim Chishti, who had foretold the birth of Akbar's son and heir Jahangir. Akbar is shown here seated on the cushion in the center overseeing the construction of the city. The image is contained in the *Akbarnama*, a book of illustrations Akbar commissioned to officially chronicle his reign. (Victoria & Albert Museum/The Bridgeman Art Library)

jizya A poll tax on non-Muslims.

What characterized the cultural flowering of the Islamic empires?

How were non-Muslims treated in the Islamic empires?

How did shifts in global trading patterns affect the Islamic empires?

What factors led to the decline of central power in the Islamic empires?

535

religious toleration and cultural cosmopolitanism extended further. He ordered the destruction of some Hindu temples and tried to curb Sikhism. Aurangzeb's attempts to enforce rigid Islamic norms proved highly unpopular with the majority of his subjects and aroused resistance that weakened Mughal rule.

How did shifts in global trading patterns affect the Islamic empires?

It has widely been thought that a decline in the wealth and international importance of the Muslim empires could be directly attributed to the long-term shift in trading patterns that resulted from the discoveries of European explorers. The argument is that new sea routes enabled Europeans to acquire goods from the East without using Muslim intermediaries, thus leading directly and indirectly to the eclipse of the Ottomans, Safavids, and

Map 20.3 India, 1707–1805 In the eighteenth century Mughal power gradually yielded to the Hindu Marathas and to the British East India Company.

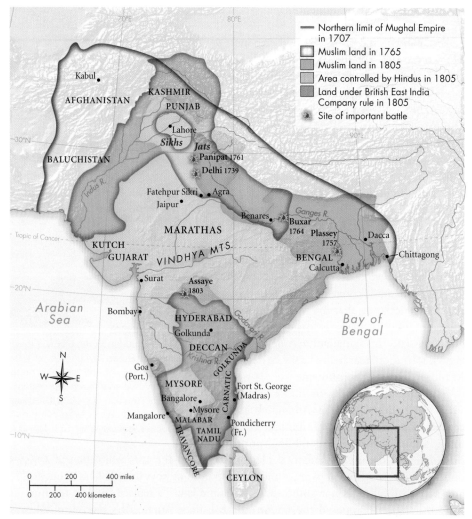

Mughals. Recent scholars have challenged these ideas as too simplistic. Turkish, Persian, and Indian merchants remained very active as long-distance traders into the eighteenth century and opened up many new routes themselves. Moreover, it was not until the eighteenth century that there were many signs of political decline in the three Islamic empires. As well, government revenue came more from taxes on farmers than from trade.

Agriculture benefited from the spread of new crops, such as coffee and sugar, from elsewhere in the Old World, but New World crops like potatoes and sweet potatoes played a relatively minor role in the economy and do not seem to have fueled population increases as rapid as those in western Europe and East Asia.

Still, the importance of trade to the economies of the three Islamic empires should not be discounted. Over the centuries covered in this chapter, trading patterns and practices evolved, and European penetration increased.

European Rivalry for Trade in the Indian Ocean

Shortly before Babur's invasion of India, the Portuguese had opened the subcontinent to Portuguese trade. In 1510 they established the port of Goa on the west coast of India as their headquarters and through an aggressive policy took control of Muslim shipping in the Indian Ocean and Arabian Sea, charging high fees to let ships through. As a result, they controlled the spice trade over the Indian Ocean for almost a century.

In 1602 the Dutch formed the Dutch East India Company with the goal of wresting the spice trade from the Portuguese. In 1685 they supplanted the Portuguese in Ceylon (Sri Lanka). The scent of fabulous profits also attracted the English. With a charter signed by Queen Elizabeth, eighty London merchants organized the British East India Company. In 1619 Emperor Jahangir granted a British mission important commercial concessions. Soon, by offering gifts, medical services, and bribes to Indian rulers, the British East India Company was able to set up twenty-eight coastal forts/trading posts. By 1700 the company had founded the cities that became Madras and Calcutta (today called Chennai and Kolkata), and they had taken over Bombay (today Mumbai), which had been a Portuguese possession (Map 20.3).

The British called their trading posts **factory-forts**. The term *factory* did not signify manufacturing; it designated the walled compound containing the residences, gardens, and offices of British East India Company officials and the warehouses where goods were stored before being shipped to Europe. The company president exercised political authority over all residents.

Factory-forts existed to make profits from Asian-European trade, which was robust due to growing European demand for Indian and Chinese wares. The European middle classes wanted Indian textiles, which were colorful, durable, cheap, and washable. The upper classes desired Chinese wallpaper

factory-forts A term first used by the British for their trading post at Surat that was later applied to all European walled settlements in India.

English Dress Made of Indian Printed Cotton Cloth Early British traders in India were impressed with the quality of the textiles made there and began ordering designs that would be popular with the English. This dress, created around 1770–1780 in England, is made of printed cotton (chintz) from the southeastern part of India. Chintz became so popular in England that it was eventually banned because it was threatening local textile industries. (© Victoria and Albert Museum, London/V&A Images)

What characterized the cultural flowering of the Islamic empires?

How were non-Muslims treated in the Islamic empires?

How did shifts in global trading patterns affect the Islamic empires?

What factors led to the decline of central power in the Islamic empires?

537

and porcelains as well as Indian silks and brocades. Other Indian goods in demand included pepper and other spices, sugar, and opium. To pay for these goods, the British East India Company sold silver, copper, zinc, lead, and fabrics to the Indians. Profits grew even larger after 1700, when the company began to trade with China.

Merchant Networks in the Islamic Empires

The shifting trade patterns associated with European colonial expansion brought no direct benefit to the Ottomans and the Safavids, whose merchants could now be bypassed by Europeans seeking goods from India, Southeast Asia, or China. Yet merchants from these Islamic empires often proved adaptable, finding ways to benefit from the new trade networks.

In the case of India, the appearance of European traders led to a rapid increase in overall trade, helping Indian merchants and the Indian economy. Block-printed cotton cloth, produced by artisans working at home, was India's chief export. Through an Islamic business device that involved advancing payment to artisans, banker-brokers supplied the material for production and money for the artisans to live on while they worked; the cloth brokers specified the quality, quantity, and design of the finished products. This procedure resembles the later English "domestic" or "putting-out" system (see page 609), for the very good reason that the English took the idea from the Indians.

From the Indian region of Gujarat, Indian merchant bankers shipped their cloth worldwide: across the Indian Ocean to Aden and the Muslim-controlled cities on the east coast of Africa; across the Arabian Sea to Muscat and Hormuz and up the Persian Gulf to the cities of Persia; up the Red Sea to the Mediterranean; by sea also to Malacca, Indonesia, China, and Japan; by land across Africa to Ghana on the west coast; and to Astrakhan, Poland, Moscow, and even the Russian cities on the distant Volga River. Indian businessmen had branch offices in many of these places, and all this activity produced fabulous wealth for some Indian merchants. Some scholars have compared India's international trade in the sixteenth century with that of Italian firms, such as the Medici. Indian trade actually extended over a far wider area, however.

Armenian Brass Bowl The inscription on this bowl dates it to 1616 and places it in New Julfa, the Armenian quarter of Isfahan. It would have been used by an Armenian Christian priest to wash his hands. (© Ana A. Melikian 2007)

Throughout Muslim lands both Jews and Christians were active in commerce. A particularly interesting case involves the Armenian Christians in the Safavid Empire in the sixteenth to eighteenth centuries. Armenian merchants had been trading from their base in Armenia for centuries and were especially known for their trade in Persian silk. When the Portuguese first appeared on the western coast of India in 1498 and began to settle in south India, they found many Armenian merchant communities already there. A few decades later Akbar invited Armenians to settle in his new capital, Agra. In 1603 Shah Abbas captured much of Armenia, taking it from the Ottomans. Because defending this newly acquired border area was difficult, he forced the Armenians to move more deeply into Persia. Among them was the merchant community of Julfa, which was moved to a new suburb of Isfahan that was given the name New Julfa.

Surviving letters and account books have allowed scholars to reconstruct the expanding trading networks of the Armenian merchants—networks that stretched from Venice and Amsterdam in western Europe, Moscow in Russia, Ottoman-controlled Aleppo and Smyrna, to all the major trading cities of India and even regions further east, including Guangzhou in southern China and Manila in the Philippines. Kinship connections were regularly used to cement commercial relations, and members of the community living in these scattered cities would return to New Julfa to marry, creating new kinship connections. Business, though, was conducted through contracts. The merchant about to take a journey would borrow a sum of money to purchase goods and would contract to pay it back with interest on his return.

The Armenian merchants would sail on whatever ships were available, including Dutch and Italian ones. The goods they dealt in included silver, gold, precious stones, indigo and other dyestuffs, silk, cotton cloth, and tea. The merchants often could speak half a dozen languages and were comfortable in both Islamic and Christian lands. In India Armenian merchants reached an agreement with the British East India Company that recognized their rights to live in company cities and observe their own religion. By the 1660s they had settled in Manila, and a few decades later they entered what is now Malaysia and Indonesia. By the end of the seventeenth century a small group of Armenian merchants had crossed the Himalayas from India and established themselves in Lhasa, Tibet. By the mid-eighteenth century they had also settled in the Dutch colony of Batavia (Indonesia).

In the mid-eighteenth century the Armenian community lost its center in New Julfa because of religious persecution by a zealous shah, and the community scattered. Still, Armenian merchants remained prominent in many trading centers, including Russia, the Mediterranean, and especially India, well into the nineteenth century.

From the British East India Company to the British Empire in India

Britain's presence in India began with the British East India Company and its desire to profit from trade. Managers of the company in London discouraged all unnecessary expenses and financial risks, and they thus opposed missionary activities or interference in local Indian politics. Nevertheless, the company responded to political instability in India in the early eighteenth century by extending political control. When warlords appeared or an uprising occurred, people from the surrounding countryside flocked into the company's factory-forts, which gradually came to exercise political authority over the territories around them. The company's factories evolved into defensive installations manned by small garrisons of native troops—known as sepoys—trained in Western military weapons and tactics.

sepoys The native Indian troops who were trained as infantrymen.

Britain eventually became the dominant foreign presence in India, despite challenges from the French. The French arrived in India in the 1670s and established factories in Bengal, Pondicherry, and elsewhere. They made allies of Indian princes and built an army of

What characterized the cultural flowering of the Islamic empires?

How were non-Muslims treated in the Islamic empires?

How did shifts in global trading patterns affect the Islamic empires?

What factors led to the decline of central power in the Islamic empires?

539

native troops who were trained as infantrymen. From 1740 to 1763, Britain and France were engaged in a tremendous global struggle, and India, like North America in the Seven Years' War, became a battlefield and a prize. The French won land battles, but English sea power proved decisive by preventing the landing of French reinforcements. The Treaty of Paris of 1763 recognized British control of much of India, marking the beginning of the British Empire in India.

How was Britain to govern so large a territory? Eventually, the East India Company was pushed out of its governing role because the English Parliament distrusted the company, believing it was corrupt. The Regulating Act of 1773 created the office of governor general to exercise political authority over the territory controlled by the company. The India Act of 1784 required that the governor general be chosen from outside the company, and it made company directors subject to parliamentary supervision.

Implementation of these reforms fell to three successive governors, Warren Hastings, (r. 1774–1785), Lord Charles Cornwallis (r. 1786–1794), and the marquess Richard Wellesley (r. 1797–1805). Hastings sought allies among Indian princes, laid the foundations for the first Indian civil service, abolished tolls to facilitate internal trade, placed the salt and opium trades under government control, and planned a codification of Muslim and Hindu laws. Cornwallis introduced the British style of property relations, whereby the rents of tenant farmers supported the landlords. Wellesley was victorious over local rulers who resisted British rule, vastly extending British influence in India. Like most nineteenth-century British governors of India, Wellesley believed that British rule strongly benefited the Indians.

Quick Review

How did the Islamic empires respond and adapt to the shifts in global commerce caused by European expansion?

What factors led to the decline of central power in the Islamic empires?

By the end of the eighteenth century, all three of the major Islamic empires were on the defensive and losing territory (Map 20.4). They faced some common problems—succession difficulties, financial strain, and loss of military superiority—but their circumstances differed in significant ways as well.

The first to fall was the Safavid Empire. Persia was exceptionally difficult to govern, and it did not have the revenue base to maintain the sort of standing armies that the Ottomans and the Mughals had. Decline in the strength of the army encouraged increased foreign aggression. In 1722 the Afghans invaded from the east, seized Isfahan, and were able to repulse an Ottoman invasion from the west. In Isfahan thousands of officials and members of the shah's family were executed. In the following century some potential leaders emerged, but none were able to reunite all of Persia. In this political vacuum, Shi'a religious institutions grew stronger.

The Ottoman Empire also suffered from poor leadership. Early Ottoman practice had guaranteed that the sultans would be forceful men. The sultan's sons gained administrative experience as governors of provinces and military experience on the battlefield as part of their education. After the sultan died, any son who wanted to succeed had to contest his brothers to claim the throne, after which the new sultan would have his defeated brothers executed. Although bloody, this system led to the succession of capable, determined men. After Suleiman's reign, however, the tradition was abandoned. To prevent threats of usurpation, sons of the sultan were brought up in the harem and confined there as adults. They were denied roles in government. The result was a series of rulers who were incom-

Map 20.4 **The Muslim World, ca. 1700** The three great Islamic empires were adjacent to each other and of similar physical size. Many of their other neighbors were Muslim as well.

petent or minor children, leaving power in the hands of high officials and the mothers of the heirs. Political factions formed around viziers, military leaders, and palace women. In the contest for political favor, the devshirme was abandoned, and political and military ranks were filled by Muslims.

The Ottoman Empire's military strength also declined. The defeat of the Turkish fleet by the Spanish off the coast of Greece at Lepanto in 1571 marked the loss of Ottoman dominance in the Mediterranean, and the empire's political and military setbacks continued. By the terms of a peace treaty with Austria signed at Karlowitz (1699), the Ottomans lost the major European provinces of Hungary and Transylvania, along with the tax revenues they had provided. Also, the Ottoman armies were depending more on mercenaries, and they did not keep up with the innovations in drill, command, and control that were then transforming European armies. From the late seventeenth century Ottoman armies began losing wars and territory along both northern and eastern borders. In 1730 the empire gave up territory along its eastern border. And in 1774 it lost the lands on the northern

What characterized the cultural flowering of the Islamic empires?

How were non-Muslims treated in the Islamic empires?

How did shifts in global trading patterns affect the Islamic empires?

What factors led to the decline of central power in the Islamic empires?

541

bank of the Black Sea to Russia. In North Africa the local governors came to act more independently, sometimes starting hereditary dynasties.

In Mughal India the old Turkish practice of letting heirs fight for the throne persisted, leading to frequent struggles over succession, but also to strong rulers. Yet military challenges proved daunting there as well. After defeating his father and brothers, Aurangzeb pushed the conquest of the south. The stiffest opposition came from the Marathas, a militant Hindu group centered in the western Deccan. From 1681 until his death in 1707, Aurangzeb led repeated sorties through the Deccan. He took many forts and won several battles, but total destruction of the Maratha guerrilla bands eluded him.

Aurangzeb's death led to thirteen years of succession struggles, shattering the empire. Mughal provincial governors began to rule independently, giving only minimal allegiance to the throne at Delhi. Meanwhile, the Marathas pressed steadily northward, constituting the gravest threat to Mughal authority. In 1857 the Mughal Dynasty came to an end.

In 1739 the Persian adventurer Nadir Shah invaded India, defeated the Mughal army, looted Delhi, and after a savage massacre carried off a huge amount of treasure. When Nadir Shah withdrew to Afghanistan, he took with him the Mughal government's prestige. Constant skirmishes between the Afghans and the Marathas for control of the Punjab and northern India ended in 1761 at Panipat, where the Marathas were crushed by the Afghans. At that point, India no longer had a state strong enough to impose order on the subcontinent or check the penetration of the Europeans.

In all three empires economic difficulties also put strain on the state. A long period of peace in the late sixteenth century and again in the mid-eighteenth century, as well as a decline in the frequency of visits of the plague, led to a doubling of the population. Increased population, coupled with the "little ice age" of the mid-seventeenth century, meant that the land could not sustain so many people; nor could the towns provide jobs for the thousands of agricultural workers who fled to them. The return of demobilized soldiers aggravated the problem. Inflation, famine, and widespread revolts resulted. The economic center of gravity shifted from the capital to the provinces, and politically the empire began to decentralize as well. Power was seized by local notables and military strongmen at the expense of central government officials. There was a positive side to increasing provincial autonomy, however, because it drew more people into political participation, thus laying a foundation for later nationalism. At the time, however, it was perceived in negative terms.

Quick Review

Why did the Islamic empires find it more and more difficult to defend themselves against external threats in the seventeenth and eighteenth centuries?

Connections

FROM 1300 TO 1800 and from North Africa to India, Islamic civilization thrived under three dynastic houses: the Ottomans, the Safavids, and the Mughals. All three empires had a period of expansion when territory was enlarged, followed by a high point politically and culturally, and later a period of contraction, when territories broke away. Two of the empires had large non-Muslim populations. India, even under Mughal rule, remained a predominantly Hindu land, and the Ottomans, in the process of conquering the Balkans, acquired a population that was predominantly Greek Orthodox Christians. Though all three states supported Islam, the Safavids took Shi'a teachings as orthodox, and the other two favored Sunni teachings. At the cultural level, the borders of these three states were porous, and people, ideas, art motifs, languages, and trade flowed back and forth.

In East Asia the fifteenth through eighteenth century also saw the creation of strong, prosperous, and expanding states, though in the case of China (under the Qing Dynasty) and Japan (under the Tokugawa Shogunate) the eighteenth century was a cultural high point, not a period of decline. The Qing emperors were Manchus, from the region northeast of China proper, reminiscent of the Mughals, who began in Afghanistan. As in the Islamic lands, during these centuries the presence of European powers became an issue in East Asia, though the details were quite different. Although one of the commodities that the British most wanted was the tea produced in China, Britain did not extend political control in China the way it did in India. Japan managed to refuse entry to most European traders after finding their presence and their support for missionary activity disturbing. The next chapter takes up these developments in East Asia.

- **For a list of suggested readings for this chapter, visit** *bedfordstmartins.com/mckayworldunderstanding*.

- **For primary sources from this period, see** *Sources of World Societies*, Second Edition.

- **For Web sites, images, and documents related to topics in this chapter, see Make History at** *bedfordstmartins.com/ mckayworldunderstanding*.

Chapter 20 Study Guide

To do these exercises online, go to bedfordstmartins.com/mckayworldunderstanding.

 Step 1

GETTING STARTED

Below are basic terms about this period in global history. Can you identify each term below and explain why it matters?

TERMS	WHO (OR WHAT) AND WHEN	WHY IT MATTERS
Ottomans, p. 520		
Anatolia, p. 520		
sultan, p. 520		
viziers, p. 523		
devshirme, p. 523		
janissaries, p. 523		
concubine, p. 523		
shah, p. 525		
Safavid, p. 525		
Qizilbash, p. 525		
ulama, p. 526		
Mughal, p. 526		
jizya, p. 535		
factory-forts, p. 537		
sepoys, p. 539		

Step 2

MOVING BEYOND THE BASICS

The exercise below requires a more advanced understanding of the chapter material. Compare and contrast the empires of the Ottomans, Safavids, and Mughals by filling in the chart below with descriptions of key aspects of each empire. When you are finished, consider the following questions: What role did military expansion play in all three empires? How did each imperial government use religion to reinforce and legitimize its rule? Why did slaves come to play such important roles in the Islamic empires?

	GOVERNMENT AND MILITARY	CULTURE AND RELIGION	RELATIONS WITH NON-MUSLIMS	ROLE OF SLAVES
Ottomans				
Safavids				
Mughals				

PUTTING IT ALL TOGETHER

Now that you've reviewed key elements of the chapter, take a step back and try to see the big picture. Remember to use specific examples from the chapter in your answers.

ORIGINS AND ORGANIZATION OF THE ISLAMIC EMPIRES

- How did Turkish culture and practices shape each of the empires?
- What common factors help explain the success of all three empires?

CULTURE AND SOCIETY OF THE ISLAMIC EMPIRES

- What role did religion play in the expansion and rule of each of the empires?
- What values and beliefs were reflected in the culture of the Islamic empires?

THE ISLAMIC EMPIRES IN THE SEVENTEENTH AND EIGHTEENTH CENTURIES

- What impact did European incursions have on the economies of the Islamic empires?
- What internal factors contributed to the decline of the Islamic empires? What about external factors?

LOOKING BACK, LOOKING AHEAD

- What connections between the peoples of the Islamic empires would you expect to persist long after the onset of imperial decline? Why?

In Your Own Words Imagine that you must explain Chapter 20 to someone who hasn't read it. What would be the most important points to include and why?

21

Continuity and Change in East Asia

1400–1800

The four centuries from 1400 to 1800 were a time of growth and dynamic change throughout East Asia. Although both China and Japan suffered periods of war, each ended up with expanded territories. The age of exploration brought New World crops to the region, leading to increased agricultural output and population growth. It also brought new opportunities for foreign trade and new religions. Another link between these countries was the series of Japanese invasions of Korea in the late sixteenth century, which led to war between China and Japan.

In China, the native Ming Dynasty brought an end to Mongol rule. Under the Ming, China saw agricultural reconstruction, commercial expansion, and the rise of a vibrant urban culture. In the early seventeenth century, after the Ming Dynasty fell into disorder, the non-Chinese Manchus founded the Qing Dynasty (1644–1911) and added Taiwan, Mongolia, Tibet, and Xinjiang to their realm. The Qing Empire thus was comparable to the other multiethnic empires of the early modern world, such as the Ottoman, Russian, and Habsburg Empires.

Kabuki Actor Urban entertainment flourished in Japan during the Tokugawa Shogunate. This late-eighteenth-century woodblock print was made for the many fans of a Kabuki actor who specialized in performing female roles. (Private Collection/Photo © Boltin Picture Library/The Bridgeman Art Library)

In the Japanese islands the fifteenth century saw the start of civil war that lasted a century. At the end of the sixteenth century a commoner, Hideyoshi (HEE-deh-YOH-shee), became the supreme ruler. After his death, power was seized by Tokugawa Ieyasu (toe-koo-GAH-wuh ee-yeh-YAH-soo). Under the Tokugawa Shogunate (1603–1867), Japan restricted contact with the outside world and social mobility among its own people. Yet Japan thrived, as agricultural productivity increased and a lively urban culture developed.

Chapter Preview

▶ What sort of state and society developed in China under the Ming?

▶ How did the Manchus build on Ming accomplishments?

▶ How did war and political instability shape Japan in the Middle Ages?

▶ What was life like in Japan during the Tokugawa peace?

▶ How did the arrival of Europeans change the Asian maritime sphere?

What sort of state and society developed in China under the Ming?

The story of Ming China begins with the rise of Zhu Yuanzhang (JOO-yoowan-JAHNG)—known as Taizu—to the position of emperor. He proved to be one of the most despotic emperors in Chinese history. Still, peace brought prosperity and a lively urban culture. By the beginning of the seventeenth century, however, the Ming government was beset by fiscal, military, and political problems.

The Rise of Zhu Yuanzhang and the Founding of the Ming Dynasty

Ming Dynasty The Chinese dynasty in power from 1368 to 1644; it marked a period of agricultural reconstruction, foreign expeditions, commercial expansion, and a vibrant urban culture.

The founder of the **Ming Dynasty**, Zhu Yuanzhang (1328–1398), began life in poverty during the last decades of the Mongol Yuan Dynasty. When he was only sixteen years old, his father, oldest brother, and that brother's wife all died. With no relatives to turn to, Zhu Yuanzhang asked a monastery to accept him as a novice. The monastery itself was short of funds, and the monks soon sent Zhu out to beg for food. For three or four years he wandered through central China.

A few years later, in 1351, members of a religious sect known as the Red Turbans rose in rebellion against the government. The Red Turbans met with considerable success, even defeating Mongol cavalry. When the temple where Zhu Yuanzhang was living was burned down in the fighting, Zhu joined the rebels and rose rapidly.

Zhu and his followers developed into brilliant generals, and gradually they defeated one rival after another. In 1356 Zhu took the city of Nanjing and made it his base. In 1368 his armies took Beijing, and Zhu Yuanzhang declared himself emperor of the Ming ("Bright") Dynasty. As emperor, he was known as Taizu (TIGH-dzoo) or the Hongwu emperor.

Taizu started his reign wanting to help the poor. To lighten the weight of government taxes and compulsory labor, he ordered a full-scale registration of cultivated land and population so that these burdens could be assessed more fairly. He also tried persuasion. He issued instructions to be read aloud to villagers, telling them to be obedient to their parents, live in harmony with their neighbors, work contentedly at their occupations, and refrain from evil.

Although in many ways anti-Mongol, Taizu retained some Yuan practices. One was setting up provinces as the administrative layer between the central government and the prefectures (local governments a step above counties). Another was hereditary service obligations for both artisan and military households. Any family classed as a military household had to supply a soldier at all times, replacing those who were injured, who died, or who deserted.

Taizu had deeply ambivalent feelings about men of education and sometimes humiliated them in open court, even having them beaten. His behavior was so erratic that it is most likely that he suffered from some form of mental illness. When literary men began to avoid official life, Taizu made it illegal to turn down appointments or to resign from office. He began falling into rages that only the empress could stop, and after her death in 1382 no one could calm him. In 1376 Taizu had thousands of officials killed because they were found to have taken shortcuts in their handling of paperwork related to the grain

Ming China, ca. 1600

Chapter 21 Continuity and Change in East Asia • 1400–1800

548

CHAPTER LOCATOR

What sort of state and society developed in China under the Ming?

tax. In 1380 Taizu concluded that his chancellor was plotting to assassinate him, and thousands only remotely connected to the chancellor were executed. From then on, Taizu acted as his own chancellor, dealing directly with the heads of departments and ministries.

The next important emperor, called Chengzu or the Yongle emperor (r. 1403–1425), was also a military man. One of Taizu's younger sons, he took the throne by force from his nephew and often led troops into battle against the Mongols. Like his father, Chengzu was willing to use terror to keep government officials in line.

Early in his reign, Chengzu decided to move the capital from Nanjing to Beijing, which had been his own base as a prince and the capital during Mongol times. Constructed between 1407 and 1420, Beijing was a planned city. The main outer walls were forty feet high and nearly fifteen miles around, pierced by nine gates. Inside was the Imperial City, with government offices, and within that the palace itself, called the Forbidden City, with close to ten thousand rooms.

The areas surrounding Beijing were not nearly as agriculturally productive as those around Nanjing. To supply Beijing with grain, the Yuan Grand Canal connecting the city to the rice basket of the Yangzi River regions was broadened, deepened, and supplied with more locks and dams. The 15,000 boats and the 160,000 soldiers of the transport army who pulled loaded barges from the towpaths along the canal became the lifeline of the capital.

Chapter Chronology

1368–1644	Ming Dynasty in China
1405–1433	Zheng He's naval expeditions
1407–1420	Construction of Beijing as Chinese capital
1467–1600	Period of civil war in Japan
ca. 1500–1600	Increased availability of books for general audiences in China
1549	First Jesuit missionaries land in Japan
1557	Portuguese set up trading base at Macao
1603–1867	Tokugawa Shogunate in Japan
1615	Battle of Osaka leads to persecution of Christians in Japan
1629	Tokugawa government bans actresses from the stage
1639	Japan closes its borders
1644–1911	Qing Dynasty in China
1793	Lord Macartney's diplomatic visit to China

Problems with the Imperial Institution

Taizu had decreed that succession should go to the eldest son of the empress or to the son's eldest son if the son predeceased his father, the system generally followed by earlier dynasties. In Ming times, the flaws in this system became apparent as one mediocre, obtuse, or erratic emperor followed another.

Because Taizu had abolished the position of chancellor, emperors turned to secretaries and eunuchs to manage the paperwork. Eunuchs were essentially slaves. Many boys and young men were acquired by dubious means, often from non-Chinese areas in the south, and after they were castrated, they had no option but to serve the imperial family. Society considered eunuchs the basest of servants, and Confucian scholars heaped scorn on them. Yet Ming emperors, like rulers in earlier dynasties, often preferred the always compliant eunuchs to high-minded, moralizing civil service officials.

In Ming times the eunuch establishment became huge. By the late fifteenth century the eunuch bureaucracy had grown as large as the civil service, each with roughly twelve thousand positions. After 1500 the eunuch bureaucracy grew even more rapidly, and by the mid-sixteenth century seventy thousand eunuchs were in service throughout the country. Tension between the two bureaucracies was high. In 1420 Chengzu set up a eunuch-run secret service to investigate cases of suspected corruption and sedition in the regular bureaucracy. Eunuch control over vital government processes, such as appointments, became a severe problem.

In hope of persuading emperors to make reforms, many Ming officials risked their careers and lives by speaking out. For example, in 1519, when an emperor announced plans to make a tour of the southern provinces, over a hundred officials staged a protest by kneeling in

Forbidden City The palace complex in Beijing, commonly called the Forbidden City, was built in the early fifteenth century when the capital was moved from Nanjing to Beijing. Audience halls and other important state buildings are arranged on a north-south axis with huge courtyards between them, where officials would stand during ceremonies. (www.chinahighlights.com. Photo: Virginia Zhang)

front of the palace. The emperor ordered the officials to remain kneeling for three days, then had them flogged; eleven died. The Confucian tradition celebrated these acts of political protest as heroic. Rarely, however, did they succeed in moving an emperor to change his mind.

Although the educated public complained about the performance of emperors, no one proposed alternatives to imperial rule. High officials were forced to find ways to work around uncooperative emperors, but they were not able to put in place institutions that would limit the damage an emperor could do. Knowing that strong emperors often acted erratically, many high officials came to prefer weak emperors who let them take care of the government.

The Mongols and the Great Wall

Although in Ming times the Mongols were never united in a pan-Mongol federation, groups of Mongols could and did raid. Twice they threatened the dynasty: in 1449 the khan of the western Mongols captured the Chinese emperor, and in 1550 Beijing was surrounded by the forces of the khan of the Mongols in Inner Mongolia. Fearful of anything that might strengthen the Mongols, Ming officials were reluctant to grant any privileges to Mongol leaders, such as trading posts along the borders. Instead, they wanted the different groups of Mongols to trade only through the formal tribute system. When trade was finally liberalized in 1570, friction was reduced.

Two important developments shaped Ming-Mongol relations: the construction of the Great Wall and closer relations between Mongolia and Tibet. The Great Wall was built as a compromise when Ming officials could agree on no other way to manage the Mongol threat. The wall extends about 1,500 miles from northeast of Beijing into Gansu province. In the eastern 500 miles, the wall averages about 35 feet high and 20 feet across, with lookout towers every half mile.

Whether the wall did much to protect Ming China from the Mongols is still debated. Perhaps of more significance was the spread of Tibetan Buddhism among the Mongols.

CHAPTER LOCATOR

What sort of state and society developed in China under the Ming?

Tibet in this period was largely ruled by the major Buddhist monasteries. When Tibetan monasteries needed military assistance, they asked competing Mongol leaders for help, and many struggles were decided by Mongol military intervention. The Tibetan Buddhist Tsong-kha-pa (1357–1419) founded the Yellow Hat or Gelug-pa sect, whose heads later became known as the Dalai Lamas. In 1577 the third Dalai Lama accepted the invitation of Altan Khan to visit Mongolia, and the khan declared Tibetan Buddhism to be the official religion of all the Mongols. The Dalai Lama gave the khan the title "King of Religion," and the khan swore that the Mongols would renounce blood sacrifice. When the third Dalai Lama's reincarnation was found to be the great-grandson of Altan Khan, the ties between Tibet and Mongolia became even stronger.

The Examination Life

In sharp contrast to Europe in this era, Ming China had few social barriers. Although China had no hereditary, titled aristocracy, it did have an elite whose status was based above all on government office acquired through education. Unlike in many European countries of the era, China's merchants did not become a politically articulate bourgeoisie. Instead, the politically active class was that of the scholars who Confucianism taught should aid the ruler in running the state. With the possible exception of the Jewish people, no people have respected learning as much as the Chinese. Merchants tried to marry into the scholar class in order to rise in the world.

Thus, despite the harsh and arbitrary ways in which the Ming emperors treated their civil servants, educated men were eager to enter the government. Reversing the policies of the Mongol Yuan Dynasty, the Ming government recruited almost all of its officials through **civil service examinations**. Candidates had to study the Confucian classics and the interpretations of them by the twelfth-century Neo-Confucian scholar Zhu Xi (joo shee; 1130–1200), whose teachings were declared orthodox. To become officials, candidates had to pass examinations at the prefecture, the provincial, and the capital levels. To keep the wealthiest areas from dominating the exams, quotas were established for the number of candidates that each province could send on to the capital.

Of course, boys from well-to-do families had a significant advantage because their families could start their education with tutors at age four or five, though less costly schools were becoming increasingly available as well. Families that for generations had pursued other careers—for example, as merchants or physicians (see "Individuals in Society: Tan Yunxian, Woman Doctor," page 552)—had more opportunities than ever for their sons to become officials through the exams. Most of those who attended school stayed only a few years, but students who seemed most promising moved on to advanced schools where they would practice essay writing and study the essays of men who had succeeded in the exams.

The examinations at the prefecture level lasted a day and drew hundreds if not thousands of candidates. Successful candidates moved on to the provincial examinations, which were major local events. From five thousand to ten thousand candidates descended on the provincial capital and filled up its hostels. Candidates would show up a week in advance to present their credentials and gather the supplies they needed to survive in their small exam cells. To prevent cheating, no written material could be taken into the cells, and candidates were searched before being admitted. During the sessions candidates had time to write rough drafts of their essays, correct them, and then copy neat final versions.

After the papers were handed in, clerks recopied them and assigned them numbers to preserve anonymity. The grading generally took about twenty days, and most candidates stayed in the vicinity to await the results. Those few who passed (generally from 2 to 10 percent) were invited to the governor's compound for a celebration. They could not spend long celebrating, however, because they had to begin preparing for the capital exams, less than a year away.

civil service examinations
A highly competitive series of tests held at the prefecture, province, and capital levels to select men to become officials.

How did the Manchus build on Ming accomplishments?

How did war and political instability shape Japan in the Middle Ages?

What was life like in Japan during the Tokugawa peace?

How did the arrival of Europeans change the Asian maritime sphere?

551

THE GRANDMOTHER OF TAN YUNXIAN (tahn Yunshyen) (1461–1554) was the daughter of a physician, and her husband had married into her home to learn medicine himself. At least two of their sons — including Yunxian's father — passed the civil service examination and became officials, raising the social standing of the family considerably. The grandparents wanted to pass their medical knowledge down to someone, and because they found Yunxian very bright, they decided to teach it to her.

Yunxian married and raised four children but also practiced medicine, confining her practice to women. At age fifty she wrote an autobiographical account, *Sayings of a Female Doctor*. In the preface she described how, under her grandmother's tutelage, she had first memorized the *Canon of Problems* and the *Canon of the Pulse*. Then when her grandmother had time, she asked her granddaughter to explain particular passages in these classic medical treatises.

Yunxian began the practice of medicine by treating her own children, asking her grandmother to check her diagnoses. When her grandmother was old and ill, she gave Yunxian her notebook of prescriptions and her equipment for making medicines, telling her to study them carefully. Later, Yunxian herself became seriously ill and dreamed of her grandmother telling her on what page of which book to find the prescription that would cure her. When she recovered, she began her medical career in earnest.

Yunxian's book records the cases of thirty-one patients she treated, most of them women with chronic complaints rather than critical illnesses. Many of the women had what the Chinese classed as women's complaints, such as menstrual irregularities, repeated miscarriages, barrenness, and postpartum fatigue. Some had ailments that men too could suffer, such as coughs, nausea, insomnia, diarrhea, rashes, and swellings. Like other literati physicians, Yunxian regularly prescribed herbal medications. She also practiced moxibustion, the technique of burning moxa (dried artemisia) at specified points on the body with the goal of stimulating the circulation of *qi* (life energy). Because the physician applying the moxa had to touch the patient, male physicians could not perform moxibustion on women.

Yunxian's patients included working women, and Yunxian seems to have thought that their problems often sprang from overwork. One woman came to her because she had had vaginal bleeding for three years. When questioned, the woman told Yunxian that she worked all day with her husband at their kiln making bricks and tiles. Yunxian's diagnosis was overwork, and she gave the woman pills to replenish her yin. A boatman's wife came to her complaining of numbness in her hands. When the woman told Yunxian that she worked in the wind and rain handling the boat, the doctor advised some time off. In another case Yunxian explained to a servant girl that she had gone back to work too soon after suffering a wind damage fever.

By contrast, when patients came from upper-class families, Yunxian believed negative emotions were the source of their problems, particularly if a woman reported that her mother-in-law had scolded her or that her husband had recently brought a concubine home. Yunxian told two upper-class women who had miscarried that they lost their babies because they had hidden their anger, causing fire to turn inward and destabilize the fetus.

Tan Yunxian herself lived a long life, dying at age ninety-three.

Source: Based on Charlotte Furth, *A Flourishing Yin: Gender in China's Medical History, 960–1665* (Berkeley: University of California Press, 1999), pp. 285–295.

QUESTIONS FOR ANALYSIS

1. Why do you think Tan Yunxian treated only women? Why might she have been more effective with women patients than a male physician would have been?
2. What do you think of Yunxian's diagnoses? Do you think she was able to help many of her patients?

Tan Yunxian would have consulted traditional herbals, like this one, with sketches of plants of medicinal value and descriptions of their uses. (Wellcome Library, London)

CHAPTER LOCATOR

What sort of state and society developed in China under the Ming?

Everyday Life in Ming China

For civil servants and almost everyone else, everyday life in Ming China followed patterns established in earlier periods. The family remained central to most people's lives, and almost everyone married. Beyond the family, people's lives were shaped by the type of work they did and where they lived.

Large towns and cities proliferated in Ming times. In these urban areas small businesses manufactured textiles, paper, and luxury goods such as silks and porcelains. The southeast became a center for the production of cotton and silks; other areas specialized in the grain and salt trades and in silver. Merchants could make fortunes moving these goods across the country.

Printing was invented in Tang times (618–907) and had a great impact on the life of the educated elite in Song times (960–1279), but not until Ming times did it transform the culture of the urban middle classes. By the late Ming period publishing houses were putting out large numbers of books aimed at general audiences. These included fiction, reference books of all sorts, and popular religious tracts. By the sixteenth century more and more books were being published in the vernacular language (the language people spoke), especially short stories, novels, and plays. Ming vernacular short stories depicted a world much like that of their readers, full of shop clerks and merchants, monks and prostitutes, students and matchmakers.

The full-length novel made its first appearance during the Ming period. The plots of the early novels were heavily indebted to story cycles developed by oral storytellers over the

Popular Romance Literature Women were among the most avid readers of the scripts for plays, especially romantic ones like *The Western Chamber*, a story of a young scholar who falls in love with a well-educated girl he encounters by chance. In this scene, the young woman looks up at the moon as her maid looks at its reflection in the pond. Meanwhile, her young lover scales the wall. This multicolor woodblock print, made in 1640, was one of twenty-one created to illustrate the play. (Museum für Ostasiatische Kunst, Köln, Inv.-No. R 61,2 [No. 11]. Photo: Rheinisches Bildarchiv, Köln)

How did the Manchus build on Ming accomplishments?

How did war and political instability shape Japan in the Middle Ages?

What was life like in Japan during the Tokugawa peace?

How did the arrival of Europeans change the Asian maritime sphere?

553

course of several centuries. *Water Margin* is the episodic tale of a band of bandits, while *The Romance of the Three Kingdoms* is a work of historical fiction based on the exploits of the generals and statesmen contending for power at the end of the Han Dynasty. *Plum in the Golden Vase* is a novel of manners about a lustful merchant with a wife and five concubines. Competing publishers brought out their own editions of these novels, sometimes adding new illustrations or commentaries.

The Chinese found recreation and relaxation in many ways besides reading. The affluent indulged in an alcoholic drink made from fermented and distilled rice, and once tobacco was introduced from the Americas, both men and women took up pipes. Plays were also very popular. The Jesuit missionary Matteo Ricci, who lived in China from 1583 to 1610, described resident troupes in large cities and traveling troupes that "journey everywhere throughout the length and breadth of the country" putting on plays. The leaders of the troupes would purchase young children and train them to sing and perform.

More than bread in Europe, rice supplied most of the calories of the population in central and south China. (In north China, wheat, made into steamed or baked bread or into noodles, served as the dietary staple.) In the south, terracing and irrigation of mountain slopes, introduced in the eleventh century, had increased rice harvests. Other innovations also brought good results. Farmers began to stock the rice paddies with fish, which continuously fertilized the rice fields, destroyed malaria-bearing mosquitoes, and enriched the diet. Farmers also cultivated cotton, sugarcane, and indigo for the commercial market. New methods of crop rotation allowed for continuous cultivation and for more than one harvest per year from a single field.

The Ming rulers promoted the repopulation and colonization of war-devastated regions through reclamation of land and massive transfers of people. Immigrants to these areas received large plots and exemption from taxation for many years. Reforestation played a dramatic role in the agricultural revolution. In 1391 the Ming government ordered 50 million trees planted in the Nanjing area to produce lumber for the construction of a maritime fleet. In 1392 each family holding colonized land in Anhui province had to plant two hundred mulberry, jujube, and persimmon trees. In 1396 peasants in the present-day provinces of Hunan and Hubei in central China planted 84 million fruit trees. Historians have estimated that 1 billion trees were planted during Taizu's reign.

Increased food production led to steady population growth and the multiplication of markets, towns, and small cities. Larger towns had permanent shops; smaller towns had periodic markets. They sold essential goods—such as pins, matches, oil for lamps, candles, paper, incense, and tobacco—to country people from the surrounding hamlets. Markets usually included moneylenders, pawnbrokers, a tearoom, and sometimes a wine shop where tea and rice wine were sold and entertainers performed. Tradesmen carrying their wares on their backs and craftsmen—carpenters, barbers, joiners, locksmiths—moved constantly from market to market.

Ming Decline

Beginning in the 1590s the Ming government was beset by fiscal, military, and political problems. The government went nearly bankrupt helping defend Korea against a Japanese invasion (see page 566). Then came a series of natural disasters: floods, droughts, locusts, and epidemics ravaged one region after another. At the same time, a "little ice age" brought a drop in average temperatures that shortened the growing season and reduced harvests. In areas of serious food shortages, gangs of ex-soldiers began scouring the countryside in search of food. Once the gangs had stolen all their grain, hard-pressed farmers joined them just to survive. The Ming government had little choice but to try to increase taxes to deal with these threats, but the last thing people needed was heavier taxes.

554   **Chapter 21 Continuity and Change in East Asia • 1400–1800**

CHAPTER LOCATOR

What sort of state and society developed in China under the Ming?

Adding to the hardship was a sudden drop in the supply of silver. In place of the paper money that had circulated in Song and Yuan times, silver ingots came into general use as money in Ming times. Much of this silver originated in either Japan or the New World and entered China as payment for the silk and porcelains exported from China (see page 428). When events in Japan and the Philippines led to disruption of trade, silver imports dropped. This led to deflation in China, which caused real rents to rise. Soon there were riots among urban workers and tenant farmers. In 1642 a group of rebels cut the dikes on the Yellow River, causing massive flooding. A smallpox epidemic soon added to the death toll. In 1644 the last Ming emperor, in despair, took his own life when rebels entered Beijing, opening the way for the start of a new dynasty.

Quick Review
Did the Ming government play much of a role in promoting China's growth and prosperity during this period? How so?

How did the Manchus build on Ming accomplishments?

The next dynasty, the Qing Dynasty (1644–1911), was founded by the Manchus, a non-Chinese people who were descended from the Jurchens. In the late sixteenth century the Manchus began expanding their territories, and in 1644 they founded the Qing (ching) Dynasty, which brought peace and in time prosperity. Successful Qing military campaigns extended the borders into Mongol, Tibetan, and Uighur regions, creating a multiethnic empire that was larger than any earlier Chinese dynasty.

Qing Dynasty The dynasty founded by the Manchus that ruled China from 1644 to 1911.

The Rise of the Manchus

In the Ming period the Manchus lived in dispersed communities in what is loosely called Manchuria (the northeast of modern-day China). In the more densely populated southern part of Manchuria, the Manchus lived in close contact with Mongols, Koreans, and Chinese (Map 21.1). They were not nomads but rather hunters, fishers, and farmers. Like the Mongols, they had a strongly hierarchical social structure, with elites and slaves. Slaves, often Korean or Chinese, were generally acquired through capture. Villages were often at odds with each other over resources, and men did not leave their villages without arming themselves. Interspersed among these Manchu settlements were groups of nomadic Mongols who lived in tents.

The Manchus credited their own rise to Nurhaci (1559–1626). Over several decades, he united the Manchus and expanded their territories. Like Chinggis Khan, who had reorganized the Mongol armies to reduce the importance of tribal affiliations, Nurhaci created a new social basis for his armies in units called banners. Each banner was made up of a set of military companies and included the families and slaves of the soldiers. Each company had a hereditary captain. Over time new companies and new banners were formed, and by 1644 there were eight each of Manchu, Mongol, and Chinese banners. When new groups were defeated, their members were distributed among several banners to lessen their potential for subversion.

banners Units of the Qing army, composed of soldiers, their families, and slaves.

The Manchus entered China by invitation of the Ming general Wu Sangui, himself a native of southern Manchuria, who was near the eastern end of the Great Wall when he heard that the rebels had captured Beijing. The Manchus proposed to Wu that they join forces and liberate Beijing. Wu opened the gates of the Great Wall to let the Manchus in, and within a couple of weeks they occupied Beijing. When the Manchus made clear that they intended to conquer the rest of the country and take the throne themselves, Wu and

Map 21.1 The Qing Empire, ca. 1800

The sheer size of the Qing Empire in China almost inevitably led to its profound cultural influence on the rest of Asia.

ANALYZING THE MAP How many different cultural groups are depicted? Which occupied the largest territories? Where was crop agriculture most prevalent?

CONNECTIONS What geographical and political factors limited the expansion of the Qing Empire?

many other Chinese generals joined forces with them. Before long, China was again under alien rule. However, most of the political institutions of the Ming Dynasty were taken over relatively unchanged, including the examination system.

After peace was achieved, population growth took off. Between 1700 and 1800 the Chinese population seems to have nearly doubled, from about 150 million to over 300 million. Population growth during the eighteenth century has been attributed to many factors: global warming that extended the growing season, expanded use of New World crops, slowing of the spread of new diseases that had accompanied the sixteenth-century expansion of global traffic, and the efficiency of the Qing government in providing relief in times of famine.

Competent and Long-Lived Emperors

For more than a century, China was ruled by only three rulers, each of them hardworking, talented, and committed to making the Qing Dynasty a success. Two, the Kangxi and Qianlong emperors, had exceptionally long reigns.

**Chapter 21 Continuity and Change
in East Asia • 1400–1800**

556

CHAPTER LOCATOR

What sort of state and society developed in China under the Ming?

Kangxi (r. 1661–1722) proved adept at meeting the expectations of both the Chinese and the Manchu elites. Kangxi (KAHNG-shee) could speak, read, and write Chinese, and he made efforts to persuade educated Chinese that the Manchus had a legitimate claim to rule, even trying to attract Ming loyalists who had been unwilling to serve the Qing. He undertook a series of tours of the south, where Ming loyalty had been strongest, and he held a special exam to select men to compile the official history of the Ming Dynasty.

Kangxi's son and heir, the Yongzheng emperor (r. 1722–1735), was also a hardworking ruler who took an interest in the efficiency of the government. Because his father had lived so long, he did not come to the throne until his mid-forties and reigned only thirteen years. His successor, however, the Qianlong emperor (r. 1736–1796), like Kangxi had a reign of sixty years.

Qianlong (chyan-loong) understood that the Qing's capacity to hold the multiethnic empire together rested on their ability to appeal to all those they ruled. Besides speaking Manchu and Chinese, Qianlong learned to converse in Mongolian, Uighur, Tibetan, and Tangut, and he addressed envoys in their own languages. He became as much a patron of Tibetan Buddhism as of Chinese Confucianism. He initiated a massive project to translate the Tibetan Buddhist canon into Mongolian and Manchu and had huge multilingual dictionaries compiled.

To demonstrate to the Chinese scholar-official elite that he was a sage emperor, Qianlong worked on affairs of state from dawn until early afternoon and then turned to reading, painting, and calligraphy. He was ostentatious in his devotion to his mother, visiting her daily and tending to her comfort with all the devotion of the most filial Chinese son.

Through Qianlong's reign, China remained an enormous producer of manufactured goods and led the way in assembly-line production. The government operated huge textile factories, but some private firms were even larger. Hangzhou had a textile firm that gave work to four thousand weavers, twenty thousand spinners, and ten thousand dyers and finishers. The porcelain kilns at Jingdezhen employed the division of labor on a large scale and were able to supply porcelain to much of the world. The growth of the economy benefited the Qing state, and the treasury became so full that the Qianlong emperor was able to cancel taxes on several occasions.

Imperial Expansion

The Qing Dynasty put together a multiethnic empire that was larger than any earlier Chinese dynasty. Taiwan was acquired in 1683 after Qing armies pursued a rebel there. Mongolia was acquired next. In 1696 Kangxi led an army into Mongolia, and within a few years Manchu supremacy was accepted there. Cannon and muskets gave Qing forces military superiority over the Mongols, who were armed only with bows and arrows. Thus the Qing could dominate the steppe cheaply, effectively ending two thousand years of Inner Asian military advantage.

In the 1720s the Qing established a permanent garrison of banner soldiers in Tibet. By this time, the expanding Qing and Russian Empires were nearing each other. In 1689 the Manchu and the Russian rulers approved a treaty defining their borders in Manchuria and regulating trade. Another treaty in 1727 allowed a Russian ecclesiastical mission to reside in Beijing and a trade caravan to make a trip from Russia to Beijing once every three years.

The last region to be annexed was Chinese Turkestan (the modern province of Xinjiang). The Qing won the region in the 1750s through a series of campaigns against Uighur and Dzungar Mongol forces.

Quick Review
What innovations were introduced by the first three Qing emperors? What Ming policies and institutions did they retain?

How did war and political instability shape Japan in the Middle Ages?

In the twelfth century Japan entered an era that can be compared to Europe's feudal age. The Kamakura Shogunate (1185–1333) had its capital in the east, at Kamakura. It was succeeded by the Ashikaga Shogunate (1336–1573), which returned the government to Kyoto (KYOH-toh) and helped launch, during the fifteenth century, the great age of Zen-influenced Muromachi culture. The sixteenth century brought civil war over succession to the shogunate.

Muromachi Culture

The headquarters of the Ashikaga shoguns were on Muromachi Street in Kyoto, and the refined and elegant style that they promoted is often called Muromachi culture. The shoguns patronized Zen Buddhism, the school of Buddhism associated with meditation and mind-to-mind transmission of truth. Because Zen monks were able to read and write Chinese, they often assisted the shoguns in handling foreign affairs.

Zen ideas of simplicity permeated the arts. The Silver Pavilion built by the shogun Yoshimasa (r. 1449–1473) epitomizes Zen austerity. A white sand cone constructed in the temple garden was designed to reflect moonlight. Yoshimasa was also influential in the development of the tea ceremony. Aesthetes celebrated the beauty of imperfect objects, such as plain or misshapen cups or pots. Spare monochrome paintings fit into this aesthetic, as did simple asymmetrical flower arrangements.

The shoguns were also patrons of the **Nō theater**. Nō drama originated in popular forms of entertainment. It was transformed into high art by Zeami (1363–1443), an actor and playwright who also wrote on the aesthetic theory of Nō. Nō was performed on a bare stage with a pine tree painted across the backdrop. One or two actors wearing brilliant brocade robes would perform, using stylized gestures and stances. The actors would be accompanied by a chorus and a couple of musicians playing drums and flute. Zeami argued that the most meaningful moments came during silence, when the actor's spiritual presence allowed the audience to catch a glimpse of the mysterious and inexpressible.

Nō theater A type of Japanese theater in which performers convey emotions and ideas as much through gestures, stances, and dress as through words.

Civil War

Civil war began in Kyoto in 1467 as a struggle over succession to the shogunate. Rival claimants and their followers used arson as their chief weapon and burned down temples and mansions, destroying much of the city and its treasures. Once Kyoto was laid waste, war spread to outlying areas. When the shogun could no longer protect cities, merchants banded together to hire mercenaries. In the political vacuum, the Lotus League, a commoner-led religious sect, set up a commoner-run government that collected taxes and settled disputes. In 1536, during eight days of fighting, the powerful Buddhist monastery Enryakuji attacked the League and its temples, burned much of the city, and killed men, women, and children thought to be believers.

In these confused and violent circumstances, power devolved to the local level, where warlords, called **daimyo** (DIGH-mee-oh), built their power bases. Unlike earlier power holders, these new lords were not appointed by the court or shogunate and did not send taxes to absentee overlords. Instead they seized what they needed and used it to build up their territories and recruit more samurai. To raise revenues they surveyed the land and

daimyo Regional lords in Japan; many had built their power by seizing what they needed and promoting irrigation and trade to raise revenues.

558 Chapter 21 Continuity and Change in East Asia • 1400–1800

CHAPTER LOCATOR

What sort of state and society developed in China under the Ming?

promoted irrigation and trade. Many of the most successful daimyo were self-made men who rose from obscurity.

The violence of the period encouraged castle building. The castles were surrounded by moats and walls made from huge stones. Inside a castle was a many-storied keep. Though relatively safe from incendiary missiles, the keeps were vulnerable to Western-style cannon, introduced in the 1570s. Many of the castles had splendid living quarters for the daimyo.

The Victors: Nobunaga and Hideyoshi

The first daimyo to gain a predominance of power was Oda Nobunaga (1534–1582). A samurai of the lesser daimyo class, he recruited followers from masterless samurai who had been living by robbery and extortion. After he won control of his native province in 1559, he immediately set out to extend his power through central Japan. A key step was destroying the military power of the great monasteries. To raise revenues, he promoted trade by eliminating customs barriers and opening the little fishing village of Nagasaki to foreign commerce; it soon became Japan's largest port.

Reunification campaign

Campaign against Korea

Hideyoshi's Campaigns in Japan and Korea, 1537–1598

In 1582, in an attempted coup, Nobunaga was forced by one of his vassals to commit suicide. His general and staunchest adherent, Toyotomi Hideyoshi (1537–1598), avenged him and continued the drive toward unification of the daimyo-held lands.

Like the Ming founder, Hideyoshi was a peasant's son who rose to power through military talent. In a few short years, he brought all of Japan under his control. Hideyoshi soothed the vanquished daimyo as Nobunaga had done—with lands and military positions—but he also required them to swear allegiance and to obey him down to the smallest particular. For the first time in over two centuries, Japan had a single ruler.

Hideyoshi did his best to ensure that future peasants' sons would not be able to rise as he had. His great sword hunt of 1588 collected weapons from farmers, who were no longer allowed to wear swords. Restrictions were also placed on samurai; they were prohibited from leaving their lord's service or switching occupations. To improve tax collection, Hideyoshi ordered a survey of the entire country. His surveys not only tightened tax collection but also registered each peasant household and tied the peasants to the land. With the country pacified, Hideyoshi embarked on an ill-fated attempt to conquer Korea and China that ended only with his death, discussed below (see page 566).

Quick Review
Who were the daimyo and how did their status and power reflect conditions during Japan's Middle Ages?

What was life like in Japan during the Tokugawa peace?

On his deathbed, Hideyoshi set up a council of regents to govern during the minority of his infant son. The strongest regent was Hideyoshi's long-time supporter Tokugawa Ieyasu (1543–1616), who ruled vast territories around Edo (AY-doh; modern-day Tokyo). In 1600

How did the Manchus build on Ming accomplishments?

How did war and political instability shape Japan in the Middle Ages?

What was life like in Japan during the Tokugawa peace?

How did the arrival of Europeans change the Asian maritime sphere?

559

Map 21.2 Tokugawa Japan, 1603–1867 The lands that the shogunate directly controlled were concentrated near its capital at Edo. The daimyo of distant places, such as the island of Kyushu, were required to make long journeys to and from Edo every year.

at Sekigahara, Ieyasu smashed a coalition of daimyo defenders of the heir and began building his own government. In 1603 he took the title "shogun." The Tokugawa Shogunate that Ieyasu fashioned lasted until 1867. This era is also called the Edo period after the location of the shogunate, starting Tokyo's history as Japan's most important city (Map 21.2).

Tokugawa Government

In the course of the seventeenth century the Tokugawa shoguns worked to consolidate relations with the daimyo. In a scheme resembling the later residency requirements imposed by Louis XIV in France (see page 440) and Peter the Great in Russia (see page 449), Ieyasu set up the alternate residence system, which compelled the lords to live in Edo every other year and to leave their wives and sons there—essentially as hostages. This arrangement had obvious advantages: the shogun could keep tabs on the daimyo, control them through their wives and children, and weaken them financially with the burden of maintaining two residences.

The peace imposed by the Tokugawa Shogunate brought a steady rise in population. To maintain stability, the early Tokugawa shoguns froze social status. Laws rigidly prescribed what each class could and could not do. Nobles, for example, were strictly forbidden to walk through the streets or lanes in places where they had no business to be. Daimyo were prohibited from moving troops outside their frontiers, making alliances, and coining money. As intended, these rules protected the Tokugawa shoguns from daimyo attack and helped ensure a long era of peace.

The early Tokugawa shoguns also restricted the construction and repair of castles—symbols, in Japan as in medieval Europe, of feudal independence. Continuing Hideyoshi's policy, the Tokugawa regime enforced a policy of complete separation of samurai and peas-

Tokugawa Shogunate The Japanese government founded by Tokugawa Ieyasu that lasted from 1603 until 1867; it is also called the Edo period because the shogunate was located at Edo.

alternate residence system Arrangement in which lords lived in Edo every other year and left their wives and sons there as hostages.

560

Chapter 21 Continuity and Change in East Asia • 1400–1800

CHAPTER LOCATOR

What sort of state and society developed in China under the Ming?

Interior of Nijo Castle To assert control over the imperial court and the city of Kyoto, Tokugawa Ieyasu built palace-like Nijo Castle there in 1601–1603. He had the sliding doors painted by leading artists of the period, making the castle as elegant as the imperial palace. (From Fujioka Michio, *Genshoku Nihon no Bijutsu*, Vol. 12: Shiro to Shoin [Tokyo: Shogakkan, 1968])

ants. Samurai were defined as those permitted to carry swords. They had to live in castles (which evolved into castle-towns), and they depended on stipends from their lords, the daimyo. Samurai were effectively prevented from establishing ties to the land, so they could not become landholders. Likewise, merchants and artisans had to live in towns and could not own land. Japanese castle-towns evolved into bustling, sophisticated urban centers.

After 1639 Japan limited its contacts with the outside world because of concerns about both the loyalty of subjects converted to Christianity by European missionaries and about the imperialist ambitions of European powers (discussed below). However, China remained an important trading partner and source of ideas. For example, Neo-Confucianism gained a stronger hold among the samurai-turned bureaucrats. The period also saw the development of a school of native learning that rejected Buddhism and Confucianism as alien and tried to identify a distinctly Japanese sensibility.

Commercialization and the Growth of Towns

During the civil war period, warfare seems to have promoted social and economic change, much as it had in China during the Warring States Period (403–221 B.C.E.). Trade grew, and greater use was made of coins imported from Ming China. Markets began appearing at river crossings, at the entrances to temples and shrines, and at other places where people congregated. Towns and cities sprang up all around the country, some of them around the new castles. Traders and artisans began forming guilds. Foreign trade also flourished, despite chronic problems with pirates who raided the Japanese, Korean, and Chinese coasts (see page 566).

Recent scholarship demonstrates that the Tokugawa era witnessed the foundations of modern Japanese capitalism: the development of a cash economy, the use of money to make more money, the accumulation of large amounts of capital for investment in factory or technological enterprises, the growth of business ventures operating over a national network of roads, and the expansion of wage labor. These developments occurred simultaneously with, but entirely independent of, similar changes in Europe.

In most cities, merchant families with special privileges from the government controlled the urban economy. Frequently, a particular family dominated the local trade in a particular product and then branched out into other businesses and into other regions.

Japanese merchant families also devised distinct patterns and procedures for their business operations. What today is called "family-style management principles" determined the age of apprenticeship (between eleven and thirteen); the employee's detachment from past social relations and adherence to the norms of a particular family business; salaries; seniority as the basis of promotion, although job performance at the middle rungs determined who reached the higher ranks; and the time for retirement. All employees in a family business were expected to practice frugality, resourcefulness, self-denial, and careful accounting. These values formed the basis of what has been called the Japanese "industrious revolution." They help to explain how, after the Meiji (MAY-jee) Restoration of 1867 (see page 707), Japan was able to industrialize rapidly and compete successfully with the West.

In the seventeenth century underemployed farmers and samurai, not to mention the ambitious and adventurous, thronged to the cities. As a result, Japan's cities grew tremendously. Kyoto became the center for the manufacture of luxury goods like lacquer, brocade, and fine porcelain. Osaka was the chief market, especially for rice. Edo was a center of consumption by the daimyo, their vassals, and government bureaucrats. Both Osaka and Edo reached about a million residents.

Two hundred and fifty towns came into being in this period. Most ranged in size from 3,000 to 20,000 people, but a few, such as Hiroshima, Kagoshima, and Nagoya, had populations of between 65,000 and 100,000. In addition, perhaps two hundred towns along the main road to Edo emerged to meet the needs of men traveling on the alternate residence system. In the eighteenth century perhaps 4 million people, 15 percent of the Japanese population, resided in cities or towns.

The Life of the People in the Edo Period

The Tokugawa shoguns brought an end to civil war by controlling the military. Stripped of power and required to spend alternate years at Edo, many of the daimyo and samurai passed their lives in idle pursuit of pleasure, spending extravagantly. Eighteenth-century Japanese novels, plays, and histories portray the samurai engrossed in tavern brawls and sexual orgies. These temptations, as well as more sophisticated pleasures and the heavy costs of maintaining alternate residences at Edo, gradually bankrupted the warrior class.

All major cities contained places of amusement for men — teahouses, theaters, restaurants, and houses of prostitution. Poor parents sometimes sold their daughters to entertainment houses (as they did in China and medieval Europe), and the most attractive or talented girls, trained in singing, dancing, and conversational arts, became courtesans, later called geishas (GAY-shuhz), "accomplished persons."

kabuki theater A popular form of Japanese drama that brings together dialogue, dance, and music to tell stories. The actors wear colorful costumes and dramatic makeup.

Another form of entertainment in the cities was **kabuki theater**, patronized by both merchants and samurai. An art form created by townspeople, kabuki originated in crude, bawdy skits dealing with love and romance. Performances featured elaborate costumes, song, dance, and poetry. Because actresses were thought to corrupt public morals, the Tokugawa government banned them from the stage in 1629. From that time on, men played all the parts.

Cities were also the center for commercial publishing. As in contemporary China, the reading public eagerly purchased fiction and the scripts for plays. Ihara Saikaku (1642–1693) wrote stories of the foibles of townspeople in such books as *Five Women Who Loved*

562 Chapter 21 Continuity and Change in East Asia • 1400–1800

CHAPTER LOCATOR

What sort of state and society developed in China under the Ming?

Picturing the Past

Interior View of a Theater

Complex kabuki plays, which dealt with heroes, loyalty, and tragedy and which included music and dance, became the most popular form of entertainment in Tokugawa Japan for all classes. Movable scenery and lighting effects made possible the staging of storms, fires, and hurricanes.
(Tokyo National Museum/image: TNM Image Archives)

ANALYZING THE IMAGE How many people are performing in this scene? Are there more men or women in the audience? How do you distinguish them? Are any of the men samurai?

CONNECTIONS What connections do you see between the popularity of kabuki plays and other aspects of Japanese life in this period?

Love and *The Life of an Amorous Man*. The art of color woodblock printing also was perfected during this period. Many of the surviving prints, made for a popular audience, depict the theater and women of the entertainment quarters.

Almost as entertaining was watching the long processions of daimyo, their retainers, and their luggage as they passed back and forth to and from Edo twice a year. The shogunate prohibited travel by commoners, but they could get passports to take pilgrimages, visit relatives, or seek the soothing waters of medicinal hot springs. Setting out on foot, groups of villagers would often take detours from their authorized journey to visit Osaka or Edo to sightsee or attend the theater.

According to Japanese tradition, farmers deserved respect. In practice, however, peasants were often treated callously. It was government policy to tax them to the level of bare

How did the Manchus build on Ming accomplishments?

How did war and political instability shape Japan in the Middle Ages?

What was life like in Japan during the Tokugawa peace?

How did the arrival of Europeans change the Asian maritime sphere?

563

subsistence, and during the seventeenth and eighteenth centuries the extravagant lifestyles of the daimyo and upper-level samurai were paid for by raising taxes on their subordinate peasants, from 30 or 40 percent of the rice crop to 50 percent. Not surprisingly, this angered peasants, and peasant protests became chronic during the eighteenth century. For example, oppressive taxation provoked eighty-four thousand farmers in the province of Iwaki to revolt in 1739; after widespread burning and destruction, their demands for lower taxes were met. Natural disasters also added to the peasants' misery. In 1783 Mount Asama erupted, spewing volcanic ash that darkened the skies all summer; the resulting crop failures led to famine. When famine recurred again in 1787, commoners rioted for five days in Edo, smashing merchants' stores and pouring sake and rice into the muddy streets.

This picture of peasant hardship tells only part of the story. Agricultural productivity increased substantially during the Tokugawa period. Peasants who improved their lands and increased their yields continued to pay the same assessed tax and could pocket the surplus as profit. As those without land drifted to the cities, peasants left in the countryside found ways to improve their livelihoods. At Hirano near Osaka, for example, more than half of the arable land was sown in cotton. The peasants ginned the cotton locally before transporting it to wholesalers in Osaka. In many rural places, as many peasants worked in the manufacture of silk, cotton, or vegetable oil as in the production of rice.

In comparison to farmers, merchants had a much easier life, even if they had no political power. By contemporary standards anywhere in the world, the Japanese mercantile class lived well. While few merchants possessed truly fabulous wealth, many lived in comfort, if not luxury.

Within a village, some families would be relatively well-off, others barely able to get by. The village headman generally came from the richest family, but he consulted a council of elders on important matters. Women in better-off families were much more likely to learn to read than women in poor families. Daughters of wealthy peasants studied penmanship, the Chinese classics, poetry, and the proper forms of correspondence, and they rounded out their education with travel. By contrast, girls from middle-level peasant families might have had from two to five years of formal schooling, but their education focused on moral instruction intended to instill virtue.

By the fifteenth and sixteenth centuries Japan's family and marriage systems had evolved in the direction of a patrilocal, patriarchal system more like China's, and Japanese women had lost the prominent role in high society that they had occupied during the Heian period. It became standard for women to move into their husbands' homes, where they occupied positions subordinate to both their husbands and their mothers-in-law. In addition, elite families stopped dividing their property among all of their children; instead they retained it for the sons alone or increasingly for a single son who would continue the family line. Marriage, which now had greater consequence, also had a more public character and was marked by greater ceremony. Wedding rituals involved both the

Edo Craftsman at Work Less than 3 inches tall, this ivory figure shows a parasol maker seated on the floor (the typical Japanese practice) eating his lunch, his tools by his side.
(Private Collection/Photo © Boltin Picture Library)

exchange of betrothal gifts and the movement of the bride from her parents' home to her husband's home. She brought with her a trousseau that provided her with clothes and other items she would need for daily life, but not with land, which would have given her economic autonomy. On the other hand, her position within her new family was more secure, for it became more difficult for a husband to divorce his wife. She also gained authority within the family. If her husband was away, she managed family affairs. If her husband fathered children with concubines, she was their legal mother.

A peasant wife shared responsibility for the family's economic well-being with her husband. If of poor or middling status, she worked alongside her husband in the fields, doing the routine work while he did the heavy work. If they were farmhands and worked for wages, the wife invariably earned a third or a half less than her husband. Wives of prosperous farmers never worked in the fields, but they reeled silk, wove cloth, helped in any family business, and supervised the maids. When cotton growing spread to Japan in the sixteenth century, women took on the jobs of spinning and weaving it. Whatever their economic status, Japanese women, like women everywhere in the world, tended the children.

How was divorce initiated, and how frequent was it? Customs among the upper class differed considerably from peasant practices. Among the elite, the husband alone could initiate divorce. For the wife, divorce carried a stigma, but she could not prevent it or insist on keeping her children. Widows and divorcées of the samurai elite were expected not to remarry. Among the peasant classes, by contrast, divorce seems to have been fairly common. A poor woman wanting a divorce could simply leave her husband's home. It was also possible to secure divorce through a temple. If a married woman entered the temple and performed rites there for three years, her marriage bond was dissolved.

> **Quick Review**
> What steps did the Tokugawa government take to prevent a return to the social and political instability of the Middle Ages?

How did the arrival of Europeans change the Asian maritime sphere?

In the period 1400–1800, maritime trade and piracy connected China and Japan to each other and also to Korea, Southeast Asia, and Europe. All through the period China and Japan traded extensively with each other as well as with Korea. During the fifteenth century China launched overseas expeditions. Japan was a major source of pirates. In the sixteenth century European traders appeared, eager for Chinese porcelains and silks. Christian missionaries followed, but despite initial successes, they were later banned in both Japan and China. Political changes in Europe changed the international makeup of the European traders in East Asia, with the dominant groups first the Portuguese, next the Dutch, and then the British.

Zheng He's Voyages

Early in the Ming period the Chinese government tried to revive the tribute system of the Han (202–220 C.E.) and Tang Dynasties (618–907), when China had dominated East Asia and envoys had arrived from dozens of distant lands. To invite more countries to send missions, the third Ming emperor (Chengzu or Yongle) authorized a series of voyages to the Indian Ocean under the command of the Muslim eunuch Zheng He (1371–1433; see also the "Individuals in Society" feature on page 410).

How did the Manchus build on Ming accomplishments?

How did war and political instability shape Japan in the Middle Ages?

What was life like in Japan during the Tokugawa peace?

How did the arrival of Europeans change the Asian maritime sphere?

565

The seven voyages that Zheng led between 1405 and 1433 followed old Arab trade routes. Each expedition involved hundreds of ships and from twenty thousand to thirty-two thousand men. Their itineraries included stops in Vietnam, Malaysia, Indonesia, Sri Lanka, India, and, in the later voyages, Hormuz (on the coast of Persia) and East Africa (see Map 16.1 on page 411). At each stop Zheng He went ashore to visit rulers, transmit messages of China's peaceful intentions, and bestow lavish gifts. Rulers were invited to come to China or send envoys, and they were offered accommodation on the return voyages. Near the Straits of Malacca, Zheng He's fleet battled Chinese pirates, bringing them under control. Zheng He made other shows of force as well, deposing rulers deemed unacceptable in Java, Sumatra, and Sri Lanka.

On the return of these expeditions, the Ming emperor was delighted by the exotic things the fleet brought back, such as giraffes and lions from Africa, fine cotton cloth from India, and gems and spices from Southeast Asia. Still, these expeditions were not voyages of discovery; they followed established routes and pursued diplomatic rather than commercial goals.

Why were these voyages abandoned? Officials complained about their cost and modest returns. As a consequence, after 1474, all of the remaining ships with three or more masts were broken up and used for lumber. Chinese did not pull back from trade in the South China Sea and Indian Ocean, but the government no longer promoted trade, leaving the initiative to private merchants and migrants.

Piracy and Japan's Overseas Adventures

One goal of Zheng He's expeditions was to suppress piracy, which had become a problem all along the China coast. Already in the thirteenth century social disorder and banditry in Japan had expanded into seaborne banditry, some of it within the Japanese islands around the Inland Sea (Map 21.3), but also in the straits between Korea and Japan. Japanese "sea bandits" would raid the Korean coast, seizing rice and other goods to take home. In the sixteenth century bands would attack and loot Chinese coastal cities or hold them hostage for ransom. As maritime trade throughout East Asia grew more lively, sea bandits, not all of them Japanese, also took to attacking ships to steal their cargo.

Possibly encouraged by the exploits of these bandits, Hideyoshi, after his victories in unifying Japan, decided to extend his territory across the seas. In 1590, Hideyoshi sent a letter asking the Koreans to allow his armies to pass through their country, declaring that his real target was China. He also sent demands for submission to countries of Southeast Asia and to the Spanish governor of the Philippines.

In 1592 Hideyoshi mobilized 158,000 soldiers and 9,200 sailors for his invasion, and he equipped them with muskets and cannon, which had recently been introduced into Japan. His forces overwhelmed Korean defenders and reached Seoul within three weeks and Pyongyang in two months. A few months later, in the middle of winter, Chinese armies arrived to help defend Korea, and Japanese forces were pushed back from Pyongyang. A stalemate lasted till 1597, when Hideyoshi sent new troops. This time the Ming army and the Korean navy were more successful in resisting the Japanese. For years the Korean navy had to defend against Japanese pirates, and it was able to keep the Japanese from supplying or reinforcing their troops. In 1598, after Hideyoshi's death, the Japanese army withdrew, but Korea was left devastated. (See "Listening to the Past: Keinen's Poetic Diary of the Korea Campaign," page 568.)

After recovering from the setbacks of these invasions, Korea began to advance socially and economically. During the Choson Dynasty (1392–1910), the Korean elite (the yangban) turned away from Buddhism and toward strict Neo-Confucian orthodoxy. As agricultural productivity improved, the population grew from about 8 million in 1600 to 14 million in 1810. With economic advances slavery declined. Between 1750 and 1790 the slave

566 Chapter 21 Continuity and Change in East Asia • 1400–1800

CHAPTER LOCATOR

What sort of state and society developed in China under the Ming?

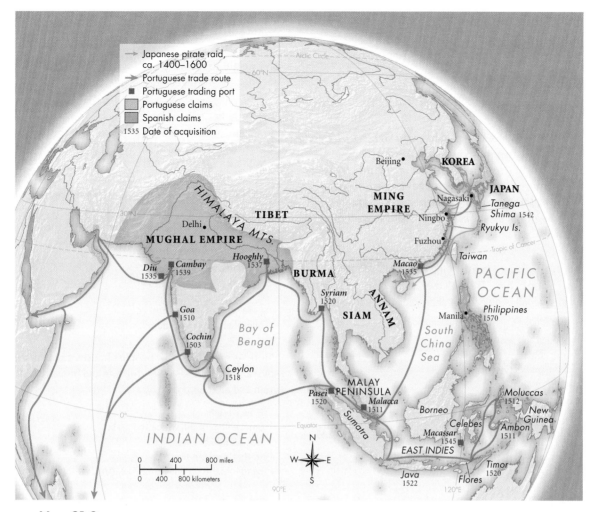

Map 21.3 East Asia, ca. 1600 Pirates and traders often plied the same waters as seaborne trade grew in the sixteenth century. The Portuguese were especially active in setting up trading ports.

population dropped from 30 percent to 5 percent of the population. The hold of the yangban elite, however, remained strong.

Europeans Enter the Scene

In the sixteenth century Portuguese, Spanish, and Dutch merchants and adventurers began to participate in the East Asian maritime world. The trade between Japan, China, and Southeast Asia was very profitable, and the European traders wanted a share of it. They also wanted to develop trade between Asia and Europe.

The Portuguese and Dutch were not reluctant to use force to gain control of trade, and they seized many outposts along the trade routes, including Taiwan. Moreover, they made little distinction between trade, smuggling, and piracy. In 1521 the Ming tried to ban the Portuguese from China. Two years later an expeditionary force commissioned by the Portuguese king to negotiate a friendship treaty defeated its mission by firing on Chinese warships near Guangzhou. In 1557, without informing Beijing, local Chinese officials decided that the way to regulate trade was to allow the Portuguese to build a trading post near the mouth of the Pearl River. The city they built there—Macao—became the first destination for Europeans going to China until the nineteenth century.

How did the Manchus build on Ming accomplishments?

How did war and political instability shape Japan in the Middle Ages?

What was life like in Japan during the Tokugawa peace?

How did the arrival of Europeans change the Asian maritime sphere?

567

LISTENING TO THE PAST

Keinen's Poetic Diary of the Korea Campaign

The Buddhist priest Keinen (1534?–1611) was ordered in 1597 to accompany the local daimyo on Hideyoshi's second campaign in Korea and spent seven months there. As a Buddhist, he did not revel in military feats but rather deplored the death and suffering that he observed. Adopting the time-honored form of the poetic diary, Keinen ends each day's entry with a short poem. The excerpt quoted here begins about six weeks after he left home.

❝ Eighth month, 4th day. Every one is trying to be the first off the ship; no one wants to lag behind. They fall over each other in trying to get at the plunder, to kill people. It is a sight I cannot bear to see.

> A hubbub rises
> as from roiling clouds and mist
> where they swarm about
> in their rage for the plunder
> of innocent people's goods.

VIII.5. They are burning the houses. As I watched them go up in smoke, I thought that my own existence was like this and was seized by sympathy.

> The "Red Country" is
> what they call it, but black is
> the smoke that rises
> from the burning houses
> where you see flames flying high.

VIII.6. The very fields and hillsides have been put to the fire, not to speak of the forts. People are put to the sword, or they are shackled with chains and bamboo tubes choking the neck. Parents sobbing for their children, children searching for their parents — never before have I seen such a pitiable sight.

> The hills are ablaze
> with the cries of soldiers
> intoxicated
> with their pyrolatry —
> the battleground of demons.

VIII.7. Looking at the various kinds of plunder amassed by them all, I formed a desire for such things. Could I really be like this, I thought, and felt ashamed. How can I attain salvation like this, I thought.

> How ashamed I am!
> For everything that I see
> I form desires —
> a creature of delusions,
> my mind full of attachments.

On the same day, as I exerted myself in reflections on my spiritual state, I felt myself more and more ashamed. And yet the Buddha has vowed not to give weight to the weightiest of evil deeds, not to abandon the most abandoned and intemperate!

> Unless it be through
> reliance on the vow of
> Amida Buddha,
> who could obtain salvation
> with such wicked thoughts as mine?

VIII.8. They are carrying off Korean children and killing their parents. Never shall they see each other again. Their mutual cries — surely this is like the torture meted out by the fiends of hell.

> It is piteous;
> when the four fledglings parted,*
> it must have been thus —
> I see the parents' lament
> over their sobbing children.

VIII.11. As night fell, I saw people's houses go up in smoke. They have lost everything to the fire, all their grain and all their property.

> How wretched it is!
> Smoke lingers still where the grain
> was burned and wasted;
> so that is where I lay my
> head tonight: on the scorched earth.

VIII.13. His lordship has set up camp about five leagues this side of Namwon. Unless this fortress is taken, our prospects are dubious; so we are to close in and invest it this evening. The word is that fifty or sixty thousand soldiers from Great Ming are garrisoning the place.

> We'll solve the challenge
> posed even by this fortress
> of the Red Country! —
> The troops rejoice to hear this,
> and they rest their weary feet.

VIII.14. Rain has been falling steadily since the evening. It comes down in sheets, like a waterfall. We have put up a makeshift tent covered with oil paper only, and it is frightening how the rain pours in. It is impossible to sleep. I had to think of the story "The Devil at One Gulp" in *Tales of Ise.*† The night described in that tale must have been just like this.

> Inexorably,
> fearsome torrents beating down
> remind me of that

568

Chapter 21 Continuity and Change
in East Asia • 1400–1800

CHAPTER LOCATOR   What sort of state and
society developed in
China under the Ming?

dreadful night when the devil
at one gulp ate his victim.

VIII.15. The fortress is to be stormed
before dawn tomorrow. Fascines of
bamboo have been distributed to the
assault troops. The sun was about to set
as they worked their way close in, right up
against the edge of the castle's bulwarks,
and gunfire opened up from the several
siege detachments, accompanied by
arrows shot from short-bows. Unthinkable
numbers of men were killed. As I saw them
dying:

> From the fortress, too,
> from their short-bows, too.
> How many killed? Beyond count
> is the number of the dead.

The castle fell to the assault in the course
of the night. Lord Hishu's troops were
the first inside the walls. Needless to say,
he is to get a vermilion-seal letter of
commendation.

VIII.16. All in the fortress were slaughtered, to the last man and woman.
No prisoners were taken. To be sure,
a few were kept alive for exchange
purposes.

> How cruel! This world
> of sorrow and inconstancy
> does have one constant —
> men and women, young and old
> die and vanish; are no more.

VIII.17. Until yesterday they did not know
that they would have to die; today, they
are transformed into the smoke of
impermanence, as is the way of this world
of constant change. How can I be
unaffected by this!

> Look! Everyone, look!
> Is this, then, to be called the human condition? —
> a life with a deadline,
> a life with a limit: today. 🎴

Source: *Sources of Japanese Tradition*, by Wm. Theodore de
Bary, Donald Keene, George Tanabe, and Paul Varley.
Copyright © 2001 by Columbia University Press. Reproduced
with permission of the publisher.

*An allusion to the proverbial tale of a mother bird's sorrow at
her fledglings' departure to the four directions.

Although the Japanese invasion failed, some of the warriors who fought in it were
celebrated, like Kato Kiyomasa, shown here fighting a tiger in the hills of Korea. (Courtesy,
Stephen Turnbull)

†This is a story of an abduction that ends badly. The lady in question, seques-
tered in a broken-down storehouse to keep her safe from the elements on a dark
and stormy night, is devoured "at one gulp" by an ogre who dwells there.

QUESTIONS FOR ANALYSIS

1. Buddhism teaches the impermanence of phenomena, the need to
   let go of attachments, and it opposes the taking of life. Can any of
   Keinen's responses be identified as specifically Buddhist?
2. Does Keinen's use of poetry seem natural, or do you think it seems
   forced?
3. What would be the purpose of bringing a Buddhist priest opposed
   to killing on a military campaign?

How did the Manchus
build on Ming
accomplishments?

How did war and
political instability shape
Japan in the Middle Ages?

What was life like in
Japan during the
Tokugawa peace?

How did the arrival of
Europeans change the
Asian maritime sphere?

569

Dutch in Japan The Japanese were curious about the appearance, dress, and habits of the Dutch who came to the enclave of Deshima to trade. In this detail from a long hand scroll, Dutch traders are shown interacting with a Japanese samurai in a room with Japanese tatami mats on the floor. Note also the Western musical instruments. (Private Collection/The Bridgeman Art Library)

European products were not in demand in China, but silver was. Japan had supplied much of China's silver, but with the development of silver mines in the New World, European traders began supplying large quantities of silver to China, allowing the expansion of China's economy.

Chinese were quick to take advantage of the new trading ports set up by European powers. In Batavia harbor (now Jakarta, Indonesia) Chinese ships outnumbered those from any other country by two or three to one. Manila, under Spanish control, and Taiwan and Batavia, both under Dutch control, all attracted thousands of Chinese colonists.

A side benefit of the appearance of European traders was New World crops. Sweet potatoes, maize, peanuts, tomatoes, chili peppers, tobacco, and other crops were quickly adopted in East Asia. Sweet potatoes and maize in particular facilitated population growth because they could be grown on land previously thought unsuitable for cultivation.

Christian Missionaries

The Spanish and Portuguese kings supported missionary activity, and merchant vessels soon brought Catholic missionaries to East Asia. The first to come were Jesuits, from the

Chapter 21   Continuity and Change
in East Asia • 1400–1800

570

CHAPTER LOCATOR

What sort of state and
society developed in
China under the Ming?

order founded by Ignatius Loyola in 1534 to promote Catholic scholarship and combat the Protestant Reformation.

The Jesuit priest Francis Xavier had worked in India and the Indies before China and Japan attracted his attention. In 1549 he landed on Kyushu, Japan's southernmost island (see Map 21.2). After he was expelled by the local lord, he traveled throughout western Japan as far as Kyoto, proselytizing wherever warlords allowed. He soon made many converts among the poor and even some among the daimyo. Xavier then set his sights on China but died on an uninhabited island off the China coast in 1552.

Other missionaries carried on his work, and by 1600 there were three hundred thousand baptized Christians in Japan. Most of them lived on Kyushu, where the shogun's power was weakest and the loyalty of the daimyo most doubtful. In 1615 bands of Christian samurai supported Tokugawa Ieyasu's enemies at the Battle of Osaka. A couple of decades later, thirty thousand peasants in the heavily Catholic area of northern Kyushu revolted. The Tokugawa shoguns thus came to associate Christianity with domestic disorder and insurrection. Accordingly, what had been mild persecution of Christians became ruthless repression after 1639. Foreign priests were expelled or tortured, and thousands of Japanese Christians suffered crucifixion.

Meanwhile, in China the Jesuits concentrated on gaining the linguistic and scholarly knowledge they would need to convert the educated class. In 1601 the Jesuit Matteo Ricci was given permission to reside in Beijing, where he made several high-placed conversions. He also interested educated Chinese men in Western geography, astronomy, and Euclidean mathematics.

Ricci and his Jesuit successors believed that Confucianism was compatible with Christianity, since both shared similar concerns for morality and virtue. The Franciscan and Dominican mendicant orders that arrived in China in the seventeenth century disagreed with the Jesuit position. In 1715 religious and political quarrels in Europe led the pope to decide that the Jesuits' accommodating approach was heretical. Angry at this insult, the Kangxi emperor forbade all Christian missionary work in China.

Missionary Publication To appeal to a Chinese audience, the Jesuits illustrated some of their publications in a distinctly Chinese style. This book illustration shows Mary during the annunciation in a Chinese-style room with a Chinese landscape painting on the wall, and the descent from Heaven of the angel Gabriel signaled in Chinese fashion by stylized clouds. (Courtesy, Archivum Romanum Societatis Iesu [ARSI], Rome)

Learning from the West

Although both China and Japan ended up prohibiting Christian missionary work, other aspects of Western culture were seen as useful. The closed-country policy that Japan instituted in 1639 restricted Japanese from leaving the country and kept European merchants in small enclaves. Still, Japanese interest in Europe did not disappear. Through the Dutch

How did the Manchus build on Ming accomplishments?

How did war and political instability shape Japan in the Middle Ages?

What was life like in Japan during the Tokugawa peace?

How did the arrival of Europeans change the Asian maritime sphere?

571

enclave of Deshima on a tiny island in Nagasaki harbor, a stream of Western ideas and inventions trickled into Japan in the eighteenth century. Western writings, architectural illustrations, calendars, watches, medicine, weapons, and paintings deeply impressed the Japanese.

In China, too, both scholars and rulers showed an interest in Western learning. The Kangxi emperor frequently discussed scientific and philosophical questions with the Jesuits at court. When he got malaria, he accepted the Jesuits' offer of the medicine quinine. In addition, he had translations made of a collection of Western works on mathematics and the calendar. The court was impressed with the Jesuits' skill in astronomy and quickly appointed them to the Board of Astronomy. In 1674 the emperor asked them to re-equip the observatory with European instruments. European painting, architecture, firearms, and mechanical clocks also were widely admired.

Admiration was not one-sided. In the early eighteenth century China enjoyed a positive reputation in Europe. Voltaire wrote of the rationalism of Confucianism and saw advantages to the Chinese political system. Chinese medical practice also drew European interest. One Chinese practice that Europeans adopted was "variolation," an early form of smallpox inoculation.

The Shifting International Environment in the Eighteenth Century

The East Asian maritime world underwent many changes from the sixteenth to the eighteenth centuries. As already noted, the Japanese pulled back their own traders and limited opportunities for Europeans to trade in Japan. In China the Qing government limited trading contacts with Europe to Guangzhou in the far south in an attempt to curb piracy. Portugal lost many of its bases to the Dutch, and by the eighteenth century the British had become as active as the Dutch. In the seventeenth century the British and Dutch sought primarily porcelains and silk, but in the eighteenth century tea became the commodity in most demand. By the end of the century tea made up 80 percent of Chinese exports to Europe.

By the late eighteenth century Britain had become a great power and did not see why China should be able to dictate the terms of trade. Wanting to renegotiate its relations with China, in the 1790s King George III sent Lord George Macartney on a mission to secure a place for British traders to live near the tea-producing areas, negotiate a commercial treaty, create a desire for British products, arrange for diplomatic representation in Beijing, and open Japan and Southeast Asia to British commerce. He traveled with an eighty-four-person entourage and six hundred cases packed with British goods that he hoped would impress the Chinese court and attract trade. The only member of the British party able to speak Chinese, however, was a twelve-year-old boy who had learned a bit of the language by talking with Chinese passengers on the long voyage.

After Lord Macartney arrived in Guangzhou in 1793, he proceeded overland. Because he would not perform the kowtow (kneeling on both knees and bowing his head to the ground), he was denied a formal audience in the palace. He was permitted to meet more informally with the Qianlong emperor, but no negotiations followed this meeting because Qianlong saw no merit in Macartney's requests. The Qing court was as intent on maintaining the existing system of regulated trade as Britain was intent on doing away with it.

kowtow The ritual of kneeling on both knees and bowing one's head to the ground performed by children to their parents and by subjects to the Chinese ruler.

Quick Review
How did maritime links connect Japan, China, and Korea prior to the seventeenth century, and how did European intrusions alter these connections?

572 Chapter 21 Continuity and Change in East Asia • 1400–1800

CHAPTER LOCATOR

What sort of state and society developed in China under the Ming?

Connections

DURING THE FOUR CENTURIES from 1400 to 1800, the countries of East Asia became increasingly connected. On the oceans trade and piracy linked them, and for the first time a war involved all three East Asian countries. In all three this was a time of economic advance. At the same time, their cultures and social structures were in no sense converging. The elites of the three countries were very different: in both Korea and Japan elite status was hereditary, while in China the key route to advancement involved doing well on a written examination. In Japan the samurai elite were warriors, but in China and Korea the highest prestige went to men of letters. The Japanese prints that capture many features of Japanese cities show a world distinct from anything in China and Korea.

By the end of this period, East Asian countries found themselves in a rapidly changing international environment, mostly because of revolutions occurring far from their shores. The next two chapters take up the story of these revolutions, first the political ones in America, France, and Haiti, and then the Industrial Revolution that began in Britain. In time these revolutions would profoundly alter East Asia as well.

- **For a list of suggested readings for this chapter, visit** *bedfordstmartins.com/mckayworldunderstanding*.

- **For primary sources from this period, see** *Sources of World Societies*, Second Edition.

- **For Web sites, images, and documents related to topics in this chapter, see Make History at** *bedfordstmartins.com/mckayworldunderstanding*.

How did the Manchus build on Ming accomplishments?

How did war and political instability shape Japan in the Middle Ages?

What was life like in Japan during the Tokugawa peace?

How did the arrival of Europeans change the Asian maritime sphere?

573

Chapter 21 Study Guide

To do these exercises online, go to bedfordstmartins.com/mckayworldundersanding.

 Step 1

GETTING STARTED
Below are basic terms about this period in global history. Can you identify each term below and explain why it matters?

TERMS	WHO (OR WHAT) AND WHEN	WHY IT MATTERS
Ming Dynasty, p. 548		
civil service examinations, p. 551		
Qing Dynasty, p. 555		
banners, p. 555		
Nō theater, p. 558		
daimyo, p. 558		
Tokugawa Shogunate, p. 560		
alternate residence system, p. 560		
kabuki theater, p. 562		
kowtow, p. 572		

 Step 2

MOVING BEYOND THE BASICS
The exercise below requires a more advanced understanding of the chapter material. Compare and contrast Qing China and Tokugawa Japan by filling in the chart below with descriptions of key aspects of each empire: social and economic developments, nature and role of elites, and relations with Europeans. When you are finished, consider the following questions: How would you explain the prosperity enjoyed by both empires during the seventeenth and eighteenth centuries? How did elites gain status and power in each empire? Why were both the Japanese and the Chinese wary of Europeans? How and why did Japanese and Chinese society and culture diverge in this period?

	SOCIAL AND ECONOMIC DEVELOPMENTS	NATURE AND ROLE OF ELITES	RELATIONS WITH EUROPEANS
Qing China			
Tokugawa Japan			

PUTTING IT ALL TOGETHER
Now that you've reviewed key elements of the chapter, take a step back and try to see the big picture. Remember to use specific examples from the chapter in your answers.

CHINA UNDER THE MING AND THE QING

- How did Ming officials manage the government when emperors were incompetent? How did this ultimately contribute to the Ming's decline?
- How did the Qing respond to the challenge of ruling a multiethnic empire?

WAR AND PEACE IN JAPAN

- How did the role of the samurai in Japanese society and government change between 1400 and 1800?
- What explains the emergence of a vibrant urban culture during the Tokugawa Shogunate?

THE ASIAN MARITIME SPHERE

- What do Zheng He's voyages tell us about Chinese attitudes toward overseas trade, expansion, and international relations?
- Why did both the Japanese and Chinese have mixed feelings about European culture? What did they admire? What did they dislike and fear?

LOOKING BACK, LOOKING AHEAD

- What explains the cultural divergence between China and Japan in this period?
- What trends in the relationship between Asia and Europe were emerging by the end of this period? How did Asian governments respond to the changes that were beginning to take place?

In Your Own Words Imagine that you must explain Chapter 21 to someone who hasn't read it. What would be the most important points to include and why?

Revolutions in the Atlantic World

1775–1815

Revolution rocked the Atlantic world in the last decades of the eighteenth century. As trade goods, individuals, and ideas circulated in ever greater numbers across the Atlantic Ocean, debates and events in one locale soon influenced those in another. Enlightenment ideals of freedom and equality flourished, inspiring reformers in many places to demand an end to the old ways. At the same time, wars fought for dominance of the Atlantic economy left European governments weakened by debt, making them vulnerable to calls for reform.

The revolutionary era began in North America in 1775. Then in 1789 France became the leading revolutionary nation. It established first a constitutional monarchy, then a radical republic, and finally an empire that would last until 1815. During this period of constant domestic turmoil, French armies violently exported revolution throughout much of Europe.

Inspired both by revolutionary ideals and by internal colonial conditions, the slaves in the French colony of Saint-Domingue rose up in 1791. Their rebellion would eventually lead to the creation of the independent nation of Haiti in 1804. The relationship between Europe and its colonies was fundamentally altered by this wave of revolution and by subsequent independence movements in Spanish North America. In Europe and its colonies abroad, the world of modern politics was born.

Liberty The figure of Liberty bears a copy of the Declaration of the Rights of Man and of the Citizen and a pike to defend them. The painting hung in France's Jacobin club until its fall from power. (Nanine Vallain, *La Liberté*, oil on canvas, 1794/Musée de la revolution française de Vizille, © Conseil général de l'Isère/Domaine de Vizille)

Chapter Preview

▶ What factors combined to spark revolutions in the Atlantic world?

▶ How did American colonists forge a new, independent nation?

▶ What were the causes and consequences of the French Revolution?

▶ How and why did the French Revolution take a radical turn?

▶ How did Napoleon assume control of France and much of Europe?

▶ What led to the creation of the independent state of Haiti in 1804?

What factors combined to spark revolutions in the Atlantic world?

No one cause lay behind the revolutions in the Atlantic world. However, certain important factors helped set the stage for reform. Among them were fundamental social and economic changes as well as political crises that eroded state authority. Another significant cause of revolutionary fervor was the impact of political ideas derived from the Enlightenment. Finally, and perhaps most important, financial crises generated by war expenses crippled European states and allowed abstract discussions of reform to become pressing realities.

Social Change

Eighteenth-century European society was still legally divided into groups with special privileges, such as the nobility and the clergy, and groups with special burdens, such as the peasantry. Nobles in France enjoyed not only exemption from taxation but also exclusive rights, such as the right to hunt game and bear swords. In most countries, various middle-class groups—professionals, merchants, and guild masters—enjoyed privileges that allowed them to monopolize all sorts of economic activity.

Traditional privileges persisted in societies undergoing dramatic and destabilizing change. Due to increased agricultural production, Europe's population rose rapidly after 1750, and its cities and towns swelled in size. Inflation kept pace with demography, making it ever more difficult for urban people to find affordable food and living space.

The growth of the economy created new inequalities between rich and poor. While the poor struggled with rising prices, investors in overseas trade or rural manufacturing reaped great profits. Old distinctions between landed aristocracy and city merchants began to fade as enterprising nobles put money into trade and rising middle-class bureaucrats and merchants bought landed estates and noble titles. Marriages between nobles and wealthy, educated commoners (often called the *bourgeoisie* [boorzh-wah-ZEE] in France) served both groups' interests, and a mixed-caste elite began to take shape. In the context of these changes, ancient privileges seemed inappropriate and unjust to many observers.

The Three Estates French inhabitants were legally divided into three orders, or estates: the clergy, the nobility, and everyone else. In this political cartoon from 1789 a peasant of the third estate struggles under the weight of a happy clergyman and a plumed nobleman. The caption—"Let's hope this game ends soon"—sets forth a program of reform that any peasant could understand. (Réunion des Musées Nationaux/Art Resource, NY)

578

Chapter 22   Revolutions in the Atlantic World • 1775–1815

CHAPTER LOCATOR

What factors combined to spark revolutions in the Atlantic world?

Another social change involved the racial regimes established in European colonies to enable and protect slavery. By the late eighteenth century European law accepted that only Africans and people of African descent were subject to slavery. Even free people of color were subject to special laws restricting their property and their personal liberty. Racial privilege conferred a new dimension of entitlement on European settlers in the colonies, and they used extremely brutal methods to enforce it. The contradiction between slavery and the Enlightenment ideals of liberty and equality was all too evident to slaves and free people of color.

Growing Demands for Liberty and Equality

In addition to destabilizing social changes, the ideals of liberty and equality helped fuel revolutions in the Atlantic world. In the eighteenth century, the call for liberty was first of all a call for individual human rights. Supporters of the cause of individual liberty (who became known as "liberals" in the early nineteenth century) demanded freedom of worship, an end to censorship, and freedom from arbitrary laws and from judges who simply obeyed orders from the government. The Declaration of the Rights of Man and of the Citizen, issued at the beginning of the French Revolution, proclaimed that "Liberty consists in being able to do anything that does not harm another person." In the context of the monarchical and absolutist forms of government then dominating Europe, this was a truly radical idea.

The call for liberty was also a call for a new kind of government. Reformers believed that the people had sovereignty—that is, that the people alone had the authority to make laws limiting an individual's freedom of action. In practice, this system of government meant choosing legislators who represented the people and were accountable to them. Monarchs might retain their thrones, but their rule should be constrained by the will of the people.

Equality was a more ambiguous idea. Eighteenth-century liberals argued that, in theory, all citizens should have identical rights and liberties and that the nobility had no right to special privileges based on birth. However, they accepted a number of distinctions. First, most eighteenth-century liberals believed that equality between men and women was neither practical nor desirable. Second, few questioned the inequality between blacks and whites.

Finally, liberals never believed that everyone should be equal economically. Great differences in wealth and income between rich and poor were perfectly acceptable, so long as every free white male had a legally equal chance at economic gain. However limited they appear to modern eyes, these demands for liberty and equality were revolutionary, given that a privileged elite had long existed with little opposition.

The two most important thinkers to use Enlightenment goals of personal freedom and legal equality to justify liberal self-government were John Locke and the baron de Montesquieu. Locke maintained that England's political tradition rested on "the rights of Englishmen" and on representative government through Parliament. He argued that if a government oversteps its proper function of protecting the natural rights, it becomes a tyranny. Montesquieu, too, believed that powerful "intermediary groups"—such as the judicial nobility of which he was a proud member—offered the best defense of liberty against despotism.

Chapter Chronology

1715–1774	Reign of Louis XV in France
1743–1803	Life of Toussaint L'Ouverture
1756–1763	Seven Years' War
1763	Treaty of Paris
1774–1792	Reign of Louis XVI in France
1775	Thomas Paine publishes *Common Sense*
1775–1783	American Revolution
1789–1799	French Revolution
1790	Edmund Burke publishes *Reflections on the Revolution in France*
1791–1804	Haitian Revolution
1792	Mary Wollstonecraft publishes *A Vindication of the Rights of Woman*
1799–1814	Reign of Napoleon Bonaparte in France

How did American colonists forge a new, independent nation?

What were the causes and consequences of the French Revolution?

How and why did the French Revolution take a radical turn?

How did Napoleon assume control of France and much of Europe?

What led to the creation of the independent state of Haiti in 1804?

579

The belief that representative institutions could defend their liberty and interests appealed powerfully to the bourgeoisie. Yet liberal ideas about individual rights and political freedom also appealed to members of the nobility, at least in western Europe and as formulated by Montesquieu. Representative government did not mean democracy. Rather, liberals envisioned voting for representatives as being restricted to men who owned property—those with "a stake in society." The blurring of practical distinctions between landed aristocrats and wealthy commoners meant that there was no clear-cut opposition between nobles and non-nobles on political issues.

Revolutions thus began with aspirations for equality and liberty among the social elite. Soon, however, dissenting voices emerged as some revolutionaries became frustrated with the limitations of classical liberal notions of equality and liberty, and they clamored for a fuller realization of these concepts. Depending on location, their demands included political rights for women and free people of color, the emancipation of slaves, and government regulation to guarantee fair access to resources and to impose economic equality. The age of revolution was thus characterized as much by conflicts over how far reform should go as by the arguments for change that launched this age in the first place.

The Seven Years' War

The roots of revolutionary ideology could be found in the writings of Locke or Montesquieu, but it was a series of events—political, economic, and military—that created the conditions in which ideology could be translated into radical action. One of the most important was the global conflict known as the Seven Years' War (1756–1763).

The war's battlefields stretched from central Europe to India to North America, pitting a new alliance of England and Prussia against the French and Austrians. Its origins were in conflicts left unresolved at the end of the War of the Austrian Succession in 1748 (see page 447). In central Europe, Austria's Maria Theresa vowed to win back Silesia, which Prussia took in the war of succession, and to crush Prussia, thereby re-establishing Habsburg leadership in German affairs. By the end of the Seven Years' War Maria Theresa had almost succeeded, but Prussia survived with its boundaries intact.

Unresolved tensions also lingered in North America, particularly regarding the border between the French and British colonies. The encroachment of English settlers into territory claimed by the French in the Ohio Valley resulted in skirmishes that soon became war. At first the French prevailed, scoring major victories until 1758. Then, the British diverted resources from the war in Europe, using superior sea power to destroy the French fleet and choke off French commerce around the world. In 1759 the British took Quebec, sealing the fate of France in North America.

Treaty of Paris The 1763 peace treaty that ended the Seven Years' War, according vast French territories in North America and India to Britain and Louisiana to Spain.

British victory on all colonial fronts was ratified in the 1763 **Treaty of Paris**. Canada and all French territory east of the Mississippi River passed to Britain, and France ceded Louisiana to Spain as compensation for Spain's loss of Florida to Britain. France also gave up most of its holdings in India, opening the way to British dominance on the subcontinent (Map 22.1).

By 1763 Britain had realized its goal of monopolizing a vast trading and colonial empire, but at a tremendous cost in war debt. France emerged from the conflict humiliated and broke, but with its profitable Caribbean colonies intact. In the aftermath of war, both British and French governments had to raise taxes to repay loans, raising a storm of protest and demands for fundamental reform. Since the Caribbean colony of Saint-Domingue remained French, revolutionary turmoil in the mother country would directly affect its population. The seeds of revolutionary conflict in the Atlantic world were thus sown.

Quick Review
How did war, and the costs of war, create opportunities to turn calls for reform into revolutions?

580   **Chapter 22 Revolutions in the Atlantic World • 1775–1815**

CHAPTER LOCATOR

What factors combined to spark revolutions in the Atlantic world?

Map 22.1 European Claims in North America and India Before and After the Seven Years' War, 1755–1763 As a result of the war, France lost its vast territories in North America and India. In an effort to avoid costly conflicts with Native Americans living in the newly conquered territory, the British government in 1763 prohibited colonists from settling west of the Appalachian Mountains. One of the few remaining French colonies in the Americas, Saint-Domingue (on the island of Hispaniola) was the most profitable plantation in the New World.

How did American colonists forge a new, independent nation?

Increased taxes were one factor behind colonial protests in the New World, where the era of liberal political revolution began. After revolting against their home country, the thirteen mainland colonies of British North America succeeded in establishing a new unified government. In founding a government firmly based on liberal principles, the Americans set an example that would have a forceful impact on France and its colonies.

The Origins of the Revolution

The high cost of the Seven Years' War doubled the British national debt. Anticipating further expenses to defend newly conquered territories, the British government broke with tradition and announced that they would maintain a large army in North America and tax the colonies directly. In 1765 Parliament passed the Stamp Act, which levied taxes on a long list of commercial and legal documents, diplomas, newspapers, almanacs, and playing cards.

These measures seemed perfectly reasonable to the British, for a much heavier stamp tax already existed in Britain, and proceeds from the tax were to fund the defense of the colonies. Nonetheless, the colonists vigorously protested the Stamp Act by rioting and by boycotting British goods. Thus Parliament reluctantly repealed it.

This dispute raised important political questions. To what extent could the British government reassert its power while limiting the authority of elected colonial bodies? Who had the right to make laws for Americans? The British government replied that Americans were represented in Parliament, albeit indirectly (like most British people), and that Parliament ruled throughout the empire. Many Americans felt otherwise, believing that only colonial political institutions had the right to make laws for colonists. Thus British colonial administration and parliamentary supremacy came to appear as grave threats to existing American liberties.

Americans' resistance to these threats was fed by the great degree of independence they had long enjoyed. In British North America, no powerful established church existed, and religious freedom was taken for granted. Colonial assemblies made the important laws, which were seldom overturned by the British government. Also, the right to vote was much more widespread than in England.

Moreover, greater political equality was matched by greater social and economic equality, at least for the free population. No hereditary nobility exercised privileges over peasants and other social groups. Instead, independent farmers dominated colonial society. This was particularly true in the northern colonies, where the revolution originated.

In 1773 disputes over taxes and representation flared up again. Under the Tea Act of that year, the British government permitted the East India Company to ship tea from China directly to its agents in the colonies rather than through London middlemen, who sold to independent merchants in the colonies. Thus the company secured a profitable monopoly on the tea trade, and colonial merchants were excluded. The price on tea was actually lowered for colonists, but the act generated a great deal of opposition because of the monopoly it gave to the East India Company.

In protest, Boston men had a rowdy Tea Party in which they boarded East India Company ships and threw tea from them into the harbor. In response, the so-called Coercive Acts of 1774 closed the port of Boston, curtailed local elections, and expanded the royal governor's power. County conventions in Massachusetts protested the measures, and other colonial assemblies soon joined in the denunciations. In September 1774, the First Continental Congress met in Philadelphia to consider the colonial response. The more radical members of this assembly argued successfully against concessions to the English crown. The British Parliament also rejected compromise, and in April 1775 fighting between colonial and British troops began at Lexington and Concord.

Commemorative Teapot Manufacturers were quick to bring products to the market celebrating weighty political events, like this British teapot heralding "Stamp Act Repeal'd." By purchasing such items, ordinary people could champion political causes of the day and bring public affairs into their private lives. (Gift of Richard C. Manning/Peabody Essex Museum, Salem, Massachusetts. Acquired 9/16/1933)

CHAPTER LOCATOR   What factors combined to spark revolutions in the Atlantic world?

Independence from Britain

As fighting spread, the colonists moved slowly toward open calls for independence. The uncompromising attitude of the British government and its use of German mercenaries did much to dissolve loyalties to the home country and to unite the separate colonies. *Common Sense* (1775), a brilliant attack by the recently arrived English radical Thomas Paine (1737–1809), also mobilized public opinion in favor of independence.

On July 4, 1776, the Second Continental Congress adopted the Declaration of Independence. Written by Thomas Jefferson and others, this document listed the tyrannical acts committed by George III (r. 1760–1820) and confidently proclaimed the natural rights of mankind and the sovereignty of the American states. The Declaration of Independence in effect universalized the traditional rights of English people and made them the rights of all mankind.

Loyalist Strength in the Colonies, ca. 1774–1776

Seeing an opportunity for revenge against the British for the humiliating defeats of the Seven Years' War, France supplied the rebels with guns and gunpowder from the beginning of the conflict. In 1778 the French government offered a formal alliance to the Americans, and in 1779 and 1780 the Spanish and Dutch declared war on Britain. Catherine the Great of Russia helped organize the League of Armed Neutrality to protect neutral shipping rights and succeeded in hampering Britain's naval power. Thus by 1780 Britain was engaged in an imperial war against most of Europe as well as the thirteen colonies. In these circumstances, and in the face of severe reverses in India, in the West Indies, and at Yorktown in Virginia, a new British government decided to cut its losses and end the war. Under the Treaty of Paris of 1783, Britain recognized the independence of the thirteen colonies and ceded all its territory between the Allegheny Mountains and the Mississippi River to the Americans.

Declaration of Independence The 1776 document in which the American colonies declared independence from Great Britain and recast traditional English rights as universal human rights.

Framing the Constitution

The liberal program of the American Revolution was consolidated by the federal Constitution, the Bill of Rights, and the creation of a national republic. Assembling in Philadelphia in the summer of 1787, the delegates to the Constitutional Convention were determined to end the period of economic depression, social uncertainty, and leadership under a weak central government that had followed independence. The delegates thus decided to grant the federal, or central, government important powers: regulation of domestic and foreign trade, the right to tax, and the means to enforce its laws.

Strong rule would be placed squarely in the context of representative self-government. Senators and congressmen would be the lawmaking delegates of the voters, and the president of the republic would be an elected official. Authority within the central government was distributed across three different branches—the executive, legislative, and judicial branches—that would systematically balance one another, preventing one interest from gaining too much power. The power of the federal government would in turn be checked by that of the individual states.

When the results of the secret deliberations of the Constitutional Convention were presented to the states for ratification, a great public debate began. The opponents of the proposed Constitution—the Antifederalists—charged that the framers of the new document had taken too much power from the individual states and made the federal government

Antifederalists Opponents of the American Constitution who felt it diminished individual rights and accorded too much power to the federal government at the expense of the states.

How did American colonists forge a new, independent nation?

What were the causes and consequences of the French Revolution?

How and why did the French Revolution take a radical turn?

How did Napoleon assume control of France and much of Europe?

What led to the creation of the independent state of Haiti in 1804?

583

too strong. Moreover, many Antifederalists feared for the individual freedoms for which they had fought. To overcome these objections, the Federalists promised to spell out these basic freedoms as soon as the new Constitution was adopted. The result was the first ten amendments to the Constitution. These amendments, ratified in 1791, formed an effective Bill of Rights to safeguard the individual.

The early American republic also sought to advance the rights of African Americans, and many free people of color voted in elections to ratify the Constitution. Congress banned slavery in federal territory in 1789, then the export of slaves from any state, and finally, in 1808, the import of slaves to any state. These early measures, along with voting rights for free people of color, were eroded in the early nineteenth century as abolitionist fervor waned.

The American Constitution and the Bill of Rights exemplified the great strengths and the limits of what came to be called classical liberalism. Liberty meant individual freedoms and political safeguards. Liberty also meant representative government but did not necessarily mean democracy, with its principle of one person, one vote. Equality meant equality before the law, not equality of political participation or wealth. It did not mean equal rights for women, slaves, or indigenous peoples.

Quick Review
What role did issues of taxation and political representation play in causing the American Revolution?

What were the causes and consequences of the French Revolution?

No country felt the consequences of the American Revolution more deeply than France. Hundreds of French officers served in America and were inspired by the experience. French intellectuals and publicists engaged in passionate analysis of events in the former colonies. The American Revolution undeniably fueled dissatisfaction with the old monarchical order in France. Yet the French Revolution did not mirror the American example. It was more radical and more complex, more influential and more controversial. For Europeans and most of the rest of the world, it was the great revolution of the eighteenth century, the revolution that opened the modern era in politics.

Breakdown of the Old Order

As did the American Revolution, the French Revolution had its immediate origins in the financial difficulties of the government. The efforts of the crown to raise taxes to meet the expenses of the War of the Austrian Succession and the Seven Years' War were thwarted by the high courts, known as the parlements. The noble judges of the parlements resented this threat to their exemption from taxation and decried the government's actions as a form of royal despotism. When renewed efforts to reform the tax system met a similar fate in 1776, the government was forced to finance its enormous expenditures during the American war with borrowed money. As a result, the national debt soared. By the 1780s fully 50 percent of France's annual budget went to interest payments on the ever-increasing debt. Another 25 percent went to maintain the military, while 6 percent was absorbed by the royal family and the court at Versailles. This was an impossible financial situation.

Nor could the king and his ministers print money and create inflation to cover their deficits. Unlike England and Holland, which had far larger national debts relative to their populations, France had no central bank, no paper currency, and no means of creating credit. Therefore, when a depressed economy and a lack of public confidence made it increasingly difficult for the government to obtain new loans in 1786, it had no alternative

Key Events of the French Revolution

NATIONAL ASSEMBLY (1789–1791)

May 5, 1789	Estates General meets at Versailles
June 17, 1789	Third estate declares itself the National Assembly
June 20, 1789	Tennis Court Oath
July 14, 1789	Storming of the Bastille
July–August 1789	Great Fear
August 4, 1789	Abolishment of feudal privileges
August 27, 1789	Declaration of the Rights of Man and of the Citizen
October 5, 1789	Women march on Versailles; royal family returns to Paris
July 1790	Civil Constitution of the Clergy establishes a national church; Louis XVI agrees to a constitutional monarchy
June 1791	Royal family is arrested trying to flee France

LEGISLATIVE ASSEMBLY (1791–1792)

April 1792	France declares war on Austria
August 1792	Mob attacks the palace; Legislative Assembly takes Louis XVI prisoner

NATIONAL CONVENTION (1792–1795)

September 1792	National Convention abolishes monarchy and declares France a republic
January 21, 1793	Louis XVI is executed
February 1793	France declares war on Britain, Holland, and Spain
March 1793	Struggle between Girondists and the Mountain
1793–1794	Reign of Terror
July 1794	Robespierre executed; Thermidorian reaction begins

THE DIRECTORY (1795–1799)

1799	Napoleon seizes power

but to try increasing taxes. Because France's tax system was unfair and out-of-date, increased revenues were possible only through fundamental reforms. Such reforms were guaranteed to create social and political unrest.

Despite all of this, the French monarchy would probably have prevailed had Louis XV lived longer, but he died in 1774. The new king, Louis XVI (r. 1774–1792), was a shy twenty-year-old with good intentions. The eager-to-please monarch Louis waffled on political reform and the economy, and he proved unable to quell the rising storm of opposition.

The Formation of the National Assembly

Spurred by a depressed economy and falling tax receipts, Louis XVI's minister of finance proposed to impose a general tax on all landed property as well as to form provincial assemblies to help administer the tax, and he convinced the king to call an assembly of notables in 1787 to gain support for the idea. The assembled notables, mainly important noblemen and high-ranking clergy, declared that such sweeping tax changes required the approval of the **Estates General**, the representative body of all three estates, which had not met since 1614.

Facing imminent bankruptcy, the king tried to reassert his authority. He dismissed the notables and established new taxes by decree. The judges of the Parlement of Paris promptly

Estates General Traditional representative body of the three estates of France that met in 1789 in response to imminent state bankruptcy.

How did American colonists forge a new, independent nation?

What were the causes and consequences of the French Revolution?

How and why did the French Revolution take a radical turn?

How did Napoleon assume control of France and much of Europe?

What led to the creation of the independent state of Haiti in 1804?

585

declared the royal initiative null and void. When the king tried to exile the judges, a tremendous wave of protest swept the country. Frightened investors refused to advance more loans to the state. Finally in July 1788, Louis XVI bowed to public opinion and called for a spring session of the Estates General.

As its name indicates, the Estates General was a legislative body with representatives from the three orders of society: the clergy, nobility, and commoners. Following centuries-old tradition each order met separately to elect delegates, first at a local and then at a regional level.

The petitions for change drafted in advance of the Estates General showed a surprising degree of consensus about the key issues confronting the realm. In all three estates, voices spoke in favor of replacing absolutism with a constitutional monarchy in which laws and taxes would require the consent of the Estates General in regular meetings. There was also the strong feeling that individual liberties would have to be guaranteed by law and that economic regulations should be loosened.

On May 5, 1789, the delegates gathered in Versailles for the opening session of the Estates General. Despite widespread hopes for serious reform, the Estates General was almost immediately deadlocked due to arguments about voting procedures. Controversy had begun during the electoral process itself, when the government confirmed that, following precedent, each estate should meet and vote separately. During the lead-up to the Estates General, critics had demanded a single assembly dominated by the third estate. (See "Listening to the Past: Abbé de Sieyès, 'What Is the Third Estate?'" page 588.) The government conceded that the third estate should have as many delegates as the clergy and the nobility combined, but then upheld a system granting one vote per estate instead of one vote per person. This meant that the two privileged estates could always outvote the third, even if the third estate had a majority by head count.

The issue came to a crisis in June 1789 when delegates of the third estate refused to meet until the king ordered the clergy and nobility to sit with them in a single body. Finally, after six weeks, a few parish priests began to go over to the third estate, which on June 17 voted to call itself the National Assembly. On June 20 the delegates of the third estate moved to a large indoor tennis court where they swore the famous Oath of the Tennis Court, pledging not to disband until they had been recognized as a national assembly and had written a new constitution.

The king's response was disastrously ambivalent. On June 23 he made a conciliatory speech to a joint session in which he urged reforms, and four days later he ordered the three estates to meet together. At the same time, Louis called an army toward the capital to bring the delegates under control, and on July 11 he dismissed his finance minister and other more liberal ministers. It appeared that the monarchy was prepared to renege on its promises for reform and to use violence to restore its control.

National Assembly French representative assembly formed in 1789 by the delegates of the third estate and some members of the clergy, the second estate.

Popular Uprising and the Rights of Man

While delegates at Versailles were pressing for political rights, economic hardship gripped common people in the towns and countryside. Conditions were already tough, due to the disastrous financial situation of the Crown. A poor grain harvest in 1788 caused the price of bread to soar suddenly and inflation spread quickly through the economy. As a result, demand for manufactured goods collapsed, and many artisans and small traders lost work.

Against this background of poverty and political crisis, the people of Paris entered decisively onto the revolutionary stage. At the beginning of July, knowledge spread of the massing of troops near Paris. On July 14, 1789, several hundred people stormed the Bastille (ba-STEEL), a royal prison, to obtain weapons and gunpowder for the city's defense. Faced

The Tennis Court Oath, June 20, 1789 Painted two years after the event shown, this dramatic painting by Jacques-Louis David depicts a crucial turning point in the early days of the Revolution. On June 20 delegates of the third estate arrived at their meeting hall in the Versailles palace to find the doors closed and guarded. Fearing the king was about to dissolve their meeting by force, the deputies reassembled at a nearby indoor tennis court and swore a solemn oath not to disperse until they had been recognized as the National Assembly. (Musée de la Ville de Paris, Musée Carnavalet, Paris/Giraudon/The Bridgeman Art Library)

with popular violence, Louis soon announced the reinstatement of his finance minister and the withdrawal of troops from Paris. The National Assembly was now free to continue its work without the threat of royal military intervention.

Just as the laboring poor of Paris had been roused to a revolutionary fervor, in the summer of 1789, throughout France peasants began to rise in insurrection against their lords. Fear of marauders and vagabonds hired by vengeful landlords — called the Great Fear by contemporaries — seized the rural poor and fanned the flames of rebellion.

Faced with chaos, the National Assembly responded to peasant demands with a surprise maneuver on the night of August 4, 1789. By a decree of the assembly, all the old noble privileges were abolished along with the tithes paid to the church. From this point on, French peasants would seek mainly to protect and consolidate this victory.

Having granted new rights to the peasantry, the National Assembly moved forward with its mission of reform. On August 27, 1789, it issued the Declaration of the Rights of Man and of the Citizen, guaranteeing equality before the law, representative government for a sovereign people, and individual freedom. This revolutionary credo was disseminated throughout France, the rest of Europe, and around the world.

The National Assembly's declaration had little practical effect for the poor people of Paris. The economic crisis worsened after the fall of the Bastille, as aristocrats fled the country

How did American colonists forge a new, independent nation?

What were the causes and consequences of the French Revolution?

How and why did the French Revolution take a radical turn?

How did Napoleon assume control of France and much of Europe?

What led to the creation of the independent state of Haiti in 1804?

587

In the flood of pamphlets that appeared after Louis XVI's call for a meeting of the Estates General, the most influential was written in 1789 by a Catholic priest named Emmanuel Joseph Sieyès. In "What Is the Third Estate?" the abbé Sieyès vigorously condemned the system of privilege that lay at the heart of French society. The term privilege *combined the Latin words for "private" and "law." In Old Regime France, no one set of laws applied to all; over time, the monarchy had issued a series of particular laws, or privileges, that enshrined special rights and entitlements for select individuals and groups. Noble privileges were among the weightiest.*

Sieyès rejected this entire system of legal and social inequality. Deriding the nobility as a foreign parasite, he argued that the common people of the third estate, who did most of the work and paid most of the taxes, constituted the true nation. His pamphlet galvanized public opinion and played an important role in convincing representatives of the third estate to proclaim themselves a National Assembly in June 1789. Sieyès later helped bring Napoleon Bonaparte to power, abandoning the radicalism of 1789 for an authoritarian regime.

❝ 1. What is the Third Estate? Everything.
2. What has it been until now in the political order? Nothing.
3. What does it want? To become something.

. . . What is a Nation? A body of associates living under a *common* law and represented by the same *legislature*.

Is it not more than certain that the noble order has privileges, exemptions, and even rights that are distinct from the rights of the great body of citizens? Because of this, it [the noble order] does not belong to the common order, it is not covered by the law common to the rest. Thus its civil rights already make it a people apart inside the great Nation. It is truly *imperium in imperio* [a law unto itself].

As for its *political* rights, the nobility also exercises them separately. It has its own representatives who have no mandate from the people. Its deputies sit separately, and even when they assemble in the same room with the deputies of the ordinary citizens, the nobility's representation still remains essentially distinct and separate: it is foreign to the Nation by its very principle, for its mission does not emanate from the people, and by its purpose, since it consists in defending, not the general interest, but the private interests of the nobility.

The Third Estate therefore contains everything that pertains to the Nation and nobody outside of the Third Estate can claim to be part of the Nation. What is the Third Estate? EVERYTHING. . . .

By Third Estate is meant the collectivity of citizens who belong to the common order. Anybody who holds a legal privilege of any kind leaves that common order, stands as an exception to the common law, and in consequence does not belong to the Third Estate. . . . It is certain that the moment a citizen acquires privileges contrary to common law, he no longer belongs to the common order. His new interest is opposed to the general interest; he has no right to vote in the name of the people. . . .

In vain can anyone's eyes be closed to the revolution that time and the force of things have brought to pass; it is none the less real. Once upon a time the Third Estate was in bondage and the noble order was everything that mattered. Today the Third is everything and nobility but a word. Yet under the cover of this word a new and intolerable aristocracy has slipped in, and the people has every reason to no longer want aristocrats. . . .

What is the will of a Nation? It is the result of individual wills, just as the Nation is the aggregate of the individuals who compose it. It is impossible to conceive of a legitimate association that does not have for its goal the common security, the common liberty, in short,

and the luxury market collapsed. Foreign markets also shrank, and unemployment among the urban working class grew. In addition, the poor could no longer look to the church, which had been stripped of its tithes, for aid.

On October 5 some seven thousand women marched the twelve miles from Paris to Versailles and invaded the National Assembly, demanding action. Interrupting a delegate's speech, an old woman defiantly shouted into the debate, "Who's that talking down there? Make the chatterbox shut up. That's not the point: the point is that we want bread."[1] Hers was the genuine voice of the people, essential to any understanding of the French Revolution.

The women invaded the royal apartments, killed some of the royal bodyguards, and searched for the queen, Marie Antoinette, who was widely despised for her frivolous and supposedly immoral behavior. Quick action saved the royal family, but the only way to calm the disorder was for the king to live closer to his people in Paris, as the crowd demanded.

588 | **Chapter 22 Revolutions in the Atlantic World • 1775–1815**

CHAPTER LOCATOR   What factors combined to spark revolutions in the Atlantic world?

This bust, by the sculptor Pierre Jean David d'Angers, shows an aged and contemplative Sieyès reflecting, perhaps, on his key role in the outbreak and unfolding of the French Revolution. (Erich Lessing/Art Resource, NY)

ties of wealth or ability are like the inequalities of age, sex, size, etc. In no way do they detract from the *equality* of citizenship. These individual advantages no doubt benefit from the protection of the law; but it is not the legislator's task to create them, to give privileges to some and refuse them to others. The law grants nothing; it protects what already exists until such time that what exists begins to harm the common interest. These are the only limits on individual freedom. I imagine the law as being at the center of a large globe; we the citizens without exception, stand equidistant from it on the surface and occupy equal places; all are equally dependent on the law, all present it with their liberty and their property to be protected; and this is what I call the *common rights* of citizens, by which they are all alike. All these individuals communicate with each other, enter into contracts, negotiate, always under the common guarantee of the law. If in this general activity somebody wishes to get control over the person of his neighbor or usurp his property, the common law goes into action to repress this criminal attempt and puts everyone back in their place at the same distance from the law. . . .

It is impossible to say what place the two privileged orders [the clergy and the nobility] ought to occupy in the social order: this is the equivalent of asking what place one wishes to assign to a malignant tumor that torments and undermines the strength of the body of a sick person. It must be *neutralized*. We must re-establish the health and working of all organs so thoroughly that they are no longer susceptible to these fatal schemes that are capable of sapping the most essential principles of vitality. ”

Source: *The French Revolution and Human Rights: A Brief Documentary History*, pp. 65, 67, 68–70. Edited, Translated, and with an Introduction by Lynn Hunt. © 1996 by Bedford/St. Martin's. Reprinted by permission of the publisher.

QUESTIONS FOR ANALYSIS

1. What criticism of noble privileges does Sieyès offer? Why does he believe nobles are "foreign" to the nation?
2. How does Sieyès define the nation, and why does he believe that the third estate constitutes the nation?
3. What relationship between citizens and the law does Sieyès envision? What limitations on the law does he propose?

the public good. No doubt each individual also has his own personal aims. He says to himself, "protected by the common security, I will be able to peacefully pursue my own personal projects, I will seek my happiness where I will, assured of encountering only those legal obstacles that society will prescribe for the common interest, in which I have a part, and with which my own personal interest is so usefully allied." . . .

Advantages which differentiate citizens from one another lie outside the purview of citizenship. Inequali-

Liberal elites brought the revolution into being and continued to lead politics. Yet the people of France were now roused and would henceforth play a crucial role in the unfolding of events.

A Constitutional Monarchy and Its Challenges

The day after the women's march on Versailles, the National Assembly followed the king to Paris, and the next two years, until September 1791, saw the consolidation of the liberal revolution. In June 1790 the National Assembly abolished the nobility and in July the king swore to uphold the as-yet-unwritten constitution. The king remained the head of state, but all lawmaking power now resided in the National Assembly, elected by the wealthiest half of French males. The constitution finally passed in September 1791 was the first in French history. It broadened women's rights to seek divorce, to inherit property, and to obtain financial support for illegitimate children from fathers, but excluded women from political office and voting.

This decision was attacked by a small number of men and women who believed that the rights of man should be extended to all French citizens. Olympe de Gouges (1748–1793), a self-taught writer and woman of the people, protested the evils of slavery as well as the injustices done to women. In September 1791 she published her "Declaration of the Rights of Woman." De Gouges's position found little sympathy among leaders of the revolution, however.

In addition to ruling on women's rights, the National Assembly replaced the complicated patchwork of historic provinces with eighty-three departments of approximately equal size. Monopolies, guilds, and workers' associations were prohibited, and barriers to trade within France were abolished in the name of economic liberty. Thus the National Assembly applied the spirit of the Enlightenment in a thorough reform of France's laws and institutions.

The National Assembly also imposed a radical reorganization on religious life. It granted religious freedom to the small minority of French Jews and Protestants. Furthermore, in November 1789 it nationalized the Catholic Church's property and abolished monasteries, using the revenue to back a new paper currency, the assignat (A-sigh-nat).

In July 1790, with the Civil Constitution of the Clergy, the National Assembly established a national church with priests chosen by voters. It then forced the Catholic clergy to take an oath of loyalty to the new government. The pope formally condemned this measure and only half of French priests swore the oath. Many sincere Christians, especially those in the countryside, were also upset by these changes in the religious order. The attempt to remake the Catholic Church, like the abolition of guilds and workers' associations, sharpened the conflict between the educated classes and the common people that had been emerging in the eighteenth century.

Quick Review
What were the goals of the leaders of the 1789 French Revolution, and what kind of state did they hope to create?

How and why did the French Revolution take a radical turn?

When Louis XVI accepted the National Assembly's constitution in September 1791, the Revolution's most constructive and lasting reforms were in place. The turmoil of the Revolution, however, was far from over. A much more radical stage lay ahead, one that would bring war with foreign powers, terror at home, and a transformation in France's government.

The International Response

The outbreak and progress of revolution in France produced great excitement and a sharp division of opinion in Europe and the United States. On the one hand, liberals and radicals saw a mighty triumph of liberty over despotism. On the other hand, conservative leaders such as British statesman Edmund Burke (1729–1797) were troubled by the aroused spirit of reform. In 1790 Burke published *Reflections on the Revolution in France*, in which he predicted that reform like that occurring in France would lead only to chaos and tyranny.

One passionate rebuttal came from a young writer in London, Mary Wollstonecraft (1759–1797). Incensed by Burke's book, Wollstonecraft (WOOL-stuhn-kraft) wrote *A*

Vindication of the Rights of Man (1790). Two years later, she published *A Vindication of the Rights of Woman* (1792). As de Gouges had one year before her, Wollstonecraft demanded equal rights for women. Considered very radical for the time, the book became a founding text of the feminist movement.

The kings and nobles of continental Europe, who had at first welcomed the revolution in France as weakening a competing power, now feared its impact. In June 1791 Louis XVI and Marie Antoinette were arrested and returned to Paris after trying unsuccessfully to slip out of France. To the monarchs of Austria and Prussia, the arrest of a crowned monarch was unacceptable. Two months later they issued the Declaration of Pillnitz, which professed their willingness to intervene in France to restore Louis XVI's rule if necessary. It was expected to have a sobering effect on revolutionary France without causing war.

But the crowned heads of Europe misjudged the situation. The new French representative body, called the Legislative Assembly, that convened in October 1791 had completely new delegates and a different character. Still prosperous, well-educated middle-class men, the delegates were younger and less cautious than their predecessors. Many of them belonged to the political Jacobin club. Such clubs had proliferated in Parisian neighborhoods since the beginning of the revolution, drawing men and women to debate the political questions of the day.

The Jacobins and other deputies reacted with patriotic fury to the Declaration of Pillnitz. They said that if the kings of Europe were attempting to incite war against France, then "we will incite a war of people against kings."[2] In April 1792 France declared war on Francis II, the Habsburg monarch.

France's crusade against tyranny went poorly at first. Prussian forces joined Austria against the French, whose armies broke and fled. The Legislative Assembly declared the country in danger, and volunteers rallied to the capital. In this wartime atmosphere, rumors of treason by the king and queen spread in Paris. On August 10, 1792, a revolutionary crowd attacked the royal palace at the Tuileries (TWEE-luh-reez), while the king and his family fled for their lives to the nearby Legislative Assembly. Rather than offering refuge, the Assembly suspended the king from all his functions, imprisoned him, and called for a legislative and constitutional assembly to be elected by universal male suffrage.

Jacobin club A political club during the French Revolution to which many of the deputies of the Legislative Assembly belonged.

The Second Revolution and the New Republic

The fall of the monarchy marked a rapid radicalization of the Revolution, a phase that historians often call the second revolution. In late September 1792 the new, popularly elected National Convention, which replaced the Legislative Assembly, proclaimed France a republic, a nation in which the people, instead of a monarch, held sovereign power.

All the members of the National Convention were republicans, and at the beginning almost all belonged to the Jacobin club of Paris. But the Jacobins themselves were increasingly divided into two bitterly opposed groups—the Girondists and the Mountain, led by Maximilien Robespierre (1758–1794) and another young lawyer, Georges Jacques Danton.

This division emerged clearly after the National Convention overwhelmingly convicted Louis XVI of treason. The Girondists accepted his guilt but did not wish to put the king to death. By a narrow majority, the Mountain carried the day, and Louis was executed on January 21, 1793. Marie Antoinette would be put to death later that year. But both the Girondists and the Mountain were determined to continue the war. The Prussians had been stopped at the Battle of Valmy on September 20, 1792. French armies then invaded Savoy and captured Nice, moved into the German Rhineland, and by November 1792 were occupying the entire Austrian Netherlands (modern Belgium).

Everywhere they went, French armies of occupation spread revolutionary ideology and found support among some peasants and middle-class people. But French armies also lived

Girondists A moderate group that fought for control of the French National Convention in 1793.

Mountain Led by Robespierre, the French National Convention's radical faction, which seized legislative power in 1793.

How did American colonists forge a new, independent nation?

What were the causes and consequences of the French Revolution?

How and why did the French Revolution take a radical turn?

How did Napoleon assume control of France and much of Europe?

What led to the creation of the independent state of Haiti in 1804?

591

off the land, requisitioning food and supplies and plundering local treasures. The liberators therefore looked increasingly like foreign invaders. Meanwhile, international tensions mounted. In February 1793 the National Convention, at war with Austria and Prussia, declared war on Britain, Holland, and Spain as well.

Groups within France added to the turmoil. Peasants in western France revolted against being drafted into the army, with the Vendée region of Brittany emerging as the epicenter of revolt. Devout Catholics, royalists, and foreign agents encouraged their rebellion.

In March 1793, with the National Convention deadlocked in a struggle between members of the Mountain and the more moderate Girondists, the laboring poor of Paris once again emerged as the decisive political factor. The laboring poor and the petty traders were often known as the **sans-culottes** (san-koo-LAHT, "without breeches") because their men wore trousers instead of the knee breeches of the aristocracy and the solid middle class. They demanded radical political action to guarantee them their daily bread. The Mountain, sensing an opportunity to outmaneuver the Girondists, joined with sans-culottes activists to engineer a popular uprising. On June 2, 1793, armed sans-culottes invaded the Convention and forced its deputies to arrest twenty-nine Girondist deputies for treason. All power passed to the Mountain.

sans-culottes The laboring poor of Paris, so-called because the men wore trousers instead of the knee breeches of the aristocracy and middle class; the term came to refer to the militant radicals of the city.

Areas of French Insurrection, 1793

The Convention also formed the Committee of Public Safety in April 1793 to deal with the threats from within and outside France. The committee, which Robespierre led, held dictatorial power to deal with the national emergency, allowing it to use whatever force necessary to defend the Revolution. Moderates in leading provincial cities revolted against the committee's power and demanded a decentralized government. Counter-revolutionary forces in the Vendée won significant victories, and the republic's armies were driven back on all fronts. By July 1793 only the areas around Paris and on the eastern frontier were firmly held by the central government. Defeat seemed imminent.

Total War and the Terror

A year later, in July 1794, the central government had reasserted control over the provinces, and the Austrian Netherlands and the Rhineland were once again in French hands. This remarkable change of fortune was due to the revolutionary government's success in harnessing the explosive forces of a planned economy, revolutionary terror, and modern nationalism in a total war effort.

Robespierre and the Committee of Public Safety advanced on several fronts in 1793 and 1794. First, in September 1793 Robespierre and his coworkers established a planned economy. Rather than let supply and demand determine prices, the government set maximum allowable prices for key products. Though the state was too weak to enforce all its price regulations, it did fix the price of bread in Paris at levels the poor could afford.

The people were also put to work, mainly producing arms and munitions for the war effort. The government told craftsmen what to produce, nationalized many small workshops, and requisitioned raw materials and grain. Through these economic reforms the second revolution produced an emergency form of socialism.

Reign of Terror The period from 1793 to 1794, during which Robespierre's Committee of Public Safety tried and executed thousands suspected of treason and a new revolutionary culture was imposed.

Second, while radical economic measures supplied the poor with bread and the armies with weapons, the **Reign of Terror** (1793–1794) enforced compliance with republican beliefs and practices. Special revolutionary courts responsible only to Robespierre's Committee of Public Safety tried "enemies of the nation" for political crimes. As a result, some forty

592 **Chapter 22 Revolutions in the Atlantic World • 1775–1815**

CHAPTER LOCATOR

What factors combined to spark revolutions in the Atlantic world?

Des Têtes! _ du Sang! _ la Mort! _ à la Lanterne! à la Guillotine!. _ point de Reine! _ Je suis la Déesse de la Liberté! _ l'égalité! _ que Londres soit brulé! _ que Paris soit Libre! _ Vive la Guillotine! _

A PARIS BELLE.

Picturing the Past

Contrasting Visions of the Sans-Culottes

These two images offer profoundly different representations of a sans-culotte woman. The image on the left was created by a French artist, while the image on the right is English. The French words above the image on the right read in part, "Heads! Blood! Death! . . . I am the Goddess of Liberty! . . . Long Live the Guillotine!" (Bibliothèque nationale de France)

ANALYZING THE IMAGE How would you describe the woman on the left? What qualities does the artist seem to ascribe to her, and how do you think these qualities relate to the sans-culottes and the Revolution? How would you characterize the facial expression and attire of the woman on the right? How does the inclusion of the text contribute to your impressions of her?

CONNECTIONS What does the contrast between these two images suggest about differences between French and English perceptions of the sans-culottes and of the French Revolution? Why do you think the artists have chosen to depict women?

thousand French men and women were executed or died in prison. Presented as a necessary measure to save the republic, the Terror was a weapon directed against all suspected of opposing the revolutionary government.

In their efforts to impose unity, the Jacobins suppressed women's participation in political debate. On October 30, 1793, the National Convention declared that "The clubs and popular societies of women, under whatever denomination are prohibited." Among those convicted of sedition was writer Olympe de Gouges, who was executed in November 1793.

Beyond imposing political unity by force, the Terror also sought to bring the Revolution into all aspects of everyday life. The government sponsored revolutionary art and songs as well as new secular festivals to encourage republican virtue. The government attempted to rationalize daily life by adopting the decimal system for weights and measures and a new calendar based on ten-day weeks. Another important element of this cultural revolution was the campaign of de-Christianization, which aimed to eliminate Catholic symbols and beliefs.

How did American colonists forge a new, independent nation?

What were the causes and consequences of the French Revolution?

How and why did the French Revolution take a radical turn?

How did Napoleon assume control of France and much of Europe?

What led to the creation of the independent state of Haiti in 1804?

593

The third and perhaps most decisive element in the French republic's victory over the First Coalition was its ability to draw on the power of patriotic dedication to the nation. With a common language and history, reinforced by the ideas of popular sovereignty and democracy, large numbers of French people were stirred by a common loyalty. This was the birth of modern nationalism, which emerged fully throughout Europe in the nineteenth century.

The all-out mobilization of French resources under the Terror combined with the fervor of nationalism to create a new kind of army. After August 1793 all unmarried young men were subject to the draft, and by January 1794 French armed forces outnumbered those of their enemies almost four to one.[3] Well-trained, well-equipped, and constantly indoctrinated, by spring 1794 French armies were victorious on all fronts. The republic was saved.

The Thermidorian Reaction and the Directory

Military success led Robespierre and the Committee of Public Safety to relax the emergency economic controls, but they extended the political Reign of Terror. In March 1794 Robespierre's Terror wiped out many of his critics. Two weeks later Robespierre sent long-standing collaborators whom he believed had turned against him, including Danton, to the guillotine. A group of radicals and moderates in the Convention, knowing that they might be next, organized a conspiracy. They howled down Robespierre when he tried to speak to the National Convention on July 27, 1794—a date known as 9 Thermidor according to France's newly adopted republican calendar. The next day it was Robespierre's turn to be guillotined.

Thermidorian reaction A reaction to the violence of the Reign of Terror in 1794, resulting in the execution of Robespierre and the loosening of economic controls.

The Execution of Robespierre Completely wooden except for the heavy iron blade, the guillotine was painted red for Robespierre's execution, a detail not captured in this black-and-white engraving of the 1794 event. Large crowds witnessed the execution in a majestic public square in central Paris, then known as the Place de la Revolution and now called the Place de la Concorde (Harmony Square). (Snark/Art Resource, NY)

After the demise of Robespierre, the respectable middle-class lawyers and professionals who had led the liberal revolution of 1789 reasserted their authority. This period of Thermidorian reaction, as it was called, harkened back to the beginnings of the Revolution, rejecting radicalism in favor of moderate policies that favored property owners. In 1795 the National Convention abolished many economic controls, let prices rise sharply, and severely restricted the local political organizations through which the sans-culottes exerted their strength.

In 1795 the middle-class members of the National Convention wrote yet another constitution to guarantee their economic position and political supremacy. As in previous elections, the mass of the population voted only for electors, whose number was cut back to men of substantial means. Electors then voted for members of a reorganized Legislative Assembly to replace the National Convention and

Chapter 22 Revolutions in the
594 Atlantic World • 1775–1815

CHAPTER LOCATOR

What factors combined to spark revolutions in the Atlantic world?

for key officials throughout France. The new assembly also chose a five-man executive body called the Directory.

The Directory continued to support French military expansion, but war was no longer so much a crusade as a response to economic problems. Large, victorious French armies reduced unemployment at home. However, the French people quickly grew weary of the corruption and ineffectiveness that characterized the Directory. This general dissatisfaction revealed itself in the national elections of 1797, which returned a large number of conservative and even monarchist deputies. The members of the Directory, fearing for their skins, used the army to nullify the elections and began to govern dictatorially. Two years later Napoleon Bonaparte ended the Directory in a coup d'état (koo day-TAH) and substituted a strong dictatorship for a weak one.

Quick Review
How did war between France and many of its neighbors shape the French Revolution from 1792 on?

How did Napoleon assume control of France and much of Europe?

For almost fifteen years, from 1799 to 1814, France was in the hands of a military dictator. Napoleon Bonaparte (1769–1821) realized the need to put an end to civil strife in France in order to create unity and consolidate his rule. And he did. But Napoleon saw himself as a man of destiny, and the glory of war and the dream of universal empire proved irresistible.

Napoleon's Rule of France

Born on the Mediterranean island of Corsica into an impoverished noble family, Napoleon left home and became a lieutenant in the French artillery in 1785. After a brief and unsuccessful adventure fighting for Corsican independence in 1789, he returned to France as a French patriot and a revolutionary. Rising rapidly in the new army, Napoleon was placed in command of French forces in Italy and won brilliant victories there in 1796 and 1797. His next campaign, in Egypt, was a failure, but Napoleon returned to France before the fiasco was generally known, and his reputation remained intact.

Napoleon soon learned that some prominent members of the legislature were plotting against the Directory. The dissatisfaction of these plotters stemmed not so much from the fact that the Directory was a dictatorship as from the fact that it was a weak dictatorship.

The young Napoleon, nationally revered for his heroism, was an ideal choice for the strong ruler the conspirators were seeking. Thus they and Napoleon organized a takeover. On November 9, 1799, they ousted the Directors, and the following day soldiers disbanded the legislature. Napoleon was named first consul of the republic, and a new constitution consolidating his position was overwhelmingly approved in a plebiscite in December 1799.

The essence of Napoleon's domestic policy was to use his personal popularity to maintain order and end civil strife. He did so by working out unwritten agreements with powerful groups in France whereby the groups received favors in return for loyal service. Napoleon's bargain with the middle class was codified in the famous Civil Code of March 1804, also known as the **Napoleonic Code**, which reasserted two of the fundamental principles of the Revolution of 1789: equality of all male citizens before the law and absolute security of wealth and private property.

At the same time, Napoleon built on the bureaucracy inherited from the Revolution and the former monarchy to create a thoroughly centralized state and applied his diplomatic skills to healing the Catholic Church in France so that it could serve as a bulwark of

Napoleonic Code French civil code promulgated in 1804 that reasserted the 1789 principles of the equality of all male citizens before the law and the absolute security of wealth and private property.

social stability. Napoleon and Pope Pius VII (pontificate 1800–1823) signed the Concordat of 1801. Under this agreement the pope gained the right for French Catholics to practice their religion freely, but Napoleon gained political power: his government now nominated bishops, paid the clergy, and exerted great influence over the church in France. Thus, religious reconciliation went hand-in-hand with political centralization.

The domestic reforms of Napoleon's early years were his greatest achievement, and much of his legal and administrative reorganization has survived in France to this day. More generally, Napoleon's domestic initiatives gave the great majority of French people a sense of stability and national unity.

But order and unity had a price: authoritarian rule. Women lost many of the gains they made in the 1790s. Under the new Napoleonic Code, women were regarded as dependents of either their fathers or their husbands. In other restrictions, free speech and freedom of the press were curtailed, and the occasional elections were thoroughly controlled by Napoleon and his government. After 1810 political suspects were held in state prisons, as they had been during the Terror.

Napoleon's Expansion in Europe

After coming to power in 1799 Napoleon sent peace feelers to Austria and Britain, the two remaining members of the Second Coalition that had been formed against France in 1798. When these overtures were rejected, French armies led by Napoleon decisively defeated the Austrians. Subsequent treaties with Austria in 1801 and Britain in 1802 consolidated France's hold on the territories its armies had won up to that point.

In 1802 Napoleon was secure but still driven to expand his power. Aggressively redrawing the map of Germany so as to weaken Austria and encourage the secondary states of southwestern Germany to side with France, Napoleon tried to restrict British trade with all of Europe. He then plotted to attack Britain, but his Mediterranean fleet was destroyed by Lord Nelson at the Battle of Trafalgar on October 21, 1805. Renewed fighting had its advantages, however, for the first consul used his high status as a military leader to have himself proclaimed emperor in late 1804.

Austria, Russia, and Sweden joined with Britain to form the Third Coalition against France shortly before the Battle of Trafalgar. Yet the Austrians and the Russians were no match for Napoleon, who scored a brilliant victory over them at the Battle of Austerlitz in December 1805. Russia decided to pull back, and Austria accepted large territorial losses in return for peace as the Third Coalition collapsed.

Napoleon then reorganized the German states to his liking. In 1806 he established the German Confederation of the Rhine, a union of fifteen German states minus Austria, Prussia, and Saxony. Naming himself "protector" of the confederation, Napoleon firmly controlled western Germany.

Napoleon's intervention in German affairs alarmed the Prussians, who mobilized their armies. In October 1806 Napoleon attacked them and won two more brilliant victories at Jena and Auerstädt. The war with Prussia, now joined by Russia, continued into the following spring. After Napoleon's armies won another victory, Alexander I of Russia was ready to negotiate for peace. In the treaties of Tilsit in 1807, Prussia lost half of its population through

German Confederation of the Rhine, 1806

Chapter 22   Revolutions in the
596   Atlantic World • 1775–1815

CHAPTER LOCATOR

What factors combined to spark revolutions in the Atlantic world?

land concessions, while Russia accepted Napoleon's reorganization of western and central Europe and promised to enforce Napoleon's economic blockade against British goods.

The Grand Empire and Its End

Increasingly, Napoleon saw himself as the emperor not just of France, but of a Grand Empire that included virtually all of Europe. After 1806 both satellites and allies were expected to support Napoleon's Continental System, a blockade in which no ship coming from Britain or her colonies was allowed to dock at any port controlled by the French. It was intended to halt all trade between Britain and continental Europe, thereby destroying the British economy and its military force.

The impact of the Grand Empire on the peoples of Europe was considerable. In the areas incorporated into France and in the satellites, Napoleon abolished feudal dues and serfdom. Yet he had to put the prosperity and special interests of France first in order to safeguard his power base. Levying heavy taxes in money and men for his armies, Napoleon came to be regarded more as a conquering tyrant than as an enlightened liberator. Thus French rule sparked patriotic upheavals and encouraged the growth of reactive nationalism.

The first great revolt occurred in Spain. In 1808 a coalition of Catholics, monarchists, and patriots rebelled against Napoleon's attempts to make Spain a French satellite. French armies occupied Madrid, but the foes of Napoleon fled to the hills and waged uncompromising

Grand Empire The empire over which Napoleon and his allies ruled, encompassing virtually all of Europe except Great Britain and Russia.

Continental System A blockade imposed by Napoleon to halt all trade between continental Europe and Britain, thereby weakening the British economy and military.

Francisco Goya, *The Third of May 1808* Spanish master Francisco Goya created a passionate and moving indictment of the brutality of war in this painting from 1814, which depicts the close-range execution of Spanish rebels by Napoleon's forces in May 1808. Goya's painting evoked the bitterness and despair of many Europeans who suffered through Napoleon's invasions. (Erich Lessing/Art Resource, NY)

How did American colonists forge a new, independent nation?

What were the causes and consequences of the French Revolution?

How and why did the French Revolution take a radical turn?

How did Napoleon assume control of France and much of Europe?

What led to the creation of the independent state of Haiti in 1804?

597

Map legend:
- French empire
- Dependent states
- Allied with Napoleon
- ✳ French victory
- ✳ French defeat

Mapping the Past

Map 22.2 Napoleonic Europe in 1812

At the height of the Grand Empire in 1810, Napoleon had conquered or allied with every major European power except Britain. But in 1812, angered by Russian repudiation of his ban on trade with Britain, Napoleon invaded Russia with disastrous results. Compare this map with Map 17.2 (page 444), which shows the division of Europe in 1715.

ANALYZING THE MAP How had the balance of power shifted in Europe from 1715 to 1812? What changed, and what remained the same? What was the impact of Napoleon's wars on Germany, the Italian peninsula, and Russia?

CONNECTIONS Why did Napoleon achieve vast territorial gains where Louis XIV did not?

598 Chapter 22 Revolutions in the Atlantic World • 1775–1815

CHAPTER LOCATOR

What factors combined to spark revolutions in the Atlantic world?

guerrilla warfare. Events in Spain sent a clear warning: resistance to French imperialism was growing.

Yet Napoleon pushed on. By 1810, it was clear that the Continental System was a failure. Instead of harming Britain, the system provoked Britain to set up a counter-blockade, which created hard times for French artisans and the middle class. Perhaps looking for a scapegoat, Napoleon turned on Alexander I of Russia, who in 1811 openly repudiated Napoleon's war of prohibitions against British goods.

Napoleon's invasion of Russia began in June 1812. Originally, he planned to winter in the Russian city of Smolensk if Alexander did not sue for peace. However, after reaching Smolensk Napoleon recklessly pressed on toward Moscow (Map 22.2). The Battle of Borodino that followed was a draw, and the Russians retreated in good order. Alexander ordered the evacuation of Moscow, which the Russians then burned in part, and he refused to negotiate. Finally, after five weeks in the scorched and abandoned city, Napoleon ordered a disastrous retreat. The Russian army, the Russian winter, and starvation cut Napoleon's army to pieces.

Leaving his troops to their fate, Napoleon raced to Paris to raise another army. Meanwhile, Austria and Prussia deserted Napoleon and joined Russia and Britain. Less than a month later, on April 4, 1814, a defeated Napoleon abdicated his throne. After this unconditional abdication, the victorious allies exiled Napoleon to the island of Elba off the coast of Italy.

In February 1815 Napoleon escaped from Elba. Landing in France, he issued appeals for support and marched on Paris. French officers and soldiers who had fought so long for their emperor responded to the call, and once more Napoleon took command. But Napoleon's gamble was a desperate long shot, for the allies were united against him. At the end of a frantic period known as the Hundred Days, they crushed his forces at Waterloo on June 18, 1815, and imprisoned him on the island of St. Helena, off the western coast of Africa.

> **Quick Review**
> How did Napoleon build on the developments of the 1790s to create a powerful, expansionist dictatorship in France?

What led to the creation of the independent state of Haiti in 1804?

The events that led to the creation of the independent nation of Haiti constitute the third chapter of the revolutionary era in the Atlantic world. Prior to 1789 Saint-Domingue, the French colony that was to become Haiti, reaped huge profits through a system of slave-based plantation agriculture. News of revolution in France lit a powder keg of contradictory aspirations among white planters, free people of color, and slaves. While revolutionary authorities debated how far to extend the rights of man on Saint-Domingue, slaves took matters into their own hands, rising up to claim their freedom. Ultimately, their revolt succeeded and in 1804 Haiti became the first nation in history to claim its freedom through slave revolt.

Revolutionary Aspirations in Saint-Domingue

On the eve of the French Revolution, Saint-Domingue—the most profitable of all Caribbean colonies—was rife with social tensions. The colony, which occupied the western third of the island of Hispaniola, was inhabited by a variety of social groups who resented and mistrusted one another. The European population included French colonial officials, wealthy plantation owners and merchants, and poor immigrants. Vastly outnumbering the white population were the colony's five hundred thousand slaves, along with a sizable population of free people of African and mixed African and European descent. Members of this last group referred to themselves as free people of color.

The 1685 Code Noir (Black Code) that set the parameters of slavery had granted free people of color the same legal status as whites. From the 1760s on, however, colonial administrators began restricting their rights, and by the time of the French Revolution, myriad aspects of free coloreds' lives were ruled by discriminatory laws.

The political and intellectual turmoil of the 1780s, with its growing rhetoric of liberty, equality, and fraternity, raised new challenges and possibilities for each of Saint-Domingue's social groups. For slaves, who constituted approximately 90 percent of the population, news of abolitionist movements in France led to hopes that they might gain their freedom. Free people of color looked to reforms in Paris as a means of gaining political enfranchisement and reasserting equal status with whites. Infuriated by talk of abolition and determined to protect their way of life, white elites looked to revolutionary ideals of representative government for the chance to gain control of their own affairs, as had the American colonists before them.

The National Assembly frustrated the hopes of all these groups. Cowed by colonial representatives who claimed that support for free people of color would result in slave insurrection and independence, the Assembly refused to extend French constitutional safeguards to the colonies. At the same time, the committee also reaffirmed French monopolies over colonial trade, thereby angering planters as well. Like the American settlers before them, the colonists chafed under the rule of the mother country.

In July 1790 Vincent Ogé (aw-ZHAY; ca. 1750–1791), a free man of color, returned to Saint-Domingue from Paris determined to win rights for his people. He raised an army and sent letters to the new Provincial Assembly of Saint-Domingue demanding political rights for all free citizens. But Ogé's demands were refused, so he and his followers turned to armed insurrection. After initial victories, his army was defeated, and Ogé was killed. Revolutionary leaders in Paris were more sympathetic to Ogé's cause. In May 1791, the National Assembly granted political rights to free people of color born to two free parents who possessed sufficient property. However, when news of this legislation arrived in Saint-Domingue, the colonial governor refused to enact it. Violence now erupted between groups of whites and free coloreds in parts of the colony.

The Outbreak of Revolt

Just as the sans-culottes helped push forward more radical reforms in France, the second stage of revolution in Saint-Domingue also resulted from decisive action from below. In August 1791 slaves, who had witnessed the confrontation between whites and free coloreds for over a year, took events into their own hands.

Revolts began on a few plantations on the night of August 22. Within a few days the uprising had swept much of the northern plain, creating a slave army that quickly grew in size and strength. During the next month slaves attacked and destroyed hundreds of sugar and coffee plantations.

On April 4, 1792, as war loomed with the European states, the National Assembly issued a decree extending full citizenship rights, including the right to vote, to free black men and free men of color. The Assembly hoped this measure would win the loyalty of free blacks and their aid in defeating the slave rebellion.

Warfare in Europe soon spread to Saint-Domingue (Map 22.3). Since the beginning of the slave insurrection, the Spanish colony of Santo Domingo, just to the east of Saint-Domingue, had supported rebel slaves. In early 1793 the Spanish began to bring slave leaders and their soldiers into the Spanish army. Toussaint L'Ouverture (TOO-sahn LOO-vair-toor; 1743–1803), a freed slave who had joined the revolt, was named a Spanish officer. In September the British navy blockaded the colony, and invading British troops captured

600 Chapter 22 Revolutions in the Atlantic World • 1775–1815

CHAPTER LOCATOR

What factors combined to spark revolutions in the Atlantic world?

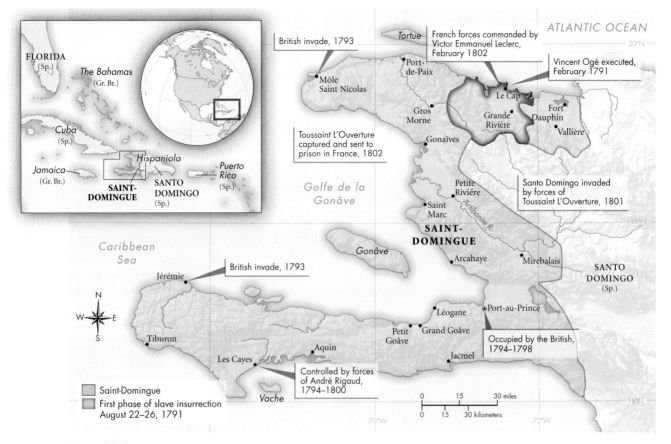

Map 22.3 The War of Haitian Independence, 1791–1804 Neighbored by the Spanish colony of Santo Domingo, Saint-Domingue was the most profitable European colony in the Caribbean. In 1791 slave revolts erupted in the north near Le Cap, which had once been the capital. In 1770 the French had transferred the capital to Port-au-Prince, which in 1804 became capital of the newly independent Haiti.

French territory on the island. For the Spanish and British, revolutionary chaos provided a tempting opportunity to capture a profitable colony.

Desperate for forces to oppose France's enemies, commissioners sent by the newly elected National Convention promised freedom to slaves who fought for France. By October 1793 they had abolished slavery throughout the colony. On February 4, 1794, the Convention ratified the abolition of slavery and extended it to all French territories, including the Caribbean colonies of Martinique and Guadeloupe.

The tide of battle began to turn when Toussaint L'Ouverture and his army of four thousand well-trained soldiers switched sides. By 1796 the French had regained control of the colony, and L'Ouverture had emerged as the key leader of the combined slave and free colored forces. (See "Individuals in Society: Toussaint L'Ouverture," page 602.) In May 1796 he was named commander of the western province of Saint-Domingue (see Map 22.3). The increasingly conservative nature of the French government during the Thermidorian reaction, however, threatened to undo the gains made by former slaves and free people of color.

The War of Haitian Independence

With Toussaint L'Ouverture acting increasingly as an independent ruler of the western province of Saint-Domingue, another general, André Rigaud (1761–1811), set up his own government in the southern peninsula. Tensions mounted between L'Ouverture and Rigaud.

How did American colonists forge a new, independent nation?

What were the causes and consequences of the French Revolution?

How and why did the French Revolution take a radical turn?

How did Napoleon assume control of France and much of Europe?

What led to the creation of the independent state of Haiti in 1804?

601

INDIVIDUALS IN SOCIETY

Toussaint L'Ouverture

LITTLE IS KNOWN OF THE EARLY LIFE of Saint-Domingue's brilliant military and political leader Toussaint L'Ouverture. He was born in 1743 on a plantation outside Le Cap owned by the Count de Bréda. According to tradition, L'Ouverture was the eldest son of a captured African prince from modern-day Benin. Toussaint Bréda, as he was then called, occupied a privileged position among slaves. Instead of performing backbreaking labor in the fields, he served his master as a coachman and livestock keeper. He also learned to read and write French and some Latin, but he was always more comfortable with the Creole dialect.

During the 1770s the plantation manager emancipated L'Ouverture, who subsequently leased his own small coffee plantation, worked by slaves. He married Suzanne Simone, who already had one son, and the couple had another son during their marriage. In 1791 he joined the slave uprisings that swept Saint-Domingue, and he took on the *nom de guerre* ("war name") L'Ouverture, meaning "the opening." L'Ouverture rose to prominence among rebel slaves allied with Spain and by early 1794 controlled his own army. A devout Catholic who led a frugal and ascetic life, L'Ouverture impressed others with his enormous physical energy, intellectual acumen, and air of mystery. In 1794 he defected to the French side and led his troops to a series of victories against the Spanish. In 1795 the National Convention promoted L'Ouverture to brigadier general.

Over the next three years L'Ouverture successively eliminated rivals for authority on the island. First he freed himself of the French commissioners sent to govern the colony. With a firm grip on power in the northern province, L'Ouverture defeated General André Rigaud in 1800 to gain control in the south. His army then marched on the capital of Spanish Santo Domingo on the eastern half of the island, meeting little resistance. The entire island of Hispaniola was now under his command.

With control in his hands, L'Ouverture was confronted with the challenge of building a post-emancipation society, the first of its kind. The task was made even more difficult by the chaos wreaked by war, the destruction of plantations, and bitter social and racial tensions. For L'Ouverture the most pressing concern was to re-establish the plantation economy. Without revenue to pay his army, the gains of the rebellion could be lost. He therefore encouraged white planters to return and reclaim their property. He also adopted harsh policies

toward former slaves, forcing them back to their plantations and restricting their ability to acquire land. When they resisted, he sent troops across the island to enforce submission. L'Ouverture's 1801 constitution reaffirmed his draconian labor policies and named L'Ouverture governor for life, leaving Saint-Domingue as a colony in name alone. In June 1802 French forces arrested L'Ouverture and jailed him at Fort de Joux in France's Jura Mountains near the Swiss border. He died of pneumonia on April 7, 1803, leaving his lieutenant, Jean Jacques Dessalines, to win independence for the new Haitian nation.

QUESTIONS FOR ANALYSIS

1. Toussaint L'Ouverture was both slave and slave owner. How did each experience shape his life and actions?
2. What did L'Ouverture and Napoleon Bonaparte have in common? How did they differ?

Equestrian portrait of Toussaint L'Ouverture. (Réunion des Musées Nationaux/Art Resource, NY)

While L'Ouverture was a freed slave of African descent, Rigaud belonged to the free colored elite. This elite resented the growing power of former slaves, who in turn accused them of adopting the racism of white settlers. Civil war broke out between the two sides in 1799, when L'Ouverture's forces, led by his lieutenant, Jean Jacques Dessalines (1758–1806), invaded the south. Victory over Rigaud in 1800 gave L'Ouverture control of the entire colony.

602

Chapter 22 Revolutions in the Atlantic World • 1775–1815

CHAPTER LOCATOR

What factors combined to spark revolutions in the Atlantic world?

This victory was soon challenged by Napoleon, who ordered his brother-in-law, General Charles-Victor-Emmanuel Leclerc (1772–1802), to lead an expedition to the island to crush the new regime. In 1802 Leclerc landed in Saint-Domingue and ordered the arrest of Toussaint L'Ouverture. The rebel leader was deported to France, along with his family, where he died in 1803.

It was left to L'Ouverture's lieutenant, Jean Jacques Dessalines, to unite the resistance, and he led it to a crushing victory over French forces. On January 1, 1804, Dessalines formally declared the independence of Saint-Domingue and the creation of the new sovereign nation of Haiti, the name used by the pre-Columbian inhabitants of the island.

Haiti, the second independent state in the Americas and the first in Latin America, was born from the first successful large-scale slave revolt in history. Haitian independence had fundamental repercussions for world history, helping spread the idea that liberty, equality, and fraternity must apply to all people. The next phase of Atlantic revolution soon opened in the Spanish American colonies.

> **Quick Review**
> How did revolution in France lead to revolution in Haiti?

Connections

THE ATLANTIC WORLD was the essential context for the great revolutionary wave of the late eighteenth century. The movement of peoples, commodities, and ideas across the Atlantic Ocean in the eighteenth century created a world of common debates, conflicts, and aspirations. Moreover, the high stakes of colonial empire heightened competition among European states, leading to a series of wars that generated crushing costs for overburdened treasuries. For both the British in their North American colonies and the French at home, the desperate need for new taxes weakened government authority and opened the door to revolution. In turn, the ideals of the French Revolution inspired slaves and free people of color in Saint-Domingue, thus opening the promise of liberty, equality, and fraternity to people of all races.

The chain reaction did not end with the birth of an independent Haiti in 1804. The next chapter of liberation movements took place in Spanish America in the following decades (see Chapter 27). On the European continent throughout the nineteenth and early twentieth centuries, periodic convulsions occurred as successive generations struggled over political rights first proclaimed by the generation of 1789 (see Chapter 24). Meanwhile, as dramatic political events unfolded, a parallel economic revolution was gathering steam. This was the Industrial Revolution, originating around 1750 and accelerating through the end of the eighteenth century (see Chapter 23). After 1815 the twin forces of industrialization and democratization would combine to transform Europe and the world.

- **For a list of suggested readings for this chapter, visit** *bedfordstmartins.com/mckayworldunderstanding*.

- **For primary sources from this period, see** *Sources of World Societies*, Second Edition.

- **For Web sites, images, and documents related to topics in this chapter, see Make History at** *bedfordstmartins.com/ mckayworldunderstanding*.

Chapter 22 Study Guide

To do these exercises online, go to bedfordstmartins.com/mckayworldundunderstanding.

 Step 1

GETTING STARTED
Below are basic terms about this period in global history. Can you identify each term below and explain why it matters?

TERMS	WHO (OR WHAT) AND WHEN	WHY IT MATTERS
Treaty of Paris, p. 580		
Declaration of Independence, p. 583		
Antifederalists, p. 583		
Estates General, p. 585		
National Assembly, p. 586		
Jacobin club, p. 591		
Girondists, p. 591		
Mountain, p. 591		
sans-culottes, p. 592		
Reign of Terror, p. 592		
Thermidorian reaction, p. 594		
Napoleonic Code, p. 595		
Grand Empire, p. 597		
Continental System, p. 597		

Step 2

MOVING BEYOND THE BASICS
The exercise below requires a more advanced understanding of the chapter material. Examine the four main phases of the French Revolution by filling in the chart below with descriptions of the leaders and key groups that shaped important developments, the policies and reforms initiated during each phase, and the groups that gained and lost the most as a result of those policies. When you are finished, consider the following questions: How did the nature of the Revolution change between 1789 and 1799? What role did violence play in the transition between each phase of the Revolution? What were the longest lasting consequences of the Revolution? Whose vision of the Revolution came closest to becoming a reality?

	LEADERS AND KEY GROUPS	POLICIES AND REFORMS	WINNERS AND LOSERS
The First Revolution: 1789–1791			
The Second Revolution: 1791–1794			
The Directory: 1795–1799			
Napoleonic France: 1799–1815			

PUTTING IT ALL TOGETHER

Now that you've reviewed key elements of the chapter, take a step back and try to see the big picture. Remember to use specific examples from the chapter in your answers.

THE AGE OF REVOLUTIONS BEGINS

- How did social, economic, ideological, and fiscal problems combine to spark the age of revolutions?
- How did the relative social and political equality enjoyed by white inhabitants of the British North American colonies shape the American Revolution?

THE FRENCH REVOLUTION

- What role did the poor people of France play in shaping the French Revolution? At what points did they take control of events from elite and middle-class leaders?
- How was violence used as a political tool during the period of the Second Revolution? What justifications were offered for its use? In your opinion, how valid were these justifications?

THE NAPOLEONIC ERA AND THE HAITIAN REVOLUTION

- Should Napoleon be considered a "revolutionary"? Why or why not?
- How did the people of Saint-Domingue react to the news of revolution in France? How would you explain their reaction? How did the French Revolution contribute to increasing social and political tensions in Saint-Domingue?

LOOKING BACK, LOOKING AHEAD

- What was revolutionary about the age of revolution? How did the states that emerged out of the eighteenth-century revolutions differ from the states that predominated in previous centuries?
- In what sense did the age of revolution mark the beginning of modern politics in Europe and the Americas?

In Your Own Words Imagine that you must explain Chapter 22 to someone who hasn't read it. What would be the most important points to include and why?

23

The Revolution in Energy and Industry

1760–1850

While the revolutions of the Atlantic world and in France were opening a new political era, another revolution was beginning to transform economic and social life. The Industrial Revolution began in Great Britain around the 1780s and started to influence continental Europe after 1815. Quite possibly only the development of agriculture during Neolithic times had a comparable impact and significance. Non-European nations began to industrialize after 1860, with the United States and Japan taking an early lead.

The Industrial Revolution profoundly modified much of human experience. It changed patterns of work, transformed the social class structure and the way people thought about class, and eventually altered the international balance of political power. In time, the Industrial Revolution also helped ordinary people gain a higher standard of living as the widespread poverty of the preindustrial world was gradually reduced.

Unfortunately, improvement in the European standard of living was limited until about 1850 for at least two reasons. First, even in Britain, only a few key industries experienced a technological revolution. Second, rapid growth in population threatened to eat up the growth in production and to leave most individuals poorer than ever. Industrialization drew on British profits from Atlantic trade, including slavery. Even more important were the consequences of early industrialization in Britain and on the European continent, which allowed Europeans to increase their economic and political dominance over other nations.

Young Factory Worker
Children composed a substantial element of the workforce in early factories, where they toiled long hours in dangerous conditions. Boys working in glass-bottle factories, like the youth here, stoked blazing furnaces with coal and learned to blow glass. (© Boume Gallery, Reigate, Surrey, UK/The Bridgeman Art Library)

Chapter Preview

▶ How and why did Britain industrialize between 1780 and 1850?

▶ When and how did industrialization spread beyond Britain?

▶ What were the social consequences of industrialization?

How and why did Britain industrialize between 1780 and 1850?

The Industrial Revolution began in Britain, the nation created by the formal union of Scotland, Wales, and England in 1707. Britain pioneered not only in industrial technology but also in social relations and urban living. Just as France was the trailblazer in political change, Britain was the leader in economic development, and it must therefore command special attention.

Origins of the British Industrial Revolution

It is generally agreed that industrial changes in Britain grew out of a long process of development. The scientific revolution and Enlightenment fostered a new worldview that embraced progress and the role of research and experimentation in understanding and mastering the natural world. In the economic realm, the seventeenth-century expansion of English woolen cloth exports throughout Europe brought commercial profits and high wages. By the eighteenth century the expanding Atlantic economy was also serving Britain well. Britain's colonial empire, augmented by a strong position in Latin America and in the African slave trade, provided raw materials like cotton and a growing market for British manufactured goods (see Chapter 18).

Agriculture also played an important role in bringing about the Industrial Revolution in Britain. English farmers were second only to the Dutch in productivity in 1700, and they were continually adopting new methods of farming. The result, especially before 1760, was a period of bountiful crops and low food prices. The ordinary English family no longer had to spend almost everything it earned just to buy bread, allowing for more spending on manufactured goods. Moreover, in the eighteenth century the members of the average British family were redirecting their labor away from unpaid work for household consumption toward work for wages that they could spend on goods, a trend reflecting the increasing commercialization of the entire European economy. In Britain, rising urbanization and high wages both reflected these developments and spurred them forward.

As manufacturing expanded to supply both foreign and British customers, the domestic market for raw materials was well-positioned to meet the growing demands of manufacturers. In an age when it was much cheaper to ship goods by water than by land, no part of England was far from navigable water. Beginning in the 1770s a canal-building boom enhanced this advantage. Rivers and canals provided easy movement of England's and Wales's enormous deposits of iron and coal, resources that would be critical raw materials in Europe's early industrial age. Nor were there any tariffs within the country to hinder trade, as there were in France before 1789 and in politically fragmented Germany.

Finally, Britain had long had a large class of hired agricultural laborers. These rural wage earners were

Cottage Industry and Transportation in Eighteenth-Century England

Industrial areas
- ■ Coal deposit
- ○ Metal goods
- ■ Woolen cloth
- — Canals, 1800
- — Navigable rivers

SCOTLAND

Newcastle

North Sea

Manchester · Sheffield

Birmingham · *Iron*

WALES

Iron

Bath · *Iron*

London

Exeter

English Channel

relatively mobile—compared to village-bound peasants in France and western Germany, for example—and along with cottage workers they formed a potential industrial labor force for capitalist entrepreneurs.

All these factors combined to initiate the Industrial Revolution, a term first coined in the 1830s to describe the burst of major inventions and technical changes in certain industries. This technical revolution went hand in hand with an impressive quickening in the annual rate of industrial growth in Britain. Whereas industry had grown at only 0.7 percent between 1700 and 1760 (before the Industrial Revolution), it grew at the much higher rate of 3 percent between 1801 and 1831 (when industrial transformation was in full swing).[1]

The First Factories

The pressures to produce more goods for a growing market and to reduce the labor costs of manufacturing were directly related to the first decisive breakthrough of the Industrial Revolution: the creation of the world's first large factories in the British cotton textile industry. Technological innovations in the manufacture of cotton cloth led to a new system of production and social relationships. The putting-out system involved a merchant who loaned, or "put out," raw materials to cottage workers who processed the raw materials in their own homes and returned the finished products to the merchant.

During the eighteenth century this system was used across Europe, but most extensively in Britain. There, pressured by growing demand, the system's limitations began to outweigh its advantages for the first time. This was especially true in the British textile industry after about 1760. There was always a serious imbalance in textile production based on cottage industry: the work of four or five spinners was needed to keep one weaver steadily employed. Cloth weavers constantly had to try to find more thread and more spinners.

There was another problem, at least from the merchant-capitalist's point of view. Scattered rural labor was extremely difficult to control. Cottage workers tended to work in spurts. After they got paid on Saturday afternoon, the men in particular tended to drink and carouse for two or three days. Productivity suffered, and by the end of the week many weavers had to work feverishly to make their quota. If they did not succeed, there was little the merchant could do. The merchant-capitalist's search for more efficient methods of production intensified.

The breakthrough came with the application of improved spinning technology to the production of cotton textiles. Cotton textiles had first been imported into Britain from India, and by 1760 a tiny domestic cotton industry had emerged in northern England. After many experiments over a generation, a gifted carpenter and jack-of-all-trades, James Hargreaves, invented his cotton-spinning jenny about 1765. At almost the same moment, a barber-turned-manufacturer named Richard Arkwright invented (or possibly pirated) another kind of spinning machine, the water frame. These breakthroughs produced an

Chapter Chronology

ca. 1765	Hargreaves invents spinning jenny; Arkwright creates water frame
1769	Watt patents modern steam engine
ca. 1780–1850	Industrial Revolution and accompanying population boom in Great Britain
1799	Combination Acts passed in England
1805	Egypt begins process of modernization
1810	Strike of Manchester, England, cotton spinners
ca. 1815	Industrial gap between continental Europe and England widens
1824	British Combination Acts repealed
1830	Stephenson's *Rocket*; first important railroad
1830s	Industrial banks promote rapid industrialization of Belgium
1833	Factory Act passed in England
1834	German *Zollverein* created
1842	Mines Act passed in England
1844	Engels, *The Condition of the Working Class in England*
1850s	Japan begins to adopt Western technologies; industrial gap widens between the West and the world
1851	Great Exhibition held at Crystal Palace in London
1860s	Germany and the United States begin to rapidly industrialize

Industrial Revolution A term first coined in the 1830s to describe the burst of major inventions and economic expansion that took place in certain industries, such as cotton textiles and iron, between 1780 and 1850.

How and why did Britain industrialize between 1780 and 1850? When and how did industrialization spread beyond Britain? What were the social consequences of industrialization?

Woman Working a Spinning Jenny The loose cotton strands on the slanted bobbins shown in this illustration of Hargreave's spinning jenny passed up to the sliding carriage and then on to the spindles in back for fine spinning. The worker, almost always a woman, regulated the sliding carriage with one hand, and with the other she turned the crank on the wheel to supply power. By 1783 one woman could spin a hundred threads at a time. (Mary Evans Picture Library/The Image Works)

spinning jenny A simple, inexpensive, hand-powered spinning machine created by James Hargreaves in 1765.

water frame A spinning machine created by Richard Arkwright that had a capacity of several hundred spindles and used waterpower; it therefore required a larger and more specialized mill—a factory.

explosion in the infant cotton textile industry in the 1780s. By 1790 the new machines were producing ten times as much cotton yarn as had been made in 1770.

Hargreaves's **spinning jenny** was simple, inexpensive, and powered by hand. In early models from six to twenty-four spindles were mounted on a sliding carriage, and each spindle spun a fine, slender thread. Now it was the weaver who could not keep up with the vastly more efficient spinner.

Arkwright's **water frame** employed a different principle. It quickly acquired a capacity of several hundred spindles and was driven by waterpower. The water frame thus required large specialized mills, factories that employed as many as one thousand workers from the very beginning. It did not completely replace cottage industry, however, for the water frame could spin only a coarse, strong thread, which was then put out for respinning on hand-powered cottage jennies. Around 1790 a hybrid machine invented by Samuel Crompton proved capable of spinning very fine and strong thread in large quantities. Gradually, all cotton spinning was concentrated in large-scale factories.

As a consequence of these revolutionary developments, cotton goods became much cheaper, and they were increasingly bought by all classes. Families using cotton in cottage industry were freed from their constant search for adequate yarn from scattered part-time spinners, since all the thread needed could be spun in the cottage on the jenny or obtained from a nearby factory. The wages of weavers, now hard-pressed to keep up with the spinners, rose markedly until about 1792. As a result, large numbers of agricultural laborers became hand-loom weavers, while mechanics and capitalists sought to invent a power loom to save on labor costs. This Edmund Cartwright achieved in 1785. But the power looms of the factories worked poorly at first, and hand-loom weavers continued to receive good wages until at least 1800.

Unfortunately, working conditions in the early cotton factories were less satisfactory than those of cottage weavers and spinners, and adult workers were reluctant to work in them. Therefore, factory owners often turned to young children who had been abandoned by their parents and put in the care of local parishes. Apprenticed as young as five or six years of age, such children were forced by law to labor for their "masters" for as many as fourteen years. Housed, fed, and locked up nightly in factory dormitories, the young workers labored thirteen or fourteen hours a day for little or no pay. Harsh physical punishment maintained brutal discipline.

The creation of the world's first modern factories in the British cotton textile industry in the 1770s and 1780s, which grew out of the putting-out system of cottage production, was a major historical development. Both symbolically and substantially, the big new cotton mills marked the beginning of the Industrial Revolution in Britain. By 1831 the largely mechanized cotton textile industry accounted for fully 22 percent of the country's entire industrial production.

The Steam Engine Breakthrough

In the eighteenth century, population growth and deforestation combined to create an energy crisis in western Europe. The shortage of energy had become particularly severe in Britain. Wood, a basic raw material and the primary source of heat for all homes and industries, was in ever-shorter supply. Processed wood (charcoal) was the fuel that was mixed with iron ore in the blast furnace to produce pig iron. The iron industry's appetite for wood was enormous, and by 1740 the British iron industry was stagnating.

As this early energy crisis grew worse, Britain looked to coal as an alternative to its vanishing wood. Coal was first used in Britain in the late Middle Ages as a source of heat. By 1640 most homes in London were heated with coal, and it was also used in industry to provide heat for making beer, glass, soap, and other products. The breakthrough came when industrialists began to use coal to produce mechanical energy and to power machinery.

As more coal was produced, mines were dug deeper and deeper, and they were constantly filling with water. Mechanical pumps, usually powered by animals, had to be installed. Such power was expensive and bothersome. In an attempt to overcome these disadvantages, Thomas Savery in 1698 and Thomas Newcomen in 1705 invented the first primitive **steam engines**. Both engines burned coal to produce steam, which was then used to operate a pump. By the early 1770s many such engines were operating successfully in English and Scottish mines.

In 1763 James Watt (1736–1819) was drawn to a critical study of the steam engine. Watt was employed at the time by the University of Glasgow as a skilled craftsman making scientific instruments, and in 1763 he was called on to repair a Newcomen engine being used in a physics course. After a series of observations, Watt saw that the Newcomen engine could be improved by adding a separate condenser. This splendid invention, patented in 1769, greatly increased the efficiency of the steam engine.

The coal-burning steam engine of Watt and his followers was the Industrial Revolution's most fundamental advance in technology. For the first time in history, humanity had, at least for a few generations, almost unlimited power at its disposal. For the first time, inventors and engineers could devise and implement all kinds of power equipment to aid people in their work.

The steam engine was quickly put to use in several industries in Britain. It drained mines and made possible the production of ever more coal to feed steam engines elsewhere. The steam-power plant began to replace waterpower in the cotton-spinning mills during the 1780s, contributing greatly to that industry's phenomenal rise. Steam also took the place of waterpower in flour mills, in the malt mills used in breweries, in the flint mills supplying the pottery industry (see "Individuals in Society: Josiah Wedgwood," page 612), and in the mills exported by Britain to the West Indies to crush sugarcane.

Coal and steam power promoted important breakthroughs in other industries. The British iron industry was radically transformed. Starting around 1710, ironmakers began to use coke — a smokeless and hot-burning fuel produced by heating coal to rid it of water and impurities — to smelt pig iron. After 1770 the adoption of steam-driven bellows in blast furnaces allowed for great increases in the quantity of pig iron produced by British

steam engines A breakthrough invention by Thomas Savery in 1698 and Thomas Newcomen in 1705 that burned coal to produce steam, which was then used to operate a pump; the early models were superseded by James Watt's more efficient steam engine, patented in 1769.

INDIVIDUALS IN SOCIETY

Josiah Wedgwood

AS THE MAKING OF CLOTH AND IRON WAS revolutionized by technical change and factory organization, so too were the production and consumption of pottery. Acquiring beautiful tableware became a craze for eighteenth-century consumers, and continental monarchs often sought prestige in building royal china works. But the grand prize went to Josiah Wedgwood, who wanted to "astonish the world."

The twelfth child of a poor potter, Josiah Wedgwood (1730–1795) grew up in the pottery district of Staffordshire in the English Midlands, where many tiny potteries made simple earthenware utensils for sale in local markets. Having grown up as an apprentice in the family business inherited by his oldest brother, Wedgwood struck off on his own in 1752. Soon manager of a small pottery, Wedgwood learned that new products recharged lagging sales. Studying chemistry and determined to succeed, Wedgwood spent his evenings experimenting with different chemicals and firing conditions.

In 1759, after five years of tireless efforts, Wedgwood perfected a beautiful new green glaze. Now established as a master potter, he opened his own factory and began manufacturing teapots and tableware finished in his green and other unique glazes, or adorned with printed scenes far superior to those being produced by competitors. Wedgwood's products caused a sensation among consumers, and his business quickly earned substantial profits. Subsequent breakthroughs, including ornamental vases imitating classical Greek models and jasperware for jewelry, contributed greatly to Wedgwood's success.

Competitors were quick to copy Wedgwood's new products and sell them at lower prices. Thus Wedgwood and his partner Thomas Bentley sought to cultivate an image of superior fashion, taste, and quality in order to develop and maintain a dominant market position. They did this by first capturing the business of the trend-setting elite. In one brilliant coup the partners first sold a very large cream-colored dinner set to Britain's queen, which they quickly christened "Queen's ware" and sold as a very expensive, must-have luxury to English aristocrats. Equally brilliant was Bentley's suave expertise in the elegant London showroom selling Wedgwood's imitation Greek vases, which became the rage after the rediscovery of Pompeii and Herculaneum in the mid-eighteenth century.

Above all, once Wedgwood had secured his position as the luxury market leader, he was able to successfully extend his famous brand to the growing middle class, capturing an enormous mass market for his "useful ware." Thus when sales of a luxury good grew "stale," Wedgwood made tasteful modifications and sold it to the middling classes for twice the price his competitors could charge. This unbeatable combination of mass appeal and high prices brought Wedgwood great fame all across Europe and enormous wealth.

A workaholic with an authoritarian streak, Wedgwood contributed substantially to the development of the factory system. In 1769 he opened a model factory on a new canal he had promoted. With two hundred workers in several departments, Wedgwood exercised tremendous control over his workforce, imposing fines for many infractions, such as being late, drinking on the job, or wasting material. He wanted, he said, to create men who would be like "machines" that "cannot err." Yet Wedgwood also recognized the value in treating workers well. He championed a division of labor that made most workers specialists who received ongoing training. He also encouraged employment of family groups, who were housed in company row houses with long narrow backyards suitable for raising vegetables and chickens. Paying relatively high wages and providing pensions and some benefits, Wedgwood developed a high-quality labor force that learned to accept his rigorous discipline and carried out his ambitious plans.

QUESTIONS FOR ANALYSIS

1. How and why did Wedgwood succeed?
2. Was Wedgwood a good boss or a bad one? Why?
3. How did Wedgwood exemplify the new class of factory owners?

Josiah Wedgwood (top right) perfected jasperware, a fine-grained pottery usually made in "Wedgwood blue" with white decoration. This elegant cylindrical vase (right), decorated in the form of a miniature Roman household altar, was destined for the luxury market. (portrait: Down House, Kent, Darwin Heirlooms Trust; vase: Image copyright © The Metropolitan Museum of Art/Art Resource, NY) ironmakers. In the 1780s Henry Cort developed the puddling furnace, which allowed pig iron to be refined in turn with coke.

Cort also developed steam-powered rolling mills, which were capable of spewing out finished iron in every shape and form. The economic consequence of these technical innovations was a great boom in the British iron industry. In 1740 annual British iron production was only 17,000 tons. With the spread of coke smelting and the impact of Cort's inventions, production had reached 260,000 tons by 1806. In 1844 Britain produced 3 million tons of iron. Once scarce and expensive, iron became the cheap, basic, indispensable building block of the economy.

Rocket The name given to George Stephenson's effective locomotive that was first tested in 1830 on the Liverpool and Manchester Railway at sixteen miles per hour.

Crystal Palace The location of the Great Exhibition in 1851 in London, an architectural masterpiece made entirely of glass and iron.

The Coming of the Railroads

The coal industry had long been using rails to move coal wagons. Rails reduced friction and allowed a horse or a human being to pull a heavier load. Thus, once a rail capable of supporting a heavy locomotive was developed in 1816, all sorts of experiments with steam engines on rails went forward. In 1830 George Stephenson's *Rocket* sped down the track of the just-completed Liverpool and Manchester Railway at sixteen miles per hour. The line from Liverpool to Manchester was a financial as well as a technical success, and within twenty years a variety of private companies had completed the main trunk lines of Great Britain (Map 23.1). Other countries were quick to follow (Figure 23.1).

The significance of the railroad was tremendous. It dramatically reduced the cost and uncertainty of shipping freight over land. This advance had many economic consequences. Previously, markets had tended to be small and local; as the barrier of high transportation costs was lowered, markets became larger and even nationwide. Larger markets encouraged larger factories with more sophisticated machinery in a growing number of industries. Such factories could make goods more cheaply and gradually subjected most cottage workers and many urban artisans to severe competitive pressures. In all countries, the construction of railroads created a strong demand for unskilled labor and contributed to the growth of a class of urban workers.

Industry and Population

In 1851 London hosted an industrial fair called the Great Exhibition in the newly built **Crystal Palace**. For visitors, one fact stood out: Britain was the "workshop of the world." Britain alone produced two-thirds of the world's coal and more than half of its iron and cotton cloth. More generally, in 1860 Britain produced a remarkable 20 percent of the entire world's output of industrial goods, whereas it had

Map 23.1 **The Industrial Revolution in England, ca. 1850** Industry concentrated in the rapidly growing cities of the north and the center of England, where rich coal and iron deposits were close to one another.

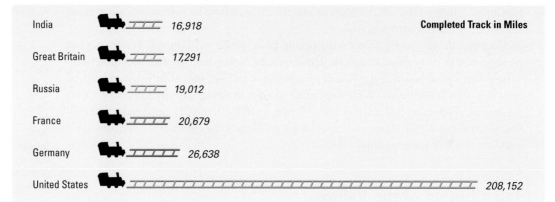

		Completed Track in Miles
India		16,918
Great Britain		17,291
Russia		19,012
France		20,679
Germany		26,638
United States		208,152

Figure 23.1 Railroad Track Mileage, 1890 Steam railroads were first used by the general public for shipping in England in the 1820s, and they quickly spread to other countries. The United States was an early adopter of railroads and by 1890 had surpassed all other countries in miles of track, as shown in this figure.

produced only about 2 percent of the world total in 1750.[2] Experiencing revolutionary industrial change, Britain became the first industrial nation (see Map 23.1).

As the British economy significantly increased its production of manufactured goods, the gross national product (GNP) rose roughly fourfold between 1780 and 1851. At the same time, the population of Britain boomed, growing from about 9 million in 1780 to almost 21 million in 1851. Thus, growing numbers consumed much of the increase in total production.

Although the question is still debated, many economic historians believe that rapid population growth in Great Britain was not harmful because it facilitated industrial expansion. More people meant a more mobile labor force, with a wealth of young workers in need of employment and ready to go where the jobs were. Contemporaries were much less optimistic. In his *Essay on the Principle of Population* (1798), Thomas Malthus (1766–1834) examined the dynamics of human populations. Starting with the assertion that population would always tend to grow faster than the food supply, Malthus concluded that the only hope of warding off such "positive checks" to population growth as war, famine, and disease was "prudential restraint." That is, young men and women had to limit the growth of population by marrying late in life. But Malthus was not optimistic about this possibility.

Crystal Palace Souvenir More than 6 million visitors from all over Europe marveled at the Great Exhibition of the Works of Industry of All the Nations, popularly known as the Crystal Palace Exhibition. It is no surprise that people bought millions of souvenirs picturing the Crystal Palace. The handsome depiction shown here brightened the lid of a ceramic pot. (Fitzwilliam Museum, Cambridge University, UK/Bridgeman Giraudon/The Bridgeman Art Library)

Economist David Ricardo (1772–1823) spelled out the pessimistic implications of Malthus's thought. Ricardo's depressing iron law of wages posited that because of the pressure of population growth, wages would always sink to subsistence level. That is, wages would be just high enough to keep workers from starving.

Malthus, Ricardo, and their followers were proved wrong in the long run. However, until the 1820s, or even the 1840s, contemporary observers might reasonably have concluded that the economy and the total population were racing neck and neck, with the outcome very much in doubt. There was another problem as well. Perhaps workers, farmers, and ordinary people did not get their rightful share of the new wealth. Perhaps only the rich got richer, while the poor got poorer or made no progress. We turn to this great issue after looking at the process of industrialization outside of Britain.

iron law of wages Theory proposed by English economist David Ricardo suggesting that the pressure of population growth prevents wages from rising above the subsistence level.

Quick Review
What developments were most important to the acceleration of British industrialization?

When and how did industrialization spread beyond Britain?

As new technologies and organization of labor began to revolutionize production in Britain, other countries took notice and began to emulate its example. Imitating Britain's success was hampered by the particular economic and social conditions of each country, many of whose peoples resisted attempts at drastic change. Yet by the end of the nineteenth century, several European countries as well as the United States and Japan had industrialized their economies to a considerable, but variable, degree.

National and International Variations

Comparative data on industrial production in different countries over time help give us an overview of what happened. Table 23.1 presents a comparison of how much industrial product was produced, on average, for each person in a given country in a given year. All the numbers are expressed in terms of a single index number of 100, which equals the per capita level of industrial goods in Great Britain (and Ireland) in 1900. Every number in the table is thus a percentage of the 1900 level in Britain and is directly comparable with other numbers. The countries are listed in roughly the order that they began to use large-scale, power-driven technology.

What does this overview tell us? First, one sees in the first column that in 1750 all countries were fairly close together, including non-Western areas such as China and India. Both China and India had been extremely important players in early modern world trade. However, the column headed 1800 shows that Britain had opened up a noticeable lead over all countries by 1800, and that gap progressively widened as the British Industrial Revolution accelerated to 1830 and reached full maturity by 1860.

Second, the table shows that the countries of continental Europe and the United States began to emulate the British model successfully over the nineteenth century, with significant variations in the timing and in the extent of industrialization. Belgium, achieving independence from the Netherlands in 1831 and rich in iron and coal, led in adopting Britain's new technology, and it experienced a truly revolutionary surge between 1830 and 1860. France developed factory production more gradually. Its slow but steady growth was overshadowed by the spectacular rise of Germany and the United States after 1860 in what has been termed the "second industrial revolution." In general, eastern and southern Europe began the process of modern industrialization later than northwestern and

TABLE 23.1 Per Capita Levels of Industrialization, 1750–1913

	1750	1800	1830	1860	1880	1900	1913
Great Britain	10	16	25	64	87	100	115
Belgium	9	10	14	28	43	56	88
United States	4	9	14	21	38	69	126
France	9	9	12	20	28	39	59
Germany	8	8	9	15	25	52	85
Austria-Hungary	7	7	8	11	15	23	32
Italy	8	8	8	10	12	17	26
Russia	6	6	7	8	10	15	20
China	8	6	6	4	4	3	3
India	7	6	6	3	2	1	2

Note: All entries are based on an index value of 100, equal to the per capita level of industrialization in Great Britain in 1900. Data for Great Britain include Ireland, England, Wales, and Scotland.

Source: P. Bairoch, "International Industrialization Levels from 1750 to 1980," *Journal of European Economic History* 11 (Spring 1982): 294, U.S. Journals at Cambridge University Press. Reprinted by permission.

central Europe. Nevertheless, these regions made real progress in the late nineteenth century, as growth after 1880 in Austria-Hungary, Italy, and Russia suggests.

Finally, the late but substantial industrialization in eastern and southern Europe meant that all European states as well as the United States managed to raise per capita industrial levels in the nineteenth century. These increases stood in stark contrast to the decreases that occurred at the same time in many non-Western countries, most notably in China and India as Table 23.1 shows. European countries industrialized to a greater or lesser extent even as most of the non-Western world stagnated. Japan, which is not included in this table, stands out as an exceptional area of non-Western industrial growth in the second half of the nineteenth century. After the forced opening of the country to the West in the 1850s, Japanese entrepreneurs began to adopt Western technology and manufacturing methods, resulting in a production boom by the late nineteenth century (see Chapter 26). Differential rates of wealth- and power-creating industrial development, which heightened disparities within Europe, also greatly magnified existing inequalities between Europe and the rest of the world (see Chapter 25).

The Challenge of Industrialization in Continental Europe

The different patterns of industrial development suggest that the process of industrialization was far from automatic. To be sure, throughout Europe the eighteenth century was an era of agricultural improvement, population increase, expanding foreign trade, and growing cottage industry. Thus, when the pace of British industry began to accelerate in the 1780s, continental businesses began to adopt the new methods as they proved their profitability. British industry enjoyed clear superiority, but at first the European continent was close behind.

By 1815, however, the situation was quite different. No wars in the early industrial period had been fought on British soil, so Britain did not experience nearly as much physical destruction or economic dislocation as Europe did. Rather, British industry maintained the momentum of the 1780s and continued to grow between 1789 and 1815. On the European continent, by contrast, the upheavals that began with the French Revolution caused severe economic disruption. War severed communications with Britain, handicapping con-

Map 23.2 Continental Industrialization, ca. 1850

Although continental countries were beginning to make progress by 1850, they still lagged far behind Britain. For example, continental railroad building was still in an early stage, whereas the British rail system was essentially complete (see Map 23.1). Coal played a critical role in nineteenth-century industrialization both as a power source for steam engines and as a raw material for making iron and steel.

ANALYZING THE MAP Locate the major exposed (that is, known) coal deposits in 1850. Which countries and areas appear rich in coal resources, and which appear poor? Is there a difference between northern and southern Europe?

CONNECTIONS What is the relationship between known coal deposits and emerging industrial areas in continental Europe? In England (see Map 23.1)?

tinental efforts to use new British machinery and technology. Thus France and the rest of Europe were further behind Britain in 1815 than in 1789.

This widening gap made it more difficult, if not impossible, for other countries to follow the British pattern after peace was restored in 1815. Above all, in the newly mechanized industries, British goods were being produced very economically, and these goods had come to dominate world markets. In addition, British technology had become so advanced and complicated that few engineers or skilled technicians outside England understood it. Moreover, the technology of steam power had grown much more expensive. It involved large investments in the iron and coal industries and, after 1830, required the existence of railroads. Continental business people had great difficulty finding the large sums of money the new methods demanded, and laborers bitterly resisted the move to working in factories. All these factors slowed the spread of modern industry (Map 23.2).

After 1815, however, European countries had at least three important advantages. First, most had a rich tradition of putting-out enterprise, merchant capitalists, and skilled urban artisans. Such a tradition gave their firms the ability to adapt and survive in the face of new market conditions. Second, continental capitalists did not need to develop their own technicians and advanced technology. Instead, they could simply "borrow" what they needed from Great Britain. European countries such as France and Russia also had a third asset that many non-Western areas lacked in the nineteenth century: they had strong, independent governments that did not fall under foreign political control. These governments would eventually use the power of the state to promote industry and catch up with Britain.

Agents of Industrialization

The British realized the great value of their technical discoveries and tried to keep their secrets to themselves. Until 1825 it was illegal for artisans and skilled mechanics to leave Britain; until 1843 the export of textile machinery and other equipment was forbidden. Many talented, ambitious workers, however, slipped out of the country illegally and introduced the new methods abroad.

One such man was William Cockerill, a Lancashire carpenter. He and his sons began building cotton-spinning equipment in French-occupied Belgium in 1799. In 1817 the most famous son, John Cockerill, built a large industrial enterprise in Liège in southern Belgium, which produced machinery, steam engines, and then railway locomotives. He also established modern ironworks and coal mines. Cockerill's plants became an industrial nerve center for the gathering and transmitting of industrial information across Europe. Many skilled British workers came to work for Cockerill, bringing with them the latest industrial plans and secrets from Britain.

A second agent of industrialization consisted of talented entrepreneurs such as Fritz Harkort (1793–1880), a pioneer in the German machinery industry. Serving in England as a Prussian army officer during the Napoleonic wars, Harkort concluded that Germany had to match England's industrial achievements as quickly as possible. To this end, he set up shop in the Ruhr Valley with the goal of producing steam engines.

Lacking skilled laborers, Harkort turned to England for experienced mechanics. Getting materials was also difficult. He had to import the thick iron boilers that he needed from England at great cost. In spite of all these problems, Harkort succeeded in building and selling engines, although his enterprise proved a financial disaster for himself and his partners.

Entrepreneurs like Harkort were obviously exceptional. Most continental businesses adopted factory technology slowly, and handicraft methods lived on. Indeed, continental industrialization usually brought substantial but uneven expansion of handicraft industry in both rural and urban areas for a time. Artisan production of luxury items grew in France as the rising income of the international middle class created increased foreign demand.

Government Support and Corporate Banking

Another major force in the spread of industrialization throughout Europe was government, which often helped business people in continental countries to overcome some of their difficulties. Tariff protection was one such support, and it proved to be important. For example, after Napoleon's wars ended in 1815, France was suddenly flooded with cheaper and better British goods. The French government responded by laying high tariffs on many British imports in order to protect the French economy. After 1815 continental governments bore the cost of building roads and canals to improve transportation. They also bore to a significant extent the cost of building railroads.

tariff protection A government's way of supporting and aiding its own economy by laying high taxes on imported goods from other countries, as when the French responded to cheaper British goods flooding their country by imposing high tariffs on some imported products.

The career of German journalist and thinker Friedrich List (1789–1846) reflects government's greater role in industrialization on the European continent than in England. List considered the growth of modern industry of the utmost importance because manufacturing was a primary means of increasing people's well-being and relieving their poverty. Moreover, List was a dedicated nationalist. To promote industry was to defend the nation.

The practical policies that List focused on were railroad building and the tariff. List supported the formation of a customs union, or *Zollverein* (TSOL-feh-rign), among the separate German states. Such a tariff union came into being in 1834, allowing goods to move between the German member states without tariffs, while erecting a single uniform tariff against other nations. List wanted a high protective tariff, which would encourage infant industries, allowing them to develop and eventually hold their own against their more advanced British counterparts. By the 1840s List's economic nationalism, designed to protect and develop the national economy, had become increasingly popular in Germany and elsewhere.

economic nationalism Policies aimed at protecting and developing a country's economy.

Finally, banks, like governments, also played a larger and more creative role on the continent than in Britain. Previously, almost all banks in Europe had been private. Because of the possibility of unlimited financial loss, banks generally avoided industrial investment as being too risky.

In the 1830s two important Belgian banks pioneered in a new direction. They received permission from the government to establish themselves as corporations enjoying limited liability. That is, if the bank went bankrupt, stockholders could now lose only their original investments in the bank's common stock, and they could not be forced to pay for additional losses out of other property they owned. Limited liability helped these Belgian banks attract investors. They mobilized impressive resources for investment in big companies and successfully promoted industrial development.

Similar corporate banks became important in France and Germany in the 1850s and 1860s. Usually working in collaboration with governments, corporate banks established and developed many railroads and many companies working in heavy industry, which were also increasingly organized as limited liability corporations.

The combined efforts of skilled workers, entrepreneurs, governments, and industrial banks meshed successfully between 1850 and the financial crash of 1873. As a result, rail networks were completed in western and much of central Europe, and the leading continental countries mastered the industrial technologies that had first been developed in Great Britain. In the early 1870s Britain was still Europe's most industrial nation, but a select handful of countries were closing the gap that had been opened by the Industrial Revolution.

The Situation Outside of Europe

The Industrial Revolution did not extend outside of Europe prior to the 1870s, with the exception of the United States and Japan, both early adopters of British practices. In many countries, national governments and pioneering entrepreneurs did make efforts to adopt the technologies and methods of production that had proved so successful in Britain, but they fell short of transitioning to an industrial economy. For example, in Russia the government brought steamships to the Volga River and a railroad to the capital, St. Petersburg, in the first decades of the nineteenth century. By midcentury entrepreneurs had established steam-powered cotton factories using imported British machines. However, these advances did not lead to overall industrialization of the country. Instead, Russia confirmed its role as provider of raw materials, especially timber and grain, to the West.

Egypt similarly began an ambitious program of modernization in the first decades of the nineteenth century, which included the use of imported British technology and experts in textile manufacture and other industries (see page 684). These industries, however, could not compete with lower-priced European imports. Like Russia, Egypt fell back on agricultural exports to European markets, like sugar and cotton.

Such examples of faltering efforts at industrialization could be found in many other places around the world. Where European governments maintained direct or indirect control, they acted to maintain colonial markets as sources for their own products, rather than encouraging the spread of industrialization. In India millions of poor textile workers lost their livelihood because they could not compete with industrially produced British cottons. The arrival of railroads in India in the mid-nineteenth century served the purpose of agricultural rather than industrial development. Latin American countries (discussed in Chapter 27) were distracted from economic concerns by the early-nineteenth-century wars of independence. By the mid-nineteenth century they had adopted steam power for sugar and coffee processing, but as elsewhere these developments led to increased reliance on agricultural crops for export, not a rise in industrial production. As in India, the arrival of cheap British cottons destroyed the pre-existing textile industry that had employed many men and women.

Quick Review

How and why did industrialization on the European continent and outside of Europe differ from industrialization in Britain?

What were the social consequences of industrialization?

In Britain, industrial development brought new social relations and intensified long-standing problems between capital and labor. A new group of factory owners and industrial capitalists arose. These men and women and their families strengthened the wealth and size of the middle class. The demands of modern industry also created a much larger group, the factory workers.

The growth of new occupational groups in industry led to the development of a new overarching interpretation—a new paradigm—regarding social relationships. Briefly, this paradigm argued that individuals were members of economically determined classes that had conflicting interests. Accordingly, the comfortable, well-educated "public" of the eighteenth century came increasingly to see itself as the middle class, and the "people" gradually transformed themselves into the modern working class. And if this paradigm was more of a deceptive simplification than a fundamental truth for some critics, it appealed to many because it seemed to explain what was happening. Therefore, conflicting classes existed, in part, because many individuals came to believe they existed and developed an appropriate sense of class feeling—what Marxists call class-consciousness (see page 639).

class-consciousness An individual's sense of class differentiation.

The New Class of Factory Owners

Most early industrialists drew upon their families and friends for labor and capital, but they came from a variety of backgrounds. Many were from well-established merchant families with rich networks of contacts and support. Others were artisans and skilled workers of exceptional ability. Members of ethnic and religious groups who had suffered discrimination in the traditional occupations jumped at the new chances. Scots, Quakers, and other Protestant dissenters were tremendously important in Britain; Protestants and Jews dominated banking in Catholic France.

As factories and firms grew larger, opportunities declined, at least in well-developed industries. It became considerably harder for a gifted mechanic to start a small enterprise and end up as a wealthy manufacturer. In Britain by 1830 and in France and Germany by 1860,

Ford Maddox Brown, *Work*
This midcentury painting provides a rich and realistic visual representation of the new concepts of social class that became common by 1850. (Birmingham Museums and Art Gallery/The Bridgeman Art Library)

ANALYZING THE IMAGE Describe the different types of work shown. What different social classes are depicted, and what kinds of work and leisure are the members of the different social classes engaged in?

CONNECTIONS What does this painting and its title suggest about the artist's opinion of the work of common laborers?

leading industrialists were more likely to have inherited their enterprises, and they were financially much more secure than their struggling parents had been. They also had a greater sense of class-consciousness; they were fully aware that ongoing industrial development had widened the gap between themselves and their workers.

The wives and daughters of successful businessmen found fewer opportunities for participation in Europe's increasingly complex business world. Rather than contributing as vital partners in a family-owned enterprise, as many middle-class women had done, they were increasingly valued for their ladylike gentility. Writers, economists, and politicians increasingly asserted that middle-class ladies should concentrate on their proper role as wife and mother.

The New Factory Workers

From the beginning, the Industrial Revolution had its critics. Among the first were the romantic poets. William Blake (1757–1827) called the early factories "satanic mills" and protested against the hard life of the London poor. Some handicraft workers—notably the Luddites, who attacked factories in northern England in 1812 and after—smashed the

Luddites Group of handicraft workers who attacked factories in northern England in 1812 and after, smashing the new machines that they believed were putting them out of work.

new machines, which they believed were putting them out of work. Doctors and reformers wrote of problems in the factories and new towns.

This pessimistic view was reinforced by Friedrich Engels (1820–1895), the future revolutionary and colleague of Karl Marx. After studying conditions in northern England, this young middle-class German published in 1844 *The Condition of the Working Class in England*. The new poverty of industrial workers was worse than the old poverty of cottage workers and agricultural laborers, according to Engels. The culprit was industrial capitalism, with its relentless competition and constant technical change. Engels's extremely influential charge of middle-class exploitation and increasing worker poverty was embellished by Marx and later socialists.

Meanwhile, other observers believed that conditions were improving for the working people. In 1835 in his study of the cotton industry, Andrew Ure wrote that conditions in most factories were not harsh and were even quite good. Edwin Chadwick, a government official well acquainted with the problems of the working population, detected an increase in worker's purchasing power. Nevertheless, those who thought conditions were getting worse for working people were probably in the majority.

The most recent scholarship confirms the view that the early years of the Industrial Revolution were hard ones for British workers. There was little or no increase in the purchasing power of the average British worker from about 1780 to about 1820. Only after 1820, and especially after 1840, did real wages rise substantially, so that the average worker earned and consumed roughly 50 percent more in real terms in 1850 than in 1770.[3] In short, there was considerable economic improvement for workers throughout Great Britain by 1850, but that improvement was hard won and slow in coming.

This important conclusion must be qualified, however. First, the number of hours in the average workweek increased. Thus, to a large extent, workers earned more because they worked more. In England nonagricultural workers labored about 250 days per year in 1760 as compared to 300 days per year in 1830.

Second, the wartime decline in the average worker's real wages and standard of living from 1792 to 1815 had a powerful negative impact on workers. These difficult war years, with more unemployment and sharply higher prices for bread, were formative years for the new factory labor force, and they colored the early experience of modern industrial life in somber tones.

Another way to consider the workers' standard of living is to look at the goods they purchased. Again the evidence is somewhat contradictory. Speaking generally, workers ate somewhat more food of higher nutritional quality as the Industrial Revolution progressed. Clothing improved, but housing for working people probably deteriorated somewhat. In short, per capita use of specific goods supports the position that the standard of living of the working classes rose, at least moderately, after the long wars with France.

Work in Early Factories

The first factories were cotton mills, which began functioning in the 1770s along fast-running rivers and streams, and they were often located in sparsely populated areas. Cottage workers, accustomed to the putting-out system, were reluctant to work in the new factories even when they received relatively good wages. In a factory, workers had to keep up with the machine and follow its relentless tempo. Moreover, they had to show up every day, on time, and work long hours under the constant supervision of demanding overseers, and they were punished systematically if they broke the work rules.

Cottage workers were not used to that kind of life and discipline. All members of the family worked hard and long, but in spurts, setting their own pace. On Saturday afternoon the head of the family delivered the week's work to the merchant manufacturer and got paid. Saturday night was a time of relaxation and drinking, especially for the men.

Workers at a U.S. Mill Female workers at a U.S. cotton mill in 1890 take a break from operating belt-driven weaving machines to pose for this photograph, accompanied by their male supervisor. The first textile mills, established in the 1820s in Massachusetts, employed local farm girls. As competition intensified, conditions deteriorated and the mills increasingly relied on immigrant women who had few alternatives to the long hours, noise, and dangers of factory work. By 1900, more than one million women worked in factories in the United States. (Courtesy of George Eastman House, International Museum of Photography and Film, GEH neg. 14250)

Also, early factories resembled English poorhouses, where totally destitute people went to live at public expense. The similarity between large brick factories and large stone poorhouses increased the cottage workers' fear of factories and their hatred of factory discipline. It was cottage workers' reluctance to work in factories that prompted the early cotton mill owners to turn to abandoned and pauper children for their labor. As we have seen, these owners contracted with local officials to employ large numbers of such children, who had no say in the matter.

Working Families and Children

By the 1790s the early pattern was rapidly changing. The use of pauper apprentices was in decline, and in 1802 it was forbidden by Parliament. Many more textile factories were being built, mainly in urban areas, where they could use steam power rather than waterpower and attract a workforce more easily than in the countryside. As a result, people came from near and far to work in the cities, both as factory workers and as laborers, builders, and domestic servants. Yet as they took these new jobs, working people did not simply give in and accept the new system of labor. Rather, they helped modify the system by carrying over old, familiar working traditions.

For one thing, workers often came to the mills and the mines as family units. This was how they had worked on farms and in the putting-out system. The mill or mine owner bargained with the head of the family and paid him or her for the work of the whole family. The preservation of the family as an economic unit in the factories from the 1790s on made the new surroundings more tolerable. Parents disciplined their children, making firm measures socially acceptable, and directed their upbringing. The presence of the whole family meant that children and adults worked the same long hours. Adult workers were not particularly interested in limiting the minimum working age or hours of their children as long as family members worked side by side. Only when technical changes threatened to place control and discipline in the hands of impersonal managers and overseers did adult workers protest against inhuman conditions in the name of their children.

Some enlightened employers and social reformers in Parliament definitely felt otherwise. They argued that more humane standards were necessary, and they used widely circulated parliamentary reports to influence public opinion. For example, Robert Owen (1771–1858), a successful manufacturer in Scotland, testified in 1816 before an investigating committee on the basis of his experience. He argued that employing children under ten years of age as factory workers was "injurious to the children, and not beneficial to the proprietors."[4]

Factory Act of 1833 English law that led to a sharp decline in the employment of children by limiting the hours that children over age nine could work and requiring younger children to attend factory-run elementary schools.

The reformers most significant early accomplishment was the Factory Act of 1833. It limited the factory workday of children between nine and thirteen to eight hours and that of adolescents between fourteen and eighteen to twelve hours. Children under nine were to be enrolled in the elementary schools that factory owners were required to establish. The employment of children declined rapidly. Thus the Factory Act broke the pattern of whole families working together in the factory because efficiency required standardized shifts for all workers.

Ties of blood and kinship were important in other ways in Great Britain in the formative years between about 1790 and 1840. Many manufacturers and builders hired workers through subcontractors. Subcontractors in turn hired and fired their own workers, many of whom were friends and relations. Ties of kinship were particularly important for newcomers, who often traveled great distances to find work. Many urban workers in Great Britain were from Ireland. Forced out of rural Ireland by population growth and deteriorating economic conditions from 1817 on, Irish in search of jobs took what they could get. Like many other immigrant groups held together by ethnic and religious ties, the Irish worked together, formed their own neighborhoods, and not only survived but also thrived.

The Sexual Division of Labor

The era of the Industrial Revolution witnessed major changes in the sexual division of labor. In preindustrial Europe most people worked in family units. By tradition, certain jobs were defined by gender, but many tasks might go to either sex. Family employment carried over into early factories and subcontracting, but by the 1830s it was collapsing as child labor was restricted and new attitudes emerged. A different sexual division of labor gradually arose to take its place. By 1850 the man was emerging as the family's primary wage earner, while the married woman found only limited job opportunities. Increasingly, women were expected to concentrate their efforts in the home.

separate spheres A gender division of labor with the wife at home as mother and homemaker and the husband as wage earner.

This new pattern of separate spheres had several aspects. First, all studies agree that married women from the working classes were much less likely to work full-time for wages, although they often earned small amounts doing putting-out handicrafts at home and taking in boarders. Second, when married women did work for wages outside the house, they usually came from the poorest families. Third, these poor married or widowed women were joined by legions of young unmarried women, who worked full-time but only in certain jobs, of which textile factory work, laundering, and domestic service were particularly important. Fourth, all women were generally confined to low-paying, dead-end jobs. Evolving gradually, but largely in place by 1850, the new sexual division of labor in Britain constituted a major development in the history of women and of the family.

If the reorganization of paid work along gender lines is widely recognized, there is no agreement on its causes. One school of scholars sees little connection with industralization and finds the answer in sexist attitudes that predated the economic transformation. These scholars stress the role of male-dominated craft unions in denying working women access to good jobs. Other scholars, stressing that the gender roles of women and men can vary enormously with time and culture, look more to a combination of economic and biological factors in order to explain the emergence of a sex-segregated division of labor.

Three ideas stand out in this more recent interpretation. First, the new and unfamiliar discipline of the clock and the machine was especially hard on married women of the laboring classes. Above all, relentless factory discipline conflicted with child care in a way that labor on the farm or in the cottage had not. A female factory worker could mind a child of seven or eight working beside her, but she could no longer pace herself through pregnancy or breast-feed her baby on the job. Thus a working-class woman had strong incentives to concentrate on child care within her home if her family could afford it.

Second, running a household in conditions of primitive urban poverty was an extremely demanding job in its own right. There were no supermarkets or public transportation. Shopping and feeding the family constituted a never-ending challenge. Thus, taking on a brutal job outside the house had limited appeal for the average married woman from the working class.

Third, why were the young, generally unmarried women who did work for wages outside the home segregated and confined to certain "women's jobs"? No doubt the desire of males to monopolize the best opportunities and hold women down provides part of the answer. Yet as some feminist scholars have argued, sex-segregated employment was also a collective response to the new industrial system. Previously, at least in theory, young people worked under a watchful parental eye. The growth of factories and mines brought unheard-of opportunities for girls and boys to mix on the job, free of familial supervision. Thus segregation of jobs by gender was partly an effort by older people to help control the sexuality of working-class youths.

Investigations into the British coal industry before 1842 provide a graphic example of this concern. (See "Listening to the Past: The Testimony of Young Mine Workers," page 626.) The middle-class men leading the inquiry, who expected their daughters and wives to pursue ladylike activities, were horrified at the sight of girls and women working without shirts, which was a common practice because of the heat, and they quickly assumed the prevalence of licentious sex with the male miners, who also wore very little clothing. In fact, most girls and married women worked for related males in a family unit that provided considerable protection and restraint. Yet many witnesses from the working class also believed that the mines were inappropriate and dangerous places for women and girls. The Mines Act of 1842 prohibited underground work for all women and girls as well as for boys under ten.

Some women who had to support themselves protested against being excluded from coal mining, which paid higher wages than most other jobs open to working-class women. But provided they were part of families that could manage economically, the girls and the women who had worked underground were generally pleased with the law. In explaining her satisfaction in 1844, one mother of four provided real insight into why many married working women accepted the emerging sexual division of labor:

Mines Act of 1842 English law prohibiting underground work for all women and girls as well as for boys under ten.

> *While working in the pit I was worth to my [miner] husband seven shillings a week, out of which we had to pay 2½ shillings to a woman for looking after the younger children. I used to take them to her house at 4 o'clock in the morning, out of their own beds, to put them into hers. Then there was one shilling a week for washing; besides, there was mending to pay for, and other things. The house was not guided. The other children broke things; they did not go to school when they were sent. . . . Then when I came home in the evening, everything was to do after the day's labor, and I was so tired I had no heart for it. . . . It is all far better now, and I wouldn't go down again.*[5]

LISTENING TO THE PAST

The Testimony of Young Mine Workers

The use of child labor in British industrialization quickly attracted the attention of humanitarians and social reformers. This interest led to investigations by parliamentary commissions, which resulted in laws limiting the hours and the ages of children working in large factories. Designed to build a case for remedial legislation, parliamentary inquiries gave large numbers of workers a rare chance to speak directly to contemporaries and to historians.

The moving passages that follow are taken from testimony gathered in 1841 and 1842 by the Ashley Mines Commission. Interviewing employers and many male and female workers, the commissioners focused on the physical condition of the youth and on the sexual behavior of workers far underground. The subsequent Mines Act of 1842 sought to reduce immoral behavior and sexual bullying by prohibiting underground work for all women and girls (and for boys younger than ten).

Mr. Payne, Coal Master

❝ That children are employed generally at nine years old in the coal pits and sometimes at eight. In fact, the smaller the vein of coal is in height, the younger and smaller are the children required; the work occupies from six to seven hours per day in the pits; they are not ill-used or worked beyond their strength; a good deal of depravity exists but they are certainly not worse in morals than in other branches of the Sheffield trade, but upon the whole superior; the morals of this district are materially improving; Mr. Bruce, the clergyman, has been zealous and active in endeavoring to ameliorate their moral and religious education. . . . ❞

Ann Eggley, Hurrier, 18 Years Old

❝ I'm sure I don't know how to spell my name. We go at four in the morning, and sometimes at half-past four. We begin to work as soon as we get down. We get out after four, sometimes at five, in the evening. We work the whole time except an hour for dinner, and sometimes we haven't time to eat. I hurry [move coal wagons underground] by myself, and have done so for long. I know the corves [small coal wagons] are very heavy, they are the biggest corves anywhere about. The work is far too hard for me; the sweat runs off me all over sometimes. I am

very tired at night. Sometimes when we get home at night we have not power to wash us, and then we go to bed. Sometimes we fall asleep in the chair. Father said last night it was both a shame and a disgrace for girls to work as we do, but there was naught else for us to do. I began to hurry when I was seven and I have been hurrying ever since. I have been 11 years in the pits. The girls are always tired. I was poorly twice this winter; it was with headache. I hurry for Robert Wiggins; he is not akin to me. . . . We don't always get enough to eat and drink, but we get a good supper. I have known my father go at two in the morning to work . . . and he didn't come out till four. I am quite sure that we work constantly 12 hours except on Saturdays. We wear trousers and our shifts in the pit and great big shoes clinkered and nailed. The girls never work naked to the waist in our pit. The men don't insult us in the pit. The conduct of the girls in the pit is good enough sometimes and sometimes bad enough. I never went to a day-school. I went a little to a Sunday-school, but I soon gave it over. I thought it too bad to be confined both Sundays and week-days. I walk about and get the fresh air on Sundays. I have not learnt to read. I don't know my letters. I never learnt naught. I never go to church or chapel; there is no church or chapel at Gawber, there is none nearer than a mile. . . . I have never heard that a good man came into the world who was God's son to save sinners. I never heard of Christ at all. Nobody has ever told me about him, nor have my father and mother ever taught me to pray. I know no prayer; I never pray. ❞

Patience Kershaw, Age 17

❝ My father has been dead about a year; my mother is living and has ten children, five lads and five lasses; the oldest is about thirty, the youngest is four; three lasses go to mill; all the lads are colliers, two getters and three hurriers; one lives at home and does nothing; mother does nought but look after home.

All my sisters have been hurriers, but three went to the mill. Alice went because her legs swelled from hurrying in cold water when she was hot. I never went to day-school; I go to Sunday-school, but I cannot read or write; I go to pit at five o'clock in the morning and

The Early Labor Movement in Britain

Many kinds of employment changed slowly during and after the Industrial Revolution in Great Britain. In 1850 more British people still worked on farms than in any other occupation. The second-largest occupation was domestic service. Thus many old, familiar jobs outside industry lived on and provided alternatives for individual workers. This helped ease the transition to industrial civilization.

This illustration of a girl dragging a coal wagon was one of several that shocked public opinion and contributed to the Mines Act of 1842. (© British Library Board, B.S. REF.18 volume 17, 65)

come out at five in the evening; I get my breakfast of porridge and milk first; I take my dinner with me, a cake, and eat it as I go; I do not stop or rest any time for the purpose; I get nothing else until I get home, and then have potatoes and meat, not every day meat. I hurry in the clothes I have now got on, trousers and ragged jacket; the bald place upon my head is made by thrusting the corves; my legs have never swelled, but sisters' did when they went to mill; I hurry the corves a mile and more under ground and back; they weigh 300 cwt.;* I hurry 11 a day; I wear a belt and chain at the workings to get the corves out; the putters [miners] that I work for are *naked* except their caps; they pull off all their clothes; I see them at work when I go up; sometimes they beat me, if I am not quick enough, with their hands; they strike me upon my back; the boys take liberties with me, sometimes, they pull me about; I am the only girl in the pit; there are about 20 boys and 15 men; all the men are naked; I would rather work in mill than in coal-pit. 〃

Isabel Wilson, Coal Putter, 38 Years Old

〃 When women have children thick [fast] they are compelled to take them down early. I have been married 19 years and have had 10 bairns [children]; seven are in life. When on Sir John's work was a carrier of coals, which caused me to miscarry five times from the strains, and was gai [very] ill after each. Putting is no so oppressive; last child was born on Saturday morning, and I was at work on the Friday night.

Once met with an accident; a coal brake my cheek-bone, which kept me idle some weeks. I have wrought below 30 years, and so has the guid man; he is getting touched in the breath now.

None of the children read, as the work is no regular. I did read once, but no able to attend to it now; when I go below lassie 10 years of age keeps house and makes the broth or stir-about. 〃

Source: *Voices of the Industrial Revolution: Selected Readings from the Liberal Economists and Their Critics*, pp. 87–90, edited by J. Bowditch and C. Ramsland. Copyright © 1961, 1989 by the University of Michigan. Reprinted by permission of the publisher.

*An old English unit of weight equaling 112 pounds.

QUESTIONS FOR ANALYSIS

1. How does Payne's testimony compare with that of Ann Eggley and Patience Kershaw?
2. Describe the work of Eggley, Kershaw, and Wilson. What strikes you most about the testimonies of these workers?
3. The witnesses were responding to questions from middle-class commissioners. What did the commissioners seem interested in? Why?

Within industry itself, the pattern of artisans working with hand tools in small shops remained unchanged in many trades, even as others were revolutionized by technological change. For example, the British iron industry was completely dominated by large-scale capitalist firms by 1850. Yet the firms that fashioned iron into small metal goods, such as tools, tableware, and toys, employed on average fewer than ten wageworkers who used handicraft skills. The survival of small workshops gave many workers an alternative to factory employment.

Working-class solidarity and class-consciousness developed in small workshops as well as in large factories. In the northern factory districts, anticapitalist sentiments were frequent by the 1820s. Commenting in 1825 on a strike in the woolen center of Bradford and the support it had gathered from other regions, one paper claimed with pride that "it is all the workers of England against a few masters of Bradford."[6] Modern technology and factory organization had created a few versus the many.

The transformation of some traditional trades by organizational changes, rather than technological innovations, could by themselves also create ill will and class feeling. In 1799 Parliament passed the Combination Acts, which outlawed unions and strikes. In 1813 and 1814 Parliament repealed the old and often disregarded law of 1563 regulating the wages of artisans and the conditions of apprenticeship. As a result of these and other measures, certain skilled artisan workers found aggressive capitalists ignoring traditional work rules and trying to flood their trades with unorganized workers to beat down wages.

The capitalist attack on artisan guilds and work rules was bitterly resented by many craftworkers, who subsequently played an important part in Great Britain and in other countries in gradually building a modern labor movement. The Combination Acts were widely disregarded by workers. Skilled craftsmen continued to take collective action, and societies of skilled factory workers also organized unions. Unions sought to control the number of skilled workers, to limit apprenticeship to members' own children, and to bargain with owners over wages.

In the face of widespread union activity, Parliament repealed the Combination Acts in 1824, and unions were tolerated, though not fully accepted, after 1825. The next stage in the development of the British trade-union movement was the attempt to create a single large national union. This effort was led not so much by working people as by social reformers such as Robert Owen. Owen, a self-made cotton manufacturer (see page 624), had pioneered in industrial relations by combining firm discipline with concern for health and safety. After 1815 he experimented with cooperative and socialist communities, including one at New Harmony, Indiana. Then in 1834 Owen organized one of the largest and most visionary of the early national unions, the Grand National Consolidated Trades Union.

When Owen's and other grandiose schemes collapsed, the British labor movement moved once again after 1851 in the direction of craft unions. These unions won real benefits for members by fairly conservative means and thus became an accepted part of the industrial scene.

British workers also engaged in direct political activity in defense of their own interests. After the collapse of Owen's national trade union, many working people went into the Chartist movement, which sought political democracy. The key Chartist demand was that all men be given the right to vote. Workers were also active in campaigns to limit the workday in factories to ten hours and to permit duty-free importation of wheat into Great Britain to secure cheap bread. Thus working people developed a sense of their own identity and played an active role in shaping the new industrial system. They were neither helpless victims nor passive beneficiaries.

The Impact of Slavery

Another mass labor force of the Industrial Revolution was made up of the millions of slaves who toiled in European colonies in the Caribbean and in North and South America. Historians have long debated the extent to which revenue from slavery contributed to Britain's achievements in the Industrial Revolution. They now agree that profits from colonial plantations and slave trading were a small portion of British income in the eighteenth century and were probably more often invested in land than in industry.

Nevertheless, the impact of slavery on Britain's economy was much broader than direct profits alone. In the mid-eighteenth century the need for items to exchange for colonial cotton, sugar, tobacco, and slaves stimulated demand for British manufactured goods in the Caribbean, North America, and West Africa. Britain's dominance in the slave trade also led to the development of finance and credit institutions that would help early industrialists obtain capital for their businesses. The British Parliament abolished the slave trade in 1807 and freed all slaves in British territories in 1833, but by 1850 most of the cotton processed by British mills was supplied by the coerced labor of slaves in the southern United States. Thus, the Industrial Revolution cannot be detached from the Atlantic world and the misery of slavery it included.

Quick Review
How did working men and women respond to the challenges posed by industrialization?

Connections

FOR MUCH OF ITS HISTORY, Europe lagged behind older and more sophisticated civilizations in China and the Middle East. There was little reason to predict that the West would one day achieve world dominance. And yet by 1800 Europe had broken ahead of the other regions of the world in terms of wealth and power, a process historians have termed "the Great Divergence."[7]

One important prerequisite for the rise of Europe was its growing control over world trade, first in the Indian Ocean in the sixteenth and seventeenth centuries and then in the eighteenth-century Atlantic world. Acquisition of New World colonies—itself the accidental result of explorers seeking direct access to the rich Afroeurasian trade world—brought Europeans new sources of wealth and raw materials as well as guaranteed markets for their finished goods. A second crucial factor in the rise of Europe was the Industrial Revolution, which by dramatically increasing the pace of production and distribution while reducing their cost, allowed Europeans to control other countries first economically and then politically. Britain dominated this process at first, but was soon followed by other European nations. By the middle of the nineteenth century the gap between Western industrial production and standards of living and those of the non-West had grown dramatically, bringing with it the economic dependence of non-Western nations, meager wages for their largely impoverished populations, and increasingly aggressive Western imperial ambitions (see Chapter 25). In the late nineteenth century non-Western countries began to experience their own processes of industrialization. Today's world is witnessing a surge in productivity in China, India, and other non-Western nations, leading many to question how long Western economic leadership will endure.

- **For a list of suggested readings for this chapter, visit** *bedfordstmartins.com/mckayworldunderstanding*.

- **For primary sources from this period, see** *Sources of World Societies*, Second Edition.

- **For Web sites, images, and documents related to topics in this chapter, see Make History at** *bedfordstmartins.com/ mckayworldunderstanding*.

Chapter 23 Study Guide

To do these exercises online, go to bedfordstmartins.com/mckayworldundunderstanding.

GETTING STARTED

Below are basic terms about this period in global history. Can you identify each term below and explain why it matters?

TERMS	WHO (OR WHAT) AND WHEN	WHY IT MATTERS
Industrial Revolution, p. 609		
spinning jenny, p. 610		
water frame, p. 610		
steam engines, p. 611		
Rocket, p. 613		
Crystal Palace, p. 613		
iron law of wages, p. 615		
tariff protection, p. 618		
economic nationalism, p. 619		
class-consciousness, p. 620		
Luddites, p. 621		
Factory Act of 1833, p. 624		
separate spheres, p. 624		
Mines Act of 1842, p. 625		
Combination Acts, p. 628		

MOVING BEYOND THE BASICS

The exercise below requires a more advanced understanding of the chapter material. Examine the changes brought on by the process of industrialization by filling in the chart below with descriptions of key aspects of work and home life for cottage and factory workers. When you are finished, consider the following questions: How did the relationship between home and work life change as industrialization progressed? How did changes in work patterns reshape gender relations? How did industrialization change the way that workers thought about themselves and their communities?

	COTTAGE INDUSTRY	FACTORY WORK
Nature of Work		
Work and Gender		
Work and Children		
Relationship to Home Life		
Identity/Class-consciousness		

PUTTING IT ALL TOGETHER

Now that you've reviewed key elements of the chapter, take a step back and try to see the big picture. Remember to use specific examples from the chapter in your answers.

THE INDUSTRIAL REVOLUTION IN BRITAIN

- What advantages help explain Britain's early industrialization? How did those advantages combine to spark the Industrial Revolution?
- How did British innovators solve the eighteenth-century energy crisis? How did their solution help transform the British economy?

INDUSTRIALIZATION IN CONTINENTAL EUROPE

- Compare and contrast conditions in continental Europe before and after 1815. What made conditions after 1815 more favorable to industrialization than conditions before 1815?
- What role did government play in continental industrialization? How did continental governments work with private individuals and companies to promote economic development?

RELATIONS BETWEEN CAPITAL AND LABOR

- How did ideas about "women's work" change as a result of industrialization?
- What is class-consciousness? How did industrialization help produce a new sense among workers of their own social identity?

LOOKING BACK, LOOKING AHEAD

- How did developments between 1600 and 1800 contribute to the rise of Europe to world dominance in the nineteenth century?

- Argue for or against the following proposition: "Given contemporary trends, the dominance of the West in the nineteenth and twentieth centuries should be seen as a temporary aberration, rather than as a fundamental and permanent shift in the global balance of power."

In Your Own Words Imagine that you must explain Chapter 23 to someone who hasn't read it. What would be the most important points to include and why?

24

Ideologies of Change in Europe

1815–1914

Europe's momentous economic and political transformation began in the late eighteenth century with the Industrial Revolution in England and then the French Revolution. Until about 1815 these economic and political revolutions were separate, involving different countries and activities and proceeding at very different paces. After peace returned in 1815, economic and political changes tended to fuse, reinforcing each other and bringing about what historian Eric Hobsbawm has called the dual revolution. Gathering strength, the dual revolution transformed Europe and had a powerful impact on the rest of the world.

The dual revolution also stimulated the growth of new ideas and powerful ideologies. The most important of these were revitalized conservatism and three ideologies of change—liberalism, nationalism, and socialism. All played critical roles in the political and social battles of the era and in the great popular upheaval that eventually swept across Europe in the revolutions of 1848. These revolutions failed, however, giving way to nation building in the 1860s. Redrawing the political geography of central Europe and uniting first Italy and then Germany, European political leaders and middle-class nationalists also began to deal effectively with some of the problems posed by rapid urbanization. Additionally, European leaders encouraged their peoples to put their faith in a responsive national state. At the same time, the triumph of nationalism promoted rivalries between states and peoples, and in the twentieth century it brought an era of tragedy and decline in Europe.

Christabel Pankhurst, Militant Suffragette
Christabel Pankhurst led the British Women's Social and Political Union, whose motto was "deeds, not words." Women in Britain, along with many other countries, gained the right to vote in the years immediately after World War I. (© Daily Mail/Rex/Alamy)

Chapter Preview

▶ How was European conservatism challenged between 1815 and 1848?

▶ What led to the revolutions of 1848 and why did they fail?

▶ How did nation building transform Italy, Germany, and Russia?

▶ How did urbanization impact cities, society, and ideas?

▶ How did nationalism and socialism shape politics before 1914?

How was European conservatism challenged between 1815 and 1848?

The triumph of revolutionary economic and political forces was by no means certain as the Napoleonic era ended. With the war over, conservative aristocratic monarchies of Russia, Prussia, Austria, and Great Britain—known as the Quadruple Alliance—met at the **Congress of Vienna** to fashion a general peace settlement. The great challenge for political leaders in 1814 was to construct a settlement that would last and not sow the seeds of another war. Their efforts were largely successful and contributed to a century unmarred by destructive generalized war (Map 24.1).

In the years following the peace settlement intellectuals and social observers sought to understand the revolutionary changes that had occurred and were still taking place. Almost all of these basic ideas were radical. In one way or another, the new ideas rejected conservatism, with its stress on tradition, a hereditary monarchy, and a strong landowning aristocracy. Radical thinkers developed and refined alternative visions—alternative ideologies—and tried to convince society to act on them.

Congress of Vienna A meeting of the Quadruple Alliance—Russia, Prussia, Austria, and Great Britain—and France held in 1814–1815 to fashion a general peace settlement that attempted to redraw Europe's political map after the defeat of Napoleonic France.

The European Balance of Power

With the restoration of monarchy in France, the allies were prepared to be lenient toward their former foe. The first Peace of Paris gave France the boundaries it possessed in 1792, which were larger than those of 1789, and France did not have to pay any war reparations.

In their moderation toward France, the allies were motivated by self-interest and traditional ideas about the balance of power. To the peacemakers, especially to Klemens von Metternich (1773–1859), Austria's foreign minister, the balance of power meant an inter-

Adjusting the Balance
The Englishman on the left uses his money to counterbalance the people that the Prussian and the fat Metternich are gaining in Saxony and Italy. Alexander I sits happily on his prize, Poland. This cartoon captures the essence of how the educated public thought about the balance-of-power diplomacy resulting in the Treaty of Vienna. (Bibliothèque nationale de France)

LA BALANCE POLITIQUE.

national equilibrium of political and military forces that would discourage aggression by any combination of states or, worse, the domination of Europe by any single state. The Quadruple Alliance members, therefore, agreed to meet periodically to discuss their common interests and to consider appropriate measures to maintain peace in Europe. This agreement marked the beginning of the European "congress system," which lasted long into the nineteenth century.

Coerced Conservatism After 1815

The peace settlement's domestic side was much less moderate. In 1815, under Metternich's leadership, Austria, Prussia, and Russia embarked on a crusade against the ideas and politics of the dual revolution. Metternich's policies dominated the entire German Confederation of thirty-eight independent German states, which the Vienna peace settlement had called into being (see Map 24.1). It was through the German Confederation that Metternich had the repressive Carlsbad Decrees issued in 1819. These decrees required the member states to root out subversive ideas in their universities and newspapers, and a permanent committee was established to investigate and punish any liberal or radical organizations.

Born into the landed nobility, Metternich defended his class and its privileges. Like many European conservatives of his time, he believed that liberalism (see below), as embodied in revolutionary America and France, had been responsible for a generation of war. He blamed liberal revolutionaries for stirring up the lower classes, which he believed desired nothing more than peace and quiet.

Because liberals believed that each national group had a right to establish its own independent government, the quest for national self-determination posed a grave threat to the Habsburgs' Austrian Empire. It was a dynastic state dominated by Germans but containing many other national groups. As a result, the multinational state that Metternich served was both strong and weak. It was strong because of its large population and vast territories; it was weak because of its many and potentially dissatisfied nationalities. In these circumstances, Metternich virtually had to oppose liberalism and nationalism, for Austria was unable to accommodate those ideologies of the dual revolution.

Liberalism and the Middle Class

The principal ideas of liberalism — liberty and equality — were by no means defeated in 1815. (This form of liberalism is often called "classical liberalism" and should not be confused with modern American liberalism, which usually favors government programs to meet social needs and to regulate the economy.) First realized successfully in the American Revolution and then achieved in part in the French Revolution, liberalism demanded representative government and equality before the law. The idea of liberty also meant specific individual freedoms: freedom of the press, freedom of speech, freedom of assembly, and freedom from arbitrary arrest. In Europe, only France and Great Britain had

Chapter Chronology

ca. 1790s–1840s	Romantic movement in literature and the arts
1814–1815	Congress of Vienna
1832	Reform Bill in Britain
ca. 1840s–1890s	Realism is dominant in Western literature
1845–1851	Great Famine in Ireland
1848	Revolutions in France, Austria, and Prussia; Marx and Engels, *The Communist Manifesto*; first public health law in Britain
1854–1870	Development of germ theory
1859	Darwin, *On the Origin of Species by the Means of Natural Selection*
1859–1870	Unification of Italy
1861	Freeing of Russian serfs
1866–1871	Unification of Germany
1873	Stock market crash spurs renewed anti-Semitism in central and eastern Europe
1883	First social security laws to help workers in Germany
1890–1900	Massive industrialization surge in Russia
1905	Russo-Japanese War; revolution in Russia
1906–1914	Social reform in Great Britain

dual revolution A term that historian Eric Hobsbawm used for the economic and political changes that tended to fuse and reinforce each other after 1815.

liberalism A philosophy whose principal ideas were equality and liberty; liberals demanded representative government and equality before the law as well as such individual freedoms as freedom of the press, freedom of speech, freedom of assembly, and freedom from arbitrary arrest.

Great Powers

- Great Britain
- France
- Kingdom of Prussia
- Austrian Empire
- Russian Empire
- Boundary of the German Confederation

Map 24.1 Europe in 1815

In 1815 Europe contained many different states, but after the defeat of Napoleon international politics was dominated by the five Great Powers: Russia, Prussia, Austria, Great Britain, and France. (The number rises to six if one includes the Ottoman Empire.)

ANALYZING THE MAP Trace the political boundaries of each Great Power, and compare their geographical strengths and weaknesses. What territories did Prussia and Austria gain as a result of the war with Napoleon?

CONNECTIONS How did Prussia's and Austria's territorial gains contribute to the balance of power established at the Congress of Vienna? What other factors enabled the Great Powers to achieve such a long-lasting peace?

realized much of the liberal program in 1815. Even in those countries, liberalism had not fully succeeded.

Liberalism faced more radical ideological competitors in the early nineteenth century. Opponents of liberalism especially criticized its economic principles, which called for unrestricted private enterprise and no government interference in the economy. This philosophy was popularly known as the doctrine of laissez faire (lay-say FEHR).

Scottish philosopher Adam Smith (see page 475) posited the idea of a free economy in 1776 in opposition to mercantilism and its attempt to regulate trade. Smith argued that freely competitive private enterprise would result in greater income for everyone. In early-nineteenth-century Britain this economic liberalism was embraced most enthusiastically by business groups and thus became a doctrine associated with business interests.

In the early nineteenth century liberal political ideals also became more closely associated with narrow class interests. Early-nineteenth-century liberals favored representative government, but they generally wanted property qualifications attached to the right to vote. In practice this meant limiting the vote to well-to-do males.

As liberalism became increasingly identified with the middle class after 1815, some intellectuals and foes of conservatism felt that liberalism did not go nearly far enough, calling for universal voting rights, at least for males, and for democracy. These democrats and republicans were more radical than the liberals, and they were more willing to endorse violent upheaval to achieve goals.

> **laissez faire** A doctrine of economic liberalism that emphasizes unrestricted private enterprise and no government interference in the economy.

The Growing Appeal of Nationalism

Nationalism was a second radical ideology in the years after 1815. Early advocates of the "national idea" argued that the members of each ethnic group (although the term *ethnic group* was not used at the time) had its own genius and its own cultural unity, which were manifested especially in a common language, history, and territory. In fact, such cultural unity was more a dream than a reality as local dialects abounded, historical memory divided the inhabitants of the different states as much as it unified them, and a variety of ethnic groups shared the territory of most states.

Nevertheless, European nationalists sought to make the territory of each people coincide with well-defined boundaries in an independent nation-state. It was this political goal that made nationalism so explosive in central and eastern Europe after 1815, when there were either too few states (Austria, Russia, and the Ottoman Empire) or too many (the Italian peninsula and the German Confederation), and when different peoples overlapped and intermingled.

The nationalist vision triumphed in the long run partly because the development of complex industrial and urban society required better communication between individuals and groups.[1] The development of a standardized national language that was spread through mass education created at least a superficial cultural unity. Nation-states also emerged because those who believed in the new ideology wanted to create "imagined communities," communities seeking to bind inhabitants around the abstract concept of an all-embracing national identity. Thus nationalists and leaders brought citizens together with emotionally charged symbols and ceremonies, such as ethnic festivals and flag-waving parades that celebrated the imagined nation of spiritual equals.[2]

Between 1815 and 1850 most people who believed in nationalism also believed in either liberalism or radical democratic republicanism. A common faith in the creativity and nobility of the people was perhaps the single most important reason for the linking of these two concepts. Liberals and especially democrats saw the people as the ultimate source of all good government. Early nationalists usually believed that every nation, like every citizen, had the right to exist in freedom and to develop its character and spirit. Yet early nationalists also stressed the differences among peoples. Thus while European nationalism's

> **nationalism** The idea that each people had its own genius and its own specific unity, which manifested itself especially in a common language and history, and often led to the desire for an independent political state.

Building German Nationalism As popular upheaval in France spread to central Europe in March 1848, Germans from the solid middle classes came together in Frankfurt to draft a constitution for a new united Germany. (akg-images)

main thrust was liberal and democratic, below the surface lurked ideas of national superiority and national mission that eventually led to aggression and conflict.

The Birth of Socialism

socialism A backlash against the emergence of individualism and the fragmentation of society, and a move toward international cooperation and a sense of community; the key ideas were economic planning, greater economic equality, and state regulation of property.

Socialism, the new radical doctrine after 1815, began in France. Early French socialist thinkers were acutely aware that the political revolution in France, the rise of laissez faire, and the emergence of modern industry in England were transforming society. They were disturbed because they saw these trends as fomenting selfish individualism and division within communities. There was, they believed, an urgent need for a further reorganization of society to establish cooperation and a new sense of community.

Early French socialists believed in economic planning. Inspired by the price controls and other emergency measures implemented in revolutionary France (see Chapter 22), they argued that the government should rationally organize the economy and help the poor. Socialists also believed that government should regulate private property or that private property should be abolished and replaced by state or community ownership.

One of the most influential early socialist thinkers was Henri de Saint-Simon (1760–1825). A proponent of industrial development, the key to progress, in his view, was proper social organization that required the "parasites"—the royal court, the aristocracy, lawyers, churchmen—to give way, once and for all, to the "doers"—the leading scientists, engineers, and industrialists. The doers would carefully plan the economy, guide it forward, and improve conditions for the poor.

Charles Fourier (1772–1837), another influential French thinker, envisaged a socialist utopia of self-sufficient communities. An early proponent of the total emancipation of women, Fourier also called for the abolition of marriage, free unions based only on love, and sexual freedom.

It was left to Karl Marx (1818–1883) to establish firm foundations for modern socialism. Marx had studied philosophy at the University of Berlin before turning to journalism and economics. In 1848 the thirty-year-old Karl Marx and the twenty-eight-year-old Friedrich Engels (1820–1895; see page 622) published *The Communist Manifesto*, which became the bible of socialism.

Marx argued that middle-class interests and those of the industrial working class were inevitably opposed to each other. In Marx's view one class had always exploited the other, and, with the advent of modern industry, society was split more clearly than ever before: between the middle class—the **bourgeoisie** (boor-ZHWAH-zee)—and the modern working class—the **proletariat**.

Just as the bourgeoisie had triumphed over the feudal aristocracy, Marx predicted that the proletariat would conquer the bourgeoisie in a violent revolution. For Marx, class identity trumped national identity. While a tiny majority owned the means of production and grew richer, the ever-poorer proletariat was constantly growing in size and in class-consciousness, a dynamic that would inevitably lead to revolution. In Marx's view, that revolutionary moment was imminent.

bourgeoisie The well-educated, prosperous, middle-class groups.

proletariat The Marxist term for the modern working class.

> **Quick Review**
> How did new alternative ideologies challenge the conservative notion of the state?

What led to the revolutions of 1848 and why did they fail?

As liberal, national, and socialist forces battered the conservatism of 1815, pressure built up. In some countries change occurred gradually and peacefully, but in 1848 revolutionary political and social ideologies combined with economic crisis to produce a vast upheaval. Great Britain, France, Austria, and Prussia all experienced variations on this basic theme between 1815 and 1848.

Liberal Reform in Great Britain

The landowning aristocracy dominated eighteenth-century British society, but that class was neither closed nor rigidly defined. Basic civil rights were guaranteed, but only about 8 percent of the population could vote for representatives to Parliament. By the 1780s there was growing interest in some sort of reform, but the French Revolution threw the British aristocracy into a panic, and after 1815 it was determined to defend its ruling position.

Only in 1832 did a surge of popular protest convince the king and lords to give in. The Reform Bill of 1832 had profound significance, increasing the number of voters and moving British politics in a democratic direction. Thus the pressures building in Great Britain were temporarily released without revolution or civil war.

A major reform had been achieved peacefully, and continued reform within the system appeared difficult but not impossible. In 1847 the Tories passed the Ten Hours Act, which limited the workday for women and young people in factories to ten hours. Passage of the act demonstrated that Tory aristocrats were willing to compete vigorously with the middle class for working-class support. This healthy competition was a crucial factor in Great Britain's peaceful evolution in the nineteenth century.

The people of Ireland did not benefit from this political competition. Long ruled as a conquered people, most of the population was made up of Irish Catholic peasants who rented their land from a tiny minority of Church of England Protestants. Ruthlessly exploited and growing rapidly in numbers, the Irish peasantry around 1800 lived under abominable conditions.

In spite of terrible conditions, Ireland's population continued to increase, caused in part by the extensive cultivation of the potato. The potato crop failed in 1845, 1846, 1848, and 1851 in Ireland and throughout much of Europe. The general result in Europe was high food prices, suffering, and, frequently, social upheaval. In Ireland the result was widespread starvation and mass fever epidemics. Total population losses were staggering. Fully one million emigrants fled the famine between 1845 and 1851, going primarily to the United States and Great Britain. The Great Famine, as this tragedy came to be known, intensified anti-British feeling and promoted Irish nationalism.

Revolutions in France

Louis XVIII's Constitutional Charter of 1814 protected the economic and social gains made by sections of the middle class and the peasantry in the French Revolution, and it permitted great personal freedom. The charter was anything but democratic, however. Only a tiny minority of males had the right to vote for the legislative deputies who, with the king and his ministers, made the nation's laws.

Although Louis Philippe (r. 1830–1848) accepted the Constitutional Charter of 1814, the situation in France remained fundamentally unchanged. Republicans, democrats, social reformers, and the poor of Paris were bitterly disappointed. The government's refusal to consider electoral reform heightened a sense of class injustice among shopkeepers and urban working people, and it eventually touched off a popular revolt in Paris in February 1848. Barricades went up, and Louis Philippe quickly abdicated.

The revolutionaries were firmly committed to a truly popular and democratic republic. In practice, building such a republic meant giving the right to vote to every adult male, and this was quickly done. Revolutionary compassion and sympathy for freedom were expressed in the freeing of all slaves in French colonies, the abolition of the death penalty, and the establishment of national workshops as an alternative to capitalist employment for unemployed Parisian workers.

Yet there were profound differences within the revolutionary coalition in Paris, and the socialism promoted by radical republicans frightened not only the middle and upper classes but also the peasants, many of whom owned land. When the French masses voted for delegates to the new Constituent Assembly in late April 1848, they elected a majority of moderate republicans who opposed any further radical social measures.

After the elections, this clash of ideologies—of liberal capitalism and socialism—became a clash of classes and arms. When the government dissolved the national workshops in Paris, workers rose in a spontaneous and violent uprising. After three terrible "June Days" and the death or injury of more than ten thousand people, the republican army stood triumphant in a sea of working-class blood and hatred.

The revolution in France thus ended in spectacular failure. The February coalition of the middle and working classes had in four short months become locked in mortal combat. In place of a generous democratic republic, the Constituent Assembly completed a constitution featuring a strong executive. This allowed Louis Napoleon, nephew of Napoleon Bonaparte, to win a landslide victory in the December 1848 election.

Picturing the Past

The Triumph of Democratic Republics

This French illustration offers an opinion of the initial revolutionary breakthrough in 1848. The peoples of Europe, joined together around their respective national banners, are achieving republican freedom, which is symbolized by the Statue of Liberty and the discarded crowns. The woman wearing pants at the base of the statue — very radical attire — represents feminist hopes for liberation. (Musée de la Ville, Paris/Giraudon/The Bridgeman Art Library)

ANALYZING THE IMAGE How many different flags can you count and/or identify? How would you characterize the types of people marching and the mood of the crowd?

CONNECTIONS What do the angels, Statue of Liberty, and discarded crowns suggest about the artist's view of the events of 1848? Do you think this illustration was created before or after the collapse of the revolution in France? Why?

President Louis Napoleon at first shared power with a conservative National Assembly. But in 1851 Louis Napoleon dismissed the Assembly and seized power in a coup d'état. A year later he called on the French to make him hereditary emperor, and 97 percent voted to do so in a national plebiscite. Louis Napoleon — proclaimed Emperor Napoleon III — then ruled France until 1870. Gradually his government became less authoritarian as he liberalized his empire.

The Revolutions of 1848 in Central Europe

Throughout central Europe the news of the upheaval in France prompted demands from liberals for written constitutions, representative government, and greater civil liberties from authoritarian regimes. When governments hesitated, popular revolts followed. Urban

Street Fighting in Berlin, 1848 This contemporary lithograph portrays a street battle on March 18, 1848, between Prussian troops loyal to King Frederick William IV and civilian men and women demonstrators. The king withdrew his troops the following day rather than kill anymore of his "beloved Berliners." Revolutionaries across Europe often dug up paving stones and used them as weapons. The tricolor flag achieved prominence during the revolution as the symbol of a united and democratic Germany. (akg-images)

workers and students served as the shock troops, but they were allied with middle-class liberals and peasants. In the face of this united front, monarchies collapsed. The popular revolutionary coalition then broke down as it had in France.

The revolution in the Austrian Empire began in 1848 in Hungary, where nationalistic Hungarians demanded national autonomy, full civil liberties, and universal suffrage. When Viennese students and workers also took to the streets and peasant disorders broke out, the Habsburg emperor Ferdinand I (r. 1835–1848) capitulated and promised reforms and a liberal constitution. The coalition of revolutionaries was not stable, however. When the monarchy abolished serfdom, the newly free peasants lost interest in the political and social questions agitating the cities.

The revolutionary coalition was also weakened and ultimately destroyed by conflicting national aspirations. In March the Hungarian revolutionary leaders pushed through an extremely liberal, almost democratic, constitution. But the Hungarian revolutionaries also sought to create a unified, centralized Hungarian nation. To the minority groups that formed half of the population—the Croats, Serbs, and Romanians—such unification was completely unacceptable. Each felt entitled to political autonomy and cultural independence. Likewise, Czech nationalists based in Bohemia and the city of Prague came into conflict with German nationalists. Thus conflicting national aspirations within the Austrian Empire enabled the monarchy to play off one ethnic group against the other.

The monarchy's first breakthrough came in June when the army crushed a working-class revolt in Prague. In October the predominantly peasant troops of the regular Austrian army attacked the student and working-class radicals in Vienna and retook the city. Thus the determination of Austria's aristocracy and the loyalty of its army were the final ingredients in the triumph of reaction and the defeat of revolution.

When Ferdinand I abdicated in favor of his young nephew, Franz Joseph (see page 660), only Hungary had yet to be brought under control. Another determined conservative, Nicholas I of Russia (r. 1825–1855), obligingly lent a hand. In June 1849, Russian troops poured into Hungary and subdued the country. For a number of years the Habsburgs ruled Hungary as a conquered territory.

After Austria, Prussia was the largest and most influential German kingdom. Prior to 1848, the goal of middle-class Prussian liberals had been to reshape Prussia into a liberal constitutional monarchy, which would transform the German Confederation into a unified nation. When the artisans and factory workers in Berlin exploded in March 1848 and joined with the middle-class liberals in the struggle against the monarchy, Prussian King Frederick William IV (r. 1840–1861) caved in. On March 21 he promised to grant Prussia a liberal constitution and to transform Prussia into a new national German state.

A self-appointed committee of liberals from various German states met in Frankfurt in May 1848 and began writing a federal constitution for a unified German state. This National Assembly completed drafting a liberal constitution in March 1849 and elected King Frederick William of Prussia emperor of the new German national state. By early 1849, however, Frederick William had reasserted his royal authority, contemptuously refusing to accept the "crown from the gutter." When Frederick William tried to get the small monarchs of Germany to elect him emperor, Austria balked. Supported by Russia, Austria forced Prussia to renounce all its unification schemes in late 1850. Attempts to unite the Germans—first in a liberal national state and then in a conservative Prussian empire—had failed completely.

Quick Review
What common factors led to the outbreak of revolution in France, Austria, and Prussia in 1848?

How did nation building transform Italy, Germany, and Russia?

Louis Napoleon's triumph in 1848 and his authoritarian rule in the 1850s provided Europe's old ruling classes with a new model in politics. To what extent might the expanding urban middle classes and even portions of the working classes rally to a strong and essentially conservative national state that also promised change? In central Europe, a resounding answer came with the national unification of Italy and Germany.

The Russian empire also experienced profound political crises in this period, but they were unlike those in Italy or Germany because Russia was already a vast multinational state built on military conquest and absolutist rule by Russian elites. It became clear to the Russian leaders that they had to embrace the process of modernization, defined narrowly as the changes that enable a country to compete effectively with the leading countries at a given time.

modernization The changes that enable a country to compete effectively with the leading countries at a given time.

Map 24.2 The Unification of Italy, 1859–1870 The leadership of Sardinia-Piedmont, nationalist fervor, and Garibaldi's attack on the kingdom of the Two Sicilies were decisive factors in the unification of Italy.

Cavour, Garibaldi, and the Unification of Italy

Italy had never been a united nation prior to 1850. A battleground for the Great Powers after 1494, Italy was reorganized in 1815 at the Congress of Vienna. Austria received Lombardy and Venetia. Sardinia and Piedmont fell under the rule of an Italian monarch, and Tuscany shared north-central Italy with several smaller states. The papacy ruled over central Italy and Rome, while a branch of the Bourbons ruled Naples and Sicily (Map 24.2).

After 1815 the goal of a unified Italian nation captured the imaginations of many Italians, but there was no agreement on how it could be achieved. After the turmoil of 1848, a frightened Pope Pius IX (r. 1846–1878) turned against most modern trends, including national unification. At the same time, Victor Emmanuel, king of independent Sardinia, retained the moderate liberal constitution he granted under duress in March 1848. To the Italian middle classes Sardinia (see Map 24.2) appeared to be a liberal, progressive state ideally suited to achieve the goal of national unification.

Sardinia had the good fortune of being led by Count Camillo Benso di Cavour. Embracing economic liberalism, Cavour's national goals were limited and realistic. Until 1859 he sought unity only for the states of northern and perhaps central Italy in a greatly expanded kingdom of Sardinia.

In the 1850s Cavour worked out a secret diplomatic alliance with Napoleon III, and in July 1858 he goaded Austria into attacking Sardinia. The combined Franco-Sardinian forces were victorious, but Napoleon III decided on a compromise peace with the Austrians in July 1859. Sardinia would receive only Lombardy, the area around Milan. Cavour resigned in a rage.

Popular revolts and Italian nationalism salvaged Cavour's plans. While the war against Austria raged in the north, dedicated nationalists in central Italy had risen and driven out their rulers. Cavour returned to power in early 1860, and the people of central Italy voted overwhelmingly to join a greatly enlarged kingdom of Sardinia. Cavour had achieved his original goal of a north Italian state (see Map 24.2).

For superpatriots such as Giuseppe Garibaldi (1807–1882), the job of unification was still only half done. A poor sailor's son, Garibaldi personified the romantic revolutionary nationalism of 1848. Having led a unit of volunteers to several victories over Austrian troops in 1859, Garibaldi emerged in 1860 as an independent force in Italian politics. (See "Individuals in Society: Giuseppe Garibaldi," page 646.)

Secretly supported by Cavour, Garibaldi conceived a bold plan to "liberate" the kingdom of the Two Sicilies. Landing on the shores of Sicily in May 1860, Garibaldi's guerrilla band of a thousand Red Shirts inspired the Sicilian peasantry to rise in rebellion. Outwitting the royal army, Garibaldi captured Palermo, crossed to the mainland, and prepared to attack Rome and the pope. But Cavour quickly sent Sardinian forces to occupy most of the Papal States (but not Rome) and to intercept Garibaldi. When Garibaldi and Victor Emmanuel rode through Naples to cheering crowds, they symbolically sealed the union of north and south.

The new kingdom of Italy, which did not include Venice until 1866 or Rome until 1870, was a parliamentary monarchy under Victor Emmanuel, neither radical nor democratic. Only a small minority of Italian males had the franchise. Despite political unity, the propertied classes and the common people were divided. A great social and cultural gap separated the progressive industrializing north from the stagnant agrarian south.

Bismarck and German Unification

In the aftermath of 1848, the German states, particularly Austria and Prussia, were locked in a political stalemate, each seeking to block the power of the other within the German Confederation. At the same time, powerful economic forces were undermining the political status quo. Modern industry was growing rapidly within the German customs union, or *Zollverein*, founded in 1834 to stimulate trade. By 1853 all the German states except Austria had joined the customs union, and a new Germany excluding Austria was becoming an economic reality.

Prussia had emerged from the upheavals of 1848 with a parliament of sorts, which was in the hands of the liberal middle class by 1859. When Prussia's King William I (r. 1861–1888) pushed to raise taxes and increase the defense budget to double the army's size, parliament pushed back. Parliament rejected the military budget in 1862, and the liberals triumphed in new elections. King William then called on Count Otto von Bismarck (1815–1898) to head a new ministry and defy the parliament.

When Bismarck took office as chief minister in 1862, he declared that the government would rule without parliamentary consent. He lashed out at the middle-class opposition: "The great questions of the day will not be decided by speeches and resolutions . . . but by blood and iron." Bismarck had the Prussian bureaucracy go right on collecting taxes even though the parliament refused to approve the budget, and he reorganized the army.

In 1866 Bismarck launched the Austro-Prussian War with the intent of expelling Austria from German politics. The war lasted only seven weeks, and the reorganized Prussian

INDIVIDUALS IN SOCIETY

Giuseppe Garibaldi

WHEN GIUSEPPE GARIBALDI (1807–1882) visited England in 1864, he received the most triumphant welcome ever given to any foreigner. Honored and feted by politicians and high society, he also captivated the masses. An unprecedented crowd of a half-million people cheered his carriage through the streets of London. These ovations were no fluke. In his time, Garibaldi was probably the most famous and most beloved figure in the world.* How could this be?

A rare combination of wild adventure and extraordinary achievement partly accounted for his demigod status. Born in Nice, Garibaldi went to sea at fifteen and sailed the Mediterranean for twelve years. At seventeen his travels took him to Rome, and he was converted in an almost religious experience to the "New Italy, the Italy of all the Italians." As he later wrote in his bestselling *Autobiography*, "The Rome that I beheld with the eyes of youthful imagination was the Rome of the future—the dominant thought of my whole life."

Sentenced to death in 1834 for his part in a revolutionary uprising in Genoa, Garibaldi barely escaped to South America. For twelve years he led a guerrilla band in Uruguay's struggle for independence from Argentina. "Shipwrecked, ambushed, shot through the neck," he found in a tough young woman, Anna da Silva, a mate and companion in arms. Their first children nearly starved in the jungle while Garibaldi, clad in his long red shirt, fashioned a legend as a fearless freedom fighter.

After he returned to Italy in 1848, the campaigns of his patriotic volunteers against the Austrians in 1848 and 1859 mobilized democratic nationalists. The stage was set for his volunteer army to liberate Sicily against enormous odds, astonishing the world and creating a large Italian state. Garibaldi's achievement matched his legend.

A brilliant fighter, the handsome and inspiring leader was an uncompromising idealist of absolute integrity. He never drew personal profit from his exploits, continuing to milk his goats and rarely possessing more than one change of clothing. When Victor Emmanuel offered him lands and titles after his great victory in 1861, even as the left-leaning volunteers were disbanded and humiliated, Garibaldi declined, saying he could not be bought off. Returning to his farm on a tiny rocky island, he denounced the government without hesitation when he concluded that it was betraying the dream of unification with its ruthless rule in the south. Yet even after a duplicitous Italian government caused two later attacks on Rome to fail, his faith in the generative power of national unity never wavered. Garibaldi showed that ideas and ideals count in history.

Above all, millions of ordinary men and women identified with Garibaldi because they believed that he was fighting for them. They recognized him as one of their own and saw that he remained true to them in spite of his triumphs, thereby ennobling their own lives and

Giuseppe Garibaldi, the charismatic leader, shown in an 1856 engraving based on a photograph. (Bettmann/Corbis)

aspirations. Welcoming runaway slaves as equals in Latin America, advocating the emancipation of women, introducing social reforms in the south, and pressing for free education and a broader suffrage in the new Italy, Garibaldi the national hero fought for freedom and human dignity. The common people understood and loved him for it.

*Denis Mack Smith, *Garibaldi: A Great Life in Brief* (New York: Alfred A. Knopf, 1956), pp. 136–147; and Denis Mack Smith, "Giuseppe Garibaldi," *History Today*, August 1991, pp. 20–26.

QUESTIONS FOR ANALYSIS

1. Why was Garibaldi so famous and popular?
2. Nationalism evolved and developed in the nineteenth century. How did Garibaldi fit into this evolution? What kind of a nationalist was he?

646   Chapter 24   Ideologies of Change
in Europe • 1815–1914

CHAPTER LOCATOR   How was European conservatism challenged between 1815 and 1848?

Map 24.3 The Unification of Germany, 1866–1871 This map shows how Prussia expanded and a new German Empire was created through two wars, the Austro-Prussian War of 1866 and the Franco-Prussian War of 1870–1871.

army defeated Austria decisively. In the aftermath of the war, the mainly Protestant states north of the Main River were grouped in the new North German Confederation, led by an expanded Prussia (Map 24.3). Each state retained its own local government, but the federal government—William I and Bismarck—controlled the army and foreign affairs.

Bismarck then asked the Prussian parliament to approve after the fact all of the government's "illegal" spending between 1862 and 1866. Most of the liberals jumped at the chance to cooperate. With German unity in sight, they legalized the government's spending. The constitutional struggle in Prussia was over, and the German middle class accepted the monarchical authority and aristocratic superiority that Bismarck represented.

The final act in the drama of German unification followed quickly with a patriotic war with France. The apparent issue—whether a distant relative of Prussia's William I might become king of Spain—was only a diplomatic pretext. By 1870, alarmed by their powerful new neighbor on the Rhine, French leaders had decided on a war to teach Prussia a lesson.

German forces under Prussian leadership were victorious at Sedan on September 1, 1870. Three days later French patriots in Paris proclaimed yet another French republic and vowed to continue fighting. But after five months, in January 1871, a starving Paris surrendered, and France accepted Bismarck's harsh peace terms. By this time the south German states had agreed to join a new German Empire. As in the 1866 constitution, the Prussian king and his ministers had ultimate power in the new German Empire, and the lower house of the legislature was elected by universal male suffrage.

The Franco-Prussian War released an enormous surge of patriotic feeling in Germany. The new German Empire had become Europe's most powerful state, and most Germans now imagined themselves the fittest and best of the European species. Semi-authoritarian nationalism and a "new conservatism," which was based on an alliance of the propertied classes and sought the active support of the working classes, had triumphed in Germany.

The Modernization of Russia

In the 1850s Russia was a poor agrarian society with a rapidly growing population. Then the Crimean War of 1853 to 1856, arising out of a dispute with France over who should protect certain Christian shrines in the Ottoman Empire, brought crisis. France and Great Britain, aided by Sardinia and the Ottoman Empire, inflicted a humiliating defeat on Russia.

Military defeat showed that Russia had fallen behind western Europe in many areas. Moreover, the war had caused hardship and raised the specter of massive peasant rebellion. Military disaster thus forced the new tsar, Alexander II (r. 1855–1881), and his ministers along the path of rapid social change and general modernization.

The first and greatest of the reforms was the freeing of the serfs in 1861. The emancipated peasants received, on average, about half of the land. Yet they had to pay fairly high prices for their land, which was owned collectively by peasant villages. Thus the effects of the reform were limited. More successful was reform of the legal system, which established independent courts and equality before the law.

Russia's greatest strides toward modernization were economic rather than political. Rapid railroad construction to 1880 enabled agricultural Russia to export grain

The Crimean War, 1853–1856

and thus earn money for further industrialization. Industrial suburbs grew up around Moscow and St. Petersburg, and a class of modern factory workers began to take shape.

In 1881 Alexander II was assassinated, and the reform era came to an abrupt end. Political modernization remained frozen until 1905, but economic modernization continued in the industrial surge of the 1890s. Under the leadership of Sergei Witte (suhr-GAY VIH-tuh), the minister of finance, the government doubled Russia's railroad network by the end of the century and promoted Russian industry with high protective tariffs.

By 1900 Russia was catching up with western Europe and expanding its empire in Asia. By 1903 Russia had established a sphere of influence in Chinese Manchuria and was eyeing northern Korea. When the protests of equally imperialistic Japan were ignored, the Japanese launched an attack on Russian forces in Manchuria in February 1904. After Japan scored repeated victories, Russia was forced in September 1905 to accept a humiliating defeat.

The Russian Revolution of 1905

Area of peasant unrest
• Major strikes and mutinies

St. Petersburg
Moscow
RUSSIA
Warsaw
Black Sea

Military disaster in East Asia brought political upheaval at home. On January 22, 1905, workers protesting for improved working conditions and higher wages were attacked by the tsar's troops outside the Winter Palace. This event, known as Bloody Sunday, set off a wave of strikes, peasant uprisings, and troop mutinies across Russia. The revolutionary surge culminated in October 1905 in a general strike, which forced the government to capitulate. The tsar, Nicholas II (r. 1894–1917), issued the **October Manifesto**, which granted full civil rights and promised a popularly elected Duma (DOO-muh; parliament) with real legislative power.

Under the new constitution Nicholas II retained great powers and the Duma had only limited authority. The efforts of middle-class liberals, the largest group in the newly elected Duma, to cooperate with the tsar's ministers soon broke down. In 1907 Nicholas II and his reactionary advisers rewrote the electoral law so as to increase greatly the weight of the propertied classes. On the eve of World War I, Russia was partially modernized, a conservative constitutional monarchy with a peasant-based but industrializing economy.

October Manifesto The result of a great general strike in Russia in October 1905, it granted full civil rights and promised a popularly elected Duma (parliament) with real legislative power.

> **Quick Review**
> How did political conservatives build powerful nation-states in Italy and Germany? How did Russia try to catch up with these states?

How did urbanization impact cities, society, and ideas?

After 1850, as identification with the nation-state was becoming a basic organizing principle in Europe, urban growth continued unchecked. Rapid urban growth worsened long-standing overcrowding and unhealthy living conditions. Officials, reformers, and scientists worked tirelessly to address these challenges, and eventual success with urban problems encouraged people to put their faith in a responsive national state.

Taming the City

The steam engine freed industrialists from dependence on the energy of fast-flowing streams and rivers so that by 1800 there was every incentive to build new factories in cities, which had better shipping facilities as well as a large and ready workforce. Therefore, as industry grew, there was also a rapid expansion of already overcrowded and unhealthy cities.

In the 1820s and 1830s people in Britain and France began to worry about the condition of their cities. Parks and open areas were almost nonexistent, and highly concentrated urban populations lived in extremely unsanitary and unhealthy conditions, with open drains and sewers flowing alongside or down the middle of unpaved streets.

The urban challenge eventually brought an energetic response from a generation of reformers. The most famous early reformer was Edwin Chadwick, a British official. Chadwick became convinced that disease and death actually caused poverty and that disease could be prevented by cleaning up the urban environment.

Collecting detailed reports from local officials and publishing his findings in 1842, Chadwick argued that sewers were both more cost-effective than communal outhouses and

King Cholera This 1852 drawing from *Punch* tells volumes about the unhealthy living conditions of the urban poor. In the foreground children play with a dead rat and a woman scavenges a dung heap. Cheap rooming houses provide shelter for the frightfully overcrowded population. Such conditions and contaminated water spread deadly cholera epidemics from India throughout Europe in the 1800s. (© British Library Board, P.P. 5270 vol. 23, 139)

much more sanitary. In 1848 Chadwick's report became the basis of Great Britain's first public health law, which created a national health board and gave cities broad authority to build modern sanitary systems. Such sanitary movements won dedicated supporters in the United States, France, and Germany from the 1840s on.

Perhaps the most important breakthrough in sanitation and disease prevention was the development of the **germ theory** of disease by Louis Pasteur (1822–1895). By 1870 the work of Pasteur and others had clearly demonstrated the connection between germs and disease. Over the next twenty years researchers identified the organisms responsible for disease after disease. These discoveries led to the development of a number of effective vaccines. Surgeons also applied the germ theory in hospitals, sterilizing not only the wound but everything else — hands, instruments, clothing — that entered the operating room.

The achievements of the bacterial revolution coupled with the public health movement saved millions of lives, particularly after about 1890. In England, France, and Germany death rates declined dramatically, and diphtheria, typhoid, typhus, cholera, and yellow fever became vanishing diseases in the industrializing nations.

More effective urban planning after 1850 also improved the quality of urban life. France took the lead during the rule of Napoleon III (1848–1870). In the baron Georges Haussmann (1809–1884), Napoleon III found an authoritarian planner capable of bulldozing both buildings and opposition. In twenty years Paris was transformed by slum clearance, new streets and housing, parks and open spaces, and good fresh water. The rebuilding of Paris stimulated modern urbanism throughout Europe, particularly after 1870.

The development of mass public transportation was also of great importance in the improvement of urban living conditions. In the 1870s many European cities authorized pri-

germ theory The idea that disease is caused by the spread of living organisms that can be controlled.

vate companies to operate horse-drawn streetcars, which had been developed in the United States. Then in the 1890s countries in North America and Europe adopted another American transit innovation, the electric streetcar. Electric streetcars were cheaper, faster, more dependable, and more comfortable than their horse-drawn counterparts. Electric streetcars also gave people of modest means access to improved housing, as the still-crowded city was able to expand and become less congested.

New Social Hierarchies and the Middle Classes

By 1850 at the latest, working conditions were improving. Moreover, real wages were rising for the mass of the population, and they continued to do so until 1914. With increased wages, the rigid class structures of Old Regime Europe began to break down. Greater economic rewards for the average person did not eliminate hardship and poverty, however, nor did they significantly narrow the gap between the rich and the poor.

The great gap between rich and poor endured, in part, because industrial and urban development made society more diverse and less unified. Society had not split into two sharply defined opposing classes, as Marx had predicted. Instead, economic specialization created more new social groups than it destroyed, with one group or subclass blending into another in a complex, confusing hierarchy.

The diversity and range within the urban middle class were striking as the twentieth century opened, and it is meaningful to think of a confederation of middle classes loosely united by occupations requiring mental, rather than physical, skill. As the upper middle class, composed mainly of successful business families, gained in income and progressively lost all traces of radicalism, they were almost irresistibly drawn toward the aristocratic lifestyle. Next came the much larger, much less wealthy, and increasingly diversified middle middle class. Here one found moderately successful industrialists and merchants, professionals in law and medicine, and midlevel managers of large public and private institutions. The expansion of industry and technology created a growing demand for experts with specialized knowledge, and engineers, architects, chemists, accountants, and surveyors first achieved professional standing in this period. At the bottom were independent shopkeepers, small traders, and tiny manufacturers — the lower middle class. Industrialization and urbanization also diversified the lower middle class and expanded the number of white-collar employees. White-collar employees were propertyless, but generally they were committed to the middle class and to the ideal of moving up in society.

The middle classes were loosely united by a shared code of expected behavior and morality. This code stressed hard work, self-discipline, and personal achievement. Men and women who fell into crime or poverty were generally assumed to be responsible for their own circumstances. In short, the middle-class person was supposed to know right from wrong and to act accordingly.

The People and Occupations of the Working Classes

About four out of five Europeans belonged to the working classes at the turn of the twentieth century. Many of them were small landowning peasants and hired farm hands. This was especially true in eastern Europe.

The urban working classes were even less unified and homogeneous than the middle classes. In the first place, economic development and increased specialization expanded the traditional range of working-class skills, earnings, and experiences. In the second place, skilled, semiskilled, and unskilled workers developed widely divergent lifestyles and cultural values, and their differences contributed to a keen sense of social status and hierarchy within the working classes.

Highly skilled workers, who made up about 15 percent of the working classes, became known as the labor aristocracy. This group included construction bosses, factory foremen, members of the traditional highly skilled handicraft trades that had not yet been placed in factories, as well as new kinds of skilled workers such as shipbuilders and railway locomotive engineers. Thus the labor elite remained in a state of flux as individuals and whole crafts moved in and out of it.

Below the labor aristocracy stood the complex world of semiskilled and unskilled urban workers. A large number of the semiskilled were factory workers who earned good wages and whose relative importance in the labor force was increasing. Below the semiskilled workers was a larger group of unskilled workers that included day laborers such as longshoremen, wagon-driving teamsters, and maids. Many of these people had real skills and performed valuable services, but they were unorganized and divided. The same lack of unity characterized street vendors and market people — self-employed workers who competed with each other and with the established lower-middle-class shopkeepers.

To make ends meet, many working-class wives had to find employment in the "sweated industries." These industries resembled the old putting-out and cottage industries of earlier times, and they were similar to what we call sweatshops today. The women normally worked at home and were paid by the piece. Sweating became a catch-all word denoting meager wages, hard labor, unsanitary and dangerous working conditions, and harsh treatment, often by a middleman who had subcontracted the work.

Across the face of Europe drinking remained unquestionably the favorite working-class leisure-time activity. Generally, however, heavy problem drinking declined in the late nineteenth century as drinking became more public and social. Cafés and pubs became increasingly bright, friendly places.

The two other leisure-time passions of the working classes were sports and music halls. The second half of the nineteenth century saw the rise of modern spectator sports, of which racing and soccer were the most popular. Music halls and vaudeville theaters, the working-class counterparts of middle-class opera and classical theater, were enormously popular throughout Europe.

The Changing Family

Industrialization and the growth of modern cities also brought great changes to women's lives. These changes were particularly consequential for married women, and most women did marry in the nineteenth century.

After 1850 the work of most wives continued to become increasingly distinct and separate from that of their husbands. Husbands became wage earners in factories and offices; wives tended to stay home, manage households, and care for children. As economic conditions improved, only married women in poor families tended to work outside the home. The ideal became separate spheres (see page 624), the strict division of labor by sex. This rigid division meant that married women faced great obstacles if they needed or wanted to work outside the home. Well-paying jobs were off-limits to women, and a woman's wage was almost always less than a man's, even for the same work.

Middle-class women lacked legal rights and faced discrimination in education and employment. Thus organizations founded by middle-class feminists campaigned for legal equality as well as for access to higher education and professional employment. In the later nineteenth century middle-class women scored some significant victories, such as the 1882 law giving English married women full property rights. Socialist women leaders usually took a different path. They argued that the liberation of working-class women would come only with the liberation of the entire working class through revolution. In a general way these different approaches to women's issues reflected the diversity of classes in urban society.

652

Chapter 24   Ideologies of Change
in Europe • 1815–1914

CHAPTER LOCATOR

How was European
conservatism challenged
between 1815 and 1848?

As the ideology and practice of rigidly separate spheres narrowed women's horizons, their control and influence in the home became increasingly strong throughout Europe in the later nineteenth century. Among the English working classes, for example, the wife generally determined how the family's money was spent. All the major domestic decisions were hers. (See "Listening to the Past: Mrs. Beeton's Guide for Running a Victorian Household," page 654.)

The woman's guidance of the household went hand in hand with the increased emotional importance of home and family. The home she ran was idealized as a warm shelter in a hard and impersonal urban world. Husbands and wives were expected to have emotional ties to each other, and mothers were expected to have powerful feelings toward their children. Among the middle and upper classes, marriages in the late nineteenth century were increasingly based on personal preference. Among the working classes, young people often began working or left home when they reached adolescence, so they had greater independence in their decisions about who to marry.

Medical doctors in both Europe and the United States began to study sexual desires and behavior more closely, and to determine what was considered "normal" and "abnormal." Same-sex attraction, labeled "homosexuality" for the first time, was identified as a "perversion." Governments seeking to promote a healthy society as a way of building up their national strength increasingly regulated prostitution, the treatment of venereal disease, and access to birth control in ways that were shaped by class and gender hierarchies.

Medical science also turned its attention to motherhood, and a wave of specialized books on child rearing and infant hygiene instructed middle-class women on how to be better mothers. Social reformers, some of them women, attempted to instruct working-class women in this new "science of motherhood," but, often working at a "sweated" trade or caring for boarders within their own homes, poorer women had little time for new mothering practices. Similarly, when Europeans established colonial empires, the wives of missionaries and officials sometimes tried to change child-rearing practices of local peoples.

Women in industrializing countries also began to limit the number of children they bore. This revolutionary reduction in family size, in which the comfortable and well-educated classes took the lead, was founded on the parents' desire to improve their economic and social position and that of their children. A young German skilled worker with one child spoke for many in his class when he said, "We want to get ahead, and our daughter should have things better than my wife and sisters did."[3]

Science for the Masses

The intellectual achievements of the scientific revolution (see Chapter 18) had resulted in few practical benefits, and theoretical knowledge had also played a relatively small role in the Industrial Revolution in England. But breakthroughs in industrial technology stimulated basic scientific inquiry as researchers sought to explain how such things as steam engines and blast furnaces actually worked. The result from the 1830s onward was an explosive growth of fundamental scientific discoveries that were increasingly transformed into material improvements for the general population.

The triumph of science and technology had at least three significant consequences. First, though ordinary citizens continued to lack detailed scientific knowledge, everyday experience and innumerable articles in newspapers and magazines impressed the importance of science on the popular mind. Second, as science became more prominent in popular thinking, the philosophical implications of science formulated in the Enlightenment spread to broad sections of the population. Natural processes appeared to be determined by rigid laws, leaving little room for either divine intervention or human will. Third, the methods of science acquired unrivaled prestige after 1850. For many, the union of careful experiment and abstract theory was the only reliable route to truth and objective reality.

The growth of the middle class in the second half of the nineteenth century resulted in sharper divisions of labor according to sex. More and more husbands were now going off each morning to their jobs in factories and offices, while their wives remained at home to manage the household. But life in a middle-class Victorian household was often quite different from the homes in which these women had been raised. Many a wife faced a steep learning curve as she learned to manage servants, purchase and use new gadgets and appliances, handle large household budgets, and present herself, her children, and her home in a comfortable and respectable middle-class light.

Fortunately, there were many how-to manuals and guides that these wives could refer to for answers about nearly anything related to the home. One of the most popular of these how-to manuals in England was Mrs. Beeton's Book of Household Management. *Compiled and edited by Isabella Mary Beeton (1836–1865), this book offered advice on such wide-ranging topics as the management of children, dealing with servants, making a will, emergencies and doctors, taxes, fashion, animal husbandry, and shopkeepers. The book was also popularly referred to as "Mrs. Beeton's Cookbook" because over 900 of the 1,100 plus pages contained recipes. The excerpt that follows comes from the section on "The Mistress."*

❝ 1. As With the Commander of an Army, or the leader of any enterprise, so is it with the mistress of a household. Her spirit will be seen through the whole establishment; and just in proportion as she performs her duties intelligently and thoroughly, so will her domestics follow in her path. Of all those requirements, which more particularly belong to the feminine character, there are none which take a higher rank, in our estimation, than such as enter into a knowledge of household duties; for on these are perpetually dependent the happiness, comfort, and well-being of a family. . . .

2. Early Rising is One Of The Most Essential Qualities which enter into good Household Management, as it is not only the parent of health, but of innumerable other advantages. Indeed, when a mistress is an early riser, it is almost certain that her house will be orderly and well-managed. On the contrary, if she remain in bed till a late hour, then the domestics, who, as we have before observed, invariably partake somewhat of their mistress's character, will surely become sluggards. . . .

4. Cleanliness Is Also Indispensable To Health, and must be studied both in regard to the person and the house, and all that it contains. Cold or tepid baths should be employed every morning, unless, on account of illness or other circumstances, they should be deemed objectionable. . . .

5. Frugality And Economy Are Home Virtues, without which no household can prosper. . . . We must always remember that it is a great merit in housekeeping to manage a little well. . . . Economy and frugality must never, however, be allowed to degenerate into parsimony and meanness. . . .

14. Charity And Benevolence Are Duties which a mistress owes to herself as well as to her fellow-creatures. . . . Visiting the houses of the poor is the only practical way really to understand the actual state of each family; and although there may be difficulties in following out this plan in the metropolis and other large cities, yet in country towns and rural districts these objections do not obtain. Great advantages may result from visits paid to the poor; for there being, unfortunately, much ignorance, generally, amongst them with respect to all household knowledge, there will be opportunities for advising and instructing them, in a pleasant and unobtrusive manner, in cleanliness, industry, cookery, and good management.

15. In Marketing, That The Best Articles Are The Cheapest, may be laid down as a rule; and it is desirable, unless an experienced and confidential housekeeper be kept, that the mistress should herself purchase all provisions and stores needed for the house. If the mistress be a young wife, and not accustomed to order "things for the house," a little practice and experience will soon teach her who are the best trades people to deal with, and what are the best provisions to buy.

16. A Housekeeping Account-book should invariably be kept, and kept punctually and precisely. . . . The housekeeping accounts should be balanced not less than once a month; so that you may see that the money you have in hand tallies with your account of it in your diary. . . .

---

evolution The idea, applied by Charles Darwin, that concluded that all life had gradually evolved from a common origin; as applied by thinkers in many fields, the idea stressed gradual change and continuous adjustment.

Living in an era of rapid change, nineteenth-century thinkers in Europe were fascinated with the idea of evolution and dynamic development. The most influential of all nineteenth-century evolutionary thinkers was Charles Darwin (1809–1882). Darwin came to doubt the general belief in a special divine creation of each species of animal. Instead, he concluded in *On the Origin of Species by the Means of Natural Selection* (1859), all life had gradually evolved from a common ancestral origin in an unending "struggle for survival." According to Darwin's theory of evolution, small, random variations within

654 Chapter 24 Ideologies of Change in Europe • 1815–1914

CHAPTER LOCATOR   How was European conservatism challenged between 1815 and 1848?

The publication of cookbooks and household guides proliferated in the nineteenth century. Mrs. Beeton's bestselling guide offered housekeeping tips and a wealth of recipes for the homemaker to share with her family. (Graphic Arts Division, Department of Rare Books and Special Collections, Princeton University Library)

18. In Obtaining A Servant's Character, it is not well to be guided by a written one from some unknown quarter; but it is better to have an interview, if at all possible, with the former mistress. By this means you will be assisted in your decision of the suitableness of the servant for your place, from the appearance of the lady and the state of her house. Negligence and want of cleanliness in her and her household generally, will naturally lead you to the conclusion, that her servant has suffered from the influence of the bad example.

19. The Treatment Of Servants is of the highest possible moment, as well to the mistress as to the domestics themselves. On the head of the house the latter will naturally fix their attention; and if they perceive that the mistress's conduct is regulated by high and correct principles, they will not fail to respect her. If, also, a benevolent desire is shown to promote their comfort, at the same time that a steady performance of their duty is exacted, then their respect will not be unmingled with affection, and they will be still more solicitous to continue to deserve her favour. . . .

48. Of The Manner Of Passing Evenings At Home, there is none pleasanter than in such recreative enjoyments as those which relax the mind from its severer duties, whilst they stimulate it with a gentle delight. Where there are young people forming a part of the evening circle, interesting and agreeable pastime should especially be promoted. It is of incalculable benefit to them that their homes should possess all the attractions of healthiest amusement, comfort, and happiness; for if they do not find pleasure there, they will seek it elsewhere. It ought, therefore, to enter into the domestic policy of every parent, to make her children feel that home is the happiest place in the world; that to imbue them with this delicious home-feeling is one of the choicest gifts a parent can bestow. . . .

54. Such Are The Onerous Duties which enter into the position of the mistress of a house, and such are, happily, with a slight but continued attention, of by no means difficult performance. She ought always to remember that she is the first and the last, the Alpha and the Omega in the government of her establishment; and that it is by her conduct that its whole internal policy is regulated. 🔊

Source: Isabella Mary Beeton, ed., *Beeton's Book of House Management* (London: S.O. Beeton, 1863), pp. 1–2, 5–7, 17, 18–19.

QUESTIONS FOR ANALYSIS

1. In what ways might the mistress of the household be considered like the commander of an army?
2. How important is outward appearance — to guests, servants, and the outside world — for the Victorian mistress of a household?
3. What advice does Mrs. Beeton give for the well-being and happiness of children?
4. Some scholars consider Mrs. Beeton a feminist. Do you agree with that assessment? Why?

individuals in one species allowed them to acquire more food and better living conditions and made them more successful in reproducing, thus passing their genetic material to the next generation. When a number of individuals within a species became distinct enough that they could no longer interbreed successfully with others, they became a new species.

Darwin provoked, and continues to provoke, resistance, particularly because he extended his theory to humans. Despite the criticism, however, Darwin's theory had a powerful and

What led to the revolutions of 1848 and why did they fail? | How did nation building transform Italy, Germany, and Russia? | How did urbanization impact cities, society, and ideas? | How did nationalism and socialism shape politics before 1914?

655

Madrid in 1900 This wistful painting of a Spanish square on a rainy day, by Enrique Martínez Cubells y Ruiz (1874–1917), includes a revealing commentary on how scientific discoveries transformed urban life. Coachmen wait atop their expensive hackney cabs for a wealthy clientele, while modern electric streetcars that carry the masses converge on the square from all directions. In this way the development of electricity brought improved urban transportation and enabled the city to expand to the suburbs. (Museo Municipal, Madrid/The Bridgeman Art Library)

Social Darwinism The application of the theory of biological evolution to human affairs; it sees the human race as driven to ever-greater specialization and progress by an unending economic struggle that determines the survival of the fittest.

many-sided influence on European thought and the European middle classes. His findings reinforced the teachings of secularists such as Marx, who dismissed religious belief in favor of agnostic or atheistic materialism. Many writers also applied the theory of biological evolution to human affairs. Herbert Spencer (1820–1903), an English philosopher, saw the human race as driven forward to ever-greater specialization and progress by an economic struggle that efficiently determines the "survival of the fittest." The idea that human society also evolves, and that the stronger will become powerful and prosperous while the weaker will be conquered or remain poor became known as Social Darwinism. Powerful nations used this ideology to justify nationalism and expansion, and colonizers to justify imperialism.

Not only did science shape society, but society also shaped science. As nations asserted their differences from one another, they sought "scientific" proof for those differences, which generally meant proof of their own superiority. European and American scientists, anthropologists, and physicians measured skulls, brains, and facial angles to prove that whites were more intelligent than other races, and that northern Europeans were more advanced than southern Europeans, perhaps even a separate "Nordic race" or "Aryan race." Africans were described and depicted as "missing links" between chimpanzees and Europeans, and they were occasionally even displayed as such in zoos and fairs. This scientific racism extended to Jews, who were increasingly described as a separate and inferior race, not a religious group.

Cultural Shifts

The French Revolution kindled the belief that radical reconstructions of politics and society were also possible in cultural and artistic life. The most significant expression of this belief in the early nineteenth century was the romantic movement. In part a revolt against classicism and the Enlightenment, romanticism was characterized by a belief in emotional exuberance, unrestrained imagination, and spontaneity in both art and personal life. Romanticism crystallized fully in the 1790s, primarily in England and Germany, and gained strength until the 1840s. Great individualists, romantic artists believed the full development of each person's unique human potential to be the supreme purpose in life.

One of the greatest romantic painters in France, Eugène Delacroix (oe-ZHEHN deh-luh-KWAH; 1798–1863), was a romantic master of dramatic, colorful scenes that stirred the emotions. He was fascinated with remote and exotic subjects (see *Massacre at Chios*, page 658). Yet he was also a passionate spokesman for freedom.

It was in music that romanticism realized most fully and permanently its goals of free expression and emotional intensity. Abandoning well-defined structures, great romantic composers, such as Ludwig van Beethoven (1770–1827), used a wide range of forms to create musical landscapes and evoke powerful emotion.

Nowhere was the break with classicism more apparent than in romanticism's general conception of nature. Classicism was not particularly interested in nature. The romantics, in contrast, were enchanted by nature. For some it was awesome and tempestuous, while others saw nature as a source of spiritual inspiration.

The study of history became a romantic passion. History was the key to a universe that was now perceived to be organic and dynamic, not mechanical and static as the Enlightenment thinkers had believed. Historical studies supported the development of national aspirations and encouraged entire peoples to seek in the past their special destinies.

Romanticism found a distinctive voice in poetry. William Wordsworth (1770–1850) was the leader of English romanticism. In 1798 Wordsworth and his fellow romantic poet Samuel Taylor Coleridge (1772–1834) published their *Lyrical Ballads*, which abandoned flowery classical conventions for the language of ordinary speech. Wordsworth described his conception of poetry as the "spontaneous overflow of powerful feeling recollected in tranquility." Victor Hugo (1802–1885) was France's greatest romantic master in both poetry and prose. His powerful novels exemplified the romantic fascination with fantastic characters, strange settings, and human emotions.

In central and eastern Europe, literary romanticism and early nationalism often reinforced each other. Romantics turned their attention to peasant life and transcribed the folk songs, tales, and proverbs that the cosmopolitan Enlightenment had disdained. The brothers Jacob and Wilhelm Grimm were particularly successful at rescuing German fairy tales from oblivion. In the Slavic lands romantics played a decisive role in converting spoken peasant languages into modern written languages.

Beginning in the 1840s, romanticism gave way to a new artistic genre, realism, which continued to dominate Western culture and style until the 1890s. Realist writers believed that literature should depict life exactly as it is. Forsaking poetry for prose and the personal, emotional viewpoint of the romantics for strict scientific objectivity, the realists simply observed and recorded.

The major realist writers focused on creating fiction based on contemporary everyday life. Beginning with a dissection of the middle classes, from which most of them sprang, many realists eventually focused on the working classes, especially the urban working classes.

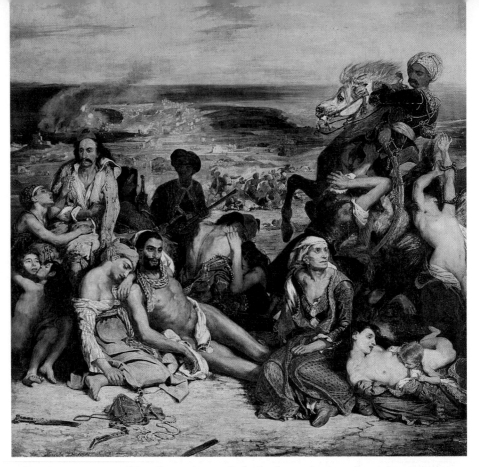

Delacroix, *Massacre at Chios* The Greek struggle for freedom and independence won the enthusiastic support of liberals, nationalists, and romantics. The Ottoman Turks were portrayed as cruel oppressors who were holding back the course of history, as in this moving masterpiece by Delacroix. (Réunion des Musées Nationaux/Art Resource, NY)

The realists put a microscope to many unexplored and taboo subjects—sex, strikes, violence, alcoholism—shocking many middle-class critics.

The realists' claims of objectivity did not prevent the elaboration of a definite worldview. Realists such as the famous French novelist Emile Zola (1840–1902) and English novelist Thomas Hardy (1840–1928) were strict determinists. They believed that human beings, like atoms, are components of the physical world and that all human actions are caused by unalterable natural laws: heredity and environment determine human behavior; good and evil are merely social conventions.

Quick Review
What were the social and cultural consequences of industrialization and urbanization in the second half of the nineteenth century?

How did nationalism and socialism shape politics before 1914?

After 1871 Europe's heartland was organized into strong national states. Only on Europe's borders—in Ireland and Russia, in Austria-Hungary and the Balkans—did people still strive for national unity and independence. Nationalism served as a new unifying principle. At the same time, socialist parties grew rapidly, alarming many prosperous and conservative citizens. Governing elites manipulated national feeling to create a sense of unity to divert attention from underlying class conflicts, and increasingly channeled national sentiment in an antiliberal and militaristic direction. This policy helped manage domestic conflicts, but only at the expense of increasing the international tensions that erupted in World War I.

Trends in Suffrage

There were good reasons why ordinary people felt increasing loyalty to their governments in central and western Europe. More people could vote. By 1914 universal male suffrage had become the rule rather than the exception. This development had as much psychological as political significance. Ordinary men felt they were becoming "part of the system."

Women also began to demand the right to vote. The women's suffrage movement achieved its first success in the western United States, and by 1913 women could vote in twelve states. In Europe, Norway gave the vote to most women in 1914. Suffragettes had little success elsewhere before 1914, but they prepared the way for getting the vote in many countries immediately after World War I.

As the right to vote spread, politicians and parties in national parliaments usually represented the people more responsively. The multiparty system prevailing in most countries meant that parliamentary majorities were built on shifting coalitions, which gave political parties leverage to obtain benefits for their supporters. Governments also passed laws to alleviate general problems, thereby acquiring greater legitimacy and appearing more worthy of support.

The German Empire

The new German Empire was a federal union of Prussia and twenty-four smaller states. The separate states conducted much of the everyday business of government. Unifying the whole was a strong national government with a chancellor — Bismarck until 1890 — and a popularly elected parliament called the Reichstag. Although Bismarck refused to be bound by a parliamentary majority, he pragmatically sought the backing of whichever coalition of political parties would support his policies.

As for socialism, Bismarck tried to stop its growth in Germany because he feared its revolutionary language and allegiance to a movement transcending the nation-state. In 1878 he pushed through a law outlawing the Social Democrats, but he was unable to force socialism out of existence. Bismarck's essentially conservative nation-state then pioneered social measures designed to win working-class support. In 1883 the Reichstag approved a national social security system that was the first of its kind anywhere.

Under Kaiser William I (r. 1861–1888), Bismarck had, in effect, managed the domestic and foreign policies of the state. In 1890 the new emperor, William II (r. 1888–1918), eager to rule in his own right, forced Bismarck to resign. Following Bismarck's departure, the Reichstag passed new laws to aid workers and to legalize socialist political activity. German foreign policy changed as well, and mostly for the worse (see pages 752–754).

Republican France

Although Napoleon III's reign made some progress in reducing antagonisms between classes, the Franco-Prussian war undid these efforts, and in 1871 France seemed hopelessly divided once again. The republicans who proclaimed the Third Republic in Paris defended the city with great heroism for weeks, until they were starved into submission by German armies in January 1871. When national elections then sent a large majority of conservatives and monarchists to the National Assembly, France's leaders decided they had no choice but to surrender Alsace and Lorraine to Germany. The traumatized Parisians exploded in patriotic frustration and proclaimed the Paris Commune in March 1871.

In response, the National Assembly ordered the French army into Paris and brutally crushed the Commune. Twenty thousand people died in the fighting. As in June 1848, it was Paris against the provinces. Out of this tragedy France slowly formed a new national unity before 1914.

The moderate republicans sought to preserve their creation by winning the loyalty of the next generation. Trade unions were fully legalized, and France acquired a colonial empire. More important, a series of laws between 1879 and 1886 established free compulsory elementary education for both girls and boys, thereby greatly reducing the role of parochial Catholic schools that had long been hostile to republicanism. In France and throughout the world the general expansion of public education served as a critical nation- and nationalism-building tool in the late nineteenth century.

Although the educational reforms of the 1880s disturbed French Catholics, many of them rallied to the republic in the 1890s, and tensions between church and state eased. Unfortunately, the Dreyfus affair changed all that. In 1894 Alfred Dreyfus, a Jewish captain in the French army, was falsely accused and convicted of treason. In 1898 and 1899 the case split France apart. On one side was the army, which had manufactured evidence against Dreyfus, joined by anti-Semites and most of the Catholic establishment. On the other side stood the civil libertarians and most of the more radical republicans.

This battle, which eventually led to Dreyfus's being declared innocent, revived militant republican feeling against the church. Between 1901 and 1905 the government severed all ties between the state and the Catholic Church. In France only the growing socialist movement, with its very different but thoroughly secular ideology, stood in opposition to patriotic republican nationalism.

Dreyfus affair A divisive case in which Alfred Dreyfus, a Jewish captain in the French army, was falsely accused and convicted of treason. The Catholic Church sided with the anti-Semites against Dreyfus; after Dreyfus was declared innocent, the French government severed all ties between the state and the church.

Great Britain and the Austro-Hungarian Empire

The development of Great Britain and Austria-Hungary, two leading but quite different powers, throws a powerful light on the dynamics of nationalism in Europe before 1914. At home Britain passed a series of voting rights bills between 1832 and 1884 that culminated in universal male suffrage. Between 1906 and 1914, the Liberal Party substantially raised taxes on the rich to pay for national health insurance, unemployment benefits, old-age pensions, and a host of other social measures. The state was integrating the urban masses socially as well as politically.

On the eve of World War I, however, the unanswered question of Ireland brought Great Britain to the brink of civil war. The terrible Irish famine fueled an Irish revolutionary movement. Thereafter the English slowly granted concessions, but they refused to give Ireland self-government. In 1910 Irish nationalists in the British Parliament supported the Liberals in their domestic agenda. In 1913 they received a home-rule bill for Ireland in return.

Ireland and Britain, however, still faced the prospect of civil war. The Irish Catholic majority in the southern counties wanted home rule, but the Irish Protestants in the northern counties of Ulster vowed to resist it. Unable to resolve the conflict as World War I started in August 1914, the British government postponed indefinitely the whole question of Irish home rule.

The dilemma of conflicting nationalisms in Ireland helps one appreciate how desperate the situation in the Austro-Hungarian Empire had become by the early twentieth century. After 1848 Hungary was ruled as a conquered territory, and Emperor Franz Joseph (r. 1848–1916) and his bureaucracy tried hard to centralize the state and Germanize the language and culture of the different nationalities.

Following its defeat by Prussia in 1866, a weakened Austria was forced to establish the so-called dual monarchy. The empire was divided in two, and the nationalistic Magyars gained

Bills Leading to Universal Male Suffrage in Britain
1832: Solid middle-class males enfranchised
1867: All middle-class males and the best-paid male workers enfranchised
1884: All adult males enfranchised

virtual independence for Hungary. Still, the disintegrating force of competing nationalisms continued unabated, and the Austro-Hungarian Empire was progressively weakened and eventually destroyed by the conflicting national aspirations of its different ethnic groups.

Jewish Emancipation and Modern Anti-Semitism

Revolutionary changes in political principles and the triumph of the nation-state brought equally revolutionary changes in Jewish life in western and central Europe. Beginning in France in 1791, Jews gradually gained their civil rights throughout Europe, although progress was slow and uneven. Legal equality led to greater economic opportunities, and by 1871 a majority of Jews in western and central Europe had improved their economic situations and entered the middle classes.

Vicious anti-Semitism reappeared after the stock market crash of 1873, beginning in central Europe. Drawing on long traditions of religious intolerance, this hostility also drew on modern ideas about Jews as a separate race. Modern anti-Semitism whipped up resentment against Jewish achievement and Jewish "financial control," while fanatics claimed that the Jewish race posed a biological threat to the German people. Anti-Semitic beliefs were particularly popular among conservatives, extremist nationalists, and people who felt threatened by Jewish competition.

Anti-Semites also created modern political parties. In Austrian Vienna in the early 1890s, Karl Lueger (LOO-guhr) and his "Christian socialists" used fierce anti-Semitic rhetoric to

"The Expulsion of the Jews from Russia" So reads this postcard, correctly suggesting that Russian government officials often encouraged popular anti-Semitism and helped drive many Jews out of Russia in the late nineteenth century. The road signs indicate that these poor Jews are crossing into Germany, where they will find a grudging welcome and a meager meal at the Jolly Onion Inn. Other Jews from eastern Europe settled in France and Britain, thereby creating small but significant Jewish populations in both countries for the first time since they had expelled most of their Jews in the Middle Ages. (Alliance Israelite Universelle, Paris/Archives Charmet/The Bridgeman Art Library)

help win striking electoral victories. Lueger appealed especially to the German-speaking lower middle class—and to an unsuccessful young artist named Adolf Hitler. In response to spreading anti-Semitism, a Jewish journalist named Theodor Herzl (1860–1904) turned from German nationalism to advocate Jewish political nationalism, or **Zionism**, and the creation of a Jewish state.

Before 1914 anti-Semitism was most oppressive in eastern Europe, where Jews also suffered from terrible poverty. In the Russian empire, where there was no Jewish emancipation and 4 million of Europe's 7 million Jewish people lived in 1880, officials used anti-Semitism to channel popular discontent away from the government. In 1881–1882 a wave of violent pogroms commenced in southern Russia. The police and the army stood aside while peasants assaulted Jews and looted and destroyed their property. Official harassment continued in the following decades, and some Russian Jews turned toward self-emancipation and the vision of a Zionist settlement in the Ottoman province of Palestine. Large numbers also emigrated to western Europe and the United States.

The Socialist Movement

Socialism appealed to large numbers of working men and women in the late nineteenth century, and the growth of socialist parties after 1871 was phenomenal. By 1912 the German Social Democratic Party, which espoused Marxist ideology, had millions of followers and was the Reichstag's largest party. Socialist parties also grew in other countries, and Marxist socialist parties were linked together in an international organization.

Yet socialism was not as radical and revolutionary in these years as it sometimes appeared. As socialist parties grew and attracted large numbers of members, they looked more and more toward gradual change and steady improvement for the working class and less and less toward revolution. Workers themselves were progressively less inclined to follow radical programs for several reasons. As workers gained the right to vote and won real benefits, their attention focused more on elections than on revolutions. Workers were also not immune to nationalistic patriotism, even as they loyally voted for socialists. Nor were workers a unified social group. Perhaps most important of all, workers' standard of living rose steadily after 1850, and the quality of life improved substantially in urban areas.

The growth of labor unions reinforced this trend toward moderation. In the early stages of industrialization, modern unions were considered subversive bodies and were generally prohibited by law. In Great Britain new unions that formed for skilled workers after 1850 avoided radical politics and concentrated on winning better wages and hours for their members through collective bargaining and compromise. After 1890 unions for unskilled workers developed in Britain.

After most legal harassment was eliminated in 1890, German union membership skyrocketed from only about 270,000 in 1895 to roughly 3 million in 1912. The German trade unions and their leaders were thoroughgoing revisionists. **Revisionism** was an effort by various socialists to update Marxist doctrines to reflect the realities of the time. The socialist Eduard Bernstein (1850–1932) argued in his *Evolutionary Socialism* in 1899 that Marx's predictions of ever-greater poverty for workers had been proved false. Therefore, Bernstein suggested, socialists should reform their doctrines and win gradual evolutionary gains for workers through legislation, unions, and further economic development.

Moderation found followers elsewhere. In France, socialist leader Jean Jaurès (1859–1914) formally repudiated revisionist doctrines in order to establish a unified socialist party, but he remained at heart a gradualist. Questions of revolutionary versus gradualist policies split Russian Marxists.

Socialist parties in other countries had clear-cut national characteristics. Russians and socialists in the Austro-Hungarian Empire tended to be the most radical. In Great Britain

Zionism The movement toward Jewish political nationhood started by Theodor Herzl.

revisionism An effort by various socialists to update Marxist doctrines to reflect the realities of the time.

the socialist but non-Marxist Labour Party formally committed to gradual reform. In Spain and Italy anarchism, seeking to smash the state rather than the bourgeoisie, dominated radical thought and action.

In short, socialist policies and doctrines varied from country to country. Socialism itself was to a large extent "nationalized." This helps explain why almost all socialist leaders supported their governments when war came in 1914.

Quick Review
Why did Europeans across the social and political spectrum come to feel a greater identification with the nation-state in the last decades of the nineteenth century?

Connections

MUCH OF WORLD HISTORY in the past two centuries can be seen as the progressive unfolding of the dual revolution. Europe in the nineteenth century, and Asia, Latin America, and Africa more recently, underwent interrelated economic and political transformations. Although defeated in 1848, the new political ideologies associated with the French Revolution triumphed after 1850. Nationalism, with its commitment to the nation-state, became the most dominant of the new ideologies. National movements brought about the creation of unified nation-states in two of the most fractured regions in Europe, Germany and Italy.

After 1870 nationalism and militarism, its frequent companion, touched off increased competition between the major European powers for raw materials and markets for manufactured goods. As discussed in the next chapter, during the last decades of the nineteenth century Europe colonized nearly all of Africa and large areas in Asia. In Europe itself nationalism promoted a bitter, almost Darwinian competition between states, threatening the very progress and unity it had helped to build. In 1914 the power of unified nation-states turned on itself, unleashing an unprecedented conflict among Europe's Great Powers. Chapter 28 tells the story of this First World War.

Nationalism also sparked worldwide challenges to European dominance by African and Asian leaders who fought to liberate themselves from colonialism, and it became a rallying cry in nominally independent countries like China and Japan, whose leaders sought complete independence from European and American influence and a rightful place among the world's leading nations. Chapters 25, 26, 32, and 33 explore these developments. Likewise, Chapter 34 discusses how the problems of rapid urbanization and the huge gaps between rich and poor caused by economic transformations in America and Europe in the 1800s are now the concern of policymakers in Africa, Asia, and Latin America.

Another important ideology of change, socialism, remains popular in Europe, but it never accomplished more than democratically electing socialist parties to office in some countries. Marxist revolutions that took absolute control of entire countries, as in Russia, China, and Cuba, had to wait until the twentieth century.

- **For a list of suggested readings for this chapter, visit** *bedfordstmartins.com/mckayworldunderstanding*.

- **For primary sources from this period, see** *Sources of World Societies*, Second Edition.

- **For Web sites, images, and documents related to topics in this chapter, see Make History at** *bedfordstmartins.com/mckayworldunderstanding*.

Chapter 24 Study Guide

To do these exercises online, go to bedfordstmartins.com/mckayworldunderstanding.

 Step 1

GETTING STARTED
Below are basic terms about this period in global history. Can you identify each term below and explain why it matters?

TERMS	WHO (OR WHAT) AND WHEN	WHY IT MATTERS
Congress of Vienna, p. 634		
dual revolution, p. 635		
liberalism, p. 635		
laissez faire, p. 637		
nationalism, p. 637		
socialism, p. 638		
bourgeoisie, p. 639		
proletariat, p. 639		
modernization, p. 643		
October Manifesto, p. 649		
germ theory, p. 650		
evolution, p. 654		
Social Darwinism, p. 656		
Dreyfus affair, p. 660		
Zionism, p. 662		
revisionism, p. 662		

Step 2

MOVING BEYOND THE BASICS
The exercise below requires a more advanced understanding of the chapter material. Examine the new ideologies that shaped European history in the nineteenth century by filling in the chart below with the key characteristics and beliefs associated with liberalism, conservatism, nationalism, and socialism. When you are finished, consider the following questions: Why did liberals tend to support nationalist movements and conservatives tend to resist them? How did the socialist diagnosis of the problem of nineteenth-century Europe differ from the liberal diagnosis? How were each of these four ideologies shaped by memories of the French Revolution?

	KEY CHARACTERISTICS AND BELIEFS
Liberalism	
Conservatism	
Nationalism	
Socialism	

PUTTING IT ALL TOGETHER

Now that you've reviewed key elements of the chapter, take a step back and try to see the big picture. Remember to use specific examples from the chapter in your answers.

REACTION AND REVOLUTION

- What were the goals of the participants in the Congress of Vienna? How did their experience of the French Revolution and the Napoleonic Wars shape their vision of postwar Europe?

- What explains the near simultaneous eruption of revolution across Europe in 1848? How did revolution in one country help trigger revolution in another? Why did all of the revolutions of 1848 fail?

NATION BUILDING IN ITALY, GERMANY, AND RUSSIA

- How did Bismarck use war to promote German unification under Prussian leadership? How did he use war to tame his domestic opponents?

- What did Russian leaders mean by "modernization"? How successful were their modernization efforts?

LATE NINETEENTH-CENTURY SOCIETY, CULTURE, AND POLITICS

- What explains the increasing social diversity of nineteenth-century Europe? What were the economic and political implications of this diversity?

- How did governments across Europe work to cement the loyalty of their citizens in the late nineteenth century? How effective were their efforts?

LOOKING BACK, LOOKING AHEAD

- How did nineteenth-century nation-states differ from their eighteenth-century counterparts? What role did industrialization and new political ideologies play in producing the differences you note?

- In what sense were the societies and states that developed in nineteenth-century Europe "modern"? What fundamental features of contemporary nation-states emerged in the period covered in this chapter?

In Your Own Words Imagine that you must explain Chapter 24 to someone who hasn't read it. What would be the most important points to include and why?

25

Africa, Southwest Asia, and the New Imperialism

1800–1914

While industrialization and nationalism were transforming society in Europe and the neo-European countries (the United States, Canada, Australia, New Zealand, and, to an extent, South Africa), Western society itself was reshaping the world. European commercial interests went in search of new sources of raw materials and markets for their manufactured goods. At the same time, millions of Europeans and Asians picked up stakes and emigrated abroad. What began as a relatively peaceful exchange of products with Africa and Asia in the early nineteenth century had transformed by the end of the century into a frenzy of imperialist occupation and domination that had a profound impact on both the colonizers and the colonized.

Sengbe Pieh Enslaved in 1839, Pieh led a revolt on the slave ship *Amistad*. Charged with mutiny and murder, the U.S. Supreme Court found the slaves innocent because they had been illegally captured and sold. They returned to their native Sierra Leone as free men. (New Haven Colony Historical Society)

The political annexation of territory in the 1880s—the "new imperialism," as it is often called by historians—was the capstone of Western society's underlying economic and technological transformation. More directly, Western imperialism rested on a formidable combination of superior military might and strong authoritarian rule, and it posed a brutal challenge to African and Asian peoples. Different societies met this Western challenge in different ways and with changing tactics, as we shall see. Nevertheless, by 1914 non-Western elites in many lands were rallying their peoples and leading an anti-imperialist struggle for dignity and genuine independence that would triumph after 1945.

Chapter Preview

▶ How did slavery, Islam, and imperialism shape Africa's development?

▶ What were the causes and consequences of European empire building?

▶ How and why did Ottoman and Egyptian leaders reform their states?

▶ How did Western industrialization change the world economy?

▶ What explains global migration patterns in this period?

How did slavery, Islam, and imperialism shape Africa's development?

From the beginning of the nineteenth century to the global depression of the 1930s, the different regions of Africa experienced gradual but monumental change. The long-standing transatlantic slave trade declined and practically disappeared by the late 1860s. In the early nineteenth century Islam expanded its influence in a long belt south of the Sahara, but Africa generally remained free of European political control. After about 1880 further Islamic expansion to the south stopped, but the pace of change accelerated as France and Britain led European nations in a "scramble for Africa" that would establish colonial regimes across the continent.

Trade and Social Change

palm oil A West African tropical product often used to make soap; the British encouraged its cultivation as an alternative to the slave trade.

The most important development in West Africa before the European conquest was the decline of the Atlantic slave trade and the simultaneous rise of the export of palm oil and other commodities. A major break with the past, the shift in African foreign trade marked the beginning of modern economic development in sub-Saharan Africa.

Although the trade in African people was a worldwide phenomenon, the transatlantic slave trade between Africa and the Americas became the most extensive and significant portion of it (see pages 506–512). The forced migration of millions of Africans intensified after 1700, and especially after 1750 (see Figure 19.2, page 514). Increasing demand for labor resulted in rising prices for African slaves in the eighteenth century. Some African merchants and rulers who controlled exports profited, but in the long run the slave trade resulted in instability and warfare, decimated the population, and destroyed local economies.

Until 1700, and perhaps even 1750, most Europeans considered the African slave trade a legitimate business activity. After 1775 a broad campaign to abolish slavery developed in Britain. British women played a critical role in this movement, denouncing the immorality of human bondage and stressing the cruel treatment of female slaves and slave families. The abolitionist movement also argued for a transition to legitimate (non-slave) trade, to end both the transatlantic slave trade and the internal African slave systems. In 1807 Parliament declared the slave trade illegal. Britain then established the antislavery West Africa Squadron, using its navy to seize the ships of the slave runners.

British action had a limited impact at first. Britain's West Africa squadron intercepted fewer than 10 percent of all slave ships, and the demand for slaves remained high on the plantations of Cuba and Brazil until the 1850s and 1860s. Nonetheless, over time, as more nations, including the United States, joined Britain in outlawing the slave trade, the shipment of human cargo slackened along the West African coast. At the same time the ancient but limited shipment of slaves across the Sahara and from the East African coast into the Indian Ocean and through the Red Sea expanded dramatically. Only in the 1860s did this trade begin to decline rapidly. As a result of these shifting currents, exports of slaves from all of West Africa across the Atlantic declined from an estimated 6.5 million persons in the eighteenth century to 3.9 million in the nineteenth century. Yet total exports of slaves from all regions of sub-Saharan Africa declined less than half as fast in the same years, from 7.4 million to 6.1 million.[1] The abolitionist vision of "legitimate" commerce in tropical products quickly replacing illegal slave exports was not realized.

Nevertheless, beginning in West Africa, trade in tropical products did make steady progress, for several reasons. First, with Britain's support and encouragement, palm oil sales from West Africa to Britain surged. Second, the sale of palm oil served the self-interest of industrializing Europe. Manufacturers used palm oil to lubricate machines, and from palm

668 Chapter 25 Africa, Southwest Asia, and the New Imperialism • 1800–1914

CHAPTER LOCATOR

How did slavery, Islam, and imperialism shape Africa's development?

oil they made the first good, cheap soap and other cosmetics. Third, the production of peanuts for export also grew rapidly, in part because both small, independent African farmers and their families and large-scale enterprises could produce peanuts for the substantial American and European markets.

Finally, powerful West African rulers and warlords who had benefited from the Atlantic slave trade succeeded in redirecting some of their slaves into the production of goods for world markets. This was possible because slavery and slave markets remained strong in sub-Saharan Africa, as local warfare and slave raiding continued to enslave large numbers of men, women, and children. Thus, the slow decline of the transatlantic slave trade coincided with the most intensive use of slaves within Africa.

At the same time, a new group of African merchants did rise to handle legitimate trade, and some grew rich. Women were among the most successful of these merchants. Although there is a long tradition of the active involvement in trade of West African women, the arrival of Europeans provided new opportunities. The African wife of a European trader served as her husband's interpreter and learned all aspects of his business. When the husband died, as European men invariably did in the hot, humid, and mosquito-infested areas of tropical West Africa, the African wife inherited his commercial interests, including his inventory and his European connections. Many such widows used their considerable business acumen to make small fortunes.

By the 1850s and 1860s legitimate African traders, flanked by Western-educated African lawyers, teachers, and journalists, formed an emerging middle class in the coastal towns of West Africa. This tiny middle class provided new leadership that augured well for the region's future. Unfortunately for West Africans, in the 1880s and 1890s African business leadership gave way to imperial subordination.

Chapter Chronology

1805–1848	Muhammad Ali modernizes Egypt
1808–1839	Mahmud II rules Ottoman state and enacts reforms
1809	Usuman founds Sokoto caliphate
1830	France begins conquest of Algeria
1839–1876	Western-style reforms (Tanzimat) in Ottoman Empire
1860s	Transatlantic slave trade declines rapidly
1869	Completion of Suez Canal
1876	Europeans take financial control in Egypt after Ottoman state declares partial bankruptcy
1880	Western and central Sudan unite under Islam
1880–1900	Most of Africa falls under European rule
1880–1914	Height of new imperialism in Asia and Africa
1881	Ahmed Arabi leads revolt against foreign control of Egypt
1884–1885	Berlin Conference
1899	Kipling, "The White Man's Burden"; Amin, *The Liberation of Women*
1899–1902	South African War
1902	Hobson, *Imperialism*
1908	Young Turks seize power in Ottoman Empire

Islamic Revival and Expansion in Africa

By the early eighteenth century Islam had been practiced throughout the Sudanic Savanna—the vast belt of flat grasslands across Africa below the southern fringe of the Sahara—for five hundred to a thousand years, depending on the area. The cities, political rulers, and merchants in many small states were Muslim. Yet the peasant farmers and migratory cattle raisers—the vast majority of the population—generally remained true to traditional animist beliefs and practices. Many Muslim rulers shared some of these beliefs and did not try to convert their subjects in the countryside or enforce Islamic law.

Beginning in the eighteenth century and gathering strength in the early nineteenth century, a powerful Islamic revival brought reform and revolutionary change from within to the western and eastern Sudan. In essence, Muslim scholars and fervent religious leaders arose to wage successful **jihads**, or religious wars, against both animist rulers and Islamic states that they deemed corrupt. The new reformist rulers believed that African cults and religious practice could no longer be tolerated, and they often effected mass conversions of animists to Islam.

jihad Religious war waged by Muslim scholars and religious leaders against both animist rulers and Islamic states that they deemed corrupt.

What were the causes and consequences of European empire building?

How and why did Ottoman and Egyptian leaders reform their states?

How did Western industrialization change the world economy?

What explains global migration patterns in this period?

669

Pears' Soap Advertisement

Andrew Pears began making his transparent soap in London in 1789. Starting in the late 1800s, it was marketed worldwide as a product symbolizing progress in advancing Europe's "civilizing mission." In 1910 the Lever brothers, William and James, bought Pears's company and sold Pears' Soap along with their own brands, including Sunlight, Lifebuoy, and Lux. These soaps were made with palm oil from Lever plantations in the Congo and the Solomon Islands. Pears' Soap is still made today, in India. (North Wind Picture Archives/Alamy)

ANALYZING THE IMAGE Which elements or words in this advertisement suggest the Western ideal of "civilization"? Which elements or words are used to describe non-Europeans?

CONNECTIONS How might the English phrase "Cleanliness is next to Godliness" relate to this advertisement? How can Pears' Soap lighten "the white man's burden" and brighten "the dark corners of the earth"?

The first step towards lightening

The White Man's Burden

is through teaching the virtues of cleanliness.

Pears' Soap

is a potent factor in brightening the dark corners of the earth as civilization advances, while amongst the cultured of all nations it holds the highest place—it is the ideal toilet soap.

Sokoto caliphate Founded in 1809 by Usuman dan Fodio, this African state was based on Islamic history and law.

The most important of these revivalist states, the Sokoto caliphate, illustrates the pattern of Islamic revival in Africa. It was founded by Usuman dan Fodio (1754–1817), a Muslim teacher who first won followers among both the Fulani herders and the Hausa peasants in the Muslim state of Gobir in the northern Sudan. After his religious community was attacked by Gobir's rulers, Usuman launched the jihad of 1804. Young religious students and discontented Fulani cattle raisers formed the backbone of the fighters, who succeeded in overthrowing the Hausa rulers and inspired more jihads in the Sudan. In 1809 Usuman established the new Sokoto caliphate, which was consolidated by his son Muhammad Bello as a vast decentralized state in Nigeria (see Map 25.1).

The triumph of the Sokoto caliphate had profound consequences for Africa and the Sudan. First, the caliphate was based on Islamic history and law, which gave sub-Saharan Africa a sophisticated written constitution that earlier preliterate states had never achieved. This government of laws, rather than men, provided stability and made Sokoto one of the most prosperous regions in tropical Africa. Second, because of Sokoto and other revivalist

670 Chapter 25 Africa, Southwest Asia, and the New Imperialism • 1800–1914

CHAPTER LOCATOR

How did slavery, Islam, and imperialism shape Africa's development?

Colonial presence, 1914

Legend:
- British
- French
- German
- Italian
- Portuguese
- Belgian
- Spanish
- Independent African states
- Afrikaner republic

SPANISH MOROCCO
Madeira Is. (Portugal)
Tangier
Canary Is. (Spain)
Casablanca
Algiers
TUNISIA
MOROCCO
Tripoli
Cyrene
IFNI
RIO DE ORO
ALGERIA
LIBYA
Cairo
EGYPT
Aswan
Tropic of Cancer
ARABIA
Mediterranean Sea
S A H A R A
Senegal R.
FRENCH WEST AFRICA
Niger R.
GAMBIA
PORTUGUESE GUINEA
SIERRA LEONE
Freetown
IVORY COAST
GOLD COAST
TOGOLAND
NORTHERN NIGERIA
L. Chad
Monrovia
LIBERIA
S. NIGERIA
KAMERUN
FRENCH EQUATORIAL AFRICA
Fernando Po. (Spain)
SPANISH GUINEA
São Tomé (Portugal)
ATLANTIC OCEAN
CABINDA
Omdurman
Khartoum
ANGLO-EGYPTIAN SUDAN
Fashoda
ERITREA
Adowa
FRENCH SOMALILAND
BRITISH SOMALILAND
ETHIOPIA
ITALIAN SOMALILAND
Red Sea
Blue Nile R.
White Nile R.
Nile R.
Uele R.
Congo R.
CONGO FREE STATE
BRITISH EAST AFRICA
L. Victoria
GERMAN EAST AFRICA
L. Tanganyika
Mombasa
Zanzibar (Gr. Br.)
INDIAN OCEAN
Equator
ANGOLA
NORTHERN RHODESIA
L. Nyasa
NYASALAND
MOZAMBIQUE
Zambezi R.
SOUTHERN RHODESIA
MADAGASCAR
GERMAN SOUTHWEST AFRICA
BECHUANALAND
TRANSVAAL
ORANGE FREE STATE
NATAL
Isandhlwana
SWAZILAND
UNION OF SOUTH AFRICA
BASUTOLAND
Cape Town
20°S
Tropic of Capricorn

Colonial presence, 1878

ALGERIA
EGYPT
SAHARA
SENEGAL
Nile R.
Niger R.
Congo R.
ANGOLA
MOZAMBIQUE
ORANGE FREE STATE (Afrikaner)
TRANSVAAL (Afrikaner)
CAPE COLONY
NATAL

0 250 500 miles
0 250 500 kilometers

Mapping the Past

Map 25.1 The Partition of Africa

The European powers carved up Africa after 1880 and built vast political empires.

ANALYZING THE MAP What European countries were leading imperialist states in Africa, and what lands did they hold? What countries maintained political independence?

CONNECTIONS The late nineteenth century was the high point of European imperialism. What were the motives behind the rush for land and empire in Africa?

What were the causes and consequences of European empire building?

How and why did Ottoman and Egyptian leaders reform their states?

How did Western industrialization change the world economy?

What explains global migration patterns in this period?

671

states, Islam became much more widely and deeply rooted in sub-Saharan Africa than ever before. By 1880 the entire western and central Sudan was united in Islam. Finally, Islam had always approved of slavery for non-Muslims and Muslim heretics, and "the *jihads* created a new slaving frontier on the basis of rejuvenated Islam."[2] In 1900 the Sokoto caliphate had at least 1 million and perhaps as many as 2.5 million slaves. Among all modern slave societies, only the American South had more slaves, about 4 million in 1860.

Islam also expanded in East Africa, in large part because of the efforts of Sayyid Said (r. 1804–1856), the imam of Oman. Reviving his family's lordship of the African island of Zanzibar and eventually moving his capital from southern Arabia to Zanzibar in 1840, Sayyid Said (sa-EED sa-EED) gained control of most of the Swahili-speaking East African coast. Said concentrated the shipment of slaves to the Ottoman Empire and Arabia through Zanzibar. In addition, he successfully encouraged Indian merchants to develop slave-based clove plantations in his territories. Thus, from the 1820s on Arab merchants and adventurers pressed far into the interior in search of slaves and ivory, establishing small Muslim states as they did so. The Arab immigrants brought literacy, administrative skills, and increased trade and international contact, as well as the intensification of slavery, to East Africa.

The Scramble for Africa, 1880–1914

Between 1880 and 1914 Britain, France, Germany, Belgium, Spain, and Italy worried that they would not get "a piece of that magnificent African cake" (in King Leopold II of Belgium's graphic phrase), scrambled for African possessions as if their national livelihoods were at stake. By 1914 only Ethiopia in northeast Africa and Liberia on the West African coast remained independent (see Map 25.1).

In addition to the general causes underlying Europe's imperialist burst after 1880 (see pages 677–680), certain events and individuals stand out. First, as the antislavery movement succeeded in shutting down the Atlantic slave trade by the late 1860s, the persistence of slavery elsewhere attracted growing attention in western Europe and the Americas. Through the publications of Protestant missionaries such as David Livingstone from Scotland, antislavery activists learned of the horrors of slavery and the slave trade in Africa. The public was led to believe that European conquest and colonization would end this human tragedy by bringing, in Livingstone's famous phrase, "Commerce, Christianity, and Civilization" to Africa.

Leopold II of Belgium (r. 1865–1909) also played a crucial role. His agents signed treaties with African chiefs and planted Leopold's flag along the Congo River. In addition, Leopold intentionally misled leaders of the other European nations to gain their support by promising to promote Christianity and civilization in his proposed Congo Free State. By 1883 Europe had caught "African fever," and the race for territory was on.

To bring some order to this competition, Premier Jules Ferry of France and Chancellor Otto von Bismarck of Germany arranged a European conference on Africa in Berlin in 1884–1885. The Berlin Conference, to which Africans had not been invited, established the principle that European claims to African territory had to rest on "effective occupation" in order to be recognized by other states. A nation could establish a colony only if it had effectively taken possession of the territory through signed treaties with local leaders and had begun to develop it economically.

In addition to developing rules for imperialist competition, participants at the Berlin Conference also promised to end slavery and to bring Christianity and civilization to Africa. In truth, however, these ideals ran a distant second to, and were not allowed to interfere with, their primary goal of commerce—holding on to their old markets and exploiting new ones.

Berlin Conference A meeting of European leaders held in 1884–1885 to lay down basic rules for imperialist competition in sub-Saharan Africa.

The Berlin Conference coincided with Germany's emergence as an imperial power. In 1884 and 1885 Bismarck's Germany established **protectorates** over a number of small African kingdoms and societies in Togoland, Kamerun, southwest Africa, and, later, East Africa (see Map 25.1). In acquiring colonies, Bismarck cooperated with France's Jules Ferry against the British. (See "Listening to the Past: A French Leader Defends Imperialism," page 678.) The French expanded into West Africa and formed a protectorate on the Congo River. As for the British, they began enlarging their West African enclaves and pushed northward from the Cape Colony and westward from the East African coast.

Pushing southward from Egypt, which the British had seized control of in 1882 (see page 000), the British were blocked in the eastern Sudan by fiercely independent Muslims, who had felt the full force of Islamic revival. In 1881 a pious local leader, Muhammad Ahmad (1844–1885), led a revolt against foreign control of Egypt. In 1885 his army took the city of Khartoum, forcing the British to retreat to Cairo. Ten years later a British force returned, building a railroad to supply arms and reinforcements as it went. Finally, in 1898 these troops met their foe at Omdurman, where Sudanese Muslims armed with spears charged time and time again, only to be cut down by the recently invented machine gun. In the end eleven thousand Muslim fighters lay dead. Only twenty-eight Britons had been killed.

All European nations resorted to some violence to exert control over land, resources, and people in their colonies. In no colony, however, was the violence and brutality worse than in Leopold II's Congo Free State. Rather than promoting Christianity and civilization, the European companies operating in the Congo Free State introduced slavery, unimaginable savagery, and terror. Missionaries and other religious leaders were not even allowed into the colony, for fear of their reporting the horrors they would witness there.

Profits in the Congo Free State came first from the ivory trade, but in the 1890s, when many of the elephant herds in the Congo had been decimated, a new cash crop arose to take ivory's place. In the mid-1880s a northern Irishman named John Dunlop developed a process to make inflatable rubber tires. Other scientific developments soon followed, and new uses for rubber were found, which caused a worldwide boom in the demand for raw rubber. As it happened, the Congo Free State was a rich source of wild rubber vines. By the mid-1890s rubber was the colony's major income producer. Violence and brutality increased exponentially as the European appetite for rubber became insatiable. Europeans and their well-armed mercenaries terrorized entire regions, cutting off hands, feet, and heads and wiping out whole villages to make it clear to the Africans that they must either work for the Europeans or die. In the early 1900s, human rights activists such as Edmund

Brutality in the Congo No Africans suffered more violent and brutal treatment under colonial rule than those living in Belgian King Leopold the II's Congo Free State. When not having their hands, feet, or heads cut off as punishment, Africans were whipped with *chicottes*, whips made of dried hippopotamus hide. Some Congolese were literally whipped to death. (Courtesy, Anti-Slavery International, London)

protectorate An autonomous state or territory partly controlled and protected by a stronger outside power.

Morel exposed the truth about the horrific conditions in the Congo Free State, and in 1908 Leopold was forced to turn over his private territory to Belgium as a colony, the Belgian Congo.

Southern Africa in the Nineteenth Century

The development of southern Africa diverged from the rest of sub-Saharan Africa in important ways. Whites settled in large numbers, modern capitalist industry took off, and British imperialists had to wage all-out war.

In 1652 the Dutch East India Company established a supply station at Cape Town for Dutch ships sailing between Amsterdam and Indonesia. The colony gradually expanded, and when the British took possession of the colony in the Napoleonic wars, the Cape Colony included about twenty thousand free Dutch citizens and twenty-five thousand African slaves, with substantial mixed-race communities on the northern frontier of white settlement.

After 1815 powerful African chiefdoms, Dutch settlers—first known as Boers, and then as **Afrikaners**—and British colonial forces waged a complicated three-cornered battle to build strong states in southern Africa. Of critical importance, the Zulu leader Shaka (r. 1818–1828) revolutionized African warfare and managed to create the largest and most powerful African society in southern Africa in the nineteenth century. The Zulu armies often destroyed their African enemies completely, sowing chaos and sending refugees fleeing in all directions. Shaka's wars also led to the consolidation of the Zulu, Tswana, Swazi, and Sotho peoples into stronger states in southern Africa. By 1880 these states were largely subdued by Dutch and British invaders, but only after many hard-fought frontier wars.

Beginning in 1834 the British gradually abolished slavery in the Cape Colony and introduced color-blind legislation (whites and blacks were equal before the law) to protect African labor. In 1836 about ten thousand Afrikaner cattle ranchers and farmers, who resented the British colonial officials and missionaries treating blacks as equals after abolishing slavery, began to make their so-called Great Trek northward into the interior. In 1845 another group of Afrikaners joined them north of the Orange River. Over the next thirty years Afrikaner and British settlers reached a mutually advantageous division of southern Africa. The British ruled strategically valuable coastal colonies, and the Afrikaners controlled their ranch-land republics in the interior. The Zulu, the Xhosa, and other African peoples lost much of their land.

The discovery of incredibly rich deposits of diamonds in 1867 and of gold in the 1880s revolutionized the economy of southern Africa, making possible large-scale industrial capitalism and transforming the lives of all its peoples. Small-scale white and black diamond diggers soon gave way to Cecil Rhodes (1853–1902) and the powerful financiers behind his De Beers mining company. Extraction of the deep-level gold deposits discovered in 1886 in the Afrikaners' Transvaal republic required big foreign investment, European engineering expertise, and an enormous labor force. By 1888 Rhodes's firm monopolized the world's diamond industry.

The mining bonanza whetted the appetite of British imperialists led by the powerful Rhodes. Between 1889 and 1893 Rhodes used missionaries and a front company chartered by the British government to force African chiefs to accept British protectorates, and he managed to add Southern and Northern Rhodesia (modern-day Zimbabwe and Zambia) to the British Empire. Rhodes and the imperialist clique then succeeded in starting the South African War of 1899–1902 (also known as the Anglo-Boer War), Britain's greatest imperial campaign on African soil.

The long and bitter war divided whites in South Africa, but South Africa's blacks were the biggest losers. The British had promised the Afrikaners representative government in

Afrikaners Descendants of the Dutch settlers in the Cape Colony in southern Africa.

674 Chapter 25 Africa, Southwest Asia, and the New Imperialism • 1800–1914

CHAPTER LOCATOR

How did slavery, Islam, and imperialism shape Africa's development?

The Struggle for South Africa, 1878

- Boer republics
- British territory
- ⚔ Battle

KALAHARI DESERT

TRANSVAAL

ZULULAND

ORANGE FREE STATE

NATAL

CAPE COLONY

Cape Town

ATLANTIC OCEAN

INDIAN OCEAN

return for surrender in 1902, and they made good on their pledge. In 1910 the Cape Colony; the former Afrikaner colony Natal (nuh-TAL), which had been annexed by the British in 1843; and the two Afrikaner republics formed a new self-governing Union of South Africa. After the peace settlement, because whites—21.5 percent of the total population in 1910—held almost all political power in the new union and because the Afrikaners outnumbered the English-speakers, the Afrikaners began to regain what they had lost on the battlefield. South Africa, under a joint British-Afrikaner government within the British Empire, began the creation of a modern segregated society that culminated in an even harsher system of racial separation, or apartheid, after World War II.

Colonialism's Impact After 1900

By 1900 much of black Africa had been conquered—or, as Europeans preferred to say, "pacified"—and a system of colonial administration was taking shape. In general, this system weakened or shattered the traditional social order and challenged accepted values.

The self-proclaimed political goal of the French and the British—the principal foreign powers—was to provide good government for their African subjects, especially after World War I. "Good government" meant, above all, law and order. It meant strong, authoritarian government, which maintained a small army and built up an African police force to put down rebellion, suppress ethnic warfare, and protect life and property. Good government required a modern bureaucracy capable of taxing and governing the population. Many African leaders and their peoples had chosen not to resist the invaders' superior force, and others stopped fighting and turned to other, less violent means of resisting colonial rule. Thus the goal of law and order was widely achieved.

Colonial governments demonstrated much less interest in providing basic social services. Expenditures on education, public health, hospitals, and other social services increased after the First World War but still remained small. Europeans feared the political implications of mass education and typically relied instead on the modest efforts of state-subsidized mission schools. Moreover, they tried to make even their poorest colonies pay for themselves. Thus salaries of government workers normally absorbed nearly all tax revenues.

Economically, the colonial goal was to draw the African interior into the world economy on terms favorable to the dominant Europeans. The key was railroads linking coastal trading centers to outposts in the interior. Cheap, dependable transportation facilitated easy shipment of raw materials out and manufactured goods in. Railroads had two other important outcomes: they allowed the quick movement of troops to put down local unrest, and they allowed many African peasants to earn wages for the first time.

The focus on economic development and low-cost rule explained why colonial governments were reluctant to move decisively against slavery within Africa. Officials feared that an abrupt abolition of slavery where it existed would disrupt production and lead to costly revolts by powerful slaveholding elites. Thus colonial regimes settled for halfway measures designed to satisfy humanitarian groups in Europe and also make all Africans, free or enslaved, participate in a market economy and work for wages. Even this cautious policy was enough for many slaves to boldly free themselves by running away, and it facilitated a rapid decline of slavery within Africa. At the same time, colonial governments often imposed taxes, payable in labor or European currency, to compel Africans to work for their white overlords. In some regions, particularly in West Africa, African peasants found it advantageous to voluntarily shift to export crops on their own farms. Overall, the result

A Missionary School A Swahili schoolboy leads his classmates in a reading lesson in Dar es Salaam in German East Africa before 1914, as portraits of Emperor William II and his wife look down on the classroom. Europeans argued that they were spreading the benefits of a superior civilization with schools like this one, which is unusually well-built and furnished because of its strategic location in the capital city. (Ullstein Bilderdienst/The Granger Collection, New York)

of these developments was an increase in wage work and production geared to the world market and a decline in nomadic herding and traditional self-sufficient farming of sustainable crops.

In sum, the imposition of bureaucratic Western rule and the gradual growth of a world-oriented cash economy after 1900 had a revolutionary impact on large parts of Africa. The experiences of the Gold Coast and British East Africa, two very different African colonies, dramatically illustrate variations on the general pattern.

The British established the Gold Coast colony in 1821. Over the remainder of the century they extended their territorial rule inland from the coast. This angered the powerful Asante kingdom in the interior, which also wanted control of the coast. After a series of Anglo-Asante wars beginning in 1824, British troops finally forced the Asante kingdom to accept British protectorate status in 1902. The large territory the British then controlled is essentially today's nation of Ghana.

Precolonial local trade was vigorous and varied, and palm oil exports were expanding. Into this economy British colonists subsequently introduced the production of cocoa beans for the world's chocolate. Output rose from a few hundred tons in the 1890s to 305,000 tons in 1936. Independent peasants and African businessmen and businesswomen were mainly responsible for the spectacular success of cocoa-bean production. African entrepreneurs even built their own roads, and they sometimes reaped big profits.

The Gold Coast also showed the way politically and culturally. The westernized black professional and business elite took full advantage of opportunities provided by the fairly

676 Chapter 25   Africa, Southwest Asia, and the New Imperialism • 1800–1914

CHAPTER LOCATOR

How did slavery, Islam, and imperialism shape Africa's development?

enlightened colonial regime. The black elite was the main presence in the limited local elections permitted by the British, for few permanent white settlers established themselves in West Africa.

Across the continent in the colony of British East Africa (modern Kenya), events unfolded differently. In West Africa Europeans had been establishing trading posts since the 1400s and carried on a complex slave trade for centuries. In East Africa there was very little European presence, until after the scramble for Africa in the 1880s. Once the British started building their strategic railroad from the Indian Ocean across British East Africa in 1901, however, foreigners from Great Britain and India moved in to exploit the situation. Indian settlers became shopkeepers, clerks, and laborers in the towns. British settlers dreamed of turning East Africa into a "white man's country" like Southern Rhodesia or the Union of South Africa. They saw the local population as nothing more than cheap labor for their estates and plantations. British East Africa's blacks thus experienced much harsher colonial rule than did their fellow Africans in the Gold Coast.

> **Quick Review**
> What role did slavery play in shaping Africa's development in the nineteenth century, both before and after the European "scramble for Africa"?

What were the causes and consequences of European empire building?

Western expansion into Asia and Africa reached its apex between about 1880 and 1914. In those years the leading European nations continued to send money and manufactured goods to both continents, and they also rushed to create or enlarge vast political empires abroad. This frantic political empire building contrasted sharply with the economic penetration of non-Western territories between 1816 and 1880, which had left a China or a Japan "opened" but politically independent (see Chapter 26). Noting this difference, contemporaries described this latest wave of European expansion as the **new imperialism**.

new imperialism The late-nineteenth-century drive by European countries to create vast political empires abroad.

Causes of the New Imperialism

Many factors contributed to the West's late-nineteenth-century rush for territory in Africa and Asia, and it is little wonder that controversies have raged over interpretation of the new imperialism. But despite complexity and controversy, basic causes are clearly identifiable.

Economic motives played an important role in the extension of political empires, especially of the British Empire. By the late 1870s France, Germany, and the United States were industrializing rapidly behind rising tariff barriers. Great Britain was losing its industrial leadership and facing increasingly tough competition in foreign markets. In this new economic situation Britain came to more highly value its old possessions, especially India. When in the 1880s European continental powers began to grab unclaimed territories, the British followed suit. They feared that France and Germany would seal off their empires with high tariffs and that future economic opportunities would be lost forever.

The overall economic gains of the new imperialism proved limited before 1914. The new colonies were too poor to buy much, and they offered few immediately profitable investments. Nonetheless, colonies became important for political and diplomatic reasons. Each leading European country saw them as crucial to national interests and international prestige. (See "Listening to the Past: A French Leader Defends Imperialism," page 678.)

Colonial rivalries reflected the increasing aggressiveness of Social Darwinian theories of brutal competition among races (see page 656). As one prominent English economist

Although Jules Ferry (1832–1893) first gained political prominence as an ardent champion of secular public education, he was most famous for his empire building. While he was French premier in 1880–1881 and again in 1883–1885, France occupied Tunisia, extended its rule in Indonesia, seized Madagascar, and penetrated the Congo. Criticized by conservatives, socialists, and some left-wing republicans for his colonial expansion, Ferry defended his policies before the French National Assembly and also elaborated a philosophy of imperialism in his writings.

In a speech to the Assembly on July 28, 1883, portions of which follow, Ferry answered his critics and summarized his three main arguments with brutal honesty. Note that Ferry adamantly insisted that imperial expansion did not weaken France in its European struggle with Germany, as some opponents charged, but rather that it increased French grandeur and power. Imperialists needed the language of patriotic nationalism to be effective.

❝ *M. Jules Ferry:* Gentlemen, . . . I believe that there is some benefit in summarizing and condensing, in the form of arguments, the principles, the motives, and the various interests by which a policy of colonial expansion may be justified; it goes without saying that I will try to remain reasonable, moderate, and never lose sight of the major continental interests which are the primary concern of this country. What I wish to say, to support this proposition, is that in fact, just as in word, the policy of colonial expansion is a political and economic system; I wish to say that one can relate this system to three orders of ideas: economic ideas, ideas of civilization in its highest sense, and ideas of politics and patriotism.

In the area of economics, I will allow myself to place before you, with the support of some figures, the considerations which justify a policy of colonial expansion from the point of view of that need, felt more and more strongly by the industrial populations of Europe and particularly those of our own rich and hard working country: the need for export markets. Is this some kind of chimera? Is this a view of the future or is it not rather a pressing need, and, we could say, the cry of

our industrial population? I will formulate only in a general way what each of you, in the different parts of France, is in a position to confirm. Yes, what is lacking for our great industry, drawn irrevocably on to the path of exportation by the [free trade] treaties of 1860, what it lacks more and more is export markets. Why? Because next door to us Germany is surrounded by barriers, because beyond the ocean, the United States of America has become protectionist, protectionist in the most extreme sense. . . .

Gentlemen, there is a second point, . . . the humanitarian and civilizing side of the question. On this point the honorable M. Camille Pellatan has jeered in his own refined and clever manner; he jeers, he condemns, and he says "What is this civilization which you impose with cannonballs? What is it but another form of barbarism? Don't these populations, these inferior races, have the same rights as you? Aren't they masters of their own houses? Have they called upon you? You come to them against their will, you offer them violence, but not civilization." There, gentlemen, is the thesis; I do not hesitate to say that this is not politics, nor is it history: it is political metaphysics. ("Ah, Ah" *on far left.*)

. . . Gentlemen, I must speak from a higher and more truthful plane. It must be stated openly that, in effect, superior races have rights over inferior races. (*Movement on many benches on the far left.*)

M. Jules Maigne: Oh! You dare to say this in the country which has proclaimed the rights of man!

M. de Guilloutet: This is a justification of slavery and the slave trade! . . .

M. Jules Ferry: I repeat that superior races have a right, because they have a duty. They have the duty to civilize inferior races. . . . (*Approval from the left. New interruptions from the extreme left and from the right.*)

. . . M. Pelletan . . . then touched upon a third point, more delicate, more serious, and upon which I ask your permission to express myself quite frankly. It is the political side of the question. The honorable M. Pelletan, who is a distinguished writer, always

argued in 1873, the "strongest nation has always been conquering the weaker . . . and the strongest tend to be best." Thus European nations, which were seen as racially distinct parts of the dominant white race, had to seize colonies to show they were strong and virile. Moreover, since racial struggle was nature's inescapable law, the conquest of "inferior" peoples was just. Social Darwinism and harsh racial doctrines fostered imperialist expansion.

So did the industrial world's unprecedented technological and military superiority. Three aspects were crucial. First, the machine gun provided a huge advantage in fire power. Second, newly discovered **quinine** proved effective in controlling attacks of malaria, which had previously decimated Europeans in the tropics whenever they left coastal enclaves and

quinine An agent that proved effective in controlling attacks of malaria, which had previously decimated Europeans in the tropics.

CHAPTER LOCATOR   How did slavery, Islam, and imperialism shape Africa's development?

comes up with remarkably precise formulations. I will borrow from him the one which he applied the other day to this aspect of colonial policy.

"It is a system," he says, "which consists of seeking out compensations in the Orient with a circumspect and peaceful seclusion which is actually imposed upon us in Europe."

I would like to explain myself in regard to this. I do not like this word, "compensation," and, in effect, not here but elsewhere it has often been used in a treacherous way. If what is being said or insinuated is that any government in this country, any Republican minister could possibly believe that there are in any part of the world compensations for the disasters which we have experienced [in connection with our defeat in the Franco-Prussian War of 1870–1871], an injury is being inflicted . . . and an injury undeserved by that government. (*Applause at the center and left.*) I will ward off this injury with all the force of my patriotism! (*New applause and bravos from the same benches.*)

Gentlemen, there are certain considerations which merit the attention of all patriots. The conditions of naval warfare have been profoundly altered. ("Very true! Very true!")

At this time, as you know, a warship cannot carry more than fourteen days' worth of coal, no matter how perfectly it is organized, and a ship which is out of coal is a derelict on the surface of the sea, abandoned to the first person who comes along. Thence the necessity of having on the oceans provision stations, shelters, ports for defense and revictualling. (*Applause at the center and left. Various interruptions.*) And it is for this that we needed Tunisia, for this that we needed Saigon and the Mekong Delta, for this that we need Madagascar, that we are at Diégo-Suarez

Jules Ferry, French politician and ardent imperialist.
(Bettmann/Corbis)

and Vohemar [two Madagascar ports] and will never leave them! (*Applause from a great number of benches.*) Gentlemen, in Europe as it is today, in this competition of so many rivals which we see growing around us, some by perfecting their military or maritime forces, others by the prodigious development of an ever growing population; in a Europe, or rather in a universe of this sort, a policy of peaceful seclusion or abstention is simply the highway to decadence! Nations are great in our times only by means of the activities which they develop; it is not simply "by the peaceful shining forth of institutions" (*interruptions on the extreme left and right*) that they are great at this hour.

. . . [The Republican Party] has shown that it is quite aware that one cannot impose upon France a political ideal conforming to that of nations like independent Belgium and the Swiss Republic; that something else is needed for France: that she cannot be merely a free country, that she must also be a great country, exercising all of her rightful influence over the destiny of Europe, that she ought to propagate this influence throughout the world and carry everywhere that she can her language, her customs, her flag, her arms, and her genius. (*Applause at center and left.*) 〞

Source: Speech before the French National Assembly, July 28, 1883. Reprinted in R. A. Austen, ed., *Modern Imperialism: Western Overseas Expansion and Its Aftermath, 1776–1965* (Lexington, Mass.: D. C. Heath, 1969), pp. 70–73.

QUESTIONS FOR ANALYSIS

1. What was Jules Ferry's economic argument for imperial expansion? Why had colonies recently gained greater economic value?
2. How did Ferry's critics attack the morality of foreign expansion? How did Ferry try to claim the moral high ground in his response?
3. What political arguments did Ferry advance? How would you characterize his philosophy of politics and national development?

ventured into mosquito-infested interiors. Third, the introduction of steam power and the international telegraph permitted Western powers to quickly concentrate their military might in a given area when it was needed. Steamships reduced the time and expense of journeys to far-flung colonies. Small steamboats could travel back and forth along the coast and also carry goods up and down Africa's great rivers. Likewise, train cars pulled by steam engines replaced the thousands of African porters hitherto responsible for carrying raw materials from the interior to the coast.

Social tensions and domestic political conflicts also contributed to overseas expansion. Conservative political leaders often manipulated colonial issues in order to divert popular attention from domestic conflicts and to create a false sense of national unity. Thus imperial propagandists relentlessly stressed that colonies benefited workers as well as capitalists, and they encouraged the masses to glory in foreign triumphs.

Finally, special-interest groups in each country were powerful agents of expansion. Shipping companies wanted lucrative subsidies. White settlers wanted more land, and missionaries and humanitarians wanted to spread religion and stop the slave trade. Military men and colonial officials foresaw rapid advancement and high-paid positions in growing empires. The actions of such groups pushed the course of empire forward.

A "Civilizing Mission"

Imperialists did not rest the case for empire solely on naked conquest and a Darwinian racial struggle or on power politics and the need for navy bases on every ocean. They developed additional "moral" arguments for expansion.

A favorite idea was that Europeans and Americans could and should "civilize" supposedly primitive non-Western peoples. According to this view, Africans and Asians would receive the benefits of modern economies, cities, advanced medicine, and higher standards of living and eventually might be ready for self-government and Western democracy.

Another argument was that imperial government protected colonized peoples from ethnic warfare and the slave trade within Africa, as well as from exploitation by white settlers and business people. Thus the French spoke of their sacred "civilizing mission." In 1899 Rudyard Kipling (1865–1936), who wrote extensively on Anglo-Indian life and was perhaps the most influential British writer of the 1890s, exhorted Westerners to unselfish service in distant lands in his poem "The White Man's Burden":

> *Take up the White Man's Burden—*
> *Send forth the best ye breed—*
> *Go bind your sons to exile*
> *To serve your captives' need,*
> *To wait in heavy harness,*
> *On fluttered folk and wild—*
> *Your new-caught, sullen peoples*
> *Half-devil and half-child.*[3]

white man's burden The idea that Europeans could and should civilize more primitive nonwhite peoples and that imperialism would eventually provide nonwhites with modern achievements and higher standards of living.

Written in response to America's seizure of the Philippines after the Spanish-American War, Kipling's poem and his concept of a **white man's burden** won wide acceptance among those who supported America's imperial ambitions. It was an important factor in the decision to rule, rather than liberate, the Philippines after the Spanish-American War (see page 733). Like their European counterparts, these Americans believed that their civilization had reached unprecedented heights and that they had unique benefits to bestow on all "less-advanced" peoples.

Imperialists claimed that peace and stability under European control would permit the spread of Christianity. In Africa Catholic and Protestant missionaries competed with Islam south of the Sahara, seeking converts and building schools. Some peoples, such as the Ibo in Nigeria, became highly Christianized. Such occasional successes in black Africa contrasted with the general failure of missionary efforts in the Islamic world and in much of Asia.

Critics of Imperialism

The expansion of empire aroused sharp criticism. J. A. Hobson (1858–1940), in his *Imperialism*, contended that the rush to acquire colonies was due to the economic needs

680 Chapter 25 Africa, Southwest Asia, and the New Imperialism • 1800–1914

CHAPTER LOCATOR

How did slavery, Islam, and imperialism shape Africa's development?

of unregulated capitalism. Moreover, Hobson argued, the quest for empire diverted popular attention away from domestic reform and the need to reduce the great gap between rich and poor at home. These and similar arguments had limited appeal because most people were sold on the idea that imperialism was economically profitable for the homeland.

Hobson and many Western critics struck home, however, with their moral condemnation of whites imperiously ruling nonwhites. Kipling and his kind were lampooned as racist bullies whose rule rested on brutality, racial contempt, and the Maxim machine gun.

Critics charged Europeans with applying a degrading double standard and failing to live up to their own noble ideals. At home Europeans had won or were winning representative government, individual liberties, and a certain equality of opportunity. In their empires Europeans imposed military dictatorships on Africans and Asians, forced them to work involuntarily, and discriminated against them shamelessly. Only by renouncing imperialism and giving captive peoples the freedom idealized in Western society would Europeans be worthy of their traditions.

African and Asian Resistance

To peoples in Africa and Asia, Western expansion represented a profoundly disruptive assault with many consequences. Everywhere it threatened traditional ruling classes, economies, and ways of life. Christian missionaries and European secular ideologies challenged established beliefs and values. African and Asian societies experienced crises of identity and a general pattern of reassertion, although the details of each people's story varied substantially.

Often the initial response of African and Asian rulers was to try to drive the unwelcome foreigners away, as in China and Japan (see Chapter 26). Violent antiforeign reactions exploded elsewhere again and again, but the superior military technology of the industrialized West almost invariably prevailed. In addition, European rulers gave special powers and privileges to some individuals and groups from among the local population. These local elites recognized the imperial power realities in which they were enmeshed, and used them to maintain or gain authority over the masses. Some concluded that the West was superior in certain ways and that it was therefore necessary to reform and modernize their societies by copying some European achievements. This process of maintaining domination through providing advantages to a select few is referred to as hegemony, and it explains why relatively small numbers of Europeans were able to maintain control over much larger populations without constant rebellion and protest.

Nevertheless, imperial rule was in many ways an imposing edifice built on sand. Support for European rule among the conforming and accepting millions was shallow and weak. Thus the conforming masses followed with greater or lesser enthusiasm a few determined personalities who came to oppose the Europeans. Such leaders always arose, both when Europeans ruled directly and when they manipulated native governments, for at least two basic reasons.

First, the nonconformists—the eventual anti-imperialist leaders—developed a burning desire for human dignity. They came to feel that such dignity was incompatible with foreign rule. Second, potential leaders found in the Western world the ideologies and justification for their protest. They echoed the demands of anti-imperialists in Europe and America that the West live up to its own liberal political ideals. Above all, they found themselves attracted to the nineteenth-century Western ideology of nationalism, which asserted that every people—or at least every European people—had the right to control its own destiny (see Chapter 24). After 1917 anti-imperialist revolt would find another weapon in Lenin's version of Marxist socialism.

Quick Review
What was new about the "new imperialism," and how did Africans and Asians respond to it?

What were the causes and consequences of European empire building?

How and why did Ottoman and Egyptian leaders reform their states?

How did Western industrialization change the world economy?

What explains global migration patterns in this period?

681

How and why did Ottoman and Egyptian leaders reform their states?

Stretching from West Africa into southeastern Europe and across Southwest Asia all the way to the East Indies, Islamic civilization competed successfully and continuously with western Europe for centuries. But beginning in the late seventeenth century, the rising absolutist states of Austria and Russia began to challenge the greatest Muslim state, the vast Ottoman Empire, and gradually to reverse Ottoman rule in southeastern Europe. In the nineteenth century European industrialization and nation building further altered the long-standing balance of power, and Western expansion eventually posed a serious challenge to Muslims everywhere.

In close contact with Europe and under constant European pressure, the ruling elites both in the Ottoman Empire and in Egypt, a largely independent Ottoman province, sought to resist European encroachment by launching reform and modernization efforts. The results of all these pressures and the momentous changes they brought were profound and paradoxical. On the one hand, the Ottoman Empire and Egypt achieved considerable modernization on Western lines. On the other hand, these accomplishments never came fast enough to offset the growing power and appetite of the West. The Islamic heartland in Southwest Asia and North Africa increasingly fell under foreign control.

Decline and Reform in the Ottoman Empire

In 1750 the relationship between the Ottomans and the Europeans was still one of roughly equal strength. In the later eighteenth century this situation began to change quickly and radically. The Ottomans fell behind western Europe in science, industrial skill, and military technology. Absolutist Russia pushed southward between 1768 and 1774. The danger that the Great Powers of Europe would gradually conquer the Ottoman Empire and divide up its vast territories was real.

Caught up in the Napoleonic wars and losing more territory to Russia, the Ottomans were forced to grant Serbia local autonomy in 1816. In 1821 the Greeks revolted against Ottoman rule, and in 1830 they won their national independence. Facing uprisings by their Christian subjects in Europe, the Ottomans also failed to defend their Islamic provinces in North Africa. In 1830 French armies began their conquest of the province of Algeria. By 1860 two hundred thousand European colonists had settled among the Muslim majority, whose number had been reduced to about 2.5 million by the war against the French and related famines and epidemics.

Ottoman weakness reflected the decline of the sultan's "slave army," the so-called janissary corps (see page 523). With time, the janissaries—boys and other slaves raised in Turkey as Muslims, then trained to serve in the elite corps of the Ottoman infantry— became a corrupt and privileged hereditary caste. They resisted any military innovations that might undermine their high status.

A transformation of the army was absolutely necessary to battle the Europeans more effectively and enhance the

Ottoman Decline in the Balkans, 1818–1830

sultanate's authority within the empire. The empire was no longer a centralized military state. Instead, local governors were becoming increasingly independent, pursuing their own interests and even seeking to establish their own governments and hereditary dynasties.

Sultan Selim III (r. 1789–1807) understood these realities, but when he tried to reorganize the army, the janissaries refused to use any "Christian" equipment. In 1807 they revolted, and Selim was executed in a palace revolution, one of many that plagued the Ottoman state. The reform-minded Mahmud II (r. 1808–1839) proceeded cautiously, picking loyal officers and building his dependable artillery corps. In 1826 his council ordered the janissaries to drill in the European manner. As expected, the janissaries revolted and charged the palace, where they were mowed down by the waiting artillery corps.

The destruction and abolition of the janissaries came too late to stop the rise of Muhammad Ali, the Ottoman governor in Egypt. In 1831 his French-trained forces occupied the Ottoman province of Syria and appeared ready to depose Mahmud II. The Ottoman sultan survived, but only by securing the intervention of Britain, Russia, and Austria. The Ottomans were saved again in 1839 after their forces were routed trying to drive Muhammad Ali from Syria. Russian diplomatic efforts, British and Austrian naval blockades, and threatened military action convinced Muhammad Ali to return Syria to the Ottomans. European powers preferred a weak and dependent Ottoman state to a strong and revitalized Muslim entity under a dynamic leader such as Muhammad Ali.

Realizing their precarious position, in 1839 liberal Ottoman statesmen launched an era of radical reforms. Known as the Tanzimat (literally, regulations or orders), these reforms were designed to remake the empire on a western European model. The new decrees called for the equality of Muslims, Christians, and Jews before the law and in business, security of life and property, and a modernized administration and military. New commercial laws allowed free importation of foreign goods, as British advisers demanded, and permitted foreign merchants to operate freely throughout an economically dependent empire. Under heavy British pressure, slavery in the empire was drastically curtailed, though not abolished completely. Of great significance, growing numbers among the elite and the upwardly mobile embraced many aspects of Western culture.

Intended to bring revolutionary modernization such as that experienced by Russia under Peter the Great (see page 449) and by Japan in the Meiji era (see page 707), the Tanzimat permitted partial recovery. Yet the Ottoman state and society failed to regain its earlier strength for several reasons. First, implementation of the reforms required a new generation of well-trained and trustworthy officials, and that generation did not exist. Second, the liberal reforms failed to halt the growth of nationalism among Christian subjects in the Balkans (see Chapter 28), which resulted in crises and defeats that undermined all reform efforts. Third, the reforms did not curtail the appetite of Western imperialism, and European bankers gained control of Ottoman finances.

Finally, the elaboration—at least on paper—of equal rights for citizens and religious communities did not create greater unity within the state. Religious disputes increased, worsened by the relentless interference of the Great Powers. Moreover, many conservative Muslims detested the religious reforms, which they saw as a departure from Islamic tradition and holy law. These Islamic conservatives became the strongest supporters of Sultan Abdülhamid (r. 1876–1909), who abandoned the model of European liberalism in his long and repressive reign.

The combination of declining international power and conservative tyranny eventually led to a powerful resurgence of the modernizing impulse among idealistic Turkish exiles in Europe and young army officers in Istanbul. These patriots, the so-called Young Turks, seized power in the revolution of 1908. Failing to stop the rising tide of anti-Ottoman nationalism in the Balkans, the Young Turks helped to prepare the way for the birth of modern secular Turkey after the defeat and collapse of the Ottoman Empire in World War I (see pages 768–770).

Tanzimat A set of radical reforms designed to remake the Ottoman Empire on a western European model.

Young Turks Fervent patriots who seized power in the revolution of 1908, forcing the conservative sultan to implement reforms; they helped pave the way for the birth of modern secular Turkey.

Egypt: From Reform to British Occupation

Egypt was conquered by the Ottoman Turks in the early sixteenth century. In 1798 French armies under the young general Napoleon Bonaparte invaded Egypt and occupied the territory for three years as part of France's war with Britain. Into the power vacuum left by the French withdrawal stepped another ambitious general, Muhammad Ali (1769–1849).

First appointed governor of Egypt by the Turkish sultan, Muhammad Ali set out to build his own state on the strength of a large, powerful army organized along European lines. He also reformed the government and promoted modern industry. (See "Individuals in Society: Muhammad Ali," page 685.) European intervention prevented him from toppling the Ottoman sultan, but by the time of his death in 1849, Muhammad Ali had established a strong and virtually independent Egyptian state within the Turkish empire.

To pay for a modern army and industrialization, Muhammad Ali encouraged the development of commercial agriculture geared to the European market. This development had profound social implications. Egyptian peasants had been poor but largely self-sufficient, growing food on state-owned land. Offered the possibility of profits from export agriculture, high-ranking officials and members of Muhammad Ali's family began carving large private landholdings out of the state domain, and they forced the peasants to grow cash crops for European markets. Thus, estate owners "modernized" agriculture, to the detriment of the peasants' well-being.

Egyptian Travel Guide Ismail's efforts to transform Cairo were fairly successful. As a result European tourists could more easily visit the country that their governments dominated. Ordinary Europeans were lured to exotic lands by travel books like this colorful "Official Guide" to an exhibition on Cairo held in Berlin. (Private Collection/Archives Charmet/The Bridgeman Art Library)

Muhammad Ali's policies of modernization attracted growing numbers of Europeans to Egypt. Europeans served as army officers, engineers, doctors, government officials, and police officers. Others worked in trade, finance, and shipping. Above all, Europeans living in Egypt combined with landlords and officials to continue the development of commercial agriculture geared to exports. By 1900 about two hundred thousand Europeans lived in Egypt, where they enjoyed important commercial and legal privileges and formed an economic elite.

Muhammad Ali's grandson Ismail (r. 1863–1879) was a westernizing autocrat. Educated at France's leading military academy, he dreamed of using European technology and capital to modernize Egypt and build an empire in northeastern Africa. He promoted cotton production, and exports to Europe soared. Ismail also borrowed large sums, and with his support the Suez Canal was completed by a French company in 1869, shortening the voyage from Europe to Asia by thousands of miles. Young Egyptians educated in Europe spread new skills; and Cairo acquired modern boulevards and Western hotels. As Ismail proudly declared, "My country is no longer in Africa, we now form part of Europe."[4]

A host of writers, intellectuals, and religious thinkers responded to the novel conditions with innovative ideas that had a powerful impact in Egypt and other Muslim societies. Three influential figures who represented broad families of thought were especially significant. The teacher and writer Jamal al-Din al-Afghani (1838/39–1897) preached Islamic regeneration and defense against Western Christian aggression. Regeneration, he argued, required the purification of religious belief, the unity of all Muslim peoples, and a revolutionary overthrow of corrupt Muslim rulers and foreign exploiters. The more moderate Muhammad Abduh (1849–1905) also searched for Muslim rejuvenation. Abduh concluded that Muslims should return to

684 Chapter 25 Africa, Southwest Asia, and the New Imperialism • 1800–1914

CHAPTER LOCATOR

How did slavery, Islam, and imperialism shape Africa's development?

THE DYNAMIC LEADER MUHAMMAD ALI (1769–1849) stands across the history of modern Egypt like a colossus. Yet the essence of the man remains a mystery, and historians vary greatly in their interpretations of him. Sent by the Ottomans, with Albanian troops, to oppose the French occupation of Egypt in 1799, Muhammad Ali maneuvered skillfully after the French withdrawal in 1802. In 1805 he was named pasha, or Ottoman governor, of Egypt. Only the Mamluks remained as rivals. Originally an elite corps of Turkish slave-soldiers, the Mamluks had become a semifeudal military ruling class living off the Egyptian peasantry. In 1811 Muhammad Ali offered to make peace, and he invited the Mamluk chiefs and their retainers to a banquet in Cairo's Citadel. As the unsuspecting guests processed through a narrow passage, his troops opened fire, slaughtering all the Mamluk leaders.

After eliminating his foes, Muhammad Ali embarked on a program of radical reforms. He reorganized agriculture and commerce, reclaiming most of the cultivated land for the state domain, which he controlled. He also established state agencies to monopolize, for his own profit, the sale of agricultural goods. Commercial agriculture geared to exports to Europe developed rapidly, especially after the successful introduction of high-quality cotton in 1821. Canals and irrigation systems along the Nile were rebuilt and expanded.

Muhammad Ali used his growing revenues to recast his army along European lines. He recruited French officers to train the soldiers. As the military grew, so did the need for hospitals, schools of medicine and languages, and secular education. Young Turks and some Egyptians were sent to Europe for advanced study. The ruler boldly financed factories to produce uniforms and weapons, and he prohibited the importation of European goods so as to protect Egypt's infant industries. In the 1830s state factories were making one-fourth of Egypt's cotton into cloth. Above all, Muhammad Ali drafted Egyptian peasants into the military for the first time, thereby expanding his army to 100,000 men. It was this force that conquered the Ottoman province of Syria, threatened the sultan in Istanbul, and triggered European intervention. Grudgingly recognized by his Ottoman overlord as Egypt's hereditary ruler in 1841, Muhammad Ali nevertheless had to accept European and Ottoman demands to give up Syria and abolish his monopolies and protective tariffs. The old ruler then lost heart; his reforms languished, and his factories disappeared.

In the attempt to understand Muhammad Ali and his significance, many historians have concluded that he was a national hero, the "founder of modern Egypt." His ambitious state-building projects — hospitals, schools, factories, and the army — were the basis for an Egyptian reawakening and eventual independence from the Ottomans' oppressive foreign rule. Similarly, state-sponsored industrialization promised an escape from poverty and Western domination, which was foiled only by European intervention and British insistence on free trade.

A growing minority of historians question these views. They see Muhammad Ali primarily as an Ottoman adventurer. In their view, he did not aim for national independence for Egypt, but rather "intended to carve out a small empire for himself and for his children after him."* Paradoxically, his success, which depended on heavy taxes and brutal army service, led to Egyptian nationalism among the Arabic-speaking masses, but that new nationalism was directed against Muhammad Ali and his Turkish-speaking entourage. Continuing research into this leader's life will help to resolve these conflicting interpretations.

*K. Fahmy, *All the Pasha's Men: Mehmed Ali, His Army, and the Making of Modern Egypt* (Cambridge, U.K.: Cambridge University Press, 1997), p. 310.

QUESTIONS FOR ANALYSIS

1. Which of Muhammad Ali's actions support the interpretation that he was the founder of modern Egypt? Which actions support the opposing view?
2. After you have studied Chapter 26, compare Muhammad Ali and the Meiji reformers in Japan. What accounts for the similarities and differences?

Muhammad Ali, the Albanian-born ruler of Egypt, in 1839 (Mary Evans Picture Library/ The Image Works)

What were the causes and consequences of European empire building? | **How and why did Ottoman and Egyptian leaders reform their states?** | How did Western industrialization change the world economy? | What explains global migration patterns in this period?

685

the purity of the earliest, most essential doctrines of Islam and reject later additions that could limit Muslim creativity. This would permit a flexible, reasoned approach to change, social questions, and foreign ideas.

Finally, the writer Qasim Amin (1863–1908) represented those who found inspiration in the West in the late nineteenth century. In his influential book *The Liberation of Women* (1899), Amin argued forcefully that superior education for European women had contributed greatly to the Islamic world's falling far behind the West. The rejuvenation of Muslim societies, therefore, required greater equality for women.

Egypt changed rapidly during Ismail's rule, but his projects were enormously expensive. By 1876 the Egyptian government could not pay the interest on its colossal debt. Rather than let Egypt go bankrupt and repudiate its loans, France and Great Britain intervened to protect the European investors who held the Egyptian bonds. They forced Ismail to appoint French and British commissioners to oversee Egyptian finances so that the Egyptian debt would be paid in full. This meant that Europeans were going to determine the state budget and in effect rule Egypt.

Foreign financial control evoked a violent nationalistic reaction among Egyptian religious leaders, intellectuals, and army officers. In 1879, under the leadership of Colonel Ahmed Arabi, they formed the Egyptian Nationalist Party. Continuing diplomatic pressure, which forced Ismail to abdicate in favor of his weak son, Tewfiq (r. 1879–1892), resulted in bloody anti-European riots in Alexandria in 1882. In response, the British fleet bombarded Alexandria, and a British expeditionary force decimated Arabi's forces and occupied all of Egypt. The British remained in Egypt until 1956, ruling the country through a puppet government.

In Egypt the British abandoned what some scholars have called the "imperialism of free trade," which was based on economic penetration and indirect rule. They accepted a new model for European expansion in the densely populated lands of Africa and Asia. Such expansion was based on military force, political domination, and a self-justifying ideology of beneficial reform. This model, which was also adopted in varying ways by other European colonial powers in the age of the new imperialism, was to predominate in the British colonies from the 1880s until 1914.

The Suez Canal, 1869

Quick Review

Why did the reform efforts of Ottoman and Egyptian leaders meet with only limited success?

How did Western industrialization change the world economy?

In the course of the nineteenth century the Industrial Revolution expanded and transformed economic relations across the face of the earth. As a result the world's total income grew as never before, and international trade boomed. Western nations used their superior military power to force non-Western nations to open their doors to Western economic interests, and the largest share of the new wealth flowed to the West, resulting in a stark division between rich and poor countries.

686

Chapter 25 Africa, Southwest Asia, and the New Imperialism • 1800–1914

CHAPTER LOCATOR

How did slavery, Islam, and imperialism shape Africa's development?

The Rise of Global Inequality

From a global perspective, the ultimate significance of the Industrial Revolution was that it allowed those regions of the world that industrialized in the nineteenth century to increase their wealth and power enormously in comparison with those that did not. A gap between the industrializing regions and the nonindustrializing or Third World regions (mainly Africa, Asia, and Latin America) opened and grew steadily throughout the nineteenth century. Moreover, this pattern of uneven global development became institutionalized, built into the structure of the world economy.

The explanation for this disparity between industrializing regions and nonindustrializing regions has generated a great deal of debate. One school of interpretation stresses that the West used science, technology, capitalist organization, and even its critical worldview to create its wealth. Another school argues that the West used its political and economic power to steal much of its riches, continuing its rapacious colonialism in the nineteenth and twentieth centuries.

These issues are complex, and there are few simple answers. As noted in Chapter 23, the wealth-creating potential of technological improvement and more intensive capitalist organization was great. At the same time, the initial breakthroughs in the late eighteenth century rested in part on Great Britain's having already used political force to dominate a substantial part of the world economy. In the nineteenth century other industrializing countries joined with Britain to extend Western dominion over the entire world economy. Unprecedented wealth was created, but most of it flowed to the West and its propertied classes and to a tiny non-Western elite of cooperative rulers, landowners, and merchants.

Third World A term that refers to the nonindustrialized nations of Africa, Asia, and Latin America as a single unit.

The World Market

The nineteenth century saw an enormous increase in international commerce, a development that summed up the growth of an interlocking world economy centered in Europe. Great Britain, with its vast colonial empire, played a key role in using trade to tie the world together economically. The technological breakthroughs of the Industrial Revolution encouraged British manufacturers to seek export markets around the world. After Parliament repealed laws restricting the importation of grain in 1846, Britain also became the world's leading importer of foreign goods. Free access to Britain's market stimulated the development of mines and plantations in Africa and Asia.

The growth of trade was facilitated by the conquest of distance. The earliest railroad construction occurred in Europe and in America north of the Rio Grande; other parts of the globe saw the building of rail lines after 1860. Wherever railroads were built, they drastically reduced transportation costs, opened new economic opportunities, and called forth new skills and attitudes.

Much of the railroad construction undertaken in Africa, Asia, and Latin America connected seaports with inland cities and regions, as opposed to linking and developing cities and regions within a country. Thus railroads dovetailed with Western economic interests, facilitating the inflow and sale of Western manufactured goods and the export and development of local raw materials.

The power of steam also revolutionized transportation by sea. Steam power, long used to drive paddle wheelers on rivers, began to supplant sails on the oceans of the world in the late 1860s. Passenger and freight rates tumbled, and the shipment of low-priced raw materials from one continent to another became feasible.

The revolution in land and sea transportation helped European settlers take vast, thinly populated territories and produce agricultural products and raw materials for sale in Europe. Improved transportation enabled Asia, Africa, and Latin America to export not only

What were the causes and consequences of European empire building? | How and why did Ottoman and Egyptian leaders reform their states? | **How did Western industrialization change the world economy?** | What explains global migration patterns in this period?

687

Indigo

The extract of leaves from a small bush that are carefully fermented in vats and processed into cakes of pigment, indigo has been highly prized since antiquity. It dyes all fabrics, does not fade with time, and yields tints ranging from light blue to the darkest purple-blue. Used primarily today as a dye for blue jeans, indigo has been used throughout history as a dye for textiles, as a pigment for painting, and for medicinal and cosmetic purposes.

Widely grown and used in Asia, indigo trickled into Europe from western India in the High Middle Ages but was very expensive. Woad — an inferior homegrown product — remained Europe's main blue dye until the opening of a direct sea route to India by the Portuguese in 1498 reconfigured the intercontinental trade in indigo, as it did for many Asian products. Bypassing Muslim traders in the Indian Ocean, first Portuguese and then Dutch and English merchants and trading companies supplied European dyers and consumers with cheaper, more abundant indigo.

In the early seventeenth century indigo became one of the British East India Company's chief articles of trade, and it was exported from India to Europe more than ever before. As European governments adopted mercantilist policies, they tried to control trade and limit the flow of gold and silver abroad for products like indigo. The result was a second transformation in the global trade in indigo.

Europeans established indigo plantations in their American colonies, and by the first half of the eighteenth century only small quantities of indigo continued to reach Europe from peasant producers in western India. Large indigo plantations in Brazil, Guatemala, Haiti and the Caribbean, and South Carolina depended on slaves brought from Africa, as did the entire Atlantic economy in the eighteenth century.

In the late eighteenth century the geography of the indigo trade shifted dramatically once again: production returned to India, now largely controlled by the British. Why did this happen? Political upheaval in the revolutionary era played a key role. American independence left South Carolina outside Britain's mercantilist system; the slave rebellion in Haiti in 1791 decimated some of the world's richest indigo producers; and Britain's continental blockades cut off Spain and France from their colonies. On the economic side, the takeoff in the British textile industry created surging demand for indigo. Thus in the 1780s the British East India Company hired experienced indigo planters from the West Indies to develop indigo production in Bengal. Leasing lands from Indian *zemindars* (landlords who doubled as tax collectors), British planters coerced Bengali peasants into growing indigo, which the planters processed in their "factories." Business expanded rapidly, as planters made — and lost — fortunes in the boom-and-bust cycles characteristic of commodity production in the nineteenth century.

In 1859 Bengali peasants revolted and received unexpected support from British officials advocating free-market contracts and recourse to the courts to settle disputes. As peasants pressed their case against the outraged planters, Indian professionals and intellectuals joined their cause. Winning freer and more equitable contracts, the rural-urban alliance created in the "Indigo Disturbances" marked a key step in the growth of nationalism in Bengal, a leading force in the subsequent drive for Indian independence.

Even as the Indigo Disturbances agitated Bengal, industrializing Europe discovered on its doorstep a completely new source of colorants: thick, black coal tar. This residue, a noxious byproduct of the destructive distillation of soft coal for the gas used in urban lighting and heating, was emerging as the basic material for the chemistry of carbon compounds and a new synthetic dye industry. British, German, and French chemists synthesized a small number of dyes between 1856 and 1869, when the first synthetic dye replaced a natural dye.

the traditional tropical products, but also new raw materials for industry, such as jute, rubber, cotton, and coconut oil. (See "Global Trade: Indigo," above.)

Intercontinental trade was facilitated by the building of the Suez and Panama Canals. Investment in modern port facilities made loading and unloading cheaper and faster. Finally, transoceanic telegraph cables inaugurated rapid communications among the financial centers of the world and linked world commodity prices in a global network.

The growth of trade and the conquest of distance encouraged Europeans to make massive foreign investments beginning about 1840. Most of the capital exported did not go to European colonies or protectorates in Asia and Africa. About three-quarters of total European investment went to other European countries, the United States and Canada, Australia and New Zealand, and Latin America. Europe found its most profitable opportunities for investment in construction of the railroads, ports, and utilities that were necessary to settle and develop the lands of extensive European expansion.

Quick Review

What connection was there between globalization and growing regional income inequality in the nineteenth century?

688 Chapter 25 Africa, Southwest Asia, and the New Imperialism • 1800–1914

CHAPTER LOCATOR

How did slavery, Islam, and imperialism shape Africa's development?

Map 25.2 The Indigo Trade

Thereafter, German researchers and Germany's organic chemical companies built an interlocking global monopoly that produced more than 90 percent of the world's synthetic dyes.

Indigo was emblematic of this resounding success. Professor Adolf Bayer first synthesized indigo in 1880. But an economically viable process required many years of costly, systematic research before two leading German companies working together achieved their objective in 1897. Producers' groups in India slashed indigo prices drastically, but to no avail. Indian exports of natural indigo plummeted from nineteen thousand tons in 1895 to only one thousand tons in 1913. Synthetic indigo claimed the global market, German firms earned super profits, and Indian peasants turned to different crops. Today, nearly all the indigo produced in the world is synthetic, although limited production of natural indigo still occurs in India, as well as in parts of Africa and South America.

What explains global migration patterns in this period?

Global economic expansion was accompanied by the movement of millions of people in one of history's greatest migrations: the so-called **great migration**. In the early eighteenth century the world's population entered a period of rapid growth that continued unabated through the nineteenth and twentieth centuries. All of the world's regions experienced population growth, but growth in the industrialized world was the most rapid. As a result, Europeans and peoples of predominately European origin jumped from about 22 percent of the world's total in 1850 to a high of about 38 percent in 1930.

The growing number of Europeans was a driving force behind emigration and Western expansion. The rapid increase in numbers led to relative overpopulation in area after area

great migration The mass movement of people from Europe in the nineteenth century; one reason that the West's impact on the world was so powerful and many-sided.

What were the causes and consequences of European empire building?   How and why did Ottoman and Egyptian leaders reform their states?   How did Western industrialization change the world economy?   What explains global migration patterns in this period?

689

migration chain The movement of peoples in which one strong individual blazes the way and others follow.

great white walls Discriminatory laws built by Americans and Australians to keep Asians from settling in their countries in the 1880s.

British East African Railway Poster Europeans constructed railroads in most of their African colonies to haul raw materials from the interior to coastal ports and to transport colonial officials, white settlers, and foreign tourists. Britain's East African railroad line from Kampala, Uganda, to the Kenyan port city of Mombasa was one of the most famous and most romanticized. Indians from British India did much of the construction and then remained in Kenya to form substantial Indian communities. U.S. President Theodore Roosevelt rode this train while on his 1909 African safari. (National Archives, London/HIP/Art Resource, NY)

in Europe. Overpopulation led to migration, and more than 60 million people left Europe over the course of the nineteenth century, primarily for the rapidly growing "areas of European settlement" — North and South America, Australia, New Zealand, and Siberia (see Chapter 27).

The European migrant was most often a small peasant landowner or a village craftsman whose traditional way of life was threatened by too little land, estate agriculture, and cheap factory-made goods. The vast majority of migrants were young and often unmarried. Many European migrants returned home after some time abroad.

Ties of family and friendship played a crucial role in the movement of peoples. Many people from a given province or village settled together in rural enclaves or tightly knit urban neighborhoods thousands of miles away. Very often a strong individual — a businessman, a religious leader — would blaze the way, and others would follow, forming a **migration chain**.

Many young European men and women were spurred to leave by a spirit of revolt and independence. In Sweden and Norway, in Jewish Russia and Italy, these young people felt frustrated by the small privileged classes that often controlled both church and government and resisted demands for change and greater opportunity. Migration slowed when the economic situation improved at home, or when people began to win basic political and social reforms, such as the right to vote and social security.

A substantial number of Asians — especially Chinese, Japanese, Indians, and Filipinos — also responded to population pressure and rural hardship with temporary or permanent migration. At least 3 million Asians moved abroad before 1920. Most went as indentured laborers to work on the plantations or in the gold mines of Latin America, southern Asia, Africa, California, Hawai'i, and Australia (see Chapter 26). White estate owners often used Asians to replace or supplement blacks after the suppression of the Atlantic slave trade.

Such migration from Asia would undoubtedly have grown to much greater proportions if planters and mine owners had had their way. But usually they did not. Asians fled the plantations and gold mines as soon as possible, seeking greater opportunities in trade and towns. There they came into conflict with white settlers in areas of European settlement. These settlers demanded a halt to Asian immigration. By the 1880s Americans and Australians were building **great white walls** — discriminatory laws designed to keep Asians out.

The general policy of "whites only" in the lands of large-scale European settlement meant that Europeans and people of European ancestry reaped the main benefits of the great migration. By 1913 people in Australia, Canada, and the United States all had higher average incomes than did people in Great Britain, still Europe's wealthiest nation. This, too, was part of Western global dominance.

Within Asia and Africa the situation was different. Migrants from south China frequently settled in Dutch, British, and French colonies of Southeast Asia, where they es-

CHAPTER LOCATOR   How did slavery, Islam, and imperialism shape Africa's development?

tablished themselves as peddlers and small shopkeepers (see Chapter 26). These "overseas Chinese" gradually emerged as a new class of entrepreneurs and office-workers. Traders from India and modern-day Lebanon performed the same function in much of sub-Saharan Africa after the European seizure in the late nineteenth century. Thus in some parts of Asia and Africa the business class was both Asian and foreign, protected and tolerated by Western imperialists who found these business people useful.

Quick Review
Who participated in the great migration, and what were their motives for migration?

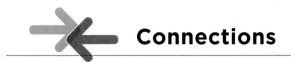

Connections

BY THE END OF THE NINETEENTH CENTURY broader industrialization across Europe increased the need for raw materials and markets, and with it came a rush to create or enlarge vast political empires abroad. The new imperialism was aimed primarily at Africa and Asia, and in the years before 1914 the leading European nations not only created empires abroad but also continued to send massive streams of migrants, money, and manufactured goods around the world. (The impact of this unprecedented migration is taken up in the next two chapters.) This political empire building contrasted sharply with the economic penetration of non-Western territories between 1816 and 1880, which had left China and Japan "opened" but politically independent, as Chapter 26 will show.

European influence also grew in the Middle East. Threatened by European military might, modernization, and Christianity, Turks and Arabs tried to implement reforms that would assure their survival and independence but also to retain key aspects of their cultures, particularly Islam. Although they made important advances in the modernization of their economies and societies, their efforts were not enough to overcome Western imperialism. With the end of World War I and the collapse of the Ottoman Empire, England and France divided much of the Middle East into colonies and established loyal surrogates as rulers in other, nominally independent countries. Chapter 29 will take up the story of these developments.

Easy imperialist victories over weak states and poorly armed non-Western peoples encouraged excessive pride and led Europeans to underestimate the fragility of their accomplishments. Imperialism also made nationalism more aggressive and militaristic. As European imperialism was dividing the world after the 1880s, the leading European states were also dividing themselves into two opposing military alliances. As Chapter 28 will show, when the two armed camps stumbled into war in 1914, the results were disastrous. World War I set the stage for a new anti-imperialist struggle in Africa and Asia for equality and genuine independence (see Chapters 32 and 33).

- **For a list of suggested readings for this chapter, visit** *bedfordstmartins.com/mckayworldunderstanding*.

- **For primary sources from this period, see** *Sources of World Societies*, Second Edition.

- **For Web sites, images, and documents related to topics in this chapter, see Make History at** *bedfordstmartins.com/mckayworldunderstanding*.

Chapter 25 Study Guide

To do these exercises online, go to bedfordstmartins.com/mckayworldunderstanding.

Step 1

GETTING STARTED

Below are basic terms about this period in global history. Can you identify each term below and explain why it matters?

TERMS	WHO (OR WHAT) AND WHEN	WHY IT MATTERS
palm oil, p. 668		
jihad, p. 669		
Sokoto caliphate, p. 670		
Berlin Conference, p. 672		
protectorate, p. 673		
Afrikaners, p. 674		
new imperialism, p. 677		
quinine, p. 678		
white man's burden, p. 680		
Tanzimat, p. 683		
Young Turks, p. 683		
Third World, p. 687		
great migration, p. 689		
migration chain, p. 690		
great white walls, p. 690		

Step 2

MOVING BEYOND THE BASICS

The exercise below requires a more advanced understanding of the chapter material. Examine the "New Imperialism" of the late nineteenth century by filling in the chart below with descriptions of the causes, motives, and characteristics of Western expansion before and after 1880. When you are finished, consider the following questions: What role did economic and political motives play in Western expansion before and after 1880? How did the nature of Western domination change after 1880? How would you explain the changes you note?

	CAUSES AND MOTIVES	KEY CHARACTERISTICS
Western Expansion Before 1880		
Western Expansion After 1880		

692

PUTTING IT ALL TOGETHER

Now that you've reviewed key elements of the chapter, take a step back and try to see the big picture. Remember to use specific examples from the chapter in your answers.

THE NEW IMPERIALISM

- How did Western pressure shape African development before 1880? How about after 1880?

- How did Westerners justify imperialism? How did Western critics of imperialism challenge such justifications?

MODERNIZATION AND REFORM IN THE ISLAMIC HEARTLAND

- How did Ottoman and Egyptian leaders use Western ideas and culture to resist Western domination?

- Should the modernization efforts of the Ottomans and Egyptian be deemed "failures"? Why or why not?

GLOBALIZATION, INDUSTRIALIZATION, AND MIGRATION

- Who benefitted the most from the economic growth and globalization of the nineteenth century? Why?

- Compare and contrast European and Asian migration during the nineteenth century. What important differences do you note? What common factors help explain the movements of both groups of migrants?

LOOKING BACK, LOOKING AHEAD

- What place did Europe have in the world economy in 1750? What about 1900? How would you explain the differences you note?

- What connections might one make between nineteenth-century European imperialism and the disastrous wars that befell Europe in the first half of the twentieth century?

In Your Own Words Imagine that you must explain Chapter 25 to someone who hasn't read it. What would be the most important points to include and why?

26

Asia in the Era of Imperialism

1800–1914

During the nineteenth century the societies of Asia underwent enormous changes as a result of population growth, social unrest, and the looming presence of Western imperialist powers. By the end of the century, most of the southern tier of Asia had been colonized by Western powers. Most of these colonies became tied to the industrializing world as exporters of agricultural products or raw materials. The Western presence brought benefits, especially to educated residents of major cities, where the colonizers often introduced modern public health, communications, and educational systems. Still, cultural barriers between the colonizers and the colonized were huge, and the Western presence rankled. The West relied on force to conquer and rule, and it treated non-Western peoples as racial inferiors.

Rammohun Roy The expansion of British power in India posed intellectual and cultural challenges to the native elite. Among those who rose to this challenge was writer and reformer Rammohun Roy. (V&A Images, London/Art Resource, NY)

Not all the countries in Asia were reduced to colonies. Although Western powers put enormous pressures on China and exacted many concessions from it, China remained politically independent. Much more impressively, Japan became the first non-Western country to use nationalism to transform itself and thereby meet the many-sided challenge of Western expansion. Japan emerged from the nineteenth-century crisis stronger than any other Asian nation, becoming the first non-Western country to industrialize successfully. By the end of this period Japan had become an imperialist power itself, making Korea and Taiwan its colonies.

Chapter Preview

▶ What were the consequences of British rule for India?

▶ Why were most but not all Southeast Asian societies colonized?

▶ What factors contributed to China's decline in the nineteenth century?

▶ How did Japan respond to the challenges posed by the West?

▶ Why did people move into and out of Asia in the nineteenth century?

▶ What common experiences did Asian societies share in this era?

What were the consequences of British rule for India?

Arriving in India on the heels of the Portuguese in the seventeenth century, the British East India Company outmaneuvered French and Dutch rivals and was there to pick up the pieces as the Mughal Empire decayed during the eighteenth century (see pages 540–542). By 1757 the company had gained control over much of India. During the nineteenth century the British government replaced the company, progressively unified the subcontinent, and harnessed its economy to British interests.

The Evolution of British Rule

In 1818 the British East India Company controlled territory occupied by 180 million Indians. In India the British ruled with the cooperation of local princely allies, whom they could not afford to offend. To assert their authority, the British disbanded and disarmed local armies, introduced simpler private property laws, and enhanced the powers of local princes and religious leaders, both Hindu and Muslim. The British administrators, backed by British officers and native troops, were on the whole competent and concerned about the welfare of the Indian peasants. Slavery was outlawed and banditry suppressed, and new laws designed to improve women's position in society were introduced.

The last armed resistance to British rule occurred in 1857. By that date the British military presence in India had grown to include two hundred thousand Indian sepoy troops and thirty-eight thousand British officers. The sepoys were well trained and armed with modern rifles. In 1857 groups of them, especially around Delhi, revolted in what the British called the **Great Mutiny** and the Indians called the **Great Revolt**. The sepoys' grievances were many, ranging from the use of fat from cows (sacred to Hindus) and pigs (regarded as filthy by Muslims) to grease rifle cartridges to high tax rates and the incorporation of low-caste soldiers into the army. The insurrection spread rapidly throughout northern and central India before it was finally crushed.

Thereafter, although princely states were allowed to continue, Britain ruled India much more tightly. Moreover, the British in India acted more like an occupying power and mixed less with the Indian elite. After 1858 India was ruled by the British Parliament in London and administered by a civil service in India, the upper echelons of which were all white. In 1877 Queen Victoria adopted the title empress of India, and her image became a common sight in India.

Great Mutiny/Great Revolt
The terms used by the British and the Indians, respectively, to describe the last armed resistance to British rule in India, which occurred in 1857.

The Great Mutiny/Great Revolt, 1857

CHINA
TIBET
NEPAL
Delhi
INDIA
GOA (Port.)
Arabian Sea
Bay of Bengal
Ceylon

☐ Under British control
☐ Area of rebellion

The Socioeconomic Effects of British Rule

The impact of British rule on the Indian economy was multifaceted. In the early stages, the British East India Company expanded agricultural production, creating large plantations. Early crops were opium to export to China (see page 702) and tea to substitute for imports from China. During the nineteenth century India also exported cotton fiber, silk, sugar, jute, coffee, and other agricultural commodities to be processed elsewhere. Clearing land for tea and coffee plantations, along with massive commercial logging operations, led to extensive deforestation.

To aid the transport of goods, people, and information, the colonial administration invested heavily in India's infrastructure. By 1855 India's major cities had all been linked by telegraph and railroads, and postal service was being extended to local villages. By 1870 India had the fifth-largest rail network in the world. Irrigation also received attention, and by 1900 India had the world's most extensive irrigation system.

At the same time, Indian production of textiles suffered a huge blow. Britain imported India's raw cotton but exported machine-spun yarn and machine-woven cloth, displacing millions of Indian hand-spinners and hand-weavers. By 1900 India was buying 40 percent of Britain's cotton exports. Not until 1900 were small steps taken toward industrializing India.

As the economy expanded the standard of living of the poor did not see much improvement. Tenant farming and landlessness increased with the growth in plantation agriculture. Increases in production were eaten up by increases in population. There was also a negative side to improved transportation. As Indians traveled more widely by rail, disease spread, especially cholera, which is transmitted by exposure to contaminated water. Pilgrims' bathing in and drinking from sacred pools and rivers worsened this problem.

The British and the Indian Educated Elite

The Indian middle class probably gained more than the poor from British rule, because they were the ones to benefit from the English-language educational system Britain established in India. Missionaries also established schools with Western curricula, and 790,000 Indians

Chapter Chronology

1825	King Minh Mang outlaws teaching of Christianity in Vietnam
1830	Dutch institute Culture System in Indonesia
1839–1842	Opium War
1851–1864	Taiping Rebellion in China
1853	Commodore Perry opens Japanese ports to foreign trade
1857	Great Mutiny/Great Revolt by Indian sepoys against British rule
1858	British Parliament begins to rule India
1859–1885	Vietnam becomes a colony of France
1867	Meiji Restoration in Japan
1869	Suez Canal opens
1872	Universal public schools established in Japan
1885	Foundation of Indian National Congress
1894-1895	Japan defeats China in Sino-Japanese War and gains control of Taiwan
1898	United States takes control of Philippines from Spain
1900	Boxer Rebellion in China
1904	Japan attacks Russia and starts Russo-Japanese War
1910	Korea becomes a province of Japan
1912	China's monarchy is replaced by a republic

Wooden Model of a Colonial Courtroom The judge, an officer with the British East India Company who is seated on a chair with his top hat on the table, presides over a courtroom filled with Indian assistants seated on the floor and the plaintiffs and defendants in the case standing. Notice the attention the Indian craftsman paid to the details of the dress and hats of each of the figures in this 20-inch-long wooden model. (© Victoria and Albert Museum, London/V&A Images)

Why were most but not all Southeast Asian societies colonized?

What factors contributed to China's decline in the nineteenth century?

How did Japan respond to the challenges posed by the West?

Why did people move into and out of Asia in the nineteenth century?

What common experiences did Asian societies share in this era?

697

Mapping the Past

Map 26.1 Asia in 1914

India remained under British rule, while China precariously preserved its political independence. The Dutch Empire in modern-day Indonesia was old, but French control of Indochina was a product of the new imperialism.

ANALYZING THE MAP Consider the colonies of the different powers on this map. What European countries were leading imperialist states, and what lands did they hold? Can you see places where colonial powers were likely to come into conflict with each other?

CONNECTIONS Do the sizes of the various colonial territories as seen on this map adequately reflect their importance to the countries that possessed them? If not, what else should be taken into account in thinking about the value of these sorts of colonial possessions?

were attending some 24,000 schools by 1870. High-caste Hindus came to form a new elite profoundly influenced by Western thought and culture.

By creating a well-educated, English-speaking Indian elite and a bureaucracy aided by a modern communication system, the British laid the groundwork for a unified, powerful state. Britain placed under the same general system of law and administration the various peoples of the subcontinent who had resisted one another for centuries. It was as if Europe had been conquered and united in a single great empire. University graduates tended to

698

Chapter 26 Asia in the Era of
Imperialism • 1800–1914

CHAPTER LOCATOR

What were the
consequences of British
rule for India?

look on themselves as Indians more than as residents of separate states and kingdoms, a necessary step for the development of Indian nationalism.

Some Indian intellectuals sought to reconcile the values of the modern West and their own traditions. Rammohun Roy (1772–1833), who had risen to the top of the native ranks in the British East India Company, founded a college that offered instruction in Western languages and subjects. He also founded a society to reform traditional customs and espoused a modern Hinduism centered on the *Upanishads* (oo-PAH-nih-shahds), the ancient sacred texts of Hinduism.

The more that Western-style education was developed in India, the more the inequalities of the system became apparent to educated Indians. Indians were eligible to take the examinations for entry into the elite Indian Civil Service, the bureaucracy that administered the Indian government, but the exams were given in England. Thus, in 1870 only 1 of the 916 members of the service was Indian. In other words, no matter how Anglicized educated Indians became, they could never become the white rulers' equals. The top jobs, the best clubs, the modern hotels, and even certain railroad compartments were reserved for whites. Most of the British elite considered all Indians to be racially inferior. For example, when the British Parliament in 1883 was considering a bill to allow Indian judges to try white Europeans in India, the British community rose in protest and defeated the measure.

The peasant masses might accept such inequality as the latest version of age-old class and caste hierarchies, but the well-educated, English-speaking elite eventually could not. They had studied not only Milton and Shakespeare but also English traditions of democracy, liberty, and national pride.

In the late nineteenth century the colonial ports of Calcutta, Bombay, and Madras became centers of intellectual ferment. In these and other cities, newspapers in English and in regional languages gained influence. Lawyers trained in English law began agitating for Indian independence. By 1885, when a group of educated Indians came together to found the Indian National Congress, demands were increasing for the equality and self-government that had already been granted white-settler colonies such as Canada and Australia (see Chapter 27). The Congress Party called for more opportunities for Indians in the Indian Civil Service and reallocation of the government budget from military expenditures to the alleviation of poverty. They advocated unity across religious and caste lines, but most members were upper-caste, Western-educated Hindus.

Defending British possessions in India became a key element of Britain's foreign policy during the nineteenth century and led to steady expansion of the territory Britain controlled in Asia. By 1852, the kingdom of Burma had been annexed. British trade between India and China went through the Strait of Malacca, making that region strategically important. Britain created a base in the area at Singapore, later expanding into Malaya (now Malaysia) in the 1870s and 1880s. In both Burma and Malaya, Britain tried to foster economic development, building railroads and promoting trade. So many laborers were brought into Malaya for the expanding mines and plantations that its population came to be approximately one-third Malay, one-third Chinese, and one-third Indian.

Indian Civil Service The bureaucracy that administered the government of India. Entry into its elite ranks was by examinations that Indians were eligible to take but that were offered only in England.

Indian National Congress A political association formed in 1885 that worked for Indian self-government.

Quick Review
What steps did Britain take to expand and develop India's economy, and who benefited most from such efforts?

Why were most but not all Southeast Asian societies colonized?

At the beginning of the nineteenth century only a small part of Southeast Asia was under direct European control. Spain administered the Philippines, and the Dutch controlled Java. By the end of the century most of the region would be in foreign hands.

The Dutch East Indies

Although the Dutch presence in the East Indies dated back to the seventeenth century, in 1816 the Dutch ruled little more than the island of Java. Thereafter they gradually brought almost all of the 3,000-mile-long archipelago under their political authority. In extending their rule, the Dutch, like the British in India, brought diverse peoples with different languages and distinct cultural traditions into a single political entity (Map 26.1).

Taking over the Dutch East India Company in 1799, the Dutch government modified the company's loose control of Java and gradually built a modern bureaucratic state. Javanese resistance to Dutch rule led to the bloody Java War (1825–1830). In 1830, after the war, the Dutch established a particularly exploitive policy called the Culture System. Under this system, Indonesian peasants were forced to plant a fifth of their land in export crops, especially coffee and sugar, to turn over to the Dutch as tax. In 1870 Dutch liberals succeeded in eliminating some of the system's most coercive elements, but the practical effects were limited because Dutch and Javanese officials still worked together to make sure the flow of goods continued.

At the end of the nineteenth century the Dutch began to encourage Western education in the East Indies. The children of local rulers and privileged elites, much like their counterparts in India, encountered new ideas in Dutch-language schools. They began to question the long-standing cooperation of local elites with Dutch colonialism, and they searched for a new national identity. Thus anticolonial nationalism began to take shape in the East Indies in the early twentieth century, and it would blossom after World War I.

Java War The 1825–1830 war between the Dutch government and the Javanese, fought over the extension of Dutch control of the island.

Mainland Southeast Asia

Unlike India and Java, mainland Southeast Asia had escaped European rule during the eighteenth century. In 1802 the Nguyen Dynasty came to power in Vietnam, putting an end to thirty years of peasant rebellion and civil war. Working through a centralizing scholar bureaucracy fashioned on the Chinese model, the Nguyen (gwin) Dynasty energetically built irrigation canals, roads and bridges, and impressive palaces in Hue (hway), the new capital city. Yet construction placed a heavy burden on the peasants drafted to do the work, and it contributed to a resurgence of peasant uprisings.

Roman Catholic missionaries from France posed a second, more dangerous threat to Vietnam's Confucian ruling elite. The king and his advisers believed that Christianity would undermine Confucian moral values and the unity of the Vietnamese state. In 1825 King Minh Mang (r. 1820–1841) outlawed the teaching of Christianity, and soon his government began executing Catholic missionaries and Vietnamese converts. In response, in 1859–1860 a French naval force seized Saigon and three surrounding provinces in southern Vietnam, making that part of Vietnam a French colony. In 1884–1885 France launched a second war against Vietnam and conquered the rest of the country. Laos and Cambodia were added to form French Indochina in 1887. In all three countries the local rulers were left on their thrones, but France dominated and tried to promote French culture.

After the French conquest, Vietnamese patriots continued to resist the colonial occupiers with a combination of loyalty to Confucian values and intense hatred of foreign rule. After Japan's victory over Russia in 1905 (see page 712), a new generation of nationalists saw Japan as a model for Vietnamese revitalization and freedom.

In all of Southeast Asia, only Siam succeeded in preserving its independence. Siam was sandwiched between the British in Burma and the French in Indochina. Siam's King Chulalongkorn (r. 1868–1910) took advantage of this situation to play the two competitors off each other. He outlawed slavery and implemented modernizing reforms that centralized the government so that it could more effectively control outlying provinces coveted

Nguyen Dynasty The last Vietnamese ruling house, which lasted from 1802 to 1945.

IN THE MID-SEVENTEENTH CENTURY, A CHINESE merchant immigrated to the Philippines and married a woman who was half Chinese, half Philippine. Because of anti-Chinese animosity, he changed his name to Mercado, Spanish for "merchant."

Mercado's direct patrilineal descendant, José Rizal (1861–1896), was born into a well-to-do family that leased a plantation from Dominican friars. Both of his parents were educated, and he was a brilliant student himself. In 1882, after completing his studies at the Jesuit-run college in Manila, he went to Madrid to study medicine. During his ten years in Europe he not only earned a medical degree in Spain and a Ph.D. in Germany but he also found time to learn several European languages and make friends with scientists, writers, and political radicals.

While in Europe, Rizal became involved with Philippine revolutionaries and contributed numerous articles to their newspaper, *La Solidaridad*, published in Barcelona. Rizal advocated making the Philippines a province of Spain, giving it representation in the Spanish parliament, replacing Spanish friars with Filipino priests, and making Filipinos and Spaniards equal before the law. He spent a year at the British Museum doing research on the early phase of the Spanish colonization of the Philippines. He also wrote two novels.

The first novel, written in Spanish, was fired by the passions of nationalism. In satirical fashion, it depicts a young Filipino of mixed blood who studies for several years in Europe before returning to the Philippines to start a modern secular school in his hometown and to marry his childhood sweetheart. The church stands in the way of his efforts, and the colonial administration proves incompetent. The novel ends with the hero being gunned down after the friars falsely implicate him in a revolutionary conspiracy. Rizal's own life ended up following this narrative surprisingly closely.

In 1892 Rizal left Europe, stopped briefly in Hong Kong, and then returned to Manila to help his family with a lawsuit. Though he secured his relatives' release from jail, he ran into trouble himself. Because his writings were critical of the power of the church, he made many enemies, some of whom had him arrested. He was sent into exile to a Jesuit mission town on the relatively primitive island of Mindanao. There he founded a school and a hospital, and the Jesuits tried to win him back to the church. He kept busy during his four years in exile, not only teaching English, science, and self-defense, but also maintaining his correspondence with scientists in Europe. When a nationalist secret society rose in revolt in 1896, Rizal, in an effort to distance himself, volunteered to go to Cuba to help in an outbreak of yellow fever. Although he had no connections with the secret society and was on his way across the ocean, Rizal was arrested and shipped back to Manila.

Tried for sedition by the military, Rizal was found guilty. When handed his death certificate, Rizal struck out the words "Chinese half-breed" and wrote "pure native." He was publicly executed by a firing squad in Manila at age thirty-five, making him a martyr of the nationalist cause.

QUESTIONS FOR ANALYSIS

1. Did Rizal's comfortable family background contribute to his becoming a revolutionary?
2. How would Rizal's European contemporaries have reacted to his opposition to the Catholic Church?

After Rizal's death, his portrait was used to inspire patriotism. (Cover of "The Filipino Teacher," December 1908. Courtesy, Museo Santisima Trinidad)

by the imperialists. Independent Siam gradually developed a modern centralizing state similar to those constructed by Western imperialists in their Asian possessions.

The Philippines

The United States became one of the imperialist powers in Asia when it took the Philippines from Spain in 1898. Under the Spanish, Roman Catholic churches were established, and Spanish priests able to speak the local languages became the most common intermediaries between local populations, who rarely could speak Spanish, and the new rulers. The government of Spain encouraged Spaniards to colonize the Philippines through the *encomienda* system (see page 000): Spaniards who had served the Crown were rewarded with grants giving them the exclusive right to control public affairs and collect taxes in a specific locality of the Philippines. A local Filipino elite also developed, aided by the Spanish introduction of private ownership of land. Manila developed into an important entrepôt in the galleon trade between Mexico and China, and this trade also attracted a large Chinese community, which handled much of the trade within the Philippines.

Spain did not do much to promote education in the Philippines. In the late nineteenth century, however, wealthy Filipinos began to send their sons to study abroad, and a movement to press Spain for reforms emerged among those who had been abroad. When the Spanish cracked down on critics, a rebellion erupted in 1896 (see "Individuals in Society: José Rizal," page 701). It was settled in 1897 with Spanish promises to reform.

In 1898 war between Spain and the United States broke out in Cuba (see page 733), and in May the American naval officer Commodore George Dewey sailed into Manila Bay and sank the Spanish fleet anchored there. Dewey called on the Philippine rebels to help defeat the Spanish forces, but when the rebels declared independence, the U.S. government refused to recognize them. U.S. forces fought the Philippine rebels, and by the end of the insurrection in 1902 the war had cost the lives of 5,000 Americans and about 200,000 Filipinos. In the following years, the United States introduced a form of colonial rule that included public works and economic development projects, improved education and medicine, and in 1907 an elected legislative assembly.

Quick Review
How did the Dutch, French, and Americans expand their presence in Southeast Asia in the nineteenth century?

What factors contributed to China's decline in the nineteenth century?

In 1800 China was the most populous country in the world, its products were in great demand in foreign countries, and its borders had recently been expanded. A century later China's world standing had sunk precipitously. In 1900 foreign troops marched into China's capital to protect foreign nationals, and more and more Chinese had come to think that their government, society, and cultural values needed to be radically changed.

The Opium War

The Qing (Manchu) emperors, who had been ruling China since 1644 (see pages 555–557), permitted Europeans to trade only at the port of Guangzhou (Canton) and only through licensed Chinese merchants. Initially, the balance of trade was in China's favor. Great Britain and the other Western nations used silver to pay for tea, since they had not been able to find anything that the Chinese wanted to buy. By the 1820s, however, the British had found something the Chinese would buy: opium. Grown legally in British-occupied India, opium was smuggled into China, where its use and sale were illegal. Huge profits and the cravings of addicts led to rapid increases in sales, from 4,500 chests a year in 1810 to 10,000 in 1830 and 40,000 in 1838. At this point it was China that suffered a drain of silver, since it was importing more than it was exporting.

To deal with this crisis, the Chinese government dispatched Lin Zexu to Guangzhou in 1839. He dealt harshly with Chinese who purchased opium, seized the opium stores of British merchants, and sent formal complaints to the British government. When Lin pressured the Portuguese to expel the uncooperative British from their trading post at Macao, the British settled on the barren island of Hong Kong.

The British responded to the new Chinese policies by flexing its military muscles. With the encouragement of their merchants in China, the British sent an expeditionary force from India with forty-two warships, many of them leased from the major opium trader, Jardine, Matheson, and Company. With its control of the seas, the British easily shut down key Chinese ports and forced the Chinese to negotiate. Dissatisfied with the resulting agreement, the British sent a second, larger force, which took even more coastal cities, including Shanghai. This **Opium War** was settled at gunpoint in 1842, with a series of treaties highly favorable to Britain.

The treaties satisfied neither side. China continued to refuse to accept foreign diplomats at its capital in Beijing, and the expansion of trade fell far short of Western expectations. Between 1856 and 1860 Britain and France renewed hostilities with China, occupying Beijing. Another round of harsh treaties gave European merchants and missionaries greater privileges and forced the Chinese to open several more cities to foreign trade. Large areas

The Opium War Treaties
Five ports opened to international trade
Tariff on imported goods fixed at 5 percent
War reparation of 21 million ounces of silver imposed on China
Hong Kong ceded to Britain
British subjects in China answerable only to British law
Privileges granted by China to other nations extended automatically to Britain

Opium War The 1839–1842 war between the British and the Chinese over limitations on trade and the importation of opium into China.

Treaty of Nanjing The settlement reached by Britain and China in 1842 was written in both English and Chinese. The chief negotiators of both sides signed the document, and the seals of both countries were placed on it. The Chinese seal was impressed with red ink in the traditional way, while the British used wax. (The National Archives, UK)

Why were most but not all Southeast Asian societies colonized? | **What factors contributed to China's decline in the nineteenth century?** | How did Japan respond to the challenges posed by the West? | Why did people move into and out of Asia in the nineteenth century? | What common experiences did Asian societies share in this era?

703

concessions Large areas of Chinese treaty ports that were leased in perpetuity to foreign powers.

Internal Problems

China's problems in the nineteenth century were not all of foreign origin. By 1850 China had more than 400 million people. As the population grew, farm size shrank, forests were cleared, and surplus labor suppressed wages. When the best parcels of land were all occupied, conflicts over rights to water and tenancy increased. Hard times also led to increased female infanticide, as families felt that they could not afford to raise more than two or three children and saw sons as necessities. A shortage of marriageable women resulted, reducing the incentive for young men to stay near home. Some became bandits, others boatmen, carters, sedan-chair carriers, and, by the end of the century, rickshaw pullers.

These economic and demographic circumstances led to some of the most destructive rebellions in China's history. The worst was the **Taiping Rebellion** (1851–1864), in which some 20 million people lost their lives, making it one of the bloodiest wars in world history.

Taiping Rebellion A massive rebellion by believers in the religious teachings of Hong Xiuquan, begun in 1851 and not suppressed until 1864.

Chinese Rebellions, 1851–1900

The Taiping (TIGH-ping) Rebellion was initiated by Hong Xiuquan (hong show-chwan; 1814–1864), a failed applicant for the civil service. Influenced by a religious vision and by Christian tracts, Hong became convinced that he was Jesus's younger brother, assigned a divine mission to annihilate devils. He soon gathered followers, whom he instructed to destroy idols and ancestral temples, give up opium and alcohol, and renounce foot binding and prostitution. In 1851 he declared himself king of the Heavenly Kingdom of Great Peace (Taiping), an act of open insurrection.

By 1853 the Taiping rebels, as Hong's followers were known, had moved north and established their capital at the major city of Nanjing, which they held onto for a decade. From this base they set about creating a utopian society based on the equalization of landholdings and the equality of men and women.

Christian missionaries quickly concluded that the Christian elements in Taiping doctrines were heretical and did not help the rebels. To suppress the Taipings, the Manchus had to turn to Chinese scholar-officials, who raised armies on their own, revealing that the Manchus were no longer the mighty warriors they had been when they had conquered China two centuries earlier.

The Self-Strengthening Movement

After the various rebellions were suppressed, forward-looking reformers began addressing the Western threat. Under the slogan "self-strengthening," they set about modernizing the military along Western lines. Recognizing that guns and ships were merely the surface manifestations of the Western powers' economic strength, some of the most progressive reformers also initiated new industries, which in the 1870s and 1880s included railway lines, steam navigation companies, coal mines, telegraph lines, and cotton spinning and weaving factories.

These measures drew resistance from conservatives, who thought copying Western practices was compounding defeat. Yet knowledge of the West gradually improved with more

China's First Railroad Soon after this 15-mile-long railroad was constructed near Shanghai in 1876 by the British firm of Jardine and Matheson, the provincial governor bought it in order to tear it out. Many Chinese of the period saw the introduction of railroads as harmful not only to the balance of nature but also to people's livelihoods, since the railroads eliminated jobs in transport like dragging boats along canals or driving pack horses. (Private Collection)

translations and travel in both directions. Newspapers covering world affairs began publication in Shanghai and Hong Kong. By 1880 China had embassies in London, Paris, Berlin, Madrid, Washington, Tokyo, and St. Petersburg.

Despite the enormous effort put into trying to catch up, China was humiliated yet again at the end of the nineteenth century. First came the discovery that Japan had so successfully modernized that it posed a threat to China (see pages 799–801). Then, in 1894 Japanese efforts to separate Korea from Chinese influence led to the brief Sino-Japanese War in which China was decisively defeated even though much of its navy had been purchased abroad at great expense. In the peace negotiations, China ceded Taiwan to Japan, agreed to a huge indemnity (compensation for war expenses), and gave Japan the right to open factories in China. China's helplessness in the face of aggression led to a scramble among the European powers for concessions and protectorates in China. At the high point of this rush in 1898, it appeared that the European powers might actually divide China among themselves, the way they had recently divided Africa.

Republican Revolution

China's humiliating defeat in the Sino-Japanese War in 1895 led to a renewed drive for reform. In 1898 a group of educated young reformers gained influence over the twenty-seven-year-old Qing emperor. They proposed redesigning China as a constitutional monarchy with modern financial and educational systems. For three months the emperor issued a series of reform decrees. But the Manchu establishment and the empress dowager, who had dominated the court for the last quarter century, felt threatened and not only suppressed the reform movement but imprisoned the emperor as well. Hope for reform from the top was dashed.

A period of violent reaction swept the country, reaching its peak in 1900 with the uprising of a secret society that foreigners dubbed the **Boxers**. The Boxers blamed China's ills on foreigners, especially the missionaries who traveled throughout China telling the Chinese that their beliefs were wrong and their customs backward. After the Boxers laid siege to the foreign legation quarter in Beijing, a dozen nations including Japan sent troops to lift the siege. In the negotiations that followed, China had to accept a long list of heavy penalties.

Boxers A Chinese secret society that blamed the country's ills on foreigners, especially missionaries, and rose in rebellion in 1900.

Hong Kong Tailors In 1872 the newspaper *Shenbao* was founded in Shanghai, and in 1884 it added an eight-page weekly pictorial supplement. Influenced by the pictorial press then popular in Europe, it depicted both news and human interest stories, both Chinese and foreign. This scene shows a tailor shop in Hong Kong where Chinese tailors use sewing machines and make women's clothes in current Western styles. To Chinese readers, men making women's clothes and placing them on bamboo forms would have seemed as peculiar as the style of the dresses. (From *Dianshizhai huabao*, a Shanghai picture magazine, 1885 or later)

1911 Revolution The uprising that brought China's monarchy to an end.

After this defeat, gradual reform lost its appeal. More and more Chinese were studying abroad and learning about Western political ideas, including democracy and revolution. The most famous was Sun Yatsen (1866–1925). Sent by his peasant family to Hawai'i, he learned English and then continued his education in Hong Kong. From 1894 on, he spent his time abroad organizing revolutionary societies and seeking financial support from overseas Chinese. The plot that finally triggered the collapse of China's imperial system is known as the **1911 Revolution**. Army officers fearful that their connections to the revolutionaries would be exposed staged a coup and persuaded the provincial governments to secede. The powers behind the child emperor (who had ascended to the throne at the age of three in 1908) agreed to his abdication, and at the beginning of 1912 China's long history of monarchy came to an end, to be replaced by a republic modeled on Western political ideas. China had escaped direct foreign rule but would never be the same.

Quick Review
How did external pressures along with internal conflicts and problems contribute to China's decline?

How did Japan respond to the challenges posed by the West?

While China's standing in the world plummeted, Japan's was rising. European traders and missionaries first arrived in Japan in the sixteenth century, but in the early seventeenth century the Japanese government expelled them. It limited trade to a single port (Nagasaki), where only the Dutch were allowed, and forbade Japanese to travel abroad. Because Japan's

706 Chapter 26 Asia in the Era of Imperialism • 1800–1914

CHAPTER LOCATOR   What were the consequences of British rule for India?

land and population were so much smaller than China's, the Western powers never expected much from Japan as a trading partner and did not press it as urgently. Still, the European threat was part of what propelled Japan to modernize.

The "Opening" of Japan

Wanting to play a greater role in the Pacific, the United States decided to force the Japanese to share their ports and behave as a "civilized" nation. In 1853 Commodore Matthew Perry steamed into Edo (now Tokyo) Bay and demanded diplomatic negotiations with the emperor. Some Japanese samurai (members of the warrior class) urged resistance, but senior officials knew what had happened in China and how defenseless their cities would be against naval bombardment. Under threat of gunboat diplomacy, and after consulting with the daimyo (major lords), the officials signed a treaty with the United States that opened two ports and permitted trade.

Japan at this time was a complex society. The emperor was a figurehead. For more than two hundred years real power had been in the hands of the Tokugawa shogun (see pages 560–561). The country was divided into numerous domains, each under a daimyo. Each daimyo had under him samurai, who had hereditary stipends and privileges. After two centuries of peace, there were many more samurai than were needed to administer or defend the country, and many lived very modestly. They were proud, however, and felt humiliated by the sudden American intrusion and the unequal treaties that the Western countries imposed. Some began agitating against the shogunate under the slogan "Revere the emperor and expel the barbarians."

When foreign diplomats and merchants began to settle in Yokohama after 1858, radical samurai reacted with a wave of antiforeign terrorism and antigovernment assassinations. The Western response was swift and unambiguous. Much as the Western powers had sent troops to Beijing a few years before, they now sent an allied fleet of American, British, Dutch, and French warships to demolish key Japanese forts, further weakening the power and prestige of the shogun's government.

gunboat diplomacy The imposition of treaties and agreements under threat of military violence, such as the opening of Japan to trade after Commodore Perry's demands.

The Meiji Restoration

In 1867 a coalition of reform-minded daimyo led a coup that ousted the Tokugawa Shogunate. The samurai who led this coup declared a return to direct rule by the emperor, not practiced in Japan for more than six hundred years. This emperor was called the Meiji (MAY-jee) emperor and this event the Meiji Restoration.

The domain leaders who organized the coup, called the Meiji Oligarchs, used the boy emperor to win over both the lords and the commoners. During the emperor's first decade on the throne, the leaders carried him around in hundreds of grand imperial processions so that he could see his subjects and they him. The emerging press also worked to keep its readers informed of the young emperor's actions and their obligations to him. Real power remained in the hands of the oligarchs.

The battle cry of the Meiji reformers had been "strong army, rich nation." How were these goals to be accomplished? In an about-face, the determined but flexible leaders of Meiji Japan dropped their antiforeign attacks. Convinced that they could not beat the West until they had mastered the secrets of its military and industrial might, they initiated a series of measures to reform Japan along modern Western lines. In 1868 an imperial declaration promised that "Deliberative assemblies shall be widely established and all matters decided by public discussion" and that "Knowledge shall be sought throughout the world so as to strengthen the foundations of imperial rule."[1] Within four years a delegation was

Meiji Restoration The 1867 ousting of the Tokugawa Shogunate that "restored" the power of the Japanese emperors.

Why were most but not all Southeast Asian societies colonized?

What factors contributed to China's decline in the nineteenth century?

How did Japan respond to the challenges posed by the West?

Why did people move into and out of Asia in the nineteenth century?

What common experiences did Asian societies share in this era?

707

traveling the world to learn what made the Western powers strong. Its members examined everything from the U.S. Constitution to the factories, shipyards, and railroads that made the European landscape so different from Japan's.

Japan under the shoguns had been decentralized, with most of the power over the population in the hands of the daimyos. By elevating the emperor, the oligarchs were able to centralize the government. In 1871 they abolished the domains and merged the domain armies. Following the example of the French Revolution, they declared everyone equal and stripped the samurai (7 to 8 percent of the population) of their privileges. Not surprisingly, some samurai rose up against their loss of privileges, but these uprisings were uncoordinated and ineffective.

Several leaders of the Meiji Restoration, in France on a fact-finding mission during the Franco-Prussian War of 1870–1871, were impressed by the active participation of French citizens in the defense of Paris. For Japan to survive in the hostile international environment, they concluded, ordinary people had to be trained to fight. Consequently, a conscription law, modeled on the French law, was issued in 1872. Like French law, it exempted first sons. To improve the training of soldiers, the new War College was organized along German lines, and German instructors were recruited to teach there. Young samurai were trained to form the new professional officer corps. The success of this approach was demonstrated first in 1877, when the professionally led army of draftees crushed a major rebellion by samurai.

Many of the new institutions established in the Meiji period reached down to the local level. Schools open to all were rapidly introduced after 1872. Teachers were trained in newly established teachers' colleges, where they learned to inculcate discipline, patriotism, and morality. Another modern institution that reached the local level was a national police force. In 1884 police training schools were established in every prefecture, and within a few years one- or two-man police stations were set up throughout the country. The new policemen not only dealt with crime but also enforced public health rules, conscription laws, and codes of behavior.

In time these new laws and institutions brought benefits, but at the local level they were often perceived as oppressive. Protests became very common against everything from conscription and the Western calendar to the new taxes to pay for the new schools.

In 1889 Japan became the first non-Western country to adopt the constitutional form of government. The constitution, however, was handed down from above, drafted by the top political leaders and issued in the name of the emperor. A commission sent abroad to study European constitutional governments had come to the conclusion that the German constitutional monarchy would provide the best model for Japan, rather than the more democratic governments of the British, French, and Americans. Japan's new government had a two-house parliament, called the Diet. The upper house of lords was drawn largely from former daimyo and nobles, and the lower house was elected by a limited electorate (about 5 percent of the adult male population in 1890). Although Japan now had a government based on laws, it was authoritarian rather than democratic. The emperor had the right to appoint the prime minister and cabinet. He did not have to ask the Diet for funds because wealth assigned to the imperial house was entrusted to the Imperial Household Ministry, which was outside the government's control.

Cultural change during the Meiji period was as profound as political change. The influential author Fukuzawa Yukichi began urging Japan to pursue "civilization and enlightenment," by which he meant Western civilization. (See "Listening to the Past: Fukuzawa Yukichi, Escape from Asia," page 710.) Fukuzawa advocated learning Western languages and encouraged Japan to learn from the West in order to catch up with it. Soon Japanese were being told to conform to Western taste, eat meat, wear Western-style clothes, and drop customs that Westerners found odd, such as married women blackening their teeth.

Industrialization

The leaders of the Meiji Restoration, wanting to strengthen Japan's military capacity, promoted industrialization. The government recruited foreign experts to help with industrialization, and Japanese were encouraged to go abroad to study science and engineering.

The government played an active role in getting railroads, mines, and factories started. Japan's coal mines had produced only 390,000 tons in 1860, but by 1900 this output had risen to 5 million tons. Introducing the mechanical reeling of silk gave Japan a strong price advantage over China in the sale of silk, and Japan's total foreign trade increased tenfold from 1877 to 1900. The next stage was to develop heavy industry. The huge indemnity exacted from China in 1895 was used to establish the Yawata Iron and Steel Works. The third stage of Japan's industrialization would today be called import substitution. Factories such as cotton mills were set up to help cut the importation of Western consumer goods.

Most of the great Japanese industrial conglomerates known as *zaibatsu* (zigh-BAHT-dzoo), such as Mitsubishi, got their start in this period, often founded by men with government connections. Sometimes the government set up plants that it then sold to private investors at bargain prices. Successful entrepreneurs were treated as patriotic heroes.

As in Europe, the early stages of industrialization brought hardship to the countryside. Farmers often rioted as their incomes failed to keep up with prices or as their tax burdens grew. Workers in modern industries were no happier, and in 1898 railroad workers went on strike for better working conditions and overtime pay. Still, rice production increased, death rates dropped as public health was improved, and the population grew from about 33 million in 1868 to about 45 million in 1900.

Picturing the Past

Japan's First Skyscraper

Meiji Japan's fascination with things Western led to the construction of Western-style buildings. Japan's first elevator made possible this twelve-story tower built in Tokyo in 1890. Situated in the entertainment district, it was filled with shops, theaters, bars, and restaurants. (Edo-Tokyo Museum. Image: TNM Image Archives/Tokyo Metropolitan Foundation for History and Culture Image Archives)

ANALYZING THE IMAGE Locate all the people in this picture. How are they dressed? What are they doing?

CONNECTIONS Keeping in mind that the building in this picture was built in 1890, what connections would you draw between the politics of the period and this visual celebration of a new style of architecture?

Why were most but not all Southeast Asian societies colonized?

What factors contributed to China's decline in the nineteenth century?

How did Japan respond to the challenges posed by the West?

Why did people move into and out of Asia in the nineteenth century?

What common experiences did Asian societies share in this era?

709

Fukuzawa Yukichi was one of the most prominent intellectuals and promoters of westernization in Meiji Japan. His views on domestic policy were decidedly liberal, but he took a hard-line approach to foreign affairs. His ruthless criticism of Korea and China published on March 16, 1885, can be read as inviting colonialism. In 1895, ten years after writing this call to action, he rejoiced at Japan's victory over China in their conflict over Korea.

❝ Civilization is like an epidemic of measles. The current measles in Tokyo, which has advanced eastwards from Nagasaki in western Japan, seems to have begun to claim more victims with the arrival of springtime. Will we be able now to find a means of checking this epidemic? It is obvious that we have no way to do so. We cannot put up effective resistance, even against an epidemic that carries with it only harm; much less against civilization, which is always accompanied by both harm and good, but by more good than harm.

Though our land of Japan is situated on the Eastern edge of Asia, the spirit of its people has already shaken off the backwardness of Asia to accept the civilization of the West. Unfortunately, however, we have two neighboring countries, one being called China, the other called Korea. The people of these two countries are no different from us Japanese people in having been brought up since olden times in the Asian culture and customs, and yet, whether because they are of another racial origin, or because, while similar in culture and customs, differ from us in the main lines of their traditional education, a comparison of the three countries, Japan, China, and Korea, reveals that the latter two resemble each other more closely than they do Japan. The people of those two countries do not know how to go about reforming and making progress, whether individually or as a country. It is not that they have not seen or heard of civilized things in the present world of facile communication; yet what their eyes and ears perceive have failed to stimulate their minds, and their emotional attachment to ancient manners and customs has changed little for the past hundreds and thousands of years. In this lively theater of civilization, where things change daily, they still speak of education in terms of Confucianism, cite humanity, justice, civility, and wisdom as their principles of school education, are completely obsessed only with outward appearance, are in reality not only ignorant of truths and principles but so extreme in their cruelty and shamelessness that for them morality is completely non-existent, and yet are as arrogant as if they never gave a thought to self-examination.

In our view, these countries have no likelihood of maintaining their independence in the current tide of civilization's eastward advance. Let there not be the slightest doubt that, unless they are fortunate enough to have motivated men appear in their lands who, as a first step to improve the condition of their countries will plan such a great enterprise of overall reform of their governments as our Restoration was, and succeed in altering their people's minds through political reforms, those countries will meet their doom in but a few years, with their territories divided among the civilized countries of the world. The reason is that China and Korea, confronted by an epidemic of civilization comparable to measles, are impossibly trying to ward it off, despite its inevitability, by shutting themselves up in a room, with the result being that they are cutting off their supply of fresh air and asphyxiating themselves. Though mutual help between neighboring countries has been likened to the relationship between the lips and the teeth, China and Korea of today cannot be of any assistance at all to our country of Japan.

Japan as an Imperial Power

During the course of the Meiji period, Japan became an imperial power, making Taiwan and Korea into its colonies. Taiwan had been a part of China for two centuries; Korea had been an independent country with a unified government since 668. The conflicts that led to Japanese acquisition of both of them revolved around Korea.

In the second half of the nineteenth century Korea found itself caught between China, Japan, and Russia, each trying to protect or extend its sphere of influence. Westerners also began demanding that Korea be "opened." Korea's first response was to insist that its foreign relations be handled through Beijing. Matters were complicated by the rise in the 1860s of a religious cult, the Tonghak movement, that had strong xenophobic elements. Thus, like China in the same period, the Korean government faced simultaneous internal and external threats.

710

Chapter 26 Asia in the Era of Imperialism • 1800–1914

CHAPTER LOCATOR   What were the consequences of British rule for India?

Fukuzawa Yukichi. (Fukuzawa Memorial Center for Modern Japanese Studies, Keio University)

laws, the western man will suppose Japan too to be a lawless country. When he finds that the gentlemen of China and Korea are too deeply infatuated to know what science is, the western scholar will think that Japan too is a land of Yin-Yang and the Five Elements. When the Chinese display their servility and shamelessness, they obscure the chivalrous spirit of the Japanese. When the Koreans employ cruel means of physical punishment, the Japanese too are surmised to be just as inhuman. Such examples are too numerous to count. This may be compared to the case in which most of those in a string of houses within a village or town are foolish, lawless, cruel, and inhuman; an occasional family that heeds what is just and right will be eclipsed by the other's evil and its virtue will never be noticed. It is indeed not infrequent that something similar happens in our foreign relations and indirectly interferes with them. This should be regarded a great misfortune for our country of Japan.

To plan our course now, therefore, our country cannot afford to wait for the enlightenment of our neighbors and to cooperate in building Asia up. Rather, we should leave their ranks to join the camp of the civilized countries of the West. Even when dealing with China and Korea, we need not have special scruples simply because they are our neighbors, but should behave toward them as the westerners do. One who befriends an evil person cannot avoid being involved in his notoriety. In spirit, then, we break with our evil friends of Eastern Asia. **"**

Civilized western man is not without a tendency to regard all three countries as identical because of their geographic proximity and to apply his evaluation of China and Korea to Japan also. For example, when he finds that the governments of China and Korea are old-fashioned autocracies without abiding

Source: Centre for East Asian Cultural Studies, comp., *Meiji Japan Through Contemporary Sources*, Vol. 3, 1869–1894 (Tokyo: Centre for East Asian Cultural Studies, 1972), pp. 129–133, modified. Used with permission of Toyo Bunko.

QUESTIONS FOR ANALYSIS

1. What does Fukuzawa mean by "civilization"?
2. How does Fukuzawa's justification of colonialism compare to Europeans' justification of it during the same period?

In 1871 the U.S. minister to China took five warships to try to open Korea, but left after exchanges of fire resulted in 250 Koreans dead without any progress in getting the Korean government to make concessions. Japan tried next and in 1876 forced the Korean government to sign an unequal treaty and open three ports to Japanese trade. On China's urging, Korea also signed treaties with the European powers in an effort to counterbalance Japan.

Over the next couple of decades reformers in China and Japan tried to encourage Korea to adopt its own self-strengthening movement, but Korean conservatives did their best to undo reform efforts. In 1894, when the religious cult rose in a massive revolt, both China and Japan sent military forces, claiming to come to the Korean government's aid. They ended up fighting each other instead in what is known as the Sino-Japanese War (see page 705). With Japan's decisive victory, it gained Taiwan from China and was able to make Korea a protectorate.

In this same period Japan was competing aggressively with the leading European powers for influence and territory in China, particularly in the northeast (Manchuria). There Japanese and Russian imperialism met and collided. In 1904 Japan attacked Russian forces and, after its 1905 victory in the bloody **Russo-Japanese War**, emerged with a valuable foothold in China—Russia's former protectorate over Port Arthur (see Map 26.1).

Japanese Expansion, 1875–1914

■ Japan in 1875
■ Territory acquired by 1910
□ Sphere of Japanese influence

Russo-Japanese War The 1904–1905 war between Russia and Japan fought over imperial influence and territory in northeast China (Manchuria).

Japan also steadily strengthened its hold on Korea. In 1907 the Japanese forced the Korean king to abdicate in favor of his feeble-minded son. Korean resistance to Japan's actions was suppressed in bloody fighting, and in 1910 Korea was formally annexed as a province of Japan.

Japan's victories over China and Russia changed the way European nations looked at Japan. Through negotiations Japan was able to eliminate special legal protections for foreigners in 1899 and gain control of its own tariffs in 1911. Within Japan, the success of the military in raising Japan's international reputation added greatly to its political influence.

Quick Review
How did Japan's leaders use Western ideas and innovations to help meet the challenge posed by expansionist Western powers?

Why did people move into and out of Asia in the nineteenth century?

The nineteenth century was marked by extensive movement of people into, across, and out of Asia. In no earlier period had so many Europeans lived in Asia or so many Asians taken up residence in other countries. This vast migration both resulted from and helped accelerate the increasing integration of the world economy (see pages 686–691). At the same time, the movement of people helped quicken the pace of cross-cultural exchange.

Westerners to Asia

Imperialism brought Westerners to Asia in unprecedented numbers. By the early 1900s significant expatriate communities had formed in most Asian countries—the largest in India. Especially after the opening of the Suez Canal in 1869, British working in India were accompanied by their wives and children, who would return to Britain every few years on leave. By the eve of World War I, hundreds of thousands of expatriates lived in India, many since birth.

Beginning in 1809 British recruits to the British East India Company and subsequently to the Indian Civil Service were required to learn at least one Indian language fluently, but that did not mean that they mixed freely with Indians. The trend, especially after the Great Revolt of 1857 (see page 696), was for the British to live separately from the Indians in their own enclaves. Indian servants handled most of colonists' dealings with local Indians.

China was not under colonial occupation and so did not have as many foreign civil servants and soldiers in its cities, but it did attract more missionaries than any other Asian country. Unlike the British civil servants in India, missionaries had no choice but to mix with the local population, finding the best opportunities for conversion among ordinary poor Chinese. Although most missionaries devoted themselves to preaching, over the course of the nineteenth century more and more worked in medicine and education.

Missionaries helped spread Western learning at their schools. For their elementary schools, missionaries produced textbooks in Chinese on a full range of subjects. They also translated dozens of standard works into Chinese, especially in the natural sciences, mathematics, history, and international law. Most of this activity was supported by contributions sent from America and Britain.

Missionaries in China had more success in spreading Western learning than in gaining converts. By 1900 fewer than a million Chinese were Christians. Ironically, although Western missionaries paid much less attention to Korea, Christianity took much stronger root there, and today about 25 percent of the Korean population is Christian. Catholic missionaries also had some success in Vietnam after the French occupied the country and extended protection to them.

Asian Emigration

In the nineteenth century Asians, like Europeans, left their native countries in unprecedented numbers (Map 26.2). As in Europe, both push and pull factors prompted people to leave home. On the push side, between 1750 and 1900 world population grew rapidly, in many places tripling. Not surprisingly, the two largest Asian countries, China and India, were the leading exporters of people in search of work or land. On the pull side were the new opportunities created by the flow of development capital into previously underdeveloped areas. In many of the European colonies in Asia and Africa the business class came to consist of both Asian and European migrants. Asian diasporas formed in many parts of the world, with the majority in Asia itself, especially Southeast Asia.

For centuries people had emigrated from China in search of new opportunities. Chinese from the southern coastal regions came to form key components of mercantile communities throughout Southeast Asia. Chinese often assimilated in Siam and Vietnam, but they rarely did so in Muslim areas such as Java, Catholic areas such as the Philippines, and primitive tribal areas such as northern Borneo. In these places, distinct Chinese communities emerged.

With the growth in trade that accompanied the European expansion, Chinese began to settle in the islands of Southeast Asia in larger numbers. After Singapore was founded by the British in 1819, Chinese rapidly poured in, soon to become the dominant ethnic group. In British-controlled Malaya, some Chinese built great fortunes in the tin business, while others worked in the mines. There the Chinese community included old overseas families, Malay speakers who had long lived in the Portuguese city of Malacca, and a much larger number of more recent immigrants, most of whom spoke Cantonese. Chinese also settled in the Spanish-controlled Philippines and in Dutch-controlled Indonesia. By 1900 more than five hundred thousand Chinese were living in the Dutch East Indies.

Discovery of gold in California in 1848, Australia in 1851, and Canada in 1858 encouraged Chinese to book passage to those places (see Chapter 27). In California few arrived soon enough to strike gold, but they soon found other work. Thousands laid railroad tracks, and others took up mining in Wyoming and Idaho. In 1880 more than a hundred thousand Chinese men and three thousand Chinese women were living in the western United States.

Indian entrepreneurs were attracted by the burgeoning commerce of Southeast Asia, though not in quite as large numbers as the Chinese. Indians also moved outside Asia, especially to areas under British control. The bulk of Indian emigrants were indentured laborers, recruited under contract. The rise of indentured labor from Asia was a direct result of the outlawing of the African slave trade in the early nineteenth century by Britain and the United States. Sugar plantations in the Caribbean and elsewhere needed new sources of

indentured laborers Laborers who in exchange for passage agreed to work for a number of years, specified in a contract.

Why were most but not all Southeast Asian societies colonized?

What factors contributed to China's decline in the nineteenth century?

How did Japan respond to the challenges posed by the West?

Why did people move into and out of Asia in the nineteenth century?

What common experiences did Asian societies share in this era?

713

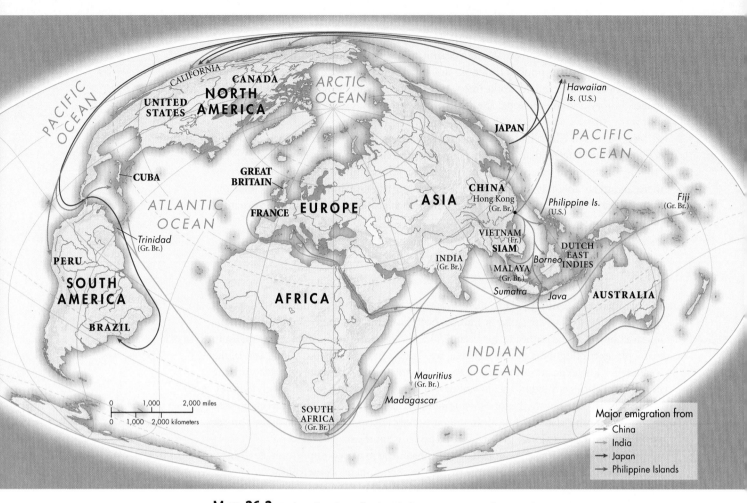

Map 26.2 Emigration Out of Asia, 1820–1914 As steamships made crossing oceans quicker and more reliable, many people in Asia left their home countries to find new opportunities elsewhere. European imperialism contributed to this flow, especially by recruiting workers for newly established plantations or mines. Many emigrants simply wanted to work a few years to build their savings and planned to return home. Often, however, they ended up staying in their new countries and forming families there.

workers, and Indian laborers were recruited to replace blacks. By 1870 more than half a million Indians had migrated to Mauritius (in the southern Indian Ocean, east of Madagascar) and to the British Caribbean, especially Trinidad. After the French abolished slavery in 1848, they recruited workers from India as well. Later in the century, many Indians emigrated to British colonies in Africa, the largest numbers to South Africa. Indentured Indian laborers—who were often treated little better than slaves—built the railroad in East Africa. Malaya, Singapore, and Fiji also received many emigrants from India.

In areas outside the British Empire, China offered the largest supply of ready labor. Starting in the 1840s contractors arrived at Chinese ports to recruit labor for plantations and mines in Cuba, Peru, Hawai'i, Sumatra, South Africa, and elsewhere. In the 1840s, for example, the Spanish government actively recruited Chinese laborers for the plantations of Cuba.

India and China sent more people abroad than any other Asian countries during this period, but they were not alone. As Japan started to industrialize, its cities could not absorb all those forced off the farms, and people began emigrating in significant numbers, many to Hawai'i and later to South America. Emigration from the Philippines also was substantial, especially after it became a U.S. territory in 1898.

714

Chapter 26 Asia in the Era of
Imperialism • 1800–1914

CHAPTER LOCATOR

What were the
consequences of British
rule for India?

Canadian Immigration Certificate This certificate proved that the eleven-year-old boy in the photograph had a legal right to be in Canada, as the $500 head tax required for immigration of Chinese had been paid. The head tax on Chinese immigrants introduced in 1885 started at $50, but it was raised to $100 in 1900 and to $500 in 1903. Equal to about what a laborer could earn in two years, the tax succeeded in its goal of slowing the rate of Asian immigration to Canada. (Library and Archives Canada)

Asian migration to the United States, Canada, and Australia—the primary destinations of European emigrants—would undoubtedly have been greater if it had not been so vigorously resisted by the white settlers in those regions. In 1882 Chinese were barred from becoming American citizens, and the immigration of Chinese laborers was suspended.

Most of the Asian migrants discussed so far were illiterate peasants or business people, not members of traditional educated elites. By the beginning of the twentieth century, however, another group of Asians was going abroad in significant numbers: students. Indians and others in the British colonies usually went to Britain, Vietnamese and others in the French colonies to France, and so on. Chinese eager to master modern learning most commonly went to Japan, but others went to Europe and the United States, as did Japanese students. Most of these students traveled abroad to learn about Western science, law, and government in the hope of strengthening their own countries. On their return they contributed enormously to the intellectual life of their societies, increasing understanding of the modern Western world and also becoming the most vocal advocates of overthrowing the old order and driving out the colonial masters.

Among the most notable of these foreign-educated radicals were Mohandas Gandhi (1869–1948) and Sun Yatsen (see page 706). Sun developed his ideas about the republican form of government while studying in Hawai'i and Hong Kong. Gandhi, after studying law in Britain, took a job in South Africa, where he became involved in trying to defend the interests of the Indians who lived and worked there. It was in South Africa that he developed the ideas and strategies he would employ in the fight for Indian independence.

Quick Review
How did global economic developments shape Asian migration patterns in the nineteenth century?

Why were most but not all Southeast Asian societies colonized?

What factors contributed to China's decline in the nineteenth century?

How did Japan respond to the challenges posed by the West?

Why did people move into and out of Asia in the nineteenth century?

What common experiences did Asian societies share in this era?

715

What common experiences did Asian societies share in this era?

The European concept of Asia encourages us to see commonalities among the countries from India east. Although to Westerners it may seem natural to think about Japan and Indonesia as part of the same region, the world looked very different from the perspective of the peoples of these countries. In fact, at the start of the nineteenth century the societies in this region varied much more than those of any other part of the world. In the temperate zones of East Asia the old established monarchies of China, Japan, and Korea were all densely populated and boasted long literary traditions and traditions of unified governments. They had ties to each other that dated back many centuries and shared many elements of their cultures. South of them, in the tropical and subtropical regions, cultures were more diverse. India was just as densely populated as China, Japan, and Korea, but politically and culturally less unified, with several major languages and dozens of independent rulers reigning in kingdoms large and small, not to mention the growing British presence. In both India and Southeast Asia, Islam was much more important than it was in East Asia, although there was a relatively small Muslim minority in China. All of the countries with long written histories and literate elites were at a great remove from the thinly populated and relatively primitive areas without literate cultures and sometimes even without agriculture, such as some of the islands of the Philippines and Indonesia.

The nineteenth century gave the societies of Asia more in common in that all of them in one way or another had come into contact with the expanding West. Still, the Western powers did not treat all of the countries the same way. Western powers initially wanted manufactured goods such as Indian cotton textiles and Chinese porcelains from the more developed Asian societies. At the beginning of the nineteenth century Britain had already gained political control over large parts of India and was intent on forcing China to trade on terms more to its benefit. It paid virtually no attention to Korea and Japan, not seeing in them the same potential for profit. The less developed parts of Asia also attracted increasing Western interest, not because they could provide manufactured goods, but because they offered opportunities for Western development, much as the Americas had earlier.

The West that the societies of Asia faced during the nineteenth century was itself rapidly changing, and the steps taken by Western nations to gain power in Asia naturally also changed over time. Western science and technology were making rapid advances, which gave European armies progressively greater advantages in weaponry. The Industrial Revolution made it possible for countries that industrialized early, such as Britain, to produce huge surpluses of goods for which they had to find markets, shifting their interest in Asia from a place to buy goods to a place to sell goods. Britain had been able to profit from its colonization of India, and this profit both encouraged it to consolidate its rule and invited its European rivals to look for their own colonies. For instance, rivalry with Britain led France to seek colonies in Southeast Asia not only for its own sake but also as a way to keep Britain from extending its sphere of influence any further.

There were some commonalities in the ways Asian countries responded to pressure from outside. In the countries with long literary traditions, often the initial response of the established elite was to try to drive the unwelcome foreigners away. This was the case in China, Japan, and Korea in particular. Violent antiforeign reactions exploded again and again, but the superior military technology of the industrialized West almost invariably prevailed. After suffering humiliating defeats, some Asian leaders insisted on the need to preserve their cultural traditions at all costs. Others came to the opposite conclusion that the West was indeed superior in some ways and that they would have to adopt European ideas or techniques for their own purposes. As nationalism took hold in the West, it found a receptive audience among the educated elites in Asia. How could the assertion that every people had the right to control its own destiny not appeal to the colonized?

Whether they were colonized or not, most countries in Asia witnessed the spread of new technologies between 1800 and 1914. Railroads, telegraphs, modern sanitation, and a wider supply of inexpensive manufactured goods brought fundamental changes in everyday life not only to lands under colonial rule, such as India and Vietnam, but also, if less rapidly, to places that managed to remain independent, such as China and Japan. In fact, the transformation of Japan between 1860 and 1900 was extraordinary. By 1914 Japan had urban conveniences and educational levels comparable to those in Europe.

Quick Review
How did the challenge posed by expansionist Western powers create similarities in the development of Asian societies in the nineteenth century?

Connections

THE NINETEENTH CENTURY brought Asia change on a much greater scale than did any earlier century. Much of the change was political—old political orders were ousted or reduced to tokens by new masters, often European colonial powers. Old elites found themselves at a loss when confronted by the European powers with their modern weaponry and modern armies. Cultural change was no less dramatic as the old elites pondered the differences between their traditional values and the ideas that seemed to underlie the power of the European states. In several places ordinary people rose in rebellion, probably in part because they felt threatened by the speed of cultural change. Material culture underwent major changes as elites experimented with Western dress and architecture and ordinary people had opportunities to travel on newly built railroads. Steamships, too, made long-distance travel easier, facilitating the out-migration of people seeking economic opportunities far from their countries of birth.

In the Americas, too, the nineteenth century was an era of unprecedented change and movement of people. Colonial empires were being overturned there, not imposed as they were in Asia in the same period. Another sharp contrast is that the Americas and Australia (discussed in the next chapter) were on the receiving end of the huge migrations taking place, while Asia, like Europe, was much more an exporter of people. The Industrial Revolution brought change to all these areas, though in the old countries of Asia the negative effects of this revolution were more often felt as traditional means of making a living disappeared. Intellectually, in both Asia and the Americas the ideas of nationalism and nation building shaped how people, especially the more educated, thought about the changes they were experiencing.

- **For a list of suggested readings for this chapter, visit** *bedfordstmartins.com/mckayworldunderstanding*.

- **For primary sources from this period, see** *Sources of World Societies*, Second Edition.

- **For Web sites, images, and documents related to topics in this chapter, see Make History at** *bedfordstmartins.com/mckayworldunderstanding*.

Chapter 26 Study Guide

To do these exercises online, go to bedfordstmartins.com/mckayworldunderstanding.

 Step 1

GETTING STARTED

Below are basic terms about this period in global history. Can you identify each term below and explain why it matters?

TERMS	WHO (OR WHAT) AND WHEN	WHY IT MATTERS
Great Mutiny/Great Revolt, p. 696		
Indian Civil Service, p. 699		
Indian National Congress, p. 699		
Java War, p. 700		
Nguyen Dynasty, p. 700		
Opium War, p. 703		
concessions, p. 704		
Taiping Rebellion, p. 704		
Boxers, p. 705		
1911 Revolution, p. 706		
gunboat diplomacy, p. 707		
Meiji Restoration, p. 707		
Russo-Japanese War, p. 712		
indentured laborers, p. 713		

Step 2

MOVING BEYOND THE BASICS

The exercise below requires a more advanced understanding of the chapter material. Compare and contrast the experiences of India, China, and Japan in the era of imperialism by filling in the chart below with descriptions of the nature and extent of Western intervention, the economic impact of the Western presence, and the efforts of the peoples of each society to respond to and resist Western expansion. When you are finished, consider the following questions: What connections can you make between the nature of Western intervention and its economic impact in each society? What about between the nature of Western intervention and the response to the Western challenge that developed in each society?

	NATURE OF WESTERN INTERVENTION	ECONOMIC IMPACT	RESPONSE AND RESISTANCE
India			
China			
Japan			

Step 3

PUTTING IT ALL TOGETHER

Now that you've reviewed key elements of the chapter, take a step back and try to see the big picture. Remember to use specific examples from the chapter in your answers.

INDIA AND SOUTHEAST ASIA

- What motives underlay British efforts to shape India's society and economy? What role did Indians play in implementing British policy?

- Why was Siam able to resist colonization while much of the rest of Southeast Asia was not?

CHINA AND JAPAN

- Why was Japan so much more successful than China at resisting Western domination?

- Argue for or against the following statement. "By the end of the nineteenth century, Japan had become, for all intents and purposes, a Western imperial power."

REGIONAL TRENDS

- How did global economic and political developments influence Asian migration patterns in the nineteenth century?

- How did conflicts between "modernizers" and "traditionalists" shape the development of Asian societies in the nineteenth century?

LOOKING BACK, LOOKING AHEAD

- How did Europeans' desire to gain access to the wealth of Asia shape world history from 1500 to 1900?

- What connections might one make between the events of the second half of the nineteenth century and the role of Japan in regional and world affairs in the first half of the twentieth century?

In Your Own Words Imagine that you must explain Chapter 26 to someone who hasn't read it. What would be the most important points to include and why?

27

Nation Building in the Americas and Australia

1770–1914

In the Americas and in Australia, as in Europe, the nineteenth century was a period of nation building as well as industrial and commercial growth. Unlike in Europe, the century was also a time of geographical expansion and large-scale in-migration.

At the end of the eighteenth century Canada and the countries of South America remained colonies. The infant United States was a small and unproven experiment in democracy. The island continent of Australia served as a dumping ground for English criminals. The nineteenth century brought revolutions, civil wars, and foreign invasions, among other challenges. In some countries abolishing slavery was achieved with great difficulty. Yet by 1914 all the countries were not only politically independent but also stronger and richer than they had been in 1800.

Many issues crosscut the histories of all these countries in the long nineteenth century: nation building, nationalism, urbanization, racism, regional separatism, new technologies, territorial expansion, new trading patterns, and new constitutional governments, to name just a few. Yet the outcomes by 1914 were strikingly different. The United States had become a major industrial power and a stable democracy. Canada and Australia also had stable democratic governments, but their economies remained predominantly agricultural. Most of the countries of Latin America suffered political instability, and their economies did not fare as well in the emerging world trade system.

Acoma Indian, ca. 1905 Native Americans found their world under assault during the nineteenth century, as the United States expanded its territory and encouraged settlers to farm lands where Indians had long lived. (Library of Congress LC-USZ62-69902)

Chapter Preview

▶ How did Latin American nations fare after independence?

▶ How did the United States become a world power?

▶ What factors shaped the development of Canada?

▶ How did Australia evolve from penal colony to nation?

▶ What common forces shaped the Americas and Australia?

How did Latin American nations fare after independence?

In 1800 Spain controlled a vast American empire, one that still provided the mother country with considerable wealth (Map 27.1). Spain believed that the riches of the Americas existed for its benefit, a stance that fostered bitterness and the desire for independence in the colonies. Between 1806 and 1825 the Spanish colonies in Latin America were convulsed by upheavals that ultimately resulted in the dissolution of the empire.

The Creoles—people of Spanish descent born in the Americas (see page 484)—resented the economic and political dominance of the peninsulares (puh-nihn-suh-LUHR-ayz), as the colonial officials and other natives of Spain or Portugal were called. A tiny minority, peninsulares controlled the rich export-import trade, intercolonial trade, and mining industries. The Creoles wanted to supplant the peninsulares as the ruling class and, more generally, to free themselves from Spain and Portugal. They had little interest in improving the lot of the Indians, the mestizos (meh-STEE-zohz) of mixed Spanish and Indian background, or the mulattos of mixed Spanish and African heritage.

> **Creoles** People of Spanish descent born in the Americas.
>
> **peninsulares** A term for natives of Spain and Portugal.

Over the course of the nineteenth century, the countries of Latin America developed into national states. The predominant factors in this evolution were the heritage of colonial exploitation, a neocolonial economic structure, massive emigration from Europe and Asia, and the fusion of Amerindian, Caucasian, African, and Asian peoples.

The Origins of the Revolutions Against Colonial Powers

The Latin American movements for independence drew strength from unfair taxation and trade policies, Spain's declining control over its Latin American colonies, racial and class discrimination, and the spread of revolutionary ideas. By the eighteenth century the Spanish colonies had become self-sufficient producers of foodstuffs, wine, textiles, and consumer goods, though Spain maintained monopolies on alcohol and tobacco and the colonies traded with each other.

Spain's humiliating defeat in the War of the Spanish Succession (1701–1713; see page 444) prompted demands for sweeping reform of all of Spain's institutions, including its colonial policies and practices. To improve administrative efficiency, Charles III (r. 1759–1788) carved the region of modern Colombia, Venezuela, and Ecuador out of the vast viceroyalty of Peru; it became the new viceroyalty of New Granada with its capital at Bogotá. The Crown also created the viceroyalty of Rio de la Plata (present-day Argentina) with its capital at Buenos Aires (see Map 27.1).

Additionally, Spain adopted free-trade policies (allowing trade without government interference) in order to compete with Great Britain

Don Juan Joachin Gutierrez Altamirano Velasco, ca. 1752 In this painting by Miguel Cabrera, the pleated cuffs on Velasco's shirt, the richly embroidered and very expensive coat, the knee breeches, the tricorn hat, the plaque of titles, and the coat of arms on the wall all attest to the proud status of this member of the peninsulares, the most powerful element in colonial Mexican society. (Miguel Cabrera, Mexican, 1695–1768, oil on canvas, 81⁵⁄₁₆ x 53½. Brooklyn Museum of Art, Museum Collection Fund, and the Dick S. Ramsay Fund 52.166.1)

and Holland in the great eighteenth-century struggle for empire. In Latin America these actions stimulated the production of crops that were in demand in Europe: coffee in Venezuela; sugar in the Caribbean; hides, leather, and salted beef in the Rio de la Plata viceroyalty. Between 1778 and 1788 the volume of Spain's trade with the colonies soared, possibly by as much as 700 percent.[1]

Colonial manufacturing, which had been growing steadily, suffered a heavy blow under free trade. Colonial products could not compete with their cheaper Spanish counterparts. In the Rio de la Plata region heavy export taxes and light import duties shattered the wine industry. Madrid's tax reforms also aggravated discontent. Like Great Britain, Spain believed its colonies should bear some of the costs of their own defense. Accordingly, Madrid raised the prices of its monopoly products — tobacco and liquor — and increased sales taxes on many items. As a result, protest movements in Latin America, like those in British North America a decade earlier, claimed that the colonies were being unfairly taxed.

Political conflicts beyond the colonies also helped to drive aspirations for independence. The French Revolution and Napoleonic wars, which involved France's occupation of Spain and Britain's domination of the seas, isolated Spain from Latin America. As Spain's control over its Latin American colonies diminished, foreign traders, especially from the United States, swarmed into Spanish-American ports.

Racial, ethnic, and class privileges also fueled discontent. At the end of the eighteenth century colonists complained bitterly that only peninsulares were appointed to the colonies' highest judicial bodies and to other positions in the colonial governments. From 1751 to 1775 only 13 percent of appointees to the judicial bodies were Creoles.[2]

From a racial standpoint, the makeup of Latin American societies is one of the most complicated in the world. Because few European women immigrated to the colonies, Spanish men formed relationships with Indian and African women, while African men deprived of black women sought Indian women. The result was a population composed of every possible combination of Indian, Spanish, and African blood.

Spanish theories of racial purity rejected people of mixed blood, particularly those of African descent. Peninsulares and Creoles reinforced their privileged status by showing contempt for people who were not white. Moreover, owners of mines, plantations, and factories had a vested interest in keeping blacks and Indians in servile positions. Nevertheless, nonwhites in Latin America did experience some social mobility in the colonial period, certainly more than nonwhites in the North American colonies experienced. The army and the church seem to have offered the greatest opportunities for social mobility. Many black slaves gained their freedom by fleeing to the jungles or mountains, where they established self-governing communities.

A final factor contributing to rebellion was Enlightenment ideas, which had been trickling into Latin America for decades (see Chapter 18). North American ships calling at South American ports introduced the subversive writings of Thomas Paine and Thomas Jefferson. In 1794 the Colombian Antonio Nariño translated and published the French Declaration of the Rights of Man and of the Citizen. By 1800 the Creole elite throughout

Chapter Chronology

1770	James Cook lands in Australia and claims land for British crown
1774	Quebec Act grants religious freedom to French Canadians
1778–1788	Height of Spain's trade with its colonies
1780	Tupac Amaru II leads rebellion in Peru
1780–1825	Wars of independence in Latin America
1786	British government establishes a penal colony at Botany Bay, Australia
1791	Constitution Act in Canada divides the province of Quebec in two
1803	United States purchases Louisiana Territory from France
1804	Haiti achieves independence from France and becomes the first black republic
1845	First use of term *manifest destiny* in United States; Texas and Florida admitted into United States
1861–1865	U.S. Civil War
1865–1877	U.S. Reconstruction
1867	Dominion of Canada formed
1883–1894	Mexican land laws put most land into the hands of a few individuals
1898	Spanish-American War
1901	Commonwealth of Australia formed
1904	United States secures the rights to build and control the Panama Canal
1914	Panama Canal completed

Before independence

Spanish colonies
- Viceroyalty of New Spain
- Viceroyalty of New Granada
- Viceroyalty of Peru and Audencia of Chile
- Viceroyalty of Rio de la Plata

Portuguese colonies
- Viceroyalty of Brazil

✕ Silver mine

In 1830

1811 Year independence gained

☐ Colony

Mapping the Past

Map 27.1 Latin America in ca. 1780 and 1830

By 1830 almost all of Central America, South America, and the Caribbean islands had won independence. Note that the many nations that now make up Central America were unified when they first won independence from Mexico. Similarly, modern Venezuela, Colombia, and Ecuador were still joined in Gran Colombia.

ANALYZING THE MAP Compare the boundaries of the Spanish and Portuguese colonies in ca. 1780 with the boundaries of the independent states in 1830. How did these boundaries change, and which regions experienced the most breakup?

CONNECTIONS Why did Pan-Americanism fail?

CHAPTER LOCATOR

How did Latin American nations fare after independence?

Latin America was familiar with liberal Enlightenment political thought, and the Creoles wanted the "rights of man" extended to themselves.

Resistance, Rebellion, and Independence

The mid-eighteenth century witnessed frequent Andean Indian rebellions against the Spaniards' harsh exploitation. In 1780, under the leadership of a descendant of the Inca rulers who took the name Tupac Amaru II, a massive insurrection exploded. Indian chieftains from the Cuzco region (see Map 27.1) gathered a powerful force of Indians and people of mixed race. Rebellion swept across highland Peru. Before peace was restored two years later, a hundred thousand people lay dead, and vast amounts of property were destroyed. Although Spanish rule was not ended, the government enacted limited reforms. The revolts also raised elite fears of racial and class warfare.

As news of the rebellion of Tupac Amaru II trickled northward, it helped stimulate the 1781 Comunero Revolution in the New Granada viceroyalty (see Map 27.1). In this revolution an Indian peasant army commanded by Creole captains marched on Bogotá. Dispersed by the ruling Spanish, who made promises they did not intend to keep, the revolt in the end did little to improve the Indians' lives.

Much more than the revolts in Peru and New Granada, the successful revolution led by Toussaint L'Ouverture (1743–1803) in Haiti aroused elite fears of black revolt and class warfare (see pages 599–603 and Map 22.3). In 1804 Haiti declared its independence, becoming the second nation (after the United States) in the Western Hemisphere to achieve self-rule. The revolt was also the first successful uprising of a non-European people against a colonial power, and it sent waves of fear through the upper classes in both Europe and Latin America.

In 1808 Napoleon Bonaparte deposed the Spanish king Ferdinand VII and placed his own brother on the Spanish throne. Creoles in Latin America argued that the removal of the legitimate king shifted sovereignty to the people—that is, to themselves. The Creoles who led the various movements for independence did not intend a radical redistribution of property or a reconstruction of society. They merely rejected the authority of the Spanish crown.

The great hero of the movement for independence was Simón Bolívar (1783–1830), a very able general who is considered the Latin American George Washington. Bolívar's victories over the royalist armies won him the presidency of Gran Colombia (formerly the New Granada viceroyalty) in 1819. He dreamed of a continental union and in 1826 summoned a conference of the American republics at Panama. The meeting achieved little, however. The territories of Gran Colombia splintered (see Map 27.1), and a sadly disillusioned Bolívar went into exile. Under Spain, Mexico had been united with Central America as the Viceroyalty of New Spain. In the 1830s, after independence, regional separatism resulted in New Spain's breakup into five separate countries. In South America, too, the old colonies were divided, not amalgamated. The failure of Pan-Americanism isolated individual countries, prevented collective action, and later paved the way for the political and economic intrusion of the United States and other powers.

Brazil followed a different path to independence from Portugal. When Napoleon's troops entered Portugal, the royal family fled to Brazil and made Rio de Janeiro the capital of the Portuguese Empire. The new government immediately lifted the old mercantilist restrictions and opened Brazilian ports to the ships of all friendly nations. The king returned to Portugal in 1821, leaving his son Pedro in Brazil as regent. Under popular pressure, Pedro proclaimed Brazil's independence in 1822, issued a constitution, and even led resistance against Portuguese troops. He accepted the title Emperor Pedro I (r. 1822–1831). Even though Brazil was a monarchy, Creole elites dominated society as they did elsewhere in Latin America. The reign of his successor, Pedro II (r. 1831–1889), witnessed the expansion of the coffee industry, the beginnings of the rubber industry, and massive immigration.

The Aftermath of Independence

The Latin American wars of independence, over by 1825, differed from the American Revolution in important ways. First, they lasted much longer, and outside powers provided no help, leaving those involved weary and divided. Second, many of the peninsulares returned to Europe instead of remaining in Latin America to build new nations, as most North American colonists had. Also, although the Creole elites followed the example of the United States by creating written constitutions, these governments excluded much of the population from political participation. To a large degree the local elites took over exploiting the peasantry from the old colonial elites. Small independent farmers of the sort who became common in the United States and Canada did not gain a comparable place in Latin America. The new governments also largely confirmed the wealth of the Roman Catholic Church and its authority over the people, not adopting separation of church and state.

The newly independent nations had difficulty achieving political stability when the wars of independence ended. Between 1836 and 1848 Mexico lost half of its territory to the United States, and other countries, too, had difficulty defending themselves from their neighbors. The Creole leaders of the revolutions had no experience in government, and the wars left a legacy of military, not civilian, leadership.

In many Latin American countries, generals ruled. In Argentina, Juan Manuel de Rosas (r. 1835–1852) assumed power amid widespread public disorder and ruled as dictator. In Mexico, liberals declared a federal republic, but incessant civil strife led to the rise of the dictator Antonio López de Santa Anna (1794–1876) in the mid-nineteenth century. Likewise in Venezuela, strongmen, dictators, and petty aristocratic oligarchs governed from 1830 to 1892.

On occasion, the ruling generals were charismatic military leaders who were able to attract mass support for their governments. In Venezuela, José Antonio Páez (1790–1873) was able to present himself as a patron of the common man and maintain his popularity even though his economic policies favored the elite. Some rulers were of common origins. In

Latin America, ca. 1760–1900

1759–1788	Reign of Spain's Charles III; administrative and economic reforms
1780–1825	Wars of independence against Spain
1781	Comunero Revolution in New Granada
1791–1804	Haitian Revolution
1822	Proclamation of Brazil's independence by Portugal
1826	Call by Simón Bolívar for Panama conference on Latin American union
ca. 1870–1929	Latin American neocolonialism
1876–1911	Porfirio Díaz's control of Mexico
1880–1914	Massive emigration from Europe and Asia to Latin America
1888	Emancipation of slaves in Brazil; final abolition of slavery in Western Hemisphere
1898	Spanish-American War; end of Spanish control of Cuba; transfer of Puerto Rico and the Philippines to the United States

Mexico, Benito Juárez (1806–1872), a Zapotec Indian, was something of an exception to the generalization that Creoles had a tight hold on power. Juárez was a strong advocate of democracy. He led efforts to reduce the power of the Catholic Church and later led resistance to the "emperor" imposed by Napoleon III in 1862. Between 1858 and his death in 1872 Juárez served five terms as president of Mexico.

The economic lives of most Latin American countries were disrupted during the years of war. Armies were frequently recruited by force, and when the men were demobilized, many did not return home. The consequent population dislocation hurt agriculture and mining. Guerrilla warfare disrupted trade and communications, and the seizure of private property for military use ruined many people.

On the positive side, the push for independence speeded abolition of slavery. The destruction of agriculture in countries such as Mexico and Venezuela caused the collapse of the plantation system, and fugitive slaves could not be recaptured. Generals on both sides offered slaves their freedom in exchange for military service. Still, Cuba and Brazil did not free their slaves until 1886 and 1888, respectively.

Although the edifice of racism persisted in the nineteenth century, Latin America offered blacks greater economic and social mobility than did the United States. One reason is that the Creole elite in Latin America viewed race mixture as a civilizing process that diminished and absorbed the dark and "barbarous" blood of Africans and Indians. In Latin America, light-skinned people of color could rise economically and socially in a way not available to those with darker skins. (See "Listening to the Past: Mary Seacole on Her Early Life," page 728.)

Neocolonialism and Its Socioeconomic Effects

At first, political instability discouraged foreign investment in Latin America's newly independent nations. But with the general expansion of world trade after 1870 and the development of stable dictatorships, foreign investors turned to Latin America for raw materials and basic commodities to supply industrializing Europe and the United States. Modern business enterprises, often owned by foreign capitalists, led the way. These firms usually specialized in a single product that could be shipped through the growing international network of railroads, ports, and ocean freighters.

In Mexico, for example, North American capital supported the production of hemp, sugar, bananas, and rubber, frequently on American-owned plantations, and British and American interests backed the development of tin, copper, and gold mining. British capital financed Argentina's railroads, meatpacking industry, and utilities; Chile's copper and nitrate industries (nitrate is used in the production of pharmaceuticals and fertilizers); and Brazil's coffee, cotton, and sugar production. By 1904 Brazil produced 76 percent of the world's coffee. The extension of railroads also attracted outside entrepreneurs. (See "Individuals in Society: Henry Meiggs, Promoter and Speculator," page 730.)

Thus, by the turn of the century, the Latin American nations were active participants in the international economic order, but foreigners controlled most of their industries, and their governments used force when they felt their economic interests were threatened. This form of economic domination is often called neocolonialism. Perhaps the best example was the U.S.-financed building of the Panama Canal. In 1904 Americans secured the rights to control the Panama Canal, connecting the Atlantic and Pacific Oceans, on their own terms. This monumental construction project wasn't completed until 1914 and took the lives of thousands of workers. The United States retained control of the Panama Canal Zone until 1999.

Another distinctive feature of neocolonialism was that each country's economy revolved around only one or two products: sugar in Cuba, nitrates and copper in Chile, meat in

neocolonialism Term referring to the political and economic systems that perpetuated Western economic domination of nations after their political independence.

Mary Seacole was born in Jamaica in 1805, the daughter of a Scottish soldier and a local Jamaican Creole woman. She learned folk medical treatment from her mother, who ran a boarding house, and gradually took to running hotels and to working as a nurse herself. During the Crimean War she volunteered to go to the Crimea to treat wounded soldiers. Shortly afterward, in 1857, she wrote an autobiography, an excerpt of which follows.

❝ I was born in the town of Kingston, in the island of Jamaica, some time in the present century. . . . I am a Creole, and have good Scotch blood coursing in my veins. My father was a soldier, of an old Scotch family; and to him I often trace my affection for a camp-life, and my sympathy with what I have heard my friends call "the pomp, pride, and circumstance of glorious war." Many people have also traced to my Scotch blood that energy and activity which are not always found in the Creole race, and which have carried me to so many varied scenes: and perhaps they are right. I have often heard the term "lazy Creole" applied to my country people; but I am sure I do not know what it is to be indolent. . . .

My mother kept a boarding-house in Kingston, and was, like very many of the Creole women, an admirable doctress; in high repute with the officers of both services, and their wives, who were from time to time stationed at Kingston. It was very natural that I should inherit her tastes; and so I had from early youth a yearning for medical knowledge and practice which has never deserted me. . . .

[After returning to Kingston from a trip in 1825], I nursed my old indulgent patroness in her last long illness. After she died, in my arms, I went to my mother's house, where I stayed, making myself useful in a variety of ways, and learning a great deal of Creole medicinal art, until I couldn't find courage to say "no" to a certain arrangement timidly proposed by Mr. Seacole, but married him, and took him down to Black River, where we established a store. Poor man! He was very delicate; and before I undertook the charge of him, several doctors had expressed most unfavorable opinions of his health. I kept him alive by kind nursing and attention as long as I could; but at last he grew so ill that we left Black River, and returned to my mother's house at Kingston.

Within a month of our arrival there he died. This was my first great trouble, and I felt it bitterly. For days I never stirred — lost to all that passed around me in a dull stupor of despair. If you had told me that the time would soon come when I should remember this sorrow calmly, I should not have believed it possible: and yet it was so. I do not think that we hot-blooded Creoles sorrow less for showing it so impetuously; but I do think that the sharp edge of our grief wears down sooner than theirs who preserve an outward demeanor of calmness, and nurse their woe secretly in their hearts. . . .

In the year 1850, the cholera swept over the island of Jamaica with terrible force. . . . While the cholera raged, I had but too many opportunities of watching its nature, and from a Dr. B—, who was then lodging in my house, received many hints as to its treatment which I afterwards found invaluable.

Early in the same year my brother had left Kingston for the Isthmus of Panama, then the great high-road to and from golden California, where he had established a considerable store and hotel. Ever since he had done so, I had found some difficulty in checking my reviving disposition to roam, and at last persuading myself that I might be of use to him (he was far from strong), I resigned my house into the hands of a cousin, and made arrangements to journey to Chagres. . . .

All my readers must know — a glance at the map will show it to those who do not — that between North America and the envied shores of California stretches a little neck of land, insignificant-looking enough on the map, dividing the Atlantic from the Pacific. By crossing this, the travellers from America avoided a long, weary, and dangerous sea voyage round Cape Horn, or an almost impossible journey by land.

But that journey across the Isthmus, insignificant in distance as it was, was by no means an easy one. It seemed as if nature had determined to throw every conceivable obstacle in the way of those who should seek to join the two great oceans of the world. . . .

When, after passing Chagres, an old-world, tumble-down town, for about seven miles, the steamer reached

---

Argentina, coffee in Brazil. Consequently, a sharp drop in world demand for a product could devastate the export sector, and with it, the nation's economic well-being.

Many of the workers on the plantations producing export products were Indians or mestizos. In the United States and Canada, Indians were pushed out of the way when their land was taken from them. In Latin America, by contrast, many more of them were kept in place and incorporated into the social system as subordinated workers, especially on large plantations called haciendas (ah-see-EN-dahz).

haciendas Large landed estates.

Navy Bay, I thought I had never seen a more luckless, dreary spot. . . . It seemed as capital a nursery for ague and fever as Death could hit upon anywhere, and those on board the steamer who knew it confirmed my opinion. As we arrived a steady down-pour of rain was falling from an inky sky; the white men who met us on the wharf appeared ghostly and wraith-like, and the very negroes seemed pale and wan. The news which met us did not tempt me to lose any time in getting up the country to my brother. According to all accounts, fever and ague, with some minor diseases, especially dropsy, were having it all their own way at Navy Bay, and, although I only stayed one night in the place, my medicine chest was called into requisition. But the sufferers wanted remedies which I could not give them — warmth, nourishment, and fresh air. Beneath leaky tents, damp huts, and even under broken railway wagons, I saw men dying from sheer exhaustion. Indeed, I was very glad when, with the morning, the crowd, as the Yankees called the bands of pilgrims to and from California, made ready to ascend to Panama. . . .

It was not so easy to hire a boat as I had been led to expect. The large crowd had made the boatmen somewhat exorbitant in their demands. . . . There were several reasons why I should engage one for my own exclusive use, instead of sharing one with some of my traveling companions. In the first place, my luggage was somewhat bulky; and, in the second place,

The first edition of Mary Seacole's *Wonderful Adventures* appeared in London in 1857 with her picture on the cover. (© Museum of London)

my experience of travel had not failed to teach me that Americans (even from the Northern States) are always uncomfortable in the company of colored people, and very often show this feeling in stronger ways than by sour looks and rude words. I think, if I have a little prejudice against our cousins across the Atlantic — and I do confess to a little — it is not unreasonable. I have a few shades of deeper brown upon my skin which shows me related — and I am proud of the relationship — to those poor mortals whom you once held enslaved, and whose bodies America still owns. And having this bond, and knowing what slavery is; having seen with my eyes and heard with my ears proof positive enough of its horrors — let others affect to doubt them if they will — is it surprising that I should be somewhat impatient of the airs of superiority which many Americans have endeavored to assume over me? Mind, I am not speaking of all. I have met with some delightful exceptions. ❞

Source: Mary Seacole, *Wonderful Adventures of Mrs. Seacole in Many Lands* (London: Blackwood, 1857), pp. 1–17.

QUESTIONS FOR ANALYSIS

1. How does Mary Seacole understand race?
2. How does she understand disease? What were the health problems that she saw as most serious?
3. What audience do you think Seacole is attempting to address in her autobiography?

The late nineteenth century witnessed ever-greater concentrations of land in ever fewer hands. In places like the Valley of Mexico in southern Mexico, a few large haciendas controlled all the land. Under the 1876–1911 dictatorship of General Porfirio Díaz, the Mexican government enacted a series of laws that facilitated the expropriation of Indian ancestral lands by wealthy elites and business interests. As a result of the policies of Díaz (who was overthrown in the Mexican Revolution that started in 1910), vast stretches of land — in one case, 12 million acres — came into the hands of private individuals. Debt peonage

How did the United States become a world power?　　What factors shaped the development of Canada?　　How did Australia evolve from penal colony to nation?　　What common forces shaped the Americas and Australia?

729

Henry Meiggs, Promoter and Speculator

ALL THROUGHOUT THE AMERICAS IN THE nineteenth century opportunities beckoned. Henry Meiggs, born in upstate New York in 1811, responded to several of them, building and losing fortunes in Brooklyn, San Francisco, Chile, and Peru.

Meiggs, with only an elementary school education, began work at his father's shipyard. He soon started his own lumber business and did well until he lost everything in the financial panic of 1837. He rebuilt his business, and when gold was discovered in California in 1848, he filled a ship with lumber and sailed around Cape Horn to San Francisco, where he sold his cargo for $50,000, twenty times what he had paid for it. He then entered the lumber business, organizing crews of five hundred men to fell huge Californian redwoods and bring them to his steam sawmills. As his business flourished, he began speculating in real estate, which led to huge debts when the financial crisis of 1854 hit. In an attempt to save himself and his friends, Meiggs forged warrants for more than $900,000; when discovery of the fraud seemed imminent, he sailed with his wife and children for South America.

Although at one point Meiggs was so strapped for cash that he sold his watch, within three years of arriving in Chile, he had secured his first railway contract, and by 1867 he had built about 200 miles of rail lines in that country. In 1868 he went to Peru, which had less than 60 miles of track at the time. In the next nine years he would add 700 more.

Meiggs was not an engineer, but he was a good manager. He recruited experienced engineers from abroad and arranged purchase of foreign rolling stock, rails, and ties, acting as a promoter and developer. Much of the funding came from international investors in Peruvian bonds.

The most spectacular of the rail lines Meiggs built was Peru's Callao-Lima-Oroya line, which crosses the Andes at about seventeen thousand feet above sea level, making it the highest standard gage railway in the world. Because water was scarce in many areas along the construction site, it had to be transported up to workers, who were mostly local people. Dozens of bridges and tunnels had to be built, and casualties were high. Eight hundred people were invited to the banquet that marked the beginning of work on the Oroya Railway. Meiggs drummed up enthusiasm at the event by calling the locomotive the "irresistible battering ram of modern civilization."

In Peru Meiggs became known for his extravagance and generosity, and some charged that he bribed Peruvian officials on a large scale to get his projects approved. He was a good speaker and loved to entertain lavishly. In one example of his generosity, he distributed thousands of pesos and soles to the victims of the earthquake of 1868. He also contributed to the beautification of Lima by tearing down an old wall and putting a seven-mile-long park in its place.

Always the speculator, in 1877 Meiggs died poor, his debts exceeding his assets. He was beloved, however, and more than twenty thousand Peruvians, many of whom had labored on his projects, attended his funeral at a Catholic church in Lima.

QUESTIONS FOR ANALYSIS

1. What accounts for the changes in fortune that Meiggs experienced?
2. Were the Latin American governments that awarded contracts to Meiggs making reasonable decisions?
3. Should it matter whether Meiggs had to bribe officials to get the railroads built? Why?

The challenges in building the Callao-Lima-Oroya railroad across the Andes can be imagined from this picture of one of its many bridges. (From Elio Galessio, *Ferrocarriles del Perú: Un viaje a través de su Historia.* Reproduced with permission of the author)

also became common: landowners paid their laborers not in cash but in vouchers redeemable only at the landowner's store, where high prices and tricky bookkeeping kept the peons permanently in debt.

peons Low-status laborers.

The Impact of Immigrants from Europe, Asia, and the Middle East

The involvement of foreign business interests in Latin America encouraged European and American immigration to the region in the second half of the nineteenth century. Asia and the Middle East were also significant sources of immigrants to Latin America. For example, in the late nineteenth and early twentieth centuries large numbers of Japanese arrived in Brazil, and by 1920 Brazil had the largest Japanese community in the world outside of Japan. From the Middle East, Lebanese, Turks, and Syrians also entered Brazil. Between 1850 and 1880, 144,000 South Asian laborers went to Trinidad, 39,000 to Jamaica, and smaller numbers to the islands of St. Lucia, Grenada, and St. Vincent as indentured servants. Perhaps one-third returned to India, but the rest stayed, saved money, and bought small businesses or land. Cuba had received 500,000 African slaves between 1808 and 1865. When slavery was abolished in 1886, some of the work in the sugarcane fields was done by Chinese indentured servants, who followed the same pattern as the South Asian migrants who had gone to Trinidad. Likewise, the abolition of slavery in Mexico led to the arrival of thousands of Chinese bonded servants.

Immigration helped fuel urbanization, and Portuguese, Italian, French, Chinese, and Japanese immigrants gave an international flavor and a more vigorous tempo to Latin American cities. By 1914 Buenos Aires in particular had emerged as one of the most cosmopolitan cities in the world, with a population of 3.6 million. Elegant shops near the Plaza de Mayo catered to the expensive tastes of the elite upper classes, who constituted about 5 percent of the population. By contrast, the thousands of immigrants who toiled twelve

Buenos Aires, 1894 When this photo was taken, Buenos Aires was already a cosmopolitan city, with a population of more than 600,000, and its streets looked much like streets in European cities of the time. (Archivo General de la Nación, Buenos Aires)

hours a day, six days a week, on docks and construction sites and in meatpacking plants were crowded into the city's one-room tenements.

Despite such difficult living conditions, immigrants' dreams of rapid economic success in the New World often came true. The first generation almost always did manual labor, but its sons often advanced to upper-blue-collar or white-collar jobs. The sons of successful Genoese or Neapolitan immigrants typically imitated the dress, manners, and values of the Creole elite.

Immigrants brought wide-ranging skills that helped develop industry and commerce. In Argentina, Italian and Spanish settlers stimulated the expansion of the cattle industry and the development of the wheat and shoe industries. In Brazil, Swiss immigrants built the cheese business, Italians gained a leading role in the coffee industry, and Japanese pioneered the development of the cotton industry. In Peru, Chinese laborers built the railroads, and in sections of large cities such as Lima, the Chinese came to dominate the ownership of shops and restaurants. European immigrants also brought anarchist and socialist ideas and became involved in union organizing.

The vast majority of migrants were unmarried males; seven out of ten people who landed in Argentina between 1857 and 1924 were single males between thirteen and forty years old. There, as in other South American countries, many of those who stayed sought Indian or other low-status women, leading to further racial mixing.

The creation of independent nations in Latin America did little to improve the position of the poor. Neocolonialism had a modernizing influence on commerce and industry, but it further concentrated wealth. Spanish and Portuguese merchants who returned to the Iberian Peninsula were replaced by British and U.S. businessmen. Just as the United States waged wars against the Indians (see pages 733–734) and pushed its frontier westward, so Brazil, Venezuela, Ecuador, Peru, and Bolivia expanded into the Amazonian frontier at the expense of indigenous peoples. Likewise, Mexico, Chile, and Argentina had their "Indian wars" and frontier expansion. Racial prejudice kept most of the South American black population in a wretched socioeconomic position until well past 1914. European immigrants, rather than black plantation workers, gained the urban jobs. In 1893, 71.2 percent of the working population of São Paulo was foreign-born.

Quick Review

Why did political independence lead so infrequently to economic independence in Latin America?

How did the United States become a world power?

Americans carried an unbounded optimism about the future into the nineteenth and twentieth centuries. Until 1860 most eastern states limited voting rights to property holders or taxpayers, but suffrage was gradually expanded to include most adult white males. The movement toward popular democracy accelerated as the young nation, confident of its "manifest destiny," pushed relentlessly across the continent. As settlers moved into new territories, the industrializing North and the agricultural South came into conflict over extending slavery into these lands. The ensuing Civil War (1861–1865) cost six hundred thousand American lives — more than any other war the nation has fought. Yet the victory of the North preserved the federal system and strengthened the United States as a nation.

The years between 1865 and 1917 witnessed the transformation of the United States into a major industrial power, a process that was facilitated to a great degree by the arrival of millions of immigrants. Most of the social and cultural phenomena seen in western Europe in this period (see Chapter 24) — such as improved sanitation, mass transit, faith in science, and strong identification with the nation — occurred also in the United States.

Manifest Destiny and Its Consequences for Native Americans

In an 1845 issue of the *United States Magazine and Democratic Review*, editor John L. O'Sullivan declared that foreign powers were trying to prevent American annexation of Texas in order to impede "the fulfillment of our manifest destiny to overspread the continent allotted by Providence for the free development of our yearly multiplying millions." O'Sullivan was articulating a sentiment prevalent in the United States since early in its history: that God had foreordained the nation to cover the entire continent. After a large-circulation newspaper picked up the phrase manifest destiny, it was used on the floor of Congress and soon entered the language as a catchword for and justification of expansion.

In 1789, fewer than 4 million people inhabited the thirteen states on the eastern seaboard. By 1861, the United States stretched across the continent and had 31 million inhabitants. During the colonial period, pioneers pushed westward to the Appalachian Mountains. After independence, westward movement accelerated. The eastern states claimed all the land from the Atlantic Ocean to the Mississippi River, but two forces blocked immediate expansion. The Indians, trying to save their lands, allied with the British in Canada to prevent further American encroachment. In 1794 Britain agreed to evacuate border forts in the Northwest Territory, roughly the area north of the Ohio River and east of the Mississippi, and thereby end British support for the Indians. A similar treaty with Spain paved the way for southeastern expansion.

Events in Europe and the Caribbean led to a massive increase in American territory. In 1800 Spain ceded the Louisiana Territory—the land between the Mississippi River and the Rocky Mountains—to France. Three years later Napoleon sold it to the United States for only $12 million. Spain, preoccupied with rebellions in South America, sold the Florida Territory to the U.S. government, and beginning in 1821 American settlers poured into the Mexican territory of Texas. Southern politicians, fearing that Texas would become a refuge for fugitive slaves, pressured President John Tyler to admit Texas to the United States. The admission of Florida as the twenty-seventh state and Texas as the twenty-eighth state in 1845 meant the absorption of large numbers of Hispanic people into the United States.

The acquisition of Texas's 267,339 square miles (making it a fifth larger than France) whetted American appetites for the rest of the old Spanish Empire in North America. Exploiting Mexico's political instability, President James Polk goaded Mexico into war. Mexico suffered total defeat and in the 1848 Treaty of Guadalupe Hidalgo surrendered its remaining claims to Texas, yielded New Mexico and California to the United States, and recognized the Rio Grande as the international border. A treaty with Great Britain in 1846 had already recognized the American settlement in the Oregon Territory, so with the new lands from Mexico the continent had been acquired. Then, in 1898 a revolt in Cuba against an incompetent Spanish administration had consequences beyond "manifest destiny." Inflamed by press reports of Spanish atrocities, public opinion swept the United States into war. The Spanish-American War lasted just ten weeks and brought U.S. control over Cuba, the Philippine Islands, and Puerto Rico. The United States had become a colonial power.

The people who were native to this vast continent fared poorly under manifest destiny. Government officials sometimes manipulated the Indians by gathering a few chiefs, plying them with whiskey, and then inducing them to hand over the tribes' hunting grounds. Sometimes officials exploited rivalries among tribes or used bribes. By these methods, William Henry Harrison, superintendent of the Indians of the Northwest Territory and a future president, got some Native Americans to cede 48 million acres (Map 27.2). He had the full backing of President Jefferson.

The policy of pushing the Indians westward across the Mississippi accelerated during Andrew Jackson's presidency (1829–1837). Thousands of Delawares, Shawnees, and Wyandots, tricked into moving from east of the Mississippi River to reservations west of

manifest destiny The belief that God had foreordained Americans to cover the entire continent.

Treaty of Guadalupe Hidalgo The 1848 treaty between the United States and Mexico in which Mexico ceded large tracts of land to the United States in exchange for $15 million.

How did the United States become a world power? | What factors shaped the development of Canada? | How did Australia evolve from penal colony to nation? | What common forces shaped the Americas and Australia?

733

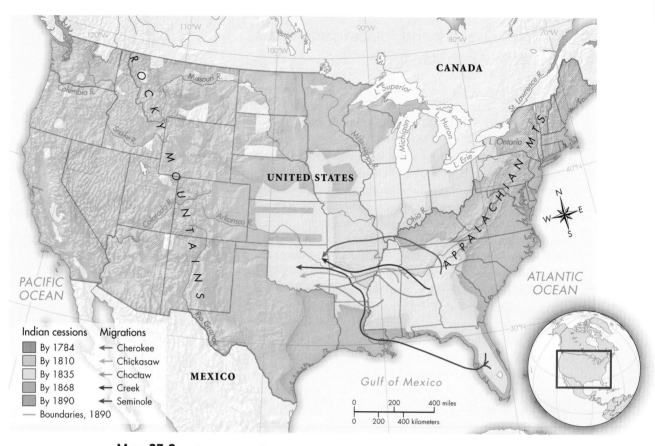

Map 27.2 Indian Cession of Lands to the United States, 1784–1890 Forced removal of the Creeks, Cherokees, and Chickasaws to reservations in Oklahoma led to the deaths of thousands of Native Americans on the Trail of Tears, as well as to the destruction of their cultures.

Missouri, died of cholera and measles during the journey. The survivors found themselves hopelessly in debt for supplies and farming equipment. The state of Georgia, meanwhile, was nibbling away at Cherokee lands, which were theoretically protected by treaty with the U.S. government. When gold was discovered on the Cherokee lands, a gold rush took place. The Creek, Cherokee, and other tribes were rounded up, expelled, and sent beyond the western boundaries of Missouri and Arkansas. Cherokee Chief John Ross, in a 1935 letter to Congress, movingly appealed, "We are deprived of membership in the human family! We have neither land, nor home, nor resting place, that can be called our own."[3]

The mid-nineteenth century saw a steady flow of white settlers westward past the Mississippi River into the Great Plains, home to many Indians. The U.S. Army, in the name of protecting the migrants, fought the Indians and slaughtered the buffalo on which they depended for food, shelter, and clothing. The federal government's policy was to confine indigenous people to reservations, where malnutrition and disease took a terrible toll.

In 1868, after pursuing a policy of total war on the Plains Indians, General W. T. Sherman brokered the Treaty of Fort Laramie. This treaty promised that the United States would close western forts and grant the Sioux and Cheyenne permanent control of their ancestral lands in the Dakotas: the Black Hills as well as the area between the Platte River and the Bighorn Mountains. A few chiefs signed; many did not. In 1874 gold was discovered in the Black Hills, and prospectors flooded into the area. By 1875 whites outnumbered Indians there, violating the terms of the treaty. During the course of the nineteenth century, while the number of white residents skyrocketed from 4.3 million to 66.8 million, the number of Indians steadily declined to a recorded 237,196 in 1900.

Women's Roles in White Settlements

Generally speaking, the settlers' lives blurred sex roles. It fell to women to make homes out of crude log cabins that had no windows or doors or out of tarpaper shacks with mud floors. Considered the carriers of "high culture," women organized whatever educational, religious, musical, and recreational activities the settlers' society possessed. Women also had to defend their homes against prairie fires and Indian attacks. These burdens were accompanied by frequent pregnancies and, often, the need to give birth without medical help or even the support of other women.

Influenced by ideas then circulating in England, some women began promoting rights for women. At the Seneca Falls Convention in 1848, they demanded equal political and economic rights. Others promoted women's education and opened women's colleges. It was not until 1920, however, that women in the United States got the right to vote.

England remained an important cultural influence in other spheres besides women's rights and abolition. Many books published in London were quickly reprinted in the United States once copies arrived, and education beyond the elementary level usually involved reading classics of English literature. Meanwhile, in the American South, rights to an education and other freedoms were withheld from another group of citizens: blacks.

Black Slavery in the South

In 1619, as one solution to the chronic labor shortage in North America, Dutch traders brought the first black people to Virginia as prisoners (white indentured servants who worked for a term of years was another solution). In the early eighteenth century, with the expansion of rice cultivation in the Carolinas and tobacco farming in Virginia and Maryland, planters demanded more laborers. Between 1720 and 1770, black prisoners poured into the Southern colonies. From 1730 through 1760, white fears of black revolts pushed colonial legislatures to pass laws that established blacks' legal position as property of whites, enshrining the slave system in law.

The American Revolution did not bring liberty to slaves. The framers of the Constitution treated private property as sacrosanct and viewed slaves as property. Antislavery sentiment was growing, however, and states from Delaware north eventually outlawed slavery. In 1809 the United States followed Britain's lead in outlawing the importation of slaves. Nevertheless, white planters and farmers had a material and psychological interest in maintaining black bondage, which brought financial profit and conferred social status and prestige.

Between 1820 and 1860, as new lands in the South and West were put to the production of cotton and sugar, the demand for labor skyrocketed. The upper South—Maryland and Virginia—where decades of tobacco farming had reduced the fertility of the soil, supplied the slaves. This period witnessed the forced migration of about 650,000 people, in many cases causing the breakup of slave families.

Despite such threats to black families, a study of the entire adult slave population of North Carolina in 1860 has shown that most slave women spent their entire adult lives in settled unions with the same husband. Planters encouraged slave marriages because large slave families were in their economic interest, especially after the end of the Atlantic slave trade. Evidence from all parts of the South reveals that, in spite of illiteracy, separated spouses tried to remain in touch with one another and, once slavery had been abolished, went to enormous lengths to reunite their families.

The Civil War and Its Impact

In the 1850s westward expansion, not moral outrage, brought the controversy over slavery to a head. As Congress created new territories, the question of whether slavery would be

Picturing the Past

Slave Auction, 1850s

In a scene outside a country tavern near a river with a Mississippi-type steamer on it, an auctioneer extols a biracial girl's qualities to a group of planters (center), while another dealer with a whip (left) brutally separates a mother from her children. The picture was intended to send an abolitionist message. (Carnegie Museum of Art, Pittsburgh. Gift of Mrs. W. Fitch Ingersoll)

ANALYZING THE IMAGE Look at the clothing the various people are wearing. What social distinctions do they convey? Is there anything else about the picture that lets you know it was intended to send an abolitionist message?

CONNECTIONS Can you think of other examples of art with social or political messages? How would this painting compare in its effectiveness?

extended to them arose again and again (Map 27.3). For years elaborate compromises were worked out, but tensions rose, fueled by increasing differences between the North and South. On the eve of the Civil War the South was overwhelmingly agricultural, while the North controlled 90 percent of the country's industrial capacity.

Abraham Lincoln, committed to checking the spread of slavery, was elected president in 1860. To protest his victory, South Carolina seceded from the Union in December of that year. Ten Southern states soon followed South Carolina's example and formed the Confederacy.

Confederacy The eleven Southern states that seceded from the United States and formed the Confederate States of America.

Lincoln declared the seceding states' actions illegal and declared war on them to preserve the Union. The years of fighting that followed took a huge toll on both sides. Thinking that it might help end the war more quickly, Lincoln issued the Emancipation Proclamation, which became effective on January 1, 1863 (two years after the abolition of serfdom in Rus-

Map 27.3 Slavery in the United States, 1861 Although many issues contributed to the tension between North and South, slavery was the fundamental, enduring force that underlay all others. Lincoln's prediction, "I believe this government cannot endure, permanently half slave and half free," tragically proved correct.

sia; see page 648). It freed slaves only in states and areas that were in rebellion against the United States and allowed slavery for convicted felons. Nevertheless, the proclamation spelled the doom of North American slavery and transformed the Civil War from a political struggle to preserve the Union into a moral crusade for the liberty of all Americans.

European and English liberals greeted the Emancipation Proclamation with joy. A gathering of working people in Manchester, England, wrote President Lincoln: "The erasure of that foul blot upon civilization and Christianity—chattel slavery—during your Presidency will cause the name of Abraham Lincoln to be honoured and revered by posterity."[4] As Lincoln acknowledged, this was a magnanimous statement, for the Civil War hurt working people in Manchester, whose factories had closed when importation of cotton from the South stopped.

The war also had important political consequences in Europe. In 1861 British and European opinion had divided along class lines. The upper classes sympathized with the American South, while the commercial classes and working people sided with the North. Thus the Northern victory was interpreted as a triumph of the democratic experiment over aristocratic oligarchy. When parliaments debated the extension of suffrage, the American example was frequently cited.

In April 1865 the Confederate general Robert E. Lee surrendered his army at Appomattox Court House in Virginia, ending the war. In his second inaugural address in 1864 Lincoln had called for "malice toward none and charity for all." Those who came to power after Lincoln was assassinated in April 1865 were less inclined to be generous toward the South.

During Reconstruction (1865–1877), the vanquished South had to adjust to a new social and economic order without slavery. Former slaves wanted land to farm, but, lacking cash, they soon accepted the sharecropping system: sharecroppers paid landowners about half of a year's crops at harvest time in return for a cabin, food, mules, seed, tools, and land.

The Fifteenth Amendment to the U.S. Constitution outlawed denying anyone the vote "on account of race, color, or previous condition of servitude," and in the early years of Reconstruction, when Northerners were in charge, many former slaves voted. However, between 1880 and 1920, after Southerners returned to power, so-called Jim Crow laws were passed to prevent blacks from voting and to enforce rigid racial segregation.

In these racist circumstances, no institution played a more positive role in the construction of a black community than the black Protestant churches. Black preachers became leaders of the black community. Throughout the South the black church provided support, security, and a sense of solidarity for its members.

Industrialization and the Formation of Large Corporations

At the beginning of the nineteenth century, providing raw materials was the central role of the United States in global trade. By the end of the century the United States had become a major manufacturing power, due in part to extensive British investment in U.S. enterprises. The flow of British funds was a consequence of Britain's own industrialization, which generated enormous wealth (see Chapter 23).

The availability of raw materials in the United States also facilitated industrialization. Huge iron ore deposits were found near the Great Lakes in 1844; oil was discovered in Pennsylvania in 1859, and oil drilling soon began; coal was also widely available.

The West also held precious metals, and the discovery of gold and silver in California, Colorado, Arizona, and Montana and on the reservations of the Sioux Indians of South Dakota (see page 734) precipitated gold and silver rushes. Even before 1900 miners had extracted $1.24 billion in gold and $901 million in silver from western mines. Many miners settled down to farm, and by 1912 the West had been won.

The federal government contributed to industrialization by turning over vast amounts of land and mineral resources to industry for development. The railroads — the foundation of industrial expansion — received 130 million acres. By 1900 the U.S. railroad system connected every part of the nation.

Between 1880 and 1920 industrial production soared. By the 1890s the United States was producing twice as much steel as Britain. Large factories replaced small ones, and Henry Ford of Detroit set up assembly lines in the automobile industry. Each person working on the line performed only one task instead of assembling an entire car, greatly increasing the speed and efficiency of production. Other new machines also had a pervasive impact. Sewing machines made cheap, varied, mass-produced clothing available for city people to buy in department stores and for country people to purchase through mail-order catalogues.

Even food production was industrialized. Grain elevators, introduced in 1850, made it possible to store much more grain, which could be transported by the growing rail system as needed. The new practice of canning meant that food did not have to be eaten immediately, and the development of refrigeration meant that meat could be shipped long distances. Factories turned out crackers, cookies, and breakfast cereals.

The national economy experienced repeated cycles of boom and bust in the late nineteenth century. Serious depressions in 1873, 1884, and 1893 slashed prices and threw many people out of work. Leading industrialists responded by establishing larger corporations and consolidating companies into huge conglomerates.

Immigrants and Their Reception

Immigrants were an important source of workers for the new American industries, and the United States attracted these newcomers from its founding. Before the Civil War most immigrants came from England, Ireland, and Germany. When the Irish potato crop was destroyed by a fungal disease leading to a horrific famine in 1845–1859, a million people fled overseas, the majority heading to the United States. Immigrants who arrived with nothing had to work as laborers for years, but in time many were able to acquire farms, especially if they were willing to move west as the country expanded.

Between 1860 and 1914, 28 million additional immigrants arrived in the United States. Industrial America developed on the labor of these people. Chinese, Scandinavian, and Irish immigrants laid thirty thousand miles of railroad tracks between 1867 and 1873 and another seventy-three thousand miles in the 1880s. At the Carnegie Steel Corporation, Slavs and Italians produced one-third of the world's total steel supply in 1900. Lithuanians, Poles, Croats, Scandinavians, Irish, and blacks entered the Chicago stockyards and built the meat-packing industry. Irish immigrants continued to operate the spinning frames and knitting machines of New England's textile mills.

Immigration fed the growth of cities. As in Europe (see Chapter 24), cities themselves were being transformed. By the early twentieth century they had electricity, sewer systems that curbed the spread of infectious diseases, and streetcars that allowed them to expand, thus reducing crowding.

Still, the working conditions that new immigrants found were often deplorable. Industrialization had created a vast class of wageworkers who depended totally on their employers for work. To keep labor costs low, employers paid workers piecemeal for the number of articles they made, and they hired women and children who could be paid much less than men. Because business owners fought in legislatures and courts against the installation of costly safety devices, working conditions in mines and mills were frightful. Workers responded with strikes, violence, and, gradually, unionization.

THE COMING MAN—JOHN CHINAMAN.

Uncle Sam introduces Eastern Barbarism to Western Civilization.

Racist Cartoon from *Harper's Weekly*, 1869 Nineteenth-century immigrants encountered terrible prejudice, as even "respectable" magazines and newspapers spewed out racism, such as this cartoon from an 1869 issue of *Harper's Weekly* that satirizes both the Irish and the Chinese as "uncivilized." The Irishman is identified by his shillelagh, a blackthorn club, here used to imply a tendency toward violence, and the Chinese man is identified by his long pigtail and his bowing, seen as a sign of his devious obsequiousness. Well into the twentieth century, being American meant being of Anglo-Saxon descent. (*Harper's Weekly*, August 28, 1869. Private Collection)

Nationalism carried different meanings in the United States than it did in Europe (see pages 637–638). It did not refer to an ancient people whose unique culture was tied to its language, as it did in Europe. Immigrants were expected to switch their loyalties to their new country and learn English. As in Europe, much was done to promote patriotism and bring people together through flag-waving parades and other emotionally charged symbols and ceremonies. The negative side of identification with the nation was nativist sentiment—that is, hostility to foreign and "un-American" looks, behavior, and loyalties—among native-born Americans. Some of this antagonism sprang from racism and religious bigotry. A great deal of the dislike of the foreign-born sprang from fear of economic competition. To most Americans, the Chinese with their exotic looks and willingness to work for very little seemed especially dangerous. Increasingly violent agitation against Asians led to race riots in California and finally culminated in the Chinese Exclusion Act of 1882, which denied Chinese laborers entrance to the country.

Quick Review
What explains the rapid industrialization and urbanization of the United States in the second half of the nineteenth century?

The severe economic depression of the 1890s also fed resentment toward immigrants. Faced with overproduction, the rich and powerful owners of mines, mills, and factories fought the organization of labor unions, laid off thousands of workers, slashed wages, and ruthlessly exploited their workers. Workers in turn feared that immigrant labor would drive salaries lower.

What factors shaped the development of Canada?

In 1608 the French explorer Samuel de Champlain (1567–1635) sailed down the St. Lawrence River (see Map 27.4) and established a trading post on the site of present-day Quebec. The fur-trading monopolies subsequently granted to Champlain by the French crown attracted settlers, and Jesuit missionaries to the Indians further increased the French population. The British, however, vigorously challenged French control of the fur trade. The mid-eighteenth-century global struggle for empire between the British and the French, known in Europe as the Seven Years' War (see pages 580–581), spilled into North America, where it was known as the French and Indian Wars. English victory was formalized in the Treaty of Paris of 1763, in which France ceded Canada to Great Britain.

For the French Canadians, who in 1763 numbered about ninety thousand, the British conquest was a tragedy. British governors replaced the French, and English-speaking merchants from Britain and the thirteen American colonies to the south took over the colony's economic affairs. The Roman Catholic Church remained, however, and played a powerful role in the political and cultural, as well as the religious, life of French Canadians. Most French Canadians were farmers, though a small merchant class sold furs and imported manufactured goods.

In 1774 the British Parliament passed the Quebec Act, which granted religious freedom to French Canadians and recognized French law in civil matters, but it denied Canadians a legislative assembly. Instead, Parliament placed power in the hands of an appointed governor and an appointed council composed of both English and French Canadians. English Canadian businessmen protested that they were being denied a basic right of Englishmen—representation.

During the American Revolution, about forty thousand Americans demonstrated their loyalty to Great Britain and its empire by moving to Canada. These "loyalists" not only altered the French-English ratio in the population but also pressed for a representative assembly. In 1791 Parliament responded with the Constitution Act, which divided the province of Quebec in two and provided for an elective assembly in each province.

Map 27.4 **The Dominion of Canada, 1871** Shortly after the Dominion of Canada came into being as a self-governing nation within the British Empire in 1867, new provinces were added. Vast areas of Canada were too sparsely populated to achieve provincial status. Alberta and Saskatchewan did not become part of the Dominion until 1905, Newfoundland only in 1949.

Not wanting to repeat the errors made in 1776, when failure to grant the thirteen colonies autonomy provoked them to declare independence, the British gradually extended home rule to Canada, beginning in 1840. During the American Civil War (1861–1865), English-American relations were severely strained, and fear of American aggression led to confederation, a loose union of the provinces, each with substantial powers. In 1867 the provinces of New Brunswick and Nova Scotia joined Ontario and Quebec to form the Dominion of Canada (Map 27.4). The Dominion Cabinet was given jurisdiction over internal affairs, while Britain retained control over foreign policy.

Believing that the U.S. Constitution left the states too strong and helped to bring on the Civil War, the framers of the Canadian constitution created a powerful central government. The first prime minister, John A. Macdonald, vigorously pushed Canada's "manifest destiny" to absorb the entire northern part of the continent. In 1870 his government purchased the vast Northwest Territories of the Hudson's Bay Company for $1.5 million. Fearful that the sparsely settled colony of British Columbia would join the United States, Macdonald lured British Columbia into the confederation with a subsidy to pay its debts and the promise of a transcontinental railroad. Likewise, the tiny, debt-ridden maritime province of Prince Edward Island was drawn into the confederation with a large subsidy. In the five short years between 1868 and 1873, through Macdonald's imagination and drive, Canadian sovereignty stretched from coast to coast. The completion of the Canadian Pacific Railroad in 1885 led to the formation of two new prairie provinces, Alberta and Saskatchewan, which in 1905 entered the Dominion. (Only in 1949 did the island of Newfoundland renounce colonial status and join the Dominion.)

Canada was thinly populated in the nineteenth century, and by 1900 still had only a little over 5 million people (as compared to 76 million in the United States). As in the

confederation A relatively loose form of union, leaving the parts with substantial powers.

United States, the native peoples were pushed aside by Canada's development plans, and their population dropped by half or more during the century, many succumbing to the newcomers' diseases. French Canadians remained the largest minority in the population. Distinctively different in language, law, and religion and fiercely proud of their culture, they resisted assimilation.

Immigration picked up in the 1890s. Some immigrants went to work in the urban factories of Hamilton, Toronto, and Montreal. However, most immigrants from continental Europe flooded the midwestern plains and soon transformed the prairies into one of the world's greatest grain-growing regions. Mining also was expanded, and British Columbia, Ontario, and Quebec produced large quantities of wood pulp, much of it sold to the United States. Canada's rivers were harnessed to supply hydroelectric power for industrial and domestic use. But Canada remained a predominantly agricultural country, with less than 10 percent of its population engaged in manufacturing (and a third of them processing timber or food).

Quick Review
How did the British experience of the Revolutionary War shape the political development of Canada?

How did Australia evolve from penal colony to nation?

In April 1770 James Cook, the English explorer, navigator, and captain of HMS *Endeavor*, dropped anchor in a wide bay about ten miles south of the present city of Sydney on the coast of eastern Australia. Because the ship's botanist, Joseph Banks, subsequently discovered thirty thousand specimens of plant life in the bay, sixteen hundred of them unknown to European science, Captain Cook called the place Botany Bay. Unimpressed by the flat landscape and its few naked inhabitants—the Aborigines, or native people—Cook sailed north along the coast (Map 27.5). On August 21, on a rock later named Possession Island, Cook formally claimed the entire land south of where he stood for Britain. Cook called the land New South Wales.

Britain populated the new land with prisoners, and their labor—as well as the efforts of their descendants and new arrivals—transformed Australia into an economically viable and increasingly independent nation. Like the other nations discussed in this chapter, Australia was not free of racial discrimination.

Botany Bay A bay on the coast of eastern Australia in which numerous specimens of plant life were discovered. It later became home to a penal colony.

New South Wales The name given to Australia by James Cook, the English explorer; today it is the name of the most populous of the six states of Australia.

A Distant Land Turned Penal Colony

The world's smallest continent, Australia has a temperate climate and little intense cold. Three topographical zones (see Map 27.5) roughly divide the continent. The Western Plateau, a vast desert and semidesert region, covers almost two-thirds of the continent. The Central Eastern Lowlands extend from the Gulf of Carpentaria in the north to western Victoria in the south. The Eastern Highlands are a complex belt of tablelands.

When Cook arrived in Australia, about three hundred thousand Aborigines lived there. A peaceful and nomadic people, the Aborigines lived entirely by food gathering, fishing, and hunting and never practiced warfare as it was understood by more technologically advanced peoples such as the Mexica (Aztecs) of Mexico or the Mandinke of West Africa. When the white settlers arrived, they occupied the Aborigine lands unopposed. Like the Indians of Central and South America, the Aborigines fell victim to European diseases and to a spiritual malaise caused by the breakdown of their tribal life.

The victory of the thirteen North American colonies in 1783 inadvertently contributed to the establishment of a colony in Australia five years later. Crime in England was increas-

Map 27.5 Australia Because of the vast deserts in western Australia, cities and industries developed mainly in the east. Australia's early geographical and cultural isolation bred a sense of inferiority. Air travel, the communications revolution, and the massive importation of Japanese products and American popular culture have changed that.

ing in the 1770s and 1780s, and the transportation of felons "beyond the seas" seemed the answer to the problem of overcrowded prisons. Until the founding of the United States in 1776, the British government had shipped about one thousand convicts annually to the North American colony of Georgia. After that became impossible, the British Cabinet approved the establishment of a penal colony at Botany Bay in 1786. In May 1787 a fleet carrying a thousand felons and their jailers sailed for Australia. On January 28, 1788, after an eight-month voyage, it landed in Sydney Cove.

Because the land at Botany Bay proved completely unsuited for agriculture and lacked decent water, the first governor, Arthur Phillip, moved the colony ten miles north to Port Jackson, later called Sydney. Announcing that those who did not work would not eat, Phillip set the prisoners to planting seeds. But most of the convicts knew nothing of agriculture, and some were too ill or too old to work. Moreover, the colony lacked draft animals and plows. Consequently, the colony of New South Wales tottered on the brink of starvation for years.

For the first thirty years of the penal colony, men far outnumbered women. Because the British government refused to allow wives to accompany their convict-husbands, prostitution flourished. Many women convicts, if not professional prostitutes when they left England, became such during the long voyage south.

exclusionists The officers and jailers who tried to establish a colonial gentry and impose rigid class distinctions from England.

emancipists The lower strata of the Australian social order in the mid-nineteenth century, made up of former convicts.

Army officers and jailers, though descended from the middle and lower middle classes, tried to establish a colonial gentry and to impose the rigid class distinctions that they had known in England. Known as **exclusionists**, these self-appointed members of the colonial gentry tried to exclude from polite society all **emancipists**, that is to say, convicts who had served their sentences and were now free (few emancipists returned to England). Deep and bitter class feeling took root.

An Economy Built on Wool, Gold, and Immigrant Labor

Governor Phillip and his successors urged the British Colonial Office to send free settlers, not just prisoners, to Australia. After the end of the Napoleonic wars in 1815 a steady stream of people relocated there. The end of the European wars also released capital for potential investment. But investment in what? What commodity could be developed and exported to England?

Immigrants explored several possibilities, but in the end wool proved the most profitable option. Australia's temperate climate is ideally suited to sheep farming. Moreover, wool production requires much land and little labor—precisely the situation in Australia. After 1820 the commercial importance of Australia exceeded its significance as a penal colony, and wool exports steadily increased.

Settlers also experimented with wheat farming. Soil deficiencies and the dry climate slowed early production, but farmers eventually developed a successful white-grained winter variety, and by 1900 wheat was Australia's second most valuable crop.

Population shortage remained a problem through the nineteenth century. In its quest for British immigrants, Australia could not compete with North America. It was just too expensive and took too long to get to Australia. To reduce the financial disincentives, the government offered immigrants free passage. Still, in the nineteenth century over 2.5 million British immigrants went to North America and only 223,000 to Australia.

In the early nineteenth century Australia's population was concentrated on the eastern coast of the continent, but the growth of sheep farming led to the opening of the interior. The Ripon Land Regulation Act of 1831, which provided land grants, attracted free settlers, and by 1850 Australia had five hun-

The "Life of Emigration" Puzzle Some of the advertising designed to attract people to move to Australia was aimed at children. The 38-piece wooden puzzle depicts the life of a family moving from Britain to Australia, from their departure to clearing ground and sheering sheep. It dates to about 1840. (Photograph Courtesy of the State Library of South Australia, S.A. Memory website)

dred thousand inhabitants. The discovery of gold in Victoria in 1851 quadrupled that number in a few years.

The gold rush led to an enormous improvement in transportation within Australia. Railroad construction, financed by British investors, began in the 1870s, and by 1890 nine thousand miles of track had been laid. The improved transportation offered by railways stimulated agricultural production.

The gold rush also provided financial backing for educational and cultural institutions. Public libraries, museums, art galleries, and universities opened in the thirty years following 1851. In keeping with the overwhelmingly British ethnic origin of most immigrants to Australia, these institutions dispensed a distinctly British culture.

On the negative side, the large numbers of Asians in the goldfields sparked bitter racial prejudice. "Colored peoples" (as nonwhites were called in Australia) adapted more easily than the British to the warm climate and worked for lower wages. Thus they proved essential to the country's economic development in the nineteenth century. Chinese and Japanese built the railroads and ran the market gardens near, and the shops in, the towns. Filipinos and Pacific Islanders labored in the sugarcane fields. Afghanis and their camels controlled the carrying trade in some areas. But fear that colored labor would lower living standards and undermine Australia's distinctly British culture triumphed. The Commonwealth Immigration Restriction Act of 1901 closed immigration to Asians and established the "white Australia policy," which remained on the books until the 1970s.

The Shaping of a Government and a National Identity

In 1850 the British Parliament passed the Australian Colonies Government Act, which allowed the four most populous colonies—New South Wales, Tasmania, Victoria, and South Australia—to establish colonial legislatures, determine voting rights, and frame their own constitutions. By 1859 all but one colony was self-governing. The provincial parliament of South Australia was probably the most democratic in the world, in that it was elected by universal manhood suffrage (that is, by all adult males) and by secret ballot. Other colonies soon adopted the secret ballot. In 1902 Australia became one of the first countries in the world to give women the vote.

The Commonwealth of Australia came into existence on January 1, 1901. From the British model, Australia adopted the parliamentary form of government in which a cabinet is responsible to the House of Commons. From the American system, Australia took the concept of decentralized government, whereby the states and the federal government share power.

> **Quick Review**
> How did the vast distance between Australia and Europe shape Australia's development?

What common forces shaped the Americas and Australia?

Looked at from the perspective of world history, the new countries of the Americas and Australia had much in common. All of them began as European colonies. All had indigenous populations who suffered from the arrival of Europeans. For all of them the nineteenth century was a period of nation building, and all had achieved self-rule by the end of the century. In all cases the languages of the colonial powers—English, French, Spanish, and Portuguese—became the languages of government after independence. All the new nations provided European financiers with investment opportunities, not only in the expansion of agricultural enterprises, but also in mines, transportation, and manufacturing. And by the end of the nineteenth century they all had become connected to the rest of the world through global trade. Another global current they all felt was nationalism, which in these countries meant mass identification with the country rather than with an ancient people and its language. All at one time or another allowed or encouraged immigration, and many had also imported slaves from Africa. Discrimination on the basis of ethnic origin and race was pervasive in all of them.

Despite so many similarities, the countries covered in this chapter were already very different by 1914. While the United States had built a strong industrial base and become one of the richest countries in the world, the economies of most of the other countries were still predominantly agricultural. While the three English-speaking countries had established strong democratic traditions, most of the countries of Latin America were controlled by narrow elites or military strongmen, with much of the population excluded from the political process. Of the countries of Latin America, only Argentina, with its temperate climate, fertile prairies, and large influx of European immigrants approached the prosperity of the United States, Canada, or Australia.

What accounts for these differences in outcomes? That the three countries that began as British colonies ended up as stable democracies strongly suggests that their common origins mattered. Even though they obtained independence in different ways, the British tradition of representative government shaped the political culture of each of the new states. By the time they achieved independence, their citizens were already accustomed to elections and local self-government. That was not true of any of the former Spanish or Portuguese colonies.

The United States also benefited from its size. That a single country was formed by the original thirteen colonies in North America and preserved through the Civil War gave the United States the advantages of substantial size from the beginning. In addition it had room to expand west into territory with many advantages—a temperate climate, navigable rivers, and abundant arable land and mineral resources. As a consequence of its original size and subsequent expansion, the United States became the largest of the new countries in population. The only country that had more land was Canada, and much of Canada's land was too far north for agriculture. If Simón Bolívar had succeeded in forming a union of the Spanish-speaking countries of South America, it might have shared some of the advantages of size that the United States had.

It was important that the United States did not long remain a supplier for Europe of raw materials and basic commodities, but was quick to industrialize. Why did the United States industrialize in the nineteenth century much more rapidly than any of the other countries of the Western Hemisphere or Australia? Many reasons can be suggested. It had ample resources such as iron, coal, petroleum, and fertile land. Also, its government put few obstacles in the way of those who built the great enterprises. At the same time, through much of the nineteenth century, the United States placed high tariffs on imports to discourage the importing of European goods and to foster its own industries. To support these industries it had no difficulty attracting both capital and immigrants from abroad. Furthermore, the United States developed a social structure that rewarded self-made men and encouraged innovation. At the beginning of the nineteenth century the most crucial advances in industrial technology were made in Europe, but by the beginning of the next century they were just as likely to come from the United States. It was the United States that introduced streetcars and Henry Ford who developed the assembly line.

Once the United States became an industrialized country, its economic advantages accelerated; its citizens had more money to buy the products of its industries, its capitalists had more income to invest, educational levels rose as the advantages of learning became clearer, it attracted more immigrants, and so on. Countries further behind could not easily catch up. In other words, by diversifying its economy early, the United States escaped the neocolonial trap.

Quick Review

What accounts for the similarities and differences between the countries covered in this chapter?

Chapter 27 Nation Building in the Americas and Australia • 1770–1914

Connections

IN THE AMERICAS AND AUSTRALIA the century or so leading up to World War I was a time of nation building. Colonial governments were overthrown, new constitutions were written, settlement was extended, slavery was ended, and immigrants were welcomed. On the eve of World War I, there was reason to be optimistic about the future of all these countries. Although wealth was very unevenly distributed, in most of them it was not hard to point to signs of progress: growing cities, expanding opportunities for education, modern conveniences.

World War I, the topic of the next chapter, affected these countries in a variety of ways. Those most deeply involved were Canada and Australia, which followed Britain into the war in 1914 and sent hundreds of thousands of men to fight, losing many in some of the bloodiest battles of the war. The United States did not join the war until 1917, but quickly mobilized several million men and in 1918 began sending soldiers and materials in huge numbers. Even countries that maintained neutrality, as all the Latin American countries other than Brazil did, felt the economic impact of the war, especially the increased demand for food and manufactured goods. For them, the war had a positive side. How the war was started, expanded, and finally concluded are the topics of the next chapter.

- **For a list of suggested readings for this chapter, visit** *bedfordstmartins.com/mckayworldunderstanding*.

- **For primary sources from this period, see** *Sources of World Societies*, Second Edition.

- **For Web sites, images, and documents related to topics in this chapter, see Make History at** *bedfordstmartins.com/mckayworldunderstanding*.

Chapter 27 Study Guide

To do these exercises online, go to bedfordstmartins.com/mckayworldunderstanding.

 Step 1

GETTING STARTED
Below are basic terms about this period in global history. Can you identify each term below and explain why it matters?

TERMS	WHO (OR WHAT) AND WHEN	WHY IT MATTERS
Creoles, p. 722		
peninsulares, p. 722		
neocolonialism, p. 727		
haciendas, p. 728		
peons, p. 731		
manifest destiny, p. 733		
Treaty of Guadalupe Hidalgo, p. 733		
Confederacy, p. 736		
confederation, p. 741		
Botany Bay, p. 742		
New South Wales, p. 742		
exclusionists, p. 744		
emancipists, p. 744		

Step 2

MOVING BEYOND THE BASICS
The exercise below requires a more advanced understanding of the chapter material. Compare and contrast the development of the United States and the independent nations of Latin America in the nineteenth century by filling in the chart below with descriptions of the nature of government and degree of democratization, economic development, and the impact of race on society. When you are finished, consider the following questions: Why did suffrage expand more quickly in the United States than in Latin America? How did the United States escape the neocolonial economic trap? Why were so many Latin American countries unsuccessful in this regard? How did race shape American societies in both South and North America?

	GOVERNMENT AND DEMOCRACY	ECONOMIC DEVELOPMENT	RACE AND SOCIETY
United States			
Latin America			

PUTTING IT ALL TOGETHER

Now that you've reviewed key elements of the chapter, take a step back and try to see the big picture. Remember to use specific examples from the chapter in your answers.

LATIN AMERICA

- How did events in Europe contribute to the emergence of independence movements in Latin America?
- Why did the new nations of Latin America so often develop into dictatorships and oligarchies?

THE UNITED STATES

- How did possibility of geographical expansion in North America shape the development of the United States?
- How did immigrants from around the world help the United States realize its economic potential?

CANADA AND AUSTRALIA

- How did a sparse population shape the development of both Canada and Australia?
- How did a common British heritage shape the development of the United States, Canada, and Australia?

LOOKING BACK, LOOKING AHEAD

- How did the process of nation building in the Americas and Australia differ from the nation building in Italy and Germany (see Chapter 24) that occurred in roughly the same time period?
- What new opportunities and challenges might the devastation of old nations of Europe in World War I have created for the new nations covered in this chapter?

In Your Own Words Imagine that you must explain Chapter 27 to someone who hasn't read it. What would be the most important points to include and why?

28

World War and Revolution

1914–1929

In the summer of 1914 the nations of Europe went willingly to war. Both peoples and governments confidently expected a short war leading to a decisive victory. They were wrong. The First World War was long, indecisive, and tremendously destructive. To the shell-shocked generation of survivors, it became simply the Great War.

In the midst of the war, in March 1917, the war-weary Russian people rebelled against their tsar, Nicholas II, forcing him to abdicate. Moderate reformists established a provisional government, but they made the fatal decision to continue the war against Germany. In November Vladimir Lenin and his Communist Bolshevik party staged a second revolution, promising an end to the war. Few then could have realized how profoundly the subsequent establishment of the first Communist state in history would shape the remainder of the twentieth century.

When the victorious Allies, led by Great Britain, France, and the United States, gathered in Paris in 1919 to write the peace, they were well-aware of the importance of their decisions. Some came to Paris seeking revenge, some came looking for the spoils of war, and others promoted nationalist causes or sought an idealistic end to war. In the end, few left Paris satisfied with the results. The peace and prosperity the delegates had so earnestly sought lasted barely a decade.

Chapter Preview

▶ How did European conflicts lead to global war?

▶ What made World War I a "total war"?

▶ How did war lead to revolution in Russia?

▶ What were the global consequences of the war?

▶ How did leaders seek to re-establish peace and stability?

▶ How were postwar anxieties reflected in art and science?

How did European conflicts lead to global war?

The First World War clearly marked a great break in the course of world history. The war accelerated the growth of nationalism in Asia (see Chapter 29), and it consolidated America's position as a global power. Yet the war's greatest impact was on Europe. Drawn into war by a system of alliances, the European combatants soon found themselves in a prolonged and destructive war. Imperialism would further expand the conflict into the Middle East, Africa, and Asia, making this a global war of unprecedented scope.

The Bismarckian System of Alliances

The Franco-Prussian War (see pages 647–648) and the unification of Germany opened a new era in international relations. By 1871 France was defeated and Bismarck had made Prussia-Germany the most powerful nation in Europe. Bismarck declared Germany a "satisfied" power that desired only peace.

But how to preserve the peace? Bismarck's first concern was to keep France diplomatically isolated and without military allies. His second concern was the threat to peace posed

Map 28.1 European Alliances at the Outbreak of World War I, 1914 By the time war broke out, Europe was divided into two opposing alliances; the Triple Entente of Britain, France, and Russia, and the Triple Alliance of Germany, Austria-Hungary, and Italy. Italy switched sides and joined the Entente in 1915.

by the conflicting interests of Austria-Hungary and Russia, particularly in the Balkans. To avoid Germany's being dragged into a great war between the two rival empires, Bismarck devised an alliance system to restrain both Russia and Austria-Hungary, to prevent conflict between them, and to isolate a hostile France.

Bismarck's balancing efforts infuriated Russian nationalists, leading Bismarck to conclude a defensive military alliance with Austria against Russia in 1879. Motivated by tensions with France, Italy joined Germany and Austria to form the Triple Alliance in 1882.

Bismarck's complicated alliance system broke down after Germany's new emperor, William II, forced Bismarck to resign in 1890. William then refused to renew Bismarck's nonaggression pact with Russia, by which both states promised neutrality if the other was attacked. This prompted France to court Russia. As a result, continental Europe was divided into two rival blocs.

Great Britain's foreign policy became increasingly crucial. After 1891 Britain was the only uncommitted Great Power. Many Germans and some Britons felt that their nations were natural allies. However, the good relations that had prevailed between Prussia and Great Britain since the mid-eighteenth century gave way after 1890 to a bitter Anglo-German rivalry.

There were several reasons for this development. Commercial rivalry between Germany and Great Britain in world markets and Germany's pursuit of colonies unsettled the British. Above all, Germany's decision in 1900 to expand greatly its battle fleet challenged Britain's long-standing naval supremacy. This decision coincided with the South African War (see page 674) between the British and the Afrikaners, which revealed widespread anti-British feeling around the world. To strengthen its global position, Britain improved its relations with the United States, concluded an alliance with Japan in 1902, and in the Anglo-French Entente of 1904 settled all outstanding colonial disputes with France.

Frustrated by Britain's closer relationship with France, Germany's leaders decided to test the entente's strength. Rather than accept a territorial payoff—a slice of French jungle somewhere in Africa or a port in Morocco—in return for French primacy in Morocco, in 1905 the Germans insisted on an international conference on the whole Moroccan question. Germany's crude bullying forced France and Britain closer together, and Germany left the conference empty-handed.

The Moroccan crisis was something of a diplomatic revolution. Britain, France, Russia, and even the United States began to view Germany as a potential threat. At the same time, German leaders began to fear encirclement. In 1907 Russia, battered by its disastrous war with Japan and the 1905 revolution, agreed to settle its territorial quarrels with Great Britain in Persia and Central Asia and signed the Anglo-Russian Agreement. The treaty served as a catalyst for the Triple Entente, the alliance of Great Britain, France, and Russia in the First World War (Map 28.1).

Germany's decision to dramatically expand its naval forces also heightened tensions. German nationalists saw a large navy as the legitimate mark of a great world power. But British leaders considered it a military challenge that forced them to spend the "People's Budget" on battleships rather than on social welfare. By 1909 Britain was psychologically,

Chapter Chronology

1914	Assassination of Archduke Francis Ferdinand; formation of Triple Entente; Ottoman Empire joins Central Powers; German victories on the eastern front
1914–1918	World War I
1915	Italy joins the Triple Entente; German submarine sinks the *Lusitania*; Japan seizes German holdings in China and expands into southern Manchuria
1916	Battles of Verdun and the Somme; Irish Easter Rebellion; German Auxiliary Service Law requires 17- to 60-year-old males to work for war effort; Rasputin murdered
1916–1918	Growth of antiwar sentiment throughout Europe
1917	United States declares war on Germany; Bolshevik Revolution in Russia
1918	Treaty of Brest-Litovsk; revolution in Germany
1918–1922	Civil war in Russia
1919	Treaty of Versailles; Freudian psychology gains popularity; Rutherford splits the atom; Bauhaus school founded
1920s	Existentialism, Dadaism, and surrealism gain prominence
1923	French and Belgian armies occupy the Ruhr
1924	Dawes Plan
1926	Germany joins League of Nations
1928	Kellogg-Briand Pact

Triple Entente The alliance of Great Britain, France, and Russia in the First World War.

if not officially, in the Franco-Russian camp. Europe's leading nations were divided into two hostile blocs, both ill-prepared to deal with upheaval in the Balkans.

The Outbreak of War

In the early twentieth century a Balkans war seemed inevitable. The reason was simple: nationalism was destroying the Ottoman Empire in Europe and threatening to break up the Austro-Hungarian Empire. Western intervention in 1878 had forced the Ottoman Empire to cede most of its territory in Europe, but it retained important Balkan holdings (Map 28.2).

By 1903 Balkan nationalism was asserting itself again. Serbia led the way, becoming openly hostile to both Austria-Hungary and the Ottoman Empire. The Slavic Serbs looked to Slavic Russia for support. In 1908, to block Serbian expansion, Austria formally annexed Bosnia and Herzegovina, with their large Serbian, Croatian, and Muslim populations. Serbia erupted in rage but could do nothing without support from its ally Russia.

Then two nationalist wars, the First and Second Balkan Wars in 1912 and 1913, finally destroyed the centuries-long Ottoman presence in Europe (see Map 28.2). This event elated the Balkan nationalists and dismayed Austria-Hungary's multinational leaders. The former hoped and the latter feared that Austria might next be broken apart.

Map 28.2 The Balkans, 1878–1914 The Ottoman Empire suffered large territorial losses after the Congress of Berlin in 1878, but remained a power in the Balkans. By 1914 ethnic boundaries that did not follow political boundaries had formed, and Serbian national aspirations threatened Austria-Hungary.

Within this tense context, Archduke Francis Ferdinand, heir to the Austro-Hungarian throne, and his wife, Sophie, were assassinated by Serbian revolutionaries on June 28, 1914, during a state visit to the Bosnian capital of Sarajevo. Austria-Hungary's leaders held Serbia responsible and presented Serbia with an unconditional ultimatum on July 23, including demands that amounted to Austrian control of the Serbian state. When Serbia replied moderately but evasively, Austria declared war on Serbia on July 28.

Of prime importance in Austria-Hungary's fateful decision was Germany's unconditional support. Germany realized that war between Austria and Russia was likely, for Russia could not stand by and watch the Serbs be crushed. Yet they also hoped that while Russia (and its ally France) would go to war, Great Britain would remain neutral.

The Schlieffen Plan

- - - Planned German offensive
← Actual German offensive
☐ Neutral nations

GREAT BRITAIN
NETHERLANDS
BELGIUM
GERMANY
Brussels
Rhine R.
LUX.
Reims
Paris
Metz
Seine R.
Marne R.
FRANCE
0   100   200 mi.
0   100   200 km
SWITZ.

Military plans and timetables, rather than diplomacy, soon began to dictate policy. On July 28 Tsar Nicholas II ordered a partial mobilization against Austria-Hungary, but almost immediately found this was impossible. Russia had assumed a war with both Austria and Germany, and it could not mobilize against one without mobilizing against the other. Therefore, on July 29 Russia ordered full mobilization and in effect declared general war. The German general staff had also prepared for a two-front war. Its Schlieffen plan called for first knocking out France with a lightning attack through neutral Belgium before turning on Russia. On August 3 German armies invaded Belgium. Great Britain declared war on Germany the following day.

Stalemate and Slaughter

When the Germans invaded Belgium in August 1914, everyone believed the war would be short. The Belgian army defended its homeland, however, and then fell back to join a rapidly landed British army corps near the Franco-Belgian border. Instead of quickly capturing Paris in a vast encircling movement, by the end of August German soldiers were advancing along an enormous front. On September 6 the French attacked a gap in the German line at the Battle of the Marne. For three days, France threw everything into the attack. Finally, the Germans fell back. France had been saved (Map 28.3).

The two stalled armies now dug in behind rows of trenches, mines, and barbed wire. Eventually an unbroken line of parallel trenches stretched over four hundred miles from the Belgian coast to the Swiss frontier. By November 1914 the slaughter on the western front had begun in earnest. Ceaseless shelling by heavy artillery supposedly "softened up" the enemy in a given area. Then young soldiers went "over the top" of the trenches in frontal attacks on the enemy's line.

The human cost of **trench warfare** was staggering; territorial gains were minuscule. The massive French and British offensives during 1915 never gained more than three miles of blood-soaked earth from the enemy. In the Battle of the Somme in the summer of 1916, the British and French gained an insignificant 125 square miles at the cost of 600,000 dead or wounded, and the Germans lost 500,000 men. British poet Siegfried Sassoon (1886–1967) wrote of the Somme offensive, "I am staring at a sunlit picture of Hell." The year 1917 was equally terrible.

On the eastern front, Russia immediately moved into eastern Germany but suffered appalling losses against the Germans at the Battles of Tannenberg and the Masurian Lakes in August and September 1914 (see Map 28.3). With the help of German forces, the

trench warfare Fighting behind rows of trenches, mines, and barbed wire; used in World War I with a staggering cost in lives and minimal gains in territory.

**Legend (top right):**
- Triple Entente and allies
- Central Powers and allies
- Greatest extent of territory gained by Germany-Austria
- German submarine war zone
- Neutral nations
- Farthest advance by Central Powers on date marked
- Farthest advance by Entente Powers on date marked
- British naval blockade
- ✷ Major battle

**Main map labels:**

NORWAY
SWEDEN
FINLAND
Helsinki
Petrograd (St. Petersburg)
ESTONIA
North Sea
Jutland 1916
DENMARK
LATVIA
Riga
COURLAND
Moscow
RUSSIA
LITHUANIA
Vilnius
Masurian Lakes 1914
E. PRUSSIA
BELARUS
GREAT BRITAIN
Kiel
GERMANY
Berlin
Farthest Russian advance, 1914
Aug. 1914
Tannenberg 1914
Warsaw
KINGDOM OF POLAND (Russia)
Brest-Litovsk
Armistice line, December 1917
March 1918
Treaty of Brest-Litovsk, March 1918
Lusitania 1915
London
NETHERLANDS
Rhine R.
BELGIUM
Armistice line, November 1918
LUXEMBOURG
Kiev
Dnieper R.
1914
Seine R.
See inset map
Paris
ALSACE-LORRAINE
Western front
GALICIA
May 1915
Farthest German military advance
Bordeaux
Loire R.
SWITZERLAND
Aug. 1917
Mar. 1918
AUSTRIA-HUNGARY
Vienna
Budapest
FRANCE
Rhône R.
Caporetto 1917
Italian front
TRANSYLVANIA
Caspian Sea
SPAIN
Ebro R.
Po R.
Adriatic Sea
Elba
ITALY
Rome
Corsica
ROMANIA
Bucharest
Danube R.
Black Sea
March 1918
Balearic Is.
Sardinia
Sarajevo
SERBIA
MONTENEGRO
BULGARIA
Nov. 1917
PERSIA
ALGERIA (Fr.)
ALBANIA
1917-1918
1916
1915
Dardanelles
Constantinople
Gallipoli 1915
Middle Eastern front
IRAQ
Al Kut 1915 1916 1917
Mar. 1918
Tunis
TUNISIA (Fr.)
Sicily
Malta
GREECE
Balkan front
OTTOMAN EMPIRE
Oct. 1918
Baghdad
Basra
Crete
Cyprus
SYRIA
Damascus
Mediterranean Sea
LIBYA (It.)
EGYPT (Gr. Br.)
Red Sea
Al Aqabah 1917

The Western Front

NETHERLANDS
Ruhr R.
Dover
Ostend
Antwerp
FLANDERS
Ghent
Rhine R.
Cologne
Ypres
Calais
Schelde R.
Brussels
Louvain
Liège
BELGIUM
Meuse R.
Armistice line, November 1918
Coblenz
English Channel
Arras
ARDENNES
LUX.
GERMANY
Somme R.
St. Quentin
Amiens
Somme
Sedan
Moselle R.
Compiègne
Aisne R.
ARGONNE FOREST
Belleau Wood
Reims
LORRAINE
St. Mihiel
Marne I
Verdun
Saar R.
Marne R.
Paris
Seine R.
Marne II
Chateau-Thierry
Châlons-sur-Marne
Nancy
Strasbourg
FRANCE
Epinal
ALSACE
Mulhouse
Basel
SWITZ.

Inset legend:
- Germany, 1914
- Greatest extent of territory gained by Germany, Sept. 1914
- Front at beginning of 1915
- German offensive, Summer 1918
- ✷ Major battle

Map 28.3 The First World War in Europe The trench war on the western front was concentrated in Belgium and northern France (inset), while the war in the east encompassed an enormous territory.

CHAPTER LOCATOR

How did European conflicts lead to global war?

Austrians reversed the Russian advances of 1914 and forced the Russians to retreat deep into their own territory in the 1915 eastern campaign.

These changing tides of victory and hopes of territorial gains brought neutral countries into the war. Italy, a member of the Triple Alliance since 1882, had declared its neutrality in 1914 on the grounds that Austria had launched a war of aggression. Then, in May 1915 Italy joined the Triple Entente of Great Britain, France, and Russia in return for promises of Austrian territory. In October 1914 the Ottoman Empire joined with Austria and Germany, by then known as the Central Powers. The following September Bulgaria followed the Ottoman Empire's lead in order to settle old scores with Serbia.

The War Becomes Global

In late 1914 the Ottoman Turks joined forces with Germany and Austria-Hungary. The Young Turks (see page 683) were pro-German because the Germans had helped reform the Ottoman armies before the war and had built important railroads, like the one to Baghdad. Alliance with Germany permitted the Turks to renounce the limitations on Ottoman sovereignty that the Europeans had imposed in the nineteenth century and also to settle old scores with Russia, the Turks' historic enemy.

The entry of the Ottoman Turks pulled the entire Middle East into the war and made it truly a global conflict. While Russia attacked the Ottomans in the Caucasus, the British protected their rule in Egypt. In 1915, at the Battle of Gallipoli, British forces tried to take the Dardanelles and Constantinople from the Ottoman Turks but were badly defeated. Casualties were high on both sides and included thousands of Australians and New Zealanders.

The British were more successful at inciting the Arabs to revolt against their Turkish overlords. The foremost Arab leader was Hussein ibn-Ali (1856–1931), who governed much of the Ottoman Empire's territory along the Red Sea, an area known as the Hejaz (see Map 29.1, page 785). In 1915 Hussein won vague British commitments for an independent Arab kingdom. The next year he revolted against the Turks, proclaiming himself king of the Arabs. He joined forces with the British under T. E. Lawrence, who in 1917 led Arab tribesmen and Indian soldiers in a successful guerrilla war against the Turks on the Arabian peninsula. In 1918 British armies totally smashed the old Ottoman state. Thus war brought revolutionary change to the Middle East (see pages 784–792).

Japan, allied with the British since 1902, used the war as an opportunity to seize Germany's holdings on the Shandong (Shantung) Peninsula and in 1915 forced China to accept Japanese control of Shandong and southern Manchuria. These actions infuriated Chinese patriots and heightened long-standing tensions between China and Japan.

War also spread to colonies in Africa and East Asia. Instead of revolting as the Germans hoped, French and British colonial subjects generally supported the allied powers. Colonized peoples provided critical supplies and fought in Europe and in the Ottoman Empire. They also helped local British and French commanders seize Germany's colonies around the globe. More than a million Africans and Asians served in the various armies of the warring powers, with more than double that number serving as porters to carry equipment.

Many of these men joined up to get clothes (uniforms), food, and money for enlisting. Others did so because colonial recruiters promised them better lives when they returned home. Most were illiterate and had no idea of why they were going or what they would experience. As one West African infantryman wrote: "We black African soldiers were very sorrowful about the white man's war. . . . I didn't really care who was right—whether it was the French or the Germans—I went to fight with the French army and that was all I knew. . . . We just fought and fought until we got exhausted and died.[1]

The war had a profound impact on these colonial troops. Fighting against and killing Europeans destroyed the impression, encouraged in the colonies, that the Europeans were

Henri de Groux, *The Assault, Verdun* An eerie portrayal by Belgian artist Henri de Groux (1867–1930) of French troops moving forward in a thick haze of smoke and perhaps clouds of diphosgene, a poisonous gas first used by the Germans at Verdun on June 22, 1916. (Musée des Deux Guerres Mondiales, Paris/The Bridgeman Art Library)

superhuman. New concepts like nationalism and individual freedoms—ideals for which the Europeans were supposedly fighting—were carried home to become rallying cries for future liberation struggles.

Another crucial development in the expanding conflict came in April 1917 when the United States declared war on Germany. American intervention grew out of the war at sea and sympathy for the Triple Entente. At the beginning of the war Britain and France established a naval blockade to strangle the Central Powers. No neutral cargo ship was permitted to sail to Germany. In early 1915 Germany launched a counter-blockade using submarines. In May a German submarine sank the British passenger liner *Lusitania*. More than a thousand people, including 139 U.S. citizens died. President Woodrow Wilson protested vigorously. Germany was forced to restrict its submarine warfare for almost two years, or face almost certain war with the United States.

Early in 1917 the German military command—confident that improved submarines could starve Britain into submission before the United States could come to its rescue—resumed unrestricted submarine warfare. This was a reckless gamble, and the United States declared war on Germany. The United States eventually tipped the balance in favor of the Triple Entente and its allies.

Quick Review

How did industrialization and globalization shape the course of World War I?

What made World War I a "total war"?

The war's impact on civilians was no less massive than on the men in the trenches. Total war mobilized entire populations, led to increased state power, and promoted social equality. It also led to dissent and a growing antiwar movement.

Mobilizing for Total War

In August 1914 most Europeans greeted the outbreak of hostilities enthusiastically, believing that their own nation was in the right and defending itself from aggression. Yet by mid-October generals and politicians had begun to realize that victory would require more than patriotism. Combatant countries desperately needed men and weapons. Change had to come, and fast, to keep the war machine from sputtering to a stop.

The change came through national unity governments that began to plan and control economic and social life in order to wage total war. Governments imposed rationing, price and wage controls, and even restrictions on workers' freedom of movement. These total war economies involved entire populations, blurring the old distinction between soldiers on the battlefield and civilians at home. (See "Listening to the Past: The Experience of War," page 760.)

Germany went furthest in developing a planned economy to wage total war. As soon as war began, the Jewish industrialist Walter Rathenau convinced the German government to set up the War Raw Materials Board to ration and distribute raw materials. Under Rathenau's direction, every useful material was inventoried and rationed. Moreover, the board launched successful attempts to produce substitutes, such as synthetic rubber and synthetic nitrates, for scarce war supplies. Food was also rationed.

Following the terrible Battles of Verdun and the Somme in 1916, military leaders forced the Reichstag to accept the Auxiliary Service Law, which required all males between seventeen and sixty to work only at jobs considered critical to the war effort. Women also worked in war factories, mines, and steel mills. Thus in Germany total war led to history's first "totalitarian" society.

France and Great Britain tended to mobilize economically for total war less rapidly and less completely than Germany, as they could import materials from their colonies and from the United States. When it became apparent that the war was not going to end quickly, however, the western Allies all began to pass laws that gave their governments sweeping powers over all areas of the nation's daily life — including industrial and agricultural production, censorship, education, health and welfare, the curtailment of civil liberties, labor, and foreign aliens.

By December 1916 the British economy was largely planned and regulated directly by the state. The Espionage Act of June 1917 and the Sedition Act of May 1918 allowed the United States government to keep groups like labor unions, political parties, and ethnic organizations under surveillance. Welfare systems of various kinds were also adopted in most of the belligerent countries. Many of these laws were revoked at war's end. Still, they set precedents and would be turned to again in response to the economic depressions of the 1920s and 1930s and World War II.

total war Practiced by countries fighting in World War I, a war in which the government plans and controls all aspects of economic and social life in order to make the greatest possible military effort.

The Social Impact

The social impact of total war was no less profound than the economic impact. The military's insatiable needs — nearly every belligerent power resorted to conscription to put

The Experience of War

World War I was a total war: it enlisted the efforts of male and female adults and children, both at home and on the battlefield. It was a terrifying and painful experience for all those involved, not the romantic endeavor it was purported to be. The documents below offer two different wartime experiences. The first is from a letter written by a German soldier fighting in the trenches. The second is from the diary of a Viennese woman. As you read both passages, think about the different ways war and its consequences were made real for these two people.

A German Soldier Writes from the Trenches, March 1915

❝ *Souchez, March 11th, 1915*

"So fare you well, for we must now be parting," so run the first lines of a soldier-song which we often sang through the streets of the capital. These words are truer than ever now, and these lines are to bid farewell to you, to all my nearest and dearest, to all who wish me well or ill, and to all that I value and prize.

Our regiment has been transferred to this dangerous spot, Souchez. No end of blood has already flowed down this hill. A week ago the 142nd attacked and took four trenches from the French. It is to hold these trenches that we have been brought here. There is something uncanny about this hill-position. Already, times without number, other battalions of our regiment have been ordered here in support, and each time the company came back with a loss of twenty, thirty or more men. In the days when we had to stick it out here before, we had 22 killed and 27 wounded. Shells roar, bullets whistle; no dugouts, or very bad ones; mud, clay, filth, shell-holes so deep that one could bathe in them.

This letter has been interrupted no end of times. Shells began to pitch close to us — great English 12-inch ones — and we had to take refuge in a cellar. One such shell struck the next house and buried four men, who were got out from the ruins horribly mutilated. I saw them and it was ghastly!

Everybody must be prepared now for death in some form or other. Two cemeteries have been made up here, the losses have been so great. I ought not to write that to you, but I do so all the same, because

the newspapers have probably given you quite a different impression. They tell only of our gains and say nothing about the blood that has been shed, of the cries of agony that never cease. The newspaper doesn't give any description either of *how* the "heroes" are laid to rest, though it talks about "heroes' graves" and writes poems and such-like about them. Certainly in Lens I have attended funeral-parades where a number of dead were buried in one large grave with pomp and circumstance. But up here it is pitiful the way one throws the dead bodies out of the trench and lets them lie there, or scatters dirt over the remains of those which have been torn to pieces by shells.

I look upon death and call upon life. I have not accomplished much in my short life, which has been chiefly occupied with study. I have commended my soul to the Lord God. It bears His seal and is altogether His. Now I am free to dare anything. My future life belongs to God, my present one to the Fatherland, and I myself still possess happiness and strength. ❞

A Viennese Woman Remembers Home Front Life

❝ Ten dekagrammes [3½ ounces] of horse-flesh per head are to be given out to-day for the week. The cavalry horses held in reserve by the military authorities are being slaughtered for lack of fodder, and the people of Vienna are for a change to get a few mouthfuls of meat of which they have so long been deprived. Horse-flesh! I should like to know whether my instinctive repugnance to horse-flesh as food is personal, or whether my dislike is shared by many other housewives. My loathing of it is based, I believe, not on a physical but on a psychological prejudice.

I overcame my repugnance, rebuked myself for being sentimental, and left the house. A soft, steady rain was falling, from which I tried to protect myself with galoshes, waterproof, and umbrella. As I left the house before seven o'clock and the meat distribution did not begin until nine o'clock, I hoped to get well to the front of the queue.

soldiers in the field — created a tremendous demand for workers. This situation — seldom, if ever, seen before 1914 — brought about momentous changes.

One such change was greater power and prestige for labor unions. Unions cooperated with war governments in return for real participation in important decisions. This entry of labor leaders into policymaking councils paralleled the entry of socialist leaders into the war governments.

A ration coupon used in the German city of Eisenberg showing Germans waiting in line for their meager rations. (akg-images)

No sooner had I reached the neighbourhood of the big market hall than I was instructed by the police to take a certain direction. I estimated the crowd waiting here for a meagre midday meal at two thousand at least. Hundreds of women had spent the night here in order to be among the first and make sure of getting their bit of meat. Many had brought with them improvised seats — a little box or a bucket turned upside down. No one seemed to mind the rain, although many were already wet through. They passed the time chattering, and the theme was the familiar one: What have you had to eat? What are you going to eat? One could scent an atmosphere of mistrust in these conversations: they were all careful not to say too much or to betray anything that might get them into trouble.

At length the sale began. Slowly, infinitely slowly, we moved forward. The most determined, who had spent the night outside the gates of the hall, displayed their booty to the waiting crowd: a ragged, quite freshly slaughtered piece of meat with the characteristic yellow fat. [Others] alarmed those standing at the back by telling them that there was only a very small supply of meat and that not half the people waiting would get a share of it. The crowd became very uneasy and impatient, and before the police on

guard could prevent it, those standing in front organized an attack on the hall which the salesmen inside were powerless to repel. Everyone seized whatever he could lay his hands on, and in a few moments all the eatables had vanished. In the confusion stands were overturned, and the police forced back the aggressors and closed the gates. The crowds waiting outside, many of whom had been there all night and were soaked through, angrily demanded their due, whereupon the mounted police made a little charge, provoking a wild panic and much screaming and cursing. At length I reached home, depressed and disgusted, with a broken umbrella and only one galosh.

We housewives have during the last four years grown accustomed to standing in queues; we have also grown accustomed to being obliged to go home with empty hands and still emptier stomachs. Only very rarely do those who are sent away disappointed give cause for police intervention. On the other hand, it happens more and more frequently that one of the pale, tired women who have been waiting for hours collapses from exhaustion. The turbulent scenes which occurred to-day inside and outside the large market hall seemed to me perfectly natural. In my dejected mood the patient apathy with which we housewives endure seemed to me blameworthy and incomprehensible. 〃

Sources: Alfons Ankenbrand, in *German Students' War Letters*, ed. A. F. Wedd (London: Methuen, 1929), pp. 72–73; *Blockade: The Diary of an Austrian Middle-Class Woman, 1914–1924*, trans. Winifred Ray (New York: Ray Long & Richard Smith, 1932), pp. 63–68.

QUESTIONS FOR ANALYSIS

1. What is the soldier's view of the war? Would you characterize it as an optimistic or pessimistic letter?
2. What similarities and differences do you see in the experience of the Viennese woman as compared to the soldier's experience?
3. Why does the Viennese woman describe the housewives as "blameworthy" or "incomprehensible"?

Women's roles also changed dramatically. In every country, large numbers of women left home and domestic service to work in industry, transportation, and offices. Women also served as nurses and doctors at the front. (See "Individuals in Society: Vera Brittain," page 762.) In general, the war greatly expanded the range of women's activities and changed attitudes toward women. Although most women were quickly let go and their jobs given back to the returning soldiers, their many-sided war effort

What made World War I a "total war"? How did war lead to revolution in Russia? What were the global consequences of the war? How did leaders seek to re-establish peace and stability? How were postwar anxieties reflected in art and science?

761

INDIVIDUALS IN SOCIETY

Vera Brittain

ALTHOUGH THE GREAT WAR UPENDED MILLIONS of lives, it struck Europe's young people with the greatest force. For Vera Brittain (1893–1970), as for so many in her generation, the war became life's defining experience, which she captured forever in her famous autobiography, *Testament of Youth* (1933).

Brittain grew up in a wealthy business family in northern England, bristling at small-town conventions and discrimination against women. Very close to her brother Edward, two years her junior, Brittain read voraciously and dreamed of being a successful writer. Finishing boarding school and beating down her father's objections, she prepared for Oxford's rigorous entry exams and won a scholarship to its women's college. Brittain also fell in love with Roland Leighton, an equally brilliant student from a literary family and her brother's best friend. All three, along with two more close friends, Victor Richardson and Geoffrey Thurlow, confidently prepared to enter Oxford in late 1914.

When war suddenly approached in July 1914, Brittain shared with millions of Europeans a thrilling surge of patriotic support for her government, a prowar enthusiasm she later played down in her published writings. She wrote in her diary that her "great fear" was that England would declare its neutrality and commit the "grossest treachery" toward France.* She seconded Roland's decision to enlist, agreeing with her sweetheart's glamorous view of war as "very ennobling and very beautiful." Later, exchanging anxious letters in 1915 with Roland in France, Vera began to see the conflict in personal, human terms. She wondered if any victory or defeat could be worth Roland's life.

Struggling to quell her doubts, Brittain redoubled her commitment to England's cause and volunteered as an army nurse. For the next three years she served with distinction in military hospitals in London, Malta, and northern France, repeatedly torn between the vision of noble sacrifice and the reality of human tragedy. She lost her sexual inhibitions caring for mangled male bodies, and she longed to consummate her love with Roland. Awaiting his return on leave on Christmas Day in 1915, she was greeted instead with a telegram: Roland had been killed two days before.

Roland's death was the first of the devastating blows that eventually overwhelmed Brittain's idealistic patriotism. In 1917, first Geoffrey and then Victor died

from gruesome wounds. In early 1918, as the last great German offensive covered the floors of her war-zone hospital with maimed and dying German prisoners, the bone-weary Vera felt a common humanity and saw only more victims. A few weeks later brother Edward—her last hope—died in action. When the war ended, she was, she said, a "complete automaton," with "my deepest emotions paralyzed if not dead."

Returning to Oxford and finishing her studies, Brittain gradually recovered. She formed a deep, restorative friendship with another talented woman writer, Winifred Holtby, published novels and articles, and became a leader in the feminist campaign for gender equality. She also married and had children. But her wartime memories were always there. Finally, Brittain succeeded in coming to grips with them in *Testament of Youth*, her powerful antiwar autobiography. The unflinching narrative spoke to the experiences of an entire generation and became a runaway bestseller. Above all, perhaps, Brittain captured the ambivalent, contradictory character of the war, when millions of young people found excitement, courage, and common purpose but succeeded only in destroying their lives with their superhuman efforts and futile sacrifices. Becoming ever more committed to pacifism, Brittain opposed England's entry into World War II.

*Quoted in the excellent study by P. Berry and M. Bostridge, *Vera Brittain: A Life* (London: Virago Press, 2001), p. 59; additional quotations are from pp. 80 and 136.

QUESTIONS FOR ANALYSIS

1. What were Brittain's initial feelings toward the war? How and why did they change as the conflict continued?
2. Why did Brittain volunteer as a nurse, as many women did? How might wartime nursing have influenced women of her generation?
3. In portraying the ambivalent, contradictory character of World War I for Europe's youth, was Brittain describing the contradictory character of all modern warfare?

Vera Brittain was marked forever by her wartime experiences. (Vera Brittain Archive, William Ready Division of Archives and Research Collections, McMaster University Library)

762   Chapter 28 World War and
Revolution • 1914–1929

CHAPTER LOCATOR   How did European conflicts lead to global war?

caused Britain, Germany, and Austria to grant them the right to vote immediately after the war.

War promoted also social equality, blurring class distinctions and lessening the gap between rich and poor. Greater equality was reflected in full employment, rationing according to physical needs, and a sharing of hardships. Society became more uniform and more egalitarian, in spite of some war profiteering.

Growing Political Tensions

During the war's first two years many soldiers and civilians supported their governments. Belief in a just cause and patriotic nationalism united peoples behind their various national leaders. Each government employed censorship and propaganda to maintain popular support.

By spring 1916, however, people were beginning to crack under the strain of total war. In April Irish nationalists in Dublin unsuccessfully tried to take advantage of this situation and rose up against British rule in the Easter Rebellion. Strikes and protest marches over inadequate food flared up on every home front. Besides the massive mutiny of Russian soldiers in 1917 that supported the revolution, nearly half of the French infantry divisions mutinied for two months after the army suffered enormous losses in the Second Battle of the Aisne in April 1917.

The Central Powers experienced the most strain. In October 1916 a young socialist assassinated Austria's chief minister. Conflicts among nationalities grew, and both Czech and Yugoslav leaders demanded autonomous democratic states for their peoples. The strain of total war was also evident in Germany. By 1917 national political unity was collapsing and prewar social conflicts re-emerging. A coalition of socialists and Catholics in the Reichstag

Picturing the Past

"Never Forget!"
This 1915 French poster with a passionate headline dramatizes Germany's brutal invasion of Belgium in 1914. The "rape of Belgium" featured prominently — and effectively — in anti-German propaganda.
(Mary Evans Picture Library/The Image Works)

ANALYZING THE IMAGE How is neutral Belgium personified? What do you think the artist's purpose was?

CONNECTIONS How did governments use propaganda and other means to unite people for the war effort?

What made World War I a "total war"? | How did war lead to revolution in Russia? | What were the global consequences of the war? | How did leaders seek to re-establish peace and stability? | How were postwar anxieties reflected in art and science?

763

called for a compromise "peace without annexations or reparations." Thus militaristic Germany, like its ally Austria-Hungary and its enemy France, began to crack in 1917. But it was Russia that collapsed first and saved the Central Powers—for a time.

How did war lead to revolution in Russia?

The 1917 Russian Revolution, directly related to the Great War, had a significance far beyond the wartime agonies of a single Allied or Central Power nation. The Russian Revolution opened a new era with a radically new prototype of state and society.

The Fall of Imperial Russia

Like their allies and their enemies, Russians had embraced war with patriotic enthusiasm in 1914. For a moment Russia was united, but soon the war began to take its toll. Unprecedented artillery barrages quickly exhausted Russia's supplies of shells and ammunition, and better-equipped German armies inflicted terrible losses. Russian soldiers were sent to the front without rifles; they were told to find their arms among the dead. The Duma, Russia's lower house of the parliament, and local governments led the effort toward full mobilization on the home front. These efforts improved the military situation, but overall Russia mobilized less effectively for total war than did the other warring nations.

The great problem was leadership. Under the constitution resulting from the 1905 revolution (see page 649), Tsar Nicholas II (r. 1894–1917) retained complete control over the bureaucracy and the army. Nicholas distrusted the Duma and rejected popular involvement. As a result, the Duma, the educated middle classes, and the masses became increasingly critical of the tsar's leadership. In response, Nicholas announced in September 1915 that he was traveling to the front to lead Russia's armies.

His departure was a fatal turning point. His wife, Tsarina Alexandra, took control of the government. She tried to rule in her husband's absence with an uneducated Siberian preacher, Rasputin, as her most trusted adviser. Rasputin gained her trust by claiming that he could stop the bleeding of her hemophiliac son Alexis. In this atmosphere of unreality, the government slid steadily toward revolution.

In desperation, three members of the high aristocracy murdered Rasputin in December 1916. In the meantime, food shortages worsened and morale declined. On March 8 a women's bread march in Petrograd (formerly St. Petersburg) started riots, which spread throughout the city. The tsar ordered troops to restore order, but discipline broke down, and the soldiers joined the revolutionary crowd. The Duma declared a provisional government on March 12, 1917. Three days later, Nicholas abdicated.

The Provisional Government

March Revolution The first phase of the Russian Revolution of 1917, in which unplanned uprisings led to the abdication of the tsar and the establishment of a transitional democratic government that was then overthrown in November by Lenin and the Bolsheviks.

The March Revolution was joyfully accepted throughout the country. After generations of authoritarianism, the provisional government established a liberal republic, rejecting further social revolution. A new government formed in May 1917, which included the socialist Alexander Kerensky, refused to confiscate large landholdings and give them to peasants, fearing that such drastic action in the countryside would only complete the disintegration of Russia's peasant army. For the patriotic Kerensky, who became prime minister in July,

764 Chapter 28 World War and Revolution • 1914–1929

CHAPTER LOCATOR   How did European conflicts lead to global war?

as for other moderate socialists, the continuation of war was still the all-important national duty.

The provisional government, however, had to share power with a formidable rival—the Petrograd Soviet (or council) of Workers' and Soldiers' Deputies. Modeled on the revolutionary soviets of 1905, the Petrograd Soviet comprised two to three thousand workers, soldiers, and socialist intellectuals. This counter- or half-government issued its own radical orders, further weakening the provisional government. Most famous of these was Army Order No. 1, issued in March 1917, which stripped officers of their authority and gave power to elected committees of common soldiers.

The order led to a total collapse of army discipline. Peasant soldiers began "voting with their feet," to use Lenin's graphic phrase. They returned to their villages to get a share of the land, which peasants were simply seizing from landowners in a great agrarian upheaval. Liberty was turning into anarchy in the summer of 1917, offering an unparalleled opportunity for the most radical and most talented of Russia's many socialist leaders, Vladimir Ilyich Lenin (1870–1924).

Petrograd Soviet A counter-government that was a huge, fluctuating mass meeting of two to three thousand workers, soldiers, and socialist intellectuals.

Lenin and the Bolshevik Revolution

Born into the middle class, Lenin became an enemy of imperial Russia when his older brother was executed for plotting to kill the tsar in 1887. As a law student Lenin studied Marxist doctrines with religious ferocity. Exiled to Siberia for three years because of socialist agitation, after his release Lenin lived in western Europe for seventeen years and developed his own revolutionary interpretations of Marxist thought.

Three interrelated ideas were central for Lenin. First, he stressed that only violent revolution could destroy capitalism. Second, Lenin believed that a socialist revolution was possible even in a country like Russia, where capitalism was not fully developed. There the industrial working class was small, but the poor peasants were also potential revolutionaries.

Third, Lenin believed that at a given moment revolution was determined more by human leadership than by vast historical laws. He called for a highly disciplined workers' party, strictly controlled by a dedicated elite of intellectuals and full-time revolutionaries like him.

Lenin's ideas did not go unchallenged by other Russian Marxists. At a Social Democratic Labor Party congress in London in 1903, Lenin demanded a small, disciplined, elitist party; his opponents wanted a more democratic party with mass membership. The Russian Marxists split into two rival factions. Lenin's camp was called Bolsheviks, or "majority group"; his opponents were Mensheviks, or "minority group."

Bolsheviks The majority group; this was Lenin's camp of the Russian party of Marxist socialism.

Key Events of the Russian Revolution

August 1914	Russia enters the war
1916–1917	Tsarist government in crisis
March 1917	March Revolution; establishment of provisional government; tsar abdicates
April 1917	Lenin returns from exile
October 1917	Bolsheviks gain a majority in the Petrograd Soviet
November 7, 1917	Bolsheviks seize power; Lenin named head of new Communist government
March 1918	Treaty of Brest-Litovsk; Trotsky becomes head of the Red Army
1918–1922	Civil war
1922	Civil war ends; Lenin and Bolshevik-Communists take control of Russia

From exile in neutral Switzerland, Lenin saw the war as a product of imperialistic rivalries and an opportunity for socialist revolution. After the March Revolution of 1917, the German government provided safe passage for Lenin across Germany and back into Russia, hoping he would undermine Russia's sagging war effort. They were not disappointed. Arriving in Petrograd on April 3, Lenin attacked at once, rejecting all cooperation with the provisional government. Lenin was a superb tactician, and throughout the summer the Bolsheviks markedly increased their popular support, while Prime Minister Kerensky's support for the war lost him all credit with the army, the only force that might have saved him and democratic government in Russia.

In October the Bolsheviks gained a fragile majority in the Petrograd Soviet. It was Lenin's supporter Leon Trotsky (1879–1940) who brilliantly executed the Bolshevik seizure of power. On November 6–7 militant Trotsky followers joined with trusted Bolshevik soldiers to seize government buildings and arrest provisional government members. At the congress of soviets a Bolshevik majority then declared that all power had passed to the soviets and named Lenin head of the new government.

Dictatorship and Civil War

The Bolsheviks proclaimed their regime a "provisional workers' and peasants' government," promising that a freely elected Constituent Assembly would draw up a new constitution. But after Bolshevik delegates won fewer than one-fourth of the seats in free elections in November, the Constituent Assembly met for only one day, on January 18, 1918. Bolshevik soldiers acting under Lenin's orders then permanently disbanded it.

Lenin acknowledged that Russia had lost the war with Germany and that the only realistic goal was peace at any price. That price was very high. Germany demanded that the Soviet government give up all its western territories, and a third of old Russia's population was surrendered in the Treaty of Brest-Litovsk (BREHST lih-TAWFSK), signed with Germany in March 1918. With peace, Lenin could now pursue his

"You! Have You Volunteered?" A Red Army soldier makes a compelling direct appeal to the ordinary citizen and demands all-out support for the Bolshevik cause in this 1920 poster by Dmitri Moor, a popular Soviet artist. Lenin recognized the importance of visual propaganda in a vast country with limited literacy, and mass-produced posters like this one were everywhere during the civil war of 1918–1922. (Stephen White, University of Glasgow)

766   Chapter 28   World War and
Revolution • 1914–1929

CHAPTER LOCATOR

How did European
conflicts lead to
global war?

- ☐ Ceded after Treaty of Brest-Litovsk, 1918
- ▨ Bolshevik territory, 1919
- ☐ Occupied by Allies, 1919
- → White Army forces
- ── Boundary of U.S.S.R., 1921

The Russian Civil War, 1917–1922

goal of absolute political power for the Bolsheviks—now renamed Communists—within Russia.

The war's end, along with the destruction of the democratically elected Constituent Assembly, revealed Bolshevik rule as dictatorship from the capital. Officers of the old army organized the so-called White opposition to the Bolsheviks in southern Russia, Ukraine, Siberia, and west of Petrograd, and by the summer of 1918 the country was plunged into civil war. The Whites came from many social groups and were united only by their hatred of the Bolsheviks—the Reds. By the end of the year, White armies were on the attack, and by October 1919 appeared poised to triumph. Yet they did not. The Red Army under Trotsky's command captured Vladivostok in October 1922 and that effectively marked the end of the civil war.

Lenin and the Red Army won for several reasons. Strategically, the Bolsheviks controlled the center, while the disunited Whites attacked from the fringes. Moreover, the poorly defined political program of the Whites did not unite all the foes of the Bolsheviks under a progressive democratic banner. Most important, the Communists developed a better army, an army for which the divided Whites were no match.

The Bolsheviks also mobilized the home front. Establishing **war communism**—the application of the total-war concept to a civil conflict—they seized grain from peasants, introduced rationing, nationalized all banks and industry, and required everyone to work. Although these measures contributed to a breakdown of normal economic activity, they also served to maintain labor discipline and to keep the Red Army supplied.

Revolutionary terror also contributed to the Communist victory. The old tsarist secret police was re-established as the Cheka. During the so-called Red Terror of 1918–1920 the Cheka sowed fear, silenced opposition, and killed tens of thousands of "class enemies."

Finally, foreign military intervention in the civil war ended up helping the Communists. After the Soviet government nationalized all foreign-owned factories without compensation and refused to pay foreign debts, Western governments began to support White armies. While these efforts did little to help the Whites' cause, they did permit the Communists to appeal to the patriotic nationalism of ethnic Russians.

war communism The application of the total-war concept to a civil conflict; the Bolsheviks seized grain from peasants, introduced rationing, nationalized all banks and industry, and required everyone to work.

> **Quick Review**
> How did World War I make the Bolsheviks' rise to power possible?

What were the global consequences of the war?

In spring 1918 the Germans launched their last major attack against France. It failed, and Germany was defeated. Austria-Hungary and the Ottoman Empire broke apart and ceased to exist. Then, as civil war spread in Russia and as chaos engulfed much of eastern Europe, the victorious Western Allies came together in Paris to establish a lasting peace.

Laboring intensively, the Allies soon worked out terms for peace with Germany and for the creation of the peacekeeping League of Nations. The 1919 peace settlement, however, turned out to be a failure. Surely this was the ultimate tragedy of the Great War that cost $332 billion and left 10 million people dead and another 20 million wounded.

The End of the War

Victory over revolutionary Russia temporarily boosted German morale, and in the spring of 1918 the German army went on the offensive in France. For a time German armies pushed forward, coming within thirty-five miles of Paris, but they never broke through. They were stopped in July at the second Battle of the Marne, where 140,000 fresh American soldiers saw action. Adding 2 million men in arms to the war effort by August, the massive American intervention decisively tipped the scales in favor of Allied victory.

By September British, French, and American armies were advancing steadily on all fronts. On October 4 the German emperor formed a new, more liberal German government to sue for peace. As negotiations over an armistice dragged on, the frustrated German people rose up. On November 3 sailors in Kiel (keel) mutinied, and throughout northern Germany soldiers and workers established revolutionary councils on the Russian soviet model. Austria-Hungary surrendered to the Allies the same day. With army discipline collapsing, the German emperor abdicated and fled to Holland. Socialist leaders in Berlin proclaimed a German republic on November 9, and they agreed to tough Allied terms of surrender. The armistice went into effect on November 11, 1918.

Military defeat brought political revolution to Austria-Hungary, as it had to Germany, Russia, and the Ottoman Empire (see pages 783–792). The independent states of Austria, Hungary, Czechoslovakia, and a larger Romania were created out of the Austro-Hungarian Empire (Map 28.4). A greatly expanded Serbian monarchy united the Slavs in the western Balkans and took the name Yugoslavia.

The Treaty of Versailles

The peace conference opened in the Versailles Palace near Paris in January 1919 with seventy delegates from twenty-seven nations. There were great expectations. A young British diplomat later wrote that the victors "were journeying to Paris . . . to found a new order in Europe. We were preparing not Peace only, but Eternal Peace."[2]

This idealism was strengthened by President Wilson's January 1918 peace proposal, the Fourteen Points, which stressed national self-determination and the rights of small countries and called for the creation of the **League of Nations**, a permanent international organization designed to protect member states from aggression and avert future wars.

League of Nations A permanent international organization established during the 1919 Paris peace conference to protect member states from aggression and avert future wars.

The real powers at the conference were the United States, Great Britain, and France. Almost immediately the three Allies began to quarrel. President Wilson insisted that the first order of business be the creation of the League of Nations. Wilson had his way, although prime ministers Lloyd George of Great Britain and especially Georges Clemenceau of France were unenthusiastic. They were primarily concerned with punishing Germany.

The "Big Three" were soon in a stalemate over what do to with Germany. Although personally inclined to make a somewhat moderate peace with Germany, Lloyd George felt pressured for a victory worthy of the sacrifices of total war. Clemenceau also wanted revenge and lasting security for France, which, he believed, required the creation of a buffer state between France and Germany, the permanent demilitarization of Germany, and vast German reparations. Wilson, supported by Lloyd George, would hear none of this, and by April the conference was deadlocked on the German question.

In the end, Clemenceau agreed to a compromise. He gave up the French demand for a buffer state in return for a formal defensive alliance with the United States and Great Britain. Thus Clemenceau appeared to win his goal of French security, as Wilson had won his of a permanent international organization.

Map 28.4 Territorial Changes in Europe After World War I

The Great War brought tremendous changes to eastern Europe. Empires were shattered, new nations were established, and a dangerous power vacuum was created by the relatively weak states established between Germany and Soviet Russia.

ANALYZING THE MAP What territory did Germany lose, and to whom? What new independent states were formed from the old Russian empire?

CONNECTIONS How were the principles of national self-determination applied to the redrawing of Europe after the war? Did this theory work out?

The **Treaty of Versailles** was the first step toward re-establishing international order. Germany's colonies were given to France, Britain, and Japan as League of Nations mandates. Germany's territorial losses within Europe were minor: Alsace-Lorraine was returned to France, and parts of Germany were ceded to the new Polish state (see Map 28.4). The treaty limited Germany's army to one hundred thousand men and allowed no new military fortifications in the Rhineland.

Treaty of Versailles The 1919 peace settlement that ended World War I; it declared Germany responsible for the war, limited Germany's army to one hundred thousand men, and forced Germany to pay huge reparations.

More harshly, the Allies declared that Germany (with Austria) was responsible for the war and had therefore to pay reparations equal to all civilian damages caused by the war. The actual reparations figure was not set, however, and there was the clear possibility that it might be set at a reasonable level when tempers had cooled in the future.

The Allies concluded separate peace treaties with the other defeated powers—Austria, Hungary, Bulgaria, and Turkey. For the most part these treaties merely ratified the existing situation in east-central Europe following the breakup of the Austro-Hungarian Empire (see Map 28.4). The Ottoman Empire was broken up, and, controversially, Britain and France extended their power in the Middle East.

Despite strong French objections, Hussein ibn-Ali's son Faisal (1885–1933) attended the Versailles Peace Conference, but his efforts to secure Arab independence came to nothing. Brushing aside Arab opposition, France received Lebanon and Syria. Britain took Iraq and Palestine, which was to include a Jewish national homeland first promised by Britain in 1917 in the Balfour Declaration (see page 786). Officially League of Nations mandates, these Allied acquisitions were one of the most imperialistic elements of the peace settlement. Another was mandating Germany's holdings in China to Japan (see page 795). The mandates system left colonial peoples in the Middle East and Asia bitterly disappointed (see Chapter 29), and demonstrated that the age of Western, and Eastern, imperialism lived on.

American Rejection of the Versailles Treaty

The 1919 peace settlement was not perfect, but for war-shattered Europe it was an acceptable beginning. Germany was punished but not dismembered. A new world organization complemented a traditional defensive alliance of victorious powers. The remaining problems could be worked out in the future.

There were, however, two great interrelated obstacles to the new global order enshrined in the settlement: Germany and the United States. Plagued by Communist uprisings, reactionary plots, and popular disillusionment with losing the war, Germany's moderate socialists and their liberal and Catholic supporters faced an enormous challenge. They needed time (and luck) if they were to establish a peaceful and democratic republic. Progress in this direction required understanding yet firm treatment of Germany by the victorious Western Allies.

In the United States, there was a quick reversion to prewar preferences for isolationism, and the U.S. Senate rejected the treaty. Wilson rejected all attempts at compromise and thereby ensured the treaty would never be ratified by the United States in any form and that the United States would never join the League of Nations. Moreover, the Senate refused to ratify Wilson's defensive alliance with France and Great Britain. America turned its back on Europe. Using U.S. action as an excuse, Great Britain also refused to ratify its defensive alliance with France. Betrayed by its allies, France stood alone, and the great hopes of early 1919 had turned to ashes by year's end.

Quick Review
What global tensions and divisions were reflected in the peace treaties that put a formal end to World War I?

How did leaders seek to re-establish peace and stability?

The Versailles settlement had established a shaky truce, not a solid peace, and the pursuit of real and lasting peace in the first half of the interwar years proved difficult for many reasons. Germany hated the Treaty of Versailles. France was fearful and isolated. Britain

770   Chapter 28   World War and
Revolution • 1914–1929

CHAPTER LOCATOR   How did European
conflicts lead to
global war?

was undependable, and the United States had turned its back on European problems. Eastern Europe was in ferment, and no one could predict the future of Communist Russia. Moreover, the international economic situation was poor and was greatly complicated by war debts and disrupted patterns of trade. Yet for a time, from 1925 to late 1929, it appeared that peace and stability were within reach.

Germany and the Western Powers

Germany held the key to lasting peace, yet all Germans believed that the Treaty of Versailles represented a harsh dictated peace and should be revised or repudiated as soon as possible. Moreover, France and Great Britain disagreed over Germany. By the end of 1919 France wanted to stress the harsh elements in the Treaty of Versailles. Most of the war on the western front had been fought on French soil, and the expected costs of reconstruction, as well as of repaying war debts to the United States, were staggering. Moreover, reparation payments could hold Germany down indefinitely, and France would realize its goal of security.

The British soon felt differently. Prewar Germany had been Great Britain's second-best market, and after the war a healthy, prosperous Germany appeared to be essential to the British economy. The British were also suspicious of France's army — the largest in Europe — and the British and French were also at odds over their League of Nations mandates in the Middle East.

In April 1921 the Allied reparations commission announced that Germany had to pay the enormous sum of 132 billion gold marks ($33 billion) in annual installments of 2.5 billion gold marks. The young German republic — known as the Weimar Republic — made its first payment in 1921. Then in 1922, wracked by rapid inflation and political assassinations and motivated by hostility and arrogance as well, the Weimar Republic announced its inability to pay more and proposed a reparations moratorium for three years.

The British were willing to accept a moratorium, but the French were not. In January 1923 armies of France and its ally Belgium occupied the Ruhr district, industrial Germany's heartland, creating the most serious international crisis of the 1920s.

Strengthened by a wave of patriotism, the German government ordered the people of the Ruhr to stop working and to nonviolently resist the French occupation. The French responded by sealing off not only the Ruhr but also the entire Rhineland from the rest of Germany, letting in only enough food to prevent starvation.

French Occupation of the Ruhr, 1923–1925

By the summer of 1923 France and Germany were engaged in a great test of wills. French armies could not collect reparations from striking workers at gunpoint. But French occupation was paralyzing Germany and its economy. The German government began to print money to pay its bills. Prices soared, and German money rapidly lost all value. Many retired and middle-class people saw their savings wiped out. Many Germans felt betrayed. They hated and blamed the Western governments, their own government, big business, the Jews, the workers, and the Communists for their misfortune. The crisis left them psychologically prepared to follow radical right-wing leaders including Adolf Hitler and the new Nazi Party.

In August 1923, as the mark fell and political unrest grew throughout Germany, Gustav Stresemann (1878–1929) became German chancellor. Stresemann adopted a compromising attitude. He called off the peaceful resistance campaign in the Ruhr and in October agreed in

What made World War I a "total war"?

How did war lead to revolution in Russia?

What were the global consequences of the war?

How did leaders seek to re-establish peace and stability?

How were postwar anxieties reflected in art and science?

771

principle to pay reparations, but he asked for a re-examination of Germany's ability to pay. The French accepted. Thus, after five years of hostility and tension, Germany and France, with the help of the British and the Americans, decided to try compromise and cooperation.

Hope in Foreign Affairs

Dawes Plan The product of the reparations commission, accepted by Germany, France, and Britain, that reduced Germany's yearly reparations, made payment dependent on German economic prosperity, and granted Germany large loans from the United States to promote recovery.

In 1924 an international committee of financial experts met to re-examine reparations. The resulting **Dawes Plan** (1924) was accepted by France, Germany, and Britain. Germany's yearly reparations were reduced and linked to the level of German economic prosperity. Germany would also receive large loans from the United States to promote German recovery. In short, Germany would get private loans from the United States and pay reparations to France and Britain, thus enabling those countries to repay the large sums they owed the United States.

This circular flow of international payments was complicated and risky, but it worked for a while. Germany's economy recovered, and U.S. loans allowed it to meet its reparations payments in 1927 and 1928, enabling France and Britain to pay the United States. Thus, the Americans belatedly played a part in the general economic settlement that facilitated the worldwide recovery of the late 1920s.

This economic settlement was matched by a political settlement. In 1925 European leaders met in Locarno, Switzerland. The European powers agreed to settle existing border disputes peacefully and entered into a number of defensive treaties. For years a "spirit of Locarno" gave Europeans a sense of growing security and stability in international affairs.

Other developments also strengthened hopes for international peace. In 1926 Germany joined the League of Nations, and in 1928 fifteen countries signed the Kellogg-Briand Pact, renouncing "war as an instrument of national policy." The pact fostered the cautious optimism of the late 1920s and also encouraged the hope that the United States would accept its international responsibilities.

Hope in Democratic Government

Mein Kampf Adolf Hitler's autobiography, published in 1925, which also contains Hitler's political ideology.

European domestic politics also offered reason to hope. During the Ruhr occupation and the great inflation, Germany's republican government appeared ready to collapse. In 1923 Communists momentarily entered provincial governments, and in November Adolf Hitler proclaimed a "national socialist revolution" in a Munich beer hall. Hitler's plot to seize government control was poorly organized and easily crushed. Hitler was sentenced to prison, where he outlined his theories and program in his book *Mein Kampf* (My Struggle, 1925). Throughout the 1920s, Hitler's National Socialist Party attracted little support.

Throughout the 1920s elections were held regularly, and as the economy boomed, republican democracy appeared to have growing support among a majority of Germans. There were, however, sharp political divisions in the country. Many unrepentant nationalists and monarchists populated the right and the army. Members of Germany's Communist Party received directions from Moscow. The working classes were divided politically, but a majority supported the socialist, but nonrevolutionary Social Democrats.

The situation in France was similar to that in Germany. Communists and socialists battled for the workers' support. After 1924 the democratically elected government rested mainly in the hands of moderate coalitions, and business interests were well represented. France's great accomplishment was rapid rebuilding of its war-torn northern region, and good times prevailed until 1930.

Britain, too, faced challenges after 1920. The wartime trend toward greater social equality continued, however, helping maintain social harmony. The great problem was unemployment, which hovered around 12 percent throughout the 1920s. However, social welfare measures such as unemployment benefits kept living standards from seriously declining, defused class tensions, and pointed the way to the welfare state Britain established after World War II.

Relative social harmony was accompanied by the rise of the Labour Party. Committed to moderate, "revisionist" socialism (see page 662), the Labour Party moved toward socialism gradually and democratically, so that the middle classes were not overly frightened as the working classes won new benefits.

The British Conservatives showed the same compromising spirit on social issues, and Britain experienced only limited social unrest in the 1920s and 1930s. In 1922 Britain granted southern, Catholic Ireland full autonomy, thereby removing another source of prewar friction. Thus developments in both international relations and domestic politics gave the leading democracies cause for cautious optimism in the late 1920s.

Quick Review
What made the 1920s a period of hope and optimism for many Western leaders?

How were postwar anxieties reflected in art and science?

When Allied diplomats met in Paris in early 1919 with their optimistic plans, most people looked forward to a return to prewar peace, prosperity, and progress. These hopes were in vain. The First World War and the Russian Revolution had mangled too many things beyond repair. Great numbers of men and women felt themselves increasingly adrift in an age of anxiety and continual crisis.

Uncertainty in Philosophy and Religion

Before 1914 most people in the West still believed in Enlightenment philosophies of progress, reason, and individual rights. Just as there were laws of science, many thinkers felt, there were laws of society that rational human beings could discover and wisely act on.

There were, however, dissenting voices. The German philosopher Friedrich Nietzsche (NEE-chuh; 1844–1900) believed that reason, democracy, progress, and respectability were outworn social and psychological constructs that suffocated self-realization and excellence. Little read during his lifetime, Nietzsche attracted growing attention in the early twentieth century.

The First World War accelerated the revolt against established certainties in philosophy. Logical positivism, often associated with Austrian philosopher Ludwig Wittgenstein (VIT-guhn-shtighn; 1889–1951), rejected most concerns of traditional philosophy—from God's existence to the meaning of happiness—and argued that life must be based on facts and observation. Others looked to existentialism for answers. Highly diverse and even contradictory, existential thinkers were loosely united in a search for moral values in a world of anxiety and uncertainty. They did not believe that a supreme being had established humanity's fundamental nature and had given life its meaning. In the words of the famous French existentialist Jean-Paul Sartre (ZHAWN-pawl SAHR-truh; 1905–1980), human beings simply exist.

The loss of faith in human reason and in continual progress led to a renewed interest in Christianity. After World War I several thinkers and theologians began to revitalize Christian fundamentals. Sometimes described as Christian existentialists, they stressed human beings' sinful nature, the need for faith, and the mystery of God's forgiveness.

existentialism The name given to a highly diverse and even contradictory philosophy that stresses the meaninglessness of existence and the search for moral values in a world of terror and uncertainty.

The New Physics

By the late nineteenth century, science was one of the main pillars supporting Western society's optimistic and rationalistic worldview. Unchanging natural laws seemed to determine physical processes and permit useful solutions to more and more problems. All this was comforting, especially to people no longer committed to traditional religious beliefs. And all this was challenged by the new physics.

An important first step toward the new physics was the discovery at the end of the nineteenth century that atoms were not stable and unbreakable. Polish-born physicist Marie Curie (1867–1934) and her French husband Pierre (1859–1906) discovered that radium constantly emits subatomic particles and thus does not have a constant atomic weight. Building on this, German physicist Max Planck (1858–1947) showed in 1900 that subatomic energy is emitted in uneven little spurts and not in a steady stream, as previously believed.

In 1905 the German-Jewish genius Albert Einstein (1879–1955) further undermined Newtonian physics. His theory of special relativity postulated that time and space are relative to the observer's viewpoint and that only the speed of light is constant for all frames of reference in the universe. In addition, Einstein's theory stated that matter and energy are interchangeable and that even a particle of matter contains enormous levels of potential energy.

Breakthrough followed breakthrough. In 1919 Ernest Rutherford (1871–1937) first split the atom. By 1944 seven subatomic particles had been identified. The implications of the new theories and discoveries were disturbing to millions of people in the 1920s and 1930s. The new universe was strange and troubling, and, moreover, science appeared distant from human experience and human problems.

Freudian Psychology

With physics presenting an uncertain universe so unrelated to ordinary human experience, questions about the power and potential of the human mind assumed special significance. The findings and speculations of psychologist Sigmund Freud (1856–1939) were particularly disturbing.

Before Freud, most psychologists assumed that human behavior was the result of rational thinking by the conscious mind. In sharp contrast, Freud concluded that human behavior was governed by three parts of the self: the **id**, **ego**, and **superego**. The irrational unconscious, which he called the id, was driven by sexual, aggressive, and pleasure-seeking desires and was locked in constant battle with the mind's two other parts: the rationalizing conscious—the ego—which mediates what a person can do, and ingrained moral values—the superego—which specify what a person should do. Thus, for Freud human behavior was a product of a fragile compromise between instinctual drives and the controls of rational thinking and moral values.

id, ego, superego Freudian terms for the primitive, irrational unconscious (id), the rationalizing conscious that mediates what a person can do (ego), and the ingrained moral values, which specify what a person should do (superego).

Twentieth-Century Literature

Western literature was also influenced by the general intellectual climate of pessimism, relativism, and alienation. Nineteenth-century novelists had typically written as all-knowing narrators, describing realistic characters in an understandable, if sometimes harsh, society. In the twentieth century many writers adopted the limited, often confused viewpoint of a single individual. Like Freud, these novelists focused on the complexity and irrationality of the human mind.

Some novelists used the stream-of-consciousness technique with its reliance on internal monologues to explore the psyche. The most famous stream-of-consciousness novel is

Ulysses, published by Irish novelist James Joyce (1882–1941) in 1922. Abandoning conventional grammar and blending foreign words, puns, bits of knowledge, and scraps of memory together in bewildering confusion, the language of *Ulysses* was intended to mirror modern life itself.

Creative writers rejected the idea of progress; some even described "anti-utopias," nightmare visions of things to come. In 1918 Oswald Spengler (1880–1936) published *The Decline of the West*, in which he argues that Western civilization was in its old age and would soon be conquered by East Asia. Likewise, T. S. Eliot (1888–1965) depicts a world of growing desolation in his poem *The Waste Land* (1922). Franz Kafka's (1883–1924) novels *The Trial* (1925) and *The Castle* (1926) portray helpless individuals crushed by inexplicably hostile forces.

Modern Architecture, Art, and Music

Like scientists and intellectuals, creative artists rejected old forms and old values after the war. Modernism in architecture, art, and music meant constant experimentation and a search for new kinds of expression.

The United States, with its rapid urban growth and lack of rigid building traditions, pioneered in the new architecture. In the 1890s the Chicago School of architects built skyscrapers and office buildings lacking almost any exterior ornamentation. The buildings of

modernism A variety of cultural movements at the end of the nineteenth century and beginning of the twentieth that rebelled against traditional forms and conventions of the past.

Picasso, *Les Demoiselles d'Avignon* Originating in memories of a brothel scene in Barcelona, this is one of the twentieth century's more influential paintings. Picasso abandoned unified perspective and depicted instead fragmented figures and distorted forms in his search for the magical violence of a pictorial breakthrough. The three faces on either side were inspired by African masks. (Digital image © The Museum of Modern Art/Licensed by Scala/Art Resource, NY/© 2011 Estate of Pablo Picasso/Artists Rights Society [ARS], New York)

Frank Lloyd Wright (1867–1959) were renowned for their creative use of wide varieties of materials, and their appearance of being part of the landscape.

In Europe architectural leadership centered in German-speaking countries. In 1919 Walter Gropius (1883–1969) founded the Bauhaus. Throughout the 1920s the Bauhaus, with its stress on functionalism and good design for everyday life, attracted enthusiastic students from all over the world.

functionalism The principle that buildings, like industrial products, should serve the purpose for which they were made as well as possible.

After 1905 art increasingly took on a nonrepresentational, abstract character. Though individualistic in their styles, "postimpressionists" and "expressionists" were united in their desire to depict unseen inner worlds of emotion and imagination. Artists such as the Dutch expressionist Vincent van Gogh (1853–1890) painted the moving vision of the mind's eye. Paul Gauguin (1848–1903), a French expressionist, moved to the South Pacific, where he found inspiration in Polynesian forms, colors, and legends.

In 1907 in Paris the famous Spanish painter Pablo Picasso (1881–1973), along with other artists, established cubism—an artistic approach concentrated on a complex geometry of zigzagging lines and sharply angled overlapping planes. In Picasso's *Les Demoiselles d'Avignon* (1907), the figures resemble large wooden African masks, presenting a radical new view of reality with a strikingly non-Western depiction of the human form. The influence of Polynesian art on Gauguin and of carved African masks on Picasso reflected the growing importance of non-Western artistic traditions in European art.

About 1910 came the ultimate stage in the development of abstract, nonrepresentational art. Artists such as the Russian-born Wassily Kandinsky (1866–1944) turned away from nature completely, producing purely abstract works. Radicalization accelerated after World War I with Dadaism and surrealism. Dadaism attacked all accepted standards of art and behavior. After 1924 many Dadaists were attracted to surrealism. Surrealists, such as Salvador Dalí (1904–1989), painted fantastic worlds of wild dreams and complex symbols.

Developments in modern music were strikingly parallel to those in painting. Composers, too, were attracted by the emotional intensity of expressionism. The dissonant rhythms and the dancers' representation of lovemaking in the ballet *The Rite of Spring* by composer Igor Stravinsky (1882–1971) practically caused a riot when first performed in Paris in 1913. Likewise, modernism in opera and ballet flourished. Led by Viennese composer Arnold Schönberg (SHUHN-buhrg; 1874–1951), some composers turned their backs on long-established musical conventions. As abstract painters arranged lines and color but did not draw identifiable objects, so modern composers arranged sounds without creating recognizable harmonies.

Movies and Radio

Cinema and radio became major industries after World War I, and standardized commercial entertainment began to replace the traditional arts and amusements of people in villages and small towns. During the First World War the United States became the dominant force in the rapidly expanding silent-film industry. Whether foreign or domestic, motion pictures became the main entertainment of the masses worldwide until after the Second World War.

Motion pictures also became powerful tools of indoctrination, especially in countries with dictatorial regimes. Lenin encouraged the development of Soviet film making, and beginning in the mid-1920s a series of epic films dramatized the Communist view of Russian history. In Germany Hitler turned to a talented woman film maker, Leni Riefenstahl (1902–2003), for a masterpiece of documentary propaganda, *The Triumph of the Will*, based on the 1934 Nazi Party rally at Nuremberg.

Radio also dominated popular culture after the war. In the 1920s, every major country established national broadcasting networks. In the United States these were privately owned and financed by advertising, as was LOR Radio Argentina, which became the first formal radio station in the world when it made its first broadcast in August 1920. In Europe, China, Japan, India, and elsewhere the typical pattern was direct government control. By the late 1930s more than three-fourths of the households in both democratic Great Britain and dictatorial Germany had at least one cheap, mass-produced radio.

Like the movies, radio was well suited for political propaganda. Dictators such as Mussolini and Hitler controlled the airwaves and could reach enormous national audiences with their speeches. In democratic countries politicians such as President Franklin Roosevelt and Prime Minister Stanley Baldwin effectively used informal "fireside chats" to bolster support.

Quick Review
How did breakthroughs in science help shape postwar thought and culture?

Connections

THE GREAT WAR has continued to influence global politics and societies more than ninety years after the guns went silent in November 1918. Anyone seeking to understand the origins of many modern world conflicts must begin by studying World War I.

The war's most obvious consequences were felt in Europe, where three empires collapsed and new states were created out of the ruins. Old European antagonisms and mistrust made the negotiation of fair and just treaties ending the war impossible, despite the best efforts of an outsider, American President Wilson, to make this a war to end all wars. In Chapter 30 we will see how the conflict contributed to a worldwide depression, the rise of totalitarian dictatorships, and a Second World War more global and destructive than the first. In the Middle East the five-hundred-year-old Ottoman Empire came to an end, allowing France and England to carve out mandated territories—including modern Iraq, Palestine/Israel, and Lebanon—that remain flashpoints for violence and political instability in the twenty-first century. Nationalism, the nineteenth-century European ideology of change, took root in Asia, partly driven by Wilson's promise of self-determination. In Chapter 29 the efforts of various nationalist leaders—Atatürk in Turkey, Gandhi in India, Mao Zedong in China, Ho Chi Minh in Vietnam, and others—to throw off colonial domination will be examined. Included there also will be a discussion of how the rise of ultranationalism in Japan led it into World War II and ultimate defeat.

America's entry into the Great War placed it on the world stage, a place it has not relinquished as a superpower in the twentieth and twenty-first centuries. Russia too eventually became a superpower, but this outcome was not so clear in 1919 as its leaders fought for survival in a vicious civil war. By the outbreak of World War II Joseph Stalin had solidified Communist power, and the Soviet Union and the United States would play leading roles in the defeat of totalitarianism in Germany and Japan. But at war's end, as explained in Chapter 31, the two superpowers found themselves opponents in a Cold War that lasted for much of the rest of the twentieth century.

- **For a list of suggested readings for this chapter, visit** *bedfordstmartins.com/mckayworldunderstanding*.

- **For primary sources from this period, see** *Sources of World Societies*, Second Edition.

- **For Web sites, images, and documents related to topics in this chapter, see Make History at** *bedfordstmartins.com/mckayworldunderstanding*.

Chapter 28 Study Guide

To do these exercises online, go to bedfordstmartins.com/mckayworldunderstanding.

Step 1

GETTING STARTED

Below are basic terms about this period in global history. Can you identify each term below and explain why it matters?

TERMS	WHO (OR WHAT) AND WHEN	WHY IT MATTERS
Triple Entente, p. 753		
trench warfare, p. 755		
total war, p. 759		
March Revolution, p. 764		
Petrograd Soviet, p. 765		
Bolsheviks, p. 765		
war communism, p. 767		
League of Nations, p. 768		
Treaty of Versailles, p. 769		
Dawes Plan, p. 772		
Mein Kampf, p. 772		
existentialism, p. 773		
id, ego, superego, p. 774		
modernism, p. 775		
functionalism, p. 776		

Step 2

MOVING BEYOND THE BASICS

The exercise below requires a more advanced understanding of the chapter material. Examine the nature and consequences of total war by filling in the chart below with descriptions of the military, political, social, and economic impact of total war. When you are finished, consider the following questions: In what ways was total war a conflict between nations, as opposed to armies? In your opinion, was the destruction of World War I truly unprecedented? How did it compare, for example, to the human and material costs of the Thirty Years' War or the Napoleonic wars?

	MILITARY	POLITICAL	SOCIAL	ECONOMIC
Impact of Total War				

PUTTING IT ALL TOGETHER

Now that you've reviewed key elements of the chapter, take a step back and try to see the big picture. Remember to use specific examples from the chapter in your answers.

WORLD WAR I

- What factors contributed to the division of Europe into two hostile blocs? Why did European leaders fail to resolve the tensions and conflicts that led to this situation?

- How did political leaders channel their nations' resources into the war effort? How did their policies affect European society and government?

THE RUSSIAN REVOLUTION

- How did the war undermine the tsarist regime in Russia? How did the tsar himself contribute to the collapse of his government?

- Compare and contrast the wartime revolutionary movements in Russia and Germany. Why were the radicals able to take power in Russia, but not in Germany?

THE POSTWAR WORLD

- What steps did Western leaders take to repair the political and economic damage of World War I? Why were the new political and economic systems they created so fragile?

- How did the experience of World War I shape Western thought and culture in the 1920s?

LOOKING BACK, LOOKING AHEAD

- Compare and contrast the peace settlements that followed the Napoleonic wars and World War I. Which was more successful? Why?

- Argue for or against the following statement: "The roots of the economic crisis and global conflicts of the 1930s and 1940s can be found in the failures of the 1920s." What evidence can you present to support your position?

In Your Own Words Imagine that you must explain Chapter 28 to someone who hasn't read it. What would be the most important points to include and why?

29

Nationalism in Asia

1914–1939

From Asia's perspective the First World War was largely a European civil war that shattered Western imperialism's united front, underscored the West's moral bankruptcy, and convulsed prewar relationships throughout Asia. Most crucially, the war sped the development of modern nationalism in Asia. Before 1914 modern nationalism had already won converts among Asia's westernized, educated elites. In the 1920s and 1930s it increasingly won the allegiance of the masses. As in nineteenth-century Europe, nationalism in Asia between 1914 and 1939 became a mass movement.

The modern nationalism movement was never monolithic. Between the outbreak of the First and Second World Wars each Asian country developed a distinctive national movement rooted in its own unique culture and history. Each nation's people created their own national reawakening, which renovated thought and culture as well as politics and economics. And as in Europe, nationalist movements gave rise to conflict both within large, multiethnic states and against other independent states in Asia.

The Asian nationalist movement witnessed the emergence of two of the true giants of the twentieth century. Mohandas Gandhi in India and Mao Zedong in China both drew their support from the peasant masses in the two most populous countries in the world. Gandhi successfully used campaigns of peaceful nonviolent resistance to British colonial rule to gain Indian independence. Mao on the other hand used weapons of war to defeat his opponents and established a modern Communist state.

Kasturba Gandhi Wife of Indian leader Mohandas Gandhi, Kasturba (1869–1944) supported Gandhi through decades of struggle for Indian independence. Here she spins cotton, part of Gandhi's campaign for Indians to free themselves from imported British goods. (© Dinodia Photo Library/The Image Works)

Chapter Preview

▶   How did World War I stimulate nationalism in Asia?

▶   What forces shaped nationalism in the Middle East?

▶   What characterized the Indian independence movement?

▶   What nationalist struggles emerged in East and Southeast Asia?

How did World War I stimulate nationalism in Asia?

Every Asian national movement sought genuine freedom from foreign imperialism. The First World War profoundly affected these aspirations by altering relations between Asia and Europe. For four years Asians watched Europeans vilifying and destroying each other. Japan's defeat of imperial Russia in 1905 (see page 648) had shown that an Asian power could beat a European Great Power; now for the first time Asians saw the entire West as divided and vulnerable.

Asian Reaction to the War in Europe

In China and Japan few people particularly cared who won the Great War. In British India and French Indochina enthusiasm was also limited, but the war's impact was unavoidably greater. Total war required the British and the French to draft their colonial subjects into the conflict, uprooting hundreds of thousands of Asians. This too had major consequences. An Indian or Vietnamese soldier who fought in France and came in contact there with democratic and republican ideas was less likely to accept foreign rule when he returned home.

The British and the French had made rash promises to gain the support of colonial peoples during the war. French representatives suggested to Syrian nationalists in 1917 that Syria would have self-government after the war. British leaders promised Europe's Jewish nationalists a homeland in Palestine, while promising Arab nationalists independence from the Ottoman Empire. In India the British were forced in 1917 to announce a new policy of self-governing institutions in order to counteract Indian popular unrest fanned by wartime inflation and heavy taxation. After the war the nationalist genie the colonial

Prince Faisal and His British Allies On board a British warship on route to the Versailles Peace Conference in 1919, Prince Faisal is flanked on his right by British officer T. E. Lawrence—popularly known as Lawrence of Arabia because of his daring campaign against the Turks. Faisal failed to win political independence for the Arabs because the British backed away from the vague pro-Arab promises they had made during the war. (Courtesy, Paul Atterbury)

powers had called on refused to slip meekly back into the bottle.

U.S. President Wilson's war aims had also raised the hopes of peoples under imperial rule. In January 1918 Wilson proposed his Fourteen Points (see page 768), whose key idea was national self-determination for the peoples of Europe and the Ottoman Empire. Wilson also recommended that in all colonial questions "the interests of native populations be given equal weight with the desires of European governments," and he seemed to call for national self-rule. This subversive message had enormous appeal for educated Asians, fueling their hopes of freedom.

The Mandates System

Although fatally weakened, Western imperialism remained very much alive in 1918, partly because President Wilson was no revolutionary. At the Versailles Peace Conference he compromised on colonial questions in order to achieve some of his European goals and the creation of the League of Nations. Also, Allied statesmen and ordinary French and British citizens were unwilling to give up their valuable colonial empires voluntarily. If pressed, Europeans said their administration was preparing colonial subjects for eventual self-rule, but only in the distant future.

The compromise at Versailles between Wilson's vague, moralistic idealism and the European preoccupation with "good administration" was a system of League of Nations mandates over Germany's former colonies and the old Ottoman Empire. Article 22 of the League of Nations Covenant, which was part of the Treaty of Versailles, assigned territories "inhabited by peoples incapable of governing themselves" to various "developed nations." "The well-being and development of such peoples" was declared "a sacred trust of civilization." The Permanent Mandates Commission, whose members came from European countries with colonies, was created to oversee the developed nations' fulfillment of their international responsibility. Thus the League elaborated a new principle—development toward the eventual goal of self-government—but left its implementation to the colonial powers themselves.

The mandates system demonstrated that Europe was determined to maintain its imperial power and influence. Bitterly disappointed patriots throughout Asia saw the mandate system for what it was, nothing more than the extension of the existing colonial system. Yet Asian patriots did not give up. They preached national self-determination and struggled to build mass movements capable of achieving freedom and independence.

In this struggle Asian nationalists were encouraged by Soviet communism. After seizing power in 1917, Lenin declared that the Asian inhabitants of the new Soviet Union were complete equals of the Russians with a right to their own development. (In actuality this equality hardly existed, but the propaganda was effective nonetheless.) The Communists also denounced European and American imperialism and pledged to support revolutionary movements in colonial countries. The example, ideology, and support of Soviet

Chapter Chronology

1916	Sykes-Picot Agreement divides Ottoman Empire; Lucknow Pact forms alliance between Hindus and Muslims in India; New Culture Movement in China begins
1917	Balfour Declaration establishes Jewish homeland in Palestine
1919	Amritsar Massacre in India; May Fourth Movement in China; Treaty of Versailles; Afghanistan achieves independence
1920	King of Syria deposed by French; Gandhi launches campaign of nonviolent resistance against British rule in India
1920s–1930s	Large numbers of European Jews immigrate to Palestine; Hebrew becomes common language
1923	Sun Yatsen allies Nationalist Party with Chinese Communists; Treaty of Lausanne ends war in Turkey; Mustafa Kemal begins to modernize and secularize Turkey
1925	Reza Shah Pahlavi proclaims himself shah of Persia and begins modernization campaign
1927	Jiang Jieshi, leader of Chinese Nationalist Party, purges his Communist allies
1930	Gandhi leads Indians on march to the sea to protest the British salt tax
1931	Japan occupies Manchuria
1932	Iraq gains independence in return for military alliance with Great Britain
1934	Mao Zedong leads Chinese Communists on Long March; Philippines gain self-governing commonwealth status from United States
1937	Japanese militarists launch attack on China; Rape of Nanjing

Permanent Mandates Commission A commission created by the League of Nations to oversee the developed nations' fulfillment of their international responsibility toward their mandates.

communism exerted a powerful influence in the 1920s and 1930s, particularly in China and French Indochina (see page 795).

Nationalism's Appeal

There were at least three reasons for the upsurge of nationalism in Asia. First, nationalism provided the most effective means of organizing anti-imperialist resistance both to direct foreign rule and to indirect Western domination. Second, nationalism called for fundamental changes and challenged old political and social practices and beliefs. As in Russia after the Crimean War, in Turkey after the collapse of the Ottoman Empire, and in Japan after the Meiji Restoration, the nationalist creed after World War I went hand in hand with acceptance of modernization by the educated elites. Modernization promised changes that would enable old societies to compete effectively with the world's leading nations. Educated elites thus used modernization to contest the influence and power of conservative traditionalists. Third, nationalism offered a vision of a free and prosperous future, and provided an ideology to ennoble the sacrifices the struggle would require.

Nationalism also had a dark side. As in Europe, Asian nationalists developed a strong sense of "we" and "they." "They" were often the enemy. European imperialists were just such a "they," and nationalist feeling generated the will to destroy European empires and challenge foreign economic domination. But, as in Europe, Asian nationalism also stimulated bitter conflicts and wars between peoples, in two different ways.

First, nationalism stimulated conflicts between relatively homogeneous peoples in large states, rallying, for example, Chinese against Japanese and vice versa. Second, it often heightened tensions between ethnic or religious groups within states, especially states with diverse populations like British India and the Ottoman Empire. Such states had been formed by authoritarian rulers, very much like the Austro-Hungarian and Russian empires before 1914. When their rigid rule declined or snapped, the different nationalistic peoples might easily quarrel, seeking to divide the existing state or to dominate the enemy "they" within its borders.

Nationalism's appeal in Asia was not confined to territories under direct European rule. The extraordinary growth of international trade after 1850 had drawn millions of Asians into the Western-dominated world economy, disrupting local markets and often creating hostility toward European businessmen. Moreover, Europe and the United States had forced even the most solid Asian states, China and Japan, to accept unequal treaties and humiliating limitations on their sovereignty. Thus the nationalist promise of genuine economic independence and true political equality with the West appealed as powerfully in old but weak states like China as in colonial territories like British India.

Quick Review
How did Western efforts to maintain and expand the colonial system contribute to the growth of Asian nationalism?

What forces shaped nationalism in the Middle East?

The most flagrant attempt to expand Western imperialism occurred in the Middle East (Map 29.1). There the British and the French successfully encouraged an Arab revolt in 1916 and destroyed the Ottoman Empire. Europeans then sought to replace Turks as principal rulers throughout the region, even in Turkey itself. Turkish, Arab, and Persian nationalists, as well as Jewish nationalists arriving from Europe, reacted violently. They struggled to win nationhood, and as the Europeans were forced to make concessions, they sometimes came into sharp conflict with each other, most notably in Palestine.

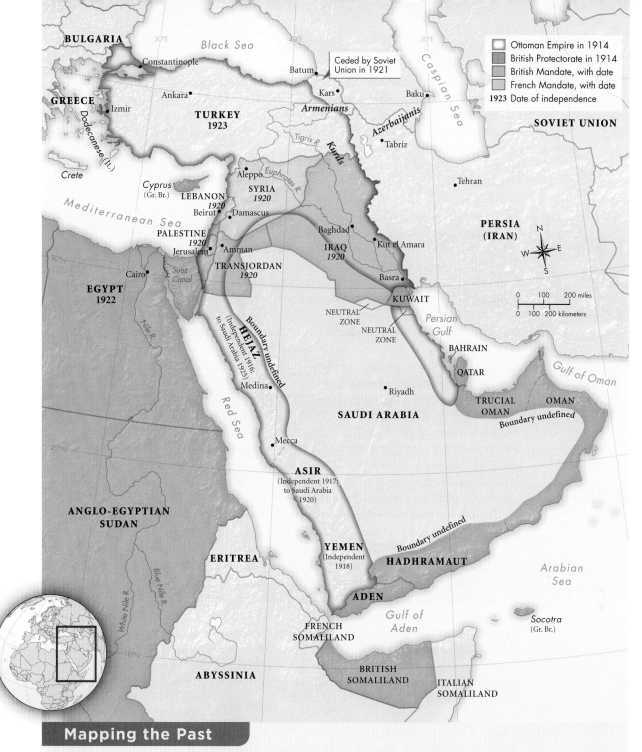

Map showing the partition of the Ottoman Empire, 1914–1923.

Legend:
- Ottoman Empire in 1914
- British Protectorate in 1914
- British Mandate, with date
- French Mandate, with date
- **1923** Date of independence

Labels on map: BULGARIA, Black Sea, Constantinople, Ankara, GREECE, Izmir, Dodecanese (It.), Crete, TURKEY 1923, Batum, *Ceded by Soviet Union in 1921*, Kars, Baku, Armenians, Azerbaijanis, Caspian Sea, SOVIET UNION, Tigris R., Kurds, Tabriz, Mediterranean Sea, Cyprus (Gr. Br.), Aleppo, Euphrates R., SYRIA 1920, LEBANON 1920, Beirut, Damascus, Tehran, PERSIA (IRAN), Baghdad, PALESTINE 1920, Jerusalem, Amman, IRAQ 1920, Kut el Amara, TRANSJORDAN 1920, Basra, Cairo, Suez Canal, EGYPT 1922, KUWAIT, NEUTRAL ZONE, NEUTRAL ZONE, Persian Gulf, BAHRAIN, QATAR, Boundary undefined, HEJAZ (Independent 1916; to Saudi Arabia 1925), Medina, Nile R., Red Sea, Riyadh, TRUCIAL OMAN, OMAN, Boundary undefined, Gulf of Oman, ANGLO-EGYPTIAN SUDAN, SAUDI ARABIA, Mecca, ASIR (Independent 1917; to Saudi Arabia 1920), White Nile R., Blue Nile R., ERITREA, YEMEN (Independent 1918), HADHRAMAUT, Boundary undefined, Arabian Sea, ABYSSINIA, ADEN, Gulf of Aden, FRENCH SOMALILAND, BRITISH SOMALILAND, ITALIAN SOMALILAND, Socotra (Gr. Br.)

Mapping the Past

Map 29.1 The Partition of the Ottoman Empire, 1914–1923

By 1914 the Ottoman Turks had been pushed out of the Balkans, and their Arab provinces were on the edge of revolt. That revolt erupted in the First World War and contributed greatly to the Ottomans' defeat. When the Allies then attempted to implement their plans, including independence for the Armenian people, Mustafa Kemal arose to forge in battle the modern Turkish state.

ANALYZING THE MAP What new countries were established as a result of the partition of the Ottoman Empire? Where were mandates established?

CONNECTIONS How might the collapse of the Ottoman Empire in World War I have contributed to the current situation in the Middle East?

The Arab Revolt

Long subject to European pressure, the Ottoman Empire failed to reform and modernize in the late nineteenth century (see pages 682–683). Declining international stature and domestic tyranny led to revolutionary activity among idealistic exiles and young army officers who wanted to seize power and save the Ottoman state. These patriots, the so-called Young Turks, succeeded in the 1908 revolution, and subsequently they were determined to hold together the remnants of the vast multiethnic empire. Defeated in the Balkan War of 1912, and stripped of practically all territory in Europe, the Young Turks redoubled their efforts in Southwest Asia. The most important of their possessions were Syria—consisting of modern-day Lebanon, Syria, Israel, the West Bank, the Gaza Strip, and Jordan—and Iraq.

For centuries the largely Arabic populations of Syria and Iraq had been tied to their Ottoman rulers by their common faith in Islam (though there were Christian Arabs as well). Yet beneath the surface, ethnic and linguistic tensions simmered between Turks and Arabs.

Young Turk actions after 1908 made the embryonic "Arab movement" a reality. The majority of Young Turks promoted a narrow Turkish nationalism. They further centralized the Ottoman Empire and extended the sway of the Turkish language, culture, and race. In 1909 the Turkish government brutally slaughtered thousands of Armenian Christians, a prelude to the wholesale massacre of more than a million Armenians during the First World War. Meanwhile, Arab discontent grew.

During World War I the Turks freely aligned themselves with the Central Powers—Germany and Austria-Hungary. As a result, the Young Turks drew all of the Middle East into what had been up to that point a European war. Arabs opposed to Ottoman rule found themselves allied with the British, who encouraged the alliance with vague promises of an independent Arab kingdom. When such a kingdom failed to emerge after the war, Arab nationalists felt bitterly betrayed by Great Britain and its allies, and this bitterness left a legacy of distrust and hatred toward the West.

Arab bitterness was partly directed at secret wartime treaties between Britain and France to divide and rule the old Ottoman Empire. In the 1916 **Sykes-Picot Agreement**, Britain and France secretly agreed that France would receive modern-day Lebanon, Syria, and much of southern Turkey, and Britain would receive Palestine, Jordan, and Iraq. The Sykes-Picot Agreement contradicted British promises concerning Arab independence after the war, and left Arab nationalists feeling cheated and betrayed.

A related source of Arab bitterness was Britain's wartime commitment to a Jewish homeland in Palestine, embodied in the **Balfour Declaration** of November 1917. Some British Cabinet members believed the Balfour Declaration would appeal to German, Austrian, and American Jews and thus help the British war effort. Others sincerely supported the Zionist vision of a Jewish homeland (see page 792), but they also believed that this homeland would be grateful to Britain and thus help maintain British control of the Suez Canal.

In 1914 Jews made up about 11 percent of the predominantly Arab population in the Ottoman territory that became, under British control, Palestine. The "National Home for the Jewish People" mentioned in the Balfour Declaration implied to the Arabs—and to the Zionist Jews as well—some kind of Jewish state that would be incompatible with majority rule.

After Faisal bin Hussein's failed efforts at Versailles to secure Arab independence (see page 770), Arab nationalists met in Damascus as the General Syrian Congress in 1919 and unsuccessfully called again for political independence. (See "Listening to the Past: Resolution of the General Syrian Congress at Damascus," page 788.) Ignoring Arab opposition, the British mandate in Palestine formally incorporated the Balfour Declaration and its commitment to a Jewish national home. In March 1920 Faisal's followers met again as

Sykes-Picot Agreement The 1916 secret agreement between Britain and France that divided up the Arab lands of Lebanon, Syria, southern Turkey, Palestine, Jordan, and Iraq.

Balfour Declaration A 1917 statement by British foreign secretary Arthur Balfour that supported the idea of a Jewish homeland in Palestine.

the Syrian National Congress and proclaimed Syria independent, with Faisal as king. A similar congress declared Iraq an independent kingdom.

Western reaction to events in Syria and Iraq was swift and decisive. A French army stationed in Lebanon attacked Syria, taking Damascus in July 1920. Faisal fled, and the French took over. Meanwhile, the British put down an uprising in Iraq and established effective control there. Western imperialism appeared to have replaced Turkish rule in the Middle East (see Map 29.1).

The Turkish Revolution

At the end of the First World War, on November 12 and 13, 1918, French and then British troops entered Constantinople to begin a five-year occupation of the Ottoman capital. A treaty forced on the helpless sultan dismembered Turkey and reduced it to a puppet state. Great Britain and France occupied parts of Turkey, and Italy and Greece claimed shares as well. In 1919 Greek armies carried by British ships landed on the Turkish coast at Smyrna, met little resistance from the exhausted Turkish troops, and advanced into the interior. Turkey seemed finished.

But Turkey produced a great leader and revived to become an inspiration to the entire Middle East. Mustafa Kemal (1881–1938), considered the father of modern Turkey, was a military man sympathetic to the Young Turk movement. After the armistice, Kemal watched with anguish the Allies' aggression and the sultan's cowardice. In early 1919 he began working to unify Turkish resistance.

The sultan, bowing to Allied pressure, initially denounced Kemal, but the cause of national liberation proved more powerful. Refusing to acknowledge the Allied dismemberment of their country, the Turks battled on through 1920 despite staggering defeats. The next year the Greeks advanced almost to Ankara, the nationalist stronghold in central Turkey. There Mustafa Kemal's forces took the offensive and won a great victory. The Greeks and their British allies sued for peace. The resulting Treaty of Lausanne (1923) abolished the hated capitulations, which since the sixteenth century had given Europeans special privileges in the Ottoman Empire (see page 535) and recognized a truly independent Turkey. Turkey lost only its former Arab provinces (see Map 29.1).

Mustafa Kemal, nicknamed Atatürk, believed Turkey should modernize and secularize along Western lines. His first moves were political. Drawing on his prestige as a war hero, Kemal called on the National Assembly to depose the sultan and establish a republic. He had himself elected president and moved the capital from Constantinople (now Istanbul) to Ankara in the Turkish heartland. Kemal savagely crushed the demands for independence of ethnic minorities like the Armenians and the Kurds, but he realistically

Treaty of Lausanne The 1923 treaty that ended the Turkish war and recognized the territorial integrity of a truly independent Turkey.

Mustafa Kemal Surnamed Atatürk, meaning "father of the Turks," Mustafa Kemal and his supporters imposed revolutionary changes aimed at modernizing and westernizing Turkish society and the new Turkish government. Dancing here with his adopted daughter at her high-society wedding, Atatürk often appeared in public in elegant European dress — a vivid symbol for the Turkish people of his radical break with traditional Islamic teaching and custom. (Hulton Archive/Getty Images)

Resolution of the General Syrian Congress at Damascus

Great Britain and France had agreed to divide up the Arab lands, and the British also had made conflicting promises to Arab and Jewish nationalists. However, President Wilson insisted at Versailles that the right of self-determination should be applied to the conquered Ottoman territories, and he sent an American commission of inquiry to Syria, even though the British and French refused to participate. The commission canvassed political views throughout greater Syria, and its long report with many documents reflected public opinion in the region in 1919.

To present their view to the Americans, Arab nationalists from present-day Syria, Lebanon, Israel, the West Bank, the Gaza Strip, and Jordan came together in Damascus as the General Syrian Congress, and they passed the following resolution on July 2, 1919. In addition to the Arab call for political independence, the delegates addressed the possibility of French rule under a League of Nations mandate and the establishment of a Jewish national home.

❝ We the undersigned members of the General Syrian Congress, meeting in Damascus on Wednesday, July 2nd, 1919, . . . provided with credentials and authorizations by the inhabitants of our various districts, Moslems, Christians, and Jews, have agreed upon the following statement of the desires of the people of the country who have elected us to present them to the American Section of the International Commission; the fifth article was passed by a very large majority; all the other articles were accepted unanimously.

1. We ask absolutely complete political independence for Syria within these boundaries. [Describes the area including the present-day states of Syria, Lebanon, Israel, the West Bank, the Gaza Strip, and Jordan.]

2. We ask that the Government of this Syrian country should be a democratic civil constitutional Monarchy on broad decentralization principles, safeguarding the rights of minorities, and that the King be the Emir Faisal, who carried on a glorious struggle in the cause of our liberation and merited our full confidence and entire reliance.

3. Considering the fact that the Arabs inhabiting the Syrian area are not naturally less gifted than other more advanced races and that they are by no means less developed than the Bulgarians, Serbians, Greeks, and Roumanians at the beginning of their independence, we protest against Article 22 of the Covenant of the League of Nations, placing us among the nations in their middle stage of development which stand in need of a mandatory power.

4. In the event of the rejection by the Peace Conference of this just protest for certain considerations that we may not understand, we, relying on the declarations of President Wilson that his object in waging war was to put an end to the ambition of conquest and colonization, can only regard the mandate mentioned in the Covenant of the League of Nations as equivalent to the rendering of economical and technical assistance that does not prejudice our complete independence. And desiring that our country should not fall a prey to colonization and believing that the American Nation is farthest from any thought of colonization and has no political ambition in our country, we will seek the technical and economical assistance from the United States of America, provided that such assistance does not exceed 20 years.

5. In the event of America not finding herself in a position to accept our desire for assistance, we will seek this assistance from Great Britain, also provided that such assistance does not infringe the complete independence and unity of our country and that the duration of such assistance does not exceed that mentioned in the previous article.

6. We do not acknowledge any right claimed by the French Government in any part whatever of our Syrian country and refuse that she should assist us or have a hand in our country under any circumstances and in any place.

7. We oppose the pretensions of the Zionists to create a Jewish commonwealth in the southern part of Syria, known as Palestine, and oppose Zionist migration to any part of our country; for we do not acknowledge their title but consider them a grave peril to our people from the national, economical, and political points of view. Our Jewish compatriots shall enjoy our common rights and assume the common responsibilities.

8. We ask that there should be no separation of the southern part of Syria, known as Palestine, nor of

abandoned all thought of winning back lost Arab territories. He then created a one-party system — partly inspired by the Bolshevik example — in order to work his will.

Atatürk's most radical changes pertained to religion and culture. Profoundly influenced by the example of western Europe, Mustafa Kemal set out, like the philosophes of the Enlightenment, to limit religious influence in daily affairs. Like Russia's Peter the Great, he employed dictatorial measures rather than reason to reach his goal. Kemal decreed a revolutionary separation of church and state. Secular law codes inspired by European models

Palestinian Arabs protest against large-scale Jewish migration into Palestine. (Roger-Viollet/Getty Images)

the littoral western zone, which includes Lebanon, from the Syrian country. We desire that the unity of the country should be guaranteed against partition under whatever circumstances.

9. We ask complete independence for emancipated Mesopotamia [today's Iraq] and that there should be no economical barriers between the two countries.

10. The fundamental principles laid down by President Wilson in condemnation of secret treaties impel us to protest most emphatically against any treaty that stipulates the partition of our Syrian country and against any private engagement aiming at the establishment of Zionism in the southern part of Syria; therefore we ask the complete annulment of these conventions and agreements.

The noble principles enunciated by President Wilson strengthen our confidence that our desires emanating from the depths of our hearts, shall be the decisive factor in determining our future; and that President Wilson and the free American people will be our supporters for the realization of our hopes, thereby proving their sincerity and noble sympathy

with the aspiration of the weaker nations in general and our Arab people in particular.

We also have the fullest confidence that the Peace Conference will realize that we would not have risen against the Turks, with whom we had participated in all civil, political, and representative privileges, but for their violation of our national rights, and so will grant us our desires in full in order that our political rights may not be less after the war than they were before, since we have shed so much blood in the cause of our liberty and independence.

We request to be allowed to send a delegation to represent us at the Peace Conference to defend our rights and secure the realization of our aspirations. 🞂🞂

Source: "Resolution of the General Syrian Congress at Damascus, 2 July 1919," from the *King-Crane Commission Report*, in *Foreign Relations of the United States: Paris Peace Conference, 1919*, 12: 780–781.

QUESTIONS FOR ANALYSIS

1. What kind of state did the delegates want?
2. How did the delegates want to modify an unwanted League of Nations mandate to make it less objectionable?
3. Did the delegates view their "Jewish compatriots" and the Zionists in different ways? Why?

replaced religious courts. State schools replaced religious schools and taught such secular subjects as science, mathematics, and social sciences.

Mustafa Kemal also struck down many entrenched patterns of behavior. Women, traditionally secluded and inferior to males in Islamic society, received the right to vote. Civil law on a European model, rather than the Islamic code, now governed marriage. Women could seek divorces, and no man could have more than one wife at a time. Men were forbidden to wear the tall red fez of the Ottoman era; government employees were ordered to wear Western clothing, erasing the visible differences between Muslims and "infidel" Europeans. The old Arabic script was replaced with a new Turkish alphabet based on Roman letters, which facilitated massive government efforts to spread literacy after 1928. Finally, in 1935, family names on the European model were introduced.

By his death in 1938, Atatürk and his supporters had consolidated their revolution. Government-sponsored industrialization was fostering urban growth and new attitudes, encouraging Turks to embrace business and science. Poverty persisted in rural areas, as did some religious discontent among devout Muslims. But like the Japanese after the Meiji Restoration, the Turkish people had rallied around the nationalist banner to repulse European imperialism and were building a modern secular nation-state.

Modernization Efforts in Persia and Afghanistan

In Persia (renamed Iran in 1935), strong-arm efforts to build a unified modern nation ultimately proved less successful than in Turkey. In the late nineteenth century Persia had also been subject to extreme foreign pressure, which stimulated efforts to reform the government as a means of reviving Islamic civilization. In 1906 a nationalistic coalition of merchants, religious leaders, and intellectuals revolted, forcing the despotic shah to grant a constitution and establish a national assembly, the Majlis.

Majlis The national assembly established by the despotic shah of Iran in 1906.

Yet the 1906 Persian revolution was doomed to failure, largely because of European imperialism. Without consulting Iran, Britain and Russia in 1907 divided the country into spheres of influence. Thereafter Russia intervened constantly. It blocked reforms, occupied cities, and completely dominated the country by 1912. When Russian power collapsed in the Bolshevik Revolution, British armies rushed into the power vacuum. By bribing corrupt Persians, Great Britain in 1919 negotiated a treaty allowing the installation of British "advisers" in every government department.

The Majlis refused to ratify the treaty, and the blatant attempt to make Persia a British satellite aroused the national spirit. In 1921 reaction against the British brought to power a military dictator, Reza Shah Pahlavi (1877–1944), who proclaimed himself shah in 1925 and ruled until 1941.

Inspired by Turkey's Mustafa Kemal, Reza Shah had three basic goals: to build a modern nation, to free Persia from foreign domination, and to rule with an iron fist. The challenge was enormous. Persia was a vast, undeveloped country. The rural population was mostly poor and illiterate, and among the Persian majority were sizable ethnic minorities with their own aspirations. Furthermore, Iran's powerful religious leaders hated Western domination but were equally opposed to a more secular, less Islamic society.

To realize his vision, the shah created a modern army, built railroads, and encouraged commerce. He won control over ethnic minorities such as the Kurds in the north and Arab tribesmen on the Iraqi border. He reduced the privileges granted to foreigners and raised taxes on the powerful Anglo-Persian Oil Company. Yet Reza Shah was less successful than Atatürk.

Because the European-educated elite in Persia was smaller than the comparable group in Turkey, the idea of re-creating Persian greatness on the basis of a secularized society attracted relatively few determined supporters. Many powerful religious leaders turned against Reza Shah, and he became increasingly greedy and tyrannical, murdering his enemies and lining his pockets. His support of Hitler's Nazi Germany (discussed in Chapter 30) also exposed Persia's tenuous and fragile independence to the impact of European conflicts.

Afghanistan Under Amanullah Khan

Afghanistan, meanwhile, was nominally independent in the nineteenth century, but the British imposed political restrictions and constantly meddled in the country's affairs. In 1919 the violently anti-British emir Amanullah (1892–1960) declared a holy war on the British government in India and won complete independence for the first time. Amanullah's subsequent modernization efforts were a failure, triggering tribal and religious revolt, civil war, and retreat from reform. Islam remained both religion and law. A powerful but primitive patriotism enabled Afghanistan to win political independence from the West, but not to build a modern society.

Gradual Independence in the Arab States

French and British mandates established at gunpoint forced Arab nationalists to seek independence by gradual means after 1920. Arab nationalists were indirectly aided by Western taxpayers, who wanted cheap—that is, peaceful—empires. As a result, Arabs won considerable control over local affairs in the mandated states, except Palestine, though the mandates remained European satellites in international and economic affairs.

In Iraq, the British chose Faisal bin Hussein, whom the French had deposed in Syria, as king. Faisal gave British advisers broad behind-the-scenes control and accepted British ownership of Iraq's oil fields. Given the severe limitations imposed on him, Faisal (r. 1921–1933) proved to be an able ruler, gaining the support of his people and encouraging moderate reforms. In 1932 he secured Iraqi independence at the price of a restrictive long-term military alliance with Great Britain.

Egypt had been occupied by Great Britain since 1882 (see page 686) and had been a British protectorate since 1914. Following intense nationalist agitation after the Great War, Great Britain in 1922 proclaimed Egypt formally independent but continued to occupy the country militarily and control its politics. In 1936 the British agreed to restrict their troops to their bases in the Suez Canal Zone.

The French compromised less in their handling of their mandated Middle East territories. Following the collapse of the Ottoman Empire after World War I, the French designated Lebanon as one of several ethnic enclaves within a larger area that became part of the French mandate of Syria. They practiced a policy of divide-and-rule and generally played ethnic and religious minorities against each other. In 1926 Lebanon became a separate republic but remained under the control of the French mandate. Arab nationalists in Syria finally won promises of Syrian independence in 1936 in return for a treaty of friendship with France.

In short, the Arab states gradually freed themselves from Western political mandates but not from the Western military threat or from pervasive Western influence. Of great importance, large Arab landowners and urban merchants increased their wealth and political power after 1918, and they often supported the Western hegemony, from which they benefited greatly. Western control of the newly discovered Arab oil fields helped to convince radical nationalists that economic independence and genuine freedom had not yet been achieved.

Arab-Jewish Tensions in Palestine

Relations between the Arabs and the West were complicated by the tense situation in the British mandate of Palestine, and that situation deteriorated in the interwar years. Both Arabs and Jews denounced the British, who tried unsuccessfully to compromise with both sides. Arab nationalist anger, however, was aimed primarily at Jewish settlers. The key issue was Jewish migration from Europe to Palestine.

A small Jewish community had survived in Palestine ever since the dispersal of the Jews in Roman times. But Jewish nationalism, known as Zionism, took shape in Europe in the late nineteenth century under the leadership of Theodor Herzl (see page 662). Herzl believed that only a Jewish state could guarantee Jews dignity and security. The Zionist movement encouraged the world's Jews to settle in Palestine, but until 1921 the great majority of Jewish emigrants preferred the United States.

After 1921 the situation changed radically. An isolationist United States drastically limited immigration from eastern Europe. Moreover, the British began honoring the Balfour Declaration despite Arab protests. Thus Jewish immigration to Palestine from turbulent Europe in the interwar years grew rapidly. In the 1930s German and Polish persecution created a mass of Jewish refugees. By 1939 the Jewish population of Palestine had increased almost fivefold since 1914 and accounted for about 30 percent of all inhabitants.

The British gradually responded to Arab pressure and tried to slow Jewish immigration. This effort satisfied neither Jews nor Arabs, and by 1938 the two communities were engaged in an undeclared civil war. On the eve of the Second World War, the frustrated British proposed an independent Palestine with the number of Jews permanently limited to only about one-third of the total population. Zionists felt themselves in grave danger of losing their dream of an independent Jewish state.

kibbutz A Jewish collective farm on which each member shared equally in the work, rewards, and defense.

Nevertheless, in the face of adversity Jewish settlers from many different countries gradually succeeded in forging a cohesive community in Palestine. Hebrew, for centuries used only in religious worship, was revived as a living language to bind the Jews in Palestine together. Despite slow beginnings, rural development achieved often remarkable results. The key unit of agricultural organization was the **kibbutz** (kih-BOOTS), a collective farm on which each member shared equally in the work, rewards, and defense. An egalitarian socialist ideology also characterized industry, which grew rapidly. By 1939 a new but old nation was emerging in the Middle East.

Quick Review
What kinds of states emerged in the Middle East in the aftermath of the collapse of the Ottoman Empire?

What characterized the Indian independence movement?

The national movement in British India grew out of two interconnected cultures, Hindu and Muslim, that came to see themselves as fundamentally different in rising to challenge British rule. Nowhere has modern nationalism's power both to unify and to divide been more strikingly demonstrated than in India.

British Promises and Repression

Indian nationalism had emerged in the late nineteenth century (see page 699), and when the First World War began, the British feared revolt. Instead, Indians supported the war effort, providing supplies, money, and soldiers. In return, the British opened more good government jobs to Indians and made other minor concessions.

As the war ground on, however, inflation, high taxes, food shortages, and a terrible influenza epidemic created widespread suffering and discontent. The prewar nationalist movement revived stronger than ever, and moderates and radicals in the Indian National Congress Party (see page 699) joined forces. Moreover, in 1916 Hindu leaders in the Congress Party formed an alliance—the **Lucknow Pact**—with India's Muslim League. The Lucknow Pact forged a powerful united front of Hindus and Muslims. It also called for putting India on equal footing with self-governing British dominions like Canada, Australia, and New Zealand.

Lucknow Pact A 1916 alliance between the Hindus leading the Indian National Congress and the Muslim League.

The British response was contradictory. On the one hand, the government announced in August 1917 that British policy in India called for the "gradual development of self-governing institutions and the progressive realization of responsible government." In late 1919 the British established a dual administration: part Indian and elected, part British and authoritarian. Such uncontroversial activities as agriculture and health were transferred from British to Indian officials. More sensitive matters like taxes, police, and the courts remained solely in British hands.

Old-fashioned authoritarian rule seriously undermined the positive impact of this reform. In 1919 the British rammed the repressive Rowlatt Acts through India's Imperial Legislative Council. These acts indefinitely extended wartime "emergency measures" designed to curb unrest and root out "conspiracy." The result was a wave of rioting across India.

Under these tense conditions a crowd of some ten thousand gathered to celebrate a Sikh religious festival in an enclosed square in the Sikh holy city of Amritsar in the northern Punjab province. Unknown to the crowd, the local English commander, General Reginald Dyer, had banned all public meetings that very day. Dyer marched his troops into the square and, without warning, ordered them to fire into the crowd. Official British records of the Amritsar Massacre list 379 killed and 1,137 wounded, but these figures remain hotly contested as being too low. Tensions flared, and India stood on the verge of more violence and repression and, sooner or later, terrorism and guerrilla war. That India took a different path to national liberation was due largely to Mohandas K. Gandhi (1869–1948).

The Roots of Militant Nonviolence

By the time of Gandhi's birth in 1869, the Indian subcontinent was firmly controlled by the British. Part of the country was ruled directly by British officials, answerable to the British Parliament in London. In each of the so-called protected states, the native prince remained the titular ruler, although he was bound to the British by unequal treaties and had to accept the "advice" of the British resident assigned to his court.

Gandhi grew up a well-to-do family in one of the small protected states north of Bombay. After his father's death, Gandhi went to study law in England, where he passed the English bar. Upon returning to India, he decided in 1893 to try a case for some wealthy Indian merchants in the colony of Natal (part of modern South Africa).

In Natal, Gandhi took up the plight of the expatriate Indian community. White plantation owners had been importing thousands of poor Indians as indentured laborers since the 1860s. Some of these Indians, after completing their contracts, remained in Natal as free persons and economic competitors. In response, the Afrikaner (of Dutch descent) and British settlers passed brutally discriminatory laws. Poor Indians had to work on plantations or return to India. Rich Indians, who had previously had the vote in Natal, lost that right in 1896. Gandhi undertook his countrymen's legal defense, and in 1897 a white mob almost lynched the "coolie lawyer."

Meanwhile, Gandhi was searching for a spiritual theory of social action. He studied Hindu and Christian teachings, and gradually developed a weapon for

Gandhi Arrives in Delhi, October 1939 A small frail man, Gandhi possessed enormous courage and determination. His campaign of nonviolent resistance to British rule inspired the Indian masses and mobilized a nation. Here he arrives for talks with the British viceroy after the outbreak of World War II. (Hulton Deutsch Collection/Corbis)

satyagraha Loosely translated as "soul force," which Gandhi believed was the means of striving for truth and social justice through love, suffering, and conversion of the oppressor.

the poor and oppressed that he called satyagraha (suh-TYAH-gruh-huh). Gandhi conceived of satyagraha, loosely translated as "soul force," as a means of striving for truth and social justice through love and a willingness to suffer the blows of the oppressor, while trying to convert the oppressor to your views of what is true. Its tactic was active nonviolent resistance.

As the undisputed leader of South Africa's Indians, Gandhi put his philosophy into action. When South Africa's white government severely restricted Asian immigration and internal freedom of movement, Gandhi organized a nonviolent mass resistance campaign. Thousands of Indian men and women marched in peaceful protest and withstood beatings, arrest, and imprisonment.

In 1914 South Africa's exasperated whites agreed to many of the Indians' demands. They passed a law abolishing discriminatory taxes on Indian traders, recognized the legality of non-Christian marriages, and permitted the continued immigration of free Indians. Satyagraha proved itself a powerful force in Gandhi's hands.

Gandhi's Resistance Campaign in India

In 1915 Gandhi returned to India. His reputation had preceded him: the masses hailed him as a mahatma, or "great soul." In 1920 Gandhi launched a national campaign of nonviolent resistance to British rule. Denouncing British injustice, he urged his countrymen to boycott British goods, jobs, and honors (such as honorary titles like baron, rai, diwān, and khan, and other awards). He told peasants not to pay taxes or buy English goods. Gandhi electrified the Indian people, initiating a revolution in Indian politics.

The nationalist movement had previously touched only the Western-educated elite. Now both the illiterate masses of village India and the educated classes heard Gandhi's call for militant nonviolent resistance. It particularly appealed to the masses of Hindus who were not members of the warrior caste or the so-called military races and who were traditionally passive and nonviolent. The British had regarded ordinary Hindus as cowards. Gandhi told them that they could be courageous and even morally superior. Gandhi made the Indian National Congress into a mass political party, welcoming members from every ethnic group and cooperating closely with the Muslim minority.

In 1922 some Indian resisters turned to violence, murdering twenty-two policemen. Savage riots broke out, and Gandhi abruptly called off his campaign. Arrested for fomenting rebellion, Gandhi told the British judge that he had committed "a Himalayan blunder to believe that India had accepted nonviolence." Released from prison after two years, Gandhi set up a commune, established a national newspaper, and set out to reform Indian society and improve the lot of the poor. For Gandhi moral improvement, social progress, and the national movement went hand in hand. Above all, Gandhi nurtured national identity, self-respect, and the courage to confront colonialism with nonviolence.

The 1920–1922 resistance campaign left the British severely shaken, but the commission formed in 1927 to consider further steps toward self-rule included no Indian members. In the meantime, Gandhi had served two years (1922–1924) of a six-year sentence for sedition, and in his absence the Indian National Congress had splintered into various factions. Indian resentment of British rule was intense and growing throughout the 1920s, and Gandhi spent the years after his release from prison quietly trying to unite the different factions. In 1929 the radical nationalists, led by Jawaharlal Nehru (1889–1964), pushed through the National Congress a resolution calling for virtual independence within a year. The British stiffened in their resolve against Indian independence, and Indian radicals talked of a bloody showdown.

India, ca. 1930

- ◼ Under direct British rule
- ◻ "Protected states" under Indian administration

Into this tense situation Gandhi reasserted his leadership, taking a hard line toward the British, but insisting on nonviolent methods. He organized a massive resistance campaign against the tax on salt, a vital commodity used by every Indian family. From March 12 to April 6, 1930, Gandhi led fifty thousand people in a march to the sea, where he made salt in defiance of the law. Over the next months the British arrested Gandhi and sixty thousand other protesters for making and distributing salt. But the protests continued, and in 1931 the frustrated and unnerved British released Gandhi from jail and sat down to negotiate with him, as an equal, over Indian self-rule. Negotiations resulted in a new constitution, the Government of India Act, in 1935, which greatly strengthened India's parliamentary representative institutions and gave Indians some voice in the administration of British India.

Despite his best efforts, Gandhi failed to heal a widening split between Hindus and Muslims. Indian nationalism, based largely on Hindu symbols and customs, increasingly disturbed the Muslim minority. Tempers mounted, and both sides committed atrocities. By the late 1930s Muslim League leaders were calling for the creation of a Muslim nation in British India. As in Palestine, the rise of conflicting nationalisms based on religion in India would lead to tragedy (see pages 877–882).

> **Quick Review**
> How did Gandhi broaden Indian nationalism beyond its Western-educated middle-class roots?

What nationalist struggles emerged in East and Southeast Asia?

Because of the efforts of the Meiji reformers, nationalism and modernization were well developed in Japan by 1914. Japan competed politically and economically with the world's leading nations, building its own empire and proclaiming its special mission in Asia. China lagged behind initially, but after 1912 the pace of nationalist development there began to quicken. Nationalism also flourished elsewhere in Asia, scoring a major victory in the Philippine Islands.

The Rise of Nationalist China

The 1911 revolution that overthrew the Qing Dynasty (see page 706) opened an era of unprecedented change for Chinese society. The central figure in the revolution was a seasoned and cunning military man, Yuan Shigai (Yüan Shih-k'ai). Called out of retirement to save the dynasty, Yuan (1859–1916) betrayed the Manchu leaders of the Qing Dynasty and convinced the revolutionaries that he could unite the country and prevent foreign intervention. Once elected president of the republic, however, Yuan concentrated on building his own power. In 1913 he dissolved China's parliament and ruled as a dictator. China's first modern revolution had failed.

The extent of the failure became apparent only after Yuan's death in 1916, when the central government in Beijing almost disintegrated. For more than a decade power resided in local military leaders, the so-called warlords. Their wars, taxes, and corruption created terrible suffering.

Foreign imperialism intensified the agony of warlordism. Japan's expansion into Shandong and southern Manchuria during World War I (see page 757) angered many in China (Map 29.2). On May 4, 1919, five thousand students in Beijing exploded against the decision of the Versailles Peace Conference to leave the Shandong Peninsula in Japanese hands. This famous incident launched the May Fourth Movement, which opposed both foreign domination and warlord government.

May Fourth Movement A Chinese nationalist movement against foreign imperialists; it began as a student protest against the decision of the Versailles Peace Conference to leave the Shandong Peninsula in the hands of Japan.

Map 29.2 **The Chinese Communist Movement and the War with Japan, 1927–1938** After urban uprisings ordered by Stalin failed in 1927, Mao Zedong succeeded in forming a self-governing Communist soviet in mountainous southern China. Relentless Nationalist attacks between 1930 and 1934 finally forced the Long March to Yan'an, where the Communists were well positioned for guerrilla war against the Japanese.

The May Fourth Movement, which was both strongly pro-Marxist and passionately anti-imperialist, looked to the October 1917 Bolshevik Revolution in Russia as a model for its own nationalist revolution. In 1923 revolutionary leader Sun Yatsen (1866–1925) decided to ally his Nationalist Party, or Guomindang, with the Communist Third International and the newly formed Chinese Communist Party. Sun, however, was no Communist. In his *Three Principles of the People*, elaborating on the official Nationalist Party ideology — nationalism, democracy, and people's livelihood — nationalism remained of prime importance: "If we do not earnestly espouse nationalism and weld together our four hundred million people into a strong nation, there is a danger of China's being lost and our people being destroyed."[1]

Sun planned to use the Nationalist Party's revolutionary army to crush the warlords and reunite China under a strong central government. When Sun unexpectedly died in 1925,

Jiang Jieshi (traditionally called Chiang Kai-shek; 1887–1975), the young Japanese-educated director of the party's army training school, took his place. In 1926 and 1927 Jiang led Nationalist armies in a successful attack on warlord governments in central and northern China. In 1928 the Nationalists established a new capital at Nanjing (Nanking).

In fact, national unification was only skin-deep. China remained a vast agricultural country plagued by foreign concessions, regional differences, and a lack of modern communications. Moreover, the uneasy alliance between the Nationalist Party and the Chinese Communist Party had turned into a bitter, deadly rivalry. Justifiably fearful of Communist subversion of the Nationalist government, Jiang decided in April 1927 to liquidate his left-wing "allies" in a bloody purge. Chinese Communists went into hiding and vowed revenge.

China's Intellectual Revolution

Nationalism was the most powerful idea in China between 1911 and 1929, but it was only one aspect of a complex intellectual revolution, generally known as the **New Culture Movement**, that hammered at traditional Chinese thought and custom, advocated cultural renaissance, and pushed China into the modern world. The New Culture Movement was founded around 1916 by young Western-oriented intellectuals in Beijing. As modernists, they provocatively advocated new and anti-Confucian virtues: individualism, democratic equality, and the critical scientific method. They also promoted the use of simple, understandable written language as a means to clear thinking and mass education. China, they said, needed a whole new culture, a radically different worldview.

New Culture Movement An intellectual revolution, sometimes called the Chinese Renaissance, that attacked traditional Chinese, particularly Confucian, culture and promoted Western ideas of science, democracy, and individualism, from around 1916 to 1923.

Picturing the Past

The Fate of a Chinese Patriot

On May 30, 1925, Shanghai police opened fire on a group of Chinese demonstrators who were protesting unfair labor practices and wages as well as the foreign imperialist presence in their country. The police killed nine people and wounded many others, touching off nationwide and international protests and attacks on foreign offices and businesses. This political cartoon shows the fate of the Chinese patriots at the hands of warlords and foreign imperialists. (© Library of Congress, LC-USZ62-99451)

ANALYZING THE IMAGE Which figures represent Chinese warlords, foreign imperialists, and Chinese patriots? What does the cartoon suggest about the fate of the Chinese demonstrators?

CONNECTIONS Why might foreign imperialists and Chinese warlords work together to put down the demonstrations?

CHAPTER LOCATOR | How did World War I stimulate nationalism in Asia? | What forces shaped nationalism in the Middle East? | What characterized the Indian independence movement? | **What nationalist struggles emerged in East and Southeast Asia?**

797

Many intellectuals thought the radical worldview China needed was Marxist socialism. Marxist socialism offered the certainty of a single all-encompassing creed. Moreover, though undeniably Western, Marxism provided a means of criticizing Western dominance, thereby salving Chinese pride. Chinese Communists could blame China's pitiful weakness on rapacious foreign capitalistic imperialism. Thus Marxism, as modified by Lenin and applied by the Bolsheviks in the Soviet Union, appeared as a means of catching up with the hated but envied West. For Chinese believers, it promised salvation soon.

Chinese Communists could and did interpret Marxism-Leninism to appeal to the masses — the peasants. Mao Zedong (Mao Tse-tung) in particular quickly recognized the impoverished Chinese peasantry's enormous revolutionary potential. A member of a prosperous, hard-working peasant family, Mao (1893–1976) converted to Marxist socialism in 1918. He began his revolutionary career as an urban labor organizer, but he soon switched his focus to tapping the revolutionary potential of rural China. Mao argued passionately in a 1927 report that "the force of the peasantry is like that of the raging winds and driving rain. . . . No force can stand in its way."[2]

Mao's first experiment in peasant revolt — the Autumn Harvest Uprising of September 1927 — was not successful, but Mao learned quickly. He advocated equal distribution of land and broke up his forces into small guerrilla groups. After 1928 he and his supporters built up a self-governing Communist soviet, centered at Ruijin (Juichin) in southeastern China, and dug in against Nationalist attacks.

China's intellectual revolution also stimulated profound changes in popular culture and family life. After the 1911 revolution Chinese women enjoyed increasingly greater freedom and equality. Foot binding was outlawed and attacked as cruel and uncivilized. Arranged marriages and polygamy declined. Women gradually gained unprecedented educational and economic opportunities. Thus rising nationalism and the intellectual revolution interacted with monumental changes in Chinese family life. (See "Individuals in Society: Ning Lao, a Chinese Working Woman," page 799.)

From Liberalism to Ultranationalism in Japan

The efforts of the Meiji reformers (see page 707) to build a powerful nationalistic state and resist Western imperialism were spectacularly successful. The Japanese, alone among Asia's peoples, had mastered modern industrial technology by 1910 and had fought victorious wars against both China and Russia. The First World War brought more triumphs. In 1915 Japan easily seized Germany's Asian holdings and held on to most of them as League of Nations mandates. The Japanese economy expanded enormously. Profits soared as Japan won new markets that wartime Europe could no longer supply.

In the early 1920s Japan seemed to make further progress on all fronts. In 1922 Japan signed a naval arms limitation treaty with the Western powers and returned some of its control over the Shandong Peninsula to China. These conciliatory moves reduced tensions in East Asia. At home Japan seemed headed toward genuine democracy. The electorate expanded twelvefold between 1918 and 1925 as all males over twenty-five won the vote. Japanese living standards were the highest in Asia. Literacy was universal.

Japan's remarkable rise was accompanied by serious problems. Japan had a rapidly growing population, but scarce natural resources. As early as the 1920s Japan was exporting manufactured goods in order to pay for imports of food and essential raw materials. Deeply enmeshed in world trade, Japan was vulnerable to every boom and bust. These economic realities broadened support for Japan's colonial empire, which was now seen by many as essential for continued economic growth.

Japan's rapid industrial development also created an imbalanced "dualistic" economy. The modern sector consisted of a handful of giant conglomerate firms, the **zaibatsu**, or "financial combines." Zaibatsu firms like Mitsubishi owned banks, mines, steel mills, cotton

zaibatsu Giant conglomerate firms in Japan.

THE VOICE OF THE POOR AND UNEDUCATED IS often muffled in history. Thus *A Daughter of Han*, a rare autobiography of an illiterate working woman as told to an American friend, offers unforgettable insights into the evolution of ordinary Chinese life and family relations.

Ning Lao was born in 1867 to poor parents in the northern city of Penglai on the Shandong Peninsula. Her foot binding was delayed to age nine, "since I loved so much to run and play." When the bandages were finally drawn tight, "my feet hurt so much that for two years I had to crawl on my knees."* Her arranged marriage at age fourteen was a disaster. She found that her husband was a drug addict ("in those days everyone took opium to some extent") who sold everything to pay for his habit. Yet "there was no freedom then for women," and "it was no light thing for a woman to leave her house" and husband. Thus Ning Lao endured her situation until her husband sold their four-year-old daughter to buy opium. Taking her remaining baby daughter, she fled.

Taking off her foot bandages, Ning Lao became a beggar. Her feet began to spread, quite improperly, but she walked without pain. And the beggar's life was "not the hardest one," she thought, for a beggar woman could go where she pleased. To better care for her child, Ning Lao became a servant and a cook in prosperous households. Some of her mistresses were concubines (secondary wives taken by rich men in middle age), and she concluded that concubinage resulted in nothing but quarrels and heartache. Hot-tempered and quick to take offense and leave an employer, the hard-working woman always found a new job quickly. In time she became a peddler of luxury goods to wealthy women confined to their homes.

The two unshakable values that buoyed Ning Lao were a tough, fatalistic acceptance of life — "Only fortune that comes of itself will come. There is no use to seek for it" — and devotion to her family. She eventually returned to her husband, who had mellowed, seldom took opium, and was "good" in those years. "But I did not miss him when he died. I had my newborn son and I was happy. My house was established. . . . Truly all my life I spent thinking of my family." Her lifelong devotion was reciprocated by her son and granddaughter, who cared for her well in her old age.

Ning Lao's remarkable life story encompasses both old and new Chinese attitudes toward family life. Her son moved to the capital city of Beijing, worked in an office, and had only one wife. Her granddaughter, Su Teh, studied in missionary schools and became a college teacher and a determined foe of arranged marriages. She personified the trend toward greater freedom for Chinese women.

Generational differences also highlighted changing political attitudes. When the Japanese invaded China and occupied Beijing in 1937, Ning Lao thought that "perhaps the Mandate of Heaven had passed to the Japanese . . . and we should listen to them as our new masters." Her nationalistic granddaughter disagreed. She urged resistance and the creation of a new China, where the people governed themselves. Leaving to join the guerrillas in 1938, Su Teh gave her savings to her family and promised to continue to help them. One must be good to one's family, she said, but one must also work for the country.

*Ida Pruitt, *A Daughter of Han: The Autobiography of a Chinese Working Woman* (New Haven, Conn.: Yale University Press, 1945), p. 22. Other quotations are from pages 83, 62, 71, 182, 166, 235, and 246.

QUESTIONS FOR ANALYSIS

1. Compare the lives of Ning Lao and her granddaughter. In what ways were they different and similar?
2. In a broader historical perspective, what do you find most significant about Ning Lao's account of her life? Why?

The tough and resilient Ning Lao (right) with Ida Pruitt.
(Reproduced with permission of Eileen Hsu-Belzer)

factories, shipyards, and trading companies, all of them closely interrelated. Zaibatsu firms wielded enormous economic power and dominated the other sector of the economy, an unorganized multitude of peasant farmers and craftsmen. The result was financial oligarchy, corruption of government officials, and a weak middle class.

Behind the façade of party politics, the old and new elites—the emperor, high government officials, big businessmen, and military leaders—were jockeying for the real power. Cohesive leadership, which had played such an important role in Japan's modernization by the Meiji reformers, had ceased to exist. By far the most serious challenge to peaceful progress was fanatical nationalism. As in Europe, ultranationalism first emerged in Japan in the late nineteenth century but did not flower fully until the First World War and the 1930s.

Japan's ultranationalists shared several fundamental beliefs. They were violently anti-Western. They rejected democracy, big business, and Marxist socialism, which they blamed for destroying the older, superior Japanese practices they wanted to restore. Reviving old myths, they stressed the emperor's godlike qualities and the samurai warrior's code of honor and obedience. Despising party politics, they assassinated moderate leaders and plotted armed uprisings to achieve their goals. Above all else, the ultranationalists preached foreign expansion. Like Western imperialists shouldering "the white man's burden," Japanese ultranationalists thought their mission was a noble one. "Asia for the Asians" was their anti-Western rallying cry.

The ultranationalists were noisy and violent in the 1920s, but it took the Great Depression of the 1930s to tip the scales decisively in their favor. The worldwide depression, which had dire consequences for many countries (see Chapter 30), hit Japan like a tidal wave in 1930. Exports and wages collapsed; unemployment and raw suffering soared. The ultranationalists blamed the system, and people listened.

Japan Against China

Among those who listened with particular care were young Japanese army officers in Manchuria, the province of northeastern China controlled by the Japanese army since its victory over Russia in 1905. Many junior Japanese officers in Manchuria came from the peasantry and were distressed by the stories of rural suffering they heard from home. They also knew the Japanese army's budget and prestige had declined in the prosperous 1920s.

The rise of Chinese nationalism worried the young officers most. This new political force, embodied in the Guomindang unification of China, challenged Japanese control over Manchuria. In response, junior Japanese officers in Manchuria, in cooperation with top generals in Tokyo, secretly manufactured an excuse for aggression in late 1931. They blew up some Japanese-owned railroad tracks near the city of Shenyang (Mukden) and then, with reinforcements rushed in from Korea, quickly occupied all of Manchuria in "self-defense."

In 1932 Japan proclaimed Manchuria an independent state and installed a puppet government. When the League of Nations condemned its aggression in Manchuria, Japan resigned in protest. Japanese aggression in Manchuria proved that the army, though reporting directly to the Japanese emperor, was an independent force subject to no outside control.

The Japanese puppet state named Manchukuo in northeast China became the model for the subsequent conquest and occupation of China and then Southeast Asia. Throughout the 1930s the Japanese worked to integrate Manchuria, along with Korea and Taiwan, into a self-sufficient economic bloc, insulated from Western power in East Asia. At home, newspapers and newsreels glorified Japan's efforts and mobilized public support for colonial empire.

For China the Japanese conquest of Manchuria was disastrous. Japanese aggression in Manchuria drew attention away from modernizing efforts. The Nationalist government promoted a massive boycott of Japanese goods but lost interest in social reform. Above all, the Nationalist government after 1931 completely neglected land reform and rural poverty.

Landownership in China was very unequal and rents were high. One study estimated that a mere 4 percent of families, usually absentee landlords living in cities, owned fully half the land. Poor peasants and farm laborers—70 percent of the rural population—owned only one-sixth of the land. As a result, peasants were heavily in debt and chronically underfed. A contemporaneous Chinese economist spelled out the revolutionary implications: "It seems clear that the land problem in China today is as acute as that of eighteenth-century France or nineteenth-century Russia." Mao Zedong agreed.

Having abandoned land reform, the Nationalists under Jiang Jieshi devoted their energies between 1930 and 1934 to great campaigns of encirclement and extermination of the Communists' rural power base in southeastern China. In 1934 they closed in for the kill, but the main Communist army broke out, beat off attacks, and retreated 6,000 miles in twelve months to a remote region on the northwestern border (see Map 29.2). Of the estimated 100,000 men and women who began the Long March, only 8,000 to 10,000 reached the final destination. There Mao built up his forces once again, established a new territorial base, and won local peasant support by undertaking land reform.

In Japan politics became increasingly chaotic. In 1937 the Japanese military and the ultranationalists were in command. Unable to force China to cede more territory in northern China, they used a minor incident near Beijing as a pretext for a general attack. This marked the beginning of what became World War II in Asia. The Nationalist government, which had just formed a united front with the Communists, fought hard, but Japanese troops quickly took Beijing and northern China. Taking the great port of Shanghai after ferocious combat, the Japanese launched an immediate attack up the Yangzi River (see Map 29.2).

Nanjing, the capital, fell to the Japanese in December 1937. Entering the city, Japanese soldiers went berserk and committed dreadful atrocities over seven weeks. They brutally murdered an estimated 200,000 to 300,000 Chinese civilians and unarmed soldiers, and raped 20,000 to 80,000 Chinese women. The "Rape of Nanjing" combined with other

Long March The 6,000-mile retreat of the Chinese Communist army to a remote region on the northwestern border of China, during which tens of thousands lost their lives.

Japanese Atrocities in China In December 1937, after the fall of the Chinese capital Nanjing, Japanese soldiers went on a horrifying rampage. These Japanese recruits are using Chinese prisoners of war as live targets in a murderous bayonet drill. Other Chinese prisoners were buried alive by their Japanese captors. (Hulton Archive/Getty Images)

Japanese atrocities to outrage world opinion. The Western Powers denounced Japanese aggression but, with tensions rising in Europe, took no action.

By late 1938 Japanese armies occupied sizable portions of coastal China (see Map 29.2). But the Nationalists and the Communists had retreated to the interior, and both refused to accept defeat. In 1939, as Europe edged toward another great war, China and Japan were bogged down in a stalemate. This conflict — called by historians the Second Sino-Japanese War (1937–1945) — provided a spectacular example of conflicting nationalisms.

Striving for Independence in Southeast Asia

The tide of nationalism was also rising in Southeast Asia. Like their counterparts in India, China, and Japan, nationalists in French Indochina, the Dutch East Indies, and the Philippines wanted political independence and freedom from foreign rule. In both French Indochina and the Dutch East Indies, they ran up against an imperialist stone wall. The obstacle to Filipino independence came from America and Japan.

The French in Indochina, as in all their colonies, rejected all calls for liberal political reforms. This uncompromising attitude stimulated the growth of an equally stubborn Communist opposition under Ho Chi Minh (1890–1969), which despite ruthless repression emerged as the dominant anti-French force in Indochina.

In the East Indies — modern Indonesia — the Dutch made some concessions after the First World War, establishing a people's council with very limited lawmaking power. But in the 1930s the Dutch cracked down hard, jailing all the important nationalist leaders. Like the French, the Dutch were determined to hold on.

In the Philippines, however, a well-established nationalist movement achieved greater success. The Spanish in the Philippines had been indefatigable missionaries. By the late nineteenth century the Filipino population was 80 percent Catholic. Filipinos shared a common cultural heritage and a common racial origin. Education, especially for girls, was advanced for Southeast Asia. Economic development helped to create a westernized elite, which turned first to reform and then to revolution in the 1890s. As in Egypt and Turkey, long-standing intimate contact with Western civilization created a strong nationalist movement at an early date.

Filipino nationalists were bitterly disillusioned when the United States, having taken the Philippines from Spain in the Spanish-American War of 1898, ruthlessly beat down a patriotic revolt and rejected Filipino independence. As the imperialist power in the Philippines, the United States encouraged education and promoted capitalistic economic development. And as in British India, an elected legislature was given some real powers. In 1919 President Wilson even promised eventual independence, though subsequent Republican administrations saw it as a distant goal.

As in India and French Indochina, demands for independence grew in the 1920s. However, it was the Great Depression that was the turning point in the movement for Filipino independence. As the United States collapsed economically in the 1930s, the Philippines suddenly appeared to be a liability rather than an asset. American farm groups lobbied for protection from cheap Filipino sugar. To protect American jobs, labor unions demanded an end to Filipino immigration. Responding to public pressure, in 1934 Congress made the Philippines a self-governing commonwealth and scheduled independence for 1944.

Like Britain and France in the Middle East, the United States was determined to hold on to its big military bases in the Philippines even as it permitted increased local self-government and promised eventual political independence. Some Filipino nationalists denounced the con-

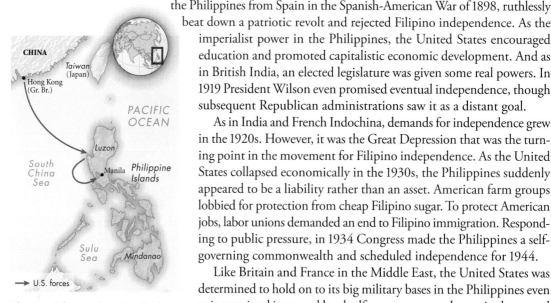

The Spanish-American War in the Philippines, 1898

tinued presence of U.S. fleets and armies. Others were less certain that the American presence was the immediate problem. Japan was fighting in China and expanding economically into the Philippines and throughout Southeast Asia. By 1939 a new threat to Filipino independence would come from Japan itself.

Quick Review
In what ways did nationalism serve as a unifying force in East and Southeast Asia? In what ways was it a divisive force?

Connections

JUST AS NATIONALISM drove politics and state building in Europe in the nineteenth century, so it took root across Asia in the late nineteenth and early twentieth centuries. While nationalism in Europe developed out of a desire to turn cultural unity into political reality and create imagined communities out of millions of strangers, in Asia nationalist sentiments drew their greatest energy from opposition to European imperialism and domination. Asian modernizers, aware of momentous advances in science and technology and of politics and social practices in the West, also pressed the nationalist cause by demanding an end to outdated conservative traditions that they argued only held back the development of modern, independent nations capable of throwing off Western domination and existing as equals with the West.

The nationalist cause in Asia took many forms and produced some of the most remarkable leaders of the twentieth century. In Chapter 32 we will discuss how nationalist leaders across Asia shaped the freedom struggle and the resulting independence according to their own ideological and personal visions. China's Mao Zedong replaced imperialist rule with one-party Communist rule. Gandhi's dream of a unified India collapsed with the partition of British India into Hindu India and Muslim Pakistan and Bangladesh. Egypt assumed a prominent position in the Arab world after World War II under the leadership of Gamal Nasser and, after a series of wars with Israel, began to play a significant role in efforts to find a peaceful resolution to the Israeli-Palestinian conflict. That conflict, however, continues unabated as nationalist and religious sentiments inflame feelings on both sides. Ho Chi Minh eventually forced the French colonizers out of Vietnam, only to face another Western power, the United States, in a long and deadly war. As described in Chapter 32, a unified Vietnam finally gained its independence in 1975, but like China, under one-party Communist control.

Japan remained an exception to much of what happened in the rest of Asia. After a long period of isolation, the Japanese implemented an unprecedented program of modernization and westernization in the late 1800s. Japan continued to model itself after the West when it took control of former German colonies as mandated territories after the Great War and occupied territory in China, Korea, Vietnam, Taiwan, and elsewhere. In the next chapter we will see how ultranationalism drove national policy in the 1930s, ultimately leading to Japan's defeat in World War II.

- **For a list of suggested readings for this chapter, visit** *bedfordstmartins.com/mckayworldunderstanding*.

- **For primary sources from this period, see** *Sources of World Societies*, Second Edition.

- **For Web sites, images, and documents related to topics in this chapter, see Make History at** *bedfordstmartins.com/ mckayworldunderstanding*.

Chapter 29 Study Guide

To do these exercises online, go to bedfordstmartins.com/mckayworldunderstanding.

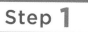

GETTING STARTED

Below are basic terms about this period in global history. Can you identify each term below and explain why it matters?

TERMS	WHO (OR WHAT) AND WHEN	WHY IT MATTERS
Permanent Mandates Commission, p. 783		
Sykes-Picot Agreement, p. 786		
Balfour Declaration, p. 786		
Treaty of Lausanne, p. 787		
Majlis, p. 790		
kibbutz, p. 792		
Lucknow Pact, p. 792		
satyagraha, p. 794		
May Fourth Movement, p. 795		
New Culture Movement, p. 797		
zaibatsu, p. 798		
Long March, p. 801		

MOVING BEYOND THE BASICS

The exercise below requires a more advanced understanding of the chapter material. Compare and contrast nationalist movements in Turkey, India, China, and Japan by filling in the table below with descriptions of four key factors that shaped the development of nationalist movements in each country: political and social context, ideology, movement goals, and internal divisions. When you are finished, consider the following questions: How did Western imperialism shape each movement? What did "reform" mean to the leaders of each movement? How did religion and ideology create divisions within Asian nationalist movements? What about conflicts between modernizers and traditionalists?

	POLITICAL AND SOCIAL CONTEXT	IDEOLOGY	MOVEMENT GOALS	INTERNAL DIVISIONS
Turkey				
India				
China				
Japan				

Chapter Preview

▶ Why did the Great Depression spread around the world?

▶ How did totalitarianism differ from conservative authoritarianism?

▶ What characterized Stalin's rule in the Soviet Union?

▶ How did Italian fascism develop?

▶ What were the goals of Hitler and his Nazi regime?

▶ What led to World War II and how did the Allies prevail?

Why did the Great Depression spread around the world?

Beginning in 1929 an exceptionally long and severe economic depression struck the entire world with ever-greater intensity, and recovery was uneven and slow. Only with the Second World War did the depression disappear in much of the world.

The social and political consequences of prolonged economic collapse were enormous and were felt worldwide. Economic depression was a major factor in Japan's aggressive empire building in the 1930s. Agricultural producers in Latin America, Asia, and Africa also suffered greatly from the collapse in prices, while urban workers faced pay cuts and high unemployment. In West Africa anticolonial nationalism attracted widespread support for the first time in the 1930s, setting the stage for strong independence movements after World War II.

In Europe and the United States the depression shattered the fragile political stability of the mid-1920s. Mass unemployment made insecurity a reality for millions of ordinary people. In desperation, people looked for leaders who would "do something." In countries around the world, they willingly supported radical attempts to deal with the crisis by both democratic leaders and dictators.

The Economic Crisis

Though economic activity was already declining moderately in many countries by early 1929, the U.S. stock market crash in October of that year really started the Great Depression. The American stock market boom of the 1920s was built on borrowed money. When

Louisville Flood Victims, 1937 During the Great Depression, the American river city Louisville, Kentucky, was hit by the worst flood in its history. The famous documentary photographer Margaret Bourke-White captured this striking image of African American flood victims lining up for bread and soup. Not only does the billboard message mock the Depression-era conditions, but the smiling white family appears to be driving its car through the line of people, instantly drawing attention to America's race and class differences. (Margaret Bourke-White/Time & Life Pictures/Getty Images)

the financial bubble burst, countless investors and speculators were wiped out in a matter of days or weeks, and the New York stock market's crash started a domino effect that hit most of the world's major stock exchanges

The financial panic in the United States triggered a worldwide financial crisis. Throughout the 1920s American bankers and investors had lent large sums to many countries, and as panic broke, New York bankers began recalling their short-term loans. Frightened citizens in the affected nations began to withdraw their savings from banks, leading to general financial chaos. The recall of American loans also accelerated the collapse in world prices, as businesses dumped goods in a frantic attempt to get cash to pay what they owed.

The financial chaos led to a general crisis of production. Between 1929 and 1933 world output of goods fell by an estimated 38 percent. As this happened, countries turned inward and tried to go it alone. Country after country followed the example of the United States, which raised protective tariffs to their highest levels ever in 1930 and tried to seal off shrinking national markets for American producers only.

Although opinions differ, two factors probably best explain the relentless slide to the bottom from 1929 to early 1933. First, the international economy lacked leadership able to maintain stability when the crisis came. Neither the seriously weakened British nor the United States — the world's economic leaders — stabilized the international economic system in 1929. Instead, Britain and the United States cut back international lending and erected high tariffs. The second factor was that in almost every country, governments cut their budgets and reduced spending when they should have run large deficits to try to stimulate their economies. After World War II such a "counter-cyclical policy," advocated by the British economist John Maynard Keynes (1883–1946), became a well-established weapon against depression. But in the 1930s economists generally regarded Keynes's prescription with horror.

Chapter Chronology

1921	New Economic Policy in Soviet Union
1922	Mussolini seizes power in Italy
1924–1929	Buildup of Nazi Party in Germany
1927	Stalin comes to power in Soviet Union
1928	Stalin's first five-year plan
1929	Start of collectivization in Soviet Union; Lateran Agreement
1929–1939	Great Depression
1931	Japan invades Manchuria
1932–1933	Famine in Ukraine
1933	Hitler appointed chancellor in Germany; Nazis begin control of state and society
1935	Mussolini invades Ethiopia
1936	Start of great purges under Stalin; Spanish civil war begins
1936–1937	Popular Front government in France
1939	Germany occupies Czech lands and invades Poland; Britain and France declare war on Germany, starting World War II
1940	Japan signs formal alliance with Germany and Italy; Germany defeats France; Battle of Britain
1941	Germany invades Soviet Union; Japan attacks Pearl Harbor; United States enters war
1941–1945	The Holocaust
1944	Allied invasion at Normandy
1945	Atomic bombs dropped on Japan; World War II ends

Mass Unemployment

The need for large-scale government spending was tied to mass unemployment. As the financial crisis led to production cuts, workers lost their jobs and had little money to buy goods. This led to still more production cuts, and unemployment soared.

Mass unemployment created immense social problems. Poverty increased dramatically. Millions of unemployed people lost their spirit, and homes and ways of life were disrupted in millions of personal tragedies. Economic distress had profound social and political implications. As workers from Manchester, England, pointed out in a 1932 appeal to city officials, "Hungry men are angry men."[1] Only strong government action could deal with the social powder keg that was preparing to explode.

Unemployment Rates in 1932
The United States: 33%
Germany: 33%
Australia: 32%
Britain: 22%

The New Deal in the United States

The Great Depression and the response to it marked a major turning point in American history. President Herbert Hoover (r. 1929–1933) and his administration initially reacted to the stock market crash and economic decline with limited action. When the full force of the financial crisis struck Europe in the summer of 1931 and boomeranged back to the United States, banks failed and unemployment soared. In 1932 industrial production fell to about 50 percent of its 1929 level.

In these circumstances Franklin Delano Roosevelt (r. 1933–1945) won a landslide presidential victory in 1932 with promises of a "**New Deal** for the forgotten man." Roosevelt's basic goal was to preserve capitalism by reforming it. Rejecting socialism and government ownership of industry, Roosevelt advocated forceful government intervention in the economy. His commitment to relief programs marked a profound shift from the traditional stress on family support and community responsibility.

Innovative programs promoted agricultural recovery. As in Asia, Africa, and Latin America, American farmers were hard hit by the Great Depression. Roosevelt's decision to leave the gold standard and devalue the dollar was designed to raise American prices and save farmers. The Agricultural Adjustment Act (1933) aimed at raising prices and farm income by limiting production. For a while, these measures worked.

Roosevelt then attacked the key problem of mass unemployment. New agencies were created to undertake a vast range of public works projects so that the federal government could employ directly as many people as financially possible. One-fifth of the entire U.S. labor force worked for one such agency, the Works Progress Administration (WPA), at some point in the 1930s, constructing public buildings, bridges, and highways.

Following the path blazed by Germany's Bismarck in the 1880s (see page 659), the U.S. government in 1935 established a national social security system with old-age pensions and unemployment benefits. The National Labor Relations Act of 1935 declared collective bargaining to be U.S. policy, and union membership more than doubled. In general, between 1935 and 1938 government rulings and social reforms chipped away at the privileges of the wealthy and tried to help ordinary people.

Despite undeniable accomplishments in social reform, the New Deal was only partly successful as a response to the Great Depression. Unemployment was still a staggering 10 million when war broke out in Europe in 1939. The New Deal brought fundamental reform, but it never did pull the United States out of the depression; it took the Second World War to do that.

The European Response to the Depression

The collapse of the American stock market in October 1929 set off a chain of economic downturns that hit Europe, particularly Germany and Great Britain, the hardest. Postwar Europe had come out of the Great War deeply in debt and in desperate need of investment capital to rebuild. The United States became the primary creditor and financier. Germany borrowed, for example, to pay Britain war reparations, and then Britain took that money and paid America back for its war debts and investment loans. When the American economy crashed, the whole system crashed with it.

Of all the Western democracies, the Scandinavian countries under socialist leadership responded most successfully to the challenge of the Great Depression. When the economic crisis struck in 1929, socialist governments in Sweden pioneered the use of large-scale deficits to finance public works projects and thereby maintain production and employment. Scandinavian governments also increased social welfare benefits, such as old-age pensions and subsidized housing. All this spending required a large bureaucracy and high taxes. Yet both private and cooperative enterprise thrived, as did democracy. Some observers saw Scan-

---

New Deal Franklin Delano Roosevelt's plan to reform capitalism through forceful government intervention in the economy.

dinavia's welfare socialism as an appealing middle way between sick capitalism and cruel communism or fascism.

In Britain, the government responded to the crisis by following orthodox economic theory. The budget was balanced, but unemployed workers received barely enough welfare to live. Nevertheless, the economy recovered considerably after 1932. This recovery reflected the gradual reorientation of the British economy. After abandoning the gold standard in 1931 and establishing protective tariffs in 1932, Britain concentrated increasingly on the national, rather than the international, market. Old export industries, such as textiles and coal, continued to decline, but new industries, such as automobiles and electrical appliances, grew. These developments encouraged British isolationism, but often had devastating economic consequences for Britain's far-flung colonies and dominions.

Because France was relatively less industrialized and more isolated from the world economy, the Great Depression came late. But once the depression hit France, it persisted throughout the 1930s. Economic stagnation both reflected and heightened an ongoing political crisis. Moderate republicanism's vital center was sapped from both sides, as both communism and fascism gained adherents.

Frightened by the Fascists' growing strength at home and abroad, French Communist, Socialist, and Radical parties formed an alliance—the **Popular Front**—for the May 1936 national elections. Following its clear victory, the Popular Front launched a far-reaching program of social reform, inspired by Roosevelt's New Deal. Popular with workers and the lower middle class, these measures were quickly sabotaged by rapid inflation and cries of revolution from Fascists and frightened conservatives. Wealthy people sneaked their money out of the country, labor unrest grew, and France entered a severe financial crisis. In June 1937, with the country hopelessly divided, the Popular Front collapsed.

Popular Front A New Deal–inspired party in France that encouraged unions and launched a far-reaching program of social reform.

Worldwide Effects

The Great Depression's magnitude was unprecedented, and its effect rippled well beyond Europe and the United States. As many of the countries and colonies of Africa, Asia, and Latin America were nearly totally dependent on one or two commodities for income, the

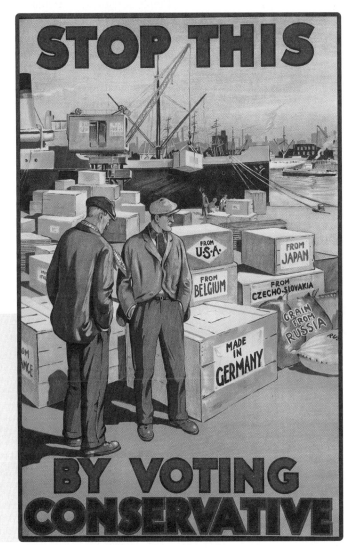

Picturing the Past

British Conservative Party Poster, 1931
This campaign poster from the 1931 British general election portrays crates and bags of goods being unloaded on English docks. (Hulton Archive/Getty Images)

ANALYZING THE IMAGE Where are the goods on the dock from? What do the Conservatives want stopped?

CONNECTIONS Was this attitude toward foreign goods unique to England? What other countries held similar views? What effect did such attitudes have on the worldwide depression?

How did totalitarianism differ from conservative authoritarianism?

What characterized Stalin's rule in the Soviet Union?

How did Italian fascism develop?

What were the goals of Hitler and his Nazi regime?

What led to World War II and how did the Allies prevail?

811

implementation of protectionist trade policies by the leading industrial nations had devastating effects. The colonies and dominions of the British Empire were among the hardest hit by the Great Depression because of their close ties to the economies of Great Britain and the United States.

While Asians were affected by the Great Depression, the consequences varied greatly by country or colony and were not as severe generally as they were elsewhere in the world. That being said, where the depression did hit, it was often severe. The price of rice fell by two-thirds between 1929 and 1932. Also crippling to the region's economies was Asia's heavy dependence on imported raw material for industrial production. With debts to local moneylenders fixed in value and taxes to colonial governments hardly ever reduced, many Asian peasants in the 1930s struggled under crushing debt and suffered severely.

In Japan the terrible suffering caused by the Great Depression caused ultranationalists and militarists to call for less dependence on global markets and the expansion of a self-sufficient empire. Such expansion began in 1931 when Japan invaded Chinese Manchuria, which became a major source of raw materials feeding Japanese industrial growth (see Chapter 29). Japan recovered more quickly from the Great Depression than any other major industrial power because of prompt action by the civilian democratic government, but the government and large corporations continued to be blamed for the economic downturn. This lack of confidence, combined with the collapsing international economic order, Europe's and America's increasingly isolationist and protectionist policies, and a growing admiration for Nazi Germany, led by the mid-1930s to the military's toppling the civilian authorities and dictating Japan's future.

The Great Depression hit the vulnerable commodities economies of Latin America especially hard. Long dependent on foreign markets, prices and exports of Latin American commodities collapsed as Europe and the United States drastically reduced their purchases and raised tariffs to protect domestic products. With their foreign sales plummeting, Latin American countries could not buy the industrial goods they needed from abroad. The global depression provoked a profound shift toward economic nationalism after 1930, as popularly based governments worked to reduce foreign influence and gain control of their own economies and natural resources. These efforts were fairly successful, but they did not bring an end to the depression. As in Hitler's Germany, deteriorating economic conditions in Latin America gave rise to dictatorships, some of them modeled along European Fascist lines (see pages 898–906).

The Great Depression was the decisive turning point in the development of African nationalism. For the first time unemployment was widespread among educated Africans. African peasants and small business people who had been drawn into world trade, and who sometimes profited from booms, also felt the agony of the decade-long bust, as did urban workers. In some areas the result was unprecedented mass protest. The Gold Coast cocoa holdups of 1930–1931 and 1937–1938 are the most famous examples (see page 908).

Quick Review

What does the Great Depression tell us about the nature and pace of globalization in the early decades of the twentieth century?

How did totalitarianism differ from conservative authoritarianism?

Both conservative and radical dictatorships arose in Europe in the 1920s and the 1930s. Although they sometimes overlapped in character and practice, they were profoundly different in essence. Conservative authoritarian regimes were joined in this period by new and frightening radical totalitarian dictatorships.

Conservative Authoritarianism

The traditional form of antidemocratic government in world history was conservative authoritarianism. Like Russia's tsars and China's emperors, the leaders of such governments relied on bureaucracies, police, and the military to control society. They forbade or limited popular participation in government, and political opposition was suppressed. Yet they had neither the ability nor the desire to control many aspects of their subjects' lives. As long as the people did not try to change the system, they often had considerable personal independence.

After the First World War, authoritarianism revived, especially in Latin America and in the less-developed eastern part of Europe. Conservative dictators also took over in Spain and Portugal. There were several reasons for this development. These lands lacked strong traditions of self-government, and many of the new states, such as Yugoslavia, were torn by ethnic conflicts. Dictatorship appealed to nationalists and military leaders as a way to repress such tensions and preserve national unity. Large landowners and the church were still powerful forces in these predominantly agrarian areas, and they often looked to dictators to save them from progressive land reform or Communist agrarian upheaval. Although some of the conservative authoritarian regimes adopted certain Fascist characteristics in the 1930s, they were concerned more with maintaining the status quo than with mobilizing the masses or forcing society into rapid change or war.

Radical Totalitarian Dictatorships

By the mid-1930s a new kind of radical dictatorship had emerged in the Soviet Union, Germany, and, to a lesser extent, Italy. These dictatorships—termed totalitarian—violently rejected liberal values and exercised unprecedented control over the masses.

Most scholars argue that totalitarianism burst on the scene with the total war effort of 1914–1918 (see Chapter 28). World War I called forth a tendency to subordinate all institutions and all classes to the state in order to achieve one supreme objective: victory.

totalitarianism A radical dictatorship that exercises complete political power and control over all aspects of society and seeks to mobilize the masses for action.

The modern totalitarian state reached maturity in the 1930s in the Stalinist Soviet Union and Nazi Germany. These and other totalitarian states were linked in their use of modern technology, particularly mass communication, to exercise complete political power and control over all aspects of society. Deviation from the norm, even in art or family behavior, could be a crime.

Unlike old-fashioned authoritarianism, modern totalitarianism was based not on an elite seeking to maintain the existing social order, but on people who had become engaged in the political process for change, most notably through commitment to nationalism and socialism. Thus totalitarian societies were fully mobilized societies moving toward a goal. As soon as one goal was achieved, another arose at the leader's command. As a result totalitarianism was an unfinished revolution in which rapid, profound change imposed from above went on forever.

There were major differences between Stalin's Communist U.S.S.R. and Hitler's Nazi Germany. Most notably, Soviet communism seized private property for the state and sought to level society by crushing the middle classes. Nazi Germany also criticized big landowners and industrialists but, unlike the Communists, did not try to nationalize private property, so the middle classes survived.

The aims of Soviet Communists were ultimately international, seeking to unite the workers of the world. Fascist leaders claimed they were interested in changing state and society on a national level only. Mussolini and Hitler used the term fascism to describe their movements' supposedly "total" and revolutionary character. Orthodox Marxist Communists argued that the Fascists were powerful capitalists who sought to destroy the revolutionary working class and thus protect their enormous profits. So while Communists and Fascists

fascism A movement characterized by extreme, often expansionist nationalism, antisocialism, a dynamic and violent leader, and glorification of war and the military.

were both committed to the overthrow of existing society, their ideologies clashed, and they were enemies.

European Fascist movements shared many characteristics, including extreme nationalism; an antisocialism aimed at destroying working-class movements; alliances with powerful capitalists and landowners; a dynamic, charismatic, and violent leader; and glorification of war and the military. Hitler and Stalin, in particular, were masters of the use of propaganda and terror. Fascists, especially in Germany, also embraced racial homogeneity, a fanatical obsession that led to the Holocaust (see page 826).

Although 1930s Japan has sometimes been called a Fascist society, most scholars disagree with this label. There were various ideological forces at work in Japan, including ultranationalism, militarism, reverence for traditional ways, and emperor worship, that contributed to the rise of a totalitarian state before the Second World War. These were all ideas that grew out of events and circumstances beginning with the Meiji Restoration in 1868 (see page 707), not from European philosophies of totalitarian government in the 1920s.

Quick Review
In what sense was totalitarianism a "modern" political ideology?

What characterized Stalin's rule in the Soviet Union?

A master of political infighting, Joseph Stalin (1879–1953) cautiously consolidated his power in the mid-1920s. Then in 1928, as the ruling Communist Party's undisputed leader, he launched the first five-year plan, an event that marked the beginning of an attempt to transform Soviet society along socialist lines. Stalin and the Communist Party used constant propaganda, enormous sacrifice, and unlimited violence and state control to establish a dynamic, modern totalitarian state in the 1930s.

five-year plan Launched by Stalin in 1928 and termed the "revolution from above," its goal was to modernize the Soviet Union and generate a Communist society with new attitudes, new loyalties, and a new socialist humanity.

From Lenin to Stalin

By spring 1921 Lenin and the Bolsheviks had won the civil war, but they ruled a shattered and devastated land. In the face of social and economic chaos, Lenin changed course. In March 1921 he announced the New Economic Policy (NEP), which re-established limited economic freedom in an attempt to rebuild agriculture and industry. Peasant producers could sell their surpluses in free markets, as could private traders and small handicraft manufacturers. Heavy industry, railroads, and banks, however, remained wholly nationalized.

New Economic Policy (NEP) Lenin's 1921 policy re-establishing limited economic freedom in an attempt to rebuild agriculture and industry in the face of economic disintegration.

The NEP was successful both politically and economically. Politically, it was a necessary but temporary compromise with the Soviet Union's peasant majority, the only force capable of overturning Lenin's government. Economically, the NEP brought a rapid return to prewar levels of industrial and agricultural production.

As the economy recovered, an intense power struggle began in the Communist Party's inner circles, for Lenin left no chosen successor when he died in 1924. The principal contenders were Stalin and Leon Trotsky. Trotsky, who had planned the 1917 takeover (see page 766) and created the Red Army, appeared to have all the advantages. Yet Stalin won because he gained the support of the party, the only genuine source of power in the one-party state.

Stalin gradually achieved absolute power between 1922 and 1927. He used the moderates to crush Trotsky, and then turned against the moderates and destroyed them as well.

Stalin's final triumph came at the party congress of December 1927, which condemned all "deviation from the general party line" formulated by Stalin.

The Five-Year Plans

The 1927 party congress marked the end of the NEP and the beginning of the era of socialist five-year plans. By 1930 economic and social change was sweeping the country. Stalin unleashed his "second revolution" for a variety of reasons. First, like Lenin, Stalin and his militant supporters were deeply committed to socialism as they understood it. Second, Stalin believed that the Soviet Union's very survival was dependent on catching up with the advanced and presumably hostile Western capitalist nations.

Domestically, there was the peasant problem. For centuries peasants had wanted to own the land, and finally they had it. Sooner or later, the Communists reasoned, the peasants would become conservative capitalists and threaten the regime. To resolve these issues, Stalin decided on a preventive war against the peasantry in order to bring it under the state's absolute control.

That war was collectivization — the forcible consolidation of individual peasant farms into large, state-controlled enterprises. Beginning in 1929 peasants were ordered to give up their land and animals and become members of collective farms. As for the kulaks, the better-off peasants, Stalin instructed party workers to "liquidate them as a class." Since almost all peasants were poor, the term *kulak* soon meant any peasant who opposed the new system.

Forced collectivization led to disaster. Many peasants slaughtered their animals and burned their crops in protest. Nor were the state-controlled collective farms more productive. Grain output barely increased, and collectivized agriculture made no substantial financial contribution to Soviet industrial development during the first five-year plan.

In Ukraine Stalin instituted a policy of all-out collectivization with two goals: to destroy all expressions of Ukrainian nationalism, and to break the will of the Ukrainian peasants so they would accept collectivization and Soviet rule. Stalin began by purging Ukraine of its intellectuals and political elite. He then set impossibly high grain quotas for the collectivized farms. This grain quota had to be turned over to the government before any peasant could receive a share. The

collectivization Stalin's forcible consolidation of individual peasant farms into large, state-controlled enterprises.

Soviet Collectivization Poster Soviet leader Joseph Stalin ordered a nationwide forced collectivization campaign from 1928 to 1933. Following Communist theory, the government created large-scale collective farms by seizing land and forcing peasants to work on it. In this idealized 1932 poster, farmers are encouraged to complete the five-year plan of collectivization, while Stalin looks on approvingly. The outcome instead was a disaster. Millions of people died in the resulting human-created famine. (Deutsches Plakat Museum, Essen, Germany/Archives Charmet/The Bridgeman Art Library)

How did totalitarianism differ from conservative authoritarianism?

What characterized Stalin's rule in the Soviet Union?

How did Italian fascism develop?

What were the goals of Hitler and his Nazi regime?

What led to World War II and how did the Allies prevail?

815

The Goals of the First Five-Year Plan
Total industrial output to increase by 250 percent
Heavy industry to grow even faster than industry as a whole
Agricultural output to increase by 150 percent
20 percent of Soviet peasants to join socialist collective farms

result was a terrible man-made famine in Ukraine in 1932 and 1933, which probably claimed 3 to 5 million lives.

Collectivization was a victory for Communist ideologues. By 1938, 93 percent of peasant families had been herded onto collective farms. Regimented as state employees and dependent on the state-owned tractor stations, the collectivized peasants were no longer a political threat.

The industrial side of the five-year plans was more successful. Soviet industry produced about four times as much in 1937 as in 1928. No other major country had ever achieved such rapid industrial growth. Heavy industry led the way, and urban development accelerated.

The sudden creation of dozens of new factories demanded tremendous resources. Funds for industrial expansion were collected from the people by means of heavy hidden sales taxes. Firm labor discipline also contributed to rapid industrialization. Trade unions lost most of their power, and individuals could not move without police permission. When factory managers needed more hands they were sent "unneeded" peasants from collective farms.

Foreign engineers were hired to plan and construct many of the new factories. Highly skilled American engineers, hungry for work in the depression years, were particularly important until newly trained Soviet experts began to replace them after 1932. Siberia's new steel mills were modeled on America's best. Thus Stalin's planners harnessed the skill and technology of capitalist countries to promote the surge of socialist industry.

Life and Culture in Soviet Society

Daily life was hard in Stalin's Soviet Union. There were constant shortages, and scarcity of housing was a particularly serious problem. A relatively lucky family received one room for all its members and shared both a kitchen and a toilet with others on the floor. Less fortunate people built scrap-lumber shacks in shantytowns.

Despite the hardships, many Communists saw themselves as heroically building the world's first socialist society while capitalism crumbled and fascism rose in the West. This optimistic belief in the Soviet Union's future also attracted many disillusioned Westerners to communism in the 1930s.

On a more practical level Soviet workers received some important social benefits, such as old-age pensions, free medical services and education, and day-care centers for children. Unemployment was almost unknown. Finally, there was the possibility of personal advancement. Rapid industrialization required massive numbers of trained experts, and a growing technical and managerial elite joined the political and artistic elites in a new upper class, whose members were rich and powerful.

Soviet society's radical transformation profoundly affected women's lives. The Russian Revolution of 1917 immediately proclaimed complete equality of rights for women. In the 1920s divorce and abortion were made easily available, and women were urged to work outside the home. After Stalin came to power, however, he played down this trend in favor of a return to traditional family values.

The most lasting changes for women involved work and education. Peasant women continued to work on farms, and millions of women now toiled in factories and heavy construction. Women entered the ranks of the better-paid specialists in industry and science. By 1950, 75 percent of all doctors in the Soviet Union were women.

Culture was thoroughly politicized through constant propaganda and indoctrination. Party activists lectured workers in factories and peasants on collective farms, while newspapers, films, and radio broadcasts recounted socialist achievements and capitalist plots.

Stalinist Terror and the Great Purges

In the mid-1930s the push to build socialism and a new society culminated in ruthless police terror and a massive purging of the Communist Party. In late 1934 Stalin's number-two man, Sergei Kirov, was mysteriously murdered. Although Stalin himself probably ordered Kirov's murder, he used the incident to launch a reign of terror.

In August 1936 sixteen prominent "Old Bolsheviks"—members of the party before the Russian Revolution of 1917—confessed to all manner of plots against Stalin in spectacular public show trials in Moscow. Then in 1937 the secret police arrested a mass of lesser party officials and newer members, torturing them and extracting confessions for more show trials. From there, the purges widened to include all of Soviet society. In all, at least 8 million people were arrested, and millions of these were executed or never returned from prisons and forced-labor camps.

Stalin recruited 1.5 million new members to take the place of those purged. Thus more than half of all Communist Party members in 1941 had joined since the purges. These new members were products of the Second Revolution of the 1930s, seeking the opportunities and rewards that party membership offered. This new generation of Stalin-formed Communists served the leader effectively until his death in 1953, and then governed the Soviet Union until the early 1980s.

> **Quick Review**
> Why did Stalin believe an almost total transformation of Soviet society was necessary?

How did Italian fascism develop?

Mussolini's Fascist movement and his seizure of power in 1922 were important steps in the rise of dictatorships between the two world wars. Mussolini and his supporters were the first to call themselves "Fascists"—revolutionaries determined to create a new kind of totalitarian state. His dictatorship contained elements of both conservative authoritarianism and modern totalitarianism.

The Seizure of Power

In the early twentieth century Italy was a liberal state with civil rights and a constitutional monarchy. But there were serious problems. Poverty was widespread, and local identification with the national state was often weak. Moreover, the papacy, many devout Catholics, conservatives, and landowners remained opposed to the middle-class lawyers and politicians who ran the country largely for their own benefit. Church-state relations were often tense. Class differences were also extreme, and by 1912 the Socialist Party's radical wing led the powerful revolutionary socialist movement.[2]

World War I worsened the political situation. Having fought on the Allied side almost exclusively for purposes of territorial expansion, Italian nationalists were disappointed with Italy's modest gains at Versailles. Workers and peasants also felt cheated: to win their support during the war, the government had promised social and land reform, which it did not deliver after the war.

The Russian Revolution energized Italy's revolutionary socialist movement, and radical workers and peasants began occupying factories and seizing land in 1920. These actions scared and mobilized the property-owning classes. Thus by 1921 revolutionary Socialists, antiliberal conservatives, and frightened property owners were all opposed—though for different reasons—to the liberal parliamentary government.

| How did totalitarianism differ from conservative authoritarianism? | What characterized Stalin's rule in the Soviet Union? | **How did Italian fascism develop?** | What were the goals of Hitler and his Nazi regime? | What led to World War II and how did the Allies prevail? |

817

Mussolini Leading a Parade in Rome Benito Mussolini was a master showman who drew on Rome's ancient heritage to promote Italian fascism. He wanted a grand avenue to stage triumphal marches with thousands of troops, so he had the Way of the Imperial Forums built through the old city. Here Mussolini rides at the head of a grand parade in 1932 to inaugurate the new road, passing the Roman Coliseum, one of the focal points along the route. (Stefano Bianchetti/Corbis)

Into these crosscurrents of unrest and fear stepped Benito Mussolini (1883–1945). Mussolini began his political career as a Socialist Party leader. Expelled from the party for supporting World War I, and wounded on the Italian front in 1917, Mussolini returned home and began organizing war veterans into a band of Fascists—from the Italian word for "a union of forces."

At first Mussolini's program was a radical combination of nationalist and socialist demands, including territorial expansion, workers' benefits, and land reform for peasants. However, when Mussolini saw that his violent verbal assaults on rival Socialists won him growing support from conservatives and the frightened middle classes, he shifted gears in 1920, exalting nation and race over class.

Mussolini and his private army of **Black**

Black Shirts A private army under Mussolini that destroyed socialist newspapers, union halls, and Socialist Party headquarters, eventually pushing Socialists out of the city governments of northern Italy.

Shirts began to grow violent. Few people were killed, but socialist newspapers, union halls, and local Socialist Party headquarters were destroyed. With the government breaking down in 1922, largely because of the chaos created by his Black Shirt bands, Mussolini stepped forward as the savior of order and property. In October 1922 a large group of Fascists marched on Rome to threaten the king and force him to appoint Mussolini prime minister. The threat worked. Victor Emmanuel III (r. 1900–1946) asked Mussolini to form a new cabinet. Thus, after widespread violence and a threat of armed uprising, Mussolini seized power "legally."

The Regime in Action

In 1924 Mussolini declared his desire to "make the nation Fascist" and imposed a series of repressive measures. Press freedom was abolished, elections were fixed, and the government ruled by decree. Mussolini arrested his political opponents, disbanded all independent labor unions, and put Fascists in control of Italy's schools. He created a Fascist youth movement, Fascist labor unions, and many other Fascist organizations. By year's end Italy was a one-party dictatorship.

Mussolini did not complete the establishment of a modern totalitarian state. His Fascist Party never destroyed the old power structure. Interested primarily in personal power, Mussolini was content to compromise with the old conservative classes that controlled the army, the economy, and the state. He controlled labor but left big business to regulate itself. There was no land reform.

Mussolini also drew increasing support from the Catholic Church. In the Lateran Agreement of 1929, he recognized the Vatican as an independent state and agreed to give the church heavy financial support. The pope in return urged Italians to support Mussolini's government.

Like Stalin, Hitler, and other totalitarian leaders, Mussolini favored a return of traditional roles for women. He abolished divorce and told women to stay at home and produce children. In 1938 women were limited by law to a maximum of 10 percent of the better-paying jobs in industry and government.

Mussolini's government passed no racial laws until 1938 and did not persecute Jews savagely until late in the Second World War, when Italy was under Nazi control. Nor did Mussolini establish a true police state. Only twenty-three political prisoners were condemned to death between 1926 and 1944. Mussolini's Fascist Italy, though repressive and undemocratic, was never really totalitarian.

Lateran Agreement A 1929 agreement that recognized the Vatican as an independent state, with Mussolini agreeing to give the church heavy financial support in return for the pope's public support.

Quick Review
What role did Italian elites play in the rise to power of Mussolini and his Fascist Party?

What were the goals of Hitler and his Nazi regime?

The most frightening dictatorship developed in Nazi Germany. While sharing some of the characteristics of Mussolini's Italian model and fascism, Nazism asserted an unlimited claim over German society and proclaimed the ultimate power of its aggressive leader, Adolf Hitler. Nazism's aspirations were truly totalitarian.

The Roots of Nazism

Nazism grew out of many complex developments, of which the most influential were extreme nationalism and racism. These two ideas captured the mind of the young Adolf Hitler (1889–1945), and he dominated Nazism until the end of World War II.

The son of an Austrian customs official, Hitler spent his childhood in small towns in Austria. He did poorly in high school and dropped out at age sixteen. He then headed to Vienna, where he was exposed to extreme Austro-German nationalists who believed Germans to be a superior people and central Europe's natural rulers.

From these extremists Hitler eagerly absorbed virulent anti-Semitism, racism, and hatred of Slavs. He developed an unshakable belief in the superiority of Germanic races and the inevitability of racial conflict. The Jews, he claimed, directed an international conspiracy of finance capitalism and Marxist socialism against German culture, German unity, and the German race. Anti-Semitism and racism became Hitler's most passionate convictions.

Hitler greeted the outbreak of the Great War as a salvation. The struggle and discipline of serving as a soldier in the war gave his life meaning, and when Germany was suddenly defeated in 1918, Hitler's world was shattered. Convinced that Jews and Marxists had "stabbed Germany in the back," he vowed to fight on.

In late 1919 Hitler joined a tiny extremist group in Munich called the German Workers' Party, which promised a uniquely German "national socialism" that would abolish the injustices of capitalism and create a mighty "people's community." By 1921 Hitler had gained absolute control of this small but growing party, now renamed the National Socialist German Worker's Party, or Nazi Party.

In late 1923 the Weimar Republic seemed on the verge of collapse. In 1925 the old Great War field marshal Paul von Hindenburg (1847–1934) became the second president of the

Nazism A movement born of extreme nationalism and racism and dominated by Adolf Hitler from 1933 until the end of World War II in 1945.

young democratic Germany. Hitler, inspired by Mussolini's recent victory, attempted an armed uprising in Munich. Despite the failure of the poorly organized plot and Hitler's arrest, Nazism had been born.

Hitler's Road to Power

At his trial Hitler violently denounced the Weimar Republic, and he gained enormous publicity. From the unsuccessful revolt, Hitler concluded that he had to come to power legally through electoral competition. He used his brief prison term to dictate *Mein Kampf* (My Struggle). Here he expounded on his basic ideas on race and anti-Semitism, the notion of territorial expansion based on "living space" for Germans, and the role of the leader-dictator, called the *Führer* (FYOUR-uhr).

The Nazis remained a small splinter group until the 1929 Great Depression shattered economic prosperity. No factor contributed more to Hitler's success than the economic crisis. Hitler began promising German voters economic as well as political and international salvation.

Hitler rejected free-market capitalism and advocated government programs to bring recovery. He pitched his speeches to middle- and lower-middle-class groups and to skilled workers. As the economy collapsed, great numbers of these people "voted their pocket-books"[3] and deserted the conservative and moderate parties for the Nazis. By 1932, the Nazis had become the largest party in the Reichstag.

Hitler and the Nazis appealed strongly to German youth. Hitler himself was only forty in 1929, and he and most of his top aides were much younger than other leading German politicians. "National Socialism is the organized will of the youth," proclaimed the official Nazi slogan. National recovery, exciting and rapid change, and personal advancement made Nazism appealing to millions of German youths.

Hitler also came to power because of the breakdown of democratic government. Germany's economic collapse in the Great Depression convinced many voters that the country's republican leaders were stupid and corrupt. Disunity on the left was another nail in the republic's coffin. The Communists refused to cooperate with the Social Democrats, even though the two parties together outnumbered the Nazis in the Reichstag.

Finally, Hitler excelled in backroom politics. In 1932 he succeeded in gaining support from key people in the army and big business who thought they could use him to their own advantage. Many conservative and nationalistic politicians thought similarly. Thus in January 1933 President von Hindenburg legally appointed Hitler, leader of Germany's largest party, as German chancellor.

The Nazi State and Society

Hitler quickly established an unshakable dictatorship. When the Reichstag building was partly destroyed by fire in February 1933, Hitler blamed the Communist Party, and he convinced President von Hindenburg to sign dictatorial emergency acts that abolished freedom of speech and assembly as well as most personal liberties. He also called for new elections in an effort to solidify his political power.

When the Nazis won only 44 percent of the votes, Hitler outlawed the Communist Party and arrested its parliamentary representatives. Then on March 23, 1933, the Nazis forced through the Reichstag the so-called Enabling Act, which gave Hitler absolute dictatorial power for four years.

After installing Nazis in top positions in the government bureaucracy, Hitler next outlawed strikes, abolished independent labor unions, and replaced independent professional

Enabling Act An act pushed through the Reichstag by the Nazis that gave Hitler absolute dictatorial power for four years.

organizations with Nazi associations. Publishing houses and universities were put under Nazi control, and students and professors publicly burned forbidden books. Modern art and architecture were ruthlessly prohibited and life became violently anti-intellectual. By 1934 a brutal dictatorship characterized by frightening dynamism and total obedience to Hitler was already largely in place.

In June 1934 Hitler ordered his elite personal guard—the SS—to arrest and shoot without trial roughly a thousand long-time Nazi storm troopers. Shortly thereafter army leaders surrendered their independence and swore a binding oath of "unquestioning obedience" to Adolf Hitler. Under Heinrich Himmler (1900–1945), the SS took over the political police, the Gestapo, and expanded its network of concentration camps.

From the beginning, German Jews were a special object of Nazi persecution. In 1935 the infamous Nuremberg Laws classified as Jewish anyone having three or more Jewish grandparents and deprived Jews of all rights of citizenship. By 1938 roughly one-quarter of Germany's half million Jews had emigrated, sacrificing almost all their property in order to leave Germany.

In late 1938 the attack on the Jews accelerated. On November 9 and 10, 1938, the Nazis initiated a series of well-organized attacks against Jews throughout Nazi Germany and some parts of Austria. This infamous event is known as Kristallnacht, or Night of Broken Glass, after the broken glass that littered the streets following the destruction of Jewish homes, shops, synagogues, and neighborhoods by German civilians and uniformed storm troopers. Many historians consider this night the beginning of Hitler's Final Solution against the Jews (see page 826), and it now became very difficult for Jews to leave Germany.

Some Germans privately opposed these outrages, but most went along or looked the other way. Although this lack of response reflected the individual's helplessness in a totalitarian state, it also reflected the strong popular support Hitler's government enjoyed.

Hitler's Popularity

Hitler had promised the masses economic recovery and he delivered. The Nazi Party launched a large public works program to pull Germany out of the depression, and in 1935 Germany turned decisively toward rearmament. Unemployment dropped steadily, and by 1938 the Nazis boasted of nearly full employment. The average standard of living increased moderately. Business profits rose sharply.

Reaching a National Audience This poster ad promotes the VE-301 receiver, "the world's cheapest radio," and claims that "All Germany listens to the Führer on the people's receiver." Constantly broadcasting official views and attitudes, the state-controlled media also put the Nazis' favorite entertainment—gigantic mass meetings that climaxed with Hitler's violent theatrical speeches—on an invisible stage for millions. (Bundesarchiv Koblenz Plak 003-022-025/Grafiker: Leonid)

How did totalitarianism differ from conservative authoritarianism?

What characterized Stalin's rule in the Soviet Union?

How did Italian fascism develop?

What were the goals of Hitler and his Nazi regime?

What led to World War II and how did the Allies prevail?

821

In contrast to those deemed "undesirable" (Jews, Slavs, Gypsies, Jehovah's Witnesses, Communists, and homosexuals), for ordinary German citizens, Hitler's government meant greater equality and more opportunities. Yet few historians today believe that Hitler and the Nazis brought about a real social revolution. The well-educated classes held on to most of their advantages, and only a modest social leveling occurred in the Nazi years. Significantly, the Nazis shared with the Italian Fascists the stereotypical view of women as housewives and mothers. Only when facing labor shortages during the war did they reluctantly mobilize large numbers of German women for office and factory work. Yet low unemployment and economic recovery coupled with an aggressive propaganda effort heralding the Nazi state's successes led to broad support for the regime.

Not all Germans supported Hitler, however, and a number of German groups actively resisted him after 1933. In the first years of Hitler's rule, the principal resisters were trade union Communists and Socialists, groups smashed by the expansion of the SS system after 1935. Catholic and Protestant churches produced a second group of opponents. Their efforts were directed primarily at preserving genuine religious life, however, not at overthrowing Hitler. Finally in 1938 and again during the war, some high-ranking army officers, who feared the consequences of Hitler's reckless aggression, plotted, unsuccessfully, against him.

Aggression and Appeasement, 1933–1939

After economic recovery and success establishing Nazi control of society, Hitler turned to the next item on his agenda: aggressive territorial expansion. In October 1933 Germany withdrew from the League of Nations, an indication of its determination to rearm in violation of the Treaty of Versailles. When in March 1935 Hitler established a general military draft and declared the "unequal" Versailles treaty disarmament clauses null and void, leaders in Britain, France, and Italy issued a rather tepid joint protest and warned him against future aggressive actions.

Italy's Ethiopian Campaign, 1935–1936

But the emerging united front against Hitler quickly collapsed. Britain adopted a policy of appeasement, granting Hitler everything he asked for in order to avoid war. British appeasement, which practically dictated French policy, was motivated by the pacifism of a population still horrified by the memory of the First World War. As in Germany, many powerful British conservatives underestimated Hitler. They believed that Soviet communism was the real danger and that Hitler could be used to stop it.

In March 1936, Hitler suddenly marched his armies into the demilitarized Rhineland, violating the Treaties of Versailles and Locarno. France would not move without British support, and Britain refused to act (Map 30.1). As Britain and France opted for appeasement and the Soviet Union watched all developments suspiciously, Hitler found powerful allies. In 1935 Mussolini attacked the independent African kingdom of Ethiopia. The Western Powers and the League of Nations condemned Italian aggression, but Hitler supported Italy energetically. In 1936 Italy and Germany established the so-called Rome-Berlin Axis. Japan, which wanted support for its occupation of Manchuria, also joined the Axis alliance.

At the same time, Germany and Italy intervened in the Spanish civil war (1936–1939), where their support helped General Francisco Franco's Fascist movement defeat republican Spain. Republican Spain's only official aid in the fight against Franco came from the Soviet Union.

In late 1937 Hitler moved forward with his plans to crush Austria and Czechoslovakia as the first step in his long-contemplated drive to the east for living space. By threatening Austria with invasion, Hitler forced the Austrian chancellor in March 1938 to put local Nazis in control of the government. The next day German armies moved in unopposed, and Austria became two provinces of Greater Germany (see Map 30.1).

Simultaneously, Hitler demanded that the pro-Nazi, German-speaking territory of western Czechoslovakia—the Sudetenland—be turned over to Germany. Once again, appeasement triumphed. In September 1938 British prime minister Arthur Neville Chamberlain (1869–1940) flew to Germany three times in fourteen days. In these negotiations, Chamberlain and the French agreed with Hitler that the Sudetenland should be ceded to Germany immediately. Sold out by the Western Powers, Czechoslovakia gave in.

Map 30.1 **The Growth of Nazi Germany, 1933–1939** Until March 1939 Hitler brought ethnic Germans into the Nazi state; then he turned on the Slavic peoples, whom he had always hated. He stripped Czechoslovakia of its independence and prepared for an attack on Poland in September 1939.

How did totalitarianism differ from conservative authoritarianism?

What characterized Stalin's rule in the Soviet Union?

How did Italian fascism develop?

What were the goals of Hitler and his Nazi regime?

What led to World War II and how did the Allies prevail?

823

Hitler's armies occupied the remainder of Czechoslovakia in March 1939. This time, there was no possible rationale of self-determination for Nazi aggression. When Hitler used the question of German minorities in Danzig as a pretext to confront Poland, Chamberlain declared that Britain and France would fight if Hitler attacked Poland. Hitler did not take these warnings seriously and pressed on.

In an about-face that stunned the world, Hitler and Stalin signed a nonaggression pact in August 1939. Each dictator promised to remain neutral if the other became involved in war. A secret protocol divided eastern Europe into German and Soviet zones "in the event of a political territorial reorganization." Stalin agreed to the pact because he distrusted Western intentions, and Hitler offered territorial gain.

For Hitler, everything was now set. On September 1, 1939, the Germans attacked Poland from three sides. Two days later, Britain and France declared war on Germany. The Second World War had begun.

Quick Review
How did Hitler gain the support of ordinary Germans, and what roles did violence and propaganda play in his rule?

What led to World War II and how did the Allies prevail?

World war broke out because Hitler's ambitions were essentially unlimited. Nazi soldiers scored enormous successes in Europe until late 1942. Hitler's victories increased tensions in Asia between Japan, whose ambitions in Asia were equally unlimited, and the United States, and prompted Japan to attack the United States. Eventually, Britain, the United States, and the Soviet Union banded together to halt the aggressors. Thus the Nazi and Japanese empires proved short-lived.

Hitler's Empire in Europe, 1939–1942

blitzkrieg "Lightning war" using planes, tanks, and trucks; first used by Hitler to crush Poland in four weeks.

Using planes, tanks, and trucks in the first example of a **blitzkrieg**, or "lightning war," Hitler's armies crushed Poland in four weeks. The Soviet Union quickly occupied the eastern half of Poland and the Baltic states of Lithuania, Estonia, and Latvia. In the west French and British armies dug in, expecting another war of attrition and economic blockade. But in spring 1940 the Nazi lightning war struck again. After occupying Denmark, Norway, and Holland, German motorized columns broke through southern Belgium and into France.

As Hitler's armies poured into France, aging marshal Henri-Philippe Pétain formed a new French government—the so-called Vichy (VIH-shee) government—and accepted defeat. By July 1940 Hitler ruled practically all of western continental Europe; Italy was an ally, the Soviet Union a friendly neutral (Map 30.2). Only Britain, led by Winston Churchill (1874–1965), remained unconquered.

To prepare for an invasion of Britain, Germany first needed to gain control of the air. In the Battle of Britain, which began in July 1940, German planes attacked British airfields and key factories. In September Hitler began indiscriminately bombing British cities in an attempt to break British morale. British aircraft factories increased production, and the people of London defiantly dug in. By September Britain was beating Germany in the air war, and Hitler gave up his plans for an immediate invasion of Britain.

Vichy France, 1940

Occupied by Germany

Annexed by Germany

Map 30.2 **World War II in Europe and Africa, 1939–1945** The map shows the extent of Hitler's empire at its height, before the Battle of Stalingrad in late 1942 and the subsequent advances of the Allies until Germany surrendered on May 7, 1945.

Hitler now turned to the creation of a vast eastern European empire for the "master race." In June 1941 Germany broke the Nazi-Soviet nonaggression pact and attacked the Soviet Union. By October Leningrad was practically surrounded, Moscow was besieged, and most of Ukraine had been conquered. But the Soviets did not collapse, and when a severe winter struck, the invaders were stopped.

How did totalitarianism differ from conservative authoritarianism?

What characterized Stalin's rule in the Soviet Union?

How did Italian fascism develop?

What were the goals of Hitler and his Nazi regime?

What led to World War II and how did the Allies prevail?

825

New Order Hitler's program, based on the guiding principle of racial imperialism, which gave preferential treatment to the Nordic peoples above "inferior" Latin peoples and, at the bottom, "sub-human" Slavs and Jews.

Stalled in Russia, Hitler nonetheless had come to rule an enormous European empire. He now began building a New Order based on the guiding principle of Nazi totalitarianism: racial imperialism. Within the New Order, the Nordic peoples—the Dutch, Norwegians, and Danes—received preferential treatment. The French, an "inferior" Latin people, occupied the middle position. At the bottom of the New Order were the harshly treated "subhumans," Jews and Slavs.

Hitler envisioned a vast eastern colonial empire where Poles, Ukrainians, and Russians would be enslaved and forced to die out while Germanic peasants would resettle the abandoned lands. Himmler and the elite SS corps, supported by military commanders and German policemen, now implemented a program of destruction in the occupied territories to create a "mass settlement space" for Germans.

The Holocaust

Holocaust The attempted systematic extermination of all European Jews and other "undesirables" by the Nazi state during World War II.

At the center of Nazi racial policy was a determination to exterminate all European Jews in the Holocaust. After the fall of Warsaw in 1939 the Nazis began forcing the Jews in the occupied territories to move to urban ghettos. The remaining German Jews were sent to occupied Poland. When war with Russia broke out in 1941, forced expulsion spiraled into extermination. Extermination was systematized in late 1941 when the SS was ordered to speed up planning for "the final solution of the Jewish question." Throughout the Nazi empire Jews were systematically arrested, packed like cattle onto freight trains, and dispatched to extermination camps.

Arriving at their destination, small numbers of Jews were sent to nearby slave-labor camps, where they were starved and systematically worked to death. (See "Individuals in Society: Primo Levi," page 827.) Most victims were taken to "shower rooms," which were actually poison gas chambers. By 1945 about 6 million Jews had been murdered.

Who was responsible for this terrible crime? Some historians lay the guilt on Hitler and the Nazi leadership, arguing that ordinary Germans had little knowledge of the extermination camps, or that those who cooperated had no alternative given the brutality of Nazi terror and totalitarian control. But in recent years many studies have revealed a much broader participation of German people in the Holocaust and popular indifference (or worse) to the Jews' fate. A similar pattern of cooperation with and acceptance of mass murder occurred in most German-occupied countries.

The Holocaust, 1941–1945

- ☐ Axis powers and their allies
- ☐ Occupied by Germany and its allies
- ■ Extermination camp
- ● Major concentration camp
- ◆ Site of mass killing
- ✦ Ghetto

Japan's Asian Empire

The Nazis did not have a monopoly on racism and racial violence. The Japanese, for their part, encouraged racial hatred of Westerners, giving free rein at home to the anti-Western ultranationalism that had risen in the 1920s and 1930s (see page 800): proclaiming Japan's liberating mission in Asia, glorifying the virtues of honor and sacrifice, and demanding absolute devotion to the semidivine emperor. (See "Listening to the Past: "Ultranationalist Pamphlet for Japanese Students," page 828.)

Abroad, by late 1938, 1.5 million Japanese troops were bogged down in China, unable to defeat the Nationalists and the Communists (see pages 800–802). In 1939, as war broke

Primo Levi, who never stopped thinking, writing, and speaking about the Holocaust. (Giansanti/ Corbis Sygma)

MOST JEWS DEPORTED TO AUSCHWITZ WERE

murdered as soon as they arrived, but the Nazis made some prisoners into slave laborers, and a few of these survived. Primo Levi (1919–1987), an Italian Jew, became one of the most influential witnesses to the Holocaust and its death camps.

Like many in Italy's small Jewish community, Levi's family belonged to the urban professional classes. The young Primo Levi graduated in 1941 from the University of Turin with highest honors in chemistry. Since 1938, when Italy introduced racial laws, he had faced growing discrimination, and two years after graduation he joined the antifascist resistance movement. Quickly captured, he was deported to Auschwitz with 650 Italian Jews in February 1944. Stone-faced SS men picked only ninety-six men and twenty-nine women to work in their respective labor camps. Levi was one of them.

Nothing had prepared Levi for what he encountered. The Jewish prisoners were kicked, punched, stripped, branded with tattoos, crammed into huts, and worked unmercifully. Hoping for some sign of prisoner solidarity in this terrible environment, Levi found only a desperate struggle of each against all and enormous status differences among prisoners. Many stunned and bewildered newcomers, beaten and demoralized by their bosses—the most privileged prisoners—collapsed and died. Others struggled to secure their own privileges, however small, because food rations and working conditions were so abominable that ordinary Jewish prisoners perished in two to three months.

Sensitive and noncombative, Levi found himself sinking into oblivion. But instead of joining the mass of the "drowned," he became one of the "saved"—a complicated surprise with moral implications that he would ponder all his life. As Levi explained in *Survival in Auschwitz* (1947), the usual road to salvation in the camps was some kind of collaboration with German power.* Savage German criminals were released from prison to become brutal camp guards; non-Jewish political prisoners competed for jobs entitling them to better conditions; and, especially troubling for Levi, a small number of Jewish men plotted and struggled for the power of life and death over other Jewish prison-

ers. Though not one of these Jewish bosses, Levi believed that he himself, like almost all survivors, had entered the "gray zone" of moral compromise. Only a very few superior individuals, "the stuff of saints and martyrs," survived the death camps without shifting their moral stance.

For Levi, compromise and salvation came from his profession. Interviewed by a German technocrat for the camp's synthetic rubber program, Levi performed brilliantly in scientific German and savored his triumph as a Jew over Nazi racism. Work in the warm camp laboratory offered Levi opportunities to pilfer equipment that could then be traded to other prisoners for food and necessities. Levi also gained critical support from three saintly prisoners who refused to do wicked and hateful acts. And he counted "luck" as essential for his survival: in the camp infirmary with scarlet fever in February 1945 as advancing Russian armies prepared to liberate the camp, Levi was not evacuated by the Nazis and shot to death like most Jewish prisoners.

After the war Primo Levi was forever haunted by the nightmare that the Holocaust would be ignored or forgotten. Always ashamed that so many people whom he considered better than himself had perished, he wrote and lectured tirelessly to preserve the memory of Jewish victims and guilty Nazis. Wanting the world to understand the Jewish genocide in all its complexity so that never again would people tolerate such atrocities, he grappled tirelessly with his vision of individual choice and moral compromise in a hell designed to make the victims collaborate and persecute each other.

*Primo Levi, *Survival in Auschwitz: The Nazi Assault on Humanity*, rev. ed. 1958 (London: Collier Books, 1961), pp. 79–84, and *The Drowned and the Saved* (New York: Summit Books, 1988). These powerful testimonies are highly recommended.

QUESTIONS FOR ANALYSIS

1. Describe Levi's experience at Auschwitz. How did camp prisoners treat each other? Why?
2. What does Levi mean by the "gray zone"? How is this concept central to his thinking?
3. Will a vivid historical memory of the Holocaust help prevent future genocide?

Ultranationalist Pamphlet for Japanese Students

In August 1941, only four months before Japan's coordinated attack on Pearl Harbor and colonial empires in Southeast Asia, Japan's Ministry of Education issued "The Way of Subjects." Required reading for high school and university students, this twenty-page pamphlet summed up the basic tenets of Japanese ultranationalism, which had become dominant in the 1930s.

As this selection suggests, ultranationalism in Japan combined a sense of mission with intense group solidarity and unquestioning devotion to a semidivine emperor. Thus Japanese expansion into Manchuria and the war in China were part of Japan's sacred calling to protect the throne and to free Asia from Western exploitation and misrule. Of course, an unknown percentage of students (and adults) did not believe that the myths of Japan's state religion were literally true. Nevertheless, they were profoundly influenced by extremist nationalism: Japanese soldiers' determination to fight to the death was a prime indicator of that influence.

❝ The way of the subjects of the Emperor issues from the policy of the Emperor and is to guard and maintain the Imperial Throne coexistent with the Heavens and the Earth. This is not an abstract principle but a way of daily practices based on history. The life and activities of the nation are all attuned to the task of strengthening the foundation of the Empire. . . .

Modern history, in a nutshell, has been marked by the formation of unified nations in Europe and their contests for supremacy in the acquisition of colonies. . . . Their march into all parts of the world paved the way for their subsequent world domination politically, economically, and culturally and led them to believe that they alone were justified in their outrageous behavior. . . .

The thoughts that have formed the foundation of Western civilization since the early modern period are individualism, liberalism, materialism, and so on. These thoughts regard the strong preying on the weak as reasonable, unstintedly promote the pursuit of luxury and pleasure, encourage materialism, and stimulate competition for acquiring colonies and securing trade, thereby leading the world to a veritable hell of fighting and bloodshed [in the First World War]. . . . [Thereafter] a vigorous movement was started by Britain, France, and

the United States to maintain the status quo by any means. Simultaneously, a movement aiming at social revolution through class conflict on the basis of thoroughgoing materialism like Communism also vigorously developed. On the other hand, Nazism and Fascism arose with great force. The basic principles of the totalitarianism in Germany and Italy are to remove the evils of individualism and liberalism.

That these [totalitarian] principles show great similarity to Eastern culture and spirit is a noteworthy fact that suggests the future of Western civilization and the creation of a new culture. Thus, the orientation of world history has made the collapse of the old world order a certainty. Japan has hereby initiated the construction of a new world order based on moral principles.

The Manchurian Affair [the Japanese invasion of Manchuria in 1931] was a violent outburst of Japanese national life long suppressed. Taking advantage of this, Japan in the glare of all the Powers made a step toward the creation of a world based on moral principles and the construction of a new order. This was a manifestation of the spirit, profound and lofty, embodied in the founding of Empire, and an unavoidable action for its national life and world mission. . . .

The general tendency of world domination by Europe and America has begun to show signs of a change since the Russo-Japanese War of 1904–05. Japan's victory attracted the attention of the entire world, and this caused a reawakening of Asiatic countries, which had been forced to lie prostrate under British and American influence, with the result that an independence movement was started.

Hopes to be free of the shackles and bondage of Europe and America were ablaze among the nations of India, Turkey, Arabia, Thailand, Vietnam, and others. This also inspired a new national movement in China. Amid this stormy atmosphere of Asia's reawakening, Japan has come to be keenly conscious of the fact that the stabilization of East Asia is her mission, and that the emancipation of East Asian nations rests solely on her efforts. . . .

Japan has a political mission to help various regions in the Greater East Asian Co-prosperity Sphere [the Japanese term for Japan's Asian empire], which are

out in Europe, the Japanese redoubled their efforts in China, implementing a savage policy of "kill all, burn all, destroy all." Japanese troops committed shocking atrocities, including the so-called Rape of Nanjing (see page 801). During Japan's war in China—the second Sino-Japanese War (1937–1945)—the Japanese are estimated to have killed 4 million Chinese people.

In August 1940 the Japanese announced the formation of a self-sufficient Asian economic zone. Although they spoke of liberating Asia from Western imperialism, their true reduced to a state of quasi-colony by Europe and America, and rescue them from their control. Economically, this country will have to eradicate the evils of their exploitation and then set up an economic structure for coexistence and co-prosperity. Culturally, Japan must strive to fashion East Asian nations to abandon their following of European and American culture and to develop Eastern culture for the purpose of contributing to the creation of a just world. The East has been left to destruction for the past several hundred years. Its rehabilitation is not an easy task. It is natural that unusual difficulties attend the establishment of a new order and the creation of a new culture. Overcoming these difficulties will do much to help in establishing a world dominated by morality, in which all nations can co-operate and all people can secure their proper positions. . . .

In Japan, the Emperors of a line unbroken for ages eternal govern and reign over it, as the Heavens and the Earth endure, since the Imperial Foundress, Amaterasu-o-Mikami, . . . caused Her grandson Ninigi-no-Mikoto to descend on the eight great countries and She commanded him, saying: "This country, fruitful and abounding in rice, is the land over which Our descendants shall rule. Go you, therefore, down and reign over it. Under you and your offspring it shall prosper as long as the Heavens and the Earth endure." . . .

The Imperial Family is [therefore] the fountain source of the Japanese nation, and national and private lives issue from this. In the past, foreign nationals came to this country only to enjoy the benevolent rule of the Imperial Family, and became Japanese subjects spiritually and by blood. The Imperial virtues are so great and boundless that all are assimilated into one. Here is the reason for the present glorious state, in which the Emperor and his subjects are harmonized into one great unit. That the myriad subjects with one mind are glad to be unified in their devotion to the Throne is the substance of the Imperial subjects.

The way of the subjects is to be loyal to the Emperor in disregard of self. . . . To serve the Emperor is its key point. Our lives will become sincere and true when they are offered to the Emperor and the state. . . . All

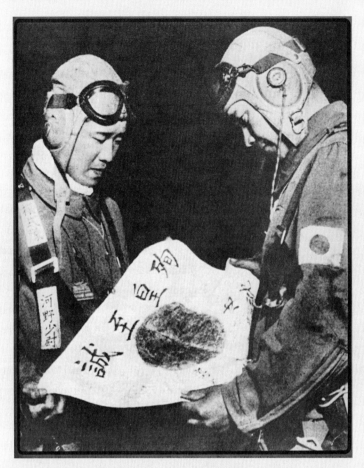

Kamikaze pilots ponder the message on the flag that they will take on their suicide mission: "All for the Emperor, we are happy to die for him." (© Keystone Pictures USA/Alamy)

must be unified under the Emperor. Herein lies the significance of national life in Japan. »

Source: "The Way of Subjects," in *Tokyo Record*, copyright © 1943 by Otto D. Tolischus and renewed 1970 by Naya G. Tolischus. Reprinted by permission of Houghton Mifflin Harcourt Publishing Company.

QUESTIONS FOR ANALYSIS

1. How does "The Way of Subjects" interpret modern history? In what ways do Western thought and action threaten Japan?
2. What is Japan's mission in Asia?
3. What is the basis of Japanese sovereignty? What is the individual's proper role in society?

intentions were to eventually rule over a vast Japanese empire. For the moment, however, Japan still depended on imports for essential materials like oil. Thus the Japanese sought alliances that might give them better access to these essential goods and also improve their position in Asia.

Seeking support for its war in China, in September 1940 Japan signed a formal alliance with Germany and Italy, and Vichy France granted the Japanese domination over northern French Indochina — from where they could attack southern China. The United

Events Leading to World War II

1919	Treaty of Versailles is signed
1921	Hitler heads National Socialist German Worker's Party (Nazis)
1922	Mussolini seizes power in Italy
1927	Stalin takes full control of the Soviet Union
1929–1939	Great Depression
1931	Japan invades Manchuria
January 1933	Hitler is appointed chancellor of Germany
March 1933	Reichstag passes the Enabling Act, granting Hitler absolute dictatorial power
October 1933	Germany withdraws from the League of Nations
1935	Nuremberg Laws deprive Jews of all rights of citizenship
March 1935	Hitler announces German rearmament
October 1935	Mussolini invades Ethiopia and receives Hitler's support
March 1936	German armies move unopposed into the demilitarized Rhineland
October 1936	Rome-Berlin Axis created
1936–1939	Spanish civil war
1937	Japan invades China
March 1938	Germany annexes Austria
September 1938	Britain and France agree to German seizure of the Sudetenland from Czechoslovakia
March 1939	Germany occupies the rest of Czechoslovakia; appeasement ends in Britain
August 1939	Nazi-Soviet nonaggression pact is signed
September 1, 1939	Germany invades Poland
September 3, 1939	Britain and France declare war on Germany

States feared that Britain would collapse if it lost its Asian colonies to Japan. Applying economic sanctions in October 1940, the United States stopped scrap iron sales to Japan and later froze all Japanese assets in the United States.

Japan's invasion of southern Indochina in July 1941 further worsened relations with the United States, which viewed this aggression as a direct threat to the Philippines and the Dutch East Indies. The United States responded by cutting off U.S. oil sales to Japan, thereby reducing Japan's oil supplies by 90 percent. Japanese leaders, increasingly convinced that war with the United States was inevitable, decided after much debate to launch a surprise attack on the U.S. fleet in Pearl Harbor in the Hawaiian Islands.

The Japanese attack at Pearl Harbor was a complete surprise but a limited success. On December 7, 1941, the Japanese sank or crippled every American battleship, but by chance all the American aircraft carriers were at sea and escaped unharmed. More important, Americans were humiliated by this unexpected defeat. Thus Pearl Harbor overwhelmed American isolationism and brought the United States into the war.

Hitler immediately declared war on the United States. Simultaneously, Japanese armies successfully attacked European and American colonies in Southeast Asia, seizing the Netherlands East Indies and the British colonies of Hong Kong, Malaya, and Singapore. After American forces surrendered the Philippines in May 1942, Japan held a vast empire in Southeast Asia and the western Pacific (Map 30.3).

Mapping the Past

Map 30.3 World War II in the Pacific

Japanese forces overran an enormous amount of territory in 1942, which the Allies slowly recaptured in a long, bitter struggle.

ANALYZING THE MAP Locate the extent of the Japanese empire in 1942, and compare it to the Japanese-controlled territory at surrender in 1945. Where was the fighting in the Pacific concentrated?

CONNECTIONS How was the course of the end of war in Europe different, and what does this suggest about the difficulties that the Allies faced in fighting the Japanese?

The Japanese claimed they were freeing Asians from Western imperialism, and they called their empire the Greater East Asian Co-Prosperity Sphere. Most local populations were glad to see the Western powers go, but Asian faith in "co-prosperity" and support for Japan steadily declined as the war went on. Although the Japanese set up anticolonial governments and promised genuine independence, real power always rested with Japanese military commanders and their superiors in Tokyo. Moreover, the Japanese never

How did totalitarianism differ from conservative authoritarianism?

What characterized Stalin's rule in the Soviet Union?

How did Italian fascism develop?

What were the goals of Hitler and his Nazi regime?

What led to World War II and how did the Allies prevail?

831

treated local populations as equals, and the occupiers exploited local peoples for Japan's wartime needs.

The Japanese often exhibited great cruelty toward prisoners of war and civilians. After the fall of Hong Kong in December 1941, for example, wounded prisoners were murdered, and there was a mass rape of nurses. Elsewhere Dutch, Indonesian, and perhaps as many as two hundred thousand Korean women were forced to provide sex for Japanese soldiers as "comfort women." Recurring cruel behavior aroused local populations against the invaders.

The Grand Alliance

Europe first policy The military strategy, set forth by Churchill and adopted by Roosevelt, that called for the defeat of Hitler in Europe before the United States launched an all-out strike against Japan in the Pacific.

While the Nazis and the Japanese built their empires, Great Britain, the United States (both vehemently anticommunist), and the Soviet Union (equally anticapitalist) joined together in an unlikely military pact called the Grand Alliance. As a first step toward building an unshakable alliance, the Grand Alliance agreed on a Europe first policy. Only after defeating Hitler would the Allies mount an all-out attack on Japan. To further encourage mutual trust, the Allies adopted the principle of the unconditional surrender of Germany and Japan. This policy cemented the Grand Alliance because it denied Germany and Japan any hope of dividing their foes.

The Grand Alliance's military resources were awesome. The United States possessed a unique capacity to wage global war with its large population and mighty industry. The British economy was totally and effectively mobilized, and the country became an important staging area for the war in Europe. As for the Soviet Union, so great was its strength that it might well have defeated Germany without Western help. In the face of the German advance, whole factories and populations were successfully evacuated to eastern Russia and Siberia. There war production was reorganized and expanded, and the Red Army was increasingly well supplied and well led. Above all, Stalin drew on the massive support of the people for what the Soviets called the "Great Patriotic War of the Fatherland."

The War in Europe, 1942–1945

The Germans renewed their offensive against the Soviet Union in 1942 and attacked Stalingrad in July. The Soviet armies counterattacked, quickly surrounding the entire German Sixth Army of 300,000 men. Hitler, who had refused to allow a retreat, suffered a catastrophic defeat. In summer 1943 the larger, better-equipped Soviet armies took the offensive and began to push the Germans back (see Map 30.2).

Not yet prepared to attack Germany directly through France, the Western Allies saw heavy fighting in North Africa (see Map 30.2). In summer 1942 British forces defeated German and Italian armies at the Battle of El Alamein (el a-luh-MAYN) in Egypt. Shortly thereafter an Anglo-American force took control of the Vichy French colonies of Morocco and Algeria.

Having driven the Axis powers from North Africa by spring 1943, Allied forces invaded Italy. War-weary Italians deposed Mussolini, and the new Italian government accepted unconditional surrender in September 1943. Italy, it seemed, was liberated. But German commandos rescued Mussolini in a daring raid and put him at the head of a puppet government. German armies seized Rome and all of northern Italy. The Allies' Italian campaign against German forces would last another two years. The German armies finally surrendered to the Allies on April 29, 1945. Two days earlier Mussolini had been captured by partisan forces. He was executed the next day.

On June 6, 1944, American and British forces under General Dwight Eisenhower landed on the beaches of Normandy, France, in history's greatest naval invasion. More than 2 mil-

CHAPTER LOCATOR

Why did the Great Depression spread around the world?

The Normandy Invasion, Omaha Beach, June 6, 1944 Airborne paratroopers landed behind German coastal fortifications around midnight, and U.S. and British forces hit several beaches at daybreak as Allied ships and bombers provided cover. U.S. troops secured full control of Omaha Beach by nightfall, but at a price of three thousand casualties. Allied air power prevented the Germans from bringing up reserves and counterattacking. (Bettmann/Corbis)

lion men and almost a half million vehicles pushed inland and broke through the German lines. In March 1945 American troops crossed the Rhine and entered Germany.

The Soviets, who had been advancing steadily since July 1943, reached the outskirts of Warsaw by August 1944. On April 26, 1945, the Red Army met American forces on the Elbe River in Germany. The Allies had closed their vise on Nazi Germany and overrun Europe. As Soviet forces fought their way into Berlin, Hitler committed suicide in his bunker, and on May 7 the remaining German commanders capitulated.

The War in the Pacific, 1942–1945

While gigantic armies clashed on land in Europe, the greatest naval battles in history decided the fate of the war in Asia. First, in the Battle of the Coral Sea in May 1942, an American carrier force halted the Japanese advance on Port Moresby in New Guinea and relieved Australia from the threat of invasion. Then, in the Battle of Midway in June 1942, American pilots sank all four of the attacking Japanese aircraft carriers and established

How did totalitarianism differ from conservative authoritarianism?

What characterized Stalin's rule in the Soviet Union?

How did Italian fascism develop?

What were the goals of Hitler and his Nazi regime?

What led to World War II and how did the Allies prevail?

833

A Hiroshima Survivor Remembers Yasuko Yamagata was seventeen when she saw the brilliant blue-white "lightning flash" that became a fiery orange ball consuming everything that would burn. Thirty years later Yamagata painted this scene, her most unforgettable memory of the atomic attack. An incinerated woman, poised as if running with her baby clutched to her breast, lies near a water tank piled high with charred corpses. (GE15-05 drawn by Yasuko Yamagata, Hiroshima Peace Memorial Museum)

Quick Review
What role did industrial production play in deciding the outcome of World War II?

overall naval equality with Japan in the Pacific (see Map 30.3).

The United States gradually won control of the sea and air as it geared up its war industry. By 1943 the United States was producing one hundred thousand aircraft a year, almost twice as many as Japan produced in the entire war. In July 1943 the Americans and their Australian allies opened an "island-hopping" campaign toward Japan. By 1944 hundreds of American submarines were decimating shipping and destroying economic links in Japan's far-flung, overextended empire.

The Pacific war was brutal and atrocities were committed on both sides.[4] Aware of Japanese atrocities in China and the Philippines, the U.S. Marines and Army troops seldom took Japanese prisoners after the Battle of Guadalcanal in August 1942, killing even those rare Japanese soldiers who offered to surrender. American forces moving across the central and western Pacific in 1943 and 1944 faced unyielding resistance, and this resistance hardened soldiers as American casualties kept rising. A product of spiraling violence, mutual hatred, and dehumanizing racial stereotypes, the war intensified as it moved toward Japan.

In June 1944 U.S. bombers began a bombing campaign of the Japanese home islands. In October 1944 American forces under General Douglas MacArthur landed on Leyte Island in the Philippines. The Japanese believed they could destroy MacArthur's troops and transport ships before the main American fleet arrived. The result was a disastrous defeat for the Japanese at the four-day Battle of Leyte Gulf. After Leyte Gulf, the Japanese navy was practically finished.

In spite of massive defeats, Japanese troops continued to fight with courage and determination, leading American commanders to the conclusion that the conquest of Japan might cost a million American casualties and possibly 10 to 20 million Japanese lives. In fact, Japan was almost helpless, its industry and cities largely destroyed by intense American bombing. Yet the Japanese seemed determined to fight on.

On August 6 and 9, 1945, the United States dropped atomic bombs on Hiroshima and Nagasaki in Japan. Mass bombing of cities and civilians, one of the terrible new practices of World War II, had led to the final nightmare — unprecedented human destruction in a single blinding flash. On August 14, 1945, the Japanese announced their surrender. The Second World War, which had claimed the lives of more than 50 million soldiers and civilians, was over.

Connections

THE INTERCONNECTEDNESS of all the world's inhabitants was demonstrated by the dramatic events of the 1930s and 1940s. First a Great Depression shook the financial foundations of the wealthiest capitalist economies and the poorest producers of raw materials and minerals. Another world war followed, bringing global death and destruction. At war's end, as we shall see in Chapter 34, the world's leaders revived Woodrow Wilson's idea of a League of Nations and formed the United Nations in 1946 to prevent such tragedies from ever reoccurring.

Although the United Nations was an attempt to bring nations together, the postwar world became more divided than ever. Chapter 31 will describe how two new superpowers—the United States and the Soviet Union—emerged from World War II to engage one another in the Cold War for nearly the rest of the century. Then in Chapters 32 and 33 we will see how a political Third World of nations in Asia, Africa, and Latin America emerged after the war. Many of them did so by turning the nineteenth-century European ideology of nationalism against its creators, breaking the bonds of colonialism.

Today we want to believe that the era of totalitarian dictatorship "can't happen again." But the truth is that horrible atrocities continue to plague the world in our time. The Khmer Rouge inflicted genocide on its people in Cambodia, and civil war led to ethnically motivated atrocities in Bosnia, Rwanda, Burundi, and Sudan, recalling the horrors of the Second World War. Today's dictators, however, are losing control over access to information—historically a cornerstone of dictatorial rule—and are being challenged and even overthrown by citizens with cell phones, cameras, and Internet connections who expose their murderous actions to the world. The 2010 and 2011 "Arab Spring," discussed in Chapter 32, offers an example of this trend.

- For a list of suggested readings for this chapter, visit *bedfordstmartins.com/mckayworldunderstanding*.

- For primary sources from this period, see *Sources of World Societies*, Second Edition.

- For Web sites, images, and documents related to topics in this chapter, see Make History at *bedfordstmartins.com/mckayworldunderstanding*.

How did totalitarianism differ from conservative authoritarianism?

What characterized Stalin's rule in the Soviet Union?

How did Italian fascism develop?

What were the goals of Hitler and his Nazi regime?

What led to World War II and how did the Allies prevail?

835

Chapter 30 Study Guide

To do these exercises online, go to bedfordstmartins.com/mckayworldunderstanding.

GETTING STARTED

Below are basic terms about this period in global history. Can you identify each term below and explain why it matters?

TERMS	WHO (OR WHAT) AND WHEN	WHY IT MATTERS
New Deal, p. 810		
Popular Front, p. 811		
totalitarianism, p. 813		
fascism, p. 813		
five-year plan, p. 814		
New Economic Policy (NEP), p. 814		
collectivization, p. 815		
Black Shirts, p. 818		
Lateran Agreement, p. 819		
Nazism, p. 819		
Enabling Act, p. 820		
blitzkrieg, p. 824		
New Order, p. 826		
Holocaust, p. 826		
Europe first policy, p. 832		

MOVING BEYOND THE BASICS

The exercise below requires a more advanced understanding of the chapter material. Examine the totalitarian regimes of the 1920s and 1930s by filling in the chart below with descriptions of the ideologies and policies of the governments of the Soviet Union, Italy, and Germany. When you are finished, consider the following questions: How did ideology shape the policies of each government? What were the most important similarities and differences between these governments?

	IDEOLOGY	SOCIAL POLICY	ECONOMIC POLICY	FOREIGN POLICY
The Soviet Union				
Italy				
Germany				

PUTTING IT ALL TOGETHER

Now that you've reviewed key elements of the chapter, take a step back and try to see the big picture. Remember to use specific examples from the chapter in your answers.

THE GREAT DEPRESSION

- Compare and contrast the response to the Great Depression in the United States, France, Britain, Germany, and the Scandinavian countries. How would you explain the similarities and differences you note?

- What light does the Great Depression shed on the nature of global economic connections in the 1920s and 1930s? How did an economic crisis that began in the United States and Europe spread to Asia, Africa, and Latin America?

THE AGE OF DICTATORS

- In your opinion, was Italy under Mussolini a totalitarian state? Why or why not?

- Compare and contrast Stalinism and Nazism. What were the most important differences between the two ideologies? How did both systems use the persecution of "outsiders" to promote loyalty and obedience to the regime?

THE SECOND WORLD WAR

- What role did race play in the German and Japanese drive for territorial expansion? Is it fair to describe World War II, in Europe and in the Pacific, as a racial war?

- In your opinion, why did the Allies win the war? What role did industrial production play in the Allied victory? What other factors were important?

LOOKING BACK, LOOKING AHEAD

- Argue for or against the following proposition: "World War II was the inevitable consequence of the destruction of World War I and the fatally flawed peace treaties produced at its conclusion." What evidence can you present to support your position?

- What similarities and differences do you see between the Great Depression of the 1930s and the global economic crisis of the early twenty-first century? Could the contemporary crisis lead to another "Age of Dictators"? Why or why not?

In Your Own Words Imagine that you must explain Chapter 30 to someone who hasn't read it. What would be the most important points to include and why?

31

Global Recovery and Division Between Superpowers

1945 to the Present

After the defeat of the Axis powers, recovery began worldwide. Hopes of peace quickly faded, however, when differences in Allied economic and political ideologies set aside during wartime came to the fore, pitting the democratic and capitalist countries of the United States and its allies, including Japan, against the Marxist Communist Soviet Union and its allies.

Despite the growing tensions of this global Cold War, the postwar decades witnessed remarkable growth and prosperity. A battered western Europe, with U.S. aid, witnessed an amazing recovery. Having avoided wartime destruction and occupation, the United States quickly converted its economies to peacetime production. After seven years of Allied occupation, Japan experienced a quick recovery that by the 1960s made it one of the world's leading economic powers. In the east, the Soviet Union sought to protect itself from future attacks from the west by occupying eastern Europe and establishing Communist dictatorships there.

In the early 1970s the global economic boom came to an end, and domestic political stability and social harmony evaporated. The collapse of communism in eastern Europe in 1989 and the end of the Cold War reinforced global integration. The result was monumental change, especially in postcommunist eastern Europe. The nations of western Europe were also transformed, as they moved toward greater unity within the European Union.

Soviet Worker Statue
An idealized Soviet worker leans forward into the new Soviet age in this example of socialist realism, an artistic style that promoted socialism and communism. Statues like this one were propaganda tools for the Soviet state. (© Eduard Talaykov)

Chapter Preview

▶ What were the causes of the Cold War?

▶ How did western Europe recover after World War II, and why did progress stall?

▶ How did the Soviet Union dominate eastern Europe in the postwar era?

▶ What factors shaped social and political developments in postwar America?

▶ How did Japan become a global power after its defeat in World War II?

▶ What opportunities and challenges did Europe face after the Cold War?

What were the causes of the Cold War?

In 1945 triumphant American and Russian soldiers embraced along the Elbe River in the heart of vanquished Germany. Yet the United States and the Soviet Union soon found themselves at loggerheads. By the end of 1947 Europe was rigidly divided, West versus East, in a Cold War eventually waged around the world.

The Origins of the Cold War

Almost as soon as the unifying threat of Nazi Germany disappeared, the Soviet Union and the United States began to quarrel. Hostility between the Eastern and Western superpowers was the logical outgrowth of military developments, wartime agreements, and long-standing political and ideological differences.

In the early phases of the Second World War, the Americans and the British avoided discussion of Joseph Stalin's war aims and the shape of the eventual peace settlement, fearing that hard bargaining might encourage Stalin to make a separate peace with Hitler. By late 1943 decisions about the shape of the postwar world could no longer be postponed. Franklin Roosevelt, Winston Churchill, and Joseph Stalin met in Teheran, Iran, in November 1943, and there the "Big Three" reaffirmed their determination to crush Germany. It was agreed that the Americans and British would launch an invasion of France. Soviet armies would liberate eastern Europe.

When the Big Three met again in February 1945 at Yalta on the Black Sea in southern Russia, the Red Army occupied most of eastern Europe and was within a hundred miles of Berlin. American-British forces had yet to cross the Rhine into Germany. Moreover, the

The Big Three In 1945 a triumphant Winston Churchill, an ailing Franklin Roosevelt, and a determined Joseph Stalin met at Yalta in southern Russia to plan for peace. Cooperation soon gave way to bitter hostility. (F.D.R. Library)

Postwar Territorial Changes in Eastern Europe

Legend:
- Lost by Germany
- Gained by Soviet Union

Chapter Chronology

1945	Yalta and Potsdam Conferences; end of World War II
1945–1952	Allied occupation of Japan
1945–1960s	Decolonization of Asia and Africa
1947	Truman Doctrine; Marshall Plan
1949	Formation of NATO
1950–1953	Korean War
1950–1970	Enormous growth of Japanese economy
1953–1964	Khrushchev implements policy of de-Stalinization in the Soviet Union
1957	Formation of Common Market
1961	Building of Berlin Wall
1962	Solzhenitsyn, *One Day in the Life of Ivan Denisovich*; Cuban missile crisis
1964	Civil Rights Act in United States
1964–1975	U.S. involvement in Vietnam War
1973	OPEC oil embargo
1985	Glasnost leads to greater freedom of speech and expression in the Soviet Union
1989	Collapse of Berlin Wall
1989–1991	Fall of communism in Soviet Union and eastern Europe
1990	Charter of Paris for a New Europe
1990–1992	Collapse of Japanese stock market
1991–2001	Civil war in Yugoslavia
1993	Formation of European Union
2000–2008	Resurgence of Russian economy under Putin
2008	Worldwide financial crisis
2009	Ratification of Treaty of Lisbon

United States was far from defeating Japan. In short, the Soviet Union's position was strong and America's was weak. At Yalta the Big Three agreed that Germany would be divided into zones of occupation and would pay the Soviet Union heavy reparations. Stalin agreed to declare war on Japan after Germany's defeat. As for Poland and eastern Europe, the Big Three reached an ambiguous compromise: eastern European governments were to be freely elected but pro-Russian.

Almost immediately this compromise broke down. Even before the conference, Communists arriving with the Red Army controlled Bulgaria and Poland. Elsewhere in eastern Europe, pro-Soviet "coalition" governments were formed, but key ministerial posts were reserved for Moscow-trained Communists.

At the postwar Potsdam Conference in July 1945, long-avoided differences over eastern Europe were finally debated. The compromising Roosevelt had died and had been succeeded by the more assertive Harry Truman (1884–1972), who now demanded free elections throughout eastern Europe. Stalin refused, convinced that a buffer zone of Communist states was crucial to the Soviet Union's security. By the middle of 1945 the United States had no way to determine political developments in eastern Europe short of war, and war was out of the question. Stalin would have his way.

West Versus East

America's response to Stalin's conception of security was to "get tough." In May 1945 Truman cut off all aid to the Soviet Union. In October he declared that the United States would never recognize any government established by force against the free will of its people. His declaration, however, applied only to Europe and to countries threatened by communism, not to British and French colonies in Asia and Africa, for example, or to Latin

American right-wing dictatorships. America's failure to support Third World liberation movements would have tragic consequences later on, particularly in Vietnam. In March 1946 former British prime minister Churchill ominously informed an American audience that an "iron curtain" had fallen across the European continent, dividing Germany and all of Europe into two antagonistic camps (Map 31.1).

Stalin quickly renewed the "ideological struggle against capitalist imperialism." France's and Italy's large, well-organized Communist Parties challenged their own governments with violent criticism and large strikes. The Soviet Union also put pressure on Iran, Turkey, and Greece, and a bitter civil war raged in China (see pages 870–871). By spring 1947 many Americans believed that Stalin was determined to export communism throughout Europe and around the world.

Truman Doctrine U.S. policy to contain communism to areas already occupied by the Red Army.

The United States responded with the **Truman Doctrine**, aimed at "containing" communism to areas already occupied by the Red Army. Truman told Congress in 1947, "I believe it must be the policy of the United States to support free people who are resisting attempted subjugation by armed minorities or by outside pressure." Then, in June, Secretary of State George C. Marshall offered Europe economic aid—the **Marshall Plan**—to help it rebuild. Stalin refused Marshall Plan assistance for all of eastern Europe, where he had established Soviet-style Communist dictatorships.

Marshall Plan American plan for providing economic aid to Europe to help it rebuild.

On July 24, 1948, Stalin blocked all highway traffic through the Soviet zone of Germany to Berlin. The Western allies responded by airlifting provisions to the West Berlin-

Map 31.1 Cold War Europe in the 1950s Europe was divided by an "iron curtain" during the Cold War. None of the Communist countries of eastern Europe were participants in the Marshall Plan.

The Korean War, 1950–1953

CHINA

SOVIET UNION

Yalu R.

Chosin Reservoir

Farthest UN advance Nov. 1950

NORTH KOREA

Pyongyang

Sea of Japan

Demilitarized zone 1953

38th Parallel

Seoul

SOUTH KOREA

Inchon landing Sept. 15, 1950

Yellow Sea

UN defensive line Sept. 1950

Pusan

JAPAN

→ North Korean invasion, June–Sept. 1950

→ UN offensive, Sept.–Nov. 1950

→ Communist Chinese offensive, Nov. 1950–Jan. 1951

ers. After 324 days the Soviets backed down: containment seemed to work. In 1949 the United States formed an anti-Soviet military alliance of Western governments: the North Atlantic Treaty Organization (NATO). Stalin countered by tightening his hold on his satellites, later united in the Warsaw Pact. Europe was divided into two hostile blocs.

As tensions rose in Europe, the Cold War spread to Asia. In 1945 Korea was divided into Soviet and American zones of occupation, which in 1948 became Communist North Korea and anticommunist South Korea. In late 1949 the Communists triumphed in China (see page 871), frightening many Americans, who saw new evidence of a powerful worldwide Communist conspiracy. When the Russian-backed Communist forces of North Korea invaded South Korea in spring 1950, Truman sent U.S. troops to lead a twenty-nation UN coalition force.

The Korean War (1950–1953) was bitterly fought. The well-equipped North Koreans conquered most of the peninsula, but the South Korean, American, and UN troops rallied and drove their foes north to the Chinese border. At that point China intervened and pushed the South Koreans and Americans back south. In 1953 a fragile truce was negotiated. Thus the United States extended its policy of containing communism to Asia, but drew back from invading Communist China and possible nuclear war.

NATO The North Atlantic Treaty Organization, an anti-Soviet military alliance of Western nations.

> **Quick Review**
> Why did tensions between the United States and the Soviet Union escalate in the years following World War II?

How did western Europe recover after World War II, and why did progress stall?

As the Cold War divided Europe into two blocs, the future appeared bleak. Yet western Europe recovered to enjoy unprecedented economic prosperity and peaceful social transformation. Then, in the early 1970s, the cycle turned abruptly, and a downturn in the world economy hit western Europe hard.

The Postwar Challenge

After the war, economic conditions in western Europe were terrible. Yet, within a few years, western Europe began to recover. Progressive Catholics and their Christian Democrat political parties were particularly influential. Socialists and Communists active in the resistance against Hitler emerged from the war with increased power and prestige, especially in France and Italy. In the immediate postwar years social welfare measures were enacted throughout much of Europe. Social reform complemented political transformation, creating solid foundations for a great European renaissance.

There were many reasons for this amazing recovery. The United States sped the process through the Marshall Plan, and as aid poured in, western Europe's battered economies began to turn the corner. Europe entered a period of unprecedented economic progress lasting into the late 1960s. Western European governments also adopted a variety of successful economic and social strategies. Postwar West Germany adopted a free-market economy while maintaining an extensive social welfare network. The French established a new kind of planning commission that set ambitious but flexible goals for the French economy, using the nationalized banks to funnel money into key industries.

European workers also contributed to the economic turnaround. They worked hard for low wages in hope of a better future. During the Great Depression few Europeans had been able to afford many of the new consumer products. Thus in 1945 the electric refrigerator, the washing machine, and the automobile were rare luxuries, and there was great potential demand, which manufacturers moved to satisfy.

Migrant laborers from the Mediterranean basin (southern Italy, North Africa, Turkey, Greece, and Yugoslavia) also played a key role in Europe's postwar recovery. They accepted the least desirable jobs for the lowest pay. Europeans assumed that rising birthrates among the majority population would eventually fill the labor shortages, so at first they labeled the migrants "guest workers" to signal their temporary status. By the 1980s, however, as millions more migrants arrived from Europe's former colonies, it was clear that their presence would be permanent. Their full integration into European society has been incomplete, creating ongoing tensions.

Finally, western European nations abandoned protectionism and gradually created a large, unified market. This historic action was part of a larger search for European unity.

Building Europe and Decolonization

Western Europe's postwar political recovery was unprecedented. Democratic governments took root throughout western Europe. The changes in Germany were especially profound. Konrad Adenauer (1876–1967), the first chancellor of postwar West Germany, was largely responsible for West Germany's remarkable recovery. Fiercely anticommunist, Adenauer brought Germany firmly into the Western capitalist camp by developing close ties with the United States and restoring relations with Great Britain and France.

A similarly extraordinary achievement was the march toward a united Europe. Many Europeans believed that only unity could forestall future European conflicts and that only a new "European nation" could reassert western Europe's influence in world affairs dominated by the United States and the Soviet Union.

European federalists focused first on economics. In 1952 France, West Germany, Italy, Belgium, the Netherlands, and Luxembourg joined together to control and integrate their coal and steel production. In 1957 the six nations of the Coal and Steel Community signed the Treaty of Rome, creating the European Economic Community, popularly known as the Common Market. The treaty's primary goal was a gradual reduction of all tariffs among the six in order to create a single market almost as large as that of the United States.

Common Market The European Economic Community created in 1957.

The Common Market was a great success, encouraging hopes of rapid progress toward political as well as economic union. In the 1960s, however, a resurgence of more traditional nationalism in France led by Charles de Gaulle, French president from 1958 to 1969, frustrated these hopes. Viewing the United States as the main threat to genuine French (and European) independence, he withdrew all French military forces from NATO, developed France's own nuclear weapons, and refused to permit majority rule within the Common Market. De Gaulle also thwarted efforts to expand the membership of the Common Market. Thus, throughout the 1960s the Common Market thrived economically but remained a union of sovereign states.

As Europe moved toward greater economic unity in the postwar era, its centuries-long overseas expansion was dramatically reversed. Between 1945 and the early 1960s almost every colonial territory gained independence. This rolling back of Western expansion — decolonization — marks one of world history's great turning points. The basic cause of imperial collapse was the rising demand by Asian and African peoples for national self-determination and racial equality (see Chapters 32 and 33).

Most Europeans viewed their empires after 1945 very differently than they had before 1914. Empires had rested on self-confidence and self-righteousness. The horrors of the Second World War destroyed such complacent arrogance and gave imperialism's opponents much greater influence in Europe. After 1945 many Europeans were willing to let go of their colonies more or less voluntarily and to concentrate on rebuilding at home.

European political and business leaders still wanted some ties with the former colonies, however. As a result, western European countries increased their economic and cultural ties with their former African colonies in the 1960s and 1970s. This situation led many critics to charge that western Europe and the United States had imposed a system of neo-colonialism designed to perpetuate Western economic domination and undermine political independence, just as the United States had subordinated the new nations of Latin America in the nineteenth century (see pages 727–731).

The Changing Class Structure and Social Reform

A more mobile and more democratic European society developed after World War II as old class barriers relaxed. Most noticeably, the structure of the middle class changed. After 1945 a new breed of managers and experts required by large corporations and government agencies replaced traditional property owners as leaders of the middle class. Members of this new middle class could give their children access to advanced education, but only rarely could they pass on the positions they had attained. Thus the new middle class, based largely on specialized skills and high levels of education, was more open, democratic, and insecure than the old propertied middle class.

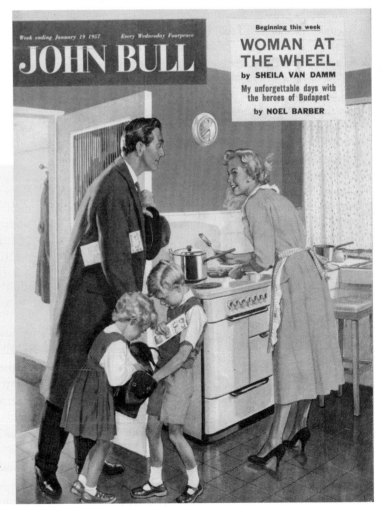

Picturing the Past

Cover of *John Bull* Magazine, January 1957

Like the *Saturday Evening Post* in America, *John Bull* portrayed English life through images and stories. This cover, published twelve years after the end of World War II, shows an English household that has fully recovered from the war, with the husband coming home to two beautiful children and a lovely wife in a modern and stylish kitchen. (Private Collection/The Advertising Archives/The Bridgeman Art Library)

ANALYZING THE IMAGE What are the members of this family doing? What clothes are they wearing, and what might this suggest about their roles within the family?

CONNECTIONS What does this magazine cover suggest about the availability of consumer goods and the desire for them after the war?

GLOBAL TRADE

Oil

Oil in its crude form is found as a liquid hydrocarbon located in certain rocks below the earth's crust. Although it is found throughout the world, the Persian Gulf and Caspian Sea areas contain about three-quarters of the world's proven reserves. The uses of crude oil are limited, but it may be refined into valuable products such as kerosene, gasoline, and fuel oil.

Oil has been used throughout history, although it did not become a worldwide commodity until the nineteenth century. In antiquity, the Sumerians and Babylonians mixed evaporated oil from tar pits with sand to make asphalt for waterproofing ships and paving roads. Islamic societies in the Middle East used small quantities of oil for lighting, although cooking fires were probably the main source of light.

In Europe, lamp oil — from animal fats and plants — was a luxury. The nineteenth century brought revolutionary changes in lighting, and by the 1840s manufacturers in coal-rich Europe were distilling coal into crude oil and gas for use in lighting. North America followed suit. The production of kerosene took off as consumers accepted the bright, clean-burning, and relatively inexpensive oil for use in their lamps.

The modern oil industry operated on a global scale from the beginning. After the late 1860s the United States exported two-thirds of its kerosene. The leading producer was John D. Rockefeller's Standard Oil, which held a monopoly on kerosene until the U.S. government broke the corporation into separate companies in 1911. Most kerosene went to Europe at first, but other markets grew rapidly. In the 1870s the Baku region on the Caspian Sea introduced drilling and created a Russian refining industry. Russian capitalists fought well-publicized "oil wars" with Standard Oil for world kerosene markets.

International differences were significant. In the United States and western Europe kerosene appealed especially to farmers and urban working people, who had previously lacked decent lighting. The affluent urban classes generally continued to use coal-distilled gas until the 1880s, when electricity from central power stations began to replace gas in elegant neighborhoods. In China peasants rejected bulk distribution and insisted on kerosene in tin cans, recycling them into valuable all-purpose containers. Russia pioneered in using oil as fuel, as the refining of heavy Baku crude yielded abundant thick "leftovers" — an excellent power source for riverboats, railroads, and factories.

During the twentieth century oil became a major fuel source as kerosene production declined. Until 1941 the explosive growth of automobiles in the United States was easily outpaced by the development of domestic oil fields, enabling the United States to sell one-third of all the oil consumed beyond its borders. In oil-poor Europe (Russia excepted), fuel oil loomed large as a strategic material. After 1919 the British government took control of the two oil companies in Iran and Iraq to guarantee supplies for Britain's military and industrial needs. Germany distilled coal into synthetic gasoline, and Hitler relentlessly pushed production of this very expensive alternative to free his war machine from dependence on foreign oil.

The international oil trade shifted dramatically after 1945. The United States, previously producing half the world's oil, became the world's largest importer. The Middle East became the world's leading exporter. At the same time, western Europe and Japan shifted from coal to oil to drive their factories and fuel their automobiles. Nevertheless, the American and British oil companies in the Middle East expanded output so rapidly — sixteen times between 1948 and 1972 — that the inflation-adjusted price for Middle Eastern oil fell substantially in these years.

Increasingly dissatisfied with their share of the profits, the main exporting countries — Iran, Iraq, Kuwait, Saudi Arabia, and Venezuela — organized the Organization of Petroleum Exporting Countries (OPEC) in 1960 to gain control of their oil resources. In 1973, during the Arab-Israeli war, OPEC engineered a fourfold price increase with enormous global consequences. The exporting states also nationalized their oil industries, reducing foreign companies to simple buyers and transporters.

The structure of the lower classes also became more flexible and open. There was a mass exodus from farms and the countryside. Meanwhile, the industrial working class ceased to expand, but job opportunities for white-collar and service employees grew rapidly. Such employees bore a greater resemblance to the new middle class of salaried specialists than to industrial workers, who themselves were also better educated and more specialized.

European governments also reduced class tensions with a series of social reforms. Many of these reforms — such as increased unemployment benefits and more extensive old-age pensions — strengthened existing social security measures. Other programs were new, such as state-run, comprehensive national health systems. Most countries introduced direct government grants that helped many poor families make ends meet. Maternity grants and inexpensive public housing for low-income families and individuals were also common.

846

Chapter 31 Global Recovery and Division
Between Superpowers • 1945 to the Present

CHAPTER LOCATOR

What were the causes
of the Cold War?

Map 31.2 The Oil Trade, ca. 1900–1975

The oil exporters used their profits to improve living standards somewhat, but vast sums went for lavish spending by the elite, and above all, the money went for expensive military hardware from the industrialized countries, which increased tensions and prolonged the terrible war between Iraq and Iran in the 1980s (see pages 890–891).

A price collapse followed the upward price revolution of the 1970s. In the 1980s and early 1990s conservation, greater efficiency, recession, environmental concerns, and significant new oil discoveries outside the Middle East eliminated much of the inflation-adjusted price increases of the 1970s. By 2002 some argued that oil was really "just another commodity." The outbreak of the Iraq War in 2003, however — followed by natural disasters such as Hurricane Katrina; instability in Nigeria, Venezuela, and other major oil-producing countries; and skyrocketing demands for oil by China and India — sent oil to nearly $150 per barrel by 2008, creating another global energy crisis.

Economic and Social Dislocation, 1970–1990

An economic crisis in the 1970s brought the postwar economic recovery to a halt. The earliest cause was the collapse of the postwar international monetary system, which since 1945 had been based on the U.S. dollar. In 1971 the dollar's value fell sharply, and inflation accelerated worldwide. Fixed rates of exchange were abandoned, and uncertainty replaced predictability in international trade and finance.

Even more damaging was the dramatic reversal in the price and availability of energy. (See "Global Trade: Oil," page 846.) In 1971 the Arab-led Organization of Petroleum Exporting Countries — OPEC — decided to reverse a decline in the crude oil price by presenting a united front against the oil companies. After the Arab-Israeli war in October 1973 (see

OPEC The Arab-led organization of countries that export oil that helps set policies and prices on its trade.

How did western Europe recover after WWII, and why did progress stall?　How did the Soviet Union dominate eastern Europe in the postwar era?　What factors shaped social and political developments in postwar America?　How did Japan become a global power after its defeat in World War II?　What opportunities and challenges did Europe face after the Cold War?　**847** page 884), OPEC placed an embargo on oil exports, and crude oil prices quadrupled in a year.

The rise in energy prices coupled with the upheaval in the international monetary system plunged the world into its worst economic decline since the 1930s. By 1976 a modest recovery was in progress, but when Iranian oil production collapsed during Iran's fundamentalist Islamic revolution in 1979 (see page 891), crude oil prices doubled again. By 1985 unemployment rates in western Europe had risen to their highest levels since the Great Depression. Global recovery was painfully slow until late 1993.

Western Europe's welfare system prevented mass suffering, but increased government spending was not matched by higher taxes, causing a rapid growth of budget deficits, national debts, and inflation. By the late 1970s a powerful reaction against government's ever-increasing role had set in. In Britain, Prime Minister Margaret Thatcher slowed government spending and privatized industry by selling off state-owned companies to private investors. Other Western governments introduced austerity measures to slow the growth of public spending and the welfare state.

Individuals felt the impact of austerity, and the threat of unemployment—or underemployment in dead-end jobs—shaped the outlook of a whole generation. Students in the 1980s were serious, practical, and often conservative.

Harder times also meant that more women entered or remained in the workforce after they married. Although attitudes related to personal fulfillment were one reason for the continuing increase—especially for well-educated upper-middle-class women—many wives in poor and middle-class families worked outside the home because of economic necessity.

Quick Review
What challenges did western Europeans face in the postwar period, and how did they respond to them?

How did the Soviet Union dominate eastern Europe in the postwar era?

Postwar economic recovery in eastern Europe proceeded along Soviet lines, and changes in the Soviet Union strongly influenced political and social developments. That trend remained true more than forty years later, when radical reform in the Soviet Union opened the door to popular revolution in the eastern European satellites—and ultimately to the collapse of the Soviet Union itself.

Stalin's Last Years

The "Great Patriotic War of the Fatherland" had fostered Russian nationalism and a relaxation of totalitarian terror. But even before war's end, Stalin was moving his country back toward rigid dictatorship. As early as 1944 Communist Party members received a new slogan: "The war on Fascism ends, the war on capitalism begins."[1] Stalin purged thousands of returning soldiers and ordinary civilians in 1945 and 1946, and he revived the terrible forced-labor camps of the 1930s. Culture and art were purged of Western influences, Orthodox Christianity again came under attack, and Soviet Jews were accused of being pro-Western and antisocialist.

Stalin reintroduced the five-year plans to cope with the enormous task of economic reconstruction. Once again heavy and military industry were given top priority, and consumer goods, housing, and collectivized agriculture were neglected. Everyday life was very hard.

Stalin then exported the Stalinist system to eastern Europe. Rigid ideological indoctrination, attacks on religion, and a lack of civil liberties were soon facts of life in the region's one-party states. Only Yugoslavia's Josip Tito (1892–1980), the popular resistance leader and

Communist Party chief, could resist Soviet domination successfully, because there was no Russian army in Yugoslavia.

Limited De-Stalinization and Stagnation

In 1953 Stalin died. Even as his heirs struggled for power, they realized that reforms were necessary because of the widespread fear and hatred of Stalin's political terrorism. They curbed secret police powers and gradually closed many forced-labor camps. Change was also necessary for economic reasons. Agriculture was in bad shape, and shortages of consumer goods were discouraging hard work and initiative. Moreover, Stalin's belligerent foreign policy had led directly to a strong Western alliance, isolating the Soviet Union.

The Communist Party leadership was badly split on just how much change to permit. Reformers, led by Nikita Khrushchev (1894–1971), argued for major innovations and won. The liberalization of the Soviet Union—labeled de-Stalinization in the West—was genuine. The Communist Party maintained its monopoly on political power, but Khrushchev shook up the party and brought in new members. Some resources were shifted from heavy industry and the military toward consumer goods and agriculture, and controls over workers were relaxed. The Soviet Union's standard of living began to improve and continued to rise substantially throughout the 1960s.

De-Stalinization created great ferment among writers and intellectuals. The writer Aleksandr Solzhenitsyn (1918–2008) created a sensation when his *One Day in the Life of Ivan Denisovich* was published in the Soviet Union in 1962. Solzhenitsyn's novel portrays life in a Stalinist concentration camp in grim detail and is a damning indictment of the Stalinist past.

Khrushchev also de-Stalinized Soviet foreign policy. "Peaceful coexistence" with capitalism was possible, he argued. But while Cold War tensions relaxed between 1955 and 1957, de-Stalinization stimulated rebelliousness in the eastern European satellites. Poland won greater autonomy in 1956 when extensive rioting brought in a new Communist government. Led by students and workers, the people of Budapest, Hungary, installed a liberal Communist reformer as their new chief in October 1956. After the new government promised free elections and renounced Hungary's military alliance with Moscow, Russian leaders ordered an invasion and crushed the revolution.

In August 1961 East Germany began construction of the Berlin Wall. Officially the wall was called the "Anti-Fascist Protection Wall." In reality the Berlin Wall, which dramatically symbolized the Iron Curtain, was necessary to prevent East Germans from "voting with their feet" by defecting to the West.

By late 1962 party opposition to Khrushchev's policies had gained momentum. De-Stalinization was seen as a dangerous threat to party authority. Moreover, Khrushchev's policy toward the West was erratic and ultimately unsuccessful. When Khrushchev ordered missiles with nuclear warheads installed in Fidel Castro's Communist Cuba in 1962, U.S. president John F. Kennedy countered with a naval blockade of Cuba. After a tense diplomatic crisis Khrushchev agreed to remove the missiles. Khrushchev was removed in a bloodless coup within two years of the Cuban missile crisis.

After Leonid Brezhnev (1906–1982) and his supporters took over in 1964, they talked quietly of Stalin's "good points," stopped further liberalization, and launched a massive arms buildup.

The Impact of Reform on Everyday Life

In the wake of Khrushchev's reforms, the 1960s brought modest liberalization and more consumer goods to eastern Europe, as well as somewhat greater national autonomy. In January 1968 reform elements in the Czechoslovakian Communist Party gained a majority

de-Stalinization The liberalization of the post-Stalin Soviet Union, led by reformer Nikita Khrushchev during his years as the head of the Soviet Union (1953–1964).

and replaced a long-time Stalinist leader with Alexander Dubček (1921–1992), whose new government launched dramatic reforms. In response, in August 1968, five hundred thousand Russian and eastern European troops occupied Czechoslovakia, and the Czech reform movement came to an end. Shortly afterward, Brezhnev declared the so-called **Brezhnev Doctrine**, according to which the Soviet Union and its allies could intervene in any socialist country whenever they saw the need.

In the aftermath of intervention in Czechoslovakia, free expression and open protest disappeared. Dissidents were blacklisted or quietly imprisoned in jails or mental institutions. Unlike in the Stalinist era, though, dictatorship was collective rather than personal, and coercion replaced uncontrolled terror. This compromise seemed to suit the leaders and a majority of the people, and the Soviet Union appeared stable in the 1970s and early 1980s.

A rising standard of living for ordinary people contributed to stability, although the economic crisis of the 1970s greatly slowed the rate of improvement, and long lines and shortages persisted. The exclusive privileges enjoyed by the Communist Party elite also reinforced the system. Ambitious individuals had tremendous incentives to do as the state wished in order to gain access to special well-stocked stores, attend superior schools, and travel abroad.

Another source of stability was the enduring nationalism of ordinary Russians. Party leaders successfully identified themselves with Russian patriotism, stressing their role in saving the motherland during the Second World War. Moreover, the politically dominant Great Russians, only half of the total Soviet population, held the top positions in the Soviet Union's non-Russian republics.

Beneath this stability, however, the Soviet Union was experiencing a social revolution. A rapidly expanding urban population abandoned its old peasant ways, exchanging them for more education, better job skills, and greater sophistication. This trend in turn helped foster the growth of Soviet public opinion. Educated people read, discussed, and formed definite ideas about social questions ranging from environmental pollution to urban transportation. These changes set the stage for the dramatic reforms of the Gorbachev era.

The Gorbachev Era

Elected as leader in 1985, Mikhail Gorbachev (b. 1931) believed in communism, but he realized that Brezhnev's reforms would not be enough to save the failing state. Importantly, Gorbachev realized that success at home required better relations with the West. Thus Gorbachev attempted to save the Soviet system with a series of reform policies he labeled democratic socialism.

The first set of reforms was intended to transform and restructure the economy. This economic restructuring, **perestroika**, permitted freer prices, more independence for state enterprises, and the setting up of some profit-seeking private cooperatives. The reforms were rather timid, however, and when the economy stalled, Gorbachev's popular support gradually eroded.

Gorbachev's bold and far-reaching campaign of openness, or **glasnost**, was much more successful. Where censorship, dull uniformity, and outright lies had long characterized public discourse, the new frankness led rather quickly to something approaching free speech and free expression.

Democratization was the third of Gorbachev's reforms, and it led to the first free elections in the Soviet Union since 1917. Democratization encouraged demands for greater autonomy by non-Russian minorities, especially in the Baltic region and in the Caucasus. But whereas China's Communist Party leaders brutally massacred similar pro-democracy demonstrators in Beijing in June 1989 (see page 873), Gorbachev drew back from repression. Thus nationalist demands continued to grow.

Finally, Gorbachev brought "new political thinking" to foreign affairs. He withdrew Soviet troops from Afghanistan in February 1989 and sought to reduce East-West tensions.

Of enormous importance, Gorbachev repudiated the Brezhnev Doctrine, pledging to respect the political choices of eastern Europe's peoples. By 1989 it seemed that the Soviet occupation of eastern Europe might gradually wither away.

The Revolutions of 1989

Instead of gradually changing, however, in 1989 a series of largely peaceful revolutions swept across eastern Europe, overturning existing Communist regimes. New governments formed dedicated to democratic elections, human rights, and national rejuvenation.

The Poles led the way. Poland had from the beginning resisted Soviet-style collectivization and had refused to break with the Roman Catholic Church. Faced with an independent agricultural sector and a vigorous church, the Communists failed to monopolize society. They also failed to manage the economy effectively and instead sent it into a nosedive by the mid-1970s. When Polish-born Pope John Paul II (1920–2005) returned to Poland to preach the love of Christ and country and the "inalienable rights of man," he electrified the Polish nation, and the economic crisis became a spiritual crisis as well.

In August 1980 scattered strikes snowballed into a working-class revolt. Led by Lech Walesa (lehk vah-LEHN-suh; b. 1943), the workers organized an independent trade union they called **Solidarity**. In response, the Communist leadership proclaimed martial law in December 1981 and arrested Solidarity's leaders. (See "Listening to the Past: A Solidarity Leader Speaks from Prison," page 852.) Though outlawed, Solidarity maintained its organization and strong popular support. By 1988 widespread labor unrest and raging inflation had brought Poland to the brink of economic collapse. Thus Solidarity pressured Poland's Communist Party leaders into legalizing Solidarity and allowing free elections in June 1989 for some seats in the Polish parliament. Solidarity won every contested seat. A month later Tadeusz Mazowiecki (b. 1927) was sworn in as the first noncommunist prime minister in eastern Europe in a generation.

Poland was soon followed by Czechoslovakia, where in December 1989 the so-called Velvet Revolution peacefully ousted Communist leaders. The Velvet Revolution grew out of massive street protests led by students and intellectuals, and it led to the election of Václav Havel (VAH-slahf HAH-vuhl; 1936-2011) as president in 1989. (See the feature "Individuals in Society: Václav Havel," page 854.)

Only in Romania was revolution violent and bloody. There Communist dictator Nicolae Ceauşescu (chow-SHES-kou; 1918–1989) ordered

Solidarity Led by Lech Walesa, a free and democratic Polish trade union that worked for the rights of workers and political reform.

Fall of the Berlin Wall A man stands atop the partially destroyed Berlin Wall flashing the V for victory sign as he and thousands of other Berliners celebrate the opening of the Berlin Wall in November 1989. Within a year the wall was torn down, communism collapsed, and the Cold War ended. (Lionel Cironneau/AP Images)

How did western Europe recover after WWII, and why did progress stall?

How did the Soviet Union dominate eastern Europe in the postwar era?

What factors shaped social and political developments in postwar America?

How did Japan become a global power after its defeat in World War II?

What opportunities and challenges did Europe face after the Cold War?

851

Solidarity built a broad-based alliance of intellectuals, workers, and the Catholic Church. That alliance was one reason that Solidarity became such a powerful movement in Poland. Another reason was Solidarity's commitment to social and political change through nonviolent action. That commitment enabled Solidarity to avoid a bloodbath in 1981 and thus maintain its structure after martial law was declared, although at the time foreign observers often criticized Lech Walesa's leadership for being too cautious and unrealistic.

Adam Michnik was one of Walesa's closest coworkers. Whereas Walesa was a skilled electrician and a devout Catholic, Michnik was an intellectual and a disillusioned Communist. Their faith in nonviolence and in gradual change bound them together. Trained as a historian but banned from teaching because of his leadership in student strikes in 1968, Michnik earned his living as a factory worker. In 1977 he joined with others to found the Committee for the Defense of Workers (KOR), which supported workers fired for striking. In December 1981 Michnik was arrested with the rest of Solidarity's leadership. While in prison, he wrote his influential Letters from Prison, *from which this essay is taken.*

❝ Why did Solidarity renounce violence? This question returned time and again in my conversations with foreign observers. I would like to answer it now. People who claim that the use of force in the struggle for freedom is necessary must first prove that in a given situation it will be effective and that force, when it is used, will not transform the idea of liberty into its opposite.

No one in Poland is able to prove today that violence will help us to dislodge Soviet troops from Poland and to remove the communists from power. The U.S.S.R. has such enormous military power that confrontation is simply unthinkable. In other words, we have no guns. Napoleon, upon hearing a similar reply, gave up asking further questions. However, Napoleon was above all interested in military victories and not building democratic, pluralistic societies. We, by contrast, cannot leave it at that.

In our reasoning, pragmatism is inseparably intertwined with idealism. Taught by history, we suspect that by using force to storm the existing Bastilles we shall unwittingly build new ones. It is true that social change is almost always accompanied by force. But it is not true that social change is merely a result of the violent collision of various forces. Above all, social changes follow from a confrontation

of different moralities and visions of social order. Before the violence of rulers clashes with the violence of their subjects, values and systems of ethics clash inside human minds. Only when the old ideas of the rulers lose this moral duel will the subjects reach for force — sometimes. This is what happened in the French Revolution and the Russian Revolution — two examples cited in every debate as proof that revolutionary violence is preceded by a moral breakdown of the old regime. But both examples lose their meaning when they are reduced to such compact notions, in which the Encyclopedists are paired with the destruction of the Bastille, and the success of radical ideologies in Russia is paired with the storming of the Winter Palace. An authentic event is reduced to a sterile scheme.

In order to understand the significance of these revolutions, one must remember Jacobin and Bolshevik terror, the guillotines of the sans-culottes, and the guns of the commissars. Without reflection on the mechanisms in victorious revolutions that gave birth to terror, it is impossible to even pose the fundamental dilemma facing contemporary freedom movements. Historical awareness of the possible consequences of revolutionary violence must be etched into any program of struggle for freedom. The experience of being corrupted by terror must be imprinted upon the consciousness of everyone who belongs to a freedom movement. [Or], as Simone Weil wrote, freedom will again become a refugee from the camp of the victors. . . .

Solidarity's program and ethos are inextricably tied to this strategy. Revolutionary terror has always been justified by a vision of an ideal society. In the name of this vision, Jacobin guillotines and Bolshevik execution squads carried out their unceasing, gruesome work.

The road to God's Kingdom on Earth led through rivers of blood.

Solidarity has never had a vision of an ideal society. It wants to live and let live. Its ideals are closer to the American Revolution than to the French. . . . The ethics of Solidarity, with its consistent rejection of the use of force, has a lot in common with the idea of nonviolence as espoused by Gandhi and Martin Luther King, Jr. But it is not an ethic representative of pacifist movements.

his security forces to slaughter thousands, thereby sparking an armed uprising. After Ceauşescu's forces were defeated, he and his wife were captured and executed by a military court.

In Hungary growing popular resistance forced the Communist Party to renounce one-party rule and schedule free elections for early 1990. Hungarians gleefully tore down the

Pacifism as a mass movement aims to avoid suffering; pacifists often say that no cause is worth suffering or dying for. The ethics of Solidarity are based on an opposite premise: that there are causes worth suffering and dying for. Gandhi and King died for the same cause as the miners in Wujek who rejected the belief that it is better to remain a willing slave than to become a victim of murder [and who were shot down by police for striking against the imposition of martial law in 1981]. . . .

But ethics cannot substitute for a political program. We must therefore think about the future of Polish-Russian relations. Our thinking about this key question must be open; it should consider many different possibilities. . . .

The Soviet state has a new leader; he is a symbol of transition from one generation to the next within the Soviet elite. This change may offer an opportunity, since Mikhail Gorbachev has not yet become a prisoner of his own decisions. No one can rule out the possibility that an impulse for reform will spring from the top of the hierarchy of power. This is exactly what happened in the time of Alexander II and, a hundred years later, under Khrushchev. Reform is always possible, even in the face of resistance by the old apparatus. . . .

So what can now happen [in Poland]?

The "fundamentalists" say, no compromises. Talking about compromise, dialogue, or understanding demobilizes public opinion, pulls the wool over the eyes of the public, spreads illusions. Walesa's declarations about readiness for dialogue were often severely criticized from this point of view. I do not share the fundamentalist point of view. . . . The logic of fundamentalism precludes any attempt to find compromise, even in the future. It harbors not only the belief that communists are ineducable but also a certainty that they are unable to behave rationally, even in critical situations — that, in other words, they are condemned to suicidal obstinacy.

This is not so obvious to me. Historical experience shows that communists were sometimes forced by circumstances to behave rationally and to agree to compromises. Thus the strategy of understanding must not be cast aside. We should not assume that a bloody confrontation is inevitable and, consequently, rule out the possibility of evolutionary, bloodless

Solidarity activist Adam Michnik in 1984, appearing under police guard in the military court that sentenced him to prison. (Wide World Photos/AP Images)

change. This should be avoided all the more inasmuch as democracy is rarely born from bloody upheavals. We should be clear in our minds about this: The continuing conflict may transform itself into either a dialogue or an explosion. The TKK [the underground Temporary Coordinating Committee of outlawed Solidarity] and [Lech] Walesa are doing everything in their power to make dialogue possible. Their chances of success will be greater if the level of self-organization of independent Polish society increases. For street lynchings, angry crowds are enough; compromise demands an organized society. **"**

Source: Adam Michnik, *Letters from Prison and Other Essays*, trans. Maya Latynski (Berkeley and Los Angeles: University of California Press, 1985), pp. 86–89, 92, 95, by permission of the University of California Press. Copyright © 1985 by The Regents of the University of California.

QUESTIONS FOR ANALYSIS

1. Are Michnik's arguments for opposing the government with nonviolent actions convincing?
2. How did Michnik's study of history influence his thinking? What lessons did he learn?
3. Analyze Michnik's attitudes toward the Soviet Union and Poland's Communist leadership. What policies did he advocate? Why?

barbed-wire "iron curtain" that separated Hungary and Austria (see Map 31.1) and opened their border to refugees from East Germany.

At the same time, a protest movement arose in East Germany. Desperately hoping to stabilize the situation, East Germany's Communist Party leaders opened the Berlin Wall in November 1989, then were swept aside. In general elections in March 1990 a

How did western Europe recover after WWII, and why did progress stall?

How did the Soviet Union dominate eastern Europe in the postwar era?

What factors shaped social and political developments in postwar America?

How did Japan become a global power after its defeat in World War II?

What opportunities and challenges did Europe face after the Cold War?

853

INDIVIDUALS IN SOCIETY

Václav Havel

ON THE NIGHT OF NOVEMBER 24, 1989, the revolution in Czechoslovakia reached its climax. Three hundred thousand people had poured into Prague's historic Wenceslas Square to continue the massive protests that had erupted a week earlier after the police savagely beat student demonstrators. Now all eyes were focused on a high balcony. There an elderly man with a gentle smile and a middle-aged intellectual wearing jeans and a sports jacket stood arm in arm and acknowledged the cheers of the crowd. "Dubček-Havel," the people roared. "Dubček-Havel!" Alexander Dubček, who represented the failed promise of reform communism in the 1960s (see page 850), was symbolically passing the torch to Václav Havel, who embodied the uncompromising opposition to communism that was sweeping the country. That very evening, the hard-line Communist government resigned, and soon Havel was the unanimous choice to head a new democratic Czechoslovakia. Who was this man to whom the nation turned in 1989?

Born in 1936 into a prosperous, cultured, upper-middle-class family, the young Havel was denied admission to the university because of his class origins. Loving literature and philosophy, he gravitated to the theater, became a stagehand, and emerged in the 1960s as a leading playwright. His plays were set in vague settings, developed existential themes, and poked fun at the absurdities of life and the pretensions of communism. In his private life, Havel thrived on good talk, Prague's lively bar scene, and officially forbidden rock 'n' roll.

In 1968 the Soviets rolled into Czechoslovakia, and Havel watched in horror as a tank commander opened fire on a crowd of peaceful protesters in a small town. "That week," he recorded, "was an experience I shall never forget."* The free-spirited artist threw himself into the intellectual opposition to communism and became its leading figure for the next twenty years. The costs of defiance were enormous. Purged and blacklisted, Havel lifted barrels in a brewery and wrote bitter satires that could not be staged. In 1977 he and a few other dissidents publicly protested Czechoslovakian violations of the Helsinki Accords on human rights, and in 1989 this Charter '77 group became the inspiration for Civic Forum, the democratic coalition that toppled communism. Havel spent five years in prison and was constantly harassed by the police.

Havel's thoughts and actions focused on truth, decency, and moral regeneration. In 1975, in a famous open letter to Czechoslovakia's Communist boss, Havel wrote that the people were indeed quiet, but only because they were "driven by fear. . . . Everyone has something to lose and so everyone has reason to be afraid." Havel saw lies, hypocrisy, and apathy undermining and poisoning all human relations in his country:

"Order has been established — at the price of a paralysis of the spirit, a deadening of the heart, and a spiritual and moral crisis in society."†

Yet Havel saw a way out of the Communist quagmire. He argued that a profound but peaceful revolution in human values was possible. Such a revolution could lead to the moral reconstruction of Czech and Slovak society, where, in his words, "values like trust, openness, responsibility, solidarity and love" might again flourish and nurture the human spirit. Havel was a voice of hope and humanity who inspired his compatriots with a lofty vision of a moral postcommunist society. As president of his country (1989–2003), Havel continued to speak eloquently on the great questions of our time.

*Quoted in M. Simmons, *The Reluctant President: A Political Life of Václav Havel* (London: Methuen, 1991), p. 91.
†Quoted ibid., p. 110.

QUESTIONS FOR ANALYSIS

1. Why did Havel oppose Communist rule? How did his goals differ from those of Dubček and other advocates of reform communism?
2. Havel has been called a "moralist in politics." Is this a good description of him? Why? Can you think of a better one?

Václav Havel, playwright, dissident leader, and the first postcommunist president of the Czech Republic. (Chris Niedenthal/Black Star)

conservative-liberal "Alliance for Germany" won and quickly negotiated an economic union with West Germany. On October 3, 1990, East and West Germany merged, forming a single nation under West Germany's constitution and laws.

The End of the Cold War and Soviet Disintegration

Germany's reunification accelerated the end of the Cold War. In November 1990 delegates from twenty-two European countries joined those from the United States and the Soviet Union in Paris and agreed to scale down their armed forces, recognize all existing borders in

Map 31.3 Russia and the Successor States After the attempt in August 1991 to depose Gorbachev failed, an anticommunist revolution swept the Soviet Union. Led by Russia and Boris Yeltsin, the republics that formed the Soviet Union declared their sovereignty and independence. Eleven of the fifteen republics then formed a loose confederation called the Commonwealth of Independent States, but the integrated economy of the Soviet Union dissolved into separate national economies, each with its own goals and policies.

How did western Europe recover after WWII, and why did progress stall?

How did the Soviet Union dominate eastern Europe in the postwar era?

What factors shaped social and political developments in postwar America?

How did Japan become a global power after its defeat in World War II?

What opportunities and challenges did Europe face after the Cold War?

855

Europe, and declare an end to confrontation and division in Europe. The **Charter of Paris for a New Europe** was for all practical purposes a general peace treaty, bringing an end to the Cold War.

Peace in Europe encouraged the United States and the Soviet Union to scrap a significant portion of their nuclear arsenals and to relax their nuclear defensive posture. For the first time in four decades Soviet and American nuclear weapons were not standing ready to destroy capitalism, communism, and life itself.

The great question then became whether the Soviet Union would also experience a popular anticommunist revolution. In the wake of a series of electoral defeats of the Communist Party, Gorbachev broke definitively with the party hardliners and asked Soviet citizens to ratify a new constitution that formally abolished the Communist Party's monopoly of political power and expanded the power of the Congress of People's Deputies. Gorbachev then convinced a majority of deputies to elect him president of the Soviet Union.

Gorbachev's eroding power and unwillingness to risk a popular election for the presidency strengthened his rival, Boris Yeltsin (1931–2007). A radical reform Communist, Yeltsin embraced the democratic movement, and in May 1990, as leader of the Russian parliament, Yeltsin announced that Russia would declare its independence from the Soviet Union. This move broadened the base of the anticommunist movement by appealing to the patriotism of ordinary Russians.

In August 1991 Gorbachev survived an attempted coup by Communist Party hardliners who wanted to preserve Communist Party power and the multinational Soviet Union. Instead, an anticommunist revolution swept the Russian Federation as the Communist Party was outlawed and its property confiscated. Yeltsin and his liberal allies declared Russia independent and withdrew from the Soviet Union. All the other Soviet republics followed suit, and the Soviet Union ceased to exist on December 25, 1991 (Map 31.3).

Quick Review
How did the Soviets try to reform society, and what led to the anticommunist revolutions of 1989?

What factors shaped social and political developments in postwar America?

The Cold War era was one of remarkable economic growth and social transformation within the United States. As America tried to contain communism around the globe, it underwent an internal transformation that led to new rights for African Americans and women, and the development of a vigorous and active counterculture. The end of the Cold War and the Soviet Union's collapse in 1991 left Americans grappling with questions about the new position of the United States as the world's only superpower.

America's Economic Boom and Civil Rights Revolution

The Second World War ended the Great Depression in the United States, bringing about a great economic boom. Unemployment practically vanished, and Americans' well-being increased dramatically. As in western Europe, the U.S. economy advanced fairly steadily for a generation.

Prosperity helps explain why postwar domestic politics consisted largely of modest adjustments to the status quo until the 1960s. The re-election in 1948 of President Harry S. Truman (r. 1945–1953) demonstrated that Americans had no interest in undoing Roosevelt's social and economic reforms. In 1952 American voters turned to General Dwight D.

Eisenhower (r. 1953–1961), a self-described moderate. In 1960 young John F. Kennedy (r. 1961–1963) revitalized the old Roosevelt coalition and modestly expanded existing liberal legislation before being struck down by an assassin's bullet in 1963.

Belatedly and reluctantly, complacent postwar America did experience a genuine social revolution: after a long struggle African Americans (and their white supporters) threw off a deeply entrenched system of segregation and discrimination. This civil rights movement advanced on several fronts. The National Association for the Advancement of Colored People (NAACP) challenged school segregation in the courts. In 1954 it won a landmark decision in the Supreme Court, which ruled in *Brown v. Board of Education* that "separate educational facilities are inherently unequal." Blacks also effectively challenged inequality by using Gandhian methods of nonviolent peaceful resistance (see page 794). In describing his principles for change, the civil rights leader Martin Luther King, Jr. (1929–1968), said that "Christ furnished the spirit and motivation, while Gandhi furnished the method."

With African American support in key Northern states, Democrat Lyndon Johnson (r. 1963–1969) won the 1964 presidential election in a landslide. He repaid liberals' support by getting enacted the 1964 Civil Rights Act, which prohibited discrimination in public services and on the job, and the 1965 Voting Rights Act, which guaranteed all blacks the right to vote.

Civil Rights Act A 1964 U.S. act that prohibited discrimination in public services and on the job.

In the mid-1960s President Johnson began an "unconditional war on poverty." With the support of Congress, Johnson's administration created a host of antipoverty projects, such as medical care for the poor and aged, free preschools for poor children, and community-action programs. Thus the United States promoted the kind of social reform that western Europe had embraced immediately after the Second World War.

Youth and the Counterculture

Economic prosperity and a more democratic class structure had a powerful impact on youth throughout North America and western Europe. The "baby boomers" born after World War II developed a distinctive youth culture that became increasingly oppositional in the 1960s, interacting with leftist thought to create a counterculture that rebelled against parents, authority figures, and the status quo.

Several factors contributed to the emergence of the international youth culture in the 1960s. First, mass communications and youth travel linked countries and continents together. Second, the postwar baby boom meant that young people formed an unusually large part of the population and therefore exercised exceptional influence on society as a whole. Third, postwar prosperity and greater equality gave young people more purchasing power than ever before. This enabled them to set their own trends and fads in everything from music to fashion to chemical stimulants to sexual behavior.

Duck and Cover American schoolchildren in the 1950s practice the "duck and cover" drill in the event of a nuclear attack by the Soviet Union. (Bettmann/Corbis)

In the late 1960s student protesters embraced romanticism and revolutionary idealism to oppose the established order. The materialistic West was hopelessly rotten, but better societies were being built in the newly independent countries of Asia and Africa, or so many young radicals believed. Thus the counterculture became linked to the Vietnam War, as politically active students became involved in what became worldwide student opposition to that war.

The Vietnam War

American involvement in Vietnam was a product of the Cold War and the ideology of containment. After Vietnam won independence from France in 1954 (see page 877), the Eisenhower administration refused to sign the Geneva Accords that temporarily divided the country into a socialist north and an anticommunist south pending national unification by means of free elections. When the South Vietnamese government declined to hold elections, Eisenhower provided military aid to help the south resist North Vietnam. President Kennedy later increased the number of American "military advisers." In 1964 President Johnson greatly expanded America's role in the Vietnam conflict.

Under Johnson, South Vietnam received massive military aid; American forces in the south grew to a half million men; and the United States bombed North Vietnam with ever-greater intensity. The undeclared war in Vietnam, fought nightly on American television, eventually divided the nation. At first, support was strong. Most Americans saw the war as part of a legitimate defense against communism. But an antiwar movement quickly emerged on college campuses. By 1967 a growing number of critics denounced the American presence in Vietnam as a criminal intrusion into a complex and distant civil war.

Criticism reached a crescendo after the Vietcong Tet Offensive in January 1968. This attack on major South Vietnamese cities failed militarily, but it resulted in heavy losses on both sides, and it belied Washington's claims that victory in South Vietnam was in sight. Within months President Johnson announced he would not stand for re-election and called for negotiations with North Vietnam.

Elected in 1968, President Richard Nixon (1913–1994) sought to disengage America gradually from Vietnam. He began a slow process of withdrawal from Vietnam in a process called "Vietnamization." Arguing that the South Vietnamese had to take full responsibility for their country and their security, he cut American forces there from 550,000 to 24,000 in four years. Nixon finally reached a peace agreement with North Vietnam in 1973 that allowed the remaining American forces to complete their withdrawal in 1975.

As Nixon worked to establish peace in Vietnam, the Watergate scandal erupted. Nixon had authorized special units to conduct domestic spying activities that went beyond the law. One such group broke into Democratic Party headquarters in Washington's Watergate building in June 1972 and was promptly arrested. Facing the threat of impeachment for trying to cover up the affair, Nixon resigned in disgrace in 1974.

The Vietnam War, 1964–1975

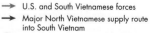

→ U.S. and South Vietnamese forces

→ Major North Vietnamese supply route into South Vietnam

✳ Important battle or action

Détente and a Return to Cold War Tensions

While America was fighting a war, in its eyes, to contain the spread of communism in Southeast Asia, relations between the Soviet Union and the United States eased somewhat in the late 1960s and early 1970s. Both sides adopted a policy for the progressive relaxation of Cold War tensions that became known as détente (day-TAHNT). The policy of détente reached its high point in 1975 when the United States, Canada, and all European nations (except Albania and Andorra) signed the Helsinki Accords. These nations agreed that Europe's existing political frontiers could not be changed by force, and they guaranteed the human rights and political freedoms of their citizens. Hopes for détente faded quickly, however, when Brezhnev's Soviet Union ignored the human rights provisions of the Helsinki Accords and in December 1979 invaded Afghanistan. Alarmed, Americans looked to NATO to thwart Communist expansion. President Jimmy Carter (r. 1977–1981) pushed NATO to apply economic sanctions to the Soviet Union, but among the European allies only Great Britain supported Carter's plan. Some observers felt the alliance had lost its cohesiveness.

Yet the Western alliance endured. The U.S. military buildup launched by Jimmy Carter was greatly accelerated by President Ronald Reagan (r. 1981–1989). The Reagan administration deployed nuclear arms in western Europe and built up the navy to preserve American power in a renewed crusade against the Soviet Union.

Reagan found conservative allies in Britain's Margaret Thatcher and in West Germany's Helmut Kohl. In the 1980s they gave indirect support to ongoing efforts to liberalize Communist eastern Europe. With the Soviet Union's collapse in 1991, the United States emerged as the world's lone superpower.

In 1991 the United States used its superpower status and military superiority after Iraq's strongman, Saddam Hussein (1937–2006), invaded Kuwait in August 1990 (see page 892). With United Nations General Assembly and Security Council consent, a U.S.-led military coalition smashed Iraqi forces. The Gulf War demonstrated the awesome power of the rebuilt and revitalized U.S. military.

détente The progressive relaxation of Cold War tensions.

Quick Review

How did American foreign policy influence social and political developments at home in the post–Cold War era, and vice versa?

How did Japan become a global power after its defeat in World War II?

Devastated and defeated, in 1945 Japan's future looked bleak. Yet Japan under American occupation from 1945 to 1952 turned from military expansion to democracy. It experienced extraordinarily successful economic development until the 1990s and in the process joined the ranks of First World nations both politically and economically.

Japan's American Revolution

Japan, like Nazi Germany, was formally occupied by all the Allies, but real power resided in American hands. General Douglas MacArthur (1880–1964) exercised almost absolute authority. MacArthur and the Americans had a revolutionary plan for defeated Japan, introducing fundamental reforms designed to make Japan a free, democratic society along American lines.

Japan's sweeping American revolution began with demilitarization and a systematic purge of convicted war criminals and wartime collaborators. The American-dictated constitution of 1946 allowed the emperor to remain the "symbol of the State." Real power resided in the Japanese Diet, whose members were popularly elected. A bill of rights granted basic civil liberties. Article 9 of the new constitution also abolished all Japanese armed forces and declared that Japan forever renounced war.

The American occupation left Japan's powerful bureaucracy largely intact and used it to implement fundamental social and economic reforms. The occupation promoted the Japanese labor movement, introduced American-style antitrust laws, and granted Japanese women equality before the law. The occupation also imposed revolutionary land reform that strengthened the small, independent peasant, who became a staunch defender of post-war democracy.

America's efforts to remake Japan in its own image were powerful but short-lived. By 1948, as China went Communist, American leaders began to see Japan as a potential Cold War ally. The American command began purging leftists and rehabilitating prewar nationalists. When the occupation ended in 1952, Japan regained independence, and the United States retained its vast military complex in Japan. Important for the Americans, Japan became the chief Asian ally of the United States in the fight against communism.

"Japan, Inc."

Japan's economic recovery, like Germany's, proceeded slowly after the war. During the Korean War, however, the economy took off and grew with spectacular speed. Japan served as a base for American military operations during the war, and billions of dollars in military contracts and aid poured into the Japanese economy. By the 1960s Japan had the third-largest economy in the world. In 1975 Japan joined France, West Germany, Italy, Great Britain, and the United States to form the G6, the world's six leading industrialized nations. In 1986 Japan's average per capita income exceeded that of the United States for the first time.

Japan's emergence as an economic superpower fascinated outsiders. Many Asians and Africans looked to Japan for the secrets of successful modernization, but some of Japan's Asian neighbors again feared Japanese exploitation. In the 1970s and 1980s some Americans and Europeans bitterly accused "Japan, Inc." of an unfair alliance between government and business and urged their own governments to retaliate.

"Japan, Inc." A nickname from the 1980s used to describe the intricate relationship of Japan's business world and government.

Japanese prosperity was, in fact, built on a government-business alliance. In a system of managed capitalism, the government decided which industries were important, then made loans and encouraged mergers to create powerful firms in those industries. Antitrust regulations introduced by the Americans were quickly scrapped, and the home market was protected from foreign competition by various measures. Big business was valued and respected because it served the national goal and mirrored Japanese society. Workers were hired for life, and employees' social lives revolved around the company. Most unions became moderate, agreeable company unions. The social and economic distance between salaried managers and workers was slight and was often breached. *Efficiency*, *quality*, and *quantity* were the watchwords.

Japan in the Post–Cold War World

The 1990s brought a sharp reversal in Japan's economic performance. From 1990 to 1992 the Japanese stock market dropped by 65 percent. The bursting of the speculative bubble crippled Japanese banks, stymied economic growth, and led to record postwar unemployment of 4.5 percent in 1998. Unemployment remained around that level through 2011. Japan also faced increasingly tough competition from its industrializing neighbors in Asia (see Chapter 32).

The global economic crisis of 2008–2009 had a seriously deleterious effect on most of the leading world economies. The crisis hurt Japan more than other countries, however, because it had still not recovered from the financial reverses of the early 1990s, and its recovery had been based not on exports but on increased domestic spending. In 2008 the economy shrank by 1.2 percent and in 2009 by 5 percent. Japan has dropped from the world's second largest economy to third—behind the United States and China.

While postwar Japanese society, with its stress on discipline and cooperation rather than individualism and competition, has generally adapted well to meet the challenges of modern industrial urban society, important long-term problems remain. These include a massive government debt, a declining population, the aging of the population, and dependence on foreign sources for the energy, forest products, and minerals needed for modern industry. An earthquake with magnitude 9.0 that struck off Japan's northeast coast on March 11, 2011, followed by a catastrophic tsunami, devastated Japan's already fragile economy and left massive destruction, death, and human misery in their wake.

> **Quick Review**
> What explains Japan's spectacular recovery from the devastation of World War II?

What opportunities and challenges did Europe face after the Cold War?

The end of the Cold War and the Soviet Union's collapse ended the division of Europe into two opposing camps. Although Europe in the 1990s remained diverse, the entire continent now shared a commitment to capitalism and democracy.

Common Patterns and Problems

In economic affairs European leaders embraced, or at least accepted, a large part of the neoliberal, free-market vision of capitalist development. This vision differed markedly from western Europe's still-dominant welfare capitalism.

Two factors were particularly important in explaining the shift to tough-minded capitalism. First, Europeans were following practices and ideologies revived in the 1980s by Reagan in the United States and Thatcher in Great Britain. Western Europeans especially took free-market prescriptions more seriously during the presidency of Bill Clinton (r. 1993–2001) because U.S. prestige and power were so high after the Cold War ended and because the U.S. economy outperformed its western European counterparts. Second, market deregulation and the privatization of state-controlled enterprises in different European countries were integral parts of the trend toward an open global economy.

The freer global economy had powerful social consequences, and global capitalism and freer markets challenged hard-won social achievements. As in the United States, many Europeans generally opposed corporate downsizing, the efforts to reduce the power of labor unions, and, above all, government plans to reduce social benefits. The reaction was particularly intense in France and Germany, where unions remained strong and socialists championed a minimum amount of change in social policies.

In the 1990s political developments across Europe also shared common patterns and problems. Most obviously, the demise of European communism brought the apparent triumph of liberal democracy everywhere. All countries embraced genuine electoral competition with elected presidents and legislatures, and they guaranteed basic civil liberties.

Recasting Russia Without Communism

In Russia politics and economics were closely intertwined as President Boris Yeltsin (r. 1991–1999) sought to create conditions that would prevent a return to communism and right

Putin and Democracy After the Soviet Union's collapse in 1991, Russia's new leaders instituted a number of democratic reforms. After taking office in 2000, however, Russian President Vladimir Putin, who worked as a KGB agent during the Soviet era, was accused of rolling back many of these measures. (ARIAIL © The State/distributed by Newspaper Enterprise Association, Inc.)

the faltering economy. In January 1992 Yeltsin initiated a program of economic shock therapy, turning thousands of factories and mines over to new private companies. Instead of reviving production, prices soared and production fell sharply. From 1992 to 2001 the Russian economy fell by almost 30 percent. In 2005 Russia's GDP (gross domestic product) was still lower than in 1991, but it grew sharply from 2003 through 2007. The global economic crisis of 2008–2009 hit Russia hard, but by late 2009 Russia's economy was recovering, aided by rising commodity and oil prices.

Rapid economic liberalization worked poorly in Russia for several reasons. With privatization, powerful state industrial monopolies became powerful private monopolies that cut production and raised prices in order to maximize profits. Powerful managers forced Yeltsin's government to hand out enormous subsidies and credits to reinforce the positions of big firms or avoid bankruptcies. Finally, the managerial elite worked with criminal elements to intimidate would-be rivals, preventing the formation of new firms.

Runaway inflation and poorly executed privatization brought a profound social revolution to Russia. A new capitalist elite acquired great wealth and power, while the vast majority of people fell into poverty. At the same time, the quality of public services and health care declined precipitously.

The 2000 election of Yeltsin's handpicked successor, President Vladimir Putin (b. 1952), ushered in a new era of "managed democracy." Putin's stress on public order and economic reform was popular, but during his seven and a half years in office, he became progressively more authoritarian. Putin consolidated his power, closing off the development of democratic pluralism and an independent legal system. Putin also supported renationalization of some industries and state regulation of energy policy and economic planning in general.

Putin's illiberal tendencies were also evident in his brutal military campaign against Chechnya (CHECH-nyuh), a tiny republic of 1 million Muslims in southern Russia (see

Map 31.3, inset) that in 1991 declared its independence from Russia. Despite widespread death and destruction, Chechen resistance to Russian domination continues, often in the form of terrorist attacks, such as a 2011 suicide bombing at Moscow's airport.

Unable to run for re-election in 2008, Putin handpicked a successor, Dmitry Medvedev, to be president, and took the position of prime minister for himself. He remains the power behind the throne in Russia and an important power broker on the world stage. In September 2011 Putin and Medvedev announced that they would be switching positions, with Putin elected president in March 2012.

Postcommunist Reconstruction in Eastern Europe

Eastern Europe had many of the same problems as Russia, and developments there were similar. The postcommunist nations worked to replace state planning and socialism with market mechanisms and private property. Western-style electoral politics also took hold, and as in Russia these politics were marked by intense battles between presidents and parliaments and by weak political parties. Ordinary citizens and the elderly were the big losers, while the young and former Communist Party members were the big winners. Capital cities such as Warsaw and Budapest concentrated wealth and opportunity; provincial centers stagnated; and industrial areas declined.

Poland, the Czech Republic, and Hungary were the most successful in making the transition. They managed to control national and ethnic tensions that might have destroyed their postcommunist reconstruction. The popular goal of "rejoining the West" was a powerful force for moderation in these countries. They hoped to find security in NATO membership, which came in 1997, and prosperity by joining western Europe's economic union.

The great postcommunist tragedy was Yugoslavia, which under Josip Tito had been a federation of republics and regions under Communist rule. After Tito's death in 1980, power passed increasingly to the sister republics, which encouraged a revival of regional and ethnic conflicts.

The revolutions of 1989 accelerated the breakup of Yugoslavia. When Serbian president Slobodan Milosevic (1941–2006) attempted to grab land from other republics and unite all Serbs in a "greater Serbia," a civil war broke out that eventually involved Kosovo, Slovenia, Croatia, and Bosnia-Herzegovina. The civil war unleashed ruthless brutality and charges of "ethnic cleansing" — genocide — against opposing ethnic groups.

From March to June 1999 the Western Powers, led by the United States, carried out heavy bombing attacks on Serbia and demanded that Milosevic withdraw Serbian armies. In 2000 the Serbs voted Milosevic out of office, and in 2001 a new pro-Western Serbian government turned him over to a war crimes tribunal in the Netherlands to stand trial for crimes against humanity.

Unity and Identity in Western Europe

The movement toward western European unity received a powerful second wind in the 1990s. French president François Mitterrand (1916–1996) and German chancellor Helmut Kohl took the lead in pushing for the monetary union of European Community members, and the Maastricht Treaty of 1992 created a single EU currency, the euro. In 1993 the European Community proudly rechristened itself the **European Union (EU)** (see Map 31.4).

Not all Europeans supported economic union. Many people resented the unending flow of rules handed down by the EU's growing bureaucracy, which sought to standardize everything from cheeses to day care. Moreover, many feared that more power in the hands of distant bureaucrats would undermine popular sovereignty and democratic control. Above all, they feared that the new Europe was being created at their expense. Joining the

European Union (EU) An economic and political alliance of twenty-seven European nations.

The European Union

- Original members, 1951
- New members, 1973
- New members, 1981
- New members, 1986
- German reunification, 1990
- New members, 1995
- New members, 2004
- New members, 2007
- Candidate countries, 2011
- € Euro Zone countries, 2011

ICELAND

NORWAY   SWEDEN

FINLAND
€

ESTONIA
€
(effective 2011)

DENMARK

North
Sea

Baltic Sea

LATVIA

LITHUANIA

RUSSIA

RUSSIAN
FEDERATION

IRELAND UNITED
€   KINGDOM

NETHERLANDS
€

BELGIUM
€

GERMANY
€

POLAND

BELARUS

LUXEMBOURG
€

CZECH
REP.

SLOVAKIA

UKRAINE

ATLANTIC
OCEAN

FRANCE
€

SWITZ.

AUSTRIA
€

HUNGARY

MOLDOVA

SLOVENIA
€

CROATIA

ROMANIA

PORTUGAL
€

SPAIN
€

ITALY
€

BOSNIA-
HERZEGOVINA

SERBIA

KOSOVO

BULGARIA

Black Sea

MONTENEGRO

MACEDONIA

ALBANIA

Mediterranean Sea

GREECE
€

TURKEY

MALTA
€

CYPRUS
€

0   200   400 miles
0   200   400 kilometers

Mapping the Past

Map 31.4 The European Union, 2011

No longer divided by ideological competition and the Cold War, much of today's Europe has banded together in a European Union.

ANALYZING THE MAP Trace the expansion of membership in the European Union. How would you characterize the most recent members? Whose membership is still pending?

CONNECTIONS Which countries are not part of the Euro Zone? What does this suggest about the euro's success in the European Union?

monetary union required governments to meet stringent fiscal standards and impose budget cuts and financial austerity. The resulting reductions in health care and social benefits hit ordinary citizens and did nothing to reduce western Europe's high unemployment rate.

Nonetheless, the successful introduction of the euro in January 2002 encouraged the EU to accelerate plans for an enlargement to the east. In 2004, the EU started admitting eastern European countries. By 2007 the EU had twenty-seven member states, including most of eastern Europe, making it the world's largest trading bloc. Future candidates for membership include Croatia, Macedonia, former members of the old Soviet Union, and Turkey.

A proposed EU constitution binding EU member states even closer together was scheduled to go into effect in 2007. First, however, it needed approval by voters in all member countries. In 2005 voters in France and Holland voted overwhelmingly against the constitution, which was replaced with the Treaty of Lisbon in 2007. The new treaty kept most of the reforms contained in the original European constitution, but it reformed the political structure of the EU bureaucracy. By November 2009 all members had approved it, and the Lisbon treaty came into force on December 1, 2009, unifying what had been a profoundly divided continent just fifty years earlier.

Quick Review
What happened after the breakup of the Soviet Union, and how did Europe as a whole respond to calls for increased unity?

 Connections

IN 1945 EUROPE LAY IN RUINS. Two new superpowers emerged to claim the mantle of global leadership: the democratic, capitalistic United States and the Communist Soviet Union. As each superpower worked to acquire allies in the new Cold War, other nations, particularly newly independent nations such as China and India, adopted non-aligned positions that denied the right of either the Soviet Union or the United States to determine the world's destiny (see Chapter 32). As western Europe hunkered down to address its domestic problems, the empires created at the end of the nineteenth century crumbled in the face of powerful independence movements in Asia (Chapter 32) and Africa (Chapter 33).

Western Europe and Japan, with massive aid packages from the United States, quickly recovered from the terrible destruction caused by the war and soon surged ahead economically. But as the next chapter discusses, the economic superpower status of the United States, Europe, and Japan faced fierce new competitors from Asia, most notably China.

By the end of the twentieth century the Cold War had ended, democratic governments had replaced the former Soviet Union and its satellite states throughout eastern Europe, and a new European Union had ended the divisions that had plagued Europe for most of the century. New divisions, however, would rise to divide Europe, this time in the form of debate concerning the growing multiethnic European society, as migrants from Africa, Asia, and the economically weaker states of eastern Europe entered the European Union both legally and illegally. Chapter 34 takes up this issue and explores the economic, political, social, and environmental challenges facing the world in the twenty-first century.

- **For a list of suggested readings for this chapter, visit** *bedfordstmartins.com/mckayworldunderstanding*.

- **For primary sources from this period, see** *Sources of World Societies*, Second Edition.

- **For Web sites, images, and documents related to topics in this chapter, see Make History at** *bedfordstmartins.com/ mckayworldunderstanding*.

Chapter 31 Study Guide

To do these exercises online, go to bedfordstmartins.com/mckayworldundunderstanding.

GETTING STARTED

Below are basic terms about this period in global history. Can you identify each term below and explain why it matters?

TERMS	WHO (OR WHAT) AND WHEN	WHY IT MATTERS
Truman Doctrine, p. 842		
Marshall Plan, p. 842		
NATO, p. 843		
Common Market, p. 844		
OPEC, p. 847		
de-Stalinization, p. 849		
Brezhnev Doctrine, p. 850		
perestroika, p. 850		
glasnost, p. 850		
Solidarity, p. 851		
Charter of Paris for a New Europe, p. 856		
Civil Rights Act, p. 857		
détente, p. 859		
"Japan, Inc.," p. 860		
European Union (EU), p. 863		

MOVING BEYOND THE BASICS

The exercise below requires a more advanced understanding of the chapter material. Compare and contrast eastern and western Europe in the postwar period by filling in the chart below with descriptions of the key social, economic, and political developments in the decades following World War II. When you are finished, consider the following questions: In what ways did eastern and western Europe diverge in the decades following World War II? In what ways did they remain connected? How did the Cold War shape European life on both sides of the iron curtain?

	SOCIETY	ECONOMY	POLITICS
Eastern Europe			
Western Europe			

PUTTING IT ALL TOGETHER

Now that you've reviewed key elements of the chapter, take a step back and try to see the big picture. Remember to use specific examples from the chapter in your answers.

COLD WAR EUROPE

- Why did cooperation between the Western Allies and the Soviet Union break down so quickly once World War II was over? Was the Cold War inevitable? Why or why not?

- How did the class structure of western and eastern Europe change after World War II? What role did government play in social change on both sides of the iron curtain?

POSTWAR AMERICA AND JAPAN

- To what extent was the counter-culture of the 1960s a product of postwar affluence? What other factors contributed to its emergence?

- How did the "managed capitalism" of postwar Japan differ from capitalism as it existed in the United States?

THE POST–COLD WAR ERA IN EUROPE

- How would you explain the pattern of post–Cold War development in eastern Europe? Why were some states more successful than others?

- What forces were behind the push toward greater European unity in the late twentieth century? What might explain the increasing reluctance of ordinary Europeans to support further steps toward unification?

LOOKING BACK, LOOKING AHEAD

- Compare and contrast Europe in 1918 and 1945. Why was Europe's recovery from war so much more successful after World War II than World War I?

- In your opinion, will Europe continue to move toward greater unification over the next several decades? Why or why not?

In Your Own Words Imagine that you must explain Chapter 31 to someone who hasn't read it. What would be the most important points to include and why?

32

Independence, Progress, and Conflict in Asia and the Middle East

1945 to the Present

While the United States and the Soviet Union faced each other in a deadly standoff during the Cold War, most people in the so-called Third World went about their daily lives. The term *Third World* has its origins in the 1950s, when many thinkers, journalists, and politicians viewed Africa, Asia, and Latin America as a single entity, different from both the capitalist, industrialized "First World" and the Communist, industrialized "Second World." Despite differences in history and culture, most Third World countries in Africa, Asia, and Latin America shared many characteristics that encouraged a common consciousness and ideology. This chapter explores the characteristics of the countries in Asia and the Middle East, while Chapter 33 covers the development of the countries of Africa and Latin America.

Nearly all the countries in Asia and the Middle East experienced political or economic domination, nationalist reaction, and a struggle for genuine independence. In the mid-twentieth century most Asian and Middle Eastern countries earned the majority of their revenues from cash crops or natural resources, particularly oil, whose production was frequently controlled and exploited by First World countries or by multinational agribusinesses. In the second half of the twentieth century a few of these countries—most notably in the oil-rich Middle East and in East Asia, where there has been successful industrialization—became important players in the global economy. In many cases, however, independence brought ethnic and religious conflict.

Iranian Green Revolution Protester An Iranian woman protests the 2009 presidential election. Demonstrators returned to the streets of Iran in February 2011, as protests erupted against authoritarian regimes across North Africa and the Middle East. (Getty Images)

Chapter Preview

▶ What explains East Asia's economic success after World War II?

▶ How have India, Pakistan, and Bangladesh fared since independence?

▶ How has religion shaped Middle Eastern politics since 1945?

What explains East Asia's economic success after World War II?

Other than Japan, most Asian countries recovered slowly after World War II. In the early 1950s the two Koreas and China were at war in the Korean peninsula, and the Vietnamese were fighting among themselves and against the French. The Nationalist Chinese were in exile in Taiwan. Hong Kong, Singapore, Indonesia, South Korea, and the Philippines were recovering from years of colonial rule and Japanese occupation. Despite these challenges, over the next forty years China and the Asian "economic tigers" developed some of the largest and fastest-growing economies in the world, but liberal democracy remained elusive.

The Communist Victory in China

The triumph of communism in China was due to many factors. Mao Zedong and the Communists had avoided pitched battles. They concentrated on winning peasant support and forming a broad anti-Japanese coalition. By reducing rents, promising land redistribution, enticing intellectuals, and spreading propaganda, they emerged in peasant eyes as the true patriots, the genuine nationalists.

With the defeat of the Japanese at the end of the Sino-Japanese War (see pages 800–801), Chinese Communists and Nationalists rushed to seize evacuated territory. Heavy fighting between the Communists and Nationalists broke out in Manchuria, and civil war began in earnest in April 1946. By 1948 the demoralized Nationalist forces were disintegrating before the better-led, more determined Communists. The following year Nationalist leader Jiang Jieshi and 2 million mainland Chinese fled to Taiwan, and in October 1949 Mao Zedong proclaimed the People's Republic of China (Map 32.1).

Between 1949 and 1954 the Communists consolidated their rule. They seized the vast land holdings of landlords and rich peasants, and they distributed the land to poor peasants. Meanwhile, at least 800,000 "class enemies" were summarily liquidated. Millions more were deported to forced-labor camps. All visible opposition from the old ruling groups was thus destroyed.

Mao and the Communists then set out to prove that China was once again a great power. This was the real significance of China's participation in the Korean War (see page 843). From 1950 to 1953 the Chinese army's ability to fight the American "imperialists" to a standstill mobilized the masses and increased Chinese self-confidence. Fighting a war in Korea did not prevent the Chinese from also expanding their territory in the west, invading Tibet in 1950, and declaring Chinese sovereignty over the country in 1951. (See "Individuals in Society: The Dalai Lama," page 928.)

Map 32.1 **The New States in Asia** Divided primarily along religious lines into two states, British India led the way to political independence in 1947.

Mao's China

China looked to the Soviet Union for inspiration in the early 1950s. Along with the gradual collectivization of agriculture, China adopted a Soviet-style five-year plan to develop large factories and heavy industry rapidly. Russian specialists built many Chinese plants, and Soviet economic aid was considerable. The first five-year plan was successful, as undeniable economic growth followed the Communists' social revolution.

In the cultural and intellectual realms, too, the Chinese followed the Soviet example. Basic civil and political rights were abolished. Temples and churches were closed, and press freedom died. The Communists enthusiastically promoted Soviet Marxist ideas concerning women and the family. Full equality, work outside the home, and state-supported child care became primary goals.

In 1958 China broke from the Marxist-Leninist course of development and began to go its own way. Mao proclaimed a Great Leap Forward in which industrial growth would be based on small-scale backyard workshops and steel mills run by peasants living in self-contained communes. The creation of a new socialist personality that rejected individualism and traditional Confucian family values, such as filial piety and acceptance of parental authority, was a second goal.

The intended great leap produced an economic disaster, as land in the countryside went untilled when peasants turned to industrial production. As many as 30 million people died in famines that swept the country in 1960–1961. When Soviet premier Nikita Khrushchev criticized Chinese policy in 1960, Mao condemned him and his Russian colleagues as detestable "modern revisionists." The Russians abruptly cut off aid, splitting the Communist world apart.

For a time, Mao lost influence, but in 1965 he staged a dramatic comeback. Fearing that China was becoming bureaucratic, capitalistic, and "revisionist" like the Soviet Union, Mao launched the Great Proletarian Cultural Revolution. He sought to purge the party and to recapture the revolutionary fervor of his guerrilla struggle (see pages 797–800). The army and the nation's young people responded enthusiastically, organizing themselves into radical cadres called Red Guards. Mao's thoughts, through his speeches and writings, were collected in the *Little Red Book*, which became holy scripture to the Red Guards.

The Red Guards sought to erase all traces of "feudal" and "bourgeois" culture and thought. Party officials, professors, and intellectuals were exiled to remote villages to purify themselves with heavy labor. Universities were shut down for years. Thousands of people died, many of them executed, and millions more were sent to rural forced-labor camps.

Chapter Chronology

1947	Separation of India and Pakistan
1948	End of British mandate in Palestine; Jews proclaim state of Israel; Mohandas Gandhi assassinated
1949–1954	Mass arrests, forced-labor camps, and Communist propaganda in China
1949–present	Harsh restrictions against religion and speech in China
1956	Nasser nationalizes Suez Canal Company
1958	Great Leap Forward in China
1964–1975	Vietnam War
1965	Great Proletarian Cultural Revolution in China
1967	Six-Day War in Israel
1970s–present	Revival of Islamic fundamentalism in the Middle East
1975–1990	Civil war in Lebanon
1979	Islamic revolution in Iran
1980–1988	Iran-Iraq War
1987	Palestinians start the intifada
1989	Chinese military puts down student revolt in Tiananmen Square
1990–1991	Persian Gulf War
1991	Congress Party in India embraces Western capitalist reforms
2001	China joins World Trade Organization
2007	Hamas establishes Palestinian Authority government
2009	Mahmoud Ahmadinejad violently suppresses protests in Iran
2010–2011	The "Arab Spring," populist uprisings and protests across the Middle East

Great Leap Forward Mao Zedong's acceleration of Chinese development in which industrial growth was to be based on small-scale backyard workshops run by peasants living in gigantic self-contained communes.

Great Proletarian Cultural Revolution A movement launched by Mao Zedong that attempted to purge the Chinese Communist Party of time-serving bureaucrats and recapture the revolutionary fervor of his guerrilla struggle.

Red Guards Radical cadres formed by young people who would attack anyone identified as an enemy of either the Chinese Communist Party or Chairman Mao.

Picturing the Past

Communist China Poster Art

One of the most popular art forms in Communist China is poster art, millions of copies of which have been printed to adorn the walls of homes, offices, factories, and businesses. Although related to socialist realism in the Soviet Union (see page 839), this uniquely Chinese version contains neither abstract, modern, or bourgeois elements nor classical Chinese art styles. Like Soviet socialist realism, such posters seek to glorify the state, its leaders, and the heroes of the ongoing revolution. The two young women in this poster wear uniforms and caps bearing the Communist red star, the five points of which represent the five components of Communist society: the youth, the army, the peasants, the workers, and the intellectuals. (Courtesy, University of Westminster Poster Collection, London)

ANALYZING THE IMAGE Who is depicted, and what are they doing? What message do you think the artist seeks to convey with this image?

CONNECTIONS What social function or application might posters such as this one have? Is this sort of expression unique to Communist societies, or can you think of examples of other types of art that promote public messages?

The Red Guards attracted enormous worldwide attention and served as an extreme model for the student rebellions in the West in the late 1960s (see page 857).

The Limits of Reform

Mao and the Red Guards succeeded in mobilizing the masses, shaking up the party, and creating greater social equality. But the Cultural Revolution also created growing chaos and a general crisis of confidence, especially in the cities. Persecuted intellectuals, technicians, and purged party officials launched a counterattack on the radicals and regained much of their influence by 1969. This shift to the right opened the door to a limited but lasting reconciliation between China and the United States in 1972, facilitated by U.S. president Richard Nixon's visit that year.

After Mao's death in 1976, Deng Xiaoping (1904–1997) and his supporters initiated a series of new policies, embodied in the campaign of the "Four Modernizations": agriculture, industry, science and technology, and national defense. China's 800 million peasants experienced the most beneficial change from what Deng called China's "second revolution." China's peasants were allowed to farm the land in small family units rather than in large collectives and to "dare to be rich" by producing crops of their choice. Peasants responded enthusiastically, increasing food production by more than 50 percent between 1978 and 1984.

The successful use of free markets in agriculture encouraged further economic experimentation. Foreign capitalists were allowed to open factories in southern China and to export Chinese products around the world. Private enterprise was also permitted in cities. China also drew on the business talent of wealthy "overseas" Chinese in Hong Kong and Taiwan who knew the world market and needed new sources of cheap labor. The Chinese economy grew rapidly between 1978 and 1987, and per capita income doubled in these years.

Most large-scale industry remained state-owned, however, and cultural change proceeded slowly. Above all, the Communist Party preserved its monopoly on political power. When the worldwide movement for greater democracy and political freedom in the late 1980s also took root in China, the government responded by banning all demonstrations and slowing the trend toward a freer economy. Inflation then soared to more than 30 percent a year. The economic reversal, the continued lack of political freedom, and the conviction that Chinese society was becoming more corrupt led China's university students to spearhead demonstrations in April 1989.

The students evoked tremendous popular support, and on May 17 more than a million people streamed into Beijing's central **Tiananmen Square** in support of their demands. The government declared martial law and ordered the army to clear the students. Masses of Chinese citizens blocked the soldiers' entry into the city for two weeks, but on June 4, 1989, tanks rolled into Tiananmen Square. At least seven hundred students died as a wave of repression, arrests, and executions descended on China.

Tiananmen Square The site of a Chinese student revolt in 1989 at which Communists imposed martial law and arrested, injured, or killed hundreds of students.

In the months after Tiananmen Square communism fell in eastern Europe, the Soviet Union broke apart, and China's rulers felt vindicated. They believed their action had preserved Communist power, prevented chaos, and demonstrated the limits of reform. After some hesitation Deng and his successor Jiang Zemin (b. 1926) reaffirmed economic liberalization. Private enterprise and foreign investment boomed in the 1990s. Consumerism was encouraged, and the living standard rose. Calls for political liberalization, however, were suppressed.

These policies continued into the twenty-first century. In 2001 China joined the World Trade Organization, giving it all the privileges and obligations of participation in the liberal global economy. Politically Communist, China now has a full-blown capitalist economy. When Europe, the United States, Japan, and many other nations faced a severe economic downturn in 2008, China's economy continued to expand. In March 2011 China replaced Japan as the world's second largest economy after that of the United States.

But China continues to have a miserable human rights record, and China's current leader, Hu Jintao (b. 1942), remains clearly committed to maintaining a strong authoritarian state. In October 2010 the Nobel Peace Prize committee awarded the prize to Chinese dissident Liu Xiaobo, a long-time democracy advocate who was then serving an eleven-year sentence for subversion. China refused to allow Liu, or anyone representing him, to go to Oslo to receive the prize, something that had happened only once before, when Hitler's Nazi Germany refused that right to Nobel Prize–winner and imprisoned pacifist Carl von Ossietzky in 1935. (See "Individuals in Society: Liu Xiaobo," page 874.)

INDIVIDUALS IN SOCIETY

Liu Xiaobo

AT THE NOBEL PEACE PRIZE CEREMONY IN OSLO on October 8, 2010, the chair reserved for the recipient, Liu Xiaobo (b. 1955) of China, was empty. Liu was serving an eleven-year prison term, and his wife, Liu Xia, was under house arrest. China blocked all news coverage of the event, including Web sites reporting on the ceremony.

Born in 1955, Liu received his Ph.D. in literature from Beijing Normal University in 1988. A highly regarded scholar and teacher, he lectured at Beijing Normal and, in the late 1980s, at Columbia University, the University of Oslo, and the University of Hawai'i. In spring 1989, when Chinese prodemocracy students began to gather in Beijing's Tiananmen Square, Liu was at Columbia. Although he had not previously involved himself in politics, Liu left the United States and returned to China in mid-May to join the students and other demonstrators. He began a hunger strike when rumors of an army crackdown filled the square.

Shortly before the Tiananmen Square massacre on June 4, 1989, Liu began to negotiate with the army to allow the protestors to peacefully leave the square. But at 1 A.M. Chinese troops and tanks moved into the square and attacked the remaining demonstrators. By 5:40 A.M. the square had been cleared. The true number of deaths and injuries in and around the square that night will never be known, but estimates range from a few hundred to a few thousand. Liu and others are widely credited with saving many lives by having negotiated a peaceful withdrawal by the students before the tanks rolled in.

Fearing arrest, Liu initially took asylum in the Australian embassy, but he went into the streets again when the government began going after, arresting, and executing demonstrators. He was arrested on June 8 and spent the next twenty months in prison.

Events at Tiananmen Square had made the previously detached academic a vocal critic of China's human rights policies. Chinese officials responded by banning all of his publications. Liu continued to write, however, and in Taiwan in 1992 he published a controversial memoir, *The Monologues of a Doomsday's Survivor*, that chronicled his involvement in and criticism of the 1989 popular democracy movement. Now constantly harassed by the government, Liu received a three-year prison sentence in 1996 for involvement in the human rights movement and for disturbing the social order. After his release Liu and his wife lived under constant police surveillance. In 2004 the police raided his home and took his computer and most of his personal papers.

Liu was a founder of the Chinese PEN Centre and served as its president from 2003 to 2007. An international organization of writers, PEN members campaign for freedom of expression and speak on behalf of writers who are being persecuted for their views.

In 2008 Liu helped write Charter 08, a Chinese human rights manifesto signed by over 350 activists and intellectuals. They issued the charter on the sixtieth anniversary of the Universal Declaration of Human Rights, a 1948 United Nations document guaranteeing all human beings certain rights, including the "four freedoms" of speech, of belief, from want, and from fear. On June 23, 2009, Liu was charged with "inciting the subversion of state power" and was sentenced in December to eleven years in prison.

The Nobel Peace Committee awarded Liu the 2010 prize "for his long and non-violent struggle for fundamental human rights in China."* In "I Have No Enemies: My Final Statement," which was read at the award ceremony, Liu wrote:

> But I still want to say to this regime, which is depriving me of my freedom, that . . . I have no enemies and no hatred. . . . I hope that I will be the last victim of China's endless literary inquisitions and that from now on no one will be incriminated because of speech. Freedom of expression is the foundation of human rights, the source of humanity, and the mother of truth. To strangle freedom of speech is to trample on human rights, stifle humanity, and suppress truth.†

*The Nobel Peace Prize 2010. Nobelprize.org. http://nobelprize.org/nobel_prizes/peace/laureates/2010/.
†Liu Xiaobo-Appell. Nobelprize.org. http://nobelprize.org/nobel_prizes/peace/laureates/2010/xiaobo-lecture.html.

QUESTIONS FOR ANALYSIS

1. Why is the Chinese government so afraid of Liu's writings?
2. What do you think Liu meant when he said in his Nobel Peace Prize statement "I have no enemies and no hatred"?

Jailed Chinese dissident and civil rights activist Liu Xiaobo in Beijing, China. (Liu Xia/epa)

The Asian "Economic Tigers"

China's exploding economy replicated the rapid industrial progress that characterized first Japan (see page 860) and then Asia's economic tigers—Taiwan, Hong Kong, Singapore, and South Korea. Both South Korea and Taiwan were underdeveloped Third World countries in the early postwar years. They also had suffered from Japanese imperialism and from destructive civil wars with Communist foes. Yet they managed spectacular turnarounds by making economic development national missions. First, radical land reform expropriated large landowners and drew small farmers into a competitive market economy. Second, pro-business governments cooperated with capitalists, opposed strikes, and protected businesses from foreign competition while securing access to the large American market. Third, both countries succeeded in preserving many cultural fundamentals even as they accepted and mastered Western technology. Last, tough nationalist leaders—Park Chung Hee (1917–1978) in South Korea and Jiang Jieshi in Taiwan—maintained political stability at the expense of genuine political democracy.

After a military coup overthrew Park in 1980, South Korea suffered under an even more authoritarian regime through the 1980s until democracy was restored at the end of the decade. South Korea's economy, however, continued to grow and expand. By the late 1990s South Korea had one of the largest economies in the world.

In 1949, after Jiang Jieshi had fled to Taiwan with his Nationalist troops and around 2 million refugees, he re-established the Republic of China (ROC) in exile. Over the next fifty years Taiwan created one of the world's most highly industrialized capitalist economies.

A large threatening cloud hangs over the island, however. As one of the founding members of the United Nations in 1945, Jiang's ROC government held one of the Security Council's five permanent seats. In 1971 the United Nations expelled the ROC, and its Security Council seat was given to the Communist People's Republic of China (mainland China). This action left Taiwan in political limbo: Should it remain the ROC or become an independent Republic of Taiwan? Meanwhile, mainland China claims authority over Taiwan, considers it part of "One China," and has threatened to attack if Taiwan declares its formal independence.

In recent years, tension surrounding the standoff between China and Taiwan has eased somewhat, and there has been increased contact between the two sides in commerce, communications, and transportation. But China continues to hold to its One China position, and the Chinese military continues to prepare for a possible invasion of the island.

The independent city-state of Singapore is the smallest of the economic tigers. It has prospered on the hard work and inventiveness of its largely Chinese population. The government, dominated by the People's Action Party, forcefully promotes conservative family values and strict social discipline. It also applies a mixture of economic planning and free-market practices, the so-called Singapore model, which has resulted in its enjoying one of the highest per capita incomes in the world since the 1990s. Despite the global economic downturn in 2008 and 2009, Singapore possessed the fastest growing economy in the world in 2010.

Hong Kong has long played a prominent role in the world economy. The British first occupied Hong Kong in 1841. Primarily a center of oceanic trade in the nineteenth century, Hong Kong turned to finance and manufacturing in the twentieth. On July 1, 1997, the United Kingdom returned Hong Kong to Chinese control. Under the

Asian "Economic Tigers"

Lights in the Night in the Eastern Hemisphere This NASA photo uniquely illustrates differences in wealth between the North and South. Human-made lights shine brightly from developed countries and heavily populated cities. Africa's continent-wide economic poverty is clearly evident, while North Korea sits in stark dark contrast to the blaze of light from South Korea and the other Asian economic tigers. (Image by Craig Mayhew and Robert Simmons, NASA GSFC)

agreement Hong Kong became a Special Administrative Region, and China promised that, under its "one country, two systems" formula, China's socialist economic system would not be imposed on Hong Kong. Although Hong Kong's economy was hurt by the global downturn in 2008 and 2009, its increasing integration with the Chinese economy has allowed it to recover more quickly than expected.

Political and Economic Progress in Southeast Asia

While many of the countries of Southeast Asia gained independence in the decade after 1945 (see Map 32.1), the attainment of stable political democracy proved a more difficult goal. In the decades after independence, governments in the Philippines, Indonesia, North and South Vietnam, Cambodia, and Burma fell to dictatorships or military juntas. (See "Listening to the Past: Aung San Suu Kyi, 'Freedom from Fear,'" page 878.) By the early twenty-first century all these countries, including most recently Burma, have been moving toward more stable governments and growing economies.

The Philippine Islands suffered greatly under Japanese occupation during the Second World War. Granted independence by the United States in 1946, the Philippines was an American-style democracy until 1972, when President Ferdinand Marcos (1917–1989) subverted the constitution and ruled as dictator. In 1986 a widespread popular rebellion forced him into exile, and Corazón Aquino (1933–2009) became the first female president. Aquino and her successors have made some progress in improving the economy. The Philippines weathered the 2008–2009 economic downturn, continuing to show modest gains in economic growth. Despite the growing economy, Communist insurgents and Muslim separatists continue to threaten the Philippines' political stability.

The Netherlands East Indies emerged in 1949 as independent Indonesia under the nationalist leader Achmed Sukarno (1901–1970). Like the Philippines, the populous new nation encompassed a variety of peoples, islands, and religions, with 85 percent of the population practicing Islam. A military coup led by General Suharto (1921–2008) forced Sukarno out in 1965. Suharto's authoritarian rule concentrated mainly on economic development. Blessed with large oil revenues, Indonesia achieved solid economic growth for a generation. Increasingly tied to the world economy, in 1997 Indonesia was devastated by a financial crisis, and Suharto was forced to resign in 1998.

After Suharto's fall, freely elected governments attacked corruption and reversed the economic decline. In 2000 Indonesia gave East Timor political independence. In 2004, in the first direct presidential elections ever held there, the Indonesians elected Susilo Bambang Yudhoyono (b. 1949) as president. Indonesia's economy grew at over 6 percent in 2007 and 2008, its fastest pace in eleven years. Economic expansion dropped to 4 percent in 2009 during the global economic crisis, but this smaller gain still made Indonesia one of only three of the world's largest economies, along with China and India, to exhibit growth.

The Reunification of Vietnam

French Indochina experienced the bitterest struggle for independence in Southeast Asia. The French tried to reimpose imperial rule there after the Communist and nationalist guerrilla leader Ho Chi Minh (1890–1969) declared an independent republic in 1945, but they were defeated in the 1954 Battle of Dien Bien Phu. At the subsequent international peace conference, French Indochina gained independence. Laos and Cambodia became separate states, and Vietnam was "temporarily" divided into two hostile sections at the seventeenth parallel pending elections to select a single unified government within two years.

The elections were never held, and a civil war soon broke out between the two Vietnamese governments, one Communist and the other anticommunist. Despite tremendous military effort in the Vietnam War by the United States in 1964–1975 (see page 858), the Communists emerged victorious in 1975. In 1986 Vietnamese Communists began to turn from central planning toward freer markets and private initiative with mixed results. The Vietnamese economy has grown 7 to 8 percent per year since 1990, but Vietnam remains one of the poorest countries in the region. Still, Communist officials are committed to a market economy, and Vietnam joined the World Trade Organization in 2007. Vietnam's Communist leaders continue to hold a monopoly on political power.

Quick Review
How have East Asian nations both contributed to and taken advantage of accelerating globalization?

How have India, Pakistan, and Bangladesh fared since independence?

The South Asian subcontinent has transformed itself no less spectacularly than has East Asia. After World War II, the newly independent nations of India, Pakistan, and Bangladesh exhibited many variations on the dominant themes of national renaissance and modernization, and ethnic and religious rivalries greatly complicated the process of renewal and development.

CHAPTER LOCATOR

What explains East Asia's economic success after World War II?

How have India, Pakistan, and Bangladesh fared since independence?

How has religion shaped Middle Eastern politics since 1945?

877

Aung San Suu Kyi, the Burmese opposition politician, spent fifteen years under house arrest between July 20, 1989, and her recent release on November 13, 2010, for her opposition to the military junta that rules Burma. After receiving a Ph.D. at the University of London in 1985, Suu Kyi returned to Burma in 1988 to lead the prodemocracy movement. A Buddhist as well as a follower of Gandhi's philosophy of nonviolence, Suu Kyi was arrested while campaigning for a peaceful transition to a democratic civilian government when Burma's leader General Ne Win retired after twenty-four years in power. In 1991, for her contributions in the struggle for human rights, Suu Kyi received the Nobel Peace Prize and the Sakharov Prize for Freedom of Thought from the European Parliament. This selection is from her "Freedom from Fear" acceptance speech for the Sakharov award.

❝ It is not power that corrupts but fear. Fear of losing power corrupts those who wield it and fear of the scourge of power corrupts those who are subject to it. Most Burmese are familiar with the four a-gati, the four kinds of corruption. Chanda-gati, corruption induced by desire, is deviation from the right path in pursuit of bribes or for the sake of those one loves. Dosa-gati is taking the wrong path to spite those against whom one bears ill will, and moga-gati is aberration due to ignorance. But perhaps the worst of the four is bhaya-gati, for not only does bhaya fear, stifle and slowly destroy all sense of right and wrong, it so often lies at the root of the other three kinds of corruption.

Just as chanda-gati, when not the result of sheer avarice, can be caused by fear of want or fear of losing the goodwill of those one loves, so fear of being surpassed, humiliated or injured in some way can provide the impetus for ill will. And it would be difficult to dispel ignorance unless there is freedom to pursue the truth unfettered by fear. With so close a relationship between fear and corruption it is little wonder that in any society where fear is rife corruption in all forms becomes deeply entrenched.

It would be difficult to dispel ignorance unless there is freedom to pursue the truth unfettered by fear. With so close a relationship between fear and corruption it is little wonder that in any society where fear is rife corruption in all forms becomes deeply entrenched. . . .

The effort necessary to remain uncorrupted in an environment where fear is an integral part of everyday existence is not immediately apparent to those fortunate enough to live in states governed by the rule of law. Just laws do not merely prevent corruption by meting out impartial punishment to offenders. They also help to create a society in which people can fulfil the basic requirements necessary for the preservation of human dignity without recourse to corrupt practices. Where there are no such laws, the burden of upholding the principles of justice and common decency falls on the ordinary people. It is the cumulative effect on their sustained effort and steady endurance which will change a nation where reason and conscience are warped by fear into one where legal rules exist to promote man's desire for harmony and justice while restraining the less desirable destructive traits in his nature.

In an age when immense technological advances have created lethal weapons which could be, and are, used by the powerful and the unprincipled to dominate the weak and the helpless, there is a compelling need for a closer relationship between politics and ethics at both the national and international levels. The Universal Declaration of Human Rights of the United Nations proclaims that "every individual and every organ of society" should strive to promote the basic rights and freedoms to which all human beings regardless of race, nationality or religion are entitled. But as long as there are governments whose authority is founded on coercion rather than on the mandate of the people, and interest groups which place short-term profits above long-term peace and prosperity, concerted international action to protect and promote human rights will remain at best a partially realized ideal. . . .

The quintessential revolution is that of the spirit, born of an intellectual conviction of the need for change in those mental attitudes and values which shape the course of a nation's development. A revolution which aims merely at changing official policies and institutions with a view to an improvement in material conditions has little chance of genuine success. Without a revolution of the spirit, the forces which produced the iniquities of the old order would continue to be operative, posing a constant threat to the process of reform and regeneration. It is not enough merely to call for freedom, democracy and human rights. There has to be a united determination to persevere in the struggle, to make sacrifices in the

The End of British India

World War II accelerated the drive toward Indian independence begun by Mohandas Gandhi (see pages 794–795). In 1942 Gandhi called on the British to "quit India" and threatened another civil disobedience campaign. He and the other Indian National Con-

At her home in Rangoon, Aung San Suu Kyi sits in front of a portrait of her father, General Aung San, founder of the Burmese independence movement. (Richard Vogel/AP Images)

courage that comes from cultivating the habit of refusing to let fear dictate one's actions, courage that could be described as "grace under pressure" — grace which is renewed repeatedly in the face of harsh, unremitting pressure.

Within a system which denies the existence of basic human rights, fear tends to be the order of the day. Fear of imprisonment, fear of torture, fear of death, fear of losing friends, family, property or means of livelihood, fear of poverty, fear of isolation, fear of failure. A most insidious form of fear is that which masquerades as common sense or even wisdom, condemning as foolish, reckless, insignificant or futile the small, daily acts of courage which help to preserve man's self-respect and inherent human dignity. It is not easy for a people conditioned by fear under the iron rule of the principle that might is right to free themselves from the enervating miasma of fear. Yet even under the most crushing state machinery courage rises up again and again, for fear is not the natural state of civilized man.

The wellspring of courage and endurance in the face of unbridled power is generally a firm belief in the sanctity of ethical principles combined with a historical sense that despite all setbacks the condition of man is set on an ultimate course for both spiritual and material advancement. It is his capacity for self-improvement and self-redemption which most distinguishes man from the mere brute. At the root of human responsibility is the concept of perfection, the urge to achieve it, the intelligence to find a path towards it, and the will to follow that path if not to the end at least the distance needed to rise above individual limitations and environmental impediments. It is man's vision of a world fit for rational, civilized humanity which leads him to dare and to suffer to build societies free from want and fear. Concepts such as truth, justice and compassion cannot be dismissed as trite when these are often the only bulwarks which stand against ruthless power. 🗎

name of enduring truths, to resist the corrupting influences of desire, ill will, ignorance and fear. . . .

Among the basic freedoms to which men aspire that their lives might be full and uncramped, freedom from fear stands out as both a means and an end. A people who would build a nation in which strong, democratic institutions are firmly established as a guarantee against state-induced power must first learn to liberate their own minds from apathy and fear. . . .

Gandhi, that great apostle of non-violence, and Aung San, the founder of a national army, were very different personalities, but as there is an inevitable sameness about the challenges of authoritarian rule anywhere at any time, so there is a similarity in the intrinsic qualities of those who rise up to meet the challenge.

Fearlessness may be a gift but perhaps more precious is the courage acquired through endeavour,

Source: Aung San Suu Kyi, *Freedom from Fear and Other Writings*, ed. Michael Aris (New York: Penguin, 2010), pp. 180–185. Copyright © 1991, 1995 by Aung San Suu Kyi and Michael Aris. Reproduced by permission of Penguin Books Ltd. and Viking Penguin, a division of Penguin Group (USA) Inc.

QUESTIONS FOR ANALYSIS

1. To whom is Aung San Suu Kyi referring when she talks about the fear of losing power?
2. How does Aung San Suu Kyi reconcile her struggle with her Buddhist faith in her reference to the four a-gati?
3. How might Aung San Suu Kyi's words apply to other regimes mentioned in this chapter, such as Egypt, China, or Iran?

gress Party leaders were jailed for most of the war. Meanwhile, the Congress Party's prime political rival skillfully seized the opportunity to increase its influence.

That rival was the **Muslim League**, led by Muhammad Ali Jinnah (1876–1948). Jinnah feared Hindu domination of an independent Indian state led by the Congress Party. Asserting in nationalist terms the right of Muslim areas to separate from the Hindu majority,

Muslim League The rival to the Indian National Congress Party, it argued for separate homelands for Muslims and Indians.

in March 1940 Jinnah called on the British government to grant the Muslim and Hindu peoples separate homelands by dividing India into autonomous national states. In Jinnah's view, Indian Hindus and Muslims constituted two completely separate cultures: "To yoke together two such nations under a single State, one as a numerical minority and the other as majority, must lead to growing discontent and final destruction of any fabric that may be so built up for the government of such a State."[1] Only a two-nation solution, in his view, would ensure the survival of the minority Muslim culture. Gandhi regarded Jinnah's two-nation theory as untrue and as promising the victory of hate over love.

Britain agreed to speedy independence for India after 1945, but conflicting Hindu and Muslim nationalisms and religious hatred led to murderous clashes between the two communities in 1946. When it became clear that Jinnah and the Muslim League would accept nothing less than an independent Pakistan, Britain proposed partition. Both sides accepted. At midnight on August 14, 1947, India and Pakistan gained political independence (Map 32.2).

In the weeks following independence communal strife exploded into an orgy of massacres and mass expulsions. Perhaps a hundred thousand Hindus and Muslims were slaughtered, and an estimated 5 million became refugees. Congress Party leaders were completely powerless to stop the wave of violence. "What is there to celebrate?" exclaimed Gandhi in reference to independence, "I see nothing but rivers of blood."[2] In January 1948 Gandhi himself was gunned down by a Hindu fanatic.

Map 32.2 The Partition of British India, 1947 Violence and fighting were most intense where there were large Hindu and Muslim minorities— in Kashmir, the Punjab, and Bengal. The tragic result of partition, which occurred repeatedly throughout the world in the twentieth century, was a forced exchange of populations and greater homogeneity on both sides of the border.

After the ordeal of independence, relations between India and Pakistan were, and continue to be, tense. Fighting over the disputed area of Kashmir, a strategically important northwestern border state with a Muslim majority annexed by India, continued until 1949 and broke out again in 1965–1966, 1971, and 1999 (see Map 32.2).

Pakistan and the Creation of Bangladesh

Pakistan's western and eastern provinces shared the Muslim faith but were separated by more than a thousand miles of Indian territory, as well as by language, ethnic background, and social custom. The Bengalis of East Pakistan constituted a majority of Pakistan's population, but they were neglected by the central government, which remained in the hands of West Pakistan's elite after Jinnah's death. In essence, East Pakistan remained a colony of West Pakistan.

Tensions escalated in the late 1960s, and in 1971 the Bengalis revolted and won their independence as the new nation of Bangladesh. For the next twenty years Bangladesh, nominally a secular parliamentary democracy, found genuine political stability elusive. It also suffered a string of natural calamities, mostly related to the country's straddling the Ganges Delta, a vast, low-lying fertile area of land that is subject to annual monsoon floods, tornados, and cyclones.

Bangladesh is the world's eighth most populous country (around 160 million), one of the most densely populated, and also one of the poorest. Still, since 1991 Bangladesh's economy has grown and diversified with a steady increase in foreign investment. The middle class has expanded, illiteracy rates have fallen, poverty has decreased, and there has been a marked improvement in gender parity in the country's schools.

Like Bangladesh, Pakistan has experienced political instability and widespread corruption, alternating between civilian and military rule since independence. From 1977 to 1988, military strongman General Muhammad Zia-ul-Haq ruled the country with a heavy hand. Zia was responsible for aiding neighboring Afghanistan following the Soviet invasion of that country in 1979, and his help eventually led to Soviet withdrawal. During the 1980s Pakistan was a close ally of the United States, but relations between the two countries became chilly in the 1990s when Pakistan refused to abandon its development of nuclear weapons. After the September 11, 2001, al-Qaeda attack on the United States (see page 932), Pakistan again became an important ally and the recipient of billions of dollars in military aid from the United States.

Although General Pervez Musharraf (b. 1943) did much to revive the Pakistani economy in the early years of his rule, in 2007 he attempted to reshape the country's Supreme Court by replacing the chief justice with one of his close allies, bringing about calls for his impeachment. Benazir Bhutto (1953–2007), who became the first female elected head of a Muslim state when she was elected prime minister in 1988, returned from exile to challenge Musharraf. While campaigning, Bhutto was assassinated on December 27, 2007. After being defeated at the polls in 2008, Musharraf resigned and went into exile in London. In the elections that followed, Asif Ali Zardari (b. 1955), the widower of Benazir Bhutto, won the presidency.

Pakistan had a population of over 170 million in 2010, a number that is expected to increase to over 250 million by 2030. It has a semi-industrialized economy, the second largest in South Asia after India, with the service sector and telecommunications growing in importance.

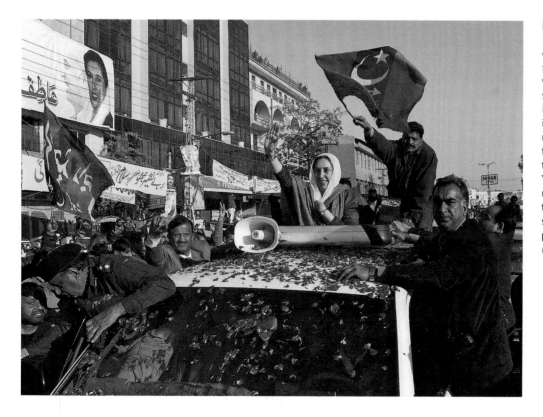

Bhutto's Assassination Pakistani presidential candidate Benazir Bhutto stands up in her campaign van just moments before she was assassinated on December 27, 2007. In the initial confusion it was reported that an assassin fired at her with a pistol and then threw a bomb. Scotland Yard investigators later determined that she died when the force of the bomb explosion slammed her head into part of the open hatch. (Mohammed Javed/AP Images)

CHAPTER LOCATOR

What explains East Asia's economic success after World War II?

How have India, Pakistan, and Bangladesh fared since independence?

How has religion shaped Middle Eastern politics since 1945?

881

Recently, there has been increasing concern about the stability and resolve of the new Pakistani government. As of 2009 around 1.7 million Afghani refugees had settled in northwest and west Pakistan. Many were suspected of being sympathetic to the Taliban and of harboring fugitive Taliban and al-Qaeda members, including the al-Qaeda leader, Osama bin Laden. These suspicions were reinforced when U.S. Special Forces killed bin Laden on May 1, 2011, in a walled compound only thirty miles from the Pakistani capital. Since 2009 the United States has increased missile strikes against supposed Taliban strongholds in Pakistan, leading to large demonstrations against the United States as well as Pakistan's government for its perceived inability to stop the attacks. Massive flooding in July 2010 and the government's slow response further weakened President Zardari's regime. The United States continues to send Pakistan massive amounts of military aid to fight the insurgents and humanitarian aid to help Pakistan recover from the floods, hoping to keep the country stable and an ally in the war in Afghanistan.

India Since Independence

Jawaharlal Nehru (1889–1964) and the Indian National Congress Party ruled India for a generation after independence and introduced major social reforms. Hindu women were granted legal equality, including the right to vote, to seek divorce, and to marry outside their castes. The constitution abolished the untouchable caste. In practice less-discriminatory attitudes toward women and untouchables evolved slowly—especially in the villages, where 85 percent of the people lived.

The Congress Party leadership tried with modest success to develop the country economically by means of democratic socialism. But population growth of about 2.4 percent per year ate up much of the increase in output. Intense poverty remained the lot of most people and encouraged widespread political corruption. The Congress Party maintained neutrality in the Cold War and sought to join with newly independent states in Asia and Africa to create a "third force" of nonaligned nations, aiming for economic and cultural cooperation. This effort culminated in the Afro-Asian Conference in Bandung, Indonesia, in 1955.

Nehru's daughter, Indira Gandhi (1917–1984; no relation to Mohandas Gandhi), became prime minister in 1966. In 1975 she subverted parliamentary democracy and proclaimed a state of emergency. Attacking dishonest officials, black marketers, and tax evaders, she also threw the weight of the government behind a heavy-handed campaign of mass sterilization to reduce population growth.

Many believed that Gandhi's emergency measures marked the end of the parliamentary democracy and Western liberties in India. Contrary to such expectations, Gandhi called for free elections. She suffered a spectacular electoral defeat in 1977, largely because of the vastly unpopular sterilization campaign and her subversion of democracy. Her successors fell to fighting among themselves, and in 1980 she won an equally stunning electoral victory.

Separatist ethnic nationalism plagued Indira Gandhi's last years in office. Democratic India remained a patchwork of religions, languages, and peoples, always threatening to further divide the country along ethnic or religious lines. Most notable were the 15 million Sikhs of the Punjab in northern India (see Map 32.2), with their own religion and a distinctive culture. Most Sikhs wanted greater autonomy for the Punjab, and by 1984 some Sikh radicals were fighting for independence. Gandhi cracked down hard, and she was assassinated by Sikhs in retaliation.

Elected prime minister in 1984 by a landslide sympathy vote, one of Indira Gandhi's sons, Rajiv Gandhi (1944–1991), showed considerable skill at effecting a limited reconciliation with a majority of the Sikh population. Under his leadership the Congress Party moved away from the socialism of his mother and grandfather. He prepared the way for market reforms, capitalist development, and Western technology and investment from 1991 onward. These reforms were successful, and since the 1990s India's economy has experienced explosive growth.

Holding power almost continuously from 1947, the Congress Party was challenged increasingly by Hindu nationalists in the 1990s. These nationalists argued forcefully that India was based, above all, on Hindu culture and religious tradition. Campaigning also for a strong Indian military, the Hindu nationalist party gained power in 1998. The new government immediately resumed testing of nuclear devices, asserting its vision of a militant Hindu nationalism. In 2004 the United Progressive Alliance (UPA), a center-left coalition dominated by the Congress Party, regained control of the government and elected Manmohan Singh (b. 1932) as prime minister.

After Pakistan announced that it had developed nuclear weapons in 1998, relations between Pakistan and India worsened. In December 2001 the two nuclear powers seemed poised for war until intense diplomatic pressure forced them to back off. In April 2005 both sides agreed to open business and trade relations and to work to negotiate a peaceful solution to the Kashmir dispute. Islamic and Hindu chauvinism remains strong, however, and tension between the two countries again increased in November 2008 when a Pakistan-based terrorist organization carried out a widespread shooting and bombing attack across Mumbai, India's largest city. Tensions remain high, and nationalist and religious extremists in both countries appear willing to carry out such attacks again.

> **Quick Review**
> What similarities do you see in the development of India, Pakistan, and Bangladesh since independence? How have they differed?

How has religion shaped Middle Eastern politics since 1945?

Throughout the vast umma (world of Islam), nationalism remained the primary political force after 1945. Anti-Western and anticommunist in most instances, Muslim nationalism generally combined a strong secular state with deep devotion to Islam. The idealistic side of Arab nationalism focused on the Pan-Arab dream of uniting all Arabs in a single nation that would be strong enough to resist the West, defeat the new state of Israel, and achieve genuine independence. This vision floundered on intense regional, ideological, and personal rivalries; thus a more practical Arab nationalism focused largely on nation building within former League of Nations mandates and European colonies.

In the very heart of this world of Islam, Jewish nationalists founded the state of Israel following the Second World War. The Zionist claim to a homeland came into sharp, and often violent, conflict with the rights and claims of the Palestinians. Religious differences, territorial claims, and the right to nationhood have been at the heart of the Israeli-Palestinian conflict since the early 1900s.

In the Muslim countries of the Middle East, nation building, often led by westernized elites, almost universally culminated in the creation of one-party dictatorships, corruption, and continued hardship for the masses. In the 1970s some Islamic preachers and devoted laypeople charged that the model of modernizing, Western-inspired nationalism had failed. These critics, labeled fundamentalists in the West, urged a return to strict Islamic principles and traditional morality. In countries like Egypt they worked to overthrow the government, which generally resulted in their movements being banned and their leaders arrested. In countries like Lebanon and Turkey they gained some political power within the secular governments. In Iran in 1979 they overthrew the secular government and created an Islamic republic.

The Arab-Israeli Conflict

Before the Second World War, Arab nationalists were loosely united in their opposition to the colonial powers and to Jewish migration to Palestine. The British had granted independence to Egypt and Iraq before the war, and the French followed suit with Syria and Lebanon in 1945. In British-mandated Palestine, the situation was volatile. Jewish settlement in Palestine (see pages 791–792) was strenuously opposed by the Palestinian Arabs and the seven independent states of the newly founded Arab League (Egypt, Iraq, Jordan, Lebanon, Saudi Arabia, Syria, and Yemen). Murder and terrorism flourished, nurtured by bitterly conflicting Arab and Jewish nationalisms.

The British announced in early 1947 their intention to withdraw from Palestine in 1948, leaving the United Nations to solve the problem of a Jewish homeland. In November 1947 the UN General Assembly passed a plan to partition Palestine into two separate states — one Arab and one Jewish (Map 32.3). The Jews accepted, and the Arabs rejected, the partition of Palestine.

When the British mandate ended on May 14, 1948, the Jews proclaimed the state of Israel. Arab countries immediately attacked the new Jewish state, but the Israelis drove off the invaders and conquered more territory. Roughly nine hundred thousand Palestinian refugees fled or were expelled from old Palestine. The war left an enormous legacy of Arab bitterness toward Israel and its political allies, Great Britain and the United States.

In Egypt the Arab defeat triggered a nationalist revolution. Colonel Gamal Abdel Nasser (1918–1970) drove out the corrupt and pro-Western king Farouk in 1952. Nasser claimed neutrality in the Cold War, but accepted Soviet aid to demonstrate Egypt's independence of the West. Relations with Israel and the West worsened, and in 1956 Nasser nationalized the European-owned Suez Canal Company. Outraged, the British and French joined forces with the Israelis and successfully invaded Egypt. The United States unexpectedly sided with the Soviets and forced the British, French, and Israelis to withdraw from Egypt.

Nasser's victory encouraged hopes of Pan-Arab political unity. Yet the Arab world remained deeply divided apart from bitter opposition to Israel and support for the right of Palestinian refugees to return to their homeland. In 1964 a loose union of Palestinian refugee groups joined together, under the leadership of Yasir Arafat (1929–2004), to form the **Palestine Liberation Organization (PLO)**.

On June 4, 1967, as Syrian and Egyptian armies massed on their borders, the Israelis made the decision to strike first. The Israelis launched a surprise air strike early on June 5 and by noon had destroyed most of the Egyptian, Syrian, and Jordanian air forces. Over the next five days Israeli armies took control of the Sinai Peninsula and the Gaza Strip from Egypt, the West Bank and East Jerusalem from Jordan, and the Golan Heights from Syria. In the Six-Day War, Israel proved itself to be the pre-eminent military force in the region, and it expanded the territory under its control threefold. After the war, Israel began to build large Jewish settlements in the Gaza Strip and the West Bank, home to millions of Palestinians.

Six years later, on Yom Kippur on October 6, 1973, the holiest day in Judaism, a coalition of Arab forces led by Syria and Egypt launched a surprise attack on Israel across the Golan Heights and the Sinai Peninsula. Despite initial setbacks, the Israelis successfully counterattacked and were closing in on Cairo and Damascus when a ceasefire ended hostilities on October 25. For the Arab world, the Yom Kippur War (or 1973 Arab-Israeli War) marked a psychological victory because of the Arab states' initial successes. The Israelis now felt less invincible than they had following the Six-Day War, and the United States recognized the need to become more actively involved in mediation and peacemaking. Efforts undertaken by U.S. president Jimmy Carter led to the Camp David Accords in 1979 that normalized relations between Egypt and Israel and that brokered the return of the Sinai Peninsula to Egypt.

Palestine Liberation Organization (PLO) Created in 1964, a loose union of Palestinian refugee groups opposed to Israel and working toward Palestinian home rule.

Map 32.3 Palestine, Israel, and the Middle East Since the British mandate expired on May 14, 1948, there have been five major wars and innumerable armed clashes in what was formerly Palestine. Through negotiations between Israel and the PLO, Jericho and the Gaza Strip were placed under Palestinian self-rule, and Israeli troops were withdrawn in 1994 (inset). In 2010–2011 a series of populist uprisings and protests spread throughout the Middle East, toppling some regimes and leading to both uncertainty and hope for democratic reform.

The Palestinian Quest for Independence

In 1987 Palestinians in the occupied territories of the Gaza Strip and the West Bank began the intifada, a prolonged campaign of rock throwing and civil disobedience against Israeli soldiers. Inspired increasingly by Islamic fundamentalists, the Palestinian uprising

intifada A popular uprising by young Palestinians against Israeli rule; the Arabic word *intifada* means "shaking off."

eventually posed a serious challenge not only to Israel but also to the secular Palestine Liberation Organization (PLO), long led from abroad by Yasir Arafat. The result was an agreement in 1993 between Israel and the PLO. Israel agreed to recognize Arafat's organization and start a peace process that granted Palestinian self-rule in Gaza and called for self-rule throughout the West Bank in five years. In return, Arafat renounced terrorism and abandoned the long-standing demand that Israel must withdraw from all land occupied in the 1967 war.

The peace process increasingly divided Israel. In 1995 a right-wing Jewish extremist assassinated Prime Minister Yitzhak Rabin (1922–1995). In 1996 a coalition of opposition parties won a slender majority. The new Israeli government limited Palestinian self-rule where it existed and expanded Jewish settlements in the West Bank. On the Palestinian side, dissatisfaction with the peace process grew. Between 1993 and 2000 the number of Jewish settlers in the West Bank doubled to two hundred thousand and Palestinian per capita income declined by 20 to 25 percent.

Failed negotiations between Arafat and Israel in 2000 unleashed an explosion of tit-for-tat violence, known as the Second Intifada, in Israel, the West Bank, and the Gaza Strip. In 2003 the Israelis began building a barrier around the West Bank, which has met with opposition from Israelis and Palestinians alike.

The death of Yasir Arafat, the PLO's long-time leader, in November 2004 marked a major turning point in the Israeli-Palestinian dispute. Mahmoud Abbas, Arafat's successor, is viewed as moderate and pragmatic, but peace talks have made little progress since he took office. In January 2006 Hamas, a radical Sunni Muslim political party, won a ma-

Israel's Wall of Separation A Palestinian man waves as he walks across the hills near Jerusalem, where Israel's wall of separation divides Israeli and Palestinian territory. Israelis argue that the wall, made of concrete and covered with razor wire, protects them from Palestinian militants and suicide bombers. Increasingly it is described by Palestinians and others as a Berlin Wall–like structure, a symbol of Israelis forcing a separation, an Israeli version of apartheid, between the two peoples. (Kevin Frayer/AP Images)

jority in the Palestinian legislature, seizing control from Abbas and the PLO. Considered by many in the West to be a terrorist organization, Hamas had gained widespread support from many Palestinians for the welfare programs it established in the West Bank and Gaza Strip.

Immediately after the Hamas victory, Israel, the United States, the European Union, and several other Western donor nations cut off all aid to the Palestinian Authority, the governing body of the West Bank and Gaza Strip established by the 1994 peace agreement. In June 2007 Hamas seized control of the Gaza Strip. Since then, economic and humanitarian conditions for Palestinians living in the Gaza Strip have deteriorated. When a "Gaza freedom flotilla" attempted to break an Israeli blockade around Gaza in May 2010, the Israeli navy intercepted the flotilla and raided the ships. Under pressure from critics around the world, Israel eased its blockade in 2010, allowing more humanitarian goods and food aid into Gaza, but the movement of people to and from Gaza remains restricted.

While Gaza remained isolated, Abbas and the Palestinian Authority formed a separate government in the West Bank. In September 2010 Israeli prime minister Benjamin Netanyahu (b. 1949) agreed to hold direct peace talks with President Abbas and the Palestinians, mediated by the U.S. Obama administration. The peace talks broke down barely three weeks after they started, as Israel resumed construction of settlement homes in the West Bank and East Jerusalem. Thus, despite years of diplomacy, war, and stalemate, the nature of a future Palestinian state remains unresolved.

Egypt: Arab World Leader

In late 1977 Egypt's president Anwar Sadat (1918–1981) made a pathbreaking official visit to Israel, leading to a peace settlement known as the Camp David Accords (see page 884). Each country gained: Egypt got back the Sinai Peninsula, which Israel had taken in the 1967 Six-Day War (see Map 32.3), and Israel obtained peace and normal relations with Egypt. Israel also kept the Gaza Strip, taken from Egypt in 1967 and home to about 1 million Palestinians. Some Arab leaders denounced Sadat's initiative, and Egypt was suspended from the Arab League from 1979 to 1989.

After Sadat's assassination by Islamic radicals in 1981, Egypt's relations with Israel deteriorated, but Egypt and Israel maintained their fragile peace as Sadat's successor as president, Hosni Mubarak (b. 1928), took office in 1981. Mubarak was a consistent supporter of Israel and a mediator for peaceful relations between Israel and the Arab world. Egypt is considered the closest Middle Eastern ally of the United States after Israel, and since the Camp David Accords the United States has given Egypt billions of dollars in development, humanitarian, and military aid.

Domestically, however, Mubarak failed to promote significant economic development and ruled with an increasingly dictatorial hand. Many of the government's critics charged that massive fraud and corruption funneled Egypt's wealth to a privileged few. Over 40 percent of the total population lived in poverty.

The human rights picture during Mubarak's thirty years in office was no better. Officially Egypt is a republic, but it has been ruled under an emergency law since 1967. Mubarak used the emergency law to create a wholly separate justice system in order to silence all opposition and to punish, torture, and kill anyone who was perceived as a threat to his rule. Demonstrations, political organizations, and even financial donations that were not approved by the government were banned under the law. Thousands of people were arrested. In May 2010 the parliament approved the law's extension for another two years.

In December 2010 demonstrations broke out in Tunisia against the authoritarian rule of President Zine Ben Ali (b. 1936), leading to his downfall on January 14, 2011. This populist revolt soon spread across North Africa and the Middle East. Dubbed the "Arab Spring," the protests spread to the streets of Cairo and other cities as Egyptians of all ages united in

Egyptian Protesters in Cairo, January 29, 2011 The Tunisian overthrow of the repressive regime of long-serving President Ben Ali on January 14, 2011, set off a wave of popular uprisings against authoritarian regimes across North Africa and the Middle East. Next to go was Egypt's Hosni Mubarak, who had ruled Egypt with an iron hand for nearly thirty years. He stepped down on February 11, 2011, after the army—including the men on the tanks in this image—joined the protesters. (Ahmed Ali/AP Images)

revolt against Mubarak's dictatorial rule. After three weeks of increasingly large demonstrations, coordinated through Facebook, Twitter, and other electronic communications networks, Mubarak stepped down as president on February 11, 2011.

Libya, located between Tunisia and Egypt, also witnessed a massive uprising against its dictatorial leader of forty-two years, Muammar Gaddafi (1942–2011). Gaddafi responded by using his army and air force to attack cities, neighborhoods, and rural areas held by opposition forces. In response to the slaughter of thousands of Libyans by Gaddafi's air force, in March 2011 the United Nations created a no-fly zone over Libya and authorized NATO forces to enforce it. After months of civil war, Gaddafi was finally killed in October 2011 by forces of the, by then, de facto Libyan government, the National Transitional Council of Libya.

A Fractured Lebanon

With the Vichy French government unable to maintain its control over Lebanon, the mandated territory gained its independence from French rule in 1943. When Lebanon became an independent nation, the unwritten National Pact included an agreement that the Lebanese president would be a Christian and the prime minister a Muslim. This arrangement was based on a 1932 census that showed a Christian majority. By the late 1960s the Lebanese Muslim population had grown significantly, and Muslims were no longer content with a Christian-controlled government and military. Their dissatisfaction came to a head in early

1975, starting with armed scrimmages between Christian and Muslim factions that resulted in the slaughter of many innocent civilians, and the escalating violence and reprisals led to a fifteen-year civil war.

In the course of the war the Lebanese army disintegrated when soldiers switched their allegiance from the national government to various sectarian militias. One of these was a hard-line group known as Hezbollah. Hezbollah condemned the Israeli invasions of Lebanon in 1978 and 1982 aimed at eradicating the Palestine Liberation Organization's control of southern Lebanon, and it had as one of its stated objectives the complete destruction of the state of Israel.

The Lebanese civil war was massively destructive. War crimes and terrorist acts were committed by all sides. Lebanon's entire infrastructure was destroyed, and Beirut in 1990 looked like the bombed-out cities of Europe after World War II. The civil war ended after Lebanon's Maronite Christian and Muslim communities agreed to a more balanced sharing of power, and by 1991 the sectarian violence had generally ceased. Israeli forces finally left Lebanon in 2000, and Syria withdrew its troops, who had been sent in by the Arab League to maintain peace, in 2005.

The 2006 Israel-Lebanon War

By 2004 Hezbollah had established virtual control over much of southern Beirut and southern Lebanon. Hezbollah members adhere to a distinct brand of Islamic theology and ideology developed by the Shi'ite Ayatollah Ruhollah Khomeini, leader of the Iranian Islamic Revolution in 1979. This connection explains the significant financial and military support that Iran provides and its powerful influence in shaping Hezbollah's policies.

On July 12, 2006, Hezbollah's hostility toward Israel erupted into what became known as the July War in Lebanon and the Second Lebanon War in Israel. By early August all sides clearly desired a way out, and with the help of the United Nations Security Council, both sides agreed to a cease-fire on August 14, 2006.

Opinions about who won and who lost the war vary, but it was costly to both sides. Hezbollah declared victory, and many in the Muslim world felt pride in Hezbollah's ability to stand up to Israel. Although Hezbollah may have won the propaganda war, there can be no doubt that the group paid dearly. It lost the elaborate infrastructure it had taken years to build in the south, and it lost the support of hundreds of thousands of Lebanese whose homes, lives, and livelihoods were destroyed by its actions. For its part, Israel also claimed victory, but it was also no better off. Israelis emerged from the war deeply troubled by a new sense of vulnerability and turned to Israeli hardliners such as Benjamin Netanyahu, who was elected prime minister in the next election.

Meanwhile, efforts to rebuild Lebanon have been ongoing. The majority of Lebanese people appear to want peace, but since 2006 Hezbollah has rearmed and has re-emerged as a political and military power. In May 2008 a Christian and former commander of the Lebanese armed forces, Michel Suleiman (b. 1948), became president. He formed a national unity government, which included Hezbollah parliament members. But in early January 2011 Hezbollah pulled out of the national coalition government, causing it to collapse. In late January Suleiman appointed a Sunni businessman, Najib Mikati, as prime minister-designate. Mikati was supported by Hezbollah and its allies in parliament, leading to widespread rioting by Sunnis across Lebanon, who viewed the action as the next step in the eventual takeover of Lebanon by the Shi'ite Hezbollah movement.

Challenges to Turkey's Secularism

Through the remainder of the twentieth century, Turkey remained basically true to Atatürk's vision of a modernized, secularized, Europeanized state (see pages 787–788). But Turkey remains a country on the border—seeking membership in the European Union of the West, while acknowledging its Islamic heritage and historical connections with the East. In the twenty-first century Turks have become increasingly divided over the future of the secular state in Turkey.

Turkey is the most secular of Islamic countries. Since the 1920s Turks have maintained a strict separation of state and religion. In the 2002 elections, however, the newly formed Justice and Development Party, or AKP, scored a stunning victory, with Abdullah Gül (b. 1950) becoming president of Turkey and Recep Erdogan (b. 1954), head of the AKP, becoming prime minister. Although the AKP campaigned as a moderate, conservative, pro-Western party, many Turks are concerned that it is intent on doing away with Turkey's secular constitution and establishing an Islamic state.

Despite this opposition the AKP continues to remain popular and win elections. During its rule, the Turkish economy has seen rapid growth, and the hyperinflation that plagued the country for three decades had fallen to around 7 percent in November 2010. Turkey weathered the 2008–2009 global economic downturn better than most countries, and its stock market in 2009 rose the most in the world after Argentina's.

A second major problem facing Turkey is its handling of its minority Kurdish population (Map 32.4). Many observers view the victory of the AKP in the 2007 elections as having been prompted by a surge in Turkish nationalism and a resurgence of conservative Muslim influence since September 11, 2001, when the West, particularly the United States, demanded a "with us or against us" position from its allies in the Middle East (see pages 927–929). When Turkey refused to participate in the invasion of Iraq in 2003 because it worried about destabilizing fragile relations with its Kurdish citizens, many in the George W. Bush administration labeled the Turks as "against" the United States and the war on terrorism.

As the situation in Iraq continued to deteriorate and as the Kurds in northern Iraq continued to push for more autonomy, Kurdish nationalists in Turkey increased their attacks on Turkish targets. In February and March 2008 the Turkish army began a military offensive against Kurds in eastern Turkey and also across the border in northern Iraq. In December 2010 the leader of the leading Kurdish independence movement, the Kurdistan Workers' Party, labeled a terrorist organization by the Turks, announced a unilateral cease-fire and suggested that the Kurds would be willing to accept a degree of Kurdish autonomy within Turkey rather than demand a separate Kurdish state.

Despite concerted efforts by leaders to meet the economic, legal, and humanitarian standards set by the EU, Turkey's pace of reform received heavy EU criticism. Even if Turkey meets all of the EU's demands, it cannot be admitted into the EU until the next round of EU membership admissions in 2013. In the meantime support within Turkey for EU membership has weakened as the economy has strengthened and Turkey's role as a regional power broker has grown.

Revolution and War in Iran and Iraq

After 1945 Iran tried to follow Turkey's example of Westernization. The new shah—Muhammad Reza Pahlavi (r. 1941–1979), the son of Reza Shah Pahlavi—angered Iranian nationalists by courting Western powers and Western oil companies. In 1953 the freely elected prime minister Muhammad Mossaddeq (1882–1967) tried to nationalize the British-owned Anglo-Iranian Oil Company, and the shah was forced to flee to Europe. However, loyal army officers, with the help of the American CIA, quickly restored the shah to his throne.

Seeking to build a powerful modern nation and ensure his own rule, the shah undermined the power bases of the traditional politicians—large landowners and religious leaders—by means of land reform, secular education, and increased power for the central government. Modernization surged forward, but at the loss of ancient values, widespread corruption, and harsh dictatorship. The result was an Islamic revolution in 1979 aimed at infusing strict Islamic principles into all aspects of personal and public life. Led by the Islamic cleric Ayatollah Ruhollah Khomeini, the fundamentalists deposed the shah and tried to build their vision of a true Islamic state.

Iran's Islamic republic frightened its neighbors. Iraq, especially, feared that Iran—a nation of Shi'ite Muslims—would succeed in getting Iraq's Shi'ite majority to revolt against its Sunni leaders (see Map 32.4). Thus in September 1980 Iraq's strongman, Saddam Hussein (1937–2006), launched a surprise attack, setting off a savage eight-year conflict.

Mapping the Past

Map 32.4 Abrahamic Religions in the Middle East and Surrounding Regions

Islam, Judaism, and Christianity, which all trace their origins back to the patriarch Abraham, have significant populations in the Middle East. Since the 1979 Iranian revolution Shi'ites throughout the region have become more militant and more strident in their demands for equality and power. One of the largest stateless ethnic groups, the Kurds, who follow various religions, has become a major player in the politics of the region, especially in Iraq and Turkey, where the group seeks Kurdish independence.

ANALYZING THE MAP Which religion dominates? Where are the largest concentrations of Jews and Christians in the Middle East located?

CONNECTIONS How have divisions between Shi'ite and Sunni Muslims contributed to war in the region?

Hussein next eyed Kuwait's great oil wealth. In August 1990 he ordered his forces to over-run Kuwait and proclaimed its annexation to Iraq. His aggression touched off the Persian Gulf War. In early 1991 his troops were chased out of Kuwait by an American-led, United Nations–sanctioned military coalition, which included Arab forces from Egypt, Syria, and Saudi Arabia.

Iran and Iraq went in different directions in the 1990s. The United Nations Security Council imposed stringent economic sanctions on Iraq as soon as it invaded Kuwait, and these sanctions continued after the Gulf War to force Iraq to destroy its weapons of mass destruction. United Nations inspectors destroyed many such weapons, but the United States charged Iraq with deceit and ongoing weapons development. An American-led invasion of Iraq in 2003 overthrew Saddam Hussein's regime (see pages 927–929).

As secular Iraq spiraled downward, Iran appeared to back away from fundamentalism. Executive power in Iran was divided between a Supreme Leader and twelve-member Guardian Council selected by high Islamic clerics, and an elected president and parliament. The Supreme Leader was a very conservative religious leader, but a growing reform move-ment pressed for a relaxation of strict Islamic decrees and elected a moderate, Mohammad Khatami (b. 1943), as president in 1997 and again in 2001. The Supreme Leader, control-ling the army and the courts, vetoed many of Khatami's reform measures and jailed some of the religious leadership's most vocal opponents.

In 2005 dubious election returns gave the presidency to an ultraconservative Islamic hardliner, Mahmoud Ahmadinejad (b. 1956). His populist speeches and actions made him popular among some elements of Iranian society, but they have also caused much anxiety and anger in the West. Despite this setback, many Iranians believe that moderate, secular reform is inevitable.

While supporters of reform may be right in the long run, the Iranian regime under Ahmadinejad has become more brutal in its opposition to internal dissent and more defi-ant in its relations with the United States and the West. Despite a failed economic policy, Ahmadinejad won re-election as president in 2009 after a strong, and bitterly contested, challenge from more moderate candidates. The government responded quickly and vio-lently to quell massive protests that broke out after news of the election results.

Iran's continued development of its nuclear program (see pages 934–935) remains the single greatest concern for leaders in the United States and Europe. They are also troubled by Iran's military and monetary support for the spread of its own Shi'ite brand of Islamic fundamentalism to countries across the Middle East in which the Shi'ite populations are either the ma-jority or make up a large minority of the people. Iran remains the primary backer of the Hamas party in the Gaza Strip and Hezbollah in Lebanon.

Quick Review

Why has religion become an increasingly important part of nationalist movements throughout the Middle East in recent decades?

Connections

SINCE THE END OF WORLD WAR II, Asia and the Middle East have undergone tremendous economic, political, and social changes. Japan's defeat and the collapse of European imperial empires allowed nationalist movements in these regions finally to begin to chart their own destinies. The newly independent countries led by China and India declared themselves to be nonaligned in the superpowers' Cold War. Most were concerned with feeding their hungry millions, rebuilding from the destruction of the war and occupation, and creating stable governments — some Communist, some part socialist and part free market, and some copying the Western model of democratic capitalism. In the Middle East, Arab leaders spoke of Pan-Arab unity but set about creating individual nations. Many of them became one-party dictatorships just as oppressive and exploitative of the masses as had been the European colonial powers and the Ottoman Turks. Decolonization in Africa and Latin America followed a similar pattern, as Chapter 33 explores.

As we will see in Chapter 34, in the decades since 1945 the United Nations has grown in importance, and that is in no small part due to the efforts of UN representatives of Asian, African, and Latin American nations who have pushed for greater efforts to deal with global problems that have the most negative impact on them, such as delivering better health services, advancing educational opportunities for boys and girls equally, ending global poverty, and cleaning up the environment. We will also look at how the growth of multinational corporations, the green revolution in agriculture, and mushrooming urbanization have had both positive and harmful effects on the world's populations.

- **For a list of suggested readings for this chapter, visit** *bedfordstmartins.com/mckayworldunderstanding*.

- **For primary sources from this period, see** *Sources of World Societies*, Second Edition.

- **For Web sites, images, and documents related to topics in this chapter, see Make History at** *bedfordstmartins.com/ mckayworldunderstanding*.

CHAPTER LOCATOR

What explains East Asia's economic success after World War II?

How have India, Pakistan, and Bangladesh fared since independence?

How has religion shaped Middle Eastern politics since 1945?

893

Chapter 32 Study Guide

To do these exercises online, go to bedfordstmartins.com/mckayworldunderstanding.

To do these exercises online, go to bedfordstmartins.com/mckayworldunderstanding.

Step 1

GETTING STARTED

Below are basic terms about this period in global history. Can you identify each term below and explain why it matters?

TERMS	WHO (OR WHAT) AND WHEN	WHY IT MATTERS
Great Leap Forward, p. 871		
Great Proletarian Cultural Revolution, p. 871		
Red Guards, p. 871		
Tiananmen Square, p. 873		
Muslim League, p. 879		
Palestine Liberation Organization (PLO), p. 884		
intifada, p. 885		

Step 2

MOVING BEYOND THE BASICS

The exercise below requires a more advanced understanding of the chapter material. Compare and contrast developments since 1945 in the world's two most populous countries—China and India—by filling in the chart below with descriptions of economic developments, political developments, and sources of internal division within each nation. When you are finished, consider the following questions: What advantages do their large populations give China and India over their smaller neighbors? What are the disadvantages of a large population? What role has government played in the economic success of each nation? How has each government responded to internal dissent and division?

	ECONOMIC DEVELOPMENT	POLITICAL DEVELOPMENT	INTERNAL DIVISIONS
China			
India			

PUTTING IT ALL TOGETHER

Now that you've reviewed key elements of the chapter, take a step back and try to see the big picture. Remember to use specific examples from the chapter in your answers.

EAST ASIA

- In your opinion, how stable is China's combination of economic liberalism and political authoritarianism? What does China's history since 1945 tell us about the likelihood of political liberalization in China in coming decades?

- What common characteristics link Asia's "economic tigers"?

SOUTH ASIA

- How has religious conflict shaped the history of South Asia since 1947?

- What challenges and opportunities do the nations of South Asia face in the early twenty-first century?

THE MIDDLE EAST

- What explains the dominant role the Israeli/Palestinian issue has played in Middle Eastern politics since 1945?

- What light do the recent histories of Turkey and Iran shed on the ambivalence many Middle Easterners feel toward westernization and modernization?

LOOKING BACK, LOOKING AHEAD

- How did Asian and Middle Eastern nationalists draw on Western ideas and models during the struggle for independence? How did attitudes toward the West in newly independent countries change in the decades after independence?

- In your opinion, in the next several decades will South and East Asia overtake Europe and North America as the dominant regions in the global economy? Why or why not?

In Your Own Words Imagine that you must explain Chapter 32 to someone who hasn't read it. What would be the most important points to include and why?

33

The Global South: Latin America and Africa

1945 to the Present

There are fifty-five countries in Africa and twenty in Latin America. There is thus room for much variety—economically, politically, and socially—when discussing the history of these two huge continents over the past hundred-plus years. As we discussed in the previous chapter, Latin America and Africa, together with East and South Asia, were considered part of the Third World during the Cold War era. There were sound reasons for this. Most of the countries sought to remain nonaligned, refusing to side with either of the two superpowers. In general they were also economically less developed—meaning less industrialized—than most of the countries in the Northern Hemisphere. Their economies were based primarily on agricultural or other raw material production.

Most Latin American countries gained their independence in the early 1800s, while sub-Saharan African countries did not break free from their colonial bonds until the 1960s and later. Still, events in many Latin American and African countries were similar in the post–World War II

Sandinista Soldier in Nicaragua Nicaraguan street art shows a female soldier of the Sandinista National Liberation Front picking coffee beans in her military camouflage. The Socialist Sandinistas ruled Nicaragua from 1979 until 1990 and then returned to power in 2006. (Thalia Watmough/aliki image library/Alamy)

era. Politically, for example, there was an initial period of democracy followed by years of harsh dictatorships. When the Soviet Union collapsed in 1991, a euphoria of democracy swept through many nations of Africa and Latin America as citizens concluded that if the Soviet dictatorship could be overthrown and representative government instituted, it could happen in their countries as well.

Chapter Preview

▶ How did Latin American states develop after World War II?

▶ What factors influenced decolonization in sub-Saharan Africa?

▶ What common features characterize independent African states since 1960?

▶ How have writers depicted the experience of the emerging world?

How did Latin American states develop after World War II?

After the Second World War Latin America experienced a many-faceted recovery, somewhat similar to that of Europe, though beginning earlier. A generation later, Latin America also experienced its own period of turbulence and crisis similar to the upheaval experienced in the Middle East and Asia. Many Latin American countries responded by establishing authoritarian military regimes. Others took Marxist paths. In the late 1980s most Latin American countries copied eastern Europe by electing civilian governments and embracing economic liberalism for the first time since the 1920s.

Picturing the Past

Juan O'Gorman, *Credit Transforms Mexico*

Emerging as an important architect in the 1930s, O'Gorman championed practical buildings and then led the movement to integrate architecture with art in postrevolutionary Mexico. These panels are from a 1965 fresco for a bank interior. (Photos: Enrique Franco-Torrijos. Courtesy, Banco Bital, S.A., Mexico City)

ANALYZING THE IMAGE What Mexican motifs are shown? How do the two panels differ in terms of lighting and mood, and what message does this imply about prerevolutionary and postrevolutionary life?

CONNECTIONS O'Gorman believed that Mexico had to preserve its cultural values in order to preserve its independence. What did he mean by this?

Economic Nationalism in Mexico and Brazil

The growth of economic nationalism was a common development throughout Latin America in much of the twentieth century. To understand the importance of genuine economic independence to Latin Americans, one must remember that Latin American countries developed as producers of foodstuffs and raw materials exported to Europe and the United States in return for manufactured goods and capital investment. Thus, Latin America became dependent on foreign markets, products, and investments. Industry did not develop, and large landowners profited the most from economic development, using their advantage to enhance their social and political power. The Great Depression further hampered development (see pages 811–812) and provoked a shift toward economic nationalism. Economic nationalism and the rise of industry were especially successful in the two largest countries of Latin America, Mexico and Brazil.

The Mexican Revolution of 1910 overthrew the elitist upper-class rule of the tyrant Porfirio Díaz and culminated in a new constitution in 1917. This radical nationalistic document called for universal suffrage, massive land reform, benefits for labor, and strict control of foreign capital. Progress was modest until 1934, when Lázaro Cárdenas (1895–1970) became president and dramatically revived the languishing revolution. Under Cárdenas many large estates were divided among small farmers or were returned undivided to Indian communities. State-supported Mexican businessmen built many small factories to meet domestic needs. In 1938 Cárdenas nationalized the petroleum industry. The 1930s also saw the flowering of a distinctive Mexican culture that proudly embraced Mexico's Indian past.

Beginning in the 1940s more moderate Mexican presidents used the state's power to promote industrialization, and the Mexican economy grew consistently through the 1970s. Agricultural production, which had always formed the basis of Latin American economies, declined as the industrial and service sectors grew. This was a time of rapid urbanization as well, with people leaving the rural areas for jobs in the cities. While the country's economic health improved, social inequities remained. The upper and middle classes reaped the lion's share of the benefits of this economic growth.

As time went on, successive Mexican governments became more authoritarian, sometimes resorting to violence to quell dissent. Mexico's growth began to slow in the mid-1970s when its president, Luis Echeverría (b. 1922), began populist economic and political reform, including nationalizing key industries and redistributing private land to peasants. Echeverría also imposed limits on foreign investments.

José López Portillo (1920–2004) succeeded Echeverría as president in 1976. During his administration significant oil fields were discovered that made Mexico the world's fourth largest oil producer. Portillo's time in office was characterized by massive corruption and rampant inflation. Before leaving office in 1982, he ordered the nationalization of Mexico's banking system. When a national debt crisis crippled economies across Latin America, Mexico was one of the worst affected.

Chapter Chronology

1937	Getúlio Vargas establishes "new state" dictatorship in Brazil
1940s–1970s	Economic growth and rapid urbanization during the "Mexican miracle"
1946–1964	Decolonization in Africa
1953–1959	Cuban Revolution
1958	Commonwealth status given to France's African territories, and all but Guinea accept
1959	Fidel Castro establishes Communist rule in Cuba
1979	Sandinistas end dictatorship in Nicaragua
1980	Blacks win long civil war with white settlers in Zimbabwe
1984	South Africa's whites grant limited parliamentary representation for nonwhites, but maintain racial segregation and discrimination
1989	South African government opens talks with ANC
1994	Nelson Mandela becomes president of South Africa; North American Free Trade Agreement; Mexican economy collapses
1999	Hugo Chávez launches socialist "Bolivarian revolution" in Venezuela
2008	Retirement of Cuban president Fidel Castro after forty-nine years as ruler
2010	Catastrophic earthquake in Haiti; United States extends 1963 trade embargo on Cuba

economic nationalism A systematic effort by Latin American nationalists to end neocolonialism and to free their national economies from American and western European influences.

Mexico's economy reached rock bottom in December 1994 when it completely collapsed and had to be rescued by a financial aid package from the United States. Through the remainder of the 1990s, however, the economy quickly recovered. Mexico's GDP rose significantly for more than a decade until the global economic downturn of 2008–2009. Mexico had a positive growth rate again in 2010 of around 5.2 percent.

Like Mexico's, Brazil's economy at the turn of the century was controlled by large landowners. Regional rivalries and deteriorating economic conditions allowed a military revolt led by Getúlio Vargas (1882–1954) to seize control of the federal government in 1930. An ardent anticommunist, Vargas established a full-fledged dictatorship known as the "new state," which was modeled somewhat along European Fascist lines, in 1937. His rule lasted until 1945. Despite his harsh treatment of opponents, he was generally popular with the masses, combining effective economic nationalism, promotion of industrialization, and moderate social reform.

After World War II modernization continued for the next fifteen years, and Brazil's economy boomed. Economic nationalism was especially vigorous under president Juscelino Kubitschek (1902–1976).

By the late 1950s economic and social progress seemed to be bringing less violent, more democratic politics to Brazil and other Latin American countries. These expectations were shaken by the Communist Cuban Revolution, and conservative leaders and military officers across Latin America took control of governments in order to block any further spread of communism. In 1961 left-wing candidate João Goulart (1919–1976) became Brazil's president. Goulart introduced a number of sweeping social and economic reforms. Goulart also tried to promote a nuclear-free Latin America; much to Washington's displeasure, he established close ties with the new Castro regime in Cuba.

In 1964 the military drove Goulart from office, and over the next twenty years the military installed a series of right-wing general-presidents. At the same time, the generals of these repressive military dictatorships oversaw political-economic reforms that promoted an economic miracle in Brazil. A slow return to democracy began in 1974, and in 1985 Brazilians elected the first civilian government in twenty years. The first decade of civilian rule was shaky, but the election of Fernando Cardoso (b. 1931) in 1994 began a string of four successful peaceful, democratic transitions of power. The election in October 2010 brought to office Brazil's first woman president, Dilma Rousseff (b. 1947).

Communist Revolution in Cuba

Achieving nominal independence in 1898 as a result of the Spanish-American War (see page 802), Cuba was practically an American protectorate until the 1930s, when a series of rulers with socialist and Communist leanings seized and lost power. Cuba's political institutions were weak and its politicians corrupt. In March 1952 Fulgencio Batista (1901–1973), a Cuban military colonel, staged a coup with American support and instituted a repressive authoritarian regime that favored wealthy Cubans and multinational corporations. Through the 1950s Cuba was one of Latin America's most prosperous countries, although enormous differences remained between rich and poor.

Cuba

The **Cuban Revolution** led by Fidel Castro (b. 1927) began in 1953. Castro's second in command, the Argentinean Marxist revolutionary Ernesto "Che" Guevara (1928–1967), and a force of guerrilla rebels finally overthrew the Cuban government on New Year's Day 1959. Castro had promised a "real" revolution, and it soon be-

Cuban Revolution The Communist revolution led by Fidel Castro that overthrew the American-backed Cuban dictator Fulgencio Batista on January 1, 1959.

Fidel Castro's March to Havana, 1959 In August 1958 Cuban rebel forces turned back a government offensive planned by Cuban president Fulgencio Batista. On January 1, 1959, after Castro's forces went on the offensive and won two major battles, Batista fled the country to the Dominican Republic. This photo shows cheering throngs of supporters greeting Castro and his men on their triumphal march to the capital. (Bettmann/Corbis)

came clear that "real" meant "Communist." Middle-class Cubans began fleeing to Miami, and Cuban relations with the Eisenhower administration deteriorated rapidly. In April 1961 U.S. president John F. Kennedy tried to use Cuban exiles to topple Castro, but Kennedy abandoned the exiles as soon as they landed ashore at the Bay of Pigs in southern Cuba.

After routing the Bay of Pigs forces, Castro moved to build an authoritarian Communist society, forming an alliance with the Soviet bloc, and using oppressive policies to silence opposition. Like Stalin's Soviet Union, Castro's Communist dictatorship was characterized by a cult of personality, and he played a central role in the exportation of Communist revolutions throughout Latin America. Castro's close ties with the Soviet Union led to the Cuban missile crisis in 1962 (see page 849), a confrontation between the United States and the U.S.S.R. over the placement of Soviet nuclear missiles in Cuba. In 1963 the United States placed a complete commercial and diplomatic embargo on Cuba that has remained in place ever since.

Under Castro's regime, human rights deteriorated dramatically. Every aspect of Cuban life was closely monitored, and any perceived opposition to the government was quickly repressed. The standard of living declined significantly following the revolution as the U.S. embargo took hold.

Between 1961 and 1991 Cuba was heavily dependent on the Soviet Union for trade, development, commercial, and military aid. Although statistics provided by the Cuban government are thought to be inflated, observers agree that Castro's government has significantly raised the educational level of all of its citizens, provided them with some of the best health care in Latin America, and organized cultural and arts programs that enjoy massive participation rates.

When the Soviet Union collapsed in 1991, Cuba entered what became known as the "special period in peacetime." Foreign economists estimate that Cuba lost 80 percent of its import and export trade and that its GDP dropped by 35 percent. The loss of oil imports from the Soviet Union effectively shut down the economy and plunged Cuba into an economic depression. Famine spread as agricultural production stopped. Cuban leaders were forced to implement a number of free-market reforms, including allowing some private ownership and self-employment. Tourism was promoted, and foreign investment encouraged. By 1999 the new measures had started to take effect. In the mid-1990s Cuba's GDP stood at around $25 billion. By 2010 it had reached an estimated $114 billion. Despite these gains, as much as one-third of Cuba's population lives in poverty.

In 2008 Raúl Castro (b. 1931) took his brother's place as Cuba's leader. He introduced a number of economic and political measures that removed many restrictions limiting daily life. Raúl Castro also expressed his desire to improve relations with the United States. For his part U.S. president Barack Obama relaxed the travel ban in 2009, allowing Cuban-Americans to freely travel to Cuba. In 2010 and again in 2011, however, Obama extended the decades-long embargo. It now is in effect until September 2012.

From Authoritarianism to Democracy in Latin America

Following Castro's seizure of power in Cuba in 1961, conflict between leftist movements and ruling elites grew, won most often by the elites and their military allies, but at the cost of imposing a new kind of conservative authoritarianism. By the late 1970s only Costa Rica, Venezuela, Colombia, and Mexico retained some measure of democratic government (Map 33.1). As in Brazil, authoritarian military juntas (groups of military officers) seized control of Argentina and Chile. Oil-rich Venezuela also went through a period of military rule, democracy, and most recently a unique brand of socialism.

In Argentina the dictatorial populist and economic nationalist Juan Perón (1895–1974) began his presidency in 1946 with widespread support, in no small measure because of the popularity of his wife, Eva Perón. (See "Individuals in Society: Eva Perón," page 904.) His rule grew increasingly oppressive, however, and when Eva died of cancer in 1953, Perón's opponents' efforts to overthrow him increased. In 1955 the military staged a coup and restored elected democratic government. Then, worried by a Perónist revival and following the Brazilian example, the army took control in 1966 and again in 1976 after a brief civilian interlude. Repression escalated following each military takeover. Argentina became a brutal military dictatorship.

Events in Chile followed a similar path. When Salvador Allende (1908–1973), the head of a coalition of Communists, Socialists, and Radicals, won a plurality in 1970, he was duly elected president by the Chilean Congress. Allende completed the nationalization of the American-owned copper companies and proceeded to socialize private industry, accelerate the breakup of landed estates, and radicalize the poor. In September 1973, with widespread conservative support and U.S. backing, the traditionally impartial army struck in a well-organized coup. As the army surrounded the presidential palace, and with thousands of his supporters under arrest or worse, Allende committed suicide. As in Argentina, the military, under the leadership of General Augusto Pinochet (1915–2006), imposed a harsh despotism.

The military governments that revived antidemocratic authoritarianism in Latin America blocked not only Marxist and socialist programs but most liberal and moderate reforms as well. The new authoritarians were, however, determined modernizers, committed to nationalism, industrialization, technology, and some modest social progress. They even promised free elections in the future. That time came in the 1980s, when another democratic wave gained momentum throughout Latin America. By the late 1980s, 94 percent of Latin Americans lived under regimes that guaranteed elections and civil liberties.

In Argentina General Leopoldo Galtieri (1926–2003) was the last president of a military-ruled government that gradually lost almost all popular support because of its "dirty war" (1976–1983) against its own citizens, in which thousands arbitrarily accused of opposing the regime were imprisoned, tortured, and murdered. In 1982, in a desperate gamble to rally the people, Argentina's military rulers seized the Falkland (or Malvinas) Islands from Great Britain. The British rout of Argentina's poorly led troops forced the humiliated generals to schedule national democratic elections in 1983. The democratically elected government

Map 33.1 Authoritarian Governments in Latin America Over the past eighty years nearly all the peoples of Latin America, including those living in Caribbean island nations, have suffered at one time or another under some type of authoritarian regime. These governments have varied in form from single individuals ruling as dictators to groups of officers governing as military juntas. Only since the 1990s have the majority of Latin American countries rejected authoritarian rule and adopted more or less democratic models of government.

prosecuted the former military rulers for their crimes and laid solid foundations for liberty and political democracy.

In the 1980s and 1990s a succession of presidents and their finance ministers put forward a range of plans to solve Argentina's economic problems. Nothing seemed to work, and in 2002 the country experienced an economic, social, and political crisis, leading Argentina to default on its foreign debt. With 60 percent of the population living below the poverty line, the government began to institute policies to grow Argentina's economy. Results were mixed, with inflation undercutting the positive effects of economic growth. A sharp downturn in Argentinean economy in 2007 was made worse by the global economic crisis of 2008–2009. Still, Argentina remains the fourth largest economy in Latin America, after Brazil, Mexico, and Venezuela.

Venezuela's history is closely linked to Simón Bolívar, a revolutionary who led independence movements against Spanish colonial rule in the early 1800s (see page 725). More recently its history has been tied to oil, which was discovered in massive deposits during World War I. Wealth from the oil gave Venezuela the highest per capita GDP in Latin America by 1935, lifting it from being one of the poorest to one of the richest countries on the continent. The military ruled Venezuela until 1958, except for a three-year period of civilian rule following World War II. In January 1958 a coalition of all the major political parties except the Communists forced out the military dictator Pérez Jiménez (r. 1952–1958). The Social Christian Party of Venezuela (COPEI) and the Democratic Action Party then controlled Venezuelan politics for the next forty years.

INDIVIDUALS IN SOCIETY

Eva Perón

EVA PERÓN WAS ONLY THIRTY-THREE WHEN SHE died of cancer on July 26, 1952, but already many Argentineans considered her a saint. The state radio broadcaster sadly announced that "today at 20:25 Eva Perón, Spiritual Leader of the Nation, entered immortality." Argentina went into official mourning; although Perón had never held an official political office, she was accorded a state funeral. Immediately following her death her corpse was embalmed, with the intention of putting it on public display forever in a planned memorial larger than the Statue of Liberty.

Often called Evita (the Spanish diminutive of Eva), she was one of five illegitimate children born near Buenos Aires to Juan Duarte and Juana Ibarguren. Duarte returned to his legitimate wife and children when Eva was a year old, leaving Juana and her children destitute and dependent on Juana's sewing for their existence. As they grew older all the children had to work, but Eva apparently also dreamed of becoming an actress.

At fifteen Eva Duarte moved to the cosmopolitan city of Buenos Aires. Although she had little formal education and no connections, she possessed great natural beauty, and soon she joined a professional theater group with which she toured nationally. She also modeled, appeared in a few movies, and then got regular employment as a character on a radio series. By 1943, although only twenty-three years old, she was one of the highest paid actresses in the country.

In 1943 Eva met widowed Colonel Juan Perón, then secretary of labor and social welfare in the military government that had seized power that year. Juan Perón had grand ambitions, intending to run for president. Eva Duarte became his partner and confidante, and she won him support among the Argentine masses. In 1945 Juan Perón and Eva Duarte were married.

A year later Perón won the presidency. Eva had gone out on the campaign trail and organized support for her husband from *los descamisados* ("the shirtless ones"), her name for Argentine's poor. When Perón assumed the presidency, Eva, though not officially appointed, became the secretary of labor. Having come from a childhood of poverty herself, she now worked tirelessly for the poor, for the working classes, and with organized labor. She instituted a number of social welfare measures and promoted a new Ministry of Health, which resulted in the creation of new hospitals and disease treatment programs. In 1948 she established the Eva Perón Welfare Foundation, which grew into an immense semiofficial welfare agency, helping the poor throughout Argentina and even contributing to victims of natural disasters in other countries.

From early on, Eva Perón had supported women's suffrage, and in September 1947 Argentine women won the right to vote. Eva then formed the Female Perónist Party, which by 1951 had five hundred thousand members. Thousands of Argentine women have credited Eva's example as a reason for their becoming involved in politics. In 1951 she seemed ready to run for vice president beside her husband. The huge base of women, the poor, and workers assured them victory. Her declining health, however, forced her to turn down the nomination. Perón won the election by over 30 percent, but when Eva died the following year, Perón's authoritarian rule and bad economic policies lost him support, and a military junta forced him into exile.

Eva Perón's life story is an amazing one, but what happened following her death is just as extraordinary. Before the massive monument intended to hold her embalmed body could be built, the military seized power, and her body disappeared. Seventeen years later the generals finally revealed that it was in a tomb in Milan, Italy. Juan Perón, living in Spain with his third wife, had the body exhumed and brought to Spain, where he kept it in his house. Perón returned to Argentina in 1973 and won the presidential election, but died the following year. His wife, Isabel Perón, succeeded him as president. Juan and Eva's bodies were briefly displayed together at his funeral and then, finally, buried.

Source: Nicholas Fraser and Marysa Navarro, *Evita: The Real Life of Eva Perón* (New York: Norton, 1976).

QUESTIONS FOR ANALYSIS

1. Why do you think Eva Perón was adored by the Argentine people when she died?
2. What were some of the welfare and government programs that Eva Perón promoted?

Eva Perón waves to supporters from the balcony of the presidential palace, Casa Rosada, in Buenos Aires, on October 17, 1951. (Clarin/AP Images)

Unlike much of the rest of Latin America that experienced military dictatorships in the 1960s, 1970s, and 1980s, Venezuela's civilian governments avoided military takeovers. Its economy grew throughout the twentieth century, and by 1970 Venezuela was the wealthiest country in Latin America and one of the twenty richest in the world. Following the 1973 global oil crisis, oil prices skyrocketed, and Venezuela's oil revenues also soared until 1978, when the GDP began to fall. This drop was exacerbated by the collapse of global oil prices in the mid-1980s.

In the 1980s and 1990s Venezuela experienced one political crisis after another as the economy declined, poverty and crime rose, and corruption, always a problem in the country, flourished. A succession of events in the late 1980s and early 1990s—including riots in Caracas in February 1989 that left as many as three thousand dead, two attempted military coups in 1992, and the impeachment of then president Carlos Pérez for corruption in 1993—led to the election of Rafael Caldera (1916–2009) as president in 1994. One of his first acts in office was to grant a pardon to Hugo Chávez (b. 1954) for his role in the first of the 1992 military coup attempts.

Chávez succeeded Caldera as president in 1998 and immediately launched a "Bolivarian revolution," which included a new constitution, adopted in December 1999, and changed the country's official name to the Bolivarian Republic of Venezuela. The new constitution guarantees, among other things, free education to all through college, universal suffrage, social security, free health care, a clean environment, gender equality, the right to property, and the rights of minorities, particularly Venezuela's native peoples, to maintain their traditional cultures, religions, and languages.

Chávez has labeled his efforts "socialism for the twenty-first century." His first action was to rid the government of the old guard and to fill positions of power with his supporters. He then moved to clean up corruption and to redistribute Venezuela's oil revenues to the poor and underprivileged through social programs outlined in the constitution. Despite a 2002 coup attempt, Chávez was re-elected to a second term in December 2006. His power base has changed significantly since his first election victory, and his Bolivarian revolution has alienated most of the upper and middle classes who used to support him. To his credit, the poverty rate in Venezuela has dropped from 55 percent before he took office in 1998 to 28 percent in 2008. It is no wonder that the poorest workers continue to support him.

Since 2006 Chávez has turned more and more toward a socialist agenda and also to a position of absolute power. Despite the human rights guarantees in the new constitution, various international organizations have condemned Chávez's human rights record, including the weakening of democratic institutions and the harassment or arrest of political opponents. Economically, Chávez has received much criticism for his overdependence on oil to fund the country's economy. In foreign relations Chávez has sought closer relations with other South American countries, while condemning the United States, globalization, and open market economies.

The most dramatic developments in Central America occurred in Nicaragua. In 1979 a Socialist political party, the Sandinista National Liberation Front (FSLN), joined with a broad coalition of liberals, Socialists, and Marxist revolutionaries to drive dictator Anastasio Somoza (1925–1980) from power. A multi-partisan junta—a coalition of political leaders—then led the country from 1979 to 1985. These leaders wanted genuine political and economic independence from the United States, as well as thoroughgoing land reform, some nationalized industry, and friendly ties with Communist countries. In a free and fair general election the FSLN candidate Daniel Ortega (b. 1945) won the presidency for his Sandinista Party with 67 percent of the vote and took office in January 1985.

The Sandinista government and its policies infuriated the Reagan administration in the United States, which sought to overthrow it by creating a counter-revolutionary mercenary army, the Contras, and supplying it with military aid funded illegally through military weapons sales to Iran. After years of civil war, the Nicaraguan economy collapsed, and the

Sandinista government's popularity eventually declined. The Sandinistas surrendered power when they were defeated in free elections by a coalition of opposition parties in 1990.

In elections in November 2006 Nicaraguans re-elected Ortega, the FSLN candidate, as president, and he continued to hold that position in 2011. He has remained an outspoken opponent of what he perceives as Western (especially American) imperialism.

The Reagan administration also helped engineer a 1986 coup in Haiti, where "Papa Doc" Duvalier, followed by his son, "Baby Doc," had for decades ruled in one of the most repressive dictatorships in the Americas, with U.S. support. Although "Baby Doc" was forced into exile, the country experienced a period of violence and disorder until semi-fair elections were held in 1994 with the help of U.S. military intervention. Over the next ten years, however, Haiti remained unstable with a succession of disputed elections and an increase in violence and human rights abuses. A rebellion broke out in 2004 in the northern part of the country and soon spread to the capital. Then president Jean-Bertrand Aristide was forced to flee the country. A United Nations Stabilization Mission was sent to Haiti following the 2004 rebellion to preserve the peace and maintain stability.

Following a round of controversial elections in May 2006, René Préval (b. 1943) became Haiti's president. Préval had some success in improving the economy over the next two years. Such modest gains lost all significance in January 2010 when Haiti, already the Western Hemisphere's poorest country, was rocked by a catastrophic magnitude 7.0 earthquake that killed as many as 316,000 people and left 1 to 2 million Haitians homeless. Although the initial reaction from the international community was swift and generous, a year later hundreds of thousands of Haitians continued to live in makeshift tent cities, basic services had not been restored, and there were regular outbreaks of cholera and other diseases due to the lack of clean water and proper sanitation. Widespread corruption, the absence of efficient government services, the inability to dispense relief aid effectively, and the failure of some donor nations to fulfill their monetary pledges for reconstruction have resulted in a slow recovery.

Pan–Latin American Unity

In the 1990s Latin America's popularly elected governments relaxed economic relations with other countries, moving decisively from tariff protection and economic nationalism toward free markets and international trade. In so doing, they revitalized their economies and registered solid gains. In 1994 Mexico joined with the United States and Canada in the North American Free Trade Agreement (NAFTA). Hoping to copy the success of the European Union, twelve South American countries (Brazil, Argentina, Paraguay, Uruguay, Venezuela, Bolivia, Colombia, Ecuador, Peru, Guyana, Suriname, and Chile) met in Cuzco, Peru, in December 2004 and signed the Cuzco Declaration, announcing the formation of the Union of South American Nations (UNSAN). The union is intended to provide a free-trade zone for its members and to compete economically with the United States and the European Community.

Quick Review

What kind of government was most prevalent in Latin America during the twentieth century, and how did this change after 1980?

What factors influenced decolonization in sub-Saharan Africa?

Most of sub-Saharan Africa won political independence fairly rapidly after World War II. The rise of independent states in sub-Saharan Africa resulted directly from both a reaction against Western imperialism and the growth of African nationalism.

The Growth of African Nationalism

Western intrusion was the critical factor in the development of African nationalism, as it had been in Asia and the Middle East. But two things were different about Africa. First, because the imperial system did not solidify in Africa until after 1900 (see pages 675–677), national movements began to come of age only in the 1920s and reached maturity after 1945. Second, Africa's multiplicity of ethnic groups, coupled with imperial boundaries that often bore no resemblance to existing ethnic boundaries, greatly complicated the development of political—as distinct from cultural—nationalism. Was a modern national state to be based on ethnic or clan loyalties? Was it to be a continent-wide union of all African peoples? Or would the multiethnic territories arbitrarily carved out by competing European empires become the new African nations? Only after 1945 did a tentative answer emerge.

A few educated West Africans in British colonies had articulated a kind of black nationalism before 1914. But the first real impetus came from the United States and the British West Indies. The most renowned participant in this "black nationalism" was W. E. B. Du Bois (1868–1963). The first black to receive a Ph.D. from Harvard, this brilliant writer and historian organized Pan-African congresses in Paris during the Versailles Peace Conference in 1919 and in Brussels in 1921. **Pan-Africanists** sought black solidarity and, eventually, a vast self-governing union of all African peoples. Jamaican-born Marcus Garvey (1887–1940) was the most influential Pan-Africanist voice in Africa. Young, educated Africans rallied to his call of "Africa for the Africans" and European expulsion from Africa.

In the 1920s many educated French and British Africans experienced a strong surge of pride and cultural nationalism. African intellectuals in Europe formulated and articulated the rich idea of *négritude*, or blackness: racial pride and self-confidence in black creativity and the black spirit. This westernized African elite pressed for better access to government

> **Pan-Africanists** People, such as W. E. B. Du Bois and Marcus Garvey, who promoted solidarity among all blacks and the eventual self-governing union of all African peoples.

Nationalism in Black Africa

1919	Du Bois organizes first Pan-African congress
1920s	Cultural nationalism grows among Africa's educated elites
1929	Great Depression brings economic hardship and discontent
1930–1931	Gold Coast farmers organize first cocoa holdups
1939–1945	World War II accelerates political and economic change
1951	Nkrumah and Convention People's Party win national elections in Ghana (former Gold Coast)
1957	Nkrumah leads Ghana to independence
1958	De Gaulle offers commonwealth status to France's African territories; only Guinea chooses independence
1960	Nigeria becomes an independent state
1966	Ghana's Nkrumah deposed in military coup
1967	Ibos secede from Nigeria to form state of Biafra
1980	Blacks rule Zimbabwe (former Southern Rhodesia) after long civil war with white settlers
1984	South Africa's whites issue cosmetic reforms but maintain racial segregation and discrimination
1989–1990	South African government begins process of reform; black leader Nelson Mandela freed from prison
1994	Nelson Mandela elected president of South Africa

jobs, modest steps toward self-government, and an end to humiliating discrimination. They claimed the right to speak for ordinary Africans and denounced the government-supported chiefs as "Uncle Toms," yet their demands remained moderate.

The mass protests that accompanied the deprivations of the Great Depression, in particular the cocoa holdups of 1930–1931 and 1937–1938, proved to be the catalyst for the development of African nationalism. Cocoa completely dominated the Gold Coast's economy. As prices plummeted after 1929, cocoa farmers refused to sell their beans to the large British firms that fixed prices and monopolized the export trade. Instead, the farmers organized cooperatives to cut back production and sell their crops directly to European and American chocolate manufacturers. The cocoa holdups succeeded in mobilizing much of the population against the foreign companies and demonstrated the power of mass organization and mass protest. Mass movements for national independence were not far behind.

cocoa holdups Mass protests in the 1930s by Gold Coast producers of cocoa who refused to sell their beans to British firms and instead sold them directly to European and American chocolate manufacturers.

Achieving Independence with New Leaders

The repercussions of the Second World War in black Africa greatly accelerated the changes begun in the 1930s. Many African soldiers who served in India had been impressed by Indian nationalism. As African mines and plantations strained to meet wartime demands, towns mushroomed into cities where ramshackle housing, inflation, and shortages created discontent and hardship.

Western imperialism also changed. Both the British and the French acknowledged the need for rapid social and economic improvement in their colonies; for the first time both began sending money and aid on a large scale. At the same time, however, the British and the French were in no rush to grant self-government. But a new breed of African leader was emerging. Impatient and insistent, these spokesmen for modern African nationalism were remarkably successful: by 1964 almost all of western, eastern, and central Africa had achieved statehood, generally without much bloodshed.

These new postwar African leaders formed an elite by virtue of their advanced European or American education, and they were profoundly influenced by Western thought. But compared with the interwar generation of educated Africans, they were more radical and humbler in social origin. Among them were former schoolteachers, union leaders, government clerks, and unemployed students, as well as lawyers and prizewinning poets.

Postwar African leaders accepted prevailing colonial boundaries to avoid border disputes and achieve freedom as soon as possible. Sensing a loss of power, traditional rulers sometimes became the new leaders' worst political enemies. Skillfully, the new leaders channeled postwar hope and discontent into support for mass political organizations. These organizations became political parties, eventually coming to power by winning the general elections that the colonial governments belatedly called to choose their successors.

Ghana Shows the Way

Perhaps the most charismatic of this generation of African leaders was Kwame Nkrumah (1909–1972). Nkrumah spent ten years studying in the United States, where he was deeply influenced by European socialists and Marcus Garvey. Under his leadership the Gold Coast—which he rechristened "Ghana"—became the first independent African state to emerge from colonialism.

Nkrumah came to power by building a radical mass party that appealed particularly to modern elements—former servicemen, market women, union members, urban toughs, and cocoa farmers. Rejecting halfway measures—"We prefer self-government with danger to servitude in tranquility"—Nkrumah and his Convention People's Party staged strikes

The Opening of Parliament in Ghana As part of an ancient ritual, two medicine men pour out sacred oil and call on the gods to bless the work of the Second Parliament and President Kwame Nkrumah, standing on the right. The combination of time-honored customs and modern political institutions was characteristic of African states after they secured independence. (Wide World Photos/AP Images)

and riots. Arrested, Nkrumah campaigned from jail and saw his party win a smashing victory in the 1951 national elections. By 1957 Nkrumah had achieved worldwide fame and influence as Ghana became independent.

After Ghana's breakthrough, independence for other African colonies followed rapidly. The main problem in some colonies, such as Algeria, was the permanent white settlers, not the colonial officials. Wherever white settlers were numerous, as in Kenya, they sought to preserve their privileged position. But only in Southern Rhodesia and South Africa were whites numerous enough to prevail for long. Southern Rhodesian whites declared independence illegally in 1965 and held out until 1980, when black nationalists won a long liberation struggle and renamed the country Zimbabwe. Majority rule in South Africa took even longer.

French-Speaking Regions

Decolonization took a somewhat different course in French-speaking Africa. The events in the French North African colony of Algeria in the 1950s and early 1960s help clarify France's attitude to its sub-Saharan black African colonies.

France tried hard to hold onto Algeria after 1945. Predominantly Arabic speaking and Muslim, Algerian nationalists were emboldened by Nasser's triumph in Egypt in 1952 and by France's defeat in Indochina in 1954 (see page 877). But Algeria's European population—known as the *pieds-noirs*—was determined to keep Algeria part of France. In November 1954 Algeria's anticolonial movement, the National Liberation Front (FLN), began a long war for independence. Besides being the most violent of the anticolonial wars in Africa, the war also nearly tore France apart as French anticolonialists fought with French pro-imperialists. Finally, in 1962, the FLN won, and Algeria became an independent state. An estimated 900,000 of the 1,025,000 Europeans and indigenous Jews fled Algeria in the first few months of 1962.

pieds-noirs The predominantly Catholic French population in the French colony of Algeria, called "black feet" because they wore black shoes instead of sandals.

National Liberation Front The victorious anticolonial movement in Algeria.

While the terrible war raged on in Algeria, France upped its aid to its sub-Saharan African colonies, but independence remained a dirty word until Charles de Gaulle came to power in 1958. Seeking to head off radical nationalists and receiving the support of moderate black leaders, de Gaulle chose a divide-and-rule strategy. He divided the French West Africa and French Equatorial Africa federations into thirteen separate governments, thus creating a "French commonwealth." Plebiscites were called in each territory to ratify the new arrangement. An affirmative vote meant continued ties with France; a negative vote signified immediate independence and a complete break with France.

De Gaulle's gamble was shrewd. The educated black elite loved France and dreaded a sudden divorce. They also wanted French aid to continue. France, in keeping with its ideology of assimilation, had given the vote to its educated colonial elite after the Second World War, and about forty Africans held French parliamentary seats after 1946. For both cultural and practical reasons, therefore, French Africa's leaders tended to be moderate and in no rush for independence. There were, however, exceptions. In Guinea, a young nationalist named Sekou Touré (1922–1984) led his people to overwhelming rejection of the new constitution in 1958.

The Belgians, long-time practitioners of paternalism coupled with harsh, selfish rule in their enormous Congo colony (see page 673), had always discouraged the development of an educated elite. When they suddenly decided to grant independence in 1959 after wild riots, the fabric of government broke down. Independence was soon followed by violent ethnic conflict, civil war, and foreign intervention. The Belgian Congo was the great exception to sub-Saharan black Africa's generally peaceful and successful transition to independence between 1957 and 1964.

Quick Review
What explains the rapidity of decolonization in post–World War II sub-Saharan Africa?

What common features characterize independent African states since 1960?

The facility with which most of black Africa achieved independence stimulated optimism in the early 1960s. But within a generation democratic government and civil liberties gave way to one-party rule or military dictatorship and widespread corruption.

The rise of authoritarian government in Africa after independence must be viewed in historical perspective. Representative institutions on the eve of independence were an imperial afterthought, and the new African countries faced tremendous challenges. Above all, ethnic divisions threatened to tear the fragile states apart. Yet this did not happen. Strong leaders used nationalism, first harnessed to throw off foreign rule, to build one-party regimes and promote unity. Unfortunately, nation building by idealistic authoritarians often deteriorated into brutal dictatorships, frequent military coups, and civil strife. Then, in the early 1990s, a powerful reaction to this decline, inspired by the eastern European revolutions, resulted in a surge of democratic protest that achieved major political gains and rekindled in part the optimism of the independence era.

Striving for National Unity

Africa's imperial legacy is more negative than positive. Although some countries left generally better legacies than others — Britain's was better than Belgium's or Portugal's, for example — overall the "civilizing mission" did more harm than good. While African states (Map 33.2) inherited varying degrees of functioning bureaucracies, well-equipped armies,

Mediterranean Sea
ATLANTIC OCEAN
INDIAN OCEAN

1960 Year independence achieved
Colonial conflict
Post-colonial conflict
Populist protests and uprisings, 2010–2011
Former ruler
Great Britain
France
Italy
Belgium
Portugal
Other

Map 33.2 Decolonization in Africa, 1947 to the Present

Most African territories achieved statehood by the mid-1960s, as European empires passed away, unlamented.

ANALYZING THE MAP How many African states achieved independence after 1945? How many experienced some sort of postcolonial conflict?

CONNECTIONS How did the imperialist legacy serve to complicate the transition to stable, independent nations in Africa and Latin America?

and some modern infrastructure—transportation, communication systems, schools, hospitals, and the like—other features of the imperialist legacy served to torment independent Africa.

The disruption of traditional life had caused real suffering and resulted in unobtainable postindependence expectations. The prevailing export economies were weak, lopsided, and concentrated in foreign hands. Technical, managerial, and medical skills were in acutely short supply. Above all, the legacy of political boundaries imposed by foreigners without regard to ethnic and cultural groupings weighed heavily on postindependence Africa. Nearly every new state encompassed a variety of peoples who might easily develop conflicting national aspirations.

Great Britain and France had granted their African colonies democratic governments as they prepared to depart. Yet belated Western-style democracy served the new multiethnic states poorly. No longer unified by the struggle for independence, political parties often coalesced along regional and ethnic lines. Many African leaders concluded that democracy threatened to destroy the existing states and to prevent social and economic progress. Thus these leaders maintained the authoritarian tradition they had inherited from the imperialists, and free elections often gave way to dictators and one-party rule.

After Ghana won its independence, for instance, Nkrumah jailed his main opponents—chiefs, lawyers, and intellectuals—and outlawed opposition parties. Nkrumah worked to build a "revolutionary" one-party state and a socialist economy. By the mid-1960s his grandiose economic projects had almost bankrupted Ghana, and in 1966 the army seized power.

The French-speaking countries also shifted toward one-party government to promote state unity and develop distinctive characteristics that could serve as the basis for statewide nationalism. Mali followed Guinea into Marxist radicalism. Senegal and the Ivory Coast stressed moderation as well as close economic and cultural ties with France.

Like Nkrumah, many of the initial leaders of one-party states were eventually overthrown by military leaders. As elsewhere, military rule in Africa was authoritarian and undemocratic. Yet military regimes generally managed to hold their countries together, and many, like their Latin American counterparts, were committed to social and economic modernization. Drawing on an educated and motivated elite, they sometimes accomplished much. As economic and social conditions stagnated and often declined in African countries from the mid-1970s to the early 1990s, however, army leaders and dictators became more and more greedy and dishonest. By the late 1980s military rulers and one-party authoritarian regimes were coming under increasing pressure to hand over power to more democratic forces.

Nigeria, Africa's Giant

Nigeria's history illustrates the difficulties of postindependence nation building. After Nigeria achieved independence in 1960, the key constitutional question was the relationship between the central government and the various regions. Ultimately Nigeria adopted a federal system, whereby the national government at Lagos shared power with three regional or state governments in the north, west, and east. Each region had a dominant ethnic group and a corresponding political party. The parties were expected to cooperate in the national parliament, and the rights of minorities were protected by law.

After independence Nigerians' bright hopes gradually dimmed because of growing ethnic rivalries. In 1967 these intense rivalries erupted into a civil war. The crisis began in 1964 when some young military officers, many of whom were Ibos from the southeast, seized the government and executed its leaders.

At first the young officers were popular, but Muslim northerners had long distrusted the non-Muslim Ibos. When the Ibo-led military council proclaimed a centralized dictatorship, frenzied mobs in northern cities massacred thousands of Ibos. When a group of northern officers then seized the national government in a countercoup, the Ibos revolted and proclaimed the independent state of Biafra in 1967.

The Biafran war lasted three years. The Ibos fought with heroic determination, believing that political independence was their only refuge from genocide. Heavily outnumbered, they were gradually surrounded. Perhaps millions starved to death as Biafra became a symbol of monumental human tragedy.

Having preserved the state in the 1960s, Nigeria's military rulers focused on building a nation in the 1970s. Although the federal government held the real power, the country was divided into nineteen small units to handle local and cultural matters. The defeated Ibos were pardoned, and Iboland was rebuilt with federal oil revenues.

Except for a couple of brief periods of civilian rule, combinations of Hausa-Fulani Muslim army officers ruled until 1998, when the brutal military dictator General Sani Abacha suddenly died, giving Nigeria renewed hope for unity and democracy. A new constitution was adopted in 1999 and that same year Nigerians voted in free elections and re-established civilian rule. The April 2003 elections marked the first civilian transfer of power in Nigeria's history, ending thirty-three years of military rule, and elections in 2007 marked the first civilian-to-civilian transfer. Democracy is still not firmly entrenched in the country, however, and corruption and mismanagement remain widespread and systemic.

Nigeria is the world's eleventh largest oil producer and a member of OPEC. From the first oil boom in the 1970s, Nigerian politicians have squandered the massive oil revenues. Also, like Venezuela, Nigeria's leaders ran up huge debts in the 1970s when oil prices were high, only to be unable to repay these loans when oil prices dropped precipitously during the 1980s oil glut. Although there should be plentiful income from oil revenues to fund social programs, Nigeria's education and health care systems have continued to decline since the liberal spending in these areas in the 1970s.

Nigeria needs to diversify its economy if it is to overcome massive poverty and become economically stable. Nigeria's leaders must also calm the religious strife that continues to divide the country. Since 2000 riots between Muslims and non-Muslims have left thousands dead in the predominately Muslim northern Nigerian states.

The Struggle in Southern Africa

Decolonization stalled after the great rush toward political independence in the early 1960s. Southern Africa remained under white minority rule, largely because of the numerical strength and determination of its white settlers.

In Portuguese Angola and Mozambique, white settlers using forced native labor established large coffee farms, and the white population increased from 70,000 to 380,000 between 1940 and the mid-1960s. As economic exploitation grew, so too did resentment. Nationalist liberation movements arose to wage unrelenting guerrilla warfare. After a coup overturned the long-established dictatorship in Portugal, African liberation forces seized control in Angola and Mozambique in 1975. Shortly thereafter a coalition of nationalist groups also won in Zimbabwe after a long struggle.

The battle in South Africa threatened to be still worse. The racial conflict in the white-ruled Republic of South Africa could be traced back in part to the outcome of the South African War (see page 675). After the British finally conquered the inland Afrikaner republics, they agreed to grant all of South Africa self-government as soon as possible. South Africa became basically a self-governing British dominion, like Canada and Australia. English and moderate Afrikaners ruled jointly and could also decide which nonwhites, if any, should vote.

In 1913 the new South African legislature passed the **Native Land Act**, which limited black ownership of land to native reserves encompassing a mere one-seventh of the country. Poor and overpopulated, the rural native reserves served as a pool of cheap, temporary black labor for white farms, mines, and factories. Legally, the black worker was only a temporary migrant who could be returned to the native reserve at will by the employer or the government. The native reserves system, combining racial segregation and indirect forced labor, formed the foundation of white supremacy in South Africa.

Some extreme Afrikaner nationalists refused to accept defeat and any British political presence. They elaborated an Afrikaner nationalist platform of white supremacy and systematic racial segregation that between 1910 and 1948 gradually won them political power from their English-speaking settler rivals. After their decisive 1948 electoral victory, Afrikaner nationalists spoke increasingly for a large majority of South African whites.

Native Land Act A 1913 South African law that limited black ownership of land to native reserves encompassing only one-seventh of the country.

South African Native Land Act of 1913

Native reserves
White South Africa

ZIMBABWE
MOZAMBIQUE
BOTSWANA
NAMIBIA
TRANSVAAL
SWAZILAND
ORANGE
FREE STATE
NATAL
LESOTHO
CAPE
PROVINCE

Greenpoint Stadium, Cape Town, South Africa This modern stadium, complete with a retractable roof, was built especially for the 2010 soccer World Cup and seats 68,000 people. The 2010 matches marked the first time the World Cup was held in Africa. South Africa's successful handling of this global event became a matter of great pride for the country and the continent. To the left of the stadium is Cape Town, with the famous Table Mountain in the distance. (AfriPics.com/Alamy)

apartheid The system of racial segregation and discrimination that was supported by the Afrikaner government in South Africa.

Once in control, successive Afrikaner governments wove the somewhat haphazard early racist measures into an authoritarian fabric of racial discrimination and inequality. This system was officially known as **apartheid**, meaning "apartness" or "separation." The population was divided into four legally unequal racial groups: whites, blacks, Asians, and racially mixed "coloureds." Although Afrikaner propagandists claimed that apartheid served the interests of all racial groups by preserving separate cultures and racial purity, most observers saw it as a way of maintaining the privileges of the white minority.

After 1940 South Africa became the most highly industrialized country in Africa. Rapid urbanization followed, but good jobs in the cities were reserved for whites. Whites lived in luxurious modern central cities. Blacks, as temporary migrants, were restricted to outlying black townships plagued by poverty, crime, and white policemen.

South Africa's white supremacy elicited many black nationalist protests from the 1920s onward. By the 1950s blacks — and their coloured, white, and Asian allies — were staging large-scale peaceful protests. A turning point came in 1960, when police at Sharpeville fired into a crowd of demonstrators and killed sixty-nine blacks. The main black nation-alist organization — the **African National Congress (ANC)** — was then outlawed but sent some of its leaders abroad to establish new headquarters. Other members, led by Nelson Mandela (b. 1918), stayed in South Africa to set up an underground army to oppose the government. Captured after seventeen months, Mandela was tried for treason and sentenced to life imprisonment. (See "Listening to the Past: Nelson Mandela, The Struggle for Freedom in South Africa," page 916.)

African National Congress (ANC) The main black nationalist organization in South Africa, led by Nelson Mandela.

By the late 1970s the white government had apparently destroyed the moderate black opposition in South Africa. Operating out of the sympathetic black states of Zimbabwe and Mozambique to the north, the militant ANC turned increasingly to armed struggle. South Africa struck back hard and forced its neighbors to curtail the ANC's guerrilla activities. Fortified by these successes, South Africa's white leaders launched a program of cosmetic "reforms" in 1984. For the first time, the 3 million coloureds and the 1 million South Africans of Asian descent were granted limited parliamentary representation. But no provision was made for any representation of the country's 22 million blacks, and laws controlling black movement and settlement were maintained.

The government's self-serving reforms provoked black indignation and triggered a massive reaction. In the segregated townships young black militants took to the streets. Heavily armed white security forces clashed repeatedly with black protesters. Between 1985 and 1989 five thousand died and fifty thousand were jailed without charges because of the political unrest.

By 1989 the white government and the black opposition had reached an impasse. Black protesters had been bloodied but not defeated, and their freedom movement had gathered worldwide support. The U.S. Congress had applied strong sanctions against South Africa in October 1986, and the European Common Market had followed. The white government still held power, but harsh repression of black resistance had failed.

The political stalemate ended in September 1989 with the election of a new state president, Frederik W. de Klerk (b. 1936). Negotiating with Nelson Mandela, whose reputation had soared during his long years in prison, de Klerk lifted the state of emergency, legalized the ANC, and freed Mandela in February 1990. Mandela then suspended the ANC's armed struggle and met with de Klerk for serious talks on South Africa's political future. They reached an agreement calling for universal suffrage, which meant black majority rule. They also guaranteed the civil and economic rights of minorities, including job security for white government workers.

Mandela was elected South Africa's first black president by an overwhelming majority in May 1994. Heading the new "government of national unity," which included de Klerk as vice president, Mandela and the South African people set about building a democratic, multiracial nation. The new constitution guaranteed all political parties some legislative seats until 1998.

The magnitude of the social and economic problems facing Mandela and his successors were truly daunting, but significant progress was made. Much still needs to be done, all under the heavy burden of the worst AIDS crisis in the world (see pages 946–947). The highly controversial ANC leader Jacob Zuma (b. 1942) became president following elections in 2009. His problematic personal life, his contentious remarks on matters such as homosexuality, and irregularities relating to his personal finances have all made him a lightning rod of debate in South Africa. Still, South Africa today has a better education system, a more viable infrastructure, and a more diversified economy than any other African country. Many people across southern Africa, and even further north, are looking to South Africa to be the economic engine that drives the continent.

Political Reform in Africa Since 1990

Democracy's triumph in South Africa was part of a broad trend toward elected civilian government that swept through sub-Saharan Africa after 1990. Political protesters rose up and forced one-party authoritarian regimes to grant liberalizing reforms and call national conferences, which often led to competitive elections and new constitutions. These changes occurred in almost all African countries.

Many factors contributed to this historic watershed. The anticommunist revolutions of 1989 in eastern Europe showed Africans that even the most well-entrenched one-party

Nelson Mandela, The Struggle for Freedom in South Africa

Many African territories won political freedom in the mid-1960s, but in South Africa the struggle was long and extremely difficult. Only in 1990 did the white government release Nelson Mandela from prison and begin negotiations with the famous black leader and the African National Congress (ANC). In 1994 Mandela and the ANC finally came to power and established a new system based on majority rule and racial equality.

Born in 1918 into the royal family of the Transkei, Nelson Mandela received an education befitting the son of a chief. But he ran away to escape an arranged marriage, experienced the harsh realities of black life in Johannesburg, studied law, and became an attorney. A born leader with a natural air of authority, Mandela was drawn to politics and the ANC. In the 1950s the white government responded to the growing popularity of Mandela and the ANC with tear gas and repression. Betrayed by an informer, Mandela was convicted of sabotage and conspiracy to overthrow the government in 1964 and sentenced to life imprisonment. Mandela defended all of the accused in the 1964 trial. The following selection is taken from his opening statement.

❝ At the outset, I want to say that the suggestion made by the State in its opening that the struggle in South Africa is under the influence of foreigners or communists is wholly incorrect. I have done whatever I did, both as an individual and as a leader of my people, because of my experience in South Africa and my own proudly felt African background, and not because of what any outsider might have said.

In my youth in the Transkei I listened to the elders of my tribe telling stories of the old days. Amongst the tales they related to me were those of wars fought by our ancestors in defence of the fatherland. . . . I hoped then that life might offer me the opportunity to serve my people and make my own humble contribution to their freedom struggle. . . .

It is true that there has often been close cooperation between the ANC and the Communist Party. But cooperation is merely proof of a common goal—in this case the removal of White supremacy—and is not proof of a complete community of interests. . . . What is more, for many decades communists were the only political group in South Africa who were prepared to treat Africans as human beings and their equals; who were prepared to eat with us, talk with us, live with us, and work with us. . . . Because of this, there are many Africans who today tend to equate freedom with communism. . . .

I turn now to my own position. I have denied that I am a communist. . . . [But] I am attracted by the idea of a classless society, an attraction which springs in part from Marxist reading and, in part, from my admiration of the structure and organization of early African societies in this country. The land, then the main means of production, belonged to the tribe. There were no rich or poor and there was no exploitation. . . .

[Unlike communists] I am an admirer of the parliamentary system of the West. . . . [Thus] I have been influenced in my thinking by both West and East. . . . [I believe] I should be absolutely impartial and objective. I should tie myself to no particular system of society other than of socialism. I must leave myself free to borrow the best from the West and from the East. . . .

Our fight is against real, and not imaginary, hardships or, to use the language of the State Prosecutor, "so-called hardships." . . . Basically, we fight against two features which are the hallmarks of African life in South Africa and which are entrenched by legislation which we seek to have repealed. These features are poverty and lack of human dignity, and we do not need communists or so-called "agitators" to teach us about these things.

South Africa is the richest country in Africa, and could be one of the richest countries in the world. But it is a land of extremes and remarkable contrasts. The Whites enjoy what may well be the highest standard of living in the world, while Africans live in poverty

regimes could be forced out. The decline of military rule in Latin America and the emerging global trend toward political and economic liberalism worked in the same direction.

The end of the Cold War also transformed Africa's relations with Russia and the United States. Both superpowers had given large-scale military and financial aid to their African allies as well as to "uncommitted" African leaders who often played one side against the other. Communism's collapse in Europe brought an abrupt end to Communist aid to Russia's African clients, leaving them weakened and much more willing to compromise with opposition movements. American involvement in Africa also declined. During the Cold War U.S. leaders had generally supported pro-Western African dictators. This interventionist policy gave way to support of free elections and civil rights in the 1990s. An example of this evolution was the end of U.S. support for the "anticommunist" General Mobutu

Nelson Mandela at the time of his imprisonment in 1964.
(Mohamed Lounes/Gamma)

and misery. . . . Poverty goes hand in hand with malnutrition and disease. . . .

The lack of human dignity experienced by Africans is the direct result of the policy of White supremacy. White supremacy implies Black inferiority. Legislation designed to preserve White supremacy entrenches this notion. . . . Because of this sort of attitude, Whites tend to regard Africans as a separate breed. They do not look upon them as people with families of their own; they do not realize that they have emotions. . . .

Africans want to be paid a living wage. Africans want to perform work which they are capable of doing, and not work which the Government declares them to be capable of. . . . Africans want a just share in the whole of South Africa; they want security and a stake in society.

Above all, we want equal political rights, because without them our disabilities will be permanent. I know this sounds revolutionary to the Whites in this country, because the majority of voters will be Africans. This makes the White man fear democracy.

But this fear cannot be allowed to stand in the way of the only solution which will guarantee racial harmony and freedom for all. It is not true that the enfranchisement of all will result in racial domination. Political division, based on color, is entirely artificial and, when it disappears, so will the domination of one color group by another. The ANC has spent half a century fighting against racialism. When it triumphs it will not change that policy.

This then is what the ANC is fighting. Their struggle is a truly national one. It is a struggle of the African people, inspired by their own suffering and their own experience. It is a struggle for the right to live.

During my lifetime I have dedicated myself to this struggle of the African people. I have fought against White domination, and I have fought against Black domination. I have cherished the ideal of a democratic and free society in which all persons live together in harmony and with equal opportunities. It is an ideal which I hope to live for and to achieve. But if need be, it is an ideal for which I am prepared to die. **"**

Source: Slightly adapted from Nelson Mandela, *No Easy Walk to Freedom: Articles, Speeches and Trial Addresses* (London: Heinemann, 1973), pp. 163, 179–185, 187–189. Reprinted by permission of the Nelson Mandela Foundation.

QUESTIONS FOR ANALYSIS

1. How does Nelson Mandela respond to the charge that he and the ANC are controlled by Communists?
2. What factors influenced Mandela's thinking? In what ways has he been influenced by "both East and West" and by his African background?
3. According to Mandela, what is wrong with South Africa? What needs to be done?
4. What are Mandela's goals for South Africa? Are his goals realistic, idealistic, or both?

Sese Seko (1930–1997) after he seized power in 1965 in Zaire (now the Democratic Republic of the Congo). Mobutu looted and impoverished his country for decades before the United States cut off aid in the early 1990s, thereby helping an opposition group topple the tyrant in 1997.

If events outside Africa established conditions favoring political reform, Africans themselves were the principal actors in the shift toward democracy. Above all, the strength of the democratic opposition rested on a growing class of educated urban Africans, for postindependence governments had enthusiastically expanded opportunities in education, especially higher education. The growing middle class of educated professionals chafed at the privilege of tiny closed elites and pressed for political reforms that would democratize social and economic opportunities. Thus after 1990 sub-Saharan Africa participated fully in the global trend toward greater democracy and human rights.

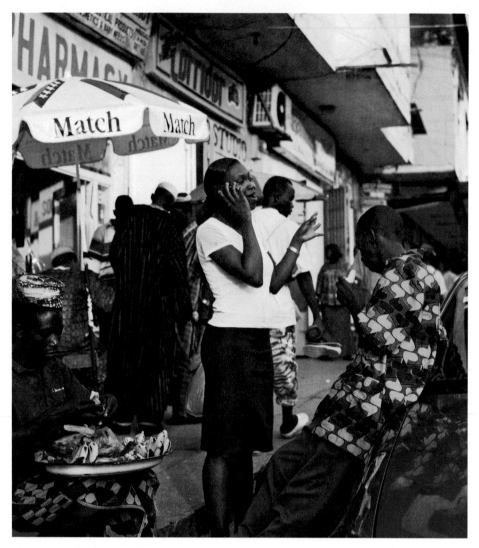

The Communications Revolution in Africa A young woman with a cell phone pressed to her ear in a street in Monrovia, Liberia, illustrates the communications revolution that has transformed economic and social life across Africa. (Tim Hetherington/Panos Pictures)

Twelve years into the twenty-first century, many African countries continue to make significant progress in the consolidation of democracy and human rights. Nonetheless, democracy is still a long struggle away in many African countries. Recent populist revolutions have brought down some of North Africa's one-party authoritarian rulers, but Eritrea, Ethiopia, Equatorial Guinea, Zimbabwe, and Swaziland have increasingly brutal dictatorships. Sudan's authoritarian Islamic rulers ended their long civil war with the Christians and animists in the south, only to have pro-government Arab militias attack Muslim ethnic Africans in the western Darfur region. The genocidal attacks have caused tens of thousands of deaths and an estimated 2 million refugees.

In January 2011, 98 percent of the electorate in southern Sudan voted to break away from Sudan and form a new country. The new country of South Sudan came into being on July 9, 2011. Unlike the generally poor countries across Africa's Sahel region, South Sudan has a major revenue source: it possesses around 80 percent of Sudan's oil wells. Nearly the entire petroleum infrastructure, however, is in the north. According to the terms of the peace agreement, Sudan and South Sudan will share oil revenues equally. There remain, however, important questions about the transparency of the process, with many in the south worrying that revenues from the sale of the refined petroleum products will not be reported properly.

Congo-Kinshasa, Rwanda, and Burundi remain perilously close to the abyss of the horrendous violence that they experienced in the 1990s. The Second Congo War in Congo-Kinshasa that began in 1998 has involved nine African nations and twenty-five armed groups, and it has affected more than half of the country's 71 million people. While peace accords supposedly brought an end to the war in 2003, there has been no end to the violence in the eastern part of the country, where the war continues. By 2007 an estimated 5.4 million had died, and hundreds of thousands more have died in the four years since, making it the world's deadliest conflict since World War II. In this war rape and sexual violence have become weapons. Although it is impossible to know precisely, observers place the number of women and young girls who have been raped by soldiers from both sides of the conflict in the tens of thousands. While the war is complex and the motivations of the many countries involved are varied, possession of the Congo's abundant natural resources—including timber, diamonds, and other minerals of all kinds in great quantities—is sought by all the combatants. While the Congo is nearly the poorest country in the world, it is arguably the richest country in the world in terms of raw minerals and other natural resources, with the total mineral value estimated at $24 trillion.

Since the Somali civil war in 1991, no central government has existed to rule over this country that bends around the Horn of Africa. In effect, there is no Somalia, which has been labeled a "failed state." Somalia has some of the worst poverty and highest rates of violence in the world. Somali pirates operating off the Horn of Africa have been seriously disrupting international shipping since 2007.

Second Congo War, 1998 to the Present

Belligerents

Riots following the questionable re-election of Mwai Kibaki (b. 1931) as president of Kenya on December 27, 2007, resulted in over 250 deaths in the first week after the election. Subsequent interethnic violence forced hundreds of thousands to flee their homes. Former UN Secretary General Kofi Annan led an effort to mediate an end to the election violence. They successfully promoted a power-sharing agreement known as the National Accord and Reconciliation Act 2008. Kenya's tourism industry was hurt by the election violence of 2007 and the global economic downturn in 2008–2009. The economy picked up again in 2010; with significant increases in the tourism, telecommunications, transport, and agricultural export industries, Kenya's GDP grew at over 4 percent in 2010.

Many of the most stable democratic countries are in southern Africa. Botswana, South Africa, Zambia, and Namibia have all made the transition from colonialism to democracy. Malawi, Nigeria, Niger, and Madagascar are also making good progress. Much of the political progress is closely linked to economic progress. As Zimbabwe's authoritarian regime under Robert Mugabe (b. 1924) has created a human rights nightmare, it has also suffered total economic collapse. More politically stable countries such as Ghana have seen their economies grow and foreign investments increase. Countries in western and central Africa may soon undergo revolutionary political and economic change as a result of the oil and natural gas boom in those regions. Chad, Mauritania, Angola, Nigeria, Gabon, São Tomé and Príncipe, Congo Brazzaville, and Equatorial Guinea could all benefit from complete economic turnarounds, and others will follow.

Quick Review
How did the legacy of imperialism shape the development of independent African states?

How have writers depicted the experience of the emerging world?

Having come of age during and after the struggle for political emancipation, numerous intellectuals embraced the vision of Third World solidarity, and some argued that genuine independence and freedom from outside control required a total break with the former colonial powers and a total rejection of Western values. This was the message of Frantz Fanon (1925–1961) in his powerful study of colonial peoples, *The Wretched of the Earth* (1961).

According to Fanon, a French-trained black psychiatrist from the Caribbean island of Martinique, decolonization is always a violent and totally consuming process whereby one "species" of men, the colonizers, is completely replaced by an absolutely different species—the colonized, the wretched of the earth.

As countries gained independence and self-rule, some writers looked beyond wholesale rejection of the industrialized powers. They too were anti-imperialist, but often also activists and cultural nationalists who applied their talents to celebrating the rich histories and cultures of their peoples. Many did not hesitate to criticize their own leaders or fight oppression and corruption.

The Nigerian writer Chinua Achebe (b. 1930) rendered these themes with acute insight and vivid specificity in his short, moving novels. Achebe sought to restore his people's self-confidence by reinterpreting the past. For Achebe, the "writer in a new nation" had a duty to help his or her people regain the dignity and self-respect they lost during the colonial period by showing them the depth and beauty of their own culture.

In *Things Fall Apart* (1958) Achebe achieved his goal by vividly bringing to life the men and women of an Ibo village at the beginning of the twentieth century, with all their virtues and frailties. Woven into the story are the proverbs and wisdom of a sophisticated people and the beauty of a vanishing world:

> *[The white man] says that our customs are bad; and our own brothers who have taken up his religion also say that our customs are bad. How do you think we can fight when our own brothers have turned against us? The white man is very clever. He came quietly and peaceably with his religion. We were amused at his foolishness and allowed him to stay. Now he has won our brothers, and our clan can no longer act like one. He has put a knife on the things that held us together and we have fallen apart.*[1]

In later novels Achebe portrays the postindependence disillusionment of many writers and intellectuals, which reflected trends in many developing nations in the 1960s and 1970s: the rulers seemed increasingly corrupted by Western luxury and estranged from the rural masses.

From the 1970s onward Achebe was active in the struggle for democratic government in Nigeria. In his novel *Anthills of the Savannah* (1989) he calls upon Africa to take responsibility and realize that widespread corruption is frustrating hopes of progress and genuine independence. Yet in recent essays and speeches he also returns to his earlier theme of the West's enduring low opinion of Africa—ever the "dark continent," the savage, non-Western "other world."

The Nobel Prize–winning novelist V. S. Naipaul, born in Trinidad in 1932 of Indian parents, also castigated governments in the developing countries for corruption, ineptitude, and self-deception. Another of Naipaul's recurring themes is the poignant loneliness and homelessness of people uprooted by colonialism and Western expansion.

Quick Review
What light do contemporary writers shed on the ongoing struggle in emerging nations for genuine social, economic, and political progress?

Connections

IN THE LAST HALF OF THE TWENTIETH CENTURY many Latin America countries broke free from their neocolonial ties with the United States and Europe. This freedom gave them the economic independence they desired to go along with the political independence they had gained in the early 1800s. Nationalist leaders in sub-Saharan Africa meanwhile were busy gathering the masses behind them to push for political independence from the colonial powers that had occupied their lands during the scramble for Africa in the late 1800s. Leaders on both continents had to decide whether to take sides in the superpower conflict of the Cold War. And when the Cold War ended, their citizens demanded more civil and human rights, democracy, and an end to corruption and rule from above.

We will see in the last chapter that the countries of Africa and Latin America played important roles in the newly formed United Nations, setting agendas in matters that were of the most concern to them: poverty, illiteracy, fair trade, globalization. The populations of these countries and those of Asia make up two-thirds of the world's citizens. In Chapter 34 we will discuss the global changes, developments, and problems that directly affect these people every day: disease, the environment, education, telecommunications, urban growth, and the agricultural revolution.

- **For a list of suggested readings for this chapter, visit** *bedfordstmartins.com/mckayworldunderstanding*.

- **For primary sources from this period, see** *Sources of World Societies*, Second Edition.

- **For Web sites, images, and documents related to topics in this chapter, see Make History at** *bedfordstmartins.com/mckayworldunderstanding*.

CHAPTER LOCATOR

How did Latin American states develop after World War II?

What factors influenced decolonization in sub-Saharan Africa?

What common features characterize independent African states since 1960?

How have writers depicted the experience of the emerging world?

921

Chapter 33 Study Guide

To do these exercises online, go to bedfordstmartins.com/mckayworldunderstanding.

 GETTING STARTED

Below are basic terms about this period in global history. Can you identify each term below and explain why it matters?

TERMS	WHO (OR WHAT) AND WHEN	WHY IT MATTERS
economic nationalism, p. 899		
Cuban Revolution, p. 900		
Pan-Africanists, p. 907		
cocoa holdups, p. 908		
pieds-noirs, p. 909		
National Liberation Front, p. 909		
Native Land Act, p. 913		
apartheid, p. 914		
African National Congress (ANC), p. 914		

 MOVING BEYOND THE BASICS

The exercise below requires a more advanced understanding of the chapter material. Compare and contrast economic and political developments since 1945 in Latin America and sub-Saharan Africa by filling in the chart below. When you are finished, consider the following questions: Why were leaders in both regions such ardent promoters of economic nationalism? How successful were their programs of economic development? Why did authoritarian regimes dominate many of the independent states of both regions for much of the twentieth century? When and why did democratization gain traction?

	ECONOMIC DEVELOPMENT	AUTHORITARIANISM AND DEMOCRATIZATION
Latin America		
Sub-Saharan Africa		

PUTTING IT ALL TOGETHER

Now that you've reviewed key elements of the chapter, take a step back and try to see the big picture. Remember to use specific examples from the chapter in your answers.

LATIN AMERICA

- What policies and practices did Latin American authoritarian leaders employ to maintain their hold on power? Why did so many dictatorships give way to democracy in the late twentieth century?

- Why was the Cuban Revolution such an important turning point in Latin American history?

SUB-SAHARAN AFRICA

- What explains the surge of African nationalism after World War II?

- What light do the recent histories of Nigeria and South Africa shed on the challenges facing sub-Saharan Africa as the region enters the twenty-first century?

INTERPRETING THE EXPERIENCES OF THE EMERGING WORLD

- How would you explain the desire among some non-Western intellectuals, such as Frantz Fanon, for a total break with the West?

- Why do you think Chinua Achebe places such a high priority on the recovery of authentic African cultures?

LOOKING BACK, LOOKING AHEAD

- How did the circumstances under which Latin American and sub-Saharan African nations gained independence shape their subsequent development?

- In your opinion, will historians look back at the twenty-first century as a century of African and Latin American progress? Why or why not?

In Your Own Words Imagine that you must explain Chapter 33 to someone who hasn't read it. What would be the most important points to include and why?

34

A New Era in World History

Communism's collapse in Europe in 1991 opened a new era in world history—one that arrived with promises of peace, democracy, and economic prosperity. Millions of people still living under repressive, authoritarian, corrupt regimes were inspired to start pressing their governments for political and human rights. (See "Individuals in Society: The Dalai Lama," page 928.) The post-1991 optimism soon faded as new tensions, conflicts, and divisions arose. Two decades later, however, the people are again taking to the streets to demand change. Africa and the Middle East have witnessed the toppling of two dictators. Perhaps more will fall, and the promises of 1991 will finally be realized.

We live in a global age. Economic cycles, international treaties and agreements, multinational organizations, and global threats connect the world's citizens in complex networks. Every day around the world billions of individuals are confronted with similarly complex global issues that impact each of them in an immediate and personal way. As we bring our history of the world's societies to a close, let us look at our interconnected planet once again, this time focusing on ordinary people and the global changes and challenges they face.

Because people living in developing nations make up at least two-thirds of the earth's population, many of the people discussed here live in the so-called Third World, where the changes and challenges of the new millennium are perhaps greatest. We should not forget, though, that there really is no Third World. There is only a set of conditions—such as poverty, disease, hunger, and unemployment—that are at their worst in the poorest or developing countries but that exist in all countries.

Indian UN Peacekeeper
More than a hundred peacekeepers were stationed in Liberia following a brutal fourteen-year civil war, and the all female unit has become a model for the stationing of other female UN peacekeepers at troubled spots around the globe. (Issouf Sanogo/AFP/Getty Images)

Chapter Preview

- ▶ How has global politics changed since 1989?

- ▶ What are the consequences of increasing global interdependence?

- ▶ What are the causes and consequences of worldwide urbanization?

- ▶ How have developments in science and technology changed the world?

- ▶ What social problems do women and children face?

How has global politics changed since 1989?

The end of the Cold War superpower confrontation brought dramatic changes to the global political situation. Yet nation-states, the traditional building blocks of global politics, continued to exist. An astonishing aspect of recent scientific and technological achievements is the lack of any corresponding change in the way the human race governs—or fails to govern—itself. Sovereign nation-states continue to reign supreme, reinforced by military power. The embryonic growth of an effective global political organization that could protect nations from themselves appears permanently arrested, although efforts to control weapons of mass destruction, global warming, and other universal threats have sometimes led to global agreements.

The United Nations

United Nations Founded in 1945, its main purpose is to maintain international peace and security; its expanded mission is to work with the international community to solve economic, social, cultural, and humanitarian problems.

Security Council The UN body that has the authority to examine international conflicts, impose economic and political penalties on an aggressor, and even use force, if necessary, to restore international peace and security.

General Assembly The second main body of the United Nations; each "peace-loving" state is eligible to join and participate in it.

The independent territorial nation-state remains the fundamental political organization in the early twenty-first century. Yet as the horrors of the conflicts of the twentieth century suggested, there was a need for a form of global authority transcending sovereign states as a way to maintain peace worldwide.

With a main purpose of maintaining international peace and security, the World War II generation founded the United Nations in San Francisco in 1945. The UN charter prohibits any member nation from using armed force except for self-defense. The charter also gives the UN Security Council the authority to examine any international conflict, impose penalties on an aggressor, and use force as necessary to restore peace and security. In theory, the Security Council has the power to police the world. In practice, however, this power is severely restricted. The Security Council's five permanent members—China, France, Great Britain, Russia (formerly the Soviet Union), and the United States—have to agree on any peacekeeping action.

Every "peace-loving" state is eligible to join the United Nations and to participate in its General Assembly. Founded with 50 members, the General Assembly comprises 193 members in 2012. Each member state, whatever its size, has one voice and one vote on all

The United Nations in Action These soldiers are part of a French battalion serving in a United Nations peacekeeping operation in Cambodia (Kampuchea), a country wracked by war and civil conflict since 1970. United Nations forces usually provide humanitarian aid as they try to preserve fragile cease-fires after warring armies agree to stop fighting. (J. F. Roussier/Sipa Press)

CHAPTER LOCATOR

How has global politics changed since 1989?

General Assembly resolutions, but General Assembly resolutions become legally binding on states only if all five permanent members of the Security Council agree to them.

During the Cold War, the original hopes for the creation of an effective world body were stymied by Security Council members, most often the Soviet Union, using their veto power to block actions they felt would harm their national interests. With the Security Council often deadlocked, the General Assembly claimed ever-greater authority. As decolonization picked up speed and the number of member states grew, a nonaligned, anticolonial African-Asian bloc emerged. Reinforced by sympathetic Latin American countries, by the mid-1960s the bloc succeeded in organizing within the General Assembly a Third World majority that concentrated on economic and social issues.

With a large numerical majority, the developing nations succeeded in broadening the organization's mission. By the 1970s United Nations committees, specialized agencies, and affiliated international organizations were studying and promoting health, labor, agriculture, industrial development, and world trade. Without directly challenging national sovereignty, Third World members of the General Assembly pressure for international cooperation in dealing with global issues, and the world's major powers sometimes go along. In 2000 the United Nations issued the "Millennium Declaration," a plan of action identifying eight goals, such as eliminating hunger, for the United Nations and member nations to reach by 2015. (See "Listening to the Past: The United Nations Millennium Project Report," page 930.)

Preemptive War in Iraq

As the Cold War ended, the United Nations participated in the 1990 Persian Gulf War (see page 892). Success in Iraq led some to believe that the United Nations could fulfill its original purpose and guarantee peace throughout the world. Failure to stop savage civil wars in Somalia in 1992 and Bosnia in the mid-1990s, however, caused the United Nations to scale back its peacekeeping ambitions.

In 2002 another crisis over Iraq brought the United Nations to the center of the world's political stage. U.S. president George W. Bush accused Iraq of rebuilding its weapons of mass destruction and claimed that the United States had the right to act preemptively to prevent a hostile attack. Iraq, impoverished by a decade of United Nations sanctions, gave no indication of plans to attack any of its neighbors or the United States. America's declaration of its right to stage a unilateral preemptive strike to prevent attack thus set a dangerous precedent, while raising questions about when and how the United Nations charter's stipulating the use of armed force would apply.

As 2002 ended UN inspectors found no weapons of mass destruction. France, Russia, China, Germany, and a majority of the smaller states argued for continued weapons inspections, and France threatened to veto any resolution authorizing an invasion of Iraq. Rather than risk this veto, the United States and Britain claimed that earlier Security Council resolutions provided ample authorization and on March 20, 2003, invaded Iraq.

Chapter Chronology

1945	United Nations founded
1945–present	Explosive growth of cities; rapid urbanization; increasing gap in wealth between rich and poor nations
1950s	Beginning of green revolution
1970	Treaty on the Non-Proliferation of Nuclear Weapons
1980s–present	HIV/AIDS global epidemic
1989	United Nations Convention on the Rights of the Child
1994	Internet becomes available to general public
1997	Chemical Weapons Convention bans the production of chemical weapons; Kyoto Protocol on global warming
2000	United Nations Millennium Project initiated
2000–2010	Warmest decade in recorded history
2001	Al-Qaeda attacks on World Trade Center and U.S. Pentagon
2003	North Korea withdraws from 1970 nonproliferation treaty; U.S.-led coalition invades Iraq; Human Genome Project completes sequencing of human genome
2004	Bombing of train station in Madrid
2005	Bombing of London subway and bus systems
2007	Assassination of Pakistani politician Benazir Bhutto
2011	United States begins troop drawdown in Afghanistan and removes troops from Iraq; bin Laden killed

What are the consequences of increasing global interdependence?

What are the causes and consequences of worldwide urbanization?

How have developments in science and technology changed the world?

What social problems do women and children face?

927

The Dalai Lama

SHORTLY BEFORE HE DIED IN 1933, Thupten Gyatso (1876–1933), the "Great Thirteenth" Dalai Lama of Tibet, had a vision of the future. He predicted that if the Tibetans did not protect their territory, their spiritual leaders would be exterminated, their property and authority would be taken away, and their people would become slaves. For fifty-seven years he had ruled over a country treated like a pawn in the "Great Game" played by Russia, Britain, and China for territory and power. He feared the Chinese the most.

After his death, a mission of high officials went in search of his successor. Tibetans believe that each succeeding Dalai Lama is the reincarnation of the previous one. In 1937 the mission came to a peasant village in northeastern Tibet to question a two-year-old boy, Tenzin Gyatso. When he passed all the tests, they took him and his family to Lhasa, the Tibetan capital. There, in 1940, he was enthroned as His Holiness the Fourteenth Dalai Lama.

In Lhasa the boy spent much of his time studying, eventually earning a doctorate in Buddhist philosophy at age twenty-five. His youth ended abruptly in October 1950, when the thirteenth Dalai Lama's vision came true: eighty thousand Chinese soldiers invaded Tibet. In November the fifteen-year-old Dalai Lama assumed full political power. In 1954 he traveled to Beijing for peace talks with Mao Zedong. Although he was impressed by Mao's promise to modernize Tibet and intrigued by socialism, he was stunned by Mao's last words to him: "But of course, religion is poison."*

This remark was deeply troubling because the Tibetans are an intensely religious people. For centuries they lived in near isolation, practiced Buddhism, and looked to the Dalai Lama as both their political and their spiritual leader. After returning to Tibet, the Dalai Lama tried to negotiate a peaceful settlement with the Chinese, to no avail. In March 1959 the Chinese army crushed a massive demonstration in Lhasa, and the Dalai Lama had to flee for his life. The Indian prime minister, Jawaharlal Nehru, gave him political asylum, and he established a Tibetan government in exile at Dharamsala, India. More than 120,000 Tibetan refugees live there today.

Since the Chinese occupation began, all but twelve of more than six thousand monasteries in Tibet have been destroyed, and thousands of sacred treasures have been stolen or sold. An estimated three thousand political or religious prisoners are in labor camps in Tibet, and the Chinese have been directly responsible for the deaths of 1.2 million Tibetans. Over 7 million Chinese settlers have poured into Tibet. Tibetan women are routinely forced to undergo sterilization or have abortions.

To counter this destruction, the Dalai Lama has campaigned for Tibetan self-determination and basic human rights. He has established programs abroad to save the Tibetan culture and language and to shelter the refugees. There are Tibetan educational systems for refugees, a Tibetan Institute of Performing Arts, agricultural settlements for refugees, and over two hundred new monasteries to preserve Tibetan Buddhism and to train new monks. In his quest for justice, the Dalai Lama travels around the world seeking support from world leaders, institutions, and common citizens. Although he describes himself as a simple Buddhist monk, few individuals in human history have spoken for the downtrodden and oppressed and for universal justice and human dignity with such moral authority.

In December 1989 the Dalai Lama received the Nobel Peace Prize. In accepting, he said that he did so on behalf of all oppressed peoples—those who struggle for freedom and work for world peace—as well as for the people of Tibet. The prize, he said, "reaffirms our conviction that with truth, courage and determination as our weapons, Tibet will be liberated. . . . Our struggle must remain nonviolent and free of hatred."†

Source: *Freedom in Exile: The Autobiography of the Dalai Lama* (London: Little, Brown, 1990).

*Tenzin Gyatso, the Dalai Lama, *My Land and My People* (New York: McGraw-Hill, 1962), p. 117.

†Nobelprize.org: The Official Web Site of the Nobel Prize. The Nobel Peace Prize 1989: The 14th Dalai Lama, Acceptance Speech. http://nobelprize.org/nobel_prizes/peace/laureates/1989/lama-acceptance.html.

QUESTIONS FOR ANALYSIS

1. In what ways do Tibet's history and the Dalai Lama's life reflect many of the major issues and events of the twentieth century?
2. The world's response to China's occupation reflects what political and economic factors?

The Dalai Lama in Germany promoting freedom for Tibet.
(Roberto Pfeill/AP Images)

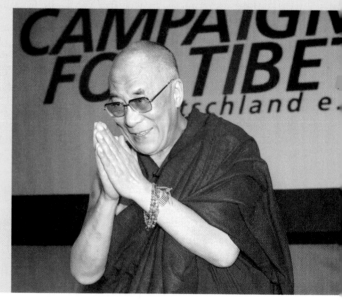

CHAPTER LOCATOR

How has global politics changed since 1989?

Iraq, ca. 2010

Areas that are predominantly
- Sunni (ca. 36%)
- Shi'ite (ca. 60%)
- Mixed
- Kurdish

Iraqi forces were quickly defeated, and President Bush announced an end to the war on May 1, 2003. Nonetheless, the United States, Britain, and their coalition allies maintained their forces in Iraq, and the country remained one of the most dangerous places on earth. So-called insurgents representing all three main factions in Iraq—Sunni Muslims, Shi'ite Muslims, and Kurds—carried out daily attacks on Iraqi military and police, government officials, religious leaders, and civilians. Estimates of Iraqi deaths since the war began through 2011 range from one hundred thousand to over 1 million.

An earthquake in world affairs, the Iraq War split the West and was partially responsible for Republican losses in the 2008 U.S. elections. Democratic presidential candidate Barack Obama campaigned on a pledge to bring American troops home. After becoming president he kept his pledge to end the American presence in Iraq. In December 2011 the last U.S. troops pulled out of Iraq.

Complexity and Violence in a Multipolar World

The sudden end of the Cold War shattered the interlocking restraints of the superpowers and their allies, removing a basic principle of global organization and order. The Cold War contributed to the ideology of Third World solidarity (see Chapter 33). Beginning in the 1980s, however, wide differences in economic performance in countries and regions undermined the whole idea of solidarity, and developing countries increasingly went their own ways.

A striking development was the growing multipolar nature of world politics. Increasingly assertive **middle powers** jockeyed for regional leadership and sometimes came into conflict. Brazil, with more than 140 million people as well as vast territory and resources, emerged as the dominant nation-state in South America. Mexico emerged as the leader of the Spanish-speaking Americas. France and a reunited Germany took the lead in European affairs. Nigeria and South Africa were the leading powers in sub-Saharan Africa. Egypt and Israel were also regional powerhouses. Iran and Iraq competed and fought for dominance in the Persian Gulf. China, India, and Japan were all leading regional powers, and several other Asian countries—notably South Korea, Indonesia, Vietnam, and Pakistan—were determined to join them. The rise of these middle powers reflected the fact that most countries were small and weak, and very few had the resources necessary to wield real power on even a regional scale.

Conflict and violence often bedeviled the emerging multipolar political system. In the 1990s civil wars in Bosnia, Kosovo, Rwanda, and Afghanistan killed over a million people and created hundreds of thousands of refugees. Since 2000, new and continuing wars have caused millions more deaths and new refugees, particularly in Sierra Leone, Liberia, the Democratic Republic of the Congo, Uganda, Afghanistan, Burundi, Somalia, Iraq, Sudan, and Angola.

Rivalries between ethnic groups are often at the heart of recent civil wars. Only about twenty states, representing about 10 percent of the world's population, are truly homogeneous. The goal of a separate state for each self-defined people—the classic nationalist goal—could lead to endless battles and to tragedy on a global scale. The peaceful reconciliation of existing states with widespread separatist aspirations is thus a mighty challenge in the twenty-first century. The challenge of separatism seems especially great in light of the fact that civil war and terrorism often have gone hand in hand.

middle powers Countries that have become increasingly assertive regional leaders after the Cold War.

What are the consequences of increasing global interdependence? | What are the causes and consequences of worldwide urbanization? | How have developments in science and technology changed the world? | What social problems do women and children face?

929

The United Nations Millennium Project Report

In September 2000 the United Nations issued a Millennium Declaration—a bold statement of values and an agenda of actions to be undertaken by the United Nations and its member nations to reach eight major goals relating to global poverty and hunger, disease, education, the environment, maternal health, child mortality, gender equality, and global partnerships by 2015. In the following speech delivered the previous April, Secretary-General Kofi Annan set out the broad framework for this plan of action, which became the United Nations Millennium Project. In January 2005 the United Nations issued a five-year report that summarized the results to date and offered strategies for meeting the goals by 2015.

❝ If one word encapsulates the changes we are living through, it is "globalisation." We live in a world that is interconnected as never before. . . . This has its dangers, of course. Crime, narcotics, terrorism, disease, weapons—all these move back and forth faster, and in greater numbers, than in the past. . . .

But the *benefits* of globalisation are obvious too: faster growth, higher living standards, and new opportunities—not only for individuals but also for better understanding between nations, and for common action.

One problem is that, at present, these opportunities are far from equally distributed. . . . A second problem is that, even where the global market does reach, it is not yet underpinned, as national markets are, by rules based on shared social objectives. . . .

So, . . . the overarching challenge of our times is to make globalisation mean more than bigger markets. To make a success of this great upheaval we must learn how to govern better, and—above all—how to govern better together.

We need to make our States stronger and more effective at the national level. And we need to get them working together on global issues—all pulling their weight and all having their say.

What are these global issues? I have grouped them under three headings, each of which I relate to a fundamental human freedom—freedom from want, freedom from fear, and the freedom of future generations to sustain their lives on this planet.

First, *freedom from want*. How can we call human beings free and equal in dignity when over a billion of them are struggling to survive on less than one dollar a day, without safe drinking water, and when half of all humanity lacks adequate sanitation? Some of us are worrying about whether the stock market will crash, or struggling to master our latest computer, while more than half our fellow men and women have much more basic worries, such as where their children's next meal is coming from. . . .

Many of these problems are worst in sub-Saharan Africa, where extreme poverty affects a higher proportion of the population than anywhere else, and is compounded by a higher incidence of conflict, HIV/AIDS, and other ills. I am asking the world community to make special provision for Africa's needs, and give full support to Africans in their struggle to overcome these problems. . . .

Within the next fifteen years, I believe we can halve the population of people living in extreme poverty; ensure that all children—girls and boys alike, particularly the girls—receive a full primary education; and halt the spread of HIV/AIDS. In twenty years, we can also transform the lives of one hundred million slum dwellers around the world. And I believe we should be able to offer all young people between 15 and 24 the chance of decent work. . . .

The second main heading in the Report is *freedom from fear*. Wars between States are mercifully less frequent than they used to be. But in the last decade *internal* wars have claimed more than five million lives, and driven many times that number of people from their homes. Moreover, we still live under the shadow of weapons of mass destruction.

Both these threats, I believe, require us to think of security less in terms of merely defending territory, and more in terms of protecting *people*. That means we must tackle the threat of deadly conflict at every stage in the process. . . .

[T]he best way to prevent conflict is to promote political arrangements in which all groups are fairly represented, combined with human rights, minority rights, and broad-based economic development. Also, illicit transfers of weapons, money or natural resources must be forced into the limelight, so we can control them better.

We must protect vulnerable people by finding better ways to enforce humanitarian and human rights law, and to ensure that gross violations do not go unpunished. National sovereignty offers vital protection to small and weak States, but it should not be a shield for crimes against humanity. In extreme cases the clash

The Terrorist Threat

terrorism The use of force or violence by a person or organized group with the intention of intimidating societies or governments, often for political purposes.

Beginning in the early 1900s and peaking in the 1960s, many nationalist movements used **terrorism** to win nationhood and political independence. Terrorist groups carried out deadly bombings, assassinations, airplane hijackings, kidnappings, and in some cases all-out war.

CHAPTER LOCATOR

How has global politics changed since 1989?

A child is immunized against disease in a remote village in Thailand, advancing one of the United Nation's Millennium Project's goals. (Peter Charlesworth/OnAsia Images)

We must face the implications of a steadily shrinking surface of cultivable land, at a time when every year brings many millions of new mouths to feed. Biotechnology may offer the best hope, but only if we can resolve the controversies and allay the fears surrounding it. . . .

We must preserve our forests, fisheries, and the diversity of living species, all of which are close to collapsing under the pressure of human consumption and destruction. In short, we need a new ethic of stewardship. We need a much better informed public, and we need to take environmental costs and benefits fully into account in our economic policy decisions. We need regulations and incentives to discourage pollution and overconsumption of nonrenewable resources, and to encourage environment-friendly practices. And we need more accurate scientific data. . . .

But, you may be asking by now, what about the United Nations? . . .

[My] Report contains a further section on renewing the United Nations. . . . But let us not forget *why* the United Nations matters. It matters only to the extent that it can make a useful contribution to solving the problems and accomplishing the tasks I have just outlined.

Those are the problems and the tasks which affect the everyday lives of our peoples. It is on how we handle *them* that the utility of the United Nations will be judged. If we lose sight of that point, the United Nations will have little or no role to play in the twenty-first century.

Let us never forget . . . that our Organisation was founded in the name of "We, the Peoples." . . . We are at the service of the world's peoples, and we must listen to them. They are telling us that our past achievements are not enough. They are telling us we must do more, and do it better. 🗨

Source: Millennium Report, presented to the United Nations by Secretary-General Kofi Annan, April 3, 2000. Reproduced by permission of the United Nations Development Program.

QUESTIONS FOR ANALYSIS

1. According to Kofi Annan, what are the benefits of globalization, and what is the primary problem with it?
2. What are the three global issues and the related three fundamental freedoms that Annan hopes the Millennium Project will address?

of these two principles confronts us with a real dilemma, and the Security Council may have a moral duty to act on behalf of the international community. . . .

Finally, we must pursue our disarmament agenda more vigorously. Since 1995 it has lost momentum in an alarming way. That means controlling the traffic in small arms much more tightly, but also returning to the vexed issue of nuclear weapons. . . .

The third fundamental freedom my Report addresses is one that is not clearly identified in the Charter, because in 1945 our founders could scarcely imagine that it would ever be threatened. I mean the freedom of future generations to sustain their lives on this planet. . . .

If I could sum it up in one sentence, I should say we are plundering our children's heritage to pay for our present unsustainable practices.

This must stop. We must reduce emissions of carbon and other "greenhouse gases," to put a stop to global warming. Implementing the Kyoto Protocol is a vital first step. . . .

This wave of terrorism receded in the 1980s as colonies gained independence and local and international police and security agencies became more effective in preventing attacks before they happened.

Generally successful in keeping ethnic nationalism under control in the West in the 1990s, many Europeans and most Americans believed that terrorism was primarily a problem

What are the consequences of increasing global interdependence?

What are the causes and consequences of worldwide urbanization?

How have developments in science and technology changed the world?

What social problems do women and children face?

931

for developing countries. In fact, terrorism had become part of a complex global pattern of violence and political conflict. As the new century opened, the global dimension of terrorism was revealed most dramatically in the United States.

On the morning of September 11, 2001, two hijacked passenger planes that departed from Boston crashed into and destroyed the World Trade Center in New York City. Shortly thereafter a third plane crashed into the Pentagon, and a fourth, believed to be headed for the White House or the U.S. Capitol, crashed into a field in rural Pennsylvania. These terrorist attacks took the lives of almost three thousand people from many countries. The United States launched a military campaign to destroy the perpetrators of the crime, Saudi-born Osama bin Laden's al-Qaeda network of terrorists and Afghanistan's reactionary Muslim government, the Taliban. Building a broad international coalition that included NATO member troops, Russia, and Pakistan, the United States joined with the Northern Alliance in Afghanistan, which had been fighting the Taliban for years. In mid-November 2001 the Taliban government collapsed. The Taliban did not go away, however, and while bin Laden was eventually killed in May 2011, the war for control of Afghanistan continues.

In December 2010 Obama significantly increased the U.S. military presence in Afghanistan, committing an additional thirty thousand forces to the sixty-eight thousand already there. The extra forces were intended to speed up the training of the Afghan Security Force so that they could take responsibility for the war. At the same time, Obama announced a troop drawdown from Afghanistan that began in 2011.

In trying to make sense of the actions of Osama bin Laden, his al-Qaeda followers, and others in this new wave of terrorism, many commentators were quick to stress the role of extreme Islamic fundamentalism as a motivating factor. But some scholars noted that recent heinous crimes had been committed by terrorists inspired by several religious faiths and sects, and they were by no means limited to Islamic extremists.[1] These scholars also noted that different terrorist movements needed to be examined in the context of underlying political conflicts and civil wars for meaningful understanding.

When this perspective is brought to the study of Osama bin Laden and al-Qaeda, two stages of their activities stand out. First, in the long, bitter fighting against the Soviet Union and the local Communists in Afghanistan, bin Laden and like-minded "holy warriors" developed terrorist skills and a narrow-minded, fanatical Islamic puritanism. They also developed a hatred of most existing Arab governments, which they viewed as corrupt, un-Islamic, and unresponsive to the needs of ordinary Muslims.

New York, September 11, 2001 Pedestrians race for safety as the World Trade Center towers collapse after being hit by jet airliners. Al-Qaeda terrorists with box cutters hijacked four aircraft and used three of them as suicide missiles to perpetrate their unthinkable crime. Heroic passengers on the fourth plane realized what was happening and forced their hijackers to crash the plane in a field. (Amy Sanetta/AP images)

CHAPTER LOCATOR

How has global politics changed since 1989?

Second, when these Islamic extremists returned home and began to organize, they met the fate of many earlier Islamic extremists and were jailed or forced into exile, often in tolerant Europe. There they blamed the United States for being the supporter and corrupter of existing Arab governments, and they organized plots against the United States—a proxy for the Arab rulers they could not reach.

Although U.S.-led forces decimated al-Qaeda camps in Afghanistan and overthrew the Taliban government, many analysts have since argued that the war on terrorism may have become more difficult as a result. Islamic extremists with only loose ties to al-Qaeda set off bombs in a Madrid train station on March 11, 2004, killing 191 and wounding over 1,800. In London on July 7, 2005, 56 people were killed and more than 700 were injured by bombs targeting the mass transit system. At least three of the bombers were British citizens of Pakistani descent with unclear links to al-Qaeda. A suicide bomber who may have had links to al-Qaeda has also been blamed for the 2007 assassination of Pakistani presidential candidate Benazir Bhutto (see page 881). Thus, the war on terrorism is no longer against just the single global network of al-Qaeda. Many loosely connected cells and movements have emerged around the world, and these groups share many of the same goals but are not answerable to al-Qaeda's leadership.

Weapons of Mass Destruction

President George W. Bush justified the U.S.-led attack on Iraq in 2003 by saying that the world needed to destroy Iraq's weapons of mass destruction. As it turned out, Iraq had no weapons of mass destruction. Still, the fear that terrorists or rogue governments might acquire such weapons reflects global concern about the danger of nuclear, chemical, and biological attacks. (See "Global Trade: Arms," page 934.)

After the bombing of Hiroshima and Nagasaki in 1945 (see page 834), the United States proposed the international control of all atomic weapons. The Soviets refused and exploded their first atomic bomb in 1949. The United States responded by exploding its first hydrogen bomb in 1952, and within ten months the Soviet Union did the same. Further scientific tests aroused worldwide fear of radioactive fallout. Concerned scientists called for a ban on atomic bomb testing.

In 1963 the United States, Great Britain, and the Soviet Union signed an agreement, eventually signed by more than 150 countries, banning nuclear tests in the atmosphere. A second step toward control was the 1970 Treaty on the Non-Proliferation of Nuclear Weapons, designed to halt their spread to non-nuclear states and to reduce stockpiles of existing bombs held by the nuclear powers. It seemed that the nuclear arms race might yet be reversed.

This outcome did not come to pass. By 1974, Britain, France, China, and India had developed nuclear weapons. Meanwhile, the nuclear arms race between the Soviet Union and the United States surged ahead after 1968, while the two sides also tried to set limits on their nuclear arsenals. The Strategic Arms Limitation Talks (SALT) in the 1970s limited the rate at which the two superpowers produced nuclear warheads, and in 1991 the United States and Russia negotiated the first Strategic Arms Reduction Treaty (START I), which eventually removed about 80 percent of existing strategic nuclear weapons. The New START treaty, signed by U.S. president Obama and Russian president Medvedev in 2010, requires the two countries to further reduce the number of their nuclear warheads by one-third.

India's nuclear blast in 1974 in turn frightened Pakistan, which regarded India as a bitter enemy, and by the mid-1980s Pakistan had the ability to produce nuclear weapons. In 1998 both India and Pakistan set off tests of their nuclear devices within weeks of each other. Since then, both India and Pakistan have continued to increase their nuclear arsenals.

In the 1950s Israel began a nuclear weapons development program, and it is generally believed to have had an arsenal of nuclear weapons since the 1980s. Israel's apparent nuclear

What are the consequences of increasing global interdependence?   What are the causes and consequences of worldwide urbanization?   How have developments in science and technology changed the world?   What social problems do women and children face?

933

GLOBAL TRADE

Arms

Arms, with unprecedented destructive powers, command billions of dollars annually on the open global marketplace. On April 16, 1953, U.S. president Dwight Eisenhower spoke about the tremendous sums the Soviet Union and the United States were spending on Cold War weapons: "Every gun that is made, every warship launched, every rocket fired signifies, in the final sense, a theft from those who hunger and are not fed, those who are cold and are not clothed."

In the approximately sixty years since Eisenhower's speech, the spending has never stopped. In 2009 global military spending exceeded $1.53 trillion; the United States accounted for nearly half of that total. Globally in 2009 the value of all conventional arms transfer agreements to developing nations was more than $45.1 billion, and deliveries totaled $17 billion. Although those numbers have been dropping since the early 1990s, global arms manufacturing and trade remains big business.

Three different categories of arms are available on the world market. The category that generally receives the most attention is nuclear, biological, and chemical weapons. After the Soviet Union collapsed, there was widespread fear that former Soviet scientists would sell nuclear technology, toxic chemicals, or harmful biological agents from old, poorly guarded Soviet labs and stockpiles to the highest bidders. Recognizing the horrific danger such weapons represent, the world's nations have passed numerous treaties and agreements limiting their production, use, and stockpiling. The most important of these are the Treaty on the Non-Proliferation of Nuclear Weapons (1970), the Biological and Toxin Weapons Convention (1972), and the Chemical Weapons Convention (1993).

A second category of arms is so-called heavy conventional weapons, such as tanks, heavy artillery, jet planes, missiles, and warships. In general, worldwide demand for these weapons declined significantly after the Cold War ended. Only a few companies located in the largest industrialized nations have the scientists, the funding, and the capacity to produce them. Because the major Soviet- and Western-bloc nations had large weapon surpluses in 1991, most of the new weapons produced in this category have been made for export. New demand comes mainly from developing nations that are not technologically or financially capable of producing such weapons, such as Pakistan, which received fourteen F-16s from the United States in the summer of 2010. New or potential NATO member states have been another significant market for the United States, Great Britain, France, and Germany. In 2003, for example, the United States sold forty-eight F-16 fighter aircraft worth $3.5 billion to Poland, while Germany received $1 billion from Greece for 170 battle tanks. Many of the former Soviet-bloc countries of eastern Europe have illegally served as points of origin or transfer points for sales to embargoed nations such as North Korea and to terrorist groups such as al-Qaeda.

The third category is small arms and light conventional weapons (SALWs). These are almost any remotely portable weapons including automatic rifles, machine guns, pistols, antitank weapons, small howitzers and mortars, Stinger missiles and other shoulder-fired weapons, grenades, plastic explosives, land mines, machetes, small bombs, and ammunition. SALWs make up the majority of weapons exchanged in the global arms trade. They also do the most harm. In the 1990s the weapons of choice in forty-seven of forty-nine major conflicts were small arms. Every year, they are responsible for over a half million deaths.

SALWs are popular because they have relatively long lives and are low-maintenance, cheap, easily available, highly portable, and easily concealable. Many can be used by child soldiers. Globally, there are around 650 million guns, about 60 percent of them owned by private citizens. Fifteen billion to twenty billion or more rounds of ammunition are produced annually. Despite widespread concern about terrorists obtaining nuclear

superiority was threatening to the Arabs. When Iraq attempted, with help from France, to develop nuclear capability in the 1980s, Israel responded suddenly, attacking and destroying the Iraqi nuclear reactor in June 1981.

The risks associated with the proliferation of nuclear weapons helped mobilize the international community and contributed to positive developments through the 1980s and 1990s. A number of nations have abandoned their nuclear weapons programs. Several of the former Soviet republics possessing nuclear arsenals returned their nuclear weapons to Russia. Nuclear watch-guard agencies monitored exports of nuclear material, technology, and missiles that could carry atomic bombs. These measures encouraged confidence in global cooperation and in the nonproliferation treaty, which was extended indefinitely in 1995.

Still, nuclear proliferation continues to threaten world peace. Iraq's attempt to build a bomb before the Gulf War highlighted the need for better ways to detect cheating. In 2003 the United States accused Iran of seeking to build nuclear missiles, and ongoing efforts by France, Germany, Britain, China, the United States, and Russia have failed to get Iran to

How has global politics changed since 1989?

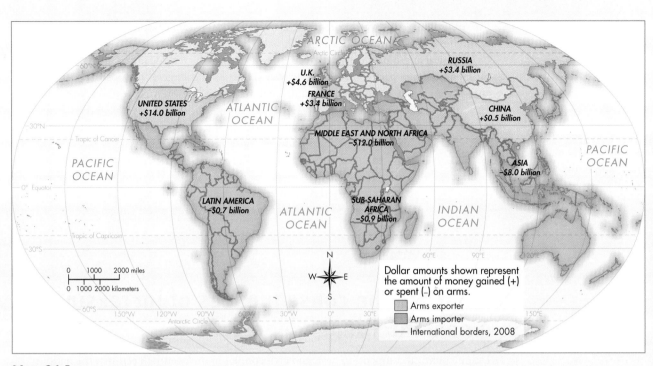

Map 34.1 The Arms Trade

or chemical weapons, terrorists on the whole favor such small conventional weapons as truck as well as car bombs and automatic rifles and pistols for assassinations, sniping, armed attacks, and massacres. One of the most deadly SALWs is the land mine. Over 110 million of them still lie buried in Afghanistan, Angola, Iran, and other former war zones, and they continue to kill or injure fifteen thousand to twenty thousand people a year.

Over ninety countries manufacture and sell SALWs, but the five permanent members of the UN Security Council — France, Britain, the United States, China, and Russia — dominate. The United States and Britain account for nearly two-thirds of all conventional arms deliveries, and these two nations plus France sometimes earn more income from arms sales to developing countries than they provide in aid.

In 2000 UN Secretary-General Kofi Annan observed that "the death toll from small arms dwarfs that of all other weapons systems — and in most years greatly exceeds the toll of the atomic bombs that devastated Hiroshima and Nagasaki. In terms of the carnage they cause, small arms, indeed, could well be described as 'weapons of mass destruction.'"*

Source: Map and data from www.controlarms.org/the_issues/movers_shakers.htm, reproduced with the permission of Oxfam GB, Oxfam House, John Smith Drive, Cowley, Oxford OX4 2JY, UK, www.oxfam.org.uk. Oxfam GB does not necessarily endorse any text or activities that accompany the materials, nor has it approved the adapted text.

*Kofi A. Annan, "Freedom from Fear," in *"We the Peoples": The Role of the United Nations in the 21st Century*, ch. 4, p. 52.

place limitations on its nuclear program. There is also the threat that enriched nuclear materials will fall into the hands of terrorist organizations. In 2001 three Pakistani nuclear scientists were arrested following allegations that they had met with Taliban and al-Qaeda representatives. Just as ominously, the father of Pakistan's nuclear weapons program, Abdul Qadeer Khan, was charged in 2004 with passing on nuclear weapons expertise and technology to Iran, Libya, and North Korea.

In 2003 long-standing tensions between North Korea and the United States reached crisis proportions over the question of nuclear arms on the Korean peninsula. In October 2006 North Korea tested its first nuclear device. In February 2007 North Korea agreed to shut down a major nuclear facility in exchange for thousands of tons of heavy fuel oil and the release of $25 million in frozen North Korean funds. In April 2009, however, North Korea ended all diplomatic talks and expelled all nuclear inspectors, and in May 2009 it successfully conducted a nuclear test. In 2010 some observers estimated that North Korea could possess a mid-range missile capable of reaching Japan with a nuclear warhead within five years. The case of North Korea illustrates the danger of atomic war in a multipolar world of intense regional rivalries.

Chemical and biological weapons of mass destruction created similar anxieties. Since the Geneva Protocol (1925) after World War I, the use of chemical weapons has been outlawed by international agreement, but the manufacture of these terrible weapons was nonetheless permitted. In 1997 most of the world's nations signed the Chemical Weapons Convention banning the production of chemical weapons and requiring the destruction of those in existence. Inspectors received the right to make surprise searches "anytime, anywhere." As of 2010 only five countries—Angola, Egypt, North Korea, Somalia, and Syria—had not signed the agreement. Nonetheless, the threat of biological or nuclear weapons falling into the hands of terrorists remains a real danger.

Quick Review
How have nation-states responded to the ongoing dangers posed by war, terrorism, and weapons of mass destruction?

What are the consequences of increasing global interdependence?

Despite political competition, war, and civil conflict in the twentieth century, the nations of the world became increasingly interdependent both economically and technologically. Dependence promoted peaceful cooperation and limited the scope of violence. Yet the existing framework of global interdependence also came under intense attack. The poor countries of the developing world—frequently referred to now as the South—charged that the North (the industrialized countries) continued to receive far more than their rightful share from existing economic relationships, which had been forged unjustly to the South's disadvantage in the era of European political domination. Critics saw strong evidence of neocolonialism in the growing importance of the North's huge global business corporations—the so-called multinationals—in world economic development.

Multinational Corporations

multinational corporations
Business firms that operate in a number of different countries and tend to adopt a global rather than a national perspective.

A striking feature of global interdependence beginning in the early 1950s was the rapid emergence of multinational corporations, business firms that operate in a number of different countries and tend to adopt a global rather than a national perspective. The rise of the multinationals was partly due to the general revival of capitalism after the Second World War, relatively free international economic relations, and the worldwide drive for rapid industrialization. Multinationals could invest huge sums of money in research and development, and they could hold monopolies on their creations. They employed advanced advertising and marketing skills to promote their products around the world. And they treated the world as one big market, coordinating complex activities across many political boundaries and escaping political controls and national policies.

The impact of multinational corporations, especially on Third World countries, has been mixed. The multinationals helped draw the developing world's elites into consumer society, and they often hired local business leaders to manage their operations abroad. Critics considered this part of the process of neocolonialism, whereby local elites were co-opted by foreign interests.

Some poor countries found ways to assert their sovereign rights over the foreign multinationals. Many foreign mining companies were nationalized by the host countries. More important, governments in the developing countries learned how to play Americans, Europeans, and Japanese off against each other and to make foreign manufacturing compa-

The Ubiquitous Multinational Corporations Under one of the most recognized advertising symbols in the world, the Marlboro Man, Buddhist monks line up to wait for daily donations in Phnom Penh, Cambodia. (Ou Neakiry/AP Images)

nies conform to some of their plans and desires. Increasingly, multinationals had to share ownership with local investors, hire more local managers, provide technology on better terms, and accept a variety of controls. Finally, having been denied the right to build manufacturing plants and industry as colonies, some newly independent countries also began to industrialize.

Industrialization and Modernization

Throughout the 1950s and 1960s the conventional wisdom among policy makers was that industrialization was the only answer to poverty and population growth. To Third World elites, the economic history of the West, Japan, and the Soviet Union seemed to validate this faith in industrialization. The wealthy countries had also been agricultural and "underdeveloped" until, one by one, the Industrial Revolution had lifted them out of poverty. Modernization theories, popular in the 1960s, assumed that all countries were following the path already taken by the industrialized nations and that the elites' task was to speed the trip. Marxism, with its industrial and urban bias, preached a similar gospel. These ideas reinforced the desire of the newly independent countries to industrialize.

Nationalist leaders believed a successful industrialization strategy required state action and enterprise along socialist lines. In Asia and Africa capitalists and private enterprise were often equated with the old rulers and colonial servitude. The reasoning was practical as well as ideological: socialism meant an expansion of steady government jobs for political and ethnic allies, and modern industry meant ports, roads, schools, and hospitals as well as factories. Only the state could afford such expensive investments.

The degree of state involvement varied considerably. A few governments, such as Communist China, tried to control all aspects of economic life. A few one-party states in Africa—notably Zambia, Ghana, and Tanzania—mixed Marxist-Leninist ideology and peasant communes in an attempt to construct a special "African socialism." At the other extreme the British colony of Hong Kong downgraded government control of the economy and emphasized private enterprise and the export of manufactured goods. Most governments assigned the state an important, even leading, role, but they also recognized private property and tolerated native (and foreign) business people. The mixed economy—part socialist, part capitalist—became the general rule in Africa and Asia.

Political leaders concentrated state investment in big, highly visible projects that proclaimed the country's independence and stimulated national pride. For example, Nasser's stupendous Aswan Dam harnessed the Nile, demonstrating that modern Egyptians could surpass even the pyramids of their ancient ancestors. These big projects testified to the prevailing faith in expensive advanced technology and modernization along European lines. Yet many of the projects were also bad investments in business terms, and they were soon abandoned when expensive parts broke or energy sources failed. Long after they had rusted or fallen into disuse, the enormous national debts incurred to pay for them remained.

By the late 1960s disillusionment with relatively rapid industrialization was spreading. While Third World industry was growing faster than ever before, Asian, African, and Latin American countries did not as a whole match the "miraculous" advances of western Europe and Japan, and the great economic gap between rich and poor nations continued to widen. Moreover, industrialization appeared least effective where poverty was most intense. All-out modern industrialization had failed as a panacea.

Agriculture and the Green Revolution

By the late 1960s widespread dissatisfaction with policies of all-out industrialization prompted a greater emphasis on rural development. Governments had neglected agriculture because feeding the masses was deceptively easy in the 1950s and early 1960s. Before 1939 the countries of Asia, Africa, and Latin America had collectively produced more grain than they consumed. After 1945, as their populations soared, they began importing ever-increasing but readily available quantities from countries like the United States. Although crops might fail in poor countries, starvation seemed a thing of the past.

However, after famines struck India in 1966 and 1967, complacency dissolved in Asia and Africa, and neo-Malthusian prophecies that population would grow faster than the food supply multiplied in wealthy nations. Paul Ehrlich, an American scientist and author of *The Population Bomb*, painted a particularly grim picture, arguing that it was too late to prevent hundreds of millions of people from starving.

Countering such nightmarish visions was the hope offered by technological improvements. Plant scientists set out to develop new genetically engineered seeds. The first breakthrough came in Mexico in the 1950s when an American-led team developed new strains of wheat that enabled farmers to double their yields, though they demanded greater amounts of fertilizer and water for irrigation. Mexican wheat production soared. Thus began the transformation of agriculture in some poor countries—the so-called green revolution.

In the 1960s an American-backed team of scientists in the Philippines developed a new hybrid "miracle rice" that required more fertilizer and water but yielded more and grew much faster than ordinary rice. It permitted the advent of year-round farming on irrigated land, making possible two to four crops a year. Asian scientists, financed by their governments, developed similar hybrids to meet local conditions.

Some Asian countries experienced rapid and dramatic increases in grain production. Farmers in India upped production more than 60 percent in fifteen years. China followed with its own highly successful version of the green revolution.

The green revolution offered new hope to the developing nations, but it was no cure-all. Initially most of its benefits flowed to large landowners and to substantial peasant farmers who could afford the necessary investments in irrigation and fertilizer. Subsequent experi-

mixed economy An economy that is part socialist and part capitalist.

neo-Malthusian Social science belief, based on the late-eighteenth-century works of Thomas Malthus, that population tends to grow faster than the food supply.

green revolution The increase in food production stemming from the introduction of high-yielding wheat, hybrid seeds, and other advancements.

CHAPTER LOCATOR

How has global politics changed since 1989?

ence in China and other Asian countries showed, however, that even peasant families with tiny farms could gain substantially. Indeed, the green revolution's greatest successes occurred in Asian countries with broad-based peasant ownership of land. The technological revolution, however, shared relatively few of its benefits with the poorest villagers, who almost never owned the land. This helps explain why the green revolution failed to spread from Mexico throughout Latin America, where 3 to 4 percent of the rural population owned 60 to 80 percent of the land.

As the practice of genetically engineered foods grew in the late twentieth and early twenty-first centuries, global opposition to the practice also grew. Many people feared that such foods would have still-unknown effects on the human body. The loss of biodiversity was also of growing concern. When one or two genetically engineered seeds replaced all of the naturally occurring local seeds in an area, food security was threatened. With a shrinking diversity of plants and animals, farmers will find it more difficult to find alternatives if the dominant hybrid seed in use becomes susceptible to a particular disease or pest or there is a significant climate change. Corporate ownership of seeds through patents is another worrisome outcome of this shrinking diversity: farmers will be dependent on a few giant multinational agribusinesses for their seeds. Finally, as mass-produced, genetically modified

Picturing the Past

Greenpeace in Thailand

The global environmental organization Greenpeace has led protests around the world against the use of genetically modified (GM) foods. Greenpeace organized this demonstration in Thailand after a government official said that he might lift a ban on such foods. The colorful genetically modified vegetables being taped off are meant to illustrate the harmful effects of GM processes on foods and the humans who ingest them. (Shailendra Yashwant/Greenpeace)

ANALYZING THE IMAGE What do the costumes suggest about the protesters' views about the effects of genetically modified foods?

CONNECTIONS What are some of the advantages and disadvantages of the scientific engineering of food crops?

foods have become cheaper, they are eaten by the poor, while the rich are able to afford organically grown, chemically free, but more expensive foods.

The Economics and Politics of Globalization

After the 1960s there was dissatisfaction in Asia, Africa, and Latin America not only with the fruits of the industrialization drive but also with the world's economic system, which critics called unjust and in need of radical change. The demand of the developing nations for a new international economic order had many causes, both distant and immediate. Critics of imperialism such as J. A. Hobson (see page 680) and Third World writers on decolonization such as Frantz Fanon (see page 920) had long charged that the colonial powers grew rich exploiting Asia, Africa, and Latin America. Beginning in the 1950s a number of writers, many of them Latin American Marxists, breathed new life into these ideas with their theory of dependency.

The poverty and so-called underdevelopment of the South, they argued, were the deliberate and permanent results of exploitation by the capitalist industrialized nations in the modern era. Poor countries produced cheap raw materials for wealthy, industrialized countries and were conditioned to buy their expensive manufactured goods. Thus the prevailing economic interdependence was the unequal, unjust interdependence of dominant and subordinate, of master and peon.

The great gap between the richest and poorest nations resulted from a combination of factors, ranging from colonial systems that limited economic development to the wealth-creating effects of continuous technological improvement in the developed countries since the Industrial Revolution. In the face of bitter poverty, unbalanced economies, and local elites that were generally more concerned about maintaining their own expensive living standards while catering to Western interests, people of the developing countries had reason for frustration and anger.

But close examination of our planet reveals a much more complex configuration than simply two sharply defined economic camps, a North and a South. By the early 1990s there were several distinct classes of nations in terms of wealth and income (Map 34.2). The former Communist countries of eastern Europe formed something of a middle-income group, as did the major oil-exporting states, which still lagged behind the wealthier countries of western Europe and North America. Latin America was much better off than sub-Saharan Africa but contained a wide range of national per capita incomes. Some of the largest and fastest-growing economies, as well as the highest standards of living, were found in South and East Asia. When one added global differences in culture, religion, politics, and historical development, the supposed clear-cut split between the rich North and the poor South broke down further. Moreover, the solidarity of the South had always been fragile, resting largely on the ideas of some Third World intellectuals and their supporters.

Thus a continuation of the global collective bargaining that first emerged in the 1970s seemed more likely than an international class war. The recurring international debt crisis illustrates the process of global bargaining. The economic dislocations of the 1970s and early 1980s worsened the problems of many developing countries, especially those that had to import oil. Growing unemployment, unbalanced budgets, and large trade deficits forced many poor countries to borrow rapidly from the wealthy industrialized nations. By the early 1980s much of the debt was short-term and could not be repaid as it came due, so it continued to build. By 2005 the world's poorest countries were spending more on debt repayments—$100 million a day—than on health care. In 2000 the United Nations Millennium Project Report made debt relief a major goal.

Efforts to bring living standards in developing countries to levels approaching those in rich industrialized countries put tremendous pressure on global resources. American scien-

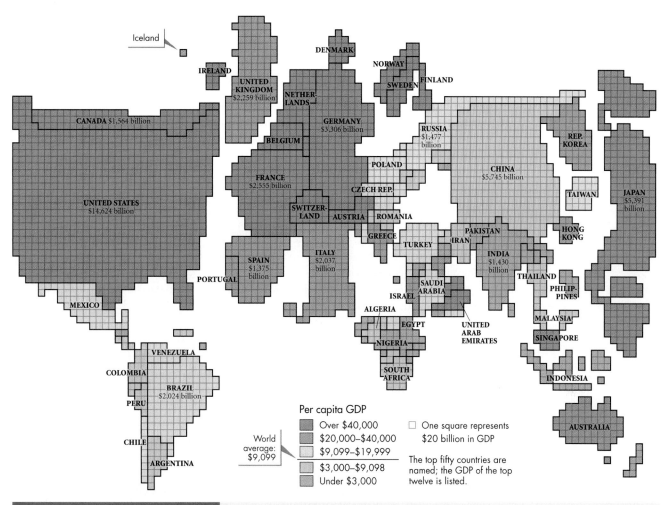

Per capita GDP

- Over $40,000
- $20,000–$40,000
- $9,099–$19,999
- $3,000–$9,098
- Under $3,000

World average: $9,099

One square represents $20 billion in GDP

The top fifty countries are named; the GDP of the top twelve is listed.

Mapping the Past

Map 34.2 The Global Distribution of Wealth, ca. 2010

This size-comparison map, arranged according to global wealth distribution, vividly illustrates the gap in wealth between the Northern and Southern Hemispheres. The two small island nations of Japan and the United Kingdom have more wealth than all the nations of the Southern Hemisphere combined, although wealth creation in India and Brazil has advanced significantly. As market capitalism expands in China, Vietnam, and other Asian countries and in Latin America and Africa, the relative size-ratios on the map will continue to change and evolve. Tiny Iceland, whose GDP is less than $20 billion, nevertheless has one of the highest per capita GDPs in the world.

ANALYZING THE MAP Which three countries are the wealthiest? Where are the poorest countries concentrated?

CONNECTIONS How were the two small nations of Japan and the United Kingdom able to acquire such enormous wealth?

tist and writer Jared Diamond, in his study of how societies succeed or fail, says it is therefore incumbent to ask how much of the traditional industrialized countries' consumer values and living standards we can afford to retain. Diamond is encouraged, however, by the decline in human fertility rates, and also because today humans have the advantage of a global communications network and a knowledge of human history that were not available to earlier generations.[2] Throughout its history, the human race has exhibited considerable skill in finding new resources and inventing new technologies. Perhaps we can learn from the achievements and mistakes made in the human past and share our finite global resources more equitably and wisely in the future.

Quick Review

Which regions have gained the most from globalization, and which have gained the least? Why?

What are the consequences of increasing global interdependence?

What are the causes and consequences of worldwide urbanization?

How have developments in science and technology changed the world?

What social problems do women and children face?

941

What are the causes and consequences of worldwide urbanization?

Perhaps no single phenomenon in the last hundred years has had a greater impact on individuals, families, and communities than the mass movement of peoples from rural areas to cities. The reasons for this migration are numerous, and the consequences for life on earth are profound.

Rapid Urbanization

Cities in Africa, Asia, and Latin America expanded at an astonishing pace after 1945. Many doubled or even tripled in size in a single decade. Rapid urbanization in the developing countries represents a tremendous historical change. In 1950 there were only eight **megacities** (5 million or more inhabitants), and just two were in developing countries. Estimates are that by 2015 there will be fifty-nine megacities, and forty-eight of them will be outside North America and Europe.

megacities Cities with populations of 5 million people or more.

What caused this urban explosion? First, the general growth of population in the developing nations was critical. Urban residents gained substantially from a medical revolution that provided improved health care but only gradually began to reduce the size of their families. Second, the pressure of numbers in the countryside encouraged millions to set out for the nearest city. More than half of all urban growth has been due to rural migration. Another factor was the desire to find jobs. Industrial jobs in the developing nations were concentrated in cities. Yet industrialization accounted for only part of the urban explosion.

Newcomers streamed to the cities even when there were no industrial jobs available, seeking any type of employment. Sociologists call this **urbanization without industrialization**. Many were pushed: large landowners found it more profitable to produce export crops, and their increasingly mechanized operations provided few jobs for agricultural laborers. The push factor was particularly strong in Latin America, with its neocolonial pattern of large landowners and foreign companies exporting food and raw materials. More generally, much migration was seasonal or temporary. Many young people left home for the city to work in construction or serve as maids, expecting higher wages and steadier work and planning to return shortly with a modest nest egg. Many young people were attracted as well by the cosmopolitan lifestyle the city offered.

urbanization without industrialization A sociological phenomenon in which newcomers stream to cities seeking work even when no industrial jobs are available.

Many of these developments were mirrored in the industrialized countries as well. But because industrialization had advanced in Europe and North America in the nineteenth and early twentieth centuries, people there had been drawn to urban areas at a much earlier date. By 1920 more Americans were already living in cities than in rural areas.

Overcrowding and Shantytowns

The late twentieth century saw a repeat of the problems associated with urbanization that had arisen in the cities of Europe and North America in the early twentieth century (see Chapter 24), but on a larger scale. Rapid population growth threatened to overwhelm urban social services. New neighborhoods often lacked running water, paved streets, electricity, and police and fire protection. As in the early days of European industrialization, sanitation was minimal in poor sections of town.

Makeshift squatter settlements were another striking manifestation of the urban housing problem. These shantytowns, also known more positively as self-help housing, sprang up when a group of urban poor "invaded" unoccupied land and quickly threw up tents or huts. Often beaten off by the police, they invaded again and again until the authorities gave up and a new squatter beachhead had been secured.

Shantytowns grew much faster than more prosperous urban areas. In most developing countries, these self-help settlements came to house up to two-fifths of the urban population. Such settlements had occasionally grown in American mining towns and in Europe, but never to the extent they did in Latin America, Asia, and Africa.

Rich and Poor

At the beginning of the twenty-first century differences in wealth between rich and poor countries, and often between rich and poor individuals within those countries, were truly staggering. At the bottom end of the global income spectrum, there were sixty-one countries in which the average person made less than $750 a year; half of the world's population—3 billion people—lived on less than $2 a day. At the other end, the wealth of the world's three richest people was greater than the GDP of the poorest forty-eight nations combined.

The gap between rich and poor was most pronounced in the towns and cities. The rich in Asia and Africa often moved into the luxurious sections previously reserved for colonial administrators and foreign business people. Particularly in Latin America, elites built fine mansions in exclusive suburbs, where they lived behind high walls with servants and armed guards.

Elites in the developing countries often had more in common with the power brokers of the industrialized nations than with their own people, and too often the partnership of the wealthy elite of a developing country with multinational companies and First World nations resulted in the developing country's experiencing economic growth without economic development. Enormous profits were being made from cash crop production or from industrial manufacturing, but few of these profits were used to benefit and raise the standard of living of the common people. Multinational companies took the majority of the profits out of the country. The remainder often went directly into the private bank accounts of the wealthy elite, who also ruled the country, in return for their maintaining stability, keeping wages low and unions out, and allowing the companies to exploit the land and people as they wished.

In general, the majority of the exploding population of urban poor earned precarious livings in a modern yet traditional bazaar economy of petty traders and unskilled labor. Here regular salaried jobs were rare and highly prized, and a complex world of tiny,

economic growth without economic development Outcome when large profits are made from cash crop production or from industrial manufacturing and few of the profits are put back into the construction of infrastructure or other efforts to raise the standard of living of the common people.

bazaar economy An economy with few salaried jobs and an abundance of tiny, unregulated businesses such as peddlers and pushcart operators.

Rich and Poor in Hong Kong Global inequalities in wealth are evident in this photo of Hong Kong that shows refugee squatter housing in the foreground and modern, affluent apartment blocks behind. As a result of rapid urbanization and peasants' having to leave their land, this stark contrast between desperately poor and comfortably wealthy is found throughout the developing world. (Brian Brake/Photo Researchers, Inc.)

unregulated businesses and service occupations predominated. Peddlers and pushcart operators hawked their wares, and sweatshops and home-based workers manufactured cheap goods for popular consumption. This bazaar economy continued to grow as migrants streamed to the cities, as modern industry provided too few jobs, and as the wide gap between rich and poor persisted.

Urban Migration and the Family

After 1945 large-scale urban migration had a profound impact on traditional family patterns in the developing countries, just as it had on families in industrialized countries earlier. Particularly in Africa and Asia, the great majority of migrants to the city were young men; women tended to stay in the villages. The result was a sexual imbalance in both places.

For rural women the consequences of male out-migration were mixed. Asian and African women had long been treated as subordinates, if not inferiors, by their fathers and husbands. Rather suddenly, they found themselves heads of households, faced with managing the farm, feeding the children, and running their own lives. African and Asian village women had to become unprecedentedly self-reliant and independent. As a result, the beginning of more equal rights and opportunities for women became readily visible in Africa and Asia.

In Latin America the pattern of migration was different. Whole families migrated much more commonly than in Asia and Africa. These families frequently belonged to the class of landless laborers, which was generally larger in Latin America than in Africa and Asia. Migration was also more likely to be permanent. Another difference was that single women were as likely as single men to move to the cities, in part because women were in high demand as domestic servants. Some women also left to escape the narrow, male-dominated villages. Even so, in Latin America urban migration seemed to have less impact on traditional family patterns and on women's attitudes than it did in Asia and Africa.

Urbanization and Agriculture

The development of multinational agribusiness and the successes of the green revolution caused millions of small farmers and peasants to leave their land and migrate to cities. This phenomenon affected farmers in developed and developing countries alike.

The decline of the family farm in the United States is as representative as any of the consequences of modern agricultural production on small farmers. The shift from small family farms to large operations owned by private farmers owning thousands of acres — factory farms producing massive quantities of livestock products — or corporate agribusinesses has dramatically altered the American labor force. Since the 1930s the percentage of farmers in the workforce has shrunk from 21 percent to 2 percent. Half of all family farms now depend on off-farm income. The result has been the death of many small towns in America and the loss of many farm-related businesses and jobs.

Why has this happened? One simple reason is that the younger generation wants to move to the city. But there are other reasons as well. As farm-related costs — land, equipment, fuel, seeds, fertilizer, irrigation — rise, it becomes more difficult for small farmers to compete with the large operations. Agribusinesses have the advantages of economy of scale and can afford larger machines to farm larger acreages, can control all phases of the process — from producing the hybrid seeds to marketing the final product — and can take advantage of international markets.

Peasants in developing countries leave the land for many of the same reasons. The major difference in developing countries, though, is that these peasant farmers are often producing subsistence crops and are forced off the land by government troops or thugs hired by large landowners or companies to make way for large cash-crop production. The loss of land can also result from peasant families' possessing no documents proving ownership of the fields they have worked for generations. In industrialized countries like the United States, farmers who leave their land have educational and employment options. In developing countries, few options are available for illiterate peasants with no skills other than rudimentary farming.

Quick Review
How has rapid urbanization changed life in the developing world?

How have developments in science and technology changed the world?

The twentieth century was a time of amazing advances in science and technology. These advances were not always positive. The great excitement over the telephone, the automobile, electricity, and the airplane was quickly tempered in 1914 by the killing machines invented and used in the Great War. Totalitarian regimes exploited new developments in mass communication for mass propaganda. No sooner had the atom been harnessed than the United States released atomic bombs over Hiroshima and Nagasaki. Yet since World War II, scientists have made tremendous progress in medicine and communication technologies, though disease and environmental issues continue to present challenges.

The Medical Revolution

The medical revolution began in the late 1800s with the development of the germ theory of disease (see page 650) and continued rapidly after World War II. Scientists discovered vaccines for polio, measles, and many other deadly diseases. The medical revolution significantly lowered death rates and lengthened life expectancies. Children became increasingly likely to survive their early years, although infant and juvenile mortality remained far higher in poor countries than in rich ones.

Since the 1980s medical science has continued to make remarkable advances. In 1979 the World Health Organization announced the worldwide eradication of smallpox. By this time, transplants of such organs as hearts, lungs, and kidneys had become routine. In 2003 scientists working on the Human Genome Project announced that they had successfully identified, mapped, and sequenced the entire genome, or hereditary information, of human beings. This knowledge gives health care providers immense new powers for preventing, treating, and curing diseases, and it makes the completion of the project one of the most important scientific developments in history.

Despite these advances, there remains a wide gap in health care availability and affordability for the rich and the poor. Thousands of people die every day in the developing world from diseases and illnesses that are curable and easily treated, like diarrhea. Deaths worldwide from HIV/AIDS are reaching epic proportions, while malaria and tuberculosis continue to be major killers of young and old alike.

Population Change: Balancing the Numbers

A less favorable consequence of the medical revolution has been the acceleration of population growth. The combined populations of Asia, Africa, and Latin America, which had grown relatively modestly from 1925 to 1950, increased from 1.7 billion to 3 billion between 1950 and 1975 and continue to grow at a similar rate.

Concerned about famine and starvation, some governments began pushing family planning and birth control to slow population growth. For a number of reasons these measures were not always successful. Islamic and Catholic religious teachings were hostile to birth

What are the consequences of increasing global interdependence? | What are the causes and consequences of worldwide urbanization? | **How have developments in science and technology changed the world?** | What social problems do women and children face?

945

control. Moreover, widespread cultural attitudes dictated that a "real man" keep his wife pregnant. There were also economic reasons for preferring large families. Farmers needed the help of children at planting and harvest times, and sons and daughters were a sort of social security system for their elders. By the 1970s and 1980s, however, population growth in the industrialized countries had begun to fall significantly. By the 1990s some European leaders were bemoaning birthrates in their countries that were below the 2.1 level needed to maintain a stable population.

The world's poor women also began to bear fewer children. Small countries such as Barbados, Chile, Costa Rica, South Korea, Taiwan, and Tunisia led the way. Between 1970 and 1975 China followed, registering the fastest five-year birthrate decline in recorded history. Then other big countries, especially in Latin America and East Asia, experienced large declines in fertility.

There were several reasons for this decline in fertility among women in the developing world. Fewer babies were dying of disease or malnutrition, so couples needed fewer births to guarantee the survival of the number of children they wanted. Also, better living conditions, urbanization, and more education encouraged women to have fewer children.

In the early 1960s the introduction of the birth control pill marked a revolution not only in birth control techniques but also in women taking control of their own fertility. Family planning was now truly possible. However, male chauvinism, religious teachings, and conservative government leaders combined in many predominately Roman Catholic countries and in most Muslim countries to control the availability and distribution of birth control methods and abortion. Birth control and abortion were most accepted in North America, Protestant Europe, the Soviet Union, and East Asia, which explains why these regions had the lowest birthrates and population growth.

Global Epidemics

One of humanity's gravest fears in the early years of the new millennium comes from the threat posed by epidemic diseases. Outbreaks in Africa of the deadly Ebola and Marburg viruses; a worldwide outbreak of severe acute respiratory syndrome, or SARS, which began in 2002; ongoing avian, or bird, flu in Asia; and "mad-cow disease," which has wreaked havoc with meat production in several countries, have all raised the frightening specter of a global recurrence of a modern Black Death.

Few diseases in world history have been more frightening, or caused more disruption of human society, than HIV/AIDS. In 2007 the Population Division of the United Nations calculated that 36 million persons globally were infected with HIV, the virus that causes AIDS. AIDS was the world's fourth-leading cause of death.

About 90 percent of all persons who die from AIDS and 86 percent of those currently infected with HIV live in sub-Saharan Africa (Map 34.3). In Africa HIV/AIDS is most commonly spread through heterosexual sex. Widespread disease and poverty are also significant factors in that Africans already suffering from other illnesses such as malaria or tuberculosis have less resistance to HIV and less access to health care for treatment.

Another critical factor contributing to the spread of AIDS in Africa is the continued political instability of many countries—particularly those in the corridor running from Uganda to South Africa. This corridor was the scene of brutal civil and liberation wars that resulted in massive numbers of refugees, a breakdown in basic health care services, and the destruction of family and cultural networks. The populations of countries along this corridor—Uganda, Rwanda, Burundi, Zaire/Congo, Angola, Zimbabwe, Mozambique, and South Africa—have been decimated by HIV/AIDS. South Africa currently has the largest number of HIV/AIDS cases in the world. Medical health experts expect that Russia, India, China, Japan, and other countries in Asia might soon overtake South Africa in reported HIV/AIDS cases.

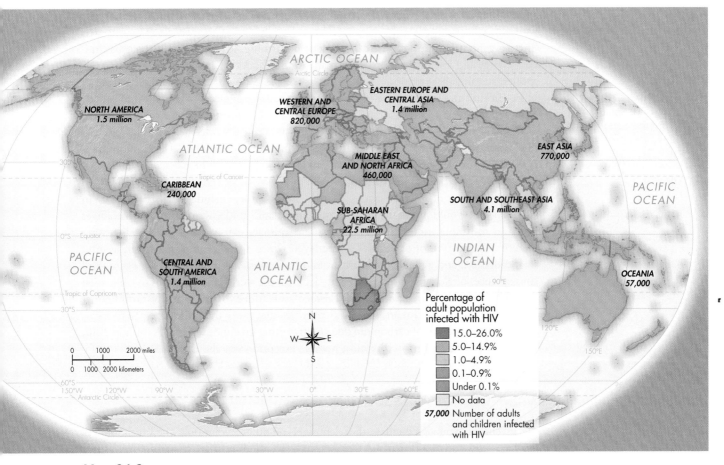

Map 34.3 People Living with HIV/AIDS Worldwide, ca. 2010 As this map illustrates, Africa has been hit the hardest by the HIV/AIDS epidemic. AIDS researchers expect that in the coming decade, however, Russia and South and East Asia will overtake and then far surpass Africa in the number of infected people. (Source: Data from World Health Organization, www.whosea.org)

Although HIV/AIDS has had a devastating impact on Africa, globally the epidemic is still at a relatively early stage. Changes in behavior will be critical to slowing the spread of AIDS in the developing world. Since 2001 relatively inexpensive AIDS drugs that are widely available in the West have been dispensed freely to many of those infected in Africa and Asia, but the availability of these drugs has generally failed to keep up with the increase in cases.

Environmentalism

The modern environmental movement began with concerns about chemical waste, rapid consumption of energy and food supplies, global deforestation, environmental degradation caused in part by sprawling megacities, and threats to wildlife. By the 1970s citizens had begun joining together in organizations such as Greenpeace and Friends of the Earth to try to preserve, restore, or enhance the natural environment.

The environmental movement is actually several different movements, each with its own agenda. American biologist and writer Rachel Carson was an early proponent of the environmental health movement. In *Silent Spring* (1962) she warned of the dangers of pesticides and pollution. Carson and others were concerned about the effects of chemicals, radiation, pollution, waste, and urban development on the environment and on human health.

The conservation movement, represented in the United States by the Sierra Club and the Audubon Society, seeks to protect the biodiversity of the planet and emphasizes the

What are the consequences of increasing global interdependence?

What are the causes and consequences of worldwide urbanization?

How have developments in science and technology changed the world?

What social problems do women and children face?

947

spiritual and aesthetic qualities of nature. The ecology movement consists of different groups with somewhat similar agendas, ranging from politically active Green Parties to Greenpeace. These organizations are concerned about global warming, toxic chemicals, the use of nuclear energy and nuclear weapons, genetically modified food, recycling, saving endangered species, sustainable agriculture, protecting ancient forests, and environmental justice.

Environmentalists today are especially concerned about **global warming**, the increase of global temperatures over time. The ten years to 2010 formed the warmest decade in recorded history, followed by the 1990s. The majority of the world's scientists believe that the increase began with the Industrial Revolution in the 1700s. The subsequent human-generated hydrocarbons produced through the burning of fossil fuels — coal, oil, natural gas — have caused a greenhouse effect.

Possible effects of global warming over the next century include a catastrophic rise in sea levels that would put many coastal cities and islands under water; ecosystem changes that may threaten various species of plants and animals; extreme and abnormal weather patterns; destruction of the earth's ozone layer, which shields the planet from harmful solar radiation; and a decline in agricultural production. Although the exact causes and consequences of global warming are being debated, the world community is so concerned that in 1997 an amendment, the Kyoto Protocol, was added to the United Nations Framework Convention on Climate Change. Countries that ratify the protocol agree to try to reduce their emissions of carbon dioxide and five other greenhouse gases. As of July 2010, 191 countries had ratified it. The most notable exception was the United States.

global warming The belief of the majority of the world's scientists that hydrocarbons produced through the burning of fossil fuels have caused a greenhouse effect that has increased global temperatures over time.

Mass Communication

The invention of moving pictures, the telephone, and other revolutionary new technologies between 1875 and 1900 prepared the way for a twentieth century of mass communications and the "information age." The global availability and affordability of radios and television sets in the 1950s introduced a second communications revolution. The transistor radio penetrated the most isolated hamlets of the developing world. Governments embraced radio broadcasting as a means of power, propaganda, and education. Though initially less common, television use expanded into nearly every country. Governments recognized the power of the visual image to promote their ideology or leader, and a state television network became a source of national pride. By the beginning of the twenty-first century television was having a profound, even revolutionary, impact everywhere. Alluring television images of high living standards and the excitement of urban life stirred powerful desires in young people, who copied Western materialism, migrated to the cities, and created a global youth culture.

The third, and perhaps greatest, communications revolution occurred with the first Apple personal computers in 1976, followed by the introduction of cell phones in 1985. Mass communications have exploded since then. Cell phones allowed individuals and nations in the developing world to bypass telephone lines, installation, and other obstacles associated with landline telephone use. Cell phones have become among the most widely owned consumer products worldwide.

The Internet has had the greatest impact on human communication. First made available to the general public in 1994, the Internet allows for instantaneous communication to anyone, anywhere with an Internet connection. The possibilities for global access to information and knowledge are seemingly infinite. Authoritarian governments have realized the threat that the Internet and Facebook, Twitter, and other social networking services pose to their power and control. The governments of China and North Korea, for example, have spent millions of dollars trying to restrict information traveling in and out of their countries over the Internet. For the first time in history, this type of censorship may prove impossible.

Quick Review
How have developing nations sought to take advantage of technological and scientific advances?

CHAPTER LOCATOR

How has global politics changed since 1989?

What social problems do women and children face?

Just as an end to slavery became the rallying cry for social reformers in the nineteenth century, modern social reformers have sought to end global inequality, racism, and sexism and to improve human and civil rights for all. We have already described many of these developments, such as the victory of the democratic movement in eastern Europe (see pages 851–855) and the end of the racist apartheid system in South Africa (see page 915). Much remains to be achieved, however, and nowhere is more worldwide attention being focused than on the advancement of human and civil rights for women and children.

Women: The Right to Equality

The feminization of poverty, the disproportionate number of women living in extreme poverty, is one of the greatest concerns facing women today. Even in the most developed countries, two out of every three poor adults are women. In the United States, for example, half of all poor families are supported by single mothers whose average income is 23 percent lower than the poverty line. There are many causes for this phenomenon. Having principal responsibility for child care, women have less time and opportunity for work, and because they have less access to health care they are often unable to work. As male labor migration increases worldwide, the number of households headed by women increases, and thus the number of families living in poverty. Job restrictions and discrimination, plus limited education, result in women having few job options except in the "informal economy" as maids, street vendors, or prostitutes.

Despite increased access to birth control, even within developed countries, birthrates remain high among poor women, especially among poor adolescents, who make up an inordinate number of the estimated 585,000 women who die every year during pregnancy and childbirth. The poorest women usually suffer most from government policies, usually legislated by men, that restrict their access to reproductive health care.

Women have made some modest gains in the workplace, but segregated labor markets remain the rule, with higher-paying jobs reserved for men. In the farm sector, women globally produce more than half of all the food that is grown and up to 80 percent of subsistence crops grown in Africa. Because this is informal labor and often unpaid, these women laborers are denied access to loans, and many of them cannot own the land they farm.

Some observers believe that violence against women is on the rise. Rape and sexual violence, long part of war, were used as weapons of war during the wars in the former Yugoslavia and in Rwanda in the early 1990s. Rape and sexual violence have been subsequently labeled crimes against humanity and are considered forms of torture and genocide. Still, they have continued to be used as weapons in conflicts in Sierra Leone, Kosovo, Afghanistan, the Democratic Republic of the Congo, and elsewhere. Domestic violence appears to be on the increase in many countries, including Russia, Pakistan, Peru, and South Africa. Forced prostitution and international female slave traffic is carried on by traffickers from such countries as Ukraine, Moldova, Nigeria, Burma, and Thailand.

Still, some progress has been made toward equality for women. New laws have been enacted, and worldwide more girls than ever before are receiving an education. More women are now allowed to vote and to hold office, and half of all the female heads of state elected since 1900 were elected after 1990. Women also are moving across and up in the workplace, holding a wider variety of jobs and more senior positions.

feminization of poverty The issue that those living in extreme poverty are disproportionately women.

What are the consequences of increasing global interdependence?

What are the causes and consequences of worldwide urbanization?

How have developments in science and technology changed the world?

What social problems do women and children face?

949

Children: The Right to Childhood

In 1989 the United Nations General Assembly adopted the Convention on the Rights of the Child, which spelled out a number of rights that are due every child. These include civil and human rights and economic, social, and cultural rights. The convention has been ratified by more countries than any other human rights treaty in world history—194 countries as of 2009. The United States and Somalia remain the only two countries in the United Nations that have not ratified it.

It is not difficult to see why such a document was necessary. Globally, a billion children live in poverty—one in every two children in the world. In the United States 16 percent of children, more than 11 million girls and boys, live in poor families with parents who earn at or below the poverty line. Worldwide, 640 million children do not have adequate shelter, 400 million do not have safe water, and 270 million receive no health care. From 10 million to 11 million children die each year before age five.

Besides poverty, the convention addresses a number of other concerns. These include children's making up half of the world's refugees, child labor and exploitation, sexual violence and sex trafficking, police abuse of street children, HIV/AIDS orphans, lack of access to education, and lack of access to adequate health care. Increasingly in the last decade, children have been recruited or kidnapped to become child soldiers. Child sexual abuse and child soldiers have become such widespread problems that the United Nations wrote two additional protocols—one on the involvement of children in armed conflicts and the other on the sale of children, child pornography, and child prostitution—that were attached to the original convention and adopted in 2000.

As the twenty-first century began, nearly a billion people were unable to read a book or sign their names. Of the 100 million children without access to primary education, 60 percent or more were girls. Most of the global literacy problems are found in the developing world. Increasing economic globalization have put pressure on all governments to improve literacy rates and to improve educational opportunities for young people. Since the 1990s more and more countries have recognized the importance of providing a minimum

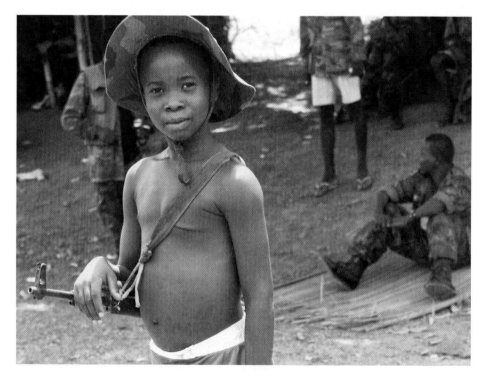

Child Soldier in Sierra Leone
This eleven-year-old boy with a rifle slung over his shoulder is a member of the Sierra Leone army and stands guard at a checkpoint during his country's civil war. Tens of thousands of boys and girls under eighteen have been used by the militaries in more than sixty countries since 2000, either as armed combatants or informally in tasks such as spying, scouting, carrying messages, and cooking. (Brennan Linsley/AP Images)

level of basic education and have made it compulsory. Globally, four in five children now participate in lower secondary education (U.S. ninth and tenth grades), but discrepancies remain wide. Many countries have 90 to 100 percent participation in at least lower secondary education, but in Africa the rate is closer to 45 percent and is only 29 percent for upper secondary (U.S. eleventh and twelfth grades). Only when countries are stable and have prosperous economies will all children receive the education they deserve.

Quick Review
What steps have global organizations taken in recent decades to protect the rights of women and children?

Connections

AFTER FORTY YEARS of superpower confrontation, the Cold War's end brought renewed hope for global peace and prosperity. If we have learned anything since 1991, however, it is that neither peace nor prosperity comes easily for the human race. New rifts and old animosities have set us at odds in ways that are just as dangerous and lethal as the Cold War differences they replaced. At the same time, as the twenty-first century enters its second decade, populist revolts in several countries across North Africa, the Middle East, and elsewhere have demonstrated that women and men are still ready to fight and die for freedom from authoritarian rule and for better lives.

A common feature of these recent revolts has been the use of the Internet, cell phones, and social networking sites. While these have proved innovative tools for political change, the most revolutionary advances in education in the developing world will also come through access to the Internet. Despite the initial costs — significant for many countries — the benefits of having even one computer connected to the Internet in each school are incalculable. Instantaneously, children get access to all the world's libraries, art galleries, museums, educational sites, and knowledge bases. Internet access does not make the playing field between rich and poor students exactly level, but it comes closer to doing so than any other development in history.

The study of world history will put these and future events in perspective. Future developments on this small planet will surely build on the many-layered foundations hammered out in the past. Moreover, the study of world history, of mighty struggles and fearsome challenges, of shining achievements and tragic failures, imparts a strong sense of life's essence: the process of change over time. Again and again we have seen how peoples and societies evolve, influenced by ideas, human passions, and material conditions. Armed with the ability to think historically, students of history are prepared to comprehend this inexorable process of change in their own lifetimes, as the world races forward toward an uncertain destiny.

- **For a list of suggested readings for this chapter, visit** *bedfordstmartins.com/mckayworldunderstanding*.

- **For primary sources from this period, see** *Sources of World Societies*, Second Edition.

- **For Web sites, images, and documents related to topics in this chapter, see Make History at** *bedfordstmartins.com/ mckayworldunderstanding*.

What are the consequences of increasing global interdependence?   What are the causes and consequences of worldwide urbanization?   How have developments in science and technology changed the world?   What social problems do women and children face?

Chapter 34 Study Guide

To do these exercises online, go to bedfordstmartins.com/mckayworldunderstanding.

To do these exercises online, go to bedfordstmartins.com/mckayworldunderstanding.

GETTING STARTED

Below are basic terms about this period in global history. Can you identify each term below and explain why it matters?

TERMS	WHO (OR WHAT) AND WHEN	WHY IT MATTERS
United Nations, p. 926		
Security Council, p. 926		
General Assembly, p. 926		
middle powers, p. 929		
terrorism, p. 930		
multinational corporations, p. 936		
mixed economy, p. 938		
neo-Malthusian, p. 938		
green revolution, p. 938		
megacities, p. 942		
urbanization without industrialization, p. 942		
economic growth without economic development, p. 943		
bazaar economy, p. 943		
global warming, p. 948		
feminization of poverty, p. 949		

MOVING BEYOND THE BASICS

The exercise below requires a more advanced understanding of the chapter material. Compare and contrast the impact of global trends on Asia, Africa, and Latin America by filling in the chart below with descriptions of the impact in the following key areas: urbanization, population growth, and technology and science. When you are finished, consider the following questions: In what ways has the social and economic history of these three regions converged in recent decades? In what ways has it diverged? How would you explain the patterns you note?

	URBANIZATION	POPULATION GROWTH	TECHNOLOGICAL AND SCIENTIFIC DEVELOPMENTS
Asia			
Africa			
Latin America			

PUTTING IT ALL TOGETHER

Now that you've reviewed key elements of the chapter, take a step back and try to see the big picture. Remember to use specific examples from the chapter in your answers.

GLOBAL POLITICS AND INTERDEPENDENCE

- What larger trends are reflected in the emergence of terrorism as a threat to nations around the world?
- What particular challenges do multinational corporations pose to developing nations?

SOCIAL, TECHNOLOGICAL, AND SCIENTIFIC CHANGE

- What connections are there between urbanization and population growth in Asia, Africa, and Latin America?
- What challenges and opportunities have been created by recent advances in science and technology?

SOCIAL REFORM AND PROGRESS

- Why do women and children remain the most vulnerable populations on the planet?
- What might explain recent findings that show increases in violence against women?

LOOKING BACK, LOOKING AHEAD

- Compare and contrast global conditions in 1900 and 2000. What are the most important differences? How would you explain them?
- A hundred years from now, will the nation-state still be the basic unit of social and political organization? Why or why not?

In Your Own Words Imagine that you must explain Chapter 34 to someone who hasn't read it. What would be the most important points to include and why?

Chapter Endnotes

Chapter 16

1. Quoted in C. M. Cipolla, *Guns, Sails, and Empires: Technological Innovation and the Early Phases of European Expansion, 1400–1700* (New York: Minerva Press, 1965), p. 132.
2. Thomas Benjamin, *The Atlantic World: Europeans, Africans, Indians and Their Shared History, 1400–1900* (Cambridge, U.K.: Cambridge University Press, 2009), pp. 35–59.
3. Quoted in C. Gibson, ed., *The Black Legend: Anti-Spanish Attitudes in the Old World and the New* (New York: Knopf, 1971), pp. 74–75.
4. Herbert S. Klein, "Profits and the Causes of Mortality," in *The Atlantic Slave Trade*, ed. David Northrup (Lexington, Mass.: D. C. Heath and Co., 1994), p. 116.
5. C. Cotton, trans., *The Essays of Michel de Montaigne* (New York: A. L. Burt, 1893), pp. 207, 210.
6. Ibid., p. 523.

Chapter 17

1. Theodore K. Rabb, *The Struggle for Stability in Early Modern Europe* (Oxford: Oxford University Press, 1975).
2. H. Kamen, "The Economic and Social Consequences of the Thirty Years' War," *Past and Present* 39 (April 1968): 44–61.
3. Quoted in John A. Lynn, *Giant of the Grand Siècle: The French Army, 1610–1715* (Cambridge, U.K.: Cambridge University Press, 1997), p. 74.
4. H. Rosenberg, *Bureaucracy, Aristocracy, and Autocracy: The Prussian Experience, 1660–1815* (Boston: Beacon Press, 1966), p. 40.
5. For a revisionist interpretation, see J. Wormald, "James VI and I: Two Kings or One?" *History* 62 (June 1983): 187–209.
6. Geoffrey Vaughn Scammel, *The First Imperial Age: European Overseas Expansion, c. 1400–1715* (London and New York: Routledge, 2002), p. 432.

Chapter 18

1. H. Butterfield, *The Origins of Modern Science* (New York: Macmillan, 1951), p. viii.
2. Ibid., p. 120.
3. Quoted in G. L. Mosse et al., eds., *Europe in Review* (Chicago: Rand McNally, 1964), p. 156.
4. See E. Fox-Genovese, "Women in the Enlightenment," in *Becoming Visible: Women in European History*, 2d ed., ed. R. Bridenthal, C. Koonz, and S. Stuard (Boston: Houghton Mifflin, 1987), esp. pp. 252–259, 263–265.
5. R. Heilbroner, *The Essential Adam Smith* (New York: W. W. Norton, 1986), p. 281.
6. Laurent Dubois and John D. Garrigus, *Slave Revolution in the Caribbean, 1789–1904* (New York: Palgrave, 2006), p. 8.
7. Orlando Patterson, *Slavery and Social Death* (Cambridge, Mass.: Harvard University Press, 1982), p. 255.
8. Erik R. Seeman, "Jews in the Early Modern Atlantic: Crossing Boundaries, Keeping Faith," in *The Atlantic in Global History, 1500–2000*, ed. Jorge Canizares-Esguerra and Erik R. Seeman (Upper Saddle River, N.J.: Pearson Prentice-Hall, 2007), p. 43.

Chapter 19

1. Quoted in R. Hallett, *Africa to 1875* (Ann Arbor: University of Michigan Press, 1970), p. 151.
2. See A. J. Russell-Wood, *The Portuguese Empire: A World on the Move* (Baltimore: Johns Hopkins University Press, 1998), pp. 35–38.
3. P. E. Lovejoy, *Transformations in Slavery: A History of Slavery in Africa* (Cambridge, U.K.: Cambridge University Press, 1992), p. 25, Table 2.1, "Trans-Saharan Slave Trade, 650–1600."
4. J. Iliffe, *Africans: The History of a Continent* (Cambridge, U.K.: Cambridge University Press, 2007), p. 77.
5. See D. Eltis, *The Rise of African Slavery in the Americas* (Cambridge, U.K.: Cambridge University Press, 2000), Chap. 3; and the review/commentary by J. E. Inikori, *American Historical Review* 106, no. 5 (December 2001): 1751–1753.
6. R. Blackburn, *The Making of New World Slavery: From the Baroque to the Modern, 1492–1800* (New York: Verso, 1998), pp. 79–80.
7. R. E. Conrad, *Children of God's Fire: A Documentary History of Black Slavery in Brazil* (Princeton, N.J.: Princeton University Press, 1983), pp. 20–23.
8. *Equiano's Travels: The Interesting Narrative of the Life of Olaudah Equiano*, ed. P. Edwards (Portsmouth, N.H.: Heinemann, 1996), pp. 23–26.
9. James A. Rawley and Stephen D. Behrendt, *The Transatlantic Slave Trade*, rev. ed. (Lincoln, Neb.: University of Nebraska Press, 2005), pp. 45–47.
10. Robert W. July, *A History of the African People* (Prospect Heights, Ill.: Waveland Press, 1998), p. 171.
11. A. G. Hopkins, *An Economic History of West Africa* (New York: Columbia University Press, 1973), p. 119.
12. P. Manning, *Slavery and African Life: Occidental, Oriental, and African Slave Trades* (New York: Cambridge University Press, 1990), pp. 22–23 and Chap. 3, pp. 38–59.

Chapter 22

1. G. Pernoud and S. Flaisser, eds., *The French Revolution* (Greenwich, Conn.: Fawcett, 1960), p. 61.
2. Quoted in L. Gershoy, *The Era of the French Revolution, 1789–1799* (New York: Van Nostrand, 1957), p. 150.
3. T. Blanning, *The French Revolutionary Wars, 1787–1802* (London: Arnold, 1996), pp. 116–128.

Chapter 23

1. N. F. R. Crafts, *British Economic Growth During the Industrial Revolution* (Oxford, U.K.: Oxford University Press, 1985), p. 32.
2. P. Bairoch, "International Industrialization Levels from 1750 to 1980," *Journal of European Economic History* 11 (Spring 1982): 269–333.
3. Crafts, *British Economic Growth*, p. 95.
4. Quoted in E. R. Pike, *"Hard Times": Human Documents of the Industrial Revolution* (New York: Praeger, 1966), p. 109.
5. Quoted in Pike, *"Hard Times,"* p. 208.

6. Quoted in D. Geary, ed., *Labour and Socialist Movements in Europe Before 1914* (Oxford, U.K.: Berg, 1989), p. 29.
7. Kenneth Pomeranz, *The Great Divergence: China, Europe, and the Making of the Modern World Economy* (Princeton, N.J.: Princeton University Press, 2000).

Chapter 24

1. E. Gellner, *Nations and Nationalism* (Oxford, U.K.: Basil Blackwell, 1983), pp. 19–39.
2. B. Anderson, *Imagined Communities: Reflections on the Origins and Spread of Nationalism,* rev. ed. (London and New York: Verso, 1991).
3. Quoted in R. P. Neuman, "The Sexual Question and Social Democracy in Imperial Germany," *Journal of Social History* 7 (Winter 1974): 281.

Chapter 25

1. P. Lovejoy, *Transformations in Slavery: A History of Slavery in Africa,* 2d ed. (Cambridge, U.K.: Cambridge University Press, 2000), p. 142.
2. Ibid., p. 15.
3. Rudyard Kipling, *The Five Nations* (London, 1903).
4. Quoted in Earl of Cromer, *Modern Egypt* (London, 1911), p. 48.

Chapter 26

1. R. Tsunoda, W. T. de Bary, and D. Keene, eds., *Sources of Japanese Tradition,* vol. 2 (New York: Columbia University Press, 1964), p. 137.

Chapter 27

1. See B. Keen and M. Wasserman, *A Short History of Latin America* (Boston: Houghton Mifflin, 1980), pp. 109–115.
2. M. Burkholder and D. S. Chandler, *From Impotence to Authority: The Spanish Crown and the American Audiencias, 1687–1808* (Columbia: University of Missouri Press, 1977), p. 145.
3. Gary E. Moulton, ed., *The Papers of Chief John Ross,* vol. 1, 1807–1839 (Norman: University of Oklahoma Press, 1985).
4. Quoted in S. E. Morison, *The Oxford History of the American People* (New York: Oxford University Press, 1965), p. 654.

Chapter 28

1. Svetlana Palmer and Sarah Wallis, eds., *Intimate Voices from the First World War* (New York: William Morrow, 2003), p. 221.

2. Quoted in H. Nicolson, *Peacemaking 1919* (New York: Grosset & Dunlap Universal Library, 1965), pp. 8, 31–32.

Chapter 29

1. Quoted in W. T. deBary, W. Chan, and B. Watson, *Sources of Chinese Tradition* (New York: Columbia University Press, 1964), pp. 768–769.
2. Quoted in B. I. Schwartz, *Chinese Communism and the Rise of Mao* (Cambridge, Mass.: Harvard University Press, 1951), p. 74.

Chapter 30

1. Quoted in S. B. Clough et al., eds., *Economic History of Europe: Twentieth Century* (New York: Harper & Row, 1968), pp. 243–245.
2. R. Vivarelli, "Interpretations of the Origins of Fascism," *Journal of Modern History* 63 (March 1991): 41.
3. W. Brustein, *The Logic of Evil: The Social Origins of the Nazi Party, 1925–1933* (New Haven, Conn.: Yale University Press, 1996), pp. 52, 182.
4. J. Dower, *War Without Mercy: Race and Power in the Pacific War* (New York: Pantheon, 1986).

Chapter 31

1. Quoted in D. Treadgold, *Twentieth Century Russia,* 5th ed. (Boston: Houghton Mifflin, 1981), p. 442.

Chapter 32

1. Syed Sharifuddin Pirzada, ed., *Foundations of Pakistan: All-India Muslim League Documents.* Vol. 2: *1924–1947* (Karachi: National Publishing House, 1970), p. 338.
2. Quoted in K. Bhata, *The Ordeal of Nationhood: A Social Study of India Since Independence, 1947–1970* (New York: Atheneum, 1971), p. 9.

Chapter 33

1. C. Achebe, *Things Fall Apart* (London: Heinemann, 2000), pp. 124–125.

Chapter 34

1. D. Rappaport, "The Fourth Wave: September 11 in the History of Terrorism," *Current History,* December 2001, pp. 419–424.
2. J. Diamond, *Collapse: How Societies Choose to Fail or Survive* (New York: Viking, 2004), pp. 524–525.

Index

A Note About the Index: Key terms and the pages where they are defined appear in boldface. Letters in parentheses following page numbers refer to:

(i) illustrations, including photographs and artifacts

(f) figures, including charts, graphs, and tables

(m) maps

(b) boxed features

Abacha, Sani (Nigeria), 912
Abbas I ("the Great," Persia), 519*(i)*, 526, 529, 532*(i)*, 539
Abbas, Mahmoud, 886–887
Abbasid caliphate (Islam), Turks and, 520
Abduh, Muhammad, 684–686
Abdülhamid (Sultan), 683
Abolition
    of English slave trade, 507, 668
    of Russian serfdom, 736–737
    of slave trade, 513, 514, 629
    in United States, 584, 668, 735–738
Aboriginal peoples. *See* Aborigines; Native Americans
Aborigines (Australia), 742
Abortion, 816, 946
Abrahamic religions, 891*(m)*
Absolutism, 439–443
    in Austria, 445, 682
    in Bohemia, 445
    in central and eastern Europe, 444–452
    in England, 452
    enlightened, 478–480
    in France, 439–442
    in Prussia, 446–447, 447–452
    in Russia, 682
    in Spain, 442–443
Abstract art, 776
Academies, of science, 471
Achebe, Chinua, 920
Acoma Indians, 721*(i)*
Adal (Muslim state), 500
Adenauer, Konrad, 844
Administration. *See also* Government
    of China, 548
    of Mughal India, 527
    of Spanish colonies, 422–423
Adolescents. *See* Young people
al-Afghani, Jamal al-Din, 684
Afghanistan
    al-Qaeda in, 933
    Amanullah Khan in, 790*(m)*, 791
    Babur in, 527
    civil war in, 929

Marathas and, 542
modernization of, 791
refugees from, 881
Safavid Empire and, 540
Soviets and, 850, 859, 880
Taliban in, 932
warfare in, 929
Africa. *See also* Slavery; Slave trade; Sub-Saharan Africa; Trans-Saharan trade; specific locations
    Asian trade with, 502*(i)*
    Christianity in, 680
    communications in, 918*(i)*
    decolonization in, 845, 906–910, 911*(m)*
    democracy in, 911–912, 918
    demography of slave trade in, 513
    disruption by imperialism, 911
    Dutch and, 459
    Europe and, 492, 663, 672–677
    First World War and, 757
    Germany and, 753
    in global South, 896
    government in, 919
    Great Depression and, 808, 811–812
    HIV/AIDS in, 946, 947, 947*(m)*
    human rights in, 918
    independence in, 906–908, 910–920
    Indians and, 538, 714
    indigo in, 689*(b)*
    Islam in, 669–672
    nationalism in, 812, 907–908
    neocolonialism in, 845
    new imperialism in, 666
    oil and natural gas in, 919
    partition of, 671*(m)*
    political reform since 1990, 915–919
    Portuguese in, 415
    resistance to imperialism in, 681
    scramble for (1880–1914), 672–674
    secondary education in, 951
    Second World War in, 825*(m)*
    slavery and, 668–669
    slave trade and, 411, 512–514
    socialism and, 937
    society in, 492, 494*(m)*
    southern, 913–915
    in Third World, 687
    trade in, 409–412
    trade routes in, 514
    urban migration and family in, 944
    warfare in, 929
    wealth gap in cities, 943
    women from, 460–461
"Africa for the Africans," 907

African Americans, 584, 735–738, 808*(i)*, 857. *See also* Africans; Blacks; Slavery
African liberation forces, in Angola and Mozambique, 913
African National Congress (ANC), 914, 915
Africans. *See also* Slavery
    in Haiti, 600
    as slaves, 425
Africanus, Leo, 496
Afrikaners (South Africa), **674**–675, 753, 793, 913
Afro-Asian Conference (Bandung, Indonesia), 882
Afroeurasia, trade in, 408, 409–412, 411*(m)*
Age-grade systems, in Senegambia, **495**
Age of anxiety, 1920s as, 773–777
Age of crisis, 17th century as, 436–439
Age of Discovery (1450–1650), 406
Agra
    Armenians in, 539
    Babur's capture of, 527
    Taj Mahal in, 529
Agribusiness, multinational, 944
Agricultural Adjustment Act (1933), 810
Agriculture. *See also* Farms and farming; Plantations
    African slavery and, 507
    in Australia, 744
    in Canada, 742
    in China, 549, 871, 873
    collectivization of, 815, 848
    consumer revolution and, 483
    in Egypt, 685*(b)*
    Great Depression and, 808, 810
    Green Revolution and, 938–940
    in India, 696–697
    Industrial Revolution and, 608
    in Japan, 564
    in Mexico, 899
    New World crops and, 537
    in Palestine, 792
    population and, 938
    Soviet, 815–816, 848, 849
    urbanization and, 944–945
    in West Africa, 498, 499
Ahmad, Muhammad, 673
Ahmad ibn-Ghazi (Adal), 500
Ahmadinejad, Mahmoud, 892
AIDS. *See* HIV/AIDS
Airplanes, in Second World War, 824
Air pollution. *See* Environment
Air pump, 467
Aisne, Second Battle of the, 763

Akbar (Mughal India), 527, 529
Armenians and, 539
building by, 529
Muslim-Hindu accommodation by, 535
Albania, 859
Alberta, in Dominion of Canada, 741, 741(m)
Alcibar, José de, 460(i)
Alcohol, working classes and, 652
Alexander I (Russia), 596, 599, 634(i)
Alexander II (Russia), 648
Alexander VI (Pope), 418
Alexandra (Russia), 764
Alexandria, riots in, 686
Alexis (Russia), 764
Algebra, 467, 470
Algeria
France and, 682, 909
Ottomans in, 521
Second World War in, 832
white settlers in, 909
Algorithm, 467
Ali (Islam), Islamic succession and, 525
Allende, Salvador, 902
Alliance(s). See also specific alliances
Axis, 822
Bismarckian system of, 752–754
after 1880s, 691
in First World War, 752–754, 752(m)
Japanese, 829–830
Lucknow Pact as, 792
Quadruple, 634
Safavid, 526
Alliance for Germany, 855
Allies (First World War), 750
at Paris Peace Conference, 767–768
Allies (Second World War), 825(m), 831(m), 832
in Japan, 838, 859–860
Normandy invasion by, 832–833, 833(i)
Alphabet, Turkish, 790
al-Qaeda, 881, 932–933
nuclear weapons and, 935
September 11, 2001, terrorist attacks by, 932, 932(i)
Alsace, 659
Alsace-Lorraine, after First World War, 769
Altan Khan (Mongolia), 551
Alternate residence system (Japan), **560**
Amanullah Khan (Afghanistan), 790(m), 791
Amaterasu-o-Mikami (god), 829(b)
Amazon River region, peoples of, 732
Ambassadors
Chinese embassies and, 705
in France, 441(i)
Amendments, to U.S. Constitution, 584
America(s). See also Latin America
Australia compared with, 745–746
colonies in, 422–427
Columbus and, 416–417, 416(m)
Creoles in, 484
European colonies in, 458–461

European conquest of, 412–427
indigo plantations in, 688(b)
naming of, 417
nation building in, 720
slaves in, 514
American Indians. See Native Americans
American Revolution, 576, 582–584
France and, 583, 584
Latin American wars of independence and, 726
liberalism and, 635
Loyalists and, 583(m), 740
Amhara, Ethiopia, Galla occupation of, 500
Amin, Qasim, 686
Amistad, 667(i)
Amritsar Massacre, 793
Amsterdam, 457(m)
Analytic geometry, 470
Anatolia, 520. See also Turkey
Ottomans in, 520
Ottomans vs. Safavids in, 521
ANC. See African National Congress
Andalusia. See also Spain
Muslims in, 521
Andes region. See also Inca Empire
Indian rebellions in, 725
Andorra, 859
Anglican Church, in England, 453, 454, 455
Anglo-Asante wars, 676
Anglo-Boer War. See South African War
Anglo-French Entente (1904), 753
Anglo-German rivalry, 753
Anglo-Iranian Oil Company, 890
Anglo-Persian Oil Company, 790
Anglo-Russian Agreement, 753
Angola, 502, 913, 919
independence for, 913
slavery and, 507, 513
warfare in, 929
Ankara, Turkey, 787
Annan, Kofi, 919, 930(b)
on arms trade, 935(b)
on United Nations Millennium Project Report, 930 (b)
Anne of Austria, 440
Annexation, of Texas, 733
Anthills of the Savannah (Achebe), 920
Anticolonialism, Great Depression and, 808
Anticommunism, 844, 856, 915–916
Antifederalists (U.S.), **583**–584
Anti-imperialism, 666, 681
Anti-Semitism. See also Jews and Judaism; Nazi Germany
Dreyfus affair and, 660
in Russia, 661(i)
Antislavery sentiment, in United States, 672, 735
Antisocialism, fascism and, 814
Antitrust regulations, in Japan, 860
Antiwar movement, in Vietnam War, 858
Anxiety. See Age of Anxiety
Apartheid, 675, **914**
Appeasement, of Hitler, 822, 823

Apple computers, 948
Apprenticeships, for children, 610–611
Aquinas. See Thomas Aquinas (Saint)
Aquino, Corazón (Philippines), 876
Arabi, Ahmed (Egypt), 686
Arabian Sea region, 426, 537
Arabic language
in Islamic empires, 528
scientific texts in, 467
Swahili from, 501
Arab-Israeli conflicts, 884, 885(m)
in 1948, 884
Six-Day War (1967) as, 884, 887
Yom Kippur War (1973) as, 846(b), 847–848, 884
Arab League, 884, 887, 889
Arab movement, 786
Arabs and Arab world. See also Islam; Jews and Judaism; Middle East; Moors; Muslims; Palestine
after First World War, 770, 782(i)
in First World War, 757
independence for, 786, 791
Islamic fundamentalism and, 932–933
Jews and, 791–792
nationalism in, 883, 884
nuclear weapons and, 934
oil and, 791
Omani Arabs and, 502
Ottoman rule in, 786
PLO and, 884
revolt by, 784, 786–787
trade and, 408
Turks and, 786
Arab Spring, 835, 887–888
Arafat, Yasir, 884, 886
Arawak language, 416
Architecture
Chicago School of, 775
gardens and, 530–532
of Islamic cities and palaces, 529
of Jahan (Mughal Empire), 529
in Mexico, 898(i)
modernism in, 775–776
tiles for, 532(i)
Argentina, 722
American financing in, 727
debt default in, 903
"dirty war" in, 902
economy in, 903
Falklands war and, 902–903
government of, 902
by 1914, 746
radio in, 776–777
in UNSAN, 906
Arguin, North Africa, Portuguese in, 415
Aristide, Jean-Bertrand, 906
Aristocracy. See Elites; Nobility
Aristotle, on universe, 466, 466(i)
Arkwright, Richard, 609, 610
Armed forces. See also Military; Soldiers; specific battles and wars
in British North America, 582

in France, 591–592, 594, 595, 596–597, 599
in Iran, 790
in Lebanon, 889
Ottoman, 682–683
in Prussia, 447
in Russia, 449
in Russian civil war, 767
Armenia and Armenian people
after First World War, 785(m)
genocide against, 786
Persia and, 539
trade and, 539
Turks and, 786, 787
Armenian Christians, Safavids and, 535, 539
Armistice, in First World War, 768
Arms and armaments. See Nuclear weapons; Weapons
Arms race. See Nuclear arms race
Arms trade, 934–935(b), 935(m)
Army Order No. 1 (Russia), 765
Arouet, François Marie. See Voltaire
Arranged marriage. See also Marriage
in China, 798, 799(b)
Art(s). See also specific art(s)
in Benin, 496, 496(i)
in France, 441
Islamic, 528–529
in Mexico, 898(i)
modernism in, 775–776
postwar anxieties in, 774–777
rococo style in, 477
romanticism in, 657
Soviet, 816, 848
Artisans
capitalists and, 628
in industry, 627–628
production by, 618
Asante kingdom, 676
Ashikaga Shogunate (Japan), 558
Ashley Mines Commission, 626(b)
Asia. See also Middle East; specific locations
African trade with, 502(i)
Christianity in, 713
Cold War in, 843, 843(m)
common experiences in societies of, 716–717
decolonization in, 845
distance from, Europe, 414
economic tigers in, 875–876
emigration from, 713–714, 714(i), 714(m)
Europeans and, 565–572, 663
European trade with, 406
First World War and, 757
Great Depression and, 808
green revolution and, 938
HIV/AIDS in, 946, 947, 947(m)
immigration to Australia from, 745
immigration to Latin America from, 731–732
imperialism in, 694
independence in, 868

indigo in, 688–689(b)
Japanese empire in, 826–832, 831(m)
migration from, 690
movement of peoples within and out of, 712–715
nationalism in, 782–784, 795–803
new imperialism in, 666
in 1914, 698(m)
Portuguese trade and, 415
resistance to imperialism in, 681
Soviet communism and, 783–784
states in, 870(m)
students from, 715
in Third World, 687
trade with, 412, 416
urban migration and family in, 944
wealth gap in cities, 943
Westerners in, 712–713
Asiento, 444(m)
Assault, The, Verdun (Groux), 758(i)
Assemblies. See also Estates (assemblies)
Dutch, 457
in France, 585–586
in Russia, 649
Assembly lines, in China, 557
Assignats (currency), 590
Assimilation, in French colonies, 910
Astrolabe, 414
Astrology, 467
Astronomy, 467
Arabic text translations of, 467
exploration and, 414
Galileo and, 469
Islamic, 532
Ptolemy on, 414, 466, 469
Atahualpa (Inca), 422
Atatürk. See Kemal, Mustafa
Atlantic Ocean region. See also Exploration; Transatlantic trade
consumerism and, 482–488
economy of, 483–484, 485(m)
English settlements in, 458
exploration of, 420
identities and communities in, 484–487
revolutions in, 576–603
slavery and, 488
slave trade in, 412
Atmospheric nuclear testing, 933
Atomic bomb, 834, 834(i), 933. See also Nuclear weapons
Auctions, slave, 736(i)
Audiencia (judges), 423
Audubon Society, 947
Auerstädt, battle at, 596
Augsburg, Peace of, 437, 438
Aung San Suu Kyi, 878–879(b), 879(i)
Aurangzeb (India), 527, 535, 542
Auschwitz, 827(b)
Austerlitz, Battle of, 596
Australia, 743(m). See also Aborigines
Americas compared with, 745–746
Asians in, 715
Chinese emigrants to, 713

Commonwealth of, 745
economy in, 744–745
First World War and, 747, 757
gold in, 745
government of, 745
Great Depression and, 809(f)
growth of, 742–745
identity in, 745
immigration to, 743, 744(i)
nation building in, 720
in 19th century, 720
by 1914, 746
as penal colony, 742–744
racism in, 742, 745
in Second World War, 833, 834
Australian Colonies Government Act (Britain, 1850), 745
Austria. See also Austria-Hungary; Habsburg Dynasty
absolutism in, 682
annexations in Balkan region, 754
anti-Semitism in, 661–662
Austrian Empire and, 635, 642–643
Bismarck alliance with, 753
dual revolution and, 635
First World War and, 755, 757, 768, 770
France and, 591, 596, 599
German unification and, 645
in Grand Alliance, 442
growth to 1748, 446(m)
Habsburg Dynasty in, 445
Hitler and, 823
Jews in, 821
nationalism and, 637
Nazi Germany and, 823
partition of Poland and, 480(m)
Prussia and, 643
in Quadruple Alliance, 634
Sardinia and, 645
in Triple Alliance, 753
War of the Austrian Succession and, 478, 580, 584
Austria-Hungary
end of, 768
First World War and, 767
Francis Ferdinand assassination and, 755
industrialization and, 616
nationalism in, 660–661, 754
before 1914, 753
socialism in, 662
Austrian Netherlands, France and, 591
Austro-Hungarian Empire. See Austria-Hungary
Austronesian language-speakers, 409
Austro-Prussian War, 645–647, 647(m)
Authoritarianism, 806. See also Dictators and dictatorships
in Africa, 912
conservative, 812, 813
in Italy, 817
in Japan, 708
in Latin America, 902–906, 903(m)
of Putin (Russia), 862–863, 862(i)

Autobiography (Garibaldi), 646(b)
Automobiles
    oil use for, 846(b)
    in United States, 846(b)
Autumn Harvest Uprising (China, 1927), 798
Auxiliary Service Law (Germany), 759
Avian influenza (bird flu), 946
Axis powers (Second World War), 822, 832, 838
Azores, 414
Azov, Russia and, 521–522
Aztec Empire. *See* Mexica (Aztec) Empire

Babur (Mughal India), 527, 535
Baby boom, 857
Babylon and Babylonia, 846(b)
Bacon, Francis, 470
Bacterial revolution, 650
Baghdad. *See also* Iraq
    Ottomans in, 523
    Safavid capture of, 526
Bahamas, 416
Baku region, oil in, 846(b)
Balanced budget, Ottoman, 523
Balance of power
    after Napoleonic wars, 634–635, 634(i)
    in 19th century, 682
Baldwin, Stanley, 777
Balfour Declaration (1917), 770, **786**, 792
Balkan region. *See also* specific locations
    1878–1914, 754(m)
    before First World War, 754–755, 754(m)
    nationalism in, 683, 754
    before 1914, 753
    Ottomans and, 520, 535, 543, 682(m), 785(m)
    slaves from, 412, 503
Balkan Wars (1912, 1913), 754, 786
Baltic region. *See also* specific locations
    Russia and, 447
    Russian capital in, 450–451
Bananas, in Africa, 498
Bandits. *See* Piracy
Bangladesh, 877, 880–882
Banker-brokers, Islamic, 538
Banking
    in Belgium, 619
    in France, 619, 844
    in Germany, 619
    Great Depression and, 809, 810
    in Japan, 860
    in Mexico, 899
Bankruptcy, in Spain, 443
Banners (Manchu army units), **555**, 557
Bantu language and people, Swahili and, 501
Barbados, 425, 458
Barber, Francis, 503
Barbosa, Duarte, 504–505(b)
Barometer, 467
Bastille, storming of, 586–587

Batavia (Jakarta, Indonesia)
    Armenian merchants in, 539
    China and, 570
Batista, Fulgencio, 900, 901(i)
Battle of Britain, 824
Battles. *See* specific battles and wars
Bauhaus, 776
Bayer, Adolf, 689(b)
Bayle, Pierre, 473
Bay of Pigs, 901
Bazaar economy, 943–944
Beattie, James, 488
Beethoven, Ludwig van, 657
Beeton, Isabella Mary, 654–655(b)
Beijing. *See also* China; Tiananmen Square
    British and French occupation of, 704
    as Chinese capital, 549, 550(i)
    Japanese in, 801
    Manchus in, 555–556
    massacre of demonstrators in, 850
    Taizu in, 548
Beirut, 889. *See also* Lebanon
Belarus, 447, 480
Belgian Congo, 674, 910. *See also* Democratic Republic of the Congo
Belgium, 824
    Africa and, 672
    Coal and Steel Community and, 844
    after First World War, 771
    in First World War, 755, 763(i)
    France and, 591
    independence of, 615
    industrialization in, 615, 618, 619
    as Spanish Netherlands, 444(m)
Bello, Muhammad, 670
Ben Ali, Zine (Tunisia), 887
Bengal, 880(m)
    French in, 539
    indigo from, 688(b)
    Mughal rule in, 527
    nationalism in, 688(b)
Bengali people, in East Pakistan, 880
Benin, 493(i), 494, 495–496
    oba of, 495, 496(i)
    white slaves in, 503
Benin City, 496
Bentley, Thomas, 612
Berbers. *See also* Moors
    as slaves, 412
Berlin. *See also* Germany
    academy of science in, 471
    blockade in, 842–843
    revolution in (1848), 642(i), 643
    in Second World War, 833
Berlin Conference (1884–1885), **672**–673
Berlin Wall, 849, 851(i), 853
Bernstein, Eduard, 662
Bhutto, Benazir, 881, 881(i), 933
Biafra, independence of, 912
Big business, in Japan, 860. *See also* Business; Japan
Bight of Benin, slaves from, 507, 512
Bight of Biafra, slaves from, 507

Big Three, 840–841, 840(i)
Bill of Rights
    in England (1689), 455
    in Japan, 860
    in United States, 583–584
Bin Laden, Osama, 932
Biodiversity, 947–948
Biological and Toxin Weapons Convention (1972), 934(b)
Biological weapons, 933–934, 936
Biology. *See also* Medicine
    Darwin and, 654–656
    human affairs and, 656
    race and, 488
Bird flu, 946
Birth control, 653, 945–946
    birthrates and, 949
    pill for, 946
Birthrates
    declining, 946
    among poor women, 949
Bismarck, Otto von, 645–648, 659, 672, 810
    alliance system of, 752–754
Black Africans, as elite, 676–677
Black Code, in Saint-Domingue, 600
Black Hills region, Indians and, 734
Black nationalism
    in Africa, 907
    Du Bois and, 907
Blackness
    cultural nationalism and, 907–908
    slavery and, 506–507
Blacks. *See also* Africa; African Americans; Slavery
    in First World War, 757
    in Latin America, 723, 727
    in Shakespeare's *Othello*, 430
    as slaves and servants, 503
    in South Africa, 913, 915
    in United States, 735–738
Black Sea region, trade in, 412
Black Shirts (Italy), **818**
Blake, William, 621
Blitzkrieg (lightning war), **824**
Blockades
    in Cuban missile crisis, 849
    in First World War, 758
    by Israel, 887
    Napoleonic, 596, 597
    of West Berlin, 842–843
Blocs, during Cold War, 843
Bloody Sunday (Russia), 649
Board of Astronomy (China), 572
Boats. *See* Ships and shipping
Body. *See* Medicine
Boers, 674
Boer War. *See* South African War
Bogotá, 725
Bohemia, Habsburg rule of, 445
Bohemian phase, of Thirty Years' War, 437
Bolívar, Simón, 725, 903
Bolivarianism, of Chávez, 905

Bolivia, 426
    in UNSAN, 906
Bolshevik Revolution (Russia, 1917),
    765–767, 796
Bolsheviks (Soviet Union), 750, **765**–766.
    See also Communist Party
Bombay (Mumbai), 699
    terrorism in, 883
Bombs and bombings. *See also* Weapons
    atomic bomb, 834, 834(i)
    of North Vietnam, 858
    in Second World War, 824, 834
    of Serbia, 863
    terrorist, 933
Bonaparte family. *See* Napoleon I;
    Napoleon III
Bonny (city), slave trade and, 512, 513
Book(s). *See also* Literature; Novels; Printing
    burning in Nazi Germany, 821
    in China, 553–554
    in Enlightenment, 476–477, 476(i)
    in France, 476(i)
    Indo-Persian, 529
    in Ottoman Empire, 533
Book of Duarte Barbosa, The (Barbosa),
    504–505(b)
Book of the Sea (Piri Reis), 532
Boom and bust cycles, 738
Borders
    of Benin, 495
    French, 442
    Ottoman-Safavid, 523, 525
    U.S.-British colonial, 733
Bosnia
    atrocities in, 835
    civil war in, 927, 929
Bosnia-Herzegovina, 754, 863
Boston Tea Party, 582
Botany Bay, 742, 743
Botswana, 919
Bougainville, Louis-Antoine de,
    486–487(b), 487(i)
Boundaries. *See* Borders
Bourbon Dynasty
    in Italy and Sicily, 644
    in Spain, 444(m)
Bourgeoisie, 578, **639**
Bourke-White, Margaret, 808(i)
Boxers (China), **705**
Boyars (Russian nobility), **447,** 448
Boyle, Robert, and Boyle's law, 471
Boys. *See also* Eunuchs; Men
    in devshirme system, 523
Brahe, Tycho, 468
Branches of government, in United States,
    583
Brandenburg, Prussia and, 445
Brandenburg-Prussia, growth to 1748,
    446(m)
Brass (city), 513
Brazil
    African slavery and, 507
    American financing in, 727

Dutch and, 459
economy in, 900
First World War and, 747
government of, 900
immigrants in, 731
independence of, 725–726
as middle power, 929
modernization of, 900
Montaigne on, 429
Portugal and, 418, 419, 423
racial mix in, 461
slavery in, 425, 506, 727
sugar and, 426, 458
Swiss immigrants in, 731
in UNSAN, 906
Bread, in France, 586
Brest-Litovsk, Treaty of, 766–767
Brezhnev, Leonid, 849, 850, 851, 859
Brezhnev Doctrine, 850
Bride wealth, 409
    in Africa, 498
    in Southeast Asia, 409
Bristol, slave trade in, 511–512
Britain. *See also* England
    African nationalism and, 908
    alliances before First World War, 753
    Battle of, 824
    Canada ceded to, 740
    Crimean War and, 648
    East Asia trade and, 572
    Egypt and, 686, 884
    Falklands and, 902–903
    First World War and, 755, 757, 770, 771,
        772–773
    foreign policy of, 699, 753
    formation of, 608
    Hong Kong and, 703, 875
    India and, 696–699, 712, 792–793,
        794–795, 878–880
    industrialists in, 620
    Iran and, 790
    Iraq and, 791
    Iraq War and, 927, 929
    Jewish immigration to Palestine and, 792
    labor unions in, 662
    liberalism in, 635–637
    liberal reform in, 639–640
    mandates of, 769, 770, 771, 884
    Middle Eastern independence from, 884
    nationalism and, 660
    navy of, 583, 596, 753
    new imperialism by, 677
    nuclear weapons of, 933
    Ottoman Empire and, 786
    Palestine and, 791–792
    Persia and, 790
    population of, 614
    post-colonial African states and, 911–912
    in Quadruple Alliance, 634
    socialism in, 662–663
    South African independence and, 913
    Spanish trade and, 722
    Suez Canal and, 786

worker movement in, 618
world economy and, 687
British Columbia, 741
British East Africa Railway, 690(i)
British East India Company, 537
    American colonies and, 582
    Armenian merchants and, 539
    British Empire and, 539–540
    British in, 712
    in India, 536(m), 696
    indigo trade by, 688(b)
British Empire. *See also* Britain; Colonies
        and colonization; England
    in Burma, 699
    economic motives in, 677
    in India, 539–540, 696–699
    in Malaya, 699
    in southern Africa, 674
British North America, colonies in, 484,
    581–584
British West Indies. *See* West Indies
British Women's Social and Political Union,
    633(i)
Brittain, Edward, 762(b)
Brittain, Vera, 762(b), 762(i)
Brown, Ford Maddox, 621(i)
Brown v. Board of Education (1954), 857
Budapest, 849, 863
Budget deficits. *See* Deficits; Finances
Buenos Aires, 722, 731(i)
    immigrants to, 731–732
Buffon, Comte de (Georges-Louis Leclerc),
    488
Buildings. *See* Architecture
Bulgaria, 841
    First World War and, 757, 770
    Ottomans in, 520
Bullion. *See also* Gold; Silver
    from South America, 499
Bureaucracy
    in China, 549
    of EU, 863, 865
    in Europe, 434
    in France, 595
    in India, 698, 699
    in Japan, 860
    Mughal, 527
    in Prussia, 447
    in Russia, 449
Burke, Edmund, 590
Burma
    Britain and, 699
    government in, 876
Bursa, Anatolia, 520
Burundi
    atrocities in, 835, 919
    Second Congo War and, 919
    warfare in, 929
Bush, George W.
    Iraq War and, 927–928
    on Turkey, 890
    weapons of mass destruction and, 927,
        933

Business. *See also* Commerce; Multinational corporations; Trade
in Japan, 562, 860
in Russia, 862
Byzantine Empire. *See also* Constantinople
Ottomans and, 520–521
Russia and, 447–448
Byzantium (city). *See* Byzantine Empire; Constantinople

Cabot, John, 420
Cabral, Pedro Alvares, 418, 507
Cabrera, Miguel, 722(i)
Cairo, 684, 684(i)
Cajamarca, 422
Calabar, 512
Calcutta (Kolkata), 537, 699
Caldera, Rafael, 905
Calicut, India, 408, 416
California
Chinese emigrants to, 713
Spain and, 483
as U.S. state, 733
Caliphs and caliphates, Sokoto, 670–672
Callao-Lima-Oroya railroad, 730, 730(i)
Calvin, John, and Calvinism, 438
Cambodia (Kampuchea). *See also* French Indochina
in French Indochina, 700
genocide in, 835
government in, 876
independence of, 877
UN peacekeeping in, 926(i)
Camp David Accords (1979), 884, 887
Canada
Asian immigration certificate for, 715(i)
Asians in, 713, 715
confederation in, 741
development of, 740–742
Dominion of, 741, 741(m)
economy in, 742
England and, 580
First World War and, 747
French cession to Britain, 740
French colonies in, 420, 442
immigration to, 714, 742
in NAFTA, 906
in 19th century, 720
by 1914, 746
population of, 741–742
Canadian Pacific Railroad, 741
Canals. *See also* Suez Canal
in Egypt, 685(b)
in England, 608
Canary Islands, 412, 425
Canning, in United States, 738
Cannons, in Japan, 559
Canon of Problems, 552
Canon of the Pulse, 552
Canton, China. *See* Guangzhou
Cape Colony, 503, 506(m), 674
Dutch hierarchy in, 505–506
slavery in, 503–504, 674

Cape of Good Hope, 415
Cape Town, 674, 914(i)
Capital (financial), in Latin America, 727
Capitalism. *See also* Industrialization; Industrial Revolution
in China, 873
after Cold War, 861
in continental Europe, 618
exploitation by, 940
Hitler on, 820
in India, 883
in Japan, 561–562, 860
merchant-capitalists and, 609
in Russia, 862
slave trade and, 512
welfare, 861
Caravan trade, trans-Saharan, 494
Caravel, 414
Carbon dioxide emissions, 948
Cárdenas, Lázaro, 899
Cardoso, Fernando, 900
Caribbean region. *See also* Haiti
Asian emigrants to, 713–714
authoritarianism in, 903(m)
Dutch and, 459
England and, 459
France and, 459, 580, 601
immigrants to, 731
Indian migrants to, 714
mixed-race progeny in, 487
slavery and, 425, 601
sugar from, 723
trade in, 484
Carlsbad Decrees (1819), 635
Carpets
in Islamic empires, 528
miniature painting and, 529
Persian, 528, 528(i)
Carson, Rachel, 947
Carter, Jimmy, 859, 884
Cartesian dualism, 470
Cartier, Jacques, 420
Cartography
exploration and, 414
of Piri Reis, 532
Cartwright, Edmund, 610
Cash economy
in colonial Africa, 676
in Japan, 561
Caspian Sea region, oil in, 846(b)
Cassava (manioc), 498
Castes. *See also* Caste system (India); Class
janissaries as, 682
Caste system (India), 697–699. *See also* Class
Sikhs and, 533
untouchables in, 882
Castle, The (Kafka), 775
Castles, in Japan, 559, 560, 561
Castro, Fidel, 849, 900–902, 901(i)
Castro, Raúl, 902
Catalonia, revolt in, 443
Catherine the Great (Russia), 478–479, 480, 583

Catholicism. *See* Roman Catholic Church
Catholic League, 437
Cattle, in Argentina, 731
Caucasus region
in First World War, 757
Russia and, 479
white slave women from, 503
Cavour, Camillo Benso di, 644–645
Ceaușescu, Nicolae, 851–852
Celebi, Abi Ahmet, 533
Cell phones, 948
Censorship, of Internet, 948
Central Africa. *See also* Africa
political and economic change in, 919
Central America. *See also* Latin America; specific locations
independence in, 724(m)
Central Asia, Turks in, 520
Central Europe
absolutism in, 444–447
Enlightenment in, 475–476
nationalism in, 637, 657
revolutions of 1848 in, 641–643
romanticism in, 657
Central government. *See* Government
Centralized government. *See also* Absolutism
in Europe, 434
in Japan, 708
Central Powers (First World War), 757, 763–764, 786
Ceramics. *See also* Pottery
in China, 502(i), 557
Cereal crops. *See* Crop(s)
Ceylon, 427, 537. *See also* Sri Lanka
Chad, 919
Chadwick, Edwin, 622, 649–650
Chamberlain, Arthur Neville, 823, 824
Champlain, Samuel de, 458, 740
Charcoal, 611
Charles I (England), 452, 453, 454
Charles I (Spain). *See* Charles V (Holy Roman Empire)
Charles II (England), 454–455, 459
Charles III (Spain), 423, 722
Charles V (Holy Roman Empire; Charles I of Spain), 424
Austria and, 445
exploration and, 417
Magellan and, 418–419
slave trade and, 425
Charter, of UN, 926
Charter '77 group (Czechoslovakia), 854(b)
Charter of Paris for a New Europe, 855–856
Chartist movement (England), 628
Châtelet, marquise du (Gabrielle-Emilie Le Tonnelier de Breteuil), 474
Chattel slavery, 495
Chávez, Hugo, 905
Chechnya, Putin and, 862–863
Cheka, 767
Chelebi, Katib, on tobacco, 530–531(b)

Chemical weapons, 933
        arms trade and, 934–935(b)
        proliferation of, 936
Chemical Weapons Convention, 934(b), 936
Chemistry, 471
Chengzu (Yongle, China), 549
Chennai. See Madras
Cherokee Indians, 734
Cheyenne Indians, 734
Chiang Kai-shek. See Jiang Jieshi
Chicago, immigrants to, 739
Chicago School of architects, 775
Childbearing, limitations on, 653
Child labor, 607(i), 610–611
        in factories, 623, 624
        in mining, 626–627(b), 627(i)
Children. See also Child labor
        books on, 653
        education for, 950–951
        in Indian Ocean region, 409
        middle class, 845
        rights of, 950–951
        sexual division of labor and, 625
        as soldiers, 950, 950(i)
        in West Africa, 498
        in workforce, 623–624
Chile
        Allende in, 902
        American financing in, 727
        government of, 902
        in UNSAN, 906
China. See also Civil service examinations;
        Examination system; Manchuria;
        Mao Zedong; Mongols; Nationalist
        China
        agriculture in, 873
        Christianity in, 571, 713
        civil war in, 842
        communism in, 796, 796(m), 797, 801,
            826, 843, 870–872
        decline in 19th century, 702–706
        economy in, 704–705, 871, 873
        in 18th century, 543
        eunuchs in, 549
        expansion of, 557
        foods in, 554
        foreigners in, 712–713
        Four Modernizations in, 873
        German holdings in, 770
        Great Wall in, 550–551
        green revolution and, 938
        human rights in, 873
        immigrants to Australia, 745
        immigrants to United States from, 739
        immigrants to Latin America, 731
        industrialization in, 615
        industry in, 873
        internal problems of, 704
        Internet in, 948
        Iraq War and, 927
        Japan and, 561, 566, 705, 757, 795,
            796(m), 800–802, 801(i), 826–828
        Korea and, 711

Korean War and, 843, 843(m)
        labor from, 714
        land in, 801
        literature in, 553–554
        under Mao, 871–872
        massacre of demonstrators in (1989),
            850, 873
        medicine in, 552(b), 552(i)
        as middle power, 929
        migrants from, 690
        military in, 548, 557
        Mongolia and, 546, 550, 557
        Mongols and, 546, 550–556
        New Culture Movement in, 797–798
        in 1914, 698(m)
        nuclear weapons of, 933
        oil use by, 846(b), 847(b)
        opium trade and, 696, 703
        Opium War in, 702–704
        patriots in, 797(i)
        peasants in, 873
        Polo and, 416
        population of, 554, 556, 704
        poster art in, 872(i)
        pottery from, 502(i)
        poverty in, 801
        printing in, 553
        Qing (Manchu) Dynasty in, 543, 546,
            555–557
        railroads in, 704, 705(i)
        recreation in, 554
        reforms in, 704–706, 872–873
        republic in, 706
        revolution in (1911), 705, 795
        romance literature in, 553(i)
        Russia and, 557, 648
        self-strengthening movement in,
            704–705
        Shandong Peninsula and, 798
        silver supply in, 555
        silver trade and, 428(b)
        Soviet Union and, 871
        Taiping Rebellion in, 704
        Tibet and, 546, 550–551, 557, 928(b)
        trade and, 557, 566, 570, 702–704
        Turkestan and, 557
        United States and, 873
        West and, 408, 572
        women in, 798, 799(b), 799(i)
        Zheng He's voyages and, 408, 410(b),
            410(i), 411(m), 565–566
Chinese Communist Party, 797, 798, 873
Chinese Exclusion Act (U.S., 1882), 740
Chinese people
        in Peru, 732
        in Philippines, 702
Chinese Renaissance, 797
Chocolate. See Cocoa holdups
Cholera, 650, 650(i), 697
Cholula, 420
Choson Dynasty (Korea), 566–567
Christendom. See Christians and Christianity
Christian existentialists, 773

Christians and Christianity, 891(m). See also
        Coptic Christianity; Jesuits; Missions
        and missionaries; Orthodox Church;
        Protestants and Protestantism;
        Roman Catholic Church; specific
        groups
        in Africa, 672
        Armenians and, 786
        in Asia, 713
        in China, 571
        in East Asia, 570–571
        in Ethiopia, 500–501
        in Japan, 572
        in Lebanon, 888–889
        in Muslim commerce, 539
        new imperialism and, 680
        in New World, 430–431
        Ottoman protection of, 520
        spread of, 413
        in Sudan, 918
        universe and, 466
        in Vietnam, 700
        voyages of exploration and, 416
Christian socialists, in Austria, 661–662
Chulalongkorn (Siam), 700–702
Church(es)
        African American Protestant, 738
        in French Revolution, 590
Churchill, Winston
        on "iron curtain," 842
        Second World War and, 824
        at wartime meetings, 840–841, 840(i)
Church of England. See Anglican Church
CIA, Iran and, 890
Cinqué, Joseph. See Pieh, Sengbe
Circumnavigation
        of globe, 419–420
        of India, 408
Cities and towns. See also Urban areas;
        Urbanization; Villages
        bombing of (Second World War), 824
        in eastern Europe, 437
        industrialization and, 649–658
        Islamic, 529
        Istanbul as, 521
        in Japan, 562
        megacities and, 942
        in Ming China, 553
        in United States, 739
        wealth gap in, 943–944
Citizens and citizenship
        Asians in United States and, 714
        Jews and, 821
City-states
        in Africa, 501, 501(m)
        Swahili, 492
Civic Forum (Czechoslovakia), 854(b)
Civil Code (Napoleon, 1804), 595
Civil Constitution of the Clergy (France),
        590
Civilization(s). See also Culture(s); Imperialism
        concept of, 680
        Western impact on, 708, 710–711(b)

Civil liberties, before Second World War, 806
Civil rights, for Jews, 661
Civil Rights Act (U.S., 1964), **857**
Civil rights movement (U.S.), 857
Civil service. *See also* Bureaucracy; Civil
    service examinations
    in China, 549
    in India, 540, 696, 699
Civil service examinations, 551
    in China, 551, 556
Civil war(s)
    in Afghanistan, 929
    atrocities during, 835
    in Bosnia, 927, 929
    in China, 842
    in England, 452–454, 454(m)
    in former Yugoslavia, 863
    in Japan, 558–559
    in Kosovo, 929
    in Lebanon, 889
    in 1990s, 929
    in Russia, 767, 767(m), 814
    in Rwanda, 929
    in Somalia, 919, 927
    in Spain, 822–823
    in United States, 732, 735–738, 741
    in Vietnam, 877
Class. *See also* Caste system; Elites
    concepts of, by 1850, 621(i)
    dietary changes and, 483
    factory owners as, 620–621
    First World War and, 763
    French estates as, 440
    hierarchies of, 651
    in India, 697–699
    in Japan, 560
    Marx on, 639
    in Mexico, 899
    after Second World War, 845–846
    social hierarchies and, 651
Class-consciousness, 620
Classical economists. *See* Ricardo, David;
    Smith, Adam
Classical liberalism, 584, 635–637
Clemenceau, Georges, 768
Clergy. *See also* Monks and monasteries
    in France, 440, 578, 578(i), 586, 590
Climate. *See also* Little ice age
    of Australia, 742
Clinton, Bill, 861
Cloth and clothing. *See also* Cotton and
    cotton industry; Silk; Textiles and
    textile industry; Weaving
    in England, 609–611
    Indian trade and, 538
    of industrial workers, 622
    weaving and, 611
Coal and coal mining. *See also* Mines and
    mining
    in China, 704
    in Japan, 709
    in United States, 738
    women in, 625

Coal and Steel Community, 844
Cockerill, William and John, 618
Cocoa, in British Africa, 676
Cocoa holdups, 812, 908
Code Noir (Black Code), in Saint-
    Domingue, 600
Codes of law. *See* Law codes
Codex Ixtlilxochitl, 407(i)
Coercive Acts (U.S., 1774), 582
Coffee
    in Brazil, 727, 728
    in India, 697
    from Latin America, 723
    slaves for industry, 507–508
Coffeehouses, 477
    in Islamic world, 533–534
Coins. *See also* Trade
    from Mexico, 429(m)
    in Spain, 443
Coke, 611–613
Colbert, Jean-Baptiste (France), 442, 458
Cold War, 835, 838
    Africa and, 916–917
    in Asia, 843, 843(i)
    détente policy and, 859
    easing of, 849
    end of, 851(i), 855–856, 929
    in Europe (1950s), 842(m)
    German reunification and, 855
    origins of, 840–843
    post–Cold War era, 838, 860–861,
      861–865
    Russia and, 916–917
    Third World in, 868, 929
    United Nations during, 843, 927
    United States and, 916–917
    Vietnam War and, 858
Coleridge, Samuel Taylor, 657
Collective bargaining
    global, 940
    in United States, 810
Collective farms, kibbutz as, 792
Collectivization, 815
    in China, 871
    in Soviet Union, 815–816, 815(i), 848
College. *See* Universities and colleges
Colombia, 722. *See also* Gran Colombia
    government of, 902
    in UNSAN, 906
Colonialism. *See also* Colonies and coloniza-
    tion; Imperialism
    impact after 1900, 675–677
Colonies and colonization
    administration of Spanish, 422–423
    in Africa, 672–677
    African independence and, 906–910
    American independence and, 581–584
    in Americas, 420, 458–461
    in Asia by Western powers, 694
    in Australia, 742–744
    British, 458, 487, 686
    decolonization and, 844–845
    Dutch, 459

    European, 663
    European influence and, 629
    First World War and, 757, 769
    French, 442, 458–459, 660, 700
    German, 753
    Great Depression and, 811–812
    Haitian revolt and, 599–603, 725
    indigo plantations in, 688(b)
    languages in, 745–746
    in Latin America, 415(m), 722–725
    lifestyle in, 459–461
    national self-rule for, 783
    in Philippines, 702
    racism in, 487, 579
    revolutions in, 576
    Second World War and, 830
    slave trade and, 628–629
    in Southeast Asia, 699–702
    Spanish, 442–443, 722
    terrorism and, 931
    in United States, 733
    wars in, 459
"Colored peoples," in Australia, 745
Columbian exchange, 424–425
Columbus, Christopher, 412, 419(i)
    voyages to Americas, 416–417, 416(m),
      418–419(b)
Combination Acts (England, 1799), **628**
"Comfort women," 832
Commerce. *See also* Business; Industrializa-
    tion; Industrial Revolution; Trade
    Dutch, 427, 457, 457(m)
    England and, 572
    in Iran, 790
    in Japan, 561–562
    in Muslim world, 539
    women in, 409
Commercial agriculture, in eastern Europe,
    437
Committee for the Defense of Workers
    (KOR), 852(b)
Committee of Public Safety (France), 592
Common Market, 844
Common people
    in France, 440
    in Japan, 564
    in Russia, 448, 449
Common Sense (Paine), 583
Commonwealth, French, 910
Commonwealth Immigration Restriction
    Act (Australia, 1901), 745
Commonwealth of Australia, 745
Commonwealth of Independent States,
    855(m)
Communication(s), 688
    in Africa, 918(i)
    mass, 948
Communism. *See also* Bolsheviks; Commu-
    nist Party; Marxism
    appeal in 1920s and 1930s, 784
    Asian nationalism and, 783–784
    in China, 796, 796(m), 801, 826, 843,
      870–872, 872(i)

in Cuba, 900–902
in eastern Europe, 841, 873
end of European, 924
in Germany, 820
in Korea, 843
Nazis and, 822
in Philippines, 877
reform, 854(b)
after Second World War, 843
in Soviet Union, 813
Truman on, 841–842
in Vietnam, 877
Communist Manifesto, The (Marx and
    Engels), 639
Communist Party. *See also* Communism;
    Marxism
    in China, 797, 798, 873
    in Czechoslovakia, 849–850
    in East Germany, 853
    in France, 811, 842
    in Germany, 820
    in Hungary, 852
    in Italy, 842
    in Poland, 851
    in Russia, 750, 767
    in Soviet Union, 814, 817, 848, 849, 856
    in Yugoslavia, 848–849
Communist Third International, 796
Community
    in Atlantic world, 484–487
    in Senegambia, 495
Company of the East Indies (France), 442
Compass, 414
Competition, Anglo-German, 753
Computers, 948
Comunero Revolution, 725
Concentration camps
    in Nazi Germany, 821
    in Soviet Union, 849
Concessions, in treaty ports, **704**
Concord, Massachusetts, fighting at, 582
Concordat of 1801, 596
Concubines, 523
    in China, 799(b)
    in Japan, 565
    Ottoman, 523
*Condition of the Working Class in England,
    The* (Engels), 622
Condorcanqui, José Gabriel. *See* Tupac
    Amaru II (Peru)
Confederacy, in U.S. South, **736–738**
Confederation of the Rhine (Germany),
    596, 596(m)
Confederations, 741
    in Canada, 741
Conflict
    in multipolar political system, 929
    rape, sexual violence, and, 949
Confucius and Confucianism, in Vietnam,
    700
Congo. *See also* Kongo kingdom
    Belgian, 674
    Congo Brazzaville, 919

Congo colony, 910
Congo Free State, 672, 673, 673(i), 674
Congo-Kinshasa, 919
    economy of, 919
    France in, 678(b)
    independence for, 910
Congo River region, 672
    slaves from, 507
Congress (U.S.), 584
Congress of Berlin (1878), 754(m)
Congress of People's Deputies (Soviet
    Union), 856
Congress of Vienna (1815), **634,** 644
Congress system, in Europe, 635
Connecticut colony, 458
Conquest. *See* Colonies and colonization;
    Exploration
Conquistadors, 420
Conscription. *See* Draft (military)
Conservatism, 635
    challenges to European (1815–1848),
        634–639
    French Revolution and, 590
Conservative authoritarianism, 812, 813,
    817
Conservative Party (England), 811(i)
Constantine IX Palaeologus (Byzantine
    Empire), 520
Constantinople. *See also* Istanbul
    First World War and, 757, 787
    Ottoman control of, 520
    Russia and, 447
Constituent Assembly
    in France, 640
    in Russia, 766
Constitution(s). *See also* Constitution (U.S.)
    in EU, 865
    in France, 589–590
    in India, 882
    in Japan, 708, 859–860
    in Nigeria, 912
    in Prussia, 643
    in Russia, 649
    in Venezuela, 905
Constitution (U.S.), 583–584
    slavery and, 735, 738
Constitution Act (England, 1791), 740
Constitutional Charter (France, 1814), 640
Constitutional Convention (U.S.), 583
Constitutionalism, 452–457
    Dutch, 455–457
    in Europe, 439
Constitutional monarchy
    in England, 452, 455
    in France, 576, 589–590
    in Russia, 649
Consumer goods
    after Second World War, 844
    in Soviet Union, 848, 849
Consumer revolution and consumerism
    Atlantic world and, 482–487, 482(i)
    in China, 873
Containment policy, 842, 843, 858

Continental Europe. *See also* Europe
    industrialization in, 615–619, 617(m)
Continental System, of Napoleon, **597**
Contraceptives. *See* Birth control
Contras, in Nicaragua, 905–906
Convention. *See* National Convention
    (France)
Conventional weapons. *See also* Weapons
    heavy, 934(b)
Convention People's Party (Ghana),
    908–909
Conversion. *See also* Missions and
    missionaries
    in New World, 430–431
    by Protestants, 431
    religious, in New World, 430–431
Convicts, in Australia, 743–744
Cook, James, 488, 742
Cookbooks, 655(i)
Copernican hypothesis, 468–469, 472
Copernicus, Nicolaus, 468, 469
Copper, 727
    nationalization of Chilean industry, 902
Coptic Christianity, in Ethiopia, **500–**501
Coral Sea, Battle of the, 833
Corn. *See* Maize
Cornwallis, Charles, 540
Coromandel coast, India, 408
Corporations. *See also* Multinational
    corporations
    agribusiness and, 944
    downsizing by, 861
    in United States, 738
Corregidores (local officials), 423
Corruption
    in Haiti, 906
    in Mexico, 899
    in Venezuela, 905
Cort, Henry, 613
Cortés, Hernando, 420, 421(i), 422
Cossacks, 448, 449, 521–522
Costa Rica, 902
Cottage industry
    in England, 608(m), 609
    vs. factory work, 622–623
Cotton and cotton industry
    in China, 704
    in England, 609–611
    factories in, 622–623
    in India, 537(i), 697
    in Japan, 564, 565
    mills for, 610
    slavery in United States and, 629
    steam power in, 611
    in West Africa, 500
Counterculture, 857–858
Counter-cyclical economic policy, 809
Counter-Reformation, 472
Counter-revolution, in France, 592
Countryside. *See* Rural areas
Coups d'état
    in Argentina, 902
    in Chile, 902

Coups d'état (continued)
    in France, 595
    in Haiti, 906
    in Portugal, 913
    in South Korea (1980), 875
    Soviet, 849, 856
    in Venezuela, 905
Court (law), in colonial India, 697(i)
Court (royal)
    in France, 441, 441(i)
    Safavid, 525(i)
Cowrie shells, for trade, **499**
Crafts
    in Japan, 564(i)
    in West Africa, 499–500
Crash (financial), in 1873, 619
Creation accounts, Diderot and, 486(b)
Credit, in France, 584
Credit Transforms Mexico (O'Gorman),
    898(i)
Creek Indians, 733
Creoles, 484, **722,** 723
    Latin American independence and,
        723–725, 726
Crimean region, 479
Crimean War, 648, 648(m)
Crimes against humanity, rape and sexual
    violence as, 949
Croatia and Croatians, 739, 754, 863, 865
Crompton, Samuel, 610
Cromwell, Oliver, 454, 459
Crop(s)
    from Americas, 546
    in Columbian exchange, 424
    consumer revolution and, 483
    in Japan, 564
    in Latin America, 723
    miracle rice as, 938
    from New World, 537, 570
    in Songhai, 497
Crop rotation, 554
Crucifixion, of Japanese Christians, 571
Crystal Palace, Great Exhibition in, **613,**
    614(i)
Cuba
    Chinese in, 714
    Columbus in, 417
    Communist Revolution in, 900–902
    independence of, 900
    lifestyle in, 901
    refugees from, 901
    slavery in, 727
    Spain and, 702, 733
    United States and, 702, 733
    U.S. travel to, 902
Cuban missile crisis, 849, 901
Cuban Revolution, 900–902, 901(i)
Cubism, 776
Cults
    in Korea, 710
    of personality, 901
    of sensibility, 477
Cultural nationalism, in Africa, 907–908

Cultural Revolution (China), 871, 872
Culture(s). *See also* Art(s); Civilization(s);
    Society
    in Asia, 716–717
    of Asian tigers, 875
    in Australia, 745
    in China, 797–798
    counterculture and, 857–858
    Enlightenment and, 473, 474(i)
    European in West Africa, 513
    after French Revolution, 657–658
    in Indian Ocean region, 409
    Islamic, 528–534
    in Japan, 558, 708
    Mexican, 899
    Soviet, 816, 848
    unity in, 637
    urban, 476–477, 476(i)
    youth, 857
Culture System (Indonesia), 700
Curie, Marie, 774
Curie, Pierre, 774
Currency. *See also* Coins; Money
    euro as, 863, 864
    in France, 584
    silver as, 428(b)
Cushitic-speaking people, in Ethiopia, 500
Customs union. *See* Zollverein
Cuzco and Cuzco region, 422, 725
Cuzco Declaration, 906
Cyprus, Ottoman expansion and, 522
Czechoslovakia
    after First World War, 768
    Nazi Germany and, 823–824, 823(m)
    Soviets and, 849–850
    Velvet Revolution in, 851, 854(b)
Czech people, nationalism of, 763
Czech Republic, in postcommunist era,
    854(i), 863

Dadaism, 776
Da Gama, Christovao, 500
Da Gama, Vasco, 415–416, 501
Dahomey, slave trade in, 513
Daily life. *See* Lifestyle
Daimyo (Japan), **558**–559, 560, 564, 707
Dalai Lama, 551, 928(b), 928(i)
D'Alembert, Jean le Rond, 475
Dalí, Salvador, 776
Damascus, General Syrian Congress (1919)
    at, 786, 788–789(b)
Danish phase, of Thirty Years' War, 437
Danton, Georges Jacques, 591, 594
Danzig, 824
Dardanelles, 757
Dar es Salaam, 502(i), 676(i)
Darfur region, 918
Darwin, Charles, 654–656
Daughter of Han, A (Ning Lao), 799(b)
David, Jacques-Louis, 587(i)
Dawes Plan (1924), **772**
D-Day. *See* Normandy, invasion in
Death camps, Nazi, 826, 827(b)

Death rates
    of African slaves, 425, 507
    lowering of, 945
De Beers mining company, 674
Debt
    British, 582
    in France, 584
    national, 848
    in Nigeria, 913
Debt crisis
    in Argentina (2002), 903
    in Latin America, 899
Debt peonage, in Mexico, 729–731
Deccan region, 542
Decentralized government, in Australia,
    745
De-Christianization, in France, 593
Decimal mathematics system, 593
Decimal point notation, 467
Declaration of Independence (U.S.), **583**
Declaration of Pillnitz, 591
Declaration of the Rights of Man and of the
    Citizen (France), 579, 587, 723
"Declaration of the Rights of Woman" (de
    Gouges), 590
Decline of the West, The (Spengler), 775
Decolonization, 844–845
    in Africa, 906–910, 911(m), 913–915
    Fanon on, 920
    UN membership and, 927
Deductive reasoning, 470
Defensive alliances. *See* Alliance(s)
Deficits
    budget, 848
    Great Depression and, 809, 810
Deforestation, 611, 697
De Gaulle, Charles, 844
    African independence and, 910
De Gouges, Olympe, 590, 592
De Humani Corporis Fabrica. See On the
    Structure of the Human Body
Deism, 475
De Klerk, Frederik W., 915
Delacroix, Eugène, 657, 658(i)
Delaware Indians, 733
Delhi, India
    architecture in, 529
    Babur's capture of, 527
Delhi sultanate, 527
Demilitarization, of Japan, 859, 860
Democracy(ies)
    in Africa, 911–912, 917, 919
    in Brazil, 900
    demise of communism and, 861
    in 1848, 641(i)
    after First World War, 772–773
    in Japan, 859–860
    in Nigeria, 913
    Putin and, 862–863, 862(i)
    after Second World War, 844
    in sub-Saharan Africa, 915–916, 917
    in United States, 584
Democratic Action Party (Venezuela), 903

Democratic Republic of the Congo, 917
    slave trade and, 513
    warfare in, 929
Democratic socialism, of Gorbachev, 850
Democratization, in Soviet Union, 850
Demography. *See also* Disease; Education;
        Population
    of African slave trade, 513
    of China, 704
Demoiselles d'Avignon, Les (Picasso), 775*(i)*,
        776
Dengel, Lebna (Ethiopia), 500
Deng Xiaoping (China), 873
Denmark, 824
Dependency theory, 940
Depressions (economic). *See also* Great
        Depression
    in United States, 738
Descartes, René, 470
Deserts, trans-Saharan trade in West Africa
        and, 494, 497
Deshima, 570*(i)*, 571
Dessalines, Jean Jacques, 602*(b)*, 603
De-Stalinization, 849
Détente policy, **859**
Determinists, in literature, 658
Developed countries, 876*(i)*. *See also*
        Industrialized powers
Developing countries. *See also* Third World
    dependency theory and, 940
    as global South, 896
    green revolution and, 938–939
    peasant migration in, 944–945
Devshirme, slave trade and, **523**
Dewey, George, 702
*Dialogue on the Two Chief Systems of the
        World* (Galileo), 469
Diamond, Jared, 941
Diamond mines, in South Africa, 674
Diarbakr, Safavid capture of, 526
Diaz, Bartholomew, 415
Díaz, Porfirio, 729, 899
Dictators and dictatorships, 806
    in Africa, 916, 918
    in Brazil, 900
    Communist, in eastern Europe, 842
    conservative, 813
    in Cuba, 901
    in France, 595
    in Germany, 777
    in Italy, 777, 818–819
    in Latin America, 726, 812, 900, 903*(m)*
    in Nazi Germany, 819, 820–821
    in 1920s and 1930s, 813–814
    radical totalitarian, 812, 813–814, 835
    in Russia, 766–767
    in Southeast Asia, 876
    Soviet, 838, 848, 850
Diderot, Denis
    Encyclopedia of, 475
    on race, 488
    "Supplement to Bougainville's Voyage,"
        486–487*(b)*, 487*(i)*

Dien Bien Phu, Battle of, 877
Diet (food). *See also* Food(s)
    in China, 554
    colonial plants and, 483
    of industrial workers, 622
Diet (Japanese parliament), 708, 860
Dimitrash (Cossacks), 521–522
Diphtheria, 650
Diplomacy. *See also* Ambassadors
    English-Chinese, 572
    before First World War, 753–754
    gunboat, 707
    between United States and Cuba, 901
Directory (French Revolution), 585, 595
Discrimination
    against Asian migrants, 690
    against Indians in South Africa, 793
    in Saint-Domingue, 600
    against women, 652
Disease. *See also* Epidemics; HIV/AIDS;
        Medicine
    in Africa, 498
    African slavery and, 507
    in Columbian exchange, 424, 425
    European in Americas, 423
    germ theory of, 945
    global epidemics and, 946–947
    in India, 697
    public health movement and, 650
Dissent, revolutionary, 580
Distribution of wealth, global, 941*(m)*
Diversification, of U.S. economy, 746
Divine right of kings
    James I (England) and, 452
    Louis XIV and, 440
Division of labor, sexual, 624–625, 652
Divorce
    in Italy, 819
    in Japan, 565
    in Soviet Union, 816
Dnieper River, 447
Doctors. *See* Medicine; Physicians
Dollar (U.S.), Great Depression and, 810
Domains, in Japan, 707, 708
Domestic system, in England, 538
Dominican Republic, 416. *See also*
        Hispaniola
Dominicans, 571
Dominion of Canada, 741*(m)*
Draft (military)
    in First World War, 759–760
    in Japan, 708
    in Nazi Germany, 822
Drama. *See* Theater
Dreyfus, Alfred, 660
Dreyfus affair, 660
Drinking. *See* Alcohol
Dualism, Cartesian, 470
Dualistic economy, in Japan, 798–800
Dual monarchy, Austria-Hungary as,
        660–661
Dual revolution, 632, 635, 663
Dubček, Alexander, 850, 854*(b)*

Dublin, 763
Du Bois, W. E. B., 907
"Duck and cover" drill, 857*(i)*
Duma (Russia), 649, 764
Dunlop, John, 673
Dutch. *See also* Dutch East Indies; East
        Indies; Holland; Netherlands
    Africa and, 674
    American Revolution and, 583
    comfort women and, 832
    commerce of, 457*(m)*
    East Asia and, 567–570, 572
    economy of, 457
    farming and, 608
    in Grand Alliance, 442
    independence for, 443, 443*(i)*, 455
    Japan and, 570*(i)*, 572, 706
    Java and, 699
    republicanism of, 452
    in 17th century, 455–457
    as trading power, 427
Dutch East India Company, 537
    in Cape Town, 504, 674
    slave trade and, 503–504
    spice trade and, 427
Dutch East Indies, 700. *See also* East Indies;
        Indonesia
    Chinese in, 713
    nationalism in, 700, 802
Dutch Empire, in 1914, 698*(m)*
Dutch Republic. *See* Dutch; United
        Provinces of the Netherlands
Dutch West India Company, 425, 459
Duvalier, "Papa" Doc and "Baby" Doc, 906
Dyer, Reginald, 793
Dyes, indigo trade and, 688*(b)*
Dynasties. *See* Empire(s); specific dynasties
Dzungar Mongols, 557

Earth (planet), Aristotle on, 466–467,
        466*(i)*
Earth-centered universe, 468
Earthquakes
    in Haiti (2010), 906
    in Japan (2011), 861
East Africa. *See also* Ethiopia
    British, 673, 677
    foreign powers in, 500–502
    German protectorates in, 673
    Islam in, 672
    labor in, 714
    in 16th century, 501*(m)*
    slave trade and, 411, 668
    societies in, 492
    trade in, 409
East Asia. *See also* specific locations
    in 1400–1800, 546
    in ca. 1600, 567*(m)*
    Christian missionaries in, 570–571
    economic success after Second World
        War, 870–877
    England and, 572
    Europe and, 543, 567–570

East Asia *(continued)*
    maritime trade in, 566–567, 567*(m)*
    nationalism in, 795–803
    West and, 571–572
Eastern Christian Church. *See* Orthodox
    Church
Eastern Europe, 824, 838, 859. *See also*
    specific locations
    absolutism in, 447–452
    authoritarianism in, 813
    Cold War and, 842*(m)*
    after communism, 863, 873
    Enlightenment in, 475
    EU membership for, 864–865
    industrialization in, 616
    Jews in, 661, 661*(i)*, 662
    nationalism in, 637, 657
    Nazi empire in, 825
    rebellions in (1950s and 1960s), 849
    revolutions of 1989 in, 851–855
    romanticism in, 657
    after Second World War, 841*(m)*, 848
    serfdom in, 436–437
    Soviets and, 838, 840, 841, 848–849,
      849–850
Eastern front, in First World War, 755
Eastern Orthodox Church. *See* Orthodox
    Church
Easter Rebellion (Ireland), 763
East Germany, 849, 853
East India Company. *See* British East India
    Company; Dutch East India
    Company
East Indies, 700, 830. *See also* Dutch East
    Indies; Indonesia
East Jerusalem, 884
East Pakistan, 880
East Timor, 877
Ebola virus, 946
Echeverría, Luis, 899
Economic crisis, of 1970s, 847–848
Economic growth without economic
    development, 943
Economic liberalism, 475
Economic nationalism, 619, 899
    in Brazil, 900
    in Latin America, 812
    in Mexico, 899–900
Economics
    counter-cyclical policy of, 809
    of globalization, 940–941
    of liberalism, 637
Economic sanctions, against Japan, 830
Economic tigers, in Asia, 870, 875–876
Economy. *See also* Capitalism; Global
    economy; Great Depression;
    Industrialization; Industrial
    Revolution; North (global);
    Socialism; South (global)
    in Africa, 513
    in Americas and Australia, 745–746
    in Argentina, 903
    of Asian tigers, 875

    in Atlantic region, 483–484, 485*(m)*
    in Australia, 744–745
    in Bangladesh, 881
    bazaar, 943
    in Brazil, 900
    in Britain, 759
    in British Empire, 699
    in British India, 696–697
    in Canada, 742
    in China, 557, 704–705, 873
    colonial, 483
    in colonial Africa, 675
    in Congo, 919
    in Cuba, 901–902
    dual revolution and, 632
    Dutch, 457
    in East Asia, 870–877
    in Egypt, 887
    in Europe, 578
    European unification and, 844
    in First World War, 759, 763
    in France, 442
    free, 637
    free-market, 844
    global, 425–427, 806, 808–809, 861,
      940–941
    Great Depression and, 806, 808–809,
      811
    growth without development, 943
    in Hong Kong, 875
    in India, 883
    in Indonesia, 877
    in Japan, 561–562, 798, 838, 860–861
    in Kenya, 919
    in Latin America, 727, 906
    in Mexico, 899, 900
    middle, 940
    mixed, 938
    Navigation Acts and, 459
    neocolonialism and, 845
    in Nicaragua, 905–906
    in Pakistan, 881
    in Philippines, 802, 876–877
    political, 475
    in political empires, 677
    in post-colonial Africa, 911
    in Russia, 648, 855*(m)*, 862
    scientific revolution and, 472
    after Second World War, 843–844
    in 17th century, 436
    in Singapore, 875
    slavery and, 628–629
    in Songhai, 497
    in South Africa, 915
    in Southeast Asia, 876–877
    Soviet, 814, 815, 850
    specialization in, 651
    in sub-Saharan Africa, 668
    in Turkey, 890
    in United States, 738, 856–857
    in Venezuela, 903, 905
    in Vietnam, 877
    in Western Europe, 847–848

    Western industrialization and, 686–688
    women in informal, 949
Ecuador, 722
    in UNSAN, 906
Edict of Nantes, 439, 441
Edo. *See* Tokyo (Edo), Japan
Edo period (Japan), 560, 562–565
Education. *See also* Intellectual thought;
    Learning; Schools
    Asian students and, 715
    for children, 950–951
    Chinese civil service examinations and,
      551
    in Cuba, 901
    discrimination against women in, 652
    in East Indies, 700
    in France, 660
    in India, 697–699
    in Japan, 564, 708
    in Nigeria, 913
    for specialized skills, 651
    in United States, 735
    for women, 477, 798
Eggley, Ann, 626*(b)*
Ego, 774
Egypt, 887–888
    Arab Spring in, 887–888
    British in, 673, 686
    fundamentalists in, 883
    independence for, 685*(b)*, 791, 884
    industrial projects in, 938
    invasion of (1956), 884
    Israel and, 884
    as middle power, 929
    modernization of, 619–620, 682
    Muhammad Ali in, 683, 684, 685*(b)*,
      685*(i)*
    Napoleon I in, 595, 684
    reforms in, 684–686
    Second World War in, 832
    tourism in, 684*(i)*
Egyptian Nationalist Party, 686
Ehrlich, Paul, 938
Einstein, Albert, 774
Eisenhower, Dwight D., 856–857, 858,
    934*(b)*
El Alamein, Battle of, 832
Elba, Napoleon exiled to, 599
Elbe River region, 833, 840
Elderly, in West Africa, 498
Elections
    after Cold War, 861
    demise of communism and, 851
    in India, 882
    in Indonesia, 877
    in Iran, 892
    in Nigeria, 912–913
Electricity, in cities, 651, 846*(b)*
Electronic communications
    in Egyptian revolution (2011), 888
    Internet and, 948
    social networking and, 948
Elements, Aristotle on, 467

Eliot, T. S., 775
Elites. *See also* Class; Nobility
    in Africa, 676–677, 908
    in Asia, 716
    in Brazil, 725–726
    colonial, 484
    in developing countries, 943
    in India, 697–699
    in Japan, 565
    in Korea, 566–567
    in Latin America, 725, 726, 902
    mixed-caste, 578
    oil profits and, 847*(b)*
    in Philippines, 702
    in Russia, 862
    Soviet, 850
    women in Enlightenment and, 477
Elizabeth I (England), 452
    revenues of, 529
Emancipation
    of Jews, 480, 661–662
    of Russian serfs, 736–737
Emancipation Proclamation (U.S.),
    736–737
Emancipists, in Australia, **744**
Embargo
    on oil, 848
    by United States on Cuba, 901
Embassies, Chinese, 705
Emerging world. *See also* Developing
    countries
    depictions of, 920
Emigration. *See also* Immigrants and
    immigration
    from Asia, 713–714, 714*(m)*
    Chinese, 408
    of German Jews, 821
    from Ireland, 640
    from Japan, 714
Emperors. *See also* Empire(s); specific rulers
    of China, 556–557
    of Japan, 707, 708, 814, 826, 828*(b),*
        829*(b),* 859
Empire(s). *See also* Imperialism; Islam;
    specific locations
    in Americas, 426–427, 722
    Austrian, 635, 642–643
    French, 576, 660
    German, 647*(m),* 648
    of Hitler, 824–826
    Islamic, 518, 520–542
    Japanese, 826–832
    maritime trade, 426*(m)*
    of Napoleon, 597–599, 598*(m)*
    Ottoman, 518, 520–525, 522*(m)*
    Portuguese, 414–416, 414*(m)*
    Russian, 648
    Second World War and, 844–845
    Spanish, 426–427
    of Timur, 520*(m)*
Empire building, new imperialism and, 489,
    677–681
Empiricism, logical, **470**

Enabling Act (Nazi Germany), **820**
Enclosure, in England, **483**
Encomienda system, 423, 423*(i),* 424
Encyclopedia (Diderot and d'Alembert), 475
Endeavor (ship), 742
Energy
    crisis over, 847*(b)*
    Industrial Revolution and, 610, 611–613
Engels, Friedrich, 621, 639
Engines, steam, 611–613
England. *See also* Britain; British Empire;
    Colonies and colonization; First
    World War; India; Mandates; Second
    World War
    abolition of slave trade and, 668
    absolutism in, 452
    Africa and, 672, 676–677
    agricultural labor in, 608–609
    agriculture in, 483
    American colonies of, 458, 581–583
    appeasement of Hitler by, 822, 823
    in Britain, 608
    Cape Town and, 674
    civil war in, 452–454, 454*(m)*
    colonial trade and, 483
    colonies of, 458, 812
    constitutionalism in, 452
    cottage industry in, 608*(m)*
    cotton industry in, 609–611
    debt in, 582
    East Asia and, 572
    exploration by, 420
    farming in, 608
    after First World War, 782–783
    foreign policy of, 753
    France and, 596
    Gibraltar and, 444*(m)*
    Glorious Revolution in, 455
    in Grand Alliance, 442, 832
    Great Depression and, 809, 809*(f),* 810,
        811, 811*(i)*
    Hitler and, 824
    India and, 580
    Indian textiles and, 537*(i)*
    indigo trade and, 688*(b)*
    industrial labor in, 618
    Industrial Revolution in, 608–615
    Ireland and, 660
    labor movement in, 626–628
    Luddites and, 621–622
    mercantilism in, 459
    Napoleon and, 596, 597, 598*(m)*
    oil use by, 846*(b)*
    Protectorate in, 454
    public health movement in, 650
    Puritans in, 452–454
    republicanism and, 452
    romanticism in, 657
    Saint-Domingue and, 600–601
    in Seven Years' War, 540, 580
    sexual division of labor in, 624
    slavery and, 628–629
    slave trade and, 459, 507, 513

    Thatcher and, 848
    transportation in, 608, 608*(m)*
    Versailles Treaty and, 768–771
    voting rights in, 660
    women's property rights in, 652
English language, in India, 697–698
Enlightened absolutism, 478–480
Enlightenment (historical period), 464,
      472–478. *See also* Enlightened
      absolutism
    in Austria, 479
    books in, 476–477, 476*(i)*
    in colonies, 484–485
    consumerism and Atlantic economy in,
      482–487
    culture of, 476–477
    in France, 473–475, 590
    industrialization and, 608
    Jewish, 473, 479–480
    late period in, 477–478
    Latin American colonies and, 723
    philosophes and, 473–475, 474*(i),* 477
    political ideas from, 475–476, 579
    in Prussia, 478
    public sphere in, 477
    race and, 488
    scientific revolution and, 466–472
    in Scotland, 475, 484
    women in, 477
Enryakuji monastery, 558
Entente, before First World War, 753
Entertainment, in Japan, 562
Entrepôts
    in Malacca, 408
    Manila as, 702
    Senegambia as, 494
    slave-trade, 513
Environment, environmentalism and,
    947–948
Epidemics. *See also* Disease; HIV/AIDS
    global, 946–947
Equality, 857
    demands for, 578–579
    in France, 587
    in Japan, 708
    for Jews, 661–662
    liberalism and, 635
    in Ottoman Empire, 683
    in United States, 584
    Voltaire on, 475
    for women, 735, 816, 949
Equatorial Guinea, 918, 919
Equiano, Olaudah, 509–510, 510*(i)*
    autobiography of, 510*(b)*
    on Middle Passage, 509–511
Erdogan, Recep, 890
Eritrea, dictatorship in, 918
Espionage Act (U.S., 1917), 759
Essay, as literary genre, 428–429
Essay Concerning Human Understanding
    (Locke), 473
Essay on the Principle of Population
    (Malthus), 614

Essays (Montaigne), 428
Estates (assemblies), in France, 584–585
Estates (classes, orders), in France, 440, 578, 578(i), 586
Estates (land), haciendas as, 728–729
Estates General (France), 440, **585**–586
Estonia, 436(i), 450
Ethiopia, 492
    Christianity in, 500–501
    dictatorship in, 918
    as independent nation, 672
    Italian invasion of, 822, 822(m)
"Ethnic cleansing," 863
Ethnic groups and ethnicity. *See also* specific groups
    in Africa, 907
    African interethnic violence and, 919
    in Austria-Hungary, 660–661
    civil wars and, 929
    Kurds as stateless, 891(m)
    in Middle East, 791
    minorities in Iran, 790
    nationalism and, 637, 929, 931–933
    race and, 427
    separatism in India and, 882
    in Turkey, 787–788
    in Yugoslavia, 863
Eunuchs
    in China, 549
    in India, 535
Euro, 863, 864
Europe. *See also* Nobility; Western world
    Africa and, 492
    Asia and, 565–572
    authoritarianism in, 813
    balance of power in, 634–635, 634(i)
    blocs in, 843
    challenges to conservatism in, 634–639
    Charter of Paris for a New Europe and, 855–856
    after Cold War, 838, 861–865
    Cold War in, 842(m)
    colonial plants in, 483
    conquest of New World by, 422–427
    crisis of 17th century in, 436–439
    East Asia and, 543, 567–570
    economy in, 578
    Egypt and, 686
    in 1815, 636(m)
    Enlightenment in, 472–478
    expansion by, 412–422, 415(m), 427–431, 434
    First World War and, 754–764, 756(m), 767–773, 769(m)
    global trade and, 406
    Great Depression and, 810–811
    Great Divergence and, 629
    ideologies in (1815–1914), 632–663
    immigrants to Latin America, 731–732
    Japan and, 571–572
    Jews in, 661–662
    mandates system in, 769, 770, 771, 783
    migrations from, 689–690

Napoleonic (1812), 596–599, 598(m)
    national states in, 658–659
    North American claims of, 581(m)
    Ottoman Empire and, 521–522
    Ottomans and, 682, 683
    population in, 578
    refugees from Algeria in, 909
    Second World War in, 825(m), 832–833
    Seven Years' War and, 580
    socialism in, 662–663
    society in, 578–579
    after Thirty Years' War, 438(m)
    unification efforts in, 844, 863–865
    voyages of exploration by, 412–422, 415(m)
European Common Market, sanctions against South Africa, 915
European Community, 863
European Economic Community. *See* Common Market
European Union (EU), 838, **863**–865
    Turkey and, 865, 890
    in 2011, 864(m)
Europe first policy, in Second World War, **832**
Eva Perón Welfare Foundation, 904(b)
Evolution, 654–655
    Diderot on, 486(b)
    human affairs and, 656
Evolutionary Socialism (Bernstein), 662
Ewuare (oba), 495
Examination system (China), 551, 556. *See also* Civil service examinations
Exchange. *See* Trade
Exclusionists (Australia), **744**
Existentialism, 773
Expansion. *See also* Colonialism; Colonies and colonization; Culture(s); Immigrants and immigration; Imperialism; Migration; New imperialism
    by China, 557
    European, 412–422, 427–431, 434, 458–459
    of France, 442
    by India, 527
    by Japan, 710–712, 712(m), 812
    of Nazi Germany, 822–824, 823(m)
    Ottoman, 520–523
    of Russia, 447(m), 479
    by Turks, 520
    by United States, 733
Expatriates, British in India, 712
Expeditions. *See* Exploration
Experimental method, Galileo and, 469
Exploration. *See also* Colonies and colonization
    of Americas, 546
    Chinese, 408, 410(b), 410(i)
    by England, 420
    European voyages of, 412–422, 415(m)
    by France, 420
    by Portugal, 412, 413

    scientific knowledge and, 467
    by Spain, 412, 413
    by Zheng He, 408, 410(b), 410(i), 411(m), 565–566
Exports. *See also* Slavery
    from Africa, Asia, and Latin America, 687–688
    Australian, 744
    colonial, 483
    from India, 696–697
    Japanese, 798
    Latin American, 728
    markets for, 687
    of oil, 846–847(b)
    of people, 713
    in slave trade, 513, 668
Expressionism, 776
Extended families, in West Africa, 498
Extermination camps, of Nazis, 826

Facebook, 948
Factories. *See also* Factory (walled compound); Workers
    in Canada, 742
    child labor in, 607(i), 610–611
    in cities, 649
    in England, 611
    industrialization and, 609–611
    in Japan, 709
    in Mexico, 899
    owners as social class, 620–621
    railroads and, 613
    Soviet, 816
    in United States, 738
    women in, 622(i)
    workers in, 620
    working conditions in, 610–611, 622–623
Factory (walled compound)
    as foreign trade center, 512, 539
    in India, 539
    use of term, 537
Factory Act (England), **of 1833, 624**
Factory-forts, 512, **537**
Factory system, Wedgwood and, 612(b)
Faisal bin Hussein (Arab leader), 782(i), 786–787, 791
Falkland Islands, Argentina and, 902–903
Families
    of American slaves, 735
    in Cape Colony, 506
    in China, 798, 799(b)
    Chinese civil service and, 551
    grants for, 846
    in Japan, 562, 565
    of Jewish people, 456(b)
    sexual division of labor and, 625
    size reduction in, 653
    Soviet, 816
    in urban areas, 652–653
    urban migration and, 944
    in West Africa, 497
    as workers, 623–624

Family planning, 945–946
Family-style management, in Japan, 562
Famines, 945
    in China, 871
    in Ireland, 660
    in Japan, 564
    in Ukraine, 815(i), 816
Fanon, Frantz, 920, 940
Farms and farming. See also Agriculture
    decline of family farm, 944
    Dutch, 608
    in England, 608
    Great Depression and, 810
    in Japan, 563–564, 709
    in Latin America, 726
    in Mexico, 899
    Soviet, 815, 848
Farouk (Egypt), 884
Fascism, 811, **813**
    Brazil and, 900
    conservative authoritarianism and, 813
    in Germany, 822
    in Italy, 817–819
    in 1920s and 1930s, 813–814
    in Spain, 822–823
Fashion, in 18th century, 482(i), 483
Fatehpur-Sikri, 529
Federal government, in United States, 583
Federalists
    European, 844
    in United States, 584
Female infanticide, in China, 704
Females. See Women
Feminists. See also Women
    in 1848, 641(i)
    Wollstonecraft and, 591
Feminization of poverty, 949
Ferdinand (Aragon), 416
Ferdinand I (Austrian Empire), 642, 643
Ferdinand I (Holy Roman Empire), 445
Ferdinand II (Holy Roman Empire), 445
Ferdinand III (Holy Roman Empire), 445
Ferdinand and Isabella (Spain). See
        Ferdinand (Aragon); Isabella
        (Castile)
Ferry, Jules (France), 672, 678–679(b),
        679(i)
Fertility, declines in, 945
Fertilizer, in developing nations, 938–939
Fifteenth Amendment (U.S.), 738
Fiji, Indians in, 714
Filipinos. See Philippines
Film. See Movies
Final Solution, of Hitler, 821, 826
Finances. See also Economy
    in France, 442, 584
    in Latin America, 727
    in Mexico, 899
Financial aid, by United States to Mexico,
        900
Financial crisis. See Economic crisis; Global
        economic crisis (2008–2009); Great
        Depression

Fireside chats, 777
First Balkan War, 754
First Battle of the Marne, 755
First Coalition, 594
First Continental Congress (U.S.), 582
First law of motion, of Kepler, 468
First World, use of term, 868
First World War, 750
    age of anxiety after, 773–777
    alliances and, 750
    American countries and, 747
    armistice for, 768
    Asian nationalism after, 782–784
    Australia and, 747
    authoritarianism after, 813
    blockade in, 758
    colonies in, 757, 770
    economies in, 759
    Europe and, 754–764, 754(m), 756(m),
        767–773, 769(m)
    experiences of, 760–761(b)
    foreign policy after, 772
    Germany and, 755, 757, 759, 768, 770,
        771–772
    global consequences of, 767–770
    globalization of, 757–758
    Irish home rule and, 660
    Japan and, 795, 798
    Middle East in, 757
    nationalism after, 784
    opening of, 755
    peace after, 770–773
    political tensions in, 763–764
    Russia in, 764
    society in, 759–763
    as total war, 759–764
    Treaty of Versailles after, 769
    United States and, 758, 768, 770
    women in, 761–763
Fish and fishing industry
    in Africa, 498
    in Americas, 420
    Dutch, 457
Five Women Who Loved Love (Ihara Saikaku),
        562–563
Five-year plans
    in China, 871
    in Soviet Union, **814,** 815–816, 816(f),
        848
Flint mills, steam power in, 611
Flooding, in China, 554
Florida, 580, 733
Flour mills, 611
Folk medicine, in Africa, 498
Food(s). See also Agriculture; Crop(s); Green
        Revolution
    in Africa, 498
    in China, 554
    Columbian exchange and, 424
    consumer revolution and, 482–483
    genetically modified, 939–940
    in United States, 738
Foot binding, in China, 798

Forbidden City (Beijing), 549, 550(i)
Forced labor
    in China, 871
    Nazis and, 826, 827(b)
    in Soviet Union, 817, 848, 849
Ford, Henry, 738
Foreigners
    in China, 712–713
    in East Africa, 500–502
    in India, 712
    in Japan, 707
    in Russia, 449
Foreign investment
    by Europe, 688
    in Latin America, 727
Foreign trade. See Trade
Fort Laramie, Treaty of, 734
Fourier, Charles, 639
"Four Modernizations," in China, 873
Fourteen Points (Wilson), 768, 783
France. See also First World War; French
        Indochina; French Revolution;
        Second World War
    absolutism in, 439–442
    Africa and, 672, 908, 909–910
    Algeria and, 682, 909
    American colonies of, 458–459
    American Revolution and, 583, 584
    artisans in, 618
    Austria and, 591
    banking in, 619
    Belgian occupation by, 591
    books in, 476(i)
    Canada and, 420, 442, 740
    cession of North American holdings by,
        459
    Coal and Steel Community and, 844
    colonial trade and, 483
    Communists in, 842
    constitutional monarchy in, 589–590
    de Gaulle in, 844
    economy in, 844
    education in, 660
    England and, 596
    EU constitution and, 865
    exploration by, 420
    finances in, 442, 584
    First Coalition against, 594
    First World War and, 755, 757, 763,
        770, 771, 782
    Germany and, 596–597
    government of, 440–442, 590
    Great Depression and, 811
    Haiti and, 599–601
    Hitler and, 822
    immigrants to Latin America from, 731
    India and, 539–540
    Indochinese independence and, 802
    industrialists in, 620
    industrialization in, 515, 618
    insurrection in (1793), 592, 592(m)
    Iraq War and, 927
    Jews in, 660, 661

France (continued)
    Lebanon and, 888
    liberalism in, 635–637
    mandates of, 769, 771, 791
    mercantilism in, 442
    Middle East and, 788(b), 791
    as middle power, 929
    monarchs in, 521, 585–586, 591–592, 634
    Napoleon I in, 595–599
    nationalism in, 660, 844
    new imperialism by, 677
    nuclear weapons of, 933
    Ottomans and, 521
    post-colonial African states and, 911–912
    Prussia and, 752–753
    public health movement in, 650
    religion in, 439, 590
    as republic, 576, 591, 659–660
    revolution of 1848 in, 640–641
    Roman Catholicism in, 660
    romanticism in, 657
    Russia and, 596, 648, 753
    in Seven Years' War, 540, 584
    social benefits in, 861
    socialism in, 638, 660
    social orders in, 440, 578, 578(i), 586
    sub-Saharan colonies of, 910
    Sykes-Picot Agreement and, 786
    tariff protection in, 618
    taxation in, 584, 585
    Versailles Treaty and, 768–771
    Vichy government in, 824, 824(m)
    Vietnam and, 700, 858
    women in, 441, 596
    workers in, 590
Franchise. See Voting and voting rights
Francis I (France), 521, 529
Francis II (Austria), 591
Franciscans, 571
Francis Ferdinand (Austria), 755
Franco, Francisco, 822–823
Franco-Prussian War, 647–648, 659
    Bismarck's policies after, 752–753
    Japanese in France during, 708
Franz Joseph (Austrian Empire), 643, 660
Fratricide, in Ottoman Empire, 523
Frederick II (the Great, Prussia), 447, 478
Frederick William (Great Elector, Branden-burg), 445–446
Frederick William I ("the Soldiers' King," Prussia), 446
Frederick William IV (Prussia and Ger-many), 642(i), 643
Free blacks, 503
Freedom(s)
    in France, 587, 596, 640
    ideas of, 579
    in U.S. Constitution, 583–584
Free markets, European economies and, 861
Freemasons, 477
Free people of color, 465(i), 584
    in Saint-Domingue, 600

Free trade. See also North American Free Trade Agreement
    imperialism of, 686
    in Latin America, 906
    Spanish, 722
French and Indian Wars. See Seven Years' War
French Canadians, 740, 742
French commonwealth, 910
French Equatorial Africa, 910
French Indochina. See also Indochina
    formation of, 700
    independence of, 877
    nationalism in, 802
    in 1914, 698(m)
    Vietnam in, 700
French phase, of Thirty Years' War, 437
French Revolution, 576, 584–595. See also Napoleon I
    Directory in, 585, 595
    Haiti and, 599–601
    liberalism and, 635
    liberties and, 579
    patriotism in, 504
    radicalization of, 590, 591–594
    Reign of Terror in, 592–593
    Second Revolution and, 591–592
    Spain after, 723
    total war during, 592–594
    women in, 588, 590, 593(i)
French West Africa, 910
Freud, Sigmund, 774
Friends of the Earth, 947
Fronde (French rebellion), **440**
Fuel. See also Coal and coal mining
    oil as, 846(b)
Fugitive slaves. See Slavery
Führer, Hitler as, 820
Fukuzawa Yukichi, 708, 710–711, 711(i)
Fulani people, 670
Functionalism, 776
Fundamentalism
    in Iran, 891, 892
    Islamic, 883, 932–933
Fur trade, 420, 458, 740

G6 nations, 860
Gabon, 919
Gaddafi, Muammar, 888
Galen (physician), medicine and, 471
Galilei, Galileo, 468(i), 469
Galla people, in Ethiopia, 500, 501
Gallipoli
    Battle of, 757
    Ottomans in, 520
Galtieri, Leopoldo, 902
Gama, Vasco da. See Da Gama, Vasco
Gandhi, Indira, 882
Gandhi, Mohandas (Mahatma), 715, 780, 793–794, 793(i)
    death of, 880
    Indian independence and, 878–879, 880
    nonviolent peaceful resistance by, 857

Gandhi, Rajiv, 882–883
Ganges River region, 880
Gao, as capital, 496
Gardens, Persia and, 530–532
Garibaldi, Giuseppe, 645, 646(b), 646(i)
Garvey, Marcus, 907
Gasoline, 846(b)
Gauguin, Paul, 776
Gays. See Homosexuality
Gaza Strip, 884
    Camp David Accords and, 887
    after First World War, 786
    Hamas in, 887
    self-rule in, 886
    Young Turks in, 786
GDP. See Gross domestic product
Gedi, Kenya, 505(b)
Gelug-pa sect. See Yellow Hat
Gender. See also Men; Sex and sexuality; Women
    in Australia, 743
    division of labor and, 624–625, 652
    urban migration and, 944
General Assembly (UN), 859, **926**–927
Generals, in Latin America, 726
General Syrian Congress (1919), Resolution of, 786, 788–789(b)
General will, Rousseau on, **477**–478
Genetically modified foods, 939–940, 939(i)
Genetics, evolution and, 655
Geneva Accords (1954), 858
Geneva Protocol (1925), 936
Genoa, trade in, 412
Genocide. See also Holocaust
    in Cambodia, 835
    in Darfur, 918
    in former Yugoslavia, 863
Geoffrin, Madame, 474(i)
Geography (Ptolemy), **414,** 416
Geography, Islamic, 532
Geometry, 467
    Descartes on, 470
George III (England), American Revolution and, 572
Georgia (U.S. state), Cherokees and, 734
German Confederation (1815), 635, 637, 643
German Confederation of the Rhine, 596, 596(m)
German Empire, 647(m), 648, 659
German Workers' Party, 819
Germany. See also First World War; Holy Roman Empire; Nazi Germany; Prussia; Second World War
    Africa and, 672
    Alsace and Lorraine to, 659
    Asian holdings of, 798
    banking in, 619
    Bismarck in, 645–648, 659, 672
    Britain and, 753
    colonies of, 753, 769
    Confederation of the Rhine in, 596(m)
    economic nationalism in, 619
    Enlightenment in, 481(b)

after First World War, 771–772, 810, 819–820

France and, 596–597

in Great Depression, 809(f), 820

as imperial power, 673

indigo trade and, 689(b)

industrialists in, 620

industrialization in, 615, 618

Iraq War and, 927

Japanese government and, 708

Jewish refugees from, 792

labor unions in, 662

mandates over former colonies of, 783

as middle power, 929

nationalism in, 638(i)

nation building in, 645–648

new imperialism by, 677

oil use by, 846(b)

public health movement in, 650

reparations after First World War and, 770, 810

republic in (1918), 768

reunification of, 855

romanticism in, 657

after Second World War, 844

social benefits in, 861

socialism in, 659

Suleiman alliance in, 521

Thirty Years' War and, 437–438

totalitarianism in First World War, 759

in Triple Alliance, 753

unification of, 643, 645–648, 647(m), 752

Versailles Treaty and, 768–771

Germ theory, 650, 945

Gestapo (Nazi Germany), 821

Ghana. *See also* Mali

African socialism and, 937

economy of, 919

England and, 676

gold in, 411

independence for, 908–909, 912

parliament in, 909(i)

Songhai and, 496

Ghettos, Jews in, 479, 826

Ghirlandaio, Ridolfo, 419(i)

Gibraltar, ceded to Britain, 444(m)

Girls. *See also* Women

in factories, 625

Japanese sale of, 562

Girondists, 591, 592

Glasnost (openness), **850**

Glassmaking, 483

Global age, politics since 1989, 926–936

Global economic crisis (2008–2009)

Japan and, 860–861

Mexico and, 900

Russia and, 862

Global economy, 425–427. *See also* Globalization; Multinational corporations

downturn of 2008–2009, 900

Great Depression and, 806, 808–809

industrialization and, 937–938

in post–Cold War era, 861

silver trade and, 428–429(b), 429(m)

Global energy crisis (2008), 847(b)

Globalization. *See also* Multinational corporations

distribution of wealth and (ca. 2010), 941(m)

economics and politics of, 940–941

of First World War, 757–758

in 1450–1600, 406

inequality and, 687

interdependence and, 936–941

urbanization and, 942–945

Global North, 940

Global South, 896, 940

Global trade. *See also* Trade

in slaves, 508–509(b)

Global warming, 948

Glorious Revolution (England), 455

Glückel of Hameln, 456(b)

GNP. *See* Gross national product

Goa, 426, 537

Godavari River, Mughal Empire and, 527

Golan Heights, 884

Gold

in Africa, 499

in Americas, 417

in Australia, 745

Chinese emigration and, 713

as currency, 429(m)

Portugal and, 501

in South America, 499

in southern Africa, 674

in United States, 713, 734, 738

in West Africa, 411

Gold Coast, 676, 812. *See also* Ghana

cocoa in, 908

colonial rule of, 676–677

factory-forts on, 512

independence for, 908–909

Gold standard, Great Depression and, 810, 811

Goods and services. *See also* Industrialization; Industrial Revolution

in 18th century, 483–484, 485(m)

from India, 537–538

in slave trade, 512

Gorbachev, Mikhail, 850–851, 856

Goulart, João, 900

Government. *See also* Absolutism; Administration; Constitutionalism; Empire(s); Representative government

in Africa, 675, 919

of Australia, 745

of Brazil, 900

of British India, 540, 696

of Canada, 740

of China, 549

conservative authoritarian, 813

of Cuba, 901

of England, 452–454

after First World War, 772–773

before First World War, 659

of France, 440–442, 590, 595–596, 640–641

Great Depression and, 809, 810–811

of Haiti, 906

of India, 882

industrialization, modernization, and, 937–938

of Iran, 892

of Japan, 559–561, 707, 708, 798–800

in Latin America, 902–906

of Lebanon, 888–889

Montesquieu on, 473–474

of Mughal India, 527, 542

of Nicaragua, 905–906

of Nigeria, 912–913

Ottoman, 523, 683

of Pakistan, 881

Pan–Latin American unity and, 906

radio and, 777

Russian provisional, 764–765

after Second World War, 844

sovereignty over multinationals by, 936–937

tariff protection by, 618

totalitarian, 813–814

of Turkey, 787–790

of United States, 583–584, 746

of Venezuela, 903–905

Voltaire on, 474–475

Government of India Act (1935), 795

Governor general, of India, 540

Goya, Francisco, 597(i)

Granada, 413

Gran Colombia, 724(m), 725

Grand Alliance (1701), 442

Grand Duchy of Moscow, 447, 521–522

Grand Empire (Napoleon), **597–599**

Grand National Consolidated Trades Union, 628

Gravitation. *See* Universal gravitation

Great Britain. *See* Britain; England

Great Depression (1930s), 808, 820, 835

African Americans in, 808(i)

African nationalism and, 808, 812, 908

Asia and, 808, 811–812

causes of, 808–809

Europe and, 810–811

Filipino independence and, 802

Japan and, 800, 812

Latin America and, 808, 811–812, 899

Second World War and, 810, 856

unemployment in, 809

United States and, 810

worldwide effects of, 811–812

"Great Divergence," 629

Great Elector. *See* Frederick William

Greater East Asian Co-Prosperity Sphere, 828–829(b), 831–832

Greater Germany, 823, 823(m)

Great Exhibition (London, 1851), 613, 614(i)

Great Famine, in Ireland, 640

Great Fear (France), 587
Great Leap Forward, 871
Great migration, global, **689**
Great Mutiny/Great Revolt (India, 1857),
    696, 696(m), 712
Great Patriotic War of the Fatherland (Soviet
    Union), 832, 848
Great Power(s)
    in 1815, 636(m)
    Ottoman Empire and, 682, 683
    Prussia as, 447
    Russia as, 449
Great Proletarian Cultural Revolution
    (China), **871,** 872
Great Revolt. *See* Great Mutiny/Great
    Revolt
Great Russians, 850
Great Trek, 674
Great Wall (China), 550–551
Great War. *See* First World War
Great white walls, for immigration, **690**
Greece, 842, 844
    revolt against Ottomans by, 682
Greek Orthodox Church. *See* Orthodox
    Church
Greenhouse gases, 948
Green Parties, 948
Greenpeace, 939(i), 947, 948
Green revolution, 938–940
    migration to cities and, 944
    protesters in Iran, 869(i)
Grenada, immigrants to, 731
Grimm, Jacob and Wilhelm, 657
Gropius, Walter, 776
Gross domestic product (GDP)
    in Cuba, 901–902
    in Mexico, 900
    in Russia, 862
    in Venezuela, 903
Gross national product (GNP), in England,
    614
Groux, Henri de, 758(i)
Guadalcanal, Battle of, 834
Guadalupe Hidalgo, Treaty of, 733
Guadeloupe, 601
Guanajuato, Mexico, mines in, 428
Guanche people, 412
Guangzhou (Canton), China, 567, 572, 702
Guerrilla warfare
    in Cuba, 900
    in South Africa, 915
Guest workers, 844
Guevara, Ernesto "Che," 900
Guilds
    capitalists and, 628
    in France, 590
Guillotine, 594(i)
Guinea
    independence in, 910
    Portugal and, 415
Gujarat and Gujaratis, 408, 499
    merchant networks and, 538
Gül, Abdullah, 890

Gulf of Guinea, kingdoms along, 494, 495
Gulf of Mexico region, 459
Gulf War, 859, 892, 927
Gunboat diplomacy, 707
Gunpowder, 414
    Ottoman use of, 521
    Safavid use of, 526
Guns. *See* Weapons
Guomindang (Kuomintang), 796, 800. *See
    also* Nationalist China
Gutierrez Altamirano Velasco, Juan Joachin,
    722(i)
Guyana, in UNSAN, 906
Gyatso, Tenzin, 928(b), 928(i)
Gyatso, Thupten, 928(b)

Habsburg Dynasty
    in Austria, 445, 447, 479, 635, 642,
        643
    France and, 440
    Maria Theresa and, 478, 479
    Ottoman Turks and, 521, 522
    Protestants and, 521
Haciendas (estates), **728**
Haiti, 416, 906. *See also* Hispaniola;
        L'Ouverture, Toussaint; Saint-
        Domingue
    coup in, 906
    earthquake in (2010), 906
    government of, 906
    independence of, 576, 599–603
    indigo and, 688(b)
    L'Ouverture and, 600–603, 602(b),
        602(i), 725
    war of independence in, 600–603,
        601(m)
Hamas party, 886–887, 892
Hameln, Chayim, 456(b)
Hameln, Lower Saxony, Glückel of, 456(b)
Hamilton, Ontario, 742
Hand-loom weavers, 610
Han Dynasty (China), trade and, 565
Hangzhou, China, 417
    textiles in, 557
Harar, Ethiopia, 500
Hardy, Thomas, 658
Hargreaves, James, 609, 610
Harkort, Fritz, 618
Harper's Weekly, racist cartoon from, 739(i)
Harrison, William Henry, 733
Harvey, William, 471
Haskalah (Jewish Enlightenment move-
    ment), **479**–480
Hastings, Warren, 540
Hausa-Fulani Muslims, 912–913
Hausaland, 494, 497
Hausa people, 497, 498, 670
Haussmann, Georges, 650
Havel, Václav, 851, 854(b), 854(i)
Hawai'i
    Chinese in, 714
    Japanese in, 714
Health. *See* Health care; Medicine

Health care. *See also* Medicine
    national systems of, 846
    in Nigeria, 913
    prevention, cures, and, 945
    in Russia, 862
Heavy conventional weapons, 934(b)
Hebrew language, in Jewish Palestine, 792
Heine, Heinrich, 456(b)
Hejaz (kingdom), 757
Heliocentric theory. *See* Sun-centered solar
    system
Helsinki Accords, on human rights, 854(b),
    859
Henry II (France), 521
Henry IV (France), 439
Henry the Navigator (Portugal), 413–414
Herbal medicine, 552(b), 552(i)
Herder, Johann Gottfried von, 488
Hereditary service obligations, in China,
    548
Heredity. *See* Inheritance
Herzegovina, 754. *See also* Bosnia-
    Herzegovina
Herzl, Theodor, 662, 792
Hezbollah, 889, 892
Hideyoshi, Toyotomi (Japan), 546, 559,
    559(m), 566
    Korean campaign of, 568–569(b)
Hierarchy. *See also* Caste system; Class
    racial, in Cape Colony, 505–506
    social, 651
    in working classes, 651–652
Higher education. *See* Universities and
    colleges
Himmler, Heinrich, 821, 826
Hindenburg, Paul von, 819–820
Hindu nationalists, in India, 883
Hindus and Hinduism
    in India, 698, 699, 792, 795
    in Mughal Empire, 527, 533, 535
Hirano, Japan, 564
Hiroshima, Japan, 562
    atomic bombing of, 834, 834(i), 933
Hispanics, in United States, 733
Hispaniola. *See also* Haiti; Saint-Domingue
    Columbus and, 416 417, 418(b)
Historical and Critical Dictionary (Bayle),
    473
History and historiography
    on responsibility for Holocaust, 826
    romantic study of, 657
Hitler, Adolf, 771, 772, 806, 814. *See also*
        Nazi Germany
    aggression by, 822–824, 823(m)
    anti-Semitism and, 662, 820
    appeasement of, 822, 823
    European empire of (1939–1942),
        824–826
    fascism and, 822
    First World War and, 819
    Holocaust and, 821, 826
    Jews and, 819
    Mein Kampf by, 820

Mussolini and, 822
New Order of, 826
popularity of, 821–822
propaganda by, 776, 777, 821*(i)*
suicide of, 833
United States and, 830
HIV/AIDS, 945, 946
children and, 950
people living with, 947*(m)*
Hobsbawm, Eric, 632, 635
Hobson, J. A., 680–681, 940
Ho Chi Minh, 802, 877
Hohenzollern family (Prussia), 444*(m)*, 445
Holland. *See also* Dutch; Dutch East
India Company; Dutch Empire;
Netherlands
EU constitution and, 865
in Second World War, 824
slaves in, 505–506
Spanish trade and, 722
Holocaust, 806, 807*(i)*, **826,** 826*(m)*,
827*(b)*
Holtby, Winifred, 762
Holy League, against Ottoman Empire,
522
Holy Office, Copernicus and, 469
Holy Roman Empire. *See also* Austrian
Empire; Charles V (Holy Roman
Empire)
Austria and, 445
religions in, 437
Holy war. *See also* Jihad (holy war)
in Afghanistan, 791
Home rule, for Ireland, 660
Homosexuality. *See also* Same-sex relations
identification of, 653
in Nazi Germany, 822
Hong Kong
as Asian tiger, 875
Britain and, 703
China and, 873
economy in, 938
pictorial press on, 706*(i)*
rich and poor in, 943*(i)*
in Second World War, 830, 832
Hongwu emperor. *See* Taizu
Hong Xiuquan (China), 704
Hoover, Herbert, 810
Horn of Africa. *See also* Africa; East Africa
slave trade in, 506
Somali pirates and, 919
Hospitals, sterilization in, 650
Household(s). *See also* Families
guides for, 654–655*(b)*, 655*(i)*
sexual division of labor and, 625
women's roles in, 653, 654–655*(b)*,
655*(i)*
House of Commons (England), 452, 454,
745
House of Orange. *See* William III of Orange
House of Representatives (U.S.), lawmaker
images in, 523
House of Trade (Spain), 422

Housing
coal for heating, 611
in 18th century, 483
of industrial workers, 622
Soviet, 816, 848
Hudson Bay territory, 459
Hue, Vietnam, 700
Hugo, Victor, 657
Huguenots, 439. *See also* Protestants and
Protestantism
Human Genome Project, 945
Human rights
in Africa, 673–674, 918
in China, 873, 874*(b)*
in Egypt, 887
Helsinki Accords on, 854*(b)*, 859
in Venezuela, 905
in Zimbabwe, 919
Humayun (Mughal India), 527
Hume, David, 475
Hungary. *See also* Austria-Hungary; Magyars
Austria and, 445, 446*(m)*
in Austria-Hungary, 660–661
after First World War, 768, 770
Habsburgs and, 445
Ottomans and, 445, 541
in postcommunist era, 863
revolutions in, 642–643, 849, 852–853
Hunger. *See also* Famines
UN on, 927
Hürrem (Ottomans), 524*(b)*, 524*(i)*
Hurricane Katrina, 847*(b)*
Hussein, Saddam, 859, 891–892
Hussein ibn-Ali, 757, 770
Hydrocarbons, 948
Hygiene. *See* Sanitation
Hyperinflation, in Turkey, 890

Iberian Peninsula. *See also* Portugal; Spain
Catholic Church in, 484
Iboland, 513
Ibo people (Nigeria), 680, 912
Ice Age, little ice age in 17th century, 436
Id, 774
Ideas. *See also* Intellectual thought
spread of revolutionary, 591–592
Identity
in Atlantic Ocean region, 484–487
in Australia, 745
consumption and, 483
Ideologies. *See also* Intellectual thought;
Philosophy; Religion(s)
communism vs. fascism and, 813–814
conservatism as, 635
Enlightenment and, 472–473
in Europe (1815–1914), 632–663
liberalism as, 584, 635–637
nationalism as, 637–638
socialism as, 638–639
Idris Alooma (Kanem-Bornu), 497
Illness. *See* Disease; Epidemics; Health care;
Medicine
Illustration, miniatures as, 528–529

Illustrators, women as, 472
Imam (leader)
of Oman, 672
Safavids and, 525
Immigrants and immigration. *See also*
Emigration; Migration
to Australia, 743, 744*(i)*
to Canada, 714, 742
in China, 554
Irish, 640
Jewish, 792
in Latin America, 731–732, 731*(i)*
single men as, 732
in United States, 732, 739–740
Impeachment, of Venezuelan president, 905
Imperial City (Beijing), 549
Imperialism. *See also* Anti-imperialism;
Colonialism; Colonies and
colonization
in Africa, 908
in Asia, 694
in China, 795
critics of, 680–681, 940
Ferry's writings and, 678–679*(b)*
of free trade, 686
by Japan, 694, 710–712, 831–832
Ottoman Empire and, 683
in Philippines, 702
resistance to, 681
Russian, 449
Second World War and, 831–832, 845
Western, 666
Imperialism (Hobson), 680–681
Imports. *See also* Trade
in France, 442
of oil, 846*(b)*
Inca Empire, 422
silver and, 428
Spanish conquest of, 422
Income. *See also* Taxation
in China, 873
Indentured labor, 713–714
in American colonies, 458
from Asia, 713–714
Indians as, 714
South Asian immigrants as, 731
Independence. *See also* Revolution(s)
for Afghanistan, 791
in Africa, 865, 908–910
American Revolution and, 581–584
Arab, 786, 791
in Asia, 865, 868
of Bangladesh, 880
for Belgian Congo, 910
of Belgium, 615
of Biafra, 912
of Cuba, 900
Dutch, 443, 443*(i)*, 455
economic, in Latin America, 899–900
of Egypt, 685*(b)*, 791
of Haiti, 599–603
of India, 699, 792–795, 880
of Indonesia, 877

Independence *(continued)*
    of Iraq, 791
    of Israel, 884
    in Latin America, 722–727, 724*(m)*,
        732, 896
    of Lebanon, 888
    in Middle East, 868
    Nigeria after, 912
    Palestinian, 885–887
    of Philippines, 702, 802, 876
    of Portugal, 443
    of Siam, 700–702
    of Sikhs, 882
    in Southeast Asia, 802–803
    in southern Africa, 913–915
    in sub-Saharan Africa, 896, 906
    of Syria, 787, 791
    of Turkey, 787–788
India. *See also* Asia; Gandhi, Mohandas;
    Mughal Empire (India)
    African settlers from, 677, 691
    Armenian merchants in, 539
    Britain and, 539–540, 580, 583, 695*(i)*,
        696–699, 712, 878–880
    British East India Company in, 536*(m)*,
        696
    building in, 529
    bureaucracy in, 698, 699
    civil service in, 540, 696, 699
    economy in, 883
    educated elite in, 697–699
    in 18th century, 536*(m)*
    emigration from, 713, 714
    English language in, 697–698
    European claims in, 581, 581*(m)*
    European trade and, 538
    France and, 580
    government under Britain, 540, 696
    Great Mutiny/Great Revolt in (1857),
        696*(m)*
    after independence, 877, 878–880,
        882–883
    independence movement in, 699,
        792–795
    indigo in, 689*(b)*
    industrialization in, 615, 620
    infrastructure in, 697
    irrigation in, 697
    languages in, 527
    march to the sea in, 795
    as middle power, 929
    migration to Africa from, 690*(i)*
    Mughal Empire in, 518, 526–527,
        527*(m)*
    Muslim-Hindu accommodation in, 535
    nationalism in, 699
    in 1914, 698*(m)*
    in ca. 1930, 794*(m)*
    nonviolence in, 793–794
    nuclear weapons in, 883, 933
    oil use by, 847*(b)*
    Pakistan and, 883
    partition of, 880*(m)*

Portugal and, 537, 539
printing in, 533
railroads in, 697
riots in, 793
self-government for, 792–793
socioeconomic effects of British rule in,
    696–697
trade in, 408
UN peacekeeper from, 925*(i)*
India Act (England, 1784), 540
Indian. *See also* India; Native Americans
    use of term, 416
Indian Civil Service, 540, 696, **699**
Indian National Congress, 699, 792, 794,
    878–879, 882, 883
Indian Ocean region, 406. *See also* Southeast
    Asia
    European trade in, 537–538
    Indian trade in, 538
    Muslim trade and, 416
    peoples and cultures of, 409
    Swahili language and people in, 501
    trade in, 408–409
Indian people, in South Africa, 793
Indies. *See also* Dutch East Indies; East
    Indies; West Indies
    westward passage to, 420
Indigenous peoples
    in Americas, 423
    in Latin America, 732
    in United States, 584
Indigo, 688*(b)*, 688–689, 689*(m)*
Indochina. *See also* Cambodia; French
    Indochina; Laos; Vietnam
    Japanese in, 829–830
    in 1914, 698*(m)*
Indonesia, 409. *See also* Batavia; Dutch East
    Indies; East Indies
    Chinese in, 713
    comfort women from, 832
    economy in, 877
    France in, 678*(b)*
    government in, 876
    independence and democracy in,
        877
    middle powers and, 929
    in 1914, 698*(m)*
    slaves from, 506
    spice trade and, 427
Inductive reasoning, 470
Industrialization. *See also* Industrial
    Revolution
    agents of, 618
    bacterial revolution and, 650
    balance of power and, 682
    in Belgium, 615, 618, 619
    comparative, 615–616, 616*(f)*
    in continental Europe, 616–619, 617*(m)*
    economic nationalism and, 619
    in Egypt, 619–620, 684
    in England, 608–615
    European influence and, 629
    factory owners and, 620–621

in Germany, 619
global, 937–938
impact of Western on world economy,
    686–688
in India, 620
in Japan, 572, 615, 619, 694, 709
labor movement and, 626–628
in Latin America, 620
Luddites and, 621–622
in Mexico, 899
national and international variations in,
    615–616, 616*(f)*
per capita levels of, 616*(f)*
population and, 613–615
in Russia, 616, 618, 619–620
sexual division of labor and, 624–625
slave trade and, 512
in South Africa, 913
Soviet, 816, 848
tariff protection and, 618
in United States, 615, 616, 738, 746
urbanization and, 649–658, 942
workers and, 621–622
worldwide, 619–620
Industrialized powers, emerging world and,
    920
Industrial Revolution, 606, **609**
    in England, 608–615
    global inequality after, 687
    slavery and, 628–629
    social consequences of, 620–629
    worldwide, 619–620
Industrial technology, 653
    in Japan, 798
Industry. *See also* Cottage industry;
    Industrialization; Industrial
    Revolution; Multinational
    corporations
    in Britain, 609–611, 616–617
    in China, 553, 704, 871, 873
    cottage, 608*(m)*
    in France, 442
    Great Depression and, 811
    immigrant contributions in Latin
        America, 732
    in Mexico, 899
    occupational groups in, 620
    Soviet, 816
    steam power in, 611–613
    in United States, 834
    in West Africa, 499–500
Inequality, racial, 857
Inertia, law of, 469
Infant mortality, in West Africa, 498
Inflation, 851
    in China, 873
    in Europe, 578
    in Mexico, 899
    in 1970s, 848
    in Russia, 862
Influenza, 423
Informal economy, women in, 948
Infrastructure, in India, 697

Inheritance, in Indian Ocean region, 409
Inland Sea (Japan), 566
Inner Asia, China and, 557
Inoculation, for smallpox, 572
Inquiry into the Nature and Causes of the Wealth of Nations (Smith), 475
Inquisition, Galileo and, 469
Inspectors, for nuclear weapons, 936
Instrument(s), scientific, 467
Instrument of Government (England), 454
Instruments of the Observatory (Mehmet), 532
Intellectuals, in China, 871, 872
Intellectual thought. *See also* Education; Philosophy; Renaissance; Scholarship; Scientific revolution
   de-Stalinization and, 849
   in Egypt, 684
   Islamic, 532–533
   in 1920s, 773–777
   of philosophes, 473–475, 474(i)
   in postindependence Africa, 920
   salons and, 474, 477
Intendant system, 423
Intercolonial trade, 483–484
Intercontinental trade, 688
Interdependence, global, 936–941
Interesting Narrative of the Life of Olaudah Equiano, The (Equiano), 510(b)
Intermarriage
   of English to Africans or Native Americans, 487
   of French traders and Wolof women, 513
International economy. *See* Global economy
International monetary system, collapse of, 847, 848
International trade. *See* Trade
Internet, 948. *See also* Electronic communications
Interracial marriage. *See also* Mixed-race peoples
   among servants, 503(i)
Intifada, 885
Intolerance, Enlightenment ideas and, 489
Invasions. *See also* Wars and warfare; specific invasions
   by Hideyoshi, 566
Investment. *See also* Foreign investment
   in Australia, 745
   by multinationals, 936
Iran. *See also* Pahlavi family; Persia
   fundamentalism in, 891, 892
   Green Revolution protester in, 869(i)
   Iran-Iraq War and, 891, 897(b)
   Islamic Revolution in (1979), 889
   Majlis in, 790
   middle powers and, 929
   modernization of, 790
   nuclear weapons and, 934–935
   oil and, 846(b)
   in OPEC, 846(b)
   revolution in (1979), 848, 889, 891
   after Second World War, 842
   women in, 869(i)

Iran-Contra affair, 905
Iran-Iraq War, 847(b), 891
Iraq, 891(m). *See also* Abbasid caliphate; Hussein, Saddam; Mesopotamia
   after First World War, 770, 786
   Gulf War and, 859, 927
   independence for, 791, 884
   Iran-Iraq War and, 891, 897(b)
   Kurds in, 890
   middle powers and, 929
   nuclear weapons and, 934
   oil and, 791, 846(b)
   Saddam Hussein in, 859
   Turkey and, 890
   in ca. 2010, 929(m)
   warfare in, 929
   weapons of mass destruction in, 927, 933
   Young Turks in, 786
Iraq War (2003–2011), 847(b), 927–929
Ireland
   England and, 453, 454, 640, 660
   home-rule bill for, 660
   immigrants to United States from, 739
   industrialization and, 615
   kinship ties of workers and, 624
   nationalism in, 763
   population of, 640
   potato blight in, 640
   rebellion in, 453
Iron and iron industry
   in England, 611, 613
   industrialization and, 611
   steam power in, 611
   in United States, 738
   workers in, 627
Iron curtain, 842, 842(m), 849
Iron law of wages, 615
Irrigation
   in developing nations, 938–939
   in Egypt, 685(b)
   in India, 697
Isabella (Castile), 416
Isfahan, 526, 529, 539, 540
   Armenian brass bowl from, 538(i)
Islam, 518, 891(m). *See also* Arabs and Arab world; Fundamentalism; Jihad; Mongols; Muslims; Ottoman Empire
   in Afghanistan, 791
   in Africa, 669–672
   in East Africa, 672
   fundamentalist, 883, 932–933
   in Iran, 848
   in Kanem-Bornu, 497
   nationalism in, 883
   in North Africa, 682
   in Ottoman Empire, 786
   regeneration of, 684
   in Senegambia, 494
   slavery and, 503, 672
   in Southwest Asia, 682
   in Sudan, 670–672, 673, 918
   in Turkey, 890

Islamic empires, 520–542. *See also* Islam; Mughal Empire; Ottoman Empire; Safavid Empire; Sufis and Sufism
   coffeehouses in, 533–534
   culture in, 528–534
   decline of, 536–537, 540–542
   intellectual thought in, 532–533
   merchant networks in, 538–539
   non-Muslims in, 534–536
   religious trends in, 532–533
   in ca. 1700, 541
   trade in, 536–540
Islamic fundamentalism, 883, 932–933
   Palestinian intifada and, 885–886
Islamic Republic of Iran. *See* Iran
Islamic Revolution (Iran), 848, 889, 891
Islamic terrorism. *See* Terrorism
"Island hopping" campaign (Second World War), 834
Ismail (Egypt), 684, 684(i), 686
Isma'il (Safavids), 525
Isolationism
   British, 811
   of United States, 830
Israel, 885(m). *See also* Jews and Judaism; Palestine
   Egypt and, 884, 887
   after First World War, 786
   founding of, 883
   Lebanon and, 889
   as middle power, 929
   nuclear weapons in, 933–934
   wall of separation in, 886, 886(i)
   Young Turks in, 786
Israel-Lebanon War (2006), 889, 889(m)
Istanbul. *See also* Constantinople
   coffeehouse in, 533
   medicine in, 532–533
   under Ottomans, 521
Italy. *See also* Second World War
   academic posts for women in, 472
   Africa and, 672
   Cavour and, 644–645
   Coal and Steel Community and, 844
   Communists in, 842
   Ethiopia invasion by, 822, 823(m)
   First World War and, 757, 817
   immigrants to Latin America, 731
   immigrants to United States from, 739
   industrialization and, 616
   Japan and, 829–830
   Jews in, 819, 827(b)
   migrant workers from, 844
   Mussolini in, 817–819
   nationalism and, 637
   nation building in, 644–645
   sciences in, 472
   trade and, 412
   in Triple Alliance, 753
   women in, 819
Ivan III ("the Great," Russia), 447
Ivan IV ("the Terrible," Russia), 447, 448, 521–522

Jackson, Andrew, 733
Jacobin club, 591
Jahan (Mughal shah), 527, 529
Jahangir (India), 527, 529, 535, 537
Jakarta, Indonesia. *See* Batavia
Jamaica
  immigrants to, 731
  slaves in, 505
James I (England), 452, 453
James II (England), 455
Jamestown, 458
Janissaries, 523, 682
Japan, 546. *See also* Pacific Ocean region;
    Second World War; Shoguns;
    Sino-Japanese War
  agriculture in, 564
  Allied occupation of, 838, 859–860
  alternate residence system in, 560
  atomic bombings of, 834, 834(i)
  atrocities in China by, 801–802, 801(i)
  Britain and, 753
  China and, 561, 566, 705, 712, 757, 795,
    796(m), 800–802
  Christian missionaries in, 571
  civil wars in, 558–559
  class in, 560
  closed-country policy in, 571–572
  commerce in, 561–562
  constitutional government in, 859–860
  constitution in, 708
  culture of, 558
  Dutch and, 570(i), 572, 706
  earthquake in (2011), 861
  economy of, 561–562, 838, 860–861,
    873
  Edo period in, 560, 562–565
  education in, 708
  in 18th century, 543
  emigration from, 714
  empire of, 826–832
  Europe and, 571–572
  expansion by, 710–712, 712(m)
  family in, 562, 565
  farming in, 563–564
  after First World War, 798
  foreigners in, 707
  German holdings in China to, 770
  government of, 559–561, 708
  Great Depression and, 812
  Hideyoshi in, 546, 559, 559(m)
  immigrants to Australia, 745
  immigrants to Brazil, 731
  imperialism by, 694, 710–712
  Indochina and, 829, 830
  industrialization in, 572, 615, 619, 709
  Korea and, 546, 554, 566, 568–569(b),
    705, 800
  League of Nations condemnation of, 800
  learning in, 561
  liberalism in, 800
  Manchuria and, 800, 822
  mandates of, 769, 798, 884
  maritime trade in, 566–567
  marriage in, 564–565
  Meiji Restoration in, 562, 708
  merchants in, 564
  middle ages in, 558–559
  as middle power, 929
  military in, 708, 709, 712, 812
  modernization of, 707–712, 717, 795
  nationalism in, 798–800
  oil and, 830, 846(b)
  outside world and, 561
  Pearl Harbor attack by, 830
  peasants in, 559, 564
  Philippines and, 876
  piracy and, 565, 566–567
  population of, 560, 709
  Portugal and, 426
  protests in, 564, 708
  "Rape of Nanjing" by, 801–802
  Russia and, 648
  samurai in, 708
  Second Sino-Japanese War in, 802, 828
  Shandong (Shantung) Peninsula and,
    757, 795, 798
  skyscraper in, 709(i)
  society in, 707
  Taiwan and, 694, 705, 800
  taxation in, 563–564
  tea in, 558
  theater in, 547(i), 558, 562, 563(i)
  Tokugawa Shogunate in, 559–565,
    560(m)
  totalitarianism in, 806, 814
  towns in, 562
  trade in, 562
  ultranationalism in, 800, 812, 814, 826,
    828–829(b)
  wealth in, 564
  Western ideas in, 707–709
  Western imperialism and, 706–707
  women in, 564–565
  Zen Buddhism in, 558
"Japan, Inc.," 860
Jardine, Matheson, and Company, 703, 705
Jaurès, Jean, 662
Java
  Dutch in, 699, 700
  Zheng He and, 566
Java War, 700
Jefferson, Thomas, 583, 723
Jehovah's Witnesses, in Nazi Germany, 822
Jena, battle at, 596
Jerusalem
  Ottomans and, 524(b)
  Six-Day War and, 884
Jesuits, 431
  in Canada, 740
  in East Asia, 570–571
  in Ethiopia, 500
Jesus Christ (Jesus of Nazareth). *See*
    Christians and Christianity
Jewish Bride, The (Rembrandt), 456(i)
Jews and Judaism, 891(m). *See also* Anti-
    Semitism; Israel
  and Arabs in Palestine, 791–792
  in Atlantic economy, 487
  Balfour Declaration and, 786
  emancipation of, 661–662
  enlightened absolutism and, 479–480
  in Enlightenment, 473
  expulsion from European countries, 661
  family life of, 456(b)
  in France, 590, 660, 661
  in Hameln, Lower Saxony, 456(b)
  Hitler and, 819, 826
  Holocaust against, 806, 807(i), 826,
    826(m), 827(b)
  in Italy, 819
  learning and, 551
  Muslim commerce and, 539
  nationalism of, 883
  Nazis and, 821, 822
  in Ottoman Empire, 535
  Pale of Settlement for, 479(m), 480
  in Palestine, 770, 782, 786, 788(b), 884
  racial ideas and, 657
  as refugees from Algeria, 909
  in Russia, 661(i), 662
  sciences and, 472
  slavery and, 412
  Soviet, 848
  in Timbuktu, 497
Jiang Jieshi (Chiang Kai-shek), 797, 870,
    875
Jiang Zemin (China), 873
Jihad (holy war), **669,** 672
Jiménez, Pérez (Venezuela), 903
Jinnah, Muhammad Ali, 879–880
Jizya (poll tax in India), **535**
John Bull (magazine), 845(i)
John Paul II (Pope), 851
Johnson, Lyndon B., 857, 858
Johnson, Samuel, black manservant of, 503
Jordan, 884
  after First World War, 786
Joseph II (Austria), 479, 480
Joyce, James, 775
Juarez, Benito, 727
Judaism. *See* Jews and Judaism
Judiciary. *See* Court (law)
Julfa, merchants in, 539
July War (Lebanon), 889
June Days (France, 1848), 640
Junkers (Prussia), **446,** 447
Juntas
  in Latin America, 902
  in Nicaragua, 905
  in Southeast Asia, 876
Jupiter (planet), moons of, 469
Justice and Development Party (AKP,
    Turkey), 890

Kabuki theater (Japan), 547(i), **562**
Kabul, Afghanistan, 527
Kafka, Franz, 775
Kagoshima, Japan, 562
Kamakura Shogunate (Japan), 558

Kamerun, 673
Kamikaze pilots, 829(i)
Kampala, Uganda, 690(i)
Kampuchea. See Cambodia
Kandinsky, Wassily, 776
Kanem-Bornu, 494, 497
Kangxi emperor (China), 556, 557, 571, 572
Kano, Nigeria (city), 497
Kant, Immanuel, 476, 488
Karlowitz, treaty at, 541
Kashmir, 880, 880(m), 883
Kasr-I-Shirim, treaty of, 523
Katsina (city), 497
Keinen (Buddhist priest, Japan), poetic diary
    of the Korea campaign, 568–569(b)
Kellogg-Briand Pact (1928), 772
Kemal, Mustafa (Atatürk), 785(m),
    787–790, 787(i)
Kennedy, John F., 849, 857, 858
    Cuban Bay of Pigs landing and, 901
Kenya, 677, 690(i)
    economy in, 919
    independence and, 909
Kepler, Johannes, 468
Kerensky, Alexander, 764–765, 766
Kerosene, 846(b)
Kershaw, Patience, 626–627(b)
Keynes, John Maynard, 809
Khan, Abdul Qadeer, 935
Khartoum, England and, 673
Khatami, Mohammad, 892
Khmer Rouge, 835
Khomeini, Ayatollah Ruhollah, 889, 891
Khrushchev, Nikita, 849, 871
Kibbutz, 792
Kiel, mutiny in, 768
Kiev (city), 447
Kievan Russia, Grand Duchy of Moscow in,
    447
Kilwa (city-state), 501, 504–505(b)
    Portuguese in, 501
King, Martin Luther, Jr., 857
Kingdom of the Two Sicilies, 645
Kings and kingdoms. See Absolutism;
    Emperors; specific rulers and
    locations
Kinship, of workers, 624
Kipling, Rudyard, 680
Kirov, Sergei, 817
Kiyomasa, Kato, 569(i)
Knowledge, specialized, 651
Kohl, Helmut, 859, 863
Kolkata. See Calcutta
Kongo kingdom, slave trade and, 513
Korea
    China and, 554
    Choson Dynasty in, 566–567
    Christianity in, 713
    comfort women from, 832
    Japan and, 546, 554, 559(m), 566,
        568–569(b), 694, 705, 710, 800
    population of, 566–567
    Russia and, 648

trade in, 711
    zones of occupation in, 843
Korean War, 843, 843(m), 860, 870
Kosovo, 863
    battle at (1389), 520
    civil war in, 929
Kowtow, 572
Kristallnacht (Night of Broken Glass), 821
Kubitschek, Juscelino (Brazil), 900
Kulaks, 815
Kunduchi pillar tomb, Chinese plates in,
    502(i)
Kuomintang Party (KMT). See Nationalist
    China
Kurdistan Workers' Party, 890
Kurds, 891(m)
    in Iran, 790
    in Iraq, 890, 929
    in Turkey, 787–788, 890
Kuwait, 892
    Iraq and, 859, 892
    Saddam Hussein and, 859
Kyoto, Japan, 558, 561(i), 562
Kyoto Protocol, 948
Kyushu, Japan, 560(m), 571

Labor. See also Division of labor; Forced
    labor; Peasants; Slavery; Wages;
    Workers; Workforce; Workplace
    African slaves as, 506–507
    agricultural, 608–609
    in Americas, 423–424
    from Asia, 713–714
    child, 607(i), 610–611
    Chinese, 873
    in continental Europe, 618
    in First World War, 760
    Great Depression and, 810
    indentured, 713–714
    indigenous Americans as, 423–424
    industrial, 609, 613
    migrant, 844
    rural, 609
    sexual division of, 624–625, 652
    slavery and, 483, 628–629, 735, 827(b)
    in southern Africa, 674
    Soviet, 816
Labor aristocracy, 652
Labor movement, in Britain, 626–628
Labor strikes
    in England, 628
    in Japan, 709
    in Russia, 649
Labor unions. See also Trade unions
    in England, 628
    in First World War, 760
    global economy and, 861
    Great Depression and, 810
    in Japan, 860
    socialism and, 662
Labour Party (England), 773
Lagos, 912
Laissez faire, 637

La Malinche. See Marina (Doña)
Lamu (city-state), 501
Land
    in Bohemia, 445
    in Brazil, 900
    in China, 554, 798, 801
    in Japan, 860
    in Latin America, 729
    in Mexico, 899
    Native American cession of, 733–734,
        734(m)
    in Ottoman Empire, 523
    in Philippines, 702
    in Russia, 449
Landlords, in eastern Europe, 437
Land mines, 935(b)
Landowners, in Latin America, 899, 900
Landscapes, gardens and, 530–532
Langport, battle at, 454
Language(s). See also specific languages
    of colonial powers, 745–746
    English, 697–698
    in Islamic empires, 528
    of Mughal Empire, 527
    in Senegambia, 495
    Turkish, 790
Laos, 700, 877. See also French Indochina
La Salle, Robert de, 459
Las Casas, Bartolomé de, 424
Lateen sail, 414
Lateran Agreement (1929), **819**
Latin America. See also America(s); specific
    locations
    authoritarianism in, 813, 902–906,
        903(m)
    colonies in, 415(m)
    Communist revolutions in, 901
    crops in, 723
    debt crisis in, 899
    economic nationalism in, 899–900
    economies in, 727, 906
    First World War and, 747
    in global South, 896
    governments in, 902–906
    Great Depression and, 808, 811–812
    green revolution in, 939
    Haitian independence and, 599–603, 725
    immigrant impact in, 731–732, 731(i)
    after independence, 726–727
    independence in, 896
    industrialization in, 620
    landowners in, 899, 900
    liberalism in, 916
    manufacturing in, 723
    mixed-race peoples in, 424(i)
    modernization in, 902
    national states in, 722
    neocolonialism in, 727–731
    by 1914, 746
    race in, 424(i), 723, 727
    revolutions in, 722–725
    in ca. 1780 and 1830, 724(m)
    society in, 723

Latin America *(continued)*
    Spanish colonies in, 722
    in Third World, 687
    trade in, 483, 727
    UN and, 927
    urban migration and family in, 944
Latitude, 414
Latvia, 450, 480
Laud, William, 453
Lausanne, Treaty of, 787
Lavater, Johann Kaspar, 481*(b)*, 481*(i)*
Law (political). *See also* Law codes; specific
    laws
    in British India, 698
    in Prussia, 478
    for women, 949
Law (scientific)
    of inertia, 469
    of Kepler, 468
    of Newton, 469–470
    of universal gravitation, 470
Law codes
    Napoleonic, 595
    Ottoman, 523
    in Turkey, 788–790
Lawrence, T. E. (Lawrence of Arabia), 757,
    782*(i)*
Leadership, of African independence
    movements, 908–909
League of Armed Neutrality, 583
League of Nations, 767, 768
    Germany and, 822
    Japan and, 798, 800
    mandates of, 769, 770, 783–784
    United States and, 770
Learning. *See also* Education; Intellectual
    thought
    Chinese people and, 551
    in Japan, 561
    Jews and, 551
    Western, 572, 713
Lebanon, 888–889
    after First World War, 770, 786
    in French Syria, 791
    fundamentalists in, 883
    immigrants to Latin America, 731
    independence of, 884, 888
    rebuilding of, 889
    Young Turks in, 786
Leclerc, Charles-Victor-Emmanuel, 603
Lee, Robert E., 737
Legislation. *See* Reform(s); specific laws
Legislative Assembly (France), 585, 591, 594
Legislatures. *See* Assemblies
Leibniz, Gottfried, 475
Leighton, Roland, 762
Leisure and recreation
    in China, 554
    of European working classes, 652
Lenin, Vladimir Ilyich, 750, 765–766
    Bolshevik revolution and, 765–766
    economy under, 814
    Marxism and, 798

Leningrad. *See also* St. Petersburg
    battle at, 825
Leo X (Pope), 496
Leopold II (Belgium), 672, 673, 674
Leopold II (Holy Roman Empire), 479
Lepanto, Battle of, 522, 541
Letters from Prison . . . (Michnik), 852–853*(b)*
Lever Brothers, palm oil and, 670*(i)*
Levi, Primo, 827*(b)*, 827*(i)*
Lexington, Massachusetts, fighting at, 582
Leyte Gulf, Battle of, 834
Lhasa, Tibet, Armenian merchants in, 539
Liberalism, 635–637
    British reforms and, 639–640
    classical, 584, 635–637
    economic, 475, 637
    French Revolution and, 590
    individual liberty and, 579–580
    in Japan, 798
    Metternich on, 635
    nationalism and, 637
    opponents of, 637
    in Sardinia, 644
    trend toward, 916
Liberal Party (England), 660
Liberation. *See also* Independence;
    Nationalism
    struggles for colonial, 757
Liberation movements, in Angola and
    Mozambique, 913
Liberation of Women, The (Amin), 686
Liberia, 918*(i)*
    as independent nation, 672
    warfare in, 929
Liberty(ies). *See also* Rights
    demands for, 579–580
    figure of, 577*(i)*
    in France, 586
    liberal supporters of, 579, 635
    in United States, 584
Libraries, 477
Libya
    nuclear weapons and, 935
    uprising in, 888
Lichtenstein, Israel, 807*(i)*
Liège, factories in, 618
Life of an Amorous Man, The (Ihara Saikaku),
    563
Lifestyle. *See also* Society; Standard of living
    in Africa, 918*(i)*
    in American colonies, 459–461
    in Asia, 717
    in Britain, 773
    of child workers, 610–611
    consumer revolution and, 482–483
    in Cuba, 901
    in 18th century, 483
    of factory workers, 622–623
    in global North and South, 940–941
    of immigrants in Latin America, 732
    of industrial immigrants, 739
    in Japan, 559–565
    of Manchus, 555

in Ming China, 553–554
in Rio, 511*(i)*
sciences and, 472
in shantytowns, 942–943
Soviet, 816, 848
urban, 649–651
in West Africa, 497–499
of working classes, 651–652
Lighting, oil used in, 846*(b)*
Lightning war. *See* Blitzkrieg
Lincoln, Abraham, 736–738
Lin Zexu (China), 703
Lisbon
    trade in, 415
    Treaty of (2007), 865
Lisowska, Aleksandra (Hürrem), 524*(b)*
List, Friedrich, 619
Literacy
    of children, 950
    in Japan, 798
Literature. *See also* specific works
    in China, 553–554, 553*(i)*
    on emerging world, 920
    in Enlightenment, 473
    essay in, 428–429
    gardens in, 531–532
    novels as, 477
    realism in, 657–658
    by Rizal, 701*(b)*
    romanticism in, 657
    of Shakespeare, 430
    Soviet, 849
    in 20th century, 774–775
Lithuania, 480
    immigrants to United States from, 739
Little ice age. *See also* Ice Age
    in 17th century, 436
    Muslim empires and, 542
Little Red Book (Mao), 871
Liu Xiaobo (China), 873, 874*(b)*, 874*(i)*
Liverpool, slave trade in, 511
Liverpool and Manchester Railway, 613
Livestock. *See also* Cattle
    breeding of, 483
Living standards. *See* Lifestyle; Standard of
    living
Livingstone, David, 672
Lloyd George, David, 768
Locarno, Treaty of, 822
Locke, John, 455, 473, 475, 579
Locomotives, 613
Lombardy, 644, 645
London
    academy of science in, 471
    Great Exhibition in, 613
    slave trade in, 511
    terrorist bombings in, 933
Longitude, 414
Long March (China), **801**
Long Parliament (England), 453
Looms. *See also* Weaving
    power, 610
López Portillo, José, 899

Lords. *See* Nobility
Lorraine, 659
    after First World War, 769
Lotus League (Japan), 558
Louis XIII (France), 440
Louis XIV (France), 435*(i),* 439–442, 441
    American colonies and, 458
    Charles II (England) and, 455
    at Versailles, 441
    wars of, 442, 459
Louis XV (France), 585
Louis XVI (France), 585–586, 590
    arrest of, 591
    execution of, 591
Louis XVIII (France), 640
Louisiana, 459, 484, 580
Louisiana Territory, 733
Louis Philippe (France), 640
Louisville, Kentucky, flood in (1937), 808*(i)*
L'Ouverture, Toussaint, 600–603, 602*(b),*
    602*(i),* 725
Low Countries. *See* Belgium; Dutch;
    Netherlands
Lower classes, 846. *See also* Working classes
Loyalists (American Revolution), 583*(m),*
    740
Loyola, Ignatius, 571
Luanda, Angola, slave trade and, 508–509
Lucknow Pact (1916), **792**
Luddites, 621–622
Lueger, Karl, 661–662
Lumber, in China, 554
Lusitania (ship), 758
Lutherans and Lutheranism, Ottomans and
    recognition of, 521
Luxembourg, Coal and Steel Community
    and, 844
Luxury goods
    demands for, 413
    trade in, 412
Luzon, Philippines, 408
Lyrical Ballads (Wordsworth and Coleridge),
    657

Maastricht Treaty (1992), 863
Macao, 426, 567, 703
MacArthur, Douglas, 834, 859
Macartney, George, 572
Macdonald, John A., 741
Macedonia (modern), 865
Machine(s)
    Luddites and, 621–622
    in United States, 738
Machine gun, 678
Madagascar, 504, 506, 919
    France and, 678*(b)*
Mad-cow disease, 946
Madeira, 414, 425
Madras (Chennai), 537, 699
Madrid, terrorist bombings in, 933
Magellan, Ferdinand, 418–420
Magnetic compass. *See* Compass
Magyars (Hungarians), 660–661

Mahdi. *See* Ahmad, Muhammad
Mahmud II (Ottomans), 683
Maize (corn), 424
    in Africa, 498
Majlis (national assembly, Iran), **790**
Malabar, 408
Malacca, 408, 426, 713
Malagasy. *See* Madagascar
Malaria, 498, 945
    Africans and, 507
    quinine and, 678–679
Malawi, 919
Malaya. *See* Malaysia
Malay Peninsula, 409, 426
Malaysia, 409
    Britain and, 699
    Chinese emigrants in, 713
    Indians in, 714
    in Second World War, 830
Maldives, 499
Male suffrage, in France, 591
Mali
    gold from, 411
    king of, 409*(i)*
    Songhai and, 496
    white slaves in, 503
Malinche, La. *See* Marina (Doña)
Malindi, 501, 505*(b)*
Malinke people, 498
Malnutrition, in Americas, 423–424
Malthus, Thomas, 614, 615
Malt mills, steam power in, 611
Malvinas Islands. *See* Falkland Islands
Mamluks (Egypt), 685
Managed capitalism, in Japan, 860
"Managed democracy," in Russia, 892
Management, family-style, 562
Manchu Dynasty. *See* Qing (Manchu)
    Dynasty
Manchukuo, 800
Manchuria
    Japan and, 712, 795, 800, 822, 828*(b)*
    Manchus in, 555
    Russia and, 648
Mandates
    in Arab world, 791
    British, 769, 770, 771, 884
    after First World War, 783–784
    French, 769, 771, 791
    Japanese, 769, 798, 884
    of League of Nations, 769, 770
    in Middle East, 791
Mandela, Nelson, 914, 915
    as president of South Africa, 915
    on the struggle for freedom, 916–917*(b),*
    917*(i)*
Mandeville, John (fictional character),
    413*(i),* 416
Mandinka people, kingdom of Mali and,
    742
Manifest destiny, 733
    of Canada, 741
    of United States, 733

Manila, 426–427, 428*(b),* 702
    China and, 570
Manioc, 498
Mansa Musa (Mali), 409*(i)*
Mantua, war over, 443
Manual labor. *See* Labor
Manuel I (Portugal), 507
Manufacturing. *See also* Factories; Industrial-
    ization; Industrial Revolution
    in Canada, 742
    in China, 557
    in England, 614
    industrialization and, 608
    in Latin America, 723
    in United States, 738
Mao Zedong (China), 780, 798, 871–872
    communism in China and, 870
    Long March and, 801
    on Soviets, 871
Maps. *See* Cartography
Marathas (militant Hindus), 536*(m),* 542
Marburg virus, 946
March Revolution (Russia), **764**–765, 766
March to the sea (India), 795
Marcos, Ferdinand, 876
Maria Theresa (Austria), 447, 478, 479*(i),*
    580
Marie Antoinette (France), 588, 591
Marie de' Medici (France), 440
Marina (Doña) (La Malinche), 421*(i)*
Maritime trade. *See also* Trade
    in China, 565–566
    commercial empires and, 426*(m)*
    Dutch, 427
    in East Asia, 566, 567*(m)*
    East-West, 565–567
    international (18th century), 572
    in Japan, 566–567
    Muslim empires and, 536–537
    Swahili, 501
Market(s)
    industrialization and, 608
    for multinationals, 936
    in West Africa, 499
    worldwide, 687–688
Marne
    first battle of, 755
    second battle of, 768
Maronite Christians, in Lebanon, 889
Marquette, Jacques, 459
Marriage. *See also* Intermarriage
    arranged (China), 798, 799*(b)*
    in Indian Ocean region, 409
    in Japan, 564–565
    by Ottoman sultan, 523
    slave, 735
    social class and, 578
    in West Africa, 497
Married women. *See also* Women
    sexual division of labor and, 624
    as workers, 652
Marshall, George C., 842
Marshall Plan, 842, 843

Martinique, 601
Marx, Karl, 639
    social hierarchies and, 651
    on working class, 621
Marxism (Marxian socialism)
    anti-imperialism and, 681
    in China, 798, 871
    on class-consciousness, 620
    in Germany, 662
    Lenin and, 765
Marxism-Leninism, China and, 798
Mary II (England), 455
Maryland, 458
Mascarene Islands, slaves in, 506
Masonic lodges, 477
Massachusetts Bay Colony, 458
Massacre at Chios (Delacroix), 658(*i*)
Massawa, 500
Mass communication, 948
    international youth culture and, 857
    totalitarianism and, 813
Masses, science for, 653–657
Mass movements, in Africa, 908
Mass production, in United States, 738
Mass settlement space, of Nazi Germany,
    826
Masurian Lakes, Battle of the, 755
Mathematical Principles of Natural Philosophy
    (Newton). See *Principia*
Mathematics
    Arabic text translations of, 467
    decimal system and, 592
    Descartes and, 470
    exploration and, 414
    Islamic, 532
    Newton and, 469–470
Mauritania, 919
Mauritius, 714
May Fourth Movement (China), **795**–796
Mazarin, Jules, 440
Mazowiecki, Tadeusz, 851
Measles, vaccine for, 945
Meat, in Argentina, 728
Meatpacking industry, in United States, 739
Mecca, coffee drinking in, 533
Mechanization. *See also* Industrialization
    of British industries, 617
Medical revolution, 945–947
Medici, Marie de', 440
Medicine, 471. *See also* Disease
    in Africa, 498
    in China, 552(*b*), 552(*i*), 572
    global epidemics and, 946–947
    Islamic, 532–533
    population change and, 945–946
    revolution in, 945–947
    sexuality studied by, 653
    in 20th century, 945–947
Mediterranean region
    Indian trade in, 538
    migrant laborers from, 844
    Ottoman control of, 521
    trade in, 412

Medvedev, Dmitry, 863
    New START treaty and, 933
Megacities, 942
Mehmet II (Ottoman sultan), 520, 535
Mehmet, Takiyuddin, 532
Meiggs, Henry, 730(*b*)
Meiji reformers, 795, 798
Meiji Restoration (Japan), 562, **707**–708
Mein Kampf (Hitler), **772**, 820
Men. *See also* Division of labor; Gender
    in Australia, 743
    in Japan, 562
    in middle class families, 653
    out-migration by, 944
    sexual division of labor and, 624–625
    in workplace, 652
Mendelssohn family
    Dorothea, 481(*b*)
    Felix, 481(*b*)
    Moses, 479–480, 481(*b*), 481(*i*)
Mendez, Alphonse, in Ethiopia, 500
Mensheviks (Russia), 765
Mercado (Chinese merchant), 701(*b*)
Mercantilism, 442, 459
    in France, 442
    free economy vs., 637
Mercenaries, Ottoman use of, 541
Merchant(s). *See also* Business; Commerce;
        Trade
    in Africa, 512, 669
    in African slave trade, 512, 513
    in China, 554
    in Indian Ocean region, 408
    Islam and, 538–539
    in Japan, 562, 564
Merchant-capitalism, 609, 618
Merchant marine, Dutch, 457
Mesopotamia, Safavids and, 526
Mestizo (mulatto class, métis) peoples, 461,
    513, 722, 728
Metals and metallurgy. *See also* Gold; Mines
        and mining; Silver
    in United States, 738
Methodists, 431
Métis (mulatto class). *See* Mestizo
Metternich, Klemens von, 634–635, 634(*i*)
Mexica (Aztec) **Empire, 420**–422, 742
    noble in, 407(*i*)
Mexican Revolution (1910), 729, 899
Mexico. *See also* Mexica (Aztec) Empire
    agriculture in, 727
    economy in, 899
    government of, 902
    green revolution in, 939
    haciendas in, 729
    land ceded to United States by, 733
    loss of territory by, 726
    as middle power, 929
    in NAFTA, 906
    in New Spain, 725
    North American capital in, 727
    peons in, 729–731
    Santa Anna in, 726

silver in, 426, 428(*b*), 429(*b*)
Spanish conquest of, 420–422
Texas and, 733
Miami, Cuban refugees in, 901
Michael Romanov, 448–449
Michnik, Adam, 852–853(*b*), 853(*i*)
Microscope, 467
Mid-Atlantic colonies, 458
Middle ages (Japan), 558–559
Middle classes, 651
    in Africa, 669, 917
    in Europe, 578
    in France, 640
    in India, 697–699
    liberalism and, 637
    Marx on, 639
    in Russia, 448
    after Second World War, 845
    social structure and, 620–621, 651
    in Soviet Union, 813
    women in, 621, 652, 654–655(*b*), 655(*i*)
Middle East, 885(*m*). *See also* Britain; France
    Abrahamic religions in, 891(*m*)
    Egyptian-Israeli relations in, 887
    European influence in, 691
    after First World War, 770
    in First World War, 757
    immigrants to Latin America, 731
    independence in, 868
    nationalism in, 784–792
    oil and, 846–847(*b*), 847(*m*)
    OPEC in, 846(*b*)
    Ottomans in, 521
    religion since 1945, 883–892
    trade and, 411–412
    Young Turks and, 786
Middlemen, in European trade, 412
Middle Passage, 508–509, 512
    Equiano on, 509–511
Middle powers, 929
Midway, Battle of, 833–834
Migrant laborers, 844
Migration. *See also* Emigration; Immigrants
        and immigration
    of Africans, 668
    to Europe, 865
    global patterns of (1850–1930), 689–691
    after Second World War, 844
    urban, 944
Migration chain, 690
Mikati, Najib, 889
Militant nonviolence, in India, 794–795
Militarism
    in Japan, 812, 814
    nationalism and, 663
Military. *See also* Armed forces; Soldiers;
        specific battles and wars
    British in China, 703
    in China, 548, 557
    devshirme system and, 523
    in Ghana, 912
    in Japan, 708, 709, 712
    in Nigeria, 912

Ottoman, 541
in Prussia, 447
totalitarianism and, 806
U.S. buildup of, 859
of United States in Philippines, 802–803
in Venezuela, 903
of Western world, 678–679
Military dictatorship, English Protectorate
as, 454
Military juntas
in Latin America, 902
in Nicaragua, 905
in Southeast Asia, 876
Military technology. *See also* Weapons
Ottoman use of, 521
"Millennium Declaration" (UN, 2000),
927, 930*(b)*
Millennium Project Report (UN),
930–931*(b)*, 931*(i)*
Mills. *See also* Cotton and cotton industry;
Factories; Textiles and textile industry
industrial, 622–623, 623*(i)*
Milosevic, Slobodan, 863
Mind-body dualism. *See* Cartesian dualism
Mines Act (England), **of 1842, 625,** 626*(i)*
Mines and mining. *See also* Coal and coal
mining; Gold; Iron and iron
industry; Silver
in Africa, 674
in Canada, 742
child labor in, 626–627*(b)*, 627*(i)*
coal and, 611
in Japan, 708
women in, 625
Ming Dynasty (China), 408, 546, **548,**
548*(m)*. *See also* Zheng He
books in, 553–554
civil service examinations and, 551
decline of, 554–555
founding of, 548–549
Japan and, 566
lifestyle under, 553–554
Mongols and, 550–551
trade and, 565–566
Minh Mang (Vietnam), 700
Miniatures, painting of, 528–529
Minimum wage, 624
Minorities. *See also* Ethnic groups and
ethnicity; specific groups
in Iran, 790
Soviet, 850
Miracle rice, 938
Missiles. *See also* Weapons
in Cuba, 849, 901
Missions and missionaries
in Africa, 672, 676*(i)*
in Americas, 424, 430–431
in China, 713
Christian in East Asia, 570–571, 571*(i)*
in India, 699
Mississippi River region, 459, 580
Mitsubishi, 709, 798–800
Mitterrand, François, 863

Mixed economy, 938
Mixed-race peoples
in American colonies, 460–461
in Latin America, 424*(i)*, 723
racism and, 487
Mobility. *See* Immigrants and immigration;
Migration; Social mobility
Mobilization
for First World War, 755
for Second World War, 806, 832
Mobutu Sese Seko (Democratic Republic of
the Congo), 916–917
Modernism, in arts, **775–776**
Modernization, 643. *See also*
Industrialization
of Afghanistan, 791
of Brazil, 900
of China, 704–705
of Egypt, 619–620, 684–686, 938
after First World War, 784
global, 937–938
of Iran, 891
of Japan, 707–712, 717, 795
in Latin America, 902
of Persia, 790
of Russia, 648–649
of Turkey, 788–790
Mogadishu (city-state), 501, 501*(m)*
Mohács, Battle of, 521
Moldava, 480
Molière (Jean-Baptiste Poquelin), 441
Mombasa (city-state), 501, 502, 690*(i)*
Monarchs and monarchies. *See also*
Absolutism; Emperors; specific rulers
and locations
end of Chinese, 706
English royal power and, 453, 455
in France, 521, 585–586, 591–592, 634
in Italy, 645
Montesquieu on, 473–474
Restoration in England and, 454–455
after Thirty Years' War, 439
Voltaire on, 474–475
Monasticism. *See* Monks and monasteries
Monetary system. *See also* Money
oil prices and, 848
after Second World War, 847
Money. *See also* Coins; Currency; Wealth
in China, 555
paper, 429*(i)*
Mongolia. *See also* Mongols
China and, 546, 550, 557
Mongols
China and, 546, 550–556, 557
empire of, 518
Russia and, 447, 479
Tibet and, 550–551
Turks and, 520
Monks and monasteries
in French Revolution, 590
in Tibet, 551
Monologues of a Doomsday's Survivor, The
(Liu Xiao), 874*(b)*

Monrovia, Liberia, 918*(i)*
Montaigne, Michel de, 428–429
Montesquieu, baron de (Charles-Louis de
Secondat), 473, 579, 580
Montezuma II (Aztec), 420, 421
Montreal, 742
Moon(s)
of Jupiter, 469
telescopic observations of, 469
Moor, Dmitri, 766*(i)*
Moors, 499. *See also* Arabs and Arab world;
Berbers; Islam; Muslims
in Shakespeare's *Othello,* 430
Morality
as argument for new imperial expansion,
680
of coffeehouses, 534
condemnation of whites ruling non-
whites, 680
of English Puritans, 454
Morel, Edmund, 673–674
Moriscos (former Muslims), expulsion from
Spain, 443
Morocco
crisis over, 753
Second World War in, 832
Songhai and, 497
Mortality. *See* Death rates
Moscow
battle at, 825
Grand Duchy of, 447, 521–522
Napoleon and, 599
principality of, 447
terrorism in, 863
Mossaddeq, Muhammad, 890
Mosul, Safavid capture of, 526
Motherhood, 653
Mothers
of African rulers, 498*(i)*
medical science and, 653
Motion
Aristotle on, 466–467
Descartes and, 470
Mountain, the (France), **591,** 592
Mount Asama, Japan, 564
Movement of peoples. *See also* Immigrants
and immigration; Migration
Asian, 712–715
Movies, 776, 948
Mozambique, 502, 913
Mrs. Beeton's Book of Household Management
(Beeton), 654–655*(b)*, 655*(i)*
Mubarak, Hosni, 887–888
Mugabe, Robert (Zimbabwe), 919
Mughal Empire (India), 518, **526–527,**
527*(m)*
architecture in, 529
authority of emperor in, 535
books in, 533
British control after, 696
decline of, 527, 536–537, 536*(m)*, 542
Islam in, 535–536
religion in, 529

Muhammad (Prophet). *See* Islam
Muhammad Ali (Egypt), 683, 684, 685(b), 685(i)
Muhammad Toure, 496
Mulattos
    in Senegambia, 513
    in Spanish Americas, 460(i), 461, 722
Multiethnicity, in European society, 865
Multiethnic states
    in China, 546, 557
    Ottoman Empire as, 786
Multiethnic territories, in Africa, 907
Multinational corporations, 936–937, 937(i)
    in agribusiness, 944
    in developing countries, 943
    neocolonialism by, 936
Multinational states
    Austria-Hungary as, 754
    German Confederation as, 635
Multiparty system, 659
Multipolar world, conflict and violence in, 929–933
Mumbai. *See* Bombay
Munich, Hitler's uprising in, 820
Muromachi culture (Japan), 558
Musa, Mansa. *See* Mansa Musa (Mali)
Muscovites, 447. *See also* Moscow
Musharraf, Pervez, 881
Music
    modernism in, 776
    romanticism in, 657
Music halls, 652
Musikiysky, Grigory, 449(i)
Muslim League, 795, **879**–880
Muslims. *See also* Arabs and Arab world;
        Fundamentalism; Islam; Islamic
        empires; Ottoman Empire
    in Africa, 500
    in Balkan region, 754
    blackness, menial slavery, and, 506
    in Ethiopia, 500
    in India, 792, 795
    Indian Ocean trade and, 416
    in Lebanon, 888–889
    in Nigeria, 912–913
    in Philippines, 877
    slavery and, 412
    trade and, 411(m)
Mussolini, Benito, 818(i)
    execution of, 832
    Fascists and, 817–819
    Hitler and, 822
    radio propaganda by, 777
Mutiny
    in Kiel, 768
    in Russia (1917), 763
Mystics, Sufis as, 520

NAACP. *See* National Association for the
        Advancement of Colored People
Nadir Shah (Persia), 542
NAFTA. *See* North American Free Trade
        Agreement

Nagasaki, 426
    atomic bombing of, 834, 933
    Western trade in, 706
Nagoya, 562
Naipaul, V. S., 920
Namibia, 919
Nanjing (Nanking), China, 549, 550(i)
    Japanese in, 801–802, 828
    Nationalist capital in, 797
    Taiping Rebellion and, 704
    Taizu in, 548
    Treaty of, 703(i)
Naples
    under Bourbons, 644
    Italian unification and, 644
Napoleon I (Bonaparte, France), 588(b), 595–599
    Continental System of, 597
    dictatorship of, 595
    in Egypt, 595, 684
    Grand Empire of, 597–599
    Haiti and, 603, 725
    law code of, 595
    rule of France by, 595–596
    in Russia, 596, 597, 598(m), 599
Napoleon III (Louis Napoleon, France), 640–641, 659
    Sardinia and, 645
    urban planning under, 650
Napoleonic Code, 595
Napoleonic wars, peace settlement after, 634
Nariño, Antonio, 723
Naseby, battle at, 454
Nasser, Gamal Abdel, 884
Natal, 675, 793
Nation(s). *See also* State (nation)
    classes by wealth and income, 940
    European grouping by, 488
National Accord and Reconciliation Act
        (2008), 919
National Assembly (France), 585, **586,**
        587, 587(i), 589–590
    on Alsace and Lorraine, 659
    Paris Commune and, 660
    Saint-Domingue revolt and, 600
National Assembly (Persia), 790
National Association for the Advancement
        of Colored People (NAACP), 857
National Convention (France), 585, 591, 592
    economy and, 594
    Haiti and, 601
    women and, 593
National debt. *See* Debt; Debt crisis
Nationalism, 637–638, 835. *See also*
        Nationalist China; Ultranationalism
    in Africa, 808, 812, 907–908
    Afrikaner, 913
    in Algeria, 909
    in Americas and Australia, 745–746
    anti-imperialism and, 681
    appeal of, 784
    Arab, 782, 791, 884

    in Austria-Hungary, 660–661
    in Austrian Empire, 642–643
    in Balkan region, 683, 754
    in Bengal, 688(b)
    in China, 800
    in East Indies, 700
    economic, 619, 812, 899–900
    in Egypt, 685(b), 791
    after 1815, 637–638
    ethnic, 929, 931–933
    in Europe, 658–659
    fascism and, 814
    First World War and, 754, 782–784
    in France, 594, 660, 844
    in French Revolution, 594
    in Germany, 638(i), 648
    in India, 699, 782–783, 794–795
    industrialization and, 937
    in Iraq, 890
    in Ireland, 660, 763
    Islamic, 883
    in Italy, 645
    in Japan, 798–800, 812, 826, 828–829(b)
    Jewish, 791–792
    liberation struggles and, 757
    in Middle East, 784–792
    militarism and, 663
    Napoleon and, 597
    national competition and, 663
    in nation-states, 663
    in Philippines, 701(b), 802
    in politics, 658–663
    problems with, 784
    romanticism and, 657
    in Southeast Asia, 802
    Soviet, 848, 850
    terrorism and, 930–931
    in Turkey, 786, 787–790
    in Ukraine, 815
    in United States, 740
Nationalist China, 795–797, 800–801, 826, 870
    as Republic of China (ROC) in exile, 875
Nationalists, Hindu, in India, 883
Nationalization
    in Chile, 902
    in Mexico, 899
    of oil industries, 846(b)
    in Soviet Union, 767
National Labor Relations Act (U.S., 1935), 810
National Liberation Front (FLN, Algeria), **909**
National self-determination, 783
National Socialist (Nazi) Party, 772, 819. *See also* Nazi Germany
National Transitional Council of Libya, 888
National unity, in Africa, 910–911
Nation building. *See also* Unification
    in Americas, 720
    in Australia, 720

balance of power and, 682
in Germany, 645–648
in Italy, 644–645
in Muslim Middle East, 883
in Russia, 648–649
Nation-states. *See also* Nationalism; State (nation)
after 1815, 637
nationalism in, 663
Native Americans
African slavery and, 507
in Canada, 740, 742
European settlement and, 423–424
fur trade and, 458
intermarriage with English, 487
land cessions by, 733–734, 734*(m)*
in Latin America, 723
in Mexico, 899
as plantation workers, 728
rebellions of Andean Indians, 725
in United States, 584
U.S. expansion and, 721*(i)*, 733–734
Native Land Act (South Africa, 1913), **913,** 913*(m)*
Native peoples. *See* Native Americans
Nativism, in United States, 740
NATO, 843, 859
Afghanistan and, 932
eastern Europe and, 863
French withdrawal from, 844
Libya and, 888
Natural gas, in Africa, 919
Natural man, 486*(b)*, 488
Natural philosophy, 466–467
science as, 464, 467
Natural resources. *See also* Raw materials
in Latin America, 812
Natural rights, Locke on, 455
Nature, in romantic arts, 657
Naval arms limitation treaty (1922), 798
Navigation, scientific revolution and, 467
Navigation Acts (England), **459**
Navy
British, 583, 596, 753
in First World War, 758
Japanese, 566
Korean, 566
Russian, 449
in Second World War, 830, 832–833, 833–834
Nazi Germany. *See also* Hitler, Adolf; Nazi Party; Second World War
aggression by, 822–824
Allied policy toward, 832
Austria and, 823
dictatorship in, 819
European empire of, 824–826
expansion by, 822–824, 823*(m)*
Hitler in, 819–822
Holocaust of, 806, 826, 826*(m)*, 827*(b)*
Japan and, 829–830
Jews in, 821
movies in, 776

New Order of, 826
propaganda in, 821*(i),* 822
resistance in, 822
Reza Shah support of, 790
society in, 820–821, 821–822
Soviet Union and, 825
totalitarianism in, 806, 813–814
women in, 822
Nazi Party, 771, 819, 820, 821
Nazism, 819–820. *See also* Nazi Germany
Nazi-Soviet nonaggression pact (1939), 824, 825
Négritude, 907. *See also* Blackness
Nehru, Jawaharlal, 794, 882
Nelson, Horatio, at Trafalgar, 596
Neocolonialism, 727, 845
in Latin America, 727–731, 732
multinationals and, 936
Neo-Confucianism, 551, 561, 566
Neo-Malthusian, 938
NEP. *See* New Economic Policy
Netanyahu, Benjamin, 887, 889
Netherlands. *See also* Dutch; Holland
agriculture in, 483
Belgian independence and, 615
Coal and Steel Community and, 844
constitutionalism in, 452
golden age of, 455
Netherlands East Indies. *See* Dutch East Indies; East Indies; Indonesia
Neutrality, in First World War Latin America, 747
New Amsterdam, 459
New Brunswick, in Dominion of Canada, 741
Newcomen, Thomas, 611
New Culture Movement (China), **797**–798
New Deal (U.S.), **810**
New Economic Policy (NEP, Soviet Union), **814,** 815
New England, 458
immigrants to, 739
Newfoundland, 420, 459
in Dominion of Canada, 741, 741*(m)*
New France, 442, 458
New Granada, 722, 725
New Harmony, Indiana, Owen's community in, 628
New Haven colony, 458
New imperialism, 666, 677–681. *See also* Imperialism
and Asia in 1914, 698*(m)*
economic gains of, 677
resistance to, 681
New Julfa, 538*(i),* 539
Newly independent countries, industrialization in, 937
New Mexico, 733
New Model Army, 453, 454
New Netherland, 459
New Order, of Nazis, **826**
New South Wales, 742

New Spain
breakup of, 725
silver from, 426
viceroyalty of, 725
New START treaty, 933
"New state," in Brazil, 900
Newton, Isaac, 469–470, 472, 473
New World, 416–417. *See also* America(s); Columbus, Christopher; Western Hemisphere
crops from, 537, 546
in East Asia, 570
impact of European conquest of, 422–427
religious conversion in, 430–431
silver from, 428–429*(b)*, 429*(m)*
New York (colony), 458
New York City, 459
September 11, 2001, attacks in, 932, 932*(i)*
New Zealand, 757
N'gazargamu (Kanem-bornu capital), 497
Nguyen Dynasty (Vietnam), **700**
Nhara (women slave traders), 513
Nicaragua
economy in, 905–906
government of, 905–906
Sandinistas in, 897*(i),* 905
Nice, France and, 591
Nicholas I (Russia), 643
Nicholas II (Russia), 649, 750, 755, 764
Nietzsche, Friedrich, 773
Niger (country), 919
Nigeria
Achebe in, 920
Biafra and, 912
democracy and, 919
government of, 912–913
Ibo people in, 680
after independence, 912
Islam in, 670
as middle power, 929
oil in, 847*(b)*
Niger River region
Benin and, 495
slave trade and, 513
Night of Broken Glass. *See* Kristallnacht
Nijo Castle (Japan), 561*(i)*
1911 Revolution (China), **706,** 795
Ning Lao, 799*(b),* 799*(i)*
Ninigi-no-Mikoto (Japanese mythology), 829*(b)*
Nitrates, 727
Nixon, Richard, 858, 873
Nkrumah, Kwame, 908–909, 909*(i),* 912
Nobel Prize
to Dalai Lama, 928*(i)*
to Liu Xiaobo, 873, 874
to Ossietzky, 873
Nobility
in France, 440, 441, 578, 578*(i),* 586, 587–588
in Hungary, 445

Nobility (continued)
    in Japan, 558–559, 560
    Junkers as, 446
    Mexica, 407(i)
    Ottomans and, 523
    representative government and, 580
    in Russia, 448, 479
Nobunaga, Oda (Japan), 559
Nonaggression pact
    Germany-Russia (1890), 753
    Germany-Russia (1939), 824, 825
Nonaligned nations, 882, 896
    UN and, 927
Non-Proliferation of Nuclear Weapons,
    Treaty on the, 933, 934(b)
Nonrepresentational art, 776
Nonviolence
    in India, 793–794
    Michnik on, 852–853(b)
    in United States, 857
Non-Western world. See also Third World
    European economic penetration of, 677
    European political movement into, 677
    industrialization in, 616
Normandy, France, invasion in (Second
    World War), 833(i)
North (global), 940. See also First World
North (U.S.), Civil War in, 732, 736–738
North Africa, 499
    end of authoritarian rule in, 918
    Islam and, 682
    migrants from, 844
    Muslims and, 521
    Ottomans and, 521, 542
    in Second World War, 825(m), 832
North America. See also Colonies and
        colonization
    American Revolution in, 576
    European claims in, 581, 581(m)
    independence in, 581–584
    Seven Years' War and, 540, 580, 740
    trade and, 459
North American Free Trade Agreement
    (NAFTA), 906
North Atlantic Treaty Organization. See
    NATO
North Carolina, slavery in, 735
Northern Alliance (Afghanistan), 932
Northern Europe, expansion of powers in,
    458–459
Northern Hemisphere, global South and,
    896
Northern Rhodesia, 674
North German Confederation, 647
North Korea, 843. See also Korea
    Internet in, 948
    nuclear weapons and, 935–936
North Vietnam, 858. See also Vietnam;
        Vietnam War
    government in, 876
Northwest Territory (U.S.), 733
Norway, in Second World War, 824
Nō theater (Japan), 558

Nova Scotia, 459
    in Dominion of Canada, 741
Novels, 477. See also Literature
    in China, 553–554
    in 20th century, 774–775
Novgorod, 447
Nuclear arms race, 933
Nuclear family, in West Africa, 498
Nuclear power. See also Nuclear weapons
    in Iran, 892
Nuclear weapons. See also Atomic bomb;
        Weapons, of mass destruction
    arms trade and, 934–935(b)
    ban on testing, 933
    in Brazil, 900
    cutbacks in, 856
    in France, 844
    in India, 883
    inspections for, 936
    non-proliferation of, 933, 934(b)
    in Pakistan, 880, 883, 933
    proliferation of, 934–936
    Reagan and, 859
    testing of, 933
Nuremberg Laws (Germany, 1935), 821
Nuremberg rally, 776
Nurhaci (Manchus), 555

Oath of the Tennis Court (France), 586,
    587(i)
Oba (king of Benin), 495, 496(i)
Obama, Barack
    Afghanistan and, 932
    Iraq War and, 929
    New START treaty and, 933
Occupation (military), of Japan, 838,
    859–860
Occupations (work)
    industrial, 620
    of Puritans, 453(i)
    sexual division of labor and, 624–625
    of working classes, 651–652
Occupation zones
    in Germany, 841
    in Korea, 843
Occupied territories, in Second World War,
    826
Oceans. See Navigation; Ships and shipping;
    specific locations
October Manifesto (Russia), 649
Ogé, Vincent, 600
O'Gorman, Juan, 898(i)
Ohio River region, English and French in,
    580
Oil
    in Africa, 919
    in Arab world, 791
    embargo on, 848
    in Indonesia, 877
    in Iran, 846(b), 848
    in Iraq, 791, 846(b)
    Japan and, 830, 846(b)
    in Mexico, 899

    in Nigeria, 913
    prices of, 847–848
    Soviet, 846(b)
    in Sudan, 918
    trade and, 846–847, 847(m)
    in United States, 738, 846(b)
    in Venezuela, 846(b), 905
"Oil wars," 846(b)
Old-age pensions, 810, 846
Old Bolsheviks, public trials of, 817
Old Regime (France), 584–585, 588(b),
    651
Old World. See Africa; Asia; Europe
Olearius, Adam, on Russian life, 450–451,
    451(i)
Oligarchy, Dutch regents as, 455–457
Omaha Beach, 833(i)
Oman, 672
Omani Arabs, 502
Omdurman, battle at, 673
"On Cannibals" (Montaigne), 429, 430
"One China," 875
One Day in the Life of Ivan Denisovich
    (Solzhenitsyn), 849
One-party government, in Africa, 912,
    937
Ontario, in Dominion of Canada, 741
On the Different Races of Man (Kant), 488
"On the Immortality of the Soul"
    (Mendelssohn), 481(b)
On the Origin of Species by the Means of
    Natural Selection (Darwin), 654
On the Revolutions of the Heavenly Spheres
    (Copernicus), 468
On the Structure of the Human Body
    (Vesalius), 471, 471(i)
OPEC (Organization of Petroleum
    Exporting Countries), 846(b),
    847–848, 913
Opium
    from India, 696
    trade in, 703
Opium War, 703
Oppenheim, Moritz, 481(i)
Orange, House of. See William III of
    Orange
Orange River region, 674
Orbits, planetary, 468
Orders (social), European classes as, 578
Oregon, Territory of, 733
Organization of Petroleum Exporting
    Countries. See OPEC
Orphans, 950
Ortega, Daniel, 905, 906
Orthodox Church
    Ottoman Empire and, 520, 543
    Stalin and, 848
Osaka, Japan, 562
    Battle of, 571
Osman (Turks), 520
Ossietzky, Carl von, 873
O'Sullivan, John L., 733
Othello (Shakespeare), 430

Ottoman Empire, 518, 520–525, 522(m)
    Arab revolt and, 786–787
    in Balkan region, 682(m)
    Crimean War and, 648
    decline of, 536–537, 540–541, 682–683
    destruction of, 767, 768, 770
    Europe and, 521–522
    expansion of, 520–523
    First World War and, 783, 785
    Habsburg Empire and, 521, 522
    Jews in, 535
    mandates in, 783
    nationalism and, 637, 754, 784–792
    partition of (1914–1923), 785(m)
    reforms in, 682–683
    religions in, 533, 535
    Safavid Empire and, 522–523, 526
    self-determination in, 783
    Young Turks in, 786
Ottomans (Ottoman Turks), **520**–523. *See
        also* Ottoman Empire
    in Egypt, 684
    in Ethiopia, 500
    in First World War, 757
    Hasbsburgs and, 445
Out-migration, gender, family, and, 944
Overcrowding, 942–943
Overpopulation, migration and, 690
Overseas Chinese, 691
Overseas expansion. *See* Expansion
Owen, Robert, 624, 628
Ozone layer, 948

Pacific Islands, immigrants to Australia
        from, 745
Pacific Ocean region
    exploration of, 419–420
    Japan and, 826–832
    Second World War in, 826–832, 831(m),
        833–834
    United States in, 707
Pacifism, Michnik on, 852–853(b)
Páez, José Antonio, 726
Pahlavi family
    Muhammad Reza Shah, 890–891
    Reza Shah, 790
Paine, Thomas, 583, 723
Painting. *See also* Art(s)
    of miniatures, 528–529
    romantic, 657
    in 10th century, 776
Pakistan. *See also* India
    Bangladesh independence and, 880–882
    Bhutto assassination in, 881(i)
    economy of, 881
    government of, 881
    independence and, 877, 880
    India and, 883
    middle powers and, 929
    nuclear weapons and, 880, 883, 933, 935
    population of, 881
    refugees in, 881
    Taliban in, 881

Palaces. *See also* Forbidden City (Beijing)
    in China, 549, 550(i)
    Islamic, 529
Pale of Settlement, 479(m), 480
Palestine, 885(m)
    Arab control of, 791
    Arab-Jewish tensions in, 791–792
    British withdrawal from, 884
    after First World War, 770, 782
    independence for, 885–887
    Israel and, 883
    Jews and, 662, 782, 786, 789, 789(b)
    Ottomans in, 521, 524(b)
    partition of, 884
**Palestine Liberation Organization (PLO),
    884,** 886, 889
Palestinian Authority, 887
Palm oil, trade in, **668**–669, 670(i)
Pan-Africanists, 907
Panama, conference in (1826), 725
Panama Canal, 688
Pan-Americanism, Latin America and, 725
Pan-Arab world, 883
Panipat, India, battle at, 527, 542
Pankhurst, Christabel, 633(i)
Pan–Latin Americanism, 906
Papacy. *See also* specific popes
    Italy and, 644
    Rome and, 644
Papal Inquisition. *See* Inquisition
Papal States, 645
Paracelsus, 471
Paraguay, in UNSAN, 906
Paris. *See also* Paris, Treaty of
    academy of science in, 471
    Bastille and, 586–587
    in Enlightenment, 477
    Franco-Prussian War and, 648
    in French Revolution, 592
    revolt of 1848 in, 640
    riots in, 586–587
    transformation of, 650
Paris, Treaty of
    in 1763, 540, **580,** 740
    in 1783, 583
Paris Commune (1871), 659–660
Paris Peace Conference (1919), 750,
        767–768
    Versailles Treaty and, 768–771
Park Chung Hee (South Korea), 875
Parlement of Paris (court), 585–586
Parliament(s). *See also* Parliament (England)
    of Australia, 745
    before First World War, 659
    in Germany, 645, 659
    Japanese Diet as, 708
Parliament (England)
    absolutism and, 452
    Charles I and, 452, 453
    in constitutional monarchy, 455
    India ruled by, 696
    liberal reforms and, 639–640
    North American colonies and, 582

    Puritans and, 454
    Restoration and, 454–455
    slave trade abolished by, 629
    workplace conditions and, 624
Partitions
    of Africa, 671(m)
    of India, 880(m)
    of Poland, 479, 480(m)
Paşa, Lütfi, 523
Pasteur, Louis, 650
Pate (city-state), 501
Paternalism, in Belgian Africa, 910
Patriotism. *See also* Nationalism
    in Afghanistan, 791
    in France, 594
    of Garibaldi, 646(b)
    in Germany, 648, 771
    Russian, 850
    in United States, 740
Patriots, in China, 797(i)
Patronage system, in France, 441
Paupers, in English workforce, 623
Payne (coal master), 626(b)
Peace. *See also* specific treaties
    after First World War, 769–773
    after Napoleonic wars, 634
    after Vietnam War, 858
Peaceful coexistence policy, 849
Peacekeeping (UN), 925(i), 926(i), 927
Peace of Augsburg, 437, 438, 521
Peace of Utrecht, 442, 444(m), 459
Peace of Westphalia, 437–438
Peace process, in Middle East, 886
Pearl Harbor, Hawaii, Japanese attack on, 830
Pears, Andrew, 670(i)
Peasants. *See also* Serfs and serfdom
    in Africa, 675
    in China, 801, 871, 873
    as European social order, 578
    in France, 578, 578(i), 587, 592, 640
    in Japan, 559, 560–561, 564, 860
    migration to cities by, 944–945
    in Russia, 448(i), 648
    in 17th century, 436–437
    slavery and, 506
    Soviet, 814, 815–816
Pedro I (Portugal), 725
Pedro II (Portugal), 725–726
Pemba (island), slaves in, 506
Penal colony, Australia as, 742–744
Pendulum clock, 467
Peninsulares, 722, 722(i), 723, 726
Pennsylvania, 458
    September 11, 2001, attacks and, 932
Pentagon, September 11, 2001, attack on, 932
Peons, in Mexico, 729–**731**
People, the, 620. *See also* Common people
People of color
    free, 465(i), 584, 600
    in Latin America, 461, 727
    in Saint-Domingue, 600
    in United States, 584
People's Action Party (Singapore), 875

People's Budget (England), 753
People's Republic of China, 875. *See also* China
Pepper, 409
Per capita income, in Japan, 860
Perestroika (economic restructuring), **850**
Pérez, Carlos, 905
Permanent Mandates Commission, 783
Perón, Eva, 902, 904*(b)*, 904*(i)*
Perón, Isabel, 904*(b)*
Perón, Juan, 902, 903*(b)*
Perry, Matthew, 707
Persia. *See also* Iran; Safavid Empire
    carpets in, 528, 528*(i)*
    gardens of, 530–532
    India and, 527
    modernization of, 790
    princess in, 519*(i)*
    Safavid Empire in, 518, 525–526
Persian Gulf region
    Indian trade and, 408, 538
    oil in, 846*(b)*
Persian Gulf War. *See* Gulf War
Persian language, 527
    in Islamic empires, 528
Persian Letters, The (Montesquieu), 473
Peru. *See also* Inca Empire
    Chinese in, 714, 732
    Meiggs in, 730*(b)*
    rebellion in, 725
    in UNSAN, 906
    viceroyalty of, 722
Pétain, Henri-Philippe, 824
Peter the Great (Russia), 449–451, 449*(i)*
    Catherine the Great and, 478
Petrograd. *See* St. Petersburg
Petrograd Soviet, 765
Petroleum industry. *See* Oil
Philip II (Spain), 419
Philip of Anjou, 442
Philippines, 409
    Chinese in, 408, 713
    economy of, 876–877
    emigration from, 714
    government in, 876
    immigrants to Australia, 745
    imperialism in, 680
    independence of, 702
    Japan and, 566
    miracle rice in, 938
    nationalism in, 701*(b)*, 802
    Rizal in, 701*(b)*, 701*(i)*
    in Second World War, 830, 834
    Spain and, 699, 702, 733
    Spanish-American War in, 802, 802*(m)*
    trade and, 426–427
    United States and, 702, 733, 830
Phillip, Arthur, 743, 744
Philosophes, 473–475, 474*(i)*, 477
Philosophy. *See also* Religion(s)
    in Enlightenment, 472–476, 477–478, 479–480
    after First World War, 773–774

Physicians. *See also* Medicine
    Islamic, 533
    in Soviet Union, 816
Physics
    Aristotelian, 466, 469
    after First World War, 774
    Galileo and, 469
    Newton and, 469–470
Picasso, Pablo, 775*(i)*, 776
Piedmont, 644
Pieds-noirs (black feet), **909**
Pieh, Sengbe (Joseph Cinqué), 667*(i)*
Pig iron, 611–613
Pill, the, 946
Pinochet, Augusto, 902
Piracy
    Chinese, 566
    in East Asia, 566, 567*(m)*
    Japan and, 565, 566–567
    Somali, 919
Piri Reis (Ottomans), maps by, 532
Pius V (Pope), Holy League of, 522
Pius VII (Pope), 596
Pizarro, Francisco, 420, 422
Plains Indians (North America), 734
Planck, Max, 774
Planetary motion. *See also* Astronomy
    laws of, 468–469
Planets. *See also* Astronomy; Earth; Universe
    orbits of, 468
Plantains, 498
Plantations. *See also* Sugar and sugar industry
    Asian labor for, 714
    in India, 696
    indigo, 688*(b)*
    in Latin America, 727, 728
    rice, 458
    sugar, 425
Plants. *See also* Agriculture; Crop(s)
    from colonies, 483
Plays. *See* Theater
Plebiscites, in French Africa, 910
PLO. *See* Palestine Liberation Organization
Plum in the Golden Vase (China), 554
Plymouth Colony, 458
Poets and poetry, romantic, 657
Pogroms, in Russia, 662
Poland
    after First World War, 769
    immigrants to United States from, 739
    Jews in, 480
    Nazi Germany and, 824
    Ottomans and, 524*(b)*
    partition of, 479, 480*(m)*
    in postcommunist era, 863
    after Second World War, 841, 849
    Second World War and, 824
    Solidarity in, 851, 852–853*(b)*
    Ukraine and, 449
Police, in Japan, 708
Polio vaccine, 945
Political economy, 475

Political parties
    in Africa, 908
    anti-Semitic, 661–662
    in Turkey, 788
Political reform, in Africa since 1990, 915–919
Politics and political thought. *See also* Government
    anti-Semites and, 661–662
    dual revolution and, 632
    in First World War, 763–764
    global (1989–), 926–936
    of globalization, 940–941
    Hitler and, 820
    nationalism and socialism in, 658–663
    Ottoman, 523
    slave trade and, 513
    in Southeast Asia, 876–877
Polk, James, 733
Poll tax
    in India, 535
    in Islamic empires, 534
Pollution. *See* Environment
Polo, Marco, 414, 416
Poltava, battle at, 449–450
Polygamy, in China, 798
Polygyny, in West Africa, 497
Polynesia, 776
Pondicherry, India, French factory in, 539–540
Poor people. *See also* Poverty
    in French Revolution, 592
    government grants to, 846
Pope(s). *See also* Papacy; specific popes
Popular Front, in France, **811**
Population
    of Africa, 514
    agriculture and, 938
    of American colonies, 733
    in Australia, 744–745
    baby boom in, 857
    of Bangladesh, 881
    Black Death and, 413
    of Britain, 614
    of Canada, 741–742
    of China, 554, 556, 704
    in Europe, 413, 578
    of indigenous Americans, 423–424
    industrialization and, 613–615
    of Ireland, 640
    in Japan, 560, 709, 861
    of Japanese cities, 562
    of Jewish Palestine, 792
    of Korea, 566–567
    medicine and, 945–946
    migration and, 690
    of Native Americans, 734
    of Pakistan, 881
    of United States, 746
    of West Africa, 507
Population Bomb, The (Ehrlich), 938
Porcelain. *See* Ceramics
Pornography, child, 950

Port(s)
 in India, 699
 in Japan, 707
Port-au-Prince, Haiti, 601(m)
Portillo, José López. See López Portillo,
 José
Port Jackson. See Sydney, Australia
Port Moresby, New Guinea, 833
Portugal. See also Iberian Peninsula; Spain
 Africa and, 496, 500
 Angola and, 913
 Brazil and, 725
 conservative authoritarianism in, 813
 Creoles and, 722
 East Asia and, 567
 expansion by, 414–416, 414(m)
 exploration by, 412, 413, 414–416
 global trade and, 426
 immigrants to Latin America, 731
 India and, 408, 537, 539
 Japan and, 426
 Macao and, 426, 567, 703
 Ottomans and, 521
 revolt in, 443
 slavery and, 425
 spice trade and, 427
 spread of Christianity and, 413
 Swahili trade and, 501–502
Postal service, in India, 697
Poster art, in China, 872(i)
Postimpressionists, 776
Potatoes
 from Americas, 424, 483
 blight in Ireland, 640, 739
Potosí, 426
 silver from, 428(b)
Potsdam Conference (1945), 841
Pottery
 in China, 502(i)
 steam power and, 611
 tile making and, 532(i)
 Wedgwood and, 612(b), 612(i)
Poverty. See also Poor people; Wealth gap
 in Africa, 876(i)
 of children, 950
 in China, 800
 in Cuba, 902
 feminization of, 949
 in France, 586
 of global South, 940
 industrial, 621
 in Latin America, 732
 in Russia, 862
 in Somalia, 919
 in Venezuela, 905
 war on, 857
 and wealth in Hong Kong, 943(i)
Power (authority)
 decline in Islamic empires, 540–542
 in Europe, 434
 in Japan, 800
 of middle and regional powers, 929
 in Muslim empires, 542

 in 17th century, 439
 of United States, 732–740
Power (energy). See Energy
Power loom, 610
Power politics, in 18th century, 461
Pragmatic Sanction, 447
Prejudice. See Anti-Semitism; Race and
 racism
Presbyterian Church, 453
Préval, René (Haiti), 906
Prices
 of oil, 847(b), 847–848
 in 17th century, 436
Prince Edward Island, 741
Principia (Newton), 469, 472, 473, 474
Printing
 in China, 553
 knowledge and, 467
 in Mughal India, 533
Prisoners of war, in Second World War, 832,
 834
Privacy, in 18th century, 483
Private enterprise, in China, 873
Private property. See Property
Privatization, in Russia, 862
Production. See also Industrialization;
 Manufacturing
 efficiency of, 609
 Great Depression and, 809, 810
 in Second World War, 832
Professions, 651
Progress
 in Asia and Middle East, 868
 Enlightenment thinkers on, 472
Proletariat, 639
Propaganda
 in movies, 776
 in Nazi Germany, 776, 821(i), 822
 on radio, 777
 Soviet, 814, 816
 in totalitarian states, 814
Property
 in Japan, 564
 women and, 652
Prosperity
 in Japan, 860
 after Second World War, 838, 857
 in United States, 856–857
Prostitution, 949
 child, 950
 government regulation of, 653
Protectionism, 844
Protective tariffs
 in France, 618
 Great Depression and, 809, 812
Protectorate, 454, 673
 in Africa, 673, 674, 676
 Cuba as, 900
 in England, 454
Protest(s). See also Independence; Revolts
 and rebellions
 in China, 549–550, 873
 cocoa holdups as, 812

 in Gold Coast, 908
 in Japan, 564, 708
 in Latin America, 723
 in Middle East, 885(m)
 in Russia, 649
 in South Africa, 915
 student, 858
 in Tunisia, 887–888
Protestants and Protestantism. See also
 Christians and Christianity; Puritans
 African Americans as, 738
 in Americas, 431
 in France, 439, 590
 in Nazi Germany, 822
 North German Confederation and, 647
 sciences and, 472
 Thirty Years' War and, 437
Protestant Union, 437
Providence colony, 458
Provinces, in China, 548
Provisional government (Russia), 764–765
Pruitt, Ida, 799
Prussia. See also Brandenburg-Prussia;
 German Empire; Germany
 absolutism in, 446–447
 Anglo-German rivalry and, 753
 Austro-Prussian War and, 645–647
 dual revolution and, 635
 Enlightenment and, 478
 France and, 599
 Franco-Prussian War and, 647–648
 French Revolution and, 591, 596–597
 in German Empire, 659
 German unification and, 645, 647–648
 in Grand Alliance, 442
 as Great Power, 447
 Hohenzollern rulers of, 444(m), 445
 in Quadruple Alliance, 634
 revolution of 1848 and, 642(i), 643
 in 17th century, 445–446
 in Seven Years' War, 580
Psychology, Freudian, 774
Ptolemy, Claudius (astronomer), 466, 469
 Geography by, **414**
Public, the, in 18th century, 620
Public health, in Japan, 709
Public health movement, 650
Public opinion, urban culture and, 850
Public services, in Russia, 862
Public sphere, 476–477, 476(i)
Public transportation, 650–651
Public works
 in Nazi Germany, 821
 projects in Great Depression, 810
Publishing. See also Book(s); Printing
 in China, 553
Puddling furnace, 613
Puerto Rico, 733
Pugachev, Emelian, 478–479
Pulaar language, 495
Punch magazine, 650(i)
Punishment. See also Justice
 Ottoman, 523

Punjab, 542, 880(m)
Purges
in China, 797
in Soviet Union, 817, 848
Puritans, 452
in England, 452–454
occupations of, 453(i)
Putin, Vladimir, 862–863, 862(i)
Putting-out system, 538, 609, 618
Pyrenees, Treaty of the, 443

Qazvin, Persia, 526
Qi (vital energy), 552(b)
Qianlong emperor (China), 556, 557, 572
Qing (Manchu) **Dynasty** (China), 543, 546, **555**–557, 556(m)
Chinese society under, 704–706
revolution against, 795
Russia and, 557
scholar-officials and, 557
Taiping Rebellion and, 704
trade and, 572, 702–704
Qinsay. *See* Hangzhou
Qizilbash Sufis, Safavid Empire and, **525,** 526, 533
Quadruple Alliance, 634, 635
Quakers, 431
Quebec, 458, 580, 740
in Dominion of Canada, 741
Quebec Act (England, 1774), 740
Queens. *See also* Monarchs and monarchies; specific rulers
in Africa, 498(i)
Quilon, India, 408
Quinine, malaria and, **678**–679
Qum, Persia, 526(m)
Qur'an, religious toleration and, 534

Rabin, Yitzhak (Israel), 886
Race and racism. *See also* Ethnic groups and ethnicity; Holocaust
African slavery and, 579
in Americas, 746
in Australia, 742, 745, 746
concept of, 427, 488
Enlightenment and, 488
equality concepts and, 579
in Fascist Italy, 819
in French colonies, 487
Harper's Weekly racist cartoon and, 739(i)
Holocaust and, 806, 826, 826(m), 827(b)
in India, 699
Japanese and, 826
Jews and, 657, 661–662, 819
in Latin America, 424(i), 723, 727
mixed-race peoples and, 487
Nazism and, 827(b)
new imperialism and, 677–678
science and, 488, 656–657
Shakespeare and, 430
in South Africa, 913, 914
in United States, 740
Race riots, in United States, 740

Racine, Jean, 441
Radical democratic republicanism, nationalism and, 637
Radicalism
in France, 576, 590, 591–594, 811
liberalism and, 635–637
after Napoleonic wars, 634
nationalism and, 637
socialism and, 638–639
Radical totalitarian dictatorships, 812, 813–814
Radio, 776–777, 821(i), 948
Radioactive fallout, 933
Railroads, 612, 613(f)
in Asia, 717
in Australia, 745
in Canada, 741
in China, 704, 705(i)
in colonial Africa, 675
in continental Europe, 617(m)
in England, 613, 613(m), 617
in India, 697
in Iran, 790
in Japan, 709
in Latin America, 727
in Russia, 648
in Third World, 687
in United States, 738
Rákóczy, Francis (Hungary), 445
Rape, 949
in Second Congo War, 919
in Second World War, 832
Rape of Nanjing, 801–802, 828
Rasputin, 764
Rathenau, Walter, 759
Rationalism, 489
of Hume, 475
Rationing, in First World War, 759, 761(i)
Raw materials
Asia and, 812
in Congo, 919
in First World War, 759
in United States, 738, 746
Razin, Stenka, 449
Reading. *See also* Education; Literacy; Literature
revolution in, 476–477
Reagan, Ronald, 859, 861
Haiti and, 906
Sandinistas and, 905–906
Realism, in literature, 657–658
Rearmament, in Nazi Germany, 821, 822
Reason and reasoning. *See also* Intellectual thought
empirical, 470
Enlightenment and, 464
inductive and deductive, 470
natural law and, 488
Rebellions. *See* Revolts and rebellions
Recessions. *See* Great Depression
Reconquista
European expansion after, 413
Ottoman support of Muslims and, 521

Reconstruction (U.S.), 738
Recreation. *See* Leisure and recreation
Red Army (Soviet Union), 766(i), 767, 814, 832, 833
Red Guards (China), **871**–872
Reds, Bolsheviks as, 767
Red Sea region, Indian trade in, 538
Red Shirts (Italy), 645
Red Terror (Soviet Union, 1918–1920), 767
Red Turbans (China), 548
Reform(s)
in Africa, 917
in Brazil, 900
in Britain, 639–640
in China, 549–550, 704–706, 872–873
in cities, 649–650
in Cuba, 901
in Egypt, 684–686, 685(b)
by French Popular Front government, 811
in India, 793, 883
in Iran, 892
in Iraq, 791
in Japan, 707–708, 795
in Korea, 711
in Latin America, 725
New Deal and, 810
in Ottoman Empire, 682–683
political, in Africa since 1990, 915–919
in Russia, 449–452, 478–479, 648
social, 843, 846, 857
in Songhai, 497
in South Africa, 915
in Soviet Union, 849, 850–851
in Spain, 722
Reform Bill (England), First (1832), 639
Refugees
Afghan in Pakistan, 881
children as, 950
Cuban, 901
Indian and Pakistani Hindus and Muslims as, 880
Jewish, 792
Palestinian, 884
Regents
Dutch, 455–457
French, 440
Regional powers, 929
Regulating Act (England, 1773), 540
Regulation. *See* Law (political)
Reichstag (Germany), 659, 759, 820
coalition in First World War, 763–764
Reign of Terror (France), **592**–594
Relativity theory, 774
Relief programs. *See also* Social welfare
in Great Depression, 810
Religion(s). *See also* Monks and monasteries; Philosophy; Secularism; specific groups
Abrahamic, 891(m)
in Afghanistan, 790
English civil war and, 452–454, 454(m)
Enlightenment and, 472–473

in France, 590
in India, 795
in Iran, 790
in Ireland, 660
Islam and, 533
in Japan, 558
Leibniz on, 475
of Mexica, 420
in Middle East since 1945, 883–892
in Ottoman Empire, 683
in Philippines, 702
sciences and, 472, 489
Shi'a Islam, 525–526
Thirty Years' War and, 437–438
in Tibet, 928(b)
in Turkey, 788–789
in Vietnam, 700
Voltaire on, 475
Religious orders, Christian, in East Asia, 571
Religious toleration
in England, 454, 455
for European Jews, 480
in France, 590
by Frederick the Great, 478
in Holland, 505
Mendelssohn, Moses, on, 481(b)
in Muslim world, 534–535
Religious wars, jihads as, 669
Rembrandt van Rijn, *Jewish Bride, The,*
456(i)
Renaissance
Chinese, 797
European, 467
Renationalization, in Russia, 862
Reparations
after First World War, 770, 771–772,
810
after Second World War, 841
Representative government. *See also*
Constitutionalism
in France, 587
ideas of, 579–580, 635
Republic(s)
in China, 706
Dutch, 455
in 1848, 641(i)
France as, 576, 591–592
in Germany, 768
in Soviet Union, 855(m)
in United States, 583–584
Republicanism, 452
in China, 705–706
Dutch, 452
in France, 811
Republic of China (ROC), 875. *See also*
Taiwan
Republic of South Africa. *See* South Africa
Republic of the Congo, slave trade and, 513
Republic of the United Provinces of the
Netherlands. *See* United Provinces of
the Netherlands
Reservations (Native American), 733–734,
738

Residency requirements, in France, Russia,
and Japan, 560
Resistance. *See also* Revolts and rebellions;
Revolution(s)
to British in India, 696, 696(m)
by Gandhi, 794–795, 857
in Latin America, 725–726
in Nazi Germany, 822
in Second World War, 843
to Western imperialism, 681
Resources. *See also* Natural resources
global, 941
wood shortages and, 611
Restoration
in England, 454–455
in France, 634
Meiji (Japan), 707–708
Reunification. *See also* Unification
of Germany, 855
of Vietnam, 877
Revisionism, socialists and, **662,** 773
Revolts and rebellions. *See also* Revolution(s)
Arab, 784, 786–787
in China, 798
in France, 440, 592, 592(m)
in Haiti, 599–603, 725, 906
in Ireland, 453
in Italy, 645
in Japan, 564
in Latin America, 724–725
in Mughal Empire, 527
against Napoleon, 597–599
in Philippines, 701(b), 702
in Russia, 449, 478–479
in Saint-Domingue, 600–603
against Spain, 443
Revolution(s). *See also* Dual revolution;
Industrial Revolution; Revolts and
rebellions; Scientific Revolution
American, 576
in Atlantic world, 576–603
in Austrian Empire, 642–643
in China (1911), 706, 795
consumer, 482–483
in Cuba, 900–902, 901(i)
dual, 632, 635
of 1848, 640–643
English Glorious Revolution, 455
in France, 576, 584–595, 640–641
in Haiti, 599–603, 725
in Hungary (1848), 642
in Hungary (1956), 849
in Iran (1979), 848, 890–891
Irish revolutionary movement and, 660
in Latin America, 722–725
Marx on, 639
medical, 945–947
Mexican (1910), 729, 899
of 1989, 851–855
in Ottoman Empire, 683
in Russia, 750, 764–767
in Turkey, 787–790
Velvet Revolution, 851, 854(b)

Revolutionary era, in America, 581–584
Reza Shah Pahlavi. *See* Pahlavi family
Rhineland
after First World War, 769, 771
France and, 591
Nazi invasion of, 822
Rhode Island colony, 458
Rhodes, Cecil, 674
Rhodesia, 674
Ribeiro, Diogo, world map of, 417(m)
Ricardo, David, 615
Ricci, Matteo, 554, 571
Rice
in Africa, 497
in Great Depression, 812
in Japan, 709
miracle rice, 938
Rice plantations, 458
Richardson, Victor, 762(b)
Richelieu, Cardinal (Armand Jean du
Plessis), 440
Riefenstahl, Leni, 776
Rigaud, André, 601–602
Rights. *See also* Human rights; Liberty(ies)
of children, 950–951
Locke on, 455
of women, 652, 735, 949
Rio de Janeiro, 511, 511(i)
Rio de la Plata, 722
goods from, 723
Rio Grande River, 733
Riots. *See also* Revolts and rebellions
in Alexandria, 686
in China, 554
in India, 793
in Japan, 564
in Venezuela, 905
Ripon Land Regulation Act (Australia,
1831), 744–745
Rite of Spring, The (Stravinsky), 776
Rizal, José, 701(b), 701(i)
Robespierre, Maximilien, 591, 592, 594,
594(i)
ROC. *See* Republic of China (ROC)
Rockefeller, John D., 846(b)
Rocket (locomotive), **613**
Rococo style, 477
Roman Catholic Church. *See also* Christians
and Christianity; Monks and
monasteries; Orthodox Church;
Religious orders
in Asia, 713
book publication and, 484–485
in Canada, 740
on Copernican hypothesis, 468
in England, 454, 455
English Puritans and, 453
Ethiopia and, 500
in France, 590, 592, 595, 660
in Latin America, 430–431
Mussolini and, 819
in Nazi Germany, 822
in Philippines, 702, 802

Roman Catholic Church (continued)
  in Poland, 851
  scientific revolution and, 472
  Thirty Years' War and, 437
  in Vietnam, 700
Romance literature, in China, 553(i)
Romance of the Three Kingdoms, The (China), 554
Romania and Romanians
  after First World War, 768
  revolution and, 851–852
Roman Inquisition. See Inquisition
Romanov family (Russia)
  Anastasia (wife of Ivan IV), 448
  Ivan IV and, 448
  Michael, 448–449
Romanticism, 657
Rome (city), 832
  Italian unification and, 645
  papacy in, 644
Rome, Treaty of (1957), 844
Rome-Berlin Axis (1936), 822
Roosevelt, Franklin Delano, 810, 840–841, 840(i)
  fireside chats by, 777
Roosevelt, Theodore, on Uganda Railway, 690(i)
Rosas, Juan Manuel de, 726
Ross, John (Cherokee), 734
Rousseau, Jean-Jacques, 477–478, 488
Rousseff, Dilma (Brazil), 900
Rowlandson, Thomas, 503(i)
Rowlatt Acts (British India, 1919), 793
Roy, Rammohun (India), 695(i), 699
Royal African Company, 425
Royal and Supreme Council of the Indies, 422–423
Royal courts. See Court (royal)
Royalty. See Monarchs and monarchies; specific rulers
Rubber industry
  in Africa, 673
  synthetic, 759
Rudolph II (Holy Roman Empire), 468
Rugs. See Carpets
Ruhr region, occupation after First World War, 771, 771(m)
Ruiters, Dierick, 495–496
Rump Parliament (England), 454
Rural areas
  in Japan, 563–564
  labor in, 609
  migration from, 846
Russia. See also Russian revolution; Soviet Union; Tsars
  abolition of serfdom in, 736–737
  absolutism in, 447–452, 682
  Africa and, 916–917
  alliance against Ottomans, 522
  American Revolution and, 584
  Anglo-Russian Agreement and, 753
  Bismarck's alliance system and, 753
  Catherine the Great in, 478–479

China and, 557
civil war in, 767, 767(m), 814
after communism, 856, 861–863
dictatorship in, 766–767
dual revolution and, 635
economy in, 648, 861–862
Estonia annexed by, 436
expansion of, 447(m), 449
before First World War, 753
First World War and, 755, 757
France and, 596, 597, 753
German account of, 450–451(b), 451(i)
as Great Power, 449
Indian trade in, 538
industrialization and, 616, 618, 619–620
Iran and, 790
Iraq War and, 927
Japan and, 648
Jews in, 661(i), 662
March Revolution in, 764–765, 766
modernization of, 648–649
Mongols and, 447
mutiny in 1917, 763
Napoleon in, 596, 597, 598(m), 599
nationalism and, 637
nation building in, 648–649
nobility in, 448
nuclear weapons and, 933
oil in, 846(b), 862
Olearius on, 450–451, 451(i)
Ottoman losses to, 541–542
partition of Poland and, 480(m)
peasants in, 448(i), 648
Peter the Great in, 449–451, 449(i)
Putin in, 862–863
in Quadruple Alliance, 634
railroads in, 648
St. Petersburg construction and, 450
serfs in, 449
socialism in, 662
spheres of influence of, 648
and successor states, 855(m)
warfare of, 450
Westernization of, 451–452
Russian Federation, 856
Russian revolution, of 1917, 480, 750, 764–766, 816
Russo-Japanese War, 712
Rutherford, Ernest, 774
Rwanda
  atrocities in, 835, 919
  civil war in, 929

Sadat, Anwar, 887
Saddam Hussein. See Hussein, Saddam
Safavid Empire (Persia), 518, 525–526, 525(i), 526(m)
  Armenian Christians in, 535, 539
  cities in, 529
  decline of, 526, 536–537, 540
  Ottomans and, 522–523, 524(b), 526
  religion in, 533
  trade in, 412

Sahara Desert region, and trans-Saharan trade in West Africa, 494, 497
Said, Sayyid (Oman), 672
Saikaku, Ihara (Japan), 562–563
Sailing. See also Ships and shipping
  lateen sail and, 414
  lives of sailors, 413
Saint-Domingue, 484, 580, 599. See also Haiti
  revolution in, 576
  Toussaint L'Ouverture and, 600–603
St. Helena, Napoleon's exile to, 599
St. Lawrence River region, 420, 740
Saint-Louis, Senegambia, 513
St. Lucia, immigrants to, 731
St. Petersburg, Russia, 451
  battle at, 825
  Lenin in, 766
  Petrograd Soviet and, 765
Saint-Simon, Henri de, 638–639
St. Vincent, immigrants to, 731
Salons, 474(i), 477
Salt, in West Africa, 499
SALT talks. See Strategic Arms Limitation Talks
SALWs. See Small arms and light conventional weapons
Samarkand, Timur from, 520
Same-sex relations, 653. See also Homosexuality
Samurai (Japan), 559, 560–561, 570(i), 708
  Christian, 571
  modernization and, 707
  taxation of, 564
  Tokugawa Shogunate and, 560–561
Sanctions, on Iraq, 892
Sandinista National Liberation Front (FSLN), 896, 897(i), 905–906
Sanitation, in cities and towns, 649–650, 650(i)
San Salvador, 416, 417
Sans-culottes (France), 592, 593(i), 594
Santa Anna, Antonio López de, 726
São Paulo, working population of, 732
São Tomé and Principe, 919
Sarajevo, Francis Ferdinand assassinated in, 755
Sardinia, 644, 645
Sarfati, Isaac, 535
SARS. See Severe acute respiratory syndrome
Sartre, Jean-Paul, 773
Saskatchewan, in Dominion of Canada, 741, 741(m)
Sassoon, Siegfried, 755
Sati (widow immolation, India), 535
Satyagraha (soul force), 794
Saudi Arabia, 884
  oil in, 846(b)
  in OPEC, 846(b)
Savanna (Africa), slave trade in, 506
Savery, Thomas, 611
Savoy, France and, 591
Saxony, Napoleon and, 596

Sayings of a Female Doctor (Tan Yunxian), 552(b)

Scandinavia
    Great Depression and, 810–811
    immigrants to United States from, 739
Schlieffen plan, 755, 755(m)
Scholar-official class (China), 557. *See also* Civil service; Civil service examinations
Scholarship. *See also* Intellectual thought
    scientific revolution and, 467
Schönberg, Arnold, 776
Schools. *See also* Education; Universities and colleges
    in Japan, 708
    missionary, in Africa, 676(i)
    segregation in, 857
Science(s). *See also* Astronomy; Mathematics; Philosophy; Scientific Revolution
    academies for, 471
    anxiety and postwar, 773–774
    environmentalism and, 947–948
    for masses, 653–657
    medical revolution and, 945
    natural philosophy as, 466–467
    race and, 427, 488
    religion and, 472
    society and, 471–472, 653–657
    Western in China, 572
    women in, 471–472
Scientific instruments, navigational, 467
Scientific method, 469, 470
Scientific revolution, 466–474, 489
    Copernican hypothesis and, 468–469
    Enlightenment and, 472–473
    industrialization and, 608
    Newton and, 469–470
    origins of, 467
    race and, 488
Scotland
    in Britain, 608
    Enlightenment in, 475, 484
    Presbyterian Church in, 453
"Scramble for Africa" (1880–1914), 672–674
Script, Turkish, 790
Seaborne trade. *See* Maritime trade; Trade
Seacole, Mary, 728–729(b), 729(i)
Secondary education, children in, 951
Second Balkan War, 754
Second Battle of the Aisne, 763
Second Battle of the Marne, 768
Second Coalition, against France, 596
Second Congo War, 919, 919(m)
Second Continental Congress (U.S.), 583
Second industrial revolution, 615–616
Second Intifada, 886
Second law of motion, of Kepler, 468
Second Lebanon War, 889
Second Revolution
    in French Revolution, 591–592
    in Soviet Union (1930s), 815, 817

Second Sino-Japanese War, 802, 828
Second Treatise of Civil Government (Locke), 455
Second World, use of term, 868
Second World War, 806
    Africa and, 825(m), 832, 908
    Allies in, 832
    atomic bomb in, 834, 834(i)
    casualties in, 806, 826, 828, 833(i), 834
    Cold War after, 840–843
    decolonization after, 844–845
    in Europe, 824–826, 825(m), 832–833
    events leading to, 822–824, 830(f)
    Great Depression and, 810
    Holocaust in, 806, 807(i), 826, 826(m), 827(b)
    Italian surrender in, 832
    occupation zones after, 841, 843
    opening of, 824–826
    in Pacific, 826–832, 831(m), 833–834
    Philippines during, 876
    recovery after, 843–848
    wartime conferences in, 840–841, 840(i)
Secret ballot, in Australia, 745
Secret police, Soviet, 767, 817, 849
Secret service, in China, 549
Secret societies, 477
Secular governments, Muslims in Middle East and, 883
Secularism, in Turkey, 788–789, 890
Security Council (UN), **926**, 927. *See also* Peacekeeping (UN); United Nations
    China on, 875
    Iraq and, 859, 892
    Israel-Lebanon War and, 889
Sedan, battle at, 648
Sedition Act (U.S, 1918), 759
Segregation
    in South Africa, 675
    in United States, 857
Sekigahara, Japan, 560
Self-determination, after First World War, 783
Self-government
    in Africa, 908
    of Australia, 745
    for India, 792–793
    in League mandates, 783
    for South Africa, 913
Self-interest, economic, 475
Self-strengthening movement, in China, 704–705
Selim I (Ottomans), 521
Selim II (Ottomans), 524(b)
Selim III (Ottomans), 683
Semiskilled workers, 652
Seneca Falls Convention, 735
Senegal, soldier from, 751(i)
Senegambia, 492, 494–495, 507, 513
Sensibility, cult of, 477
Separate spheres, 624, 653

Separation of church and state, in Latin America, 726
Separatism
    civil wars and, 929
    in India, 882
Sepoys (India), **539,** 696
September 11, 2001, terrorist attacks, 881, 932, 932(i)
Serbia
    autonomy for, 682
    First World War and, 757, 768
    Francis Ferdinand assassination and, 755
    Milosevic and, 863
    nationalism in, 754
Serbs, in Yugoslavia, 863
Serer language, 495
Serfs and serfdom. *See also* Peasants
    in Austria, 479
    in eastern Europe, 436–437
    in Estonia, 436(i)
    in Prussia, 478
    in Russia, 449, 479, 736–737
    in 17th century, 436–437
    slaves and, 506, 507
Servants. *See also* Indentured labor; Slavery
    blacks as, 503
    Islamic, 529
Service employees, 846
Service nobility, in Russia, 448
Settlement(s)
    by Europeans, 687–688
    of West Bank, 886
    by whites in Africa, 909
Seven Years' War, 484, 580
    Canada and, 740
    European claims in North American and India before and after, 581(m)
    France and, 540, 584
    India and, 540, 581(m)
    North America and, 540, 580, 581(m), 740
Severe acute respiratory syndrome (SARS), 946
Seville, 426
Sewage systems
    in English cities, 649–650
    in United States, 739
Sex and sexuality. *See also* Gender
    medical studies of, 653
Sex traffickers, 949
Sexual abuse, of children, 950
Sexual division of labor, 624–625, 652
Sexual violence, 949
    in Congo-Kinshasa, 919
Shah (Persia), **525**. *See also* Pahlavi family
    of Iran, 790, 890
    of Safavid state, 525
Shahjahanabad. *See* Delhi, India
Shaka (Zulu leader), 674
Shakespeare, William, 430
Shandong (Shantung) Peninsula, Japan and, 757, 795, 798
Shanghai, China, Japanese in, 801

Shantytowns, 942–943
Sharpeville, South Africa, police shootings in, 914
Shawnee Indians, 733
Sheep, in Australia, 744
Shenbao (newspaper), 706(*i*)
Shenyang (Mukden), 800
Sherman, W. T., 734
Shi'a (Shi'ite) Muslims, 891(*m*)
    in Iran, 891, 892
    in Iraq, 929
    in Persia, 523
    Safavid Empire and, 523, 525–526, 526(*m*), 540
    Shi'ite/Sunni split and, 533
Ships and shipping. *See also* Navy; Railroads; Trade
    in American Revolution, 583
    caravels and, 414
    in China, 566
    Dutch, 457
    in England, 608
    Ottomans and, 521
    Portuguese, 537
Shiraz, Persia, 526(*m*)
Shoa, Ethiopia, Galla occupation of, 500
Shock therapy, in Russia, 862
Shoguns (Japan)
    Kamakura, 558
    modernization and, 707
    succession to, 558
    Tokugawa, 543
Shore trading, 512
Siam. *See* Thailand (Siam)
Siberia, Russia and, 447, 449
Sicily
    under Bourbons, 644
    Italian unification and, 645
Siderus Nuncius (Galileo), 469
Sierra Club, 947
Sierra Leone
    Amistad case and, 667(*i*)
    child soldiers in, 950(*i*)
    warfare in, 929
Sieyès, Emmanuel Joseph (Abbé de), 588–589(*b*), 589(*i*)
Sigismund (Hungary), 520
Sigismund I (Poland), 524(*b*)
Sikhs, 533, 882
    Amritsar Massacre and, 793
Silent Spring (Carson), 947
Silesia, 446(*m*), 447, 478, 580
Silk, in Japan, 709
Silver
    China and, 428(*b*), 555, 703
    in Latin America, 426
    in Mexico, 426, 428(*b*), 429(*b*)
    from New Spain, 426
    trade and, 428–429(*b*), 429(*m*)
    in United States, 738
Silver Pavilion (Japan), 558
Simone, Suzanne, 602(*b*)
Sinai Peninsula, 884, 887

Singapore, 875
    as Asian tiger, 875
    Indians in, 714
    in Second World War, 830
Singapore model, 875
Singh, Manmohan, 883
Sino-Japanese War, 705, 710(*b*), 711
    Second (1937–1945), 802, 828, 870
Sioux Indians, 734
    gold and silver on reservations of, 738
Six-Day War (1967), 884, 887
Skepticism, in Enlightenment, 473, 475
Skilled workers
    in social hierarchy, 652
    unions for, 662
Skyscrapers
    in Japan, 709(*i*)
    in United States, 775
Slave army. *See* Janissaries
Slave labor camps. *See* Forced labor
Slavery. *See also* Serfs and serfdom; Slave trade
    African, 415, 425, 492, 514, 668–669
    in Americas, 514
    auction in 1850s, 736(*i*)
    blackness and, 506–507
    in Cape Colony, 503–504, 674
    in Caribbean region, 601
    colonial economies and, 483, 485(*m*)
    devshirme system and, 523
    encomienda system as, 423, 423(*i*)
    goods produced by, 483
    in Haiti, 599
    imports by destination (1501–1866), 507(*f*)
    industrialization and, 628–629
    intercolonial trade and, 483
    Islam and, 503, 672
    Jewish ownership of, 487
    in Korea, 566–567
    in Latin America, 727
    in Mughal India, 527
    in New England, 458
    Ottoman, 520, 523–525
    race and, 427
    racial regimes and, 579
    Safavid, 526
    in Saint-Domingue, 600
    in Senegambia, 495
    slaves as chattel and, 495
    in Songhai, 497
    sugar and, 425
    in United States, 584, 735–738
    in West Indies, 459
Slave trade, 497, 507, 508–509(*b*). *See also* Slavery
    abolition of, 513, 514, 629, 672
    African, 411, 512
    African society and, 512–514
    in Brazil, 511, 511(*i*)
    Britain and, 444(*m*), 459
    Dutch in, 459
    economy and, 628–629
    international, 509(*m*)

    Portugal and, 426
    Senegambia and, 494
    sugar and, 425
    suppression of, 506
    transatlantic, 503–514, 514(*f*)
    in triangle trade, 512
    in United States, 584, 735
    Venetian and Genoese, 412
    in West Africa, 668
Slavs. *See also* Baltic region
    after First World War, 768
    before First World War, 754
    as immigrants to United States, 739
    Nazis and, 822, 826
    romantics and languages of, 657
    women as slaves, 503
Sleeping sickness, 507
Slovenia, 863
Slums. *See also* Shantytowns
    clearance of, 650
Small arms and light conventional weapons (SALWs), 934–935(*b*)
Smallpox
    in Africa, 498
    in American slaves, 507
    in Americas, 423
    in China, 554
    inoculation for, 572, 945
Smith, Adam, 475, 482, 637
Smoking. *See* Tobacco
Smolensk, Napoleon and, 599
Snayers, Peeter, 443(*i*)
Soaps, palm oil for, 670(*i*)
Social Christian Party of Venezuela (COPEI), 903
Social class. *See* Class
Social Contract, The (Rousseau), 477–478
Social Darwinism, 656, 677–678
Social Democrats (Germany), 659, 662, 772, 820
Social hierarchies, 651. *See also* Hierarchy
Socialism, 638–639. *See also* Bolsheviks; Communism; Marx, Karl; Nazi Party; Soviet Union
    in Africa, 937
    anti-imperialism and, 681
    in China, 871
    democratic, 850
    egalitarian in Jewish Palestine, 792
    in England, 773
    in Europe, 658–659, 662–663
    in First World War governments, 760
    in France, 660
    in Germany, 659
    Hong Kong and, 876
    in Italy, 817
    nationalism, industrialization, and, 937
    in Scandinavia, 810–811
    after Second World War, 843
    in Venezuela, 902, 905
Socialist Party
    in France, 811
    in Italy, 817, 818

Socialist realism, Soviet, 872(i)
Socialists, after First World War, 768
Social mobility, in Latin America, 723
Social networking, 948
Social revolution
    in Soviet Union, 850
    in United States, 857
Social security system
    in Germany, 659
    in United States, 810
Social services, in colonial Africa, 675
Social welfare
    in Britain, 773
    before First World War, 753
    in Great Depression, 810–811
    after Second World War, 844
Society. *See also* Civilization(s); Culture(s);
        Elites
    in Africa, 494(m)
    Asian, 716–717
    in Brazil, 900
    in British India, 696
    changes in revolutionary era, 578–580
    in China, 704–706
    coffeehouses and, 533–534
    in Europe, 578–579
    in First World War, 759–763
    Great Depression and, 809
    impact of slave trade in Africa, 512–515
    Industrial Revolution and, 606,
        620–629
    in Japan, 707, 860, 861
    in Latin America, 723, 728
    in Mexico, 899
    migrants and European, 844
    in Nazi Germany, 820–822
    science and, 471–472, 654–657
    after Second World War, 845–846
    in Senegambia, 495
    in South Africa, 914–915
    Soviet, 816
    totalitarianism and, 813–814
    in Turkey, 789–790
    in U.S. South, 738
    Western expansion and, 679–680
    women in, 949
Society of Jesus. *See* Jesuits
Sofala (city-state), 501(m), 504(b)
    Portuguese in, 501
Soil, in Africa, 507
Sokoto caliphate, 670–672
Solar system. *See* Astronomy; Universe
Soldiers. *See also* Armed forces; Military;
        Wars and warfare; specific battles
        and wars
    children as, 950, 950(i)
    in First World War, 757
    German in First World War, 760(b)
    in Japan, 708
    Russian, 763, 765
    from Senegal, 751(i)
Solidarity movement, **851,** 852–853(b)
Solzhenitsyn, Aleksandr, 849

Somalia
    civil war in, 919, 927
    Convention on the Rights of the Child
        and, 950
    warfare in, 929
Somme, Battle of the, 755
Somoza, Anastasio, 905
Song Dynasty (China), printing in, 553
Songhai, 492, 494, 496
    economy in, 497
    empire of, 497
Sonni Ali (Songhai), 496
Sorting, in trade, **512**
Sotho people, 674
South (global), 896, 940. *See also* Develop-
        ing countries; Third World
South (U.S.)
    blacks in, 735–738
    Civil War in, 732, 735–738
    Reconstruction in, 738
    slaves in, 672
South Africa. *See also* Southern Africa
    apartheid in, 914
    Chinese in, 714
    as democracy, 919
    economic sanctions against, 915
    economy of, 915
    Gandhi in, 715, 793
    HIV-AIDS in, 946
    independence for, 913
    Indians in, 714, 793
    Mandela in, 914, 915
    as middle power, 929
    Native Land Act in, 913, 913(m)
    native reserves in, 913
    race in, 913
    soccer in, 914(i)
    Union of, 675
    whites in, 909
South African War, 674, 753, 913
South America. *See also* Latin America;
        specific locations
    bullion from, 499
    independence in, 724(m), 725
    indigo in, 689(b)
    Japanese in, 714
    Magellan and, 419
    trade and, 459
    Venezuela and, 905
South Asia. *See also* Asia; Southeast Asia;
        specific locations
    immigrants to Latin America, 731
South Carolina, in U.S. Civil War, 736
South China Sea, 408
Southeast Asia, 409. *See also* Asia; specific
        locations
    Chinese migrants in, 690, 713
    colonialism in, 699–702
    economy in, 876–877
    independence in, 802–803
    India and, 408
    Japan and, 566
    nationalism in, 795–803

peoples and cultures of, 409
political progress in, 876–877
Second World War in, 830, 831(m)
Vietnam and, 700
Southeastern Europe, Ottomans and, 682
Southern Africa. *See also* South Africa
    decolonization and, 913–915
    democracies in, 919
    development of, 674
Southern Europe. *See also* Europe
    industrialization in, 616
Southern Rhodesia, 674. *See also* Zimbabwe
    independence for, 909
    whites in, 909
South Korea, 843. *See also* Korea
    as Asian tiger, 875
    middle powers and, 929
South Sudan, 918–919
South Vietnam, 858, 876. *See also* Vietnam;
        Vietnam War
Southwest Africa, 673. *See also* Africa
Southwest Asia. *See also* Middle East
    Islam in, 682
    new imperialism in, 666
    Young Turks in, 786
Sovereignty
    in England, 455
    of governments over multinationals,
        936–937
Soviets (Russia), 765, 766
Soviet Union. *See also* Cold War; Russia;
        Second World War; Stalin, Joseph
    Afghanistan and, 850, 859, 880
    Asian nationalism and, 783
    atomic bomb and, 933
    China and, 871
    collapse of, 873, 896
    Cuba and, 849, 901–902
    de-Stalinization in, 849
    eastern Europe and, 840, 841, 848–849,
        849–850
    economy in, 814, 815–816, 848
    end of, 855(m), 856
    five-year plans in, 814, 815–816
    foreign policy of, 849, 850–851
    Gorbachev in, 850–851
    Hitler and, 825
    Hungarian revolution (1956) and, 849
    invasion by Nazi Germany, 825
    Jews in, 848
    lifestyle and culture in, 816, 848
    movies in, 776
    nationalism in, 848, 850
    Nazi-Soviet nonaggression pact and, 824,
        825
    New Economic Policy in, 814, 815
    nuclear arms race and, 933
    reforms in, 849, 850–851
    after Second World War, 842–843
    social revolution in, 850
    Spanish civil war and, 823
    Stalin in, 814–817, 848–849
    as superpower, 835

Soviet Union (continued)
  terror and purges in, 817, 848
  totalitarianism in, 806, 813–814
  women in, 816
Spain. See also Reconquista
  absolutism in, 442–443
  Africa and, 672
  American Revolution and, 583
  asiento with Britain and, 444(m)
  Chinese immigrants and, 714
  civil war in, 822–823
  colonial administration by, 422–423
  colonial trade and, 484
  Columbus and, 416
  conservative authoritarianism in, 813
  East Asia and, 567–570
  exploration by, 412, 413
  France and, 597(i)
  gardens in, 531
  Inca and, 422
  Mexico and, 420–422
  Moriscos expelled from, 443
  Napoleon and, 597–599, 597(i)
  Philippines and, 699, 702
  reconquista and, 521
  Saint-Domingue and, 601
  spread of Christianity and, 413
  U.S. expansion and, 733
  War of the Spanish Succession and, 442,
    444(m), 459
Spanish America
  colonies in, 484–485
  mulattos in, 460–461, 460(i)
Spanish-American War, Philippines and,
    680, 702, 802, 802(m)
Spanish Empire
  in Americas, 426–427, 722
  independence in, 576
  U.S. acquisitions and, 733
Spanish Netherlands (Belgium), 444(m)
Special Administrative Region, Hong Kong
    as, 876
Special-interest groups, imperialist expan-
    sion and, 680
Specialization, economic, 651
Species, Darwin on, 654–655
Speculation, in stock market, 860
Spencer, Herbert, 656
Spengler, Oswald, 775
Spheres of influence
  in Persia and Afghanistan, 790–791
  of Russia, 648
Spice trade, 413
  Dutch and, 427
  Portugal and, 537
Spinning, 609, 610, 610(i)
Spinning jenny, 609, 610
Spinoza, Baruch, 473
Spirit of Laws, The (Montesquieu), 473–474
Sports, 652
Squatter settlements, 942–943
Sri Lanka (Ceylon). See also Ceylon
  Zheng He and, 566

SS (Nazi Germany), 821, 822, 826, 827(b)
Stadholder (Dutch Republic), 457
Stalin, Joseph, 814, 824
  death of, 849
  five-year plans of, 814, 815–816
  last years of, 848–849
  after Second World War, 842–843
  Soviet Union under, 814–817
  terror and purges under, 817, 848
  at wartime meetings, 840–841, 840(i)
Stalingrad, Battle of, 825(m), 832
Stamp Act (U.S., 1765), 582, 582(i)
Standard of living
  Dutch, 457
  industrialization and, 606
  in Nazi Germany, 821
  oil prices and, 847(b)
  Soviet, 849, 850
  of workers, 622, 662
Standard Oil Company, 846(b)
START I. See Strategic Arms Reduction
    Treaty
Starvation, 945. See also Famines
  in Biafra, 912
State (nation). See also Nation(s)
  in Europe, 434
  independent African, 910–920
  industrialization, modernization, and,
    937–938
  in Latin America, 722
  after Thirty Years' War, 439
States (U.S.), 733
States General, Dutch, 457
Status. See Class; Society
Steam engine, 611
Steam power, 611–613
  in China, 704
  in factories, 611–613
  in Latin America, 620
  railroads and, 613, 614(f)
  sea transportation and, 687
  steamships and, 619, 679, 687, 714
  Western powers and, 679
Stephenson, George, 613
Sterilization, hospital sanitation and, 650
Sternpost rudder, 414
Stock market
  in Japan, 860
  in Turkey, 890
Stock market crash, of 1929, 806, 808–809
Storm troopers, in Nazi Germany, 821
Strait of Magellan, 419
Strategic Arms Limitation Talks (SALT),
    933
Strategic Arms Reduction Treaty (START 1),
    933
Stravinsky, Igor, 776
Stream-of-consciousness technique,
    774–775
Streetcars, 651
Stresemann, Gustav, 771–772
Strikes. See Labor strikes
Stuart Dynasty (England), 455

Students
  demonstrations and protests by Chinese,
    858, 873
  in 1980s, 848
Subcontractors, for workers, 624
Submarine warfare
  in First World War, 758
  in Second World War, 834
Sub-Saharan Africa. See also Africa
  decolonization in, 906–910
  democracy in, 915–916
  economic development in, 668
  French colonies in, 910
  HIV/AIDS in, 946
  independence in, 896, 906–910
  slave trade in, 668, 669
Succession
  Islamic, 525
  in Japan, 558
  in Ming China, 549
  in Mughal India, 542
  in Ottoman Empire, 540–541
  to sultans, 540–541
  War of the Austrian Succession and, 478,
    580, 584
  War of the Spanish Succession and, 442,
    444(m), 459
Sudan, 494, 496–497
  atrocities in, 835
  British and, 673
  Islam in, 669, 670–672, 673
  oil in, 918–919
  rule in, 918
  Sokoto caliphate and, 670–672
  warfare in, 929
Sudetenland, 823
Suez Canal, 686(m), 688
  Britain and, 712, 786, 791
  Egypt and, 791
Suez Canal Company, nationalization of,
    884
Suffrage. See also Voting and voting rights
  before First World War, 659
  male, 591
  in South Africa, 915
Sufis and Sufism, 520, 533
  Qizilbash Sufis, 525
Sugar and sugar industry
  in Caribbean region, 458
  from Latin America, 723, 727
  Portugal and, 415
  slavery and, 425, 507–508
  trade and, 483
Sukarno, Achmed (Indonesia), 877
Suleiman I ("the Magnificent," Ottomans),
    521, 523, 525, 529
  Hürrem and, 524(b)
  medicine and, 532–533
  succession to, 523, 524(b)
Suleiman, Michel, 889
Sultan(s), 520
  marriage and, 523
  Ottoman, 683

succession to, 540–541
Turkey and, 787
Sumatra
Chinese in, 714
Zheng He and, 566
Sumer and Sumerians, 846(b)
Sun-centered solar system, 468
Sunni Muslims, 891(m)
in Iran, 891
in Iraq, 929
Ottomans as, 523
Shi'ite/Sunni split and, 533
Sun Yatsen (China), 706, 715, 796
Superego, 774
Superpowers, 835, 859, 865
economic, 860
end of Cold War and, 929
"Supplement to Bougainville's Voyage"
(Diderot), 486–487(b), 487(i)
Supreme Leader, in Iran, 892
Supreme Sacred Congregation of the Roman
and Universal Inquisition. See Holy
Office
Suriname, in UNSAN, 906
Survival in Auschwitz (Levi), 827(b)
Survival of the fittest, 656
Su Teh (China), 799(b)
Swahili city-states, 409, 492, 500, 501–502,
505(b)
Portuguese and, 501
Swahili language and culture, **501**. *See also*
Swahili city-states
meaning of *Swahili*, 501
missionary schools and, 676
Swaziland, dictatorship in, 918
Swazi people, 674
Sweated industries, 652
Sweatshops, 652
Sweden
France and, 596
Great Depression and, 810
Russia and, 449, 450
Swedish phase, of Thirty Years' War, 437
Sweet potatoes, in Africa, 498
Sydney, Australia, 743
Sydney Cove, 742
Sykes-Picot Agreement (1916), **786**
Synthetic dye, indigo and, 688–689(i)
Synthetic rubber, 759
Syphilis, in Africa, 498
Syria. *See also* Damascus
after First World War, 770, 786
France and, 791
immigrants to Latin America, 731
independence of, 787, 791, 884
Lebanon and, 791, 889
Ottomans in, 521, 683, 685(b)
Young Turks in, 786
Syrian National Congress, 787

Tabriz, Persia, 526(m)
Taghaza, salt mining in, **496,** 499
Taino people, 416–417

Taiping Rebellion (China), **704**
Taiwan, 567
as Asian tiger, 875
China and, 546, 873, 875
Japan and, 694, 705, 710, 800
Nationalists on, 870
Taizu (China), 548. *See also* Ming Dynasty
Taj Mahal, 529
Takauji (Japan). *See* Ashikaga Shogunate
Taliban
in Afghanistan, 932, 933
nuclear weapons and, 935
in Pakistan, 881
Tamerlane. *See* Timur
Tang Dynasty (China)
printing in, 553
trade and, 565
Tannenberg, Battle of, 755
Tan Yunxian (woman doctor), 552(b), 552(i)
Tanzania, African socialism and, 937
Tanzimat (regulations), **683**
Tariff(s). *See also* Protective tariffs
in France, 442
in Germany, 619
Great Depression and, 809, 812
in Japan, 712
in United States, 746
Tariff protection, 618. *See also* Protective
tariffs
Tatars. *See also* Mongols
Crimean, 479
Taxation
of British North American colonies, 582,
582(i)
in China, 554
in England, 452
in France, 584, 585
in India, 795
in Japan, 563–564
in Mughal Empire, 535
by Napoleon, 597
in Prussia, 446
in Russia, 448, 449
in Scandinavia, 810
in Soviet Union, 816
of Spanish American colonies, 723
Tea
British tax on, in Americas, 582(i)
in China, 572
trade in, 573, 582
Tea Act (U.S., 1773), 582
Tea ceremony, in Japan, 558
Technology. *See also* Green Revolution;
Industrialization; Industrial
Revolution; Science(s)
agriculture and, 938
in Asia, 717
for exploration, 414
global inequality and, 687
green revolution and, 938, 939
industrial, 609
of mass communication, 948
military, 521

Ottomans and, 520
science for masses and, 653–657
steam engine and, 611, 612(b)
for voyages, 414
of Western world, 678–679
Teheran conference (1943), 840
Telegraph, 688
in China, 704
in India, 697
Telephone, 948
Telescope, 467, 468(i), 469
Television, 948
Vietnam War on, 858
Tempest, The (Shakespeare), 430
Ten Hours Act (England, 1847), 639–640
Tennis Court Oath (France), 586, 587(i)
Tenochtitlán, 420, 420(i), 422
Terror, the. *See* Reign of Terror
Terrorism, 930. *See also* Weapons, of mass
destruction
global violence and, 932–933, 932(i)
Islamic fundamentalist, 932–933, 932(i)
against Jews, 821
nuclear materials and, 935
Pakistan-based, 883
in Russia, 863
on September 11, 2001, 881
Soviet, 817
threat of, 930–933
understanding of, 932
Test Act (England, 1673), **455**
Testament of Youth (Brittain), 762(b)
Tet Offensive, 858
Tewfiq (Egypt), 686
Texas, annexation of, 733
Textiles and textile industry. *See also* Cloth
and clothing
in England, 609–611
in Hangzhou, China, 557
in India, 620, 697
Indian cotton and, 537(i)
in Latin America, 620
mills for, 610
in West Africa, 499–500
workers for, 622, 623(i)
Thailand (Siam)
France and, 441(i)
Greenpeace protests in, 939(i)
as independent state, 700–702
Thatcher, Margaret, 848, 859, 861
Theater
in China, 554
in France, 441
in Japan, 547(i), 558, 562, 563(i)
Thermidorian reaction (French Revolu-
tion), **594,** 594(i)
Saint-Domingue and, 601
Thermometer, 467
Things Fall Apart (Achebe), 920
Thinking. *See* Intellectual thought
Third Coalition, against France, 596
Third estate (France), 586
"Third force," of nonaligned nations, 882

Third (Communist) International, 796
Third law of motion, of Kepler, 468
Third of May 1808 (Goya), 597*(i)*
Third Republic (France), 659
Third World, 687, 835, 842
    Asian tigers and, 875
    in Cold War, 868, 929
    conditions constituting, 924
    global South and, 896, 940
    multinationals in, 936–937
    UN and, 927
    use of term, 868
    writers in, 940
Thirty Years' War, 437–438, 438*(m)*
Thomas Aquinas (Saint), 466
Three Principles of the People (Sun Yatsen), 796
Thurlow, Geoffrey, 762*(b)*
Tiananmen Square (Beijing), **873**
    student demonstrations in (1989), 850,
        873
Tibet
    China and, 546, 550–551, 557, 870
    Dalai Lama and, 551, 928*(b)*, 928*(i)*
    Mongols and, 550–551
Tile makers, 532*(i)*
Tilsit, treaties of, 596–597
Timbuktu, 492
    cosmopolitan nature of, 496–497
    Portugal and, 415
Time of Troubles, in Russia, 448–449
Timur (Tamerlane, Turks), 520
    empire of, 520*(m)*
    landscape architects of, 531
Tito, Josip, 848–849
Tlaxcala people, 420
Tobacco, 531*(i)*
    Chelebi on, 530–531*(b)*
Togoland, 673
Tokugawa Ieyasu (Japan), 546, 559–560,
    561*(i)*, 571
Tokugawa Shogunate (Japan), 543, **560,**
    560*(m)*
    lifestyle under, 559–565
    ouster of, 707
Tokyo (Edo), Japan, 559, 560, 562
    craftsmen in, 564*(i)*
    Perry in, 707
Tolerance. *See* Religious toleration
Tondibi, battle at, 497
Tonghak movement (Korea), 710
Topography, of Australia, 742
Tordesillas, Treaty of, 418
Tories (England), reform and, 639–640
Totalitarianism, 806, **813,** 835. *See also*
    Dictators and dictatorships
    in First World War Germany, 759
    in Italy, 817, 819
    radical totalitarian dictatorships and,
        813–814
    Soviet, 806, 813–814
Total war, 759, 760*(b)*
    in First World War, 759–764, 813
    in French Revolution, 592–593

Toure, Muhammad (Songhai), 496, 497
Touré, Sekou, 910
Tourism, in Egypt, 684*(i)*
Toussaint L'Ouverture. *See* L'Ouverture,
    Toussaint
Towns. *See* Cities and towns
Trade. *See also* Coins; Commerce; Maritime
    trade; Silver; Slave trade
    in Africa, 409–412
    African economy and, 513
    in Afroeurasia, 409–412, 411*(m)*
    Arab, 408
    Armenian, 539
    Asian, 565
    Asian-African, 502*(i)*
    Asian nationalism and, 784
    in Atlantic region, 482, 483–484
    in Benin, 496
    in China, 554, 557, 566, 570, 702–704
    China-West, 408
    in Cuba, 901
    Dutch, 427, 459
    in Egypt, 686
    England and, 572, 580
    European in East Asia, 567–570
    European influence and, 629
    European in Indian Ocean, 537–538
    French colonial, 458–459
    in Genoa, 412
    global, 406
    imperialism and, 686
    in India, 408, 538
    in Indian Ocean region, 408–409
    in indigo, 688–689*(b)*, 689*(m)*
    industrialization and, 608, 615
    intercolonial, 483–484
    intercontinental, 688
    international (18th century), 572
    Islamic, 536–540
    in Japan, 562
    in Korea, 711
    in Latin America, 727
    in Mali, 411
    Napoleon I and, 596, 597
    in oil, 846–847*(b)*, 847*(m)*
    in opium, 696, 702, 703
    in palm oil, 668–669
    in Philippines, 702
    precolonial African, 676
    in silver, 428–429*(b)*, 429*(m)*
    silver in China and, 554
    in slaves, 508–509*(b)*, 509*(m)*
    Swahili-Portuguese, 501
    by United States, 738
    in Venice, 412
    in West Africa, 499–500, 668–669
    world market and, 687
Trade routes
    in Africa, 514
    Europeans and East Asian, 567
    in West Africa, 499*(m)*
Trade unions. *See also* Labor unions
    in England, 628

    in France, 660
    Soviet, 816
Trading bloc, EU as, 865
Trading posts. *See also* Entrepôts
    European, 677
    factory-forts as, 512, 537
    Portuguese, 415
Trafalgar, Battle of, 596
Transatlantic trade, slave trade and, 425,
    494, 503–514, 510*(b)*, 514*(f)*, 668
Transoceanic telegraph, 688
Transplants, organ, 945
Transportation. *See also* Railroads; Steam
    power
    in Australia, 745
    in England, 608, 608*(m)*
    public, 650–651
    in West Africa, 499
Trans-Saharan trade. *See also* Africa;
    Sub-Saharan Africa
    in West Africa, 494, 497
Transvaal, 674
Transylvania
    Austria and, 445, 446*(m)*
    Ottomans and, 541
Travel
    in Egypt, 684*(i)*
    in Japan, 563
    between United States and Cuba, 902
    youth, 857
Travels in Muscovy (Olearius), 450–451*(b)*,
    451*(i)*
Travels of Marco Polo, The (Polo), 414
Travels of Sir John Mandeville, The, 413–414,
    413*(i)*
Treaties. *See also* specific treaties
    Napoleonic, 596
    with Native Americans, 734
    after Opium War, 703
    after Thirty Years' War, 437–438
Treaty ports, in China, 704
Trees, in China, 554
Trench warfare, 755
Trial, The (Kafka), 775
Trials, in Soviet Union, 817
Triangle trade, 483
    slave trade in, 512
Tributary system, in China, 565
Trinidad, 714
    immigrants to, 731
Triple Alliance, 752*(m)*, 753, 757
Triple Entente, 752*(m)*, **753**
    Italy in, 757
    United States and, 758
Triumph of the Will, The (movie), 776
Trotsky, Leon, 766, 767, 814
Truman, Harry S., 841–842, 843, 856
Truman Doctrine, 842
Tsars (Russia), 447, 448–449. *See also*
    specific rulers
Tsetse fly, 507
Tsong-kha-pa (Tibet), 551
Tsunami, in Japan (2011), 861

Tswana people, 674
Tuareg people, **499**
Tuberculosis, 945
Tuileries palace, capture of, 591
Tunisia
    demonstrations in, 887–888
    France in, 678(b)
    Ottomans in, 521
Tupac Amaru II (Peru), 725
Turkestan, China and, 557
Turkey, 683, 891(m). See also Anatolia;
        Ottoman Empire; Ottomans
    economy of, 890
    EU and, 865, 890
    after First World War, 770, 784, 787–789
    fundamentalists in, 883
    immigrants to Latin America, 731
    janissaries in, 682
    Kemal, Mustafa (Atatürk), in, 785(m),
        787–790, 787(i)
    migrant workers from, 844
    modernization of, 788–790
    nationalism in, 786, 787–790
    after Second World War, 842
    secularism in, 890
    separation of church and state in, 788–789
    tobacco in, 530
    women in, 789
    Young Turks and, 683
Turkish Empire. See Ottoman Empire
Turkish language, 527, 528
Turkish Revolution, 787–790
Turks. See also Ottoman Empire; Ottomans;
        Young Turks
    Arab revolt against, 757
    Armenians and, 786
    in Central Asia and Persia, 520
    in First World War, 757
    Mongols and, 520
    after Ottoman Empire, 786
    Persian influence on, 528
Tuscany, 644
Twitter, 948
Tyler, John, 733
Typhoid, 650
Typhus, 650

Uganda, 690(i)
    warfare in, 929
Uighur Turks, China and, 557
Ukraine, 447, 480, 825
    land in, 449
    Stalin and, 815–816
Ulama (scholars), **526**
    in India, 535
Ulster, 660
Ultranationalism, in Japan, 800, 812, 814,
        826, 828–829(b)
Ulysses (Joyce), 775
Umma (Islam), nationalism in, 883
UN. See United Nations
Unconditional surrender policy (Second
        World War), 832

Underemployment, 848
Unemployment
    benefits for, 810, 846
    in Britain, 773
    Great Depression and, 808, 809, 809(f),
        810, 856
    in Japan, 860
    oil prices and, 848
    in 17th century, 436
Unification
    of China, 797
    of Germany, 643, 645–648, 647(m), 752
    of Italy, 644–645
Unification movement, in Europe, 844,
        863
Union of South Africa, 675. See also South
        Africa
Union of South American Nations
        (UNSAN), 906
Unions. See Labor unions; Trade unions
United Kingdom. See Britain; England
United Nations (UN), 835, **926**
    China in, 875
    Convention on the Rights of the Child,
        950
    Framework Convention on Climate
        Change, 948
    Gulf War and, 859
    Iraq and, 892
    Israel and, 884
    Israel-Lebanon War and, 889
    Jiang in, 875
    Korean War and, 843
    Libya and, 888
    Millennium Project Report of,
        930–931(b), 931(i)
    organization of, 926–927
    peacekeeping by, 925(i), 926(i)
    Persian Gulf War and, 892, 927
    Population Division of, 946
    SALWs and, 935(b)
    Stabilization Mission in Haiti, 906
United Progressive Alliance (UPA, India),
        883
United Provinces of the Netherlands, 455
United States. See also American Revolution;
        Cold War; Second World War;
        Western world
    abolition of slave trade in, 668
    Afghanistan and, 932
    Africa and, 916–917
    agribusiness in, 944
    Arab fundamentalism and, 933
    Asians in, 715
    black nationalism in, 907
    blacks in, 735–738
    Britain and, 753
    British convicts and, 743
    China and, 873
    civil rights movement in, 857
    civil war in, 732, 735–738, 741
    Convention on the Rights of the Child
        and, 950

cotton mill in, 623(i)
Cuba and, 849, 900, 901, 902
détente and, 859
economy in, 856–857, 861
expansion by, 733
financial aid to Mexico from, 899
First World War and, 747, 768
government of, 583–584
Great Depression and, 808–809, 810
immigration to, 732, 739–740
imperialism and, 680, 702
independence of, 583
industrialization of, 615, 616, 738
Iraq War and, 927–929
isolationism in, 770, 830
Jewish emigrants to, 792
Korea and, 711
Korean War and, 843, 843(m)
in NAFTA, 906
nationalism in, 740
New Deal in, 810
in 19th century, 720
by 1914, 746
nuclear arms race and, 933
oil and, 846(b)
Pakistan and, 880
precious metals in, 738
prosperity of, 856–857
racism in, 740
railroads in, 614
raw materials in, 738
sanctions against South Africa, 915
after Second World War, 845
in Second World War, 758
September 11, 2001, terrorist attacks on,
        881
sexuality studied in, 653
slavery in, 584
Spanish territories and, 733
as superpower, 835, 859
Third World and, 842
unemployment in Great Depression and,
        809(f)
Versailles Treaty and, 768–771
Vietnam War and, 858, 858(m), 877
Watergate scandal in, 858
women in, 584, 735
as world power, 732–740
*United States Magazine and Democratic
        Review,* 733
Universal gravitation
    Galileo and, 469
    Kepler and, 468
    Newton on, 470
Universal suffrage, in South Africa, 915
Universe. See also Astronomy
    Aristotle on, 466–467, 466(i)
    sun- vs. earth-centered, 468
Universities and colleges. See also Education;
        Schools
    antiwar movement in, 858
    in China, 871, 873
    scientific revolution and, 467

UNSAN. *See* Union of South American Nations
Unskilled workers, 652
Untouchables, in India, 882
Upanishads (India), 699
Ural Mountains, 447
Urban VIII (Pope), 469
Urban areas. *See also* Cities and towns
    crises of poor in, 436
    Enlightenment culture in, 476–477, 476(i)
    families in, 652–653
    in Japan, 562
    labor in, 618
    middle classes in, 651–652
    migration and family in, 944
    in Ming China, 553
    Paris development and, 650
Urbanization
    agriculture and, 944–945
    immigrants and, 731
    industrialization and, 649–658
    in Mexico, 899
    in South Africa, 913
    Soviet, 816
    worldwide, 942–945
Urbanization without industrialization, 942
Uruguay, in UNSAN, 906
U.S.S.R. *See* Soviet Union
Usuman dan Fodio, 670
Utrecht, Peace of, 442, 444(m), 459

Vaccines, 945
Vacuums, 471
Valmy, Battle of, 591
Values
    in Europe and Americas, 427–431
    in Japan, 562
Van Gogh, Vincent, 776
Vargas, Getúlio, 900
Vatican. *See* Papacy
Velvet Revolution (Czechoslovakia), 851
Vendée region (France), 592
Venereal disease, 653
Venetia, 644
Venezuela, 417, 722, 724(m)
    agriculture in, 727
    Chávez in, 905
    coffee from, 723
    economy in, 903, 905
    government of, 902, 903–905
    human rights in, 905
    oil in, 846(b), 847(b), 905
    in OPEC, 846(b)
    rulers of, 726
    in UNSAN, 906
Venice
    Italy and, 645
    trade in, 412
Versailles. *See also* Paris Peace Conference (1919)
    Estates General at, 586

French court at, 441, 441(i)
    women's march to, 588–589
Versailles, Treaty of (1919), 768–771, **769,** 822
Vesalius, Andreas, 471, 471(i)
Vespucci, Amerigo, 417–418
Viceroyalties (New World), **423**
    of New Granada, 722, 725
    of New Spain, 415(m), 423, 725
    of Peru, 722
    Portuguese, 415(m)
Vichy France, 824, 824(m), 829
    Lebanon and, 888
Victor Emmanuel II (Sardinia), 644, 645
Victor Emmanuel III (Italy), 818
Victoria (England), middle classes under, 654(b)
Vienna
    anti-Semitism in, 661–662
    Ottomans and, 521
    revolution of 1848 in, 643
    Treaty of, 634(i), 635
Vietcong, 858
Vietnam, 842. *See also* French Indochina; North Vietnam; South Vietnam
    Christianity in, 713
    economy of, 877
    French in, 700
    government in, 876
    middle powers and, 929
    religion in, 700
    reunification of, 877
Vietnamization, 858
Vietnam War, 858, 858(m), 877
Villages. *See also* Cities and towns
    Manchu, 555
    in Senegambia, 495
Vindication of the Rights of Man, A (Wollstonecraft), 591
Vindication of the Rights of Woman, A (Wollstonecraft), 591
Violence. *See also* Wars and warfare
    African interethnic, 919
    antiforeign, 681
    by Europeans in Africa, 673
    against Jews, 826
    in multipolar world, 929–933
    sexual, 949
Virginia, 458
Virgin of Guadalupe, 431
Viruses, 946
Visual arts. *See* Art(s)
Vizier, 523
    in Ottoman Empire, 523
Vladivostok, 767
Voltaire (François Marie Arouet), 474–475, 474(i), 572
Voting and voting rights
    after 1815, 637
    in England, 660
    in Italy, 645
    liberals on, 580
    male suffrage in France and, 591

in South Africa, 915
    in United States, 584, 735, 857
    for women, 633(i), 659, 735, 949
    workers and, 662
Voting Rights Act (U.S., 1965), 857
Voyages
    European, 412–422, 415(m)
    navigational problems of, 467
    of Zheng He, 408, 410(b), 410(i), 411(m), 565–566

Wages
    industrialization and, 608, 622
    iron law of, 615
Wales, 608
Walesa, Lech, 851, 851(i), 852(b)
Wall of separation (Israel), 886, 887(i)
Walls. *See* Berlin Wall; Wall of separation
War College, in Japan, 708
War communism, 767
War crimes and criminals
    in Japan, 859
    Milosevic and, 863
Warlords, in China, 795, 796
War of the Austrian Succession, 478, 580, 584
War of the Spanish Succession, 442, 444(m), 459, 722
War on poverty, 857
War profiteering, in First World War, 763
War Raw Materials Board (Germany), 759
Wars and warfare. *See also* Civil war(s); Military; Military technology; Total war; Trench warfare; specific battles and wars
    children in, 950, 950(i)
    colonial, 459
    French, 442
    for Haitian independence, 601(m)
    in 1990s, 929
    Russian, 450
    Spanish, 443
Warsaw, 826, 833, 863
Warsaw Pact, 843
Warships. *See* Navy; Wars and warfare
Wars of independence. *See also* American Revolution; Independence
    in Latin America, 726
Washington, D.C., September 11, 2001, terrorist attacks in, 932
Waste Land, The (Eliot), 775
Water, as power source, 609
Water frame, 609, 610
Watergate scandal, 858
Waterloo, battle at, 599
Water Margin (China), 554
Water systems, in Islamic empires, 529
Watt, James, 611
Wayna Daga, Battle of, 500
"Way of Subjects, The" (Japan), 828(b)
Wealth. *See also* Economy
    Arab, 791
    from colonial trade, 483

Dutch, 457
global distribution of (ca. 2010), 941(m)
Great Depression and, 810, 811
inequities in, 579
in Japan, 564
and poverty in Hong Kong, 943(i)
social hierarchies and, 651
in West, 687
Wealth gap, 938
in cities and towns, 651, 943–944
in Cuba, 900
between nations, 940
Wealth of Nations. See Inquiry into the Nature and Causes of the Wealth of Nations
Weapons. *See also* Nuclear weapons
arms trade and, 934–935(b), 935(m)
in China, 557
heavy conventional, 934(b)
international inspections and, 927
of mass destruction, 927–929, 933–936
Safavid, 526
Weather, global warming and, 948
Weaving. *See also* Industrial Revolution; Textiles and textile industry
carpet, 528, 528(i)
industrialization and, 609–611
in Japan, 565
Web. *See* Internet
Weddings. *See* Marriage
Wedgwood, Josiah, 612(b), 612(i)
Weil, Simone, 852(b)
Weimar Republic, 771, 819–818
Welfare capitalism, 861
Welfare socialism, in Scandinavia, 810–811
Welfare state, 848
Welfare systems
in First World War, 759
in 1970s, 848
Wellesley, Richard, 540
West. *See* West (U.S.); Western world
West (U.S.)
movement into, 733–734, 734(m)
precious metals in, 738
West Africa. *See also* Africa; East Africa
anticolonial nationalism in, 808
black nationalism and, 907
British in, 673
European culture in, 513
families in, 498
industry in, 499–500
lifestyle in, 497–499
palm oil trade and, 668–669
societies in, 492, 494(m)
trade and, 411, 484, 499, 668–669
trade routes in, 499(m)
whites in, 677
West Bank, 884
after First World War, 786
government in, 887
self-rule in, 885
Young Turks and, 786
West Berlin, 842–843
West Coast, of Africa, 494–496

Western Africa, political and economic change in, 919
Western Chamber, The (China), 553
Western civilization. *See* Western world
Western Europe. *See also* Europe; Industrialization; Western world; specific locations
after Cold War, 838, 861
oil and, 846(b), 848
after Second World War, 843–848
unification efforts in, 844
Western front, in First World War, 755, 771
Western Hemisphere (New World), 406. *See also* America(s); Columbian exchange
Westernization
in Iran, 890–891
in Russia, 451–452, 478
in Turkey, 788–790
Western world. *See also* America(s); Europe; Imperialism; Industrialization; Western Europe
Asia and, 571–572, 712–713, 716
China and, 572, 704–705, 712–713
education of Asian students in, 715
expansion into Africa by, 677
after First World War, 771–772
India and, 697–699, 712
industrialization, world economy, and, 686–688
Japan and, 710–711(b)
new imperialism by, 666
Ottoman Empire and, 683
Russian White armies and, 767
Westerners in Asia and, 712–713
worldwide impact of, 666
West Germany, 855
Coal and Steel Community and, 844
West Indies
colonies in, 458
England and, 583
trade and, 483
West Pakistan, 880
Westphalia, Peace of, 437–438
Westward movement, in United States, 732, 733
What Is Enlightenment? (Kant), 476
"What Is the Third Estate?" (Sieyès), 588–589(b)
White-collar employees, 846
White man's burden, 680
"White Man's Burden, The" (Kipling), 680
Whites
in East Africa, 677
in India, 699
ruling nonwhites, 680
as settlers in Africa, 909
as slaves, 503, 506
in South Africa, 913, 915
Whites (Russian civil war), 767
Whites only policy, 690
White supremacy, in South Africa, 913
Widows, in India, 535

William I (Germany, Prussia), 645, 647, 659
William II (Germany), 659, 676(i), 753, 768
William III of Orange (England), 455
Wilson, Isabel, 627(b)
Wilson, Woodrow
First World War and, 758
Fourteen Points of, 768, 783
League of Nations and, 768
Philippine independence and, 802
Winter Palace (Russia), 649
Witte, Sergei, 648
Wittgenstein, Ludwig, 773
Wives, poor/middle-class, 848
Wollstonecraft, Mary, 590–591
Wolof language, 495
Woman suffrage. *See also* Voting and voting rights
before First World War, 659
Women. *See also* Division of labor; Gender; Industrialization; Industrial Revolution; Widows
as African merchants, 669
in Argentina, 904(b)
in Australia, 743
birthrate decline and, 946
childbearing by, 653
in China, 798, 799(b), 799(i)
as Chinese doctors, 552(b)
in colonies, 459–460
as comfort women, 832
education for, 477, 735
in Enlightenment, 477
equal rights for, 816, 860
in family, 652
in Fascist Italy, 819
in First World War, 761–763
Fourier on, 639
in France, 441, 588–589, 596
French Revolution and, 588, 590, 593(i)
idealization of roles, 653
in India, 696, 882
in Indian Ocean region, 409
in Iran, 869(i)
in Italy, 472
in Japan, 564–565, 860
in Japanese theater, 562
male out-migration and, 944
medical treatments for, 552(b), 552(i)
in middle class, 621, 653, 654–655(b)
in Muslim societies, 686
in Nazi Germany, 822
as prime minister, 848
rights of, 652, 735
Rousseau on, 488
in salons, 477
in sciences, 471–472
sexual division of labor and, 624–625
social problems of, 948
in Soviet Union, 816
in Turkey, 789
in United States, 584, 735
voting rights for, 633(i), 659

Women (continued)
  in West Africa, 497
  in workforce, 623(i), 652, 848
  in working class, 652
Wood, deforestation and, 611
Wool and wool industry, in Australia, 744
Wordsworth, William, 657
Work (Brown), 621(i)
Workday, 624, 628
Workers. See also Labor; Labor unions; Third
    estate; Working classes
  in factories, 620
  families of, 623–624
  in France, 590
  in French Revolution, 592
  gender of, 624–625
  Great Depression and, 809, 810
  guest, 844
  identity of, 628
  immigrant labor and, 740
  immigrants to Latin America as, 731–732
  industrialization and, 608
  in Japan, 709, 860
  labor movement and, 626–628
  in Latin America, 728
  living conditions of immigrants and,
    739
  Luddites and, 621–622
  in Poland, 851
  in Russia, 648
  after Second World War, 844
  socialism and, 662–663
  Soviet, 816, 838, 839(i)
  subcontractors for, 624
  unions and, 662
  in Venezuela, 905
  wages of, 622
Workforce
  children in, 623–624
  farmers in, 944
  women in, 623–624, 623(i), 848
Working classes
  fascism and, 814
  people and occupations of, 651–652
  after Second World War, 846
  women in English, 653
Workplace
  conditions in, 610–611, 622–624

  at Wedgwood factory, 612(b)
  women in, 949
Works Progress Administration (WPA), 810
Workweek, 622
World economy. See Global economy
World Health Organization, 945
World power, United States as, 732–740
World trade. See Global trade
World Trade Center, September 11, 2001,
    attack on, 932, 932(i)
World Trade Organization (WTO)
  China in, 873
  Vietnam in, 877
Worldview
  in China, 798
  industrialization and, 608
World War I. See First World War
World War II. See Second World War
World Wide Web. See Internet
WPA. See Works Progress Administration
Wretched of the Earth, The (Fanon), 920
Wu Sangui (China), 555
Wyandot Indians, 733

Xavier, Francis (Jesuit missionary), 571
Xhosa people, 674
Xinjiang, 546

Yalta Conference, 840–841, 841(i)
Yamagata, Yasuko, 834(i)
Yams, in Africa, 498
Yangban (Korean elites), 566
Yangzi River region, 549
Yawata Iron and Steel Works, 709
Yellow fever, 650
Yellow Hat (Gelug-pa sect), 551
Yeltsin, Boris, 855(m), 856, 861–862
Yemen, 884
Yi Dynasty (Korea). See Choson Dynasty
Yokohama, foreign settlement in, 707
Yom Kippur War (1973), 846(b), 847–848,
    884
Yongle emperor (Chengzu, China), 410(b),
    549
Yongzheng emperor, 557
Yorktown, battle at, 583
Yoruba people, Benin and, 495
Yoshimasa (Japan), 558

Young people. See also Students; Youth
    culture
  as Italian Fascists, 818
  in Nazi Germany, 820
  in working classes, 653
Young Turks, 683, 786, 787
Youth culture
  counterculture and, 857–858
  international, 857
Yuan Dynasty (China), 548
Yuan Grand Canal (China), 549
Yuan Shigai (China), 795
Yudhoyona, Susilo Bambang, 877
Yugoslavia, 813
  breakup of, 863
  creation of, 768
  ethnic conflicts in, 863
  migrant workers from, 844
  Tito in, 848–849
Yugoslav people, nationalism of, 763

Zacatecas, mines at, 428
Zaibatsu, 709, 798–800
Zaire. See Democratic Republic of the
    Congo
Zambia, 674, 919, 937
Zanzibar, 506
  Omani capital in, 672
  Portuguese in, 501
Zapotecs, Juarez as, 727
Zardari, Asif Ali, 881, 882
Zeami (Japanese actor/playwright), 558
Zemindars (landlords), 688(b)
Zen Buddhism, in Japan, 558
Zheng He (China), 408, 410(b), 410(i),
    411(m), 565–566
Zhu Xi (philosopher), 551
Zhu Yuanzhang (Taizu, China). See Taizu
Zia-ul-Haq, Muhammad, 881
Zimbabwe, 674, 919
  dictatorship in, 918
  independence for, 913
Zionism, 662, 786, 791–792, 883
Zola, Emile, 658
Zollverein (customs union), 619, 645
Zones. See Occupation zones
Zulu people, 674
Zuma, Jacob, 915

EUROPE

PS

Mediterranean Sea

SAHARA

ARABIAN
DESERT

AFRICA

Nile R.

Congo R.

Zambezi

KALAHARI
DESERT

URAL MTS.

Volga R.

Ob. R.

ASIA

GOBI

Yellow R.
(Huang He)

HIMALAYA MTS.

Ganges R.

Yangzi R.

Arabian
Sea

Bay of
Bengal

South
China
Sea

INDIAN OCEAN

PACIFIC OCEAN

AUSTRALIA

20°E   40°E   60°E   80°E   100°E   120°E   140°E   160°E

80°N

Arctic Circle

60°N

40°N

Tropic of Cancer

20°N

Equator   0°

20°S

Tropic of Capricorn

40°S

60°S

Antarctic Circle

80°S

Vegetation zones

- Tundra
- Northern forest
- Temperate forest
- Temperate grassland
- Desert and dry shrub
- Mediterranean shrub
- Mountain grassland
- Tropical grassland and savanna
- Tropical forest
- Permanent ice cover

About the Authors

John P. McKay (Ph.D., University of California, Berkeley) is professor emeritus at the University of Illinois. He has written or edited numerous works, including the Herbert Baxter Adams Prize–winning book *Pioneers for Profit: Foreign Entrepreneurship and Russian Industrialization, 1885–1913*.

Bennett D. Hill (Ph.D., Princeton University), late of Georgetown University, published *Church and State in the Middle Ages* and numerous articles and reviews, and was one of the contributing editors to *The Encyclopedia of World History*. He was also a Benedictine monk of St. Anselm's Abbey in Washington, D.C.

John Buckler (Ph.D., Harvard University), late of the University of Illinois, published numerous works, including *Theban Hegemony, 371–362 B.C.*; *Philip II and the Sacred War*; and *Aegean Greece in the Fourth Century B.C.* With Hans Beck, he most recently published *Central Greece and the Politics of Power in the Fourth Century*.

Patricia Buckley Ebrey (Ph.D., Columbia University), professor of history at the University of Washington in Seattle, specializes in China. She has published many journal articles and *The Cambridge Illustrated History of China* as well as numerous monographs. In 2010 she won the Shimada Prize for outstanding work of East Asian Art History for *Accumulating Culture: The Collections of Emperor Huizong*.

Roger B. Beck (Ph.D., Indiana University) is Distinguished Professor of African and twentieth-century world history at Eastern Illinois University. His publications include *The History of South Africa*, a translation of P. J. van der Merwe's *The Migrant Farmer in the History of the Cape Colony, 1657–1842*, and more than a hundred articles, book chapters, and reviews. He is a former treasurer and Executive Council member of the World History Association.

Clare Haru Crowston (Ph.D., Cornell University) teaches at the University of Illinois, where she is currently associate professor of history. She is the author of *Fabricating Women: The Seamstresses of Old Regime France, 1675–1791*, which won the Berkshire and Hagley Prizes. She edited two special issues of the *Journal of Women's History*, has published numerous journal articles and reviews, and is a past president of the Society for French Historical Studies.

Merry E. Wiesner-Hanks (Ph.D., University of Wisconsin–Madison) is a UWM Distinguished Professor and chair in the Department of History at the University of Wisconsin–Milwaukee. She is the senior editor of the *Sixteenth Century Journal* and the author or editor of more than twenty books, most recently *The Marvelous Hairy Girls: The Gonzales Sisters and Their Worlds* and *Gender in History*. She is the former Chief Reader for Advanced Placement World History.

About the Cover Art

Augustus Edwin John, *Head of a Jamaican Girl*, 1937
Jamaica became an English colony in 1655 and still remains part of the Commonwealth. In 1937 Augustus John (1878–1961) visited the island and painted this portrait of a Jamaican servant girl, possibly a servant at the Mona Great House hotel where he was staying. This painting and another, *Two Jamaican Girls*, are prime examples of why John was considered the leading portrait painter of his generation.